WHO'S WHO IN THE BIBLE

Two Volumes in One

Who's Who in the Old Testament
together with the Apocrypha

by Joan Comay

Who's Who in the New Testament

by Ronald Brownrigg

WINGS BOOKS
New York • Avenel, New Jersey

This book was originally published in two volumes.

Who's Who in the Old Testament copyright © MCMLXXI by Joan Comay
Who's Who in the New Testament copyright © MCMLXXI by Ronald Brownrigg
All rights reserved.
The Scripture quotations in this publication are from the *Revised
Standard Version Bible*, copyright 1946 and 1952 by the Division of
Christian Education, National Council of the Churches of Christ in the
U.S.A., and used by permission.

This edition is published by Wings Books, distributed by
Random House Value Publishing, Inc., 40 Engelhard Avenue,
Avenel, New Jersey 07001, by arrangement with Holt, Rinehart and Winston.

Random House
New York • Toronto • London • Sydney • Auckland

Manufactured in the United States of America

Who's Who in the Old Testament designed by Juanita Grout
Who's Who in the New Testament designed by Margaret Downing

Library of Congress Cataloging in Publication Data
Main entry under title:

Who's who in the Bible.

    CONTENTS: Comay, J. Who's who in the Old Testament,
together with the Apocrypha—Brownrigg, R. Who's who in
the New Testament.
    1. Bible—Biography.   1. Comay, Joan. Who's who
in the Old Testament, together with the Apocrypha.
1980.   II. Brownrigg, Ronald. Who's who in the New
Testament. 1980.
BS570.W56 1980   220.9′2[B]   80-17306
ISBN: 0-517-32170X

25 24 23 22 21 20 19 18

List of color plates
(Color plates follow page 414)

Volume One

Who's Who in the Old Testament
together with the Apocrypha

Joan Comay

Advisory editors for this volume:

Rabbi Michael Graetz,
Encyclopaedia Judaica, Jerusalem

Revd Dr Leonard Cowie, F.R.Hist.S.,
Senior Lecturer in History, Whitelands
College, London

Contents

List of maps

Author's preface

A scholar approaches the Old Testament in much the same spirit as an archaeologist attacks a site inhabited over several ages. He takes into account that the present text has evolved over a lengthy period, is woven together from different sources and has been constantly re-edited in the light of changing concepts. He will try to retrace this process – to sort out the different historical and literary strata and to interpret each element in relation to the time and place of its origin. In this way it becomes possible to analyse a biblical character in historical depth.

However, such a strictly scholastic treatment is not the intention of the present work. In general, the events relating to specific characters are set out as a straightforward narrative derived from the text, and designed to bring out the human interest of the story. In many cases, notes and comments are added that sketch in the general background or touch on the problems of interpretation that have occupied the scholars, without presuming to resolve them. It is not laid down whether each person in the Bible really existed in historical fact, or only in folk-mythology, or as fictional characters in tales written for moral purposes.

A few more points may help to explain the method of presentation:

As a rule, the biblical narrative and its historical setting are fully dealt with under the heading of the main character, while under each subordinate character the relevant events are briefly retold.

It is doubtful whether either the nations or the pagan deities mentioned in the Old Testament have a place in a Who's Who devoted to individual human beings. For convenience of reference, they have been included, but briefly.

The meanings of personal names have been given in those cases where the derivation is reasonably clear.

The following abbreviations have been used:

Acc.	Accadian		Gk.	Greek
Ass.	Assyrian		Heb.	Hebrew
Bab.	Babylonian		Pers.	Persian
Egypt.	Egyptian			

Author's preface

It is difficult to be precise about biblical dates. Generally, the older the period the more conjectural are the dates. It is essential in a work of this kind to adhere to one single chronological table and that given in the new Jerusalem Bible has been used as a basis. Where no approximate date or even century can be given the term 'date unknown' has been used. Here again no judgment is implied on the question whether the character had an historical existence or is legendary. This refers particularly to the chapters in Genesis before Abraham.

Author's acknowledgments

The author would particularly like to thank the advisory editors, Rabbi Michael Graetz and Revd Dr Leonard Cowie, who while not always in agreement with me on matters of interpretation have provided invaluable comments and suggestions. Dr Meir Gertner, of the Near and Middle Eastern Department, School of Oriental and African Studies, and his two assistants, Mr S. Sharvit and Mr J. Dean, supplied extremely helpful advice on the derivations of the names.

I am also deeply indebted to Jonathan Cowan for his research assistance with the mass of small entries; to Diane Kagan and Nomi Miller for their patient checking of quotations and references; to Elaine Varady for her artistic skill in finding appropriate illustrations; to Carta, Jerusalem, for the indispensable maps; and to Pauline Cooperstone without whose rapid and accurate typing and retyping of drafts this work could not have been completed in the given time.

As usual my long-suffering husband and children provided much-needed encouragement.

Photographic acknowledgments

The author and publishers would like to thank the following museums, institutions and photographers for supplying the illustrations reproduced on the pages listed below:

Aldus Books 40; Archives Photographiques, Paris 166, 194; Ashmolean Museum, Oxford 416 (top); Association pour la diffusion des arts graphiques et plastiques 91, 93, 165 (top); Barber Institute of Fine Arts, University of Birmingham 43; Bayerische Staatsbibliothek, Munich 276 (left); Biblioteca Medicea-Laurenziana, Florence 127 (left), 404 (bottom); Bibliothèque de l'Arsenal, Paris 414 (right); Bibliothèque Municipale, Moulins 428; Bibliothèque Nationale, Paris 31, 64, 97, 144 (left), 163 (top), 217 (top), P-8, 284, P-15, 392, Bodleian Library, Oxford 23 (bottom), 80, 148, 211, 212, 214, Bollinger Foundation 266; Werner Braun 119, 130, 215 (right), 234 (left), 270 (top), 279 (bottom), 283 (right), 324 (left), 352 (top), 376, 412 (top right); British Museum 25, 35 (right), 38, 41 (bottom), 45, 100 (bottom), 101, 109, 116, 122 (right), 125 (top), 135 (left), 149, 163 (bottom), 186 (right), 191, 196, 197, 199, 206 (right), P-7, 227, 237 (bottom), 250 (bottom), 252, 259, 271, (bottom), 282 (top), 285 (bottom), P-11, 289, 291 (right), 292, 324 (right), 325 (left), 331, 332, 336, 350 (top), 354, 360, 361, 371, 372, 390, 393, 416, (bottom); British School of Archaeology in Iraq 58; Brooklyn, New York 133, 179; Rev. Ronald Brownrigg 221; Photo Bulloz 123 (bottom); Hillel Burger 229 (left); Cairo Museum 174; Cincinnati Art Museum 402 (top); Peter Clayton 414 (left), 423; Cleveland Museum of Art 290, 304, 315; Dagon Collection, Haifa 54, 222 (top); Department of Archaeology, Hebrew University, Jerusalem 173 (right), 188, 295 (bottom), 296, 300, 391; Department of Archaeology, University of Tel Aviv 178, 187 (bottom), 253, 299, 380; Detroit Institute of Arts 323 (right); Directorate General of Antiquities, Baghdad 158; District Museum of Art, Yaroslavl, USSR 107; Ecole Biblique, Jerusalem 102 (left), 295 (top); Edinburgh University Library 240; Mary Evans Picture Library 128, 319; Fogg Art Museum, Cambridge, Mass. 90, 213; Françoise Foliot 30, 31, 59, 62, 64, 74, 97, 99 (top), 144, 154, 159 (bottom), 217 (top), 250 (top), 274 (bottom), 283 (left), 284, 291 (left), 340, P-15; Giraudon 37, 268 (bottom), 428; Haags Gemeentemuseum, The Hague 112 (top); Sonia Halliday P-1, 138 (left); David Harris 27 (left), 35 (left), 55, 91, 93, 98, 139, 142, 150, 181 (left), 207, 229 (right), 234 (right) 236, 256, 271 (top), P-10, 277 (right), 281, 282 (left), 329, 353, P-14, 373 (bottom), 378, 412 (top left), 420, 431; The Hermitage, Leningrad 401 (right); Cecil Higgins Art Gallery, Bedford 34; Hirmer Fotoarchiv 53, 275 (right); Michael Holford 124, P-13, P-16; Ikonenmuseum, Rechlinghausen P-5; Israel Department of Antiquities and Museums 39, 42, 51, 81, 86, 112 (bottom), 136, 152, 153 (right), 161 (bottom), 172, 187 (top), 201, 203, 228, 230, 234 (right), 243 (bottom), 246, 250 (left), 274 (top right), 279 (top), 309 (top), 320 (bottom), 321 (top), 322, 328 (left), 329, 334, 344, 345 (bottom), 359 (top), 369, 374, 378, 401 (left), 404 (top); Israel Government Press Office 57, 131, 137, 140 (right), 164, 170, 238, 243 (top), 245 (bottom), 275 (left), 276 (top right and bottom), 277 (left), 280, 297, 370, 426; Israel Information Service, New York 365 (bottom); Israel Museum 23 (top), 55, 85, 91, 93, P-3, 127 (right), 139, 141, 142, 165 (top), 167, 169 (top), 175 (bottom), 181 (left), 210, 225, 229 (left), 233 (bottom), 256, 271 (top), 282 (left), 301 (left), 307, 317 (right), 321 (bottom), 341, 352 (bottom), 366, 411, 431; Israel National Parks Authority 134 (top); Jerusalem Excavation Fund 287, 425; Jewish Theological Seminary, New York 405; Joint Expedition to Shechem 337; Teddy Kollek 347; Kongelige Bibliotek, Copenhagen 363; Kunsthistorischesmuseum, Vienna 427; Louvre, Paris 30, 59, 62, 66, 74, 99 (top), 144 (right), 146, 154, 159 (bottom), 250 (top), 274 (bottom), 283 (left), P-12, 291 (left), 340, 351 (top); Mansell Collection 32 (top), 75, 96, 111, 120, 138 (right), 159 (top), 173 (top left), 204, 217 (bottom), 220, 237 (top), 244, 263, 327, 346, 350 (bottom), 362, 389, 395, 399, 417; Foto Marburg 123 (top), 193, 398 (bottom), Mauritshuis, The Hague 359; Metropolitan Museum of Art, New York 46, 52, 71, 102 (right), 140 (left), 175 (top), 264 (bottom), 305, 397 (left); Middle East Archives 313; Ann Münchow 22; Elizabeth Muir 251 (bottom); Musée Condé, Chantilly 37, 122 (left); Musé de Cluny 408; Museo Arqueológico Nacional, Madrid 206 (left); Museo Civico, Turin 294, 325 (right); Museo del Prado, Madrid 160, 308; Museum of Fine Arts, Boston 77, 245 (top), 328 (right), 400; Museum of Fine Arts, Montreal 180; National Gallery, London 20, 67, 316; National Gallery of Art, Washington, D.C. 84; National Gallery of Canada, Ottawa 153 (left), P-6, 215 (left), 261 (bottom), 293; New Jersey State Museum Collection 200; Ny-Carlsberg Glyptothek, Copenhagen 302 (right); Öffentliche Kunstsammlung, Basle 310; Öst. Nationalbibliothek, Vienna 83, 105, 108, 190, 241; Oriental Institute, University of Chicago 27 (right), 110, 165 (bottom), 222 (bottom), 242, 269, 345 (top), 398 (top); Pierpont Morgan Library, New York 69, 87, 176 (left), 231, 261 (top), 274 (top left), 314, 317 (left), 326, 397 (right), 429; Leon Pomerance 306; Princeton University Press 266; Zev Radovan 32 (bottom), 41 (top), 70, 133, 135 (right), 161 (top), 169, 173, (bottom left), 176 (right), 181 (right), 210, 218, 219, 233 (top), 235 (right), 247, 267, 306 (left), 309 (bottom), 317 (right), 320 (top), 323 (left), 328 (left), 341, 349 (bottom), 373 (top), 407 (bottom), 410, 412, (bottom), 413, 418, 419, 421; Reifenberg Collection, Jerusalem 205, 407 (top), 420; Rheinisches Bildarchiv, Cologne 356 (bottom); Rijksmuseum, Leiden 223; Roger-Viollet 349 (top); Seattle Art Museum 388; Ricarda Schwerin 33, 355; Staatliche Museen, Berlin 24, 65, 118, 186 (left), 235 (left), 254, 260, P-9, 285 (top), 402 (bottom), 415; Staatsbibliothek, Bamberg 162; Staatsbibliothek, St Gallen 49; Suermondt Museum, Aachen 22; Tate Gallery, London P-4; Telegraph Colour Library P-2; Mr and Mrs Joseph Ternbach 29; Uni-Dia Verlag 264 (top); University Museum, University of Pennsylvania 79, 262, 303; Victoria and Albert Museum, London 28, 36, 124, 134 (bottom), 268 (top), 333, P-13, P-16; Walters Art Gallery, Baltimore 185, 301 (right), 302 (left); Mortimer Wheeler 78; Roger Wood 82, 270 (bottom); Robert B. Wright 125 (bottom), 356 (top).

Main Old Testament archaeological sites

LEBANON

SYRIA

Tyre

Dan

Achzib

Hazor

Golan Hts.

Acre

Galilee

Sea of Galilee

Mediterranean Sea

Carmel

Megiddo

Beth-shean

Samaria

Shechem (Nablus)

Joppa (Jaffa)

Samaria

Gezer

Bethel

Jericho

Ashdod

Jerusalem

Beit Shemesh

Ashkelon

Judea

Dead Sea

Lachish

Hebron

Gaza

Ein-gedi

Gaza Strip

Beersheba

Arad

Sodom

Negev

Mediterranean Sea

Jerusalem

Beersheba

Kadesh-barnea

Wilderness of Zin

Negev

Sinai

Dead Sea

Ezion-geber (Eilat)

SAUDI ARABIA

Gulf of Suez

Gulf of Eilat

St. Catherine

Mt. Sinai

E G Y P T

Red Sea

–·– 1967 Cease Fire Line
······ Israel Occupied Areas

0   20 miles

Introduction to the Old Testament

The Books of the Old Testament

The Old Testament contains the ancient literature of the Hebrew people. The works in it were composed and re-edited over a period of more than a thousand years, up to about the end of the 3rd century BC.

Other Near Eastern civilizations, such as the Egyptian and the Babylonian, produced religious and historical writings, legal codes, legends and folk-tales, prophecies, proverbs and poetry. But only the Hebrews wove them into a sacred anthology. What resulted was not so much an historical work in the modern sense, as a religious epic. The covenant between a small people and a universal God was the central theme, and all events were related to it. When neighbouring nations oppressed them, when the imperial armies of the ancient world trampled upon them, when they were afflicted by plague or bad harvests, it was because the Lord was angry with the Israelites for their transgressions. Even kings had to obey the Law, for it was God's Law. Perhaps for this reason, the Hebrews portrayed their own forefathers with remarkable honesty, and refused to make saints or demigods of them. Jacob can trick his old, blind father into giving him Esau's blessing; and David, the national hero, can behave shamefully over Bathsheba. It is this quality which makes the Old Testament so intensely human a chronicle.

The most venerable part of the Old Testament is the Pentateuch, or the Five Books of Moses. Its ultimate form was a blend of four early written versions: the 'J' Document, compiled in the southern kingdom of Judah in the 10th century BC; the 'E' Document, compiled in Ephraim in the northern kingdom of Israel in the 9th and 8th centuries BC; the Book of Deuteronomy (the 'D' Document), dating from the 7th century BC; and the material introduced by the priestly writers (the 'P' Document) about the time of the Exile.

Chronicles, produced about the 4th century BC, drew its material partly from Genesis, Exodus, Numbers and Joshua, and mainly from the Books of Samuel and Kings. This material was rewritten in a way that suited the Chronicler's didactic purpose. Ezra and Nehemiah are usually regarded as a continuation of Chronicles.

The final editing of the Books of Joshua, Judges, Samuel and Kings took place only in the post-Exilic period.

Introduction

These multiple sources of the Old Testament, dating from different periods and reflecting changes in religious and social ideas, explain the problems of interpretation that face biblical scholars.

The Hebrew Bible is divided into three sections: the Law (Pentateuch), the Prophets and the Writings. The Pentateuch was canonized – i.e. accepted in final form as a sacred text – about 400 BC; the Prophets about 200 BC; and the Writings about AD 90. In that year, the scope and arrangement of the Hebrew Bible was settled by the Rabbinical Council of Jamnia. This step was prompted by the destruction of Jerusalem and the Second Temple by the Romans, in AD 70.

The oldest extant edition in the Hebrew language is the Masoretic Text finalized in Tiberias in the 9th century AD ('Masorah' means tradition). This is still the standard Hebrew Bible in general use today. It is a remarkable fact that the Isaiah scrolls discovered in a Dead Sea cave in 1947 are almost identical with the Masoretic Text, although they date from ten centuries earlier.

The accepted Jewish translation into the English language is that of the Jewish Publication Society of America, published in 1914.

The Books are listed below in the order in which they appear with their abbreviations in brackets. They also have the Hebrew equivalents in brackets, except for those bearing the names of persons.

The Law (Torah)	Genesis (Gen.)	(Bereishit)
	Exodus (Exod.)	(Shemot)
	Leviticus (Lev.)	(Vayikrah)
	Numbers (Num.)	(Bamidbar)
	Deuteronomy (Deut.)	(Devarim)

The Prophets (Nevi'im)	The Earlier Prophets:	
	Joshua (Josh.)	
	Judges (Judg.)	(Shoftim)
	1 Samuel (1 Sam.)	(Shmuel Alef)
	2 Samuel (2 Sam.)	(Shmuel Beth)
	1 Kings (1 Kgs.)	(Melachim Alef)
	2 Kings (2 Kgs.)	(Melachim Beth)
	The Later Prophets:	
	Isaiah (Isa.)	
	Jeremiah (Jer.)	
	Ezekiel (Ezek.)	
	The Twelve Minor Prophets:	

Hosea (Hos.)	Nahum (Nahum)
Josel (Joel)	Habakkuk (Hab.)
Amos (Amos)	Zephaniah (Zeph.)
Obadiah (Obad.)	Haggai (Hag.)
Jonah (Jonah)	Zechariah (Zech.)
Micah (Mic.)	Malachi (Mal.)

The Writings (Ketuvim)	Psalms (Ps.)	(Tehillim)
	Proverbs (Prov.)	(Mishlei)
	Job (Job)	
	Song of Songs (S. of S.)	(Shir-ha-Shirim)
	Ruth (Ruth)	
	Lamentations (Lam.)	(Ichah)
	Ecclesiastes (Eccles.)	(Kohelet)
	Esther (Esther)	
	Daniel (Dan.)	
	Ezra (Ezra)	
	Nehemiah (Neh.)	
	1 Chronicles (1 Chr.)	(Divrei ha-Yamim Alef)
	2 Chronicles (2 Chr.)	(Divrei ha-Yamim Beth)

The Bible is known in Hebrew as the 'Tanach', a word made up of the initials of the three above sections.

By early tradition, the Hebrew Bible consisted of 'The Twenty-four Books', since Samuel, Kings, the Twelve Prophets, Ezra-Nehemiah, and Chronicles were each regarded as one Book.

The Greek Bible

In the 3rd century BC the Septuagint, a Greek translation of the Hebrew Bible, was produced in Alexandria, Egypt, for the use of the large Jewish community residing there. Egypt was then under Greek influence, being ruled by the Ptolemaic dynasty descended from one of the generals of Alexander the Great. The work is regarded as having been initiated by the king himself, and colourful legends have clustered round its obscure early history. Septuagint means the Version of the Seventy, from the number of elders who were said to have been brought from Jerusalem for the purpose. From the surviving texts, it is clearly the work of various translators, and is uneven in quality.

The Greek Bible continued to be amplified, and became the Old Testament in general use in the early Christian Church. The earliest comprehensive manuscript of the Septuagint dates from the 4th century AD. It included not only the books of the Hebrew canon, with some omissions and additions, but also additional Jewish works, mostly written in the 2nd and 1st centuries BC in Hebrew, Aramaic and Greek. These writings later became known as the Apocrypha, from a Greek word meaning 'hidden' or 'spurious'.

The Latin Bible

In the 4th century AD St Jerome, working in Bethlehem, produced the Latin translation of the Bible known as the Vulgate. He wished to limit the Old Testament to the Hebrew canon, but was overruled by the Church, and most of the Apocrypha were included, though they were termed 'deutero-canonical'. Their inclusion was confirmed by the Council of Trent (1546) and by the Vatican Council (1870). The books of the Apocrypha not accepted into the Latin Bible were 1 and 2 Esdras and the Prayer of Manasseh.

Introduction

The Latin Bible continues to be used by the Roman Catholic Church. Recently, authoritative modern translations have been published in French (*La Bible de Jérusalem*, 1956), and in English (The Jerusalem Bible, 1966).

The Protestant Bible

In his German translation of the Bible (1534), Martin Luther reverted to the opinion of St Jerome about the canon of the Old Testament. He relegated the Apocrypha to a separate section at the end of the Old Testament, since they were not holy scripture but 'good and useful for reading'.

The same attitude was taken in the early English translations, such as Wycliffe (*c*. 1382), Coverdale (1535), the Greek Bible (1539), the Geneva Bible (1560), and the Bishops' Bible (1568). These were forerunners of the Authorized Version or King James Bible, published in 1611. It became the classic English Bible, and had a profound effect on the thought and literature of the English-speaking world.

In the course of time, the Authorized Version (AV) lagged increasingly behind biblical scholarship, archaeology and the increased knowledge of ancient Hebrew and Greek. Moreover, some of its magnificent language became archaic. A Revised Version (RV) was published in 1885. After World War II a Revised Standard Version (RSV) was produced in the United States and the Old Testament section appeared in 1952. It is from the RSV that the quotations and spelling of names have been taken for the present work.

From the beginning of the 20th century, a number of translations were brought out in modern colloquial English by Protestant, Catholic and Jewish scholars. In 1947, a joint commission was set up by the Protestant Churches in the British Isles, to prepare a fresh and authoritative translation into modern English from the original sources. It was published in 1970 as the New English Bible (NEB).

In the Protestant versions, the Books of the Old Testament appear in the following order, which differs in certain respects from the arrangement in the Hebrew Bible, though the individual Books are the same.

Genesis	2 Chronicles	Daniel
Exodus	Ezra	Hosea
Leviticus	Nehemiah	Joel
Numbers	Esther	Amos
Deuteronomy	Job	Obadiah
Joshua	Psalms	Jonah
Judges	Proverbs	Micah
Ruth	Ecclesiastes	Nahum
1 Samuel	Song of Solomon	Habakkuk
2 Samuel	Isaiah	Zephaniah
1 Kings	Jeremiah	Haggai
2 Kings	Lamentations	Zechariah
1 Chronicles	Ezekiel	Malachi

To sum up: The Hebrew Bible contains thirty-nine works, regarded as constituting 'Twenty-four Books'.

In the Septuagint the Old Testament included additional books or parts of books, dating from the 2nd and 1st centuries BC.

The Latin Bible incorporated eleven of these works, known as 'deutero-canonical'.

The Protestant Bible reverted to the Hebrew canon (though not in the same order), with fifteen additional works printed separately as Apocrypha.

The physical setting

The Land of the Bible has a remarkably varied landscape. There are five distinct regions: the coastal plain, the central hill country, the Jordan valley, the plateau east of the Jordan, and the Negev in the south.

The fertile coastal plain is flat and sandy, with a good supply of water from underground springs. It was well settled from the earliest times. The northern part was occupied by the Phoenicians, and the southern part by the Philistines from the 12th century BC.

Inland from the coast are rolling limestone hills two to three thousand feet high. The Valley of Jezreel divides them into two areas – the Galilee highlands in the north, and the mountains of Samaria and Judea in the centre. The Israelites settled mainly in the hill region.

The deep Jordan Valley is part of the longest rift in the earth's surface, running across the Red Sea and into the heart of Africa. The Jordan river flows from Mount Hermon through the Sea of Galilee and ends in the Dead Sea, 1,300 feet below sea level.

East of the Jordan Valley and the Dead Sea, a steep escarpment leads to the open Transjordan plateau. In this area lay the kingdoms of Edom, Moab and Ammon, and the tribes of Reuben, Gad and part of Manasseh were settled.

The northern part of the Negev round Beersheba is a sparse plain dotted with low scrub. It becomes bleaker and more rugged further south. The Hebrew patriarchs were typical of the nomads who have inhabited this region down the ages.

The ancient route from Egypt to Mesopotamia ran via Gaza up the coastal plain, and cut through a strategic pass into the Jezreel Valley, continuing across the Jordan to Damascus. The other main route, the King's Highway, ran east of the Dead Sea and the Jordan River. It was from this side that Joshua invaded Canaan.

Chronology

GENERAL		ISRAELITE	MAIN BIBLICAL CHARACTERS
		THE CREATION AND THE FLOOD (Gen. 1-11)	ADAM and EVE NOAH
		THE PATRIARCHS AND THE SOJOURN IN EGYPT 1800-1250 BC (Gen. 12–Exod. 1)	
Egyptian domination *Middle Bronze Age: 2100-1550*	BC		
	2000		
	1800	The patriarchs in Canaan: *c.* 1800-1700	ABRAHAM, ISAAC and JACOB
Hyksos regime in Egypt: 1720-1560 New Kingdom in Egypt: 1560-715 *Late Bronze Age: 1550-1200* Tel el-Amarna Letters	1700	The Israelites in Egypt: *c.* 1700-1250	JOSEPH JOB
Rameses II: 1301-1234	1300	Israelite forced labour	
		THE EXODUS AND THE CONQUEST 1250-1200 (Exod., Lev., Num., Deut., Josh.)	
Egyptian control weakens	1250	The Exodus: *c.* 1250 The Law at Sinai The Conquest: *c.* 1220-1200	MOSES AARON JOSHUA
		THE JUDGES 1200-1030 (Judg., 1 Sam. 1-7, Ruth)	
Egypt: 20th Dynasty: *c.* 1200-1085 *Iron Age 1: 1200-900*	1200	Allocation and settlement of Israelite tribal areas: 1200-1025	
Philistines settle on Palestine coast		Wars of Ehud, Deborah, Gideon and Jephthah Exploits of Samson Migration of tribe of Dan	EHUD, DEBORAH GIDEON
Assyrian hegemony in Mesopotamia Rise of Aramean kingdoms (Damascus, Zobah, Hamath)	1100	War against Benjamin The story of Ruth Philistine victory at Apek and capture of Ark	JEPHTHAH, SAMSON RUTH
21st Egyptian Dynasty: 1085-945	1050	Samuel appears: *c.* 1040	SAMUEL

THE MONARCHY 1030-931
(1 and 2 Sam., 1 Kgs., 1 and 2 Chr.)

Left events	Date	Reign / events	Key figures
Struggle with Philistines		Reign of Saul: c. 1030-1010	SAUL
		Victories over Ammonites, Philistines, Amalekites	
		Saul and David	
		Defeat and death at Mt Gilboa	
		Reign of David: c. 1010-970	DAVID
		Capture of Jerusalem	
		Victories and expansion	
		Alliances with Hamath and Tyre	
		Revolt of Absalom	
		Solomon appointed successor	
		Reign of Solomon: c. 970-931	SOLOMON
		Building of Temple and palace	
	950	Red Sea trade route	
		Visit of Queen of Sheba	
22nd (Libyan) Dynasty in Egypt		Solomon's death and split in kingdom	
Shishak I: 945-925			

THE TWO KINGDOMS 931-587
(1 and 2 Kgs., 2 Chr., Amos, Hos., Isa., Mic., Jer.)

Left events	Date	**Israel:** 931-721	**Judah:** 931-587	Key figures
Shishak's campaign in Palestine		Jeroboam I: 931-910	Rehoboam: 931-913	JEROBOAM
		Nadab: 910-909	Abijah: 913-911	REHOBOAM
Iron Age 2: 900-600		Baasha: 909-886	Asa: 911-870	
Ben-hadad I, king of Damascus		Elah: 886-885		
		Zimri: 885		
		Omri: 885-874		OMRI
		Founds Samaria		
Ben-hadad II, king of Damascus		Ahab: 874-853	Jehoshaphat: 870-848	AHAB
Assyrian domination		Wars against		ELIJAH
Shalmaneser III: 858-824		Damascus		JEHOSHAPHAT
Victory over 12 kings at Kharkar, 853		Ahaziah: 853-852		
		Jehoram: 852-841		
Mesha, king of Moab	850		Jehoram: 848-841	ELISHA
			Ahazia: 841	
Shalmaneser III invades Palestine		Jehu: 841-814	Athalia: 841-835	JEHU
			Joash: 835-796	
		Jehoahaz: 814-798		
Ben-hadad III, king of Damascus	800	Joash: 798-783	Amaziah: 796-781	
		Jeroboam II: 783-743	Uzziah: 781-740	JEROBOAM II, UZZIAH
Tiglath-pileser III: 745-727	750			AMOS
		Zechariah: 743		HOSEA
		Shallum: 743		
Rezin, king of Damascus		Menahem: 743-738	Jotham: 740-736	ISAIAH
		Pekahiah: 738-737	Ahaz: 736-716	MICAH
		Pekah: 737-732	Rezin and Pekah	
		Tiglath-pileser occupies Galilee	besiege Jerusalem	
Shalmaneser V: 726-722		Hoshea: 732-724		
Sargon II: 721-705		**Fall of Samaria: 721**		
		Deportation of inhabitants		
Sargon defeats Egyptians at Rafiah, 720			Hezekiah: 716-687	HEZEKIAH
Sargon takes Ashdod, 711				
Sennacherib: 704-681			Shiloh tunnel	
			Assyrians invade Judah: 701	

17

Chronology

Esarhaddon: 680-669	700	Manasseh: 687-642	
Lower Egypt occupied: 671		Tribute paid to	JONAH
Ashurbanipal: 668-621	650	Assyria	TOBIT
		Amon: 642-640	JOSIAH
Fall of Nineveh, 612		Josiah: 640-609	ZEPHANIA
		Religious reforms	NAHUM
Campaign of Pharaoh Neco			
Judean defeat at Megiddo, 609		Jehoahaz: 609	JEREMIAH
		Jehoiakim: 609-598	HABAKKUK
Babylonian domination			
Battle of Carchemish – end of			
Assyrian Empire, 605			
Nebuchadnezzar: 604-562	600	Jehoiachin: 598	
		Jerusalem surrenders;	
		Jehoiachin deported	DANIEL
		Zedekiah: 598-587	
		Siege of Jerusalem:	
		589	
Siege of Tyre: 588-575		**Fall of Jerusalem: 587**	
		Deportations	
		Gedaliah assassinated	
		Judea a Babylonian	
		province	

THE EXILE AND THE RETURN
587-331 BC (Ezek., Isa. 40-55, Zeph., Nahum,
Hab., Ezra, Neh., Hag., Zech., Obad., Joel,
Mal., Esther)

		Exile in Babylonia	EZEKIEL
		Fresh deportations: 582	'SECOND ISAIAH'
	550		
Persian domination			
Cyrus, king of Medes and Persians:		Edict of Cyrus: **Return: 538**	
549-529		Foundations of Second Temple: 537	
Capture of Babylon, 539		Zerubbabel as governor	
Cambyses: 529-522			
Conquest of Egypt		Second Temple built: 520-515	
			ZERUBBABEL
Darius I: 522-486			HAGGAI
Organization of Empire			ZECHARIAH
Battle of Marathon: 490	500		
Xerxes I (Ahasuerus): 486-465			ESTHER
Defeat at Salamis: 480			JUDITH
Artexerxes I Longimanus: 465-423		Ezra's mission: 458 (if under Artaxerxes I)	
	450	Mission of Nehemiah: 445-425	EZRA
		Walls of Jerusalem rebuilt	NEHEMIAH
		Religious reforms	OBADIAH
			JOEL
Artaxerxes II Mnemon: 404-358	400	Ezra's mission: 398 (if under Artaxerxes II)	MALACHI
	350	Code of Laws	

THE HELLENISTIC PERIOD
331-63 (1 and 2 Macc., Dan. 11)

Alexander the Great
Conquests: 336-323
End of Persian Empire: 331
Ptolemaic dynasty in Egypt: 323-30
Seleucid dynasty in Syria and
Mesopotamia: 312-64

eptuagint in Alexandria	300	Judea under Ptolemies: 301-197	
	250		
ntiochus III: 223-187			
	200		
Defeats Egyptians at Panias: 198		Judea under Seleucids: 197-142	
Defeated by Romans at		Antiochus III sanctions Jewish religious	
Magnesia: 188		autonomy	
ntiochus IV Epiphanes: 175-163		Temple pillaged: 170	
Egyptian campaigns: 170, 168		Persecution of Jews: from 167	
		Mattathias starts revolt in Modi'in: 167	
		Judas Maccabeus becomes leader: 166	JUDAS MACCABEUS
		Victories of Judas: 166-164	
		Rededication of Temple: Dec. 164	
ntiochus V Eupator: 163-162			
		Lysias besieges Jerusalem: 162	
emetrius I Soter: 162-150		Judas defeated and killed: 160	
		Jonathan, high priest and ethnarch: 163-142	JONATHAN THE MACCABEE
lexander Balas: 150-145	150	Captured and killed: 143-142	
emetrius II: 145-138			
ntiochus VI: 145-142			
ryphon: 142-138			
ntiochus VII: 138-129		Simon, high priest and ethnarch: 143-134	SIMON THE MACCABEE
emetrius II: 129-125		Judea becomes autonomous: 142	
(second reign)		John Hyrcanus I, high priest and ethnarch:	
		134-104	
ompey's eastern campaigns: 66-62	100	**Pompey takes Jerusalem: 63**	

END OF HELLENISTIC PERIOD AND
BEGINNING OF ROMAN PERIOD

B The main biblical characters have been placed in the chronology as far as possible in the periods that correspond to the biblical count. This does not imply that each of them exists in history.

A

AARON *c.* 13 century BC. Brother of Moses and first high priest.

Aaron was the son of Amram and Jochebed, of the priestly tribe of Levi. He was older than his brother Moses by three years, though younger than their sister Miriam. He married Elisheba, the daughter of Amminadab of the tribe of Judah, and had four sons: Nadab, Abihu, Eleazar and Ithamar.

When the Lord ordered Moses to go to Pharaoh and ask him to let the Israelites leave Egypt, Moses pleaded that 'I am slow of speech and of tongue.' (Exod. 4:10) The Lord told him that Aaron his brother would serve as his spokesman, for 'I know that he can speak well.' (Exod. 4:14)

Aaron went into the wilderness and met Moses. The two brothers embraced, and Moses repeated the Lord's commandments. They then sent for the Israelite elders. Aaron informed them that the Lord was about to release them from their slavery, and convinced them by performing magic signs.

Moses and Aaron appeared before Pharaoh, and at first asked for permission for the Israelites to journey into the wilderness to hold a feast to their God. Pharaoh refused, and increased the burdens of the Hebrew slaves, who then blamed the brothers for these new hardships. Once again they appeared before Pharaoh to urge their plea. To impress Pharaoh with a miracle, Aaron threw down his rod and it turned into a serpent. Pharaoh sent for his sorcerers who performed the same feat 'but Aaron's rod swallowed up their rods'. (Exod. 7:12)

Aaron's role in the infliction of some of the ten plagues that followed is recorded in Exodus (Chapters 7, 8 and 9). By stretching out his rod at the behest of Moses, he brought on the first three plagues (blood, frogs and lice). Together they were involved in producing the sixth plague (boils) and the eighth one (locusts). Only Moses is mentioned in connection with the other five. Pharaoh finally yielded to the demand to 'let my people go'. Aaron was then eighty-three years old and Moses eighty.

left The Worship of the Golden Calf
(detail), by Filippino Lippi (1457-1504).

After their dramatic crossing of the Red (or Reed) Sea, the Israelites were attacked in the desert by fierce Amalekite nomads. All day Moses sat on a hill-top while Aaron and Hur stood on either side of him and held up his hands grasping the sacred rod, until the attackers were repulsed.

Moses went up Mount Sinai to receive the Ten Commandments leaving Aaron and Hur in charge of the encampment. When Moses did not appear at the appointed time, the people became rebellious and demanded of Aaron: 'Up, make us gods, who shall go before us; as for this Moses ... we do not know what has become of him.' (Exod. 32:1) Aaron told them to bring him whatever gold items they had, and he fashioned a golden calf as a tangible object of worship for them. He proclaimed a feast for the following day and the people sacrificed, ate, drank and 'rose up to play' (Exod. 32:6).

On his return, the outraged Moses smashed the stone tablets he was carrying. He destroyed the calf and upbraided Aaron, who replied defensively: 'Let not the anger of my lord burn hot; you know the people, that they are set on evil.' (Exod. 32:22)

It was after this that the Ark of the Law and the tabernacle were constructed, and Aaron and his sons ordained as priests.

Two hundred and fifty of the Israelites, led by Korah, a Levite, revolted against the leadership of Moses and Aaron, claiming that all members of the congregation were holy. The earth split open and swallowed up the mutinous group. Moses placed a stave from each of the tribes overnight in the Tabernacle, with the Levites represented by that of Aaron. Next morning, it was seen that Aaron's rod alone had sprouted blossom, 'put forth buds ... and it bore ripe almonds' (Num. 17:8). This demonstrated the special status of the priesthood and the Levites.

Before the Children of Israel entered the Promised Land, they reached Mount Hor, near the southern end of the Dead Sea. The Lord told Moses to take Aaron up the mountain, together with his son Eleazar. Aaron's vestments were placed upon Eleazar, who succeeded him as high priest. Aaron then died, at the age of one hundred and twenty-three. The Israelites mourned him for thirty days.

Aaron figures in the biblical account as sharing with Moses the receipt of God's commands, the performance of miracles, and leadership over the people. Despite this close association in authority, Aaron lacked the spiritual grandeur that made Moses the central figure of the Old Testament.

Aaron and the Priesthood

Scholars are generally of the opinion that the earlier traditions about the Exodus, as reflected in the J and E Documents, give Aaron a minor role, and do not refer to his priestly function at all. A professional priesthood was developed in Jerusalem under the monarchy, and was centred on the Temple. Two priestly orders came into being, both claiming descent from Aaron – the Zadokites, through Aaron's son Eleazar; the Aaronites, through Aaron's son Ithamar. After the Return, and under the influence of Ezra's reforms, the Zadokites became the dominant priesthood, and the Aaronites or Levites were relegated to the status of Temple servants and lesser country priests.

The special role of the priesthood, and the details of Temple worship, were elaborated in the P (priestly) Document in the post-exilic period, in about the 4th century BC. It is mainly from this late source that these themes were injected into the Books of Exodus, Leviticus and Numbers. Aaron's importance as the founder of the priesthood and the first high priest was thereby magnified in retrospect. [The main part of the story of Aaron is told in the Books of Exodus, Leviticus and Numbers.]

ABAGTHA *c.* 5 century BC. One of the seven chamberlains of Ahasuerus, king of Persia, sent to bring Queen Vashti to the king's banquet to show off her beauty. [Esther 1:10, 11]

ABDA (Heb. 'servant') **1.** *c.* 10 century BC. Father of Adoniram who was the member of King Solomon's household in charge of the levy of labour for public works. [1 Kgs. 4:6]

2. *see* OBADIAH **9.**

ABDEEL (Heb. 'servant of God') *c.* 7 century BC. Father of Shelemiah, who was ordered by King Joiakim to arrest the prophet Jeremiah and his scribe Baruch. [Jer. 36:26]

ABDI (Heb. 'servant') **1.** *c.* 10 century BC. Grandfather of Ethan, one of the chief musicians of King David. [1 Chr. 6:44]

2. *c.* 8 century BC. The father of Kish, a Levite who sanctified himself and helped cleanse the Temple in the reign of Hezekiah. [2 Chr. 29:12]

3. 5 century BC. Descendant of Elam, who divorced his non-Jewish wife in the time of Ezra. [Ezra 10:26]

ABDIEL (Heb. 'servant') *c.* 8 century BC. Father of Ahi and son of Guni, he was head of a family of Gadites

Dutch oak statue of a high priest, early 18th century. Aaron is the traditional founder of the priesthood.

living in Gilead during the period of Jeroboam II, king of Israel. [1 Chr. 5:15]

ABDON (Heb. 'servile') **1.** *c.* 12 century BC. Son of Hillel, a Pirathonite from the land of Ephraim, he judged Israel for eight years and had forty sons and thirty nephews who rode on seventy asses. [Judg. 12:13-15]

2. date unknown. Son of Shashak, a Benjaminite leader who lived in Jerusalem. [1 Chr. 8:23-25]

3. *c.* 11 century BC. Son of Jeiel, a Benjaminite leader and uncle of King Saul. [1 Chr. 8:30; 9:36]

4. *c.* 7 century BC. The son of Micah, he was sent by King Josiah to consult the prophetess Huldah. Also called Achbor. [2 Kgs. 22:12, 14; 2 Chr. 34:20]

ABEDNEGO (Bab. 'servant of Nego' [a Babylonian god]) *c.* 6 century BC. The Babylonian name given to Azariah, one of the four young men of Judah taken off to Babylon by the orders of King Nebuchadnezzar. When the four refused to worship or serve the Babylonian gods, Nebuchadnezzar, in great rage, ordered them cast into the fiery furnace. They were delivered by an angel and walked out unhurt. [Dan. 1-3]

ABEL (Heb. 'son') date unknown. The younger son of Adam and Eve. Abel was a shepherd, while his elder brother Cain became a tiller of the soil. When the two brothers came to present their offerings to the Lord, the lambs of Abel were preferred to the produce of Cain. Cain was so angry that he killed his brother Abel, thus committing the first murder recorded in the Bible.

The story of Cain and Abel is regarded as expressing

above Torah finials, a reminder of the bells which adorned the high priest's skirt. Venetian, 17th century.

left Cain killing Abel, from a 14th-century French illuminated manuscript.

the age-old strife in the Near East between the desert nomads with their flocks and herds, and the settled cultivators. The story has its roots in the primitive custom of ritual human sacrifice to propitiate the gods and ensure the fertility of the soil, on which the life of the community depended.

Clearly, the story of Cain and Abel represents a stage in human society that had evolved far beyond the primitive beginnings, and it is only in a legendary sense that the two of them were regarded as the 'children' of the first human beings. *See* CAIN [Gen. 4]

ABI (Heb. 'progenitor') *c.* 8 century BC. Daughter of Zachariah, she became the wife of Ahaz, king of Judah, and the mother of his successor, King Hezekiah. Also called Abijah. [2 Kgs. 18:2; 2 Chr. 29:1]

ABIALBON *see* ABIEL **2.**

ABIASAPH (Heb. 'father added [a son]') *c.* 13 century BC. A son of Korah and a descendant of Kohath of the tribe of Levi, he was head of a family of Korahites who went out of Egypt with Moses. When his father Korah led a rebellion against Moses and Aaron in the wilderness and died unnaturally, Abiasaph and his brothers were not punished. His descendants were keepers at the gates of the Tabernacle in the reign of King David. Also called Ebiasaph. [Exod. 6:24; 1 Chr. 6:37; 9:19]

ABIATHAR (Heb. 'father of excellence') *c.* 11 century BC. High priest during the reign of David.

Abiathar was a young priest at the sanctuary town of Nob, just outside Jerusalem, and the son of the head priest Ahimelech. When Saul heard David had been helped by them, he had all the priests of Nob rounded up and slain and the town destroyed. Only Abiathar escaped and managed to join the outlawed David in the mountains. David pledged himself to look after Abiathar: 'Stay with me, fear not; for he that seeks my life seeks your life; with me you shall be in safekeeping.' [1 Sam. 22:23]

Abiathar stayed with David throughout his guerrilla days and then came to Jerusalem with him. Here David made him one of the two high priests, the other being Zadok. At the time of Absalom's revolt, they tried to follow David from Jerusalem with the Ark, but he asked them to turn back and keep him posted of developments, using their sons as runners. After the defeat and death of Absalom, the two high priests encouraged the leaders of Judah to call for the return of David.

When David was aged and losing his hold on affairs, Abiathar supported the abortive bid of the eldest surviving prince, Adonijah, to usurp the throne. Solomon, a younger son, was crowned instead.

David died shortly after and Solomon succeeded him. Because of his loyalty and long service to David, Abiathar's life was spared. But Solomon banished him from Jerusalem: 'Go to Anathoth, to your estate.' (1 Kgs. 2:26) [1 Sam. 22:20-23; 2 Sam. 15:24; 1 Kgs. 1, 2, 4; 1 Chr. 15:11, 18:16; 24:6; 27:34]

ABIDA (Heb. 'father of knowledge') *c.* 17 century BC. Son of Midian, he was a grandson of Abraham and his wife Keturah. [Gen. 25:4; 1 Chr. 1:33]

ABIDAN (Heb. 'father of judgment') *c.* 13 century BC. Son of Gideoni and a leader of the tribe of Benjamin, he was appointed by Moses to number the tribe of Benjamin for military service and led the contingent as they marched through the wilderness. [Num. 1:11; 2:22; 7:60-65; 10:24]

ABIEL (Heb. 'God is my father') **1.** *c.* 11 century BC. Son of Zeror of the tribe of Benjamin, he was the grandfather of King Saul and of Abner his commander. [1 Sam. 9:1; 14:51]

2. *c.* 10 century BC. The Arbathite warrior in the army of King David who was distinguished for his bravery. Also called Abialbon. [2 Sam. 23:31; 1 Chr. 11:32]

ABIEZER (Heb. 'father of help') **1.** *c.* 13 century BC. A leader of the tribe of Manasseh recorded in the census

Unlike Cain, Abel was a shepherd. Mesopotamian cylinder seal, 3rd millennium BC, showing a shepherd with his flocks and household utensils, and a winged god descending to earth.

by Moses who would be given a share in the land of Israel, after the conquest of Joshua. Also called Iezer. [Num. 26:30; Josh. 17:2; 1 Chr. 7:18]

2. *c.* 10 century BC. A warrior from Anathoth in King David's army distinguished for his bravery. He commanded a division during the ninth month of each year. [2 Sam. 23:27; 1 Chr. 11:28; 27:12]

ABIGAIL (Heb. 'father of joy') **1.** *c.* 11 century BC. Wife of Nabal and later of King David.

When Samuel died, David went into the wilderness to escape King Saul. While there he learned of a man named Nabal and sent ten men to ask him for a contribution to their support, and they were rudely turned away. After this was told to Nabal's wife Abigail, who was both beautiful and wise, she realized at once that this insult would mean an attack on her husband's life. Loading up asses with food, she slipped out without telling her husband, intercepted David and his men, and pleaded with them to accept the gift. David agreed and turned back. Abigail hastened home and that night attended a party given by Nabal. Because he got drunk she was unable to tell him what she had done until next morning. He then had a heart attack and died about ten days later.

When David heard of this death he asked Abigail to become his wife, and she agreed. David fled to Gath to escape Saul's wrath, and she went with him. When the Amalekites invaded from the south she was taken prisoner, but was rescued by David. After Saul's death on the battlefield they moved to Hebron, where Abigail bore David a son called Chileab (Daniel). [1 Sam. 25; 30; 2 Sam 2:2; 3:3; 1 Chr. 3:1]

2. *c.* 11 century BC. Sister of King David and the mother of Amasa, the commander of the army of Absalom. [2 Sam. 17:25; 1 Chr. 2:16, 17]

ABIHAIL (Heb. 'father of strength') **1.** *c.* 13 century BC. Father of Zuriel, chief of the Levite family of Merarites, who were appointed to pitch their camp on the northern side of the Tabernacle and were also given the task of carrying certain parts of the Tabernacle during the wanderings in the wilderness of the children of Israel. [Num. 3:35]

2. date unknown. The wife of Abishur, a Jerahmeelite from the tribe of Judah. [1 Chr. 2:29]

3. date unknown. The son of Huri, a leader of the tribe of Gad living in the land of Bashan, east of the river Jordan. [1 Chr. 5:14]

4. *c.* 10 century BC. Mother of Mahalath, a wife of King Rehoboam of Judah, she was the daughter of David's brother Eliab. [2 Chr. 11:18]

5. *c.* 5 century BC. Father of Esther who became queen of Persia. [Esther 2:15; 9:29]

ABIHU (Heb. 'God is father') *c.* 13 century BC. Second son of Aaron and Elisheba and nephew of Moses, Abihu was chosen to become a priest in the Tabernacle

in the wilderness. Later Abihu and his elder brother Nadab burnt forbidden incense to the Lord and died immediately. [Exod. 6:23; 24:1, 9; 28:1; Levit. 10:1, 2; Num. 3:2, 4; 26:60, 61; 1 Chr. 6:3; 24:1-2]

ABIHUD (Heb. 'father of praise') *c.* 16 century BC. Son of Bela and a grandson of Benjamin. [1 Chr. 8:3]

ABIJAH (Heb. 'God is my father') **1.** *c.* 16 century BC. A son of Becher and a grandson of Benjamin, he and his family were heads of the tribe and mighty warriors. [1 Chr. 7:8]

2. *c.* 11 century BC. Son of the prophet Samuel, he and his brother Joel were judges in Beersheba and known to take bribes and act corruptly. The elders of Israel asked Samuel to give them a king to succeed Samuel rather than let his sons rule over Israel. [1 Sam. 8:2; 1 Chr. 6:28]

3. Second king of Judah after the monarchy split, he reigned 913-11 BC. Abijah was the son and successor of Rehoboam king of Judah. His mother was Maacah the daughter of Abishalom.

Abijah claimed the whole of the divided kingdom, on behalf of the house of David. He defeated the forces of Jeroboam, king of Israel, which enabled the Judeans to expand their territory and occupy the southern hills of Ephraim, including the important religious centre of Bethel.

After a brief three-year reign Abijah died, leaving a family of fourteen wives, twenty-two sons and sixteen daughters. He was succeeded by his son Asa. Also called Abijam. [1 Kgs. 14:31; 15:1-8; 1 Chr. 3:10; 2 Chr. 11:20, 22; 12:16; 13]

4. *c.* 10 century BC. The young son of Jeroboam I, king of the northern kingdom of Israel, who fell mortally

Abigail is described as a woman of 'good understanding and beautiful'. Contemporary 8th-century ivory figure from Nimrod.

sick. Jeroboam sent his wife in disguise to the prophet Ahijah to ask whether the child would live and was told that he would die as soon as she returned to the capital city of Tirzah. Ahijah's prophesy came true and all the people of Israel mourned the child's death. [1 Kgs. 14:1-17]

5. *c.* 10 century BC. A priest in the reign of King David who was responsible for the eighth turn of service in the Tabernacle in Jerusalem. [1 Chr. 24:10]

6. *see* ABI

7. 6 century BC. A priest of Judah who returned with Zerubbabel from exile in Babylon. [Neh. 12:4, 17]

8. *c.* 5 century BC. One of the priests of Judah who signed the solemn covenant in the time of Nehemiah. [Neh. 10:7]

ABIJAM *see* ABIJAH 3.

ABIMAEL (Heb. 'God is my father') date unknown. Son of Joktan and a descendant of Shem, Noah's second son. [Gen. 10:26, 28; 1 Chr. 1:20, 22]

ABIMELECH (Heb. 'the King [God] is my father')
1. *c.* 17 century BC. King of Gerar. Abraham, en route to Egypt, passed off Sarah as his sister. But when she was taken into the king's harem, the Lord warned Abimelech in a dream to return Sarah to Abraham and Abimelech sent Sarah and Abraham on their way with precious gifts. Abimelech made a pact with Abraham concerning the well at Beer-sheba, and later made arrangements with Isaac about water and grazing rights.

Abimelech, probably a successor with the same name, had a similar experience with Isaac and his wife Rebekah, who was also passed off as his sister. [Gen. 20:2-18; 21:22-32; 26:1-30]

2. *c.* 12 century BC. The son of Gideon, victor over the Midianites, and of a Canaanite woman from Shechem referred to as his concubine. On his father's death, he made a bid to become king of that region. Shechem, the main city, had a mixed population – partly Israelites and the rest native Canaanites who had remained there after Joshua's conquest. Abimelech saw the path to power through his tie with his mother's people. The elders of Shechem agreed to support him and provided him with funds – seventy pieces of silver from the treasury of the local deity, Baal-berith (Lord of the Covenant). Abimelech used this money to hire a band of cut-throats from among the town vagrants. With these mercenaries he descended on his 70 brothers, seized them and had them killed 'upon one stone' (Judg. 9:5). The only one to escape this mass fratricide was Gideon's youngest son Jotham, who managed to hide himself.

All the leading citizens of Shechem gathered at the town's meeting-place, an oak tree next to a pillar, and proclaimed Abimelech their king. Suddenly Jotham appeared on nearby Mount Gerizim and shouted down at the throng. He told them the parable of the trees that

wanted a king. The honour was accepted only by the thorny bramble, fire from which consumed the whole forest. Jotham prophesied that this would happen with Abimelech and his supporters. Before he could be seized, Jotham again made his escape.

Abimelech ruled for three years, basing himself not in Shechem itself but in the fortified place of Arumah, a few miles away in the hills. Discontent grew up among the Shechemites, and revolt was sparked by a certain Gaal, the son of Ebed, who had come into town and had gained the confidence of the local leaders. (Gaal evidently belonged to the native Canaanite stock.)

At the instance of Zebul, the governor of the town, Abimelech sent four companies of armed men to take up positions outside the town gate. In the clash that followed, some of Gaal's followers were killed and the rest were chased back as far as the city gate.

After that encounter Zebul felt strong enough to expel Gaal and his brethren from the town. Abimelech came back next day with reinforcements to take his revenge upon the rebellious city. Two companies of soldiers fell upon the people working in the fields, while Abimelech with the third company seized the city gate to cut off their retreat. He then fought his way into the city, laid it waste and killed all the inhabitants found in it. Salt was thrown on the smouldering ruins – the symbol of complete destruction.

About a thousand people were in the 'migdal' or tower of Shechem, and took refuge in the stronghold of the temple standing in it. Unable to take this strongly fortified structure by assault, Abimelech tore a branch from a tree, told his men to follow suit, and set fire to the citadel, killing everyone in it.

He then marched against the neighbouring town of Thebez, that was presumably also involved in the revolt. The townspeople shut themselves in the fortified tower. As Abimelech approached it to set it alight, a woman hurled down part of a millstone. It fell on Abimelech's head, fatally injuring him. He ordered his young armour-bearer to kill him with his sword, lest it be said that Abimelech was slain by a woman. With their leader dead, his followers scattered and returned to their homes. 'Thus God requited the crime of Abimelech, which he committed against his father in killing his seventy brothers.' (Judg. 9:56)

The ruins of the ancient citadel of Shechem have recently been excavated at the southern entrance to the valley in which Nablus (Shechem) stands. The town of Thebez probably stood on the site of the present Arab hill-town of Tubaz. [Judg. 8, 9; 2 Sam. 11:21]

3. *c.* 11 century BC. A name used perhaps erroneously in the title of Psalm 34 for Achish, the Philistine king of Gath to whom David fled from the wrath of Saul. [1 Sam. 21:10; Ps. 34:1]

4. *see* ACHISH 1.

The modern village of Abu Gosh near Jerusalem, identified as Kiriath-jearim where the Ark was kept for three months in the house of Abinadab.

ABINADAB (Heb. 'father of nobility') **1.** *c.* 11 century BC. Villager of Kiriath-jearim and a member of the tribe of Judah in whose house the Ark was placed after the Philistines had in desperation returned it to the Israelites hoping to avoid further horrors. Abinadab kept it for three months and his son Eleazer looked after it. Two other sons, Uzzah and Ahio, drove the cart that brought the Ark to Jerusalem. [1 Sam. 7:1; 2 Sam. 6:3, 4; 1 Chr. 13]

2. *c.* 11 century BC. The second son of Jesse and a brother of David, he fought in Saul's army and witnessed the slaying of Goliath by David. [1 Sam. 16:8; 17:13; 1 Chr. 2:13]

3. *c.* 11 century BC. Son of King Saul and brother of Jonathan, he was killed with his father and brother when the Philistines defeated the Israelites on Mount Gilboa in the Galilee. [1 Sam. 31:2; 1 Chr. 10:2]

ABINOAM (Heb. 'father is good') *c.* 12 century BC. Father of Barak of the tribe of Naphtali. [Judg. 4:6, 12; 5:1, 12]

ABIRAM (Heb. 'exalted father') **1.** *c.* 13 century BC. Son of Eliab, of the tribe of Reuben, he and his brother Dathan were the leading conspirators behind the rebellion of Korah against Moses while in the wilderness. The earth opened and the plotters were swallowed up. [Num. 16:1, 12, 24, 25, 27; 26:9; Deut. 11:6]

2. *c.* 9 century BC. Eldest son of Hiel of Bethel, he died because his father rebuilt Jericho, thus invoking the curse of Joshua. [1 Kgs. 16:34]

ABISHAG *c.* 10 century BC. A beautiful young Shunammite chosen to minister to King David when he was old. After David's death, his son Adonijah asked permission to marry her, and as a result of his request King Solomon had him killed, fearing this was a threat to his throne. [1 Kgs. 1:3, 15; 2:17, 21, 22]

ABISHAI (Heb. 'father of gift') *c.* 11 century BC. Eldest son of Zeruiah, King David's sister, and the brother of David's tough commander Joab, and of Asahel. He was a daring warrior utterly loyal to David and to Joab. During David's outlaw days he went with him stealthily into the camp of King Saul at Hachilah. When they reached the sleeping king, Abishai urged David to kill him but David refused to raise his hand against the Lord's anointed. When David became king, Abishai was one of the thirty mighty men who formed David's bodyguard and was second-in-command to Joab. He aided Joab in the ruthless slaying of Abner in revenge for the death of their brother Asahel, and commanded a part of Joab's army in the victorious battle against the Ammonites who had insulted King David's messengers of goodwill. He saved the king's life when David joined his men in battle against the Philistines

Abishag the Shunammite was chosen for her beauty to minister to King David in his old age. 13th-century BC ivory figure from Megiddo.

and Ishbi-benob, the giant, tried to kill him with his great spear. In one battle Abishai is credited with having killed single-handed 300 of the enemy. Loyal to David in the civil war caused by Absalom, Abishai joined in the pursuit of Sheba son of Bichri and later helped to crush the last vestige of rebellion against David who then became king again of a united Israel. He seems to have died before Joab as his name does not appear at the death of David nor at the inauguration of his son King Solomon. (1 Sam. 26; 2 Sam. 3:30; 10:10; 16:9; 18:12; 19; 20:6; 21:17; 23:18; 1 Chr. 2:16; 11:20; 18:12; 19:11, 15]

ABISHALOM (Heb. 'father of peace') *c.* 10 century BC. Father-in-law of King Rehoboam of Judah, and the father of Maacah, the king's favourite wife. Also called Absalom and Uriel. [1 Kgs. 15:2, 10; 2 Chr. 11:20; 13:2]

ABISHUA (Heb. 'father of deliverance') **1.** *c.* 16 century BC. Son of Bela and a grandson of Benjamin. [1 Chr. 8:4]
2. date unknown. Son of Phinehas and great-grandson of Aaron, the high priest, he was an ancestor of Ezra. [1 Chr. 6:4, 5, 50; Ezra 7:5]

ABISHUR (Heb. 'father of protection') date unknown. Son of Shammai and a leader of Judah, he married Abihail and had two sons. [1 Chr. 2:28]

ABITAL (Heb. 'father of dew') *c.* 10 century BC. A wife of King David and the mother of Shephatiah, one of the six sons of David born to him in Hebron. [2 Sam. 3:4; 1 Chr. 3:3]

ABITUB (Heb. 'father of goodness') date unknown. Son of Shaharaim and a leader of the tribe of Benjamin. [1 Chr. 8:11]

ABNER (Heb. 'father of light') *c.* 11 century BC. Abner, the son of Ner, was King Saul's cousin and the able commander of his army. After Saul's death in battle, Abner retired eastward across the river Jordan with the remnant of his forces, set up his camp at Mahanaim, and there proclaimed Saul's weak son Ishbosheth as king.

Abner advanced again into the territory of Benjamin and at the Pool of Gibeon, north-west of Jerusalem, he met the army of David under his commander Joab. Abner and Joab agreed on a trial of strength between twelve picked men from either side. When all these men were killed leaving the issue still undecided, general fighting broke out in which Abner's army was routed.

In their flight, Abner himself was pursued by Asahel, Joab's youngest brother. Abner shouted to him to leave him alone: 'Why should I smite you to the ground? How then could I lift up my face to your brother Joab?' (2 Sam. 2:22) Asahel persisted and Abner was forced to kill him.

Abner became angry with Ishbosheth who accused him of misconduct with one of Saul's concubines. Dis-

illusioned with the weakling he had himself made king, Abner sent messengers to make his peace with David: 'Make your covenant with me, and behold, my hand shall be with you to bring over all Israel to you.' (2 Sam. 3:12) David made one condition, that his wife Michal, Saul's daughter, should be returned to him, and Abner forced her brother Ishbosheth to agree.

Before seeing David, Abner conferred with the leaders of the northern tribes, and agreed with them to unite the country under David. The union was sealed when Abner and twenty men went to Hebron to tell David. David gave him and his retinue a feast and then Abner went off to rally all of Israel to the banner of David.

When Joab returned from an expedition, he tried without success to turn David against Abner. Joab then sent a messenger after Abner asking him to return and killed him in revenge for Joab's brother Asahel.

David was angry and shocked when he heard the news. Abner was buried at Hebron and David ordered a public funeral for him. The king himself walked behind the coffin, wept over the grave, and fasted. All the country understood that David had had no hand in Abner's murder. [1 Sam. 14:50; 17:55-8; 20:25; 26: 13-16; 2 Sam. 2-4; 1 Chr. 26:28, 27:20]

Joab stabs Abner in the back.
Illustration from the Nuremberg
Bible, 1483.

ABRAHAM (Heb. 'father is exalted') *c.* 18-16 centuries BC. First patriarch, Abraham was the founder of the Hebrew nation. In Jewish, Christian and Moslem tradition, he emerges as a father-figure – dignified, firm in his faith, humane, respected by the local rulers wherever he went. He moves slowly and majestically across the Near Eastern world of nearly four thousand

right Old Babylonian terracotta, 19th-18th centuries BC, of a patriarchal married couple of perhaps the time of Abraham and Sarah.

years ago, from Mesopotamia to Egypt. The main setting for his story is the central hill country in the Land of Canaan promised to him and his seed by God.

Abram (as he was first called) came originally from 'Ur of the Chaldeans' (Gen. 11:28), a Sumerian city in the Euphrates valley, near the head of the Persian Gulf. With his father Terah, his wife Sarai (later Sarah) and his nephew Lot, he moved up the river till they came to rest in Haran, a trading centre in northern Aram (as Syria was then called). The family settled in this area, and here Terah died.

At Haran the Lord appeared to Abram and told him to leave for 'the land that I will show you' (Gen. 12:1) where he would make of Abram 'a great nation' (Gen. 12:2).

With Sarai and Lot he travelled to Canaan, and reached Shechem (the modern Nablus). Abram built an altar there, and another near Bethel (a little north of Jerusalem). The Lord again appeared to him and said: 'To your descendants I will give this land.' (Gen. 12:7) This promise was repeated during Abram's lifetime.

There was a famine in the land, and Abram's party continued to the southwest until they arrived in Egypt, then the granary of the region.

Sarai was a beautiful woman and Abram passed her off as his sister for fear that he might otherwise be killed because of her. Reports of her looks reached Pharaoh, who had her brought into his household, generously compensating her 'brother' with servants and livestock. The Lord intervened with plagues, and when Pharaoh learnt the truth he reproachfully returned Sarai to her husband and urged them to leave. (Later, Abram had a similar experience with Abimelech, king of Gerar, a Philistine city, near Gaza.)

They returned from Egypt to the hills north of Jerusalem. Both Abram and Lot had by this time acquired large herds of cattle, and there was strife between their herdsmen over the limited grazing. Uncle and nephew agreed to part amicably and Lot, given the choice by Abram, headed eastward to the 'Jordan valley' (Gen. 13:10), where stood the two cities of Sodom and Gomorrah. Abram himself settled in the plain of Mamre outside Hebron.

The Lord revealed to Abram that he intended to destroy the wicked cities of Sodom and Gomorrah. Abram pleaded with Him to spare the cities for the sake of the good men who might be among the inhabitants, and after some bargaining, the required minimum number of righteous men was fixed at ten. But in the end even this number was not found. Abraham knew that his compassionate pleas had not helped when he saw the smoke rising from the stricken cities.

Sodom and Gomorrah were attacked by four kings from the north, and Lot was among those taken captive. Setting out in pursuit, Abram carried out a night assault near Dan, chased the enemy to a point near Damascus,

Abraham is remembered for his covenant with God. 18th-century BC Mesopotamian bronze statuette of a worshipper kneeling before his god, originally a votive for Hammurabi.

The treaty between Abraham and Abimelech at Beer-sheba ('Well of the Swearing'), from a 14th-century French illuminated Bible.

and returned with the liberated captives. He restored the plunder to the king of Sodom, refusing to accept any of it for himself. Abram was a man of peace and this rescue of Lot was his only recorded martial exploit.

Isaac and Ishmael

As Abram and Sarai had remained without issue, she proposed that he should have a child with her Egyptian maid Hagar, who bore him a son called Ishmael. When Abram was ninety-nine and Sarai ninety, the Lord appeared to him again and said that henceforth his name would be Abraham, 'for I have made you the father of a multitude of nations' (Gen. 17:5). Sarai's name was changed to Sarah ('princess'). As a physical token of Abraham's covenant with him, the Lord instructed him to circumcise himself and all members of his household, and thereafter every male infant when he was eight days old. (The 'brith millah' – covenant of the circumcision – has been religiously observed by Jews to this day.)

When the Lord told the aged Abraham that Sarah would give birth to a son, he 'fell on his face and laughed' (Gen. 17:17). One hot day Abraham sat in the doorway of his tent at Mamre and saw three strangers approaching. He went forward to offer them hospitality. They were angels who told him once more that Sarah would bear him a son. Sarah overheard this from within the tent, and she too laughed as she was well past child-bearing age. But in due course Isaac (meaning 'he laughed') was born, as had been foretold.

Abraham gave a great feast when the infant was weaned. Sarah was stung by the mockery of Hagar and her son Ishmael, and demanded that Abraham cast them out. Being a kindly man he was greatly troubled, but the Lord told him to do as Sarah had asked, at the same time reassuring him that his descendants through Ishmael would also be a great nation. Abraham provided Hagar with a supply of bread and water and she left with the boy.

Abraham journeyed southward again, into the territory of Abimelech, the Philistine king of Gerar. Trouble over a well (a vital matter in this arid area) brought the two men together in a pact of friendship, consecrated by a solemn swearing ceremony. The place where this happened was named Beersheba (the 'Well of the Swearing').

Abraham's obedience to God was now put to an agonizing test. He was commanded to slay his beloved son Isaac at a distant mountain top as a burnt-offering to the Lord. Abraham set out on his ass, taking with him Isaac, two young servants and some firewood. On the third day they neared the place. Abraham left the two servants with the ass, and continued on foot with Isaac. On the way the puzzled lad said to his father 'Behold, the fire and the wood; but where is the lamb for a burnt offering?' (Gen. 22:7) The old man evaded the question by saying the Lord would provide the lamb.

When they reached the indicated spot Abraham built an altar, placed the bound boy upon the firewood, and took up the knife. At this dread moment the voice of an angel was heard saying: 'Do not lay your hand on the lad ... for now I know that you fear God.' (Gen. 22:12) In a nearby thicket Abraham saw a ram caught by the horns, and the animal was sacrificed instead of the boy. This episode also served to symbolize the rejection in the Hebrew faith of child-sacrifice practised by pagan cults.

When Sarah died at Hebron at the age of one hundred and twenty-seven, Abraham sought a family burying place and purchased from Ephron the Hittite the Cave of Machpelah and the field in which it stood, for four hundred shekels of silver. Here Sarah was laid to rest.

Abraham, now an aged man, concerned himself with finding a wife for Isaac. He sent for the trusted old retainer who managed his household, and confided in him that he did not want Isaac to marry a local Canaanite girl. The servant was instructed to travel to the Haran area from which Abraham had come to Canaan, and to seek a bride for Isaac among his kindred there. He returned with Rebekah, the young granddaughter of one of Abraham's brothers.

Abraham took another wife, Keturah, and had a number of children by her. He appointed Isaac the heir of his possessions, while making provision for his other children, including the sons of his concubines whom he sent to dwell further to the east in order to protect Isaac. Abraham died at the age of one hundred and seventy-five and was buried with Sarah in the Cave of Machpelah in Hebron.

Abraham greets the three angels and prepares to sacrifice Isaac. Panel from the Baptistry doors, Florence, by Lorenzo Ghiberti (1378-1455).

For Jews, the story of Abraham is of national importance, for it marks their transitional beginning as a people and their divine charter to the Land of Israel. In the religious sense, it also symbolizes the break with pagan idolatry and the commitment to monotheism.

In the New Testament, Abraham is held up as the example of the godfearing and righteous man.

Abraham is more revered by Moslems than any other biblical personage, and is known in the Koran as El Khalil, the Friend of God. The Arabs still call Hebron 'El Khalil', and the Cave of Machpelah is sacred to the Moslems as well. The Jaffa Gate in the Old City of Jerusalem, from which the road to Hebron started, is inscribed with a verse from the Koran: 'There is no God but Allah, and Abraham is beloved of Him.' [Gen. 11:26-25:10]

Arabic inscription from the Koran on the Jaffa Gate in the Old City of Jerusalem: 'There is no God but Allah, and Abraham is beloved of Him.

The Cave of Machpelah and the Oak of Mamre

The traditional Cave of Machpelah in Hebron is marked by a huge fort-like structure which was built by King Herod in the 1st century BC. Its outer walls are of great stone blocks rising to a height of more than forty feet. Several additions were made during the Byzantine, Mameluke and Ottoman periods, for this Jewish burial shrine later became holy also to Christians and Moslems. The crenellated battlements and two square corner minarets are Mameluke. The southern part of the enclosure is now a mosque. It was formerly a 12th-century Crusader church, and before that a Byzantine basilica. Six cenotaphs with embroidered silk coverings are said to stand exactly above the burial places in the cave beneath that of the patriarchs and their wives: Abraham and Sarah, Isaac and Rebekah, and Jacob and Leah. A seventh is held by some to mark the resting place of Joseph. Through a grating in the floor may be glimpsed the original cave.

There are fine examples of stained-glass windows from the 12th century AD made of the famous Hebron glass.

A mile away from Machpelah, along a road running off the Bethlehem-Hebron highway, is an old oak tree, barely alive, its branches supported by iron stakes. It has been known since the 12th century AD as Abraham's Oak or the Oak of Mamre. After leaving Lot near Bethel, Abraham 'came and dwelt by the oaks of Mamre, which are at Hebron; and there he built an altar unto the Lord' (Gen. 13:18). The oak stands in the grounds of the Russian Holy Trinity Church, monastery and hospice, built at the end of the last century. [Gen. 11-25; Isa. 41:8]

ABSALOM (Heb. '[my] father is peace') **1.** c. 10 century BC. Third son of King David.

The poignant story of Absalom concerns a remarkable king caught between his duty to crush rebellion and his love for a brilliant and wayward son.

Absalom was the third son of King David, born in Hebron while David was king of Judah. His mother was Maacah. Tall and handsome, with a flowing mane of hair, 'from the sole of his foot to the crown of his head there was no blemish in him' (2 Sam. 14:25).

He first appears as the avenger of his sister Tamar, who had been violated and then cast aside by Amnon, their half-brother and David's first-born. Absalom consoled his sister and took her into his house. He carefully waited for an opportunity, and two years later arranged a sheep-shearing feast at his country estate to which he invited all David's sons. Absalom's servants, at his instructions, killed the tipsy Amnon. All the rest of the princes hurriedly mounted their mules and returned to the palace. Absalom took refuge with his grandfather, King Talmai.

When Absalom had been in exile for three years,

The Oak of Mamre near the Machpelah, also known as Abraham's Oak, is traditionally the place where Abraham met the three angels who told him Sarah would bear a son.

Joab the commander-in-chief, who was his first cousin, persuaded the king to allow the youth to return to Jerusalem. But David, so skilful in the handling of men, was inept in dealing with the son he loved. Having let him come back, he refused to see him. Absalom nursed his resentment for two years, then forced Joab to come and see him by setting his barley field alight. He demanded that Joab arrange for him to be received by the king. David agreed to this. He raised up the son who came and bowed down before him, and kissed him fondly.

On Absalom's part, this reconciliation was more apparent than real. He strove to deflect popular favour away from the king and towards himself. He would stand at the city gates, intercept inhabitants bringing their disputes for judgment and pay them flattering attention; 'so Absalom stole the hearts of the men of Israel' (2 Sam. 15:6).

After a long period of intrigue, of which David seemed unaware, Absalom decided that the time had come to make a bid for power. On a pretext, he proceeded to Hebron with two hundred armed men, while sending secret messengers to his fellow-conspirators among the different tribes to stand ready for the signal of rebellion. In Hebron he was joined by a formidable ally – Ahithophel, David's leading counsellor and a man whose political judgment was regarded as infallible.

The choice of Hebron for the start of the revolt was a shrewd move. It was Absalom's birthplace; it had been David's original capital and the inhabitants felt neglected since he had moved to Jerusalem; it was the centre of David's own tribe of Judah; and it was within easy striking distance of Jerusalem twenty miles away.

David was taken completely by surprise. He made the painful decision to gain time by abandoning Jerusalem and fleeing eastward with his household and palace guard. Absalom entered the capital unopposed. One of his first acts, on Ahithophel's advice, was to symbolize the takeover by having intercourse with the ten concubines David had left behind to take care of the household.

There were others whom the cool-headed David had persuaded to remain behind in Jerusalem, and serve his interests in the heart of Absalom's camp. There were the two high priests Abiathar and Zadok who undertook to keep David informed by using their sons as runners. Also, there was Hushai, another of David's trusted counsellors, whose task it was to gain Absalom's confidence and counteract the guidance of Ahithophel.

Even with Jerusalem in his hands, and the country rallying behind him, Absalom's seizure of power could not be secure as long as King David was at large. Ahithophel urged immediate pursuit that same night, so that David could be caught and liquidated before he had a chance to organize a counter-thrust. Ahithophel had worked too long with David to underrate his capacities. Hushai argued in favour of greater caution. David and the veteran fighters with him, Hushai pointed out, were desperate men, and dangerous 'like a bear robbed of her cubs in the field' (2 Sam. 17:8). To engage them in a hurry would entail too great a risk for Absalom's cause. He would be well advised to recruit and organize

The Forgiveness of Absalom, by William Blake (1757-1827).

Absalom

a large army from all the tribes, and then face David with overwhelming strength.

Absalom was convinced by Hushai. David thus gained the time he needed to cross the river Jordan into Gilead, and there rebuilt his forces. Ahithophel clearly perceived that the prince to whom he had defected had made a fatal blunder and that his own career was wrecked. He went home and hanged himself.

Absalom appointed as his army commander Amasa, the son of David's sister Abigail, and therefore another first cousin. In due course their troops crossed the Jordan river into Gilead, and took up positions near Ephraim. Here they were attacked and heavily defeated by David's well-trained men, familiar with the difficult terrain of woods and ridges and skilfully commanded by Joab.

In trying to escape Absalom dashed along a forest path on a mule. His thick hair caught in the overhanging branches of a great oak, and he remained dangling in the air while his mule ran away. One of Joab's men spotted him but did not dare touch him, having heard David instructing his commanders that no harm should come to Absalom. The soldier reported what he had seen to Joab, who ruthlessly plunged three darts into the body of Absalom. He was finished off by Joab's men. In this fashion Absalom's revolt, and his dream of power, came to an abrupt and bloody end.

During the battle, David had remained behind in the town of Mahanaim. Runners reached him with the tidings of victory, and his first question was for the safety of Absalom. When told that the young man was dead, he was overcome with grief, crying out repeatedly, 'O my son Absalom, my son, my son Absalom! Would I had died instead of you, O Absalom, my son, my son!' (2 Sam. 18:33) David's throne had been saved, but at a terrible personal price. [2 Sam. 3:3; 13-19; 1 Chr. 3:2]
2. *see* ABISHALOM

Achan stealing loot from the conquered city of Jericho, and the stoning of Achan, from Queen Mary's Psalter.

ACHAN (Heb. 'trouble-maker') *c.* 13 century BC. Son of Carmi and a member of the tribe of Judah. After Joshua had conquered the city of Jericho with trumpets and the shouts of the Israelites, he forbade the people to touch any of the booty but Achan disobeyed and secretly stole some of the loot. During the next battle, this time against the city of Ai, Joshua's men were routed and thirty-six of them killed. When Joshua appealed to God to tell him what he had done wrong, the wrathful Lord answered him, 'Israel has sinned; ... they have taken some of the devoted things ...' (Josh. 7:11). Joshua then assembled the twelve tribes, lots were cast to find out the guilty family. The tribe of Judah was singled out and Joshua went through them family by family until he came to Achan, who confessed that he had stolen a costly Babylonian garment and large amounts of silver and gold which he had hidden in his tent. Joshua sent his men to retrieve the stolen goods

Tradition has attached the name 'Tomb of Absalom' to this funnel-shaped Herodian edifice of the Second Temple period.

and they were spread before the Lord. Then Achan, his entire family and all his possessions, including his animals and the stolen booty were taken into the valley of Achor. 'And all Israel stoned him with stones; they burned them with fire, and stoned them with stones ... then the Lord turned from his burning anger.' (Josh. 7:25, 26) Also called Achar. [Josh. 7; 1 Chr. 2:7]

ACHAR *see* ACHAN

ACHBOR (Heb. 'mouse') **1.** date unknown. Father of Baal-hanan, one of the first kings of Edom. [Gen. 36:38, 39; 1 Chr. 1:49]

2. *c.* 7 century BC. Father of Elnathan, an officer of King Jehoiakim sent to Egypt to seize the prophet Uriah. [Jer. 26:22; 36:12]

3. *see* ABDON **4.**

ACHISH (Philistine 'the king gave') **1.** *c.* 11 century BC. The Philistine king of Gath with whom David twice took refuge. The first time he arrived alone and feigned madness for fear of being recognized. Later, David and his outlaw band were welcomed by Achish as supposed enemies of the Israelite king.

Achish made David governor of Ziklag on the border of the desert. Using this town as a base, David attacked tribes that were hostile to Israel, pretending to Achish that he was raiding towns in Judah.

The Philistines gathered their armies and marched against Israel. When the other Philistine princes saw David and his men among the soldiers of Achish, they protested that the Hebrews might defect in the battle. Achish tried to convince them that David could be trusted, but had to yield to the pressure of his allies. He apologetically asked David to return. Also called Abimelech. [1 Sam. 21:10; 27-29; Ps. 34:1]

2. *c.* 10 century BC. Son of Maoch, king of Gath in the reign of King Solomon, with whom two of Shimei's slaves sought refuge. [1 Kgs. 2:39, 40]

ACHSAH (Heb. 'anklet') *c.* 13 century BC. Achsah was the daughter of Caleb, who settled in Hebron and gave her in marriage to Othniel for capturing the neighbouring city of Debir. The shrewd Achsah got her father to add to her dowry of land 'the upper springs and the lower springs' (Josh. 15:19). [Josh. 15:16-19; Judg. 1:12-14; 1 Chr. 2:49]

ADAH (Heb. 'ornament') **1.** date unknown. Wife of Lamech and mother of Jabal and Jubal. [Gen. 4:19, 23]

2. *c.* 16 century BC. A wife of Esau, she was the daughter of Elon the Hittite. Also called Basemath. [Gen. 26:34; 36:2, 4, 10, 16]

ADAIAH (Heb. 'adorned by God') **1.** date unknown. Son of Shimei and a leader of the tribe of Benjamin living in Jerusalem. [1 Chr. 8:21]

2. date unknown. An ancestor of Maaseiah, one of the men of Judah living in Jerusalem after the return from exile in Babylon. [Neh. 11:5]

3. *see* IDDO **3.**

4. *c.* 9 century BC. Father of Maaseiah, one of the army commanders of Judah sent to overthrow Queen Athaliah and crown Joash as king. [2 Chr. 23:1]

5. *c.* 7 century BC. Father of Jedidah, the wife of King Amon of Judah and the mother of King Josiah. [2 Kgs. 22:1]

6. *c.* 5 century BC. Son of Jeroham, he was one of the first priests to serve in the Temple in Jerusalem after the return from exile in Babylon. [1 Chr. 9:12; Neh. 11:12]

7. 5 century BC. A descendant of Bani who divorced his non-Jewish wife in the time of Ezra. [Ezra 10:29]

8. 5 century BC. A son of Binnui who divorced his non-Jewish wife in the time of Ezra. [Ezra 10:39]

ADALIA (Pers. 'respectable') *c.* 5 century BC. One of the ten sons of Haman who plotted to kill all the Jews of Persia in the reign of King Ahasuerus. The plot was discovered and Haman and his sons were executed. [Esther 9:8]

ADAM (Heb. 'man') date unknown. The first human being.

In five days God created day and night; heaven, earth and the seas; sun, moon and stars; plants, fish and birds. On the sixth day He created the beasts, and then Man in His own image, male and female. The Lord told them to be fruitful and multiply, and gave them dominion over all living things. In this fashion, Chapter 1 of the Book of Genesis tells the story of creation. Man here is the human species, and not a particular individual.

In the second chapter of Genesis there is a different account of the Creation, more vivid and detailed. Though it appears after Chapter 1, this version is of earlier origin. It probably derives from the J (Jehovistic) Document, whereas Chapter 1 may be attributed to the P (priestly) Document written several centuries later by priestly writers for whom the Almighty had become a more abstract concept. In the earlier version the creation of Man is overlaid with the story of a particular man, who in Genesis 3:17 is called Adam for the first time. He has a wife called Eve 'because she was the mother of all living' (Gen. 3:20). (Eve in Hebrew is Chava, which means 'life'.)

According to this earlier and more primitive account, 'the Lord God formed man of dust from the ground, and breathed into his nostrils the breath of life' (Gen. 2:7). God put Adam in the Garden of Eden and created Eve out of one of Adam's ribs to be a helpmeet for him. Adam had been warned not to eat of the fruit of the tree of knowledge of good and evil, but the serpent tempted Eve to try the fruit and she gave some to Adam too. As a result they became ashamed of their nakedness, covered it with fig-leaves and hid from the Lord.

left Adam as lord of creation before the Fall. Panel from an ivory diptych, *c.* 400.

The Garden of Eden: illumination by Pol de Limbourg from the *Très Riches Heures* of the Duc de Berry, early 15th century.

Then God cursed the serpent saying '... upon your belly you shall go, and dust you shall eat all the days of your life' (Gen. 3:14). Human beings and serpents would henceforth be enemies. To Eve God said that she would bring forth children in sorrow, and her husband would rule over her. To Adam He said, '... cursed is the ground because of you. ... In the sweat of your face you shall eat bread till you return to the ground; ... you are dust, and to dust you shall return.' (Gen. 3:17-19) Lest they eat also of the tree of life and become immortal, Adam and Eve were driven forth from Eden and their return was barred by cherubim and a flaming sword.

The Bible states that the Garden was 'in Eden in the east' (Gen. 2:8) and the river that flowed from it parted into four: Pishon, Gihon, Tigris and Euphrates. This would place Eden somewhere in Mesopotamia – the ancient Babylonia and the modern Iraq.

After the expulsion, Adam and Eve had three sons – Cain and Abel, and much later, after Abel's murder, Seth. Adam's age when he died is given as nine hundred and thirty years. [Gen. 1-4]

Reflections on Adam and Eve

The origin of Adam's name has intrigued scholars. The account in Genesis stresses that man was formed out of the earth and would return to it. This bears out the suggestion that the Hebrew word for man, *adam*, was

God creating Adam from a lump of clay.
Illustration from William Caxton's Bible,
second half of 15th century.

derived from the Hebrew word for earth, 'adama'. The
root of both words may be connected with the Hebrew
word for 'red' – 'adom'. That would imply a reddish
soil or clay in the area where Adam was created.

The belief that the first man was created out of clay
was by no means confined to Hebrew mythology. There
were similar stories among the ancient Babylonians,
Egyptians and Greeks, and parallel folk legends among
primitive tribes in many other parts of the world, including Australian aborigines, Maoris, Africans, American
Indians and Eskimos.

Adam and Eve are the prototype of the close bond
between husband and wife: 'Then the man said, "This
at last is bone of my bones and flesh of my flesh ...".
Therefore a man leaves his father and his mother and
cleaves unto his wife, and they become one flesh.' (Gen.
2:23, 24) This emphasis on the marriage tie was remarkable in ancient times, for men were permitted to take
more than one wife, and to have children by concubines.

Granting that primal man evolved from lower species
millions of years ago, the legend of Adam and Eve continues to serve as a striking parable of the human condition. Paradise is lost; men must wrest a living by their
toil, women bear children in pain, and the grave awaits
each mortal being; all men are brothers, for Adam is
their common forefather; and all men are equal, for
they are all created in the image of God. [Gen. 2-5]

ADBEEL (Heb. 'God established') *c.* 17 century BC.
Son of Ishmael and a grandson of Abraham, he was
leader of a desert tribe. [Gen. 25:13; 1 Chr. 1:29]

ADDAN 6 century BC. A leader of Judah who returned
with Zerubbabel from exile in Babylon but could not
trace his ancestry and therefore could not prove that he
was a Jew. Also called Addon. [Ezra 2:59; Neh. 7:61]
ADDAR *see* ARD 2.
ADDON *see* ADDAN
ADIEL (Heb. 'ornament of God') **1.** date unknown.
Ancestor of Adaiah, one of the chief priests in the
Temple after the return from Babylon. [1 Chr. 9:12]
2. *c.* 11 century BC. Father of Azmaveth, the officer in
charge of King David's treasuries. [1 Chr. 27:25]
3. *c.* 8 century BC. One of the leaders of Simeon who
drove out the inhabitants from the rich Gedor valley
and settled there in the reign of King Hezekiah. [1 Chr.
4:36]
ADIN (Heb. 'delicate') **1.** date unknown. Ancestor of a
family of Judah who returned with Zerubbabel from
exile in Babylon. [Ezra 2:15; 8:6; Neh. 7:20]
2. 5 century BC. A leader of Judah who signed the
solemn covenant in the time of Nehemiah. [Neh. 10:16]
ADINA (Heb. 'delicate') *c.* 10 century BC. A warrior
from the tribe of Reuben in King David's army who
was distinguished for his bravery. [1 Chr. 11:42]
ADLAI (Heb. 'God's justice') *c.* 10 century BC. Father
of Shaphat, King David's official who was in charge of
the royal herds that fed in the valley. [1 Chr. 27:29]
ADMATHA (Pers. 'military commander') 5 century
BC. One of the seven chief princes of Persia whom King
Ahasuerus consulted when he wished to punish Queen
Vashti for disobeying his orders. [Esther 1:14]
ADNA (Heb. 'pleasure') **1.** 5 century BC. A descendant
of Pahath-moab who divorced his non-Jewish wife in
the time of Ezra. [Ezra 10:30]
2. 5 century BC. Head of a priestly family descended
from Harim in the time of Nehemiah. [Neh. 12:15]
ADNAH (Heb. 'pleasure') **1.** *c.* 11 century BC. A warrior
of the tribe of Manasseh who deserted from King Saul's
army and rallied to David at Ziklag. [1 Chr. 12:20]
2. *c.* 10 century BC. Commander of a large contingent in
the army of King Jehoshaphat of Judah. [2 Chr. 17:14]
ADONIJAH (Heb. 'my Lord is God') **1.** *c.* 10 century
BC. Fourth son of David, he was born in Hebron to
David and Haggith. When David grew old, Adonijah,
then the eldest remaining son, decided to take matters
into his own hands and have himself proclaimed king.
He conferred with Joab, David's commander-in-chief,
and with one of the high priests, Abiathar. They gave
him their support, and 'he prepared for himself chariots
and horsemen, and fifty men to run before him' (1 Kgs.
1:5).

Adonijah invited his brothers (except Solomon) and
the city notables to a feast at the spring of En-rogel,
down in the valley of Kidron outside the city walls.
Here he performed ceremonial sacrifices by the sacred
stone called the Serpent's Stone.

The opposition, led by Nathan the prophet, reacted swiftly. Bathsheba the queen was sent by Nathan to go into David's bedchamber and tell him what Adonijah was doing. She also reminded the king he had promised the throne to her son Solomon. Nathan then appeared and supported Bathsheba.

David decided to abdicate immediately in favour of Solomon and instructed Zadok the other high priest, Nathan and Benaiah the commander of the palace guard, to take Solomon on the king's own mule to the spring of Gihon, also in the valley of Kidron, and in front of the Jerusalem citizens to anoint him king: 'then blow the trumpet, and say, Long live King Solomon!' (1 Kgs. 1:34). When the noise of the crowd rejoicing at Solomon's coronation reached Adonijah's feast, and the company learned that Solomon had already replaced David as king, the guests hurriedly returned to their homes. Adonijah sought sanctuary at the altar and was spared at that time by Solomon.

After David had died and Solomon was firmly established on the throne, Adonijah asked to see Bathsheba. 'And she said, "Do you come peaceably?" He said, "Peaceably".' (1 Kgs. 2:13) He then asked her if she would intervene with her son King Solomon and ask him if he would allow Adonijah to marry Abishag the young Shunammite girl who had looked after David in his old age. Bathsheba agreed to do this. When she entered the royal chamber, Solomon treated her with great deference and seated her to the right of his throne.

But when she put forward Adonijah's request, Solomon reacted sharply. Adonijah might as well have asked for the throne, he said. (To take the wife or concubine of a dead or deposed king symbolized a claim to the succession.) King Solomon immediately sent for Benaiah and had his eldest half-brother put to death. [2 Sam. 3:4; 1 Kgs. 1-2]

2. c. 9 century BC. A Levite sent by King Jehoshaphat to teach the Law of God in the cities of Judah. [2 Chr. 17:8]

3. 5 century BC. One of the leaders of Judah in the days of Nehemiah who signed the solemn covenant to observe the Laws of God. [Neh. 10:16]

ADONIKAM (Heb. 'the Lord raised [for help]') date unknown. The ancestor of a large family that returned with Zerubbabel to Judah from exile in Babylon. [Ezra 2:13; 8:13; Neh. 7:18]

ADONIRAM (Heb. 'the Lord is exalted') c. 10 century BC. The son of Abda, he was given the unpopular task of levying the forced labour necessary for the royal building programmes. He had been appointed to this task by David and retained by Solomon. By the time Solomon died and his son Rehoboam succeeded him, the population was weary with the constant exactions. The northern tribes revolted against the new king and in the disturbances Adoniram was stoned to death. Sometimes called Adoram and Hadoram. [2 Sam. 20:24; 1 Kgs. 4:6; 5:14; 12:18, 19; 2 Chr. 10:18]

ADONIZEDEK (Heb. 'Lord of righteousness') c. 13 century BC. The king of Jerusalem who formed a military alliance with the rulers of Hebron and the foothill towns of Lachish, Eglon and Jarmuth, to attack the town of Gibeon 'for it has made peace with Joshua and with the people of Israel' (Josh. 10:4). After their defeat by Joshua, Adonizedek and the other four kings hid themselves in a cave but were discovered and put to death. Their bodies were hung on trees until sunset, when they were cut down and buried in the same cave. [Josh. 10]

ADORAM see ADONIRAM

ADRAMMELECH 1. date unknown. One of the gods of the Sepharvaim, a tribe settled by the Assyrians in Samaria after the exile of the people of Israel. Children were sacrificed to this god. [2 Kgs. 17:31]

2. c. 7 century BC. He and his brother Sharezer murdered their father Sennacherib, king of Assyria, while he was at prayer in the house of Nisroch, his god. The two sons escaped to Armenia and their brother Esarhaddon became king in 680 BC. [2 Kgs. 19:37; Isa. 37:38]

ADRIEL (Heb. 'flock of God') c. 10 century BC. Son of Barzillai and the husband of King Saul's daughter

Adonijah, fleeing from Solomon, clutched the horns of the altar. Limestone altar with 'horns' from Solomon's time, found at Megiddo.

Merab. Their five sons were executed by the Gibeonites in revenge for Saul's murder of their people. [1 Sam. 18:19; 2 Sam. 21:8]

AGAG *c.* 11 century BC. King of Amalek who was defeated in battle by King Saul. Saul wanted to spare Agag alive but the prophet Samuel 'hewed Agag in pieces' (1 Sam. 15:33) as retribution for Agag's brutality. [1 Sam. 15:8, 9, 32, 33]

AGEE (Heb. 'fugitive') *c.* 10 century BC. The father of Shammah the Hararite warrior of King David who stood his ground and killed the Philistines when everyone else had fled. [2 Sam. 23:11]

AGUR (Heb. 'gatherer') date unknown. The son of Jakeh who spoke a series of prophecies, collected in the Book of Proverbs, to Ithiel and Ucal. [Prov. 30]

AHAB (Heb. 'father's brother') **1.** Seventh king of Israel after the monarchy split, he reigned 874-53 BC. In his twenty-two years on the throne of Israel, Ahab consolidated the dynasty founded in the northern kingdom by his father Omri. He further developed the lines of policy Omri had laid down: co-existence with the southern Hebrew kingdom of Judah; partnership with the Phoenicians on the seaboard; containment of Aram-Damascus to the north-east; and the fostering of commerce and construction at home. Ahab would thus have stood high in the roster of Israelite kings, but for the one aspect of his rule which the biblical chroniclers refused to condone – religious laxity. For them, the central theme in Ahab's record was the fierce onslaught of the prophet Elijah against the alien cult fostered by his queen, Jezebel. For that reason, he is sternly dismissed as having done '... more to provoke the Lord, the God of Israel, to anger than all the kings of Israel who were before him' (1 Kgs. 16:33).

The Phoenicians inhabited the coastal plain which is today Lebanon, with their two major port cities of Sidon and Tyre. They were the most enterprising traders and seafarers in the Mediterranean, with a relatively high level of affluence and skills. Hiram, king of Tyre, had been the friend and business partner of David and Solomon, and Omri had renewed these ties with the contemporary Phoenician ruler Ethbaal. The alliance was cemented by Ahab's marriage to Ethbaal's daughter Jezebel.

She seems to have been a strong-willed woman who dominated her husband and used her position at the Samarian court to promote the Phoenician culture and religion. In the midst of this Hebrew hill-nation, dedicated to the exclusive worship of a single invisible God, there sprang up the cults of the Phoenician Baal, Melkart and the fertility goddess Ashtoreth (Astarte). At the palace Jezebel maintained as her pensioners a huge corps of some four hundred 'prophets of Baal' in the service of these alien creeds. The Bible suggests that Ahab did not merely tolerate Jezebel's activities, but

Black basalt stele of King Mesha of Moab: the inscription relates that Mesha freed Moab from domination by Israel.

took an active part in them: 'He erected an altar for Baal in the house of Baal, which he built in Samaria.' (1 Kgs. 16:32)

Ahab and Elijah

The revulsion of the faithful was focused by the austere and outspoken prophetic figure of Elijah the Tishbite, from the land of Gilead across the Jordan river. He confronted the king and sternly announced that the wrathful Lord would smite Israel with a prolonged drought: '... there shall be neither dew nor rain these years' (1 Kgs. 17:1). The prophet then escaped across the river.

Two years later, Elijah set out again to see the king. Ahab went out to meet him and greeted him with the words 'Is it you, you troubler of Israel?' (1 Kgs. 18:17) Elijah retorted that it was the royal house that troubled Israel, because they had forsaken the Lord and followed false gods. Elijah demanded an encounter with the prophets of Baal on Mount Carmel in the presence of

Israelite storehouse from the
9th century BC — the time of King Ahab —
in the upper city of Hazor.

south. Adjoining the palace grounds at Jezreel was a fine vineyard which the king was anxious to buy or exchange for another elsewhere. The owner, Naboth, was unwilling to part with it as it had been a family inheritance for a long time. Ahab sulked with frustration: 'And he lay down on his bed, and turned away his face, and would eat no food.' (1 Kgs. 21:4) Jezebel arranged for Naboth to be convicted of blasphemy and stoned to death. The ruler then became the legal owner of the property.

No sooner had Ahab taken possession of the vineyard than Elijah descended upon him and cried out: 'Have you killed, and also taken possession? ... In the place where dogs licked up the blood of Naboth shall dogs lick your own blood.' (1 Kgs. 21:19) The prophet then pronounced a curse on Ahab and all his house, predicting that they would be destroyed. The frightened king tore his clothes, dressed himself in sackcloth and fasted. The Lord noted that he had humbled himself in repentance and postponed the doom of the dynasty to Ahab's son and successor.

A black basalt stele (inscribed monument) was discovered a century ago in southern Jordan. It claims that Mesha king of Moab threw off the yoke of Israel after having paid an annual tribute to Omri and Ahab of a 'hundred thousand lambs, and the wool of a hundred thousand rams' (2 Kgs. 3:4). It was presumably to help control Moab that Jericho was refortified in Ahab's reign, after having remained an empty ruin since its destruction by Joshua.

Like his father, Ahab was an energetic builder. He developed the new hill capital of Samaria, founded by Omri. The bible mentions that he built an 'ivory house'. The excavations at Samaria have in fact produced

the people. The king complied. In the famous confrontation that then took place, the foreign priests were confounded and put to death by Elijah. After this crushing victory for the forces of monotheism, the drought broke in a great storm that came sweeping in from the sea. Ahab drove back in his chariot through the pouring rain, with the exulting prophet running ahead of him part of the way with his cloak tucked up above his knees. When Jezebel heard from Ahab what had happened she furiously swore to have Elijah killed. But the prophet once more made his escape.

Jezebel's evil influence over the king was vividly shown in the story of Naboth's vineyard. Ahab had established his winter quarters at Jezreel, a town in the valley of that name, where the climate was milder than at Samaria up in the hills some twenty-five miles to the

The forces of Assyria began to make themselves felt in the reign of Ahab. 7th-century BC Assyrian relief from Nimrod showing Assyrian forces attacking a village.

hundreds of ivory carvings that were inlaid in furniture, probably according to the Phoenician fashion of the time. Ahab extended the fortifications of strategic strongholds such as those at Hazor in the eastern Galilee and Megiddo in the Jezreel valley. The extensive stables for chariot and cavalry horses excavated at Megiddo date from his time.

The Syrian War

Ahab buttressed the alliance with Judah by marrying his daughter Athalia to Jehoram, the son and heir of King Jehoshaphat of Judah. Nevertheless, Ahab's forces were unable to block a fresh advance by King Ben-hadad II of Aram-Damascus (Syria), Israel's most oppressive enemy in that period. The Syrian army marched right to the gates of Samaria and laid siege to it. Ahab at first tried to appease Ben-hadad, then rejected his arrogant demands, saying: 'Let not him that girds on his armour boast himself as he that puts it off.' (1 Kgs. 20:11) Ahab launched a surprise attack from the city in the noonday heat. The Syrians were routed, and their king escaped on the back of a chariot horse.

Ben-hadad mustered a fresh army, and took up positions near the town of Aphek on the level ground of the Golan plateau east of the Sea of Galilee. His advisers had pointed out to him that 'their gods are gods of the hills, and so they were stronger than we; but let us fight against them in the plain, and surely we shall be stronger than they.' (1 Kgs. 20:23) This seemed sound military tactics, for the Arameans could deploy their mounted troops against the Israelite highlanders, once they were lured out of their native hills into open country. But in the pitched battle that followed the forces of Aram were again defeated. King Ben-hadad begged for his life and Ahab agreed to spare him on condition that he gave back the occupied Israelite towns and granted Israel trading rights in the bazaars of Damascus. Ahab was plunged into gloom when an unknown prophet told him he would forfeit his life as a consequence of this act of clemency.

After the king of Aram was spared, the Bible states laconically that 'For three years Syria and Israel continued without war.' (1 Kgs. 22:1) The probable explanation for this truce was that both nations were threatened by the new and formidable imperial power of Assyria, pressing down from the north. In the 'monolith inscription' which survives from the sixth year of the reign of Shalmaneser III, king of Assyria, (853 BC) he boasts of a victory against a league of twelve kings. Among them were both the king of Damascus and 'Ahab the Israelite', who was said to have brought two thousand chariots and ten thousand foot soldiers into the combined army. In fact, the common front did succeed in halting the Assyrian advance for the time being.

When the Assyrian danger receded, King Jehosha-

phat of Judah joined forces with Ahab in an expedition to retake the Israelite town of Ramoth-gilead in the land of Gilead, east of the Jordan river. Ben-hadad of Damascus had either not returned this area as he had promised when his life was spared, or he had regained it later.

With the two Hebrew monarchs sitting on thrones at the threshing floor of Samaria, the whole company of prophets appeared before them and assured them of success in the coming battle. Only one prophet was missing, Micaiah, whose unsparing utterances Ahab found hard to tolerate. Prodded by Jehoshaphat, Ahab sent for Micaiah as well. At first the prophet joined in the chorus of encouragement, but when pressed he courageously pronounced his true prediction, which was one of disaster for Ahab. The king ordered the dour pessimist to be flung into jail and kept on bread and water until his own return from the war.

All the same, Ahab's confidence was shaken. Jehoshaphat entered the battle in his royal armour, but Ahab himself was disguised in order to avoid attention. The ruse was effective for a while. The Syrian leader had commanded his troops to concentrate on the king of Israel and at first they mistook Jehoshaphat for their quarry until the Judean king gave his own battle cry. Unfortunately for Ahab, a stray arrow pierced the joint in his armour at the armpit. He ordered his charioteer to withdraw, but the battle was too fierce, and he was propped upright in the chariot facing the enemy until he died at sunset in a pool of blood. When the word spread among his followers they broke off the engagement and retreated back across the river and up to Samaria. Here Ahab was buried, 'And they washed the chariot by the pool of Samaria, and the dogs licked up his blood.' (1 Kgs. 22:38) He was succeeded by his son Ahaziah. [1 Kgs. 16-22; 2 Chr. 18]

Ivory lion of the 9th century BC found at Samaria, probably from inlaid furniture for King Ahab's 'ivory house'.

The Wrath of Ahasuerus, by the Dutch painter Jan Steen (1625/6-79).

Archaeological excavations in 1932 at Samaria brought to light remains of buildings constructed by Kings Omri and Ahab and their successors. On the summit bounded by steep slopes on three sides, Omri built a rectangular citadel, protected by a wall of square stones laid with great skill on levelled beds in the rock. The base courses of sections of this wall are well preserved. There are also remains of the lower city which was built at the same time on the more gradual southern slope of the site. In Ahab's time, or possibly some years later, a city wall of great thickness was thrown up, and sections of this may also be seen today.

Among the finds in the citadel were the carved ivories from Ahab's 'ivory house', some bearing inscriptions in ancient Hebrew script; and scores of ostraca with Hebrew writing discovered in the ruins of what was probably the royal records office. The large well-plastered reservoir found by the archaeologists may have been the 'pool of Samaria' in which was 'washed the chariot' of Ahab after his death on the battlefield at Ramoth-gilead. (1 Kgs. 22:38)
2. *c.* 6 century BC. Son of Kolaiah, he was a false prophet of Judah in the time of Jeremiah. [Jer. 29:21, 22]
AHARAH *see* EHI
AHARHEL date unknown. Son of Harum and a leader of the tribe of Judah. [1 Chr. 4:8]
AHASBAI *see* UR

AHASUERUS (Pers. 'mighty', 'eye of man') **1.** *c.* 6 century BC. Father of King Darius of Persia. [Dan. 9:1]
2. 5 century BC. King of Persia (Xerxes I) (486-65 BC), who in the third year of his reign gathered together all the leading men of his empire at Shushan (Susa), the capital. Under the influence of wine, Ahasuerus sent his court chamberlains to fetch Queen Vashti, so that her beauty could be displayed to the guests. She refused to come and the angry king, after consultation with his chief counsellors, issued a decree banning Vashti from his presence. He then searched his kingdom for a suitable queen to replace her and chose Esther, the adopted daughter of Mordecai, a Jewish court official.

Esther thwarted the evil designs of Haman the chief minister to kill all the Jews in the kingdom. Ahasuerus had Haman and his sons hanged and promoted Mordecai to chief minister. [Ezra 4:6; Esther 1-3; 6-10]
AHAZ (Heb. 'he grasped') **1.** date unknown. One of the four sons of Micah of the tribe of Benjamin and a descendant of King Saul. [1 Chr. 8:35, 36; 9:41, 42]
2. Twelfth king of Judah after the monarchy split, he reigned 736-16 BC. At the age of twenty, Ahaz succeeded his father Jotham to the throne of Judah.

In the reign of his illustrious grandfather Uzziah, the kingdom had reached the peak of its expansion and strength. Under Ahaz, Judah again declined rapidly and its borders shrank.

43

Edom, the vassal desert kingdom to the south, successfully revolted. The Philistines regained their lost territory in the coastal plain, and occupied part of the foothills. The Bible attributes these reverses to Ahaz's impiety. He indulged in pagan cults and revived the primitive custom of child sacrifice that was especially associated with the valley (gei) of Hinnom (Gehenna) skirting Jerusalem. He 'even burned his son as an offering, according to the abominable practices of the nations whom the Lord drove out. . . . And he sacrificed and burned incense on the high places, and on the hills, and under every green tree.' (2 Kgs. 16:3, 4)

The forces of Pekah, king of Israel, and Rezin, king of Aram-Damascus (Syria), invaded Judah, that had refused to join their alliance against the Assyrian threat. They failed to take Jerusalem or to depose Ahaz, but delivered a crippling military blow to Judah and withdrew, carrying with them a great deal of plunder and a number of captives.

Against a strong warning from his adviser, the great prophet Isaiah, Ahaz then decided to appeal for help to the king of Assyria. He sent messengers with gifts to Tiglath-pileser III saying: 'I am your servant and your son. Come up, and rescue me from the hand of the king of Syria and from the hand of the king of Israel, who are attacking me.' (2 Kgs. 16:7) The Assyrians were in no need of this invitation in pursuing their strategy of conquest. In the period 734-2 BC, they smashed the coalition opposing them, occupied Damascus and a large part of the territory of Israel, and thrust down the coastal plain as far as Gaza. Judah was left isolated and maintained itself intact only by submission to the Assyrians and the payment of tribute. In an inscription the Assyrian monarch lists Ahaz among the local kings in the area who delivered to him tribute in the form of 'gold, silver, tin, iron, lead . . . gorgeous raiment, the purple apparel of their land.' The latter may be a reference to the famous Tyrian purple extracted from a species of periwinkle on the seacoast, chiefly at the Israelite centre of Dor.

The Book of Kings records that Ahaz went to Damascus to pay his respects to his Assyrian overlord. He was so impressed with an altar he saw there that he sent back detailed instructions to Uriah, the priest of the Temple in Jerusalem, to have an exact replica made. When he returned Ahaz moved to another position the bronze altar erected by Solomon and installed the new one in its place. He may possibly have meant this as a gesture to the Assyrians.

After a reign of twenty years, Ahaz died and was buried in Jerusalem, but not in the royal tombs. He was succeeded by his son Hezekiah, one of the greatest of the Judean kings. [2 Kgs. 15:38; 16:1-20; 17:1; 18:1; 20:11; 23:12; 1 Chr. 3:13; 2 Chr. 27:9; 28:1-27; 29:19; Isa. 1:1; 7:1-12; 14:28; 38:8; Hos. 1:1; Mic. 1:1]

AHAZIAH (Heb. 'God sustains') **1.** Eighth king of Israel after the monarchy split, he reigned 853-2 BC. After the death of King Ahab, his eldest son Ahaziah, son of Jezebel, succeeded him briefly on the throne of Israel in Samaria. He distinguished himself only by falling through the latticework of an upper room, seriously injuring himself. He sent messengers to the shrine of the Philistine god Baal-zebub (lord of the flies) at Ekron on the coastal plain to find out whether he would recover. The prophet Elijah intercepted the messengers and angrily asked them if there was no God in Israel that they go seeking the god of Ekron? He predicted that their master would not get up again from his bed.

In a rage the king despatched a company of fifty soldiers to seize the prophet but they were killed by fire from heaven. The same thing happened to a second unit. Elijah returned to the palace with the third unit and personally repeated his dire prophesy to the king, who died soon after.

Ahaziah is also mentioned as having been rebuffed by King Jehoshaphat of Judah when he proposed that his men join the Judean sailors on the vessels plying between Ezion-geber and Ophir. This was a transparent attempt to gain a footing in the southern trade route.

Ahaziah was succeeded by his brother Jehoram. [1 Kgs. 22:51; 2 Kgs. 1; 2 Chr. 20:35, 37]

2. Sixth king of Judah after the monarchy split, he reigned in 841 BC. Ahaziah was the youngest son of King Jehoram of Judah and his queen Athaliah, daughter of King Ahab of Israel. His elder brothers were killed by Philistine and nomad raiders.

At the time that Ahaziah succeeded his father, Judah and Israel were allies in a war against the kingdom of Aram (Syria) with its capital at Damascus. Ahaziah joined King Jehoram of Israel at the battlefront, which was Ramoth-gilead east of the Jordan river. Jehoram was wounded and returned to his winter palace at Jezreel accompanied by Ahaziah. The Israelite commander Jehu staged a coup, and raced back to Jezreel, where the two kings came out to meet him unaware of the danger. Jehu killed Jehoram and then pursued Ahaziah along the Jezreel valley. The Book of Kings says that Ahaziah was wounded in this chase and took refuge in the fortress at Megiddo where he died. Chronicles says that he was caught in Samaria, brought before Jehu and slain. His body was taken to Jerusalem for burial. He had been king for only one year; the throne was now seized by his mother Queen Athaliah. Also called Jehoahaz. [2 Kgs. 8:24-29; 9:16-29; 10:13; 11:1, 2; 12:18; 13:1; 14:13; 1 Chr. 3:11; 2 Chr. 22]

AHBAN (Heb. 'brother of the intelligent') date unknown. The elder son of Abishur, a leader of the tribe of Judah, and his wife Abihail. [1 Chr. 2:29]

AHER (Heb. 'another') date unknown. A leader of the tribe of Benjamin. [1 Chr. 7:12]

AHI (Heb. 'my brother') *c.* 8 century BC. Son of Abdiel and a leader of the tribe of Gad, living east of the river Jordan. [1 Chr. 5:15]

AHIAH (Heb. 'God is my brother') 5 century BC. A leader of Judah who signed the solemn covenant in the time of Nehemiah. [Neh. 10:26]

AHIAM (Heb. 'uncle') *c.* 10 century BC. Son of Sachar the Hararite and a warrior in the army of King David distinguished for his bravery. [2 Sam. 23:33; 1 Chr. 11:35]

AHIAN (Heb. 'a [young] brother') date unknown. Son of Shemida and a leader of the tribe of Manasseh. [1 Chr. 7:19]

AHIEZER (Heb. 'brother of help') **1.** *c.* 13 century BC. Son of Ammishaddai, he was the leader of the tribe of Dan chosen by Moses to take a census and led his contingent in the army of the children of Israel. [Num. 1:12; 2:25; 7:66-71; 10:25]

2. *c.* 11 century BC. An ambidextrous archer of the tribe of Benjamin who deserted from King Saul's army and joined David at Ziklag. [1 Chr. 12:1-3]

AHIHUD (Heb. 'God is praised') **1.** date unknown. Son of Gera, a leader of the tribe of Benjamin. [1 Chr. 8:7]

2. *c.* 13 century BC. Son of Shelomi, he was a leader of the tribe of Asher chosen by Moses to help divide the land of Israel among the tribes. [Num. 34:27]

AHIJAH (Heb. 'the Lord's brother') **1.** date unknown. Son of Jerahmeel, a leader of the tribe of Judah. [1 Chr. 2:25]

2. date unknown. Descendant of Ehud, a leader of the tribe of Benjamin. Also called Ahoah. [1 Chr. 8:4, 7]

3. *c.* 11 century BC. Son of Ahitub and high priest in the reign of King Saul, he was a great-grandson of Eli. [1 Sam. 14:3, 18; 21:1; 22:9]

4. 10 century BC. A prophet from the sanctuary of Shiloh in Ephraim, Ahijah encouraged Jeroboam in his plot against the ageing King Solomon. Jeroboam was the overseer of the labour force from his tribal area that was used in the building operations in Jerusalem. There was growing dissatisfaction in the country at this time over the tax and compulsory labour burdens, and jealousy was building up among the northern tribes against the dominant position of Judah.

One day, Ahijah, wrapped in a new cloak, met Jeroboam on a deserted stretch of road outside Jerusalem, and tore his cloak into twelve pieces denoting the tribes of Israel, and handed ten of them to Jeroboam, saying: 'Take for yourself ten pieces; for thus says the Lord, the God of Israel, "Behold, I am about to tear the kingdom from the hand of Solomon, and will give you ten tribes ..."' (1 Kgs. 11:31).

Jeroboam was condemned to death by Solomon, but fled to Egypt. After Solomon died and was succeeded by his son Rehoboam, he returned, and the ten northern

The Canaanite goddess Ashtaroth, condemned by the prophet Ahijah, on an Assyrian cylinder seal.

tribes seceded, set up a separate kingdom of Israel and made Jeroboam king. Ahijah's prophecy was thus fulfilled.

The new king restored idol worship, expelled the priestly Levites, who were loyal to the House of David, and in their stead recruited priests from the common people. His infant son became critically ill and he sent the queen in disguise to consult with the prophet Ahijah and find out the fate of his child. Ahijah, now old and nearly blind, was forewarned by the Lord and immediately recognized her. He told her that her son would die, and uttered a curse against the king and all his dynasty because he had departed from the ways of the Lord. The Lord, Ahijah said, would 'utterly consume the house of Jeroboam, as a man burns up dung until it is all gone' (1 Kgs. 14:10). [1 Kgs. 11:29, 30; 12:15; 14:2, 4, 5, 6, 18; 15:29; 2 Chr. 9:29; 10:15]

5. *c.* 10 century BC. Son of Shisha, he and his brother Elihoreph were secretaries to King Solomon. [1 Kgs. 4:3]

6. *c.* 10 century BC. Father of Baasha, the army commander of Israel who usurped the throne of Israel from King Nadab. [1 Kgs. 15:27, 33; 21:22; 2 Kgs. 9:9]

7. *c.* 10 century BC. A Pelonite warrior in the army of King David distinguished for his bravery. [1 Chr. 11:36]

8. *c.* 10 century BC. The Levite appointed by King David to supervise the treasuries of precious objects dedicated to the Tabernacle. [1 Chr. 26:20]

AHIKAM (Heb. 'my brother rose up') *c.* 7 century BC. The son of Shaphan, he was a court official sent by King Josiah with Hilkiah the high priest to consult the prophetess Huldah after a 'book of the law' was discovered in the Temple. She predicted the doom of Judah.

Ahikam's son Gedaliah was appointed by Nebuchadnezzar as the governor of Judah after the fall of Jerusalem in 587 BC. [2 Kgs. 22:14; 2 Chr. 34:20; Jer. 26:24; 39:14; 40:5-16]

AHILUD (Heb. 'born of my brother') *c.* 10 century BC. Father of Jehoshaphat who was court recorder for King David and then for King Solomon. [2 Sam. 8:16; 20:24; 1 Kgs. 4:3, 12; 1 Chr. 18:15]

AHIMAAZ (Heb. 'brother of wrath') **1.** date unknown. Son of Zadok, from the line of Aaron, his descendant Azariah served as the high priest in the Temple of Solomon. [1 Chr. 6:9]

2. *c.* 11 century BC. Father of Ahinoam, one of King Saul's wives. [1 Sam. 14:50]

3. *c.* 10 century BC. Son of Zadok, King David's high priest, he guarded the Ark of God during Absalom's revolt and acted as a secret messenger for King David. [2 Sam. 15:27; 17:17-22; 18:19]

4. *c.* 10 century BC. Husband of King Solomon's daughter Basemath, he was one of King Solomon's twelve officers responsible for supplying the provisions for the royal household one month in each year. [1 Kgs. 4:15]

AHIMAN (Heb. 'my brother is a gift') **1.** *c.* 13 century BC. One of the three giants descended from Anak who were driven out of Hebron by Caleb son of Jephunneh. [Num. 13:22; Josh. 15:14; Judg. 1:10]

2. *c.* 10 century BC. A Levite gatekeeper of the Tabernacle in the reign of King David. [1 Chr. 9:17]

AHIMELECH (Heb. 'the King [God] is my brother') **1.** *c.* 11 century BC. The son of Ahitub, he was the head priest at Nob, a priestly sanctuary just outside Jerusalem. When David became a fugitive from King Saul, destitute and unarmed, he took refuge at the sanctuary. Pretending that he was on a secret mission for King Saul, David persuaded the head priest to give him some of the hallowed bread as provisions together with the sword of Goliath which had been preserved at the sanctuary.

The kindly priest was to pay a cruel price for his help to the fugitive. Beside himself with fury at David's escape, the king had all the priests of Nob rounded up and brought before him. Ahimelech protested that he had done nothing wrong. Was not David Saul's son-in-law and 'captain over your bodyguard, and is honoured in your house?' (1 Sam. 22:14)

Saul would not hear any excuses and ordered his servants to kill Ahimelech and the eighty-five other priests. The men refused to 'put forth their hand to fall upon the priests of the Lord' (1 Sam. 22:17), and the grim execution was carried out by the king's Edomite herdsman Doeg. Nob was destroyed with all its inhabitants; only Abiathar, the son of Ahimelech, escaped to join David in the mountains. [1 Sam. 21, 22]

2. *c.* 11 century BC. A Hittite soldier who joined David's army and went with him secretly by night into King Saul's camp. [1 Sam. 26:6]

AHIMOTH (Heb. 'Moth [Canaanite god] is my brother') date unknown. A leader descended from Kohath. [1 Chr. 6:25]

AHINADAB (Heb. 'noble brother') *c.* 10 century BC. Son of Iddo, he was one of the twelve officers appointed by King Solomon to supply the provisions of the royal household for one month in each year. [1 Kgs. 4:14]

AHINOAM (Heb. 'brother is good') **1.** *c.* 11 century BC. A daughter of Ahimaaz and a wife of King Saul. [1 Sam. 14:50]

2. *c.* 11 century BC. David married Ahinoam from Jezreel while he was an outlaw in the wilderness of Paran, and she was the mother of his eldest son Amnon. She, together with David's other wife Abigail and their children, were carried away from Ziklag by the Amalekites. David and his men rescued them. [1 Sam. 25:43; 27:3; 30:5; 2 Sam. 2:2; 3:2; 1 Chr. 3:1]

AHIO (Heb. 'God is my brother') **1.** date unknown. Son of Elpaal and a leader of the tribe of Benjamin. [1 Chr. 8:14]

Ahimelech gave David some of the hallowed bread from the sanctuary at Nob. Egyptian limestone temple relief from Lisht, 12th dynasty, showing food and drink offerings.

2. *c.* 11 century BC. Son of Jeiel of the tribe of Benjamin and an uncle of King Saul. [1 Chr. 8:31; 9:37]

3. *c.* 10 century BC. Son of Abinadab, he and his brother Uzzah brought the Ark of God from Kiriath-jearim to Jerusalem in the reign of King David. [2 Sam. 6:3, 4; 1 Chr. 13:7]

AHIRA (Heb. 'Ra [Egyptian god] is my brother') *c.* 13 century BC. Son of Enan, he was a leader of the tribe of Naphtali chosen by Moses to take a census of the men of Naphtali and led the contingent of his tribe in the army of the children of Israel. [Num. 1:15; 2:29; 7:78-83; 10:27]

AHIRAM *see* EHI

AHISAMACH (Heb. 'brother helps') *c.* 13 century BC. Father of Oholiab of the tribe of Dan who helped Bezalel construct the Tabernacle in the wilderness. [Exod. 31:6; 35:34; 38:23]

AHISHAHAR (Heb. 'Shahar [Canaanite god] is my brother') date unknown. Son of Bilhan and a leader of the tribe of Benjamin. [1 Chr. 7:10]

AHISHAR (Heb. 'the King [God] is my brother') *c.* 10 century BC. Superintendent of the royal palace in the reign of King Solomon. [1 Kgs. 4:6]

AHITHOPHEL (Heb. 'Thophel [God] is my brother') *c.* 10 century BC. A Gilonite who was David's leading counsellor and a man of great political judgment. When Absalom decided to unfurl the banner of revolt Ahithophel joined him in the conspiracy. David fled from Jerusalem but his trusted friend Hushai remained behind and pretended to be on Absalom's side, in order to counter Ahithophel's influence. The great adviser was regarded as so sage that 'in those days the counsel which Ahithophel gave was as if one consulted the oracle of God' (2 Sam. 16:23).

The first step Absalom took on Ahithophel's advice, after entering Jerusalem, was to have intercourse with the ten concubines David had left behind – a symbolic act of succession. Ahithophel urged immediate pursuit before David could organize a counter-thrust. He had worked too long with David to underrate his capacities. But Hushai argued in favour of greater caution. 'This time the counsel which Ahithophel has given is not good.' (2 Sam. 17:7) Absalom and the men around him were convinced by Hushai, and David thus gained the time he needed to cross the river Jordan into Gilead and there rebuilt his forces. Ahithophel perceived clearly that the prince to whom he had defected had made a fatal blunder and that his own career was wrecked '... and he set his house in order, and hanged himself' (2 Sam. 17:23) – the only suicide outside the battlefield mentioned in the Old Testament. [2 Sam. 15:31-37; 16:20-23; 17; 1 Chr. 27:33, 34; Ps. 41:9; 55:12; 109]

AHITUB (Heb. 'brother of goodness') **1.** *c.* 11 century BC. Grandson of the high priest Eli and father of Ahimelech, chief priest of King Saul. [1 Sam. 14:3; 22:9, 20]

2. *c.* 10 century BC. Father of Zadok, King David's high priest, he was an ancestor of Ezra. [2 Sam. 8:17; 1 Chr. 6:7, 8; 18:16; Ezra 7:2]

3. date unknown. Son of Amariah, he was a member of a family of high priests of Judah who served in the Temple. [1 Chr. 6:11, 12]

4. date unknown. Ancestor of Azariah, a chief priest who served in the Temple after the return from Babylon. [1 Chr. 9:11; Neh. 11:11]

AHLAI 1. date unknown. Son of Sheshan, a leader of the tribe of Judah. [1 Chr. 2:31]

2. *c.* 10 century BC. Father of Zabad, a warrior in the army of King David distinguished for his bravery. [1 Chr. 11:41]

AHOAH *see* AHIJAH **2.**

AHUMAI (Heb. 'mother's brother') date unknown. The elder son of Jahath and a leader of the tribe of Judah of the families of the Zorathites. [1 Chr. 4:2]

AHUZZAM (Heb. 'possession') date unknown. A son of Ashhur, a leader of the tribe of Judah. [1 Chr. 4:6]

AHUZZATH (Heb. 'possessions') *c.* 17 century BC. A friend of King Abimelech of Gerar who accompanied him when he made his peace covenant with Isaac. [Gen. 26:26]

AHZAI *see* JAHZERAH

AIAH (Heb. 'vulture') **1.** date unknown. Son of Zibeon and a descendant of Seir. [Gen. 36:24; 1 Chr. 1:40]

2. *c.* 11 century BC. Father of Rizpah who was King Saul's concubine. [2 Sam. 3:7; 21:8]

AKAN *see* JAAKAN

AKKUB (Heb. 'insidious') **1.** *c.* 10 century BC. A gate-keeper of the Ark in the reign of King David and an ancestor of a family of Levites who returned to Jerusalem with Zerubbabel from exile in Babylon in 538 BC. [1 Chr. 9:17; Ezra 2:42, 45; Neh. 7:45; 11:19; 12:25]

2. date unknown. Son of Elioenai of the tribe of Judah and a descendant of King David. [1 Chr. 3:24]

3. *c.* 5 century BC. A Levite who explained the Law to the people of Judah after Ezra had read out the Law of Moses in the market-place. [Neh. 8:7]

ALEMETH (Heb. 'covering') **1.** *c.* 16 century BC. Son of Becher and a grandson of Benjamin, he was a leader of the tribe and a mighty warrior. [1 Chr. 7:8]

2. date unknown. Son of Jehoaddah of the tribe of Benjamin, and a descendant of King Saul. [1 Chr. 8:36; 9:42]

ALIAH date unknown. An Edomite leader descended from Esau. Also called Alvah. [Gen. 36:40; 1 Chr. 1:51]

ALIAN (Heb. 'tall') date unknown. Son of Shobal and a leader of a Horite clan. Also called Alvan. [Gen. 36:23; 1 Chr. 1:40]

ALLON (Heb. 'oak') date unknown. Son of Jedaiah and a leader of the tribe of Simeon. [1 Chr. 4:37]

ALMODAD (Heb. 'God is friend') date unknown. Son

of Joktan and a descendant of Shem. [Gen. 10:26; 1 Chr. 1:20]

ALVAH *see* ALIAH

ALVAN *see* ALIAN

AMAL (Heb. 'labour') *c.* 16 century BC. Son of Helem and a grandson of Asher, he and his family were leaders of the tribe and mighty warriors. [1 Chr. 7:35]

AMALEK date unknown. Son of Eliphaz and a descendant of Esau, he was the traditional ancestor of the Amalekites, the fierce tribe who became bitter enemies of the children of Israel. [Gen. 36:12, 16; 1 Chr. 1:36]

AMARIAH (Heb. 'God says') **1.** date unknown. Ancestor of Athaiah, one of the first men to settle in Jerusalem after the return from exile in Babylon. [Neh. 11:4]

2. *c.* 11 century BC. Son of Meraioth the priest and father of Ahitub, his grandson was Zadok, King David's high priest. [1 Chr. 6:7, 52; Ezra 7:3]

3. *c.* 10 century BC. Son of Azariah, King Solomon's high priest, and father of Ahitub. [1 Chr. 6:11]

4. *c.* 10 century BC. A Levite descended from Hebron who served in the Tabernacle in the reign of King David. [1 Chr. 23:19; 24:23]

5. *c.* 9 century BC. High priest of King Jehoshaphat of Judah, he was chief judge in all religious matters. [2 Chr. 19:11]

6. *c.* 8 century BC. One of the Levites who helped distribute the tithes and freewill offerings among the Levites in the cities of Judah during the reign of King Hezekiah. [2 Chr. 31:15]

7. 6 century BC. A priest who returned to Judah with Zerubbabel from exile in Babylon. [Neh. 12:2, 13]

8. *c.* 6 century BC. Great-grandfather of the prophet Zephaniah. [Zeph. 1:1]

9. 5 century BC. A son of Binnui who divorced his non-Jewish wife in the time of Ezra. [Ezra 10:42]

10. 5 century BC. A leading priest of Judah who signed the solemn covenant in the time of Nehemiah. [Neh. 10:3]

AMASA 1. *c.* 10 century BC. The son of David's sister Abigail and commander of the forces of his cousin Absalom in the revolt against David. His army was defeated in Gilead and Absalom killed by Joab. David kept him as commander in place of Joab, who later treacherously stabbed him to death. His body lay in the road until one of Joab's young men dragged it into a field and spread a cloak over it. [2 Sam. 17-20; 1 Chr. 2:17]

2. *c.* 8 century BC. Son of Hadlai, he was a leader of Ephraim who urged the release of the men of Judah captured in battle by King Pekah of Israel. [2 Chr. 28:12]

AMASAI (Heb. 'burdensome') **1.** date unknown. A Levite descended from Kohath, he was the father of Mahath and an ancestor of the prophet Samuel. [1 Chr. 6:25, 35]

2. *c.* 11 century BC. Leader of a group of thirty men who

deserted from King Saul's army and joined David at Ziklag, and swore allegiance to David on behalf of his men. [1 Chr. 12:18]

3. *c.* 10 century BC. A priest who blew a trumpet during the celebrations in the reign of King David when the Ark of God was taken up to Jerusalem. [1 Chr. 15:24]

AMASHSAI (Heb. 'burdensome') *c.* 5 century BC. Son of Azarel, he was one of the first priests to settle in Jerusalem after the return from exile in Babylon in the time of Nehemiah. [Neh. 11:13]

AMASIAH (Heb. 'whom God bears') *c.* 9 century BC. Son of Zichri, he commanded a large force of men in the army of King Jehoshaphat of Judah. [2 Chr. 17:16]

AMAZIAH (Heb. 'strength of the Lord') **1.** date unknown. Son of Hilkiah, the Levite, and an ancestor of Ethan, King David's musician. [1 Chr. 6:45]

2. Ninth king of Judah after the monarchy split, he reigned 796-81 BC.

Amaziah, the son of King Joash of Judah and his wife Jehoaddan of Jerusalem, succeeded to the throne at the age of twenty-five after the murder of his father by two court officials, with the connivance of the priesthood. When he was firmly established, he had the murderers executed, though was careful to spare their children in accordance with the Mosaic injunction: 'The fathers shall not be put to death for the children, nor the children be put to death for the fathers; but every man shall die for his own sin.' (2 Kgs. 14:6)

Amaziah carried out a census of all men over twenty in his kingdom as a basis for conscripting an army. He led his forces southward and defeated the Edomites in the Valley of Salt – the canyon running down from the Dead Sea. This victory gave him control of the ancient routes to Moab, east of the Dead Sea, to the mining area of Punon in the Arabah rift and to the Gulf of Akaba. Amaziah then advanced to the north-east and captured the fortified Edomite centre of Sela (the Rock). He brought back with him to Jerusalem the stone gods of the conquered Edomites.

Amaziah now felt strong enough to send a message to King Joash of Israel, challenging him to a military trial of strength. Joash scornfully advised Amaziah not to invite trouble for his kingdom and himself. A war started, and quickly ended with the defeat of the forces of Judah at Beth-shemesh, on the western outskirts of Judah, and the capture of Amaziah himself. Joash marched up to Jerusalem, battered down a large part of the city wall and returned to Samaria, taking with him hostages and plundered treasure from the Temple and the palace. Amaziah was left in his ravaged capital.

right Amaziah conquered the Edomite city of Sela. Illustration to Ps. 59; 'Who will lead me into the strong city? Who will lead me into Edom?', from a 9th-century psalter, St Gall.

In due course a revolt broke out against Amaziah. He fled to Lachish in the lowlands near the coastal plain, where the conspirators followed and killed him. They brought his body on a horse to Jerusalem for burial.

He was succeeded by his sixteen-year-old son Uzziah. [2 Kgs. 12:21; 13:12; 14:1-21, 23: 15:3; 1 Chr. 3:12; 2 Chr. 24:27; 25; 26:1, 4]

3. *c.* 8 century BC. Father of Joshah, a leader of Simeon who settled in the rich Gedor valley in the reign of King Hezekiah. [1 Chr. 4:34]

4. *c.* 8 century BC. Priest of Bethel who complained to King Jeroboam II of the seditious comments made by the prophet Amos and asked Amos to leave the royal city of Bethel and prophesy elsewhere. [Amos 7:10-14]

AMI (Heb. 'my uncle') *c.* 10 century BC. A servant of King Solomon whose descendants returned with Zerubbabel from exile in Babylon. Also called Amon. [Ezra 2:57; Neh. 7:59]

AMITTAI (Heb. 'God of truth') *c.* 8 century BC. Father of the prophet Jonah. [2 Kgs. 14:25; Jonah 1:1]

AMMIEL (Heb. 'God is my uncle') **1.** *c.* 13 century BC. Son of Gemalli, the leader of the tribe of Dan, he was one of the twelve men sent by Moses to spy out the Promised Land. [Num. 13:12]

2. *c.* 11 century BC. Father of Machir who befriended both King David and Jonathan's lame son Mephibosheth. [2 Sam. 9:4, 5; 17:27]

3. *c.* 10 century BC. A gatekeeper of the Tabernacle in the reign of King David. [1 Chr. 26:5]

AMMIEL *see* ELIAM 1.

AMMIHUD (Heb. 'uncle [God] of praise') **1.** *c.* 13 century BC. A leader of the tribe of Ephraim and the great-grandfather of Joshua. His son was Elishama, who marched at the head of his tribe in the army of the children of Israel in the wilderness. [Num. 1:10; 2:18; 7:48-53; 10:22; 1 Chr. 7:26]

2. *c.* 13 century BC. Father of Shemuel, the leader of the tribe of Simeon appointed by Moses to share out the land of Israel among the tribes. [Num. 34:20]

3. *c.* 13 century BC. Father of Pedahel, the leader of the tribe of Naphtali appointed by Moses to share out the land of Israel among the tribes. [Num. 34:28]

4. *c.* 10 century BC. Father of Talmai, king of Geshur, to whom Absalom fled after he murdered his half-brother Amnon. [2 Sam. 13:37]

5. *c.* 6 century BC. Father of Uthai, one of the first men of Judah to settle in Jerusalem after the return from exile in Babylon. Also called Uzziah. [1 Chr. 9:4; Neh. 11:4]

AMMINADAB (Heb. 'uncle [God] of nobility') **1.** *c.* 13 century BC. Father of Nahson, a leader of the tribe of Judah, and of Elisheba, Aaron's wife. [Exod. 6:23; Num. 1:7; 2:3; 7:12-17; Ruth 4:20; 1 Chr. 2:10]

2. date unknown. Son of Kohath, the Levite, and an ancestor of the prophet Samuel. [1 Chr. 6:22]

3. *c.* 10 century BC. Son of Uzziel, he was head of a group of Levites who helped bring the Ark of God to Jerusalem in the time of King David. [1 Chr. 15:10, 11]

AMMISHADDAI (Heb. 'uncle [God] is Almighty') *c.* 13 century BC. Father of Ahiezer a Danite who was chosen by Moses to take a census of the men in his tribe fit to be soldiers in the army of the children of Israel. [Num. 1:12; 2:25; 7:66, 71; 10:25]

AMMIZABAD (Heb. 'uncle [God] has given') *c.* 10 century BC. Son of David's warrior Benaiah who later commanded his father's division. [1 Chr. 27:6]

AMMONITES A fierce people living north-east of the Dead Sea who were bitter enemies of Israel. They were the traditional descendants of Ben-Ammi, the second son of Lot through his incestuous relationship with his younger daughter. [Gen. 19:38; Num. 21:24; Deut. 2:19, 20, 37; Josh. 13:10; Judg. 3; 13; 1 Sam. 11; 14; 2 Sam. 8; 10; 11; 12; 23; 1 Kgs. 11; 14; 2 Kgs. 23; 24; 1 Chr. 11; 18; 19; 20; 2 Chr. 12; 20; 24; 27; Ezra 9:1; Neh. 2; 4; 13; Ps. 83:7; Isa. 11:14; Jer. 9; 27; 40; 41; 49; Ezek. 21; 25; Dan. 11:41; Amos 1:13; Zeph. 2:8, 9]

AMNON (Heb. 'trustworthy') **1.** *c.* 10 century BC. King David's eldest son who seduced his half-sister Tamar and was killed in revenge by her brother Absalom. [2 Sam. 3:2; 13:1-39; 1 Chr. 3:1]

2. date unknown. Son of Shimon and a leader of the tribe of Judah. [1 Chr. 4:20]

AMOK (Heb. 'deep') 6 century BC. Head of a family of priests who returned to Judah with Zerubbabel from exile in Babylon. [Neh. 12:7, 20]

AMON (Heb. 'trustworthy') **1.** date unknown. Amon was the local god for the city of Thebes. When Thebes conquered the city states of Lower Egypt in about 1700 BC, Amon became the national god of the Egyptians. He was regarded as the god of fertility and later the sun-god. [Jer. 46:25]

2. *see* AMI

3. *c.* 9 century BC. Governor of Samaria, he arrested and imprisoned the prophet Micaiah after he had foretold the disaster that would befall King Ahab of Israel at Ramoth-gilead. [1 Kgs. 22:26; 2 Chr. 18:25]

4. Fifteenth king of Judah after the monarchy split, he reigned 642-40 BC. Amon was the son of King Manasseh of Judah and of Meshullemeth daughter of Haruz of Jotbah. He succeeded his father at the age of twenty-two, and continued the idolatrous practices that had marked Manasseh's reign. After two years on the throne he was assassinated by some of his officials. The conspirators were in turn put to death by the people, and Amon's eight-year-old son Josiah succeeded to the throne. [2 Kgs. 21:18-26; 1 Chr. 3:14; 2 Chr. 33:20-25; Jer. 1:2; 25:3; Zeph. 1:1]

AMORITES (Bab. 'westerners') A powerful people in pre-biblical times, they originated from and ruled in north-west Mesopotamia. Some began infiltrating into

Canaan in the early centuries of the 2nd millennium BC, and by the time Joshua appeared they were well entrenched in the land. There was thus considerable fighting between them and the Israelites. Many of them remained after Joshua's conquest. In the time of King Solomon, they were made 'a forced levy of slaves' (1 Kgs. 9:21). [Gen. 10; 14; 15; 48; Exod. 3; 23; 33; 34; Num. 13; 21; 22; 32; Deut. 1; 2; 3; 4; 7; 20; 31; Josh. 2; 3; 5; 7; 9; 10; 11; 12; 13; 24; Judg. 1; 3; 6; 10; 11; 1 Sam. 7:14; 2 Sam. 21:2; 1 Kgs. 4; 9; 21; 1 Chr. 1:14; 2 Chr. 8:7; Ezra 9:1; Neh. 9:8; Ps. 135:11; 136:19; Amos 2:9, 10]

AMOS (Heb. 'burden') *c.* 775-50 BC. First of the literary prophets.

Amos lived in Tekoa, a village in the Judean hills about six miles south of Bethlehem. Uzziah ruled at the time in the southern kingdom of Judah and Jeroboam II in the northern kingdom of Israel. Amos was a sheep-farmer, and also gathered the fruit of the sycamore tree (a kind of fig). His first appearance as a prophet was at a festival in the town of Bethel, in the kingdom of Israel. His opening words thundered a grim

above 11th-century BC bronze stand from Megiddo, showing a priest worshipping a god seated on a throne.
below The site of Tekoa, where the prophet Amos was born.

Woe to them who lie upon beds of ivory ... said Amos in his harangue against luxury. Ivory chair-back of Amos's time from Shalmaneser V's palace at Nimrod, 8th century B.C.

warning to the merrymakers: 'The Lord roars from Zion, and utters his voice from Jerusalem; the pastures of the shepherds mourn, and the top of Carmel withers.' (Amos 1:2)

For the Hebrew kingdoms, this was a period of relative peace and prosperity. What Amos saw were the negative results of this relaxation: luxurious living for the rich, exploitation of the poor, loose moral standards, corruption in public life, and religious observance based on ritual rather than real piety. It was against these abuses that he was called upon to preach.

He also sensed that the Hebrews were blind to the Assyrian danger looming up far to the north: 'Woe to those who are at ease in Zion, and to those who feel secure on the mountain of Samaria.' (Amos 6:1)

It is hardly surprising that Amos's fierce attack on the establishment was resented. After his first appearance at Bethel, the local priest sent a complaint to King Jeroboam accusing the preacher of sedition. 'Amos has conspired against you in the midst of the house of Israel; the land is not able to bear all his words. For thus Amos has said, "Jeroboam shall die by the sword, and Israel must go into exile away from his land."' (Amos 7:10, 11)

Apparently the authorities failed to take action, and the priest himself tried to persuade Amos to leave. 'O seer, go, flee away to the land of Judah, and eat bread there, and prophesy there.' (Amos 7:12) (These words implied that Amos was one of the wandering sooth-sayers who supported themselves from the credulous.) Amos replied indignantly that he was not a prophet nor a prophet's son, but had been called by the Lord from his own regular occupations. He repeated his warning

in even fiercer terms: 'Therefore thus says the Lord: "Your wife shall be a harlot in the city, and your sons and your daughters shall fall by the sword, and your land shall be parcelled out by line; and you yourself shall die in an unclean land, and Israel shall surely go into exile away from its land."' (Amos 7:17)

The Book of Amos may be divided into three main parts.

The first two chapters deal with the Lord's punishment of the nations. He starts with the neighbouring states of Damascus, Gaza, Tyre, Edom, Ammon and Moab. Their crimes are those of war and violence. The prophet then moves closer to home. The people of the south, Judah, will be punished 'because they have rejected the law of the Lord, and have not kept his statutes' (Amos 2:4). Finally comes the turn of the citizens of Israel to whom he is speaking. Here Amos's wrath rises to a climax and the catalogue of their sins becomes specific and vivid. They are profane, immoral and above all callous and inhuman towards their fellow-men – '... they sell the righteous for silver, and the needy for a pair of shoes' (Amos 2:6).

The next three chapters are warning sermons, each starting with the phrase 'Hear this word ...'. In the remaining chapters, the threats of judgment are built around concrete symbols: the devouring grasshoppers, the consuming fire, the builder's plumbline, the basket of summer fruit and the smitten sanctuary.

In the last few verses of the Book, Amos holds out the hope of a new beginning after the destruction he has prophesied. '"Behold, the eyes of the Lord God are upon the sinful kingdom, and I will destroy it from the surface of the ground; except that I will not utterly destroy the house of Jacob," says the Lord.' (Amos 9:8) 'In that day I will raise up the booth of David that is fallen and repair its breaches, and raise up its ruins, and rebuild it as in the days of old.' (Amos 9:11)

Amos the sheep farmer is usually pictured as a blunt rustic, compared with intellectual urbanites like Isaiah and Jeremiah. It is true that he is familiar with the sights and sounds of country life. Yet at the same time he reveals a wide knowledge of contemporary events, a grasp of political and social issues, and literary skill of a high order.

In the evolving theology of the Old Testament, Amos makes a great leap forward. He is the first to propound the concept of a God who is universal and is not just the tribal deity of the Hebrews. What God demands of man is moral purity and social justice, rather than the rituals and sacrifices of organized religion: 'I hate, I despise your feasts, and I take no delight in your solemn assemblies. Even though you offer me your burnt offerings and cereal offerings, I will not accept them.' (Amos 5:21, 22)

According to Amos, God judges all nations, but has a special covenant with the Hebrews. This makes special demands on them. More than other peoples, they must observe a stern ethical and social code.

Amos was a pioneer in the unique prophetic strain woven into the history of the Hebrew kingdoms over several centuries. Men of God like Amos, Isaiah and Jeremiah served as the moral conscience of the community, and the fearless critics of its rulers. The prophetical books of the Old Testament are among the most sublime ethics and poetry the world has known. [Book of Amos]

AMOZ (Heb. 'strong') *c.* 8 century BC. Father of the prophet Isaiah. [2 Kgs. 19:2; Isa. 1:1]

AMRAM (Heb. 'uncle [God] is exalted') **1.** *c.* 13 century BC. Amram was a descendant of Levi, the third son of Jacob and Leah. He married Jochebed and had three children – Miriam, Aaron and Moses. Amram died in Egypt at the age of one hundred and thirty-seven. [Exod. 6:18-20; Num. 3:19; 26:58-59; 1 Chr. 6:2, 3; 24:20]
2. 5 century BC. A descendant of Bani who divorced his non-Jewish wife in the time of Ezra. [Ezra 10:34]

AMRAPHEL *c.* 18 century BC. Amraphel was king of Shinar and one of the four Mesopotamian kings who defeated an alliance of five local kings from the Dead Sea area in the time of Abraham. They carried off a number of captives, including Abraham's nephew Lot and much booty. Abraham pursued them and rescued the captives and booty.

None of these nine kings has been identified, nor their countries or cities except Elam. [Gen. 14]

AMZI (Heb. 'strong') **1.** date unknown. Son of Bani and descended from Merari. [1 Chr. 6:46]
2. date unknown. Ancestor of Adaiah, one of the chief priests in Jerusalem after the return from exile in Babylon. [Neh. 11:12]

ANAH (Heb. '[God] answered') **1.** date unknown. A son of Seir the Horite and a leader of an Edomite clan. [Gen. 36:20, 29; 1 Chr. 1:38]
2. 18 century BC. Father of Oholibamah who married Esau, he was an Edomite leader who discovered hot springs in the desert. [Gen. 36:2, 14, 18, 24, 25; 1 Chr. 1:40, 41]

ANAIAH (Heb. '[God] answered') **1.** 5 century BC. A leader of Judah who stood at Ezra's side when he read the Law of Moses to the people in the market-place. [Neh. 8:4]
2. 5 century BC. A leader of Judah who signed the solemn covenant in the time of Nehemiah. [Neh. 10:22]

ANAK (Heb. 'long-necked') date unknown. Anak was a very tall man, like his father Arba the legendary founder of Hebron. He founded a race of giants known as Anakim who frightened the spies of Moses by their size: '... and we seemed to ourselves like grasshoppers, and so we seemed to them' (Num. 13:33). They were driven out by Caleb when he was given Hebron and the area round it. Later Joshua swept them out of the hill-country of Canaan and practically exterminated them, though some remnants were found in Gaza, Gath and Ashdod, after Joshua's time. [Num. 13:22-33; Deut. 9:2; Josh. 15:13-15; 21:11; Judg. 1:20]

Head of an unknown ruler from Nineveh, late 3rd millennium BC. Bronze, with gold headband; the eye-sockets once held precious stones.

ANAMIM date unknown. One of the seven sons of Egypt and a grandson of Ham. [Gen. 10:13; 1 Chr. 1:11]

ANAMMELECH (Heb. 'King [God] answers') date unknown. One of the gods of the Sepharvaim, a tribe settled by the Assyrians in Samaria after the exile of the people of Israel. [2 Kgs. 17:31]

ANAN (Heb. 'cloud') 5 century BC. A leader of Judah who signed the solemn covenant. [Neh. 10:26]

ANANI (Heb. 'my cloud') date unknown. Son of Elioenai of the tribe of Judah and a descendant of King David. [1 Chr. 3:24]

ANATH (Canaanite goddess) 12 century BC. Father of Shamgar, a judge over Israel. [Judg. 3:31; 5:6]

ANATHOTH (Heb. 'answers') **1.** *c.* 16 century BC. Son of Becher and a grandson of Benjamin, he was a leader of the tribe and a mighty warrior. [1 Chr. 7:8]
2. 5 century BC. A leader of Judah who signed the solemn covenant in the time of Nehemiah. [Neh. 10:19]

ANER *c.* 18 century BC. One of Abraham's three Amorite friends who helped him defeat the five kings who had seized Abraham's nephew Lot. [Gen. 14:13-24]

ANIAM (Heb. 'I am the God') date unknown. Son of Shemida and a leader of the tribe of Manasseh. [1 Chr. 7:19]

ANTHOTHIJAH (Canaanite goddess) date unknown. Son of Shashak, a leader of the tribe of Benjamin living in Jerusalem. [1 Chr. 8:24]

ANUB date unknown. Son of Koz, a leader of the tribe of Judah. [1 Chr. 4:8]

APHIAH date unknown. An ancestor of King Saul. [1 Sam. 9:1]

APHSES *see* HAPPIZZEZ

APPAIM date unknown. Son of Nadab, a leader of the tribe of Judah. [1 Chr. 2:30, 31]

ARA date unknown. Son of Jether, a leader of the tribe of Asher and a mighty warrior. [1 Chr. 7:38]

ARAD (Heb. 'wild ox') date unknown. Son of Beriah, a leader of the tribe of Benjamin living in Jerusalem. [1 Chr. 8:15]

ARAH (Heb. 'wandering') **1.** date unknown. Son of Ulla and a leader of the tribe of Asher, his descendants returned to Judah with Zerubbabel from exile in Babylon. [1 Chr. 7:39; Ezra 2:5; Neh. 7:10]
2. 5 century BC. Father of Shecaniah, a leader of Judah, whose daughter married Tobiah, Nehemiah's enemy. [Neh. 6:18]

ARAM (Heb. 'high') **1.** date unknown. Son of Shem and a grandson of Noah, he was the traditional ancestor of the Arameans who settled in Syria. [Gen. 10:22, 23; 1 Chr. 1:17]
2. *c.* 18 century BC. Son of Kemuel and a grandson of Abraham's brother Nahor. [Gen. 22:21]
3. date unknown. Son of Shomer, a leader of the tribe of Asher and a mighty warrior. [1 Chr. 7:34]

ARAN date unknown. Son of Dishan and leader of an Edomite clan. [Gen. 36:28; 1 Chr. 1:42]

ARAUNAH *c.* 10 century BC. Owner of a threshing floor. Late in his reign King David took a census of the fighting men throughout his kingdom. But a census was considered unholy (a superstition shared by most primitive communities). The Lord's punishment was a pestilence that killed seventy thousand people. David asked for advice from the prophet Gad who said: 'Go up, rear an altar to the Lord on the threshing floor of Araunah the Jebusite.' (2 Sam. 24:18) When Araunah saw the king coming, he bowed to the ground and asked what he wanted of his servant. David explained that he had come to buy his threshing floor on which he would erect an altar to the Lord so that the plague would be arrested. Araunah, delighted at the honour, provided David with the oxen and the wood for the sacrifice and wanted to give David the floor for nothing. But David

Araunah offered his threshing sledge as wood for David's sacrifice. Wooden threshing sledge of a type used since biblical times, studded with basalt stones.

refused the gift, bought the floor and the oxen for fifty shekels of silver, built an altar on it and offered up sacrifices. The Lord repented and the pestilence stopped before it reached Jerusalem. Araunah's threshing floor later became the site of Solomon's Temple. Also called Ornan. [2 Sam. 24; 1 Chr. 21; 2 Chr. 3:1]

ARBA (Heb. 'four') date unknown. A giant of a man, he was the legendary founder of Kiriath-arba which later became known as Hebron. His descendants were tall men known as Anakim, after his son Anak, and they frightened the scouts of Moses by their size. [Gen. 35:27; Josh. 14:15; 15:13; 21:11]

ARD 1. *c.* 16 century BC. Son of Benjamin, he went down to Egypt with his grandfather Jacob. [Gen. 46:21] **2.** *c.* 16 century BC. Son of Bela and a grandson of Benjamin. Also called Addar. [Num. 26:40; 1 Chr. 8:3]

ARDON (Heb. 'fugitive') date unknown. Son of Caleb by his wife Azubah and a leader of the tribe of Judah. [1 Chr. 2:18]

ARELI (Heb. 'Ar is my God') 16 century BC. Son of Gad, he went down to Egypt with his grandfather Jacob. [Gen. 46:16; Num. 26:17]

ARIDAI (Pers. 'gift of Ari [a tribe]') *c.* 5 century BC. One of the ten sons of Haman who plotted to kill all the Jews in the Persian empire in the reign of King Ahasuerus. The plot was discovered and Haman and his sons were hanged. [Esther 9:9]

ARIDATHA (Pers. 'gift of Ari [a tribe]') *c.* 5 century BC. One of the ten sons of Haman who plotted to kill all the Jews in the Persian empire in the reign of King Ahasuerus. The plot was discovered and Haman and his sons were hanged. [Esther 9:8]

ARIEL (Heb. 'lion of God') 5 century BC. A leader of Judah sent by Ezra to Iddo, to request that Levites be sent to Jerusalem to serve in the Temple. [Ezra 8:16]

ARIOCH 1. *c.* 18 century BC. King of Ellasar and one of the four Mesopotamian kings who defeated an alliance of five local kings from the Dead Sea area in the time of Abraham. They carried off a number of captives, including Abraham's nephew Lot, and much booty. Abraham pursued them and rescued the captives and booty.

None of these nine kings have been identified, and none of their countries or cities except Elam. [Gen. 14] **2.** *c.* 6 century BC. Captain of King Nebuchadnezzar who was ordered to execute all the wise men of Babylon because none could tell Nebuchadnezzar what the dream was that troubled him. Daniel volunteered to recite and explain the dream and Arioch took him to the king. [Dan. 2:14, 24]

ARISAI (Pers. 'lives among the Ari [a tribe]') 5 century BC. One of the ten sons of Haman who plotted to kill all the Jews in the Persian empire in the reign of King Ahasuerus. The plot was discovered and Haman and his sons were hanged. [Esther 9:9]

ARMONI (Heb. 'belonging to the palace') *c.* 10 century BC. A son of King Saul by his concubine Rizpah, he was put to death by the Gibeonites in the reign of King David to avenge Saul's massacre of the tribe of Gibeon. [2 Sam. 21:8]

AROD *see* ARODI

ARODI (Heb. 'wild ass') *c.* 16 century BC. Son of Gad who went down to Egypt with his grandfather Jacob. Also called Arod. [Gen. 46:16; Num. 26:17]

ARPACHSHAD date unknown. Son of Shem and a grandson of Noah. [Gen. 10:22, 24; 11:11-13; 1 Chr. 1:17, 18, 24]

ARTAXERXES I LONGIMANUS (Gk. form of the Pers. 'brave warrior') King of Persia, 465-23 BC. King Artaxerxes of Persia received a letter from the governor of Samaria, protesting against the rebuilding of Jerusalem by the Jews, on the ground that it had always been a rebellious city. He ordered the work to be suspended.

Later, Artaxerxes's Jewish cupbearer Nehemiah obtained permission from his master to go to Jerusalem on a visit and remained for twelve years, becoming governor and rebuilding the walls of the city.

On his mission to Jerusalem, Ezra obtained a decree from Artaxerxes ordering Persian officials to assist him and authorizing a treasury grant. Ezra states that his

Persian statue of a man, 6th-4th centuries BC.

journey was in the seventh year of King Artaxerxes's reign. The sequence in the Bible suggests that the reference was to Artaxerxes I, but this gives rise to serious problems of interpretation, and some scholars maintain that the king in question was Artaxerxes II Mnemon (404-358 BC). [Ezra 4:6-24; 6:14]

ARZA *c.* 9 century BC. Superintendent of the household of King Elah of Israel in whose home the drunken king was murdered by his army commander Zimri. [1 Kgs. 16:9]

ASA (Heb. 'created') **1.** Third king of Judah after the monarchy split, he reigned 911-870 BC. Succeeding his father Abijah as king of Judah, in his long reign of forty-one years he distinguished himself both as a military commander and as a religious reformer.

Early in Asa's reign, Baasha, the king of Israel, advanced to Ramah (just north of Jerusalem) which he started to fortify. To relieve the pressure, Asa sent messengers with gifts of gold and silver to Ben-hadad I, the king of Aram-Damascus, calling for his help. Ben-hadad promptly invaded Israel, and Baasha was forced to withdraw. Asa fortified the towns shielding Jerusalem from the north, Geba and Mizpah. This settled the border between Israel and Judah for some time to come.

A new threat developed from the south. A large expeditionary force from Egyptian Sinai led by Zerah the Cushite (Ethiopian) advanced as far as Mareshah in the Shephelah, but was routed by Asa's Judean spearmen and Benjaminite archers and pursued towards Gaza.

Asa is one of the few Hebrew kings who is commended in the Bible for his pious zeal. 'And Asa did what was good and right in the eyes of the Lord his God.' (2 Chr. 14:2) He stamped out idolatrous practices and restored the Temple in Jerusalem as the centre of worship. It was decreed that unbelievers would be put to death. Asa even stripped of her dignities his grandmother Maacah. (The Bible refers to her as his mother, no doubt because she had acted as queen-mother and regent in his youth.) She had fashioned an obscene idol connected with the cult of the Phoenician fertility goddess Ashtoreth (Astarte), and Asa had this object solemnly burnt in the vale of Kidron in Jerusalem.

Asa developed a disease in the legs, probably dropsy, and there is a hint of reproof about his reliance on doctors and not on prayer alone.

He died in the forty-first year of his reign and was buried in Jerusalem, laid out on a couch 'which had been filled with various kinds of spices prepared by the perfumer's art' (2 Chr. 16:14). He was succeeded by his son Jehoshaphat. [1 Kgs. 15; 16; 22:41, 43, 46; 1 Chr. 3:10; 2 Chr. 14; 15; 16; 17:2; 20:32; 21:12; Jer. 41:9]
2. *c.* 6 century BC. Father of Berechiah, a Levite who lived in Judah after the return from exile in Babylon. [1 Chr. 9:16]

ASAHEL (Heb. 'God hath made') **1.** *c.* 11 century BC. One of the sons of Zeruiah, David's sister. Zeruiah had three sons – Joab, Abishai and Asahel. 'Now Asahel was as swift of foot as a wild gazelle.' (2 Sam. 2:18) He served in David's picked guard of thirty men, and was a commander of an army formation.

After the death of Saul, when Abner's men were routed by those of Joab, Asahel pursued the fleeing Abner, who tried to reason with him: 'Why should I smite you to the ground? How then could I lift up my face to your brother Joab?' (2 Sam. 2:22) But Asahel was determined and Abner was forced to kill him in self-defence. He was buried in Hebron in his father's tomb. Joab never forgave Abner, and later murdered him. [2 Sam. 2:18-3:30; 23:24; 1 Chr. 2:16; 11:26]
2. *c.* 9 century BC. A Levite sent by King Jehoshaphat to teach the Law of God in the cities of Judah. [2 Chr. 17:8]
3. *c.* 8 century BC. One of the Levites who supervised the bringing of tithes and offerings into the Temple in the reign of King Hezekiah. [2 Chr. 31:13]
4. 5 century BC. Father of Jonathan, one of the two leaders of Judah who were present when Ezra called on all those who had married non-Jewish women to divorce them. [Ezra 10:15]

ASAIAH (Heb. 'created by God') **1.** *c.* 10 century BC. Son of Haggaiah, a Levite descended from Merari, he helped bring the Ark of God up to Jerusalem and later served in the Tabernacle in the reign of King David. [1 Chr. 6:30; 15:6, 11]
2. *c.* 8 century BC. One of the leaders of Simeon who drove out the inhabitants of the rich valley of Gedor in the time of King Hezekiah and settled there. [1 Chr. 4:36]
3. *c.* 7 century BC. Servant of King Josiah of Judah, sent with Hilkiah the priest and Shaphan the scribe to consult the prophetess Huldah. [2 Kgs. 22:12-14; 2 Chr. 34:20]
4. *c.* 6 century BC. Head of a family of Shilonites who settled in Jerusalem after the return from exile in Babylon. [1 Chr. 9:5]

ASAPH (Heb. '[God] sustained') **1.** *c.* 10 century BC. Son of Berechiah, a Levite, he was appointed by King David as one of the principal officials in charge of the liturgical music used in the public worship in Jerusalem. In later centuries the guild of Temple singers was named after him and claimed to be his descendants. He is mentioned in the titles of twelve Psalms and some may have been composed by him. [1 Chr. 6:39; 9:15; 15:17, 19; 16:5, 7, 37; 25:1-9; 26:1; 2 Chr. 5:12; 20:14; 29:13; 35:15; Ezra 2:41; 3:10; Neh. 7:44; 11:17, 22; 12:35, 46; Ps. 50; 73-83]
2. *c.* 8 century BC. Father of Joah, the court recorder of King Hezekiah of Judah. [2 Kgs. 18:18, 37; Isa. 36:3, 22]
3. 5 century BC. Keeper of the king's forest in Persia, he

was ordered by King Artaxerxes to supply Nehemiah with wood to repair the Temple, the gates and the walls of Jerusalem. [Neh. 2:8]

ASAREL (Heb. 'Asher is the God') date unknown. Son of Jehallelel and a leader of the tribe of Judah. [1 Chr. 4:16]

ASENATH (Egypt. 'belonging to the goddess Nath') *c.* 16 century BC. Daughter of the high priest of the Egyptian temple of On, she became Joseph's wife at Pharaoh's court. They had two sons, Manasseh and Ephraim. [Gen. 41:45, 50; 46:20]

ASHARELAH (Heb. 'Asher is the God') *c.* 10 century BC. One of the sons of Asaph, King David's musician, who played musical instruments in the Tabernacle under their father's direction, and took the seventh turn of service. Also called Jesharelah. [1 Chr. 25:2, 14]

ASHBEL (Heb. 'man of Baal') *c.* 16 century BC. Son of Benjamin, he went down to Egypt with his grandfather Jacob. [Gen. 46:21; Num. 26:38; 1 Chr. 8:1]

ASHER (Canaanite deity) *c.* 16 century BC. Eighth son of Jacob. Asher was the second son of Zilpah, the maid of Jacob's wife Leah. Believing herself past childbearing age, she had given Zilpah to her husband as a concubine; Asher was born in Padan-aram where Jacob was still working as a herdsman for his father-in-law Laban.

Together with his brothers, Asher was involved in the events that led to the selling of his brother Joseph into slavery in Egypt. Later he was one of the ten sons sent by Jacob to buy corn in Egypt, where Joseph had become a leading figure at Pharaoh's court. When Jacob went to settle in Egypt with all his family, it included Asher's four sons and a daughter.

On his deathbed Jacob blessed his sons in turn. Of Asher he said: 'Asher's food shall be rich, and he shall yield royal dainties.' (Gen. 49:20)

Centuries later, in the conquest of Canaan under Joshua, the tribe of Asher was allocated the coastal area of western Galilee, from Mount Carmel to beyond the Ladder of Tyre. In fact the tribe gained control of only a small part of this territory, bordering on the plain of Acre. This fertile area of the Galilee highlands, famous for its olive groves, is reflected in the blessing of Asher by Moses: '... let him dip his foot in oil' (Deut. 33:24). [Gen. 30:13, 35:26; Deut. 33:24; Josh. 17:10, 11; Judg. 5:17; 1 Chr. 2:2; 7:30, 40; Ezek. 48:34]

ASHERAH This is the Hebrew rendering of Ashirat, the leading goddess of the Phoenician Canaanites and consort of the head of their pantheon. It represented the female principle in the fertility cult. During the reign of King Ahab, his queen, Jezebel of Tyre, who had brought her worship of the Tyrian gods to her adopted land, secured official status for 'the four hundred and fifty prophets of Baal and the four hundred prophets of Asherah' (1 Kgs. 18:19). This led to the dramatic con-

The olive groves of the territory of Asher, in the Galilee highlands.

frontation with Elijah on Mount Carmel. King Josiah destroyed the Asherah idol in Jerusalem. It is occasionally mentioned in the Bible to denote a wooden cult object. It also appears in the plural form, in both genders, as Asherim and Asheroth. [Exod. 34:13; Deut. 7:5; 12:3; 16:21; Judg. 3:7; 6:25-30; 1 Kgs. 14:15, 23; 15:13; 16:33; 18:19; 2 Kgs. 13:6; 17:10, 16; 18:4; 21:3, 7; 23:4, 6, 7, 14, 15; 2 Chr. 14:3; 15:16; 17:6; 19:3; 24:18; 31:1; 33:19; 34:3, 4, 7; Isa. 27:9; Jer. 17:2; Micah 5:14]

ASHHUR (Hittite god) date unknown. Son of Caleb the son of Hezron. [1 Chr. 2:24; 4:5]

ASHKENAZ date unknown. Son of Gomer and a grandson of Japheth. [Gen. 10:3; 1 Chr. 1:6]

ASHPENAZ *c.* 6 century BC. Chief eunuch of King Nebuchadnezzar of Babylon, whom the king commanded to pick out handsome and clever young men from among the captives of Israel and teach them the Chaldean language so that they might serve in the king's palace. [Dan. 1:3]

ASHTAROTH This is the plural Hebrew form for the Canaanite goddess Astarte, one of the dominant female deities of fertility. From the numerous 'Astarte' plaques discovered in archaeological excavations, this goddess was usually represented as naked. The name is often used as a general term for female deities of Canaan. Also called Ashtoreth. [Deut. 1:4; Josh. 9:10; 12:4; 13:12, 31; Judg. 2:13; 10:6; 1 Sam. 7:3, 4; 12:10; 31:10; 1 Kgs. 11:5, 33; 2 Kgs. 23:13; 1 Chr. 11:44]

ASHTORETH *see* ASHTAROTH

ASHVATH date unknown. Son of Japhlet, a leader of the tribe of Asher. [1 Chr. 7:33]

ASIEL (Heb. 'made by God') date unknown. Ancestor of Jehu, a warrior of the tribe of Simeon who settled in the Gedor valley in the reign of King Hezekiah. [1 Chr. 4:35]

ASNAH (Heb. 'thorn-bush') *c*. 10 century BC. Head of a family of Temple servants who returned with Zerubbabel from exile in Babylon. [Ezra 2:50]

ASPATHA (Pers. 'given by the [holy] horse') *c*. 5 century BC. One of the ten sons of Haman who plotted to kill all the Jews in the Persian empire in the reign of King Ahasuerus. The plot was discovered and he and his sons were put to death. [Esther 9:7]

ASRIEL (Heb. 'Asher is the God') **1.** *c*. 16 century BC. Son of Manasseh and a grandson of Joseph, he was a leader of the tribe. [1 Chr. 7:14]
2. *c*. 13 century BC. Head of a family of the tribe of Manasseh to whom an inheritance was given in the land of Israel. [Num. 26:31; Josh. 17:2]

ASSHUR (Heb. 'land') date unknown. Son of Shem and by tradition the ancestor of the Assyrians. [Gen. 10:22; 1 Chr. 1:17]

ASSHURIM (Heb. 'lands') *c*. 17 century BC. Son of Dedan and a near descendant of Abraham, he was a leader of a desert tribe. [Gen. 25:3]

ASSIR (Heb. 'servant of God') **1.** *c*. 13 century BC. Son of Korah, the Levite who led the revolt against Moses and Aaron in the wilderness. [Exod. 6:24; 1 Chr. 6:22]
2. date unknown. Son of Ebiasaph, a Levite descended from Kohath. [1 Chr. 6:23, 37]

ATARAH (Heb. 'crown') date unknown. Wife of Jerahmeel, a leader of the tribe of Judah, and the mother of Onam. [1 Chr. 2:26]

ATER 1. date unknown. Ancestor of a family of Judah who returned with Zerubbabel from exile in Babylon. [Ezra 2:16; Neh. 7:21]
2. date unknown. Ancestor of a family of Levites, gatekeepers of the Temple, who returned with Zerubbabel from exile in Babylon. [Ezra 2:42; Neh. 7:45]
3. 5 century BC. A leader of Judah who signed the solemn covenant in the time of Nehemiah. [Neh. 10:17]

ATHAIAH *see* UTHAI **1.**

ATHALIAH (Heb. 'God is exalted') **1.** date unknown. Son of Jeroham and a leader of the tribe of Benjamin living in Jerusalem. [1 Chr. 8:26]
2. Wife of the eighth king of Judah after the monarchy split, she reigned 841-35 BC. Athaliah was the daughter of King Ahab of Israel and his domineering Phoenician queen, Jezebel. She was married to Jehoram when he was heir to the throne of Judah, in order to strengthen the alliance between the two kingdoms.

During Jehoram's eight-year reign Athaliah promoted the cult of the Phoenician god Baal as her mother had done in Israel. She was hated by the priesthood and the people.

On Jehoram's death, he was succeeded by his youngest and only surviving son Ahaziah, who was killed a year later in the military coup of Jehu in the kingdom of Israel. On learning of her son's death, Athaliah ruthlessly had all the other royal offspring murdered and

The only woman ruler of either of the Hebrew kingdoms was Athaliah. 8th-century BC ivory from Nimrod, showing a woman seated on a throne.

seized the throne herself. However, unknown to her, Ahaziah's infant son Joash escaped death, having been rescued and hidden by his aunt Jehosheba, Ahaziah's sister. Later she handed the child to the priest Jehoiada who secretly kept him in the Temple.

When Joash was seven years old Jehoiada carried out a plot whereby the boy was crowned king in the Temple, under the protection of the royal guard. Hearing the trumpet blasts and the shouts of the crowd, Athaliah rushed to the Temple. When she saw the scene there she shouted 'Treason, treason!' The guards seized her, took her outside the Temple precincts and killed her at the Horse Gate of the palace. The crowd then smashed the temple and altar of Baal in the palace and slew Mattan, the priest of Baal.

Athaliah was the only woman to occupy the throne in either of the Hebrew kingdoms. [2 Kgs. 8:26; 11:1-20; 2 Chr. 22; 23; 24:7]

3. *c.* 5 century BC. Father of Jeshaiah who returned with Ezra from exile in Babylon. [Ezra 8:7]

ATHLAI (Heb. 'God is exalted') *c.* 5 century BC. A son of Bebai, he divorced his non-Jewish wife in the time of Ezra. [Ezra 10:28]

ATTAI (Heb. 'ready') **1.** date unknown. Son of Jarha, an Egyptian slave, and the daughter of Sheshan, a leader of Judah. [1 Chr. 2:35, 36]

2. *c.* 11 century BC. One of the warriors of the tribe of Gad who deserted from King Saul's army and joined David at Ziklag. [1 Chr. 12:11]

3. *c.* 10 century BC. Son of King Rehoboam of Judah and his favourite wife Maacah. [2 Chr. 11:20]

AZALIAH (Heb. 'God has set apart') *c.* 7 century BC. Son of Meshullam and father of Shaphan, King Josiah's secretary. [2 Kgs. 22:3; 2 Chr. 34:8]

AZANIAH (Heb. 'whom God hears') 5 century BC. Father of Jeshua a Levite who signed the solemn covenant in the time of Nehemiah. [Neh. 10:9]

AZAREL (Heb. 'God helps') **1.** *c.* 11 century BC. A Korahite warrior who deserted from King Saul's army and joined David at Ziklag. [1 Chr. 12:6]

2. *c.* 10 century BC. A Levite, son of Heman, who took the eleventh turn of service to play musical instruments in the Tabernacle in the reign of King David. Also called Uzziel. [1 Chr. 25:4, 18]

3. *c.* 10 century BC. Son of Jeroham, he was made leader

7th-century BC Assyrian relief from the palace of Ashurbanipal at Nineveh, showing musicians.

of the tribe of Dan in the reign of King David. [1 Chr. 27:22]

4. *c.* 5 century BC. Father of Amashsai, one of the chief priests in the Temple after the return from exile in Babylon. [Neh. 11:13]

5. 5 century BC. A descendant of Bani who divorced his non-Jewish wife in the time of Ezra. [Ezra 10:41]

6. 5 century BC. A Levite who played a musical instrument at the dedication of the rebuilt walls of Jerusalem in the time of Nehemiah. [Neh. 12:36]

AZARIAH (Heb. 'whom God aids') **1.** date unknown. A son of Ethan of the tribe of Judah and a grandson of Zerah, he and his family were leaders of the tribe. [1 Chr. 2:8]

2. date unknown. The son of Jehu of the tribe of Judah and the father of Helez, he was descended from the Egyptian slave Jarha whom Sheshan, a leader of Judah, gave in marriage to his daughter. [1 Chr. 2:38, 39]

3. date unknown. The son of Zephaniah the Levite and the father of Joel, he was an ancestor both of the prophet Samuel and of King David's musician Heman. [1 Chr. 6:36]

4. *see* UZZIAH **1.**

5. *c.* 10 century BC. The high priest in Israel during the reign of King Solomon, he was the son of Zadok. [1 Kgs. 4:2]

6. *c.* 10 century BC. The son of Nathan and a court official in the reign of King Solomon, he was responsible for supervising the work of the twelve officers of the king who each provided the food for the royal household for one month a year. [1 Kgs. 4:5]

7. *c.* 10 century BC. The son of Ahimaaz the priest and the father of Johanan, he was the grandfather of Azariah, high priest in King Solomon's Temple. [1 Chr. 6:9]

8. *c.* 10 century BC. Son of Johanan, the high priest in the Temple in Jerusalem in the reign of King Solomon, he was the father of Amariah and an ancestor of Ezra. [1 Chr. 6:10, 11; Ezra 7:3]

9. *c.* 10 century BC. The son of Oded and a prophet in the days of Asa, king of Judah, he told the king after his victory over Zerah the Ethiopian that God would be with him as long as he kept the commandments. [2 Chr. 15:1]

10. *c.* 9 century BC. Two sons of Jehoshaphat, king of Judah, who were put to death by their eldest brother Jehoram when he succeeded to the throne. [2 Chr. 21:2]

11. *c.* 9 century BC. Son of Jehoram, he was an army commander of Judah who joined the conspiracy led by the high priest Jehoiada to overthrow Queen Athaliah and crown Joash as king of Judah. [2 Chr. 23:1]

12. *c.* 9 century BC. Son of Obed, he was an army commander of Judah who joined the conspiracy led by the high priest Jehoiada to overthrow Queen Athaliah. [2 Chr. 23:1]

13. *c.* 8 century BC. High priest of Judah during the reign of King Uzziah, he led eighty priests into the Temple to order the king not to burn incense on the altar, a privilege reserved exclusively for the priests. Uzziah refused to listen to them but while in the act of burning the incense, he was struck by leprosy and compelled to leave the Temple. [2 Chr. 26:17-20]

14. *c.* 8 century BC. The son of Johanan and a chief of the tribe of Ephraim in the reign of Pekah, king of Israel, he ordered the men of Israel to return the Jewish captives taken in battle against the kingdom of Judah and personally fed, clothed and transported the captives back to Judah. [2 Chr. 28:12]

15. *c.* 8 century BC. The son of Jehallelel, he was a Levite who obeyed the command of Hezekiah, king of Judah, to sanctify himself and cleanse the Temple. [2 Chr. 29:12]

16. *c.* 8 century BC. The father of Joel, a Levite who obeyed the command of Hezekiah, king of Judah, to sanctify himself and cleanse the Temple. [2 Chr. 29:12]

17. *c.* 8 century BC. The chief priest of the family of Zadok in the reign of Hezekiah, king of Judah, who told the king that so much food had been donated to the Temple as tithes and offerings that the priests and Levites would have more than enough to eat. [2 Chr. 31:10]

18. *see* UZZIAH **3.**

19. *c.* 7 century BC. Son of Hilkiah, high priest of Judah in the reign of Josiah, king of Judah, he was the father of Seraiah the high priest executed by Nebuchadnezzar when the Babylonians conquered Judah. [1 Chr. 6:13, 14; Ezra 7:1]

20. *c.* 6 century BC. Son of Hoshaiah and a leader of Judah after the Babylonian conquest, he rejected the prophet Jeremiah's advice to stay in Judah and insisted that the people should flee into Egypt. [Jer. 42:3; 43:2]

21. *see* ABEDNEGO

22. *see* SERAIAH **8.**

23. *c.* 5 century BC. The son of Maaseiah the Levite, he repaired part of the walls of Jerusalem opposite his house in the time of Nehemiah. [Neh. 3:23, 24]

24. 5 century BC. A Levite who explained the Law of Moses to the people of Judah after Ezra had read it to the assembled multitude in the market-place. [Neh. 8:7]

25. 5 century BC. A priest of Judah in the time of Nehemiah who signed the covenant to observe the commands of God. [Neh. 10:2]

26. *c.* 5 century BC. A priest of Judah in the time of Nehemiah who participated in the ceremony of dedicating the rebuilt walls of Jerusalem. [Neh. 12:33]

27. *see* SERAIAH **11.**

AZAZ (Heb. 'strong') date unknown. Father of Bela and a leader of the tribe of Reuben. [1 Chr. 5:8]

AZAZIAH (Heb. 'God makes strong') **1.** *c.* 10 century BC. A Levite who played a lyre at the celebration when the Ark of God was taken up to Jerusalem in the time of King David. [1 Chr. 15:21]

2. *c.* 10 century BC. Father of Hoshea, he was leader of the tribe of Ephraim in the reign of King David. [1 Chr. 27:20]

3. *c.* 8 century BC. One of the Levites who supervised the bringing of tithes and offerings into the Tabernacle in the reign of King Hezekiah. [2 Chr. 31:13]

AZBUK (Heb. 'devastation') 5 century BC. Father of Nehemiah, the ruler of part of Beth-zur, who helped repair the walls of Jerusalem at the time of the leader Nehemiah. [Neh. 3:16]

AZEL (Heb. 'noble') date unknown. Son of Eleasah and a leader of the tribe of Benjamin, he was a descendant of King Saul. [1 Chr. 8:37, 38; 9:43, 44]

AZGAD (Heb. 'God is mighty') **1.** date unknown. Ancestor of a large family of Judah who returned with Zerubbabel from exile in Babylon. [Ezra 2:12; 8:12; Neh. 7:17]

2. 5 century BC. A leader of Judah who signed the solemn covenant in the time of Nehemiah. [Neh. 10:15]

AZIEL *see* JAAZIEL

AZIZA (Heb. 'strong') 5 century BC. A descendant of Zattu who divorced his non-Jewish wife in the time of Ezra. [Ezra 10:27]

AZMAVETH (Heb. 'strong unto death') **1.** *c.* 11 century BC. Members of the tribe of Benjamin famous for their ability to use the bow and the sling with either hand, Azmaveth and his two sons joined the exiled David when he was governor of the Philistine city of Ziklag.

After David became king of the united monarchy, he appointed Azmaveth as the royal treasurer. [2 Sam. 23:31; 1 Chr. 11:33; 12:3; 27:25]

2. date unknown. Son of Jehoaddah of the tribe of Benjamin and a descendant of King Saul. [1 Chr. 8:36; 9:42]

AZRIEL (Heb. 'help of God') **1.** date unknown. A leader of the tribe of Manasseh and a mighty warrior

living east of the river Jordan. [1 Chr. 5:24]

2. *c.* 10 century BC. Father of Jeremoth, who was leader of the tribe of Naphtali in the reign of King David. [1 Chr. 27:19]

3. *c.* 6 century BC. Father of Seraiah who was sent by King Jehoiakim of Judah to arrest the prophet Jeremiah and his scribe Baruch. [Jer. 36:26]

AZRIKAM (Heb. 'my help has arisen') **1.** date unknown. Son of Azel, a leader of the tribe of Benjamin and a descendant of King Saul. [1 Chr. 8:38; 9:44]

2. *c.* 8 century BC. Commander of the palace of King Ahaz of Judah who was killed in battle by Zichri, a warrior in the army of King Pekah of Israel. [2 Chr. 28:7]

3. *c.* 6 century BC. A Levite whose descendant Shemaiah settled in Jerusalem after the return from exile in Babylon. [1 Chr. 9:14; Neh. 11:15]

4. date unknown. Son of Neariah of the tribe of Judah and a descendant of King David. [1 Chr. 3:23]

AZUBAH (Heb. 'helped') **1.** date unknown. First wife of Caleb son of Hezron, she bore him three sons. [1 Chr. 2:18, 19]

2. *c.* 9 century BC. Wife of King Asa of Judah and mother of King Jehoshaphat his successor. [1 Kgs. 22:42; 2 Chr. 20:31]

AZZAN (Heb. 'very strong') *c.* 13 century BC. Father of Paltiel, who was leader of the tribe of Issachar chosen by Moses to help divide up the land of Israel among the tribes. [Num. 34:26]

AZZUR (Heb. 'helper') **1.** *c.* 7 century BC. Father of Hananiah of Gibeon who falsely prophesied that the exile of the leaders of Judah to Babylon would end shortly. He was condemned by Jeremiah who prophesied Hananiah's death within a year. [Jer. 28:1-17]

2. *c.* 6 century BC. Father of Jaazaniah, a leader of Judah who told the people of Jerusalem that the city would not be destroyed. [Ezek 11:1]

3. 5 century BC. A leader of Judah who signed the solemn covenant in the time of Nehemiah. [Neh. 10:17]

B

BAAL (Heb. 'lord') **1.** The chief god of the Canaanites. Baal was worshipped as the god of the elements who brought rain and made the ground fruitful, and sometimes as the god of war. Temples to Baal were established on high places throughout Israel and many of the Children of Israel worshipped there from the days of the Judges. In the reign of King Ahab, Baal-worship became the court religion and led to Elijah's confrontation with the prophets of Baal on Mount Carmel. The worshippers of Baal were later massacred by King Jehu but the influence of Baal remained throughout the period of the first Temple and brought about frequent strictures by the prophets of Israel and Judah. Bel, Belus, Baalim and Merodach were alternative names for Baal and many places were named in honour of Baal. [Num. 22:41; Judg. 2:11; 6:25; 10:10; 1 Kgs. 16:31-33; 18:18-28; 2 Kgs. 10:22; 17:16; Isa. 46:1; Jer. 50:2; 51:44]
2. *c.* 11 century BC. Son of Jeiel of the tribe of Benjamin and a kinsman of King Saul. [1 Chr. 8:30; 9:36]
3. *c.* 8 century BC. Son of Reaiah and a leader of the tribe of Reuben, his son Beerah was carried into exile by the Assyrian emperor Tiglath-pileser III. [1 Chr. 5:5]
BAAL-BERITH (Heb. 'lord of the covenant') 12 century BC. The Canaanite god of Shechem in the time of Abimelech, the rebellious son of Gideon the judge. He was also called El-berith. [Judg. 8:33; 9:4, 46]
BAAL-HANAN (Heb. 'the lord is gracious') **1.** *c.* 13 century BC. Son of Achbor, he was a king of Edom. [Gen. 36:38, 39; 1 Chr. 1:49, 50]
2. *c.* 10 century BC. The Gederite, one of King David's servants in charge of the olive and sycamore trees in the Shephelah. [1 Chr. 27; 28]
BAALIM *see* BAAL
BAALIS 6 century BC. A chief of the Ammonites in the days of Jeremiah, he sent Ishmael, son of Nethaniah, to kill Gedaliah, the Jewish governor of Judah. [Jer. 40:14]
BAAL-ZEBUB (Heb. 'lord of the flies') The name of the local god of the Philistine city of Ekron. When King Ahaziah lay sick and sent messengers to find out from this deity whether he would recover, they were waylaid by the angry prophet Elijah who upbraided them with the words: 'is it because there is no God in Israel to inquire of his word?' (2 Kgs. 1:16). Elijah then foretold

Baal, the god of thunder:
stone stele from Ras Shamra, Syria,
19th-18th centuries BC.

the king's death. [2 Kgs. 1:2, 3, 6, 16]

BAANA (Heb. 'son of God') **1.** 10 century BC. Son of Ahilud, he was one of King Solomon's twelve officers who provided food for the king for one month in the year. His area of authority included 'Taanach, Megiddo and all Beth-shean'. [1 Kgs. 4:12]

2. 10 century BC. Son of Hushai, he was one of King Solomon's twelve officers who provided food for the king for one month in the year. His area of authority included Asher and Bealoth. [1 Kgs. 4:16]

3. 5 century BC. Father of Zadok who helped repair the walls of Jerusalem in the days of Nehemiah. [Neh. 3:4]

BAANAH (Heb. 'son of God') *c.* 11 century BC. **1.** The two fierce sons of Rimmon from Beeroth, Baanah and Rechab, entered the house of Ishbosheth, Saul's son, murdered him and brought his severed head to David at Hebron, hoping to be well rewarded. The shocked David ordered his men to kill them both for having 'slain a righteous man in his own house upon his bed' (2 Sam. 4:11). Their hands and feet were cut off and they were hung up over a nearby pool. David ordered the head of Ishbosheth to be buried in the sepulchre of Abner in Hebron. [2 Sam. 4:2, 5-12]

2. 10 century BC. Father of Heled, one of King David's chosen guard of thirty. [2 Sam. 23:29; 1 Chr. 11:30]

3. 6 century BC. One of the leaders of Judah who returned with Zerubbabel from exile in Babylon. [Ezra 2:2; Neh. 7:7]

4. 5 century BC. One of the leaders of Judah who signed the covenant to observe the Laws of God in the time of Nehemiah. [Neh. 10:27]

BAARA (Heb. 'God has seen') date unknown. One of the three wives of Shaharaim of the tribe of Benjamin. [1 Chr. 8:8]

BAASEIAH (Heb. 'work of God') *c.* 10 century BC. An ancestor of Asaph, a Levite musician in the Tabernacle in the reign of King David. [1 Chr. 6:40]

BAASHA Third king of Israel after the monarchy split, he reigned 909-886 BC. While King Nadab of Israel was involved in a campaign against the Philistines, Baasha the son of Ahijah, from the tribe of Issachar, seized power in a coup and proclaimed himself king. He then put Nadab and all his offspring to death, thereby wiping out the dynasty of Jeroboam. His accession also broke the domination of the tribe of Ephraim in the northern kingdom of Israel.

Baasha invaded Judah, took Ramah on the high ground overlooking Jerusalem from the north, and started to fortify it. Asa, the king of Judah, bribed Ben-hadad the Aramean ruler to switch sides, and the Syrians invaded Israel from the north, occupying parts of Upper Galilee. Baasha was compelled to abandon the thrust on Jerusalem and rush back. During this period of weakness, the kingdom of Israel also lost its hold on the territories east of the Jordan river, including

Moab, that had been part of the empire of David and Solomon.

In spite of his military reverses Baasha retained his throne for twenty-four years. For permitting sinful conduct in religious matters, he was cursed by the prophet Jehu, the son of Hanani, and doom pronounced on his posterity.

Baasha was buried in his capital of Tirzah, north of Shechem. He was succeeded by his son Elah. [1 Kgs. 15-16; 21:22; 2 Kgs. 9:9; 2 Chr. 16; Jer. 41:9]

BAKBAKKAR 6 century BC. One of the heads of the Levite families that returned from exile in the time of Zerubbabel. [1 Chr. 9:15]

BAKBUK (Heb. 'bottle') date unknown. Ancestor of a family that returned with Zerubbabel to Judah from exile in Babylon. [Ezra 2:51; Neh. 7:53]

BAKBUKIAH 1. 6 century BC. One of the Levites who returned to Judah with Zerubbabel from captivity in Babylon. [Neh. 11:17; 12:9]

2. 5 century BC. One of the porters guarding the gates of Jerusalem in the days of Nehemiah. [Neh. 12:25]

BALAAM (Gk. from the Heb. *bilam* 'a thing swallowed', or 'ruin') *c.* 13 century BC. A Mesopotamian soothsayer.

Balaam, the son of Beor, was a noted magician who lived in Pethor. Balak the king of Moab sent dignitaries to him with a large reward, invoking his aid against the children of Israel who had pitched their tents in the plains of Moab on their way to the Promised Land. 'Come now, curse this people for me, since they are too mighty for me.' (Num. 22:6)

At first the Lord said to Balaam, 'You shall not go with them; you shall not curse the people, for they are blessed.' (Num. 22:12) He therefore refused the invitation. But when another delegation arrived, God permitted him to go, provided he spoke only the words the Lord would put in his mouth.

As he was riding on his donkey through a vineyard, the animal baulked and refused to go on, and the angry Balaam beat him. When this had happened twice more the Lord 'opened the mouth of the ass, and she said to Balaam, "What have I done to you, that you have struck me these three times?"' (Num. 22:28) Only then did Balaam see that an angel stood in their path with a raised sword in his hand. Balaam threw himself on the ground and gave a solemn undertaking to say only what the Lord wanted.

The king of Moab and his courtiers came out to meet Balaam. Next morning the whole party went up to the heights of Baal, from where the Israelite encampment could be seen in the Jordan valley far below. On Balaam's instructions seven altars were erected and sacrifices made on them. They stood at the first place where, to the king's anger and distress, Balaam blessed the Israelites instead of cursing them. This happened again when they moved on to a second and a third place. To the king's protests Balaam replied that the spirit of God had come upon him. He prophesied that 'a star shall come forth out of Jacob, and a sceptre shall rise out of Israel; it shall crush the forehead of Moab' (Num. 24:17).

Not daring to harm so powerful a soothsayer, the disappointed king returned to his palace and Balaam went home without the promised reward.

In a later story in the Book of Numbers, Balaam reappears in a completely different and more sinister context. While in their camp on the Jordan plain, the Israelites attacked and wiped out some encampments of Midianite nomads, who were held accountable for the immorality and idolatrous practices that had infected the children of Israel. Balaam was among those killed.

In blaming the Midianite women for seducing the Israelites from their faith, Moses said: 'Behold, these caused the people of Israel, by the counsel of Balaam, to act treacherously against the Lord in the matter of Peor, and so the plague came among the congregation of the Lord.' (Num. 31:16)

The apparent contrast in Balaam's behaviour in the two episodes has given rise to many ingenious explanations. It has been suggested that the stories may have derived from different biblical sources at different periods. [Num. 22-4, 31; Deut. 23:4, 5; Josh. 13:22; 24:9, 10; Neh. 13:2; Micah 6:5]

BALADAN *see* MERODACH-BALADAN

BANI (Heb. 'built') **1.** 10 century BC. A Gadite warrior in the army of King David. [2 Sam. 23:36]

2. date unknown. Son of Shemer, he was a Levite descended from Merari and an ancestor of Ethan who ministered in the Tabernacle in the reign of King David. [1 Chr. 6:46]

3. date unknown. A leader of the tribe of Judah whose descendants settled in Jerusalem after the return from exile in Babylon. [1 Chr. 9:4]

4. date unknown. The ancestor of a family who returned with Zerubbabel from exile in Babylon. [Ezra 2:10; 10:29, 34]

5. 5 century BC. The father of Rehum, a Levite who helped repair the walls of Jerusalem in the time of Nehemiah. [Neh. 3:17]

6. 5 century BC. A Levite in the days of Ezra who explained the Law of Moses to the people of Judah and later signed the covenant to observe the Laws of the Lord. [Neh. 8:7; 9:4, 5; 10:13]

7. 5 century BC. A leader of Judah who signed the covenant to observe the Laws of the Lord in the time of Nehemiah. [Neh. 10:14]

8. 5 century BC. The father of Uzzi who supervised the Temple service of his fellow Levites after the return from Babylon. [Neh. 11:22]

BARACHEL (Heb. 'God blessed') period of the patriarchs. The Buzite, member of the Ram family and father of Elihu the friend of Job. [Job 32:2, 6]

BARAK (Heb. 'lightning') *c.* 12 century BC. Israelite commander who fought against Sisera.

Barak, the son of Abinoam of the tribe of Naphtali, was chosen by the prophetess Deborah to lead the Israelites against the Canaanite general Sisera. Barak gathered his forces and took up his position on Mount Tabor. Sisera's army consisted of nine hundred chariots drawn up in battle array and he assumed that the rebellious Israelite tribesmen would melt back into their hills at this display of martial force. But Deborah said to Barak 'Up! For this is the day in which the Lord has given Sisera into your hand.' (Judg. 4:14)

As Barak and his ten thousand men rushed down the slopes of Mount Tabor, a violent rainstorm flooded the Kishon river and turned the valley into a sea of mud. Their chariots bogged down, and caught completely off-balance, the Canaanite forces were routed and wiped out. Barak pursued the fleeing Sisera and found he had been killed in her tent by Jael the Kenite woman. [Judg. 4, 5]

Balaam and the angel, from the 13th-century *Psalter of St Louis.*

BARIAH (Heb. 'son of God') date unknown. One of the five sons of Shemaiah, a descendant of David. [1 Chr. 3:22]

BARKOS (Heb. 'son of Kos [a god]') date unknown. Ancestor of a family which returned with Zerubbabel to Judah from exile in Babylon. [Ezra 2:53; Neh. 7:55]

BARUCH (Heb. 'blessed') **1.** *c.* 6 century BC. Scribe of Jeremiah.

Baruch, the son of Neriah, was the devoted disciple to Jeremiah. He witnessed the deed of transfer of a piece of land bought by Jeremiah from his cousin Hanamel. Some time later, Jeremiah sent for Baruch and dictated a scroll containing his discourses and oracles from the beginning of his ministry. Since Jeremiah had been banned from the Temple area, he sent Baruch to read out the scroll to the crowd of worshippers at the Temple on a special fast day, in the hope that the grim prophecies in it would cause the hearers to repent. Baruch was then summoned to the palace to read the book again before a meeting of officials. Disturbed at its contents, they said to Baruch, 'Go and hide, you and Jeremiah, and let no one know where you are.' (Jer. 36:19) When the enraged king, who had the scroll burnt as it was read to him, ordered their arrest, they were not to be found. At the Lord's command, Jeremiah dictated the scroll over again to Baruch, with additions.

Jerusalem fell in 587 BC and two months later Gedaliah, the governor appointed by the Babylonians, was assassinated. The group of officers loyal to Gedaliah failed to capture the murderer and fearing the Babylonian anger, fled to Egypt, taking Jeremiah and Baruch with them.

Nothing more is known of Baruch's life in Egypt, though it is probable that he remained with his beloved master Jeremiah. [Jer. 32, 36, 43, 45]

2. *c.* 5 century BC. Son of Zabbai the priest, he helped repair the walls of Jerusalem in the days of Nehemiah. He later signed the covenant to observe the Laws of God. [Neh. 3:20; 10:6]

3. *c.* 5 century BC. A leader of the tribe of Judah whose son Maaseiah was one of the first to settle in Jerusalem in the time of Nehemiah. [Neh. 11:5]

BARZILLAI (Heb. 'iron-maker') **1.** *c.* 11 century BC. The father of Adriel who married King Saul's daughter Merab. [2 Sam. 21:8]

2. *c.* 10 century BC. When David, fleeing from Absalom, crossed the Jordan river and took refuge in Gilead, Barzillai and several other notables supplied him and his followers with all their needs. They 'brought beds, basins, and earthen vessels, wheat, barley ... honey and curds and sheep and cheese from the herd, ... for they said, "The people are hungry and weary and thirsty in the wilderness."' (2 Sam. 17:28, 29)

When David returned to power, he invited Barzillai

Baruch was the faithful scribe of Jeremiah.
8th-century BC relief from Zinjirli, Syria, showing a king dictating to his scribe, who holds a scroll in his hand.

to remain with him, but the eighty-year-old Gileadite declined, saying he wanted to die among his own people. He pleaded his age and asked 'Can your servant taste what he eats or what he drinks? Can I still listen to the voice of singing men and singing women?' (2 Sam. 19:35) '... I may die in my own city, near the grave of my father and my mother.' (2 Sam. 19:37) Instead, his son Chimham stayed with David, who asked his successor Solomon to show the family kindness.

In the 6th century BC a family of priests traced their ancestry through his daughter Agia and took his name. [2 Sam. 17:27; 19:31-39; 1 Kgs. 2:7; Ezra 2:61; Neh. 7:63]

BASEMATH (Heb. 'sweet-smelling') **1.** *see* ADAH **2.**

2. *see* MAHALATH **1.**

3. *c.* 10 century BC. A daughter of King Solomon, she married Ahimaaz, one of the king's twelve officers responsible for supplying the provisions of the royal household. [1 Kgs. 4:15]

BATHSHEBA (Heb. 'daughter of the oath') *c.* 10 century BC. Wife of David and mother of Solomon. One warm moonlight night early in David's reign, he was unable to sleep and paced restlessly along the rooftop of his palace in Jerusalem. Glancing down over the parapet, he was startled to see a beautiful young woman bathing herself on a nearby roof. On making enquiries he learnt that she was the daughter of Eliam and the granddaughter of his chief counsellor, Ahithophel; and that she was married to Uriah, a Hittite officer serving under Joab in the siege of Rabbah, the capital of Ammon. Yielding to sudden temptation, David sent discreet servants to bring Bathsheba to him and made love to her. She returned inconspicuously to her own home.

A little while later she sent David a message that she had become pregnant. There was only one way to avoid scandal – to let Bathsheba's husband visit her immediately. Uriah was brought back ostensibly to report on the campaign. But he spent his time with his army comrades without going near his wife, and returned to the front after two days. On David's instructions, Joab sent Uriah on a dangerous assault in which he was killed.

When Bathsheba had completed the normal period of mourning, David married the comely young widow who in due course bore him a son. 'But the thing that David had done displeased the Lord.' (2 Sam. 11:27) Bathsheba's infant son by David fell sick and died. She bore David a second son, who was named Solomon.

When the boy grew up and David had become old and feeble, Bathsheba gained a promise that Solomon would succeed him on the throne, although he was one of David's younger sons. She and Nathan the prophet told the king that the eldest prince Adonijah was moving to usurp the throne, and David promptly had Solomon crowned as king.

After David's death, Bathsheba brought Solomon a request from Adonijah to wed Abishag the Shunammite, the comely girl who had taken care of the aged David. The young monarch treated his mother with great deference. 'And the king rose to meet her, and bowed down to her; then he sat on his throne, and had a seat brought for the king's mother; and she sat on his right.' (1 Kgs. 2:19) But the request was refused and Adonijah put to death for his presumption.

The love story of David and Bathsheba has had a strong romantic appeal down the ages. Renaissance artists delighted in painting the fair bather on the moonlit rooftop, unwittingly revealing her charms to a sleepless king. Also called Bath-shua. [2 Sam. 11:3; 12:24; 1 Kgs. 1-2; 1 Chr. 3:5; Ps. 51 (title)]

BATH-SHUA (Heb. 'daughter of wealth') **1.** *c.* 16 century BC. A daughter of a Canaanite, Shua, she married Judah and bore him three sons. [Gen. 38:2, 12; 1 Chr. 2:3]

2. *see* BATHSHEBA

BAVVAI 5 century BC. A Levite and son of Henadad, ruler of half the district of Keilah, he helped repair the walls of Jerusalem in the time of Nehemiah. [Neh. 3:18]

BAZLITH *see* BAZLUTH

BAZLUTH 6 century BC. Head of a family who returned to Judah with Zerubbabel from captivity in Babylon. Also called Bazlith. [Ezra 2:52; Neh. 7:54]

BEALIAH (Heb. 'Jehovah is the Lord') 11 century BC. One of the Benjaminite warriors who rallied to David at Ziklag when he was pursued by King Saul. [1 Chr. 12:5]

BEBAI 1. date unknown. Ancestor of a large family that returned to Judah with Zerubbabel from exile in Babylon. [Ezra 2:11; 10:28; Neh. 7:16]

2. 5 century BC. One of the signatories of the solemn covenant in the time of Nehemiah. [Ezra 8:11; Neh. 10:15]

BECHER (Heb. 'young camel') **1.** *c.* 16 century BC. Son of Benjamin and a grandson of Jacob and Rachel. [Gen. 46:21; 1 Chr. 7:6, 8]

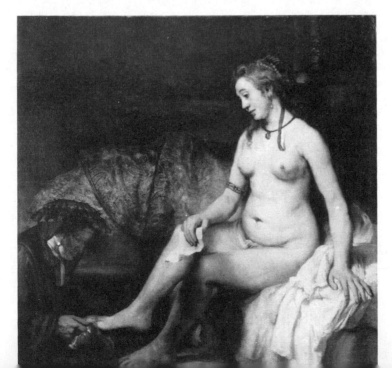

above right Belshazzar's *Feast,* by Rembrandt van Rijn (1606–69).

Bathsheba, by Rembrandt.

2. *c.* 16 century BC. Son of Ephraim and grandson of Joseph. Also called Bered. [Num. 26:35; 1 Chr. 7:20]

BECORATH (Heb. 'first fruits') *c.* 11 century BC. An ancestor of King Saul. [1 Sam. 9:1]

BEDAD (Heb. 'solitary') date unknown. Father of Hadad, king of Edom. [Gen. 36:35; 1 Chr. 1:46]

BEDAN date unknown. Son of Ulam and a descendant of Gilead of the tribe of Manasseh. [1 Chr. 7:17]

BEDEIAH (Heb. 'branch of God') 5 century BC. One of the returned exiles who divorced his non-Jewish wife in the time of Ezra. [Ezra 10:35]

BEELIADA *see* ELIADA **1.**

BEERA (Heb. 'a well') date unknown. A son of Zophah, he was a clan leader in the tribe of Asher. [1 Chr. 7:37]

BEERAH (Heb. 'a well') 8 century BC. A leader of the tribe of Reuben who was carried into captivity by Tiglath-pileser III, king of Assyria. [1 Chr. 5:6]

BEERI (Heb. 'my well') **1.** *c.* 16 century BC. Father of Judith, one of Esau's wives. [Gen. 26:34]

2. *c.* 8 century BC. Father of the prophet Hosea. [Hos. 1:1]

BEL *see* BAAL

BELA (Heb. 'destroying') **1.** date unknown. The first king of Edom, he was the son of Beor and his capital city was Dinhabah. [Gen. 36:32, 33; 1 Chr. 1:43, 44]

2. *c.* 16 century BC. Eldest son of Benjamin and a grandson of Jacob and Rachel. [Gen. 46:21; Num. 26:38, 40; 1 Chr. 7:6, 7; 8:1, 3]

3. date unknown. Son of Azaz and a leader of the tribe of Reuben. [1 Chr. 5:8]

BELSHAZZAR (Bab. 'Bel protect the king') *c.* 6 century BC. King of Babylon in the Book of Daniel.

He is described in the Book of Daniel as the son of Nebuchadnezzar and his successor on the throne of Babylon, though historically he was neither. He gave a great feast in the palace attended by all his household and a thousand of his nobles. He sent for the gold and silver vessels from the Temple in Jerusalem that Nebuchadnezzar had brought to Babylon 'and the king and his lords, his wives, and his concubines drank from them' (Dan. 5:3). Suddenly a hand appeared and wrote on the wall of the banqueting chamber the words 'MENE, MENE, TEKEL, and PARSIN' (Dan. 5:25). Nobody could understand this mysterious message and all of them were stricken with terror. The queen remembered Daniel and his ability to interpret dreams and the king sent for him. Daniel interpreted the ominous message as meaning that the king had been weighed and found wanting. He told Belshazzar that he had sinned against the Lord when he drank from the Temple vessels and 'praised the gods of silver and gold, of bronze, iron, wood, and stone, which do not see or hear or know' (Dan. 5:23). Belshazzar was assassinated that night. [Dan. 5; 7:1; 8:1]

BELTESHAZZAR *see* DANIEL

BELUS *see* BAAL

BEN-ABINADAB *c.* 10 century BC. Son-in-law of King Solomon, he was one of Solomon's twelve officers responsible for supplying the provisions of the king's household. [1 Kgs. 4:11]

BENAIAH (Heb. 'the Lord has built') **1.** *c.* 10 century BC. Captain of David's guard, Benaiah was the son of Jehoiada and came from Kabzeel in Judah. He was a brave soldier and David appointed him captain of his bodyguard. He carried out several feats of bravery such as slaying 'two ariels of Moab . . . a lion in a pit on a day when snow had fallen. And he slew an Egyptian . . .' (2 Sam. 23:20, 21). Benaiah remained loyal to David through the rebellions of Absalom and of Adonijah. When David was old he sent for him to go with Zadok the priest and Nathan the prophet to anoint Solomon as king of Israel.

On David's death Benaiah transferred his loyalties to Solomon. On the young king's orders he killed Adonijah, Joab and Shimei. Solomon through Benaiah thus succeeded in getting rid of all the men whose loyalty he doubted. Benaiah was appointed commander of the army in place of Joab. [2 Sam. 8:18; 20:23; 23:20-22; 1 Kgs. 1, 2; 4:4; 1 Chr. 11:22-24; 18:17; 27:5, 6]
2. 10 century BC. A warrior from Pirathon of the tribe of Ephraim serving in the army of King David. He was commander of the forces in the eleventh month of each year. [2 Sam. 23:30; 1 Chr. 11:31; 27:14]
3. *c.* 10 century BC. One of the Levites who played musical instruments in the Tabernacle in the reign of King David. [1 Chr. 15:18, 20]
4. *c.* 10 century BC. One of the priests who blew a trumpet before the Ark in the Tabernacle during the reign of King David. [1 Chr. 15:24; 16:6]
5. *c.* 10 century BC. Father of Jehoiada who succeeded Ahithophel as King David's counsellor. [1 Chr. 27:34]
6. 9 century BC. A Levite descended from Asaph whose grandson, Jahaziel, prophesied victory for King Jehoshaphat of Judah against the armies of the Ammonites and Moabites. [2 Chr. 20:14]
7. 8 century BC. A leader of the tribe of Simeon who drove out the inhabitants of the valley of Gedor and settled there during the reign of King Hezekiah of Judah. [1 Chr. 4:36]
8. *c.* 8 century BC. One of the Levites who supervised the bringing of tithes and offerings into the Temple in the reign of King Hezekiah. [2 Chr. 31:13]
9. *c.* 6 century BC. Father of Pelatiah who gave false counsel to the people of Judah and whose death Ezekiel prophesied. [Ezek. 11:1, 13]
10. 5 century BC. Descendant of Parosh, he married a non-Jewish wife and later divorced her in the time of Nehemiah. [Ezra 10:25]
11. 5 century BC. Descendant of Pahath-moab, he married a non-Jewish wife and later divorced her in the time of Nehemiah. [Ezra 10:30]
12. 5 century BC. Descendant of Bani, he married a non-Jewish wife and later divorced her in the time of Nehemiah. [Ezra 10:35]
13. 5 century BC. Descendant of Nebo, he married a non-Jewish wife and later divorced her in the time of Nehemiah. [Ezra 10:43]
BEN-AMMI (Heb. 'son of my people') *c.* 17 century BC. Son of the incestuous relationship between Lot and his younger daughter, Ben-ammi was the father of the Ammonites. [Gen. 19:38]

BEN-DEKER *c.* 10 century BC. One of King Solomon's twelve officers responsible for supplying the provisions of the royal household. [1 Kgs. 4:9]
BEN-GEBER (Heb. 'son of strength') *c.* 10 century BC. One of King Solomon's twelve officers responsible for supplying the provisions of the royal household. [1 Kgs. 4:13]
BEN-HADAD (Heb. 'son of Hadad [a god]') **1. Ben-hadad I** *c.* 9 century BC. When Judah was invaded and Jerusalem attacked by King Baasha of Israel, King Asa of Judah sent messengers with gifts of silver and gold to Damascus, to seek the help of Ben-hadad I, son of Tabrimmon and king of Aram, Israel's northern neighbour. Not averse to taking advantage of the quarrel between the two Hebrew kingdoms Ben-hadad invaded Israel and occupied the northern and eastern Galilee. Baasha was forced to abandon his campaign against Judah and hurry back to his capital at Tirzah. [1 Kgs. 15:18, 20; 2 Chr. 16:2-6]
2. Ben-hadad II *c.* 9 century BC. Son of Ben-hadad I. A Syrian army led by King Ben-hadad II besieged Samaria, the capital of Israel, but was routed by a surprise attack from the city. Ben-hadad escaped on a chariot horse, but was captured by King Ahab, who spared him on condition that the Galilee towns that had been occupied by his father were returned, and that Israel was given trading rights in the bazaars of Damascus.

Ahab later joined a coalition of local kings led by Ben-hadad against the Assyrians who were advancing from the north under Shalmaneser III. This advance was stopped at the battle of Karkar in 853 BC and the Assyrian danger receded.

Some years later Ben-hadad II was murdered by his army commander Hazael who seized the throne. [1 Kgs. 20; 2 Kgs. 6:24; 8:7-9]
3. Ben-hadad III *c.* 9 century BC. King of Aram-Damascus, he was the son of Hazael and succeeded his father on the throne. During his reign, the kingdom of Israel recovered the territory which Hazael had conquered from them. [2 Kgs. 13:24, 25; Jer. 49:27; Amos 1:4]
BEN-HAIL (Heb. 'son of valour') *c.* 10 century BC. One of the princes of Judah sent by King Jehoshaphat to teach the Law of God in the cities of Judah. [2 Chr. 17:7]
BEN-HANAN (Heb. 'son of grace') date unknown. A son of Shimon of the tribe of Judah. [1 Chr. 4:20]
BEN-HESED (Heb. 'son of loving kindness') *c.* 10 century BC. One of King Solomon's twelve officers responsible for supplying the provisions of the royal household. [1 Kgs. 4:10]
BEN-HINNOM *see* HINNOM
BEN-HUR (Heb. 'son of Hur [a god]') *c.* 10 century BC. One of King Solomon's twelve officers responsible for the provisions of the royal household. [1 Kgs. 4:8]

BENINU (Heb. 'our son') 5 century BC. One of the Levites in the days of Nehemiah who signed the solemn covenant. [Neh. 10:13]

BENJAMIN (Heb. 'son of the south') **1.** *c.* 16 century BC. Youngest son of Jacob.

Benjamin was born to Rachel when Jacob and his family were near Bethlehem on their way to Hebron. The dying Rachel called the baby Benoni ('son of my sorrow') but Jacob renamed him Benjamin.

He was probably too young to have taken part with his brothers in the episode which caused Rachel's elder son Joseph to be sold into slavery in Egypt. Later when there was famine in Canaan, Jacob sent ten of his sons to Egypt to buy food, but refused to let Benjamin go 'for he feared that harm might befall him' (Gen. 42:4).

Joseph, by now the most powerful man in Egypt next to Pharaoh, recognized his brothers though they did not know him. He sent them back with their grain bags full but kept Simeon as hostage for their promise to return with Benjamin, whom he was longing to see. Jacob reluctantly agreed and the brothers returned to Egypt. Joseph gave them dinner, and startled the brothers by seating them correctly according to their age. He sent food from his table to theirs and gave Benjamin five times more than the others.

When the time came to return to Hebron, Joseph commanded his steward to fill their bags with food but put his silver cup in Benjamin's sack. Joseph then sent his men after them and they were brought back under arrest for theft. Joseph upbraided them for the supposed theft and declared as a penalty that Benjamin would have to remain as his bondsman. Judah spoke up insisting that the loss of Benjamin would kill their father, and offered to remain behind instead. Ordering everyone out of the room, Joseph told his brothers who he was, and there was a tearful reunion. Joseph proposed they should fetch their father Jacob and the rest of the family and settle in Egypt. This was done, and when Jacob left Hebron with his entire family, it included the ten sons of Benjamin.

On his deathbed Jacob blessed his sons in turn. Concerning Benjamin, he forecast the martial qualities for which the tribe of that name would be renowned: 'Benjamin is a ravenous wolf, in the morning devouring the prey, and at even dividing the spoil.' (Gen. 49:27) Centuries later, in the conquest of Canaan under Joshua, the tribe of Benjamin was allocated a narrow strip across the Judean hills from the Shephelah to the Jordan valley at Jericho, with Jerusalem (still belonging to the Jebusites) just within its border. Perhaps because of Jerusalem, in the blessing attributed to Moses it is said of Benjamin: 'The beloved of the Lord, he dwells in safety by him.' (Deut. 33:13) Also called Benoni. [Gen. 35; 42-46; 49:27; Exod. 1:3; Deut. 33:12; 1 Chr. 2:2; 7:6]
2. *c.* 16 century BC. Son of Bilhan and a leader and warrior of the tribe of Benjamin. [1 Chr. 7:10]

Benjamin is brought before Joseph after the silver cup has been found in his sack. Illumination from a 13th-century French manuscript.

View of the Judean hills in the territory of the tribe
of Benjamin.

3. 5 century BC. One of the descendants of Harim who
divorced their non-Jewish wives in the time of Ezra.
[Ezra 10:32]
4. 5 century BC. One of the leaders of Judah in the time
of Nehemiah who helped repair the walls of Jerusalem
and later took part in the ceremony of dedication when
the walls had been completely rebuilt. [Neh. 3:23; 12:34]
BENO (Heb. 'his son') *c.* 10 century BC. Son of Jaaziah,
a Levite descended from Merari, he ministered in the
Tabernacle in the reign of King David. [1 Chr. 24:26, 27]
BENONI *see* BENJAMIN **1.**
BEOR (Heb. 'burning') **1.** date unknown. Father of

Bela, first king of Edom. [Gen. 36:32; 1 Chr. 1:43]
2. *c.* 13 century BC. Father of the prophet Balaam.
[Num. 22:5; 24:3, 15; 31:8; Deut. 23:4; Josh. 13:22;
24:9; Mic. 6:5]
BERA (Heb. 'son of evil') *c.* 18 century BC. A king of
Sodom who joined four other kings against Chedorlaomer, king of Elam in the time of Abraham (when he
was still called Abram). The kings of Sodom and
Gomorrah fled and fell in the vale of Siddim which was
full of bitumin pits and their flocks and possessions were
seized by the victorious enemy. After Abram succeeded
in recovering the captives and the possessions, the king

The traditional tomb of Benjamin, on the road to
Hadera. The present building was erected in the
19th century.

of Sodom offered Abram the goods as a reward but he refused to take them. [Gen. 14:1-24]

BERACAH (Heb. 'blessing') 11 century BC. One of the Benjaminite warriors who joined David at Ziklag. [1 Chr. 12:3]

BERAIAH (Heb. 'the Lord created') date unknown. A son of Shimei and a leader of the tribe of Benjamin who settled in Jerusalem. [1 Chr. 8:21]

BERECHIAH (Heb. 'God has blessed') **1.** 10 century BC. Father of Asaph, a leading singer in the religious services of King David. [1 Chr. 6:39; 15:17]

2. 10 century BC. A gatekeeper of the Ark in the time of King David. [1 Chr. 15:23]

3. 8 century BC. Son of Meshillemoth and one of the leaders of the tribe of Ephraim in the time of King Pekah of Israel and King Ahaz of Judah. When Pekah's forces attacked Judah and brought thousands of captives to Samaria, Berechiah was one of those who supported the prophet Oded against the army and insisted on freeing the captives and returning them to Judah. [2 Chr. 28:8-15]

4. date unknown. Son of Zerubbabel, a descendant of King David. [1 Chr. 3:20]

5. 6 century BC. Son of Asa the Levite, he ministered in the Temple after the return from exile in Babylon. [1 Chr. 9:16]

6. 6 century BC. Father of Zechariah the prophet. [Zech. 1:1, 7]

7. 5 century BC. Son of Meshezabel and father of Meshullam who helped repair the walls of Jerusalem in the time of Nehemiah. [Neh. 3:4, 30; 6:18]

BERED *see* BECHER 2.

BERI date unknown. Son of Zophah, one of the leaders and 'mighty warriors' (1 Chr. 7:40) of the tribe of Asher. [1 Chr. 7:36]

BERIAH (Heb. 'excellent') **1.** *c.* 16 century BC. One of the four sons of Asher and a grandson of Jacob, he accompanied his grandfather into Egypt. [Gen. 46:17; Num. 26:44, 45; 1 Chr. 7:30, 31]

2. *c.* 16 century BC. Son of Ephraim and a grandson of Jacob, he was born after some of his brothers had been killed by the men of Gath. [1 Chr. 7:23]

3. 10 century BC. Son of Shimei, one of the Levites who served in the Tabernacle in the reign of King David. [1 Chr. 23:10, 11]

4. date unknown. One of the leaders of the tribe of Benjamin living in Aijalon 'who put to flight the inhabitants of Gath'. [1 Chr. 8:13, 16]

BESAI date unknown. Ancestor of a family that returned with Zerubbabel to Judah from exile in Babylon. [Ezra 2:49; Neh. 7:52]

BESODEIAH (Heb. 'the secret of God') 5 century BC. Father of Meshullam who helped repair the Old Gate of Jerusalem in the time of Nehemiah. [Neh. 3:6]

BETHUEL (Heb. 'house of God') *c.* 18 century BC.

Father of Rebekah and Laban, and a nephew of Abraham, he gave his daughter in marriage to Abraham's son Isaac. [Gen. 22:22, 23; 24:15, 24, 47; 25:20; 28:2-5]

BETHZUR date unknown. Son of Maon and a descendant of Caleb the brother of Jerahmeel. [1 Chr. 2:45]

BEZAI 1. date unknown. Ancestor of a family who returned to Judah with Zerubbabel from captivity in Babylon. [Ezra 2:17; Neh. 7:23]

2. 5 century BC. One of the leaders of Judah who signed the solemn covenant in the time of Nehemiah. [Neh. 10:18]

BEZALEL (Heb. 'in the Lord's shadow') **1.** *c.* 13 century BC. Chief designer of the Tabernacle. Bezalel was the son of Uri, of the tribe of Judah. The Lord told Moses that Bezalel had been chosen to carry out the work on the Tabernacle: 'And I have filled him with the Spirit of God, with ability and intelligence, with knowledge and all craftmanship.' (Exod. 31:3) His gifts included work in gold, silver, stone, wood, embroidery, weaving and engraving. He designed the Tabernacle, the Ark and the furniture. Among the other gifts the Lord gave to Bezalel was the ability to teach his divinely inspired crafts and skills to others. [Exod. 31:2-11; 35:30-35; 36-39; 1 Chr. 2:20; 2 Chr. 1:5]

2. 5 century BC. A descendant of Pahath-moab who divorced his non-Jewish wife in the time of Ezra. [Ezra 10:30]

One of Bezalel's many crafts was weaving:
Egyptian funerary model of a weaving workshop,
Middle Kingdom.

BEZER (Heb. 'fortification') date unknown. Son of Zophah, he was a leader of the tribe of Asher and a brave warrior. [1 Chr. 7:37]

BICHRI (Heb. 'youthful') 10 century BC. Father of Sheba, a Benjaminite who led a revolt against King David. [2 Sam. 20:1]

BIDKAR (Heb. 'stabber') *c.* 9 century BC. The aide of Jehu son of Nimshi who assassinated King Joram of Israel and seized the throne. Bidkar threw Joram's body into the vineyard of Naboth. [2 Kgs. 9:25]

BIGTHA (Pers. 'gift of God') *c.* 5 century BC. One of the seven chamberlains of King Ahasuerus who was commanded by the drunken king on the seventh day of a feast to bring Queen Vashti before his guests to show off her beauty. [Esther 1:10]

BIGTHAN (Pers. 'gift of God') *c.* 5 century BC. One of the two doorkeepers of King Ahasuerus who conspired to kill the king. The plot was discovered and the conspirators were executed. Also called Bigthana in the Book of Esther and Gabatha in the Greek Additions to the Book of Esther, in the Apocrypha. [Esther 2:21; 6:2]

BIGTHANA *see* BIGTHAN

BIGVAI 1. 6 century BC. A leader of Judah who returned with Zerubbabel from exile in Babylon. [Ezra 2:2, 14; 8:14; Neh. 7:7, 19]
2. 5 century BC. A leader of Judah who signed the solemn covenant in the time of Nehemiah. [Neh. 10:16]

BILDAD period of the patriarchs. One of Job's friends who remonstrated with him.

Bildad the Shuhite was one of three friends who hurried to comfort Job when they heard of his afflictions. They were shocked to see his changed appearance. They 'rent their robes and sprinkled dust upon their heads toward heaven' (Job. 2:12). They sat down with him without speaking for seven days and seven nights. Then Job began to curse the day he had been born and to protest that his suffering was undeserved. Bildad and the other two tried to console him. They expressed the traditional and pious views about his suffering. Bildad asked him, 'Does God pervert justice? Or does the Almighty pervert the right? ... God will not reject a blameless man, nor take the hand of evildoers.' (Job 8:3, 20) As Job maintained his innocence, Bildad insisted that if he would only admit his faults God would forgive him: '... how can he who is born of woman be clean? Behold, even the moon is not bright and the stars are not clean in his sight.' (Job 25:4, 5)

But Job made no effort to conceal his impatience with Bildad and his other two friends, and utterly rejected their advice to bear his trials with silent fortitude. 'So these three men ceased to answer Job, because he was righteous in his own eyes.' (Job 32:1)

Finally the Lord spoke to Job out of a whirlwind and he was completely overwhelmed and humbled. Then the Lord turned on the three friends and told them that

he was angry with them for 'you have not spoken of me what is right, as my servant Job has' (Job 42:7). The Lord then instructed them to offer up a burnt sacrifice 'and my servant Job shall pray for you, for I will accept his prayer' (Job 42:8). [Job 2, 8, 18, 25, 42]

BILGAH (Heb. 'cheerfulness') **1.** 10 century BC. A priest in the reign of King David who took the fifteenth turn of service in the Tabernacle. [1 Chr. 24:14]
2. 6 century BC. A priest who returned with Zerubbabel from exile in Babylon. [Neh. 12:5, 18]

BILGAI (Heb. 'cheerfulness') 5 century BC. A priest who signed the solemn covenant in the time of Nehemiah. [Neh. 10:8]

BILHAH (Heb. 'modesty') *c.* 16 century BC. Rachel's maidservant. When Jacob married Rachel, her father Laban gave her Bilhah to be her servant. Though Jacob loved Rachel very much, she remained childless for a long time. In desperation she asked Jacob to take her handmaid 'that she may bear upon my knees, and even I may have children by her' (Gen. 30:3). Bilhah and Jacob had two sons, Dan and Naphtali, the legendary ancestors of the tribes bearing those names. She later had an illicit affair with Reuben, Jacob's eldest son by his first wife Leah. [Gen. 29:29; 30:3-8; 35:22; 37:2; 46:25; 1 Chr. 7:13]

BILHAN (Heb. 'modest') **1.** date unknown. Son of Ezer and a descendant of Esau, he was a leader of the Horites in the land of Seir. [Gen. 36:27; 1 Chr. 1:42]
2. date unknown. Son of Jediael and a leader of the tribe of Benjamin. [1 Chr. 7:10]

BILSHAN (Heb. 'eloquent') 6 century BC. A leader of Judah who returned with Zerubbabel from exile in Babylon. [Ezra 2:2; Neh. 7:7]

BIMHAL date unknown. Son of Japhlet, he was a leader of the tribe of Asher and a mighty warrior. [1 Chr. 7:33]

BINEA (Heb. 'fountain') date unknown. Son of Moza of the tribe of Benjamin and a descendant of King Saul. [1 Chr. 8:37; 9:43]

BINNUI (Heb. 'building') **1.** 6 century BC. Head of a family who returned with Zerubbabel to Judah from Babylon. [Neh. 7:15; 12:8]
2. 5 century BC. Son of Henadad, he helped rebuild the walls of Jerusalem in the time of Nehemiah. He also signed the covenant. [Neh. 3:24; 10:9]
3. 5 century BC. Father of Noadiah, the Levite, who helped weigh the holy vessels brought back to Jerusalem from Babylon in the time of Ezra. [Ezra 8:33]
4. 5 century BC. A descendant of Pahath-moab who divorced his non-Jewish wife in the time of Ezra. His sons did likewise. [Ezra 10:30, 38]

BIRSHA *c.* 18 century BC. King of Gomorrah in the days of Abraham, who with four other kings was defeated in battle by Chedorlaomer, king of Elam, and his three confederate kings. [Gen. 14:2-24]

BIRZAITH (Heb. 'son of olive tree') date unknown. Son of Malchiel and a leader of the tribe of Asher. [1 Chr. 7:31]

BISHLAM (Heb. 'son of peace') *c.* 5 century BC. A Persian official in Samaria who with others wrote to Artaxerxes I, king of Persia, protesting against the rebuilding of Jerusalem by the Jews after their return from Babylon. [Ezra 4:7]

BITHIAH (Heb. 'daughter of the Lord') date unknown. Daughter of a pharaoh who married Mered of the tribe of Judah. [1 Chr. 4:17]

BIZTHA (Pers. 'eunuch') *c.* 5 century BC. One of the seven chamberlains of King Ahasuerus who was commanded by the drunken king on the seventh day of a feast to bring Queen Vashti before his guests to show off her beauty. [Esther 1:10]

BOAZ (Heb. 'strength') *c.* 11 century BC. Husband of Ruth.

Boaz was a well-to-do landowner in the town of Bethlehem. One spring day he went to his barley field, where his servants were reaping the harvest. He noticed that behind them a comely young woman was gleaning the scattered ears left behind by the reapers. He learned on enquiry that she was Ruth, the widow of his relative Mahlon son of Elimelech, and that she had just arrived in Bethlehem from her native land of Moab with her widowed mother-in-law Naomi. Boaz spoke kindly to Ruth and praised her for her devotion to Naomi. He told her to go on gleaning his fields with his servants, where she would not be molested, and invited her to share their food and water.

At the end of the harvest Boaz spent the night on the winnowing floor after the usual feasting. Under Naomi's guidance, Ruth dressed herself in her best clothes and went to lie at the feet of the sleeping Boaz. He woke in the middle of the night and was surprised to find Ruth there. She asked him humbly to spread the edge of his cloak over her as he was a close relative. Boaz was touched and flattered by the way Ruth entrusted herself to him, when she might have gained the attention of younger men; '... for all my fellow townsmen know that you are a woman of worth' (Ruth 3:11). Concerned lest she should be seen with him, Boaz sent Ruth back to Naomi before dawn, with a cloakful of grain.

The same morning Boaz opened discussion with a kinsman who was more closely related to Elimelech. In the presence of ten elders of the town, acting as witnesses, he asked whether the other wanted to buy from Naomi the piece of land that had belonged to Elimelech, and at the same time acquire Ruth as his wife. The relative declined, and Boaz formally declared his intention to do so himself. The agreement was sealed in the customary manner of the times, by taking off and handing over one sandal.

Boaz then married Ruth. A son was born to them whom they called Obed. In due course Obed's son Jesse became the father of King David, who was therefore the great-grandson of Boaz and Ruth. [Book of Ruth; 1 Chr. 2:11, 12]

BOCHERU (Heb. 'young') date unknown. A son of Azel, he was a member of the tribe of Benjamin and a descendant of King Saul. [1 Chr. 8:38; 9:44]

BOHAN date unknown. A member of the tribe of Reuben after whom a stone was named that marked the boundary between the tribal lands of Benjamin and Judah. [Josh. 15:6; 18:17]

BUKKI (Heb. 'void') **1.** *c.* 13 century BC. Son of Jogli, he was a leader of the tribe of Dan appointed by Moses to take part in dividing the land of Israel among the tribes. [Num. 34:22]

2. date unknown. Son of Abishua, descendant of Aaron the high priest and ancestor of Ezra. [1 Chr. 6:5, 51; Ezra 7:4]

BUKKIAH (Heb. 'wasting') *c.* 10 century BC. One of the fourteen sons of Heman, Levite and musician at religious services in the time of King David, he and his sons took the sixth turn of service. [1 Chr. 25:4, 13]

BUNAH (Heb. 'discretion') date unknown. A son of Hezron of the tribe of Judah. [1 Chr. 2:25]

BUNNI (Heb. 'built') **1.** date unknown. The ancestor of the Levite Shemaiah who settled in Jerusalem in the time of Nehemiah. [Neh. 11:15]

2. 5 century BC. A Levite in the days of Ezra and Nehemiah, he participated in the service of confession on the public fast day proclaimed by Ezra and later signed the solemn covenant. [Neh. 9:4; 10:15]

BUZ 1. *c.* 18 century BC. Second son of Nahor, brother of Abraham, his descendants formed an Arabian desert tribe. [Gen. 22:21]

2. date unknown. One of the ancestors of the Gadites living on the eastern side of the Jordan river. [1 Chr. 5:14]

BUZI 6 century BC. Father of the prophet Ezekiel. [Ezek. 1:3]

C

CAIN (Heb. 'spear') date unknown. The first-born of Adam and Eve.

Cain was a tiller of the soil, while his younger brother Abel was a shepherd. When the two brothers came to make their offerings to the Lord, Abel brought young lambs while Cain brought the first-fruits of the field. God rejected Cain's offering but accepted that of Abel. Seeing Cain's wrath, the Lord gave him advice on how to control himself: 'Why are you angry, and why has your countenance fallen? If you do well, will you not be accepted? And if you do not do well, sin is couching at the door; its desire is for you, but you must master it.' (Gen. 4:6, 7) Cain remained angry. He asked Abel to come into the fields and there killed him.

The Lord asked Cain what had happened to Abel, and he replied 'I do not know; am I my brother's keeper?' (Gen. 4:9) The Lord cursed Cain and doomed him to failure as a farmer: 'When you till the ground, it shall no longer yield to you its strength.' (Gen. 4:12) Cain would henceforth become a fugitive and a wanderer across the face of the earth. Cain protested that his punishment was heavier than he could bear, and anyone who found him would slay him. God then put a mark on him so that no one would kill him.

Cain travelled to Nod, east of the Garden of Eden, where he settled down, married and had a son, called Enoch. Cain built a city and named it after his son. Enoch's son was Lamech, and among Cain's great-grandsons were Jabal, ancestor of the tent-dwelling nomads; Jubal, father of music by harp and pipe; and Tubal-cain, master of the metalsmiths.

The story of Cain and Abel derives from ancient and fragmentary traditions that may have been taken over by the Hebrews from the Kenites, the desert nomads from whom Moses acquired his wife. This may explain some of the problems scholars find in the biblical account.

One such problem is that the world of Cain is described as inhabited by other people and not just Adam and Eve and their sons. Thus, when the Lord condemned Cain to be a wanderer and a fugitive, he pleaded that 'whoever finds me will slay me' (Gen. 4:14) and the Lord put a mark on him: 'If any one slays Cain,

vengeance shall be taken on him sevenfold.' (Gen. 4:15) Cain then acquired a wife and founded a city in the land of Nod. In the condition of human societies, the story of Cain and Abel marks a stage far advanced from the primitive beginnings. It is only in a legendary sense that Cain and Abel are pictured as the 'children' of the founders of the human race.

The motive for the murder of Abel is perplexing. One theory is that it related to the primitive practice of ritual human sacrifice to propitiate the gods and secure the fertility of the soil, without which the community would starve to death. Part of the punishment for the misguided slaying was, aptly enough, that the ground desecrated by Abel's blood would no longer respond to Cain's cultivation – in other words, the effect was the opposite of that which would have been intended by the sacrifice.

It is not explained why the Lord should have put a

Mesopotamian terracotta plaque showing two men fighting, 2nd millennium BC. The first murder recorded in the Bible is that of Abel by Cain.

Cain and Abel's sacrifice; Cain killing Abel; Cain cast out; and Cain tilling the soil: panel from the gilded bronze Baptistry doors, Florence, by Lorenzo Ghiberti (1378-1455).

mark on Cain to protect him after he had killed his brother; nor is there any indication of the nature of the mark. In a number of primitive societies, it is customary to this day to mark a slayer in a special way, and to banish or isolate him. Such markings include colours painted on the body or face, tattoo marks and incisions, or smearing with mud or dung. Anthropologists surmise that the reason for this practice is to ward off trouble from the spirit of the slain man. In certain tribes even warriors who had killed an enemy in battle must be quarantined or purified afterwards. In some localities it was believed that contact with a murderer would bring misfortune and might even pollute the ground, and this would account for the distinctive marking by which a murderer could be identified on sight. Whatever the explanation for it, the mark of Cain has become a proverbial expression for blood-guilt that cannot be expiated.

However the details may be interpreted, it is clear that the story of Cain and Abel symbolizes the age-old strife in the Near East between 'the Desert and the Sown' – the nomads roaming with their tents and flocks, and the settled tillers of the soil. [Gen. 4]

CALCOL (Heb. 'nourishment') **1.** date unknown. A son of Zerah and a grandson of Judah. [1 Chr. 2:6]
2. date unknown. A son of Mahol who was considered exceptionally wise but whose wisdom was surpassed by that of King Solomon. [1 Kgs. 4:31]

CALEB (Heb. 'dog') **1.** date unknown. Brother of Jerahmeel, he was the son of Hezron and the great-grandson of Judah. His first wife Azubah bore him three sons. After her death he took a second wife, Ephrath, who bore him one son, Hur. Also called Chelubai. [1 Chr. 2:9, 18, 19, 24, 42, 46, 48-50]
2. *c.* 13 century BC. One of the twelve spies sent by Moses to reconnoitre the land of Canaan. Caleb, the son of Jephunneh, was chosen to represent the tribe of Judah when the Lord commanded Moses to send twelve men 'to spy out the land of Canaan, which I give to the people of Israel' (Num. 13:2). He and Joshua of the tribe of Ephraim came back confident and said to Moses and the people, 'Let us go up at once, and occupy it; for we are well able to overcome it.' (Num. 13:30) But the reports of the other ten were much more discouraging. The gathering was cast into gloom and grumbled at the Exodus, till the wrathful Lord decreed that they should stay wandering in the desert for forty years until that generation had died out. However, as a reward for his faith in the Lord, Caleb would survive: 'But my servant Caleb, because he has a different spirit and has followed me fully, I will bring into the land into which he went, and his descendants shall possess it.' (Num. 14:24)

When the children of Israel finally reached Canaan, Caleb, now eighty-five years of age, reminded Joshua that Moses had promised him the area he had visited as a spy. 'Then Joshua blessed him; and he gave Hebron to Caleb the son of Jephunneh for an inheritance.' (Josh. 14:13) Caleb drove out the three gigantic sons of Anak who were living there. He married his daughter Achsah to his nephew Othniel who took the neighbouring city of Debir (Kiriath-sepher). Achsah persuaded Caleb to include water sources in the land he gave her for her dowry. [Num. 13:6, 30; 14; 32:12; 34:19; Josh. 14:13, 14; 15:13-19; 21:12; Judg. 1:12-15; 1 Chr. 4:15; 6:56]

CANAAN (Heb. 'red', 'purple') date unknown. A son of Ham, he was condemned by his grandfather Noah to serve the descendants of his father's brothers Shem and Japheth. [Gen. 9:22-27; 10:6; 1 Chr. 1:8]

CAPHTORIM date unknown. A son of Egypt and a grandson of Ham, his descendants settled in Caphtor. [Gen. 10:14; 1 Chr. 1:12]

CARKAS (Pers. 'vulture') *c.* 5 century BC. One of the

seven chamberlains whom Ahasuerus, king of Persia, commanded to bring Queen Vashti to the feast he made in the third year of his reign. [Esther 1:10]

CARMI (Heb. 'vine-dresser') **1.** *c.* 16 century BC. A son of Reuben and a grandson of Jacob and Leah. [Gen. 46:9; Exod. 6:14; Num. 26:6; 1 Chr. 5:3]
2. *c.* 13 century BC. Son of Zabdi, of the tribe of Judah. His son Achan took booty following the capture and destruction of Jericho contrary to the express orders of Joshua, and was stoned to death. [Josh. 7:1, 18; 1 Chr. 2:7; 4:1]

CARSHENA (Pers. 'ploughman') 5 century BC. One of the seven princes of Persia and Media who was present at the feast of King Ahasuerus. [Esther 1:14]

CASLUHIM (Heb. 'fortified') date unknown. A son of Egypt and a grandson of Ham, from whom according to Hebrew tradition the Philistines were descended. [Gen. 10:14; 1 Chr. 1:12]

CHEDORLAOMER (Elamite 'servant of Lagamar [a god]') *c.* 18 century BC. Chedorlaomer was king of Elam, the important land east of Babylonia. He led the four Mesopotamian kings who defeated an alliance of five local kings from the Dead Sea area in the time of Abraham. They carried off a number of captives, including Abraham's nephew Lot, and much booty. Abraham pursued them and rescued the captives and booty.

None of these nine kings has been identified, and none of their countries or cities except Elam. [Gen. 14]

CHELAL (Heb. 'perfect') 5 century BC. Descendant of Pahath-moab. He divorced his non-Jewish wife in the time of Ezra. [Ezra 10:30]

CHELUB (Heb. 'basket') **1.** date unknown. Brother of Shuhah of the tribe of Judah, he was the father of Mehir. [1 Chr. 4:11]
2. 10 century BC. Father of Ezri who was the supervisor of the people who tilled the fields in the reign of King David. [1 Chr. 27:26]

CHELUBAI *see* CALEB 1.

CHELUHI 5 century BC. Descendant of Bani, he married a non-Jewish wife and later divorced her in the time of Ezra. [Ezra 10:35]

CHEMOSH date unknown. The national god of Moab and Ammon. The sacred rites to this god included human sacrifice. Mesha, king of Moab, in the hope of changing the course of the war, offered up his eldest son as a burnt offering after his defeat by the armies of Jehoram, king of Israel, and Jehoshaphat, king of Judah. [Num. 21:29; Judg. 11:24; 1 Kgs. 11:7, 33; 2 Kgs. 3:27; Jer. 48:13]

CHENAANAH (Heb. 'merchant') **1.** date unknown. Son of Bilhan of the tribe of Benjamin, he and his family were warrior leaders of the tribe. [1 Chr. 7:10]
2. 9 century BC. Father of Zedekiah, the false prophet who told Ahab, king of Israel, that he would defeat the

Hittite cylinder seal, 2nd millennium BC, showing human sacrifice. Cain's murder has been related to the primitive practice of human sacrifice.

Syrians in battle at Ramoth-gilead. [1 Kgs. 22:11, 24; 2 Chr. 18:10, 23]

CHENANI 5 century BC. A Levite who was a leading worshipper at the solemn fast day proclaimed by Ezra and Nehemiah. [Neh. 9:4]

CHENANIAH (Heb. 'made by God') **1.** 10 century BC. A Levite musician in the reign of King David, he supervised the singing of the Levites while the Ark of God was being brought to Jerusalem. [1 Chr. 15:22]

2. 10 century BC. A Levite descended from Izhar, he and his sons supervised the government administration by the judges and public officials in the reign of King David. [1 Chr. 26:29]

CHERAN date unknown. Son of Dishon and a descendant of Seir, the Horite. [Gen. 36:26; 1 Chr. 1:41]

CHERETHITES (Heb. 'executioners') 10 century BC. Part of the bodyguard of King David's army commanded by Benaiah son of Jehoiada. [2 Sam. 8:18; 15:18; 20:23; 1 Kgs. 1:38, 44; 1 Chr. 18:17]

CHESED (Heb. 'gain') *c.* 18 century BC. Fourth son of Abraham's brother Nahor and his wife Milcah. [Gen. 22:22]

CHIDON *see* NACON

CHILEAB (Heb. 'like the father') 10 century BC. Second son of King David, born in Hebron, his mother was Abigail, the Carmelitess. Also called Daniel. [2 Sam. 3:3; 1 Chr. 3:1]

CHILION (Heb. 'sickly') *c.* 11 century BC. Younger son of Elimelech of the tribe of Judah, he and his family left their native town of Bethlehem during a famine in the time of Judges and settled in Moab. Chilion and his elder brother Mahlon married Moabite women, Ruth and Orpah. After the death of Chilion and Mahlon,

Ruth went back to Bethlehem with their mother Naomi, and later married their relative Boaz. [Ruth 1:1-5]

CHIMHAM (Heb. 'longing') *c.* 10 century BC. Chimham was the son of Barzillai, the Gilead notable who befriended and helped David when he fled from Absalom's revolt. The grateful David kept Chimham at his court, and charged Solomon to be kind to Barzillai's offspring. Geruth Chimham, a place near Bethlehem, was named after him. [2 Sam. 19:37-41; Jer. 41:17]

CHISLON (Heb. 'hope') *c.* 13 century BC. A leader in the days of Moses, his son Elidad was appointed to divide the portion of the land of Israel allocated to Benjamin among the members of the tribe. [Num. 34:21]

COL-HOZEH (Heb. 'all seeing') 5 century BC. Son of Hazaiah of the tribe of Judah, his son Shallum was governor of part of Mizpah in the days of Nehemiah and repaired the gate of the fountain and the Pool of Shiloh in Jerusalem. [Neh. 3:15; 11:5]

CONANIAH (Heb. 'made by God') **1.** 8 century BC. A Levite appointed by Hezekiah, king of Judah, to supervise the bringing of offerings and tithes into the Temple. [2 Chr. 31:12, 13]

2. 7 century BC. One of the chief Levites of Judah in the reign of King Josiah who donated large quantities of cattle for the Passover offering. [2 Chr. 35:9]

CONIAH *see* JEHOIACHIN

COZBI (Heb. 'fruitful') *c.* 13 century BC. Daughter of Zur, a Midianite chief, she was brought by Zimri into the Israelite encampment in the Jordan Valley. The priest Phinehas slew them with a javelin while they were lying together in a tent. The Lord was mollified by this act and lifted the plague he had inflicted on the children of Israel for their immorality. [Num. 25:15, 18]

CUSH (Heb. 'black') **1.** date unknown. Eldest son of Ham and a grandson of Noah, he was the father of Nimrod, and by Hebrew tradition regarded as the ancestor of the Cushites, a Negro tribe which settled south of Egypt. [Gen. 10:6, 8; 1 Chr. 1:8-10]

2. *c.* 11 century BC. A Benjaminite soldier in King Saul's army who was sent in pursuit of David. [Ps. 7]

CUSHAN-RISHATHAIM *c.* 12 century BC. King of Mesopotamia, he oppressed the children of Israel and forced them to pay heavy tribute for eight years until his hold was broken by Othniel the son of Kenaz, younger brother of Caleb. [Judg. 3:8-10]

CUSHI 1. *c.* 10 century BC. A soldier in the army of King David, he was sent by Joab, David's army commander, to report to David about the death of Absalom his son and the victory of the king's army against the rebels. [2 Sam. 18:21-32]

2. *c.* 7 century BC. Great-grandfather of Jehudi, who told Baruch to read out the prophecies of Jeremiah to the leaders of Judah. [Jer. 36:14]

3. *c.* 7 century BC. Son of Gedaliah, he was the father of the prophet Zephaniah. [Zeph. 1:1]

The tomb of Cyrus the Great, king of Persia (549-29 BC), at Pasagardae. It was originally surrounded by stone columns.

CYRUS II (The Great) (Pers. 'son') King of the Medes and the Persians, 559-29 BC. Cyrus II was the son of Cambyses I, king of Anshan, and of Mandane, daughter of King Astyages of the Medes. He succeeded to the throne in 559 BC and rapidly gained control of the surrounding peoples. By 549 BC he had conquered Media. In 539 BC he defeated the Babylonian army and became the ruler of the largest empire the world had seen till then.

Cyrus was a generous conqueror, especially remembered in the Bible for his friendship towards the Jews. 'The Lord stirred up the spirit of Cyrus king of Persia' (2 Chr. 36:22), and he gave the captive Jews he found in Babylon permission to return and rebuild the Temple in Jerusalem. He suggested that those who could not

return should help by giving gold, silver, goods and animals to pay for the work. Cyrus also gave orders that the thousands of vessels of the house of the Lord, which Nebuchadnezzar had brought from Jerusalem, should be handed over to the Jews and returned to the Temple. As a result of the active interest Cyrus took in the Jews he is referred to in Isaiah as the 'shepherd' of the Lord (Isa. 44:28) or his 'anointed' (Isa. 45:1).

An excavated cylinder written in cuneiform script refers to an edict of Cyrus authorizing the return of captives 'to the other side of the Tigris'. This cylinder does not refer to the Jews as such, but is consistent with the account in the Book of Ezra. [2 Chr. 36:22, 23; Ezra 1; 4:3; 5:13-17; 6:3; Isa. 44:28; 45:1; Dan. 1:21; 6:28; 10:1]

D

DAGON (Heb. 'corn') Dagon was a Philistine god. Temples were built to him at Gaza, Ashdod and Beth-shean, and his name was incorporated in the city of Beth-dagon, in the Judean foothills. Professor W.F. Albright believes that Dagon was an Accadian god worshipped in the Euphrates valley as early as the 25th century BC.

Three events in the Old Testament took place in shrines to this god: Samson died by pulling down the temple to Dagon in Gaza; many Philistine worshippers were killed when the captured Israelite Ark was placed in the temple of Dagon at Ashdod and the statue of the god fell down; and the head of the slain King Saul was placed in the temple of Dagon at Beth-shean after the Israelite defeat on Mount Gilboa. [Josh. 15:41; Judg. 16:23-30; 1 Sam. 5; 1 Chr. 10:10]

DALAIAH *see* DELAIAH

DALPHON *c*. 5 century BC. One of the ten sons of Haman the Agagite, he joined his father's plot to eliminate all the Jews in Persia. [Esther 9:7]

DAN (Heb. 'judge') *c*. 16 century BC. Fifth son of Jacob. Dan was the elder son of Bilhah, the maid Rachel gave Jacob her husband as a concubine. Together with his brothers, he was involved in the events that led to the selling of their brother Joseph into slavery in Egypt. Later he was one of the ten sons sent by Jacob to buy

Reconstruction of the temple founded by Rameses II at Beth-shean in the 13th century BC, which remained in use until the time of King Saul.

corn in Egypt, where Joseph had become a leading figure at Pharaoh's court. When Jacob went to settle in Egypt with all his family, it included Dan's son.

On his deathbed Jacob blessed all his sons in turn, and said: 'Dan shall judge his people.' (Gen. 49:16)

In the blessing attributed to Moses, it is said: 'Dan is a lion's whelp, that leaps forth from Bashan.' (Deut. 33:22)

In the conquest of Canaan under Joshua, the small tribe of Dan was allocated an area in the foothills southwest of Ephraim. It was pushed out by Philistine pressure and resettled in the north-east corner of the country. [Gen. 30:6; 35:25; 46:23; 49:16, 17; Exod. 1:4; Num. 26:42; Deut. 33:22; Josh. 19:47; 1 Chr. 2:2]

DANIEL (Heb. 'God is my judge') **1.** *see* CHILEAB

2. *c.* 6 century BC. Hebrew official at Babylonian court. The Book of Daniel opens with King Nebuchadnezzar of Babylonia instructing his chief eunuch to select a number of boys from noble families and put them through a three-year course of instruction for service as scribes at the court. They were to be physically fit and mentally bright. Daniel was one of the four Jewish boys selected, the other three being Hananiah, Mishael and Azariah. They were given the Babylonian names of Belteshazzar, Shadrach, Meshach and Abednego.

The king ordered that the youths in training should be given food and drink from the royal table. This would have violated the religious dietary laws of the Jewish boys, so Daniel persuaded those in charge to allow them to eat only vegetables and drink only water. At first they were afraid the health of the boys would suffer and the chief eunuch would get into trouble with the king. But a ten-day trial proved they could thrive on the vegetarian diet.

Some years later, the king had a most disturbing dream. When his magicians and wise men could not interpret it he flew into a rage and ordered their death.

In a vision the king's dream was revealed to Daniel.

Daniel's companions, Shadrach, Meshach and Abednego, in the fiery furnace. Medieval drawing.

Next morning he was brought before the king, and told him that he had dreamt of a great statue. 'The head of this image was of fine gold, its breast and arms of silver, its belly and thighs of bronze, its legs of iron, its feet partly of iron and partly of clay.' (Dan. 2:32, 33) A stone came hurling out of nowhere and smashed the clay feet, at which the whole statue disintegrated into fine particles that were blown away by the wind. The stone then grew into a great mountain that filled the earth.

Daniel explained that the golden head of the statue was Nebuchadnezzar himself, and the silver, bronze, iron and clay parts represented lesser kingdoms that would succeed the Babylonian one – until all of them were swept away by the kingdom of God that would last forever.

The astounded king exclaimed: 'Truly, your God is God of gods and Lord of kings, and a revealer of mysteries, for you have been able to reveal this mystery.' (Dan. 2:47) He heaped honours and riches on Daniel, who became the chief of all the wise men and governor of the province of Babylon.

Nebuchadnezzar erected a huge golden statue and assembled all the high officials and the notables to prostrate themselves before it to 'the sound of the horn, pipe, lyre, trigon, harp, bagpipe, and every kind of music ...' (Dan. 3:5). Certain courtiers reported to the monarch that the Jews refused to join in this act of idol-worship; they referred specifically to Daniel's companions Shadrach, Meshach and Abednego who had been given official positions. The angry king ordered them to be tied up and flung into a fiery furnace. It radiated such fierce heat that the servants who thrust them in were burnt to death. The Lord sent an angel into the furnace who protected the three young Hebrews. Overwhelmed by this miracle, the king called to them to come out; '... the hair of their heads was not singed, their mantles were not harmed, and no smell of fire had come upon them' (Dan. 3:27). Nebuchadnezzar issued a decree that the mighty God of the Hebrews was to be treated with respect throughout his realm.

Nebuchadnezzar was filled with dread by another ominous dream. In it he saw a tall tree reaching up to the sky. It provided abundant fruit; the birds nested in the branches; and the animals sheltered beneath it. A 'holy one' (Dan. 4:13) came down from heaven and had the tree cut down, leaving only the stump in the ground. The king sent for Daniel, who told him that the tree stood for Nebuchadnezzar himself in all his power and glory. In order to humble him and teach him that the Lord ruled over all, he would be reduced to the level of

Ivory plaque from Megiddo, 13th-12th centuries BC, showing a winged lion. One of the beasts in Daniel's vision was a lion with eagle's wings.

an animal. He would be driven out of human society, eat grass like an ox and be drenched by the rain and dew. Daniel begged the king to repent and change his ways while there was yet time.

A year later, while the king was boasting of his might, he was attacked by a fit of madness and behaved in the way that Daniel had foretold. When he recovered his sanity he extolled God and was restored to his former greatness.

The next episode in Daniel's story concerns Belshazzar, who is described as Nebuchadnezzar's son and his successor on the throne. He gave a great feast in the palace, attended by all his household and a thousand of his nobles. His princes, wives and concubines drank wine from the vessels from the Temple in Jerusalem that Nebuchadnezzar had brought to Babylon.

Suddenly a hand appeared and wrote on the wall of the banquet chamber the words: 'MENE, MENE, TEKEL, and PARSIN' (Dan. 5:25). Nobody could understand this mysterious message and they were stricken with terror. The queen remembered Daniel and he was brought before Belshazzar. Daniel interpreted the writing on the wall as follows: 'MENE, God has numbered the days of your kingdom and brought it to an end; TEKEL, you have been weighed in the balances and found wanting; PARSIN, your kingdom is divided and given to the Medes and Persians.' (Dan. 5:26, 27, 28) (The three words are Aramaic terms denoting numbers, weight and divisions.)

That night Belshazzar was assassinated 'And Darius the Mede received the kingdom' (Dan. 5:31).

Darius made Daniel once more one of the most powerful men in the kingdom. Those who were jealous of his position tried to discredit him, but were unable to find any fault in his public service. Hoping to hit at him through his faith, they persuaded Darius to issue an edict whereby for thirty days everyone was to worship the king alone, on penalty of being thrown to the lions.

Daniel ignored the order and went on praying to the Lord three times a day in front of his window, which faced in the direction of Jerusalem. His enemies reported this to the king, who was reluctant to impose the punishment but had no option, since '. . . a law of the Medes and Persians' (Dan. 6:15) was rigid and unalterable. The distressed king had Daniel cast into the den of lions, with a prayer that the Hebrew God would save him. The entrance was blocked with a stone, and the king's seal placed upon it, together with those of his lords.

The king remained awake, fasted all night, and early next morning hurried back to the lions' pit. To his delight Daniel emerged unscathed, saying 'My God sent his angel and shut the lions' mouths, and they have not hurt me' (Dan. 6:22). The king promptly had Daniel's accusers thrown into the den, and this time there was no angel to save them. Darius too issued a proclamation calling for all his subjects to honour the God of Daniel. These simply told tales, set in the Babylon of the 6th century BC, were obviously written down centuries later, since the references to Babylonian rulers are incorrect. But the stories did bear out that God was stronger than alien rulers and would take care of the faithful. That reassurance was needed in the Judea of the 2nd century BC when the Book of Daniel was written, appropriately during the Maccabean revolt against the religious

Subject peoples bringing tribute, from the north wall at Persepolis, the city built by Darius I and his son Xerxes, 6th-5th centuries B.C.

oppression of Antiochus IV Epiphanes (*see* APOCRYPHA section). Moving from the Babylonian past to the dangerous Judean present, the author's style becomes both more sombre and more obscure. Daniel is now relating his personal visions, in which imaginary creatures symbolize the history of foreign domination of the Jews, culminating in the evils of Antiochus's rule.

In the first vision four beasts come out of the sea. They resemble a lion with eagle's wings, a bear, a leopard and a nameless and terrible monster with ten horns: '... and it had great iron teeth; it devoured and broke in pieces, and stamped the residue with its feet' (Dan. 7:7). There is a great judgment and the fourth beast is slain. The kingdom then passes permanently to the 'people of the saints of the Most High' (Dan. 7:27) and is ruled by a 'son of man' (Dan. 7:13). (The four beasts are interpreted by some as the Babylonian, Median, Persian and Seleucid Greek empires. The ten horns are the successive Seleucid kings, with Antiochus Epiphanes identified as a horn with human eyes and a boastful mouth.)

In a second vision a ram with two horns (Media and Persia) is charged from the west and overcome by a he-goat with a single horn (Greece). The horn (Alexander the Great) is replaced by four others (the successor kingdoms of his generals) and the thrusts of one horn indicate the campaigns of Antiochus. The archangel Gabriel reaffirms that the Messiah will come soon.

In the last and longest of his visions, an angel gives in enigmatic language an outline of the historical events from Alexander the Great to Antiochus Epiphanes. The account is continued into the future, when the existing regime will end in turmoil and upheaval. This collapse will receive 'a little help' – a devious reference to the revolt then in progress. In the troubles to come, the God-fearing whose names were written in the 'book of truth' will be saved, 'And many of those who sleep in the dust of the earth shall awake, some to everlasting life, and some to shame and everlasting contempt' (Dan. 12:2).

In substance, the Book of Daniel is a continuation of the Hebrew prophetic strain that developed over many centuries, and had reached its loftiest expression with Isaiah, Jeremiah and Ezekiel. [Book of Daniel]

3. 5 century BC. A priest of Judah who returned with Ezra from exile in Babylon and signed the solemn covenant. [Ezra 8:2; Neh. 10:6]

DARA date unknown. One of the five sons of Zerah and grandson of Judah. [1 Chr. 2:6]

DARDA (Heb. 'thistle') date unknown. A son of Mahol who was considered exceptionally wise but whose wisdom was surpassed by that of King Solomon. [1 Kgs. 4:31]

DARIUS (Pers. 'he who upholds the good') **1. Darius I,** king of Persia, 522-486 BC. Darius the Great, son of Hystaspes, consolidated and organized the huge Persian empire. He authorized the regional governor Tattenai to permit the Jews in Jerusalem to rebuild the Temple, with a contribution from the official tax revenues. Darius also decreed that the animals, wheat, salt, wine or oil required for the priests should be supplied daily so that prayers would be offered 'for the life of the king and his sons' (Ezra 6:10). [Ezra 4, 5, 6; Hag. 1:1, 15; 2:10; Zech. 1:1, 7; 7:1]

2. The Persian king mentioned by Nehemiah may have been Darius II (423-04 BC). [Neh. 12:22]

3. 6 century BC. According to the Book of Daniel, 'Darius the Mede' (Dan. 5:30) became king of Babylon and appointed Daniel one of the three 'presidents' (Dan. 6:2) over the whole kingdom. When the king 'planned to set him over the whole kingdom' (Dan. 6:3), the other two presidents and the princes, jealous of Daniel persuaded Darius to sign a degree that no one in the kingdom was to pray to any other god except the king for thirty days, on pain of being thrown into the lions' den. But Daniel continued to pray to the Lord three times a day. The reluctant king had Daniel thrown into the pit with the lions. The next morning, having fasted all night, the king hurried to the lions' den and to his delight Daniel emerged unscathed. Impressed with the power of the Lord, Darius had Daniel's accusers thrown into the pit and then issued a decree saying that everyone in his kingdom should fear and respect the God of Daniel: 'for he is the living God, enduring for ever' (Dan. 6:26). [Dan. 5:30; 6; 9:1; 11:1]

DARKON (Heb. 'hard') *c.* 10 century BC. A servant of King Solomon whose descendants returned with Zerubbabel from exile in Babylon. [Ezra 2:56; Neh. 7:58]

DATHAN (Heb. 'strong') *c.* 13 century BC. Son of Eliab of the tribe of Reuben, he and his brother Abiram joined a conspiracy led by Korah the Levite against the leadership of Moses and Aaron, and together with Korah and all his followers perished in an earthquake. [Num. 16:1-30; 26:9; Deut. 11:6; Ps. 106:17]

Darius I allowing the cedars of Lebanon to be cut for the rebuilding of the Temple. From a 14th-century German Bible.

The youthful David,
painting on leather
by Andrea del
Castagno (1423-57).

DAVID (possibly Heb. 'commander', 'hero') Second king of Israel, *c.* 1010-970 BC.

The small Judean town of Bethlehem was in a flurry. The prophet Samuel was coming, and the citizens did not know why. Samuel was an austere and formidable man of God, of whom the people had stood in awe for a generation. What could this sudden visit portend? When the great man arrived, the fearful elders of the town enquired, 'Do you come peaceably?' (1 Sam. 16:4) and he reassured them that he did. He had 'come to sacrifice to the Lord' (1 Sam. 16:5) and they were required to sanctify themselves and attend.

Jesse, a prosperous and respected sheep-farmer, was specially summoned to the ceremony by Samuel where he and seven of his eight sons were presented to the prophet in turn. When Jesse was asked whether these were all the sons he had, he replied that the youngest one, David, was out tending the sheep. On Samuel's insistence, David was hurriedly brought in – a ruddy, bright-eyed and attractive lad. Samuel anointed his head with oil 'and the Spirit of the Lord came mightily upon David from that day forward' (1 Sam. 16:13). The prophet returned to his home in Ramah, and Bethlehem went back to its quiet, pastoral life.

The background to Samuel's curious act was his estrangement from Saul. He had made Saul king, but turned against him when Saul refused to be an obedient puppet. Guided by the Lord, Samuel chose as the future successor to Saul a gifted but unknown boy in Bethlehem. David's experience of life till then had been confined to tending sheep in the Bethlehem hills and making up songs to accompany his harp. He was soon to be thrust into high places and stirring events, in a way which would exceed even his most poetic imaginings.

The Young David

After his final break with Samuel, Saul became increasingly subject to fits of melancholy. His worried retainers felt that music might calm the king at such times, and they sought 'a man who is skilful in playing the lyre' (1 Sam. 16:16). One of them then mentioned a lad in Bethlehem who was a skilled musician and the king asked that David be brought to him. Jesse sent him to the palace at Gibeah, bearing a farmer's modest gift of bread, a bottle of wine and a kid. Saul was charmed by young David's good looks and intelligence, and appointed him his armour-bearer. When one of Saul's black moods came upon him, David played to him on his harp 'so Saul was refreshed, and was well, and the evil spirit departed from him' (1 Sam. 16:23). Saul led out his forces against the Philistines, and Jesse's three eldest sons were mobilized. 'David went back and forth from Saul to feed his father's sheep at Bethlehem.' (1 Sam. 17:15)

One day, David was sent by his father to bring victuals from home to his brothers. Jesse prudently included a gift of ten cheeses for their commanding officer. David set out at dawn with these supplies loaded on to a small cart, probably drawn by an ass. Some twelve miles down a ravine from Bethlehem brought him to the Shephelah, the low foothills separating the Hebrews on the mountain plateau from the Philistines on the coastal plain.

In this borderland the two armies now faced each other across a narrow valley through which ran a brook. Neither side would risk an attack across the open ground and up the opposing slope. The Philistines produced a giant soldier from Gath called Goliath, clad in heavy brass armour, carrying a great sword and spear and preceded by a shield-bearer. This human tank paraded daily between the lines, taunting the Israelites and challenging them to send out a champion against him. That was the sight that met David's eyes when he entered the Israelite lines and sought out his brothers. He got talking to a group of soldiers about killing the 'uncircumcised Philistine' (1 Sam. 17:26). His eldest brother Eliab chided David, 'I know your presumption, and the evil of your heart' (1 Sam. 17:28). However, Saul heard these reports and sent for him.

David said stoutly to the king, 'your servant will go and fight with this Philistine' (1 Sam. 17:32). Saul gazed at him in astonishment and brushed aside the idea, 'for you are but a youth, and he has been a man of war from his youth' (1 Sam. 17:33). David maintained that the

9th-century BC figure
of a harpist, found
at Ashkelon.

Lord, who had helped him to slay single-handed a lion and a bear raiding his flock, would protect him against Goliath too. Moved by David's faith, Saul decided to let him try. He made David put on armour and sword, but the boy discarded them, saying he had never worn them before. Instead, he went out equipped only with a stave, a sling and his shepherd's pouch, into which he put five smooth stones carefully selected from the brook.

Goliath could hardly believe his eyes. Lumbering forward, he cried out derisively that he would carve up the youth, and feed his flesh to the birds and beasts. David's sharp tongue mocked the giant, while his nimble feet kept him well out of Goliath's reach. Waiting for the right moment, David hurled a stone from the sling and hit Goliath square in the forehead, so that he fell down stunned. Quick as a cat, David leapt towards Goliath and cut off his head with his own sword. Seeing their champion so abruptly slain, the Philistines started to flee, with the Israelite forces in hot pursuit.

Abner, Saul's general, brought David before the king, who asked him to remain in his service. Saul's son Jonathan was present, and an abiding friendship sprang up between the two men. With a typically warm-hearted gesture, Jonathan took off his own garments and put them on David, together with his sword and bow.

The Guerrilla Years

David made full use of the dazzling turn in his fortune. He was a success as a military officer, and his fame and popularity grew. When the army returned from the campaign, the women who came to greet the king with dancing and music sang that 'Saul has slain his thousands, and David his ten thousands' (1 Sam. 18:7). The king was angered and 'Saul eyed David from that day on' (1 Sam. 18:9).

In one of his evil moods, while David was playing to him, Saul twice tried to kill him with his javelin. After that he sent David on dangerous missions, hoping he might be slain in battle. Saul let David know that he would gain the hand in marriage of one of the king's daughters if he brought back the foreskins of a hundred Philistine soldiers. Instead of losing his life in the attempt, David accounted for double that number of the enemy, and returned to wed the princess Michal.

As David's prestige grew in the kingdom, Saul's resentment grew with it. He sent men to David's house to kill him, but Michal lowered him out of a window and put a dummy in his bed, pretending her husband was ill. David fled to the aged prophet Samuel in Ramah. Saul sent men to catch him, then arrived in person. Fortunately Saul, who had a strong religious streak, was caught up in the ecstasy of the company of prophets around Samuel, and David was able to escape again.

He secretly contacted Jonathan and told him 'there is but a step between me and death' (1 Sam. 20:3). Jona-

The ruins of the city of Keilah, which David saved from the Philistines, identified with Kh. Qîlā, a city mentioned in the Tel el-Amarna Letters.

than would not believe his father really meant to kill his friend. But Saul's rage when David stayed away from a court banquet left no room for doubt. Jonathan sadly agreed that David had to run for his life. The royal favourite and popular commander had become a harried fugitive.

Alone, destitute and unarmed, David reached the priestly sanctuary at Nob near Jerusalem. He pretended to be on a private mission for the king, and the head priest Ahimelech gave him loaves of the sacrificial bread as provisions, and the sword David had once taken from Goliath. (It had been preserved in the sanctuary.) The kindly priests were to pay a cruel price for this aid: the king had all the priests of Nob rounded up and slain. Only Abiathar, the son of the head priest, escaped and managed to join David in the mountains.

In his desperate flight David slipped into the Philistine city of Gath. Its king Achish was later to be his friend and protector, but now David was in the midst of the enemy. He feigned madness – 'made marks on the doors of the gate, and let his spittle run down his beard' (1 Sam. 21:13) – and got away unharmed.

Some fifteen miles north-east from Gath, David reached the hill country of Adullam, overlooking the spot where as a youth he had triumphed over Goliath. The terrain – rocky gorges, bush and hillside caves – was a natural refuge for the band of about four hundred fugitives and malcontents that now gathered around him. His parents could not share the hardships and dangers of his present life, so he put them beyond Saul's reach under the protection of the king of Moab across the Jordan river.

In the Adullam area stood the small Israelite town of Keilah. When this exposed place was raided by the Philistines, David saw a chance to secure a firm base. His lean guerrillas fell upon the Philistines and routed them; and David quartered his men in the town. On hearing this, Saul said to himself: 'God has given him into my hand; for he has shut himself in by entering a town that has gates and bars.' (1 Sam. 23:7) But David was not to be trapped. He led his men out of the comfort of city billets and back into the rugged hills.

David headed south-east past Hebron and in among the wooded ridges of Ziph. From here the Wilderness of Judah dropped steeply eastward to the Dead Sea, gleaming far below. The men of Ziph were afraid of Saul's vengeance, and hastened to reveal the presence in their area of these unwelcome bandits. David was forced to move further south to Maon, where Saul's forces caught up with him and cut him off. Saul had to

turn back to meet a new Philistine threat, and David used the welcome respite to establish himself in the bleak crags and caves overlooking the Dead Sea shore at En-gedi ('the Spring of the Wild Goat').

Saul came back with three thousand picked men to resume his obsessive search. He entered a dark cave to rest, without knowing that David and some of his men were hiding in its depths. The royal hunter was at the mercy of his quarry! Yet David, against the whispered prodding of his companions, refrained from killing 'the Lord's anointed' (1 Sam. 24:6). Instead, he stealthily cut a piece from the hem of Saul's robe.

As Saul emerged from the cave, David came out behind him and called to him. When Saul turned, David bowed himself to the ground and cried out that he had never done any harm to the king and had in fact just spared his life, as the piece of cloth bore witness. The honest and emotional Saul was much moved. 'You are more righteous than I', he exclaimed, 'for you have re-paid me good, whereas I have repaid you evil.' (1 Sam. 24:17) Saul admitted that he expected David to become king of Israel one day and begged him to spare Saul's family when that happened. Saul then withdrew his troops, while David and his men remained in their mountain fastness.

Later, however, Saul resumed his pursuit of David. One night David and his nephew Abishai stole into Saul's slumbering camp and reached the spot where the

David cuts off the edge of Saul's cloak in the cave, and then holds it up after Saul has left. From a 13th-century French manuscript.

king was sleeping on the ground. Abishai urged that Saul be killed, but David refused. Instead, they took away with them Saul's spear and water jar. From a nearby hilltop, David shouted taunts at Saul's commander Abner for failing to protect his royal master. When Saul woke and heard what had happened, he was filled with remorse, and cried out, 'behold, I have played the fool, and have erred exceedingly' (1 Sam. 26:21). He addressed David as his son and gave him his blessing. (This story may be a different version of the episode in the cave.)

Like every guerrilla leader, David was careful not to despoil the local farmers, on whose goodwill his band depended for their supplies. At shearing time David sent ten young men to a certain Nabal, a well-to-do sheep-farmer, to seek provisions. They pointed out that Nabal's flocks had been allowed to graze all winter in the hills, unmolested by David's men. Nabal rudely rebuffed them. David led his men towards Nabal's farmstead, vowing he would wipe out everyone he found there. Abigail, Nabal's attractive and clever wife, acted quickly to head them off. Without her husband's knowledge she intercepted David's party, bringing with her several asses loaded with bread, corn, mutton, wine, raisins and figs. David accepted her food and apologies, and turned back. Abigail returned to find Nabal drunk at the feast after the shearing. Next morning she told him how narrowly he had escaped David's wrath. The frightened Nabal suffered a heart attack, from which he died ten days later.

David, always susceptible to feminine beauty and intelligence, had been much attracted by Abigail. He must also have been lonely, for his wife Michal, the daughter of King Saul, had not followed him into exile but had been remarried by her father to someone else. On learning that Abigail had become a widow, David sent messengers asking her to marry him. Abigail promptly set off to join David, accompanied by five handmaidens. He also took another wife, Ahinoam, from the valley of Jezreel, about whose background nothing is known.

The years of precarious survival in the hills of southern Judea were drawing to a close. David knew he could not hold out much longer against Saul's forces. Moreover, he and his now six hundred irregulars had acquired families, which tied them down and made them yearn for a more secure life. David made a difficult decision. With his whole band, he moved westward into the coastal plain and offered his services to the leading Philistine ruler, Achish the king of Gath. What made this easier was that active warfare had died down at that time between the Israelites and their Philistine adversaries.

David was to remain the henchman of Achish for sixteen months. The king appointed him governor of the small border town of Ziklag, on the edge of the Negev desert, half-way between Gath and Beersheba. From this base David and his men carried out raids against the troublesome desert tribes as far as northern Sinai, bringing back captured sheep, cattle, donkeys and camels. To allay doubts about his loyalty, David's reports suggested that these forays were directed at the Israelites and tribes allied with them.

In due course the alliance of Philistine cities resumed the war against Israel. Their army marched north along the coastal plain and into the valley of Jezreel. Achish wanted David and his men to take an active part in the campaign. Fortunately for David, the other Philistine princes did not share Achish's trust in his able Hebrew vassal, and feared he would defect to his own people. They said 'he shall not go down with us to battle, lest in the battle he become an adversary to us' (1 Sam. 29:4). Achish rather apologetically asked David to return to Ziklag with his men.

It took them three days of forced marches to get back, only to find that in their absence the desert nomad Amalekites had raided the town and carried off the women and the children, including David's. The remaining townsmen were bitter against him and threatened to stone him. David mustered his tired men and set off into the desert in hot pursuit. Twenty miles to the south-west they reached the dry watercourse of Besor. A third of the men were too exhausted to carry on and were left behind with the baggage. Then David had a stroke of luck. His men found a young Egyptian who had been adrift in the desert for three days, after having fallen sick and been abandoned by his Amalekite master. Revived with food and water, and given a promise of protection, he led them to the Amalekite raiding party, who were spread out at their ease and making merry over their spoils. David's men fell upon them in the dusk. A number of the younger men escaped on their camels, but the rest of the encampment were wiped out. All the abducted women and children were recovered unharmed, and large flocks and herds captured. The four hundred of David's men who had taken part in this engagement objected to dividing the booty with the two hundred who had remained behind with the baggage. But David decided firmly that each serving soldier should have an equal share and made this a standing rule. On getting back to Ziklag, he sent a good number of the captured animals as gifts to towns in southern Judah that had helped him during his outlaw years. David was no doubt thinking of future prospects as well as past debts.

David in Hebron

The return to his homeland came sooner than David could have expected. There arrived at Ziklag a young Amalekite who had been serving with Saul's army in the north. He was brought before David and blurted out the dreadful news of the Israelite defeat on Mount

Gilboa. He claimed that he had himself killed King Saul at the latter's request, and produced Saul's crown and bracelet as proof. He may have expected a reward, but David ordered him to be killed, saying, 'Your blood be upon your head; for your own mouth has testified against you, saying, "I have slain the Lord's anointed"' (2 Sam. 1:16).

David was plunged in grief. Though the king had persecuted him, Saul had united and led his people for two decades and had raised the young David from obscurity to fame. Jonathan had been his closest and most faithful friend. Out of his pain David the poet composed one of the most moving laments in literature:

'Thy glory, O Israel, is slain upon thy high places!
How are the mighty fallen!
Tell it not in Gath,
publish it not in the streets of Ashkelon;
lest the daughters of the Philistines rejoice,
lest the daughters of the uncircumcised exult.
Ye mountains of Gilboa,
let there be no dew or rain upon you,
nor upsurging of the deep!
For there the shield of the mighty was defiled,
the shield of Saul, not anointed with oil. . . .
Saul and Jonathan, beloved and lovely!
In life and in death they were not divided;
they were swifter than eagles,
they were stronger than lions. . . .
I am distressed for you, my brother Jonathan;
very pleasant have you been to me;
your love to me was wonderful, passing the love of women.'
(2 Sam. 1:19-21, 23, 26)

The victory of the Philistines had given them control of northern Israel. With the remnants of his army Abner, Saul's kinsman and general, retreated east of the Jordan river, where he proclaimed as king Saul's eldest surviving son Ishbosheth, a forty-year-old weakling. David seized his chance in this confused situation. He quickly moved back across the frontier to Hebron and was accepted as king of Judah, the largest and most powerful of the Israelite tribes. At the same time, he made a gesture to Saul's memory. Having heard that the men of the town of Jabesh-gilead had retrieved the bodies of Saul and his sons and interred their bones, David sent them a message commending their act.

The united kingdom fashioned by Saul had split in two – Judah in the south and Israel in the north. It would take David many years of patient statecraft to reunite them.

The civil war between the north and the south dragged on, till Abner quarrelled with Ishbosheth and lost patience with the puppet king he had set up. Abner sent messages to David offering to help him become ruler over the whole nation. David made one demand: that

Michal, to whom he had been married in his youth, should be restored to him. Whether David still loved her or not, it was clearly of political advantage to renew his family tie with Saul's house. Afraid of Abner, her brother Ishbosheth agreed. Michal's second husband accompanied her sadly to the border.

Having obtained support for David from the elders of the tribes of Israel, Abner came on a visit to Hebron. David received him warmly, and the union was settled.

Joab had been away on a military foray during these developments. On his return, he was taken aback by the pact David had made and murdered Abner. Aghast at this bloody act, David cursed Joab and gave Abner a public funeral in Hebron.

Ishbosheth, too, was murdered by two of his officers, who brought his severed head to David, expecting to be rewarded. David had them put to death, and ordered the head of Ishbosheth to be buried in Abner's tomb.

The elders of all the tribes of Israel now came to Hebron to pledge allegiance to David saying, 'Behold, we are your bone and flesh' (2 Sam. 5:1). He had travelled a long and tortuous path since the day when the prophet Samuel had come to Bethlehem and anointed a shepherd boy's head with oil. David was now thirty years old. He was to rule over the kingdom for nearly forty years more.

Jerusalem the Capital

From the time of Joshua, who had failed to capture it, Jerusalem had remained for two and a half centuries a Jebusite enclave in Israelite territory. It was a formidable stronghold, built on a narrow spur surrounded by steep valleys on three sides – the vale of Kidron, the vale of Hinnom and the central valley (subsequently known as the Tyropoeon valley) that would later divide Solomon's Temple Mount from the Upper City. The northern approach was protected by fortifications.

David decided to take the city and make it his capital. It was centrally located between the northern and southern parts of his kingdom, and since it had never been in Israelite hands, was not identified with any one tribe.

The Jebusite defenders adopted a curious strategem. They 'said to David, "you will not come in here, but the blind and the lame will ward you off."' (2 Sam. 5:6) It has been suggested that the Jebusites were trying to shelter behind the curse that would fall upon those who dared to attack the afflicted. David's men shrank from doing so and he had to promise a reward to the first soldier who would attack in spite of the evil spell. The one who did so was the tough commander Joab himself, and the city fell.

The watchful Philistines reacted to the capture of Jerusalem by marching an army up from the coastal plain – probably through the vale of Sorek, along which the railway now runs. They reached the open ground to the south-west of Jerusalem known as the valley of

Rephaim. Here David's troops repulsed them, burning the images they left behind. When they advanced a second time, the Israelites circled round to their rear and fell upon them when the breeze rustling in the tree-tops signalled the approach of night. The fleeing enemy was chased back to the lowlands.

With his military and political hold on Jerusalem consolidated, David decided to turn it also into the religious centre of the nation, by bringing to it the sacred Ark of the Covenant. Twenty years earlier, the Ark had been returned by the Philistines, and come to rest at Kiriath-jearim, about eight miles west of Jerusalem. It was now placed on a cart drawn by two oxen, and set out to the sound of music played on harps, psalteries, timbrels, cornets and cymbals. Along the way a mishap occurred: the oxen jolted the cart, and one of the men walking beside it clutched at the Ark to steady it. He was struck dead by the Lord. The journey was suspended and the Ark was kept in a nearby house for three months. When David felt that the divine displeasure had passed, he brought the Ark to the great tent he had prepared for it in Jerusalem. He himself danced before it clad in a linen ephod, the short apron worn by priests. Michal, Saul's daughter, saw David through a window and berated him afterwards for what she regarded as unseemly conduct in public by her royal husband. David sarcastically flung these reproaches back at her. The quarrel seems to have ended their relationship, for Michal remained childless in David's prolific household.

In those days the number of women in the household was a mark of status for important men. In his outlaw years David had acquired two wives. As king in Hebron he added four more, and had six sons born to him. 'And David took more concubines and wives from Jerusalem, after he came from Hebron; and more sons and daughters were born to David.' (2 Sam. 5:13)

David proceeded to develop the new capital. The ridge on which it stood was enlarged by embankments of earth, and a palace was built with the help of David's ally, Hiram king of Tyre (present-day Lebanon), who sent him cedarwood from the Lebanon mountains, and skilled carpenters and masons.

With the kingdom united and the capital established, David started expanding the territory under Israelite control.

Saul had pushed the Philistines out of the Judean hills after the battle of Michmash. David reduced them even further, occupying Gath and Lachish and penning them into a narrow coastal strip from Gaza through Ashkelon and Ashdod to Joppa (Jaffa).

The kingdoms of Edom and Moab to the south and east of the Dead Sea were subdued, and became tribute-paying vassals. The conquest of Edom gave David access to the Gulf of Akaba that leads into the Red Sea – a maritime route later developed by his son Solomon.

The only campaigns of David treated with some detail in the Bible are those against the Ammonites and their allies, the kings of Aram (Syria). Israel had a bridgehead across the Jordan river in the land of Gilead, which had been held since Joshua by the tribe of Gad and half the tribe of Manasseh. It was a well-watered region lying between the great plateau of Moab to the south and Hauran to the north. East of it was the level country occupied by the Ammonites, with their capital at Rabbah (or Rabbath-ammon, later to become the Greek city of Philadelphia, and today Amman, the capital of the Kingdom of Jordan).

The war on this eastern front was started by an act of provocation by a new Ammonite king, Hanun. David sent him a goodwill mission, but Hanun humiliated the Israelite ambassadors by returning them with half their beards shaved and the lower half of their garments cut off. David reacted by sending his seasoned troops under Joab to attack the Ammonites, who retreated behind the walls of their city.

The Aramean king Hadadezer then sent an army

The Building of the House of King David,
by Francesco Pesellino (1422-57).

David

David and Bathsheba: etching from Marc Chagall's biblical series, 1956.

south, under his general Shobach, to the help of his Ammonite allies. David enlarged his regular forces by mobilizing the reserve militia and crossed the Jordan. The crucial battle took place at Helam (probably in the Vale of Succoth) where the Arameans were heavily defeated and Shobach was slain. Their rulers hastened to make peace with Israel, and to bring themselves under David's suzerainty. One consequence was that the Arameans 'feared to help the Ammonites any more' (2 Sam. 10:19). The following year, Joab invaded Ammon and besieged the capital Rabbah, which had a natural defensive position and was strongly fortified.

David and Bathsheba

During this siege, David had stayed behind in Jerusalem. One warm moonlit evening the sleepless king strolled on the roof of the palace and looked down to see a young woman bathing herself on a lower roof. Smitten by her beauty, David made enquiries and learnt that her name was Bathsheba, that she was the granddaughter of one of David's leading counsellors Ahithophel, and that she was married to Uriah, a Hittite officer on active service with Joab. David discreetly sent for her and made love to her. When Bathsheba let him know that she had become pregnant, David ordered that Uriah report back to him. After talking to him, David told him to go home, and sent round food from the royal kitchen. But Uriah did not rejoin his wife at all, spending that night and the next with the palace guards. Fearful of the scandal if the adultery became

known, David sent him back to the front with a sealed letter to Joab, saying, 'Set Uriah in the forefront of the hardest fighting, and then draw back from him, that he may be struck down, and die' (2 Sam. 11:15). Joab accordingly arranged for him to lead a dangerous sortie against a well-defended section of the city wall. In this engagement Uriah was killed. After the regular period of mourning Bathsheba became David's wife and bore him a son.

The prophet Nathan appeared before David and recounted a parable concerning a wealthy man and a poor one who had only one ewe lamb kept as a household pet. When a guest arrived, the rich man killed this lamb, instead of an animal from his own large flock. David cried out that the man who could do such a thing merited death. Nathan pointed at him and declared sternly 'You are the man' (2 Sam. 12:7). He added that David's child by Bathsheba would forfeit its life to redress the wrong. The child fell ill and David fasted and prayed for days, lying prostrate on the ground. But when the baby died, David rose up, broke his fast and refrained from the usual mourning, saying to his surprised retainers, 'why should I fast? Can I bring him back again? I shall go to him, but he will not return to me' (2 Sam. 12:23). Another son was born to David and Bathsheba, and was called Solomon.

David moved up to Rabbah with fresh forces and took personal command of the final successful assault. Ammon became a vassal state, and its men were put to

91

David's Empire
Early 10th century BC

ELISHAH

Aleppo

Euphrates R.
Tiphsah

Hamath

HAMATH

Arvad

Tadmor

Sumur

S
I
D
O
N
I
A
N
S

Gebal
(Byblos)

ZOBAH
Lebo-Hamath

BETH-REHOB

Sidon

ARAM-

ARAM DAMASCUS

Damascus

Izon

Tyre

Dan

Kedesh

MAACHAH

Accho

Chinnereth

G
r
e
a
t

S
e
a

Dor

Ashtaroth

Meggido

Beth-shean

Ramoth-Gilead

Shechem

Joppa

Mahanaim

AMMON

Bethel

Rabbath-
Ammon

Ashdod

Jerusalem

Gath

PHILISTINES

Hebron

Aroer

Karkor

Gaza

Dead Sea

Sharuhen

Beersheba

Kir-Moab

Zoar

MOAB

E
G
Y
P
T

Kadesh-
barnea

Bozrah

E
D
O
M

Teman

	Judah and Israel
	Conquered Kingdom
	Sphere of Influence
—·—	Border of David's Empire
······	Interior Border

0   50 miles

Ezion-geber

forced labour in stone-cutting and brick-making for David's building operations.

By now, David had carved out an empire stretching in the north beyond Damascus; in the east to the edge of the Arabian desert beyond Ammon and Moab; in the south to the Gulf of Akaba; and in the west to the Mediterranean. Some of the neighbouring rulers made treaties of friendship with him, like the king of Hamath on the Upper Euphrates; Hiram, king of Tyre, on the Phoenician coast (now Lebanon); and the king of Geshur, east of the Sea of Galilee (the Golan Heights).

Israel had become the dominant state in the area between the Nile and the Euphrates valleys. David's strategy had exploited the fact that Egypt's might had declined in the south and that of Assyria had not yet risen in the north.

David's campaigns called for an extensive army organization. The professional backbone was provided by the six hundred seasoned veterans who had been his guerrilla fighters in the early years. They were led by the two sons of David's sister Zeruiah: Joab the commander-in-chief and Abishai his deputy. Thirty of the senior officers formed a kind of army council. There were also foreign mercenaries, some of them Philistine, who had probably attached themselves to David when he was serving Achish the king of Gath.

Around this core of regulars David built up a civilian militia, its members normally being called up for a month each year. According to an unclear passage in Chronicles, 24,000 were called up each month in units supplied by the different tribes. In an emergency there might be a general mobilization of the reserves, as when David crossed the river into Gilead to halt the invading Syrian army under Shobach.

David and Absalom

As David reached the latter part of his forty-year reign, he could look with satisfaction on his achievements. The expanded kingdom was united and prosperous, and had gained peace through victory. But trouble was to descend upon him from within his own household.

The eldest of the princes, and the heir to the throne, was Amnon the son of Ahinoam. Then came Absalom the son of Maacah; and Adonijah, the son of Haggith. (The second son to be born was Chileab the son of Abigail, but he is not mentioned again and may have died as a child.)

Amnon fell in love with his half-sister Tamar, who was Absalom's sister. Pretending to be ill, he asked the king to send her to his quarters to bake some of his favourite cakes. When she refused to go to bed with him, he raped her and then had her thrown out. The dishonoured girl was taken into his home by Absalom, who swore revenge.

Two years later Absalom invited all the king's sons to a sheep-shearing feast at his farm in the hills of

David weeping for Absalom: etching from Marc Chagall's biblical series, 1956.

Ephraim. When Amnon was drunk, he was killed by the servants on Absalom's orders. The other princes rushed back to Jerusalem to tell David, while Absalom fled to his maternal grandfather, the king of Geshur. David left him banished there, but pined for the attractive son he loved so much.

After three years, the redoubtable Joab – who was David's nephew and Absalom's cousin – found a way to broach the delicate subject. He arranged for a woman from the village of Tekoa to gain an audience with the king. She pretended that she was a widow with two sons, one of whom had killed the other in a quarrel. Her kinsmen demanded that the surviving son should also be put to death. David ruled that the young man should be spared. But when the woman hinted at the parallel with his own son, David suspected that Joab had contrived the story. This Joab admitted, and was told he could fetch Absalom back to Jerusalem.

Yet David could not simply accept Absalom as if nothing had happened. The king refused to see his son, and for the next two years the prince remained in his own home, brooding over his rejection. Then, under pressure from Absalom, Joab gained him access to David, who kissed him in forgiveness.

Outwardly, father and son were now reconciled. But Absalom's resentment was already seeking the path of rebellion. His beauty and charm made him a popular figure, and he used every means to undermine David's authority and gain a following for himself. When he felt the time was ripe, Absalom raised the standard of revolt in Hebron, David's former capital, now neglected. Here he was joined by Ahithophel, David's ablest and most respected counsellor. Absalom had sent his agents to other parts of the country to prepare the ground. Now that he had come into the open, support for his cause was widespread. Absalom prepared to march on Jerusalem.

David's secure world had suddenly collapsed around him. It seems astonishing that he should have been caught so badly off his guard. But a long-established regime is always loath to believe that erosion has set in. Moreover, as a father, David could not imagine that his favourite son could plot his downfall. Now that he faced the truth, David took a prompt but painful decision – to abandon the capital to the rebels, and flee eastwards towards the Jordan river with his family and a band of his most trusted followers.

The wheel had come full circle. The illustrious monarch was once more a fugitive in the wilderness, as he had been so many years before in the time of Saul. David covered his face to hide his tears, as he led his group out of the city, across the Kidron valley and up the Mount of Olives, where he paused to pray for God's help in the dark days ahead.

His cool and resourceful mind was already at work. It was essential for him to plant a fifth column in the rebel camp. The two high priests Abiathar and Zadok had left Jerusalem with him, taking along the sacred Ark of the Covenant. He persuaded them to turn back, and to keep him informed of events, using their sons as messengers. He requested his counsellor Hushai to join Absalom and gain his confidence, in order to counteract the influence of Ahithophel. He also told his Gittite troops to return, but their captain Ittai of Gath refused, and David did not insist.

During this flight, two small incidents depressed David's spirits even more. He was met by Ziba the steward of Mephibosheth, Jonathan's crippled son whom David had protected and reared. Ziba brought two asses laden with provisions, and hinted that his master had gone over to Absalom.

Further along there appeared on the ridge above the road an old Benjaminite called Shimei, a member of the house of Saul. He pelted the party with stones and furiously cursed David as 'a man of blood' (2 Sam. 16:8) whose downfall was deserved. David said resignedly to the angry Abishai, 'Let him alone, and let him curse; for the Lord has bidden him' (2 Sam. 16:11).

East of the Jordan, David made his way to Mahanaim in the land of Gilead. Here he was heartened to find the local population had stood by him. His party had arrived 'hungry and weary and thirsty in the wilderness' (2 Sam. 17:29). They were provided with ample supplies by local leaders, and also by the son of the king of Ammon, further to the east. Having secured a base of operations, David quickly organized an army, and divided it into three formations under the command of Joab, Abishai and Ittai the Gittite.

Absalom recruited large forces, crossed the river and took up battle positions among the wooded ridges of Ephraim. Here David's trained men fell upon them and routed the hastily assembled army with heavy slaughter. Absalom himself was killed by Joab. In this inglorious fashion ended Absalom's brief and tragic rebellion.

David had yielded to the entreaties of his followers that he should stay behind in the town and not risk his person in battle. To his captains he gave one final command, 'Deal gently for my sake with the young man Absalom.' (2 Sam. 18:5)

Runners reached David at the city gate with the tidings of the victory, and his first question was 'Is it well with the young man Absalom?' (2 Sam. 18:29) When told that his beloved and wayward son was slain, he cried out in grief, 'O my son Absalom, my son, my son Absalom! Would I had died instead of you, O Absalom, my son, my son!' (2 Sam. 18:33)

Instead of a victory celebration, David declared a day of mourning. This was more than the unrepentant Joab would tolerate. Bursting into the king's room, he roughly scolded him for caring more about his enemies than his friends, and demanded that he appear before his people if he wanted to keep their allegiance. David stifled his agony and let his political instincts take charge again.

His throne had barely survived insurrection and civil war. He was still beyond the Jordan, an aging king on the eastern perimeter of a confused and divided country. He had to move warily. His return was prepared by the two high priests in Jerusalem who had remained loyal to him. David moved down the river, was ferried across and reached Gilgal on the Jericho plain, where the leaders of Judah came to meet him.

There were others who came to Gilgal. Shimei, the old Benjaminite who had shouted imprecations at the fugitive king, now came to crave pardon. David spared his life, but did not forget. Jonathan's lame son, Mephibosheth, arrived to explain that he had intended to flee with David, but had been deceived by his steward Ziba.

The eighty-year-old Gileadite notable Barzillai, who had helped David, accompanied him across the river but declined the king's invitation to settle in Jerusalem, saying he preferred to die in his home town.

The other tribes were indignant that Judah had restored the king without consulting them. Their resentment was whipped up by Sheba, a Benjaminite, who cried, 'We have no portion in David' (2 Sam. 20:1) and led a protest march out of the capital. The kingdom was again on the verge of a split. David sent troops after Sheba. Angry with Joab, he had appointed as his army commander another nephew, Amasa, who had led Absalom's forces. On the road northward in pursuit of the rebels, Amasa was intercepted and murdered by Joab, who took charge of the operation and brought back Sheba's severed head to David. After this abortive revolt, the rule of King David was firmly restored over the whole land.

The Ageing King
Little is recorded of the remaining years of David's reign.

There was a famine that lasted for three years. It was regarded as a belated punishment for Saul's slaying of a number of the inhabitants of Gibeon, an Amorite hill-town five miles north-west of Jerusalem (today the Arab village of el-Jib). The Gibeonites demanded as an act of atonement that David hand over to them seven of Saul's children and grandchildren. David felt obliged to yield up to them two sons Saul had had by Rizpah, one of his concubines, and five grandsons, the children of Saul's eldest daughter Merab. The Gibeonites hanged all seven, and after this cruel balancing of accounts the famine ended. David made peace with his troubled conscience by bringing back the bones of Saul and Jonathan from Jabesh-gilead, and having them reinterred, together with the bodies of the hanged seven, in the family tomb of Saul's father Kish.

It was during this period too that David decided to take a complete census of all the 'valiant men who drew the sword' (2 Sam. 24:9) throughout the kingdom. The tally was five hundred thousand men for Judah and eight hundred thousand for the rest of the tribes. But head-counting was considered unholy (a superstition shared by most primitive communities). The Lord's punishment was a pestilence that killed seventy thousand people. On the advice of the prophet Gad, David bought the threshing floor of Araunah the Jebusite for fifty silver shekels, built an altar on it and offered up sacrifices. The Lord repented, and the pestilence stopped before it reached Jerusalem. The threshing floor later became the site of Solomon's Temple.

The chronic border warfare with the Philistines flared up again. David was not loath to escape from the burdens of office in the capital, and once more share with his men the hardship and danger of campaigning in the field. But during the engagement 'David grew weary' (2 Sam. 21:15) and when a huge Philistine tried to kill him, he was saved by that tough professional soldier, his nephew Abishai. This narrow escape ended the career of David the warrior, for his men said to him tactfully, 'You shall no more go out with us to battle, lest you quench the lamp of Israel.' (2 Sam. 21:17)

David's vigour became dimmed by age. However many clothes were wrapped around him, he shivered with cold. His servants produced a beautiful maiden, Abishag the Shunammite, and said to David 'Let her lie in your bosom, that my Lord the king may be warm.' (1 Kgs. 1:2) A touching friendship grew up between the aging ruler and the young woman who 'became the king's nurse and ministered to him' (1 Kgs. 1:4).

David withdrew more and more from the active conduct of affairs of state. As old men are wont to do, he spent much time reflecting on his long and eventful life. The pastoral scenes of his childhood blended with the faith in God that had sustained him, and he declared that, 'When one rules justly over men, ruling in the fear of God, he dawns on them like the morning light, like the sun shining forth upon a cloudless morning, like rain that makes grass to sprout from the earth.'

The Succession of Solomon
When the king grew old, weary and secluded, the question of the succession to the throne became a pressing one. With Amnon and Absalom both dead, the handsome Adonijah was the next in line, and was regarded as the likely heir to the throne – 'all Israel fully expected me to reign' (1 Kgs. 2:15). Adonijah decided to assert his claim without waiting for the king's death. He was encouraged by Joab the commander-in-chief, and Abiathar the high priest, two of the leading men in the kingdom. They had been with David through thick and thin, from his early outlaw days. Now they wanted to ensure a smooth transition of power, and forestall the claims of Bathsheba for her son Solomon, a much younger prince.

Assured of such powerful support, Adonijah went ahead. He invited his princely brothers and the city notables to a feast at the spring of En-rogel, down in the valley of Kidron outside the city walls. Here he performed ceremonial sacrifices on the sacred Serpent's Stone. Solomon was not invited to take part – nor were Nathan the prophet, Zadok the other high priest, and Benaiah, the captain of the royal guard – all of whom were thought to be associated with Bathsheba's designs. This opposition party reacted swiftly. Bathsheba still retained a strong hold on David, and free access to him. Prompted by Nathan, she entered the king's chamber and told him Adonijah was at that moment usurping the throne he had promised her would go to her son Solomon; David should announce his own successor. Nathan appeared and supported Bathsheba.

Of all the characters of the Old Testament, David is the
one who has most caught the imagination of artists.
David, by Michelangelo (1475-1564).

David decided the time had come for him to abdicate
in favour of the sagacious young Solomon. He instructed Zadok, Nathan and Benaiah to take the youth
·on the king's own mule down to the spring of Gihon,
also in the valley of Kidron, have him anointed, 'then
blow the trumpet, and say, "Long live King Solomon!"'
(1 Kgs. 1:34) They did so, accompanied by a host of
people. When the noise of the crowd rejoicing at the
coronation reached Adonijah's company further along
the valley, and they learnt that Solomon had already
replaced David as king, the guests hurriedly returned to
their homes. Adonijah sought sanctuary at the altar,
and was spared by Solomon for the time being. The
struggle for the succession was over the same day it had
begun.

On his deathbed, David imparted his last wishes to
Solomon: 'I am about to go the way of all the earth. Be
strong, and show yourself a man' (1 Kgs. 2:2); Solomon
should follow the Lord's commandments and walk
before him in truth, as David had done. He asked
Solomon to show special kindness to the children of
Barzillai the Gileadite, and to settle accounts with Joab
and Shimei.

'Then David slept with his fathers, and was buried in
the city of David.' (1 Kgs. 2:10) After a reign of forty
years there had passed away 'the oracle of the man who
was raised on high, the anointed of the God of Jacob,
the sweet psalmist of Israel' (2 Sam. 23:1).

David is the human character most fully and vividly
presented in the Old Testament. His Hebrew bio-
graphers portrayed their hero complete with all his contradictions. The tough fighter, the shrewd statesman,
and the fond husband and father; the unworthy actions
prompted by passion or expediency; the sensitive love
of beauty, poetry and music; courage and calculation;
faith and humbleness of spirit before God – all fuse
together in a brilliant and complex man. His faults and
errors only serve to throw David's genius into relief.

In David's reign the Hebrew nation reached the peak
of its political and military strength. The united kingdom Saul put together from the Israelite tribes was
expanded by David into an empire extending from the
sea to the desert. After Solomon's death it was to split
again into the two small rival kingdoms of Israel and
Judah.

[The Story of David is told in 1 Sam. 16-31; the
Second Book of Sam.; 1 Kgs. 1, 2]

The Psalms of David

The Book of Psalms, traditionally attributed to David, is an anthology of Hebrew sacred songs and poems. It is placed in the third section of the Old Testament, the Writings ('Ketuvim'). The word 'psalms' is of Greek origin, and denotes the sound of a string instrument. The Hebrew name is 'tehillim' – praises. The themes of the psalms concern not only praise to the Lord, but also personal joy and sorrow, national redemption, festivals and historical events. Their religious fervour and literary power have given the psalms a profound influence down the ages, also in the Christian world.

There has been much dispute among scholars about the age and authorship of these poems, and about their connection with King David. They were probably composed during a thousand years or more of the biblical period. Of the 150 psalms, 73 were marked in the title 'of David' and many are in the first person. Some of these, or parts of them, appear to be of later date than David's reign. However, comparison with other Near Eastern religious poetry of about the same era suggests that some of the poems attributed to David date from his time. Whatever the experts might say, it is natural that popular belief should attribute the whole work to Israel's greatest king, a poet and musician who felt himself to be in close communion with God.

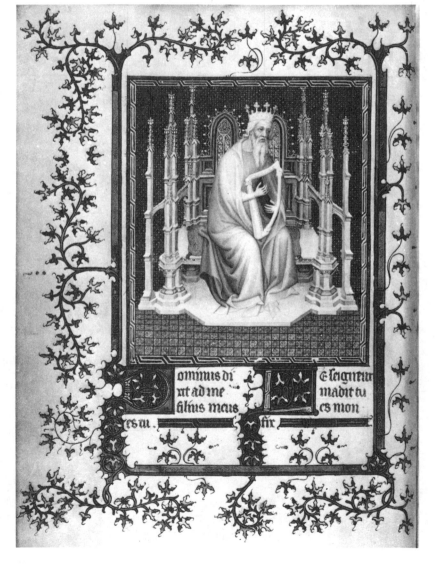

David as psalmist, from the *Psalter of the Duc de Berry*, French, early 15th century.

Reliance on the Lord's help for deliverance from enemies, sadness that life is so fleeting, the longing for peace, the concern with the future of the people of Israel, the mystic bond with Jerusalem – all these could be an authentic expression of David's own experiences and feelings. [Book of Psalms]

DEBIR (Heb. 'oracle') 13 century BC. King of Eglon, he was one of the five Amorite kings who attacked the Gibeonites after they made a pact with Israel. They were defeated by Joshua and hanged on five trees. [Josh. 10:3-26]

DEBORAH (Heb. 'bee') **1.** *c.* 17 century BC. Rebekah's nurse, she went with her mistress from Mesopotamia to Canaan where Rebekah married Isaac. Deborah stayed with Rebekah in Canaan and died in Bethel near Jerusalem where she was buried under an oak tree. [Gen. 24:59; 35:8]

2. *c.* 12 century BC. A judge and prophetess. In the Old Testament there is only one woman whose force of character and sagacity made her a leader in her own right. That was Deborah, who in the 12th century BC led a successful Israelite revolt against Canaanite domination in the northern part of the country.

The story of Deborah's triumph is told in two parallel accounts, one in prose and the other in the form of a stirring ballad or song attributed to Deborah herself. The two are not the same in all details.

Deborah was the wife of one Lappidoth, about whom nothing else is recorded. She was a 'judge', a person whose moral authority was regarded as inspired by the Lord, and was therefore accepted in the settlement of disputes. When the story opens, she is described as habitually seated under a tree between Bethel and Ramah north of Jerusalem where 'the people of Israel came up to her for judgment' (Judg. 4:5).

At that time the Israelites had for twenty years been oppressed in the north by Jabin the Canaanite, king of Hazor, because they 'did what was evil in the sight of the Lord' (Judg. 4:1). The Israelites had been unable to break the Canaanite hold on the fertile Jezreel valley, also known as the Plain of Esdraelon (today it is commonly called the 'Emek' – the 'Valley'). It stretches from west to east across the country, from behind the Carmel range down to the Sea of Galilee and the Jordan river fords.

Commanded by God, Deborah sent for Barak the son of Abinoam, from the tribe of Naphtali in the Galilee highlands. She instructed him to muster the men of Naphtali and Zebulun on the wooded slopes of Mount Tabor, a prominent hump at the north-east corner of the Jezreel valley. The prose account refers only to these two tribes as involved in the battle. However, Deborah's song indicates that she sent out a general call for help, and that contingents were also sent from her own tribe

Mount Tabor, situated at the north-east corner of the Jezreel valley, where the Israelites under Deborah defeated the Canaanite forces led by Sisera.

of Issachar, from Ephraim and Benjamin in the central hill country, and from the sub-tribe of Manasseh east of the Jordan. She poured anger on other tribes that failed to respond to her call: Gad, that stayed in Gilead beyond the Jordan; Dan, that remained working in the ships of strangers; Asher, that hung back on the sea coast; and Reuben, on the Moabite plateau of Transjordan, to whom Deborah cried, 'Why did you tarry among the sheepfolds, to hear the piping for the flocks?' (Judg. 5:16)

When summoned by Deborah to take command, Barak answered flatly: 'If you will go with me, I will go; but if you will not go with me, I will not go.' (Judg. 4:8) Deborah agreed to accompany the army.

Barak gathered his force of ten thousand men at Kedesh, his home town, probably on the plateau at the eastern end of the Jezreel valley, overlooking the Sea of Galilee. From here they moved south-west and took up positions on Mount Tabor.

Sisera assembled an army that included nine hundred chariots, and established a base at Harosheth-ha-goiim ('of the Gentiles') (Judg. 4:13), near the defile at the western end of the valley through which the Kishon river flows into Haifa Bay. From here they advanced in battle array along the open plain past the Canaanite strongholds of Megiddo and Taanach.

Sisera no doubt assumed that at this display of martial force, the rebellious Israelite tribesmen would melt back into their hills. But he failed to take into account that the Lord and the weather were on the side of his foes. A violent rainstorm came down suddenly, flooding the Kishon and turning the floor of the valley into mud, which was churned up still further by the prancing horses. With the chariots bogged down and helpless, the Israelite highlanders rushed down on them in a wild charge. Caught completely off-balance, the Canaanite forces were routed and wiped out. Sisera fled and was killed in the tent by Jael a Kenite woman.

Deborah cried in her song of triumph:
'From heaven fought the stars,
   from their courses they fought against Sisera.
The torrent Kishon swept them away,
   the onrushing torrent, the torrent Kishon.
March on, my soul, with might!' (Judg. 5:20, 21)

As a result of this victory, the power of King Jabin over the Israelites in the north was broken: 'And the land had rest for forty years.' (Judg. 5:31) [Judg. 4, 5]

DEDAN (Heb. 'low') **1.** date unknown. Son of Raamah and a descendant of Ham. [Gen. 10:7; 1 Chr. 1:9]

2. c. 17 century BC. Son of Jokshan and a grandson of Abraham. [Gen. 25:3; 1 Chr. 1:32]

DELAIAH (Heb. 'freed by God') **1.** date unknown. One of the seven sons of Elioenai, and a descendant of King David. Also called Dalaiah. [1 Chr. 3:24]

2. 10 century BC. Head of the twenty-third priestly

course in the reign of King David. [1 Chr. 24:18]

3. date unknown. Ancestor of a family that returned to Judah from captivity in Babylon with Zerubbabel. Their genealogy was lost and this was regarded as a tragedy. [Ezra 2:60; Neh. 7:62]

4. c. 6 century BC. Son of Shemaiah, he was one of the five leaders to whom Michaiah read the prophecy of Jeremiah against the kingdom of Judah, and who counselled Jeremiah and Baruch to hide themselves from King Jehoiakim. [Jer. 36:12-20, 25]

5. 5 century BC. Son of Mehetabel, he was the father of Shemaiah who was a false prophet in the days of Nehemiah. [Neh. 6:10]

DELILAH c. 12 century BC. The Philistine woman who betrayed Samson. Delilah was the daughter of a Philistine family in the valley of Sorek, near the village of Mahaneh-dan where Samson lived. When the five Philistine leaders heard that Samson was courting Delilah, they secretly visited her, and promised her eleven hundred pieces of silver from each of them, if she would pry from Samson the secret of his strength.

Three attempts to capture Samson were unsuccessful, as he had teased her by pretending he could be bound by fresh bowstrings, by new ropes or by weaving his hair into a spinning-wheel.

Delilah continued to nag him until 'his soul was vexed to death' (Judg. 16:16) and he told her the truth: because he had been a Nazarene dedicated to holiness from birth, his hair had never been cut, and therein lay his strength.

As soon as Samson fell asleep with his head in her lap, his seven locks were shaved off by a man Delilah had waiting. She woke Samson by crying out that the Philistines were upon him. He sprang up, and not knowing that his strength had gone, turned upon the men she had hidden in the room. This time they overpowered him easily, put out his eyes and brought him in triumph to Gaza.

Samson's betrayal by Delilah has become one of the most familiar tales in the Bible. [Judg. 16]

DEUEL (Heb. 'knowledge of God') c. 13 century BC. A leader of the tribe of Gad, his son Eliasaph was appointed by Moses as one of the Gadite commanders of the army of the children of Israel. Also called Renel. [Num. 1:14; 2:14; 7:42, 47; 10:20]

DIBLAIM (Heb. 'two cakes') 8 century BC. The father of Gomer, the woman who married the prophet Hosea and who symbolized the faithless wife Israel had been to God. [Hos. 1:3]

DIBRI (Heb. 'orator') date unknown. A man of the tribe of Dan whose daughter Shelomith married an Egyptian. The son of this marriage cursed God during a quarrel while the children of Israel were in the wilderness, and was put to death. [Lev. 24:11]

DIKLAH (Heb. 'palm') date unknown. Son of Joktan

Delilah tried weaving Samson's hair into a spinning wheel. 9th-century BC relief from Susa, showing a woman spinning.

and a descendant of Noah. [Gen. 10:27; 1 Chr. 1:21]

DINAH (Heb. 'judged') c. 16 century BC. The daughter of the patriarch Jacob and his wife Leah. While Jacob and his family were living near the town of Shechem (present-day Nablus) on a piece of land bought from Hamor, Shechem, the son of Hamor, fell in love with her and seduced her. Hamor sought permission from Jacob for his son to marry Dinah and further proposed that his clan and Jacob's should intermarry and merge with each other. Concealing their rage at Dinah's seduction, her brothers pretended to agree to Hamor's proposal, if 'you will become as we are and every male of you be circumcised' (Gen. 34:15). This was done, but before the men recovered from the painful operation, Jacob's sons Simeon and Levi killed all the males. 'They

slew Hamor and his son Shechem with the sword, and took Dinah out of Shechem's house.' (Gen. 34:26) When Jacob reproached them for this vindictive act they answered him, 'Should he treat our sister as a harlot?' (Gen. 34:31) [Gen. 30:21; 34; 46:15]

DIPHATH *see* RIPHATH

DISHAN (Heb. 'antelope') date unknown. A son of Seir the Horite, and an Edomite chieftain. [Gen. 36:21, 28, 30; 1 Chr. 1:42]

DISHON (Heb. 'antelope') **1.** date unknown. Son of Seir the Horite, and an Edomite chieftain. [Gen. 36:21; 1 Chr. 1:38]

2. date unknown. Son of Anah, a descendant of Seir the Horite. [Gen. 36:25; 1 Chr. 1:41]

DODAI (Heb. 'loving') 10 century BC. An Ahohite, who commanded one of King David's twelve armies, used for active service in the second month of each year. [1 Chr. 27:4]

DODANIM (Heb. 'leaders') date unknown. Son of Javan and a great-grandson of Noah, he settled along the coast of Canaan. [Gen. 10:4; 1 Chr. 1:7]

DODAVAH *see* DODAVAHU

DODAVAHU c. 9 century BC. Father of the prophet Eliezer of Mareshah who criticized King Jehoshaphat of Judah. Also called Dodavah. [2 Chr. 20:37]

DODO (Heb. 'loving') **1.** c. 12 century BC. Father of Puah of the tribe of Issachar, his grandson Tola judged Israel for twenty-three years. [Judg. 10:1]

2. 10 century BC. Father of Eleazar who was one of King David's three chief officers. [2 Sam. 23:9; 1 Chr. 11:12]

3. 10 century BC. Father of Elhanan of Bethlehem who was one of King David's chosen guard of thirty soldiers. [2 Sam. 23:24; 1 Chr. 11:26]

DOEG (Heb. 'fearful') c. 10 century BC. The Edomite who was chief herdsman to King Saul. Doeg reported to the king seeing David, who had fled from the court, being helped at the priestly sanctuary of Nob. The furious Saul ordered the priests to be killed. Since his own servants shrank from doing so, he turned to Doeg, who slew eighty-five of them. [1 Sam. 21:7; 22]

DUMAH (Heb. 'silence') c. 17 century BC. Son of Ishmael, grandson of Abraham, and founder of a desert tribe. [Gen. 25:13, 14; 1 Chr. 1:30]

Dinah's brothers killing the sons of Abimelech: illumination from a 13th-century French Bible.

E

EBAL (Heb. 'stone') **1.** date unknown. Son of Shobal and a grandson of Seir the Horite, he was an Edomite leader. [Gen. 36:23; 1 Chr. 1:40]

2. date unknown. Son of Joktan and descendant of Shem. Also called Obal. [Gen. 10:28; 1 Chr. 1:22]

EBED (Heb. 'servant') **1.** *c.* 12 century BC. Father of Gaal of the tribe of Ephraim who led an unsuccessful revolt among the people of Shechem against Abimelech, king of Shechem. [Judg. 9:26, 28, 30, 31, 35]

2. *c.* 5 century BC. Son of Jonathan, he was a leader of Judah who returned from exile in Babylon. [Ezra 8:6]

EBED-MELECH (Heb. 'king's servant') 6 century BC. The Ethiopian servant of King Zedekiah of Judah who obtained the king's permission to release the prophet Jeremiah from the pit into which he had been thrown for preaching surrender to the invading Babylonians. In return Jeremiah promised Ebed-melech that he would not be killed when the Babylonians conquered Jerusalem. [Jer. 38:7-12; 39:16]

EBER (Heb. 'beyond') **1.** date unknown. Descendant of Shem and of Noah. [Gen. 10:21, 24, 25; 1 Chr. 1:18, 19, 25]

2. *c.* 8 century BC. A leader of the tribe of Gad in Bashan, east of the river Jordan, in the time of King Jeroboam of Israel. [1 Chr. 5:13]

3. date unknown. A son of Elpaal and a leader of the tribe of Benjamin. [1 Chr. 8:12]

4. date unknown. Son of Shashak and a leader of the tribe of Benjamin living in Jerusalem. [1 Chr. 8:22]

5. 5 century BC. One of the chief priests of Judah when Joiakim was high priest in the time of Nehemiah. [Neh. 12:20]

EBIASAPH (Heb. 'God has added') **1.** *see* ABIASAPH

2. date unknown. The son of Elkanah, a Levite descended from Kohath, and the father of Assir. [1 Chr. 6:23]

ECCLESIASTES (Gk. 'the preacher') *c.* 3 century BC. The Greek form of the Hebrew word *Kohelet* – the unknown author of the biblical book known as 'Ecclesiastes'.

(See the note on 'Solomon and the Wisdom Books' at the end of the entry on SOLOMON.)

EDEN (Heb. 'pleasure') 8 century BC. Son of Joah, he was one of the Levites who obeyed King Hezekiah's command to sanctify himself and cleanse the Temple, and later he helped distribute the free-will offerings among the priests of Judah. [2 Chr. 29:12; 31:15]

EDER (Heb. 'flock') **1.** date unknown. Son of Beriah and a leader of the tribe of Benjamin. [1 Chr. 8:15]

2. *c.* 10 century BC. A Levite descended from Mushi who ministered in the Tabernacle in the reign of King David. [1 Chr. 23:23; 24:30]

EDOM *see* ESAU

EGLAH (Heb. 'heifer') *c.* 10 century BC. One of King David's wives, she bore him Ithream, David's sixth son. [2 Sam. 3:5; 1 Chr. 3:3]

EGLON (Heb. 'calf-like') *c.* 12 century BC. King of Moab, the territory east of the Dead Sea, in the time of Ehud. With the backing of the Ammonites and the Amalekites (a nomad desert tribe) Eglon pushed westward, occupied the Jericho area, and for eighteen years exacted tribute from the Israelites on the Judean highland.

He was killed at his house in Jericho by Ehud, of the tribe of Benjamin, who plunged a dagger into the belly of the fat king and escaped through the window. Finding the doors shut the servants were afraid to disturb the king and it was some time before 'they took the key

Ehud killing King Eglon of Moab: medieval manuscript illumination.

above Tel el-Farah,
the site of biblical Tirzah,
Elah's capital.

and opened them; and there lay their lord dead on the floor' (Judg. 3:25). [Judg. 3]

EGYPT date unknown. One of the four sons of Ham and a grandson of Noah, he was regarded as the legendary ancestor of the Egyptians. [Gen. 10:6, 13; 1 Chr. 1:8, 11]

EHI *c.* 16 century BC. A son of Benjamin, he went down to Egypt at the same time as his grandfather Jacob. He is mentioned only in Genesis but he may be identical with Benjamin's son Ahiram recorded in Numbers, and Aharah in the First Book of Chronicles. [Gen. 46:21; Num. 26:38; 1 Chr. 8:1]

EHUD (Heb. 'God of praise') **1.** date unknown. One of the seven sons of Bilhan and a chief of the tribe of Benjamin. [1 Chr. 7:10; 8:6]

2. *c.* 12 century BC. A Benjaminite leader and judge. Ehud the son of Gera, of the small tribe of Benjamin, was one of the judges of Israel in the period after Joshua.

The territory of Benjamin extended from the central hill region down into the Jordan valley, round Jericho. Eglon king of Moab pushed westward across the Jordan, occupied the Jericho area, and exacted tribute from the Israelites on the Judean highlands. This domination was maintained for eighteen years, and was said to be a punishment by the Lord for the lapse of the Israelites into pagan ways.

Ehud was chosen by God to deliver his people. He fashioned a short two-edged dagger and strapped it to his right thigh, where it would be concealed by his robe. (As was common among the Benjaminites, he was left-handed.) He then set out to deliver gifts to Eglon at Jericho, where the obese king was taking his ease. The tribute was presented and Ehud withdrew with his bearers. When they got to the stone quarries at Gilgal, he turned round and went back alone. Finding the king in his upper chamber where it was cool, he said he had

Noah's sons and grandsons are the traditional ancestors of the people of the Near East. Bronze head, late 2nd millennium BC, from Azerbaijan.

an important secret message to deliver. Eglon dismissed the attendants who were present. When they were alone, Ehud said that his message was from God. The king rose to his feet, at which Ehud whipped out the dagger and stabbed Eglon in the belly. Even the hilt sank into the layers of fat. Ehud locked the door from the inside and escaped through the window. Seeing the door shut, the servants thought the king was attending to his needs and were afraid to disturb him. After a while they became worried, opened the door with the key and found their royal master dead upon the floor.

Safely back in the hills, Ehud blew a horn to muster the Israelite fighting men and led them down into the Jordan valley. They seized the fords across the river to cut off the retreat of the Moabites, who were attacked and slain to the last man. 'So Moab was subdued that day under the hand of Israel. And the land had rest for eighty years.' (Judg. 3:30) [Judg. 3]

EKER (Heb. 'offspring') date unknown. Son of Ram,

leader of the tribe of Judah and the grandson of Jerahmeel. [1 Chr. 2:27]

ELA (Heb. 'oak') *c.* 10 century BC. Father of Shimei, one of King Solomon's twelve officers responsible for the king's supplies for one month in the year. [1 Kgs. 4:18]

ELAH (Heb. 'oak') **1.** date unknown. One of the Edomite leaders descended from Esau. [Gen. 36:41; 1 Chr. 1:52]

2. *c.* 13 century BC. Son of Caleb the son of Jephunneh. [1 Chr. 4:15]

3. Fourth king of Israel after the monarchy split, he reigned 886-5 BC. Elah succeeded his father Baasha as king of Israel. His reign was brief and inglorious, for within two years he was murdered while getting drunk in his steward's house. The culprit was one of his army officers, Zimri, who seized the throne. The usurper wiped out all Elah's kin, as had been foretold to Elah's father Baasha by Jehu the prophet. [1 Kgs. 16:1-14]

4. 8 century BC. Father of Hoshea, the last monarch of the northern kingdom of Israel. [2 Kgs. 15:30; 17:1; 18:1, 9]

5. 6 century BC. Son of Uzzi, he was one of the first Benjaminites to settle in Jerusalem following the return from exile in Babylon. [1 Chr. 9:8]

ELAM (Ass. 'highland') **1.** date unknown. Eldest of Shem's five sons and a grandson of Noah. [Gen. 10:22; 14:1; 1 Chr. 1:17]

2. date unknown. A head of the tribe of Benjamin. [1 Chr. 8:24]

3. 10 century BC. Fifth son of Meshelemiah, gatekeeper of King David's Tabernacle. [1 Chr. 26:3]

4. date unknown. Ancestor of a large family that returned with Zerubbabel from exile in Babylon. [Ezra 2:7; 8:7; 10:2, 26; Neh. 7:12]

5. date unknown. Ancestor of a large family that returned with Zerubbabel from exile in Babylon. [Ezra 2:31; Neh. 7:34]

6. 5 century BC. A leader of Judah who signed the solemn covenant in the days of Nehemiah. [Neh. 10:14]

7. 5 century BC. One of the priests who took part in the ceremony of dedication of the rebuilt walls of Jerusalem in the time of Nehemiah. [Neh. 12:42]

ELASAH (Heb. 'whom God made') **1.** *c.* 6 century BC. Son of Shaphan, he was sent by Jeremiah with a letter to the exiles in Babylon prophesying that they would eventually return to Judah but should meanwhile lead a full life in Babylon. [Jer. 29:3]

2. 5 century BC. A priest who divorced his non-Jewish wife in the time of Ezra. [Ezra 10:22]

EL-BERITH *see* BAAL-BERITH

ELDAAH (Heb. 'called of God') *c.* 16 century BC. Son of Midian and a grandson of Abraham and Keturah, he became leader of a tribe in the eastern desert. [Gen. 25:4; 1 Chr. 1:33]

ELDAD (Heb. 'loved by God') 13 century BC. One of the two elders of the children of Israel about whose prophecies Joshua complained to Moses. [Num. 11:26-29]

ELEAD (Heb. 'God has adorned') date unknown. One of the two sons of Ephraim who were killed by the men of Gath while trying to steal their cattle. [1 Chr. 7:21]

ELEADAH (Heb. 'God has adorned') *c.* 15 century BC. A leader of the tribe of Ephraim, he was the son of Tahath. [1 Chr. 7:20]

ELEASAH (Heb. 'made by God') **1.** date unknown. Son of Helez and a leader of the tribe of Judah. [1 Chr. 2:39, 40]

2. *c.* 9 century BC. A leader of the tribe of Benjamin and a descendant of King Saul. [1 Chr. 8:37; 9:43]

ELEAZAR (Heb. 'God has helped') **1.** *c.* 13 century BC. Eleazar was one of the priestly sons of Aaron and Elisheba, and became high priest when Aaron died on Mount Hor and Moses placed his robes on Eleazar.

He took part in Moses's census in Moab and later helped Joshua in dividing the land of Israel among the tribes of Israel. He married one of the daughters of Putiel and they had a son, Phinehas, who became high priest in the time of Joshua. Eleazar was regarded as the ancestor of most high priests and after the return from Babylon, the Zadokite priests traced their descent to him. [Exod. 6:23, 25; 28:1; Lev. 10; Num. 3:1-4, 32; 4:16; 16:37-39; 19:3, 4; 20:25, 26; 25:7-11; 26; 27; 31; 32; 34; Deut. 10:6; Josh. 14:1; 17:4; 19:51; 21:1; 22:13-32; 24:3; Judg. 20:28; 1 Chr. 6:3, 4; 9:20; 24; Ezra 7:5]

2. *c.* 11 century BC. Son of Abinadab of Kiriath-jearim, he was appointed to look after the Ark of God before it was brought up to Jerusalem. [1 Sam. 7:1]

3. 10 century BC. Son of Dodo the Ahohite, he is singled out as one of three particularly heroic warriors in the army of King David. [2 Sam. 23:9; 1 Chr. 11:12]

4. *c.* 10 century BC. A Levite descended from Mahli, he had no sons and his daughters married their kinsmen, the sons of Kish. [1 Chr. 23:21, 22; 24:28]

5. 5 century BC. Son of Phinehas the priest, he returned with Ezra to Jerusalem and helped weigh the precious vessels brought back from exile in Babylon. [Ezra 8:33]

6. 5 century BC. Descendant of Parosh who divorced his non-Jewish wife in the time of Ezra. [Ezra 10:25]

7. 5 century BC. A priest who took part in the ceremony of dedication for the rebuilt walls of Jerusalem in the time of Nehemiah. [Neh. 12:42]

ELHANAN (Heb. 'grace of God') **1.** *c.* 10 century BC. A warrior in King David's army who killed Lahmi the brother of the Philistine giant Goliath. [2 Sam. 21:19; 1 Chr. 20:5]

2. *c.* 10 century BC. Son of Dodo of Bethlehem and a mighty warrior in the armies of King David. [2 Sam. 23:24; 1 Chr. 11:26]

ELI (Heb. 'uplifted') *c.* 11 century BC. High priest at

Shiloh. Eli was a descendant of Aaron's son Ithamar and was high priest at the sanctuary of Shiloh in the period of the judges. One day he saw a woman near the altar. Her lips moved but she did not utter a sound. Thinking she was drunk, Eli advised her to 'Put away your wine from you' (1 Sam. 1:14). She explained that she was Hannah, wife of Elkanah, and had come to pray to the Lord because she was barren. Eli said to her, 'Go in peace, and the God of Israel grant your petition which you have made to him.' (1 Sam. 1:17) Soon after she bore a son, Samuel. In gratitude to the Lord she apprenticed him to the priests, 'And the boy ministered to the Lord, in the presence of Eli the priest.' (1 Sam. 2:11)

Late one night Samuel thought he heard Eli calling him. But it was the voice of the Lord who told Samuel that Eli and his household would suffer for the corruption and misdeeds of his two sons, the priests Hophni and Phinehas.

In a battle with the Philistines at Aphek at the edge of the hill country, the Israelites were defeated. The sacred Ark of the Covenant brought by Eli's sons from Shiloh was captured, and they were among the slain. The old priest, now ninety-eight years of age and almost blind, sat in the gateway to hear the story from a runner who had arrived with his clothes torn in mourning. The shock of losing both sons and the Ark was too much for him, and 'Eli fell over backward from his seat by the side of the gate; and his neck was broken and he died' (1 Sam. 4:18). [1 Sam. 1-4; 14:3; 1 Kgs. 2:27]

ELIAB (Heb. 'God is father') **1.** *c.* 13 century BC. Son of Helon and leader of the tribe of Zebulun, he was appointed by Moses to conduct the census of men in his tribe fit for war. [Num. 1:9; 2:7; 7:24-29; 10:16]

2. 13 century BC. Father of Dathan and Abiram of the tribe of Reuben who joined Korah's revolt in the wilderness against the authority of Moses and Aaron. [1 Num. 16:1, 12; 26:8, 9; Deut. 11:6]

3. *c.* 12 century BC. Son of Nahath the Levite and an ancestor of the prophet Samuel. Also called Eliel and Elihu. [1 Sam. 1:1; 1 Chr. 6:27, 34]

4. *c.* 11 century BC. Eldest brother of David. Eliab was the eldest son of Jesse and the first to be presented to the prophet Samuel when he visited Bethlehem. Samuel was told by God not to be taken in by the young man's looks or his great height 'for the Lord sees not as man sees; man looks on the outward appearance, but the Lord looks on the heart' (1 Sam. 16:7). Samuel then anointed David, the youngest son, without explaining the reason.

Eliab and two of his brothers served in the army of Saul facing the Philistines in the Valé of Elah. Jesse sent David to take them provisions and to find out how they were faring.

On hearing his young brother talking about killing the Philistine champion Goliath, Eliab turned on him

angrily: 'Why have you come down? And with whom have you left those few sheep in the wilderness? I know your presumption, and the evil of your heart.' (1 Sam. 17:28) David turned away from him and talked to other soldiers until Saul heard about the strange youth and sent for him.

Later Eliab's great-granddaughter Nahalath became the wife of Rehoboam, king of Judah. Also called Elihu. [1 Sam. 16:6; 17:28; 1 Chr. 2:13; 27:18; 2 Chr. 11:18]

5. *c.* 11 century BC. A warrior of the tribe of Gad who deserted the army of King Saul and rallied to David's support. [1 Chr. 12:9]

6. *c.* 10 century BC. One of the Levites in the reign of King David who played musical instruments when the Ark of God was brought to Jerusalem. [1 Chr. 15:18; 16:5]

ELIADA (Heb. 'God knows') **1.** *c.* 10 century BC. One of the sons of King David born to him in Jerusalem. Also called Beeliada. [2 Sam. 5:16; 1 Chr. 3:8; 14:7]

2. *c.* 10 century BC. Father of Rezon, who led bands of marauders against King Solomon. [1 Kgs. 11:23]

3. *c.* 9 century BC. A Benjaminite warrior who commanded an army in the forces of King Jehoshaphat of Judah. [2 Chr. 17:17]

ELIAHBA (Heb. 'hidden by God') *c.* 10 century BC. A soldier from Shaalbon and one of the bravest warriors in the army of King David. [2 Sam. 23:32; 1 Chr. 11:33]

ELIAKIM (Heb. 'may God raise') **1.** *c.* 8 century BC. Master of the palace under King Hezekiah of Judah. In 701 BC Sennacherib, king of Assyria invaded Judea and sent his representatives to demand the surrender of Jerusalem. A meeting took place outside the city with a delegation headed by Eliakim. No agreement was reached. The Assyrian envoy shouted out in Hebrew to influence the people on the ramparts. At one point Eliakim said, 'Pray, speak to your servants in the Aramaic language' (2 Kgs. 18:26). Hezekiah sent Eliakim with others to consult Isaiah, the prophet, whose counsel was to stand firm. The Assyrians in fact withdrew without laying siege to the city. In one of his visions, Isaiah calls Eliakim 'a father to the inhabitants of Jerusalem and to the house of Judah' (Isa. 22:21). [2 Kgs. 18:18, 26, 37; 19:2; Isa. 22:20; 36:11, 22; 37:2]

2. 5 century BC. A priest who took part in the service of dedicating the rebuilt walls of Jerusalem in the time of Nehemiah. [Neh. 12:41]

ELIAKIM *see* JEHOIAKIM

ELIAM (Heb. 'God's people') **1.** *c.* 10 century BC. Father of King David's wife Bathsheba. Also called Ammiel. [2 Sam. 11:3; 1 Chr. 3:5]

2. *c.* 10 century BC. Son of Ahithophel of Gilo, he was a mighty warrior in the army of King David. [2 Sam. 23:34]

ELIASAPH (Heb. 'God will increase') **1.** *c.* 13 century BC. A leader of the tribe of Gad, he was appointed by Moses to conduct the census of the men of Gad fit for war, and then led the contingent. [Num. 1:14; 2:14; 7:42-47; 10:20]

2. *c.* 13 century BC. Son of Lael the Levite, he was head of the family of Gershonites in the wilderness. [Num. 3:24]

ELIASHIB (Heb. 'restored of God') **1.** *c.* 10 century BC. A Levite who served in the Tabernacle in the reign of King David and was responsible for the eleventh turn of service. [1 Chr. 24:12]

2. date unknown. Son of Elioenai of the tribe of Judah and a descendant of King David. [1 Chr. 3:24]

3. 5 century BC. Father of Jehohanan in whose home Ezra fasted for the sins of the people of Judah. [Ezra 10:6]

4. 5 century BC. A Levite Temple singer who divorced his non-Jewish wife in the time of Ezra. [Ezra 10:24]

5. 5 century BC. Descendant of Zattu who divorced his non-Jewish wife in the time of Ezra. [Ezra 10:27]

6. 5 century BC. Descendant of Bani who divorced his non-Jewish wife in the time of Ezra. [Ezra 10:36]

7. 5 century BC. High priest of Judah in the days of Nehemiah, he helped rebuild the walls of Jerusalem. He was the father of Joiada. [Neh. 3:1, 20, 21; 12:10, 22; 13:28]

ELIATHAH (Heb. 'to whom God comes') *c.* 10 cen-

tury BC. Son of Heman, he and his brothers played musical instruments in the Tabernacle under their father's direction during the reign of King David. [1 Chr. 25:4, 27]

ELIDAD (Heb. 'beloved of God') *c.* 13 century BC. Son of Chislon, he was made leader of the tribe of Benjamin by Moses and ordered to divide up the inheritance of his tribe after the conquest of the land of Israel. [Num. 34:21]

ELIEHOENAI (Heb. 'eyes lifted to God') **1.** *c.* 10 century BC. Son of Meshelemiah and a gatekeeper of the Tabernacle in the reign of King David. [1 Chr. 26:3]

2. 5 century BC. Son of Zerahiah, he returned with Ezra from exile in Babylon. [Ezra 8:4]

ELIEL (Heb. 'God is my God') **1.** *see* ELIAB 3.

2. date unknown. A leader of the tribe of Manasseh living east of the river Jordan. [1 Chr. 5:24]

3. date unknown. Son of Shimei and a leader of the tribe of Benjamin living in Jerusalem. [1 Chr. 8:20]

4. date unknown. Son of Shashak of the tribe of Benjamin and a leader of the tribe living in Jerusalem. [1 Chr. 8:22]

5. *c.* 11 century BC. One of the warriors of the tribe of Gad who deserted the army of King Saul and rallied to David at Ziklag. [1 Chr. 12:11]

6. 10 century BC. The Mahavite warrior in the army of King David distinguished for his bravery. [1 Chr. 11:46]

7. 10 century BC. Another warrior in the army of King

Eliezer takes leave of Abraham and sets out to find a wife for Isaac at the well.
From the *Vienna Genesis.*

David who was distinguished for his bravery. [1 Chr. 11:47]

8. 10 century BC. Head of a family of Levites descended from Hebron who were appointed by King David to help bring the Ark of God to Jerusalem from Kiriath-jearim. [1 Chr. 15:9, 11]

9. *c.* 8 century BC. A Levite who helped supervise the bringing of tithes and offerings into the Temple in the reign of King Hezekiah. [2 Chr. 31:13]

ELIENAI (Heb. 'God is my eyes') date unknown. Son of Shimei and a leader of the tribe of Benjamin living in Jerusalem. [1 Chr. 8:20]

ELIEZER (Heb. 'help of God') **1.** *c.* 18 century BC. Steward of Abraham. [Gen. 15:2]

2. *c.* 16 century BC. Son of Becher and a grandson of Benjamin, he was a leader of his tribe. [1 Chr. 7:8]

3. *c.* 13 century BC. The younger son of Moses and Zipporah, and ancestor of Shelomoth who was in charge of the sacred gifts dedicated for the maintenance of the Tabernacle in King David's reign. [Exod. 18:4; 1 Chr. 23:15, 17; 26:25]

4. 10 century BC. A priest in the reign of King David who blew a trumpet during the celebrations when the Ark of God was brought up to Jerusalem. [1 Chr. 15:24]

5. 10 century BC. Son of Zichri, he was a leader of the tribe of Reuben in the reign of King David. [1 Chr. 27:16]

6. 9 century BC. Son of Dodavahu of Mareshah, he prophesied the doom of the ships sent by King Jehoshaphat of Judah to Tarshish in a joint venture with King Ahaziah of Israel. [2 Chr. 20:37]

7. 5 century BC. A leader sent by Ezra to Iddo in Casiphia asking him to send Levites to Jerusalem to minister in the Temple. [Ezra 8:16]

9. 5 century BC. Son of a priest, he divorced his non-Jewish wife in the time of Ezra. [Ezra 10:18]

10. 5 century BC. A Levite who divorced his non-Jewish wife in the time of Ezra. [Ezra 10:23]

11. 5 century BC. Descendant of Harim who divorced his non-Jewish wife in the time of Ezra. [Ezra 10:31]

ELIHOREPH (Heb. 'God his reward') 10 century BC. Son of Shisha, he was a secretary to King Solomon. [1 Kgs. 4:3]

ELIHU (Heb. 'he is my God') **1.** period of the patriarchs. One of Job's friends. Elihu, the son of Barachel the Buzite, sat and listened while Job's three friends argued with him. When they fell silent he made three long speeches which covered much the same ground as the others. He too expressed the view that God did not punish good men, only bad ones. If only Job would repent of his sins, God would forgive him. Elihu suggested Job should say to the Lord, 'I have borne chastisement; I will not offend any more; teach me what I do not see; if I have done iniquity, I will do it no more.' (Job 34:31, 32) To the end Job maintained his inno-

cence and demanded a fair trial with the charges against him presented in due form of law.

Elihu is not mentioned in the epilogue or elsewhere in the text and scholars suggest that the Elihu chapters were not part of the original work, but were inserted at a later date by another author [Job 32-37]

2. *see* ELIAB 3.

3. *see* ELIAB 4.

4. *c.* 11 century BC. A captain of the tribe of Manasseh who deserted the army of King Saul and rallied to David's support. [1 Chr. 12:20]

5. 10 century BC. Descendant of Obed-edom, he was a doorkeeper at the gates of the Tabernacle in Jerusalem in the reign of King David. [1 Chr. 26:7]

ELIJAH (Heb. 'my Lord is Jehovah') **1.** *c.* 9 century BC. Hebrew prophet and reformer. Of all the prophets, priests and sages in the Old Testament, none has kept so vivid a hold on the popular mind as Elijah the Prophet – 'Eliyahu ha-Navi' in Hebrew. He is described as appearing mysteriously from an unknown background, fought as a soldier of the Lord against heathen gods, championed the downtrodden, performed his miracles, and vanished up to heaven in a blazing chariot.

The first mention of Elijah is about the year 864 BC, half-way through the reign of Ahab, son of Omri, in the northern kingdom of Israel. King Omri had fostered an alliance with the coastal state of Phoenicia, and these ties of friendship were cemented by Ahab's marriage to Jezebel, daughter of Ethbaal, king of Sidon. Omri had already come under criticism from the devout for his indulgence towards the alien gods and customs of the sophisticated Phoenicians. When Jezebel became queen, she was permitted to promote these trends so actively that the Bible condemns Ahab as the wickedest of the Hebrew kings.

Shrines were openly constructed to Melkart, the Baal (god) of the Phoenicians, and to their fertility goddess Asherah (Ashtaroth, or Astarte), with a pagan temple in the palace at the new hilltop capital of Samaria. Jezebel also maintained four hundred and fifty priests or 'false prophets' of Baal and four hundred prophets of Asherah as part of her household. The Israelite priests and prophets who protested at these pagan ways were suppressed or driven out. Ahab became lax in his own religious observance, and was dominated by his wife.

Suddenly there appeared before the king a wild figure, clad only in a leather loin-cloth and a cloak of hair. He was Elijah the Tishbite, an inhabitant of Gilead, the Israelite province east of the Jordan river. He cried out a dire prediction of drought: 'As the Lord the God of Israel lives, before whom I stand, there shall be neither dew nor rain these years ...' (1 Kgs. 17:1). Before the

right Scenes from the life of the prophet Elijah. Russian icon, Yaroslav School, 17th century.

astonished king could have him arrested and punished, the prophet had gone.

Elijah escaped across the Jordan and hid himself in a desolate spot next to a stream called Cherith. Here he was brought food by the ravens and drank water from the brook until it dried up. By that time the land was gripped by the drought he had foretold as a punishment, and the spectre of famine loomed on the horizon.

At the behest of the Lord, Elijah sought refuge across the Phoenician border and reached the town of Zarephath, seven miles south of the great port-city of Sidon. Near the town gate he saw a poor widow gathering sticks for firewood. He asked her to bring him a drink of water and a piece of bread. She answered that all the food she had for her son and herself was a handful of meal in a jar and a little oil. The prophet told her not to

be afraid, for her flour and oil would by a miracle feed all three of them until the drought ended. From then on Elijah lodged in the upstairs room of the widow's humble home.

One day the boy fell ill and died. The distraught mother blamed Elijah and cried out to him: 'You have come to me to bring my sin to remembrance, and to cause the death of my son!' (1 Kgs. 17:18) Without a word, Elijah took the child in his arms, carried him up the stairs and laid him down on his own bed. Three times he stretched out on the small, inert form, praying to God to restore it to life. The child revived.

Confrontation on Mount Carmel

In the third year Elijah was told by the Lord that the drought was about to break, and he was instructed to present himself again to King Ahab. On his way to

Samaria, Elijah met Obadiah the master of the royal household, who had been sent out to search for grazing in the parched countryside. According to Obadiah, the king had hunted everywhere for Elijah, and he was most reluctant to notify Ahab of the prophet's coming; but he eventually agreed.

On receiving the message, the king himself hurried out to meet Elijah and said to him, 'Is it you, you troubler of Israel?' (1 Kgs. 18:17) Elijah flung back that it was not he but Ahab and his household that troubled Israel, for they had forsaken the Lord and worshipped Baal.

The king acceded to Elijah's demand that an assembly of the people be arranged on top of Mount Carmel, in order to witness a trial of strength between the prophet and the priests of Baal who had been brought to Samaria by Jezebel. In the presence of the king, Elijah said to the crowd, 'How long will you go limping with two different opinions? If the Lord is God, follow him; but if Baal, then follow him.' (1 Kgs. 18:21) He then proposed that the prophets of Baal should cut up a bullock and lay the pieces on firewood. He would do likewise, and they would see which divinity would send down fire to consume the sacrifice.

From morning till noon the priests leapt around their altar and cried out to Baal, but there was no answer. Elijah taunted them: 'Cry aloud, for he is a god; either he is musing, or he has gone aside, or he is on a journey, or perhaps he is asleep and must be awakened.' (1 Kgs. 18:27) As the afternoon wore on, the priests became more frenzied, slashing themselves with knives and spears in accordance with their practice until the blood flowed from them. But there was 'no voice; no one answered, no one heeded' (1 Kgs. 18:20).

Towards evening Elijah stepped forward and had the crowd draw closer to him. Using twelve stones, one for each of the tribes of Israel, he rebuilt an old altar to the Lord that had fallen to pieces. He cut up his bullock, laid the pieces on the firewood and dug a trench round the altar. He then had some of the bystanders bring buckets of water which they poured over the altar, drenching the meat and wood and filling the trench. When all was ready, Elijah called, 'Answer me, O Lord, answer me, that this people may know that thou, O Lord, art God, and that thou hast turned their hearts back.' (1 Kgs. 18:37) At that cry, fire came down on to the altar, consumed the sacrifice and the wood, and even licked up the water in the trench. The crowd shouted: 'The Lord, he is God; the Lord, he is God' (1 Kgs. 18:39) and they fell on their faces in awe.

Elijah exploited the dramatic moment to have the priests of Baal seized and dragged down to the small Kishon river in the valley below, where they were all slain.

The prophet told Ahab he could now go home for the rain was approaching. Elijah himself climbed back to the top of the ridge and crouched down with his head between his knees. His servant was sent repeatedly to a point from which he could look out to sea. The seventh time, the servant reported, 'Behold, a little cloud like a man's hand is rising out of the sea.' (1 Kgs. 18:44) Soon the sky darkened and the rain came lashing down in torrents. The king set out in his chariot for his winter palace at Jezreel, at the eastern end of the valley. The exultant prophet bounded ahead of him with his cloak tucked up around his waist.

The confrontation on Mount Carmel ranks as the most dramatic moment in the centuries of struggle between Hebrew monotheism and the seductive pagan cults that constantly eroded it.

But Elijah's victory had put him in grave peril. When the formidable Jezebel heard from Ahab what had happened, she sent a message to the prophet that by the next day he too would be put to the sword, as her priests had been. Once more he fled for his life. This time he headed southwards to Beersheba, the ancient Negeb town in the neighbouring kingdom of Judah. Here he left his servant and headed, solitary and depressed, into the barren wilderness. After walking all day he sank down exhausted under a bush of the desert broom that

Elijah's sacrifice on Mount Carmel, from the *Biblia Pauperum*, Flemish, *c.* 1400.

Elijah ran ahead of Ahab in his chariot.
Copper chariot from Tel Agrab, Iraq, c. 2800 B.C.

grows in dry gullies. Giving way to despair, he begged God to let him die.

As had happened before, his bodily needs were miraculously met. While he slept, he dreamt that an angel tapped him on the shoulder, and when he woke he found bread and water to hand. This happened a second time. On the strength of the two scanty meals, Elijah started off on a remarkable forty-day trek across broken desert terrain until he reached Mount Horeb, also known as Mount Sinai, where Moses had first received the Law from the hand of God. Elijah had obviously felt the compulsion to renew his faith at its very source, through a personal revelation from the Lord.

Spending the night in a cave, he heard the voice of God asking what he was doing there. Sadly he replied that the Children of Israel had deserted the Lord, his prophets were being put to death, and only Elijah was left clinging to his faith. For that, they wanted to kill him.

Outside the cave, the landscape was convulsed by gale, earthquake and fire. While Elijah stood in the mouth of the cave with his robe covering his face, the presence of God came to him as a 'still small voice' (1 Kgs. 19:12). The Lord told him to retrace his steps to the wilderness of Damascus. Hazael would become king in Damascus and Jehu in Israel. Their peoples would destroy each other, except for seven thousand faithful Israelites, '. . . all the knees that have not bowed to Baal, and every mouth that has not kissed him' (1 Kgs. 19:18). Elisha would continue Elijah's life work.

Passing through the Jordan valley on his way back, Elijah came upon the young Elisha ploughing on his father's land. Elijah threw his cloak over the youth, who at once accepted the call to service, and remained his faithful disciple until the end of the great prophet's life on earth.

The Scourge of Kings

Elijah was to have one final encounter with his old adversary, Ahab. The king had coveted a vineyard next to his winter palace in Jezreel, but the owner Naboth had refused to part with it. Jezebel had arranged for Naboth to be falsely convicted of blasphemy and stoned to death, whereby his property became vested in the king. When Ahab went to his newly-acquired vineyard, Elijah appeared before him and fiercely denounced him in the name of the Lord: 'Have you killed, and also taken possession?' (1 Kgs. 21:19) The prophet pronounced the doom of Ahab and his whole household, who would be wiped out. As for Jezebel, the dogs would eat her by the walls of Jezreel. Ahab rent his clothes and fasted, and at these signs of repentance, the Lord deferred the fulfilment of Elijah's curse.

After twenty-two years on the throne, Ahab was killed in battle against the Arameans at Ramoth-gilead, and was succeeded by his son Ahaziah. The following year the new king was badly injured in a fall from the balcony of his palace in Samaria. He sent messengers to consult Baal-zebub, the Philistine God who had his shrine at Ekron on the coastal plain. On the way the messengers were intercepted by Elijah who told them to say to their royal master, 'Is it because there is no God in Israel that you are sending to inquire of Baal-zebub, the god of Ekron? Therefore you shall not come down from the bed to which you have gone, but shall surely die.' (2 Kgs. 1:6)

The angry king sent an officer and fifty soldiers to seize the prophet, but they were wiped out by fire invoked by Elijah from heaven. The same thing happened to the second company of soldiers. The captain of the third detachment flung himself on his knees before Elijah and begged that his life and those of his men should be spared. Elijah accompanied them back to the palace and repeated his words in the presence of the bedridden king. Ahaziah died soon after.

Feeling his end was near, Elijah went from Gilgal to Bethel and then on to Jericho. At each place he tried to persuade Elisha not to go any further with him, but his disciple refused to be parted from him. Beyond Jericho they came to the banks of the river Jordan. Elijah rolled up his cloak and struck the water with it. It parted immediately so that they were able to cross over dryshod. Elijah then asked Elisha what he desired before his master was taken from him. Elisha answered that he wanted a double portion of Elijah's spirit.

They walked on talking when '. . . behold, a chariot of fire and horses of fire separated the two of them. And Elijah went up by a whirlwind into heaven.' (2 Kgs. 2:11) As the chariot disappeared from sight, Elisha rent his clothes, then picked up the fallen mantle of Elijah and used it to part the waters again to return across the river.

By Jewish tradition, Elijah has not died, and continues to wander the earth. He will reappear to usher in the Messiah and the final redemption of mankind.

The wonders he worked, and the strange manner of his passing, have surrounded his name with mystic properties. At the Brith Milah (circumcision) of a Jewish child it is the custom to place a chair for Elijah in the hope that he will protect the baby; at the Passover meal, an extra cup of wine is poured for Elijah, and some families draw up an empty chair at the table for him. During the service the door is flung open to let him in. One of the favourite songs of the Passover evening is:

'Elijah the Prophet
Elijah the Tishbite
Elijah the Gileadite
May he come quickly to us
With the Messiah.'

By the alchemy of time, this stern God-driven man became transmuted into a Jewish folk-legend held in popular affection. [1 Kgs. 17-19; 21; 2 Kgs. 1-3:11; 9:36-7; Mal. 4:5]

2. date unknown. Son of Jeroham and a leader of the tribe of Benjamin living in Jerusalem. [1 Chr. 8:27]

3. 5 century BC. Descendant of Harim the priest, he divorced his non-Jewish wife in the time of Ezra. [Ezra 10:21]

4. 5 century BC. A Levite descended from Elam who divorced his non-Jewish wife in the time of Ezra. [Ezra 10:26]

ELIKA 10 century BC. A mighty warrior in the armies of King David. [2 Sam. 23:25]

ELIMELECH (Heb. 'my God is King') *c.* 11 century BC. A wealthy man of Bethlehem who migrated to Moab during a famine taking with him his wife Naomi and their two sons, one of whom married Ruth. [Ruth 1:1-3]

ELIOENAI (Heb. 'eyes lifted to God') **1.** *c.* 16 century BC. Son of Becher and a grandson of Benjamin. [1 Chr. 7:8]

2. date unknown. Son of Neariah of the tribe of Judah and a descendant of King David. [1 Chr. 3:23, 24]

3. *c.* 8 century BC. One of the leaders of the tribe of Simeon who settled in the rich valley of Gedor during the reign of King Hezekiah after driving out the local inhabitants. [1 Chr. 4:36]

4. 5 century BC. Descendant of Pashhur, the priest, who divorced his non-Jewish wife in the time of Ezra. [Ezra 10:22]

5. 5 century BC. Son of Zattu the Levite, who divorced his non-Jewish wife in the time of Ezra. [Ezra 10:27]

6. 5 century BC. A priest in the time of Nehemiah who took part in the service of dedication for the rebuilt walls of Jerusalem. [Neh. 12:41]

ELIPHAL (Heb. 'judged of God') 10 century BC. Son of Ur, he was a mighty warrior in the army of King David. Also known as Eliphelet. [2 Sam. 23:34; 1 Chr. 11:35]

ELIPHAZ (Heb. 'my God is strength') **1.** *c.* 16 century BC. Eldest son of Esau and his wife Adah. [Gen. 36:4, 11, 12; 1 Chr. 1:35, 36]

2. period of the patriarchs. Eliphaz the Temanite was the eldest of Job's three friends who 'made an appointment together to come to condole with him and

Elijah ascending to heaven in a chariot, while Elisha holds the edge of his cloak. Panel from the wooden doors of S. Sabina, Rome, *c.* 1132.

above Elisha makes the axe float on the surface of the water. Drawing by Rembrandt van Rijn (1606-69).

below Elisha made the widow's oil multiply to fill all the jars she had collected. Pottery jar found at Achziv in western Galilee, 8th-6th centuries BC.

comfort him' (Job 2:11). They rent their clothes, sprinkled dust on their heads and sat with him in silence for seven days and nights.

Then Job began to curse the day he was born and to protest that his sufferings were unmerited. Eliphaz and the other two tried to console him, and expressed the traditional and pious views about his affliction: God does not punish good men, only bad ones. As Job continued to rail against God, his three friends got tired of listening to him. Eliphaz answered him angrily, 'Are you the first man that was born? Or were you brought forth before the hills?' (Job 15:7) Finally Eliphaz listed a number of uncharitable acts he falsely attributed to Job.

Job rejected all these arguments. He made no effort to conceal his impatience with Eliphaz and his friends, and utterly refused their advice to bear his trials with silent fortitude. 'So these three men ceased to answer Job, because he was righteous in his own eyes.' (Job 32:1)

Finally the Lord spoke to Job out of a whirlwind and he was completely overwhelmed and humbled. Then the Lord turned on Eliphaz: 'My wrath is kindled against you and against your two friends; for you have not spoken of me what is right, as my servant Job has.' (Job 42:7) The Lord then instructed them to 'offer up for yourselves a burnt offering; and my servant Job shall pray for you, for I will accept his prayer' (Job 42:8). [Job. 2, 4, 15, 22, 42]

ELIPHELEHU (Heb. 'who exalts God') 10 century BC. A Levite appointed by King David to play the harp during the celebrations when the Ark of God was brought to Jerusalem from Kiriath-jearim. [1 Chr. 15:18, 21]

ELIPHELET (Heb. 'God of deliverance') **1.** 10 century BC. One of King David's sons. [2 Sam. 5:16; 1 Chr. 3:8; 14:7]

2. 10 century BC. Another of King David's sons. Also called Elpelet. [1 Chr. 3:6; 14:5]

3. *see* ELIPHAL

4. *c.* 9 century BC. Son of Eshek of the tribe of Benjamin and a descendant of King Saul. [1 Chr. 8:39]

5. 5 century BC. One of the sons of Adonikam who returned with Ezra to Judah from exile in Babylon. [Ezra 8:13]

6. 5 century BC. A descendant of Hashum who divorced his non-Jewish wife in the time of Ezra. [Ezra 10:33]

ELISHA (Heb. 'God is salvation') 9 century BC. A prophet in the kingdom of Israel. Elisha was the disciple and successor of Elijah in the crusade against the religious and moral laxity of their time, especially the cult of Phoenician 'baals' (gods). Although they were equally unswerving in the cause of the Lord, there were marked differences of personality between these two holy men. Elijah was stern, forceful and solitary. Elisha could be firm when necessary; but he was a more gentle man, often living with groups of prophets and pursuing his mission by working beneficent wonders.

Elisha was the son of Shaphat, a farmer at Abel-meholah in the Jordan valley south of the Sea of Galilee. One day he was ploughing a field with a wooden plough drawn by oxen, when the noted prophet Elijah came up to him and threw his cloak over the youth. Elisha gladly accepted this symbolic call. He slaughtered two oxen, broke up the plough for firewood, and gave the farm workers a farewell meal. He then took leave of his parents and went off with the prophet.

After Elisha had faithfully served for some years, Elijah felt his end approaching. He went from Gilgal in the Jordan valley up to the sanctuary town of Bethel, and down the mountain once more to Jericho. At each place Elijah tried to persuade Elisha to remain behind, but the devoted younger man refused to do so.

From Jericho the two walked across the barren plain to the Jordan river five miles away. At this spot the stream flows quietly between reeds, bushes and flowering shrubs, before entering the Dead Sea. Some of the Jericho prophets followed them at a distance. Elijah rolled up his cloak and struck the water and it parted,

The Arab village of Solem in the Jezreel Valley has been identified with Shunem, where Elisha's room was prepared by a wealthy woman.

letting them cross dryshod to the other bank. Elijah asked whether his disciple had a final request of him. Elisha replied, 'I pray you, let me inherit a double share of your spirit.' (2 Kgs. 2:9) As they walked on conversing, a fiery chariot appeared drawn by fiery horses. Elijah stepped into the chariot and was carried up to heaven in it by a great whirlwind. Elisha sorrowfully rent his clothes, then picked up Elijah's fallen cloak and retraced his steps. At the river he used the cloak to part the water, as Elijah had done. Seeing this, the waiting prophets hailed him as the successor to Elijah and bowed down before him.

The Worker of Miracles

The men of Jericho complained to Elisha that though their town was a pleasant place to live in, the water of their spring had turned foul, making the soil barren and causing miscarriages. Elisha asked for some salt to be brought to him in a new bowl. He threw the salt into the spring and the water became wholesome again. (The spring of Ain es-Sultan, which still accounts for the lushness of the Jericho oasis, is by tradition known as the 'Spring of Elisha'. It is not surprising that this abundance of fresh water gushing out in the desolate Jordan valley was regarded as miraculous by the ancients.)

Elisha set off up the mountain to Bethel. Before he reached the town he met a gang of children who mocked at his bald head. His reaction was astonishingly harsh and curiously out of character. He lost his temper and cursed the children, at which two she-bears appeared out of the wood and mauled forty-two of them.

The stories about Elisha show him as living at times in a community of prophets in the Gilgal area, down on the plain of Jericho. Such communities were common – groups of professional holy men or mystics, usually in desert areas, living in conditions of extreme poverty assuaged only by religious ecstasy. The miracles attributed to Elisha while dwelling with the holy brothers are of a minor nature, but throw light on their way of life.

Thus, at a time of famine, they had nothing to eat except the wild plants they could gather; with a handful of meal Elisha made palatable a soup of bitter-tasting and poisonous yellow gourds that one of them had gathered.

While they were chopping down trees on the bank of the Jordan river to make themselves huts, an axe-head fell into the water. The brethren were particularly distressed because the axe had been borrowed. Elisha recovered it by getting it to float up to the surface.

When a farmer in the hills of Ephraim sent Elisha some loaves of barley bread and ears of wheat as 'first fruit' from his field, he miraculously multiplied the food in order to feed a hundred of his hungry fellow-prophets.

A destitute widow was unable to pay her husband's

debts, and the creditor claimed her two sons as his bondsmen. She had nothing in the house but a little oil in a jar. Elisha told her to collect a number of empty jars from the neighbours. All of them were miraculously filled from the single jar she had. By selling the oil she was able to redeem the debt and provide for her children and herself.

The kingdom of Moab, on the plateau east of the Dead Sea, had thrown off its allegiance to the kingdom of Israel. King Jehoram of Israel proposed to King Jehoshaphat of Judah a joint campaign against Moab. The king of Edom, a Judean vassal, was also asked to take part. They took a long detour across the 'Wilderness of Edom' past the southern end of the Dead Sea, in order to attack Moab from the south. But they ran out of water (the key to all desert campaigns) and the troops and baggage animals faced death by thirst. Elisha, who was accompanying them, told them to dig trenches in a certain wadi. By next morning the trenches had filled with water. (Flash floods are not uncommon in the area.)

From afar the Moabite sentries saw the water looking the colour of blood in the early morning light, an illusion increased by the red sandstone rock of the region. They concluded that the allies had been fighting and killing each other and rushed toward the Israelite camp to collect booty. Here they were heavily repulsed and the advance was resumed into the heart of Moab.

Elisha came to live on Mount Carmel with an attendant called Gehazi. Twenty miles away along the Jezreel valley was the small town of Shunem. On his journeys through the town, the prophet would stop for meals in the home of a well-to-do and pious woman. She and her husband built and furnished a small room for him on the roof where the holy man could rest.

Elisha consulted with his servant how he could repay the woman's kindness. The servant pointed out that she had no son and her husband was an elderly man. Elisha sent for her and told her that a son would be born to her within a year. To her great joy the prediction came true.

When the boy was grown, he went out into the fields to his father during the harvest, and was brought home complaining of a blinding headache (possibly due to sunstroke). By nightfall he had died. The bereft mother laid the body on the bed in Elisha's room and closed the door. She then went by donkey to Mount Carmel, flung herself down before the prophet, imploring him to help her. He sent Gehazi ahead with his rod to try and revive the boy and himself followed with the mother. As the laying on of the rod had not helped, the prophet stretched himself seven times over the dead child and put 'his mouth upon his mouth, his eyes upon his eyes, and his hands upon his hands' (2 Kgs. 4:34). The boy revived.

(This story parallels that of Elijah and the widow's son. It illustrates the belief that prophets inspired by God possessed a special life-force that could in suitable cases restore the dead to life.)

Naaman, the army commander of the king of Damascus, contracted the dread disease of leprosy. His wife had an Israelite slave girl who had been taken captive on one of the Aramean incursions into Israel. The girl said there was a prophet in Samaria who would be able to cure him. Carrying lavish presents and a letter from his king to Jehoram, king of Israel, asking him to cure the general, Naaman set out for Samaria with an escort. Jehoram was distressed at this unwelcome visit, fearing that the Syrians were making an impossible demand on him as a pretext to attack him. Elisha sent word that the Aramean commander be brought round to his house. The prophet did not come out to receive the foreign dignitary nor invite him in, but sent a messenger out to tell him that he should bathe seven times in the river Jordan. Naaman was angered at this curt treatment. He snorted, 'Are not Abana and Pharpar, the rivers of Damascus, better than all the waters of Israel? Could I not wash in them, and be clean?' (2 Kgs. 5:12) But his servants persuaded him to follow Elisha's advice, 'and his flesh was restored like the flesh of a little child, and he was clean' (2 Kgs. 5:14).

Naaman came back to Elisha filled with gratitude, and offered him a reward, which the prophet declined. Convinced now that the Hebrew God was the only true one, Naaman asked leave to take two mule-loads of earth back to Damascus with him, so that he could worship the Lord on Israel soil.

Elisha's servant Gehazi was overcome with greed at the thought of the rich gifts his master had spurned. He hurried after Naaman and obtained two bags of silver and two changes of clothes from him, with a concocted story about a couple of needy priests visiting Elisha. The servant hid these gains in the house, but through his occult powers Elisha knew what had happened. He told Gehazi that he may have enriched himself but at the cost of contracting the disease of which Naaman had been cured: 'So he went out from his presence a leper, as white as snow.' (2 Kgs. 5:27)

The War with Syria

In the fighting with the Arameans (Syrians), Elisha used his supernatural powers for the unexpected purpose of military intelligence. He accurately predicted the time and place of raids planned by the Arameans, so that they were constantly repulsed by the Israelite defenders. The king of Aram declared to his officers that one of them must be a traitor. They replied that the security leaks were due to the Israelite prophet Elisha, then residing in the town of Dothan, ten miles north of Samaria. Under cover of darkness an Aramean task force of chariots and cavalry penetrated as far as Dothan and surrounded the town, with instructions to capture the man of God who had become such a valuable prize.

On rising next morning and finding himself trapped, Elisha invoked the Lord's help. The Aramean troops were temporarily blinded. Elisha then told them they had come to the wrong place and offered to lead them to the man they were seeking. He guided them right into Samaria and handed them over to the king's forces before they recovered their vision. The king wanted to put them to death, but Elisha dissuaded him, pointing out that they were not really battle captives. Instead, on the prophet's advice, the raiders were fed and returned unharmed across the border. This act of clemency bore fruit in a temporary truce in the fighting.

When the Syrians under the king of Damascus later invaded Israel in force, Elisha was involved in the siege of Samaria. The city was completely cut off and famine-stricken. What little food there was fetched exorbitant prices in the market-place. The desperate King Jehoram blamed Elisha for causing all this suffering through his misplaced faith in the protection of the Lord. The prophet promised that within a day there would be an abundance of barley and flour.

During the night the Syrian army fled in panic, after the Lord had caused them to hear the sound of chariots and a great host, and they thought that Hittite and Egyptian armies had arrived to join forces with the Israelites. The siege was over, and great quantities of abandoned Syrian supplies were left in the hands of the city.

A period of peace seems to have ensued between Israel and Aram, for Elisha is next heard of in Damascus. The King Ben-hadad II was seriously ill. He heard that the renowned Israelite prophet was in his city and sent Hazael, a senior army officer, to consult him, with forty camel-loads of goods as a gift. Elisha gave a cryptic answer: the king would recover from his illness but nevertheless he was about to die.

The prophet reacted strangely to the encounter with Hazael. He seemed to go into a trance, weeping, with his face rigid and his eyes fixed. The bewildered Hazael asked him why he wept. He then predicted that Hazael would become king of Aram, and '... I know the evil that you will do to the people of Israel; you will set on fire their fortresses, and you will slay their young men with the sword, and dash in pieces their little ones, and rip up their women with child.' (2 Kgs. 8:12) The next day Hazael murdered Ben-hadad by smothering him with a wet cloth, and became king in his place. He later occupied all the Israelite territory east of the Jordan, and parts of Israel itself.

Elisha had not forgotten that King Jehoram was the son of Ahab, whose dynasty Elijah had doomed to extinction in the name of the Lord. In the twelfth year of Jehoram's reign, Israel was defending Ramoth-gilead, east of the Jordan, against the king of Aram. The king had gone back to Jezreel to recover from campaign wounds and left the front in charge of a tough and ambitious general, Jehu. Elisha sent a young disciple to inform Jehu that God had selected him to be king, and to anoint his head with oil.

Jehu dashed for Jezreel, killed the king and seized the throne. In the bloody chapter that followed, Jehu extirpated not only Queen Jezebel and all Ahab's family and supporters, but also all the priests and worshippers of the Phoenician baal-cult that Jezebel had spread. Elijah's grim prophecy had been carried out in full measure. Yet Jehu's reign was to prove that this religious purge was at the expense of the national interest. The kingdom was weakened and isolated and lost much territory. Elisha's venture in king-making had been costly.

The Prophet's Death

More than fifty years had gone by since the day when Elijah had plucked the young Elisha from his ploughing. Elisha's career since then had spanned four reigns. Jehu's grandson Joash was on the throne when the old prophet lay on his death-bed. The king came to call on him and wept over him. Elisha told him to open the east window and shoot an arrow in the direction of their old enemy Aram. Elisha prophesied that the Arameans would be defeated and turned back at Aphek, east of the Sea of Galilee. He then told the king to strike the ground with his arrows, and Joash did so three times. Elisha complained that he should have done so five or six times, then would he secure total victory; as it was, he would defeat Aram only three times. After these symbolic actions Elisha died.

A brief sequel follows in the Scriptures. Some men carrying a body for burial were surprised by Moabite marauders. They threw the body into Elisha's tomb and fled. On contact with the prophet's bones, the corpse came to life again and stood up. This story was meant to show that Elisha's powers as a worker of miracles persisted even after his death. [1 Kgs. 19; 2 Kgs. 2-9; 13]

ELISHAH (Heb. 'God saves') date unknown. Son of Javan and a descendant of Noah's son Japheth. [Gen. 10:4; 1 Chr. 1:7; Ezek. 27:7]

ELISHAMA (Heb. 'whom God hears') **1.** c. 13 century BC. Son of Ammihud and the grandfather of Joshua, he was appointed by Moses to conduct a census of the men of Ephraim fit for war and led his tribe's contingent. [Num. 1:10; 2:18; 7:48-53; 10:22; 1 Chr. 7:26]

2. 10 century BC. Son of King David. [2 Sam. 5:16; 1 Chr. 3:8; 14:7]

3. see ELISHUA

4. date unknown. Son of Jekamiah and a leader of the tribe of Judah. [1 Chr. 2:41]

5. 9 century BC. A priest in the reign of King Jehoshaphat who taught the Law of God in the cities of Judah. [2 Chr. 17:8]

6. *c.* 6 century BC. A descendant of the royal family of Judah, his grandson assassinated Gedaliah, the governor of Judah. [2 Kgs. 25:25; Jer. 41:1]

7. *c.* 6 century BC. Secretary to the leaders of Judah in the reign of King Jehoiakim, in whose room the scroll of Jeremiah's prophecies was kept before it was read to the king. [Jer. 36:12, 20, 21]

ELISHAPHAT (Heb. 'my God judged') *c.* 9 century BC. Son of Zichri, he was one of the Judean officers who on the orders of Jehoiada the high priest executed Queen Athaliah who had usurped the throne. [2 Chr. 23:1]

ELISHEBA (Heb. 'God her oath') *c.* 13 century BC. Wife of Aaron the high priest, she was the daughter of Amminadab, a leader of the tribe of Judah. [Exod. 6:23]

ELISHUA *c.* 10 century BC. Son of King David. Also called Elishama. [2 Sam. 5:15; 1 Chr. 3:6; 14:5]

ELIZAPHAN (Heb. 'my God protected') **1.** *c.* 13 century BC. A Levite head of a family of Kohathites in the

Elkanah makes his sacrifice at Shiloh. Initial from the *Bible of Stavelot*.

wilderness, he and his family were responsible for the Ark of the Tabernacle and some of its appurtenances during the wanderings of the children of Israel. [Num. 3:30; 1 Chr. 15:8; 2 Chr. 29:13]

2. *c.* 13 century BC. Son of Parnach, he was appointed by Moses to supervise the division of the part of the land of Israel allocated to Zebulun among the members of his tribe. [Num. 34:25]

ELIZUR (Heb. 'my God is my rock') *c.* 13 century BC. Son of Shedeur, Moses appointed him to conduct the census of the men of Reuben fit for war and he led the contingent of his tribe. [Num. 1:5; 2:10; 7:30-5; 10:18]

ELKANAH (Heb. 'provided by God') **1.** *c.* 13 century BC. One of the sons of Korah of the tribe of Levi who led the revolt in the wilderness against the authority of Moses and Aaron. [Exod. 6:24; 1 Chr. 6:23]

2. *c.* 13 century BC. Son of Assir and a grandson of Korah the Levite. [1 Chr. 6:23, 25, 36]

3. *c.* 12 century BC. A judge of Israel for ten years, he was an ancestor of the prophet Samuel. [1 Chr. 6:26, 35]

4. *c.* 11 century BC. Father of Samuel. Elkanah the son of Jeroham lived in Ramathaim-zophim, the hill country of Ephraim. He had two wives: Hannah who was barren and Peninnah who had several children. Hannah grieved over being childless, and Elkanah said to her: 'Hannah, why do you weep? And why do you not eat? And why is your heart sad? Am I not more to you than ten sons?' (1 Sam. 1:8) The next time the family went to the temple at Shiloh to make their annual sacrifices, she stayed behind and prayed to the Lord. Eli the high priest consoled her.

In due time Hannah bore a child she called Samuel, 'the Lord heard'. When she had weaned him she brought him to Shiloh where he was apprenticed to the priests. Elkanah and Hannah were blessed with five more children. [1 Sam. 1-2; 1 Chr. 6:27, 34]

5. *c.* 11 century BC. A warrior of the family of the Korahites who deserted the army of King Saul and rallied to David at Ziklag. [1 Chr. 12:6]

6. 10 century BC. One of the two Levites who were gatekeepers for the Ark in the reign of King David. [1 Chr. 15:23]

7. 8 century BC. Chief minister of King Ahaz of Judah, he was killed by Zichri of the tribe of Ephraim in the war between Israel and Judah. [2 Chr. 28:7]

8. date unknown. A Levite whose grandson Berechiah was one of the first to settle in Jerusalem following the return from exile in Babylon. [1 Chr. 9:16]

ELNAAM (Heb. 'God his delight') *c.* 10 century BC. Father of Jeribai and Joshaviah, two warriors in the army of King David outstanding for their bravery. [1 Chr. 11:46]

ELNATHAN (Heb. 'God hath given') **1.** 7 century BC. Father of Nehushta, the mother of King Jehoiachin of Judah. [2 Kgs. 24:8]

2. *c.* 7 century BC. Elnathan, the son of Achbor, was an official at the court of King Jehoiakim of Judah. He was sent by the king to bring back from Egypt the prophet Uriah who had predicted doom and fled.

It was Elnathan who pleaded in vain with the king not to destroy the Scroll of Jeremiah's oracles that was being read to him. [Jer. 26:22, 23; 36:25]

3. 5 century BC. Three men, each named Elnathan, leaders of the exile in Babylon, were sent by Ezra to Iddo at Casiphia requesting that he send Levites to serve in the Temple in Jerusalem. [Ezra 8:16]

ELON (Heb. 'oak tree') **1.** *c.* 16 century BC. Father of Adah and father-in-law of Esau. [Gen. 26:34; 36:2]

2. *c.* 16 century BC. Son of Zebulun and grandson of Jacob. [Gen. 46:14; Num. 26:26]

3. *c.* 12 century BC. A judge of Israel for ten years, he was buried in Aijalon. [Judg. 12:11, 12]

ELPAAL (Heb. 'God acted') date unknown. Son of Hushim, he was a leader of the tribe of Benjamin. [1 Chr. 8:11, 12, 18]

ELPELET *see* ELIPHELET **2.**

ELUZAI (Heb. 'God is my castle') *c.* 11 century BC. A Benjaminite warrior who deserted the army of King Saul and rallied to David at Ziklag. [1 Chr. 12:5]

ELZABAD (Heb. 'gift of God') **1.** *c.* 11 century BC. A warrior of the tribe of Gad who deserted the army of King Saul and rallied to David's support. [1 Chr. 12:12]

2. 10 century BC. Son of Shemaiah and a gatekeeper of the Tabernacle in the reign of King David. [1 Chr. 26:7]

ELZAPHAN (Heb. 'protected by God') *c.* 13 century BC. Son of Uzziel, a Levite descended from Kohath and a cousin of Moses, he helped remove the bodies of Nadab and Abihu from the sanctuary where they had died after burning the forbidden incense. [Exod. 6:22; Lev. 10:4]

EMIM (Heb. 'terrors') date unknown. A fierce and powerful tribe living in the land of Canaan in ancient times. [Gen. 14:5; Deut. 2:10]

ENAN (Heb. 'eyes') *c.* 13 century BC. A leader of the tribe of Naphtali, he was the father of Ahira who was appointed by Moses as commander of the tribe of Naphtali. [Num. 1:15; 2:29; 7:78, 83; 10:27]

ENOCH (Heb. 'dedicated') **1.** date unknown. Eldest son of Cain and a grandson of Adam and Eve. [Gen. 4:17, 18]

2. date unknown. Son of Jared and a descendant of Seth. [Gen. 5:18-24; 1 Chr. 1:3]

ENOSH (Heb. 'mortal') date unknown. Son of Seth, the third son of Adam. [Gen. 4:26; 5:6-11; 1 Chr. 1:1]

EPHAH (Heb. 'darkness') **1.** *c.* 16 century BC. Son of Midian and a grandson of Abraham and Keturah. [Gen. 25:4; 1 Chr. 1:33; Isa. 60:6]

2. date unknown. Caleb's concubine who bore him three sons. [1 Chr. 2:46]

3. date unknown. Son of Jahdai and a leader of the

tribe of Judah. [1 Chr. 2:47]

EPHAI (Heb. 'gloomy') 6 century BC. Father of sons who were among the army captains of Judah who rallied to the support of Gedaliah son of Ahikam when the latter was made governor of Judah by the Babylonians. [Jer. 40:8]

EPHER (Heb. 'calf') **1.** *c.* 16 century BC. Son of Midian and a grandson of Abraham and Keturah. [Gen. 25:4; 1 Chr. 1:33]

2. date unknown. Son of Ezrah of the tribe of Judah. [1 Chr. 4:17]

3. date unknown. A leader of the tribe of Manasseh living east of the river Jordan. [1 Chr. 5:24]

EPHLAL (Heb. 'judgment') date unknown. A leader of the tribe of Judah, he was descended from Perez. [1 Chr. 2:37]

EPHOD (Heb. 'clothe') *c.* 13 century BC. Father of Hanniel, a leader of the tribe of Manasseh in the time of Moses who was to supervise the division of their inheritance among the members of the tribe. [Num. 34:23]

EPHRAIM (Heb. 'fruitfulness') *c.* 16 century BC. Second son of Joseph. Ephraim, like his elder brother Manasseh, was born in Egypt where Joseph had married Asenath, the daughter of the Egyptian high priest of the temple at On.

Years later, after Joseph had brought his father Jacob and the rest of the family to Egypt, he was told his father was ill. He took Manasseh and Ephraim to Jacob's bedside to receive his blessing. The patriarch's sight was failing and when he placed his right hand on the head of Ephraim, the younger son, Joseph sought to correct him. Jacob then explained that Ephraim's descendants would be more important than those of Manasseh. Jacob gave the same importance to these two grand-children as he did to his sons and they too became founders of tribes.

In the blessing attributed to Moses, Joseph is promised great abundance and power, and it is added that 'such are the ten thousands of Ephraim' (Deut. 33:17).

In the conquest of Canaan under Joshua, the tribe of Ephraim was allocated the central hill area south of Shechem (Nablus) and extending into the coastal plain. [Gen. 41:52; 46:20; 48:1-20; 50:23; Num. 26:28; Deut. 33:17; 1 Chr. 7:20-2]

EPHRATH (Heb. 'fruitful') date unknown. A wife of Caleb, who was the son of Hezron, of the tribe of Judah and the mother of Hur. Also called Ephrathah. [1 Chr. 2:19, 50; 4:4]

EPHRATHAH *see* EPHRATH

EPHRON (Heb. 'fawn-like') *c.* 18 century BC. He was the son of Zohar a Hittite, and a landowner in Hebron from whom Abraham bought the Cave of Machpelah as a family burial place. [Gen. 23:8-20; 25:9; 49:29, 30; 50:13]

117

above Esarhaddon, king of Assyria, carved on a victory stele, holding two prisoners on leashes, probably the kings of Tyre and Egypt.

left Abraham bought the Cave of Machpelah from Ephron the Hittite. Hittite prisoners from a relief at Kadesh-on-Orontes in Syria, 13th century BC.

ER (Heb. 'watchful') **1.** *c.* 16 century BC. The eldest son of Judah. and his wife Bath-shua. Er, who married Tamar, was 'wicked in the sight of the Lord' and died suddenly without children. [Gen. 38:7; 46:12; Num. 26:19; 1 Chr. 2:3, 4]

2. *c.* 16 century BC. The son of Shelah and a grandson of Judah, he was a chief of the tribe and his descendants were renowned for their production of fine linen. [1 Chr. 4:21]

ERAN (Heb. 'watchful') *c.* 16 century BC. Son of Shuthelah and a grandson of Ephraim, he was a chief of the tribe. [Num. 26:36]

ERI (Heb. 'watching') *c.* 16 century BC. Son of Gad and

a grandson of Jacob and Zilpah. [Gen. 46:16; Num. 26:16]

ESARHADDON (Ass. 'Asshur has given a brother') King of Assyria, 680-69 BC. Esarhaddon was the son of Sennacherib and the grandson of Sargon II (the Great). He was an able monarch who expanded the Assyrian empire by the occupation of Lower Egypt in 671 BC. Manasseh, king of Judah, was one of the rulers mentioned in Assyrian records as paying tribute to him. [2 Kgs. 19:37; Ezra 4:2; Isa. 37:38]

ESAU (Heb. 'hairy, shaggy') *c.* 17 century BC. Elder son of Isaac and Rebekah.

After Isaac's wife Rebekah had been barren for

many years, she became pregnant with twins. According to the Biblical account there was conflict between the infants while they were still in the womb and it was foretold that the elder would serve the younger. The first to be born was Esau, who was covered with red hair. He was followed by Jacob, clutching his brother's heel.

Esau grew up as a skilled hunter, while Jacob became a cultivator. One day Esau returned from a hunting trip weak with hunger. He begged his brother for food, and Jacob gave him bread and red lentil soup in return for Esau's surrender of his birthright as the first-born.

At the age of forty Esau took three wives from the local Hittite people, Adah, Oholibamah and Basemath. This was a grief to his parents.

When Isaac was old and nearly blind, he asked Esau, his favourite son, to go hunting and bring him a dish of the venison he liked. He would then, he said, bestow the paternal blessing on him. Rebekah overheard this and determined to get the blessing for Jacob whom she loved best. She prepared a savoury dish of goat's meat and sent it in to her husband with Jacob, having first dressed him in one of Esau's garments and covered his hands and neck with fleece to simulate Esau's hairiness. The old man was deceived and bestowed the blessing on Jacob, declaring that he would be the head of the family after Isaac's death and his brethren would serve him.

When Esau returned and learnt what had happened, he wept bitterly, and begged his father to bless him as well. Isaac replied that Esau would have to serve his brother Jacob, but promised that Esau too would prosper and in due course become independent. Esau, his father added, would live by the sword.

The mountains of Edom, the traditional domain of Esau, seen from Eilat.

Esau hated Jacob for this betrayal and threatened to kill him. Jacob was sent away to his mother's family in Paddan-aram to escape Esau's revenge, and also to find a wife among his kinsfolk. Realizing how much his parents disapproved of Canaanite women as wives for their sons, Esau himself took another wife, Mahalath, who was the daughter of Ishmael, Isaac's half-brother.

Esau settled in the land of Seir, south of the Dead Sea. After many years had gone by, messengers arrived from Jacob, to say he had returned to Canaan with his wives and children. Esau set out to meet him, at the head of four hundred men. Jacob was fearful that the twin brother he had wronged might be coming to slay him. He therefore sent ahead many choice sheep, goats, cattle and camels as gifts for Esau.

The meeting took place near the ford of Jabbok (where the Jabbok river joins the Jordan river, to the north of Jericho). Jacob walked forward with his two wives, his two concubines, and their children, and bowed down to the ground before Esau. But his fears were unfounded. Esau ran to meet his brother and embraced him, and they kissed each other and wept.

At first Esau refused the gifts of livestock, saying he had enough animals of his own, but he was finally persuaded to accept them.

Esau wanted Jacob to return with him to the land of Seir. Jacob pleaded that he could only travel slowly as his children were of tender years and his animals were with young, and he prevailed on Esau and his men to go ahead. Jacob did not follow Esau but turned away and remained in Canaan.

Esau's character seems open and straightforward, without a trace of his brother Jacob's guile. His emotions are strong and spontaneous, whether he is weeping and pleading before his father when cheated of his blessing – or threatening to kill Jacob in revenge – or rushing to embrace his brother when they meet again in later life.

Esau is also called Edom in the Bible, and was regarded as the forefather of the Edomites, the people inhabiting the rugged semi-desert terrain of Seir or Edom, below the Dead Sea. [Gen. 25-8; 32-3; 35:1; 36; Josh. 24:4; 1 Chr. 1:34-5; Mal. 1:2-3]

ESHBAAL *see* ISHBOSHETH

ESHBAN date unknown. Son of Dishon and a grandson of Anah. [Gen. 36:26; 1 Chr. 1:41]

ESHCOL (Heb. 'cluster of grapes') *c.* 18 century BC. One of three Amorite brothers who were neighbours of Abraham at Hebron, and helped him to rescue the captured Lot.

Eshcol may have given his name to a fertile valley near Hebron from which Moses's spies brought back grapes, figs and pomegranates. [Gen. 14:13, 24; Num. 13:23, 24; 32:9; Deut. 1:24]

ESHEK (Heb. 'oppression') *c.* 9 century BC. Son of

Eleasah of the tribe of Benjamin and a descendant of King Saul. [1 Chr. 8:39]

ESHTEMOA date unknown. The Maacathite leader of the tribe of Judah whose grandmother was an Egyptian princess. [1 Chr. 4:19]

ESHTON date unknown. Son of Mehir and a leader of the tribe of Judah. [1 Chr. 4:11, 12]

ESTHER (Pers. 'star') 5 century BC. Jewish queen of King Ahasuerus (Xerxes I). The tale of Esther, the Jewish queen of King Ahasuerus of Persia (486-65), and the way she foiled the wicked designs of Haman, the Vizier (chief minister), forms one of the Books of the Old Testament. It is connected with the Feast of Purim, in early spring.

The story shows a remarkable familiarity with the atmosphere and usages of the Persian court, though there are scholastic doubts as to its authenticity. Nevertheless, this uncertainty did not prevent Purim from becoming an immensely popular Jewish folk festival, completely identified with the Book of Esther, the Megillah (scroll) of which is read in every synagogue to the accompaniment of noise and stamping at each mention of Haman's name. It is the only gay carnival of the Jewish calendar, a time for masquerades, fancy dress parades for the children, and the baking of three-cornered poppyseed cakes which are colloquially called in Hebrew 'Haman's ears'.

The Book of Esther relates that in the third year of his reign King Ahasuerus gathered together all the leading men of his empire at Shushan (Susa), the capital. On the seventh day of feasting in the palace grounds, the king, under the influence of wine, sent his court chamberlains to fetch Queen Vashti, so that her beauty could be displayed to his guests. When she refused to come, the angry king consulted his chief counsellors. They advised him to take drastic action against the queen, otherwise her example would encourage other wives to disobey their husbands. The king, they said, should issue a decree banning Vashti from his presence, and confer her position on a worthier woman.

Beautiful maidens were brought to the capital from all the provinces for a new queen to be chosen from among them. They were kept under the charge of the chief eunuch, and each of them received special beauty

Queen Esther, by Andrea del Castagno (1423-57). The story of Esther is celebrated each year at the festival of Purim.

treatment for a year with oils and spices before being brought into the king. None of them appealed to him as a suitable queen.

In Susa lived a sage and devout Jew called Mordecai, one of the exiles from Jerusalem. He had adopted as his own daughter a young orphaned cousin, Hadassah, whose Persian name was Esther, for 'the maiden was beautiful and lovely' (Esther 2:7). She was one of the girls brought to the king's palace, and so appealed to the chief eunuch that he gave her seven maids to attend on her and the best quarters in the harem. When she was summoned to the king, he was immediately attracted by her beauty and intelligence, 'so that he set the royal crown on her head and made her queen instead of Vashti' (Esther 2:17). On Mordecai's advice she did not reveal her Jewish origins.

Mordecai himself had an official position at the court. One day he overheard two of the king's chamberlains plotting to assassinate their master. He asked Esther to warn the king, who had the conspirators seized and executed. This service by Mordecai was recorded in the official court annals.

The Edict of Haman

Shortly afterwards the king appointed Haman, the Agagite, as his chief minister and gave orders that all the palace officials were to prostrate themselves before him. Mordecai alone refused to abase himself in this fashion. Haman's anger at Mordecai, the Jew, turned into hatred of the Jewish race, and a resolve to wipe it out. In the twelfth year of the reign of Ahasuerus, Haman had the magicians cast the 'pur' or sacred lot to pick a propitious day for his evil design. Haman then went to the king and denounced the Jewish minority: 'There is a certain people scattered abroad and dispersed among the peoples in all the provinces of your kingdom; their laws are different from those of every other people, and they do not keep the king's laws, so that it is not for the king's profit to tolerate them.' (Esther 3:8) He offered to pay a large sum of money into the royal treasury if he got his way – perhaps from the Jewish property that would be confiscated. The king declined the contribution but gave Haman permission to act as he saw fit about the Jews and gave him his signet ring for issuing the necessary royal decrees.

Haman had these orders drawn up, translated into all the languages of the empire and sent by special runners to the authorities in each province. On the appointed day they were to have all the local Jews slaughtered and their possessions seized.

The Jews were thrown into consternation at the news of the pending pogrom. They fasted, prayed and tore their clothes in mourning. Dressed in sackcloth, Mordecai stood in the square in front of the palace. When Esther sent to ask him what had happened, Mordecai produced a copy of Haman's edict and told her to approach the king and beg for the lives of her people.

After fasting for three days, Esther dressed herself up in her regal robes and went into the king, who was sitting on his throne. He addressed her kindly and agreed to come and dine in her quarters together with Haman. At the meal she invited them to come again the following day. Haman went home in high spirits at the unusual honour paid him. But his anger was aroused again at the sight of Mordecai in the palace square. Encouraged by his wife and friends he ordered a gallows to be constructed, intending to ask the king next morning to have Mordecai hanged on it. However, being unable to sleep the previous night, the king had called for the court records to be read to him, and came across the entry about Mordecai's having revealed the plot to assassinate him. He discovered that Mordecai's act had gone unrewarded. Thus, when Haman arrived in the morning to see the king, Ahasuerus promptly asked him 'What shall be done to the man whom the king delights to honour?' (Esther 6:6) Believing that the reference was to himself, Haman eagerly advised that such a man should be dressed in royal robes, placed upon the king's horse and led by a high official through the streets of the capital. To Haman's dismay, he was ordered to do just that for Mordecai.

When the king and Haman sat at Queen Esther's table for her second banquet, she appeared downcast, and the king asked her whether there was anything she wanted. Esther pleaded that the lives of herself and her people should be spared: 'For we are sold, I and my people, to be destroyed, to be slain, and to be annihilated.' (Esther 7:4) She then accused the terrified Haman of having organized this mass murder. Overcome with anger, the king rushed out into the garden. Haman flung himself down on the couch next to the queen and begged her to save his life. At that moment the king stalked in again and, seeing Haman on the couch, cried out: 'Will he even assault the queen in my presence, in my own house?' (Esther 7:8) The attendants seized Haman and the king ordered him to be hanged on the gallows he had constructed for Mordecai.

Haman's house and possessions were confiscated and given to Esther, while Mordecai was appointed chief minister in his place. He left the palace clothed in 'royal robes of blue and white, with a great golden crown and a mantle of fine linen and purple, while the city of Susa shouted and rejoiced' (Esther 8:15).

Esther again appeared weeping before the king and begged him to have Haman's decree cancelled. That could not be done, since Persian law made a formal edict of the ruler irrevocable even by himself. Instead Mordecai was authorized to send out another decree, which was taken on fast horses, mules and camels to all the 127 provinces of the empire. It gave the Jews the right to carry arms in self-defence. On the day Haman had appointed for their destruction, they turned on their enemies and slew them. This happened on the thirteenth day of Adar, the twelfth month by the Jewish calendar, and on the fourteenth they celebrated their survival. Mordecai, and later also Esther, sent letters to all the Jews, laying down that their deliverance from their persecutor should be commemorated each year with the Feast of Purim: 'Therefore the Jews of the villages, who live in the open towns, hold the fourteenth day of the month of Adar as a day for gladness and feasting and holiday-making, and a day on which they send choice portions to one another.' (Esther 9:19) (In walled cities the feast was held a day later because in Susa the fighting had lasted two days.) [Book of Esther]

ETAM (Heb. 'lair') date unknown. A leader of the tribe of Judah and father of Jezreel, Ishma, Idbash and their sister Hazzelelponi. [1 Chr. 4:3]

ETHAN (Heb. 'strong') **1.** *c.* 16 century BC. Son of Zerah and a grandson of Judah. [1 Chr. 2:6, 8]

2. *c.* 10 century BC. Son of Zimmah and a Levite descended from Gershom. [1 Chr. 6:42]

3. date unknown. The Ezrahite son of Mahol, famed for his wisdom which was exceeded only by that of King Solomon. [1 Kgs. 4:31; Ps. 89]

4. *c.* 10 century BC. Son of Kushaiah, one of the Levites appointed to sing while the Ark of God was brought into Jerusalem by King David. [1 Chr. 6:44; 15:17, 19]

ETHBAAL (Heb. 'man of Baal') *c.* 9 century BC. King of the great Phoenician port city of Sidon, he was father of Jezebel, who was married to Ahab, king of Israel.

The important alliance between the Israelites and the seafaring Phoenicians was started by David, developed by Solomon, and revived by Ahab's father King Omri. [1 Kgs. 16:31]

ETHNAN (Heb. 'hire') date unknown. Son of Helah and a leader of the tribe of Judah. [1 Chr. 4:7]

ETHNI (Heb. 'gift') date unknown. A Levite descended from Gershom, he was an ancestor of King David's musician, Asaph. [1 Chr. 6:41]

EVE (Heb. 'life') date unknown. The first woman. When Adam had been created and placed in the Garden of Eden, the Lord decided that he should have a helpmate. Adam was put into a deep sleep, and one of his ribs was removed and turned into a woman. Adam declared that 'This at last is bone of my bones and flesh of my flesh.' (Gen. 2:23) He called her Eve (in Hebrew 'Chava') because she was 'the mother of all living' (Gen. 3:20).

The serpent, the most subtle of the beasts, talked Eve into tasting the fruit of the tree of the knowledge of good and evil, which she gave to Adam as well. 'Then the eyes of both were opened, and they knew that they were naked; and they sewed fig leaves together and made themselves aprons.' (Gen. 3:7)

When the Lord discovered what they had done Eve pleaded that the serpent had 'beguiled' her. The Lord inflicted punishments on the serpent, on Eve and on Adam. Eve's curse was to bear children in pain and sorrow, and to be ruled by her husband.

After Adam and Eve had been expelled from the Garden of Eden she bore him three children – Cain, Abel and Seth. *see* ADAM [Gen. 3; 4:1]

EVI (Heb. 'desire') *c.* 13 century BC. One of the five chiefs of Midian slain by the army of the Children of Israel in the wilderness under Phinehas's command. [Num. 31:8; Josh. 13:21]

Esther pleads with King Ahasuerus to save the Jews. Illumination from the *Book of Hours of Anne of Montmorency*.

above Eve is shown to Adam, from the bronze doors of Hildesheim Cathedral, 11th century.

left Cylinder seal, 3rd millennium B.C, showing two figures beside a tree, from behind which appear two snakes.

below Eve: carving by Ghislebertus from Autun Cathedral, 12th century.

EVIL-MERODACH (Bab. 'man of Merodach [a god]') 6 century BC. Successor to Nebuchadnezzar as king of Babylon, he dealt kindly with King Jehoiachin of Judah whom Nebuchadnezzar had taken captive to Babylon. King Evil-merodach released Jehoiachin from prison, treated him as a distinguished guest at court, and granted him a regular allowance for the rest of his life. [2 Kgs. 25:27; Jer. 52:31]

EZBAI 10 century BC. The father of Naarai, a warrior in the army of King David. [1 Chr. 11:37]

EZBON (Heb. 'finger') **1.** *c.* 16 century BC. Son of Gad and grandson of Jacob. Also called Ozni. [Gen. 46:16; Num. 26:16]

2. *c.* 16 century BC. Son of Bela and a grandson of Benjamin. [1 Chr. 7:7]

EZEKIEL (Heb. 'the strength of God') *c.* 6 century BC. A Hebrew prophet of the Exile. Ezekiel the son of Buzi ranks as one of the three major figures among the latter prophets, together with Isaiah and Jeremiah. Above all, he is the prophet of the Babylonian exile, that started with Nebuchadnezzar's first deportations from Judah in 598 BC and was swelled with the fall of Jerusalem in 587 BC.

The record of Ezekiel's ministry covers a span of twenty-two years, starting in 593 BC. Although some of the earlier chapters have a Jerusalem setting, the majority of scholars believe that his work was wholly in Babylon, and that his apparent presence in Jerusalem was visionary.

The Book of Ezekiel is more unified and systematic than those of Isaiah and Jeremiah. It contains forty-eight chapters grouped round four themes. After an introduction describing how Ezekiel receives his call in a vision, the first part contains God's warnings and threats against the population of Judah for their faithlessness. Then come the oracles against the surrounding nations – chiefly Tyre and Egypt, and to a lesser extent

The prophet Ezekiel:
German stained-glass window,
15th century.

Sidon, Philistia, Ammon, Moab and Edom. After the fall of Jerusalem his addresses to the exiles bring a message of comfort and a promise of return to their land. The final section lays down detailed provisions for the restored Israelite state of the future, including the rebuilding of the Temple and the regulations for worship.

The Book of Ezekiel is almost devoid of biographical and personal details. It is known that he had been a priest, was one of the first group of deportees to Babylonia, and lived there in a refugee community at Tel-Abib on the river Chebar, a large irrigation canal leading from the Euphrates north of the city of Babylon. The only reference to his family is that the death of his wife on the eve of the fall of Jerusalem was for him a personal symbol of the national disaster.

What emerges from the Book is a versatile and complex mind. One part of Ezekiel is the ordained priest, deferring to the formal commandments of the Mosaic Code and absorbed by the details of temple ritual and architecture. The other Ezekiel is a mystic-prophet given to ecstatic visions and bizarre symbols. His four visions spring from the subconscious mind rather than the intellect, and are expressed in images that are precise and powerful but at times baffling. These visions found later echoes in the apocalyptic passages of Daniel and the Book of Revelations, and in such painters as Hieronymus Bosch in 15th-century Flanders, and William Blake in late 18th- and early 19th-century England.

The Four Visions

The Book of Ezekiel opens with the vision in which he receives his call from God. (He is addressed by the Lord as 'Son of man', which recurs eighty-seven times throughout the Book, though the expression is almost unknown elsewhere in the Old Testament.) He sees the Lord in a kind of chariot that moves on four creatures, each having a human form, two pairs of wings, a head with four faces – man, eagle, lion and ox – and the burnished hoofs of a calf. Above them stretches an irridescent arch. The whole tableau is bathed in blinding light and flames and the whirring of the wings is like the noise of rushing water. A hand is stretched forth towards Ezekiel holding a scroll written on both sides with words of 'lamentation and mourning and woe' (Ezek. 2:10), and he is commanded to eat the scroll, which tastes of honey. The voice of the Lord warns Ezekiel that he is being sent to minister a people 'of a hard forehead and of a stubborn heart' (Ezek. 3:7). '... nor be afraid of their words, though briars and thorns are with you and you sit upon scorpions' (Ezek. 2:6). Ezekiel records that for seven days after this revelation he was like a man stunned.

Another vision concerns the idolatrous practices which he so vehemently and constantly denounced. He feels that the hand of the Lord lifts him up by the hair

Assyrian cylinder seal showing winged and horned mythological beasts, similar to the fanciful images of Ezekiel's visions.

and transports him to Jerusalem. Through a hole in the wall, he is shown seventy elders inside the Temple, burning incense on the altars and worshipping wall reliefs of '... creeping things, and loathsome beasts, and all the idols of the house of Israel' (Ezek. 8:10). (These were apparently the sacred creatures of Assyrian and Babylonian cults.) The men are also prostrating themselves to the sun, while a group of women are weeping for the death of the Canaanite spring god Tammuz. Ezekiel then sees seven angels. Six of them are armed as soldiers while the seventh wears the white linen garb and inkhorn of a scribe. The scribe marks crosses on the foreheads of those inhabitants who are still righteous enough to be saved, and all the rest are then put to the sword.

After the fall of Jerusalem, Ezekiel has a vision of the Return in which he finds himself in a valley filled with dry bones. The Lord commands him to prophesy, and then 'there was a noise, and behold, a rattling; and the bones came together, bone to its bone ... flesh had come upon them, and skin had covered them; ... and the breath came into them, and they lived ... an exceeding great host.' (Ezek. 37:7, 8, 10)

In the twenty-fifth year of Ezekiel's exile and fourteen years after Jerusalem was destroyed, Ezekiel sees in a vision the city and the kingdom restored. He is guided round the new Temple by an angel architect equipped with a cord and a measuring rod. The detailed plans of the Temple and the adjacent structures are given, with the exact measurements of the wooden altar. (The design of the gateways, with three guard rooms on each side, was apparently modelled on the gateways to Solomon's destroyed Temple, and corresponds to the city gates excavated at Hazor, Megiddo and Gezer, dating from Solomon's time.)

The life-giving force that flows from the sanctuary is symbolized by the sacred river the celestial guide shows Ezekiel. It starts from a spring beneath the Temple and flows eastward into the Dead Sea. The waters of the river are teeming with fish and its banks are green and fruitful. (This picture would be a striking one for the prophet's audience of exiled Judeans, who would remember the bleakness of the wilderness of Judea.)

In the vision the kingdom is reunited and its boundaries restored more or less to those in David's time. Its territory is divided again among the twelve Israelite tribes, by horizontal strips without regard to geography. The ordinances are specified for sacrifices, festivals, dietary restrictions and the functions of the priests and Levites.

It was in character for Ezekiel to portray the future commonwealth with a mixture of fantasy and concrete detail. This no doubt made the hope of the Return much more tangible to the exiles in distant Babylon. His blueprint inspired those who went back in the time of Ezra and Nehemiah and laid the foundations for the Second Temple and a renewed nationhood.

Pictorial Images and Oracles

Ezekiel's love of visual imagery expressed itself at times in 'acting out' his message. This use of mime may have been connected with his disclosure that at times the Lord made him dumb.

For instance, the prophet describes the elaborate enactment of the siege and fall of Jerusalem, before the event took place. He was instructed to draw a map of the city on a clay tablet, place it on the ground, and draw round it furrows and other indications of siege. Playing the role of God, he flung out his bare arm and condemned the city. After that he lay for some time on his left side and then on his right side, to indicate the

The Solomonic gates excavated at Gezer, whose three chambers on either side correspond to Ezekiel's description of the gates of the new Temple.

periods during which first Israel and then Judah had sinned against the Lord. His next act was to cook various grains in a pot, make himself bread, and ration out this food to himself with very little water. This was done to indicate the hardship of the siege. Finally he was told to shave off his hair and his beard, to place a third of it inside the map of Jerusalem for its residents who would be slain; to spread another third around Jerusalem with a tip of a sword for the inhabitants who would be killed outside the city, and to scatter the last third to the wind for those who would be taken into exile.

On another occasion Ezekiel was told to pack a refugee's knapsack, make a hole in the wall, and go out into the dark at a time when everybody could see him. This would bring home to them the fate that awaited the sinners in Jerusalem.

On the day that Nebuchadnezzar commenced the siege of Jerusalem, Ezekiel was commanded to put flesh and bones in a cooking pot and set it on the fire. The food was reduced to cinders, the pot became red-hot but the rust and filth was not completely burnt away. This action dramatized the failure of the Lord to purge the inhabitants of Jerusalem of their wickedness and the consequent destruction of the city.

Apart from these symbolic actions, the text of the Book is studded with verbal similes and parables, mostly drawn from nature. The kingdom is compared to a vine; Babylon and Egypt are vultures, a symbol of power; the Judean kings Jehoiakim and Zedekiah are lion cubs that become man-eaters and are captured; Egypt is a crocodile; and Judah and Israel are two sticks that are tied together as a sign of reunion.

Ezekiel seems strongly attracted by a very human simile, that of the harlot. The history of Israel is told as a parable: a traveller finds a newborn girl baby by the wayside and brings her up to womanhood, but she becomes corrupted and sells her favours to neighbouring peoples. In another parable, Israel and Judah appear as two lascivious sisters who are first defiled in Egypt and then become prostitutes.

In the millennium he prophesies, Ezekiel imagines an invasion of the country by an army from the extreme north, led by King Gog of Magog, an unknown country somewhere in the Black Sea region. The barbarian hordes on horseback would sweep down on the peaceful countryside and undefended towns of Israel. But they would be destroyed by the convulsion of nature the Lord would unleash on them: '... On that day there shall be a great shaking in the land of Israel; ... and the mountains shall be thrown down, and the cliffs shall fall, and every wall shall tumble to the ground.' (Ezek. 38:19, 20) Fire, brimstone and hail would rain down on the invaders. Their corpses would be scattered over the whole country, and it would take seven months to

gather them and bury them in the steep gorge of the Arnon river, leading into the Dead Sea from the east. Their weapons would provide the Israelites with firewood for seven winters. This demonstration of the Lord's power would exalt his name among all the nations.

Ezekiel's vivid pictorial imagination is not matched by the quality of his literary style. Much of it is rather prosaic, compared to the sublime poetry of Isaiah or the fervent eloquence of Jeremiah. There are, however, passages of sharp invective, and others of brilliant descriptive power. Some of the best of these occur in the oracles against Tyre and Egypt.

It is likely that he learnt about Tyre, the great Phoenician seaport on the Mediterranean coast, from the Tyrian captives he met in Babylon. He vividly describes the city's almost impregnable location, on a rocky offshore island. (It took the Babylonians thirteen years to capture it.) Its far-ranging merchant fleet was the source of its wealth and power: 'The ships of Tarshish travelled for you with your merchandise. So you were filled and heavily laden in the heart of the seas. Your rowers have brought you out into the high seas.' (Ezek. 27:25, 26) He deplored the arrogance of its king who thought of himself as a divinity. 'Because your heart is proud, and you have said, "I am a god, I sit in the seat of the gods, in the heart of the seas", yet you are but a man, and no god ...' (Ezek. 28:2) The city-state of Tyre was like a glittering Garden of Eden. Yet no earthly city could withstand the Lord. 'They shall destroy the walls of Tyre, and break down her towers; and I will scrape her soil from her, and make her a bare rock.' (Ezek. 26:4)

The haughtiness of the ruler of Egypt is also offensive to God. 'Behold, I am against you, Pharaoh king of Egypt, the great dragon that lies in the midst of his streams, that says, "My Nile is my own; I made it." ... I will put hooks in your jaws, ... And I will cast you forth into the wilderness, you and all the fish of your streams.' (Ezek. 29:3, 5)

Ezekiel's Creed

Unlike other prophets, who stood outside the priestly establishment and were often in conflict with it, Ezekiel respected organized religious observance and established religious laws. The regulations for worship set out in his fourth vision for the future commonwealth draw a clear line between the sacred and the profane.

At the same time, Ezekiel broke with tradition by rejecting the concept of collective guilt and retribution. He asserted that each individual was solely responsible for his own actions: 'The soul that sins shall die. The son shall not suffer for the iniquity of the father, nor the father suffer for the iniquity of the son; the righteousness of the righteous shall be upon himself, and the wickedness of the wicked shall be upon himself.' (Ezek. 18:20)

The scribe Ezra: illumination from the late 9th-century *Codex Amiatanus* from Jarrow, England.

Ezekiel's religious creed has two main sources: his intense and mystical personal revelation of the glory of God; and his belief that the Hebrew nation has a holy calling which cannot be betrayed without punishment. The independence of his people has been wiped out because its covenant with God has been broken; but it will be offered a fresh start and a new covenant. 'I will take the stony heart out of their flesh and give them heart of flesh, that they may walk in my statutes and keep my ordinances and obey them; and they shall be my people, and I will be their God.' (Ezek. 11:19, 20) [Book of Ezekiel]

EZER (Heb. 'help') **1.** date unknown. Son of Seir the Horite and an Edomite leader. [Gen. 36:21, 27, 30; 1 Chr. 1:38, 42]

2. *c.* 16 century BC. One of the sons of Ephraim who was killed by the men of Gath for trying to steal their cattle. [1 Chr. 7:21]

3. date unknown. A leader of the tribe of Judah descended from Hur. [1 Chr. 4:4]

4. *c.* 11 century BC. Leader of a group of warriors of the tribe of Gad who deserted from King Saul's army and rallied to David's support. [1 Chr. 12:9]

5. 5 century BC. A priest who helped rebuild the walls of Jerusalem in the time of Nehemiah. [Neh. 3:19]

6. 5 century BC. A priest who took part in the service for the rebuilt walls of Jerusalem in the time of Nehemiah. [Neh. 12:42]

EZRA (Heb. 'help') **1.** 6 century BC. A leading priest who returned with Zerubbabel to Judah from exile in Babylon. [Neh. 12:1]

2. 5 century BC. Hebrew priest and scribe. Ezra was a Hebrew priest and scribe who played a notable role in the restoration of Judea by exiles returning from Babylonia.

The first Judean deportees, including the young King Jehoiachin, had been taken to Babylon by Nebuchadnezzar in 598 BC. Their number was swelled in 587 BC when Jerusalem was destroyed and the kingdom of Judah came to an end.

In 539 BC Babylon was captured by King Cyrus of Persia, who then became the master of the Near East. Cyrus issued a decree in 538 BC permitting the Jews to return to their homeland and rebuild it. Some forty thousand of them did so, and the Temple was restored on the original site in Jerusalem.

The community of exiles who remained in Babylon seems to have prospered under the benign Persian rule, and some of its members gained influential positions. However, they clung to their own faith and traditions encouraged by notable prophets like Ezekiel, as well as by such scholars and teachers as Ezra. They also kept in touch with their brethren in Judea, collected funds to help them and felt themselves involved with the progress

5th-century BC silver daric, a coin mentioned in Ezra 2:69, showing the Persian king with bow and arrow.

of the restoration. Ezra resolved to go to Jerusalem, investigate the conditions there, and reform the religious life of the settlers. There is reason to believe that he had attained an official position at the Persian Court, as a commissioner for the affairs of the Jewish minority. At any rate, he was able to obtain palace sponsorship and aid for his trip. The time was 458 BC in the seventh year of the reign of Artaxerxes I and eighty years after the edict of Cyrus had started the movement back to the Holy Land.

The Hebrew bible quotes in Aramaic the royal document authorizing Ezra's mission. It states that he is being sent by the king and his seven counsellors '. . . to make inquiries about Judah and Jerusalem according to the law of your God, which is in your hand' (Ezra 7:14). Any of the Israelites in the kingdom, including priests and Levites, who wish to accompany Ezra may

do so. With the official money grant, as well as voluntary offerings by Ezra's fellow-Jews, he is to buy animals to sacrifice in the Jerusalem Temple on behalf of the king. Any funds left over may be spent at Ezra's discretion. For whatever else may be necessary for the Temple, Ezra is authorized to draw on the royal treasury. The treasurers of the beyond-the-river region (west of the Euphrates) are commanded to supply Ezra with stated amounts of money, wheat, wine, oil and salt for the Temple. The priests and staff of the Temple are to be exempt from taxes. Ezra is to appoint scribes and judges to administer and teach the Jewish Law. 'Whoever will not obey the law of your God and the law of the king, let judgment be strictly executed upon him, whether for death or for banishment or for confiscation of his goods or for imprisonment.' (Ezra 7:26)

In the diary contained in Chapters 7 to 9, Ezra records that the number of persons who gathered together to accompany him numbered some fifteen hundred men, or about five thousand souls in all, divided into twelve family clans.

Ezra assembled the whole party on the banks of a river, where they camped for three days. In reviewing his mixed contingent of settlers, Ezra realized that though it included a group of priests, there were no Levites, the traditional Temple staff. He sent a deputation to Iddo, the head priest of the Jewish shrine at Casiphia, who recruited several Levite families for the expedition. Ezra chose twelve of the priests to serve as trustees of the gold and silver Temple vessels and the money donations for the Temple. They were to be responsible for handing them over at the journey's end in accordance with the inventory.

The Jerusalem Mission

On arrival in Jerusalem they rested for three days. After that the treasure was delivered at the Temple, the sacrifices were offered that the king had commanded, and Ezra's royal letter of instructions was handed over to the local authorities.

Ezra now set about promoting the central purpose of the mission – to restore strict religious observance and revive the national identity of the repatriate congregation, which had been weakened in the decades since the original Return. The most immediate and sensitive issue was that of the mixed marriages between the leading Jewish families, including priests, and the 'foreign women' belonging to other local ethnic groups. Ezra was determined to break these unions and to restore the exclusiveness of the Hebrews.

Using the powers vested in him, Ezra ordered all the men of Jerusalem and the Judean towns to attend a

left Artaxerxes telling the Jews
they can go home: engraving
by Gustave Doré (?1832-83).

mass meeting in the Temple compound within three days, on pain of exclusion from the community and confiscation of property. The gathering shivered with apprehension – and also from the heavy rain and cold. Ezra addressed them sternly, 'You have transgressed and married foreign women, ... Now then make confession ... separate yourselves from the peoples of the land and from the foreign wives.' (Ezra 10:10,11) The people sadly agreed to this drastic measure. A commission of two priests and two Levites was set up to supervise the multiple divorce proceedings which lasted for two months.

Nothing more is recorded of Ezra's actions for the next thirteen years. In the meantime a new Jewish governor, Nehemiah, had been sent to Jerusalem from the Persian court to administer what was now the province of 'Yahud'. He was an able and energetic man, who restored the fortifications of the city and increased its population by drawing on the smaller Judean towns and villages.

The time had come for Ezra to establish the religious law more firmly as the basis of daily life. He had brought with him from Babylon the codified Scriptures. On the first day of the seventh month the whole community gathered in the square at the water-gate, while Ezra, standing on a wooden dais, and in the presence of Nehemiah, the governor, read out to them the sacred book, and they wept with emotion. He called to them not to weep but to eat, drink and be glad of heart 'for this day is holy to our Lord; do not be grieved, for the joy of the Lord is your strength' (Neh. 8:10).

The next day Ezra continued the study of the Law together with the Levites and heads of families. When they read that 'the people of Israel should dwell in booths during the feast of the seventh month' (Neh. 8:14), it was decided immediately to revive the festival of Succoth (Tabernacles), commemorating the time when their ancestors were led out of Egypt by Moses and wandered for forty years in the wilderness. (In the cycle of the agricultural year this was the autumn harvest festival.) From every Judean town the menfolk went out to collect branches of olive, pine, myrtle and palm for constructing booths on the flat roof-tops and in the courtyards and public squares. The festival lasted seven days and on the eighth day another solemn assembly was held.

Ezra consolidated the religious and legal code of the small Jewish community in the Holy Land, and thereby laid the foundations for the later development of Judaism as a creed and a way of life.

Ezra and Nehemiah

The precise date of Ezra's mission to Jerusalem is problematical – in particular, whether it took place before, during or after Nehemiah's governorship, that started in 446 BC.

A present-day scribe
writing a Scroll of
the Law.

Ezra states that he made his journey in the seventh
year of the reign of Artaxerxes, but this date creates
difficulties in the sequence of events. Two other theories
have been put forward: that the word 'seventh' is a
corruption for 'thirty-seventh', so that the date of Ezra's
return would be 428 and not 458 BC; or that the monarch referred to is not Artaxerxes I Longimanus (465-
24 BC) but Artaxerxes II Mnemon (404-358 BC), which

would give 397 BC as the date for Ezra.

In their respective personal memoirs Ezra and Nehemiah do not refer to each other at all. In the third person
narrative in the Book of Nehemiah, describing the
reading of the Law by Ezra, Nehemiah's name appears
as being present, but this could have been inserted by a
later chronicler.

There is reason to believe that Ezra-Nehemiah originally formed a single Book, continuing the Book of
Chronicles and compiled by the same chronicler. That
is the way it appeared in the Greek and Latin bibles.
However, Ezra and Nehemiah were later split into two
Books in the Hebrew bible, and consequently in the
Protestant versions. This division is an unsatisfactory
one, as the most important part of Ezra's work – the
reading of the Book of the Law and the religious reforms
which followed it – remain in Chapters 8, 9 and 10 of
the Book of Nehemiah. [Books of Ezra and Nehemiah]

EZRAH (Heb. 'help') date unknown. A leader of the
tribe of Judah descended from Caleb, son of Jephunneh.
[1 Chr. 4:17]

EZRI (Heb. 'my help') *c.* 10 century BC. Son of Chelub,
he was appointed by King David to supervise the work
of tilling the soil on the royal estates. [1 Chr. 27:26]

G

GAAL (Heb. 'contempt') *c.* 12 century BC. Son of Ebed, he organized a revolt among the inhabitants of Shechem against Abimelech, king of the district of Shechem and challenged him to battle. Gaal was defeated and driven out of Shechem by the governor, Zebul. [Judg. 9:26-41]

GABBAI (Heb. 'gatherer') 5 century BC. A Benjaminite chief who settled in Jerusalem after the return from exile in Babylon. [Neh. 11:8]

GABRIEL (Heb. 'man of God') An angel who appeared to the prophet Daniel bringing him the word of God. [Dan. 8:16; 9:21]

GAD (Heb. 'fortune') **1.** *c.* 16 century BC. Seventh son of Jacob. Gad was the eldest son of Zilpah, the maid of Jacob's wife Leah. Believing herself past child-bearing age, Leah gave Zilpah to her husband as a concubine.

Together with his brothers, Gad was involved in the events that led to the selling of their brother Joseph into slavery in Egypt. Later he was one of the ten sons sent by Jacob to buy corn in Egypt where Joseph had become a leading figure at Pharaoh's court. When Jacob went to settle in Egypt with all his family, it included Gad's seven sons.

On his deathbed Jacob blessed his sons in turn. Of Gad he said, 'Raiders shall raid Gad, but he shall raid at their heels.' (Gen. 49:19)

Centuries later in the conquest of Canaan under Joshua, the tribe of Gad was allocated an extensive territory east of the Jordan on condition they took part in the conquest west of the river. In the blessing attributed to Moses, it is said that 'Gad couches like a lion .... He chose the best of the land for himself.' (Deut. 33:20, 21) [Gen. 30:11; 35:26; 46:16; 49:19; Exod. 1:4; Deut. 33:20, 21]

2. *c.* 10 century BC. A prophet in the time of King David. When David was hiding from King Saul, Gad advised him not to remain in the cave of Adullam because Saul might capture him there but to go into the land of Judah. Later, when David was king and angered the Lord by taking a census, Gad told him that God had offered him a choice of punishments – famine, military defeat or pestilence. David chose pestilence but after many thousands of people had died, he prayed to God to stop the

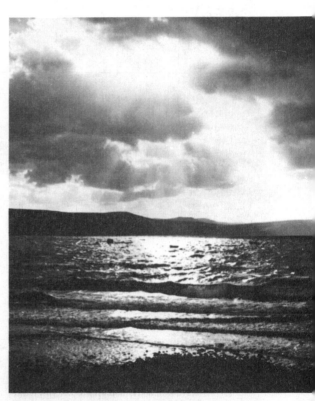

The Sea of Chinnereth (Sea of Galilee). The Gadites occupied almost the whole of the eastern Jordan Valley up to the lake.

plague and Gad came to him and told him to build an altar on the threshing floor of Araunah, the Jebusite. Gad is referred to in the Book of Chronicles as the author of a book on the acts of King David. [1 Sam. 22:5; 2 Sam. 24:11-18; 1 Chr. 21:9-19; 29:29; 2 Chr. 29:25]

GADDI (Heb. 'my fortune') *c.* 13 century BC. A leader of the tribe of Manasseh and the son of Susi, he was one of the twelve men sent by Moses to spy out the land of Israel. [Num. 13:11]

GADDIEL (Heb. 'fortune of God') *c*. 13 century BC. Son of Sodi of the tribe of Zebulun, he was one of the twelve men sent by Moses to spy out the land of Israel. [Num. 13:10]

GADI (Heb. 'my fortune') 8 century BC. Father of Menahem who assassinated King Shallum and reigned in his stead for ten years. [2 Kgs. 15:14-17]

GAHAM *c*. 18 century BC. A son of Abraham's brother Nahor by his concubine Reumah, he became the founder of a desert tribe. [Gen. 22:24]

GAHAR date unknown. Ancestor of a family of temple servants that returned with Zerubbabel to Judah from exile in Babylon. [Ezra 2:47; Neh. 7:49]

GALAL (Heb. 'God has removed [my shame]') **1.** 6 century BC. One of the first Levites to settle in Jerusalem following the return from exile in Babylon. [1 Chr. 9:15] **2.** 5 century BC. Father of Shemaiah, head of a family of Levites who served in Jerusalem after the return from Babylon in the time of Nehemiah. [1 Chr. 9:16; Neh. 11:17]

GAMALIEL (Heb. 'recompense of God') *c*. 13 century BC. Leader of the tribe of Manasseh appointed by Moses to take a census of the men of his tribe fit for war. [Num. 1:10; 2:20; 7:54-9; 10:23]

GAMUL (Heb. 'is rewarded') 10 century BC. A Levite and head of the twenty-second of the priestly course who served in the Tabernacle at the time of King David. [1 Chr. 24:17]

GARMITE *see* KEILAH

GAREB (Heb. 'potter') 10 century BC. An Ithrite, he was one of King David's outstanding warriors. [2 Sam. 23:38; 1 Chr. 11:40]

GATAM (Heb. 'small and thick') *c*. 16 century BC. A son of Eliphaz and a grandson of Esau, he was an Edomite leader. [Gen. 36:11, 16; 1 Chr. 1:36]

GAZEZ (Heb. 'sheep-shearer') **1.** *c*. 13 century BC. Son of Caleb of the tribe of Judah, by his concubine Ephah. [1 Chr. 2:46] **2.** 13 century BC. The son of Haran and a grandson of Caleb. [1 Chr. 2:46]

GAZZAM (Heb. 'wood-cutter') date unknown. Ancestor of a family of temple servants who returned with Zerubbabel to Judah from exile in Babylon. [Ezra 2:48; Neh. 7:51]

GEBER (Heb. 'man') 10 century BC. Son of Uri, he was one of the twelve officers appointed by King Solomon to supply the provisions of the royal household. [1 Kgs. 4:19]

GEDALIAH (Heb. 'God is great') **1.** 10 century BC. Son of Jeduthun, one of King David's chief musicians. Gedaliah and his brothers took the second turn of service in the Tabernacle under their father's direction. [1 Chr. 25:3, 9] **2.** *c*. 7 century BC. Grandfather of the prophet Zephaniah. [Zeph. 1:1]

3. *c*. 6 century BC. Governor of Judah. On the fall of Jerusalem in the summer of 587 BC and the capture of King Zedekiah, the Babylonians appointed Gedaliah the son of Ahikam as governor. Some of the surviving Judean officers and their men came to see him at Mizpah, just north of Jerusalem, and he urged them to co-operate with the conquerors: 'Do not be afraid because of the Chaldean officials; dwell in the land, and serve the king of Babylon, and it shall be well with you.' (2 Kgs. 25:24) This advice went unheeded. Soon after a small group of political exiles assassinated Gedaliah and fled to Egypt. [2 Kgs. 25:22-5; Jer. 39:14; 40:5-16; 41:1-10, 16; 43:6]

4. 6 century BC. Son of Pashhur, he was one of the nobles of Judah who threw Jeremiah into a pit for prophesying that those who surrendered to the Baby-lonians would be saved but those who stayed in Jeru-salem would die. [Jer. 38:1-6]

5. 5 century BC. A priest who divorced his non-Jewish wife at the request of Ezra. [Ezra 10:18]

GEDOR (Heb. 'wall') *c*. 11 century BC. One of the ten sons of Jeiel and Maachah, and an ancestor of Saul, the first king of Israel. [1 Chr. 8:31; 9:37]

GEHAZI (Heb. 'valley of vision') *c*. 9 century BC. Gehazi was the manservant of the prophet Elisha. When the prophet wanted to reward the lady of Shunem for her kindness to him, it was Gehazi who pointed out that she was childless. Elisha blessed her and the following year she gave birth to a boy. She rushed to Elisha when the child died. Gehazi was sent ahead with the prophet's staff, but the boy could not be revived till Elisha came personally and performed a miracle.

Later, after a long absence because of the drought, the woman was able to recover her property because Gehazi identified her to the king. 'My lord, O king, here is the woman, and here is her son whom Elisha restored to life.' (2 Kgs. 8:5) [2 Kgs. 4, 5, 8:5]

GEMALLI (Heb. 'my recompense from God') *c*. 13 century BC. A member of the tribe of Dan, his son Ammiel was one of the twelve spies sent by Moses to reconnoitre the land of Israel. [Num. 13:12]

GEMARIAH (Heb. 'perfected by God') **1.** *c*. 7 century BC. Son of Shaphan the scribe, he was a leader of Judah. His son Micaiah told the leaders of Jeremiah's dire prophecies about the people of Judah. [Jer. 36:10-12, 25] **2.** 6 century BC. Son of Hilkiah, he was sent from Jeru-salem with a letter of comfort from Jeremiah the prophet to the exiles in Babylon. [Jer. 29:3]

GENUBATH (Heb. 'theft') 10 century BC. Son of Hadad the Edomite who fled to Egypt after David's attack on Edom. His mother was the sister of Tahpenes, queen of Egypt, and he was brought up together with Pharaoh's sons. [1 Kgs. 11:20]

GERA (Heb. 'stranger') **1.** *c*. 16 century BC. One of the ten sons of Benjamin. [Gen. 46:21; 1 Chr. 8:3, 5, 7]

2. *c.* 16 century BC. Son of Bela and a grandson of Benjamin. Also called Heglam. [1 Chr. 8:3, 7]

3. *c.* 12 century BC. Father of Ehud who delivered the children of Israel from subservience to Eglon, king of Moab, by slaying him and then leading a successful expedition against the confused Moabites. [Judg. 3:15]

4. *c.* 10 century BC. A Benjaminite who was a member of the royal family of King Saul. His son Shimei cursed King David and threw stones at him at the time of Absalom's revolt. [2 Sam. 16:5; 19:16, 18; 1 Kgs. 2:8]

GERSHOM (Heb. 'exiled') **1.** *c.* 16 century BC. Sometimes called Gershon, he was the eldest of Levi's three sons. During the Exodus, his Levite descendants were given the task of carrying the Tabernacle, and had charge of its coverings and hangings. [Gen. 46:11; Exod. 6:16, 17; Num. 3:21-6; 4:22-6; 7:7; 10:17; 26:57; Josh. 21:6; 1 Chr. 6:43; 15:7]

2. *c.* 13 century BC. Moses's first child born to his wife Zipporah during the sojourn of Moses in Midian. Moses gave him that name for he said, 'I have been a stranger in a strange land' (Exod. 2:22). (The Hebrew

Plate found in Egypt, 5th-4th centuries BC, inscribed with the name of Geshem the Arab.

word 'ger' means a stranger.) Zipporah performed a dramatic circumcision on the boy with a sharp stone, to avert Moses being killed by God. One of Gershom's descendants served as a priest to the graven image set up by the tribe of Dan. [Exod. 2:22; 4:25; 18:3; Judg. 18:30; 1 Chr. 23:15, 16; 26:24]

3. *c.* 5 century BC. A descendant of the high priest Phinehas, he returned with Ezra to Jerusalem from the Babylonian exile. [Ezra 8:2]

GERSHON *see* GERSHOM **1.**

GESHAN date unknown. One of the six sons of Jahdai of the tribe of Judah, he was a descendant of Caleb. [1 Chr. 2:47]

GESHEM (Heb. 'rain') 5 century BC. An Arab prince who derided Nehemiah's work of rebuilding the walls of Jerusalem and tried to hinder it by spreading the rumour that the Jews would revolt against Persian rule when Jerusalem was rebuilt. He also plotted to assassinate Nehemiah. [Neh. 2:19; 6:1-6]

GETHER date unknown. One of the four sons of Aram and a grandson of Shem. [Gen. 10:23; 1 Chr. 1:17]

GEUEL (Heb. 'majesty of God') *c.* 13 century BC. Son of Machi of the tribe of Gad, he was one of the twelve spies sent by Moses to reconnoitre the land of Israel. [Num. 13:15]

GIBBAR (Heb. 'strong') date unknown. Ancestor of a family who returned with Zerubbabel to Judah from exile in Babylon. Also called Gibeon. [Ezra 2:20; Neh. 7:25]

GIBEA (Heb. 'hill') date unknown. A grandson of Caleb of the tribe of Judah. [1 Chr. 2:49]

GIBEON *see* GIBBAR

GIBEONITES Inhabitants of the town of Gibeon, north-west of Jerusalem, they made a treaty with Joshua by a ruse and thereby saved their city from attack. King Saul failed to respect the agreement and King David later made atonement for this breach. The Bible refers to them as Hivites and also as 'the remnant of the Amorites' (2 Sam. 21:2). [Josh. 9; 10; 11; 2 Sam. 21: 1-4, 9]

GIDDALTI (Heb. 'I have praised') 10 century BC. Son of Heman, one of King David's chief musicians. Giddalti and his brothers played musical instruments in the Tabernacle services under their father's direction. His family was responsible for the twenty-second turn of service. [1 Chr. 25:4, 29]

GIDDEL 1. (Heb. 'praised') 10 century BC. A servant of King Solomon whose descendants returned with Zerubbabel to Judah from exile in Babylon. [Ezra 2:56; Neh. 7:58]

2. date unknown. Ancestor of a family of Temple servants who returned with Zerubbabel from exile in Babylon. [Ezra 2:47; Neh. 7:49]

GIDEON (Heb. 'hewer') *c.* 12 century BC. Judge of Israel and military commander. The story of Gideon belongs to the period after Joshua's invasion when the Israelite tribes were struggling to hold their allotted territories against the pressure of neighbouring peoples. From time to time, a tribal leader or hero would emerge to free his people from the oppressors. These spontaneous leaders in times of stress were known as judges, since they acquired the moral authority to settle disputes.

Gideon was the fifth of the judges listed in the book of that name, and one of the most outstanding. The enemy he fought was the Midianites, one of the lean and hungry nomad tribes that roamed the uncharted wasteland of Arabia and periodically erupted into the fertile areas. Gideon's battle was one episode in the immemorial struggle between the 'Desert' and the 'Sown'. In the previous century, the Israelites themselves had been tent-dwelling nomads from the eastern desert who had fought their way into the Promised Land.

The Midianites were not the only nomads penetrating into Canaan in Gideon's time. The Bible refers to the Amalekites pressing in from the south as far as the Gaza area, and to 'the people of the East' (Judg. 6:3). They may have been driven by drought to seek food, pasture and water. Also, there was a breakdown of authority in Canaan. Egypt's control had faded, while local conflicts had weakened the security of the country against outside invaders. Earlier, Deborah's victory had relieved the pressure of local Canaanite kings on the Israelites. But the Jezreel valley region remained exposed to the camel-riding Midianite raiders from the east. By the time Gideon challenged them, they had for seven years been harassing this area, coming in across the river like locust swarms, looting, killing and destroying the harvests.

Gideon was the youngest son of Joash, a farmer of the Abiezer clan in the tribe of Manasseh. The family lived at Ophrah, in the hills between Shechem (Nablus) and the Jezreel valley. One day Gideon was threshing wheat, concealed in the winepress for fear of roving Midianite bandits. A stranger was suddenly seen sitting under a nearby oak tree. It was an angel who told him that the Lord wanted him to rescue Israel from the power of Midian. Gideon demurred, saying: '... how can I deliver Israel? Behold, my clan is the weakest in Manasseh, and I am the least in my family.' (Judg. 6:15) Gideon went into the house, prepared a young goat, made unleavened cakes and a pot of broth, and brought the food to his visitor, who asked him to place it on a rock. The angel then touched the meat and unleavened cakes with the tip of his staff. Fire sprang from the rock

The Spring of Harod in the southern Jezreel Valley, where Gideon's men made their camp.

and consumed the offering, while the angel vanished. Gideon was convinced that the message was authentic, and built an altar to the Lord on that spot.

That night the Lord commanded him to break down the local altar to Baal, to cut down the sacred grove next to it, and to sacrifice a young bullock, using the wood from the grove for the fire. This Gideon did under cover of darkness, with the help of ten servants. Next morning the townspeople learned that Gideon had destroyed the pagan altar and grove, and came to his father to demand his death. Joash retorted: 'Will you contend for Baal? ... If he is a god, let him contend for himself, because his altar has been pulled down.' (Judg. 6:31) That day his father gave Gideon the additional name of Jerubbaal, meaning 'Let Baal contend against him.' (Judg. 6:32)

The Battle of Ain Harod

The Midianites pitched their camp in the valley of Jezreel near the hill of Moreh, and Gideon issued a call to arms. First his own clan of Abiezer rallied round him, followed by the rest of the tribe of Manasseh. He then sent messengers to the three Galilee tribes of Asher, Zebulun and Naphtali and they joined him. Before proceeding further, Gideon requested the Lord to give him further signs of divine approval. Twice he put a sheep's fleece out on the threshing floor at night. The first time the fleece was soaked with dew while the ground around it remained dry; while the second time the ground was wet and the fleece dry. Since these were the proofs Gideon had requested beforehand, he was reassured.

Altogether thirty-two thousand men mustered at the spring of Harod, at the foot of Mount Gilboa on the southern edge of the Jezreel valley. The position faced the Midianite camp a few miles across the valley. Gideon set about reducing his forces drastically. The

15th-century German illustration of Gideon praying for victory in battle, with the fleece spread on the ground.

scriptural reason was that the Lord wanted the Israelites to realize that victory would be gained by his strength and not their own strength of numbers. Actually, Gideon's own battle tactics called for a small, mobile picked force rather than an unwieldy mass of men.

It was proclaimed that everyone who was fearful of battle could go home, and twenty-two thousand promptly left. The remaining ten thousand were sent to the pool at the spring, to quench their thirst. Three hundred of them did not fling themselves down on the ground and put their faces in the water like the rest, but scooped it up and lapped it out of their hands – thereby

Gideon's men drinking at the spring. Medieval manuscript illumination.

proving themselves to be wary and alert in the face of the enemy. These three hundred were then held for the operation and the rest dismissed. Gideon had pinned his faith on a commando attack at night, exploiting surprise and psychological weapons.

That night the commander carried out a personal reconnaissance. Accompanied only by his servant Purah, Gideon stole into the slumbering Midianite camp, and overheard two soldiers talking to each other. One told about a dream he had in which a loaf of barley-bread came rolling through the camp and knocked down a tent. The other interpreted the dream as prophesying that they would be defeated by the Israelites. Gideon fell to his knees in thankfulness at this good omen.

He returned to his own camp, aroused his men and organized them for the assault. He divided them into three companies of a hundred each, and issued each man with a trumpet and a lighted torch inside an empty pitcher. They crept up to the enemy camp and spread

themselves around its edge. At a given signal from Gideon, the Israelites rushed in from all sides. They shouted, 'A sword for the Lord and for Gideon!' (Judg. 7:20), blew their trumpets, smashed the pitchers and waved the torches – which were no doubt also used to set fire to the tents. The Midianites were thrown into panic and in the dark started striking each other down. They then fled in confusion down the Beth-shean valley towards the Jordan river fords.

The three hundred who carried out the attack were probably Gideon's own clansmen. The men from the other northern tribes joined in the pursuit of the fleeing Midianites. Gideon sent messengers to the tribesmen of Ephraim asking them to seize the crossing-places along the Jordan and harass the retreat. They did so, capturing two Midianite chiefs, Oreb ('the raven') and Zeeb ('the wolf'). The two were killed and their heads sent to Gideon.

The Ephraimites were indignant because Gideon had not summoned them to fight from the beginning of the battle. They were sensitive about their standing as the leading tribe in the north. Gideon soothed them down with flattery, maintaining that their role had been decisive, especially in disposing of the two Midianite leaders.

The remnant of the Midianite army streamed down the Jordan valley, managed to get across the river, and sought to escape eastward. Gideon and his three hundred crossed behind them. They reached the town of Succoth exhausted and hungry, and Gideon asked for some provisions to feed his men. He was refused, as the local inhabitants were afraid of the Midianites and distrustful of Gideon's victory claims. Referring to the

The plain at the foot of Mount Moreh, where Gideon defeated the Midianites.

Midianite kings Gideon was pursuing, they asked, 'Are Zebah and Zalmunna already in your ·hand, that we should give bread to your army?' (Judg. 8:6) (This was a reference to the practice of chopping off the hands of slain enemies, as tangible proof.) Gideon was given the same churlish rebuff at Penuel, the next town. He angrily swore to deal with them when he came back, and pressed on with the pursuit.

He caught up with the Midianites two hundred miles away at Karkor, travelling the ancient route of the nomads and caravans. Feeling that they had shaken off their pursuers and could relax, the Midianites had bivouacked in a valley between rocky ridges. Here Gideon's men again sprang a surprise attack on them and routed them, capturing the two kings.

Before returning across the Jordan, Gideon settled accounts with the two towns that had refused him help. Approaching Succoth before dawn, they caught a young man who drew up a list for them of the important men of the town, seventy-seven of them. Gideon rounded them up, showed them the two captive Midianite kings, and had them beaten with thorn-bushes. At Penuel he demolished the city tower and slew some of the men.

Interrogated by Gideon, the Midianite kings admitted to killing Israelites at Mount Tabor who had resembled Gideon and had carried themselves as proudly as princes. Gideon said they had been his own brothers; if they had been spared, he would have spared the kings. He ordered his eldest son, Jether, to kill the captives but the lad shrank from drawing his sword. As a matter of honour, the kings implored Gideon himself to strike the mortal blow, which he did.

After Gideon had broken the power of the Midianites, his own people pressed him to become king over them and establish a dynasty. Gideon refused, saying that their king was the Lord. His only request was that from the booty he should be given the gold earrings and other ornaments worn by the Midianites, as well as the gold collars of their camels. He spread a garment on to which these contributions were thrown. From the gold Gideon fashioned an ephod or sacred object that was set up in Ophrah, his home town, to commemorate his victory. But the ephod proved a snare, for the common people came from all around to worship it as an idol.

By subduing the Midianites, Gideon had won security for his people for the next generation. He himself retired to private life in Ophrah where he lived as a man of wealth and honour, with many wives who bore him seventy sons.

Gideon reached a ripe old age and on his death was buried in the tomb of his father Joash at Ophrah. Also known as Jerubbaal and Jerubbeshetho. [Judg. 6:11-39; 7; 8:4-35; 9:1, 5, 16, 19, 24, 28, 57; 1 Sam. 12:11; 2 Sam. 11:21]

GIDEONI (Heb. 'hewer') *c.* 13 century BC. Father of

Abidan who was chosen by Moses as a leader of the tribe of Benjamin. [Num. 1:11; 2:22; 7:60-5; 10:24]

GILALAI 5 century BC. A Levite musician who played at the dedication ceremony in Jerusalem in the time of Nehemiah. [Neh. 12:36]

GILEAD (Heb. 'rocky') **1.** date unknown. Son of Machir and a grandson of Manasseh, he gave his name to the area of Gilead east of the river Jordan and was the founder of the tribe of Gileadites. [Num. 26:29, 30; 27:1; 36:1; Josh. 17:1-3; 1 Chr. 2:21-3; 5:14; 7:14, 17]

Gold earring from the late Canaanite period. Gideon made a sacred image from the gold earrings of the Midianites.

2. *c.* 12 century BC. Father of Jephthah, one of the judges of Israel. [Judg. 11:1, 2]

3. date unknown. Son of Michael, recorded in the genealogy of the tribe of Gad. [1 Chr. 5:14]

GINATH (Heb. 'garden') *c.* 9 century BC. Father of Tibni who contested the throne of Israel with Omri after the death of King Zimri, and was eventually put to death by Omri. [1 Kgs. 16:21, 22]

GINNETHOI 6 century BC. The head of a priestly family that returned to Judah with Zerubbabel from exile in Babylon. [Neh. 12:4]

GINNETHON 5 century BC. Head of a priestly family who returned to Judah from captivity in Babylon, he signed the solemn covenant in the time of Nehemiah. [Neh. 10:6; 12:16]

GISHPA *c.* 5 century BC. One of the two Levites who supervised the work of the Temple servants after the return from exile in Babylon. [Neh. 11:21]

GOG 1. date unknown. The son of Shemaiah and a

leader of the tribe of Reuben. [1 Chr. 5:4]

2. date unknown. The symbolic leader of Meshech and Tubal whom Ezekiel prophesied would join forces with other nations against, the land of Israel 'in the latter years' (Ezek. 38:8) and be utterly destroyed in the ensuing battle. [Ezek. 38; 39:1-16]

GOLIATH *c.* 11 century BC. The Philistine slain by David.

King Saul and his army faced the Philistine troops in the Vale of Elah across a narrow valley, through which ran a stream. Neither side would risk an attack. In this stalemate, the Philistines produced a fearsome champion named Goliath, from the city of Gath, a giant of a man clad in brass helmet and armour, equipped with a massive spear and sword, and preceded by a shield bearer. Every day he paraded up and down between the lines scornfully challenging any Israelite soldier to meet him in single combat. Goliath cried out, 'choose a man for yourselves, and let him come down to me. If he is able to fight with me and kill me, then we will be your servants: but if I prevail against him and kill him, then you shall be our servants and serve us.' (1 Sam. 17:8, 9)

Saul was in a humiliating position, for he had no man who could match the giant in size and strength. At this point David, the shepherd lad, arrived in the camp with provisions for his brothers, and prevailed on Saul to let him face Goliath. The giant was dumbfounded when the Israelite 'champion' who came out to fight him was a mere youth armed only with a stave, a sling and a pouch into which he put a few round pebbles from the brook. He bellowed at David, 'Am I a dog, that you come to me with sticks? ... Come to me, and I will give

your flesh to the birds of the air and to the beasts of the field.' (1 Sam. 17:43, 44)

In the combat, Goliath's vastly superior power was pitted against David's nimbleness and unorthodox tactics. Each time the giant lumbered forward, David slipped out of reach towards his own lines. When the sweating Goliath paused, David's sling whipped round and the stone hit his opponent square in the forehead, so that he fell down stunned. In a flash David leapt upon him, and using Goliath's sword, severed his head. Overcome with dread at this abrupt end, the Philistines turned and fled, with the Israelites pursuing them across the border.

The story of David and Goliath has remained the classic parable of superior odds being overcome by faith, daring and skill. [1 Sam. 17; 21:9; 22:10]

GOMER (Heb. 'ember') **1.** date unknown. Eldest son of Japheth and a grandson of Noah. Ezekiel prophesied that Gomer's descendants would be destroyed in the battle 'in the latter years' (Ezek. 38:8) between Gog and Israel. [Gen. 10:2, 3; 1 Chr. 1:5, 6; Ezek. 38:6]

2. *c.* 8 century BC. Wife of the prophet Hosea, Gomer was the daughter of Diblaim. She was a loose woman but bore him three children to whom he gave names of bitter rejection. Hosea divorced her but continued to love her and at some later stage appeared to have forgiven her and taken her back. She is obviously a symbol of the relation between God and Israel. [Hos. 1:3]

GUNI 1. *c.* 16 century BC. One of the four sons of Naphtali, and the head of the Gunite family. [Gen. 46:24; Num. 26:48; 1 Chr. 7:13]

2. *c.* 8 century BC. A leader of the tribe of Gad and the father of Abdiel. [1 Chr. 5:15]

The Valley of Elah in the Shephelah, where David defeated Goliath.

H

HAAHASHTARI date unknown. Son of Ashhur and a leader of the tribe of Judah. [1 Chr. 4:6]

HABAIAH (Heb. 'God hides') date unknown. Ancestor of a family of priests who returned with Zerubbabel to Judah from exile in Babylon but were barred from officiating as priests because their genealogy could not be satisfactorily traced. Also called Hobaiah. [Ezra 2:61; Neh. 7:63]

HABAKKUK (Ass. 'basil plant') *c.* end of 7 century BC. A Hebrew prophet in the kingdom of Judah. Habakkuk probably lived in Jerusalem in the last phase of the kingdom of Judah. The short prophetical Book bearing his name has been dated soon after the defeat of the Egyptians by the Babylonians at Carchemish in 605 BC, when Nebuchadnezzar became the new master of the Near East.

Basalt relief from Carchemish showing soldiers, 9th-8th centuries BC.

Statue of the prophet Habakkuk, carved on the exterior of Genoa Cathedral.

Fragment of one of the Dead Sea Scrolls, a commentary on the Book of Habakkuk.
Written about the 1st century BC.

The first part of the Book is a dialogue between the prophet and God, in the form of two complaints answered by two oracles. The reflective Habakkuk is troubled by what appears to be divine indifference to evil and oppression: '... the law is slacked and justice never goes forth. For the wicked surround the righteous, so justice goes forth perverted.' (Hab. 1:4) The Lord indicates that worse is yet to come, and vividly describes the coming invasion of the Chaldeans (Babylonians), '... that bitter and hasty nation, who march through the breadth of the earth, to seize habitations not their own' (Hab. 1:6). They are an arrogant people who scoff at kings and princes, and scoop up prisoners like sand. Their horses are swifter than leopards and fiercer than wolves in the dark.

The prophet returns to his protest that God should not permit his people to suffer unjustly. 'Thou who art of purer eyes than to behold evil and canst not look on wrong, why dost thou look on faithless men, and art silent when the wicked swallows up the man more righteous than he?' (Hab. 1:13)

God does not explain, but instructs the prophet to write down his vision on clay tablets and to wait patiently for its fulfilment, which will come without fail.

The middle part of the Book contains five curses, each starting with the words 'Woe to him'. Their common theme is that the oppressor will himself suffer what he does to others. The Babylonians are described as plunderers and exploiters, killers and drunkards. The many peoples they have ruined cry out against them. 'Woe to him who builds a town with blood, and founds a city on iniquity!' (Hab. 2:12) They make for themselves dumb idols of wood and stone; 'But the Lord is in his holy temple; let all the earth keep silence before him.' (Hab. 2:20)

The Book ends with a psalm or hymn that appears to be taken from the Temple liturgy. It extols the power and the glory of the Lord, from whom comes salvation for his people. The prophet reaffirms his own faith: 'God, the Lord, is my strength; he makes my feet like hinds' feet, he makes me tread upon my high places.' (Hab. 3:19)

One of the Dead Sea Scrolls discovered by Bedouin shepherds in 1947 was a Hebrew commentary on the Book of Habakkuk, written about the 1st century BC. The writer finds an analogy between the Babylonians of Habakkuk and the Romans who were the master race of his own time. [Book of Habakkuk]

HABAZZINIAH (Heb. 'the Lord has made me rich') 7 century BC. A leader of the Rechabites who was invited by Jeremiah to drink wine with him but firmly refused because of his pledge. [Jer. 35:3]

HACALIAH (Heb. 'waits for God') 5 century BC. Father of Nehemiah. [Neh. 1:1; 10:1]

HACHMONI (Heb. 'wise') c. 10 century BC. Father of Jehiel who was a friend of King David's sons. Also called 'the Hachmonite'. [1 Chr. 11:11; 27:32]

HACHMONITE see HACHMONI

HADAD (Heb. 'sharp') **1.** c. 18 century BC. The sixth son of Ishmael. [Gen. 25:15; 1 Chr. 1:30]

2. (name of a god) date unknown. Son of Bedad, he was king of the desert kingdom of Edom and defeated the Midianites in Moab. [Gen. 36:35; 1 Chr. 1:46]

3. c. 10 century BC. A son of the royal house of Edom, he escaped as a child when David and Joab conquered the Edomites and slew every male. He was brought up in Egypt at Pharaoh's court and married the queen's sister. When Hadad heard that both David and Joab were dead, he returned to his hill kingdom whence he made raids on Israel. [1 Kgs. 11:14-22]

Abraham's servant Hagar came from Egypt. Egyptian funerary model of a servant girl, from Thebes, 22nd-20th centuries BC.

HADAD *see* HADAR

HADADEZER (Heb. 'Hadad is help') *c.* 10 century BC. Son of Rehob, he was king of Zobah, at that time the leading state in the Aram-Syrian area to the north-east of Israel. Hadadezer was defeated by David, and Zobah became a vassal-state paying tribute to Israel.

Later Hadadezer sent an army into Transjordan under his general Shobach. It was again defeated by David, and the Aramean kingdoms remained under Israelite domination. [2 Sam. 8; 10:16, 19; 1 Kgs. 11:23; 1 Chr. 18:3-11]

HADAR (Heb. 'grandeur') date unknown. King of Edom, he married Mehetabel and set up his capital in the city of Pau or Pai. Also called Hadad. [Gen. 36:39; 1 Chr. 1:50]

HADASSAH *see* ESTHER

HADLAI *c.* 8 century BC. A chief of the tribe of Ephraim and the father of Amasa who objected to holding the men of Judah as prisoners of Pekah, king of Israel. [2 Chr. 28:12]

HADORAM (Heb. 'Hadad is exalted') **1.** date unknown. Son of Joktan and a descendant of Shem. [Gen. 10:26, 27; 1 Chr. 1:21]

2. *c.* 10 century BC. Taskmaster over forced labour in the reign of King Rehoboam, he was stoned to death by the people of Israel as a sign of rebellion against Rehoboam's authority. [2 Chr. 10:18]

3. *see* ADONIRAM

4. *see* JORAM **1.**

HAGAB (Heb. 'locust') date unknown. Ancestor of a family of Temple servants who returned with Zerubbabel to Judah from exile in Babylon. [Ezra 2:46]

HAGABA *see* HAGABAH

HAGABAH (Heb. 'locust') date unknown. Ancestor of a family of Temple servants who returned with Zerubbabel to Judah from exile in Babylon. Also called Hagaba. [Ezra 2:45; Neh. 7:48]

The Negev desert, into which Abraham sent Hagar and her son, Ishmael.

HAGAR (('one who fled') *c.* 18 century BC. Sarah's Egyptian slave-maid. The story of Hagar is one of the most human and poignant in the Old Testament.

Her mistress Sarah proposed to Abraham that he should have a child by Hagar since she herself was barren and old. (Such a suggestion was not regarded as unusual by the customs of that time, which permitted a man to have more than one wife and as many concubines as his wealth and inclination allowed.)

When Hagar conceived, Sarah became jealous. She complained to Abraham that Hagar now despised her. Abraham replied (as any husband would) that she should deal with her servant herself. Sarah vented her resentment on Hagar, who finally ran away into the desert. At a well near Beersheba, an angel of the Lord prevailed upon her to go back, promising that she would bear a son and he would father 'a great nation'. Hagar returned and gave birth to Ishmael. Abraham was then eighty-six years old.

Obverse and reverse of a Persian silver coin minted in Jerusalem, 6th-4th centuries BC, showing the imperial eagle and the Aramaic name for Judah: *Yehud*.

When Sarah's own son Isaac was born, Ishmael was more than thirteen, and fresh friction arose between the two women. At the feast Abraham gave for Isaac's weaning, the ninety-year-old Sarah felt that Hagar and Ishmael were mocking her and demanded of Abraham that he cast them out, 'for the son of this slave woman shall not be heir with my son'. Caught between his angry wife and his paternal feelings for Ishmael, Abraham could not this time avoid the issue, and sought the Lord's counsel. He was told to do as Sarah wanted, but Abraham was reassured that no harm would come to Hagar and Ishmael. Early in the morning Abraham gave Hagar a supply of bread and water and sent them away.

Hagar and the boy wandered in the Beersheba desert till the water was used up. Unable to bear watching her son die, Hagar left him crying under a bush and moved a bowshot away, where she wept in anguish. The angel of God called out to her from heaven and told her not to fear, for God had heard the voice of the lad. She looked up and saw a well of water nearby, and thus they were saved.

They remained in the part of the Sinai desert known as the wilderness of Paran. When Ishmael grew up Hagar had a wife brought for him from her own country, Egypt.

Ishmael is regarded by the Arabs as their ancestor, and there is a Moslem legend that he and his mother Hagar are buried in the sacred Ka'aba in Mecca. [Gen. 16; 21; 25:12]

HAGGAI (Heb. 'festal') 6 century BC. Post-exilic Hebrew prophet who played a part in the life of Jerusalem after the return of the Jews from Babylonian captivity in the time of Cyrus, king of Persia.

In the summer of 520 BC Haggai and his fellow-prophet Zechariah succeeded by their moral pressure in getting work resumed on the destroyed Temple. Haggai linked the struggles of the community to the fact that the Lord's house still remained a ruin. It was for that reason that their harvests were poor, and their fields drought-stricken. If they wanted prosperity to be restored, he told them, 'Go up to the hills and bring wood and build the house' (Hag. 1:8).

In the short Book bearing his name, Haggai's thoughts went beyond the immediate aim of reconstructing the Temple. He predicted the coming of a day of divine judgment – 'and to overthrow the throne of kingdoms; I am about to destroy the strength of the kingdoms of the nations and overthrow the chariots and their riders; and the horses and their riders shall go down, every one by the sword of his fellow.' (Hag. 2:22) When that liberation came, the Jews would again be an independent nation, and perhaps Zerubbabel the leader of the returnees would be their king. The new Temple would then shine with a glory greater than that of Solomon's Temple. [Ezra 5:1; Book of Haggai]

HAGGEDOLIM (Heb. 'the great') 5 century BC. Father of Zabdiel. [Neh. 11:14]

HAGGI (Heb. 'festive') *c.* 16 century BC. A son of Gad, he went down to Egypt at the same time as his grandfather, Jacob. [Gen. 46:16; Num. 26:15]

HAGGIAH (Heb. 'Lord's feast') *c.* 10 century BC. A Levite from the family of Merari, whose descendants were appointed by King David to conduct the musical service in the Tabernacle. [1 Chr. 6:30]

HAGGITH (Heb. 'festive') *c.* 10 century BC. A wife of King David and the mother of Adonijah. [2 Sam. 3:4; 1 Kgs. 1:5, 11; 2:13; 1 Chr. 3:2]

HAGRI (Heb. 'who fled') *c.* 10 century BC. Father of Mibhar, a warrior in the armies of King David. [1 Chr. 11:38]

HAKKATAN (Heb. 'the little one') *c.* 5 century BC. Father of Johanan who returned with Ezra to Judah from exile in Babylon. [Ezra 8:12]

HAKKOZ (Heb. 'thorn') **1.** *c.* 10 century BC. A priest in the reign of King David, who took the seventh turn of service in the Tabernacle. [1 Chr. 24:10]

2. date unknown. Ancestor of a family of priests who returned with Zerubbabel from exile in Babylon. Perhaps the same as the grandfather of Meremoth. [Ezra 2:61; Neh. 3:4, 21; 7:63]

HAKUPHA (Heb. 'bent') date unknown. Ancestor of a family of Temple servants who returned with Zerubbabel from exile in Babylon. [Ezra 2:51; Neh. 7:53]

HALLOHESH (Heb. 'enchanter') 5 century BC. One of the leaders of Judah in the days of Nehemiah who signed the covenant to observe the Laws of God. His son Shallum ruled over half of the district of Jerusalem. [Neh. 3:12; 10:24]

HAM (Heb. 'hot') date unknown. Second son of Noah. Ham and his wife were in the ark with Noah and the rest of the family. After the great flood had subsided, Noah had become a farmer and planted a vineyard. One day, Ham saw his father lying naked in a drunken stupor in his tent, and he went to tell his two brothers race. He obtained permission from the king to deal with the Jewish minority and had a royal decree despatched to the authorities throughout the empire, ordering them to slaughter all their Jews on a certain day the court magicians selected by lot as propitious.

The Jews were thrown into consternation at the news of the impending pogrom. Mordecai instructed his niece, now Queen Esther, to intercede with the king. Ahasuerus agreed to dine with her together with Haman, who was gratified at the unusual honour but complained, 'Yet all this does me no good, so long as I see Mordecai the Jew sitting at the king's gate.' (Esther 5:13) His wife Zeresh and friends then suggested that he should build a gallows and persuade the king to have Mordecai hanged on it.

That night the king was unable to sleep and had the court records read to him. He came across an entry that Mordecai had foiled a plot on the king's life. Next morning the king asked Haman what he would do for a man he wanted to honour. Haman, thinking it was for himself, suggested that such a man should be led through the city square on the king's horse, and dressed in royal robes with a crown on his head. To his dismay, he was told to arrange such honours for Mordecai.

At dinner with Queen Esther, she accused Haman of having organized a mass murder against the Jews and pleaded for the lives of her people. The king in a rage rushed into the garden. The terrified Haman flung himself down on the couch and begged the queen to save his life. At that moment the king stalked in again and thinking that Haman was assaulting the queen, ordered the attendants to seize him. 'So they hanged Haman on the gallows which he had prepared for Mordecai.' (Esther 7:10) Ahasuerus gave Haman's house to Queen Esther, and Mordecai was appointed chief minister in his place. [Esther 3:1-9:24]

HAMMATH (Heb. 'hot spring') date unknown. An ancestor of Rechab. [1 Chr. 2:55]

HAMMEDATHA (Pers. 'given by the moon') *c.* 5 century BC. Father of Haman whom the Persian king Ahasuerus made his chief minister. [Esther 3:1; 8:5; 9:10]

HAMMOLECHETH (Heb. 'who is queen') *c.* 16 century BC. Daughter of Machir and the granddaughter of Manasseh. [1 Chr. 7:18]

HAMMUEL (Heb. 'God's protection') date unknown. Son of Mishma and a leader of the tribe of Simeon. [1 Chr. 4:26]

HAMOR (Heb. 'ass') *c.* 16 century BC. A Hivite chief who ruled over the area of the city of Shechem in the days of Jacob. His son, also named Shechem, raped Jacob's daughter Dinah and then asked Hamor to obtain her family's consent to his marrying Dinah. Hamor suggested to Jacob's sons that the two families should trade together and intermarry and that his son

15th-century Italian Hebrew manuscript showing the sons of Haman hanging from a tree.

what he had seen. Shem and Japheth promptly took a garment, entered the tent backwards so as not to see their father's nakedness, and covered him. When Noah awoke and heard what had happened, he blessed Shem and Japheth but cursed Ham: 'a slave of slaves shall he be to his brothers' (Gen. 9:25).

Ham had four sons, Egypt, Canaan, Cush and Put, who were the legendary founders of these countries and peoples. [Gen. 5:32; 6:10; 7:13; 9:18-27; 10:1, 6, 20; 1 Chr. 1:4, 8; 4:40; Ps. 78:51; 105:23, 27; 106:22]

HAMAN *c.* 5 century BC. Chief minister of King Ahasuerus. Haman the Agagite, son of Hammedatha, was made the chief minister of King Ahasuerus of Persia, who commanded all the king's staff and courtiers to bow down before him. Everyone obeyed except Mordecai the Jew who also served at the court. Haman's anger at Mordecai turned into a hatred of the Jewish

Shechem should marry their sister Dinah. The brothers agreed provided that Hamor, Shechem and the entire male population of the city would be circumcised. The people of Shechem agreed. However, while Hamor, Shechem and the males of Shechem were recovering from the operation, Simeon and Levi, two of Dinah's brothers, rushed into the city, killed all the males and looted their property. [Gen. 33:19; 34; Josh. 24:32; Judg. 9:28]

HAMRAN *see* HEMDAN

HAMUL (Heb. 'pity') date unknown. Son of Perez and a grandson of Judah, his descendants were an important branch of the tribe of Judah. [Gen. 46:12; Num. 26:21; 1 Chr. 2:5]

HAMUTAL (Heb. 'protection') *c.* 7 century BC. Daughter of Jeremiah of Libnah, she became the wife of Josiah, king of Judah, and the mother of Jehoahaz and Zedekiah, kings of Judah. [2 Kgs. 23:31; 24:18; Jer. 52:1]

HANAMEL (Heb. 'given of God') *c.* 7 century BC. Son of Shallum and a cousin of the prophet Jeremiah, he asked Jeremiah to redeem a plot of land for seventeen shekels of silver to demonstrate his faith that the people of Judah would eventually return in peace to their land. [Jer. 32:7-12]

HANAN (Heb. 'merciful') **1.** date unknown. Son of Shashak and a chief of the tribe of Benjamin living in Jerusalem. [1 Chr. 8:23]

2. date unknown. A son of Azel of the tribe of Benjamin and a descendant of King Saul. [1 Chr. 8:38; 9:44]

3. *c.* 10 century BC. Son of Maachah and a warrior in the army of King David distinguished for his bravery. [1 Chr. 11:43]

4. date unknown. Ancestor of a family of Temple servants who returned to Judah with Zerubbabel from exile in Babylon. [Ezra 2:46; Neh. 7:49]

5. *c.* 6 century BC. Son of Igdaliah, a man of God, his sons had a room in the Temple where the prophet Jeremiah met the Rechabites. [Jer. 35:4]

6. 5 century BC. A Levite who helped explain the Law to the people of Judah after Ezra had read it to them. He later signed the solemn covenant. [Neh. 8:7; 10:10]

7. 5 century BC. Two of the leaders of Judah with the same name who signed the covenant to keep the Laws of God, in the days of Nehemiah. [Neh. 10:22; 10:26]

8. 5 century BC. Son of Zaccur, the Levite, he was one of four trustworthy men appointed by Nehemiah to distribute the offerings among the priests and Levites. [Neh. 13:13]

HANANI (Heb. 'gracious') **1.** *c.* 9 century BC. Father of Jehu, he was a holy man who reproved King Asa of Judah for entering into an alliance with Syria instead of relying only on the Lord. The king had him flung into prison. [1 Kgs. 16:1, 7; 2 Chr. 16:7; 19:2; 20:34]

2. *c.* 10 century BC. A son of Heman, King David's

musician, he and his fourteen brothers played musical instruments in the Tabernacle. Hanani was responsible for the eighteenth turn of service. [1 Chr. 25:4, 25]

3. 5 century BC. Descendant of Immer the priest, he divorced his non-Jewish wife in the time of Ezra. [Ezra 10:20]

4. 5 century BC. Brother of Nehemiah, he came to Nehemiah in the Persian palace at Shushan and told him that the people living in Judah were in great poverty, that the walls of the city were broken and the gates burned down. Later after the walls of the city were rebuilt, Nehemiah made Hanani keeper of the gates of Jerusalem together with Hananiah, the governor of the palace. [Neh. 1:2; 7:2]

5. 5 century BC. A priest who played musical instruments in the dedication service for the rebuilt walls of Jerusalem in the time of Nehemiah. [Neh. 12:36]

HANANIAH (Heb. 'the Lord is gracious') **1.** date unknown. A son of Shashak and a leader of the tribe of Benjamin living in Jerusalem. [1 Chr. 8:24]

2. *c.* 10 century BC. A son of King David's musician, Heman, he and his brothers played musical instruments in the Tabernacle services under their father's direction; and Hananiah was responsible for the sixteenth turn of service. [1 Chr. 25:4, 23]

3. *c.* 8 century BC. An army commander of Uzziah, king of Judah.]2 Chr. 26:11]

4. *c.* 7 century BC. Hananiah the son of Azzur was a prophet from Gibeon and appeared in the Temple before Zedekiah the king, the priests and the people, in the time of Jeremiah. The Lord, he proclaimed, had broken the yoke of the king of Babylon; within two years the holy vessels carried off by Nebuchadnezzar would be returned, and the Lord would bring back Jehoiachin, the captive king of Judah, with all the other Judean deportees.

Jeremiah disagreed with him, but Hananiah illustrated his point with a symbolic act. He smashed the yoke that Jeremiah had taken to wearing, and prophesied in the name of the Lord: 'Even so will I break the yoke of Nebuchadnezzar king of Babylon from the neck of all the nations ...' (Jer. 28:11). Jeremiah answered the false prophet, 'Listen, Hananiah, the Lord has not sent you and you have made this people trust in a lie.' (Jer. 28:15) Jeremiah prophesied that Hananiah would be dead within the year. He died two months later. [Jer. 28]

5. *c.* 6 century BC. Father of Zedekiah who was a leader of Judah to whom Jeremiah's prophecy of doom was read. [Jer. 36:12]

6. *c.* 6 century BC. The grandfather of Irijah, a Benjaminite army captain who arrested the prophet Jeremiah on a charge of defecting to the Chaldeans. [Jer. 37:13]

7. *see* SHADRACH

Hannah's prayer for
a son, from a medieval
Greek Bible.

8. 6 century BC. Son of Zerubbabel who led the children of Israel from exile in Babylon back to Judah. [1 Chr. 3:19, 21]

9. *c.* 5 century BC. A descendant of Bebai who divorced his non-Jewish wife in the time of Ezra. [Ezra 10:28]

10. 5 century BC. A perfumer who helped rebuild the walls of Jerusalem in the time of Nehemiah. [Neh. 3:8]

11. 5 century BC. Son of Shelemiah and a leader of Judah who helped rebuild the walls of Jerusalem in the days of Nehemiah. [Neh. 3:30]

12. 5 century BC. Governor of the renovated king's palace in Jerusalem in the days of Nehemiah, he was jointly responsible with Nehemiah's brother Hanani for opening and closing the gates of the city. [Neh. 7:2]

13. 5 century BC. One of the leaders of Judah in the time of Nehemiah who signed the covenant to obey the Laws of God. [Neh. 10:23]

14. 5 century BC. A chief priest of Judah when Joiakim was high priest in the time of Nehemiah. [Neh. 12:12]

15. 5 century BC. A chief priest of Judah in the days of Nehemiah, he blew a trumpet at the dedication ceremony for the rebuilt walls of Jerusalem. [Neh. 12:41]

HANNAH (Heb. 'grace') *c.* 11 century BC. Mother of the prophet Samuel.

Hannah lived in the town of Ramathaim-zophim, in the hill country of Ephraim. She grieved at being childless and her husband Elkanah was unable to console her. His other wife Peninnah taunted Hannah.

The next time the family went to Shiloh on the pilgrimage, she stayed longer and prayed to the Lord to give her children. Eli, the chief priest, saw the woman's lips moving, though she did not utter a sound. Deciding she was drunk he reproached her. Hannah explained her trouble, and vowed that if God 'wilt give to thy maidservant a son, then I will give him to the Lord all the days of his life' (1 Sam. 1:11). Eli encouraged her to believe that the Lord would grant her prayer.

In due time Hannah bore a child which she called Samuel, 'the Lord heard'. When she had weaned him she took him with her to Shiloh, together with a gift of three bullocks, flour and a bottle of wine, and left him with Eli.

Though Hannah had five other children she never forgot her first-born. Each year she made him a coat and brought it to him when she came on the annual pilgrimage. [1 Sam. 1; 2]

HANNIEL (Heb. 'grace of God') **1.** *c.* 13 century BC. Son of Ephod, he was the leader of the tribe of Manasseh appointed by Moses to help divide the land of Canaan among the children of Israel. [Num. 34:23]

2. date unknown. Son of Ulla of the tribe of Asher, he was a great warrior and a leader of the tribe. [1 Chr. 7:39]

HANOCH (Heb. '[God's] follower') **1.** *c.* 16 century

Hannah's prayer was answered by the birth of Samuel. Mesopotamian terracotta of a mother nursing a child, 7th-6th centuries BC.

BC. Son of Midian and a grandson of Abraham and Keturah. [Gen. 25:4]

2. *c.* 16 century BC. Eldest son of Reuben, he went down to Egypt at the same time as his grandfather Jacob. [Gen. 46:9; Exod. 6:14; Num. 26:5; 1 Chr. 5:3]

HANUN (Heb. 'gracious') **1.** *c.* 10 century BC. King of the Ammonites, he received a message of condolence from David on the death of his father King Nahash. Hanun 'took David's servants, and shaved off half the beard of each, and cut off their garments in the middle, at their hips, and sent them away' (2 Sam. 10:4). This insult was regarded as an invitation to a war, in which Joab, David's commander, defeated the Ammonites and their Aramean allies. [2 Sam. 10; 1 Chr. 19]

2. 5 century BC. A Judean who repaired the Valley Gate of Jerusalem in the time of Nehemiah. [Neh. 3:13]

3. 5 century BC. Son of Zalaph, he repaired part of the walls of Jerusalem in the time of Nehemiah. [Neh. 3:30]

HAPPIZZEZ (Heb. 'hasty') *c.* 10 century BC. A priest in the reign of King David who took the eighteenth turn of service in the Tabernacle. [1 Chr. 24:15]

HARAN (Heb. 'mountainous') **1.** *c.* 18 century BC. Brother of Abraham and Nahor, he died at an early age and left three children, Lot, Milcah and Iscah. [Gen. 11:26-32]

2. date unknown. Son of Caleb and Ephah and a leader of the tribe of Judah. [1 Chr. 2:46]

3. *c.* 10 century BC. Son of Shimei, a Levite descended from Gershon. [1 Chr. 23:9]

HARBONA *c.* 5 century BC. One of the seven chamberlains of King Ahasuerus who was commanded by the drunken king on the seventh day of a feast to bring Queen Vashti before his guests to show off her beauty. Later he told the king of the gallows Haman had prepared for Mordecai. [Esther 1:10; 7:9]

HAREPH (Heb. 'sharp') date unknown. Son of Hur, he was a leader of Judah and regarded as the founder of Beth-gader. [1 Chr. 2:51]

HARHAIAH 5 century BC. Father of Uzziel, a goldsmith, who helped repair the walls of Jerusalem in the time of Nehemiah. [Neh. 3:8]

HARHAS *c.* 7 century BC. Ancestor of Shallum, the husband of the prophetess Huldah. Also called Hasrah. [2 Kgs. 22:14; 2 Chr. 34:22]

HARHUR date unknown. Ancestor of a family of Temple servants who returned with Zerubbabel to Judah from captivity in Babylon. [Ezra 2:51; Neh. 7:53]

HARIM (Heb. 'dedicated to God') **1.** *c.* 10 century BC. A priest who served in the Tabernacle during the reign of King David. [1 Chr. 24:8]

2. 6 century BC. Head of a family who returned with Zerubbabel to Judah from exile in Babylon. One of his sons, Malchijah, helped rebuild the walls of Jerusalem in the days of Nehemiah. [Ezra 2:32; 10:31; Neh. 3:11; 7:35]

3. date unknown. Ancestor of a family who returned to Judah with Zerubbabel from exile in Babylon. Some of his descendants married foreign wives. [Ezra 2:39; 10:21; Neh. 7:42; 12:15]

4. 5 century BC. A chief priest of Judah in the time of Nehemiah who signed the covenant to observe the Laws of God. [Neh. 10:5]

5. 5 century BC. A leader of Judah who signed the covenant to observe the Laws of God in the time of Nehemiah. [Neh. 10:27]

HARIPH (Heb. 'sharp') **1.** *see* JORAH

2. 5 century BC. He was a leader of Judah at the time of Nehemiah who signed the covenant to observe the Laws of God. [Neh. 10:19]

HARNEPHER (Heb. 'God is good') date unknown. One of the five sons of Zophah of the tribe of Asher, he was a leader of the tribe and a mighty warrior. [1 Chr. 7:36]

HAROEH (Heb. 'seer') date unknown. Son of Shobal, a leader of the tribe of Judah. Also called Reaiah. [1 Chr. 2:52; 4:2]

HARSHA date unknown. Ancestor of a family of Temple servants who returned with Zerubbabel from exile in Babylon. [Ezra 2:52; Neh. 7:54]

HARUM (Heb. 'high') date unknown. Father of Aharhel of the tribe of Judah. [1 Chr. 4:8]

HARUMAPH (Heb. 'slit-nosed') 5 century BC. Father of Jedaiah who helped rebuild the walls of Jerusalem in the time of Nehemiah. [Neh. 3:10]

HARUZ (Heb. 'gold') *c.* 7 century BC. Father of Meshullemeth and the grandfather of Amon, king of Judah. [2 Kgs. 21:19]

HASADIAH (Heb. 'beloved of God') 6 century BC. A son of Zerubbabel who led the return to Judah from captivity in Babylon. [1 Chr. 3:20]

HASHABIAH (Heb. 'considered') **1.** date unknown. Son of Amaziah, a Levite, descended from Merari. [1 Chr. 6:45]

2. *c.* 10 century BC. A son of Jeduthun, one of King David's musicians, he and his brothers were taught to play the harp in the thanksgiving service in the Tabernacle, and he had the twelfth rota in the service. [1 Chr. 25:3, 19]

3. *c.* 10 century BC. A Levite of one of the Hebronite families who served King David on the west bank of the river Jordan. [1 Chr. 26:30]

4. *c.* 10 century BC. Son of Kemuel, and head of the tribe of Levi in the reign of King David. [1 Chr. 27:17]

5. *c.* 7 century BC. A chief Levite who donated large quantities of cattle for the special Passover service celebrated by King Josiah of Judah. [2 Chr. 35:9]

6. date unknown. Son of Bunni, the Levite, his great-grandson Shemaiah returned to Jerusalem in the days of Nehemiah and ministered in the Tabernacle. [1 Chr. 9:14; Neh. 11:15]

7. 5 century BC. A leader of the priests who answered Ezra's call to return to Jerusalem to serve in the Tabernacle. He and his family helped bring back the treasure and the precious vessels from Babylon, and later he became a priest. [Ezra 8:19, 24; Neh. 12:21]

8. 5 century BC. Descendant of Parosh, he returned from exile in Babylon with Ezra. [Ezra 10:25]

9. 5 century BC. A chief Levite of Judah and ruler of half of the district of Keilah, he helped repair the walls of Jerusalem and signed the solemn covenant in the time of Nehemiah. [Neh. 3:17; 10:11; 12:24]

10. 5 century BC. Son of Mattaniah, the Levite, his grandson Uzzi supervised the service of the Levites in Jerusalem in the days of Nehemiah. [Neh. 11:22]

HASHABNAH (Heb. 'regarded') 5 century BC. A leader of Judah who signed the covenant to observe the Laws of God in the time of Nehemiah. [Neh. 10:25]

HASHABNEIAH (Heb. 'God has considered me')
1. 5 century BC. Father of Hattush who helped repair the walls of Jerusalem in the time of Nehemiah. [Neh. 3:10]

2. 5 century BC. A Levite who exhorted the people of Judah to praise God on the fast day proclaimed by Ezra and to confess their sins. [Neh. 9:5]

HASHBADDANAH 5 century BC. A leader of Judah who stood at the side of Ezra when he read the Law of Moses to the people. [Neh. 8:4]

HASHEM see JASHEN

HASHUBAH (Heb. 'important') c. 6 century BC. A son of Zerubbabel who led the return to Judah from captivity in Babylon. [1 Chr. 3:20]

HASHUM 1. date unknown. Ancestor of a family who returned with Zerubbabel from exile in Babylon. Seven of his descendants married non-Jewish wives whom they later divorced. [Ezra 2:19; 10:33; Neh. 7:22]

2. 5 century BC. A leader of Judah who stood at the side of Ezra when he read the Law of Moses to the people in the market-place. [Neh. 8:4]

3. 5 century BC. One of the leaders of Judah who signed the covenant in the time of Nehemiah to observe the Laws of God. [Neh. 10:18]

HASRAH see HARHAS

HASSENAAH see SENAAH

HASSENUAH (Heb. 'hated') **1.** date unknown. Ancestor of Sallu, one of the first Benjaminites to settle in Jerusalem after the return from exile in Babylon. [1 Chr. 9:7]

2. c. 5 century BC. Father of Judah, the deputy governor of Jerusalem after the return from exile in Babylon. [Neh. 11:9]

HASSHUB (Heb. 'respected') **1.** 5 century BC. Father of Shemaiah, one of the Levites who settled in Jerusalem after the return from exile in Babylon. [1 Chr. 9:14; Neh. 11:15]

2. 5 century BC. Descendant of Pahath-moab, he helped

Relief of Hazael, king of Aram, inscribed with his name in Aramaic.

repair the walls of Jerusalem in the time of Nehemiah. [Neh. 3:11]

3. 5 century BC. A man of Judah who helped repair the walls of Jerusalem in the time of Nehemiah. [Neh. 3:23]

4. 5 century BC. A leader of Judah who signed the covenant to observe the Laws of God in the time of Nehemiah. [Neh. 10:23]

HASSOPHERETH see SOPHERETH

HASUPHA (Heb. 'stripped') date unknown. Ancestor of a family of Temple servants who returned with Zerubbabel from exile in Babylon. [Ezra 2:43; Neh. 7:46]

HATHACH c. 5 century BC. The servant of Queen Esther who brought her Mordecai's message of how Haman planned to destroy the Jews. [Esther 4:5-10]

HATHATH (Heb. 'fear') 12 century BC. Son of Othniel, leader of the tribe of Judah. [1 Chr. 4:13]

HATIPHA (Heb. 'captive') date unknown. Ancestor of a family of Temple servants who returned with Zerubbabel to Judah from exile in Babylon. [Ezra 2:54; Neh. 7:56]

HATITA date unknown. Ancestor of a family of gate-keepers of the Temple who returned to Judah with Zerubbabel from exile in Babylon. [Ezra 2:42; Neh. 7:45]

HATTIL (Heb. 'talkative') c. 10 century BC. One of

King Solomon's servants whose descendants returned to Judah with Zerubbabel from exile in Babylon. [Ezra 2:57; Neh. 7:59]

HATTUSH 1. 6 century BC. One of the priests who returned with Zerubbabel to Judah from exile in Babylon. [Neh. 12:2]

2. 5 century BC. Son of Shemaiah of the tribe of Judah and a descendant of King David, he returned with Ezra from exile in Babylon. [1 Chr. 3:22; Ezra 8:2]

3. 5 century BC. Son of Hashabneiah, he helped repair the walls of Jerusalem in the days of Nehemiah. [Neh. 3:10]

4. 5 century BC. One of the priests of Judah in the days of Nehemiah who signed the covenant to observe the Laws of God. [Neh. 10:4]

HAVILAH (Heb. 'stretch of sand') **1.** date unknown. Son of Cush and a grandson of Ham. [Gen. 10:7; 1 Chr. 1:9]

2. date unknown. Son of Joktan and a descendant of Shem. [Gen. 10:29; 1 Chr. 1:23]

HAZAEL (Heb. 'God sees') *c.* 9 century BC. King of Aram (Syria). When Elisha was on a visit to Damascus, the sick King Ben-hadad II told Hazael, then a senior Syrian commander: 'Take a present with you and go to meet the man of God, and inquire of the Lord through him, saying, "Shall I recover from this sickness?"' (2 Kgs. 8:8) Hazael went off to meet Elisha, taking with him forty camels loaded with all the good things of Damascus. Elisha gave him a cryptic answer: the king would recover from his illness but was about to die. The prophet then seemed to go into a trance and began to weep, explaining that Hazael would become king and do great evil to the children of Israel. The next day Hazael smothered his master and seized the throne.

At this time Assyrian pressure ebbed, and Aram (Damascus) under Hazael became the dominant power in the Palestine-Syrian area. The kingdom of Israel became a feeble vassal of Damascus, and all its territory east of the Jordan was occupied by the ruthless Hazael. The kingdom of Judah also had to pay him heavy tribute, which he received from King Joash at Gath in the coastal plain about 815 BC. [1 Kgs. 19:15-17; 2 Kgs. 8:8-15; Amos 1:4]

HAZAIAH (Heb. 'whom God sees') 6 century BC. Son of Adaiah of the tribe of Judah, his grandson Maaseiah settled in Jerusalem in the time of Nehemiah. [Neh. 11:5]

HAZARMAVETH (Heb. 'Moth [a god]'s court') date unknown. Son of Joktan and a great-grandson of Shem. [Gen. 10:26; 1 Chr. 1:20]

HAZIEL (Heb. 'vision of God') *c.* 10 century BC. A Levite leader descended from Shimei, he was appointed by King David to minister in the Tabernacle. [1 Chr. 23:9]

HAZO *c.* 18 century BC. Son of Nahor and Milcah and a nephew of Abraham. [Gen. 22:22]

HAZZELELPONI (Heb. 'coming shadows') date unknown. Descendant of Judah, she was the sister of Jezreel, Ishma and Idbash. [1 Chr. 4:3]

HEBER (Heb. 'alliance') **1.** date unknown. Son of Beriah and a grandson of Asher, he was one of seventy descendants of Jacob who went with him into Egypt. [Gen. 46:17; Num. 26:45; 1 Chr. 7:31, 32]

2. *c.* 12 century BC. A Kenite descended from Moses's father-in-law Jethro, and the husband of Jael. [Judg. 4:11-21; 5:24]

3. date unknown. Descendant of Ezrah of the tribe of Judah, and the father of Soco. [1 Chr. 4:18]

4. date unknown. Son of Elpaal and a leader of the tribe of Benjamin living in Jerusalem. [1 Chr. 8:17, 18]

HEBRON (Heb. 'league') **1.** *c.* 13 century BC. A descendant of Kohath of the tribe of Levi, and an uncle of Moses. [Exod. 6:18; Num. 3:19, 27; 1 Chr. 6:2, 18; 15:9; 23:12, 19; 24:23]

2. date unknown. Son of Mareshah, and a leader of the tribe of Judah. [1 Chr. 2:42, 43]

HEGAI *c.* 6 century BC. Eunuch of King Ahasuerus of Persia into whose custody were given all the maidens who were candidates to become Queen of Persia. He showed special favour to Esther. [Esther 2:3, 8, 15]

HEGLAM *see* GERA 2.

HELAH (Heb. 'necklace') date unknown. One of the two wives of Ashhur, father of Tekoa, a leader of the tribe of Judah. [1 Chr. 4:5, 7]

HELDAI (Heb. 'mole') **1.** *c.* 10 century BC. Commander of a division in King David's army in the twelfth month of each year. [1 Chr. 27:15]

2. 6 century BC. One of the Judeans who returned from exile in Babylon. God commanded the prophet Zechariah to take them into the house of Josiah, son of Zephaniah and place a crown on Joshua, son of Jehozadak, the high priest. [Zech. 6:10, 14]

HELEB *see* HELED

HELED (Heb. 'passing') *c.* 10 century BC. Son of Baanah, he was a warrior in the army of King David. Also called Heleb. [1 Chr. 11:30; 2 Sam. 23:29]

HELEK (Heb. 'portion') date unknown. A leader of the tribe of Manasseh descended from Gilead. [Num. 26:30; Josh. 17:2]

HELEM (Heb. 'strength') date unknown. Brother of Shemer and a leader of the tribe of Asher. [1 Chr. 7:35]

HELEZ (Heb. 'strong') **1.** date unknown. Son of Azariah and father of Eleasah, he was descended from Jarha, an Egyptian servant who married the daughter of a leader of Judah. [1 Chr. 2:39]

2. *c.* 10 century BC. A warrior in the army of King David described as the 'Paltite' in the Second Book of Samuel and the 'Pelonite' in the First Book of Chronicles, where he is said to be of the tribe of Ephraim and commander of King David's army in the seventh month. [2 Sam. 23:26; 1 Chr. 11:27; 27:10]

HELKAI (Heb. 'portion') *c.* 6 century BC. Head of a family of priests, descended from Meraioth, in the days of King Jeoiakim. [Neh. 12:15]

HELON (Heb. 'strong') *c.* 13 century BC. Father of Eliab, a leader of the tribe of Zebulun who was appointed by Moses to take a census of the men of his tribe fit for war and led the contingent in the army of the children of Israel. [Num. 1:9; 2:7; 7:24, 29; 10:16]

HEMAN (Heb. 'trusty') **1.** date unknown. Son of Lotan and a grandson of Seir, the Horite. Also called Homan. [Gen. 36:22; 1 Chr. 1:39]
2. date unknown. Son of Zerah and a grandson of Judah, he was known as the Ezrahite. [1 Chr. 2:6; Ps. 88]
3. date unknown. Son of Mahol, he was a wise man whose wisdom was exceeded only by that of King Solomon. [1 Kgs. 4:31]
4. *c.* 16 century BC. Son of Joel and a grandson of Samuel, he was a Levite musician in the time of King David, who led his fourteen sons in the service in the Tabernacle. [1 Chr. 6:33; 15:17, 19; 16:41, 42; 25:1, 4-6; 2 Chr. 5:12; 29:14; 35:15]

HEMDAN date unknown. Son of Dishon and a descendant of Seir the Horite. Also called Hamran. [Gen. 36:26; 1 Chr. 1:41]

HENADAD (Heb. 'favour of Hadad') date unknown. Ancestor of a family of Levites who helped supervise the work of repairing the Temple in the time of Zerubbabel. [Ezra 3:9; Neh. 3:18, 24; 10:9]

HEPHER (Heb. 'pit') **1.** *c.* 16 century BC. A son of Gilead and a grandson of Manasseh, he was father of Zelophehad. In the Book of Joshua he is described as a son of Manasseh. [Num. 26:32, 33; 27:1; Josh. 17:2, 3]
2. date unknown. Son of Ashhur of the tribe of Judah and his wife Naarah. [1 Chr. 4:6]
3. *c.* 10 century BC. A warrior in the armies of King David, he was distinguished for his bravery. [1 Chr. 11:36]

HEPHZIBAH (Heb. 'my delight is in her') *c.* 8 century BC. Wife of King Hezekiah and the mother of King Manasseh. [2 Kgs. 21:1]

HERESH (Heb. 'carpenter') 6 century BC. A Levite descended from Asaph who settled in Jerusalem after the return from exile in Babylon. [1 Chr. 9:15]

HETH date unknown. Son of Canaan and a grandson of Ham, he was the acknowledged ancestor of the Hittite tribe. [Gen. 10:15; 23:7; 25:10; 1 Chr. 1:13]

HEZEKIAH (Heb. 'strength of God') **1.** Thirteenth king of Judah after the monarchy split, he reigned 716-687 BC.

Hezekiah was the son of King Ahaz of Judah and Abijah. He succeeded his father on the throne at the age of twenty-five. Judah at that time was shrunken in size, a mere satellite of Assyria – a small bark kept afloat on rough seas by two remarkable men: King Hezekiah, and the great prophet-statesman Isaiah.

For a number of years Hezekiah was careful to avoid giving offence to the Assyrians, and devoted himself to strengthening his kingdom. His first task was to restore the force and purity of the Hebraic religion and cleanse it of the idolatrous practices that had been prevalent in his father's reign. The local shrines or 'high places' (2 Kgs. 21:3) around the country were closed down, as were the street shrines Ahaz had erected in various parts of Jerusalem. The Temple was cleaned out, reconsecrated and restored to its primacy as the national centre of worship. From all over Judah, the people gathered in Jerusalem for the Passover as had been the custom before; and the king also sent special messengers to the towns of conquered Israel, now an Assyrian province, inviting them to worship once more in Jerusalem. In all the long array of the kings of Judah and Israel, Hezekiah is one of the very few who are commended on religious grounds. He received powerful backing from Isaiah, who was concerned with the spiritual health of the nation rather than with Temple rituals.

Hezekiah also streamlined the administration and tax-gathering structure of the kingdom, and built stables and large storehouses in which he amassed wealth for the state treasury in the form of grain, wine, oil and livestock. The border areas were consolidated and expanded, especially on the frontier with Philistia, in the western Negev as far as the town of Gerar, and southwards in the direction of Mount Seir (Edom).

The Assyrian Invasion

The defences of Jerusalem, and its capacity to withstand siege, were of special concern to Hezekiah: he 'built up all the wall that was broken down, and raised towers upon it, and outside it he built another wall; and he strengthened the Millo in the city of David. He also made weapons and shields in abundance. And he set

King Hezekiah burning idols, from a 16th-century English manuscript.

combat commanders over the people . . .' (2 Chr. 32:5, 6) The most vital step the king took concerned the water supply, a step to ensure access to the water source from inside the city in time of siege, and to deny access by the enemy. The only natural spring was that of Gihon, emerging from a cave outside the city wall. Hezekiah had a six-hundred-yard tunnel constructed from the spring through the rock of the hillside and underneath the south-eastern part of the city wall to discharge into a reservoir called the Pool of Siloam [Shiloah]. At the same time the cave at the source was sealed up so as to

prevent the enemy from using or tampering with the water supply. The tunnel has remained intact to this day.

In 704 BC the Assyrian ruler Sargon II died and was succeeded by Sennacherib. At that time Assyrian supremacy was being challenged from two directions, Babylonia and Egypt. The king of Babylon sent envoys to Jerusalem to stimulate the spirit of rebellion against Assyria. For its part Egypt incited the Philistine towns against their Assyrian masters, in order to regain its own traditional influence. The banner of revolt was raised in the Philistine city of Ashkelon. Hezekiah took the calculated risk of joining in the anti-Assyrian movement, and played a leading role in it. Isaiah apparently felt serious misgivings about this venture into power-politics. The event proved him right.

In 701 BC, after the defeat of Babylon, Sennacherib marched an army down the coastal plain and easily suppressed the Philistine rebels as well as routing Egyptian forces that had come to their aid. He then turned his attention to Judah. According to the Assyrian records, he occupied forty-six Judean towns, deported a great number of inhabitants and took a huge amount

left Relief from Sennacherib's palace at Nineveh, showing Israelite prisoners with musical instruments being led into captivity after the siege of Lachish.

below Israelite prisoners being led off by Assyrian soldiers: from Sennacherib's palace at Nineveh.

of booty. As for Hezekiah, Sennacherib records: '... himself, I imprisoned in Jerusalem, his residence, like a bird in a cage.'

The main Assyrian force was thrown against the strategic fortified city of Lachish in the foothills east of Gaza. In his palace at Nineveh Sennacherib afterwards had a detailed bas-relief made, depicting in four panels the siege and capture of Lachish. These panels have survived nearly intact, and provide one of the most graphic descriptions ever found of an ancient battle.

Realizing the ill-fated rebellion was over, Hezekiah sent a message of submission to Sennacherib at Lachish: "I have done wrong; withdraw from me; whatever you impose on me I will bear.' (2 Kgs. 18:14) The Assyrian ruler exacted a tribute of three hundred talents of silver and thirty talents of gold, which exhausted the treasury of the palace and the Temple.

But Sennacherib was not satisfied with tribute alone. He sent one of his chief aides with a detachment of troops to demand the surrender of Jerusalem. A meeting took place outside the city where Hezekiah was represented by the master of the palace, the official scribe and the herald. No agreement was reached. The Assyrian envoy shouted out in Hebrew to the spectators on the ramparts that their king was deluding them if he relied on their God to save them: had all the other peoples conquered by Assyria, including the kingdom of Israel, been saved by their deities?

The king and his ministers were thrown into fear and confusion by these threats, and Isaiah was consulted. The prophet's counsel was that they should stand firm and resist the demand to open the gates. Isaiah said: 'Therefore thus says the Lord concerning the king of Assyria, He shall not come into this city ... By the way that he came, by the same he shall return.' (2 Kgs. 19:32, 33) Sennacherib did not in fact lay siege to Jerusalem but withdrew his forces – the Bible suggests they were smitten by a sudden plague and returned to Nineveh. After this deliverance Judah reverted to its vassal status.

Not long after, Hezekiah became deathly ill with ulcers which, on the Lord's advice, were cured with a fig poultice. Hearing of his sickness, the king of Babylon sent an envoy with a letter and gift affecting solicitude for Hezekiah's health. The king received the envoy warmly, and showed him round the palace, the treasure-house, the armoury and the city. When Isaiah heard about this visit he predicted grimly that Judah would be destroyed in the future by the Babylonians. The king shrugged his shoulders and remarked, 'Why not, if there will be peace and security in my days?' (2 Kgs. 20:19)

The remaining fourteen years of Hezekiah's reign were uneventful. When he died 'all Judah and the inhabitants of Jerusalem did him honour' (2 Chr. 32:33). He was succeeded by his son Manasseh. [2 Kgs. 16:20; 18; 19; 20; 21:3; 1 Chr. 3:13; 4:41; 2 Chr. 28:27; 29; 30; 31; 32; 33:3; Prov. 25:1; Isa. 1:1; 36; 37; 38; 39; Jer. 15:4; 26:18, 19; Hos. 1:1; Mic. 1:1]

The Siloam Inscription

A discovery ninety years ago confirmed the biblical record concerning Hezekiah's measures to ensure the water supply of Jerusalem when faced by the threat of siege by Sennacherib. The Bible says that Hezekiah 'made the pool and the conduit and brought water into the city' (2 Kgs. 20:20). He also 'closed the upper outlet of the waters of Gihon and directed them down to the west side of the city of David' (2 Chr. 32:30). Gihon, the main source of the city's water, lay at the foot of what in Hezekiah's time was the eastern wall of Jerusalem, and Hezekiah's tunnel brought the water by gravity flow to a reservoir inside the city at its south-western point.

The discovery in 1880 concerned an inscription in the rock wall of the tunnel on how it was excavated. The language is perfect classical Hebrew prose, its content, script and style pointing to the reign of Hezekiah. The words are inscribed on a prepared surface of the wall, so that it looks like the surface of a tablet, but the upper part of the inscription was missing. However, six lines remained, and they describe how the tunnel was dug by two teams of miners starting at opposite ends, working towards each other and meeting in the middle. The

The tunnel, now excavated, built by King Hezekiah in the 8th century BC to bring the waters of the Spring of Gihon into the city of Jerusalem.

plaque, now in the Istanbul Museum, is known as the 'Siloam Inscription', and in its standard English translation it reads as follows:

'. . . when [the tunnel] was driven through. And this was the way in which it was cut through: – while . . . [were] still . . . axe[s], each man toward his fellow, and while there were still three cubits to be cut through, [there was heard] the voice of a man calling to his fellow, for there was an overlap in the rock on the right [and on the left]. And when the tunnel was driven through, the quarrymen hewed [the rock], each man toward his fellow, axe against axe; and the water flowed from the spring toward the reservoir for 1,200 cubits, and the height of the rock above the head[s] of the quarrymen was 100 cubits.'

2. date unknown. Father of Amariah and an ancestor of the prophet Zephaniah. [Zeph. 1:1]

3. date unknown. Father of Ater whose family returned with Zerubbabel to Judah from exile in Babylon. [Ezra 2:16; Neh. 7:21]

4. 5 century BC. A leader of Judah in the days of Nehemiah who signed the covenant to observe the Laws of God. [Neh. 10:17]

HEZION (Heb. 'light') *c.* 10 century BC. Father of Tabrimmon and grandfather of Ben-hadad I, king of Aram. [1 Kgs. 15:18]

HEZIR (Heb. 'boar') **1.** *c.* 10 century BC. A priest during the reign of King David responsible for the seventeenth turn of service in the Tabernacle. [1 Chr. 24:15]

2. 5 century BC. A leader of Judah who signed the covenant to observe the Laws of God in the time of Nehemiah. [Neh. 10:20]

HEZRO *c.* 10 century BC. A Carmelite warrior in the armies of King David. [2 Sam. 23:35; 1 Chr. 11:37]

HEZRON 1. *c.* 16 century BC. A son of Reuben, he went down to Egypt with his grandfather Jacob. [Gen. 46:9; Exod. 6:14; Num. 26:6; 1 Chr. 5:3]

2. date unknown. Elder son of Perez and a grandson of Judah, he was an ancestor of King David. [Gen. 46:12; Num. 26:21; Ruth 4:18, 19; 1 Chr. 2:5, 9, 18, 21, 24, 25; 4:1]

HIDDAI (Heb. 'leader') *c.* 10 century BC. One of King David's warriors who came from the 'brooks of Gaash' (2 Sam. 23:30). Also called Hurai. [2 Sam. 23:30; 1 Chr. 11:32]

HIEL (Heb. 'God lives') *c.* 9 century BC. Born in Bethel in the time of King Ahab, he rebuilt the city of Jericho which had been destroyed by Joshua. Hiel's two sons, Abiram and Segub, died in fulfilment of Joshua's curse upon the man who rebuilt Jericho. [Josh. 6:26; 1 Kgs. 16:34]

HILKIAH (Heb. 'God's portion') **1.** date unknown. A Levite descended from Merari, he was an ancestor of Ethan the musician of King David. [1 Chr. 6:45]

2. *c.* 10 century BC. Son of Hosah the Levite, he and his family served in the Tabernacle during the reign of King David. [1 Chr. 26:11]

3. *c.* 8 century BC. Father of Eliakim, head of King Hezekiah's household. [2 Kgs. 18:18, 26, 37; Isa. 22:20; 36:3, 22]

4. *c.* 7 century BC. The high priest in the time of King Josiah, he found a 'book of the law' (2 Kgs. 22:8) during the renovations to the Temple. The king was distressed at finding out from the book that the Laws of Moses were being neglected, and sent Hilkiah and four others to consult the prophetess Huldah, who predicted a grim fate for the Israelites. Hilkiah and his fellow-priests were ordered to destroy profane vessels and to purify the Temple. [2 Kgs. 22:4-14; 23:4, 24; 1 Chr. 6:13; 9:11; 2 Chr. 34:9-22; Ezra 7:1]

5. *c.* 7 century BC. Father of the prophet Jeremiah, he was a priest in Anathoth in the territory of Benjamin, and may have been a descendant of Abiathar, the priest banished to Anathoth by King Solomon. [Jer. 1:1, 2]

6. *c.* 6 century BC. Father of Gemariah whom King Zedekiah sent to Babylon with a message to the Emperor Nebuchadnezzar. [Jer. 29:3]

7. 6 century BC. A head priest who returned with Zerubbabel from exile in Babylon. His descendant Hashabiah was one of the chief priests of Judah when Joiakim was high priest. [Neh. 12:7, 21]

8. *c.* 5 century BC. A leader of Judah who stood on the right side of Ezra when he read from the Law of Moses to the people of Judah after the return from Babylon. [Neh. 8:4]

HILLEL (Heb. 'praise') *c.* 12 century BC. Father of Abdon who was judge over Israel eight years. [Judg. 12:13, 15]

HINNOM date unknown. A man or family whose name was given to a valley at the southern and western edges of Jerusalem. It was here that child sacrifices were offered and the name Gehenna was derived from the word Gei (Heb. 'valley of') Hinnom. The valley is also called Ben-hinnom. [Josh. 15:8; 18:16; 2 Kgs. 23:10; 2 Chr. 28:3; 33:6; Neh. 11:30; Jer. 7:31, 32]

HIRAH (Heb. 'noble') *c.* 16 century BC. An Adullamite shepherd and friend of Judah who was sent to find Judah's daughter-in-law Tamar. [Gen. 38:1, 20-2]

HIRAM (Heb. 'my brother is exalted') **1.** *c.* 10 century BC. Hiram was king of Tyre on the Phoenician coast in succession to Abibaal. When David established Jerusalem as his capital, Hiram 'sent messengers to David, and cedar trees, also carpenters and masons who built David a house' (2 Sam. 5:11). A warm friendship existed between the two men 'for Hiram always loved David' (1 Kgs. 5:1).

Solomon also made an agreement with Hiram for the supply of cedar and for logs and gold for the building of the Temple, in exchange for wheat and olive oil. To balance accounts, Solomon ceded to Hiram twenty

Phoenician portrait mask from Achziv, 10th-6th centuries BC, possibly from the time of Hiram.

towns in Galilee. Another joint venture was the trade in the Red Sea area through the port of Ezion-geber (modern Eilat). 'And Hiram sent with the fleet his servants, seamen who were familiar with the sea, together with the servants of Solomon.' (1 Kgs. 9:27) Also called Huram. [2 Sam. 5:11; 1 Kgs. 5:1-18; 9:11-27; 10:11-22; 1 Chr. 14:1; 2 Chr. 8:2-18; 9:10, 21]

2. *c.* 10 century BC. Hiram was the son of a widow from the tribe of Naphtali and his father was a man of Tyre. Solomon sent to Tyre for him in connection with the building of the Temple, 'and he was full of wisdom, understanding, and skill, for making any work in bronze' (1 Kgs. 7:14). Hiram cast the two great bronze pillars in front of the Temple, also the 'sea' (1 Kgs. 7:23), a great metal basin mounted on the backs of twelve oxen, and all the smaller basins and Temple implements. Also called Huram and Huram-abi. [1 Kgs. 7; 2 Chr. 2:13; 4-11, 16]

HITTITES An ancient Canaanite tribe descended from Heth who were driven out of the land of Canaan by the children of Israel under Joshua. [Gen. 10:15; 25:9; Exod. 23:23; Deut. 7:1; Josh. 3:10; 2 Sam. 11:3]

HIVITES 13 century BC. An ancient Canaanite tribe most of whom were driven out of Canaan by the children of Israel under Joshua. [Exod. 23:23; Deut. 7:1; Josh. 3:10; 1 Chr. 1:15]

HIZKI (Heb. 'strong') date unknown. Son of Elpaal and a leader of the tribe of Benjamin living in Jerusalem. [1 Chr. 8:17]

HIZKIAH (Heb. 'my strength is God') date unknown. Son of Neariah of the tribe of Judah and a descendant of King David. [1 Chr. 3:23]

HOBAB *see* JETHRO

HOBAIAH *see* HABAIAH

HOD (Heb. 'splendour') date unknown. Son of Zophah, he was a leader of the tribe of Asher and a mighty warrior. [1 Chr. 7:37]

HODAVIAH (Heb. 'praise') **1.** date unknown. A leader of a portion of the tribe of Manasseh living east of the river Jordan. [1 Chr. 5:24]

2. date unknown. Son of Hassenuah, the Benjaminite, his grandson Sallu returned to Jerusalem from captivity in Babylon in the time of Nehemiah. [1 Chr. 9:7]

3. date unknown. Ancestor of a family of Levites who returned to Judah with Zerubbabel from captivity in Babylon. Also called Hodevah. [Ezra 2:40; Neh. 7:43]

4. date unknown. Son of Elioenai of the tribe of Judah and a descendant of King David. [1 Chr. 3:24]

HODESH (Heb. 'new moon') date unknown. Third wife of Shaharaim of the tribe of Benjamin who bore him seven sons. [1 Chr. 8:9]

HODEVAH *see* HODAVIAH **3.**

HODIAH (Heb. 'splendour of God') **1.** date unknown. A leader of the tribe of Judah, he was the grandfather of Keilah the Garmite and Eshtemoa the Maacathite. [1 Chr. 4:19]

2. 5 century BC. A Levite in the time of Ezra who explained the Law to the assembled people of Judah on the public fast day, and who called upon the people to praise God and confess their sins. He also signed the covenant to observe the Laws of God. [Neh. 8:7; 9:5; 10:10]

3. 5 century BC. Another Levite who signed the covenant to observe the Laws of God. [Neh. 10:13]

4. 5 century BC. A leader of Judah who also signed the covenant to obey the Laws of God. [Neh. 10:18]

HOGLAH (Heb. 'partridge') *c.* 13 century BC. One of the five daughters of Zelophehad who appealed to Moses, claiming their father's patrimony since he had no sons. [Num. 26:33; 27:1; 36:11; Josh. 17:3]

HOHAM *c.* 13 century BC. Hoham, king of Hebron, made an alliance with four other Amorite kings to attack the city of Gibeon for having made a peace treaty with Joshua. Defeated by Joshua, the five kings hid themselves in a cave but were discovered. Later they were taken out, put to death, and buried in the same cave. [Josh. 10]

HOMAM *see* HEMAN **1.**

HOPHNI *c.* 11 century BC. Hophni and his brother Phinehas were priests at the sanctuary of Shiloh, where their father Eli was the chief priest. They abused their office by seducing women who came to the Temple, and by taking for themselves the best part of the sacrificial meat. Eli remonstrated with them, but they took no notice.

The two priests were sent with the Ark of the Covenant to rally the Israelite forces being hard pressed in

The prophet Hosea, from a series of anonymous Italian drawings of famous men, c. 1450.

went through a decline marked by political assassinations and moral and religious laxity. Hosea vigorously denounced these evils, particularly the prevailing idol-worship, and prophesied the disasters that would come as a punishment from the Lord.

Nothing is known about Hosea's personal life, except for his own revelations about his disastrous family life. He was married to Gomer, the daughter of Diblaim, who turned out to be a loose woman, 'a wife of harlotry' (Hos. 1:2). To the three children she bore, he gave names of bitter rejection: Jezreel, after the valley where Jehu, founder of the hated royal house, had carried out his bloody coup; Loruhamah, 'not pitied' (Hos. 1:8); Loammi, 'not of my people' (Hos. 1:9). The two latter names at least suggest that he did not regard them as his own offspring. He probably divorced Gomer by the formal declaration that 'she is not my wife, and I am not her husband' (Hos. 2:2). But he continued to love his erring wife, and at some later stage appeared to have forgiven her and taken her back.

His domestic experience strongly influenced Hosea's concept of the Lord's relationship with His people. He saw Israel as a spouse betraying God her husband, and committing adultery with pagan cults. Israel would be

battle by the Philistines at Aphek. The Israelites were defeated and the Ark captured, and Hophni and Phinehas were among the slain. The shock of their death and the loss of the Ark killed their aged father. [1 Sam. 1:3; 2:34; 3:13; 4:11]

HOPHRA *see* PHARAOH **10.**

HORAM (Heb. 'hill') *c.* 13 century BC. King of Gezer, he went to the aid of the town of Lachish when it was besieged by Joshua and was defeated. [Josh. 10:33]

HORI (Heb. 'noble') **1.** date unknown. Eldest son of Lotan and a grandson of Seir, the Horite. [Gen. 36:22; 1 Chr. 1:39]

2. *c.* 13 century BC. Father of Shaphat of the tribe of Simeon, one of the twelve men sent by Moses to spy out the Promised Land. [Num. 13:5]

HORITES Inhabitants of Seir, the north-west region of Edom, south of the Dead Sea. They took their name from Hori, grandson of Seir who gave his name to the territory. (Modern scholars consider that the Horites were Hurrians whose original home was in the mountains of Armenia and who then thrust down into northern Mesopotamia. Some of them moved south into Edom in the early centuries of the 2nd millennium BC.) [Gen. 14:6; 36:20, 21, 29, 30; Deut. 2:12, 22]

HOSAH (Heb. 'refuge') *c.* 10 century BC. A Levite descended from Merari, he was gatekeeper at the west gate of the Tabernacle during the reign of King David. [1 Chr. 16:38; 26:10, 11, 16]

HOSEA (Heb. 'salvation') *c.* 8 century BC. A Hebrew prophet in the Kingdom of Israel. Hosea, the son of Beeri, prophesied in the northern kingdom of Israel for a period starting towards the end of the reign of Jeroboam II (783-43 BC). From the death of that illustrious king until the fall of Samaria in 721 BC, the kingdom

Silver Canaanite idol: the worship of Canaanite idols was denounced by Hosea.

punished and driven out by God, but one day she would purge herself of sin and be forgiven.

Hosea fiercely attacked the Canaanite practices which crept into the 'high places', the local shrines on hilltops and under sacred trees. He was caustic too about the golden calves introduced into the sanctuaries of Bethel and Dan by the breakaway northern kingdom of Israel. Hosea did not hesitate to attack the priesthood for failing to set an example to the people: 'I reject you from being a priest to me. And since you have forgotten the law of your God, I also will forget your children.' (Hos. 4:6)

But the prophet does not call for mere observance of the formal tenets of religion. For him, true faith is a matter of the heart and not of external ritual: 'For I desire steadfast love and not sacrifice, the knowledge of God, rather than burnt offerings.' (Hos. 6:6) Hosea here struck a note that was echoed by Isaiah and Jeremiah and became one of the basic themes of the Hebrew prophetic strain.

In a period of turbulence in the Near East, Hosea warned the rulers of his little land against seeking safety in weapons or in alliances with great powers: 'Ephraim is like a dove, silly and without sense, calling to Egypt, going to Assyria.' (Hos. 7:11) Only faith in God could save his people from destruction.

Hosea has been regarded as a fierce prophet of disaster, who told his fellow-countrymen that 'they sow the wind, and they shall reap the whirlwind' (Hos. 8:7). But his God of wrath was also a God of love and mercy, who felt about his chosen people like a father does about a son whom he held in his arms in infancy, and is reluctant to punish. He is a God who says: 'I will not execute my fierce anger, I will not again destroy Ephraim; for I am God and not man, the Holy One in your midst.' (Hos. 11:9) The Book of Hosea ends with an idyllic picture of future happiness for the Israelites, when they have been reconciled with the Lord. 'O Ephraim, what have I to do with idols? It is I who answer and look after you. I am like an evergreen cypress.' (Hos. 14:8) [Book of Hosea]

HOSHAIAH (Heb. 'helped by God') **1.** 6 century BC. Father of Azariah, a leader of Judah in the time of Jeremiah. [Jer. 42:1; 43:2]
2. 5 century BC. A leader of Judah in the time of Nehemiah who led half the princes of Judah at the ceremony of dedicating the walls of Jerusalem. [Neh. 12:32]

HOSHAMA (Heb. 'when God hears') *c.* 6 century BC. Seventh son of Jeconiah of the royal house of Judah and a descendant of King David. [1 Chr. 3:18]

HOSHEA (Heb. 'salvation') **1.** *see* JOSHUA **1.**
2. *c.* 10 century BC. Son of Azaziah, he was head of the tribe of Ephraim in the days of King David. [1 Chr. 27:20]

Plaque from Ashkelon, showing three naked women, probably temple harlots.

Growth of Assyrian Empire

Shalmaneser III 858-824 BC
Tiglath-pileser III 745-727 BC
Esarhaddon 680-669 BC
Ashurbanipal 668-621 BC

0   100 miles

3. Nineteenth and last king of Israel after the monarchy split, he reigned 732-24 BC. Hoshea, son of Elah, was the last king of Israel before the kingdom was finally engulfed by the rising tide of Assyrian imperialism.

Already in the reign of his predecessor, Pekah, the Assyrian forces had invaded Israel, occupied the Galilee, the coastal district and the Transjordan territory of Gilead, and converted them into provinces under Assyrian governors. Hoshea had then murdered Pekah and replaced him on the throne. Whether this was done with the connivance of the Assyrians is not clear, but what is clear is that Hoshea was a puppet king subservient to his Assyrian masters, and paying tribute to them. That was the price for retaining the nominal independence of a rump kingdom that had shrunk to little more than the capital Samaria and the Ephraim hill-region around it.

After the death of the Assyrian monarch Tiglath-pileser III, Hoshea made a rash attempt to throw off the Assyrian yoke by invoking the rival imperial power of Egypt. The new Assyrian ruler, Shalmaneser V, reacted by invading what was left of Israel, capturing and imprisoning Hoshea, and laying siege to the capital Samaria. Its surrender in 721 BC and the deportation of its inhabitants marked the end of the northern kingdom of Israel. [2 Kgs. 15:30; 17:1-6; 18:1, 9, 10]

4. 5 century BC. A leader of Israel who signed the covenant to observe the Laws of God in the time of Nehemiah. [Neh. 10:23]

HOTHAM (Heb. 'seal') **1.** date unknown. Son of Heber and a leader of the tribe of Asher. [1 Chr. 7:32] **2.** c. 11 century BC. Father of two of King David's distinguished warriors, Shama and Jeiel. [1 Chr. 11:44]

HOTHIR (Heb. 'fullness') c. 10 century BC. Son of Heman, King David's musician. He and his brothers played musical instruments in the Tabernacle service under their father's direction, and Hothir was responsible for the twenty-first turn of service. [1 Chr. 25:4, 28]

HUL date unknown. Son of Aram and a grandson of Shem. [Gen. 10:23; 1 Chr. 1:17]

HULDAH (Heb. 'weasel') c. 7 century BC. Huldah, a

155

respected prophetess, was the wife of Shallum, keeper of the royal wardrobe. King Josiah sent a deputation to consult with her on what was to be done about the 'book of the law' (2 Kgs. 22:8) found during the repairs to the Temple. She replied: 'Thus says the Lord, Behold, I will bring evil upon this place and upon its inhabitants . . . . Because they have forsaken me and have burned incense to other gods . . .' (2 Kgs. 22:16, 17) However, Josiah himself would die in peace. [2 Kgs. 22:14-20; 2 Chr. 34:22-8]

HUPHAM *see* HUPPIM 1.

HUPPAH (Heb. 'covered') *c.* 10 century BC. A leader of the priestly family who took the thirteenth rota of service in the Tabernacle in the reign of King David. [1 Chr. 24:13]

HUPPIM 1. *c.* 16 century BC. Son of Benjamin, he went down to Egypt with his grandfather Jacob. Also called Hupham. [Gen. 46:21; Num. 26:39]
2. date unknown. A descendant of Benjamin and a leader of the tribe. [1 Chr. 7:12, 15]

HUR (Heb. 'noble') **1.** *c.* 13 century BC. Hur was one of the children of Israel in the desert. In the battle against the Amalekites, Moses had to keep his rod lifted 'and Aaron and Hur held up his hands, one on one side, and the other on the other side; so his hands were steady until the going down of the sun' (Exod. 17:12).

Later when Moses went up Mount Sinai, he left Aaron and Hur in charge of the encampment.

Because of his intimacy with Moses and Aaron, Jewish tradition holds that he was the husband of Miriam, their eldest sister. [Exod. 17:10-12; 24:14]
2. *c.* 13 century BC. Grandfather of Bezalel of the tribe of Judah, and a descendant of Hezron or Perez. [Exod. 31:2; 35:30; 38:22; 1 Chr. 2:19, 20, 50; 4:1-4; 2 Chr. 1:5]
3. *c.* 13 century BC. One of the five Midianite kings killed by the children of Israel in the wilderness on their way to the land of Israel. [Num. 31:8; Josh. 13:21]
4. *c.* 5 century BC. Father of Rephaiah, the ruler of half of Jerusalem in the time of Nehemiah, who helped rebuild the walls of Jerusalem. [Neh. 3:9]

HURAI *see* HIDDAI

HURAM (Heb. 'my brother is exalted') **1.** date unknown. Son of Bela and a grandson of Benjamin. [1 Chr. 8:5]
2. *see* HIRAM **1.**
3. *see* HIRAM **2.**

HURAM-ABI *see* HIRAM **2.**

HURI (Heb. 'noble') date unknown. Son of Jaroah and a grandson of Gilead of the tribe of Gad. [1 Chr. 5:14]

HUSHAH (Heb. 'haste') date unknown. Son of Ezer and a leader of the tribe of Judah, he was descended from Hur. [1 Chr. 4:4]

HUSHAI (Heb. 'my brother's gift') *c.* 11 century BC. Hushai the Archite (from a village west of Bethel) was an intimate friend and adviser of King David. When David fled from Jerusalem after the revolt of Absalom, Hushai came to join him 'with his coat rent and earth upon his head' (2 Sam. 15:32). David persuaded him to remain behind and gain Absalom's confidence. In this way he would be able to counteract the advice that would be given by Ahithophel, David's leading counsellor who had gone over to Absalom's camp.

When Absalom entered Jerusalem he was surprised to be met by Hushai who greeted him warmly: 'Long live the king! Long live the king!' (2 Sam. 16:16) Absalom took him to task for having deserted David: 'Is this your loyalty to your friend? Why did you not go with your friend?' (2 Sam. 16:17) Hushai answered him by explaining that his duty was to serve the man chosen by the Lord and the people of Israel, and Absalom took him at his word.

Absalom knew that even with Jerusalem in his hands his power could not be secure as long as David was at large and free to strike back. He asked for advice. Ahithophel urged immediate pursuit that same night so that David could be caught before he had a chance to organize a counter-thrust. Hushai argued in favour of greater caution. To engage David and his men in a hurry would entail too great a risk for Absalom's cause. 'And Absalom and all the men of Israel said, "The counsel of Hushai the Archite is better than the counsel of Ahithophel."' (2 Sam. 17:14) Hushai then sent a trusted runner to David telling him not to spend that night on the Jericho plain but to cross the Jordan, where he could rebuild his forces. Realizing that Absalom had made a fatal blunder and that his own career was wrecked, Ahithophel went home and hanged himself.

Hushai thus successfully carried out the task entrusted to him by David. The gratitude of David's house was reflected in the fact that Hushai's son Baana was later appointed by King Solomon as the commissioner in charge of one of the twelve administrative and tax districts of the king. [2 Sam. 15:32, 37; 16:16-18; 17:5-16; 1 Kgs. 4:16; 1 Chr. 27:33]

HUSHAM (Heb. 'haste') date unknown. The Yemanite king of Edom. [Gen. 36:34, 35; 1 Chr. 1:45, 46]

HUSHIM (Heb. 'haste') **1.** *c.* 16 century BC. Son of Dan and the grandson of Jacob and Bilhah, he went down with Jacob into Egypt. Also called Shuham. [Gen. 46:23; Num. 26:42]
2. date unknown. A leader of the tribe of Benjamin descended from Aher. [1 Chr. 7:12]
3. date unknown. One of the wives of Shaharaim, a leader of the tribe of Benjamin. [1 Chr. 8:8, 11]

I

IBHAR (Heb. 'he will choose') *c.* 10 century BC. A son born to King David in Jerusalem. [2 Sam. 5:15; 1 Chr. 3:6; 14:5]

IBNEIAH (Heb. 'God builds') 5 century BC. Son of Jeroham, he was one of the first men of Benjamin to settle in Jerusalem after the return from exile in Babylon. [1 Chr. 9:8]

IBNIJAH (Heb. 'God builds') date unknown. Ancestor of Ibneiah, one of the first men of Benjamin to settle in Jerusalem after the return from exile in Babylon. [1 Chr. 9:8]

IBRI (Heb. 'Hebrew') *c.* 10 century BC. A Levite descended from Merari, he served in the Tabernacle in the reign of King David. [1 Chr. 24:27]

IBSAM (Heb. 'balsam') *c.* 16 century BC. Son of Tola and a grandson of Issachar, he was a leader of the tribe and a mighty warrior. [1 Chr. 7:2]

IBZAN *c.* 12 century BC. Judge of Israel for seven years, he succeeded Jephthah. His sixty children married outside the tribe of Zebulun. [Judg. 12:8-10]

ICHABOD (Heb. 'inglorious') *c.* 11 century BC. Grandson of Eli and son of Phinehas a corrupt priest, he was born after the death of his father and grandfather. His mother lived long enough to call her son Ichabod – because the 'glory has departed from Israel' (1 Sam. 4:21) – and then she herself died. [1 Sam. 4:21; 14:3]

IDBASH (Heb. 'honey-sweet') date unknown. A leader of the tribe of Judah. [1 Chr. 4:3]

IDDO (Heb. 'God's friend') **1.** 10 century BC. Father of Ahinadab, one of King Solomon's twelve officers responsible for supplying the provisions of the royal household. [1 Kgs. 4:14]
2. *c.* 10 century BC. Son of Zechariah, he was appointed by King David as ruler of the half-tribe of Manasseh in Gilead, east of the Jordan. [1 Chr. 27:21]
3. date unknown. Son of Joah, a Levite, he was descended from Gershom. Also called Adaiah. [1 Chr. 6:21, 41]
4. *c.* 10 century BC. The seer who prophesied against the kings Jeroboam, Rehoboam and Abijah. His writings are referred to in the Second Book of Chronicles but have not survived to our day. [2 Chr. 9:29; 12:15; 13:22]
5. *c.* 6 century BC. Father of Berechiah and grandfather

of the prophet Zechariah, who describes him as a prophet. In the Book of Ezra he is described as Zechariah's father. [Ezra 5:1; 6:14; Zech. 1:1, 7]
6. 6 century BC. A priest of Judah who returned with Zerubbabel from exile in Babylon. His descendant, Zechariah, was one of the chief priests in the days of Nehemiah. [Neh. 12:4, 16]
7. 5 century BC. A leader of Judah and chief of the exiles at Casiphia, at Ezra's request he sent priests and Levites to serve in the Tabernacle in Jerusalem. [Ezra 8:17]

IEZER *see* ABIEZER **1.**

IGAL (Heb. 'may God redeem') **1.** *c.* 13 century BC. Son of Joseph, he represented the tribe of Issachar among the twelve spies chosen by Moses. He was one of the majority of the spies who felt that the Canaanite people who lived there in their walled cities were too strong for the Israelites to drive out. [Num. 13:7-33]
2. *c.* 10 century BC. Son of Nathan of Zobah, he was a warrior in the armies of King David. Also known as Joel. [2 Sam. 23:36; 1 Chr. 11:38]
3. *c.* 5 century BC. A son of Shemaiah of the tribe of Judah and a descendant of King David. [1 Chr. 3:22]

IGDALIAH (Heb. 'may God be glorified') *c.* 6 century BC. Father of Hanan, he is described by the prophet Jeremiah as 'a man of God' and his descendants occupied rooms in the vicinity of the Temple. [Jer. 35:4]

IKKESH (Heb. 'stubborn') *c.* 10 century BC. Father of Ira, who was a heroic warrior and one of David's twelve army commanders. [2 Sam. 23:26; 1 Chr. 11:28; 27:9]

ILAI (Heb. 'exalted') *c.* 10 century BC. An Ahohite warrior in the army of King David, distinguished for his bravery. Also known as Zalmon the Ahohite. [2 Sam. 23:28; 1 Chr. 11:29]

IMLAH (Heb. 'full') *c.* 9 century BC. Father of the prophet Micaiah consulted by Ahab and Jehoshaphat, kings of Israel and Judah. [1 Kgs. 22:8, 9; 2 Chr. 18:7, 8]

IMMANUEL (Heb. 'God is with us') *c.* 8 century BC. The symbolic name given by Isaiah to the child he predicted would be born unto the royal family of Judah, and who would choose good and reject evil. [Isa. 7:14]

IMMER (Heb. 'lamb') **1.** *c.* 10 century BC. Head of a family of priests who served in the Tabernacle in the reign of King David. [1 Chr. 9:12; 24:14; Ezra 2:37; 10:20; Neh. 3:29; 7:40; 11:13]

2. *c.* 7 century BC. Father of Pashhur, the chief priest in the Temple who beat the prophet Jeremiah and put him in the stocks. [Jer. 20:1]

IMNA date unknown. Son of Helem, he and his family were leaders of the tribe of Asher and mighty warriors. [1 Chr. 7:35]

IMNAH (Heb. 'may God defend') **1.** *c.* 16 century BC. Son of Asher, he went down to Egypt at the same time as his grandfather Jacob. [Gen. 46:17; Num. 26:44; 1 Chr. 7:30]

2. *c.* 8 century BC. Father of Kore, the Levite responsible for distributing the tithes and offerings in the reign of King Hezekiah. [2 Chr. 31:14]

IMRAH (Heb. 'stubborn') date unknown. Son of Zophah, he and his family were leaders of the tribe of Asher and mighty warriors. [1 Chr. 7:36]

IMRI (Heb. 'my lamb') **1.** date unknown. An ancestor of Uthai who was one of the first members of the tribe of Judah to return to Jerusalem after the Babylonian exile. [1 Chr. 9:4]

2. 5 century BC. Father of Zaccur who helped rebuild the walls of Jerusalem in the time of Nehemiah. [Neh. 3:2]

IOB *c.* 16 century BC. Son of Issachar, he went down to Egypt with his grandfather Jacob. Also called Jashub. [Gen. 46:13; 1 Num. 26:24; 1 Chr. 7:1]

IPHDEIAH (Heb. 'may God redeem') date unknown. Son of Shashak, he was one of the leaders of the tribe of Benjamin living in Jerusalem. [1 Chr. 8:25]

IR *see* IRI

IRA 1. *c.* 10 century BC. A court officer of King David and a priest of Israel. [2 Sam. 20:26]

2. *c.* 10 century BC. Son of Ikkesh of Tekoa, he was one of the warriors in King David's army distinguished for his bravery and appointed one of the twelve commanders. [2 Sam. 23:26; 1 Chr. 11:28; 27:9]

3. *c.* 10 century BC. An Ithrite in the army of King David, distinguished for his bravery. [2 Sam. 23:38; 1 Chr. 11:40]

IRAD (Heb. 'fleet') date unknown. Son of Enoch and a grandson of Cain. [Gen. 4:18]

IRAM date unknown. An Edomite leader descended from Esau. [Gen. 36:43; 1 Chr. 1:54]

IRI *c.* 16 century BC. Son of Bela and a grandson of Benjamin, he and his brothers were leaders of the tribe of Benjamin and mighty warriors. Also known as Ir, the father of Shuppim and Huppim. [1 Chr. 7:7, 12]

IRIJAH (Heb. 'may God see') *c.* 6 century BC. Son of Shelemiah, he was an army captain in Jerusalem in the days of King Zedekiah who imprisoned the prophet Jeremiah after accusing him of deserting to the Babylonian army. [Jer. 37:13]

IRNAHASH (Heb. 'serpent city') date unknown. Son

of Tehinnah, a leader of the tribe of Judah. [1 Chr. 4:12]

IRU *c.* 13 century BC. Son of Caleb, and a leader of the tribe of Judah. [1 Chr. 4:15]

ISAAC (Heb. 'he laughed') *c.* 18-16 centuries BC. The second patriarch son of Abraham.

Abraham was ninety-nine years old when the Lord told him that his barren wife Sarah would bear him a son. According to the account in Genesis, Abraham laughed in his heart, and Sarah was also bitterly amused because she was ninety and long past child-bearing age. The son was called Isaac (Hebrew *Yitzchak*) meaning 'he laughed'.

When Isaac was a young lad, Abraham's obedience to God was put to a fearful test. He was told to take the boy to a distant mountain top and sacrifice him to the Lord. They set out with two young servants and a load of firewood. When they neared the place, the servants and the ass were left behind and father and son went forward on foot. Isaac asked, 'Behold, the fire and the wood; but where is the lamb for a burnt offering?' (Gen. 22:7) Abraham replied evasively that the Lord would provide the lamb.

At the spot for the sacrifice, Abraham erected an altar, arranged the wood on it, and laid the bound boy

Parthian relief showing a winged angel about to sacrifice a ram, 1st-2nd centuries AD.

above Mosaic showing Abraham offering hospitality to the three angels and his sacrifice of Isaac, from S. Vitale, Ravenna, 6th century AD.

on top. When he stretched his hand for the knife an angel of the Lord intervened, and a ram that was seen in a nearby thicket was sacrificed instead of Isaac.

Stricken in years, Abraham concerned himself with finding a wife for Isaac, then forty years old. Abraham did not want him to marry a local Canaanite girl, so he sent a trusted servant to his own kinsmen in Haran (northern Syria). The servant returned with Rebekah, the daughter of Abraham's nephew. One evening Isaac was strolling through the fields when he saw the camel caravan approaching. Rebekah modestly veiled herself and alighted to greet him. 'Then Isaac brought her into the tent, and took Rebekah, and she became his wife; and he loved her. So Isaac was comforted after his mother's death.' (Gen. 24:67)

Nearing the end of his days, Abraham declared that Isaac would be the heir to his estate. To avoid trouble later, Abraham gave gifts to the sons he had had by concubines and sent them to live further east. Abraham died and was buried next to Sarah in the Cave of Machpelah by Isaac and his half-brother Ishmael, the son of Hagar, Sarah's Egyptian slave-maid.

At first Rebekah was barren but after Isaac had appealed to the Lord, she gave birth to twins. The first to be born was Esau, covered with red hair, and then Jacob, clutching his brother's heel.

There was a famine in the land and Isaac started moving with his flocks and herds towards Egypt, as his father Abraham had done in an earlier famine. He reached Gerar, ruled over by his father's friend (or his friend's namesake) Abimelech. Here the Lord appeared to him and told him not to go down to Egypt but to stay

above Mesopotamian terracotta of a husband and wife, 22nd-21st centuries BC.

159

Isaac blessing Jacob, by the Spanish painter
Jusepe de Ribera (1591-1652).

in that area. The Lord recalled his covenant with Abraham and repeated to Isaac the promise that he would be blessed and multiply and the land would belong to his seed. So Isaac remained in Gerar.

As Abraham had done with Sarah, Isaac passed Rebekah off as his sister for fear that he might be killed for her sake, as she too was fair to look upon. Looking through a window Abimelech saw Isaac and Rebekah together and realized they were husband and wife. He was angry at first at the deception but gave orders that anyone who molested them would be put to death.

Isaac re-opened the wells that Abraham had dug in this area and that had been filled in again. He reaped good crops from his sowing; his herds and flocks multiplied and he became wealthy and important. This aroused local envy. At Abimelech's suggestion, Isaac moved further away, though remaining in the region of Gerar and Beersheba. Again he located and restored some of Abraham's wells. There was friction with local shepherds over two of these watering places, but at the third, Rehoboth, they were left in peace. Isaac said, 'For now the Lord has made room for us, and we shall be fruitful in the land.' (Gen. 26:22) Isaac built an altar at Beersheba as his father had done.

Isaac's Blessing

Being aged and practically blind, Isaac sent for his favourite son Esau who was a skilled hunter. He asked him to take his quiver and bow, shoot a deer and prepare some of the venison he loved. He would then bless

him before he died. Rebekah overheard this, and determined to secure the blessing for Jacob whom she loved more. She told Jacob to slaughter two young goats, made a savoury stew of the meat, and sent it in to Isaac with Jacob pretending to be Esau. To make the deception more effective, she covered Jacob's smooth hands and neck with bits of the fleece of the slain kids (for Esau was a hairy man) and she put Esau's garment on Jacob. Isaac was suspicious at first, saying, 'The voice is Jacob's voice, but the hands are the hands of Esau.' (Gen. 27:22) But when he asked Jacob to come near and kiss him, the smell of the fields clinging to Esau's garment convinced him. He then gave Jacob his blessing, declaring that he would be the head of the family when Isaac died and his brethren would serve him.

Esau came in with the venison he had prepared for his father, and Isaac realized he had been deceived. But he could not now take back the blessing bestowed on Jacob. Esau, wailing with anger and grief, pressed Isaac to bless him as well. The old man replied that Esau would have to serve Jacob, but he too would prosper and become independent.

Fearing that Esau would kill Jacob in revenge, Rebekah persuaded Isaac to send Jacob to her brother Laban in Haran so that he too should marry someone of his own kin.

Isaac died at the age of one hundred and eighty and was buried by his twin sons Esau and Jacob in the Cave

The traditional site of the tombs of the patriarchs at Hebron, bought by Abraham, lies under this building with its mixture of Herodian, Byzantine, Crusader and Moslem architectural styles.

of Machpelah at Hebron, with his father and mother and his wife Rebekah.

Of the three patriarchs, Isaac is a less striking figure than either his father Abraham or his son Jacob.

In the dramatic episode of the sacrifice, he shows a touching faith and docility towards his father. In his later life, moving through the southland with his flocks, he stays in his father's footsteps, re-digging Abraham's abandoned wells. As soon as there is friction with the local inhabitants, he chooses to move elsewhere.

In his old age, he is not only deceived by his wife and his son Jacob, but seems helpless to undo the wrong done to the first-born son Esau, cheated of the paternal blessing.

The character that emerges from the story is not strong, but benign, pious and gentle. [Gen. 17-28]

Pottery from the Middle Bronze Period – the age of the patriarchs – recently excavated at Tel Dan (Laish).

ISAIAH (Heb. 'God's salvation') *c*. second half of 8 century BC. A Hebrew prophet in the kingdom of Judah. Isaiah the son of Amoz was the greatest of the Hebrew prophets, and the author of the most sublime religious poetry in the Old Testament. The force and beauty of his message is best appreciated in the original Hebrew, a terse and sonorous language, rich in concrete similes.

Isaiah was born in Jerusalem about 765 BC. At the age of twenty-five he had a vision of God: 'In the year that King Uzziah died I saw the Lord sitting upon a throne, high and lifted up; and his train filled the temple .... And I heard the voice of the Lord saying, "Whom shall I send, and who will go for us?" Then I said, "Here am I! Send me."' (Isa. 6:1, 8) From that day he devoted himself to the vocation of prophecy.

The Hebrew prophets were inspired men who preached the word of God and fearlessly attacked the evils of men, not even sparing kings. They acted as the moral conscience of the community. Being able to predict future events was not their main attribute. The discourses of some of them were preserved and later collected in separate books of the Bible.

The little that is known about Isaiah is contained in the book that bears his name, and from the parallel account in the Second Book of Kings. It appears that he was a man of position in the capital, with access to the king and a voice in affairs of state. He had a wife and two sons, both of whom are given symbolic names: Shear-jashub ('the remnant will return') and Maher-shalal-hash-baz ('the booty and shame are imminent' – a reference to the impending doom of Samaria). His prophecies covered about half a century, during the reigns of the Judean kings Jotham, Ahaz and Hezekiah.

His whole life was bound up with Jerusalem, that 'faithful city' he loved and chided. In his vision of the future it was from this city, remote in the Judean hills, that men would gain inspiration: '... and many peoples shall come, and say: "Come, let us go up to the mountain of the Lord, to the house of the God of Jacob; that he may teach us his ways and that we may walk in his paths." For out of Zion shall go forth the law, and the word of the Lord from Jerusalem.' (Isa. 2:3)

It was a turbulent period in the history of the Near East. The two small Hebrew kingdoms, Israel and Judah, often at odds with each other, were being caught up in the clash of empires. In Isaiah's time, the dominant power was Assyria, located on the Upper Orontes river in Mesopotamia. Four times in Isaiah's life the Assyrian cohorts rolled southward 'like a wolf on the fold' (Byron), threatening the small states in their path.

left Isaiah's vision: 11th-century German manuscript illumination reflecting the apocalyptic nature of Isaiah's imagery.

above Isaiah's vision of the celestial Jerusalem has persisted through the ages: 15th-century manuscript illumination.

below Isaiah lived at a time of Assyrian invasion. Assyrian bronze relief from the palace of Shalmaneser III, 858 BC, showing unveiled women prisoners.

The northern kingdom of Israel was wiped out with the fall of Samaria in 721 BC. In Judah's struggle to survive, its rulers sought to insure the kingdom by makeshift alliances. Isaiah strongly disapproved of this game of power politics. As a statesman, he did not believe that Judah's safety lay in pacts of expediency. As a man of deep religious conviction, he insisted on faith in God alone. He saw the enemy before the gate as an instrument of God's will, to punish the chosen people for its transgressions.

Soon after Ahaz came to the throne of Judah, Pekah king of Israel and Rezin king of Aram-Damascus formed an alliance in an attempt to halt the Assyrian advance. They wanted Ahaz to join them, and when he refused they invaded Judah to depose him. When they reached Jerusalem, there was panic in the city. The king sent to consult Isaiah, who replied firmly, 'do not fear, and do not let your heart be faint because of these two smouldering stumps of firebrands ...' (Isa. 7:4). The Lord would not permit the attempt to succeed.

Against Isaiah's counsel, Ahaz sent messengers with gifts to the king of Assyria, asking for his help. The Assyrians advanced, took Damascus, and occupied part of Israel. The pressure was relieved on Judah, but she remained a subservient vassal of Assyria.

Thirty years later, King Hezekiah joined in a revolt against the Assyrians, who marched to quell it. Isaiah derided Hezekiah's feverish preparations for the defence of Jerusalem: '... and you saw that the breaches of the city of David were many, and you collected the waters of the lower pool, and you counted the houses of Jerusalem, and you broke down the houses to fortify the wall.... But you did not look to him who did it, or have regard for him who planned it long ago.' (Isa. 22:9–11)

Isaiah was even more scornful of the mission Hezekiah sent to Egypt to gain support against the Assyrians. ' "Woe to the rebellious children," says the Lord, "who carry out a plan, but not mine.... Therefore shall the protection of Pharaoh turn to your shame, and the shelter in the shadow of Egypt to your humiliation." ' (Isa. 30:1, 3) He pointed out that 'The Egyptians are men, and not God; and their horses are flesh, and not spirit' (Isa. 31:3).

In 701 BC the Assyrian monarch Sennacherib swept through Judah and demanded the surrender of Jerusalem. It was again Isaiah who persuaded Hezekiah to stand firm: 'Therefore thus says the Lord concerning the king of Assyria, He shall not come into this city or shoot an arrow there.... By the way that he came, by the same he shall return.... For I will defend this city to save it.' (2 Kgs. 19:32-4)

A pestilence struck the camp of the Assyrians and they withdrew. The deliverance of Jerusalem was regarded as a divine miracle.

The Message of Isaiah

In vivid phrases Isaiah foretold the fate of each of Judah's enemies. About Babylon he thundered: 'wild beasts will lie down there, and its houses will be full of howling creatures; ... Fallen, fallen is Babylon; and all the images of her gods he has shattered to the ground.' (Isa. 13:21; 21:9)

Phoenician winepress, 9th-6th centuries BC. 'No more shall they tread wine in the winepresses' said Isaiah in his oration against the nations.

Isaiah's strongest invective however was reserved for his own people. They were a 'sinful nation, a people laden with iniquity, offspring of evildoers ...' (Isa. 1:4). 'How the faithful city has become a harlot, she that was full of justice! Righteousness lodged in her, but now murderers. Your silver has become dross, your wine mixed with water.' (Isa. 1:21, 22)

Isaiah railed against religious hypocrisy: 'What to me is the multitude of your sacrifices? says the Lord; I have had enough of burnt offerings of rams and the fat of fed beasts; ... When you spread forth your hands, I will hide my eyes from you; even though you make many prayers, I will not listen; your hands are full of blood.' (Isa. 1:11, 15) What the Lord wanted, he said, was not rituals and prayers but simply that each man should 'cease to do evil, learn to do good' (Isa. 1:16, 17).

It was not only the prophets of humble origin, like Amos and Hosea, that lashed out against the greed and luxury of the establishment and the exploitation of the poor. This social concern was deeply indebted in the Hebrew prophetic strain, and was shared by men of birth and position like Isaiah and Jeremiah. Isaiah abhorred the ostentation and moral laxity he saw around him, especially at the court. 'Your princes are rebels and companions of thieves. Every one loves a bribe and runs after gifts. They do not defend the fatherless, and the widow's cause does not come to them.' (Isa. 1:23)

He had no respect for men of property as such: 'Woe to those who join house to house, who add field to field.' (Isa. 5:8)

He was especially caustic about ladies of fashion who were solely concerned with their own beauty and adornment. He stripped them of their finery in one of the most precise and biting passages in the Bible: 'Because the daughters of Zion are haughty and walk with outstretched necks, glancing wantonly with their eyes, mincing along as they go, tinkling with their feet; the Lord will smite with a scab the heads of the daughters of Zion, and the Lord will lay bare their secret parts. In that day the Lord will take away the finery of the anklets, the headbands, and the crescents; the pendants, the bracelets, and the scarfs; the head-dresses, the armlets, the sashes, the perfume boxes, and the amulets; the signet rings and nose rings; the festal robes, the mantles, the cloaks and the handbags; the garments of gauze, the linen garments, the turbans, and the veils. Instead of perfume there will be rottenness; and instead of a girdle, a rope; and instead of well-set hair, baldness; and instead of a rich robe, a girding of sack-cloth; instead of beauty, shame.' (Isa. 3:16-24)

Isaiah's Prayer,
etching from Marc Chagall's
biblical series, 1956.

Isaiah's pessimism about the pending fate of his country was tempered by hope. It was not God's design to destroy utterly his chosen but erring people. Some would survive and would return to Zion and to righteousness. 'In that day the remnant of Israel and the survivors of the house of Jacob will no more lean upon him that smote them, but will lean upon the Lord, the Holy One of Israel, in truth. A remnant will return, the remnant of Jacob, to the mighty God.' (Isa. 10:20, 21)

The Immanuel passage in Chapter 7 is celebrated but its meaning is obscure. It opens with the words: 'Behold, a young woman shall conceive and bear a son, and shall call his name Immanuel. He shall eat curds and honey when he knows how to refuse the evil and choose the good.' (Isa. 7:14, 15) The name Immanuel means in Hebrew 'God is with us' which was very relevant to Isaiah's argument at the time with King Ahaz about resistance to the invasion by Pekah, king of Israel. The Hebrew word translated in the Authorized Version as 'virgin' was 'almah', which means a young woman,

Isaiah criticized the daughters of Zion for their
fine clothes: ivory plaque showing a
woman dressed in rich garments, from
Megiddo, 13th century BC.

165

single or married. Nevertheless Christian theologians regard the passage as a prediction of the birth of Jesus. The same applies to another famous passage in Chapter 9: 'For to us a child is born, to us a son is given; and the government will be upon his shoulder, and his name will be called "Wonderful Counsellor, Mighty God, Everlasting Father, Prince of Peace." ' (Isa. 9:6) To the Jews, the promised Messiah is yet to come.

The ideal world of Isaiah's Messianic kingdom is one in which man and nature at long last live in peace and brotherhood. 'The wolf shall dwell with the lamb, and the leopard shall lie down with the kid, and the calf and the lion and the fatling together, and a little child shall lead them.' 'They shall not hurt or destroy in all my holy mountain; for the earth shall be full of the knowledge of the Lord as the waters cover the sea.' (Isa. 11:6, 9)

When the United Nations was born into a war-weary human race, it was fitting that on a stone wall facing the entrance to its building in New York there should be inscribed Isaiah's vision of a better world: '... and they shall beat their swords into ploughshares, and their spears into pruning hooks; nation shall not lift up sword against nation, neither shall they learn war any more.' (Isa. 2:4)

The Second Isaiah

The Book of Isaiah is a compilation that reached its present form many centuries after the prophet's time. Of its sixty-six chapters, the first thirty-five are undoubtedly the authentic voice of the great prophet, with perhaps some scattered additions by his disciples.

Chapters 36 to 39 correspond to Chapters 18 and 20 of the Second Book of Kings and are devoted mainly to the story of the Assyrian threat to Jerusalem in 701 BC in the reign of King Hezekiah. Isaiah is referred to in the third person, and these chapters may have been composed in part by his disciples.

From the beginning of Chapter 40, one is suddenly transferred into a work of consolation relating to the exile in Babylon after the fall of Jerusalem in 587 BC, more than a century after Isaiah. The thought and style are still lofty, but the language is gentler and more diffuse. The tone is set by the opening words of Chapter 40:

'Comfort, comfort my people, says your God, speak tenderly to Jerusalem, and cry to her that her warfare is ended, that her iniquity is pardoned, that she has received from the Lord's hand double for all her sins. A voice cries: "In the wilderness prepare the way of the Lord, make straight in the desert a highway for our God." ' (Isa. 40:1-3)

left Isaiah, the prophet of a Messianic kingdom of peace and love. from Souillac, France, 12th century.

For a long time, the scholars have been perplexed by this strange transition. Had Isaiah's vision projected itself forward more than a century, after the calamity of which he had so often warned? Or did the second part of the Book of Isaiah contain the utterances of an unknown comforter-prophet close in spirit to Isaiah, though removed from him in time?

For the last 150 years, the problem of the Second Isaiah, or Deutero-Isaiah, has been one of the central themes of Biblical dispute. Modern scholarship, how-ever, has come to accept that the second part was not the work of the great 8th-century prophet. This view seems to have been scientifically verified by a rather unexpected instrument of biblical research. In 1970 a lecturer at the Haifa Technion obtained his doctorate at the Hebrew University of Jerusalem for a thesis based on a computer analysis of the Book of Isaiah. On such criteria as word frequency and sentence con-struction, the statistics showed odds of 100,000 to 1 against the two parts having derived from the same author.

Dividing the authorship has clarified the message. The later part of the Book (at any rate Chapters 40-55) was written not only by a different prophet, but in a profoundly different historical context. The original Isaiah addressed himself to his fellow-citizens in a Jewish State. The later unknown prophet preached to a community uprooted from its homeland and flung down onto the alien soil of the Babylonian diaspora. What mattered at that stage was that the Israelites should cling to their identity and ancestral faith until they should return.

The authorities tend to regard Chapters 56-66 as relating to a still later period, after the return and the reconstruction of the Temple – that is, in the period of Ezra and Nehemiah. If so, this 'Third Isaiah' may be the work of disciples of the Second Isaiah, whose style and thought are generally maintained, though the set-ting appears to be Jerusalem and no longer the Baby-lonian exile. [Book of Isaiah]

The Dead Sea Scrolls

On 29 November 1947, Dr Eleazar Sukenik, Professor of Archaeology at the Hebrew University in Jerusalem, bought three scrolls through an Armenian dealer in the Old City. They turned out to be some two thousand years old, older than any Hebrew biblical documents known till then.

Five years later, Dr Sukenik's son and successor, Professor Yigael Yadin, bought four more scrolls that had been in the possession of the Syrian Metropolitan of the Monastery of St Mark in the Old City of Jerusalem.

These priceless manuscripts had been discovered in 1946 by Bedouin shepherds in a cave overlooking the Dead Sea. They had belonged to a Jewish sect living

about the 1st century BC in a nearby monastery at Qumran on the shore of the Dead Sea, close to the freshwater springs of Ein Feshka. The remains of the monastery have been excavated, and thousands of fragments of other scrolls have been gathered from the floor of the original cave, and other caves in the vicinity.

The scrolls include:

Isaiah (MS 1) (complete and in good state of preservation)
Isaiah (MS 2) (incomplete and in poor state of preservation)
The Thanksgiving Scroll
The War of the Sons of Light and Darkness
Habbakuk Commentary
Manual of Discipline
Genesis Apocryphon (formerly called the Lamech Scroll).

Two copper scrolls were also found, and purport to describe a number of places where a great quantity of gold and silver treasure was buried.

The complete Isaiah scroll (MS 1) is 24 feet long, and is made of seventeen leather sheets sewn to each other with linen thread. It contains all sixty-six chapters, set out in fifty-four columns. The scribe made a number of mistakes, which he corrected later, while several pas-sages carelessly omitted by him were later added by someone else.

The second Isaiah scroll (MS 2) was very difficult to unroll, for the columns were stuck together and the leather parchment partially decomposed. It could be

The Shrine of the Book in Jerusalem which houses the Dead Sea Scrolls. The Isaiah Scroll consisting of seventeen leather sheets sewn together, is wound round the central drum.

partly deciphered by the use of infra-red photography.

Before the discovery of these scrolls, the earliest known version of the Hebrew Bible was the Masoretic Text, completed in the 9th century AD. Written a thousand years earlier, the Isaiah scrolls are nearly identical with the Masoretic version.

The Dead Sea Scrolls are on display in the specially built Shrine of the Book at the Israel Museum in Jerusalem.

ISCAH (Heb. 'who looks') *c.* 18 century BC. Daughter of Abraham's brother Haran. [Gen. 11:29]

ISHBAH (Heb. 'praising') date unknown. A leader of the tribe of Judah, he was the father of Eshtemoa. [1 Chr. 4:17]

ISHBAK *c.* 18 century BC. A son of Abraham and his wife Keturah, he became a desert chief east of Canaan. [Gen. 25:2; 1 Chr. 1:32]

ISHBI-BENOB (Heb. 'man sitting in Nob') *c.* 10 century BC. A Philistine giant who, armed with a new sword, sought to kill David but was himself killed by Abishai. [2 Sam. 21:16]

ISHBOSHETH (Heb. 'a man of shame') *c.* 11 century BC. The fourth son of Saul. When Saul was killed in battle, his commander-in-chief Abner took Ishbosheth, Saul's forty-year-old son, over the Jordan to Mahanaim and made him king. David had meanwhile become king of Judah, with his capital in Hebron. A long-drawn conflict developed between north and south.

One day Ishbosheth took Abner to task for having an affair with Rizpah, one of Saul's concubines. Abner was furious. He lost patience with the puppet king he had set up and made his peace with David. David insisted on the return of Saul's daughter Michal who had been his first wife. Her brother Ishbosheth sent her with Abner, ignoring the distress of the second husband Saul had given her.

Ishbosheth heard that Abner had been murdered and 'his courage failed, and all Israel was dismayed' (2 Sam. 4:1). Two of Saul's officers, Baanah and his brother Rechab, decided to murder Ishbosheth. At noon, while the king lay on his bed, they managed to get to his room and 'they smote him' (2 Sam. 4:7). The brothers then hacked off his head and escaped. Expecting a reward they brought the head to David at Hebron. The shocked David turned on them for having slain 'a righteous man in his own house upon his bed' (2 Sam. 4:11), and commanded his men to kill them. He then had the head of Ishbosheth buried in the tomb of Abner in Hebron. The way was now open for David to become ruler over the whole kingdom. Also called Eshbaal. [2 Sam. 2:8, 10, 12; 3:1; 4; 1 Chr. 8:33; 9:39]

ISHHOD (Heb. 'famed') *c.* 15 century BC. Son of Hammolecheth who was the sister of Gilead, a leader of the tribe of Manesseh. [1 Chr. 7:18]

ISHI (Heb. 'saving') **1.** date unknown. Son of Appaim

of the tribe of Judah, and the father of Sheshan, a leader of the tribe. [1 Chr. 2:31]

2. date unknown. A leader of the tribe of Judah, descended from Caleb. [1 Chr. 4:20]

3. date unknown. One of the leaders of the tribe of Manasseh living east of the Jordan and a mighty warrior. [1 Chr. 5:24]

4. *c.* 8 century BC. Head of a family of Simeon in the days of King Hezekiah of Judah. [1 Chr. 4:42]

ISHMA date unknown. A leader of the tribe of Judah. [1 Chr. 4:3]

ISHMAEL (Heb. 'God hears') **1.** *c.* 18 century BC. Son of Abraham by Hagar.

When Sarah's Egyptian slave Hagar became pregnant by Abraham, Sarah's jealousy was aroused. Hagar fled into the desert, but the angel of the Lord persuaded her to return. He told her that she would bear a son called Ishmael and that 'He shall be a wild ass of a man, his hand against every man and every man's hand against him' (Gen. 16:12).

When Ishmael was thirteen, he was circumcised together with his father Abraham and the other males of the household, as a physical mark of the covenant between God and Abraham.

In her old age, Sarah bore a son Isaac. She felt Hagar was mocking her, and in order to placate his wife, Abraham sent Hagar and Ishmael away. They wandered in the desert, and when their water was finished Hagar left the boy under a shrub to die. But they were saved by the miraculous appearance of a well.

They settled down in that part of the Sinai desert known as the wilderness of Paran, where Ishmael became a noted archer. His mother obtained a wife for him from her own native land, Egypt. Ishmael had twelve sons, who became the 'princes' of the tribes (rather like the sons of Jacob who are identified with the twelve Tribes of Israel). Ishmael died at the age of one hundred and thirty-seven years.

By Jewish and Moslem tradition Ishmael came to be regarded as the ancestor of the nomad desert tribes, particularly those inhabiting the area from the Sinai desert across the Negev to southern Jordan. The Hebrews considered themselves superior to these primitive (and usually hostile) desert kinsmen, descended from the common forefather Abraham. The Arabs on their part venerate Ishmael as their forefather, and there is a Moslem legend that he and his mother Hagar are buried in the sacred Ka'aba at Mecca. It is interesting that in some Arab tribes male children are circumcised at the age of thirteen, as Ishmael was in the Bible story. [Gen. 16, 17, 25, 36:3; 1 Chr. 1:28-31]

2. date unknown. Son of Azel of the tribe of Benjamin and a descendant of King Saul. [1 Chr. 8:38; 9:44]

3. *c.* 9 century BC. Father of Zebadiah who was in charge of King Jehoshaphat's affairs. [2 Chr. 19:11]

left Ishmael took
an Egyptian wife.
Limestone statuette
of a kneeling
woman from Egypt,
12th dynasty.

ten men, attacked and killed Gedaliah and the Jews
and the Chaldeans who were with him ...' (2 Kgs.
25:25). The following day, before anyone knew of the
murder, eighty men arrived at Mizpah, bringing offerings for the Temple. Ishmael lured them into Gedaliah's
house where he and his men killed them and threw their
bodies into a cistern. Only ten men were allowed to live
as they promised to show Ishmael where great stores
of wheat, barley, oil and honey were hidden. Ishmael
then took prisoner everyone left at Mizpah and set out
to cross the Jordan river to the Ammonites.

When the news of Ishmael's crimes reached the other
army commanders, headed by Johanan, they set out
with a force and caught up with Ishmael at Gibeon.
As soon as the prisoners saw Johanan, they broke away
and joined him but Ishmael and eight men escaped and
crossed the river. Johanan, fearing he and his comrades
would be blamed for Ishmael's crimes, fled to Egypt,
taking Jeremiah and Baruch with him. [2 Kgs. 25:23-25;
Jer. 40, 41]

6. 5 century BC. Son of Pasphur, the priest, he divorced
his non-Jewish wife in the time of Ezra. [Ezra 10:22]

ISHMAIAH (Heb. 'may God hear') **1.** *c.* 11 century
BC. A mighty warrior of Gibeon who deserted from the
army of King Saul and rallied to David at Ziklag. [1
Chr. 12:4]

2. *c.* 10 century BC. Son of Obadiah, he was appointed
by King David as ruler over the tribe of Zebulun. [1
Chr. 27:19]

ISHMERAI (Heb. 'God guards') date unknown. Son
of Elpaal, he was a leader of the tribe of Benjamin living
in Jerusalem. [1 Chr. 8:18]

ISHPAH date unknown. Son of Beriah, he was a
leader of the tribe of Benjamin living in Jerusalem. [1
Chr. 8:16]

ISHPAN date unknown. Son of Shashak, he was a
leader of the tribe of Benjamin living in Jerusalem. [1
Chr. 8:22]

ISHVAH (Heb. 'resembles') *c.* 16 century BC. Son of
Asher, he went down to Egypt with his grandfather
Jacob. [Gen. 46:17; 1 Chr. 7:30]

ISHVI (Heb. 'quiet') **1.** *c.* 16 century BC. Son of Asher,
he went down to Egypt at the same time as his grandfather Jacob. [Gen. 46:17; Num. 26:44; 1 Chr. 7:30]

2. *c.* 11 century BC. Son of King Saul and a younger
brother of Jonathan. [1 Sam. 14:49]

ISMACHIAH (Heb. 'may God support') *c.* 9 century
BC. A Levite who supervised the bringing of offerings
and tithes to the Temple in the reign of Hezekiah, king
of Judah. [2 Chr. 31:13]

ISRAEL *see* JACOB

ISSACHAR (Heb. 'rewarded') **1.** *c.* 16 century BC.
Issachar was the ninth son of Jacob and the fifth son
born to Leah. Thinking she was past childbearing age,
his mother had given her maid Zilpah to Jacob as a

Ishmael was saved in the desert by
the miraculous appearance of a well.
The nomads of Sinai still depend
on wells for their water.

4. *c.* 9 century BC. Son of Jehohanan, he was one of the
five army commanders of Judah to obey the orders of
the high priest Jehoiada to crown Joash king and
execute Queen Athaliah who had usurped the throne.
[2 Chr. 23:1]

5. *c.* 6 century BC. The murderer of Gedaliah, governor
of Jerusalem.

Ishmael, the son of Nethaniah, was a member of the
royal house of Judah. After the fall of Jerusalem and
the appointment by the Babylonians of Gedaliah as
governor, Ishmael and a group of commanders, still
roaming the countryside with their men, came to see
him in his residence at Mizpah, just north of Jerusalem.
Gedaliah urged them to co-operate with the Babylonian
conquerors. But two months later Ishmael 'came with

The fertile eastern end of the Jezreel Valley which was given to the tribe of Issachar.

concubine, so when this child was born she said, 'God has given me my hire because I gave my maid to my husband.' (Gen. 30:18) Together with his brothers he was involved in the events that led to the selling of their brother Joseph into slavery in Egypt. Later he was one of the ten sons sent by Jacob to buy corn in Egypt, where Joseph had become a leading figure at the court of Pharaoh. When Jacob went to settle in Egypt with all his family it included Issachar and his four sons.

On his deathbed Jacob blessed all his sons in turn, and said, 'Issachar is a strong ass, crouching between the sheepfolds.' (Gen. 49:14)

In the blessing attributed to Moses, it is said: 'They shall call peoples to their mountain; there they offer right sacrifices.' (Deut. 33:19)

In the conquest of Canaan under Joshua, the tribe of Issachar was allocated an area across the eastern end of the valley of Jezreel. [Gen. 30:18; 35:23; 46:13; 49:14; Exod. 1:3; 1 Chr. 2:1; 7:1]

2. *c.* 10 century BC. Seventh son of Obed-edom, a Levite, who, like his father and his family, was a gate-keeper of the Tabernacle in the reign of King David. [1 Chr. 26:5]

ISSHIAH (Heb. 'there is God') **1.** date unknown. The son of Izrahiah and a leader of the tribe of Issachar. [1 Chr. 7:3]

2. *c.* 11 century BC. One of the soldiers who deserted from the army of King Saul and joined David at Ziklag. [1 Chr. 12:6]

3. *c.* 10 century BC. A Levite descended from Uzziel who ministered in the Tabernacle in the reign of King David. [1 Chr. 23:20; 24:25]

4. *c.* 10 century BC. A Levite descended from Rehabiah who served in the Tabernacle in the reign of King David. [1 Chr. 24:21]

ISSHIJAH (Heb. 'there is God') 5 century BC. A descendant of Harim who divorced his non-Jewish wife in the time of Ezra. [Ezra 10:31]

ITHAI (Heb. 'God is with me') *c.* 10 century BC. A Benjaminite warrior in the army of King David distinguished for his bravery. Also called Ittai. [2 Sam. 23:29; 1 Chr. 11:31]

ITHAMAR (Heb. 'island of the palm tree') *c.* 13 century BC. Youngest son of Aaron and Elisheba, he was consecrated as a priest by Moses together with his father and his three brothers. He was given the task of listing the gifts brought for the tabernacle, and of supervising its transport and erection.

Ithamar became the founder of a line of priests, though it was smaller than that of his brother Eleazar. The priest Eli traced his ancestry to Ithamar. His descendants came back from exile in Babylon with Ezra. [Exod. 6:23; 28:1; 38:21; Lev. 10:6, 16; Num. 3:2, 4; 4:28, 33; 7:8; 26:60; 1 Chr. 6:3, 24:1-6]

ITHIEL (Heb. 'God is with me') **1.** date unknown. An ancestor of Sallu, one of the first Benjaminites to settle in Jerusalem after the return from exile in Babylon. [Neh. 11:7]

2. date unknown. One of the two men to whom Agur, son of Jakeh, directed his teachings. [Prov. 30:1]

ITHMAH *c.* 10 century BC. A Moabite warrior who fought in the armies of King David and was distinguished for his bravery. [1 Chr. 11:46]

ITHRA *see* JETHER **5.**

ITHRAN 1. date unknown. Son of Dishon and a grandson of Seir the Horite. [Gen. 36:26; 1 Chr. 1:41]

2. date unknown. Son of Zophah and a leader of the tribe of Asher. [1 Chr. 7:37]

ITHREAM (Heb. 'populous') *c.* 10 century BC. Son of King David and his wife Eglah, he was born in Hebron. [2 Sam. 3:5; 1 Chr. 3:3]

ITTAI (Heb. 'with me') **1.** *c.* 10 century BC. A Philistine who joined David in exile, when Absalom staged his revolt against his father David. His followers included a detachment of six hundred Gittites from the Philistine city of Gath, led by Ittai. David tried to persuade Ittai to return 'for you are a foreigner, and also an exile' (2 Sam. 15:19). Ittai answered with a ringing declaration of loyalty: '... wherever my lord the king shall be, whether for death or for life, there also will your servant be.' (2 Sam. 15:21) So Ittai and his men joined David at Mahanaim in the land of Gilead across the Jordan river. When David reorganized his forces to meet Absalom, he divided his army into three parts and placed them under the command of Joab, Abishai and Ittai. Absalom was defeated and killed and David's kingdom saved. [2 Sam. 15:19-22; 18:2-12]

2. *see* ITHAI

IZHAR (Heb. 'oil') *c.* 13 century BC. Son of Kohath and head of an important family of Levites who served in the Tabernacle in the wilderness. Izhar's son Korah led a rebellion against Moses and Aaron. [Exod. 6:18; Num. 3:19, 27; 16:1; 1 Chr. 6:2, 18, 38; 23:12, 18]

IZLIAH date unknown. Son of Elpaal and a leader of the tribe of Benjamin living in Jerusalem. [1 Chr. 8:18]

IZRAHIAH (Heb. 'may God shine forth') date unknown. Son of Uzzi of the tribe of Issachar, he and his family were mighty warriors and leaders of the tribe. [1 Chr. 7:3]

IZRI *see* ZERI

IZZIAH 5 century BC. A descendant of Parosh, he divorced his non-Jewish wife in the time of Ezra. [Ezra 10:25]

J

JAAKAN date unknown. A descendant of Seir the Horite who became an Edomite leader. Also called Akan. [Gen. 36:27; 1 Chr. 1:42]

JAAKOBAH (Heb. 'will protect') *c.* 8 century BC. One of the leaders of the tribe of Simeon in the reign of King Hezekiah of Judah, who drove out the native population from the Gedor valley and settled there. [1 Chr. 4:36]

JAALA (Heb. 'wild goat') *c.* 10 century BC. A servant of King Solomon whose descendants returned with Zerubbabel from exile in Babylon. Also called Jaalah. [Ezra 2:56; Neh. 7:58]

JAALAH *see* JAALA

JAAREOREGIM *see* JAIR 3.

JAARESHIAH date unknown. Son of Jeroham, he was a leader of the tribe of Benjamin living in Jerusalem. [1 Chr. 8:27]

JAASIEL (Heb. 'made by God') **1.** *c.* 10 century BC. The Mezobaite warrior in the armies of King David distinguished for his bravery. [1 Chr. 11:47]
2. *c.* 10 century BC. Son of Abner, he was leader of the tribe of Benjamin in the reign of King David. [1 Chr. 27:21]

JAASU (Heb. 'created') 5 century BC. One of the descendants of Bani who divorced his non-Jewish wife in the time of Ezra. [Ezra 10:37]

JAAZANIAH (Heb. 'may God hear') **1.** *c.* 6 century BC. One of the four army captains who promised loyalty to Gedaliah when the Babylonians made him governor of Judah. Also called Jezaniah. [2 Kgs. 25:23; Jer. 40:8]
2. 6 century BC. Head of the ascetic family of Rechabites in the days of the prophet Jeremiah who refused to drink wine with him, holding to his vow of abstinence. [Jer. 35:3]
3. *c.* 6 century BC. Son of Shaphan, he was one of the seventy elders of Israel seen by the prophet Ezekiel committing idolatry in a cellar in the Temple building. Jaazaniah is the only person mentioned by name and was probably the most important of them. [Ezek. 8:11]
4. *c.* 6 century BC. Son of Azzur, he was one of the men condemned by Ezekiel for their false prophecies concerning Judah. [Ezek. 11:1]

JAAZIAH (Heb. 'may God strengthen') *c.* 10 century

Onyx seal, 10th-6th centuries BC, with the inscription: '[belonging] to Ya'azanyahu, servant of the king'. This may refer to Jaazaniah.

BC. A Levite whose descendants served in the Tabernacle during the reign of King David. [1 Chr. 24:26, 27]

JAAZIEL (Heb. 'may God strengthen') *c.* 10 century BC. A Levite in the reign of King David who played a musical instrument when the Ark of God was brought to Jerusalem. Also called Aziel. [1 Chr. 15:18, 20]

JABAL (Heb. 'stream') date unknown. Son of Lamech and his wife Adah, he is described as 'the father of those that dwell in tents and have cattle'. [Gen. 4:20]

JABESH (Heb. 'dry') *c.* 8 century BC. Father of Shallum, one of the last kings of Israel. [2 Kgs. 15:10, 13-14]

JABEZ (Heb. 'sorrow') date unknown. A leader of the tribe of Judah and a pious man, he is described as being 'more honourable than his brothers'. [1 Chr. 4:9, 10]

JABIN (Heb. 'he understands') **1.** *c.* 13 century BC. Jabin was the Canaanite king of Hazor in the north of the country who organized a confederation of local kings to fight against the Israelites. They met at the Waters of Merom but, with the Lord's help, Joshua defeated them. Then Joshua 'turned back at that time, and took Hazor, and smote its king with the sword' (Josh. 11:10). [Josh. 11:1-15]

2. *c.* 12 century BC. The Canaanite king of Hazor in the time of the Judges who oppressed the Israelites and whose general Sisera was defeated by Deborah and Barak. 'And the hand of the people of Israel bore harder and harder on Jabin the king of Canaan.' (Judg. 4:24) [Judg. 4; Ps. 83:9]

JACAN (Heb. 'affliction') date unknown. Head of a family of the tribe of Gad living in Bashan. [1 Chr. 5:13]

Bronze plaque from Hazor, 16th-13th centuries BC, showing a Canaanite man, possibly of the time of King Jabin.

JACHIN (Heb. 'established') **1.** *c.* 16 century BC. A son of Simeon and grandson of Jacob and Leah. Also called Jarib. [Gen. 46:10; Exod. 6:15; Num. 26:12; 1 Chr. 4:24]

2. *c.* 10 century BC. A priest in the Tabernacle in the reign of King David, he took the twenty-first turn of service. [1 Chr. 24:17]

3. 5 century BC. A priest living in Jerusalem in the days of Nehemiah. [1 Chr. 9:10; Neh. 11:10]

above left Jabal, 'the father of those that dwell in tents and have cattle': relief from Florence Cathedral.

left Wadi Limon in northern Galilee, possibly the place where Joshua and the Israelites routed Jabin, king of Hazor.

JACOB (Heb. 'supplanted') *c.* 16 century BC. Third patriarch.

After years of childlessness, Isaac's wife Rebekah had twin sons. While still in their mother's womb 'The children struggled together' (Gen. 25:22). Esau, the first-born, was at birth covered with red hair. He grew up to be a hunter and the favourite of his father. Jacob was born clutching his brother's heel. (The Hebrew name *Ya'acov* is derived from *ekev*, 'the heel of the foot'.) He became a herdsman and cultivator and his mother loved him more than she did Esau.

Isaac and he blessed Jacob saying: 'Let peoples serve you, and nations bow down to you. Be lord over your brothers.' (Gen. 27:29) Esau hated Jacob because of the stolen blessing and threatened to kill him after Isaac's death. Rebekah felt it would be prudent to get Jacob out of the way. She persuaded Isaac to send the young man to her brother Laban in Haran (northern Syria) where he would find a bride among Laban's daughters, instead of marrying a Canaanite girl as Esau had already done.

On his way northward from Beersheba to his uncle

far left Egyptian stele, 13th century BC, bearing the only mention in Egyptian writing of the name 'Israel', first given to Jacob by the angel.

left Jacob was a tiller of the soil. Egyptian model of a man ploughing, 21st-18th centuries BC.

below The Gezer Calendar, 925 BC, which divides the year into the agricultural periods of sowing, hoeing, harvesting, etc., including one month for resting.

One day Esau came back from hunting, faint with hunger. In exchange for a meal of bread and red lentil soup, Jacob obtained from Esau his birthright, that is, his rights as the eldest son.

When Isaac was old and practically blind, he sent for Esau and asked him to go hunting, and to prepare a dish of venison, which Isaac loved. He would then bestow the paternal blessing on Esau. Rebekah overheard this, and decided to obtain the blessing for Jacob instead. She sent Jacob to select two kids from the flock, cooked them to taste like venison and told Jacob to take them into his father, pretending to be Esau. Jacob demurred, pointing out that 'My brother Esau is a hairy man, and I am a smooth man.' (Gen. 27:11) To overcome this difficulty Rebekah wrapped pieces of the fleece of the kids over his hands and the back of his neck and dressed him in Esau's garments.

Even after Isaac had touched Jacob, he was still suspicious and said, 'The voice is Jacob's voice, but the hands are the hands of Esau.' (Gen. 27:22) But the smell of the field clinging to Esau's clothes satisfied approaching with her father's sheep. Jacob introduced himself, kissed his cousin and helped her draw water for the sheep. Rachel ran and told Laban, who came out to embrace this kinsman from a distant land.

Jacob fell in love with Rachel who was 'beautiful and lovely' (Gen. 29:17); but he was told he would have to work for seven years for her father before he could marry her. At the end of that time Laban arranged a wedding feast. Jacob spent the wedding night with his bride and was shocked to find next morning that Laban had substituted for Rachel her older and plainer sister, Leah. When reproached, Laban claimed that by the custom of his country the elder daughter should be wedded first. Jacob was allowed to marry Rachel as well a week later, on undertaking to work another seven years for his father-in-law.

When that period had gone by, Jacob continued to

Jacob's dream, from a 13th-century Parisian manuscript. On the right, Jacob makes his sacrifice.

When Jacob arrived in the land of the 'people of the east', he saw a well covered over by a stone. This present-day well works on the same principle.

Laban, the weary Jacob sank down on the ground to sleep at night, with his head against a stone. Here he dreamt he saw a ladder rising up to heaven, with angels going up and down on it. The Lord stood at the top and spoke to him, reaffirming the promise made to Abraham that his seed would multiply. 'Behold, I am with you and will keep you wherever you go, and will bring you back to this land.' (Gen. 28:15) Jacob woke from this dream and said with awe, 'Surely the Lord is in this place; and I did not know it. . . . This is none other than the house of God, and this is the gate of heaven.' (Gen. 28:16, 17) Early next morning he set up and anointed with oil the stone that had served as his pillow and called the place Bethel ('the House of the Lord'). It was the same spot where Abraham had earlier made a sacrifice to the Lord. Bethel remained a holy place for the Israelites. The site is some twelve miles north of Jerusalem off the main highway.

The Stay in Haran

Jacob went on his way and reached Haran. He stopped at a well where flocks of sheep were waiting to be watered. In answer to his question the shepherds said they knew Laban and pointed out his daughter Rachel

serve Laban. As payment he asked to be allowed to keep for himself all the speckled and streaked goats, and all the dark-coloured sheep. Laban agreed to these terms but that day sent off with his sons all the animals marked in such a way. Jacob cut wands of poplar, hazel and chestnut trees, peeled white streaks in them and stuck them at the watering troughs. As a result of the visual suggestion, the goats conceived at the trough were born speckled or streaked. Jacob used this device to breed from the stronger animals, leaving the offspring of the weaker ones to Laban. After several years, Jacob owned large flocks of his own and acquired his own servants, camels and asses. It was not surprising that Laban and his sons resented the fact that Jacob had gained so much of the family wealth.

By now twenty years had gone by since Jacob had first met Rachel at the well, and he decided the time had come to return to his own country. He departed quietly when Laban was away sheep-shearing and moved southward towards Canaan with his two wives, his two concubines (the handmaids of his wives) and his children mounted on camels, and his flocks.

At this time Jacob had eleven sons and one daughter. The children of Leah were Reuben, Simeon, Levi, Judah, Issachar, Zebulun and Dinah; Leah's maid Zilpah bore Gad and Asher; the two sons of Bilhah, Rachel's maid, were Dan and Naphtali; Rachel herself gave birth to Joseph, after she had been childless for many years.

When Laban discovered that Jacob had gone, he and his kinsmen set out in pursuit. They caught up with Jacob's caravan seven days later in the mountains of Gilead, east of the Jordan river. Laban protested against the surreptitious way Jacob had gone off with his daughters and his grandchildren. He also accused Jacob of stealing the 'teraphim', the images of his household gods. Jacob indignantly denied this charge and invited Laban to go through his tents. He did not know that the images had been taken by Rachel, who hid them in the saddlebag of her camel and sat upon them while her father searched in vain. Rachel and Leah had felt cheated of their dowries by their father: 'Are we not regarded by him as foreigners? For he has sold us, and he has been using up the money given for us.' (Gen. 31:15)

Jacob and Laban agreed to part in peace, and in accordance with custom, sealed their pact by assembling a heap of stones, and partaking of food together upon them. Jacob called the place Galeed ('the heap of witness'), which explains the name of Gilead given to that region.

Laban and his party turned back, and Jacob continued southward. He had a vision of a host of angels welcoming him and called the place Mahanaim ('hosts' or 'camps'). Jacob's party descended from the plateau of Gilead into the deep gorge of the Jabbok river, a tributary flowing into the lower Jordan. His family and retainers crossed at the ford before sundown, but Jacob lingered behind and suddenly found himself wrestling in the dark with a mysterious stranger. The struggle continued until daybreak, when the other tried to get away, but Jacob held on to him until he obtained his blessing. The stranger said to Jacob that henceforth he would be known as Israel ('who prevails with God') 'for you have striven with God and with men, and have prevailed' (Gen. 32:28). During the fight Jacob's adversary had struck the inside of his thigh, causing the sinew to shrink. (Since then Jews are forbidden to eat that sinew in animals.) Jacob called the place Peniel ('the face of God').

This strange experience at the ford is related by some scholars to the primitive legends of river gods that accost travellers, but that, like all spirits, must vanish again before dawn.

Jacob's twin brother Esau had settled in the land of Seir, the rugged, semi-arid country of Edom to the east and south of the Dead Sea. Jacob sent messengers to inform Esau that he had returned, and suggesting that they meet. The messengers came back to report that Esau was advancing towards him with four hundred men, and Jacob was afraid that his wronged brother was seeking revenge. He turned to the Lord for protection; but also sent ahead a large number of choice sheep, goats, cattle and camels to placate Esau. Jacob divided his servants and the rest of his flock into two groups, so that if Esau attacked one group, the other might escape.

His fears proved groundless. When Esau arrived, Jacob bowed down to the ground before him: 'But Esau ran to meet him, and embraced him, and fell on his neck and kissed him, and they wept.' (Gen. 33:4) After Jacob had presented his women and children, Esau courteously declined the gift of livestock, saying he already had enough animals of his own. Jacob insisted that he keep them as a mark of goodwill.

Return to Canaan

Esau invited his brother to return with him to Seir but Jacob pleaded that he had to travel slowly because of his young children and the lambs. Esau rode ahead, but Jacob did not follow, continuing instead on his way to Canaan. He lived for some while at Succoth ('booths'), at the edge of the Jordan valley; then he moved across the river to Shalem, near the town of Shechem (present-day Nablus) in the hills of Samaria. Here he bought a parcel of land from Hamor, the leader of the local Hivite clan, and erected an altar on it.

Jacob's daughter Dinah became friendly with the local girls and was seen by Hamor's son Shechem, who seized and raped her. Hamor sought permission from Jacob for Shechem to marry Dinah, and further proposed that his clan and Jacob's should intermarry and merge with each other. Concealing their rage at Dinah's seduction, her brothers pretended to agree to Hamor's proposal provided that he, Shechem and all the other males of their clan would first be circumcised, as the Israelites were. This was done, but before the men had recovered from the painful operation, Jacob's sons Simeon and Levi killed them all and despoiled the town.

Jacob bitterly reproached his two sons for this bloody act of vengeance, and was afraid it would arouse the population of the surrounding area against them. He decided to move to the sanctuary at Bethel, twelve miles further south. But first he insisted that all the members of his household should purify themselves, change their clothes, and surrender to him their idolatrous images and magic amulets, which he buried under

Tel Beersheba. Here Jacob offered a sacrifice and the Lord promised to go down with him to Egypt and to bring his people up again.

an oak tree at Shechem. To his relief, the local inhabitants did not pursue or attack him during this anxious journey – perhaps because word of the killing at Shechem had already spread, and they were afraid. At Bethel, Jacob restored the altar he had erected twenty years previously, after his dream of the ladder ascending to heaven.

They proceeded on their way towards Hebron, where the aged Isaac, Jacob's father, was still alive. Near Bethlehem, Rachel died in giving birth to a boy, whom Jacob named Benjamin ('son of my right hand'). Rachel was buried there, and Jacob erected a pillar as a monument over her grave.

Soon after, Isaac died at the age of a hundred and eighty and his two sons, Jacob and Esau, buried him in the Cave of Machpelah, the family tomb. This was the last time the twin brothers saw each other.

Jacob's favourite son was Joseph, born in his old age of his beloved Rachel, and the youngest of the twelve brothers except for the baby Benjamin. His father pampered him and dressed him in a coat of many colours; but he incurred the envy and dislike of his brothers.

When Joseph was seventeen, Jacob sent him to find his brothers, who had trekked northwards with the flocks in search of pasture. They sold the youth to a passing caravan, stained his coat with the blood of a slaughtered kid and produced it to Jacob, saying they had found it in the fields. Jacob assumed that Joseph had been killed by a wild beast, and mourned him in deep grief.

Many years later, during a famine, Jacob sent his ten sons to Egypt to buy wheat, keeping at home young Benjamin. Pharaoh's powerful governor allowed them to buy the wheat only on the undertaking that they would return with their younger brother. Simeon was held in Egypt as a hostage. They had no inkling that the governor was their long-lost brother Joseph. Jacob refused to part with Benjamin. However, when they had consumed the food brought from Egypt and the famine continued, his sons prevailed upon him to yield. This time Joseph revealed his identity to the brothers, and there was a tearful reunion. Joseph proposed they should fetch Jacob and the rest of the family from Canaan and settle in the fertile Egyptian province of Goshen, in the eastern corner of the Nile delta. He would then be able to care for them in the five years of famine which he knew were still to come. Pharaoh gave his approval, and ordered that wagons should be provided for the purpose.

Jacob at first refused to believe that the youth thought slain so long ago had suddenly reappeared in Egypt. Persuaded by the sight of the wagons and the lavish gifts of food Joseph had sent, the old man said simply, 'It is enough; Joseph my son is still alive; I will go and see him before I die.' (Gen. 45:28)

Three generations of Jacob's family, numbering seventy souls, set out from Hebron together with his servants, flocks, herds and household goods. They stopped at Beersheba where Jacob's father Isaac had dwelt, and here he offered parting sacrifices to God before leaving the land of Canaan. The Lord renewed to him the promise first made to his grandfather Abraham, saying: '. . . do not be afraid to go down to Egypt; for I will there make of you a great nation. I will go down with you to Egypt, and I will also bring you up again.' (Gen. 46:3, 4)

(This promise of a return was to be redeemed some four centuries later in the time of Moses.)

They crossed the Sinai desert and reached Goshen. Judah was sent to inform Joseph, who came by chariot to meet them and flung himself weeping on his father's neck. Joseph presented his father and five of his brothers to Pharaoh, on whom Jacob bestowed a blessing. Pharaoh was told that Joseph's family had been shepherds and cattle-men for generations, and suggested that they might take charge of the royal flocks.

Jacob dwelt for seventeen years in Goshen. Having heard that his father was failing, Joseph went to see him, and took with him his two sons Manasseh and Ephraim. Jacob adopted the boys as his own.

On his deathbed Jacob gathered all his sons around him and charged them to bury him with his forefathers in Canaan. The celebrated blessing attributed to him is composed of vivid poetic similes, and refers to the qualities in each of his twelve sons that would distinguish the Israelite tribe named after him:

Reuben, the first born, was dignified but unstable as water.

Simeon and Levi were cruel and angry men.

Judah was a lion's whelp and would rule.

Zebulun would dwell on the coast and be a seafarer.

Issachar was strong as an ass and would serve others.

Dan would judge his people.

Gad would be overcome but would win in the end.

Asher would be a successful tiller of the soil.

Naphtali was a hind let loose (a venturesome spirit).

Joseph was a fruitful bough, blessed by the Almighty.

Benjamin would be as aggressive as a wolf.

Jacob died at the age of one hundred and forty-seven, and Joseph arranged to have his body embalmed by Egyptian physicians. An impressive funeral caravan

14th-century BC limestone relief of an old man from Egypt, where Jacob died at the age of one hundred and forty-seven.

The Death of Jacob: drawing by
Rembrandt van Rijn, dated 1640-2.

wound its way out of Egypt and included all Jacob's
sons and, as a special mark of respect, members of
Pharaoh's household and other leading Egyptians. It
reached Hebron where Jacob was interred in the Cave
of Machpelah, together with Abraham and Sarah,
Isaac and Rebekah, and Jacob's first wife Leah. Joseph
returned to Pharaoh's court and his brothers to their
homes in Goshen.

The Character of Jacob

Jacob belongs to the patriarchal, pastoral society from
which the Hebrew people originated two thousand
years before the Christian era. Like his grandfather
Abraham and his father Isaac, he was a tent-dwelling
nomad who moved slowly in search of grazing and
water, with his wives and concubines, his many
children, his servants, flocks and herds.

Later writers – including the learned rabbis of the
Talmud – were hard put to explain the contradictions
in Jacob's character. By the standards of a later age,
it was embarrassing that so respected a patriarch should
in his youth have outwitted his brother, his father and
his uncle for his own gain. But the ancient chroniclers
of the Old Testament made no attempt to idealize their
forefathers. The deviousness of the young Jacob did

not seem wicked to the nomad world in which he lived,
nor did it detract from his stature or his many virtues.

The Bible calls Jacob an 'ish tam' – a plain or quiet
man. In all his long life he was peaceable and never
resorted to violence – on the contrary he was fearful
lest his aggrieved and more turbulent brother Esau
might attack him. He submitted to Laban's substitution of Leah for Rachel, and agreed to work another
seven years for the latter. His diligence and skill in
tending his father-in-law's flocks greatly increased their
numbers and value. To his wives and children Jacob
was kind and affectionate, with a tender love for
Rachel and for Joseph and Benjamin, the two sons
she bore him in his old age.

Above all, Jacob inherited from Abraham and Isaac
their intimate communion with God, and the promise
that Canaan would belong to their seed. With Jacob
this covenant was singularly marked by his dream at
Bethel, and by his wrestling with the angel at the ford
of Jabbok. Jacob's devotion to God made him spurn
the household images and magic amulets to which
members of his family clung. (At Shechem he made
them bury all these objects under a tree and purify
themselves.)

Jacob has a pivotal role in the Hebrew saga. The twelve Israelite tribes that occupied Canaan from Joshua's conquest traced their descent and their names back to his sons. The Hebrews were referred to collectively as the House of Jacob or the Children of Israel. The name of the biblical kingdom of Israel was adopted for the newly-proclaimed State of Israel in 1948. [Gen. 25; 27-37; 42; 45-50]

JADA (Heb. '[God] has cared') date unknown. Younger son of Onam and a leader of the tribe of Judah. [1 Chr. 2:28, 32]

JADDAI (Heb. 'God's friend') 5 century BC. A descendant of Nebo who divorced his non-Jewish wife in the time of Ezra. [Ezra 10:43]

JADDUA (Heb. 'known') **1.** 5 century BC. A leader of Judah who signed the covenant to follow the Laws of God in the time of Nehemiah. [Neh. 10:21]
2. 5 century BC. Son of Jonathan, a Levite of Judah after the return from exile in Babylon. [Neh. 12:11, 22]

JADON (Heb. 'he will judge') 5 century BC. A Meronothite who helped rebuild the walls of Jerusalem in the time of Nehemiah. [Neh. 3:7]

JAEL (Heb. 'deer') *c.* 12 century BC. A Kenite woman who killed Sisera.

Jael was the wife of Heber, a Kenite, whose family had peaceful relations with Jabin, king of Hazor. After the defeat of Jabin's army under Sisera by the Children of Israel, inspired by the prophetess Deborah and led by Barak, Sisera escaped eastward and came to Heber's encampment. Jael came out and invited him into her tent, gave him milk to drink, covered him up and stood

Jael was a tent-dweller like the Bedouin of Sinai, seen here with their flocks of goats at Wadi el-Arish.

Miniature churn found at Azor. The drink Jael gave Sisera would have been from a skin similar in shape to this.

guard outside. After he fell asleep she 'took a tent peg ... and drove the peg into his temple' (Judg. 4:21). When Barak came in pursuit of Sisera, Jael showed him Sisera lying dead in her tent.

According to Deborah's song of victory, Jael struck Sisera down when he came to her tent door and not while he was sleeping inside the tent. Neither account offers any explanation for her deed. [Judg. 4:17-22; 5:24-27]

JAHATH (Heb. 'may [God] allay his fear') **1.** date unknown. Son of Reaiah of the tribe of Judah. [1 Chr. 4:2]
2. date unknown. A Levite descended from Gershom. [1 Chr. 6:20, 43]
3. *c.* 10 century BC. Eldest son of Shimei the Levite, he served in the Tabernacle in the reign of King David. [1 Chr. 23:10, 11]
4. *c.* 10 century BC. Son of Shelomoth, the Levite, he served in the Tabernacle in the reign of King David. [1 Chr. 24:22]
5. 7 century BC. A Levite descended from Merari, he supervised the work of repairing the Temple in the days of King Josiah. [2 Chr. 34:12]

JAHAZIEL (Heb. 'seen of God') **1.** *c.* 10 century BC. A warrior of the tribe of Benjamin who left the army of King Saul and joined David at Ziklag. [1 Chr. 12:4]

2. *c.* 10 century BC. A priest who blew a trumpet during the celebrations following the bringing of the Ark of God to Jerusalem in the reign of King David. [1 Chr. 16:6]

3. *c.* 10 century BC. A descendant of Hebron, he and his family were leaders of the tribe of Levi who served in the Tabernacle. [1 Chr. 23:19; 24:23]

4. *c.* 9 century BC. Son of Zechariah of the tribe of Levi who prophesied that King Jehoshaphat would win a great victory against the invading armies of Moab and Ammon without needing to fight since God would fight the battle on Judah's behalf. His prophecy came true for the invading armies attacked each other and destroyed themselves. [2 Chr. 20:14-17]

5. 5 century BC. Father of Shecaniah who returned to Judah with Ezra from exile in Babylon. [Ezra 8:5]

JAHDAI (Heb. 'God leads') date unknown. A leader of the tribe of Judah descended from Caleb. [1 Chr. 2:47]

JAHDIEL (Heb. 'may God cause to rejoice') date unknown. A leader and warrior of the half-tribe of Manasseh east of the river Jordan. [1 Chr. 5:24]

JAHDO (Heb. 'joyful') date unknown. Son of Buz, a leader of the tribe of Gad living in Bashan east of the river Jordan. [1 Chr. 5:14]

JAHLEEL (Heb. 'waiting for God') *c.* 16 century BC. A son of Zebulun who went down to Egypt with his grandfather Jacob. [Gen. 46:14; Num. 26:26]

JAHMAI (Heb. 'guarded') date unknown. Son of Tola and a grandson of Issachar, he was one of the leaders of the tribe and a mighty warrior. [1 Chr. 7:2]

JAHZEEL (Heb. 'may God grant a portion') *c.* 16 century BC. A son of Naphtali, he went down to Egypt with his grandfather Jacob. Also called Jahziel. [Gen. 46:24; Num. 26:48; 1 Chr. 7:13]

JAHZEIAH (Heb. 'may God see') 5 century BC. Son of Tikvah, he was present when Ezra called on those inhabitants of Judah who had married non-Jewish wives to divorce them. [Ezra 10:15]

JAHZERAH date unknown. Ancestor of Maasai, who was one of the first priests to settle in Jerusalem after the return from exile in Babylon. Also called Ahzai. [1 Chr. 9:12; Neh. 11:13]

JAHZIEL *see* JAHZEEL

JAIR (Heb. 'enlightened') **1.** date unknown. Son of Manasseh and a grandson of Joseph, his descendants took possession of Gilead and Bashan, east of the river Jordan and called the territory Havvoth-jair in his honour. [Num. 32:41; Deut. 3:14; Josh. 13:30; 1 Kgs. 4:13]

2. *c.* 12 century BC. The eighth judge of Israel who ruled for twenty-two years. Born in Gilead he had thirty sons who rode on thirty asses and ruled over thirty

cities in Gilead called Havvoth-jair. [Judg. 10:3-5]

3. *c.* 10 century BC. Father of Elhanan who killed one of the Philistine giants. Also called Jaareoregim. [2 Sam. 21:19; 1 Chr. 20:5]

4. date unknown. Son of Segub of the tribe of Judah, he was ruler over twenty-three cities in the land of Gilead. [1 Chr. 2:22]

5. *c.* 5 century BC. An ancestor of Mordecai. [Esther 2:5]

JAKEH (Heb. 'pious') date unknown. Father of Agur whose words appear in the thirtieth chapter of Proverbs. [Prov. 30]

JAKIM (Heb. 'established') **1.** date unknown. A son of Shimei, he was a leader of the tribe of Benjamin living in Jerusalem. [1 Chr. 8:19]

2. *c.* 10 century BC. A priest in the reign of King David who was responsible for the twelfth turn of service in the Tabernacle. [1 Chr. 24:12]

JALAM (Heb. 'young') *c.* 16 century BC. Son of Esau and Oholibamah, he became a leader of a desert tribe in Edom. [Gen. 36:5, 14, 18; 1 Chr. 1:35]

JALON (Heb. 'seeks shelter [in God]') date unknown. One of the four sons of Ezrah of the tribe of Judah. [1 Chr. 4:17]

JAMIN (Heb. 'lucky') **1.** *c.* 16 century BC. A son of Simeon, he went down to Egypt with his grandfather Jacob. [Gen. 46:10; Exod. 6:15; Num. 26:12; 1 Chr. 4:24]

2. date unknown. Son of Ram and a grandson of Jerahmeel, he was a leader of the tribe of Judah. [1 Chr. 2:27]

3. 5 century BC. A leader of Judah who explained the law of Moses to the people after Ezra had read out the law in the market-place. [Neh. 8:7]

JAMLECH (Heb. 'God gives dominion') *c.* 8 century BC. One of the leaders of the tribe of Simeon, in the reign of King Hezekiah of Judah, who drove out the indigenous population from the Gedor valley and settled there instead. [1 Chr. 4:34]

JANAI (Heb. 'answered') date unknown. A leader of the tribe of Gad living in Bashan, east of the river Jordan. [1 Chr. 5:12]

JAPHETH (Heb. 'he enlarges') date unknown. Third son of Noah, Japheth and his family were in the ark with Noah during the great flood. When Noah was in a drunken sleep, Japheth and Shem discreetly 'covered the nakedness of their father' (Gen. 9:23). As a result Noah blessed Japheth and told him he would 'enlarge', that is, have many descendants.

He had seven sons: Gomer, Magog, Madai, Javan, Tubal, Meshech and Tiras. These sons became the legendary founders of northern peoples that inhabited areas from the Caspian Sea to the Greek islands. [Gen. 5:32; 6:10; 7:13; 9:18-27; 10:1-5; 1 Chr. 1:4-5]

JAPHIA (Heb. 'splendour') **1.** *c.* 13 century BC. King of Lachish in the days of Joshua, he joined the Canaanite alliance against Joshua and was defeated in battle and executed. [Josh. 10:3, 23]

2. *c.* 10 century BC. One of the sons of King David born to him in Jerusalem. [2 Sam. 5:15; 1 Chr. 3:7; 14:6]

JAPHLET (Heb. 'delivered') date unknown. Eldest son of Heber, he was a leader of the tribe of Asher and a mighty warrior. [1 Chr. 7:32, 33]

JARAH (Heb. 'honeycomb') date unknown. Son of Ahaz of the tribe of Benjamin, a descendant of King Saul. Also known as Jehoaddah. [1 Chr. 8:36; 9:42]

JARED (Heb. 'descent') date unknown. Father of Enoch and the grandfather of Methuselah. [Gen. 5:15-20; 1 Chr. 1:2]

JARHA date unknown. An Egyptian servant who married the daughter of his master Sheshan, a leader of Judah. [1 Chr. 2:34, 35]

JARIB (Heb. 'God defends') **1.** see JACHIN 1.

2. 5 century BC. A leader of Judah sent by Nehemiah to Iddo, with instructions to bring Levites to Jerusalem to serve in the Temple. [Ezra 8:16]

3. 5 century BC. One of the priests who divorced his non-Jewish wife in the time of Ezra. [Ezra 10:18]

JAROAH (Heb. 'is relieved') date unknown. Son of Gilead of the tribe of Gad, he was a leader of the tribe living east of the river Jordan. [1 Chr. 5:14]

JASHEN (Heb. 'sleeping') *c.* 10 century BC. Father of Jonathan, a warrior in the armies of King David distinguished for his bravery. Also called Hashem. [2 Sam. 23:32; 1 Chr. 11:34]

JASHOBEAM (Heb. 'to whom the people turn') *c.* 10 century BC. Son of Zabdiel, he was one of David's veteran commanders, and famous for killing with his spear three hundred Philistines in one battle. When the army was reorganized he was put in charge of one of the monthly contingents of conscripts. [1 Chr. 11:11; 12:6; 27:2]

JASHUB (Heb. 'he turns') 5 century BC. One of the descendants of Bani who divorced his non-Jewish wife in the time of Ezra. [Ezra 10:29]

JASHUB see IOB

JATHNIEL (Heb. 'God-given') *c.* 10 century BC. Fourth son of Meshelemiah, a Levite, he and his family were gatekeepers of the Tabernacle in the reign of King David. [1 Chr. 26:2]

JAVAN (Heb. 'Greece') date unknown. Son of Japheth and a grandson of Noah, he was regarded by the Hebrews as the legendary father of the Greeks. [Gen. 10:2, 4; 1 Chr. 1:5, 7]

JAZIZ *c.* 10 century BC. The Hagrite officer of King David responsible for the royal flocks of sheep. [1 Chr. 27:30]

JEATHERAI date unknown. A Levite descended from Gershom, he was an ancestor of Asaph, the musician of King David. [1 Chr. 6:21]

JEBERECHIAH (Heb. 'may God bless') *c.* 8 century BC. Father of Zechariah, one of Isaiah's two witnesses to his prophecies of conquest by the Assyrian armies. [Isa. 8:2]

JEBUSITES date unknown. An ancient tribe of warriors living in Canaan, they ruled over Jerusalem until they were defeated in battle by King David. [Deut. 7:1; Josh. 11:3; 2 Sam. 5:6-10]

JECOLIAH (Heb. 'God is mighty') *c.* 8 century BC. Wife of Amaziah, king of Judah, and mother of his successor Uzziah. [2 Kgs. 15:2; 2 Chr. 26:3]

JECONIAH see JEHOIACHIN

JEDAIAH (Heb. 'known by God') **1.** date unknown. Son of Shimri and father of Allon of the tribe of Simeon. [1 Chr. 4:37]

2. *c.* 10 century BC. A priest who took the second turn of service in the Tabernacle in the reign of King David. [1 Chr. 24:7; Ezra 2:36; Neh. 7:39; 11:10]

3. *c.* 6 century BC. One of the first priests to settle in Jerusalem after the return from exile in Babylon. [1 Chr. 9:10; Neh. 12:6, 7, 19, 21]

4. 6 century BC. One of the leaders of Judah who returned from exile in Babylon in the days of the prophet Zechariah. He was ordered by Zechariah to provide gold and silver for a crown to be put ởn the head of Joshua, son of Jehozadak, the high priest, who would rebuild the Temple. Jedaiah and his colleagues were then instructed to keep the crowns in the Temple as a memorial of the event. [Zech. 6:10-14]

5. 5 century BC. Son of Harumaph, he helped repair the walls of Jerusalem in the time of Nehemiah. [Neh. 3:10]

JEDIAEL (Heb. 'known of God') **1.** *c.* 16 century BC. A son of Benjamin, he and his family were leaders of the tribe. [1 Chr. 7:6, 10]

2. *c.* 11 century BC. One of the eight leaders of the tribe of Manasseh who left the army of King Saul and joined David at Ziklag. [1 Chr. 12:20]

3. *c.* 10 century BC. Son of Shimri and brother of Joha, he and his brother were warriors in the armies of King David, distinguished for their bravery. [1 Chr. 11:45]

4. 10 century BC. Second son of Meshelemiah, a Korahite of the tribe of Levi, he and his family were gatekeepers of the Tabernacle in the reign of King David. [1 Chr. 26:2]

JEDIDAH (Heb. 'beloved') *c.* 7 century BC. Wife of King Amon of Judah and mother of King Josiah. [2 Kgs. 22:1]

JEDIDIAH see SOLOMON

JEDUTHUN (Heb. 'praiseworthy') *c.* 10 century BC. Temple choir leader, he was a Levite and came from the town of Netophah. In the time of David he was put in charge of the sacred music of the Temple service, while his sons were made keepers of the gate to the Temple. Jeduthun's choir sang to the accompaniment of harps, lutes and cymbals. In Solomon's Temple, when the priests came out of the Holy Place, Jeduthun and his sons were among the levitical singers standing to the east of the altar. He is mentioned as being the leader of one of the three music guilds. 'Ethan' is mentioned in some accounts in connection with Temple music and scholars have suggested that this might be a variant of the name of Jeduthun.

The family of Jeduthun is also listed among those taking part in Temple services in the reigns of Hezekiah and Josiah, and among those who returned from exile in Babylon. [1 Chr. 9:16; 16:38-42; 25:1, 3; 2 Chr. 5:12; 29:14; 35:15; Neh. 11:17; Titles of Pss. 39, 62, 77]

JEHALLELEL (Heb. 'who praises God') **1.** date unknown. A descendant of Caleb, the son of Jephunneh. [1 Chr. 4:16]

2. *c.* 8 century BC. Father of Azariah, a priest of Judah in the reign of King Hezekiah, who helped cleanse the Temple. [2 Chr. 29:12]

JEHDEIAH (Heb. 'may God cause to rejoice') **1.** *c.* 10 century BC. Son of Shubael, he was a Levite who served in King David's Tabernacle. [1 Chr. 24:20]

2. *c.* 10 century BC. An official of King David responsible for the king's herds of asses. [1 Chr. 27:30]

JEHEZKEL (Heb. 'may God strengthen') *c.* 10 century BC. A priest in the reign of King David responsible for the twentieth rota of service in the Tabernacle. [1 Chr. 24:16]

JEHIAH (Heb. 'may God live') *c.* 10 century BC. One of the two gatekeepers for the Ark in King David's Tabernacle. [1 Chr. 15:24]

JEHIEL (Heb. 'may God live') **1.** *c.* 10 century BC. One of the Levites who played musical instruments for the services in the Tabernacle during the reign of King David. [1 Chr. 15:18, 20; 16:5]

2. *c.* 10 century BC. Eldest son of Ladan the Levite, he and his family took charge of the gifts collected for the building of the Temple. [1 Chr. 23:8; 29:8]

3. *c.* 10 century BC. Son of Hachmoni, he was a tutor to the sons of King David. [1 Chr. 27:32]

4. *c.* 9 century BC. One of the sons of King Jehoshaphat of Judah who was put to death by his brother Jehoram when he became king. [2 Chr. 21:2]

5. *c.* 8 century BC. One of the Levites in the reign of King Hezekiah of Judah who supervised the bringing of offerings and tithes to the Temple. [2 Chr. 31:13]

6. *c.* 7 century BC. A leader of Judah who donated large numbers of animals for the special Passover offering proclaimed by King Josiah. [2 Chr. 35:8]

7. 5 century BC. Father of Obadiah, a leader of Judah who returned from exile in Babylon. [Ezra 8:9]

8. 5 century BC. Father of Shecaniah who publicly confessed to Ezra that many men of Judah had married non-Jewish wives. [Ezra 10:2]

9. *c.* 5 century BC. One of the sons of Harim the priest,

he divorced his non-Jewish wife in the time of Ezra. [Ezra 10:21]

10. *c.* 5 century BC. One of the sons of Elam, he divorced his non-Jewish wife in the time of Ezra. [Ezra 10:26]

JEHIELI (Heb. 'may my God live') *c.* 10 century BC. Son of Ladan, and an ancestor of Gershon, he was a Levite, assigned a post in the sanctuary in the time of King David. [1 Chr. 26:21]

JEHIZKIAH (Heb. 'may God show his strength') *c.* 8 century BC. Son of Shallum, he was one of the leaders of Ephraim who clothed and fed the men of Judah captured by the army of Pekah, king of Israel, and returned them to Judah. [2 Chr. 28:12]

JEHOADDAH *see* JARAH

JEHOADDAN (Heb. 'God waters') *c.* 9 century BC. Wife of Joash, king of Judah, and mother of his successor Amaziah. Also called Jehoaddin. [2 Kgs. 14:2; 2 Chr. 25:1]

JEHOADDIN *see* JEHOADDAN

JEHOAHAZ (Heb. 'God possessed') **1.** *see* AHAZIAH **2.**

2. Eleventh king of Israel after the monarchy split, he reigned 814-798 BC.

Jehoahaz succeeded his father Jehu on the throne of Israel at a time when that kingdom was in decline. Before the end of Jehu's reign, the territories east of the Jordan river had been lost to Israel's aggressive northern neighbour Aram (Syria) with its capital at Damascus. Under Jehoahaz, the Israelites became even more dominated by King Hazael of Aram and his predecessor King Ben-hadad II. Israel's army dwindled to ten thousand foot-soldiers, fifty horsemen and ten chariots. Late in this reign, some relief from the Aramean pressure was afforded when Aram had to face a fresh threat from the rising Assyrian empire further north. 'Therefore the Lord gave Israel a saviour, so that they escaped from the hand of the Syrians.' (2 Kgs. 13:5)

Jehoahaz reigned for seventeen years and was buried in the capital Samaria. He was succeeded by his son Joash. Also called Joahaz. [2 Kgs. 10:35; 13:1-10, 22-5; 14:1, 8, 17; 2 Chr. 25:17, 25]

3. The seventeenth king of Judah after the monarchy split, he reigned for three months in 609 BC. Jehoahaz was the son of King Josiah of Judah and Hamutal, daughter of Jeremiah from Libnah. He succeeded to the throne after his father was killed in the battle against the Egyptian forces at Megiddo. The Egyptian Pharaoh Neco, who was now trying to consolidate his position in Syria, summoned Jehoahaz to his headquarters in Riblah. When he arrived, Neco arrested him, put him in chains, deposed him as king and deported him to Egypt, where he died. Neco appointed Jehoahaz's half-brother Eliakim to the throne of Judah, changing his name to Jehoiakim. Jehoahaz is also called Shallum by the prophet Jeremiah. [2 Kgs. 23:30-34; 2

Limestone relief from Lower Egypt, 16th dynasty, showing the Pharaoh Neco (right) before the goddess Hathor (left). The inscription reads: '[I give] you every country . . . .

Chr. 36:1-4; Jer. 22: 10-12]

JEHOASH *see* JOASH **7.** and **8.**

JEHOHANAN (Heb. 'given by God') **1.** 10 century BC. Sixth son of Meshelemiah, a Levite. Together with his family he was a gatekeeper of the Tabernacle during the reign of King David. [1 Chr. 26:3]

2. 9 century BC. An army commander of Jehoshaphat, king of Judah. [2 Chr. 17:15]

3. 9 century BC. Father of Ishmael who helped overthrow Queen Athaliah and set up Joash as king of Judah. [2 Chr. 23:1]

4. 5 century BC. Son of Eliashib. Ezra went into Jehohanan's chamber to pray after deciding that all those who had taken non-Jewish wives should divorce them. [Ezra 10:6]

5. 5 century BC. One of the four sons of Bebai who divorced his non-Jewish wife in the time of Ezra. [Ezra 10:28]

6. 5 century BC. Son of Tobiah, one of the conspirators who tried to prevent Nehemiah from rebuilding the walls of Jerusalem. [Neh. 6:18]

7. 5 century BC. One of the chief priests of Judah when Joiakim was high priest in the time of Nehemiah. [Neh. 12:13]

8. 5 century BC. One of the eight priests who sang hymns of praise at the dedication service for the rebuilding of the walls of Jerusalem in the time of Nehemiah. [Neh. 12:42]

JEHOIACHIN (Heb. 'God appointed') Nineteenth king of Judah after the monarchy split, he reigned for three months in 598 BC.

Jehoiachin was the son of King Jehoiakim of Judah and of Nehushta, daughter of Elnathan from Jerusalem. Just after succeeding his father, he had to surrender to a Babylonian army led by Nebuchadnezzar. The Babylonian troops carried out vindictive reprisals. The king of Judah and his household were taken to Babylon as captives, together with the leading men of Judah, the army officers and the craftsmen and smiths: 'none remained, except the poorest people of the land' (2 Kgs. 24:14). The palace and the Temple were plundered and their treasure removed.

Nebuchadnezzar installed on the throne of Judah Jehoiachin's uncle Mattaniah, whose name was changed to Zedekiah. According to Jeremiah, the people of Judah continued to regard Jehoiachin as their legitimate ruler and believed he would return. The Second Book of Kings relates that thirty-seven years after his removal Jehoiachin was released from prison by a new ruler in Babylon, who treated him well and 'put off his prison garments. And every day of his life he dined regularly at the king's table.' (2 Kgs. 25:29) The records found in the basement of the palace of Nebuchadnezzar in Babylon mention Jehoiachin, his five sons and a number of Judeans in lists of captives who were issued with rations from the king's stores. Also called Jeconiah and

185

Cuneiform tablet listing the rations
supplied to King Jehoiachin and his
family while prisoners of the
Babylonian king, Nebuchadnezzar.

Jehoiada died at a very advanced age and as a tribute
was buried 'in the city of David among the kings,
because he had done good in Israel, and toward God
and his house' (2 Chr. 24:16). He was succeeded as high
priest by his son Zechariah. [2 Kgs. 11, 12; 2 Chr. 23;
24:1-22]

4. *c.* 6 century BC. A priest in the time of Jeremiah who
was succeeded by Zephaniah, son of Maaseiah. [Jer.
29:26]

5. *see* JOIADA **2.**

JEHOIAKIM (Heb. 'God established') Eighteenth
king of Judah after the monarchy split, he reigned
609-598 BC.

Jehoiakim was the son of King Josiah of Judah
and of Zebidah, daughter of Pedaiah from Rumah.
When Josiah was defeated and killed by the Egyptians
in the battle of Megiddo, he was succeeded by his
son Jehoahaz. Three months later the Egyptian king
Neco deposed Jehoahaz and instead appointed his
twenty-five-year-old half-brother Eliakim as a puppet
ruler whose name was changed to Jehoiakim. He
had to pay a heavy tribute in gold and silver to his
Egyptian masters which he raised by imposing a levy
on his subjects. Nevertheless he built himself a palace
and the prophet Jeremiah railed at him for doing this
at a time of national distress.

At the battle of Carchemish in 605 BC, the Babylonians wrested control of the area from Egypt. Three

In 599 BC Nebuchadnezzar invaded Judah..
The *Babylonian Chronicle* states that Jerusalem
fell on 15-16 March 197 BC.

Coniah. [2 Kgs. 24:6-17; 25:27-30; 1 Chr. 3:16, 17; 2
Chr. 36:8-9; Esther 2:6; Jer. 22:24, 28; 24:1; 37:1; 52:31;
Ezek. 1:2]

JEHOIADA (Heb. 'the Lord knoweth') **1.** 10 century
BC. Father of Benaiah, a warrior in the army of King
David, he deserted from King Saul's army and rallied
to King David at Hebron bringing with him 3,700 men.
[2 Sam. 8:18; 20:23; 23:20, 22; 1 Kgs. 1:8, 26, 32, 36, 38,
44; 2:25, 29, 34-5, 46; 4:4; 1 Chr. 11:22, 24; 18:17; 27:5]
2. 10 century BC. Son of Benaiah and an adviser to King
David. [1 Chr. 27:34]

3. *c.* 9 century BC. High priest in Jerusalem, he hid
the young prince Joash when King Ahaziah's mother
Athaliah murdered his children and seized the throne.
When the boy was seven, Jehoiada 'brought out
the king's son, and put the crown upon him, and
gave him the testimony ... and they clapped their
hands and said, "Long live the king!"' (2 Kgs. 11:12)
Hearing the trumpet blasts Athaliah rushed to the
Temple. The guards seized her and upon orders from
Jehoiada took her out of the Temple and killed her.

above Capital from the excavations at Ramat Rahel, which revealed a Judean citadel of the late 7th-early 6th centuries BC.

years later, Jehoiakim rebelled against Babylonian control. At first troops were sent against him from the neighbouring vassal states east of the Jordan: Ammon, Moab and Edom. Apparently they did not crush the rebellion because in 597 BC Nebuchadnezzar himself led an army against Judah. But before he arrived Jehoiakim died, after reigning for eleven years, and was succeeded by his son Jehoiachin.

In 1958 an archaeological dig was begun at Ramat Rahel on the southern outskirts of Jerusalem. The remains of a royal Judean citadel were discovered that date back to the end of the 7th century BC and the beginning of the 6th century and a seal was found of the steward to King Jehoiakim. An inner citadel was uncovered with a hewn stone casemate wall in which there were the remains of fine masonry and decorative capitals similar to those found in the royal palaces at Samaria and Megiddo. The ten-foot-thick outer wall of the citadel was of rough stone. [2 Kgs. 23:34-7; 24:1-6; 1 Chr. 3:15-16; 2 Chr. 36:4-8; Jer. 1:3; 22:18-24; 24:1; 25:1; 26:1, 21-3; 27:20; 28:4; 35:1; 36:1, 9, 20-32; 37:1; 45:1; 46:2; 52:2; Dan. 1:1-2]

JEHOIARIB (Heb. 'defended by God') **1.** *c.* 10 century BC. Head of a family of priests in the days of King David, he took the first turn of service in the Tabernacle. [1 Chr. 24:7]

2. *see* JOIARIB **1.**

JEHONADAB *see* JONADAB

JEHONATHAN (Heb. 'given by God') **1.** *c.* 9 century BC. One of the Levites sent by Jehoshaphat, king of Judah, to teach the Law of God to the people of Judah. [2 Chr. 17:8]

2. 5 century BC. Descended from Shemaiah, he was

The citadel at Ramat Rahel had hewn casemate walls consisting of an inner and outer wall linked by partitions for added strength.

one of the chief priests of Judah when Joiakim was high priest in the last years of Nehemiah. [Neh. 12:18]
JEHORAM (Heb. 'God is exalted') **1.** *c.* 9 century BC. A priest sent by King Jehoshaphat to teach the Law of God to the people of Judah. [2 Chr. 17:8]
2. Ninth king of Israel after the monarchy split, he reigned 852-41 BC.

Jehoram, son of King Ahab and his Phoenician queen Jezebel, succeeded his elder brother Ahaziah on the throne of Israel. Towards the end of Ahab's rule, King Mesha of Moab successfully revolted against Israel's control of his country, the mountain plateau east of the Dead Sea. Jehoram organized a military expedition against Moab in alliance with King Jehoshaphat of Judah and the king of Edom, a vassal of Judah. They made a detour round the southern end, through the 'Wilderness of Edom', and ran out of water, but were saved by a miracle performed by the prophet Elisha. The expedition moved into Moab, plundering and destroying, but retreated again.

After this abortive attempt to reconquer Moab, the rest of Jehoram's reign was involved in the chronic war with Israel's northern neighbour, the kingdom of Aram (Syria) with its capital at Damascus. An Aramean army under King Ben-hadad II pushed into Israel and besieged the capital, Samaria. The city was so powerfully fortified that Ben-hadad could not take it by storm and settled down to starving it into surrender. Inside the walls there was severe famine, and the dwindling supplies were sold at huge prices. Walking along the city wall one day the king was stopped by two quarrelling women, who had agreed to eat their respective children. The child of the one had been killed and eaten, and its mother bitterly accused the other of breaking the bargain by hiding her son. The king tore his clothes in horror and the passers-by noticed that he wore sackcloth next to his skin in grief for the sufferings of his people.

The king's anguish made him turn on Elisha who was in the city. He threatened to kill the man of God, saying, 'This trouble is from the Lord! Why should I wait for the Lord any longer?' (2 Kgs. 6:33) Unshaken in his faith the prophet predicted that by the following day there would be an abundance of food being sold cheaply in the market place.

That night some lepers who had stolen into the enemy camp found it empty. At dawn Jehoram sent out a reconnaissance patrol of two men mounted on two of the last five surviving horses. The scouts came back to confirm that the Arameans had fled during the night and a trail of abandoned baggage and discarded clothes led all the way to the fords over the Jordan river. The townspeople surged out to fall upon the abandoned stores and supplies.

In the twelfth year of Jehoram's reign, he was defend-

ing Ramoth-gilead in the mountains east of the Jordan river, against Hazael who had become king of Aram. Ahaziah, the king of Judah, had joined him in this campaign. Wounded by the Arameans, Jehoram handed over the command to his general, Jehu, and went back to his winter palace at Jezreel to recover. Jehu was encouraged by Elisha to make himself king and wipe out the house of Ahab which the prophet regarded as sinful. He leapt into his chariot, and with a troop of his men made a fifty-mile dash from the front across the Jordan valley to Jezreel. Jehoram went out in a chariot to meet Jehu, with King Ahaziah of Judah accompanying him in another chariot. Jehoram innocently called out to him: 'Is it peace, Jehu?' The soldier flung back: 'What peace can there be, so long as the harlotries and the sorceries of your mother Jezebel are so many?' (2 Kgs. 9:22) Realizing they were faced with treason, the two kings swung their chariots round and tried to escape. Jehu brought Jehoram down with an arrow between the shoulder blades, killing him instantly. Jehu ordered the body to be flung onto the ground of Naboth's vineyard nearby, recalling that many years before he had heard Elijah cursing Jehoram's father Ahab at that spot.

Jehu then hunted down the Judean king and afterwards massacred all Jehoram's family, including his mother Jezebel, as well as all the prophets of Baal. In this way the dynasty founded by Omri, Jehoram's grandfather, came to a bloody end. Also called Joram. [2 Kgs. 1:17; 3; 8:16, 28, 29; 9; 2 Chr. 22:5-7]
3. Fifth king of Judah after the monarchy split, he reigned 848-1 BC.

Jehoram, the eldest son, succeeded his father Jehoshaphat on the throne of Judah at the age of thirty-two. Jehoshaphat had bequeathed a large part of his treasures to his other six sons as well and had allocated certain towns to them. Jehoram promptly murdered all of them and also some of the court ministers. Before then Jehoram had married Athaliah, the daughter of King Ahab of Israel and his queen Jezebel, in order to cement an alliance between the two Hebrew kingdoms. The military reverses in Jehoram's reign and

Small ivory carving from Hazor, 9th century BC — the time of King Jehoram of Judah — showing a figure kneeling in idol-worship.

his own painful end are attributed to his indulgence towards foreign gods, under Athaliah's influence.

When the vassal territory of Edom to the south broke away and once more proclaimed its own king, Jehoram led an unsuccessful military expedition with chariots to conquer it. His forces were encircled and cut off by the Edomites and had to break out in a night attack, in order to escape. With the loss of Edom went the profitable trading route to Arabia and the Red Sea area through the port of Ezion-geber (Eilat), that had been revived by Jehoshaphat.

The weakness of Judah at this time laid it open to raids by the Philistines on the coastal plain to the west, and by nomad tribes from the south. They reached Jerusalem, killed the king's wives and children, and carried off a great deal of plunder. The only survivor of the royal household was Jehoram's youngest son, Ahaziah. The Bible links the wiping out of the royal family with a letter from Elijah in which the doom of Jehoram and his house is prophesied. It is possible that the king and the army were away in the north at the time, engaged together with the forces of Israel and other local rulers in a collective effort to stop the Assyrian advance.

After a reign of eight years, Jehoram died from a disease of the bowels. The text says pointedly that nobody regretted his passing and that he was buried in Jerusalem but not in the tomb of the kings.

Jehoram was succeeded by Ahaziah. Also called Joram. [2 Kgs. 1:17; 8:16-29; 12:18; 1 Chr. 3:11; 2 Chr. 21:1-16; 22:1-11]

JEHOSHABEATH see JEHOSHEBA

JEHOSHAPHAT (Heb. 'God has judged') **1.** *c.* 10 century BC. Son of Ahilud, he served as recorder of chronicles to King David and King Solomon. [2 Sam. 8:16; 20:24; 1 Kgs. 4:3; 1 Chr. 18:15]
2. *c.* 10 century BC. Son of Parvah, he was one of the twelve officers of King Solomon responsible for supplying provisions for the royal household. [1 Kgs. 4:17]
3. *c.* 9 century BC. Father of Jehu, the army commander who seized the throne of Israel from King Jehoram. [2 Kgs. 9:2, 14]
4. Fourth king of Judah after the monarchy split, he reigned 870-48 BC. Jehoshaphat, the son of King Asa and Azubah daughter of Shilhi, succeeded his father at the age of thirty-five and continued Asa's religious reforms. He destroyed many of the local hill-shrines, and restored the central authority of the Temple in Jerusalem. Five senior officials, eight Levites and two priests were sent round the country as instructors in the Book of the Law. Later, the king personally toured the towns of his realm 'and brought them back to the Lord, the God of their fathers' (2 Chr. 19:4). He appointed local judges, warning them that they should not respect rank nor take gifts. In Jerusalem, Jehoshaphat

established a central judicial body and appointed its members from among the priests, the Levites and the heads of leading families. He also strengthened the security of the kingdom, by reorganizing the army and fortifying strategic towns.

For most of Jehoshaphat's long reign, Judah was at peace with its neighbours and enjoyed rising prosperity. In its customary didactic spirit, the Book of Chronicles states that because of the king's piety the Lord instilled 'dread' into neighbouring peoples. Jehoshaphat collected tribute from the Philistines in gifts and silver, and from nomad Arabian tribes in sheep and goats.

The intervention of the Lord frustrated an incursion by a 'great multitude' of Ammonites, Moabites and hill-men from Edom. They came up into the Hebron hills from the direction of the Dead Sea. The king and a panic-stricken congregation gathered in the Temple and prayed for divine help. One of the Levites, possessed by 'the spirit of the Lord', told them not to fear but to march out towards the invaders. They did so with cantors chanting in the vanguard. The Lord caused the invading bands to turn and fight each other. When the Israelites reached the spot, they saw nothing but corpses and spoil. It took three days to collect the booty.

A more mundane reason for prosperity was the revival of trade with the Red Sea region, through the port of Ezion-geber (Eilat) at the head of the Gulf of Akaba. As in Solomon's time a century earlier, the Judeans became middlemen in the lucrative commerce between Arabia and the Mediterranean coast.

The Bible relates that Jehoshaphat tried to emulate Solomon by constructing 'ships of Tarshish' (1 Kgs. 22:48), but they came to grief in the Gulf of Akaba – presumably shipwrecked in a storm.

In spite of clerical disapproval, Jehoshaphat fostered an alliance with the other Hebrew kingdom, Israel. His crown prince, Jehoram, was married to Athaliah, the daughter of King Ahab. Jehoshaphat came to visit Ahab in Samaria and agreed to join in a campaign to recover Ramoth-gilead, in the highlands east of the Jordan from Aram-Damascus. But he wished to know that the venture had the Lord's blessing. Ahab assembled an impressive gathering of four hundred prophets, who appeared before the two kings sitting in state on thrones outside the city gates. All of them predicted victory against the Arameans.

One prophet, Micaiah, failed to come. He was sent for, and when pressed to speak the truth, predicted that Ahab would be killed in the battle and Israel would be 'scattered upon the mountains, as sheep that have no shepherd' (2 Chr. 18:16). To avert his fate Ahab went into battle in disguise, while Jehoshaphat in his full kingly armour was mistaken for Ahab until he gave his own battle-cry. When Ahab was killed by a stray arrow, the Israelites retreated and Jehoshaphat returned home to Jerusalem.

Jehoshaphat took part in another military expedition jointly with Ahab's son Jehoram (who succeeded his brother Ahaziah). It was directed against King Mesha of Moab, who had rebelled against the suzerainty of Israel. Together with the vassal king of Edom, they made a detour through the desert below the Dead Sea, to attack Moab from the south.

When the army ran out of water, the three kings appealed to the prophet Elisha, who was accompanying them. He rebuffed Jehoram, but agreed to help them out of respect for the God-fearing Jehoshaphat. Elisha's instructions to dig trenches produced water and they were able to defeat the enemy forces and invade Moab. However, the Israelite army did not secure their hold on the country and eventually withdrew to their own borders.

Jehoshaphat was succeeded by his son Jehoram. [1 Kgs. 15:24; 22:1-51; 2 Kgs. 1:17; 3:1-14; 8:16; 12:18; 1 Chr. 3:10; 2 Chr. 17-21]

JEHOSHEBA (Heb. 'oath of God') *c.* 9 century BC. Daughter of Joram, king of Judah, she hid her nephew Joash to prevent his being killed by his grandmother Athaliah who had seized the throne and murdered all her other grandchildren. Also known as Jehoshabeath. [2 Kgs. 11:2; 2 Chr. 22:11]

JEHOZABAD (Heb. 'given by God') **1.** *c.* 10 century BC. Son of Obed-edom, he and his family were gatekeepers of the Tabernacle in the reign of King David. [1 Chr. 26:4]

2. *c.* 9 century BC. An army commander of Jehoshaphat, king of Judah. [2 Chr. 17:18]

3. 8 century BC. A servant of Joash, king of Judah, who assassinated the king and buried the body in Jerusalem. He was executed by Amaziah, who succeeded his father as king of Judah. [2 Kgs. 12:21; 2 Chr. 24:26]

JEHOZADAK (Heb. 'Jehovah is righteous') *c.* 6 century BC. A priest descended from Zadok who went into exile at the time of Nebuchadnezzar, he was father of the high priest Jeshua. Also called Jozadak. [1 Chr. 6:14, 15; Ezra 3:2, 8; 10:18; Hag. 1:1, 12, 14; 2:2, 4; Zech. 6:11]

JEHU (Heb. '[man] of God') **1.** date unknown. Son of Obed and a leader of the tribe of Judah. [1 Chr. 2:38]

2. *c.* 11 century BC. A Benjaminite warrior who left the army of King Saul and rallied to David at Ziklag. [1 Chr. 12:3]

3. *c.* 9 century BC. Jehu, a prophet, son of Hanani, he foretold the doom of King Baasha of Israel. Years later, when King Jehoshaphat of Judah returned from the battlefield where King Ahab was killed, Jehu went out to greet him. [1 Kgs. 16:1; 2 Chr. 19:1-3]

4. Tenth king of Israel after the monarchy split, he reigned 841-14 BC.

King Joram, son of Ahab, was engaged in the defence of Ramoth-gilead, in the mountains east of the Jordan river, against the forces of Aram-Damascus (Syria). He handed over the command of the front to his general Jehu, and went back to his winter palace at Jezreel to recover from campaign wounds. Here he was joined by his ally, King Ahaziah of Judah.

The prophet Elisha now instigated a revolt against the king. He sent a young disciple who poured holy oil on Jehu's head and told him the Lord had appointed him to be king of Israel and to wipe out the sinful house of Ahab. When Jehu told them what had happened, his brother officers instantly hailed him spreading their

Jehu's men massacre the sons of King Ahab, from an 11th-century German Bible. In the background, Jehu hands a note to a messenger, and in the foreground the heads of Ahab's sons are piled up in a chest.

cloaks for him on the steps and having trumpets sounded. Jehu then leapt into his chariot and with a mounted escort set out on a fifty-mile dash for Jezreel.

The sentry on the tower of Jezreel reported that he saw a troop of men approaching in the distance, and that '... the driving is like the driving of Jehu the son of Nimshi; for he drives furiously' (2 Kgs. 9:20). The unsuspecting Joram then had his chariot brought round and himself drove out to meet his army commander with his guest the king of Judah in another chariot accompanying him. When they reached Jehu and Joram gave him the customary greeting: 'Is it peace?' he was taken aback at the rude answer: 'What peace can there be, so long as the harlotries and the sorceries of your mother Jezebel are so many?' (2 Kgs. 9:22) At Joram's shout of 'Treachery, O Ahaziah!' (2 Kgs. 9:23), the two kings spun their chariots round and tried to get away. An arrow from Jehu's bow hit the fleeing Joram between the shoulder blades and killed him on the spot. Jehu told Bidkar, his aide, to throw the king's body into Naboth's vineyard nearby, where Ahab had been cursed by Elijah. Jehu then chased after Ahaziah who had fled up the Jezreel valley. The king, wounded during the pursuit, sought refuge in the fortress of Megiddo, where he died.

Jehu now went looking for the hated Jezebel, the mother of King Joram. She was expecting him, and with the stiff pride of a king's daughter she had carefully made up her face and dressed her hair and stood waiting at an upstairs window of the palace. Jehu ordered her servants to throw her down and drove over her bloodstained body. Later, after he had eaten and drunk, he ordered her buried, for despite her end, 'she is a king's daughter' (2 Kgs. 9:34). But the dogs had already eaten her flesh as Elijah had foretold.

The slaying of the two kings by Jehu had robbed the notables in Samaria of the will to resist, and they were terrified of the ruthless usurper. On receipt of a written challenge from Jehu to Ahab's sons, they replied submitting themselves to Jehu's will. He wrote a second letter demanding that by the following day they should bring to him at Jezreel the heads of Ahab's seventy sons. The word 'heads', in Hebrew 'roshim', may have been ambiguous, meaning 'leaders', but the panicky authorities in the capital took his behest literally. They slew Ahab's sons, put their heads in baskets and sent them to Jehu. He had them placed in two heaps at the city gate. Next morning he appeared there and said to the people, 'You are innocent. It was I who conspired against my master, and slew him; but who struck down all these?' (2 Kgs. 10:9)

The blood-bath was far from over. In Jezreel, Jehu butchered all of King Joram's household including his close friends and his priests. Jehu then set out for Samaria. Along the way he killed a party of kinsmen of the slain King Ahaziah of Judah. In Samaria Jehu wiped out all the remaining members of Ahab's family.

Now firmly in the saddle Jehu set himself to crushing the worship of Baal in the country – the purpose for which the prophet Elisha had originally engineered his coup. Jehu disguised his intentions. Giving out that he would personally offer sacrifice in the great temple of Baal in Samaria, he ordered that all the priests and devotees of the cult from the whole kingdom should assemble there. Armed men waiting outside were turned loose on them, and all of them were killed. The temple and altar were demolished and the images of the god were taken out and burnt. The ruins of the building were converted into a latrine.

By this gory military coup, Jehu not only started a new dynasty but wrenched the country into the religious reformation that had been prepared by the work of Elijah and Elisha.

Jehu remained on the throne for twenty-eight years. Having dealt with the religious issue, the Bible pays little attention to the other events of his reign. It was in fact a period of rapid decline in the fortunes of the kingdom, and of drastic shrinkage of its territory. Phoenicia and Judea had been antagonized, and Hazael, king of Aram-Damascus, now occupied all the Israelite territory east of the Jordan. Jehu was left ruling over not much more than the hill-country of Ephraim. According to Assyrian records, Shalmaneser III marched at this time across Israel to a headland on the coast, probably Mount Carmel.

The Israelite King Jehu pays homage to Shalmaneser III, king of Assyria, in a scene from an Assyrian black stone obelisk, c. 841 BC.

The decline of Israel reached its lowest ebb towards the end of Jehu's reign and that of his son Jehoahaz. Jehu may have been a seasoned soldier, bold and ruthless in seizing power, but he showed no capacity for statesmanship. [1 Kgs. 19:16, 17; 2 Kgs. 9; 10; 12:1; 13:1; 14:8; 15:12; 2 Chr. 22:7-9; 25:17; Hos. 1:4]

5. *c*. 8 century BC. Son of Joshibiah, he was one of the leaders of the tribe of Simeon in the reign of King Hezekiah who drove out the inhabitants of the rich Gedor valley and dwelt there instead. [1 Chr. 4:35]

JEHUBBAH (Heb. 'hidden') date unknown. Son of Shemer and a member of the tribe of Asher. [1 Chr. 7:34]

JEHUCAL (Heb. 'God sustains') *c*. 6 century BC. Son of Shelemiah, he was an official of the court and carried a personal message from King Zedekiah to Jeremiah asking the prophet to pray for him. Also called Jucal. [Jer. 37:3; 38:1]

JEHUDI (Heb. 'Judean') 6 century BC. Son of Nethaniah, he was sent to Baruch, the scribe of the prophet Jeremiah, to ask him to read Jeremiah's prophecies to the leaders. Later Jehoiakim, king of Judah, sent Jehudi to fetch the scroll of Jeremiah's prophecies and as Jehudi read from the scroll the king burnt it piece by piece. [Jer. 36:14-23]

JEHUEL (Heb. 'may God live') 8 century BC. A Levite, descendant of Heman, he sanctified himself so that he could cleanse the Temple during the reign of Hezekiah. [2 Chr. 29:14]

JEIEL (Heb. 'God's treasure') **1.** date unknown. Head of a family of the tribe of Reuben and a leader of the tribe. [1 Chr. 5:7]

2. date unknown. Leader of the tribe of Benjamin living in Gibeon, and ancestor of Saul. [1 Chr. 8:29; 9:35]

3. *c*. 10 century BC. Son of Hotham, he and his brother Shama were warriors in the army of King David distinguished for their bravery. [1 Chr. 11:44]

4. *c*. 10 century BC. A Levite in the reign of King David who played musical instruments to accompany the bringing of the Ark of God to Jerusalem, and took part in the services in the Tabernacle. [1 Chr. 15:18, 21; 16:5]

5. *c*. 9 century BC. Ancestor of the Levite Jahaziel who prophesied a great victory for King Jehoshaphat of Judah over the invading armies of Moab, Ammon and Seir. [2 Chr. 20:14]

6. *c*. 8 century BC. Secretary to King Uzziah, he kept the records of the numbers of troops in the army of Judah. [2 Chr. 26:11]

7. *c*. 7 century BC. A leading Levite in the reign of King Josiah of Judah who donated large quantities of cattle for the Passover offering. [2 Chr. 35:9]

8. 5 century BC. A son of Nebo who divorced his non-Jewish wife in the time of Ezra. [Ezra 10:43]

JEKAMEAM (Heb. 'who gathers') *c*. 10 century BC.

A descendant of Hebron, he was one of the Levites who served in the Tabernacle in the reign of King David. [1 Chr. 23:19; 24:23]

JEKAMIAH (Heb. 'established by God') **1.** date unknown. Son of Shallum and a leader of the tribe of Judah. [1 Chr. 2:41]

2. 6 century BC. Son of Jeconiah of the tribe of Judah and a descendant of King David. [1 Chr. 3:18]

JEKUTHIEL (Heb. 'may God sustain') date unknown. Father of Zanoah and a leader of the tribe of Judah. [1 Chr. 4:18]

JEMIMAH (Heb. 'dove') period of the Patriarchs. Job's eldest daughter born after his trials and tribulations had ended and his fortune restored. [Job. 42:14]

JEMUEL (Heb. 'day of God') *c*. 16 century BC. A son of Simeon, he went down to Egypt with his grandfather Jacob. Also called Nemuel. [Gen. 46:10; Exod. 6:15; Num. 26:12; 1 Chr. 4:24]

JEPHTHAH (Heb. 'set free') *c*. 12 century BC. A judge in Israel and leader of the war against the Ammonites.

In the period of the Judges, Jephthah was born in the land of Gilead of a father who was also called Gilead, and a mother who was a harlot. His half-brothers by his father's lawful wife drove him away, lest he should share the inheritance with them. Jephthah fled eastward to the land of Tob, on the edge of the desert. Here he became leader of a robber band of destitute men who had gathered round him. He became known as a skilled and daring fighter, 'a mighty warrior' (Judg. 11:1).

The elders of Gilead sought him out and urged him to lead their forces against the Ammonites, who were encroaching on their territory. Jephthah retorted with some bitterness: 'Did you not hate me, and drive me out of my father's house? Why have you come to me now when you are in trouble?' (Judg. 11:7) He agreed to accept the appointment on condition that if they were victorious, he would remain the tribal leader. The undertaking was solemnly endorsed at Mizpah ('watch-tower') where the Israelite defenders had mustered.

On assuming command, Jephthah at first attempted to come to terms with the Ammonites by peaceful means. He sent a delegation to their king, proposing that their forces be withdrawn. In his reply, the Ammonite ruler laid claim to all the Israelite territory in Transjordan to the south of Gilead, between the Arnon and Jabbok rivers, occupied by the tribes of Gad and Reuben. Jephthah sent his envoys back to prove that there was no historical basis for this claim, since the Children of Israel under Moses had taken the area from the Amorites under King Sihon, who had barred their transit. Since then the Israelites had lived in these territories for three hundred years: 'why did you not recover them within that time? I therefore have not sinned against you, and you do me wrong by making war on me.' (Judg. 11:26, 27)

The king of Ammon rejected Jephthah's diplomatic overtures, and hostilities broke out. Jehpthah marched south in a wide sweep to attack the Ammonites from the rear. Before going into battle, he took a vow that if he won he would sacrifice to the Lord 'whoever comes forth from the doors of my house to meet me, when I return victorious . . .' (Judg. 11:31).

With the Ammonites repulsed, Jephthah returned in triumph. To his horror, the first person who came to meet him was his daughter, an only child, dancing to the sound of timbrels. Jephthah tore his clothes and cried out in grief; but even his daughter agreed that his sacred oath could not be broken. At her request, 'he sent her away for two months; and she departed, she and her companions, and bewailed her virginity upon the mountains' (Judg. 11:38). On her return, the sacrifice was carried out. From this tragic episode the custom arose for the young women to go out each year for four days, mourning Jephthah's daughter.

A quarrel now broke out between the men of Gilead and the tribe of Ephraim across the river. The Ephraimites advanced eastward into Gilead, but Jephthah drove them back towards the river and sent detachments ahead to cut them off at the fords. Those men who sought to cross and denied that they were Ephraimites were asked to say the word *Shibboleth*, which means an 'ear of wheat'. If they pronounced it *Sibboleth*,

according to the tribal dialect of Ephraim, they were slain on the spot. Thousands of Ephraimites lost their lives in this ill-advised expedition.

Jephthah judged for six years and on his death was buried in one of the towns of his native Gilead. [Judg. 11, 12; 1 Sam. 12:11]

JEPHUNNEH (Heb. 'favourably regarded') **1.** *c.* 13 century BC. Father of Caleb, he was a leader of the tribe of Judah. [Num. 13:6; 14:6; 30, 38; Deut. 1:36; 1 Chr. 4:15]

2. date unknown. Eldest son of Jether, he was a leader of the tribe of Asher and a mighty warrior. [1 Chr. 7:38]

JERAH (Heb. 'moon') date unknown. One of Joktan's thirteen sons and a descendant of Shem. [Gen. 10:26; 1 Chr. 1:20]

JERAHMEEL (Heb. 'God's mercy') **1.** date unknown. The eldest son of Hezron and a leader of the tribe of Judah, he was one of the most prominent of the early leaders of the tribe. [1 Chr. 2:9, 25-7, 42]

2. 10 century BC. Son of Kish, a Levite descended from Merari, he ministered in the Tabernacle in the reign of King David. [1 Chr. 24:29]

3. *c.* 6 century BC. One of the officers sent by King Jehoiakim of Judah to arrest the prophet Jeremiah and his scribe Baruch. [Jer. 36:26]

JERED (Heb. 'descent') date unknown. An ancestor of the members of the tribe of Judah that invaded the valley of Gedor. [1 Chr. 4:18]

JEREMAI (Heb. 'exalted') 5 century BC. A descendant of Hashum who divorced his non-Jewish wife in the time of Ezra. [Ezra 10:33]

JEREMIAH (Heb. 'God will elevate') **1.** date unknown. A leader of half of the tribe of Manasseh who dwelt in Bashan east of the river Jordan. [1 Chr. 5:24]

2. 11 century BC. One of the Benjaminite warriors who deserted from King Saul's army and joined David at Ziklag. [1 Chr. 12:4]

3. *c.* 11 century BC. Two of the eleven captains of the tribe of Gad who deserted from King Saul's army and joined David at Ziklag. [1 Chr. 12:10, 13]

4. *c.* 7 century BC. Father of Hamutal, the wife of Josiah, king of Judah. [2 Kgs. 23:31]

5. 7-6 century BC. Hebrew prophet. Jeremiah and Isaiah were the two giants of Hebrew prophecy, next to Moses himself. They lived in Jerusalem a century apart, in the turbulent period that saw the two small Hebrew kingdoms wiped out with the fall of Samaria in 721 BC and that of Jerusalem in 587 BC. Both men were caught up in the political events of their time.

Like Amos, Hosea, Isaiah and Micah before him,

Relief from Saqqara in Egypt,
c. 1550-1200 BC, showing women dancing
to the music of timbrels.

Jeremiah was a God-driven man, fearlessly denouncing the religious laxity and social ills of the nation, and warning of the disasters that would follow. With no other prophet, however, has the inner conflict behind the stern message been so revealed. Jeremiah's agony was echoed more than two thousand years later in the words of Shakespeare's Hamlet:

'The times are out of joint – oh cursed spite
that ever I was born to put them right.'

Jeremiah was born in the village of Anathoth, in the territory of Benjamin, three miles north-east of Jerusalem. This was one of the towns set aside for the priestly tribe of the Levites in the time of Joshua. Jeremiah's father Hilkiah was also a priest, and the boy was no doubt reared in a devout and quiet home. At about eighteen, he felt the call to follow the vocation of a prophet:

'Then the Lord put forth his hand and touched my mouth; and the Lord said to me, "Behold, I have put my words in your mouth.

' "See, I have set you this day over nations and over kingdoms, to pluck up and to break down, to destroy and to overthrow, to build and to plant." ' (Jer. 1:9, 10)

This took place about 627 BC, in the thirteenth year of Josiah's reign. Josiah carried out a sweeping religious reformation, stamping out idolatry and restoring the Temple in Jerusalem as the central sanctuary of the nation. In 622 BC a 'book of the law' was discovered in the Temple (probably an early version of the Book of Deuteronomy), and it became the focus of the reform movement. Curiously, Jeremiah seemed hardly involved in this development. The forms and rituals of organized worship meant little to him – 'the false pen of the scribes has made it into a lie' (Jer. 8:8). For Jeremiah, faith was an intensely personal matter, and God would judge each man by what was in his heart: 'I the Lord search the mind and try the heart, to give to every man according to his ways, according to the fruit of his doings.' (Jer. 17:10)

The Outspoken Preacher

In 609 BC the good King Josiah was killed in battle against an Egyptian army at the pass of Megiddo. He was succeeded by his son Jehoahaz, whom the Egyptian Pharaoh Neco deposed a few months later in favour of Jehoiakim, another son of Josiah. For some years the kingdom remained subservient to Egypt, while it slid back into religious and moral laxity. Jeremiah's outspoken criticisms brought him into continual trouble with the authorities.

Soon after the beginning of Jehoiakim's reign,

left The prophet Jeremiah grasping his scroll: detail of an early 12th-century sculpture from Moissac, France.

Jeremiah planted himself in the courtyard of the Temple and addressed the crowd of worshippers that had gathered from all over the country. He shocked them by a diatribe in which he swore that if they did not mend their ways, God would destroy the very sanctuary itself. 'Will you steal, murder, commit adultery, swear falsely, burn incense to Baal, and go after other gods that you have not known, and then come and stand before me in this house, which is called by my name, and say, "We are delivered!" – only to go on doing all these abominations?' (Jer. 7:9, 10)

The crowd swarmed round him, and some of the priests and people seized hold of him shouting, 'Thou shalt surely die.' Hearing the excitement, some of the king's officials immediately came over from the palace and sat down at the Temple gate to conduct an enquiry. Jeremiah's eloquence persuaded the officials that he had conveyed a message from God calling for repentance while there was yet time. The elders who were present started invoking precedents one way or the other. Some recalled that in the reign of Hezekiah a century earlier, the prophet Micah had made similar predictions which had led to repentance rather than punishment of the prophet. But others spoke of Uriah, another prophet who had recently been put to death by King Jehoiakim for similar statements. Jeremiah might have suffered the same fate but for the protection of an important man of the court, Ahikam, whose father had been the royal scribe at the time of Josiah's reforms.

Before a crowd of priests and citizens in the valley of Hinnom, Jeremiah denounced their pagan practices, and dramatically smashed an earthenware jar crying out, 'Thus says the Lord of hosts: So will I break this people and this city as one breaks a potter's vessel, so it can never be mended.' (Jer. 19:11)

Jeremiah returned to the city, stood in the court of the Temple and addressed the crowd, shouting out in God's name: 'Behold, I am bringing upon this city and upon all its towns all the evil that I have pronounced against it, because they have stiffened their neck, refusing to hear my words.' (Jer. 19:15)

The angry priest Pashhur had the prophet beaten and then put in the stocks which were at the upper gate to the Temple. Next day, when Pashhur released him, Jeremiah was totally unrepentant. He repeated that the city would be destroyed and plundered and all its inhabitants carried off to Babylon. 'And you, Pashhur, and all who dwell in your house, shall go into captivity; to Babylon you shall go; and there you shall die, and there you shall be buried, you and all your friends, to whom you have prophesied falsely.' (Jer. 20:6)

Pressure from Babylon

For centuries the Near East had been dominated by the imperial might of Assyria. That period was now coming to an end. In 612 BC the great capital city of

Nineveh was captured by the Babylonians. In 605 BC Nebuchadnezzar of Babylon defeated the Egyptian army of Neco at Carchemish, and became the new overlord of Judah and its neighbours.

Jeremiah's preaching acquired a new note of urgency. For twenty-three years he had called for repentance and prophesied disaster without any effect. With the advent of Babylon, he saw this threat as imminent. Before the citizens of Jerusalem he proclaimed: 'This whole land shall become a ruin and a waste, and these nations shall serve the king of Babylon seventy years.' (Jer. 25:11)

Jeremiah had acquired a devoted disciple and scribe, Baruch, the son of Neriah. He sent for Baruch and dictated a scroll containing his discourses and oracles from the beginning of his ministry. Soon after, there was a special fast day on which people gathered from near and far for prayers in the Temple. Since Jeremiah had been banned from the Temple area (probably after the quarrel with the priest Pashhur), he sent Baruch to read out the scroll to the crowd of worshippers, in the hope that the grim prophecies in it would cause the hearers to repent.

Baruch did this, and then found himself summoned to the palace to read the book again before a meeting of the palace officials. Disturbed at its contents, they advised Baruch to take his master and go into hiding. They then informed the king, who was in his chamber keeping himself warm in front of a brazier. He ordered his secretary Jehudi to read the document to him. Each time a few columns had been read, he hacked that piece off in a rage with the scribe's knife and threw it on the fire until the whole scroll was burned. He then ordered Jeremiah and Baruch to be arrested, but they were not to be found. At the Lord's command Jeremiah dictated the scroll over again to Baruch, with additions.

Some two years later in 602 BC, Jehoiakim joined in a revolt of several vassal kingdoms against the rule of Babylon. At first Nebuchadnezzar tried to quell it with local levies from the subject kingdoms east of the Jordan. When this did not succeed he marched with a Babylonian army against Judah.

The Rechabite community had taken refuge in Jerusalem from the Babylonian troops. They were a fundamentalist sect of desert nomads, living by the injunctions of an ancestor Jonadab, the son of Rehab, that they should not live in houses, till the soil or touch wine. Jeremiah tested them by bringing them into a chamber of the Temple and offering them glasses of wine which were rejected. He then held them up as an

Nineveh, like Sodom and Gomorrah, became typified as an example of the 'wicked city'. *The Fall of Nineveh*, engraving by John Martin (1789-1854).

Scribes taking dictation from an Assyrian officer; one writes with a pen on leather, the other with a stylus on clay. Relief from the palace of King Tiglath-pileser III at Nimrod, *c.* 8th century BC.

example of fidelity to tradition, as opposed to the lax ways of the Jerusalemites.

Jeremiah lashed out at the spendthrift and impious king who had brought calamity upon his people and said, 'With the burial of an ass he shall be buried, dragged and cast forth beyond the gates of Jerusalem.' (Jer. 22:19) In poignant terms, the prophet described the horrors of war and siege that would attend the decline and fall of Judah.

By the time the Babylonians reached Jerusalem, Jehoiakim was dead and succeeded by his son Jehoiachin (598 BC). The young king surrendered the city and was carried off into captivity in Babylon together with the queen mother, the royal household and three thousand leading citizens of the kingdom. The king's uncle Zedekiah was appointed as ruler by Nebuchadnezzar.

A spirit of revolt against the colonial rule of Babylon continued to simmer under the surface in Judah and the other states in the region. Jeremiah was opposed to the militants, and urged submission until the Lord in his own good time should break the hold of Babylon and bring back their captured brothers. Given to the use of dramatic symbols in his preaching, he walked about with a wooden yoke on his neck. He not only addressed his message to the people but also to the rulers of Edom, Moab, Ammon, Tyre and Sidon, through their ambassadors in Jerusalem, warning that armed resistance would lead to the destruction of their countries.

A leading priest and prophet, Hananiah, the son of

Azzur, proclaimed that within two years the Lord would smash Babylon and restore the captives, together with all the sacred vessels that had been removed from the Temple by order of Nebuchadnezzar. He too illustrated his point by a symbolic act. He smashed Jeremiah's yoke and proclaimed in God's name: 'Even so will I break the yoke of Nebuchadnezzar king of Babylon from the neck of all the nations...' (Jer. 28:11). Jeremiah predicted that this false prophet would be dead within the year. Two months later this came to pass.

In another metaphor used by Jeremiah a basket of good figs denoted the exiles in Babylon whom God would look after and bring back, while a basket of rotten figs stood for King Zedekiah and his nobles who would be discarded.

About this time King Zedekiah sent an official delegation to Babylon. Two of its members were friends of Jeremiah, and he sent with them a remarkable letter to the small community of Israelites that had been brought there as captives together with the young King Jehoiachin. Jeremiah begged them to be patient, and not to be deluded by the false prophets among them who were promising them a speedy return home. He repeated that their exile would last seventy years, but in the end God would bring them back in peace. Meanwhile, they should settle down, lead constructive lives and try to be on good terms with the authorities.

'Build houses and live in them; plant gardens and eat their produce.

'Take wives and have sons and daughters; take wives

197

for your sons, and give your daughters in marriage, that they may bear sons and daughters; multiply there, and do not decrease.

'But seek the welfare of the city where I have sent you into exile, and pray to the Lord on its behalf, for in its welfare you will find your welfare.' (Jer. 29:5, 6, 7)

As for those who remained behind in Jerusalem, their evil-doing would be punished by the 'sword, famine, and pestilence' (Jer. 29:17).

This specific counsel drew a sharp reaction from one of the priests in Babylon called Shemaiah. He wrote a letter of protest to Zephaniah, the chief priest of the Temple in Jerusalem, demanding that Jeremiah should be severely disciplined. When Jeremiah was called in and had the protest read to him, he retorted that because Shemaiah had prophesied falsely, God would not let him or his family take part in the return of the exiles to Jerusalem.

The Fall of Jerusalem

In 589 BC King Zedekiah took the step that Jeremiah had so gravely feared. He joined in an uprising against Babylon. Once more Nebuchadnezzar invaded the country and laid siege to Jerusalem. The king sent priests to Jeremiah, asking him to intercede with the Lord for the safety of the city. The prophet's answer was a grim one. God had decided that the faithless city would fall to the enemy. The only way its inhabitants could save themselves was to surrender.

The siege dragged on, until suddenly it was lifted. The Babylonian forces were diverted to meet an advance by an Egyptian army under the Pharaoh Hophra.

With the enemy at the gate, the king and the well-to-do citizens had made a solemn covenant in the Temple to free all their Hebrew slaves. They now broke their word and enslaved them again, at which Jeremiah expressed great indignation.

During this break in the siege, Jeremiah came to be regarded as a pacifist and a quisling, who should be suppressed in the public interest. When he tried to leave the city to attend to some family property in his native village, he was arrested as a deserter by the sentry at the gate and flung into an underground cell, where he remained shut up for a long period of time.

The king sent for him and asked anxiously whether he had received any message from God. Jeremiah answered: 'There is.' Then he said, 'You shall be delivered into the hand of the king of Babylon.' Moreover: 'What wrong have I done to you or your servants or this people, that you have put me in prison?' (Jer. 37:17, 18) The king gave orders he should be moved to the court of the guard and be brought a fresh loaf of bread each day from the 'bakers' street'.

But pressure was brought on the king by senior officials and priests on the ground that Jeremiah's words were undermining the morale of the army. The

prophet was handed over to them and they had him lowered into a muddy cistern and left to die. He was rescued by one of the palace eunuchs, Ebed-melech, the Ethiopian. The distressed slave ran to tell the king what had happened to the prophet and was given three servants to help him pull Jeremiah out with ropes. For this act, the Lord promised that Ebed-melech would be saved from the Babylonians.

The siege was renewed and nearly two years later, in the summer of 587 BC, the starving city fell. A month later the Babylonian commander had the Temple, the palace and most of the buildings razed. The inhabitants were either killed or rounded up and deported to Babylon. King Zedekiah escaped with some of his soldiers, but was captured and killed.

Nebuchadnezzar had given orders that Jeremiah should be spared and treated well. The Babylonian commander located him among the shackled prisoners awaiting deportation. He had him released, and gave him permission to go to Babylon if he wished or to remain anywhere in the country. Jeremiah went to Mizpah, just north of Jerusalem, to his friend Gedaliah, whom the Babylonians had appointed as governor of Judah.

Two months later, Gedaliah was assassinated. A group of Judean patriots loyal to Gedaliah failed to catch the murderer, and fearing that they would be blamed, fled to Egypt to seek political asylum there. Jeremiah was taken with them together with his scribe Baruch.

Little is known about the last period of the prophet's life in Egypt. It is mentioned that he predicted the invasion of Egypt by Nebuchadnezzar, an event that took place. There is also a record of an assembly at which Jeremiah remonstrated with the Judean refugees in Egypt for worshipping alien gods, and addressed himself particularly to the women who made offerings to the heavenly bodies. His audience replied with some bitterness that the ancestral faith had not saved their homeland.

There is a dubious tradition that Jeremiah met his end by being stoned to death.

Jeremiah's Personality and Beliefs

The Book of Jeremiah contains fifty-two chapters, not in a very orderly sequence. It is compiled of various elements. Roughly, the first half consists of the prophet's oracles, sermons and divine messages against Jerusalem and Judah, in the reigns of Jehoiakim and Zedekiah. In addition, there is a group of poetic but hard-hitting 'Oracles against the Nations': chiefly Babylon, but also Egypt, the Philistines, the Phoenicians, Moab, Ammon, Edom, Elam and the Arabian tribes. 'The clamour will resound to the ends of the earth, for the Lord has an indictment against the nations; he is entering into judgment with all flesh, and the wicked he will put to the sword, says the Lord.' (Jer. 25:31)

In the second part of the Book there are a number of geographical narratives about Jeremiah, probably recorded by his disciple Baruch. They are interspersed with revealing personal confessions by the prophet himself.

From the narratives and the confessions Jeremiah emerges as a lonely and sensitive figure. With no other character in the Old Testament is there so moving a revelation of inner conflict.

At an early age, Jeremiah seemed cut off from the fabric of ordinary life. He states that God told him not to get married and have children, since the times were wicked and the people around him doomed. For this reason he was not to share in the mourning or rejoicing of his fellowmen. He was even denied 'the voice of mirth and the voice of gladness' (Jer. 16:9).

As solitary people with a country upbringing tend to do, he communed with nature, and had an affinity with the world of birds. 'Even the stork in the heavens knows her times; and the turtledove, swallow and crane keep the time of their coming.' (Jer. 8:7) He noted the partridge sitting on its eggs and 'the dove that nests in the sides of the mouth of a gorge' (Jer. 48:28).

Plagued by self-doubt, Jeremiah was at times overcome by a sense of futility about his mission: 'O Lord, do not thy eyes look for truth? Thou hast smitten them, but they felt no anguish; thou hast consumed them, but they refused to take correction. They have made their faces harder than rock.' (Jer. 5:3) At first he was naive enough to believe that if the poor and ignorant failed to respond, he would get a hearing from people of standing and education; 'I will go to the great, and will speak to them; for they know the way of the Lord.'

(Jer. 5:5) He was soon disillusioned.

Jeremiah suffered acutely from the ill-will and rejection he seemed to bring upon himself. 'Woe is me, my mother, that you bore me, a man of strife and contention to the whole land! I have not lent, nor have I borrowed, yet all of them curse me.' (Jer. 15:10) He cries out to the Lord, 'Why is my pain unceasing, my wound incurable, refusing to be healed?' (Jer. 15:18) His reactions fluctuate between a human desire to be revenged on his persecutors, a need for reassurance from his divine master, and an urge to withdraw into a 'wayfarer's shelter'. But his life's work was a compulsion from which there was no escape: '. . . there is in my heart as it were a burning fire shut up in my bones.' (Jer. 20:9)

Jeremiah served an uncompromising God, who demanded repentance – otherwise 'Those who are for pestilence, to pestilence, and those who are for the sword, to the sword; those who are for famine, to famine, and those who are for captivity, to captivity.' (Jer. 15:2) But the prophet delivered this stern message without self-righteousness. He was torn by compassion and was driven to intercede with God even for wrongdoers and enemies. Three times he mentions that the Lord rebukes him for such weakness. 'As for you, do not pray for this people, or lift up cry or prayer for them, and do not intercede with me, for I do not hear you.' (Jer. 7:16) During the great drought in the time of King Jehoiakim, he is sickened at the sight of dead men lying in the fields and hungry people in the city, and remonstrates with God himself: 'Hast thou utterly rejected Judah? Does thy soul loathe Zion? Why has thou smitten us so that there is no healing for us? We looked for peace, but no good came; for a time of healing, and behold, terror.' (Jer. 14:19)

The pacifism and the counsels of surrender which

A wall relief showing Ashurbanipal's 7th-century BC Arab wars. Jeremiah's prophecies must be seen against this background of war and invasion.

so provoked Jeremiah's fellow-citizens in time of siege sprang from a genuine physical horror of war and bloodshed. 'My anguish! my anguish! I writhe in pain! Oh, the walls of my heart! My heart is beating wildly; I cannot keep silent; for I hear the sound of the trumpet, the alarm of war.' (Jer. 4:19) Jeremiah is a prophet who proclaims disaster, and then cries out that 'nor have I desired the day of disaster' (Jer. 17:16). The man of peace comes through clearly in the letter he writes to the exiles in Babylon.

Jeremiah is perplexed by the problem of retribution: 'Righteous art thou, O Lord, when I complain to thee; yet I would plead my case before thee. Why does the way of the wicked prosper? Why do all who are treacherous thrive?' (Jer. 12:1) This vain effort to reconcile faith and reason reached its fullest biblical expression in the Book of Job. It is a theme which has dominated recent centuries, which have witnessed the rationalist, scientific onslaught on religion.

In general the great prophet of the 7th century BC is curiously akin in spirit to the modern world. He lived in a confused and insecure time, in which the old values were crumbling and even a man of God could be assailed by doubt and a sense of alienation from society. With it all, Jeremiah clung to a vision of a happier world beyond disaster, where men would have entered into a new covenant with God: 'For I will satisfy the weary soul, and every languishing soul I will replenish.' (Jer. 31:25) [Book of Jeremiah]

The Lamentations of Jeremiah

The Book known as 'The Lamentations of Jeremiah' is a sombre work consisting of five dirges on the fall of Jerusalem and the exile, each composed on an acrostic pattern. The mood is set by the opening verses:

'How lonely sits the city that was full of people!
How like a widow has she become,
she that was great among the nations!' (Lam. 1:1)

'Judah has gone into exile because of affliction
and hard servitude;
she dwells now among the nations,
but finds no resting place.' (Lam. 1:3)

The Vulgate Bible of St Jerome, following the Greek Bible, inserted an introduction: 'When Israel had been taken into captivity and Jerusalem had become a Wilderness, it happened that the Prophet Jeremiah sat down in tears: he uttered this lamentation over Jerusalem.' The work was printed immediately following the Book of Jeremiah.

Protestant Bibles maintained the title 'The Lamentations of Jeremiah', and the position straight after the Book of Jeremiah, but deleted the introduction.

The Hebrew Bible did not connect this book with Jeremiah and inserted it in the section of 'Writings', not in the section of 'Prophets'.

Both the literary pattern and certain specific pas-

And mine eyes a fountain of tears:
serigraph of the prophet Jeremiah
by Ben Shahn.

sages in the text make the attribution to Jeremiah untenable.

Lamentations is recited by Jews on the fast day of the Ninth of Av, commemorating the destruction of Jerusalem. It was used by Christians in the Holy Week liturgy. [Book of Lamentations]

6. c. 6 century BC. Son of Habazziniah, he was the father of Jaazaniah the Rechabite who refused to drink wine with the prophet Jeremiah. [Jer. 35:3]

7. 6 century BC. A chief priest of Judah who returned with Zerubbabel from exile in Babylon. [Neh. 12:1, 12]

8. 5 century BC. A priest who signed the solemn covenant in the time of Nehemiah. [Neh. 10:2]

9. 5 century BC. A leader of Judah who participated in the ceremony of dedicating the rebuilt walls of Jerusalem in the time of Nehemiah [Neh. 12:34]

JEREMOTH (Heb. ('Moth [a god] established') **1.** date unknown. Son of Becher and a grandson of Benjamin, he and his family were leaders of the tribe and mighty warriors. [1 Chr. 7:8]

2. date unknown. Son of Mushi, he was a Levite descended from Merari. Also called Jerimoth. [1 Chr. 23:23; 24:30]

3. date unknown. Descendant of Elpaal and a leader of the tribe of Benjamin. [1 Chr. 8:14]

4. see JERIMOTH 4.

5. 10 century BC. Son of Azriel, he was appointed by

King David to lead the tribe of Naphtali. [1 Chr. 27:19]

6. 5 century BC. One of the descendants of Elam who divorced his non-Jewish wife in the time of Ezra. [Ezra 10:26]

7. 5 century BC. Son of Zattu who divorced his non-Jewish wife in the time of Ezra. [Ezra 10:27]

8. 5 century BC. A descendant of Bani who divorced his non-Jewish wife in the time of Ezra. [Ezra 10:29]

JERIAH (Heb. 'God has established') date unknown. The eldest son of Hebron, the Levite, and a descendant of Kohath. Also known as Jerijah. [1 Chr. 23:19; 24:23; 26:31]

JERIBAI (Heb. 'my adversary') *c.* 10 century BC. Son of Elnaam, he and his brother Joshaviah were warriors in the armies of King David and distinguished for their bravery. [1 Chr. 11:46]

JERIEL (Heb. 'God has established') date unknown. A son of Tola and a grandson of Issachar, he and his family were leaders of the tribe and mighty warriors. [1 Chr. 7:2]

JERIJAH *see* JERIAH.

JERIMOTH (Heb. 'Moth [a god] established') **1.** *c.* 16 century BC. Son of Bela and grandson of Benjamin, he and his family were leaders of the tribe and mighty warriors. [1 Chr. 7:7]

2. *see* JEREMOTH 2.

3. *c.* 11 century BC. A Benjaminite warrior who deserted from King Saul's army and rallied to David at Ziklag. [1 Chr. 12:5]

4. *c* 10 century BC. A son of Heman, King David's musician, Jerimoth and his brothers played music in the Tabernacle under their father's direction, and he was responsible for the fifteenth turn of service. Also called Jeremoth. [1 Chr. 25:4, 22]

5. *c.* 10 century BC. Father of Mahalath, who was the wife of King Rehoboam of Judah. [2 Chr. 11:18]

6. *c.* 8 century BC. A Levite who supervised the bringing of offerings and tithes into the Temple in the reign of Hezekiah, king of Judah. [2 Chr. 31:13]

JERIOTH (Heb. 'tents') date unknown. One of the two wives of Caleb, son of Hezron, of the tribe of Judah. [1 Chr. 2:18]

JEROBOAM (Heb. 'the people increased').

1. Jeroboam I First king of Israel after the monarchy split, he reigned 931-10 BC.

During Solomon's building operations in Jerusalem, he appointed Jeroboam the son of Nebat and Zeruah as overseer of the labour force from his tribal area of Ephraim. At the time there was growing disaffection in the country over the tax and compulsory labour burdens, while the northern tribes were also jealous of the dominant position of Judah.

Jeroboam started plotting against the king, and was encouraged by Ahijah, a priest from the sanctuary of Shiloh in Ephraim. The priest stopped him one day on a deserted stretch of road and went through the symbolic act of tearing his cloak into twelve pieces (denoting the tribes of Israel) and handing ten of them to Jeroboam. Condemned to death by Solomon, Jeroboam fled to Egypt, where he was given political asylum by the Pharaoh Shishak.

On Solomon's death his son Rehoboam succeeded to the throne. The northern tribes seceded, setting up a separate kingdom of Israel. Jeroboam returned from Egypt and was elected its first ruler. The great Hebrew realm of David and Solomon had broken up into two small and quarrelling successor states.

Jeroboam at first resided in Shechem. After a period at Penuel across the Jordan river, he set up his perman-

Excavations at Tel Dan have uncovered a royal gateway and paved court from the time of Jeroboam I.

ent capital in Tirzah, seven miles north-east of Shechem. It was an ancient town in beautiful surroundings and commanded both the highway through the hills and the road down to the Jordan ford at Adam (Damia).

Jeroboam consciously set about fostering the separate identity of Israel. Since religion played a vital role in the life of the nation, it was essential for him to wean his subjects away from Solomon's Temple. 'If this people go up to offer sacrifices in the house of the Lord at Jerusalem, then the heart of this people will turn again to their lord, to Rehoboam king of Judah, and they will kill me.' (1 Kgs. 12:27)

He revived the traditional sanctuaries at Bethel near his southern border and Dan in the extreme north, and set up golden calves in them, as Aaron had done in the desert. He expelled the priestly Levites, who were loyal to the House of David, and in their stead recruited priests from the common people to serve at the two main shrines and the local 'high places'.

Scriptural disapproval was vividly expressed in the person of an unnamed 'man of God' from Judah who condemned the king beside the altar at Bethel, on which burnt-offerings had just been made. Jeroboam pointed at the man and ordered him to be arrested, but the king's outstretched arm became paralysed and he could not move it. At the same moment the altar flew apart and the ashes on it were scattered to the winds. The shaken monarch expressed repentance and his arm was healed.

Jeroboam ran into more religious reaction from an unexpected quarter. His son Abijah became critically ill and he sent the queen to the shrine at Shiloh to consult with the priest Ahijah, without disclosing who she was. The priest was old and nearly blind but, forewarned by the Lord, he immediately identified the woman as Jeroboam's wife. He told her pitilessly that her son would die, and uttered a curse against the king and all his house. The Lord would 'utterly consume the house of Jeroboam, as a man burns up dung until it is all gone' (1 Kgs. 14:10).

When Jeroboam had been on the throne for four years, the country was invaded by the Pharaoh Shishak. The biblical account mentions only his threat to Jerusalem. But Shishak's own version was preserved in the great bas-relief carved into the southern wall of the temple of Amon at Karnak. From this it appears that his forces swept through the kingdom of Israel and returned by the coast.

Jeroboam reigned for twenty-two years, and was succeeded by his son Nadab. [1 Kgs. 11:26-40; 12; 13; 14:1-30; 15:1, 6, 7, 9, 25, 29, 30, 34; 16:2, 3, 7, 19, 26; 2 Kgs. 3:3; 9:9; 10:29, 31; 13:2, 11; 14:24; 15:9, 28; 17:21, 22; 23:15; 2 Chr. 9:29; 10:2-15; 11:4, 14; 12:15; 13:1-20]

2. Jeroboam II Thirteenth king of Israel after the monarchy split, he reigned 783-43 BC. He was the son of Joash and the fourth ruler of the dynasty founded by Jehu.

After a period of decline, Joash had started to recover some of the territory lost to Israel's northern neighbour and hereditary enemy, the kingdom of Aram (Syria) with its capital at Damascus. Jeroboam continued this expansion, until his northern and eastern borders again reached those carved out by King David, when Israelite power had been at its peak. Jeroboam's control extended in Transjordan from Hamath (northern Syria) down to the Dead Sea. At the same time, the sister kingdom of Judah also expanded, regaining control of Edom on both sides of the Wadi Arabah down to the Gulf of Akaba.

Jeroboam's conquests were accompanied by a

The Divided Monarchy in days of Jeroboam II and Uzziah 800 BC

marked rise in living standards, and a burst of constructive energy within the kingdom. He added new buildings to the hill-top capital of Samaria, which Omri had founded almost a century earlier. The prophet Amos railed against the luxury and selfishness of the well-to-do class and its lack of concern for the poor. He also attacked the false sense of security that arose from the lack of outside pressure: 'Woe to those who are at ease in Zion, and to those who feel secure on the mountain of Samaria.' (Amos 6:1) His prediction of pending disaster came true a generation later when Samaria was taken by an invading Assyrian army and the kingdom of Israel came to an end.

Jeroboam died after forty-one years on the throne and was succeeded by his son Zechariah. [2 Kgs. 13:13; 14:16-29; 15:1, 8; 1 Chr. 5:17; Hos. 1:1; Amos 1:1; 7:9-11]

8th-century seal found at Megiddo with the inscription:
[belonging] to Shema, servant of Jeroboam', thought
to refer to Jeroboam II.

JEROHAM (Heb. 'God will have mercy') **1.** date unknown. Son of Elihu of the tribe of Levi, he was the
father of Elkanah and grandfather of Samuel. [1 Sam.
1:1; 1 Chr. 6:27, 34]
2. date unknown. A leader of the tribe of Benjamin
living in Jerusalem. [1 Chr. 8:27]
3. *c.* 11 century BC. A leader of Benjamin whose sons
Joelah and Zebadiah left the army of King Saul and
joined David at Ziklag. [1 Chr. 12:7]
4. *c.* 10 century BC. Father of Azarel who was appointed
ruler over the tribe of Dan in the reign of King David.
[1 Chr. 27:22]
5. *c.* 9 century BC. Father of Azariah, one of the army
commanders of Judah who, on the instructions of the
high priest Jehoiada, enthroned Joash as king and
executed Queen Athaliah who had usurped the throne.
[2 Chr. 23:1]
6. 5 century BC. Father of Ibneiah of the tribe of Benjamin who settled in Jerusalem in the days of Nehemiah.
[1 Chr. 9:8]
7. 5 century BC. Father of the priest Adaiah who served
in the Temple in Jerusalem in the time of Nehemiah.
[1 Chr. 9:12; Neh. 11:12]
JERUBBAAL *see* GIDEON
JERUBBESHETH *see* GIDEON
JERUSHA (Heb. 'inheritance') *c.* 8 century BC.
Daughter of Zadok, she was the wife of Uzziah, King
of Judah, and the mother of King Jotham. Also known
as Jerushah. [2 Kgs. 15:33; 2 Chr. 27:1]
JERUSHAH *see* JERUSHA
JESHAIAH (Heb. 'saved') **1.** date unknown. Father
of Ithiel of the tribe of Benjamin, his descendants
settled in Jerusalem in Nehemiah's time. [Neh. 11:7]
2. *c.* 10 century BC. A son of King David's musician
Jeduthun. Jeshaiah and his brothers played in the
Tabernacle under their father's direction and he took

the eighth turn of service. [1 Chr. 25:3, 15]
3. *c.* 10 century BC. Descendant of Rehabiah, he was
a Levite responsible for keeping the treasures captured
by King David in battle, which were dedicated to the
Tabernacle. [1 Chr. 26:25]
4. 6 century BC. A son of Hananiah of the tribe of
Judah, and the grandson of Zerubbabel, he was a
descendant of King David. [1 Chr. 3:21]
5. 5 century BC. Son of Athaliah and a descendant of
Elam, he returned with Ezra from exile in Babylon.
[Ezra 8:7]
6. 5 century BC. A Levite descended from Merari who
returned to Jerusalem to minister in the Tabernacle in
the time of Ezra. [Ezra 8:19]
JESHARELAH *see* ASHARELAH
JESHEBEAB (Heb. 'father's place') *c.* 10 century
BC. A priest of Israel during the reign of King David,
he was responsible for the fourteenth turn of service in
the Tabernacle. [1 Chr. 24:13]
JESHER (Heb. 'right') date unknown. One of the
three sons of Caleb, son of Hezron, and a leader of the
tribe of Judah. [1 Chr. 2:18]
JESHISHAI (Heb. 'son of old age') date unknown.
Son of Jahdo of the tribe of Gad, he was a leader of the
tribe living in Gilead. [1 Chr. 5:14]
JESHOHAIAH (Heb. 'bowed') *c.* 8 century BC. A
leader of the tribe of Simeon who drove out the
inhabitants of the rich valley of Gedor and settled
there. [1 Chr. 4:36]
JESHUA (Heb. 'saviour') **1.** *c.* 10 century BC. A priest
in the reign of King David, he took the ninth turn of
service in the Tabernacle. [1 Chr. 24:11]
2. *c.* 8 century BC. A priest in the reign of Hezekiah,
he was responsible for the distribution of the holy offerings among the priests in their cities in Judah. [2 Chr.
31:15]
3. *c.* 6 century BC. Head of a family descended from
Pahath-moab who returned with Zerubbabel from exile
in Babylon. [Ezra 2:6; Neh. 7:11]
4. 6 century BC. Head of a family of priests who returned from Babylon with Zerubbabel. [Ezra 2:36;
Neh. 7:39]
5. 6 century BC. Head of a family of Levites who
returned with Zerubbabel from Babylon. [Ezra 2:40;
Neh. 12:8]
6. 6 century BC. The son of Jozadak, he was high priest
in the time of Zerubabbel, and is symbolically crowned
in the Book of Zechariah. Also known as Joshua. [Ezra
3:2; 10:18; Hag. 1:1, 12, 14; 2:2, 4; Zech. 3:1, 3; 6:11]
7. 5 century BC. Father of Jozabad, a Levite in the days
of Ezra. [Ezra 8:33]
8. 5 century BC. Father of Ezer, the ruler of Mizpah,
who repaired part of the wall of Jerusalem in the time
of Nehemiah. [Neh. 3:19]
9. 5 century BC. One of the leaders of Judah who

explained the Law of Moses to the people in the market-place after Ezra had read it to them. He called upon the people to confess their sins on the public fast day proclaimed by Ezra. [Neh. 8:7; 9:4]

10. 5 century BC. Son of Azaniah, he was one of the Levites who signed the solemn covenant in the time of Nehemiah. [Neh. 10:9]

JESHURUN (Heb. 'upright') Symbolic name for the Children of Israel in the Book of Deuteronomy. [Deut. 32:15; 33:5, 26; Isa. 44:2]

JESIMIEL (Heb. 'God will set up') c. 8 century BC. One of the leaders of the tribe of Simeon in the days of King Hezekiah, he drove the occupants out of the rich Gedor valley and settled there. [1 Chr. 4:36]

JESSE (Heb. 'the Lord is') c. 11 century BC. Father of David, Jesse was a resident of Bethlehem. He was the grandson of Ruth and Boaz and the father of eight sons, of whom David was the youngest. On a visit to Bethlehem the prophet Samuel received Jesse and his sons and anointed David without explaining why.

Later, when three of his sons were in Saul's army, Jesse sent provisions to them with David, and included a gift of ten cheeses for their commanding officers.

When David had fled from Saul, he sent his father and mother to Moab for safety.

Two of Jesse's daughters, Zeruiah and Abigail, were the mothers of famous warriors. [Ruth 4:17, 22; 1 Sam. 16; 17:12-58; 20:27-31; 22; 25:10; 2 Sam. 20:1; 23:1; 1 Kgs. 12:16; 1 Chr. 2:12, 13; 10:14; 12:18; 29:26; 2 Chr. 10:16; 11:18; Isa. 11:1, 10]

JETHER (Heb. 'who excels') **1.** c. 12 century BC. Eldest son of Gideon, the judge, he was commanded to kill the captured Midianite kings Zebah and Zalmunna. But Jether was young and afraid, so his father slew them. [Judg. 8:20]

2. date unknown. Son of Jada and a leader of the tribe of Judah who died childless. [1 Chr. 2:32]

3. date unknown. One of the four sons of Ezrah of the tribe of Judah. [1 Chr. 4:17]

4. date unknown. A leader of the tribe of Asher and a mighty warrior. [1 Chr. 7:38]

5. c. 10 century BC. The husband of King David's sister Abigail, he was the father of Amasa who was killed by David's army commander Joab. Jether is described as an Israelite and as an Ishmaelite. Also called Ithra. [2 Sam. 17:25; 1 Kgs. 2:5, 32; 1 Chr. 2:17]

Moses at the well with the daughters of Jethro : fresco by Sandro Botticelli (c. 1446-1510), in the Sistine Chapel, Vatican.

JETHETH date unknown. One of the chiefs of Edom descended from Esau. [Gen. 36:40; 1 Chr. 1:51]

JETHRO (Heb. 'excellence') *c.* 13 century BC. Moses's father-in-law. Jethro was a priest, and leader of a Midianite tribe known as Kenites, who lived in the Sinai desert.

When Moses fled from Egypt after killing Pharaoh's overseer, he lived with Jethro, married his daughter Zipporah, and tended his sheep.

Years later, when Moses was again in the Sinai desert leading the Children of Israel, his father-in-law came to visit him at the Rephidim camp. Moses was delighted to see Jethro and told him how the Lord had delivered them out of the hands of the Egyptians. Jethro said, 'Now I know that the Lord is greater than all gods.' (Exod. 18:11) Jethro offered a burnt sacrifice to God, and Aaron and all the elders came to have a meal with him.

Jethro advised Moses to appoint judges to whom he would teach the laws and delegate some of the work, leaving only the difficult cases for himself. 'Then Moses let his father-in-law depart, and he went his way to his own country.' (Exod. 18:27)

Some scholars have suggested that Jethro, also known as Hobab or Reuel, acted as a guide to Moses in the Sinai desert. Others think that Hobab was Jethro's son. [Exod. 3:1; 4:18; 18:1-12; Num. 10:29; Judg. 1:16; 4:11]

JETUR *c.* 18 century BC. Son of Ishmael and a grandson of Abraham, he was a desert chieftain. [Gen. 25:15; 1 Chr. 1:31; 5:19]

JEUEL (Heb. 'treasured') **1.** 5 century BC. A descendant of Zerah of the tribe of Judah, he was head of a family who settled in Jerusalem in the time of Nehemiah. [1 Chr. 9:6]

2. date unknown. A Levite whose ancestors took part in the purification of the Temple in the time of Hezekiah. [2 Chr. 29:13]

3. 5 century BC. An exile who returned to Judah with Ezra and helped to rebuild Jerusalem. [Ezra 8:13]

JEUSH 1. (Heb. 'may God help') *c.* 17 century BC. A son of Esau and Oholibamah, and an Edomite leader. [Gen. 36:4, 14, 18; 1 Chr. 1:35]

2. date unknown. Grandson of Jediael of the tribe of Benjamin, he was a leader of the tribe. [1 Chr. 7:10]

3. *c.* 10 century BC. A son of Shimei, a Levite. Jeush and his brother Beriah did not have many sons, therefore, in David's census, they counted as one family. [1 Chr. 23:10, 11]

4. *c.* 10 century BC. Son of King Rehoboam of Judah and his wife Mahalath. [2 Chr. 11:19]

5. *c.* 9 century BC. Son of Eshek of the tribe of Benjamin and a descendant of King Saul. [1 Chr. 8:39]

JEUZ (Heb. 'assembler') date unknown. Son of Shaharaim and his wife Hodesh, he was a leader of the tribe of Benjamin. [1 Chr. 8:10]

JEZANIAH *see* JAAZANIAH 1.

JEZEBEL (Heb. 'chaste') *c.* 9 century BC. Phoenician wife of King Ahab of Israel.

Jezebel was the daughter of Ethbaal, king of Sidon, and was married to Ahab, son and successor of Omri, king of Israel. She was a strong-willed woman who clearly dominated her husband. She fostered in Israel the worship of Melkart, the Phoenician 'baal' (god), and Ashtaroth, the goddess of fertility. Four hundred and fifty priests or 'prophets' of Baal were maintained by Jezebel in the capital Samaria, as part of her household. Shrines to her native gods sprang up on the hill-tops, and a temple to Baal was constructed in the palace. It was said that the king himself was drawn into the alien forms of worship. Those Israelite priests who resisted these inroads into the ancestral faith were eliminated or driven into hiding.

7th-century BC terracotta idols found at Judean sites. The hands under the breasts signify a fertility cult.

Alabaster statue of a Phoenician god,
found at Galera. Jezebel was
condemned in the Bible for her introduction
of Phoenician idol-worship.

The resistance was led by the prophet Elijah. In a contest of faith on Mount Carmel, Elijah triumphed over Jezebel's priests, and all of them were slain. The furious Jezebel wanted to have Elijah put to death but he managed to escape southward into the desert.

Ahab coveted the vineyard of Naboth next to the winter palace at Jezreel, but the owner refused to part with it. Taking matters into her own hands, Jezebel sent letters in Ahab's name and over his royal seal to the local leaders in Jezreel. They were to arrest Naboth on charges of blasphemy against God and the king, and to have him stoned to death on the evidence of two false witnesses. This judicial murder was carried out. By law, the condemned man's property then passed into the hands of the king. Once more Elijah appeared, and prophesied that Ahab and all his household would be destroyed and 'The dogs shall eat Jezebel within the bounds of Jezreel.' (1 Kgs. 21:23)

A tough army commander called Jehu murdered Ahab's son, King Jehoram, and seized the throne. Jezebel met her death with stiff pride: when Jehu came through the gate of the palace in Jezreel, he saw her standing drawn up at the window with her eyes and face made up and her hair carefully dressed. She called out contemptuously to him, 'Is it peace, you Zimri, murderer of your master?' (2 Kgs. 9:31) (Zimri was another army officer who had murdered an earlier king, Elah, and seized power.) Jehu shouted out to the attendants of the queen-mother to hurl her down from the window, and they obeyed him; '... some of her blood spattered on the wall and on the horses, and they trampled on her.' (2 Kgs. 9:33)

9th-century BC Phoenician ivory from
Nimrod, showing a woman with painted face
framed in a window.

After Jehu had eaten and drunk in the palace, he told his servants to go and bury Jezebel's body, since she was after all a king's daughter. They reported that all they had found left of the corpse was the skull, hands and feet. Jehu declared that this was the fulfilment of Elijah's prediction that the dogs would eat her.

The biblical editors felt obvious revulsion for Jezebel, whose gruesome end is related almost with gusto. She remains the most notorious of all Old Testament characters, and her name has become a symbol of female depravity. [1 Kgs. 16:31; 18:4, 13, 19; 19:1, 2; 21:5-25; 2 Kgs. 9:22, 30-37]

JEZER (Heb. 'God's creature') c. 16 century BC. A son of Naphtali, he went down to Egypt with his grandfather Jacob. [Gen. 46:24; Num. 26:49; 1 Chr. 7:13]

JEZIEL *c.* 11 century BC. Son of Azmaveth, a Benjaminite, he could shoot an arrow with either hand. He and his brother joined David at Ziklag. [1 Chr. 12:3]

JEZRAHIAH (Heb. 'may God sparkle') 5 century BC. Leader of the singers at the dedication service for the rebuilt walls of Jerusalem in the days of Nehemiah. [Neh. 12:42]

JEZREEL (Heb. 'may God sow') **1.** date unknown. A leader of the tribe of Judah. [1 Chr. 4:3]

2. *c.* 8 century BC. Son of the prophet Hosea, his name symbolized the destruction of the dynasty of Jehu, king of Israel, in the valley of Jezreel, the place where Jehu had originally seized the throne. [Hos. 1:4]

JIDLAPH (Heb. 'weeping') *c.* 18 century BC. Son of Abraham's brother Nahor. [Gen. 22:22]

JOAB (Heb. 'God his father') **1.** date unknown. Son of Seraiah of the tribe of Judah, he was head of a family of craftsmen. [1 Chr. 4:14]

2. *c.* 11 century· BC. Commander-in-chief to King David. David's eldest sister, Zeruiah, had three sons – Joab, Abishai and Asahel, all of whom became professional soldiers. Joab and Abishai may have been a little older than their uncle David, the youngest of Jesse's sons.

Joab was a tough, brave and skilful army commander, intensely loyal to his master, ruthless towards his enemies, and jealous of rivals to the point of murder. He shared David's fortunes over some half a century, from the time that David fled from Saul's hostility. The common hardships and dangers, and the tight comradeship of a fugitive band, forged bonds between uncle and nephew which David was later unable to break, even when he had been given good cause to rid himself of Joab.

When David became king of Judah in Hebron, after Saul's death, he appointed Joab commander-in-chief of his forces. At the pool of Gibeon, north-west of Jerusalem, the forces of Joab and Saul's general Abner confronted each other. They agreed to a trial of strength between twelve picked men on each side. When all these men were killed in a single combat, leaving the issue undecided, general fighting broke out in which Abner's men were routed. The fleeing Abner reluctantly slew Joab's youngest brother Asahel who pursued him. At sunset Joab and his soldiers caught up with Abner's party and agreed to withdraw in order to avoid more bloodshed. But Joab had a score to settle with Abner.

Joab returned from a successful foray with his men and was taken aback to discover that in his absence David had made a pact with Abner to reunite the kingdom. Joab tried to persuade David that Abner had deceived him, and had come only to spy. When

The water cistern at Gibeon (el-Jib), where the forces of Joab and Abner met.

this had no effect he sent messengers after Abner to bring him back to Hebron, and waited for him at the entrance to the town. Here 'Joab took him aside into the midst of the gate to speak with him privately, and there he smote him in the belly, so that he died, for the blood of Asahel his brother.' (2 Sam. 3:27)

The horrified David ordered a state funeral for Abner and himself led the mourning. 'These men the sons of Zeruiah,' David complained, 'are too hard for me.' (2 Sam. 3:39) In spite of that, Joab and his brother Abishai remained in David's service.

Joab was sent to capture Jerusalem, which had remained a Jebusite stronghold. At the critical stage of the attack, the Jebusite defenders brought the blind and the lame out on the walls to bar the way. The superstitious Israelite soldiers shrank back from this pathetic human barricade. David offered promotion to the first soldier who would defy the curse. The one who did so was the commander-in-chief Joab himself, and the city fell. David's tough-minded general feared neither military adversaries nor evil spells.

Joab led an expedition of picked Israelite troops against Raboth-Ammon, the capital city of Hanum, king of Ammon, who had formed a military coalition against David. Joab found himself trapped between the Ammonites drawn up in battle array before their city, and a mobile force of Syrian chariots and cavalry on his southern flank. He acted quickly and boldly. With one half of his men he attacked the Syrian force, while the other half of the Israelite troops under the command of his brother Abishai held the Ammonites at bay. The Syrians were repulsed, and the Ammonite troops retreated into their city.

The next year, the Israelite army under Joab again marched into Ammon, and laid siege to the capital Rabbah. It was during this siege that Joab received a sealed letter from the king concerning Uriah, a Hittite officer serving at the front. The letter said: 'Set Uriah in the forefront of the hardest fighting and then draw back from him, that he may be struck down, and die.' (2 Sam. 11:15) Joab could not know the reason for this extraordinary order – that David was having a love affair with Uriah's wife Bathsheba who had conceived a child by him. But Joab carried out his master's wishes without question. Uriah was sent to lead a rash attack on the walls and was killed.

Joab captured the key citadel controlling the water supply of Rabbah. He proposed that David himself move up with fresh troops for the final assault 'lest I take the city, and it be called by my name' (2 Sam. 12:28). In this way Joab demonstrated that his king's renown mattered more than his own.

Joab and David's Sons

Three years after David's favourite son Absalom murdered his elder brother Amnon and fled into exile, it was Joab who tried to bring about a reconciliation. He did not presume to broach so sensitive a subject directly. Instead he brought before the king a woman from the town of Tekoah who pretended one of her sons had killed the other. When David's compassion had been aroused she referred to his own banished son. The king relented and sent Joab to fetch Absalom back to Jerusalem.

But the conflict between father and son had not been resolved. Absalom launched a rebellion, and Joab was one of the loyal group that fled with David. In the crucial battle that later took place in the woods of Ephraim, east of the Jordan river, David's forces under Joab's command defeated those of Absalom. David had instructed his commanders that no harm should come to his rebellious son but it was not in Joab's nature to spare even a kinsman who had risen against

his master. Finding Absalom dangling in mid-air because his flowing hair had become entangled with an overhanging oak branch, Joab cold-bloodedly plunged three darts into his body and ordered his men to finish him off.

Joab roughly upbraided David for giving way to grief, and demanded that he show himself in public if he did not want to lose the support of his people. David pulled himself together but could not forgive Joab. He confirmed the appointment as army commander in Joab's place of Amasa, another nephew who had led Absalom's army.

As he had done many years before with Abner, Joab approached Amasa in feigned friendship, and suddenly stabbed him to death. Joab then assumed command again, pursued Sheba who had led a Benjaminite revolt against David, and returned with his severed head.

David became old and ailing, and his eldest surviving son Adonijah made an attempt to usurp the throne. Joab threw his powerful support behind Adonijah's claim. But his new master's cause collapsed when David renounced the throne in favour of a younger prince, Solomon, the son of Bathsheba. Joab's life was in danger. On his deathbed David referred to Joab's slaying of Abner and Amasa and charged Solomon, 'do not let his grey head go down to Sheol in peace' (1 Kgs. 2:6).

Joab sought sanctuary at the altar, but on King Solomon's instructions Benaiah, the captain of the palace guard, sought him out there and killed him, 'and he was buried in his own house in the wilderness' (1 Kgs. 2:34). Thus Joab paid with his blood for his deeds of violence, and for wavering at the end in his lifelong devotion to David. [1 Sam. 26:6; 2 Sam. 2:13-32; 3:22-31; 8:16; 10:7-14; 11:1-25; 12:26-7; 14:1, 2, 19-33; 17:25; 18:2-29; 19:1, 5, 13; 20:7-23; 23:18, 24, 37; 24:2-9; 1 Kgs. 1:1-41; 2:5, 22, 28-35; 11:15, 16; 1 Chr. 2:16; 11:6, 8, 20, 26, 39; 18:15; 19:8-15; 20:1; 21:3-6; 27:7, 24, 34]

3. 6 century BC. Head of a family descended from Pahath-moab that returned to Judah with Zerubbabel from exile in Babylon. [Ezra 2:6; 8:9; Neh. 7:11]

JOAH (Heb. 'brother of God') **1.** date unknown. Son of Zimmah, he was a Levite descended from Gershom. [1 Chr. 6:21]

2. c. 10 century BC. Son of Obed-edom, he and his family were gatekeepers of the Tabernacle in the reign of King David. [1 Chr. 26:4]

3. c. 8 century BC. Son of Asaph, he was court recorder

at the time of the Assyrian siege of Jerusalem, and together with two others delivered the Assyrian terms to King Hezekiah. [2 Kgs. 18:18-37]

4. *c.* 8 century BC. One of the Levites who obeyed King Hezekiah's command to sanctify themselves and cleanse the Temple. [2 Chr. 29:12]

5. *c.* 7 century BC. Son of Joahaz, he was court recorder for Josiah, king of Judah, and one of the three men responsible for the repair of the Temple. [2 Chr. 34:8]

JOAHAZ (Heb. 'held by God') **1.** *see* JEHOAHAZ **2.**

2. *c.* 7 century BC. Father of Joah, who was court recorder for Josiah, king of Judah. [2 Chr. 34:8]

JOASH (Heb. 'given by God') **1.** date unknown. A son of Becher and a grandson of Benjamin, he and his nine brothers were leaders of the tribe and mighty warriors. [1 Chr. 7:8]

2. date unknown. Son of Shelah and a leader of the tribe of Judah, he and his brother Saraph were rulers in Moab. [1 Chr. 4:22]

3. *c.* 12 century BC. Father of Gideon. Joash worshipped the idol Baal, but Gideon destroyed the altar Joash had made to Baal and cut down the grove next to it. When his townsmen ordered Joash to kill his son for destroying the idol, Joash answered: 'Will you contend for Baal?... If he is a god, let him contend for himself. ...' (Judg. 6:31) [Judg. 6:11, 29-31; 8:29, 32]

4. *c.* 11 century BC. One of the men of Benjamin who left the army of King Saul and rallied to David at Ziklag. [1 Chr. 12:3]

5. *c.* 10 century BC. The supervisor of the royal oil vats in the reign of King David. [1 Chr. 27:28]

6. *c.* 9 century BC. Son of King Ahab of Israel, he was commanded by his father to imprison the prophet Micaiah. [1 Kgs. 22:26; 2 Chr. 18:25]

7. Eighth king of Judah after the monarchy split, he reigned 835-796 BC.

Joash was the son of King Ahaziah of Judah and Zibiah of Beersheba. When he was still an infant his father was killed in the revolt of Jehu in the kingdom of Israel. His grandmother Athaliah, who was the daughter of the domineering Phoenician Queen Jezebel, then had all the royal offspring murdered and seized the throne herself. The only one to escape was Joash, who was taken away and hidden by his aunt Jehosheba. She handed him over to the priest Jehoiada who secretly kept him in the Temple and cared for him.

When the child was seven years old, Jehoiada had him crowned king in the Temple under the protection of the palace guard and then presented him to the excited crowd. Athaliah rushed to the scene and was killed by the guards.

In the twenty-third year of Joash's reign, he became aware that the voluntary offerings for the renovation of the Temple were not being used for the intended purpose. He ordered them collected in a special chest

at the entrance to the Temple, checked under the supervision of the king's officials and paid over directly to the contractors and workmen.

The priesthood lost its influence on the throne with Jehoiada's death, and the king had Jehoiada's son Zechariah, also a priest, executed for making trouble.

During Joash's reign King Hazael of Aram-Damascus marched across Israel and advanced on Jerusalem. Joash was able to save the city only by handing over to the Arameans a crippling ransom, for which the treasuries of the Temple and the palace had to be virtually emptied. It may have been this display of impotence in the face of an external enemy that led to Joash's downfall. He was murdered by two of his palace officials after he had been forty years on the throne. He was succeeded by his son Amaziah. Also called Jehoash. [2 Kgs. 11; 12; 13:1, 10; 14:1, 3, 13, 17, 23; 1 Chr. 3:11; 2 Chr. 22:11; 24:1-24; 25:23, 25]

8. Twelfth king of Israel after the monarchy split, he reigned 798-83 BC. Joash was the grandson of Jehu and the son of Jehoahaz. He came to the throne at a time when Israel's northern neighbour Aram-Damascus (Syria) had come to dominate it, and had stripped it of much of its territory.

At the beginning of his reign, Joash went to visit the aged prophet Elisha, then on his deathbed. The prophet told him to open the eastern window and shoot an arrow in the direction of the enemy, Aram. He did so; and this, predicted Elisha, was a symbol of the victory he would gain. The prophet then told the king to strike the ground with the remaining arrows, and reproved him when Joash stopped after the third strike, which meant that his victory would be incomplete: 'You should have struck five or six times; then you would have struck down Syria until you had made an end of it, but now you will strike down Syria only three times.' (2 Kgs. 13:19)

Joash did not conquer Aram but he won three battles against the Syrian forces and was able to regain the towns his father had lost.

King Amaziah of Judah achieved some success against Edom, and sent a boastful challenge to the king of Israel. Joash replied, 'why should you provoke trouble so that you fall, you and Judah with you?' (2 Kgs. 14:10) But Amaziah would not heed the warning. At the battle of Beth-shemesh, on the Israel-Judah border, Amaziah's forces were defeated by Joash who marched on Jerusalem and attacked it, breaking down part of the city wall. He retired to Samaria, taking with him hostages, gold and silver vessels from the Temple, and much of the royal treasure.

Joash died after a reign of sixteen years and was succeeded by his son Jeroboam II. Also called Jehoash. [2 Kgs. 13:9-25; 14:1-27; 2 Chr. 25:17-25; Hos. 1:1; Amos 1:1]

JOB period of the Patriarchs. Central character of the Book of Job.

According to a popular folk-tale dating back to the period of the Hebrew Patriarchs, Job was a prosperous and righteous notable living 'in the land of Uz', probably Edom, south of the Dead Sea. He suffered a number of afflictions to test his faith in God, and proved himself steadfast. This simple story was used by an unknown genius of the 5th or 4th century BC as a framework for a dramatic poem which is one of the great masterpieces of literature. Its theme was the reason for human suffering, and it raised profound questions about divine justice. In both form and content, the Book of Job does not resemble any other portion of the Scriptures.

The original narrative is briefly told in prose in a Prologue and Epilogue. The main body of the Book is the most sustained poetry in the Old Testament, and the only biblical work that is cast in dramatic form. It contains the debates between Job and three of his friends, and is climaxed by a confrontation between Job and God himself.

The Prologue pictures Job as a man who was 'blameless and upright, one who feared God, and turned away from evil' (Job 1:1). He was blessed with seven sons and three daughters, and an abundance of live-stock: seven thousand sheep, three thousand camels, five hundred yoke of oxen and five hundred she-asses. Each of the sons in turn would give a family feast and then Job would gather them all together to offer a sacrifice at dawn, lest any one of them had unwittingly sinned.

One day in the heavenly council, the Lord asked Satan whether in the course of his earthly journeys he had come across the pious Job. Satan replied sarcastically that it was easy for a rich and successful man to be God-fearing. 'But put forth thy hand now, and touch all that he has, and he will curse thee to thy face.' (Job 1:11) The Lord agreed that Satan should put Job to the test, provided his person was not touched.

The following day Job's donkeys and camels were carried off by marauders, and his sheep were killed in a hailstorm. What was worse, the roof of his eldest son's house collapsed during a gale, when all his children were gathered there, and none of them was left alive. Job went into mourning, but uttered no word of protest against the Lord.

Satan maintained that Job would react otherwise if he were afflicted in his own body. The Lord gave Satan permission to try Job further, provided his life was spared.

Job then broke out in dreadful sores from head to

Two illustrations from a 15th-century
Italian manuscript of the Book of Job,
showing (above) Job's servants and animals,
and (below) Job's servants and
animals being killed.

left Job: etching by Ernst Fuchs, 1963.
The name Job has become a synonym for patience
in the face of suffering.

foot. As he sat in the ash-pit and scraped at himself with a sharp piece of broken pottery, his wife cried out bitterly: 'Do you still hold fast your integrity? Curse God, and die.' (Job 2:9)

Job replied that she was a foolish woman. If they accepted happiness from God, must they not accept sorrow too?

Word of Job's misfortunes reached three of his friends – Eliphaz of Teman, Bildad of Shuah and Zophar of Naamah. (These were towns in Edom.) They came to call on Job and were shocked to find he could hardly be recognized. For seven days and nights they sat with him without speaking.

At this point the Prologue ends, and the main poem begins, with Job cursing his own existence. 'Let the day perish wherein I was born, and the night which said, A man-child is conceived.' (Job 3:3)

Job Protests his Innocence

His friends try to console him, and express the traditional and pious views about his sufferings. God does not punish good men, only bad ones. If evil-doers seem to prosper for a while, their sins will soon catch up with them: '... that the exulting of the wicked is short, and the joy of the godless but for a moment' (Job 20:5). Good people may also suffer, but then nobody is wholly pure and innocent, not even an angel, while man is inherently frail. Job should put his trust in God and appeal to him in humility, then all will be well. 'For he wounds, but he binds up; he smites, but his hands heal.' (Job 5:18)

As Job continues to rail against God, his three friends lose patience with him. Bildad asks him angrily, 'How long will you say these things, and the words of your mouth be a great wind? Does God pervert judgment? Or does the Almighty pervert the right?' (Job 8:2, 3) Zophar also chides him: 'Should a multitude of words go unanswered and a man full of talk be vindicated? Should your babble silence men, and when you mock, shall no one shame you?' (Job 11:2, 3) They suggest that if Job is afflicted, he must be a sinful man, and his protests must be prompted by a guilty conscience. Eliphaz even lists a number of uncharitable acts he falsely attributes to Job.

Job makes no effort to conceal his own exasperation with his friends, whom he calls 'miserable comforters' and 'physicians of no value'. 'Hold your peace,' he storms at them, 'Let me have silence, and I will speak, and let come on me what may.' (Job 13:13) Why should they torment him with their lectures? God does not need them to plead for him. To Bildad's strictures he retorts with irony: 'How you have helped him who has no power! How you have saved the arm that has no strength! How have you counselled him who has no wisdom.' (Job 26:2, 3)

He rejects their advice to bear his trials with silent

fortitude. 'But I would speak to the Almighty, and I desire to argue my case with God.... Behold, he will slay me ... I will defend my ways to his face.' (Job 13:3, 15)

Job recalls what a good life he used to have and how respected he was. Now everyone shuns him, and youths spit in his face whose fathers he would not have put with his sheep-dogs: 'those whom I loved have turned against me. My bones cleave to my skin and to my flesh.... Have pity on me, have pity on me, O you my friends, for the hand of God has touched me!' (Job 19:19, 20, 21)

Mournfully Job reflects on the futility of life: 'Man that is born of a woman is of few days, and full of trouble. He comes forth like a flower, and withers; he flees like a shadow, and continues not.' (Job 14:1, 2)

Over and over again, Job protests his innocence, and demands of God to 'make me understand how I have erred.' (Job 6:24) Has he been guilty of vanity or deceit, lusted after other women, failed to respect the rights of his servants, or to take care of the poor or needy? Has he sought after riches, or secretly worshipped pagan gods, or wished evil on his enemies, or

above Job's vision of the sea-serpents.
below Job with his three friends (left), and messengers bringing news of disasters (right).
15th-century Italian manuscript.

Job

turned away strangers from his door, or engaged in unfair dealings?

He is ready to account for all his actions, provided they are weighed in an even balance. What he demands is a fair trial, with the charges against him presented in due form of law. Yet how can he expect justice if God is both accuser and judge? A trial between God and himself is an unequal contest. God's power is absolute, his decrees are final, and there is no way to appeal against them. 'For he is not a man, as I am, that I might answer him, and we should come to trial together.' (Job 9:32)

He wants to defend himself, but who will get him a hearing? God is far away, and cannot be reached. 'Oh, that I knew where I might find him, that I might come even to his seat! I would lay my case before him and fill my mouth with arguments ... I cry to thee and thou dost not answer me; I stand, and thou dost not heed me.' (Job 23:3, 4; 30:20) In despair, Job asks whether God really cares about a world in which wicked men prosper and the poor go naked and hungry.

At one point Job becomes weary of seeking justice, and only wants to be left alone like a hired servant that must finish his day's work and then rest. Yet at the end he once more affirms that he is guiltless, and defiantly calls upon the Lord to hand him the list of charges against him, so that he may wear it as a badge of honour.

A new character now appears, Elihu the son of Barachel the Buzite. An introductory paragraph explains that as a young man he had kept quiet in the presence of his elders. But he could not accept the fact that Eliphaz, Bildad and Zophar had ceased to argue with Job. There follow three long speeches, in which Elihu covers much the same ground as Job's three friends, adding little in the way of fresh argument. (It is suggested that the Elihu chapters are of a later date. Elihu is not mentioned elsewhere in the Book; the style and language do not rise to the same heights; and the intervention separates Job's final plea from God's reply to him, thereby disrupting the natural flow of the dialogue.)

After Job has finished speaking, the Lord answers him out of the whirlwind, by putting questions of his own. 'Who is this that darkens counsel by words without knowledge? Gird up your loins like a man, I will question you, and you shall declare to me. Where were you when I laid the foundation of the earth?... When the morning stars sang together, and all the sons of God shouted for joy?' (Job 38:2, 3, 4, 7)

What does Job know about control of the seas, the coming of the dawn, the snow and hail, thunder, lightning and rain, the movements of the stars, and the ways of the animals and birds? 'Shall a fault-finder contend with the Almighty? He who argues with God, let him answer it.' (Job 40:2)

When the Morning Stars sang together and all the Sons of God shouted for Joy: illustration to the Book of Job by William Blake (1757-1827).

Job was overwhelmed at the presence of the Lord, and humbled at the majestic and mysterious workings of the universe. He accepted that there were matters beyond his comprehension: 'Therefore I have uttered what I did not understand, things too wonderful for me, which I did not know.... I had heard of thee by the hearing of the ear, but now my eye sees thee; therefore I despise myself, and repent in dust and ashes.' (Job 42:3, 5, 6)

With the main work ended by Job's submission to God, a short prose epilogue picks up the original folktale again, and furnishes it with a happy ending. Eliphaz, Bildad and Zophar are admonished. Job is restored to his position, and given double the wealth he lost before. All his kinsmen and friends come to pay their respects and bring gifts. Again he produces seven sons and three beautiful daughters called Jemimah, Keziah and Keren-happuch. He lives to see his descendants to the fourth generation, and dies at the ripe age of one hundred and forty.

213

Job makes his sacrifice to the Lord
and his cattle are restored:
15th-century Italian manuscript. After his trials,
Job's riches were restored twofold.

The author of the Book of Job was one of the boldest and most original religious thinkers and literary masters ever to have existed. He was as familiar with the intellectual heritage of his time as with the life of the desert, and he did not hesitate to challenge and probe accepted beliefs. The identity of the man who penned Job's immortal dialogue with God and his fellow-men remains one of the unresolved mysteries of the Old Testament. [Book of Job]

JOBAB 1. date unknown. Son of Zerah of Bozrah, he was the second king of Edom. [Gen. 36:33, 34; 1 Chr. 1:44, 45]

2. date unknown. Son of Joktan and a descendant of Shem. [Gen. 10:29; 1 Chr. 1:23]

3. date unknown. Son of Shaharaim, he was a leader of the tribe of Benjamin. [1 Chr. 8:9]

4. date unknown. Son of Elpaal, he was a leader of the tribe of Benjamin. [1 Chr. 8:18]

5. *c.* 13 century BC. King of Madon who joined a Canaanite alliance against Joshua and was defeated in battle at the Waters of Merom. [Josh. 11:1]

JOCHEBED (Heb. 'the Lord is glory') *c.* 13 century BC. Jochebed, one of the Children of Israel living in Egypt, was married to Amram a Levite, and had a daughter Miriam and two sons, Aaron and Moses. Her son Moses was born just after Pharaoh had decreed that all Jewish male infants should be killed. She hid him for three months and then she made him a 'basket made of bulrushes, and daubed it with bitumen and pitch; and she put the child in it' (Exod. 2:3). Jochebed put the baby among the bulrushes at the edge of the river, where the Egyptian princess came daily to bathe. When she found it, Miriam came forward and suggested her mother as a nurse for the child. [Exod. 2:1-10; 6:20; Num. 26:59]

JOED (Heb. 'witnessed') date unknown. Son of Pedaiah of the tribe of Benjamin and grandfather of Sallu, one of the first Benjaminites to settle in Jerusalem after the return from exile in Babylon. [Neh. 11:7]

JOEL (Heb. 'the Lord is God') **1.** date unknown. A leader of the tribe of Reuben. [1 Chr. 5:4, 8]

2. date unknown. A leader of the tribe of Gad who settled in the land of Bashan, east of the river Jordan. [1 Chr. 5:12]

3. date unknown. Son of Azariah, a Levite descended from Kohath, he was an ancestor of the prophet Samuel. Also called Shaul. [1 Chr. 6:24, 36]

4. date unknown. A descendant of Uzzi and a leader of the tribe of Issachar. [1 Chr. 7:3]

5. *c.* 11 century BC. Elder son of the prophet Samuel, he and his brother Abijah were judges in Beersheba. They were known to be corrupt and to take bribes, and the people of Israel demanded a king partly because Samuel's sons were unfit to succeed him [1 Sam. 8:2; 1 Chr. 6:28, 33]

6. *c.* 10 century BC. A Levite descended from Gershom, he was placed in charge of the treasuries in the Tabernacle in the reign of King David. [1 Chr. 23:8; 26:22]

7. *see* IGAL **2.**

8. *c.* 10 century BC. Head of the Levites descended from Gershom, who helped to carry the Ark of God to Jerusalem from Kiriath-jearim at the orders of King David. [1 Chr. 15:7, 11, 17]

9. *c.* 10 century BC. Son of Pedaiah, he was ruler of half of the tribe of Manasseh in the reign of King David. [1 Chr. 27:20]

10. *c.* 8 century BC. One of the leaders of the tribe of Simeon in the reign of King Hezekiah who drove out the population of the fertile Gedor valley and settled there. [1 Chr. 4:35]

11. *c.* 8 century BC. One of the Levites who obeyed King Hezekiah's command to sanctify themselves and cleanse the Temple. [2 Chr. 29:12]

12. 5 century BC. One of the descendants of Nebo who divorced his non-Jewish wife in the time of Ezra. [Ezra 10:43]

13. 5 century BC. Son of Zichri, he was the overseer of the Benjaminites who settled in Jerusalem in the time of Nehemiah. [Neh. 11:9]

14. *c.* 5 century BC. A Hebrew prophet in the Kingdom of Judah. The short prophetic Book of Joel, son of Pethuel, appears from its contents to have been written in Judah in the post-exilic period, probably near 400 BC. Its four chapters fall into two distinct parts. In the first two chapters the country is ravaged by a locust swarm, which the prophet regards as heralding the 'day of the Lord'. The last two chapters describe the judgment executed against enemy nations on that day. The language and style are among the finest in the prophetical writings.

The prophet Joel, from a series
of anonymous Italian drawings of
famous men, c. 1450.

Early commentators on the Bible, both Jewish and Christian, regarded the locust swarm in the Book of Joel as merely a symbolic image, set out with poetic hyperbole. But modern scholars have caught up with the facts of nature and indicated that it is also a realistic picture. Vast swarms of these insects (sometimes covering hundreds of square miles) emerge from their desert breeding grounds in Africa, the Middle East and parts of Asia and can lay waste a whole countryside in a matter of hours. Anyone who has witnessed this terrifying scourge will recognize in Joel's account a documentary record of unequalled precision and literary power.

The three stages of the insect's development, the great cloud darkening the sun and the stars, the noise of the whirring wings and chomping jaws, the fertile landscape turned into a bleached and burnt-up wasteland, even the resemblance of the locust head to that of a horse – all these have a startling realism.

'The land is like the garden of Eden before them, but after them a desolate wilderness, and nothing escapes them.... As with the rumbling of chariots, they leap

on the tops of the mountains, like the crackling of a flame of fire devouring the stubble, like a powerful army drawn up for battle.... They leap upon the city, they run upon the walls; they climb up into the houses, they enter through the windows like a thief. The earth quakes before them, the heavens tremble. The sun and the moon are darkened, and the stars withdraw their shining.' (Joel 2:3, 5, 9, 10)

Convinced that the day of the Lord is at hand, Joel calls upon the people to repent, with fasting, weeping and mourning. It must be a true inward return to God: 'And rend your hearts and not your garments' (Joel 2:13). He demands that everyone meet in solemn assembly, from the elders to the infants at the breast, even to the bride and bridegroom. Then the Lord will bring good autumn and spring rains so that the land will be restored to fertility and the famine will be over. 'The threshing floors shall be full of grain, the vats shall overflow with wine and oil.' (Joel 2:24)

In Joel's apocalyptic vision in the second part of the Book, it is predicted that on the day of the Lord, he will restore Judah and Jerusalem and punish the nations that have oppressed His people. They will be gathered together in the valley of Jehoshaphat near Jerusalem, and the judgment of the Lord upon them will be accompanied by portents in heaven and earth.

'Blow the trumpet in Zion' (Joel 2:1). The trumpet in this case was probably the ram's horn still used on the High Holy Days.

'The sun shall be turned to darkness, and the moon to blood.' (Joel 2:31) Egypt will be desolated and Edom become a wilderness, for shedding the blood of innocent Jews. Tyre and Sidon will suffer for plundering the Jews and for selling their sons and daughters into slavery.

After this judgment a new era will dawn, in which 'I will pour out my spirit on all flesh; your sons and your daughters shall prophesy, your old men shall dream dreams, and your young men shall see visions.' (Joel 2:28). It will be a time when Judah will be a green and pleasant land and Jerusalem a Jewish holy city, 'for the Lord dwells in Zion' (Joel 3:21). [Book of Joel]

JOELAH *c.* 11 century BC. Son of Jeroham of Gedor, he and his brother were among the Benjaminites to desert the army of King Saul and rally to David's support. [1 Chr. 12:7]

JOEZER (Heb. 'God aided') *c.* 11 century BC. A Benjaminite who left the army of King Saul and joined David at Ziklag. [1 Chr. 12:6]

JOGLI (Heb. 'my redemption') *c.* 13 century BC. Father of Bukki, the leader of the tribe of Dan in the time of Moses appointed to help divide up the land of Israel. [Num. 34:22]

JOHA 1. *c* 10 century BC. Son of Shimri, he and his brother Jediael were warriors in the army of King David and were distinguished for their bravery. [1 Chr. 11:45]
2. date unknown. A son of Beriah, he and his family were leaders of the tribe of Benjamin living in Jerusalem. [1 Chr. 8:16]

JOHANAN (Heb. 'God's mercy') **1.** *c.* 11 century BC. One of the archers of the tribe of Benjamin who deserted from King Saul's army and joined David at Ziklag. [1 Chr. 12:4]
2. *c.* 11 century BC. One of the eleven warriors of the tribe of Gad who left the army of King Saul and joined David in the wilderness. [1 Chr. 12:12]
3. *c.* 10 century BC. Son of Azariah, a descendant of Aaron the priest. [1 Chr. 6:9, 10]
4. *c.* 8 century BC. Father of Azariah who was one of the four leaders of the tribe of Ephraim to demand the release of the soldiers of Judah whom the army of Pekah, king of Israel, had captured in battle. [2 Chr. 28:12]
5. *c.* 7 century BC. Eldest son of Josiah, king of Judah. He may be identical with Jehoahaz who succeeded his father as king. [2 Kgs. 23:30, 31; 1 Chr. 3:15]
6. *c.* 6 century BC. Johanan the son of Kareah was one of the Judean officers left in the field after the fall of Jerusalem. They pledged their loyalty to Gedaliah, who had been appointed governor. He advised them to co-operate with the Babylonians and to go out into the abandoned countryside, gather the summer fruits, and make wine and oil for themselves.

A few months later Johanan warned Gedaliah that another officer, Ishmael, was plotting against him. Gedaliah brushed aside the threat and was assassinated. Johanan and his men pursued Ishmael and engaged him at Gibeon, but Ishmael fled to Ammon. Afraid of Babylonian reprisals, Johanan and his men took refuge in Egypt, carrying with them Jeremiah, his scribe Baruch, and Gedaliah's family. [2 Kgs. 25:23; Jer. 40:8-16; 41:11-16; 42:1-8; 43:2-5]
7. 5 century BC. One of the seven sons of Elioenai of the tribe of Judah, and a descendant of King David. [1 Chr. 3:24]
8. 5 century BC. Son of Hakkatan and a descendant of Azgad, he was a leader of Judah who returned with Ezra from Babylon. [Ezra 8:12]
9. 5 century BC. Son of Eliashib and one of the chief Levites in the time of Nehemiah. [Neh. 12:22, 23]

JOIADA (Heb. 'favoured') **1.** 6 century BC. Son of Eliashib the high priest. One of his sons married the daughter of Sanballat, the enemy of Nehemiah. Also called Jehoiada. [Neh. 12:10, 11, 22; 13:28]
2. 5 century BC. Son of Paseah, he helped repair the old gate of Jerusalem at the time of Nehemiah. [Neh. 3:6]

JOIAKIM (Heb. 'exalted') 5 century BC. Son of Jeshua, the priest, and father of Eliashib, he was high priest in the Temple during the time of Ezra and Nehemiah. [Neh. 12:10, 12, 26]

JOIARIB (Heb. 'defended') **1.** 6 century BC. Father of Jedaiah and a chief priest who returned to Judah with Zerubbabel from exile and lived in Jerusalem. Also called Jehoiarib. [1 Chr. 9:10; Neh. 11:10; 12:6, 19]
2. 5 century BC. One of the men of 'insight' sent by Ezra to Iddo with a request to provide Levites to minister in the Temple. [Ezra 8:16]
3. date unknown. Son of Zechariah of the tribe of Judah. Maaseiah, one of his descendants, was one of the first men of Judah to settle in Jerusalem following the return from exile in Babylon. [Neh. 11:5]

JOKIM (Heb. 'exalted') date unknown. Son of Shelah and a leader of the tribe of Judah. [1 Chr. 4:22]

JOKSHAN (Heb. 'birdcatcher') *c.* 17 century BC. A son of Abraham by his wife Keturah, he was a desert chieftain. [Gen. 25:2, 3; 1 Chr. 1:32]

JOKTAN (Heb. 'small') date unknown. Younger son of Eber and a great-grandson of Shem. [Gen. 10:26-9; 1 Chr. 1:19, 20]

JONADAB (Heb. 'the Lord is bounteous') *c.* 9 century BC. The son of Rechab, Jonadab, a Kenite, like his father was a member of an ascetic nomad clan that refused to touch wine, live in settled abodes or cultivate the soil. He supported Jehu in his revolt against the corrupt Ahab and in the religious reforms he carried out. Jeremiah held up Jonadab and his sons as examples of faithful followers of the Lord: to the house of the

The Lord speaks to Jonah; Jonah cast out of the ship; and Jonah swallowed by a sea-monster: from the *Paris Psalter*.

Rechabites 'Jeremiah said "Thus says the Lord of hosts ... Jonadab the son of Rechab shall never lack a man to stand before me."' (Jer. 35:19) Also called Jehonadab. [2 Kgs. 10:15-23; Jer. 35]

JONAH (Heb. 'dove') *c.* 8 century BC. Hebrew prophet. The story of Jonah, the reluctant prophet and hapless mariner, is a brief droll fable. Yet it carries a message serious enough to warrant inclusion among the prophetical books of the Bible. The message is that God's compassion extends to all his creatures, whether Jew or Gentile, human or animal.

According to a one-sentence reference in the Second Book of Kings, there was a prophet in the time of King Jeroboam II of Israel called Jonah, the son of Amittai, and he came from the village of Gath-hepher in the Galilee, near Nazareth. Nothing more is known of him outside the Book named after him. The Book opens with the Lord saying to him: 'Arise, go to Nineveh, that great city, and cry against it; for their wickedness has come up before me.' (Jonah 1:2) Nineveh on the Tigris river was the capital of the Assyrian empire. For the Hebrews, it was a byword for luxury and dissipation, so that the prophet Nahum could cry out about it: 'Woe to the bloody city, all full of lies and booty ... all who hear the news of you clap their hands over you. For upon whom has not come your unceasing evil?' (Nahum 3:1, 19) The city fell to the Babylonians in 612 BC but the legends of its depravity would have been fresh in the minds of the Jews when the story of Jonah was written.

Jonah shirked the unwelcome assignment, and tried to run away. He went to the seaport of Joppa (modern Jaffa) 'and he found a ship going to Tarshish; so he paid the fare, and went on board' (Jonah 1:3). (Tarshish was probably a Phoenician trading post and iron-smelting centre in Spain.)

The Lord unleashed a violent storm, and the ship threatened to founder. The frightened sailors lightened the vessel by throwing the cargo overboard, and each of them prayed to his own deity. Finding Jonah asleep in the hold, the boatswain angrily woke him and told him to invoke the help of his God.

In desperation the crew drew lots to find out whether the ship was in danger for having a guilty man on board, and the lot fell to Jonah. They questioned him about his background, and he admitted he was a Hebrew fleeing from the Lord. The storm was on his account, and if they threw him into the sea it would become calm.

The sailors were reluctant to consign their passenger to a watery death and rowed hard to reach land, but the wind and waves were too strong. Then, begging Jonah's God to forgive them, they threw him overboard and the storm at once subsided. The fearful sailors offered a sacrifice and made vows to the Lord to appease him.

God sent a great fish to swallow Jonah, who remained alive in its belly for three days before being vomited up on the shore. While in the belly of the fish, Jonah offered up a psalm in praise of the Lord who had rescued him from drowning when 'The waters closed in over me, the deep was round about me; weeds were wrapped about my head.' (Jonah 2:5)

God renewed his call to Jonah to go and preach in Nineveh. This time the prophet obeyed. He entered

Jonah swallowed by a great fish: detail from the Brescia Casket, ivory, 4th century AD.

the city and proclaimed that it would be destroyed within forty days. From the king downwards the inhabitants repented and put on sackcloth. A royal decree was issued ordering a fast for men and animals alike, and calling on all the citizens to renounce their evil ways in the hope that God would spare them. The Lord relented and the doom of the city was averted.

Jonah was indignant at this unexpected result of his mission, and complained to the Lord that he might as well be dead. Refusing to believe that the city would really be spared, he left it and sat down some distance away, waiting to see what would happen.

The Lord arranged for a castor-oil plant to grow rapidly next to Jonah so that it would give him shade. But at dawn the next day God sent a worm to attack the plant, and it withered. The sun beat down on Jonah's head and a scorching east wind added to his misery. He fainted and again wished for death. God brushed aside his self-pity and derided him for being upset about a plant which had cost him no labour, had sprouted in one night and had perished the next day. Should God then not spare the great city of Nineveh with 120,000 people and many animals?

All the average person knows about Jonah is that he was swallowed by a whale. The rationalists of the nineteenth century were quick to point out that the inside of a whale's throat has a kind of net built into it, so that it can swallow small fish but not large humans. Therefore, they said, the Bible could not be believed. But, contrary to popular belief, the Bible does not talk of a whale (a creature unknown in the Mediterranean) but of a 'great fish' which is a literal translation of the Hebrew *dag gadol*. [2 Kgs. 14:25; Book of Jonah]

JONATHAN (Heb. 'given by God') **1.** *c.* 13 century BC. The grandson of Moses and the son of Gershom, he was a priest who served the citizens of Dan when they built their city and set up graven images that had been made by Micah. [Judg. 18:30, 31]

2. *c.* 11 century BC. Eldest son of King Saul.

Jonathan, son of Saul and Ahinoam, is one of the most open-hearted and likeable human beings in the Bible. It was his misfortune to be caught in the feud between the two men closest to him: his father King Saul and his friend and brother-in-law David.

Jonathan was a daring and successful young officer in Saul's army, and skilled at archery, for which the men of the tribe of Benjamin were noted: '... the bow of Jonathan turned not back ...' (2 Sam. 1:22). He first distinguished himself early in Saul's reign in the attack on the Philistine garrison at Geva, north of Jerusalem. Two thousand Israelites under the king's command cut the garrison off from the rear, while Jonathan led a thousand men in a frontal assault that wiped it out.

The Philistines reacted swiftly. They sent a strong army of chariots, horsemen and foot soldiers back into the hills and occupied Michmash, another nearby town. The Israelites fled and Saul was left in a desperate situation with only a remnant of six hundred men. A personal exploit by Jonathan saved the situation. Taking only his young armour-bearer with him, he climbed up above a rocky pass, and surprised and killed a platoon of Philistine soldiers moving through it. Exaggerated

Tel Michmas, not far from Jerusalem, has been identified as Michmash where Jonathan routed the Philistines.

accounts of this sudden attack spread through the Philistine army and threw it into a panic. The Israelites attacked and were able to rout the enemy. This unexpected victory at Michmash was the turning point in Saul's military campaigns.

Ignorant of Saul's orders that his pursuing troops should eat nothing, Jonathan did. 'I tasted a little honey with the tip of the staff that was in my hand,' (1 Sam. 14:43) thereby offending the Lord. Saul reluctantly decreed that his son should die but relented when the people appealed on behalf of their popular hero.

When the young David was brought before Saul after he had slain Goliath, 'the soul of Jonathan was knit to the soul of David, and Jonathan loved him ...' (1 Sam. 18:1). Jonathan impulsively stripped off his own armour and gave it to David together with his sword and bow.

Later Saul came to hate David and tried to kill him. David fled from the court, and secretly contacted Jonathan. Saul even hurled his spear at his own son when Jonathan pleaded for David.

Through a pre-arranged signal, the two friends met again in a lonely field, and Jonathan sadly agreed that

David was forced to leave and go into hiding. They swore eternal loyalty and took a moving and tearful farewell of each other.

In the defeat of the Israelite army by the Philistines on Mount Gilboa, Jonathan was slain together with his father and his two younger brothers. Their bodies were mutilated and hung on the wall of the nearby city

Tel Beth-shean, where the bodies of Saul, Jonathan and his two younger brothers were hung by the Philistines after the battle on Mount Gilboa.

of Beth-shean. The men of Jabesh-gilead, across the Jordan river, stole up at night, took down the bodies and buried them under a tamarisk tree in their own town.

David, still in exile, poured his anguish into the immortal lament for his beloved friend: 'I am distressed for you, my brother Jonathan; very pleasant have you been to me; your love to me was wonderful, passing the love of women.' (2 Sam. 1:26) [1 Sam. 13; 14; 18-20; 23; 31; 2 Sam. 1:4-26; 4:4; 9:1-7; 21:7-14]

3. *c.* 10 century BC. Son of Abiathar the priest, he supported King David during Absalom's revolt, and later brought the news to Adonijah that King David had appointed Solomon his successor to the throne. [2 Sam. 15:27, 36; 17:17, 20; 1 Kgs. 1:42, 43]

4 *c.* 10 century BC. Son of Shimei who was the brother of King David, he killed a Philistine giant at Gath, who had six fingers on each hand and six toes on each foot. He may be identical with Jonathan described as King David's uncle. [2 Sam. 21:21; 1 Chr. 20:7]

5. *c.* 10 century BC. A warrior in the armies of King David distinguished for his bravery. He is described both as the son of Shammah the Hararite and of Shagee the

Hararite. [2 Sam. 23:32, 33; 1 Chr. 11:34]

6. *c.* 10 century BC. Son of Uzziah, he was in charge of all treasuries in towns and villages outside Jerusalem in the time of King David. [1 Chr. 27:25]

7. *c.* 10 century BC. Uncle of King David, he educated the sons of the king. He may be identical with Jonathan, son of Shimei, the brother of David. [1 Chr. 27:32]

8. 6 century BC. Son of Joiada the Levite, he and his family returned with Zerubbabel from exile in Babylon. [Neh. 12:11]

9. *c.* 6 century BC. A scribe in whose house the prophet Jeremiah was held prisoner at the order of the leaders of Judah. [Jer. 37:15, 20; 38:26]

10. 5 century BC. A chief priest of Judah when Joaikim was high priest in the last years of Nehemiah. [Neh. 12:14]

11. date unknown. Younger son of Jada, of the tribe of Judah [1 Chr. 2:32, 33]

12. 5 century BC. Father of Ebed who returned with Ezra to Judah from exile in Babylon. [Ezra 8:6]

13. 5 century BC. Son of Asahel, he was with Ezra when the latter called on the men of Judah to divorce their non-Jewish wives. [Ezra 10:15]

14. 5 century BC. Father of Zechariah, a priest who played musical instruments at the dedication ceremony for the rebuilding of the walls of Jerusalem in the time of Nehemiah. [Neh. 12:35]

JORAH (Heb. 'rain') 6 century BC. Head of a family who returned to Judah with Zerubbabel from exile in Babylon. Also called Hariph. [Ezra 2:18; Neh. 7:24]

JORAI (Heb. 'taught') date unknown. A leader of the tribe of Gad living in Bashan, east of the river Jordan. [1 Chr. 5:13]

JORAM (Heb. 'exalted') **1.** *c.* 10 century BC. Son of Toi, king of Hamath, he was sent by his father to congratulate King David on defeating Hadadezer, king of Zobah, who had fought with Toi in many battles. Joram brought David vessels of gold, silver and brass as gifts which David dedicated to God. Also called Hadoram. [2 Sam. 8:10; 1 Chr. 18:10]

2. *c.* 10 century BC. The grandfather of Shelomoth, the priest responsible for all the treasures captured by King David in battle and dedicated to the Tabernacle. [1 Chr. 26:25]

3. *see* JEHORAM **2.**

4. *see* JEHORAM **3.**

JOSEPH (Heb. 'may [God] add [children]') *c.* 16 century BC. Eleventh son of Jacob. Down the ages, novelists and painters have dwelt on the romantic story of Joseph, the Israelite lad from Canaan who became the most powerful man at the court of the Egyptian Pharaoh.

The patriarch Jacob was married to Leah and Rachel, the daughters of his uncle Laban, for whom he worked. Jacob had ten sons by Leah and by two concubines, and

was already an old man when Rachel bore her first child, Joseph. Soon after Jacob had returned to his own country, Canaan, Rachel died giving birth to the last of Jacob's sons, Benjamin. The family settled in Hebron.

The boy Joseph was pampered by his father, who made him a coat of many colours as a special mark of favour. This was resented by his older brothers. They were made angrier still when Joseph bore tales about them to Jacob, and when he claimed to have dreams in which the whole family bowed down to him.

One day Jacob sent Joseph, then seventeen years old, to locate his brothers pasturing the flocks near Shechem (Nablus), and to bring him word about them. Joseph caught up with them further north, in the broad valley of Dothan (near the present Jenin). When they saw him coming, they conspired to get rid of him, and tell their father that Joseph had been slain by a wild beast – 'and we shall see what will become of his dreams' (Gen. 37:20). Reuben, the eldest, persuaded the others not to kill him but to leave him at the bottom of an empty well, intending to return to save him. This they did, after stripping him of his coloured coat. While they were eating their food, a party of Ishmaelites came by on camels on their way to Egypt with a load of spices from Gilead. The brothers discussed selling Joseph as a slave to this caravan but were forestalled by some passing Midianite merchants who pulled Joseph out of the well and sold him to the Ishmaelites 'for twenty shekels of silver' (Gen. 37:28). (There is some discrepancy in the narrative here, possibly due to different sources having been combined.)

Reuben came to release Joseph and found he had vanished. Reuben returned in great distress to tell the other brothers, who dipped Joseph's coat in the blood of a kid and reported to their father that they had found the garment in a field, suggesting that Joseph had been torn to pieces by some wild animal.

Joseph's Rise to Power

In Egypt, the young Joseph was bought by Potiphar, the captain of Pharaoh's guard. In the course of time, Joseph showed such ability and diligence that Potiphar put him in charge of his household and all his affairs. Joseph was 'handsome and good-looking' (Gen. 39:6) and his master's wife tried to seduce him. He firmly rejected her advances. One day she clutched him by his coat and he fled, leaving the garment in her hand. The spurned woman had her revenge. She told her husband that the Hebrew slave he had brought into the house had tried to violate her, and produced his robe as proof. The angry Potiphar threw Joseph into prison. Joseph gained the trust of the head warden, who put him in charge of the other prisoners.

Pharaoh's chief cupbearer and head baker offended their master and were flung into the gaol. One morning

above The pit into which Joseph was cast by his brothers would have been much the same as this present-day one.
left Joseph sold to Potiphar (above), and Potiphar's wife attempting to seduce Joseph (below). Detail from the ivory chair of Archbishop Maximianus, Ravenna, 6th century AD.

Joseph noticed they were downcast and he asked them what was wrong. It appeared they were troubled about the meaning of the dreams they had had the night before. (In Egypt it was believed that dreams foretold the future.) Joseph said, 'Do not interpretations belong to God? Tell them to me, I pray you.' (Gen. 40:8) The cupbearer had dreamt he had filled his master's cup from the grapes of three vines. Joseph told him that in three days' time he would be released and restored to his position. The baker had dreamt he bore three white baskets on his head and the food in the topmost one was eaten by birds. Joseph foretold that in three days' time he would be hanged. Both predictions proved correct. Once free, however, the cupbearer forgot his promise to intercede with Pharaoh on Joseph's behalf.

Two years later, Pharaoh himself was disturbed by dreams which none of the magicians at the court was able to interpret. The cupbearer then told him about his own experience in prison with the Hebrew slave. Pharaoh had Joseph taken out of the dungeon and brought before him, after he had been shaved, bathed, and provided with clean clothes.

In his dream Pharaoh had seen seven fat cows come out of the river and graze in a meadow. They were followed by seven emaciated cows who devoured the fat ones while remaining just as thin themselves. He also saw seven fat ears of wheat on one stalk, and seven withered ears that devoured the fat ones. Joseph declared, 'The dream of Pharaoh is one; God has revealed to Pharaoh what he is about to do.' (Gen. 41:25) There would be seven years of plenty, which would then be wiped out by seven years of severe famine. He advised Pharaoh to find 'a man discreet and wise, and set him over the land of Egypt' (Gen. 41:33) to collect one-fifth

Miniature set of twelve granaries from a tomb at el-Kas in Upper Egypt, 3rd century B.C.

of the crops in the good years and store them as a state reserve, to tide over the lean years.

Pharaoh was so impressed by Joseph that he decided to vest power in him. Joseph now became the most important man in the kingdom after Pharaoh himself. He wore the king's own signet ring and rode in the second chariot in the royal procession. Pharaoh gave him the Egyptian name of Zaphnathpaaneah ('says the god: he will live'), and arranged for him to marry Asenath, the daughter of the high priest of the temple

The cows of Pharaoh's dream had a religious significance for the Egyptians: relief from the Temple of Rameses II at Abydos, 13th century B.C., showing a cow led as a sacrificial offering.

Egyptian relief from Horemheb, showing starving Canaanite nomads begging to enter Egypt.

at On. At the age of thirty, after thirteen years as a slave in Egypt, Joseph the Hebrew had become governor of the strongest nation in the region.

During the next seven years there were rich harvests in the Nile Valley. Under Joseph's direction, officials gathered one-fifth of each crop and accumulated wheat in great granaries constructed in all the cities. The period of plenty came to an end, and famine smote the whole region. Joseph started selling wheat to the population from his storehouses after their private reserves had been consumed. When their money gave out, he accepted their livestock in payment. After that, food was bartered for land, all of which became Pharaoh's property, except that of the priests, who were given free rations. Joseph was now able to carry out a programme of agrarian reform. Free land and seed were distributed to the peasants; they delivered one fifth of the crop to Pharaoh as a tax and retained the rest for their own needs.

The Brothers in Egypt

The Land of Canaan had also been struck by crop failures and famine. Jacob sent his sons to Egypt to buy corn, keeping at home only the youngest one, Benjamin. The brothers bowed down humbly before the resplendent and powerful governor who controlled all food supplies. Joseph did not reveal that he had recognized them, but spoke roughly to them, accusing them of being spies. In pleading their innocence, they told him about their background, and about their aged father and youngest brother at home in Canaan. Joseph was overcome with longing to see his dear mother's other child, Benjamin.

After keeping them locked up for three days, Joseph said he would release the brothers and let them go home with corn for their families, provided they proved their story by returning with the youngest. Meanwhile one of them would have to remain in Egypt as a hostage. The brothers discussed the matter among themselves in their own language, not realizing that the governor who had spoken to them through an interpreter was able to understand them. When they asked themselves whether their present troubles were not due to their evil treatment of their young brother many years before, Joseph had to turn away to conceal his feelings. Simeon, the second eldest, was bound and left behind. The others loaded their asses with the corn they had bought, and started out on the long journey home. Stopping at an inn that night, they were even more perturbed when one of the brothers opened a sack of corn to feed the animals and discovered in it the money he had paid for it. On opening the other sacks when they arrived home, the rest of the purchase money was found. (They could not know that this had been done on Joseph's instructions as a gesture to his family.)

Back in Hebron, they told Jacob all that had befallen them, including the detention of Simeon by the Egyptian governor, and his demand that Benjamin be produced to him. Jacob at first refused to let Benjamin go to Egypt, as he still grieved over the loss of Rachel's other son, Joseph. He had to yield, however, when the wheat was used up, and his sons insisted they dared not return to buy more food unless Benjamin went with them. Jacob told them to take back the money found in the sacks, with a gift for the Egyptian lord of 'a little balm and a little honey, gum, myrrh, pistachio nuts, and almonds' (Gen. 43:11).

This time Joseph received them graciously, asked after their father, and sent them round to his home. They were full of apprehension till Joseph's steward reassured them and told them they were to be his master's guests for the midday meal, and brought Simeon to join them. When Joseph arrived, they gave him the gift from Jacob, and introduced Benjamin. Again, Joseph had to leave the room to hide his tears. In the dining room the brothers were seated in the exact order of their ages, much to their astonishment. The Egyptians of the household sat separately, for they would 'not eat bread with the Hebrews' (Gen. 43:32). Joseph, who sat alone, had choice morsels from his own table served to the brothers, with the largest portion for Benjamin. The atmosphere became relaxed and merry.

The brothers set out again for home in good spirits, with the fresh supply of corn they had bought. But Joseph was still trying to keep Benjamin with him. This time he not only had the money put in again with the wheat, but ordered his silver divining-cup to be concealed in Benjamin's sack. Joseph sent his steward after the brothers, who were accused of theft and dumbfounded when the cup was found. Joseph scolded them and ordered that Benjamin be held back as his retainer. After a moving plea by Judah, Joseph abandoned any further pretence. Sending everyone else out of the chamber he told his amazed brothers who he was. He did not hold against them what they had done to him in his youth, saying it was God's will that he should become lord over Egypt and be able to save his family. He told them there were still five hungry years ahead. They should fetch their father Jacob, together with all their households and flocks, and come to settle in the land of Goshen (the north-east corner of the fertile Nile delta) where Joseph would take care of them.

Pharaoh was pleased to hear that Joseph's brethren had appeared. He approved the plan to settle the family in Goshen and ordered that wagons should be provided to bring them from Canaan. Joseph added a supply of provisions for the journey, loaded on asses.

When Jacob was persuaded that the wondrous tale brought by his sons was true he exclaimed, 'It is enough: Joseph my son is still alive; I will go and see him before I die.' (Gen. 45:28) His descendants at that time numbered seventy souls. Joseph came to meet the party in Goshen, and there was an emotional reunion between the aged patriarch and his long-lost son.

Joseph brought his father and five of his brothers to the court and presented them to Pharaoh, who was interested to learn they were skilled shepherds and suggested they might take care of the royal flocks. With great dignity Jacob gave Pharaoh his blessing.

When Jacob had lived seventeen years in Egypt and had reached the age of one hundred and forty-seven, Joseph was told that his father was ill. He took Manasseh and Ephraim, the two sons born to him by his Egyptian wife Asenath, and brought them to receive his father's blessing. Jacob was already bedridden and his sight was failing. When the old man placed his right hand on the head of Ephraim, the younger son, Joseph sought to correct him, but Jacob explained that Ephraim's descendants would be more important than those of Manasseh, the elder of the two. Jacob adopted the boys as his own children, to share equally with his sons. Jacob then said to Joseph, 'Behold, I am about to die, but God will be with you, and will bring you again to the land of your fathers.' (Gen. 48:21)

Joseph had promised that his father would be buried in the family tomb in Hebron. He had the Egyptian physicians embalm Jacob's body, and a long funeral procession wended its way across the desert. It included all Jacob's sons, also Egyptian dignitaries as a mark of respect.

The brothers now feared that, with their father dead and buried, Joseph would take his revenge on them. But he said to them, 'Fear not, for am I in the place of God?' (Gen. 50:19)

Joseph lived to see his great-grandchildren and died at the age of one hundred and ten. His body too was embalmed, and remained in Egypt at his request for centuries until Moses led the Children of Israel back to the Promised Land. They brought Joseph's bones with them, in accordance with Joseph's deathbed wish, and when they had settled in Canaan, they buried them 'at Shechem, in the portion of ground which Jacob bought ... for a hundred pieces of money' (Josh. 24:32). Nevertheless, a tradition grew up that one of the large tombs in the Cave of Machpelah in Hebron was that of Joseph. [Gen. 30:24-5; 33:2, 7; 35:24; 37-50; Exod. 1:5-8; 13:19; Josh. 24:32. There are other references in Num., Deut., Josh., Judg., 2 Sam., 1 Kgs., 1 Chr., Pss., Ezek., Amos, Obad.]

2. *c.* 13 century BC. Father of Igal of the tribe of Issachar who was one of the twelve men sent by Moses to spy out the land of Canaan. [Num. 13:7]

3. *c.* 10 century BC. A son of Asaph, King David's musician. He and his family played musical instruments in the Tabernacle, Joseph taking the first rota of service. [1 Chr. 25:2, 9]

4. 5 century BC. One of the descendants of Bani who divorced his non-Jewish wife in the time of Ezra. [Ezra 10:42]

5. 5 century BC. A priest descended from Shebaniah, he was one of the chief priests of Judah when Joiakim was high priest towards the end of Nehemiah's lifetime. [Neh. 12:14]

JOSHAH (Heb. 'God has given') *c.* 8 century BC. Son of Amaziah, he was one of the leaders of the tribe of Simeon in the reign of King Hezekiah who drove out the native population from the rich Gedor valley and settled there. [1 Chr. 4:34]

JOSHAPHAT (Heb. 'God has judged') **1.** *c.* 10 century BC. A Mithnite warrior in the army of King David distinguished for his bravery. [1 Chr. 11:43]

2. *c.* 10 century BC. A priest in the time of King David who blew the trumpet at the celebration when the Ark was brought to Jerusalem. [1 Chr. 15:24]

JOSHAVIAH (Heb. 'may God settle') *c.* 10 century BC. Son of Elnaam, he and his brother Jeribai were warriors in the army of King David distinguished for their bravery. [1 Chr. 11:46]

JOSHBEKASHAH (Heb. 'dwells in trouble') *c.* 10 century BC. One of the sons of Heman who played music in the Tabernacle in the time of King David. He and his family took the seventeenth turn of service. [1 Chr. 25:4, 24]

JOSHIBIAH (Heb. 'may God settle') *c.* 8 century BC. Father of Jehu, one of the leaders of the tribe of Simeon who settled in the Gedor valley in the reign of King Hezekiah. [1 Chr. 4:35]

19th-century French lithograph of Shechem (Nablus), where Joseph's bones were buried.

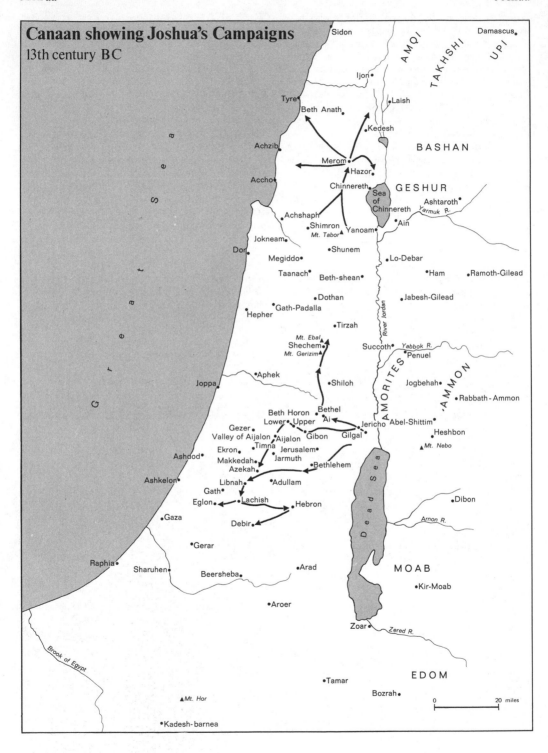

Canaan showing Joshua's Campaigns
13th century BC

Sidon

AMQI   TAKHSHI   UPI   Damascus

Ijon

Tyre   Beth Anath   Laish

Achzib   Kedesh   BASHAN

Accho   Merom   Hazor   GESHUR
Chinnereth   Sea of Chinnereth   Ashtaroth
Achshaph   Yarmuk R.
Shimron   Yanoam   Ain
Jokneam   Mt. Tabor
Dor   Shunem   Lo-Debar
Megiddo   Ham   Ramoth-Gilead
Taanach   Beth-shean   Jabesh-Gilead
Dothan
Gath-Padalla
Hepher   River Jordan
Tirzah
Mt. Ebal   Succoth   Yabbok R.
Shechem   Penuel
Mt. Gerizim   AMORITES
Aphek   Shiloh   Jogbehah   AMMON
Joppa   Bethel   Rabbath - Ammon
Beth Horon   Ai   Jericho   Abel-Shittim
Lower   Upper   Gibon   Gilgal   Heshbon
Gezer   Aijalon
Valley of Aijalon   Jerusalem   Mt. Nebo
Ekron   Timna   Jarmuth
Ashdod   Makkedah   Bethlehem
Azekah   Dibon
Ashkelon   Libnah   Adullam
Gath   Dead Sea
Eglon   Lachish   Hebron
Gaza   Debir   Arnon R.
Gerar
Raphia   Arad   MOAB
Sharuhen   Beersheba   Kir-Moab
Aroer
Zoar   Zered R.
Brook of Egypt   EDOM
Tamar
Bozrah   0   20 miles
Mt. Hor
Kadesh-barnea

Great Sea

JOSHUA (Heb. 'God is salvation') **1.** 13 century BC. Successor to Moses and leader of the Israelite invasion of Canaan. Moses had taken the Children of Israel out of bondage in Egypt, led them for forty years in their desert wanderings, and moulded them into an organized community based on the legal and religious code he taught them. But Moses himself was not permitted to enter the Promised Land with them. That role was reserved for his disciple and successor Joshua the son of Nun, an Ephraimite. He commanded the invasion and conquest of Canaan in a series of brilliant campaigns, and then dealt with its partition between the Israelite tribes.

Nothing is known of Joshua's early life or family. The first mention of him is some two months after the Israelites had left Egypt and had come to a place called Rephidim, in the southern part of the Sinai Peninsula, on the way to Mount Sinai. Here they were attacked by a tribe of Amalekites, fierce desert nomads. The Israelites had not yet developed any regular system of self-defence. The young Joshua must already have attracted attention as a potential military commander; Moses sent for him and told him to pick a number of men and lead the defence, which he did successfully.

During the sojourn at Mount Sinai, Joshua is mentioned incidentally several times, always in connection with Moses – as if to establish an early link between him and the great leader he was to succeed. Thus Joshua was present when Moses first approached the holy mountain with Aaron and seventy elders, and he is referred to as the 'servant' of Moses (Exod. 24:13). When Moses came down from Mount Sinai with the tablet of the Law, and approached the camp where the Israelites were worshipping the golden calf, Joshua was with him and drew his attention to the strange sounds in the distance. Again, Joshua was said to be in the newly-constructed Tabernacle (tent of worship) when Moses first communed there with the Lord.

The Israelites moved northwards from Mount Sinai, and came to rest at the oasis of Kadesh-barnea. Here they were at the southern edge of their destination, the Land of Canaan. Moses sent forward a scouting party to spy out the land. It consisted of twelve picked men, one from each of the tribes, and Joshua was the representative of his tribe, Ephraim.

After a forty-day trip through the hill country of Canaan as far as Syria and back, the spies returned safely to Kadesh-barnea. They described a populated land, with fortified cities. Of the twelve scouts, only Caleb of the tribe of Judah, supported by Joshua, urged that the Israelites should push forward into Canaan. They said, 'The land, which we passed through to spy it out, is an exceedingly good land ... a land which flows with milk and honey.' (Num. 14:7, 8) But the people were plunged into gloom by the report, and railed against Moses. The Lord decreed that since they

had shown so little trust in him, they would remain wandering in the desert for forty years, and none of them would reach the Promised Land except for Joshua and Caleb.

For a generation the Israelites lived the lives of desert nomads, with the oasis of Kadesh-barnea as their tribal centre. They then moved round the southern end of the Dead Sea, and occupied most of the territory east of the Jordan river.

Feeling that his task was done and that death was approaching, Moses handed over the leadership to Joshua, who had been selected by the Lord as a man 'full of the spirit of wisdom' (Deut. 34:9). At a solemn ceremony in the Tabernacle, Moses laid his hands upon Joshua and charged him with the task of leading the Israelites into the Promised Land.

The Invasion of Canaan

They were now encamped in the Jordan Valley opposite Jericho. Joshua gave careful thought to his invasion strategy. He had a good idea of the nature of the country and its inhabitants from his recollections of the scouting party nearly forty years before, and from fresh intelligence reports he now gathered.

Canaan was a corridor between the great empires in the river-basins of the Nile and the Euphrates. It was a land divided up by hills, valleys and streams, and its inhabitants lived in a number of little city-states, each under its own local chieftain or 'king'. For several

Before Joshua's conquest, Canaan was divided into a number of city-states. 15th-century BC limestone statue of a king from Alalakh in present-day Syria.

centuries, it was under the sway of Egypt. By the time of Joshua, the protective power of Egypt had declined, and Canaan was weak and disunited. The local kings bickered with each other, though they might form shifting coalitions against an outside enemy. Joshua was able to exploit these political conditions.

It was clear to Joshua that the Israelites had a better chance of gaining control of the hill country than of the plains. The hills were sparsely inhabited, being mostly grazing slopes and low woods and bushes, with only a few cities: Hebron, Jerusalem, Bethel, Ai and Shechem. Down in the flat, open plains, the poorly-armed foot-soldiers could be mowed down by the horse-chariots of the Canaanites.

Joshua's most severe military obstacle was the massive fortifications of the Canaanite cities. In the report he and the other spies had brought back to Moses in Kadesh-barnea, they had stressed that 'the cities are fortified and very large' (Num. 13:28). It was not surprising that these desert tent-dwellers should be discouraged. The existing remains of that period show that the stone walls of Gezer, for instance, were thirteen feet thick; while Jericho had double brick walls, the outer one six feet and the inner one twelve feet thick.

The conventional means of subduing a fortified city were to scale the walls, or to breach them with battering rams, or to tunnel underneath them, or to starve the inhabitants into submission by a lengthy siege. Joshua lacked the military resources for these methods. The Israelites could succeed with the aid of a miracle

Canaanite pottery mould for bronze weapons, with two axes in place, 2000-1500 BC, found at Tel Balatah.

(Jericho), or a ruse (Ai), or in cases where the enemy force had already been routed in open battle (Lachish and Hazor). A number of major cities remained unconquered at that time – for instance, Jerusalem, Gezer, Megiddo, Beth-shean, Gaza, Ashkelon, Ashdod, Ekron and Gath. Joshua had to compensate for inferiority in numbers and weapons by the fitness, courage and religious zeal of his desert fighters, and by resourceful generalship: surprise attacks, night marches and stratagems.

The Fall of Jericho and Ai

The first objective was to cross the river and establish a bridge-head beyond it. The strategic key was the city of Jericho, five miles west of the fords. Joshua sent two men to spy out the city. They found lodging with Rahab, a prostitute whose dwelling was 'built into the city wall' (Josh. 2:15). She hid them and helped them to escape down a rope from her window.

On the appointed day the Israelites struck camp and moved forward to the river. The Lord said to Joshua: 'This day I will begin to exalt you in the sight of all Israel, that they may know that, as I was with Moses, so I will be with you.' (Josh. 3:7) It was the time of the winter harvest at the end of the rainy season, and the Jordan flood-waters overflowed its banks. The priests were sent ahead with the Ark of the Law. When they reached the edge of the water, its flow was suddenly blocked higher up. The priests remained standing in the centre of the river-bed until all the Israelites had passed over. Camp was pitched that night at Gilgal, between the river and Jericho. Here Joshua had twelve stones from the Jordan set up in a circle, as a memorial to the miraculous crossing.

At Gilgal the Lord commanded that all the male Israelites should be circumcised, as this had not been done when they had been born in the forty years of wandering. The Lord said, 'This day I have rolled away

Bronze Canaanite figure of Reshef, god of war, 2000-1500 BC, from Megiddo. He wears a Hittite style of girdle.

the reproach of Egypt from you.' (Josh. 5:9) The manna which had nourished them in the desert ceased to appear, as they could now eat of the produce of the land. For the first time in Canaan, they celebrated the Passover Feast, recalling their deliverance from bondage in Egypt. It was here too that Joshua met an angel of the Lord in the guise of a warrior holding a drawn sword. He had come 'as commander of the army of the Lord' (Josh. 5:14), and Joshua was much heartened.

The inhabitants of Jericho had shut themselves in behind the seemingly impregnable walls of their city. Its fall was brought about in a remarkable manner, in accordance with divine instructions. Each morning for

slopes that led up to the hill country nearly four thousand feet above. The most direct route was to the Jebusite city of Jerusalem, but it was strongly fortified, and the ascent steep and exposed. A longer but easier approach lay to the right, up a canyon to the city of Ai, some twelve miles north of Jerusalem. A reconnaissance patrol reported that the town had comparatively few inhabitants and was lightly held, so that a relatively small force of two or three thousand men could take it. This was attempted, but the Israelites were repulsed and chased down the mountain, thirty-six men being killed.

Joshua was disconcerted by his first setback, and

Vessel in the shape of
a man's head, middle Canaanite
period, from Jericho.

The ancient mound of
Jericho, with the oasis in
the background.

six days, the Israelite force circled silently once round Jericho, with seven priests in their midst carrying the Ark and blowing on ram's horns. On the seventh day they went round seven times. The priests blew a long final note, and at a given signal from Joshua all the Israelites gave forth a loud shout. The city walls tumbled down, and the fighting men rushed straight in from all sides. They put all the inhabitants to the sword except for Rahab and her family, whom the two young spies she had sheltered took into safety. Jericho was then burnt to the ground.

From the Jericho plain, Joshua now faced the barren

feared that the news of it would spread through Canaan and discredit the Israelites as a fighting force. 'O Lord, what can I say, when Israel has turned their backs before their enemies!' (Josh. 7:8) He rent his clothes, prostrated himself in the Tabernacle and sought to know what had gone wrong. The answer was that someone in the Israelite camp had broken the ban against taking spoil in Jericho, and until that crime was expiated the Lord would not help them. Early next morning, Joshua had lots drawn among all the tribes, and by elimination the guilty person was found – Achan of Judah. He confessed to looting a valuable Babylonian robe, two hundred shekels of silver and a bar of gold, and burying them in the floor of his tent. Achan, his family and animals were taken to the nearby valley of Achor and stoned to death, while his possessions were burnt.

Joshua took the second assault on Ai more seriously. This time he used his complete army, and worked out a careful battle plan designed to lure the defenders out of the walls and into the open. An advance force of five thousand men was sent up the mountain under cover of darkness, and concealed themselves in low ground just to the west of Ai, between it and the city of Bethel a mile away. Next morning Joshua and the rest of his men appeared to the north of the town, facing it across a ravine. The king of Ai ordered his troops to attack, and Joshua's men fled, with the enemy in pursuit, being drawn further and further away from their city. Then, at a given moment, Joshua raised his javelin in the air as a signal, and the ambush group lying in wait in the west dashed into the undefended city and set it alight. They then fell on the men of Ai from the rear, while those who had pretended to flee turned round and attacked from the front. The enemy army, unexpectedly caught in this pincer movement, was overcome and wiped out. The king was captured and hanged and the remaining inhabitants of the city killed. Unlike the orders at Jericho, no ban was put on taking booty at Ai. The town itself was razed, but the cattle and spoils were taken.

The ruins of Ai (which in Hebrew means 'ruin'), north of Jericho.

Campaigns in the South and North

Joshua now held a religious ceremony on Mount Ebal above Shechem. He built an altar of unhewn stone, made sacrifices to the Lord, and solemnly read out the Laws handed down by Moses, in the presence of all the congregation including 'the women, and the little ones, and the sojourners who lived among them' (Josh. 8:35).

At the edge of the hill-plateau some six miles north-west of Jerusalem was the town of Gibeon. It stood on a strategic height looking westward towards the coast, and controlled the route down into the valley of Aijalon in the Shephelah (lowlands). Gibeon led a confederation of four towns in the vicinity, belonging to the Hivites, one of the local Canaanite peoples. It now stood directly in the path of the Israelite advance, and was fearful that it might suffer the fate of Ai, seven miles away.

The Gibeonite elders resorted to guile. They dressed themselves in worn clothes and sandals, and loaded their donkeys with stale bread, patched wineskins, and old sacks. In this guise they came to the Israelite base camp at Gilgal and told Joshua they had travelled a long way from their distant home to make a treaty, since they had heard the Lord would make the Israelites masters of the country. Their story was believed, and oaths of mutual friendship were sworn. A few days later the truth came out. The Israelites were angry at being tricked but were obliged to abide by their oath

The five kings being dragged out of their hiding place to be killed by Joshua's men:
13th-century French illuminated manuscript.

and left the Gibeonites unharmed. Joshua told them they would be punished in the future by serving as menials in the Israelite sanctuary, 'hewers of wood and drawers of water for the congregation' (Josh. 9:27).

Gibeon's pact with the Israelites undermined the security of all southern Canaan. Adonizedek, king of Jerusalem, formed a hurried military alliance with Hebron and the foothill towns of Lachish, Eglon and Jarmuth. He sent messages to their kings to 'Come up to me, and help me, and let us smite Gibeon; for it has made peace with Joshua and with the people of Israel.' (Josh. 10:4) They besieged Gibeon, whose elders sent urgent calls for help to the Israelite camp at Gilgal. After a forced night march Joshua broke the siege and drove the enemy troops pell-mell down the mountain pass into the vale of Aijalon. During this flight the hapless Canaanites were battered by a savage hailstorm, and 'there were more who died because of the hail-stones than the men of Israel killed with the sword.' (Josh. 10:11) Fearing that his beaten foe might escape and reorganize under cover of the approaching dark-ness Joshua prayed: 'Sun, stand thou still at Gibeon, and thou Moon in the valley of Aijalon.' (Josh. 10:12) Having been granted this extension of time, he was able to press home his victory.

The five defeated kings hid themselves in a cave but were discovered and shut in with a large boulder while their forces were pursued by the Israelites. Later they were pulled out and put to death, and their bodies hung on trees until sundown, when they were cut down and buried in the same cave.

After this breakthrough, Joshua's force swept through the foothills, capturing and destroying one town after another: Azekah, Makkedah, Libnah, Lachish, Eglon, Hebron and Debir. In this rapid campaign, the Israelites had gained control of the hill country south of Jerusalem, and the strategic defiles from the lowlands into the hills.

The scene of action now shifted to northern Canaan. The most important of the kings in that region was Jabin of Hazor, a large city in the Huleh Valley of eastern Galilee, astride the 'way of the sea' from Egypt to Damascus. Jabin rallied the neighbouring rulers to form a united front against the Israelites. They con-centrated a large army, including a number of the formidable Canaanite chariots, at the Waters of Merom in the hills near the Sea of Galilee. Here Joshua engaged them in battle and defeated them. He then captured and burnt Hazor.

The Areas of Settlement

After these successful military campaigns in the south and the north, the time had come to allocate defined districts of settlement to each of the tribes.

The men of Reuben, Gad and part of Manasseh were now allowed to return to the lands on the Trans-jordan plateau which Moses had agreed to let them have before they had crossed the river with Joshua. Reuben and Gad occupied what had been the Amorite kingdom of Sihon, up to the Jabbok river; and the Machir branch of the tribe of Manasseh settled in the land of Gilead, between the Jabbok and Yarmuk rivers. The Joseph tribes remained in possession of an area in the centre – Ephraim south of Shechem, and the remainder of Manasseh from Shechem northwards to the valley of Jezreel.

Judah was allotted the area south of Jerusalem, with

Hebron as its main centre. Hebron itself was given to Caleb and his family.

That left seven tribes for whom provision had to be made. Joshua sent out a team of three persons from each tribe to survey the territory not yet allocated. They were to 'describe the land in seven divisions and bring the description here to me.' (Josh. 18:6) On the basis of their report tribal areas were marked out, and lots drawn for them at a gathering of the people called by Joshua at the sanctuary at Shiloh. Benjamin's portion was a narrow belt of hill-country just north of Jerusalem. Dan was given a strip of foothills and coastal plain to the west of Benjamin. Simeon remained in the northern Negev round Beersheba. The north was divided between Asher (western Galilee), Naphtali and Zebulun (eastern and central Galilee), and Issachar (the eastern Jezreel and the Beth-shean valley). (See map below.)

Israelite Division of Canaan according to tribes

13-12th centuries BC

It is a moot point how much of the land of Canaan was actually conquered and occupied by the Israelites in Joshua's time. In one passage it is claimed that 'Joshua took the whole land, according to all that the Lord had spoken to Moses; and Joshua gave it for an inheritance to Israel according to their tribal allotments. And the land had rest from war.' (Josh. 11:23) But this statement was more rhetorical than factual. That the conquest was neither rapid nor complete is clear from

other passages in the Books of Joshua and Judges, from subsequent history, and from archaeological excavation. After a list is given of thirty-one defeated kings west of the Jordan, the Lord says to Joshua: 'You are old and advanced in years, and there remains yet very much land to be possessed.' (Josh. 13:1)

East of Jordan, five Canaanite kingdoms remained intact: Edom and Moab in the south round the Dead Sea; Ammon in the centre; and Geshur and Maachah east and north-east of the Sea of Galilee. The extreme north of Canaan, extending into what is now Syria and Lebanon, remained occupied by the Amorites. The southern coastal plain, soon to be occupied by the Philistines, stayed unconquered. The northern part of the coastal plain also remained in Canaanite hands, and was settled by the Phoenicians. In the middle of the Israelite territories, there were strongly fortified cities that could not be subdued – such as Jerusalem, which was taken by David two centuries later; Gezer, which fell to David's son Solomon; and the line of Canaanite strongholds along the Jezreel Valley, such as Megiddo and Beth-shean. These facts are borne out by the subsequent history of these cities, and by archaeological evidence.

Generally, it was easier for the Israelites to establish themselves in the hills. Their settlement of this difficult terrain was helped by two technological advances. Iron tools could be obtained from their more developed neighbours, and with these implements it was easier to clear hillsides of trees and boulders than with those made of softer bronze (a mixture of copper and tin). Furthermore, they learned to hold rain-water in rock cisterns lined with a plaster that was waterproof, thus becoming less dependent on local wells. Israelite building methods were still primitive, but unlike the Canaanites they were a patriarchal rural society dispersed in small communities, and not in walled cities.

When the Israelites tried to penetrate the plains they ran into trouble. 'And the Lord was with Judah; and he took possession of the hill country, but he could not drive out the inhabitants of the plain, because they had chariots of iron.' (Judg. 1:19) The tribes of Zebulun and Asher failed to gain control of the coastal strip allotted to them north of Acre. The elders of Manasseh and Ephraim complained to Joshua that they were cramped in a mountainous zone without enough land on which to subsist. 'The hill country is not enough for us.' (Josh. 17:16) Joshua told them to make more room for themselves by clearing the natural woods which then covered these hills.

The territory allotted to the tribe of Dan extended right into the coastal plain towards Jaffa. It was unable to hold it but was pushed out, and moved northwards to settle in the eastern Galilee near Mount Hermon. 'The Amorites pressed the Danites back into the hill country, for they did not allow them to come down to the plain.' (Judg. 1:34)

In the partition of the country, the tribe of Levi was not allotted an area of its own, since it carried out religious duties for the whole nation: 'the Lord God of Israel is their inheritance.' (Josh. 13:33) Instead, the Levites were granted a number of towns scattered through the territory of the other tribes, with some grazing land round each town.

Six cities were designated as places of refuge for persons who had killed someone inadvertently. In these cases the city authorities could admit them, and they would be safe from the blood feud. There were three such towns east of the Jordan in the areas of Reuben, Gad and Manasseh; and three west of the Jordan: Hebron (in Judah), Shechem (in Manasseh) and Kadesh (in Naphtali).

At the age of one hundred and ten Joshua felt his end was near. He assembled all the important men of the tribes at Shechem, and in a moving farewell address urged them to fear and obey the Lord who had done so much for them and to resist the temptation to inter-marry with the Canaanites and be contaminated by their pagan cults.

above The traditional burial place of Joshua at Khirbet Tibna, near Lod.

above Late Canaanite ivory from Megiddo, showing a ruler, with servants, warriors and captives.

Joshua died and was buried at Timnath-serah, his personal estate in the territory of the tribe of Ephraim to which he belonged. This burial place has never been identified, though tradition links it with an ancient tomb at Khirbet Tibna, in the hills twelve miles north-east of Lod. Also called Hoshea. [Exod. 17, 24, 32, 33; Num. 11, 13, 14, 26, 27, 32, 34; Deut. 1, 3, 31, 34; Book of Joshua; Judg. 1, 2; 1 Kgs. 16:34]

Archaeology and the Conquest

The experts have argued for generations about the account of the Israelite conquest given in the Book of Joshua. The main problem concerns the most dramatic episode in the story – the fall of Jericho.

Jericho is regarded as the oldest inhabited city in the world. It is in the Jordan Valley just north of the Dead Sea. In the middle of a bleak plain 800 feet below sea-level, a spring of fresh water gushes out of the ground, and has created an oasis filled with lush tropical vege-tation. Close by, remains of a stone wall, a tower and a moat have been excavated that date back 9,000 years – that is, nearly 6,000 years before Joshua, and thirty centuries before any city fortifications found elsewhere.

The archaeological evidence suggests that Jericho was destroyed by earthquake and fire in about the 14th century BC. Walls were toppled; houses were burnt; and the charred remains were found of wheat and other foodstuffs. The available data put the devastation of Jericho a hundred years or more before Joshua's in-vasion in the 13th century BC. It was restored and re-settled only several centuries later, in the period of the

Hebrew monarchy. This time gap remains an unresolved puzzle. One theory is that the city may have been taken by Hebrew or kindred tribes at an earlier date, and the event was later attributed to Joshua. Others accept the Bible story, and suggest that the walls destroyed in Joshua's time were erected of brick on top of earlier stone walls, thus confusing the chronology.

Another problem arises over the story of the fall of Ai. According to some archaeologists – if they have correctly identified the site – it was destroyed a thousand years before Joshua. (The Hebrew word *Ai* means 'ruin'.) The town of Bethel then developed little more than a mile away from the site of Ai, and was in turn destroyed about the time of Joshua. It was later restored, and became an important Israelite centre. It is assumed, therefore, that the biblical story of the capture of Ai really related to Bethel, and that the two places were confused by later compilers of the Bible.

On the other hand, the excavated tel of Hazor, in the Huleh Valley north of the Sea of Galilee, fits perfectly into the biblical account. This city was well known in antiquity, being located on the regular route from Egypt across Canaan to Mesopotamia. It is mentioned a number of times in Egyptian records from the 19th to 13th centuries BC, particularly in the famous

Basalt potter's wheel found at Hazor.

Aerial photograph of the tel of Hazor, which occupies 183 acres.

Tel el-Amarna Letters, from the Egyptian royal archives of the 14th century BC.

The Bible records that Joshua 'burned Hazor with fire' (Josh. 11:11) for Hazor 'was the head of all those kingdoms'(Josh. 11:11). The excavations carried out between 1955 and 1959 showed that part of the site contained the remains of a well-built Canaanite city, with houses and a canalization system. The floors of the houses in the uppermost stratum were littered with pottery of the Mycenean type definitely belonging to the 13th century BC, and the city in this stratum was destroyed by fire and never again resettled. The high mound at the southern end of the site revealed similar evidence of the last Canaanite settlement in the 13th century BC. Here, however, there was evidence of subsequent settlement, including remarkable remains of structures and fortifications built by King Solomon in the 10th century BC.

Further corroboration of the Book of Joshua came to light in the excavations at Lachish. The city occupied a strategic location, guarding the approach to the Hebron hills and Jerusalem from the south. Its Canaanite stage came to an end when it was destroyed in the 13th century BC, which would correspond to the period of Joshua.

2. *c.* 11 century BC. An inhabitant of Beth-shemesh in the days of the prophet Samuel. The Ark of God remained in his field on its return from the Philistines. [1 Sam. 6:14, 18]

3. *c.* 7 century BC. Governor of Judah in the days of King Josiah. [2 Kgs. 23:8]

4. *see* JESHUA **6.**

JOSIAH (Heb. 'God-healed') **1.** Sixteenth king of Judah after the monarchy split, he reigned 640-09 BC. Josiah was the son of King Amon of Judah and of Jedidah, daughter of Adaiah of Bozkath. He was eight years old when he succeeded his father on the throne.

In the eighteenth year of Josiah's reign, the high priest Hilkiah showed Shaphan, the royal scribe, a 'Book of the Law' which he had discovered in the Temple during the renovations ordered by the king. (It was probably an early version of the Book of Deuteronomy.) Shaphan read the sacred work to his royal master, who was filled with consternation at finding how far the religious practices of his time had strayed from God's commandments. The prophetess Huldah was consulted, and revealed that the wrathful Lord would destroy Judah, though not in the lifetime of the devout Josiah.

The king called a great assembly in the Temple of '... the priests and the prophets, all the people, both small and great,' (2 Kgs. 23:2) and read the whole Book to them. He then carried out sweeping reforms. The Temple was purged of all heathen altars and cult objects, particularly those belonging to the Assyrian worship of the sun, the moon and the stars. These

The pass guarded by the fortress of Megiddo, where King Josiah was mortally wounded.

objects were solemnly burnt in the valley of Kidron below the city wall. The practice of child sacrifice in the valley of Hinnom (Gehenna) west of the city was stopped 'that no one might burn his son or his daughter as an offering to Molech' (2 Kgs. 23:10). The idolatrous priests were killed, the pagan house of male prostitutes was pulled down and the local shrines outside Jerusalem were destroyed and defiled by burning human bones on them.

When this purge had been completed from Geba to Beersheba, Josiah summoned the whole country to a great Passover celebration in Jerusalem in the reconsecrated Temple. Thousands of lambs, kids and bullocks were slaughtered for the occasion. 'For no such passover had been kept since the days of the judges. . . .' (2 Kgs. 23:22)

It is noteworthy that Josiah included in these activities areas of the northern kingdom of Israel that had been conquered and annexed by Assyria a century earlier. Two other great powers were contending for the domination slipping out of the Assyrian grasp: Babylonia and Egypt. In 612 BC the army of the Babylonians and Medes defeated the Assyrians, and captured Nineveh the capital. At this point Pharaoh Neco of Egypt led an army to the assistance of the Assyrians, in order to stem the rising might of Babylon and to regain Egypt's traditional hold of Syrian and Israelite territory. Josiah tried to frustrate this design. In 609 BC, as the Egyptian army marched across the country along the ancient Via Maris ('way of the sea'). Josiah

Assyrian cylinder seal showing a god and two worshippers drinking. Above are the sun, moon and star symbols, whose worship Josiah prohibited in the Temple.

intercepted it at the key pass of Megiddo. His forces were defeated and he himself mortally wounded. He was rushed back by chariot to Jerusalem where he died. 'All Judah and Jerusalem mourned for Josiah.' (2 Chr. 35:24)

Josiah was succeeded by his son Jehoahaz. [1 Kgs. 13:2; 2 Kgs. 21:24, 26; 22; 23:1-34; 1 Chr. 3:14, 15; 2 Chr. 33:25; 34; 35; 36:1; Jer. 1:1-3; 3:6; 22:11, 18; 25:1, 3; 26:1; 27:1; 35:1; 36:1, 2, 9; 37:1; 45:1; 46:2; Zeph. 1:1]
2. *c.* 6 century BC. Son of Zephaniah, from whom gold and silver were to be taken to make a crown for Jeshua, the high priest. [Zech. 6:10]

JOSIPHIAH (Heb. 'may God add') 5 century BC. A leader of Judah who returned with Ezra from exile in Babylon. [Ezra 8:10]

JOTHAM (Heb. 'God is upright') **1.** *c.* 12 century BC. A judge of Israel.

One of Gideon's sons was Abimelech, whose mother was a concubine from the city of Shechem. When his father died. Abimelech had his seventy brothers murdered with the support of his mother's kinsmen, and declared himself king of the region. The only one to escape was Jotham, the youngest one, who managed to hide himself.

The leaders of Shechem gathered in the town meeting-place to proclaim Abimelech king. Jotham suddenly appeared on the top of Mount Gerizim, overlooking

The slopes of Mount Gerizim on which Jotham made his warning speech.

the city, and shouted, 'Listen to me, you men of Shechem, that God may listen to you.' (Judg. 9:7) He then told them the following parable. One day the trees decided to elect a king, and offered the position to the olive tree. It refused, saying, 'Shall I leave my fatness, by which gods and men are honoured, and go to sway over the trees?' (Judg. 9:9) They then turned to the fig tree, who replied, 'Shall I leave my sweetness and my good fruit... ?' (Judg. 9:11) The vine, when invited, said, 'Shall I leave my wine which cheers gods and men...?' (Judg. 9:13) Only the useless bramble accepted. 'If in good faith you are anointing me king over you, then come and take refuge in my shade....' (Judg. 9:15) But fire came from the thorny branches of the bramble and burnt the whole forest.

Did they think, went on Jotham, that they had served Gideon's memory well by killing seventy of his sons in order to make Abimelech king? He reminded them that his father had risked his life for Shechem, when he delivered the city from the Midianites. Jotham prophesied: 'let fire come out from Abimelech, and devour the citizens of Shechem ... and devour Abimelech.' (Judg. 9:20)

Having uttered his words of doom, Jotham dashed away and escaped again. He took refuge at Beer, a place distant from Shechem, where he could be out of reach of his half-brother Abimelech. Jotham's double prophecy came true three years later. Abimelech crushed a revolt in Shechem by killing all the people and sacking the town. The following day he moved against the neighbouring town of Thebez which had also taken part in the rebellion. Here he was killed by a millstone dropped on his head by a woman from the city wall. [Judg. 9]

2. Eleventh king of Judah after the monarchy split, he reigned 740-36 BC.

Jotham was the eldest son of the illustrious King Uzziah of Judah and Jerusha, the daughter of Zadok. During the late years of his reign Uzziah suffered from leprosy and remained secluded in his quarters. Jotham acted as a co-regent and administered the kingdom under his father's direction. When Uzziah died, Jotham became king in his own right. He continued his father's successful policies that maintained military strength and economic prosperity. The Bible mentions that Jotham constructed the upper gate of the Temple and carried out considerable work on the city wall. He also added to the number of towns that his father had fortified. Jotham defeated the kingdom of Ammon in Trans-jordan and for three successive years exacted from the Ammonites a heavy tribute of silver, wheat and barley.

Upon his death he was succeeded by his son Ahaz. [2 Kgs. 15:5, 7, 30, 32-8; 16:1; 1 Chr. 3:12; 5:17; 2 Chr. 26:21, 23; 27; Isa. 1:1; 7:1; Hos. 1:1; Mic. 1:1]

3. date unknown. A son of Jahdai and a leader of the tribe of Judah. [1 Chr. 2:47]

JOZABAD (Heb. 'given by God') **1.** *c.* 11 century BC. A Benjaminite warrior who deserted from King Saul's army and joined David at Ziklag. [1 Chr. 12:4]

2. *c.* 11 century BC. Two army commanders of the tribe of Manasseh who left the army of King Saul and rallied to David on his way to Ziklag. [1 Chr. 12:20]

3. *c.* 8 century BC. One of the Levites who supervised the bringing of offerings and tithes into the Temple in the reign of King Hezekiah. [2 Chr. 31:13]

4. *c.* 7 century BC. A Levite who donated large quantities of cattle for the Passover offering in the reign of King Josiah of Judah. [2 Chr. 35:9]

5. 5 century BC. Son of Jeshua, he was one of the Levites present when the gold and silver brought back from Babylon at Ezra's command was weighed in the Temple. [Ezra 8:33]

6. 5 century BC. A son of Pashhur the priest who divorced his non-Jewish wife in the time of Ezra. [Ezra 10:22]

7. 5 century BC. One of the Levites who divorced his non-Jewish wife in the time of Ezra. [Ezra 10:23]

8. 5 century BC. A Levite who explained the Law to the people of Judah after Ezra had read out the Law of Moses in the market-place. [Neh. 8:7]

9. 5 century BC. A leader of the Levites who settled in Jerusalem in the days of Nehemiah and was a supervisor of the Temple. [Neh. 11:16]

JOZACAR (Heb. 'the Lord remembered') *c.* 9 century BC. Son of Shimeath, he was one of the royal servants who murdered King Joash of Judah and was later put to death by Joash's son, Amaziah. Also called Zabad. [2 Kgs. 12:21; 2 Chr. 24:26]

JOZADAK *see* JEHOZADAK

JUBAL (Heb. 'sound') date unknown. Son of Lamech and Adah and a descendant of Cain, he was the first musician. [Gen. 4:21]

JUCAL *see* JEHUCAL

JUDAH (Heb. 'God will lead') **1.** *c.* 16 century BC. Fourth son of Jacob.

Judah was the fourth son of Jacob's first wife Leah

Carving of Jubal, father of musicians, from the bell tower of Florence Cathedral, based on the designs of Giotto and Andrea Pisano.

and was born in Paddan-aram where Jacob was working for his father-in-law Laban. Together with his brothers, Judah was involved in the events that led to their brother Joseph becoming a slave in Egypt. It was Judah's idea to sell Joseph to a passing caravan of Midianite traders rather than to let him die in the well into which they had lowered him: ' "let not our hand be upon him, for he is our brother, our own flesh." And his brothers heeded him.' (Gen. 37:27)

Judah married a Canaanite woman called Bath-shua who had three sons. The eldest was Er and later Judah

Mesopotamian musician entertaining a group of diners, mother-of-pearl inlaid in bitumen, 3rd millennium BC.

Judah

married him to Tamar, but Er died soon after without a child. Judah told Onan, Er's brother, to take Tamar so that according to tradition he would 'perform the duty of a brother-in-law to her, and raise up offspring for your brother.' (Gen. 38:8) But Onan refused to have children that would not be considered his and offended the Lord by spilling his semen on the ground, and he too died. Tamar disguised herself as a prostitute and lured Judah to bed with her and became pregnant. When Judah discovered who she was, he blamed himself because he should have given Tamar to his next son. Tamar had twin sons by Judah.

Later Judah was one of the ten sons sent by Jacob to buy corn in Egypt where Joseph had become a leading figure at Pharaoh's court. Joseph longed to see his full brother Benjamin and insisted that he be brought on the next journey. Joseph then accused Benjamin of stealing a silver cup and as a punishment demanded that Benjamin be left behind as his retainer. Judah made a moving plea, saying that this would kill their father Jacob. Finally Joseph disclosed his identity to his brothers and a tearful reunion took place.

Years later, when Joseph had brought his father Jacob and the rest of the family to Egypt, it included Judah's remaining three sons. Jacob sent Judah ahead

The mountainous region around Jerusalem, which was allotted to the tribe of Judah.

to tell Joseph he was coming so that he could come to meet him.

On his deathbed Jacob blessed all his sons in turn. Of Judah he said: 'The sceptre shall not depart from Judah, nor the ruler's staff from between his feet, until he comes to whom it belongs...' (Gen. 49:10). The blessing of Moses asks the Lord to intercede on behalf of Judah against its enemies. In the conquest of Canaan under Joshua, the tribe of Judah was allocated extensive territory that included the Hebron hill district south of Jerusalem. As Jacob's blessing had foretold, Judah became the dominant Israelite tribe, and produced the royal house of David. [Gen. 29:35; 35:23; 37:26, 27; 38; 43; 44; Exod. 1:2; Num. 26:19; Deut. 33:7; Ruth 4:12; 1 Chr. 2; 4; 5; 9; Neh. 11:24]

2. *c.* 6 century BC. A Levite who returned to Jerusalem with Zerubbabel from exile in Babylon, and supervised the thanksgiving service in the Tabernacle. [Neh. 12:8]

3. *c.* 5 century BC. A Levite who divorced his non-Jewish wife in the time of Ezra. [Ezra 10:23]

4. *c.* 5 century BC. Son of Hassenuah, he was deputy supervisor of the tribe of Benjamin in Jerusalem in the time of Nehemiah. [Neh. 11:9]

5. 5 century BC. A Levite who played musical instruments at the dedication ceremony for the rebuilt wall of Jerusalem in the time of Nehemiah. [Neh. 12:34]

6. *c.* 5 century BC. One of the leaders of Judah who participated in the dedication ceremony for the rebuilt wall of Jerusalem in the time of Nehemiah. [Neh. 12:36]

JUDITH (Heb. 'from Judah') *c.* 16 century BC. Wife of Esau. Judith, daughter of Beeri, was a Hittite woman whom Esau married, to the distress of his parents Isaac and Rebekah. [Gen. 26:34-5]

JUSHAB-HESED (Heb. 'may covenant be restored') 6 century BC. A son of Zerubbabel of the tribe of Judah and a descendant of King David. [1 Chr. 3:20]

The territory of Judah extended to the Dead Sea area: general view of the region east of Rosh Zohar.

K

KADMIEL (Heb. 'before God') **1.** 6 century BC. Head of a family of Levites descended from Hodaviah who returned with Zerubbabel to Judah from exile in Babylon. He and his sons helped repair the Temple in Jerusalem. [Ezra 2:40; 3:9; Neh. 7:43; 12:8]
2. 5 century BC. One of the eight Levites who led the prayers at the public fast day proclaimed by Ezra, he was also a signatory of the solemn covenant, and conducted the thanksgiving services in the Temple. [Neh. 9:4, 5; 10:9; 12:24]

KAIWAN A star god. [Amos 5:26]

KALLAI (Heb. 'runner') *c.* 5 century BC. Head of a priestly family in the time of Nehemiah. [Neh. 12:20]

KAREAH (Heb. 'bold') 6 century BC. Father of Johanan, one of the army commanders who rallied to Gedaliah when he became governor of Judah. [2 Kgs. 25:23; Jer. 40:8, 13, 15, 16; 41:11, 13, 14, 16; 42:1, 8; 43:2, 4, 5]

KEDAR (Heb. 'blackness') *c.* 17 century BC. Son of Ishmael and father of the tribe of Kedar. [Gen. 25:13; 1 Chr. 1:29; Ezek. 27:21]

KEDEMAH *c.* 17 century BC. Son of Ishmael and a desert chieftain. [Gen. 25:15; 1 Chr. 1:31]

KEILAH date unknown. A leader of the tribe of Judah and known as 'the Garmite'. [1 Chr. 4:19]

KELAIAH 5 century BC. A Levite who divorced his non-Jewish wife in the days of Ezra. He explained the Law to the people after Ezra had read it to them; and was among the signatories to the covenant to observe the Laws of the Lord. Also called Kelita. [Ezra 10:23; Neh. 8:7; 10:10]

KELITA *see* KELAIAH

KEMUEL (Heb. 'raised by God') **1.** *c.* 18 century BC. Son of Abraham's brother Nahor. [Gen. 22:21]
2. *c.* 13 century BC. Leader of the tribe of Ephraim at the time of Moses, he helped divide the Promised Land among the tribes. [Num. 34:24]
3. 10 century BC. Father of Hashabiah who was head of the tribe of Levi in the reign of King David. [1 Chr. 27:17]

KENAN (Heb. 'owner') date unknown. Son of Enosh and a great-grandson of Adam, he was the father of Mahalalel. [Gen. 5:9, 12; 1 Chr. 1:2]

KENAZ 1. *c.* 16 century BC. Son of Eliphaz and a grandson of Esau, he was an Edomite leader. [Gen. 36:11, 15, 42; 1 Chr. 1:36, 53]
2. *c.* 13 century BC. Brother of Caleb the son of Jephunneh, he was father of Othniel and a leader of the tribe of Judah. [Josh. 15:17; Judg. 1:13; 3:9, 11; 1 Chr. 4:13]
3. *c.* 13 century BC. Son of Elah and grandson of Caleb the son of Jephunneh. [1 Chr. 4:15]

KENITES A desert clan from the tribes of Midian, their main base was the territory south and south-east of Akaba, but they also wandered throughout Sinai. Moses's father-in-law Jethro, a Midianite priest, was also called a Kenite. After the Israelite conquest and the death of Joshua, members of the clan came north and dwelt peaceably in Judah. Jael, who killed the Canaanite general, Sisera, with a tent peg, was the wife of Heber, the Kenite. Both King Saul and King David dealt kindly with them. The ascetic clan of Rechab, who were commended by the prophet Jeremiah, were descendants of the Kenites. [Gen. 15:19; Num. 24:21; Judg. 1:16; 4:11, 17; 5:24; 1 Sam. 15:6; 27:10; 30:29; 1 Chr. 2:55]

KEREN-HAPPUCH (Heb. 'horn of beauty') period of the Patriarchs. Youngest daughter born to Job after the Lord had redressed his fortunes. [Job. 42:14]

KEROS (Heb. 'crooked') date unknown. Ancestor of a family of Temple servants who returned with Zerubbabel to Judah from exile in Babylon. [Ezra 2:44; Neh. 7:47]

KETURAH (Heb. 'incense') *c.* 17 century BC. Abraham's third wife; he married her after Sarah's death. [Gen. 25:1; 1 Chr. 1:32]

KEZIAH (Heb. 'cassia') period of the Patriarchs. The second daughter born to Job after the Lord had redressed his fortunes. [Job. 42:14]

KISH (Heb. 'bow') **1.** date unknown. One of the ten sons of Jeiel, the father of Gibeon, and his wife Maachah. [1 Chr. 8:30; 9:36]
2. 11 century BC. Father of King Saul, Kish was the son of Abiel of the tribe of Benjamin and a wealthy landowner. The loss of his asses and Saul's search for them led to Saul's meeting with the prophet Samuel and his anointing as king. [1 Sam. 9:1, 3; 10:11, 21;

Korah was swallowed up by the earth for his part in the rebellion against the authority of Moses. Persian miniature, 1306 AD.

14:51; 2 Sam. 21:14; 1 Chr. 8:33; 9:39; 21:1; 26:28]

3. 10 century BC. A Levite descended from Merari, he was the father of Jerahmeel, a Levite in the time of King David. [1 Chr. 23:21, 22; 24:29]

4. 8 century BC. Son of Abdi and one of the Levites who obeyed the command of King Hezekiah to sanctify themselves and cleanse the Temple. [2 Chr. 29:12]

5. date unknown. Ancestor of Mordecai, cousin of Queen Esther. [Esther 2:5]

KISHI *see* KUSHAIAH

KITTIM date unknown. Son of Javan and a great-grandson of Noah. [Gen. 10:4; 1 Chr. 1:7]

KOA (Heb. 'male camel') *c.* 6 century BC. A leader of the Chaldeans whom Ezekiel prophesied would attack and destroy Judah. [Ezek. 23:23]

KOHATH (Heb. 'assembly') *c.* 16 century BC. The second son of Levi, he went down to Egypt at the same time as his grandfather Jacob. Kohath was head of an important family of Levites which included Moses and Aaron, and which served in the Tabernacle in the wilderness, and later served in the Temple. [Gen. 46:11; Exod. 6:16, 18; Num. 3:17, 19, 27; 26:57; Josh. 21:4-42; 1 Chr.; 2 Chr.]

KOHELET (Heb. 'the preacher') *c.* 3 century BC. The unknown author of the biblical book known as 'Ecclesiastes'. (See the note on 'Solomon and the Wisdom Books' at the end of the entry on SOLOMON.)

KOLAIAH (Heb. 'voice of God') **1.** date unknown. A leader of the tribe of Benjamin whose descendant Sallu was one of the first Benjaminites to settle in Jerusalem after the return from exile in Babylon. [Neh. 11:7]

2. 6 century BC. Father of Ahab, one of the false prophets in the days of Jeremiah who favoured King Zedekiah's revolt against Babylon. [Jer. 29:21]

KORAH (Heb. 'baldness') **1.** *c.* 16 century BC. Son of Esau and an Edomite leader. [Gen. 36:5, 14, 18; 1 Chr. 1:35]

2. *c.* 16 century BC. Son of Eliphaz and a grandson of Esau. [Gen. 36:16]

3. *c.* 15 century BC. Son of Hebron and a leader of the tribe of Judah. [1 Chr. 2:43]

4. *c.* 13 century BC. Son of Izhar a Levite, he rebelled against Moses and Aaron, together with Dathan and Abiram and two hundred and fifty leaders, saying, 'You have gone too far! For all the congregation are holy.' (Num. 16:3) Moses retorted: 'You have gone too far, sons of Levi.' (Num. 16:7) The Lord told Moses and Aaron to move away from the leaders of the revolt, 'And the earth opened its mouth and swallowed them up, with their households.' (Num. 16:32) The two hundred and fifty supporters were then killed by fire from the Lord [Exod. 6:21; 24; Num. 16:1-49; 26:9-11; 27:3; 1 Chr. 6:22, 37; 9:19]

KORE (Heb. 'quail') **1.** 10 century BC. Son of Ebiasaph the Levite and a descendant of Korah, his son Shallum served in the Tabernacle in Jerusalem in the time of King David. [1 Chr. 9:19; 26:1]

2. 8 century BC. Son of Imnah the Levite, he was responsible for the distribution of the freewill offerings in the Temple during the reign of King Hezekiah. [2 Chr. 31:14]

KOZ (Heb. 'thorn') date unknown. A leader of the tribe of Judah. [1 Chr. 4:8]

KUSHAIAH (Heb. 'bow') 10 century BC. Son of Abdi, a descendant of Merari, and father of Ethan, a Levite musician who played in the procession when King David brought the Ark of the Lord to Jerusalem. Also called Kishi. [1 Chr. 6:44; 15:17]

L

LAADAH *c.* 16 century BC. Son of Shelah and a grandson of Judah, he was the father of Mareshah and his descendants were famous as the makers of fine linen. [1 Chr. 4:21]

LABAN (Heb. 'white') *c.* 18 century BC. Jacob's father-in-law. Laban lived in the city of Nahor in northern Mesopotamia, with his father Bethuel and his sister Rebekah. He took part with his father in the negotiations for Rebekah's marriage to Isaac.

A generation later the young Jacob was sent by his mother Rebekah to stay with Laban in order to escape the resentment of his brother Esau, and to find himself a wife among his own people. After Jacob had worked seven years for the hand of Laban's younger daughter, Laban managed to substitute the elder and plainer sister Leah at the wedding. Jacob was obliged to work another seven years for Rachel.

Jacob served Laban twenty years, then decided to return to his own family. Laban agreed that Jacob should keep for himself as wages all the speckled and streaked goats and all the dark-coloured sheep. But the following day Laban sent off with his sons all the animals marked in such a way. His greediness was foiled by Jacob who, with the Lord's help, turned the best of Laban's flocks into speckled and streaked animals.

When Jacob left, Laban pursued him, protested at the removal of his daughters and grandchildren and accused Jacob of stealing the images of his household gods. Jacob indignantly denied the charge and invited Laban to go through his tents. He did not know that the images had been taken by Rachel, who sat on them while her father searched in her tent.

Laban proposed a covenant of friendship and Jacob agreed. They sealed their pact in accordance with

Scenes from the story of Laban and Jacob, from the *Vienna Genesis*.

custom by assembling a heap of stones and Laban said, 'The Lord watch between you and me, when we are absent one from the other.' (Gen. 31:49) Next morning he blessed his daughters and departed. [Gen. 24; 25; 27:32; 46:18, 25]

LADAN 1. *c.* 16 century BC. Son of Tahan of the tribe of Ephraim, he was the father of Ammihud. [1 Chr. 7:26]

2. *see* LIBNI **2.**

LAEL (Heb. 'of God') *c.* 13 century BC. A prominent Levite in the days of Moses, his son Eliasaph was leader of the family of Gershonites. [Num. 3:24]

LAHAD date unknown. Son of Jahath of the tribe of Judah and a member of the family of Zorathites. [1 Chr. 4:2]

LAHMI (Heb. 'warrior') *c.* 10 century BC. Brother of Goliath, he was a Philistine warrior killed in battle by Elhanan, son of Jair. [1 Chr. 20:5]

LAISH (Heb. 'lion') *c.* 10 century BC. Father of Palti to whom King Saul gave his daughter Michal in marriage, even though she was already David's wife. [1 Sam. 25:44; 2 Sam 3:15]

LAMECH (Heb. 'strong') **1.** date unknown. A descendant of Cain, his two wives Adah and Zillah bore him three sons and a daughter. He boasted to his wives of his vengeful killing of those who had injured him. [Gen. 4:18-24]

2. date unknown. Father of Noah and the son of Methuselah. [Gen. 5:25-31]

LAPPIDOTH (Heb. 'torches') *c.* 12 century BC. Husband of Deborah the prophetess and judge. [Judg. 4:4]

LEAH (Heb. 'gazelle') *c.* 18 century BC. Wife of Jacob. Leah and Rachel were the daughters of Laban who lived in the city of Nahor in Mesopotamia. 'Leah's eyes were weak, but Rachel was beautiful and lovely.' (Gen. 29:17) When Jacob, Laban's nephew, arrived in search of a wife, he fell in love with Rachel and worked seven years to earn her, but on the night of the wedding Laban substituted Leah and Jacob was forced to work another seven years for Rachel. Leah bore him six sons

– Reuben, Simeon, Levi, Judah, Issachar and Zebulun, and a daughter Dinah. When Leah found she could not have any more children, she gave Jacob her maid Zilpah who had two sons, Gad and Asher. Leah was acknowledged as one of the matriarchs of Israel. She was buried in the family tomb in the Cave of Machpelah in Hebron, before Jacob went down to join his sons in Egypt. [Gen. 29:16-35; 30:16-24; 33:1-3; 46: 15, 18; 49:31; Ruth 4:11]

LEBANA (Heb. 'white') *c.* 6 century BC. Head of a family who returned to Judah with Zerubbabel from exile in Babylon. [Ezra 2:45; Neh. 7:48]

LEBANAH *see* LEBANA

LECAH *c.* 15 century BC. Son of Er and a descendant of Judah. [1 Chr. 4:21]

LEHABIM (Heb. 'flames') date unknown. One of the eight sons of Egypt and a grandson of Ham. [Gen. 10:13; 1 Chr. 1:11]

LEMUEL (Heb. 'dedicated') date unknown. King of Maasa mentioned in the Book of Proverbs, who was taught by his mother that kings should not waste their energies pursuing women or taking strong drink but should 'judge righteously', and look after the poor and needy. [Prov. 31:1-9]

LETUSHIM (Heb. 'hammered') *c.* 16 century BC. Son of Dedan and a great-grandson of Abraham and Keturah. [Gen. 25:3]

LEUMMIM (Heb. 'nations') *c.* 16 century BC. Son of Dedan and a great-grandson of Abraham and Keturah. [Gen. 25:3]

LEVI (Heb. 'joined') *c.* 16 century BC. Levi, born in Haran, in the fertile crescent, was the third son of Jacob by his wife Leah. Together with his brothers, he was involved in the events that led to the selling of their brother Joseph into slavery in Egypt.

When Jacob was living at Shalem, his daughter Dinah was seduced by Shechem, a local young man. The father came and asked for Dinah's hand in marriage for Shechem. Jacob and his sons, concealing their rage, agreed provided that Shechem, his father and all the men in his town were circumcised. This

Priests receiving offerings, from a 13th-century BC Egyptian relief from the Temple of Rameses II at Abydos.

The Ark of the Law, candelabra and other ritual objects: mosaic floor from the synagogue at Hamath-Tiberias, 3rd-4th centuries AD.

was done, but before the men could recover from the painful operation, Levi and his brother Simeon killed them all.

Later Levi was one of the ten sons sent by Jacob to buy corn in Egypt where Joseph had become a leading figure at Pharaoh's court.

When Jacob went to settle in Egypt with all his family, included were Levi and his three sons Gershon, Kohath and Merari.

On his deathbed Jacob blessed all his sons in turn but remembering the reprisal of Levi and Simeon over the seduction of their sister, he said: 'Cursed be their anger, for it is fierce; and their wrath, for it is cruel! I will divide them in Jacob and scatter them in Israel.' (Gen. 49:7)

The Levites were given no single territory after the conquest of Canaan under Joshua but were allocated forty-eight cities surrounded by pasture land. Six of these were to be cities of refuge – three in Canaan and three east of the river Jordan.

Levi's descendants through his son Kohath were Moses and Aaron who became the founder of the priestly line. His descendants through his sons Gershon and Merari became the Temple servants and were called

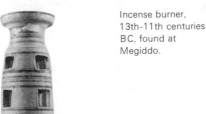

Incense burner, 13th-11th centuries BC, found at Megiddo.

Levites. [Gen. 29:34; 34:25-30; 35:23; 46:11; 49:5; Exod. 1:2; 6:16; Num. 3:17; 16:1; 26:59; 1 Chr. 2:1; 6:1-47; Ezra 8:18]

LIBNI (Heb. 'whiteness') **1.** date unknown. Son of Mahli and a grandson of Merari. One of his descendants, Asaiah, served in the Tabernacle in the reign of King David. [1 Chr. 6:29]
2. *c.* 10 century BC. A Levite descended from Gershon he was appointed by King David to minister in the Tabernacle. Also called Ladan. [Exod. 6:17; Num. 3:18; 1 Chr. 6:17, 20; 23:7; 26:21]

LIKHI (Heb. 'learned') *c.* 13 century BC. One of the four sons of Shemida, a leader of the tribe of Manasseh. [1 Chr. 7:19]

LO-AMMI (Heb. 'not my people') *c.* 8 century BC. Second son of the prophet Hosea and his wife Gomer, the name is symbolic of God's rejection of his people Israel for their sins. [Hos. 1:9]

LO-RUHAMAH (Heb. 'not pitied') *c.* 8 century BC. Daughter of the prophet Hosea and his wife Gomer, the name is symbolic of God's decision not to have mercy on Israel but to exile them for their sins. [Hos. 1:6]

LOT (Heb. 'a covering') *c.* 18-16 centuries BC. Nephew of Abraham.

Lot was the son of Abraham's deceased brother Haran, and migrated with him to Canaan. Abraham and Lot prospered, but strife broke out between their herdsmen over the limited grazing in the hill country of Canaan. It was agreed that Lot would move further east to the well-watered 'plain of Jordan'.

Lot made his home in Sodom, and was among the captives taken by four raiding kings from the north. Abraham organized a pursuit force and brought Lot back together with the other captives and the plunder.

One evening Lot invited two strangers to return home with him for the night, and protected them from a mob demanding their surrender. They disclosed to Lot that they were angels sent by the Lord to destroy the two

Lot, his daughters and his wife escaping from the burning city of Sodom: painting by Raphael (1483-1520).

evil cities of Sodom and Gomorrah, and they urged him to flee with his family. His sons-in-law did not take the story seriously, and refused to leave. At dawn, Lot, his wife and their two unmarried daughters set out for the small nearby town of Zoar. The Lord then destroyed the two cities with fire and brimstone. Though Lot's family were warned not to look back, his wife did so, and was turned into a pillar of salt. Lot and the two daughters later left Zoar for the mountains.

The daughters believed that no one else was left alive in the world, and in order to 'preserve the seed of our father' they plied Lot with wine and when he was too drunk to know what he was doing, they seduced him. As a result the first daughter gave birth to Moab, from whom the Moabites were descended; and the second daughter gave birth to Ben-ammi, the forefather of the Ammonites.

The story of Sodom and Gomorrah probably derives

Lotan

from an earthquake or volcanic convulsion that may have devastated the Dead Sea area about the time of the patriarchs. The physical setting for the story is spectacular. The steel-blue surface of the Dead Sea lies in a deep and desolate rift thirteen hundred feet below sea-level – the lowest inhabited spot on the earth. The shore is overlooked from the west by cliffs of salt and limestone, and local legend identifies one of the odd salt projections as Lot's wife. [Gen. 11:27; 13; 18; 19]

LOTAN (Heb. 'hidden') date unknown. Eldest son of Seir the Horite, he was an Edomite leader. [Gen. 36:20, 22, 29; 1 Chr. 1:38, 39]

LUD date unknown. One of Shem's five sons and a grandson of Noah. [Gen. 10:22; 1 Chr. 1:17; Isa. 66:19; Ezek. 27:10]

LUDIM date unknown. One of the eight sons of Egypt and a grandson of Ham. [Gen. 10:13]

Ludim

Ludim was the traditional father of the Libyans. 12th-century BC Egyptian glazed tile showing a Libyan.

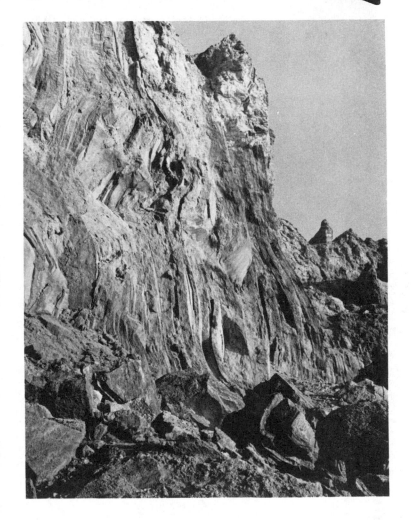

Cliffs near Sodom. It was landscape like this which probably gave rise to the story of Lot's wife.

M

MAACAH 1. *c.* 18 century BC. Son of Abraham's brother Nahor by his brother's concubine Reumah. [Gen. 22:24]

2. date unknown. Concubine of Caleb son of Hezron, she bore him five sons who were all leaders of Judah. [1 Chr. 2:48]

3. date unknown. Wife of Machir, the son of Manasseh. She is also called his sister. [1 Chr. 7:15, 16]

4. date unknown. Wife of Jeiel, one of the leaders of Benjamin living in Gibeon. [1 Chr. 8:29; 9:35]

5. *see* MAOCH

6. *c.* 10 century BC. Father of Hanan, a warrior in King David's army distinguished for his bravery. [1 Chr. 11:43]

Pottery incense burner with two figurines of the goddess Ashtaroth, 13th-11th centuries BC, found at Megiddo.

7. *c.* 10 century BC. Father of Shephatiah who was ruler over the tribe of Simeon in the reign of King David. [1 Chr. 27:16]

8. *c.* 10 century BC. Wife of King David, she was the daughter of King Talmai of Geshur and the mother of Absalom. [2 Sam. 3:3; 1 Chr. 3:2]

9. *c.* 10 century BC. Mother of King Asa of Judah, whom he removed from her royal position because she worshipped the idol Asherah. [1 Kgs. 15:10, 13; 2 Chr. 15:16]

10. *c.* 10 century BC. Daughter of Abishalom, she was the favourite wife of King Rehoboam of Judah and mother of his successor Abijah. Also called Micaiah, where her father is given as Uriel. [1 Kgs. 15:2; 2 Chr. 11:20-22; 13:2]

MAADAI (Heb. 'ornament') 5 century BC. A descendant of Bani who divorced his non-Jewish wife in the time of Ezra. [Ezra 10:34]

MAADIAH (Heb. 'ornament') 6 century BC. A priest of Judah who returned with Zerubbabel from exile in Babylon. Also called Moadiah. [Neh. 12:5, 17]

MAAI (Heb. 'merciful') 5 century BC. A Levite who played a musical instrument at the dedication of the rebuilt walls of Jerusalem in the time of Nehemiah. [Neh. 12:36]

MAASAI (Heb. 'works of God') *c.* 6 century BC. Son of Adiel, he was one of the priests who returned to Judah from exile in Babylon and settled in Jerusalem. [1 Chr. 9:12]

MAASEIAH (Heb. 'work of God') **1.** *c.* 10 century BC. A Levite who served as porter at the gates of the Tabernacle when King David brought the Ark of God to Jerusalem, and played musical instruments during the celebrations. [1 Chr. 15:18, 20]

2. *c.* 9 century BC. Son of Adaiah, Maaseiah was one of five army commanders of Judah who, under the instructions of the high priest Jehoiada, proclaimed Joash king of Judah and executed his grandmother Queen Athaliah who had usurped the throne. [2 Chr. 23:1-15]

3. *c.* 8 century BC. An officer of Uzziah, king of Judah, who supervised the organization of the king's army. [2 Chr. 26:11]

4. *c.* 8 century BC. Son of Ahaz, king of Judah, he was killed by Zichri of the tribe of Ephraim when the armies of Israel and Syria invaded Judah. [2 Chr. 28:7]

5. *c.* 7 century BC. The governor of Jerusalem in the reign of Josiah, king of Judah. [2 Chr. 34:8]

6. *c.* 6 century BC. Father of the priest Zephaniah, who was sent by King Zedekiah of Judah to the prophet Jeremiah to ask whether God would help him against Nebuchadnezzar, king of Babylon. [Jer. 21:1; 29:25; 37:3]

7. *c.* 6 century BC. Father of Zedekiah who was accused by Jeremiah of prophesying lies in the name of God. [Jer. 29:21]

8. *c.* 6 century BC. Son of Shallum, he was a doorkeeper at the entrance to the Temple in the time of Jeremiah. [Jer. 35:4]

9. 5 century BC. A descendant of Jeshua the priest, he divorced his non-Jewish wife in the time of Ezra. [Ezra 10:18]

10. 5 century BC. A descendant of Harim the priest, he divorced his non-Jewish wife in the time of Ezra. [Ezra 10:21]

11. 5 century BC. A descendant of Pashhur, he divorced his non-Jewish wife in the time of Ezra. [Ezra 10:22]

12. 5 century BC. A descendant of Pahath-moab, he divorced his non-Jewish wife in the time of Ezra. [Ezra 10:30]

13. *c.* 5 century BC. Father of Azariah who helped repair the walls of Jerusalem in the time of Nehemiah. [Neh. 3:23]

14. 5 century BC. One of the leaders of Judah who stood at Ezra's right hand when he read out the Law of Moses to the people in the market-place. [Neh. 8:4]

15. 5 century BC. One of the Levites sent by Ezra to explain the Law of Moses to the people of Judah after Ezra had read it aloud. [Neh. 8:7]

16. 5 century BC. One of the leaders of Judah who signed the solemn covenant in the time of Nehemiah. [Neh. 10:25]

17. *c.* 5 century BC. Son of Baruch, he was one of the first men of Judah to settle in Jerusalem after the return from exile in Babylon. [Neh. 11:5]

18. *c.* 5 century BC. Son of Ithiel, he was one of the first men of Benjamin to settle in Jerusalem after the return from exile in Babylon. [Neh. 11:7]

19. 5 century BC. A priest who blew a trumpet at the dedication of the rebuilt walls of Jerusalem in the time of Nehemiah. [Neh. 12:41]

20. 5 century BC. A priest who participated in the dedication of the rebuilt walls of Jerusalem in the time of Nehemiah. [Neh. 12:42]

MAAZ (Heb. 'wrath') date unknown. A son of Ram and the grandson of Jerahmeel, he was a leader of the tribe of Judah. [1 Chr. 2:27]

MAAZIAH (Heb. 'God is a refuge') **1.** 10 century BC.

A priest in Jerusalem responsible for the twenty-fourth and last turn of service in the Tabernacle in the reign of King David. [1 Chr. 24:18]

2. 5 century BC. A priest who signed the solemn covenant in the time of Nehemiah. [Neh. 10:8]

MACHBANNAI *c.* 11 century BC. One of the eleven warriors of the tribe of Gad who left the army of King Saul and joined David at Ziklag. [1 Chr. 12:13]

MACHBENAH date unknown. Son of Sheva, a leader of the tribe of Judah. [1 Chr. 2:49]

MACHI (Heb. 'decrease') *c.* 13 century BC. A leader of the tribe of Gad, his son Geuel was sent by Moses to spy out the Promised Land. [Num. 13:15]

MACHIR (Heb. 'sold') **1.** date unknown. Son of Manasseh and his Aramite concubine, he and his tribe seized the land of Gilead east of the river Jordan from the Amorites, and Moses confirmed their possession of

View of the Gilead region in the Jordan valley, allotted to the tribe of Manasseh.

this territory in the division of the Promised Land among the tribes of Israel. [Gen. 50:23; Num. 26:29; 27:1; 32:39, 40; 36:1; Deut. 3:15; Josh. 13:31; 17:1, 3; Judg. 5:14; 1 Chr. 2:21-23; 7:14-17]

2. *c.* 10 century BC. Son of Ammiel from Lo-debar in Gilead, with whom Mephibosheth, son of Jonathan, hid after David became king of Israel, fearing that as a grandson of King Saul he would be killed. Machir brought large quantities of food and equipment to the army of King David at Mahanaim east of the river Jordan, during Absalom's civil war against David. [2 Sam. 9:4; 17:27]

MACHNADEBAI 5 century BC. A son of Bihnui who divorced his non-Jewish wife in the time of Ezra. [Ezra 10:40]

MADAI date unknown. Son of Japheth and a grandson of Noah, he was traditionally regarded as the father of the Medes. [Gen. 10:2; 1 Chr. 1:5]

MAGBISH (Heb. 'gathering') date unknown. Ancestor of a large family that returned with Zerubbabel from exile in Babylon. [Ezra 2:30]

MAGDIEL (Heb. 'God's choice gift') date unknown. An Edomite chieftain descended from Esau. [Gen. 36:43; 1 Chr. 1:54]

MAGOG date unknown. Magog is mentioned as one of the seven sons of Japheth and a grandson of Noah. Magog was not clearly identified with any nation or territory, but vaguely came to represent a fierce warrior people (possibly the Scythians) that swept southwards to harass the populations of the fertile crescent. This no doubt inspired Ezekiel's vision of the millennium in which Israel was to be invaded by a horde of fierce warriors from the north led by Gog from the land of Magog.

Under the influence of the Book of Ezekiel, 'Gog and Magog' became symbolic names for the heathen who would unsuccessfully try to destroy the Lord's future kingdom. [Gen. 10:2; 1 Chr. 1:5; Ezek. 38:2; 39:6]

MAGPLASH 5 century BC. A chief of Judah who signed the solemn covenant in the time of Nehemiah. [Neh. 10:20]

MAHALALEL (Heb. 'God's praise') **1.** date unknown. Son of Kenan and a descendant of Seth. [Gen. 5:12-17; 1 Chr. 1:2]
2. date unknown. Ancestor of Athaiah, one of the first men of Judah to settle in Jerusalem after the return from exile in Babylon. [Neh. 11:4]

MAHALATH (Heb. 'harp') **1.** c. 16 century BC. A wife of Esau, she was the daughter of Ishmael. Also called Basemath. [Gen. 28:9; 36:3]
2. c. 10 century BC. A wife of King Rehoboam of Judah, she was the daughter of Jerimoth and a granddaughter of King David. [2 Chr. 11:18]

MAHARAI (Heb. 'swift') c. 10 century BC. A distinguished warrior in the army of King David, he was an army commander in the tenth month of each year. [2 Sam. 23:28; 1 Chr. 11:30; 27:13]

MAHATH 1. date unknown. Son of Amasai of the tribe of Levi, he was the father of Elkanah. [1 Chr. 6:35]
2. c. 8 century BC. A Levite who supervised the bringing of tithes and offerings into the Temple in the reign of King Hezekiah. [2 Chr. 29:12; 31:13]

MAHAZIOTH (Heb. 'visions') c. 10 century BC. Youngest son of King David's musician Heman, he and his brothers played musical instruments in the Tabernacle under their father's direction, and Mahazioth was responsible for the twenty-third turn of service. [1 Chr. 25:4, 30]

MAHER-SHALAL-HASH-BAZ (Heb. 'the booty and the shame are imminent') c. 8 century BC. Symbolic name for the son of Isaiah, signifying the impending destruction of the kingdom of Israel. [Isa. 8:1, 3]

MAHLAH 1. c. 13 century BC. One of the five daughters of Zelophehad who claimed a share of their father's estate from Moses since their father had no sons. [Josh. 17:3; Num. 26:33; 27:1; 36:11]
2. date unknown. Son of Hammolecheth who was the sister of Gilead, the leader of the tribe of Manasseh. [1 Chr. 7:18]

MAHALI see MAHLI 1.

MAHLI (Heb. 'sick') **1.** date unknown. Elder son of Merari and a grandson of Levi, his descendants were assigned special duties in the Temple. Also called Mahali. [Exod. 6:19; Num. 3:20; 1 Chr. 6:19, 29; 23:21; 24:26, 28; Ezra 8:18]
2. date unknown. Son of Mushi and a prominent Levite whose descendants served in the Tabernacle in the reign of King David. Nephew of Mahli **1**. [1 Chr. 6:47; 23:23; 24:30]

MAHLON (Heb. 'sickly') c. 11 century BC. Elder son of Elimelech and Naomi of the tribe of Judah, Mahlon and his brother Chilion left their home in Bethlehem during a famine in the days of the judges and settled in Moab. They married Moabite wives, Ruth and Orpah, but after ten years Mahlon and Chilion died, and Naomi returned to Bethlehem with her daughter-in-law Ruth. [Ruth 1:1-5; 4:9, 10]

MAHOL (Heb. 'dance') date unknown. Father of Ethan, Heman, Calcol and Darda, all of whom were famed for their wisdom. [1 Kgs. 4:31]

MAHSEIAH (Heb. 'God is my refuge') c. 7 century BC. Grandfather of Baruch, Jeremiah's faithful scribe, and of Seraiah, King Zedekiah's quartermaster. [Jer. 32:12; 51:59]

MALACHI (Heb. 'my messenger') c. middle of 5 century BC. Post-exilic Hebrew prophet. It is generally considered that Malachi is not a name, but a Hebrew word meaning 'my messenger'. It is taken from the sentence in the text, 'Behold, I send my messenger to prepare the way before me'. (Mal. 3:1) This prophet appeared in Jerusalem about the middle of the 5th century BC, when the second Temple built in the time of Zerubbabel had already been in existence for some while, but Nehemiah had not yet carried out his religious reforms.

The book of Malachi indicates that the morale of the Jewish settlers in and around Jerusalem was at a low ebb at that time. There is mention of lean harvests, drought and locust swarms. The earlier hopes that an independent and flourishing Jewish commonwealth would follow the restoration of the Temple had not been realized. Judea remained a struggling and obscure corner of the Persian empire. The prophet complains about the religious slackness, the moral erosion, and the cynicism that prevailed in it.

The priests are taken to task for accepting blemished offerings contrary to the law, and treating the Lord with a disrespect they would not dream of showing to the local Persian governor: 'When you offer blind animals in sacrifice, is that no evil? And when you offer those those that are lame or sick, is that no evil? Present that to your governor; will he be pleased with you or show you favour?' (Mal. 1:8)

As for the people, they have sinned by divorcing the Jewish wives they married in their youth and taking foreign wives. They fail to bring their tithes and dues for the support of the Temple. When reproached, they openly doubt whether there is anything to gain by fidelity to the Lord and strict observance of his tenets.

The Lord has always kept his covenant with the Children of Israel, and set his face against their enemies, such as the Edomites to the south. His patience is now exhausted. A day of reckoning will soon come when the wrongdoers will be punished and only the faithful preserved. But the Lord is compassionate and will give to everyone a chance to repent.' Behold, I will send you Elijah the prophet before the great and terrible day of the Lord comes. And he will turn the hearts of fathers to their children and the hearts of children to their fathers, lest I come and smite the land with a curse.' (Mal. 4:5, 6)

Malachi is the last work in the collection of the Twelve Minor Prophets, and therefore brings to an end the prophetical books of the Old Testament. [Book of Malachi]

MALCAM (Heb. 'their king') **1.** see MOLECH.

2. date unknown. One of the four sons of Shaharaim and Hodesh of the tribe of Benjamin. [1 Chr. 8:9]

MALCHIAH (Heb. 'God is my king') **1.** c. 6 century BC. Owner of a dungeon in Jerusalem into which the leaders of Judah cast the prophet Jeremiah. [Jer. 38:6]

2. see MALCHIJAH 3.

MALCHIEL (Heb. 'God is my king') date unknown. Younger son of Beriah and the grandson of Asher. Also described as the father of Birzaith. [Gen. 46:17; Num. 26:45; 1 Chr. 7:31]

MALCHIJAH (Heb. 'God is king') **1.** date unknown. Son of Ethni, a Levite, he was the father of Baaseiah, and his descendant Asaph was one of the chief musicians of King David. [1 Chr. 6:40]

2. c. 10 century BC. A priest who took the fifth turn of service in the Tabernacle in the reign of King David. [1 Chr. 24:9]

3. c. 6 century BC. Father of Pashhur the priest, who was sent by King Zedekiah of Judah to consult the prophet Jeremiah and who later cast Jeremiah into a dungeon. His descendants were among the first men of Judah to return from exile in Babylon. Also called Malchiah. [1 Chr. 9:12; Neh. 11:12; Jer. 21:1; 38:1]

4. 5 century BC. A descendant of Parosh who divorced his non-Jewish wife in the time of Ezra. [Ezra 10:25]

5. 5 century BC. Descendant of Harim, he divorced his non-Jewish wife, and helped repair part of the walls of Jerusalem in the time of Nehemiah, [Ezra 10:31; Neh. 3:11]

6. 5 century BC. Son of Rechab, he rebuilt the Dung Gate of Jerusalem in the time of Nehemiah. [Neh. 3:14]

7. 5 century BC. Son of a goldsmith, he helped repair the walls of Jerusalem in the days of Nehemiah. [Neh. 3:31]

8. 5 century BC. A leader who stood at the left hand of Ezra when he read from the Law of Moses to the people of Judah in the market-place. [Neh. 8:4]

9. 5 century BC. One of the priests who signed the solemn covenant in the time of Nehemiah. [Neh. 10:3]

10. 5 century BC. A priest who blew a trumpet during the service of dedication of the rebuilt walls of Jerusalem in the time of Nehemiah. [Neh. 12:42]

MALCHIRAM (Heb. 'my king is exalted') 6 century BC. A son of Jehoiachin, the last king of Judah. [1 Chr. 3:18]

MALCHISHUA (Heb. 'king of salvation') 11 century BC. Third son of King Saul and his wife Ahinoam, he was killed in battle by the Philistines with his brothers Jonathan and Abinadab. [1 Sam. 14:49; 31:2; 1 Chr. 8:33; 9:39; 10:2]

MALLOTHI (Heb. 'fullness') c. 10 century BC. One of the fourteen sons of Heman, King David's musician. He and his brothers played musical instruments under their father's direction and his sons took the nineteenth turn of service in the Tabernacle. [1 Chr. 25:4, 26]

MALLUCH (Heb. 'ruling') **1.** date unknown. A Levite descended from Merari, he was the father of Abdi and his descendant Ethan was a musician in the Tabernacle in the reign of King David. [1 Chr. 6:44]

2. 6 century BC. A priest of Judah who returned with Zerubbabel from exile in Babylon. Also known as Malluchi. [Neh. 12:2, 14]

3. 5 century BC. A descendant of Bani who divorced his non-Jewish wife in the time of Ezra. [Ezra 10:29]

4. 5 century BC. A descendant of Harim who divorced his non-Jewish wife in the time of Ezra. [Ezra 10:32]

5. 5 century BC. A priest who signed the solemn covenant in the time of Nehemiah. [Neh. 10:4]

6. 5 century BC. A leader of Judah who signed the solemn covenant in the time of Nehemiah. [Neh. 10:27]

MALLUCHI see MALLUCH 2.

MAMRE (Heb. 'strength') c. 18 century BC. An Amorite leader who gave his name to the plain near Hebron where Abraham lived. [Gen. 14:13-24; 23:19]

MANAHATH date unknown. Second son of Shobal and a grandson of Seir the Horite, who had a city near Jerusalem named after him. [Gen. 36:23; 1 Chr. 1:40]

MANASSEH (Heb. 'forgetting') **1.** c. 16 century BC Elder son of Joseph.

Manasseh, like his younger brother Ephraim, was born in Egypt where Joseph had married Asenath, the daughter of the Egyptian high priest of the temple at On.

When Jacob was old and ailing, Joseph brought Manasseh and Ephraim to his father's bedside to receive the patriarch's blessing. Jacob's sight was failing and when he placed his right hand on the head of the younger son Ephraim instead of on Manesseh, Joseph sought to correct him. Jacob then explained that Ephraim's descendants would be more important than those of Manasseh. Jacob gave the same importance to these two grandchildren as he did to his sons, and they too became the founders of tribes.

In the conquest of Canaan under Joshua, the tribe of Manasseh was allocated a large area that stretched from the coastal plain across the central hill area round Shechem (Nablus) to the Jordan valley, with one sub-tribe east of the Jordan.

Bronze ritual model of an offering to the sun god, 12th century BC, from Susa.

The tel of Ta'anach mentioned in the Book of Joshua as belonging to the territory of Manasseh.

In the blessing of Moses, Joseph is promised great abundance and power, and it is added that 'such are the thousands of Manasseh' (Deut. 33:17). [Gen. 41:51; 48:1-20; 50:23; Num. 26:28, 29-34; 32:39-41; 36:1; Deut. 3:13; 33:17; Josh. 13:31; 17:1-3; 1 Kgs. 4:13; 1 Chr. 7:14-17]

2. Fourteenth ruler of Judah after the monarchy split, he reigned 687-42 BC.

The son of King Hezekiah of Judah and his wife Hephzibah. He was twelve years old when he came to the throne and reigned for forty-five years. A reaction against Hezekiah's religious reforms set in under Manasseh, for which he is denounced in the Bible. Heathen cults were restored and pagan altars and images were introduced even into the Temple. The indignant prophets cried that the Lord 'will wipe Jerusalem as one wipes a dish, wiping it and turning it upside down.' (2 Kgs. 21:13) The account in Chronicles states that Manasseh was carried off in chains to Babylon. He then repented of his sins and was restored to Judah where he purified the Temple and strengthened the walls. A more prosaic explanation is given in Assyrian records, which include Manasseh in a group of vassal kings summoned to Nineveh, apparently in order to extract more tribute from them. He was

Cuneiform tablet recording the Assyrian King Esarhaddon's campaigns of 680-69 BC.

succeeded by his son Amon. [2 Kgs. 20; 21; 23; 24:3; 1 Chr. 3:13; 2 Chr. 32:33; 33:1-23; Jer. 15:4]

4. 5 century BC. A descendant of Pahath-moab who divorced his non-Jewish wife in the time of Ezra. [Ezra 10:30]

5. 5 century BC. A descendant of Hashum who divorced his non-Jewish wife in the time of Ezra. [Ezra 10:33]

MANOAH (Heb. 'rest') c. 12 century BC. Father of Samson whose birth was foretold by an angel. [Judg. 13:2-24]

MAOCH c. 10 century BC. Father of Achish, king of Gath, to whom David fled with all his family when pursued by King Saul. Also called Maacah. [1 Sam. 27:2; 1 Kgs. 2:39]

MAON (Heb. 'dwelling') date unknown. Son of Shammai and the father of Beth-zur, he was a leader of the tribe of Judah. [1 Chr. 2:45]

MARA see NAOMI

MARESHAH (Heb. 'hill-top') **1.** date unknown. Son of Caleb of the tribe of Judah and a nephew of Jerahmeel. [1 Chr. 2:42]

2. date unknown. Son of Laadah and a leader of the tribe of Judah. [1 Chr. 4:21]

MARSENA 5 century BC. One of the seven princes of Persia and Media who sat at the table of King Ahasuerus. [Esther 1:14]

MASH date unknown. One of the four sons of Aram and a grandson of Shem. [Gen. 10:23]

MASSA c. 17 century BC. Son of Abraham's son Ishmael, he was a leader of a desert clan. [Gen. 25:14; 1 Chr. 1:30]

MATRED date unknown. Mother of Mehetabel, the wife of Hadar, king of Edom. [Gen. 36:39; 1 Chr. 1:50]

MATRI (Heb. 'rain') date unknown. Head of a family of Benjaminites, he was an ancestor of King Saul. [1 Sam. 10:21]

MATTAN (Heb. 'gift') **1.** c. 9 century BC. The priest of the idol Baal in Jerusalem appointed by Athaliah, queen of Judah. When the high priest Jehoiada successfully organized the overthrow and execution of Queen Athaliah, the people of Judah destroyed the temple of Baal and slew Mattan in front of the altars to Baal. [2 Kgs. 11:18; 2 Chr. 23:17]

2. c. 6 century BC. Father of Shephatiah who cast the prophet Jeremiah into prison for prophesying that Jerusalem would fall into the hands of the Babylonians. [Jer. 38:1]

MATTANIAH (Heb. 'God's gift') **1.** c. 10 century BC. A son of Heman, one of King David's musicians. He and his brothers sang and played musical instruments under their father's direction, and he was appointed to the ninth turn of service in the Tabernacle. [1 Chr. 25:4, 16]

2. c. 8 century BC. A Levite descended from Asaph who cleansed and sanctified the Temple at the com-

mand of Hezekiah, king of Judah. [2 Chr. 29:13]

3. see ZEDEKIAH **3.**

4. date unknown. Son of Mica and a descendant of Asaph, one of King David's chief musicians, he was a Levite who settled in Jerusalem following the return from exile in Babylon. He was the ancestor of Jahaziel, son of Zechariah, who prophesied that Jehoshaphat, king of Judah, would defeat the armies of Moab, Ammon and Mount Seir without having to do battle. [1 Chr. 9:15; 2 Chr. 20:14; Neh. 11:17, 22; 12:8]

5. 5 century BC. Son of Elam who divorced his non-Jewish wife in the time of Ezra. [Ezra 10:26]

6. 5 century BC. Son of Zattu who divorced his non-Jewish wife in the time of Ezra. [Ezra 10:27]

7. 5 century BC. A descendant of Pahath-moab who divorced his non-Jewish wife in the time of Ezra. [Ezra 10:30]

8. 5 century BC. A descendant of Bani who divorced his non-Jewish wife in the time of Ezra. [Ezra 10:37]

9. 5 century BC. A Levite who was a gatekeeper of the Temple in Jerusalem when Joiakim was high priest in the time of Nehemiah. [Neh. 12:25]

10. 5 century BC. Son of Micaiah of the tribe of Levi and a descendant of Asaph, King David's musician, he was the father of Shemaiah and his descendant Zechariah blew a trumpet at the dedication service for the rebuilt walls of Jerusalem. [Neh. 12:35]

11. 5 century BC. A leader of the tribe of Levi, his grandson Hanan administered the treasuries of Judah in the time of Nehemiah. [Neh. 13:13]

MATTATTAH c. 5 century BC. A descendant of Hashum who divorced his non-Jewish wife in the time of Ezra. [Ezra 10:33]

MATTENAI (Heb. 'gift of God') **1.** 5 century BC. Descended from the family of Hashum, he divorced his non-Jewish wife in the time of Ezra. [Ezra 10:33]

2. 5 century BC. A descendant of Bani, he divorced his non-Jewish wife in the time of Ezra. [Ezra 10:37]

3. 5 century BC. Head of a priestly family of Judah descended from the priest Joiarib, he served during the period that Joiakim was high priest in the time of Nehemiah. [Neh. 12:19]

MATTITHIAH (Heb. 'gift of God') **1.** c. 10 century BC. A Levite who served as a gatekeeper of the Tabernacle in the reign of King David and played the harp in the festivities when the Ark was brought to Jerusalem. [1 Chr. 15:18, 21; 16:5]

2. c. 10 century BC. Son of Jeduthun, a musician of King David, Mattithiah and his brothers, under their father's direction, played the harp in the thanksgiving services, and took the fourteenth turn of service in the Tabernacle. [1 Chr. 25:3, 21]

3. 6 century BC. Eldest son of Shallum, a Levite descended from Kohath, in the time of Zerubbabel, he was responsible for the baking of flat cakes which were among the food offerings prepared for the Temple. [1 Chr. 9:31]

4. 5 century BC. A descendant of Nebo who divorced his non-Jewish wife in the time of Ezra. [Ezra 10:43]

5. 5 century BC. A leader of Judah who stood at the right hand of Ezra when he read the Law of Moses to the people in the market-place. [Neh. 8:4]

MEBUNNAI *see* SIBBECAI

MEDAD (Heb. 'measure') *c.* 13 century BC. A leader of Israel, he began to prophesy in the wilderness and Joshua asked Moses to stop him; whereupon Moses replied that he wished all Israel were prophets. [Num. 11:26, 27]

MEDAN (Heb. 'strife') *c.* 17 century BC. Son of Abraham by his wife Keturah, he was a leader of a desert tribe. [Gen. 25:2; 1 Chr. 1:32]

MEHETABEL (Heb. 'God does good') **1.** date unknown. Daughter of Matred who became the wife of Hadar (Hadad) king of Edom. [Gen. 36:39; 1 Chr. 1:50]
2. 5 century BC. Father of Shemaiah who was a false prophet in the time of Nehemiah. [Neh. 6:10]

MEHIDA 6 century BC. Head of a family of Temple servants who returned with Zerubbabel to Judah from exile in Babylon. [Ezra 2:52; Neh. 7:54]

MEHIR (Heb. 'price') date unknown. Son of Chelub, a leader of the tribe of Judah, he was the father of Eshton. [1 Chr. 4:11]

MEHUJAEL (Heb. 'smitten') date unknown. Son of Irad he was a descendant of Cain, and the father of Methuselah. [Gen. 4:18]

MEHUMAN (Pers. 'true') 5 century BC. One of the seven chamberlains of King Ahasuerus who was commanded by the drunken king on the seventh day of a feast to bring Queen Vashti before his guests to show off her beauty. [Esther 1:10]

MELATIAH (Heb. 'saved') 5 century BC. One of the Gibeonites who helped repair the walls of Jerusalem in the time of Nehemiah. [Neh. 3:7]

MELCHIZEDEK (Heb. 'king of righteousness') *c.* 18 century BC. King of Salem. When Abraham returned from rescuing his nephew Lot from the four kings who had carried him off, Melchizedek welcomed them with bread and wine. Abraham gave him a tenth of the spoil.

Scholars think that Salem might well have been Jerusalem, which is called Salem in Psalm 76:2 and in the 14th century BC Tel el-Amarna tablets is called Uru-salim.

In Psalm 110:4 Melchizedek is a symbol of an ideal priest-king. [Gen. 14:18-28; Ps. 110:4]

MELECH (Heb. 'king') date unknown. Son of Micah of the tribe of Benjamin and a descendant of Jonathan, the son of King Saul. [1 Chr. 8:35; 9:41]

MEMUCAN (Pers. 'dignified') *c.* 5 century BC. One of the seven princes of Persia and Media who sat at the table of King Ahasuerus, and who advised the king to replace Queen Vashti by another. The advice was accepted. [Esther 1:14; 16, 21]

MENAHEM (Heb. 'comforter') Sixteenth king of Israel after the monarchy split. He reigned 743-38 BC. Menahem, son of Gadi, possibly the governor of the former capital Tirzah, marched to Samaria, deposed and slew the usurper Shallum and seized power himself. Resistance to his authority from several towns in the area was brutally suppressed.

Menahem preserved Israel from being overrun by the Assyrian forces only by agreeing to paying Tiglath-pileser a huge tribute of one thousand talents of silver. He raised this sum by a levy of fifty shekels of silver

Assyrian wall relief
showing soldiers and
a war chariot.

from every man of property in the kingdom. The Assyrian inscription which relates the campaigns of Tiglath-pileser refers to Menahem of Samaria among those rulers from whom tribute was collected. A number of ostraca found in the ruins of Samaria dealing with the collection of oil and wine in the kingdom may relate to this tribute.

Menahem was succeeded by his son Pekahiah. [2 Kgs. 15:14-22]

MEONOTHAI (Heb. 'my dwellings') *c.* 12 century BC. A leader of the tribe of Judah and a son of Othniel, he was the father of Ophrah. [1 Chr. 4:14]

MEPHIBOSHETH (Heb. 'contender against shame') **1.** *c.* 10 century BC. Son of Jonathan, he was five years old when his father and grandfather Saul were killed on Mount Gilboa. Fleeing with the rest of the Israelites, Mephibosheth fell and was crippled in both feet.

When David was proclaimed king he sent for Ziba, a servant of Saul, and asked him if any of Saul's family was left. Ziba told him about Jonathan's crippled son and David, instead of having him killed as was the practice, not only spared his life but gave him all of Saul's personal possessions and moved him into the royal palace. The lame Mephibosheth, overcome by David's generosity, bowed down in front of him and said humbly, 'What is your servant, that you should look upon a dead dog such as I?' (2 Sam. 9:8) David appointed Ziba and all his family the servants of Mephibosheth and the boy was brought up with David's own sons.

After the revolt of Absalom, David was forced to flee from Jerusalem and while leaving the city was met by Ziba who brought him two asses laden with provisions for his journey. When David asked Ziba about his master, Ziba suggested indirectly that Mephibosheth had stayed behind because he was siding with Absalom. David was saddened by this desertion but later when he returned to Jerusalem after the defeat of Absalom, Mephibosheth met him with happiness at his safe return. David asked him why he had not fled and he explained that Ziba had maligned him, that he had mourned the king's departure but was now overjoyed at his return. David forgave him but divided Saul's property between Mephibosheth and Ziba in payment for the servant's loyalty to the king. Also called Meribbaal. [2 Sam. 4:4; 9:6-13; 16:1-4; 19:24-30; 21:7; 1 Chr. 8:34, 9:40]

2. *c.* 10 century BC. A son of King Saul by his concubine Rizpah, he was one of seven descendants of King Saul who were handed over to the Gibeonites by King David to be hanged as revenge for Saul's slaying of many of the Gibeonites. [2 Sam. 21:8]

MERAB (Heb. 'increasing') 11 century BC. Eldest daughter of King Saul and his wife Ahinoam, she was promised to the man who killed Goliath the Philistine. When David came to claim her he found Saul had given her to Adriel and he was given her sister Michal. Later when David became king, he handed over Merab's five sons to the Gibeonites to be killed in expiation of Saul's crimes against them, and in the belief that the current famine would cease. [1 Sam. 14:49; 18:17-19]

MERAIAH (Heb. 'rebellion') 5 century BC. Head of a priestly family in Judah when Joiakim was high priest in the time of Nehemiah. [Neh. 12:12]

MERAIOTH (Heb. 'rebellious') **1.** date unknown. Son of Zerahiah of the tribe of Levi and the father of Amariah, he was an ancestor of Ezra the scribe. [1 Chr. 6:6, 7, 52; Ezra 7:3]

2. date unknown. Father of Zadok and son of Ahitub,

a priest in the Temple, he was an ancestor of Azariah, a priest who settled in Jerusalem in the time of Ezra. [1 Chr. 9:11; Neh. 11:11]

3. *see* MEREMOTH **2.**

MERARI (Heb. 'bitter') *c.* 16 century BC. A son of Levi, he accompanied his grandfather Jacob when he went down to Egypt. His sons Mahli and Mushi and their families joined Moses in the Exodus, and their descendants became priests in the Temple in Jerusalem. [Gen. 46:11; Exod. 6:16-19; Num. 3:17-36; 4:29-45; 7:8; 10:17; 26:57; Josh. 21:7-40; 1 Chr. 6:1-77; 9:14; 15:6, 17; 23:6, 21; 24:26, 27; 26:10, 19; 2 Chr. 29:12; 34:12; Ezra 8:19]

MERED (Heb. 'revolt') date unknown. Son of Ezrah of the tribe of Judah, he was a descendant of Caleb, son of Jephunneh. [1 Chr. 4:17]

MEREMOTH (Heb. 'heights') **1.** 5 century BC. Son of Uriah, he was a priest who returned after the exile, and counted and weighed the gold and precious vessels in the Temple which had been brought back from Babylon; he helped repair the walls of Jerusalem. [Ezra 8:33; Neh. 3:4, 21]

Ostraca from the excavations at Arad, 9th-6th centuries BC, with the name 'Meremoth' in Hebrew.

2. 6 century BC. A priest who returned with Zerubbabel to Judah from exile in Babylon, he was related to Helkai, the head of a priestly family when Joiakim was high priest in the time of Nehemiah. Also called Meraioth. [Neh. 12:3, 15]

3. 5 century BC. A descendant of Bani who divorced his non-Jewish wife in the time of Ezra. [Ezra 10:36]

4. 5 century BC. A priest who signed the covenant to observe the Commandments of God in the time of Nehemiah. [Neh. 10:5]

MERES (Pers. 'lofty') *c.* 5 century BC. One of the seven princes of Persia and Media who sat at the table of King Ahasuerus. [Esther 1:14]

MERIBBAAL *see* MEPHIBOSHETH 1.

MERODACH *see* BAAL

MERODACH-BALADAN (Ass. 'Merodach [a god] has given a son') *c.* 8 century BC. King of Babylonia, he sent a present to the ailing king Hezekiah of Judah. The king showed the messenger the treasures of the Temple and palace, at which Isaiah the prophet grimly predicted that all these treasures would be despoiled by the Babylonians.

Merodach-baladan was defeated by Sargon the Great of Assyria, made a brief comeback, and was driven out by Sennacherib. [2 Kgs. 20:12; Isa. 39:1]

MESHA (Heb. 'freed') **1.** date unknown. Son of Shaharaim and his wife Hodesh, he was a leader of the tribe of Benjamin. [1 Chr. 8:9]

2. *c.* 9 century BC. King of Moab, the kingdom on the plateau east of the Dead Sea. In the reign of King Omri of Judah and most of the reign of his son Ahab, Moab was a vassal state of Judah. The tribute she paid was in sheep and wool, since Moab was grazing country.

Mesha carried out a successful revolt, as he relates on the black basalt stele (inscribed monument) that was discovered in southern Jordan a century ago.

Later, King Jehoram of Israel and King Jehoshaphat of Judah invaded Moab from the south and devastated the country. Besieged in his last stronghold, Mesha in desperation sacrificed his son to the Moabite god Chemosh. This drastic act seemed to turn the tide, for the Israelite forces retreated. [2 Kgs. 1:1; 3:4, 5, 27]

MESHACH (Pers. 'who is unto Aku, the moon-god') *c.* 6 century BC. The Babylonian name given to Mishael, one of the four young princes of Judah taken off to Babylon by the orders of King Nebuchadnezzar. When the four refused to worship or serve the Babylonian gods, Nebuchadnezzar, in great rage, ordered them cast into the fiery furnace. They were delivered by an angel and walked out unhurt. [Dan. 1-3]

MESHECH (Heb. 'drawn out') **1.** date unknown. Son of Japheth and a grandson of Noah, his descendants were a tribe of warriors. [Gen. 10:2; 1 Chr. 1:5; Ezek. 27:13; 32:26; 38:2; 39:1]

2. date unknown. Son of Shem, he was a grandson of Noah. [1 Chr. 1:17]

far left 8th-century BC boundary stone, showing Merodach-baladan and an official.

left Lapis lazuli carving of the Babylonian god Merodach (or Marduk), an alternative name for Baal, 9th century BC.

MESHELEMIAH *see* SHALLUM **4.**

MESHEZABEL (Heb. 'God saves') **1.** 5 century BC. Father of Berechiah and the grandfather of Meshullam, he helped repair the walls of Jerusalem in the time of Nehemiah. [Neh. 3:4]

2. 5 century BC. A leader of Judah who signed the solemn covenant in the time of Nehemiah. [Neh. 10:21]

3. 5 century BC. A leader of Judah in the time of Nehemiah, he was the father of Pethahiah, adviser to the Persian king. [Neh. 11:24]

MESHILLEMITH (Heb. 'repaid') date unknown. Son of Immer, and the father of Meshullam and Ahazai, one of his descendants was Maasai who settled in Jerusalem after the return from exile in Babylon. Also called Meshillemoth. [1 Chr. 9:12; Neh. 11:13]

MESHILLEMOTH (Heb. 'repaid') **1.** *c.* 8 century BC. Father of Berechiah of the tribe of Ephraim, a leader of the kingdom of Israel, who called upon his men to release the prisoners of Judah whom they had captured in the war between King Pekah of Israel and Ahaz, king of Judah. [2 Chr. 28:12]

2. *see* MESHILLEMITH

MESHOBAB 8 century BC. A leader of the tribe of Simeon in the days of Hezekiah, king of Judah, who drove out the inhabitants of the rich valley of Gedor and settled there. [1 Chr. 4:34]

MESHULLAM (Heb. 'rewarded') **1.** date unknown. A chief of the tribe of Gad in the lands of Gilead and Basham east of the river Jordan. [1 Chr. 5:13]

2. date unknown. Son of Elpaal, a leader of the tribe of Benjamin living in Jerusalem. [1 Chr. 8:17]

3. *c.* 7 century BC. Grandfather of Shaphan, a scribe who was sent by Josiah, king of Judah, to tell the high priest Hilkiah to hand over the silver collected for the repair of the Temple to the workmen. [2 Kgs. 22:3]

4. *c.* 7 century BC. A Levite descended from Kohath, he was a supervisor of the work of repairing the Temple in the reign of Josiah, king of Judah. [2 Chr. 34:12]

5. date unknown. Son of Zadok, the priest, he was the father of Hilkiah and the grandfather of Azariah, head of a priestly family who returned from exile in Babylon and settled in Jerusalem. [1 Chr. 9:11; Neh. 11:11]

6. date unknown. Son of Meshillemith the priest, he was an ancestor of Maasai, a priest who settled in Jerusalem after the return from Babylon. [1 Chr. 9:12]

7. 6 century BC. Son of Zerubbabel who led the return to Judah from exile in Babylon. [1 Chr. 3:19]

8. 5 century BC. Father of Sallu, he was a Benjaminite who settled in Jerusalem after the return from Babylon. [1 Chr. 9:7; Neh. 11:7]

9. 5 century BC. Son of Shephathiah, he was a prominent Benjaminite who settled in Jerusalem after the return from Babylon. [1 Chr. 9:8]

10. 5 century BC. A leader of Judah in exile in Babylon, he was sent by Ezra to Iddo, ruler of Casiphia, to bring priests and Levites to Jerusalem to serve in the Temple. [Ezra 8:16]

11. 5 century BC. A leader of Judah who was present when Ezra called upon the people of Judah to divorce their non-Jewish wives. [Ezra 10:15]

12. 5 century BC. A descendant of Bani who divorced his non-Jewish wife in the time of Ezra. [Ezra 10:29]

13. 5 century BC. Son of Berechiah and the grandson of Meshezabel, he was a leader of Judah who helped repair the walls of Jerusalem in the time of Nehemiah. His daughter married Jehohanan, the son of Tobiah, and although Tobiah was against the work of rebuilding Jerusalem, he gained many supporters among the leaders of Judah because of his relationship with Meshullam. [Neh. 3:4, 30; 6:18]

14. 5 century BC. Son of Besodeiah, he helped repair the Old Gate as part of the work of rebuilding the walls of Jerusalem in the time of Nehemiah. [Neh. 3:6]

15. *c.* 5 century BC. A leader who stood at the left hand of Ezra when he read out the Law of Moses to the people of Judah in the market-place. [Neh. 8:4]

16. 5 century BC. A priest of Judah who signed the solemn covenant in the time of Nehemiah. [Neh. 10:7]

17. 5 century BC. A leader of Judah who signed the solemn covenant in the time of Nehemiah. [Neh. 10:20]

18. 5 century BC. Head of a priestly family when Joiakim was high priest in the time of Nehemiah. [Neh. 12:13]

19. 5 century BC. Head of a priestly family descended from Ginnethon when Joiakim was high priest in the time of Nehemiah. [Neh. 12:16]

20. 5 century BC. A Levite who was a porter at the gates of the Temple when Joiakim was high priest in Jerusalem in the time of Nehemiah. [Neh. 12:25]

21. 5 century BC. A leader of Judah who took part in the dedication of the rebuilt walls of Jerusalem in the time of Nehemiah. [Neh. 12:33]

MESHULLEMETH (Heb. 'rewarded') *c.* 7 century BC. Wife of Manasseh, king of Judah, and the mother of Amon who inherited the throne. She was the daughter of Haruz of Jotbah. [2 Kgs. 21:19]

METHUSELAH (Heb. 'man of the javelin') date unknown. Methuselah was the son of Mehujael and, according to the Old Testament, lived to the ripe old age of nine hundred and sixty-nine years. He is thus the oldest person in the Bible, and the proverbial symbol of longevity. At the age of one hundred and eighty-seven, he had his first son, Lamech, who was the father of Noah. Methuselah had many other children. Also called Methushael. [Gen. 4:18; 5:21-7; 1 Chr. 1:3]

METHUSHAEL *see* METHUSELAH

MEUNIM (Heb. 'dwelling') *c.* 10 century BC. A Temple servant whose descendants returned with Zerubbabel from exile in Babylon. [Ezra 2:50; Neh. 7:52]

MEZAHAB (Heb. 'gilded') date unknown. Grandfather of Mehetabel, the wife of King Hadar of Edom. [Gen. 36:39; 1 Chr. 1:50]

MIBHAR (Heb. 'chosen') *c.* 10 century BC. Son of Hagri, he was a warrior in the armies of King David distinguished for his bravery. [1 Chr. 11:38]

MIBSAM (Heb. 'perfumed') **1.** *c.* 17 century BC. Son of Abraham's son Ishmael, he was a leader of a desert tribe. [Gen. 25:13; 1 Chr. 1:29]

2. *c.* 16 century BC. Son of Simeon, he was a grandson of Jacob. [1 Chr. 4:25]

MIBZAR (Heb. 'fort') date unknown. An Edomite leader, he was descended from Esau. [Gen. 36:42; 1 Chr. 1:53]

MICA (Heb. 'who is like God?') **1.** *c.* 10 century BC. Son of Mephibosheth, he was a grandson of Jonathan. Also called Micah. [2 Sam. 9:12; 1 Chr. 8:34]

2. *c.* 10 century BC. Son of Zabdi and grandson of Asaph, he was a Levite who lived in Judah. [1 Chr. 9:15; Neh. 11:17, 22]

3. 5 century BC. A Levite who signed the solemn covenant in the time of Nehemiah. [Neh. 10:11]

MICAH (Heb. 'who is like God?') **1.** *c.* 12 century BC. He was a man who lived in the hill country of Ephraim and stole eleven hundred pieces of silver from his mother. When she cursed the thief, Micah gave her back the money. She blessed him and consecrated the money to the Lord, but gave two hundred pieces to a silversmith with which to make a graven image. Micah set up an altar to the idol and installed one of his sons as the priest, until a wandering Levite from Bethlehem arrived at the house and Micah took him in as priest in place of his son.

At that time the tribe of Dan was dissatisfied with their inheritance and sent out five men to search for a better place. They came to Micah's house and recognizing the Levite, asked him whether their expedition would be successful and he assured them that it would.

Later when six hundred men of Dan set out to conquer Laish in the extreme north of the country, they stopped at Micah's house and took away the idol and the Levite who served it. Micah and some of his neighbours chased after them but the Danites threatened them and they returned home. The men of Dan took Laish, changed the name of the city to Dan and set up Micah's graven image for themselves. [Judg. 17, 18]

2. date unknown. Son of Shimei, he was a leader of the tribe of Reuben who lived east of the river Jordan in the land of Gilead. [1 Chr. 5:5]

3. *c.* 10 century BC. A descendant of Uzziel, he was a leader of the tribe of Levi who ministered in the

Micah fashioned a silver idol. Silver figurine of a female deity found at Nahariya, 18th-16th centuries BC.

Tabernacle in the reign of King David. [1 Chr. 23:20; 24:24, 25]

4. *see* MICA **1.**

5. *c.* 8 century BC. Hebrew prophet of the kingdom of Judah. Micah prophesied in Judah in the first half of the 8th century BC during the reigns of Jotham, Ahaz and Hezekiah. He was therefore a contemporary of Isaiah in Jerusalem, and came a little after the prophets Amos and Hosea in the northern kingdom of Israel.

Micah came from the small country town of Moresheth in the fertile foothills of the Shefelah, which faced across the coastal plain towards the Mediterranean. At its back rose the Judean hills, in which Jerusalem lay a day's journey away. The place is marked on the Madeba mosaic floormap of the 6th century AD with the words 'Moresheth, from which came Micah, the prophet'.

Like Amos, another village son, Micah uses rural imagery, such as the sheaves brought to the threshing floor and the jackals howling at night. He detests the capital cities of Samaria and Jerusalem, which symbolize for him the luxury and graft that have corrupted the body of the nation and aroused God's anger.

He says of Jerusalem, 'your rich men are full of violence; your inhabitants speak lies, and their tongue is deceitful in their mouth.' (Mic. 6:12) In stinging terms he foretells the city's destruction: 'Therefore because of you Zion shall be ploughed as a field; Jerusalem shall become a heap of ruins.' (Mic. 3:12) As for the northern hill capital of Samaria, with its idols and sacred prostitutes, 'I will pour down her stones into the valley, and uncover her foundations. All her images shall be beaten to pieces.' (Mic. 1:6, 7)

Micah is a prophet of social protest, the spokesman of poor and simple men exploited by the upper classes. He denounced the greedy and hypocritical Establishment – 'Its heads give judgment for a bribe, its priests teach for hire, its prophets divine for money: yet they lean upon the Lord and say, "Is not the Lord in the midst of us? No evil shall come upon us."' (Mic. 3:11) He rails against the swindling merchants with their false scales and weights, and against the landowners who 'covet fields, and seize them' (Mic. 2:2).

Like other prophets, Micah believes that true faith comes from the heart, and not from formal sacrifices. 'Will the Lord be pleased with thousands of rams, with ten thousands of rivers of oil?... what does the Lord require of you but to do justice, and to love kindness, and to walk humbly with your God?' (Mic. 6:7, 8)

Micah looks forward from the sinful and troubled present to the future Messianic kingdom, where the remnant of Israel will be gathered together and live in peace, where every man will sit under his vine and his fig tree: 'For out of Zion shall go forth the law,

and the word of the Lord from Jerusalem.' (Mic. 4:2) (This phrase also appears in Isaiah 2:3.) [Isa. 2:3; Jer. 26:18; Book of Micah]

6. *c.* 7 century BC. Father of Abdon who was a leader of Judah sent by King Josiah to the prophetess Huldah to find out what would happen to the people of Judah. Also called Micaiah. [2 Kgs. 22:12; 2 Chr. 34:20]

MICAIAH (Heb. 'who is like God?') **1.** *see* MAACAH **10.**

2. *c.* 9 century BC. A Hebrew prophet in the time of Ahab. Micaiah was one of the many professional prophets or holy men who frequented Samaria, the capital of the kingdom of Israel.

Jehoshaphat king of Judah joined forces with Ahab king of Israel to retake the Israelite town of Ramothgilead in the land of Gilead, east of the Jordan river. The two monarchs sat on thrones at the entrance to Samaria while a large group of prophets appeared before them and assured them of success in the coming battle. The pious Jehoshaphat was not satisfied and asked if there were not another prophet they might ask. Grudgingly Ahab admitted that 'There is yet one man by whom we may enquire of the Lord, Micaiah, the son of Imlah; but I hate him, for he never prophesies good concerning me, but evil.' (1 Kgs. 22:8)

Micaiah was sent for and at first joined sarcastically in the chorus of encouragement. But when pressed by Ahab he courageously foretold defeat and the death of the king. The leader of the other prophets hit Micaiah in the face and the angry Ahab ordered the bluntspoken pessimist to be flung into jail and kept on bread and water until his own safe return from the battle. Micaiah's prophecy of disaster came true, but it is not recorded what became of the prophet. [1 Kgs. 22]

3. *c.* 9 century BC. A leader of Judah whom King Jehoshaphat sent out to teach the Law of God to the people. [2 Chr. 17:7]

4. *c.* 7 century BC. Son of Gemariah, a leader of Judah in the reign of King Jehoiakim, he heard the prophecies of Jeremiah from his scribe Baruch and had them reread to all the leaders. [Jer. 36:11, 13]

5. date unknown. Son of Zaccur the priest, one of his descendants, Zechariah, son of Jonathan, blew a trumpet at the dedication of the walls of Jerusalem in the time of Nehemiah. [Neh. 12:35]

6. *see* MICAH **6.**

7. 5 century BC. A Levite priest who took part in the ceremony for the dedication of the rebuilt walls of Jerusalem in the time of Nehemiah. [Neh. 12:41]

MICHAEL (Heb. 'who is like God?') **1.** *c.* 13 century BC. A leader of the tribe of Asher, his son Sethur was one of the twelve men sent by Moses to spy out the Promised Land. [Num. 13:13]

2. date unknown. A leader of the tribe of Gad who settled in Bashan east of the river Jordan. [1 Chr. 5:13]

3. date unknown. Son of Jeshishai, he was a leader of the tribe of Gad who lived in Gilead east of the river Jordan. [1 Chr. 5:14]

4. date unknown. Son of Baaseiah of the tribe of Levi and the father of Shimea, he was an ancestor of Asaph, King David's musician. [1 Chr. 6:40]

5. date unknown. Son of Izrahiah, he and his brothers were leaders of the tribe of Issachar and mighty warriors. [1 Chr. 7:3]

6. date unknown. Son of Beriah, he was a leader of the tribe of Benjamin living in Jerusalem. [1 Chr. 8:16]

7. *c.* 11 century BC. One of the six captains of thousands of the tribe of Manasseh who joined the army of David at Ziklag, he became a commander of his army. [1 Chr. 12:20]

8. *c.* 10 century BC. Father of Omri who was made ruler of the tribe of Issachar in the reign of King David. [1 Chr. 27:18]

9. *c.* 9 century BC. Son of Jehoshaphat, king of Judah, he was killed by his brother Jehoram who inherited the kingdom. [2 Chr. 21:2]

10. 5 century BC. A descendant of Sephatiah, his son Zebadiah returned to Judah from Babylon. [Ezra 8:8]

11. By tradition, one of the four great archangels, he was the special protector of the Hebrews. Though angels appear many times in the Old Testament as messengers of the Lord, it is only after the exilic period and the Babylonian influence that they are referred to by name. In Daniel's last vision the angel about whom he is told is referred to as 'Michael, the great prince who has charge of your people.' (Dan. 12:1) [Dan. 10:13, 21, 12:1]

MICHAL (Heb. 'who is like God?') *c.* 11 century BC. Younger daughter of King Saul, Michal fell in love with David, and Saul had to agree to the match when David performed the set task of killing two hundred Philistines.

When Saul tried to kill David, he fled to his house, and Michal helped him escape his pursuers by lowering him out of a window at night. Michal then 'took an image and laid it on the bed and put a pillow of goat's hair at its head, and covered it with clothes.' (1 Sam. 19:13) Saul was furious at the escape.

During the years that David spent as an outlaw, Saul gave Michal in marriage to Phalti, the son of Laish. After Saul's death, his general Abner first supported his weak son Ishbosheth, then made overtures to David, who demanded the return of Michal. Ishbosheth was forced to agree. Abner escorted her to David at Hebron, and ordered her weeping husband to turn back.

The resumed marriage does not seem to have been a success. Michal remained out of sympathy with David and his ambitions. On the day the Ark of God was brought to Jerusalem, Michal watched the excite-

ment through a window of the palace and saw the king 'leaping and dancing before the Lord; and she despised him in her heart.' (2 Sam. 6:16) When he came in she mocked him for the exhibition he had made of himself. David, thoroughly angry, reminded her that he had been chosen by the Lord instead of her father to be king over Israel. 'And Michal the daughter of Saul had no child to the day of her death.' (2 Sam. 6:23) [1 Sam. 14:49; 18:20-28; 19:11-17; 25:44; 2 Sam. 3:13, 14; 6:16-23; 1 Chr. 15:29]

MICHRI (Heb. 'precious') *c.* 6 century BC. Father of Uzzi of the tribe of Benjamin whose grandson Elah settled in Jerusalem following the return from exile in Babylon. [1 Chr. 9:8]

MIDIAN (Heb. 'strife') *c.* 17 century BC. A son of Abraham by his wife Keturah and the legendary father of the Midianites who warred against the children of Israel. [Gen. 25:2-3; 1 Chr. 1:32]

MIJAMIN (Heb. 'with good luck') **1.** *c.* 10 century BC. A priest in charge of the sixth turn of service in the Tabernacle in the reign of King David. [1 Chr. 24:9]

2. 6 century BC. A priest who returned with Zerubbabel to Judah from exile in Babylon. [Neh. 12:5]

3. 5 century BC. A descendant of Parosh who divorced his non-Jewish wife in the time of Ezra. [Ezra 10:25]

4. 5 century BC. One of the priests who signed the solemn covenant in the time of Nehemiah. [Neh. 10:7]

MIKLOTH (Heb. 'staves') date unknown. Son of Jeiel and a leader of the tribe of Benjamin. [1 Chr. 8:32; 9:37, 38]

MIKNEIAH (Heb. 'possessed by God') *c.* 10 century BC. A Levite who played musical instruments when the Ark of God was brought up to Jerusalem at the orders of King David. [1 Chr. 15:18, 21]

MILALAI (Heb. 'God said') 5 century BC. A priest who followed after Ezra playing a musical instrument during the dedication service for the rebuilt walls of Jerusalem. [Neh. 12:36]

MILCAH (Heb. 'queen') **1.** *c.* 18 century BC. The wife of Abraham's brother Nahor, her son Bethuel was the father of Rebekah who married Abraham's son Isaac. [Gen. 11:29; 22:20; 24:15, 24, 47]

2. *c.* 13 century BC. One of the five daughters of Zelophehad who claimed a share of their father's estate since their father had no sons. [Num. 26:33; 27:1; 36:11; Josh. 17:3]

MILCOM *see* MOLECH

MINIAMIN (Heb. 'right hand') **1.** *c.* 8 century BC. A Levite in the days of Hezekiah, king of Judah, he distributed the tithes and offerings to the priests in the cities of Judah. [2 Chr. 31:15]

2. 5 century BC. One of the heads of the priestly families when Joiakim was high priest in the time of Nehemiah, who blew a trumpet at the dedication of the rebuilt walls of Jerusalem. [Neh. 12:17, 41]

MIRIAM (Heb. 'bitterness') **1.** *c.* 13 century BC. The daughter of Amram and Jochebed, she was the sister of Moses and Aaron and probably the eldest of the three. When Pharaoh's daughter found the infant Moses in the reeds, Miriam, who was keeping watch over the baby, suggested to the princess that she could find a wetnurse for the child and brought her mother to the palace.

After the crossing of the water during the Exodus and the death of the Egyptians, Miriam led the women in

Detail from the 14th-century Spanish *Golden Haggadah*. Miriam and the Israelite women dance with the timbrel to celebrate the drowning of Pharaoh's army.

the ceremonial dance and song of gratitude. But when Moses married an Ethiopian woman, she and Aaron criticized him in such a fashion that it disclosed their jealousy of his leadership. Miriam was struck by leprosy and the Exodus was delayed until Moses had interceded for her with the Lord and she was cured and allowed to return to the encampment. She died and was buried in Kadesh-barnea in the wilderness. [Exod. 15:20-21; Num. 12:1-15; 20:1; 26:59; Deut. 24:9; 1 Chr. 6:3; Mic. 6:4]

2. date unknown. The daughter of Mered of the tribe of Judah. [1 Chr. 4:17]

MIRMAH (Heb. 'fraud') date unknown. A son of Shaharaim, who was a leader of the tribe of Benjamin. [1 Chr. 8:10]

MISHAEL (Heb. 'who is God's') **1.** *c.* 13 century BC. Son of Uzziel of the tribe of Levi, and an uncle of Moses and Aaron, he and his brother Elazphan were ordered by Moses to remove the bodies of Aaron's sons Nadab and Abihu from the Tabernacle after they had been struck dead for offering forbidden incense to the Lord. [Exod. 6:22; Lev. 10:4]

2. *see* MESHACH

3. 5 century BC. A leader of Judah who stood at the left hand of Ezra as he read out the Law of God to the people. [Neh. 8:4]

MISHAM (Heb. 'the Lord is [my] uncle') date unknown. One of the sons of Elpaal, a leader of the tribe of Benjamin. [1 Chr. 8:12]

MISHMA (Heb. 'hearing') **1.** *c.* 17 century BC. Son of Abraham's son Ishmael, he was leader of a desert tribe. [Gen. 25:13-14; 1 Chr. 1:30]

2. date unknown. Son of Mibsam and father of Hammuel of the tribe of Simeon. [1 Chr. 4:25, 26]

MISHMANNAH (Heb. 'fatness') *c.* 11 century BC. One of the warriors of the tribe of Gad who deserted from King Saul's army and joined David at Ziklag. [1 Chr. 12:10]

MISPAR (Heb. 'number') *c.* 6 century BC. A leader of Judah who returned to Jerusalem with Zerubbabel from exile in Babylon. Also called Mispereth. [Ezra 2:2; Neh. 7:7]

MISPERETH *see* MISPAR

MITHREDATH (Pers. 'given by Mithra') **1.** *c.* 6 century BC. Treasurer of Cyrus, king of Persia, he was ordered to hand over to Sheshbazzar all the gold, silver and precious vessels which had been plundered from the Temple in Jerusalem. [Ezra 1:8]

2. *c.* 5 century BC. A Persian official in Jerusalem in the days of Ezra, he was one of several conspirators to write a letter to Artaxerxes, king of Persia, falsely accusing the Jews of rebuilding the walls of Jerusalem in order to organize a rebellion against the king and stop paying dues to him. [Ezra 4:7]

MIZZAH *c.* 16 century BC. Son of Reuel and a grandson of Esau, he was an Edomite chieftain. [Gen. 36:13, 17; 1 Chr. 1:37]

MOAB (Heb. 'progeny of a father') *c.* 18 century BC. Son of Lot by his incestuous relationship with his daughter after the destruction of the two cities Sodom and Gomorrah, he is regarded by Hebrew tradition as the ancestor of the Moabites who lived east of the Jordan river. [Gen. 19:37]

MOADIAH *see* MAADIAH

MOLECH The national god of the Ammonites.

This god was worshipped by offering up human sacrifices, usually a child from the family. Worship of Molech was expressly forbidden to the Children of Israel in the Book of Leviticus. Nevertheless, some of them worshipped Molech at various times and King Solomon permitted altars to be built to him. Later, Josiah, king of Judah, as part of the purification of Judah, deliberately defiled the holy places for the worship of Molech. Also known as Moloch, Milcom and Malcam, which suggests identification with the tribal god of the Ammonites. [Lev. 18:21; 1 Kgs. 11:5, 7; 2 Kgs. 23:10, 13; Isa. 30:33; Jer. 32:35; Zeph. 1:5]

MOLID (Heb. 'begetter') date unknown. The younger son of Abishur of the tribe of Judah and his wife Abihail. [1 Chr. 2:29]

MOLOCH *see* MOLECH

MORDECAI (Heb. 'consecrated to Merodach') *c.* 5 century BC. Cousin and guardian of Esther.

Mordecai was a devout Jew and an exile from Jerusalem, who lived in Shushan (Susa) the capital of the Persian Empire. He had adopted as his own daughter a young orphaned cousin whose Persian name was Esther. She was chosen by King Ahasuerus to be his queen, and Mordecai advised her not to disclose the fact that she was Jewish.

Mordecai had an official position at the court. One day he heard two of the king's eunuchs plotting to assassinate their master. He asked Esther to warn the king, who had the conspirators seized and executed. This service by Mordecai was recorded in the court annals.

Mordecai fell foul of Haman, the chief minister, by refusing to bow down to him. Haman determined to kill not only Mordecai but all the Jews. He persuaded the king to let him destroy them on the ground that they did not keep the king's laws, and a day of execution was fixed. Mordecai told Esther to intercede with the king. He received her kindly and agreed to dine with her together with Haman.

Haman's wife and friends advised him to prepare a gallows and to persuade the king the following day to let Mordecai be hanged.

That night the king was sleepless and had the court annals read to him. He came across the entry about Mordecai having foiled the plot against the king and discovered that the act had gone unrewarded. He summoned Haman and without disclosing the name, asked him how he would set about paying honour to someone. Thinking it was himself, Haman proposed that the person be conducted through the city square dressed in royal robes with a crown on his head, and seated on the king's horse. To his utter dismay, Haman was ordered to carry out this ceremony for Mordecai.

That night at dinner, Queen Esther denounced Haman and accused him of having organized the mass

Silver statue of a Persian warrior of Mordecai's time, 5th century BC.

murder of her people. 'So they hanged Haman on the gallows which he had prepared for Mordecai.' (Esther 7:10) Mordecai was then appointed chief minister in Haman's place. Since by Persian law Haman's decree could not be revoked, Mordecai was authorized to send out another decree giving the Jews the right to carry arms in self-defence. On the day Haman had appointed for their destruction, they turned on their enemies and slew them. Mordecai and Esther sent letters to all the Jews, saying that their deliverance should be commemorated every year with the Feast of Purim.

The king advanced Mordecai until 'Mordecai the Jew was next in rank to King Ahasuerus, and he was great among the Jews...and spoke peace to all his people.' (Esther 10:3)

The story appears non-historical, since no Persian ruler is known to have had a queen called Esther, a chief minister called Haman, or a Jewish counsellor called Mordecai. [Book of Esther]

above Persian soldiers and captives:
Achaemenid seal impression,
5th century BC.

below *The Triumph of Mordecai* by
Filippino Lippi (1457-1504).

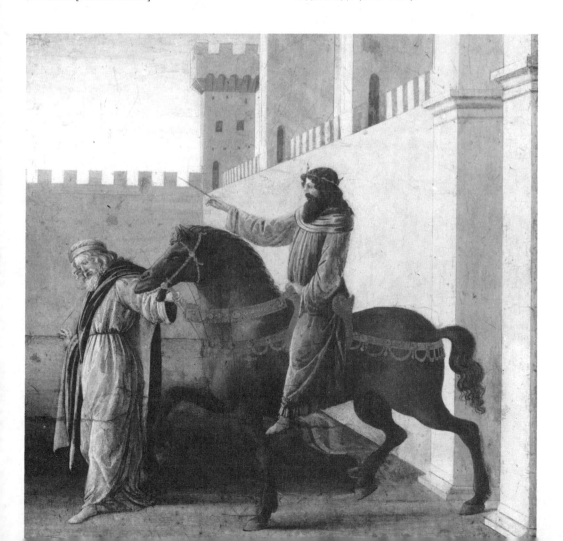

MOSES (Heb. 'to draw out') *c.* 13 century BC. The great Hebrew leader and lawgiver. Moses is the most majestic figure in the old Testament. His role was so central that the Pentateuch was called the Five Books of Moses, and the code of religious laws, the Law of Moses. To Jews he has remained for all time *Moshe Rabbenu –* 'Moses our Teacher'. No one else in the Old Testament

had the same close relationship with God. As it was written, 'the Lord used to speak to Moses face to face, as a man speaks to his friend' (Exod. 33:11).

The story opens in Egypt. Jacob and his family had settled as a pastoral clan in the land of Goshen in the north-east corner of the Nile delta. Here their descendants lived and prospered for four centuries, till 'there arose a new king over Egypt, who did not know Joseph' (Exod. 1:8). (This was possibly the Pharaoh Rameses II, in the 13th century BC – the greatest builder in Egyptian history.) He decided that the Children of Israel had become too numerous and strong. He turned them into slave labourers, and put them to work under Egyptian taskmasters on the construction of two treasure cities, Pithom and Rameses, 'And made their lives bitter with hard service, in mortar and brick, and in all kinds of work in the field.' (Exod. 1:14) When this did not reduce their numbers, Pharaoh ordered the Hebrew midwives to kill every male infant at birth. The midwives evaded this decree on the pretext that 'the Hebrew women are not like the Egyptian women; for they are vigorous and are delivered before the midwife comes to them.' (Exod. 1:19) The frustrated ruler then charged his people to throw the male babies into the river, and drown them.

Amram and Jochebed, the parents of Moses, were of the priestly house of Levi. When the child was born, his mother kept him hidden for three months. She then enclosed him in a basket woven of rushes and sealed with pitch, and concealed him among the reeds at the river's edge.

Pharaoh's daughter came to bathe at this spot and when she saw the basket she sent a maid to fetch it. On opening it, the baby started crying and the princess felt pity for it, realizing that it was one of the Hebrew children her father had ordered killed. Moses's elder sister Miriam had been posted a little distance away to watch. She approached the princess and offered to find a Hebrew nurse to suckle the child. This was agreed, and she ran off to fetch Moses's mother. When he was older, Pharaoh's daughter adopted him and gave him the name of Moses, 'Because I drew him out of the water.' (Exod. 2:10) (The Hebrew form, *Moshe*, means 'to draw out'.)

The boy grew up at the royal court but remained aware of his Hebrew origin. One day Moses, now a

left Basalt stele of Rameses II (1301-1234 BC) found at Beth-shean, showing Rameses (right) and the god Amon-Re (left).

right Moses receiving the Tablets of the Law: detail from the floor of Siena Cathedral by Beccafumi. In the foreground the Israelites melt their jewelry to fashion the golden calf.

above Egyptian wall-painting of slave labour being used for building, from the tomb of Rekh-mi-Re, Thebes, 15th century BC.
below Egyptian builders' tools from the 15th century BC, found in the Temple of Deir el-Bahri.

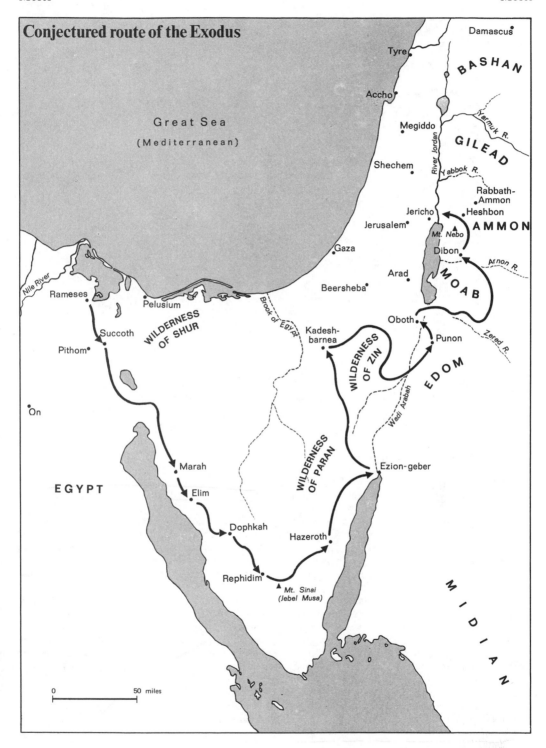

Conjectured route of the Exodus

Damascus

BASHAN

Tyre

Accho

Great Sea
(Mediterranean)

Megiddo

GILEAD

Yarmuk R.

River Jordan

Shechem

Yabbok R.

Rabbath-
Ammon

Jericho   Heshbon

Jerusalem   AMMON

Gaza

Mt. Nebo

Dibon

Arnon R.

MOAB

Beersheba

Arad

Oboth

Nile River

Rameses

Pelusium

Brook of Egypt

Kadesh-
barnea

WILDERNESS
OF ZIN

Punon

Zered R.

Pithom

Succoth

WILDERNESS
OF SHUR

Wadi Arabah

EDOM

On

WILDERNESS
OF PARAN

Marah

Ezion-geber

EGYPT

Elim

Dophkah

Hazeroth

Rephidim

Mt. Sinai
(Jebel Musa)

MIDIAN

0   50 miles

Moses found in the Nile by Pharaoh's daughter: 3rd-century wall-painting from Dura-Europos, Syria.

grown man, went off alone to find out what was happening to his kinsmen. He saw an Egyptian overseer flogging an Israelite slave. Thinking himself unobserved, Moses slew the Egyptian and buried his body in the sand. Next day he intervened in a fight between two Israelites and was alarmed when one of them said pointedly: 'Who made you a prince and a judge over us? Do you mean to kill me, as you killed the Egyptian?' (Exod. 2:14) Report of his deed reached Pharaoh, and he had to flee for his life eastward into the Sinai desert.

Pausing to rest at a well, Moses assisted some young women to water their flocks. When they told their father Jethro (or Reuel) about the helpful stranger at the well, he invited Moses to eat with them. Jethro was the priest of a tribe of desert nomads from Midian. Moses remained with him and married one of his seven daughters, Zipporah. She bore him a son whom he called Gershom, since Moses was a stranger (Heb. *ger*) in a strange land.

Moving deep into the desert in search of pasture for

his father-in-law's flocks, Moses came to the mountain of Horeb (or Sinai). He turned aside to examine a strange sight: a bush that was burning without being consumed. God's voice came out of the bush commanding him to halt and remove his shoes, as he was on holy ground. Moses was told that he had been chosen to lead his brethren out of their oppression and bring them to the Promised Land. Moses shrank from this task, saying: 'Who am I that I should go to Pharaoh, and bring the sons of Israel out of Egypt?' (Exod. 3:11) To reassure him, the name of the Lord ('Jehovah') was revealed to Moses, and he was given certain magic signs to impress Pharaoh and the Israelites: turning his staff into a snake, making his hand white with leprosy and turning water into blood. Still reluctant, Moses pointed out that 'I am slow of speech and of tongue'. (Exod. 4:10) The Lord became impatient with him, and replied that his brother Aaron could be his spokesman.

Moses took leave of Jethro and set out with his wife,

his eldest son Gershom and his newly-born second son Eliezer. Along the way Moses became ill, and Zipporah circumcised the infant with a sharp flint in the belief that her husband would die if the rite were neglected.

Let My People Go

Aaron came to meet Moses and was told what the Lord required of them. They called together the Israelite elders, and in Moses's presence Aaron conveyed the Lord's message and performed the magic signs. The people were convinced that God was about to liberate them and sank down in worship.

Moses and Aaron then gained an audience with the reigning Pharaoh (probably the successor of the ruler from whom Moses had fled). In the name of the God of Israel they requested him to 'Let my people go' (Exod. 5:1). They did not dare suggest that the Israelites would leave the country for good. Instead, they claimed that sacrifices had to be made to their God at a place three days' journey into the wilderness.

Pharaoh bluntly rejected the request. He charged the Israelites with laziness, and issued instructions that they should no longer be supplied with straw for making bricks. They would have to seek their own straw, without lowering their daily output. The people reproached Moses for having added to their hardships, and Moses complained to the Lord that his mission had only done harm. 'For since I came to Pharaoh to speak in thy name, he has done evil to this people, and thou hast not delivered thy people at all.' (Exod. 5:23) The Lord declared that he had hardened Pharaoh's heart in order that 'the Egyptians shall know that I am the Lord, when I stretch forth my hand upon Egypt and bring out the people of Israel from among them' (Exod. 7:5).

The whole of Egypt now experienced a series of plagues, except for the land of Goshen where the Israelites lived. As each plague became intolerable Pharaoh agreed to let Moses's people go, but changed his mind when the affliction stopped.

First, Aaron and Moses smote the water of the Nile with the rod and it turned to blood before the eyes of Pharaoh and his court. 'And the fish in the Nile died; and the Nile became foul, so that the Egyptians could not drink water from the Nile; and there was blood throughout all the land of Egypt.' (Exod. 7:21)

When Pharaoh refused to give way, frogs came swarming out of the river and spread everywhere, as Moses had warned Pharaoh they would, crawling 'into your house, and into your bedchamber and on your bed, and into the house of your servants and of your people, and into your ovens and your kneading bowls.' (Exod. 8:3)

The third plague was one of lice which sprang from the dust and infected man and beast alike. There followed swarms of flies; cattle disease; an epidemic of

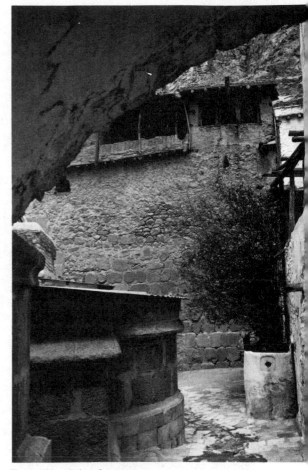

The traditional site of the burning bush in St Catherine's Monastery, Sinai.

boils; a fierce hailstorm that smashed the trees and flattened the crops; vast clouds of locusts that devoured all growing things; and three days of pitch darkness.

The tenth calamity was the most dreadful of all – the slaying of the first-born. The Lord commanded Moses and Aaron that on the fourteenth day of the month, at dusk, each Israelite family should slaughter a lamb or kid and roast its flesh for a sacrificial meal. 'In this manner you shall eat it: your loins girded, your sandals on your feet, and your staff in your hand; and you shall eat it in haste. It is the Lord's passover.' (Exod. 12:11) Blood from the slaughtered animal was to be daubed on the lintel and doorposts so that the Lord would recognize and pass over Hebrew homes, while smiting the Egyptians.

At midnight the first-born died in every Egyptian

above Moses sends the plague of locusts,
from the *Nuremberg Bible*, 1483.

below Egyptian war chariot from the Temple of
Rameses III at Medinet Habu, 12th century B.C.

Egyptian soldiers man a fortress on the coast;
on the left one of them is drowned in the sea.
12th-century BC relief from the Temple of Rameses III
at Medinet Habu.

top left The inhospitable landscape of the Sinai.

top right The resin exuded from the tamarisk tree is believed by many to have been the manna eaten by the Israelites.

left The Springs of Moses in Sinai, traditionally the place where Moses struck the rock to bring forth water.

family, and even among the domestic animals. There was grief and panic throughout the country. That same night Pharaoh sent for Moses and Aaron and begged them to leave at once with their people, together with all their herds, flocks and possessions. The Egyptians handed over to them jewels and other valuables to speed their departure.

They set out at once from the city of Rameses that their forced labour had helped to build. In fulfilment of an ancient promise, the remains of Joseph were carried with them for burial in Canaan. 'Four hundred and thirty years', says the Bible (Exod. 12:41), had passed since their ancestor Jacob had first come to live in Egypt. Forty years of wandering lay ahead of them before they would reach their journey's end. Moses was at this time eighty years old and his brother Aaron eighty-three.

Each year Jews commemorate the Exodus in the seven-day spring festival of Passover, as enjoined in Exod. 10. They eat 'matzot' (flat cakes of unleavened bread) to recall the haste with which their ancestors departed. At the 'Seder' or ceremonial meal, bitter herbs are the symbol of the bondage in Egypt, and a roasted shank-bone represents the paschal lamb eaten that fateful night.

above 7th-century BC sherd with Hebrew writing referring to a commandment in Ex. 22 : 26.

left Moses receiving the Tablets of the Law and giving them to the Israelites. 9th-century Carolingian manuscript.

271

In the Wilderness

The great highway from Egypt to Canaan and beyond lay along the Mediterranean coast of the Sinai desert. From the edge of the Nile delta to Gaza it was but a week's march for armies or trading caravans. But that direct and well-travelled route was the most dangerous for the Israelites; and the coastal plain of Canaan to which it led was held by hostile inhabitants. A mob of runaway slaves would not have been able to fight its way through to the Promised Land. So Moses turned away from the coastal road 'lest the people repent when they see war, and return to Egypt' (Exod. 13:17). Instead, they headed south-east, towards the open desert.

The first halt was at Succoth, thirty-two miles from the city of Rameses, and the next at Etham on the edge of the desert. They were trying to move as fast as they could, fearing that Pharaoh would pursue them. 'And the Lord went before them by day in a pillar of a cloud to lead them along the way, and by night in a pillar of fire to give them light, that they might travel by day and night.' (Exod. 13:21)

Their haste was warranted. Pharaoh's courtiers said to him, 'What is this we have done, that we have let Israel go from serving us?' (Exod. 14:5) He set out in pursuit with a mobile force that included six hundred chariots. When the Israelites saw them coming, they trembled with fear and cried out to Moses, 'Is it because there are no graves in Egypt that you have taken us away to die in the wilderness?' (Exod. 14:11) They were at this time at the edge of the Reed Sea (incorrectly translated into English as the 'Red Sea'). Nothing but a miracle could save them. At the Lord's behest, Moses stretched out his hand over the sea and a strong east wind pushed the water aside, so that the Children of Israel were able to cross dry-shod to the other side. Dashing after them, Pharaoh's chariots were engulfed for 'the waters returned' (Exod. 14:28), and men and horses were drowned. (This may have happened in the area of the Bitter Lakes, through which the Suez Canal now passes.)

When the Israelites 'saw the Egyptians dead upon the sea shore' (Exod. 14:30), they sang a song of thankfulness to the Lord, while Moses's sister Miriam played on a timbrel (tambourine) and led the women in dance.

The elation of their new-found freedom was short-lived. They now entered the wilderness of Shur in the Sinai peninsula – a wasteland of sand and gravel, intersected with limestone ridges and dry watercourses, in the beds of which a little sparse scrub could be found for the flocks. The sun scorched them by day and the cold was sharp at night.

The chief problem was water. After trekking for three days, they reached a spring of brackish water at Marah (which means 'bitter'). Moses threw a certain bush into the water which made it drinkable. A day's march further on they were able to camp in the oasis of Elim, 'where there were twelve springs of water and seventy palm trees' (Exod. 15:27). Soon they ran out of food and railed at Moses and Aaron for taking them away from the 'flesh pots' (Exod. 16:3) of Egypt. The Lord would come to the rescue, Moses promised, and would provide 'in the evening flesh to eat and in the morning bread to the full' (Exod. 16:8). Flocks of migrating quails sank down to rest among the scrub at night and could easily be snared (as the desert Arabs do today).

In the early morning, when the dew vanished, the ground was strewn with manna, and 'it was like coriander seed, white, and the taste of it was like wafers made with honey.' (Exod. 16:31) Moses told them the manna was bread from the Lord. They were to gather and prepare just enough to satisfy their hunger, for what was not eaten would go bad in the heat of the day. On the sixth day a double portion could be gathered, and would remain fresh over the Sabbath. (It has been suggested that the manna may have been the resin-like substance that is exuded by the tamarisk trees in the desert, and drops on the ground when dry.)

The Israelites moved deeper into the southern part of the Sinai desert and came to Rephidim. Once more they were without water, and complained loudly. Moses was told by the Lord to gather the elders together and in their presence smite a rock. He did so and fresh water gushed out. Moses called the place 'Massah and Meribah' ('testing and contention') (Exod. 17:7).

They now faced a human threat, being attacked by a party of Amalekites, fierce desert raiders. The Israelites were not yet organized or trained to fight. Moses sent for Joshua the son of Nun, a young Ephraimite, and told him to select and lead a group of Israelite defenders. Moses himself climbed to the top of a hill together with Aaron and Hur (traditionally Moses's brother-in-law); and from here they witnessed the battle. While Moses held up his hands with the sacred rod, the Israelites gained, but they were pushed back when his arms dropped from weariness. His two companions seated him on a stone and, standing on either side of him, held his arms raised in the air until nightfall, when the battle was won and the Amalekites routed. Moses built an altar to the Lord.

In the third month after leaving Egypt, the Israelites reached the wild and rugged terrain of the wilderness of Sinai. In its centre a cluster of gaunt granite peaks of a dark-red colour rose to a height of eight thousand feet, with deep canyons around them. The Israelites camped on the open ground before a peak called Mount

Sinai or Mount Horeb. It was here that Moses had heard the voice of the Lord from the burning bush many years before. Jethro now came to see Moses, bringing Zipporah and their two sons, who had been on a visit to her family. Moses welcomed the old man warmly, and they sat for a long time in the tent talking about all the wondrous things that had happened since Moses had gone back to Egypt. The Midianite priest exclaimed: 'Now I know that the Lord is greater than all gods.' (Exod. 18:11) Jethro offered a sacrifice on the Hebrew altar and Moses invited the elders to a feast in his honour.

Jethro was present next day while Moses gave judgment in the disputes and claims brought before him. In the evening Jethro offered his son-in-law some sage advice. It was too burdensome for Moses to deal personally with every trivial matter, while scores of people stood around awaiting their turn. Why should Moses not delegate authority to able men, and put each in charge of a fixed number of persons? Moses agreed, and appointed 'rulers of thousands, of hundreds, of fifties, and of tens. And they judged the people at all times; hard cases they brought to Moses.' (Exod. 18:25, 26) Moses charged them to 'judge righteously between a man and his brother or the alien that is with him. You shall not be partial in judgment; you shall hear the small and the great alike; you shall not be afraid of the face of man, for the judgment is God's.' (Deut. 1:16-17)

Having instigated this system of admin.stration, Jethro took his leave and returned to his own land.

The Ten Commandments

It was timely for Moses to be relieved of routine duties, for the Lord was about to call on him to fulfil a loftier purpose. The stage was set for one of the most awesome moments in human history: the handing down of the Law on Mount Sinai.

God called Moses up to the mountain and instructed him to tell the Children of Israel that if they would keep his covenant 'you shall be to me a kingdom of priests and an holy nation' (Exod. 19:6). They were ordered to wash and purify themselves for two days, and on the third day they gathered before the mountain that was covered with a thick cloud. Out of it came thunder, lightning and the loud blasts of a trumpet. 'And Mount Sinai was wrapped in smoke, because the Lord descended upon it in fire; and the smoke of it went up like the smoke of a kiln, and the whole mountain quaked greatly.' (Exod. 19:18) Then the voice of God rolled forth, solemnly pronouncing the Ten Commandments:

'I am the Lord your God, who brought you out of the land of Egypt, out of the house of bondage.

'You shall have no other gods before me. You shall not make for yourself a graven image . . .

'You shall not take the name of the Lord your God in vain . . .

'Remember the sabbath day, to keep it holy. Six days you shall labour, and do all your work; but the seventh day is a sabbath to the Lord your God . . .

'Honour your father and your mother . . .

'You shall not kill.

'You shall not commit adultery.

'You shall not steal.

'You shall not bear false witness against your neighbour.

'You shall not covet your neighbour's house . . . or anything that is your neighbour's.' (Exod. 20:2-17)

A number of other laws were then made known to Moses. He built a stone altar with twelve pillars representing the twelve tribes of Israel, and instructed young men to sacrifice oxen on it. Moses read out 'the book of the covenant' (Exod. 24:7) and sprinkled the blood of the sacrifices on the people as 'the blood of the covenant which the Lord has made with you in accordance with all these words' (Exod. 24:8).

He then left Aaron and Hur in charge of the encampment and disappeared into the cloud that still covered the mountain. There he remained for forty days and forty nights, communing with the Lord. At the end of that time God gave him 'two tables of the testimony, tables of stone, written with the finger of God' (Exod. 31:18).

Down in the camp, the Israelites had lost faith when Moses failed to reappear. They came in a body to Aaron and said, 'Up, make us gods, who shall go before us; as for this Moses, the man who brought us up out of the land of Egypt, we do not know what has become of him.' (Exod. 32:1) Aaron felt obliged to appease them. He asked for all the gold earrings worn by the men and women, melted them down, and moulded a golden calf. The people made burnt-offerings to it, and they sang, feasted and danced naked around it.

On the mountain the Lord told Moses what his 'stiff-necked people' (Exod. 32:9) were doing, and threatened to destroy them. Moses pleaded for them, and the Lord relented. But when Moses came down and saw the spectacle with his own eyes, he was seized with rage and dashed the two stone tablets to the ground, breaking them. Moses threw the golden calf into the fire, ground it up, mixed it with water and made the Israelites swallow it. He upbraided Aaron, who tried to defend himself, saying, 'you know the people, that they are set on evil' (Exod. 32:22). Moses felt a drastic purge was needed. He rallied round him the men from the priestly tribe of Levi (to which he and Aaron belonged) and ordered them to put to the sword a large number of the idol-worshippers.

above Bull worship was common in the Near East: 11th-century BC Assyrian cylinder seal showing worshippers before a bull on an altar.

This painful experience left Moses with a sense of failure, and he asked the Lord to relieve him of the leadership. The reply was that the journey to the Promised Land should continue as before. Moses again ascended the sacred mountain, carrying two stone tablets he had hewed to replace those smashed. Once more he stayed there forty days and nights without food or water. When he returned with 'the words of the covenant, the ten commandments' (Exod. 34:28) engraved on the tablets for the second time, Aaron and the Israelites observed that his face shone with such light that 'they were afraid to come near him' (Exod. 34:30).

The Lord had given Moses precise instructions for the construction of an Ark of acacia wood covered with gold, and a tabernacle with an open-air altar. They were to form a portable temple for the Israelites' wandering life.

above The Israelites melted down their jewelry to make the golden calf. Gold jewelry of the late Canaanite period, from Tel el-Ajjul.

below Mesopotamian religious procession headed by a standard-bearer carrying the effigy of a bull. Shell set in bitumen, mid-3rd millennium BC.

Acacia tree in the Negev: the Ark was
made from acacia wood.

Moses and Aaron supervise a sacrifice before the Ark:
12th-century Greek manuscript.

The Ark containing the tablets of the Law was placed
in the Tabernacle, which was consecrated by Moses in
the presence of all the people. As long as the pillar of
cloud or of fire stood still over the Tabernacle, it was
a sign that the Israelites should remain at that spot
until the pillar moved forward again.

Before the Israelites set out once more, Moses adopted two measures to increase their cohesion and their
self-defence: a military census and a marching order.
The census covered men of military age from twenty
upwards, 'all in Israel who are able to go forth to war'
(Num. 1:3), except for the Levites who were exempted
because of their religious duties. The order in which
Moses organized the tribes for travel gave each family
clan its fixed position. The Levites were in the centre of
a square, carrying the Ark, the Tabernacle and other
sacred objects. On each of the four sides a group of
three tribes formed up around a standard. The start of
the march was marked by a series of trumpet blasts.

Moses prevailed on his Midianite brother-in-law
Hobab to come with the Israelites as guide, since he
was born and bred in the desert and familiar with it:
'for you know how we are to encamp in the wilderness,
and you will serve as eyes for us.' (Num. 10:31)

From Sinai to Kadesh

In the second month of the second year the Children of
Israel moved northward from Mount Sinai towards
the wilderness of Paran, in the central plateau of the
Sinai peninsula. Soon trouble broke out again, this time
over the monotonous diet of manna. As refugees are
apt to do, they became nostalgic for the land they had
fled. Tearfully they asked, 'O that we had meat to eat!
We remember the fish we ate in Egypt for nothing, the
cucumbers, the melons, the leeks, the onions, and the
garlic.' (Num. 11:4, 5)

Moses felt weary of leading the discontented community he had brought out of slavery. He said to the
Lord: 'I am not able to carry all this people along, the
burden is too heavy for me. If thou will deal thus with
me, kill me at once . . .' (Num. 11:14, 15) At this cry of
distress, the Lord saw that Moses needed help in carrying the burden. He had Moses summon seventy elders
to the Tabernacle, and inspired them, so that they would
serve as a council to share responsibility with him. As
for the people's demand for flesh, the Lord taught them
a lesson. Huge flocks of quail were blown inland from
the sea and piled up all round the camp. For two days
the Israelites gorged themselves on the meat of the birds
until they fell violently ill and a number of them died.

At their next camping place Aaron and Miriam
started speaking against Moses, of whom they had
become jealous. The Lord was angry at this attack, and
Miriam was stricken with leprosy. Moses prayed that
she be forgiven, and she recovered after seven days of
isolation in the desert outside the camp. Oddly enough
Aaron was not punished – perhaps because of his
priestly role.

The Israelites resumed their journey northward, and
came to rest at Kadesh-barnea, a green and well-
watered oasis some fifty miles south of Beersheba.
They were now nearing the southern rim of Canaan,
but it was for them unknown country. Moses decided
to send into it a scouting party of twelve picked men,
one from each tribe to 'see what the land is, and whether
the people who dwell in it are strong or weak, whether
they are few or many' (Num. 13:18) – also, whether the
inhabitants lived in fortified towns or in tents, and
whether the soil was fertile.

The spies crossed the Negev, passed Arad on the
plateau above the Dead Sea, and travelled through the

The scouts sent by Moses to spy out
the Promised Land brought back a bunch of grapes
on a pole. Early 14th-century German manuscript.

central hill country of Canaan. The party reached
Kadesh safely after a forty-day trip and reported that
Canaan was truly a land flowing with milk and honey.
Nevertheless 'the people who dwell in the land are
strong and the cities are fortified and very large; and
besides, we saw the descendants of Anak there.' (Num.
13:28) (*Anak* is Hebrew for 'giant'.) They also reported
on the Amalekites who dwelt in the arid south of
Canaan, and the Hittites, Jebusites, Amorites and
other peoples in the settled areas further north. As
Moses had requested, they brought back specimens of
the fruit they had seen: figs, pomegranates and a bunch
of grapes so large that it had to be carried on a pole
slung between two men. They had picked it near Hebron
at the brook of Eshcol, a name which means 'grape-
cluster'.

One of the scouts, Caleb of the tribe of Judah, proposed that in spite of the dangers they should advance
into the country without delay and trust the Lord to
help them overcome resistance. He was supported only
by Joshua from the tribe of Ephraim. The other ten
were much more discouraging. They submitted 'an
evil report of the land ... that devours its inhabitants;
all the people that we saw in it are men of great stature
... and we seemed to ourselves like grasshoppers.'
(Num. 13:32, 33) The gathering that listened to the
report was cast into gloom. What was the good of
bringing them to the Promised Land, they said, in order
to be slain in it? It would be better to find a new leader
who would take them back to Egypt. A wrathful Lord
decreed that for their lack of belief in Him, they would
stay wandering in the desert for forty years, till that
generation had died out, except for Joshua and Caleb.

The Children of Israel now settled down for some
decades to the life of nomad shepherds and cattle-herders

roaming the wilderness of Zin, with their base at the
oasis. 'So you remained at Kadesh many days.' (Deut.
1:46) During this period Moses developed the religious
code and the rituals of worship. The stern discipline
with which observance was enforced was illustrated by
the case of the man who gathered sticks for firewood on
the Sabbath and was ordered to be stoned to death.

The leadership of Moses and Aaron was challenged
by a revolt – all the more serious because it started with
their own tribe of Levi, which was dedicated to priestly
duties. It was led by the Levite Korah the son of Izhar,
together with two Reubenite brothers, Dathan and
Abiram, and they were supported by two hundred and
fifty respected men. Punishment was swift. The earth

above The wilderness of Zin in the Negev.

below The river Jordan, which Moses crossed in order
to enter Canaan from the east.

Tel Arad in the Negev,
previously thought to be the Arad
mentioned in Numbers.

The Israelites were attacked by the Midianites,
a camel-riding tribe. The camel remains the basic
form of transport in the desert.

split open and swallowed up the three rebel leaders with
their households. The two hundred and fifty supporters
were consumed by fire from the Lord. Moses felt the
need of some act to bolster the status of Aaron and the
priests. He collected and placed in the Tabernacle a
stave from each of the tribes, with the Levites represented by Aaron's own rod. When they were taken out and
shown to the people next morning, it was seen that
Aaron's stave had sprouted with blossom and borne
almonds.

Miriam, the sister of Moses and Aaron, died at
Kadesh and was buried there.

Onward to Canaan

After nearly forty years had gone by, most of them
spent at Kadesh, the time had come to resume the march
towards the Promised Land. Unable to penetrate
Canaan from the south, the Israelites now set out on a
lengthy detour in order to enter from the east, across
the Jordan river. The route northward into Transjordan lay along the ancient caravan route known as
the King's Highway. Moses sent messengers to the
king of Edom, to say, 'Now let us pass through your
land. We will not pass through field or vineyard, neither
will we drink water from a well; we will go along the
King's Highway, we will not turn aside to the right
hand or to the left, until we have passed through your
territory.' (Num. 20:17) The king refused, and Moses
thought it prudent to bypass Edom from the west,
travelling up the great rift of Wadi Araba towards the
Dead Sea. On the way, Aaron died on top of Mount
Hor where he had been taken by Moses and by Aaron's
son Eleazar, who succeeded him as high priest.

The Israelites now had a taste of the warfare that
lay ahead. They were attacked and a number of them
killed and captured by Canaanites from Arad, that lies
on the plateau west of the Dead Sea. Further on, they
passed through a region infested with venomous snakes
and some of them were bitten. Moses stuck a brass
serpent on a pole, and looking at it served as a magic
cure for snake bite.

From the southern end of the Dead Sea, they turned
eastward into the mountains, through the precipitous
valley of Zered that divided Edom from Moab. They
emerged on the plateau and skirted round Moab to the
deep gorge of the river Arnon that entered the Dead
Sea from the east.

The country north of the Arnon had recently been
conquered by the Amorites under King Sihon. He also
refused the Israelites passage and attacked them. He
was defeated and his capital Heshbon occupied. The
advance continued northward into the fertile land of
Gilead, up to the Yarmuk river. Og, the giant king of
Bashan (the Golan Heights) gave them battle and was
repulsed. Thus ended the first phase of the Israelite
invasion.

The Israelites started to cohabit with Moabite
women, and were drawn into the cult of the local deity,
the Baal of Peor. The Lord smote them with a plague
but was mollified by the act of an outraged priest called
Phinehas, son of Eleazar and grandson of Aaron. He
seized a javelin, rushed into a tent where an Israelite
was lying with a Midianite woman and with one blow
transfixed them both.

The camel-riding Midianites in the region seem to

have been involved in this Israelite immorality. An Israelite expedition was sent against them, with a thousand men from each tribe. They wiped out the Midianite encampments with religious zeal, sparing only the young girls. Moses ruled on the division of the captured livestock: half to the fighting men and half to the rest of the community, with special shares for the priesthood.

Another census was taken and showed that none of the men of the Exodus was left alive, except for Joshua, Caleb and Moses himself. A new breed of Israelites had grown up as free men, hardened by the rigours of desert life and disciplined by the laws Moses had taught them. Out of the craven and unruly bondsmen that had emerged from Egypt, Moses had in forty years moulded a small but stalwart nation, ready to meet its destiny in the Promised Land. He was not to share that destiny; his own task was nearly done.

The Death of Moses

In three farewell addresses, recorded in the Book of Deuteronomy, Moses recalled for the Israelites the story of their wandering; expanded their religious and legal code; and instructed them about their coming settlement in Canaan. He climaxed his religious exhortations with the 'Shema Yisrael' – 'Hear, O Israel' – which has remained to this day the most celebrated prayer in the Jewish liturgy.

To a desert-weary people Moses painted a pleasant picture of the country they were about to enter:

'For the Lord your God is bringing you into a good land, a land of brooks of water, of fountains and springs flowing forth in valleys and hills, a land of wheat and barley, of vines and fig trees and pomegranates, a land of olive trees and honey, a land in which you will eat bread without scarcity, in which you will lack nothing, a land whose stones are iron, and out of whose hills you can dig copper.' (Deut. 8:7-9)

Moses composed a song of praise to God, whom he had served so humbly and faithfully, and gave his blessing to each of the tribes in turn.

He asked the Lord to appoint a new leader to whom he could hand over his charge 'that the congregation of the Lord may not be as sheep which have no shepherd' (Num. 27:17). It was indicated that Moses's successor would be Joshua the son of Nun, 'a man in whom is the spirit' (Num. 27:18).

At a solemn ceremony in the Tabernacle before Eleazar the High Priest and all the congregation, with the presence of the Lord in a pillar of cloud over the door, Moses laid his hands upon Joshua and said, 'Be strong and of good courage; for you shall go with this people into the land which the Lord has sworn to their fathers to give them; and you shall put them in possession of it.' (Deut. 31:7)

The men of Reuben and Gad asked whether they could remain in the territory east of the river. They were herdsmen, and these rolling uplands would give good grazing for their cattle and sheep. Moses rebuked them: 'Shall your brethren go to the war while you sit here? Why will you discourage the heart of the people of Israel from going over into the land which the Lord has given them? Thus did your fathers, when I sent them from Kadesh-barnea to see the land.' (Num. 32:6-8) A compromise was reached. They would establish their families and herds in Transjordan, cross the river with the other tribes to fight their way into Canaan, and return when it had been subdued. Part of the tribe of Manasseh joined in this arrangement, as they were attracted by the wooded ridges and fertile dales of Gilead, and wanted to settle there.

Before he died, Moses was given a distant view of the Promised Land from 'Mount Nebo, to the top of Pisgah, which is opposite Jericho' (Deut. 34:1). On a height jutting out from the great escarpment, Moses stood with his back to the Moab plateau, stretching away to the empty desert beyond the eastern horizon. Before him a tremendous panorama unfolded. Thousands of feet below glittered the Dead Sea, the lowest body of water on the earth's surface. Beyond it rose the dun-coloured rampart of the Judean desert, with Jerusalem and Hebron and other Canaanite cities hidden behind its rim. To the right, the Jordan river looped snake-like through lush green banks. And the Lord said: 'I have let you see it with your eyes, but you shall not go over there.' (Deut. 34:4)

After this single view Moses died and was buried by the Lord 'in the valley in the land of Moab, opposite Beth-peor; but no man knows the place of his burial to this day' (Deut. 34:6). At his death he was a hundred and twenty years old, but 'his eye was not dim, nor his natural force abated' (Deut. 34:7). For thirty days the Children of Israel wept and mourned for the great leader and teacher they had lost, 'And there has not arisen a prophet since in Israel like Moses, whom the Lord knew face to face.' (Deut. 34:10).

[There are references to Moses throughout the Old Testament. His history is given: Exod. 2-40; Book of Numbers; Deut. 1-34.]

The Law of Moses

The body of Hebrew legislation in the Pentateuch was developed over many centuries from many sources, and constituted a unique code. Whatever similarities of detail there might have been with other ancient codes, such as that of Hammurabi in Babylon, the Law of Moses had nothing in common with them in its religious beliefs or in its humanism.

The central message is the monotheism which the Hebrew people were the first to expound – the worship of one single, invisible and just God, and the rejection of every form of idolatry and paganism. The first and most important of the Ten commandments was:

'You shall have no other gods before me.' (Exod. 20:3)

But the Mosaic Code goes far beyond religious observance in the narrow sense. It deals with political, social and family affairs in a progressive spirit well in advance of its period. For example: there must be no arbitrary exercise of power; even a king must fear God and obey the law, 'that his heart may not be lifted up above his brethren, and that he may not turn aside from the commandment, either to the right hand or to the left' (Deut. 17:20).

Justice must be impartially administered, for rich and poor alike:

'You shall appoint judges and officers in all your towns which the Lord your God gives you, according to your tribes; and they shall judge the people with righteous judgment.

'You shall not pervert justice; you shall not show partiality; and you shall not take a bribe, for a bribe blinds the eyes of the wise, and subverts the cause of the righteous.' (Deut. 16:18-19)

Special protection is extended to the needy and the under-privileged, to fugitive slaves, debtors, hired servants, orphans, widows and foreigners. Women must be respected, and a slander against the chastity of a wife is a crime. Even the ox may not be muzzled while it is treading the grain on the threshing floor, and the mother-bird must be spared if eggs are collected from

Pottery vessel in the shape of a pomegranate, 10th-6th centuries BC. Pomegranates were among the fruit in Moses's description of the Promised Land.

her nest. There must be fair practices in commerce – 'a full and just weight you shall have, a full and just measure you shall have' (Deut. 25:15). Men shall be exempted from military service if they have recently built a house, planted a vineyard or betrothed a wife, or are faint-hearted. Always, in his dealings with others, the Hebrew must say to himself: 'Love the sojourner therefore; for you were sojourners in the land of Egypt.' (Deut. 10:19)

For century after century, the Jewish rabbis and sages discussed and refined the Laws of Moses. Their commentaries were gathered together in the huge tomes of the Talmud, which a learned man might study all his life without exhausting them. In this fashion was shaped the distinctive outlook and way of life which the Jewish people carried with them to all the countries of their dispersion. Through Christianity, the Hebrew code profoundly influenced the civilization of the Western world.

MOZA (Heb. 'departing') **1.** date unknown. A son of Caleb of the tribe of Judah, and his concubine Ephah. [1 Chr. 2:46]

2. date unknown. Son of Zimri of the tribe of Benjamin and a descendant of King Saul. [1 Chr. 8:36, 37; 9:42]

MUPPIM (Heb. 'serpent') *c.* 16 century BC. One of the ten sons of Benjamin and a grandson of Jacob, he went down to Egypt at the same time as Jacob. He is also known as Shephupham and Shephuphan. [Gen. 46:21; Num. 26:39; 1 Chr. 8:5]

MUSHI (Heb. 'deserted') date unknown. Younger son of Merari and a grandson of Levi, his descendants were assigned special duties in the Tabernacle in the wilderness in the days of Moses. [Exod. 6:19; Num. 3:20; 4:29-31; 1 Chr. 6:47; 23:21, 23; 24:30]

Present-day celebration of Succoth, the festival that commemorates the Exodus of the Jews out of Egypt.

N

NAAM (Heb. 'pleasant') *c.* 13 century BC. Son of Caleb the son of Jephunneh and a leader of the tribe of Judah. [1 Chr. 4:15]

NAAMAH (Heb. 'pleasing') **1.** date unknown. Daughter of Lamech and Zillah, and the sister of Tubal-cain. [Gen. 4:22]

2. *c.* 10 century BC. A princess of Ammon who was the wife of King Solomon and the mother of Rehoboam who succeeded him as king of Israel. [1 Kgs. 14:21, 31; 2 Chr. 12:13]

NAAMAN (Heb. 'pleasantness') **1.** *c.* 16 century BC. A son of Benjamin and a grandson of Jacob and Rachel, he went down to Egypt at the same time as Jacob. In the Book of Numbers and in the First Book of Chronicles, Naaman is described as a grandson of Benjamin the son of Bela. [Gen. 46:21; Num. 26:40; 1 Chr. 8:4]

2. date unknown. Son of Ehud and a leader of the tribe of Benjamin, he was head of a family in Geba carried off in exile to Manahath. [1 Chr. 8:7]

3. *c.* 9 century BC. Commander of the Syrian army in the time of King Ben-hadad II, he contracted the dread disease of leprosy. His wife had an Israelite slave who had been taken captive on one of the Syrian incursions into Israel. The girl said there was a prophet called Elisha in Samaria who could cure him. Carrying lavish presents and a letter from his king to Jehoram, king of Israel, Naaman set out for Samaria with a military escort. Jehoram was very distressed at this unwelcome visit, fearing that the Syrians were making an impossible demand on him as a pretext to attack him. Elisha, hearing the story, sent word that the Syrian commander should be brought round to his house. The prophet did not come out to receive the foreign dignitary nor invite him in, but sent a messenger out to tell him that he should bathe seven times in the river Jordan. Naaman was enraged at this curt treatment and snorted that the rivers of Damascus were better than all the waters of Israel and why should he not wash in them. But his staff persuaded him to follow Elisha's advice and he was cured.

Naaman came back to Elisha and offered him a reward which the prophet declined. Now convinced that the Hebrew God was the only true one, Naaman asked leave to take two mule-loads of earth back to Damascus with him so that he could worship the Lord on Israelite soil. He also asked Elisha if the Lord would forgive him if, in the course of his duties to his master the king, he accompanied him to worship at the temple to Rimmon. Elisha told him to go in peace.

Elisha's servant Gehazi was overcome with greed at the thought of the rich gifts his master had spurned. He hurried after Naaman and with a concocted story about a couple of needy priests visiting Elisha, obtained from him two bags of silver and two changes of clothing. When he returned he hid these things in his house, but through his occult powers Elisha knew what had happened. He told Gehazi he may have enriched himself but at the cost of contracting the leprosy of which Naaman had been cured. [2 Kgs. 5]

NAARAH (Heb. 'young girl') date unknown. One of the two wives of Ashhur a leader of the tribe of Judah. [1 Chr. 4:5, 6]

NAARAI *see* PAARAI

The Jordan river, shown here south of the Sea of Galilee, in which Naaman bathed seven times.

NABAL (Heb. 'fool') *c.* 11 century BC. Nabal was a wealthy sheep farmer who lived in Carmel in the Hebron hills with his attractive and intelligent wife Abigail. At shearing time a group of ten young men called on him, asking for provisions for David, then leader of a band of outlaws. They pointed out that Nabal's sheep had grazed all winter unmolested. Nabal answered rudely: 'Who is David? Who is the son of Jesse? There are many servants nowadays who are breaking away from their masters.' (1 Sam. 25:10) David was furious when he heard the story and set out with four hundred men, vowing he would wipe out everyone he found at Nabal's farmstead. He was headed off by Abigail who slipped out to meet him with provisions. On returning, she found her husband drunk from the feast given to celebrate the sheep-shearing. Next morning she told him how narrowly he had escaped David's wrath. The frightened Nabal suffered a heart attack from which he died ten days later. On hearing about this, David sent her a proposal of marriage, which she accepted. [1 Sam. 25:3-39; 27:3; 30:5; 2 Sam. 2:2]

NABOTH (Heb. 'fruits') *c.* 9 century BC. Naboth the Jezreelite had a vineyard adjoining the grounds of the winter palace of King Ahab of Israel. Ahab asked Naboth to give him the vineyard in exchange for another one, or to sell it to him, as he wanted it for a vegetable garden. But Naboth answered Ahab, 'The Lord forbid that I should give you the inheritance of my fathers.' (1 Kgs. 21:3)

Naboth was murdered by King Ahab so that the king could take possession of his vineyard. A present-day vineyard in Israel.

Queen Jezebel arranged for Naboth to be charged and convicted of blasphemy, on false evidence. 'So they took him outside the city, and stoned him to death with stones.' (1 Kgs. 21:13) Ahab was then entitled to take possession of the vineyard, presumably because the property of criminals was held to be forfeited to the ruler. [1 Kgs. 21:1-18; 2 Kgs. 9:25, 26]

NACON (Heb. 'ready') *c.* 10 century BC. Owner of the threshing floor where the oxen stumbled while carrying the Ark to Jerusalem and where Uzzah was killed. Also called Chidon. [2 Sam. 6:6; 1 Chr. 13:9]

NADAB (Heb. '[God] is willing') **1.** *c.* 13 century BC. Eldest son of Aaron the high priest, Nadab and his brothers held priestly office with their father Aaron. After the Tabernacle had been completed, Nadab and Abihu burnt forbidden incense before the Lord and were instantly killed. [Exod. 6:23; 24:1, 9; 28:1; Lev. 10:1, 52; Num. 3:2, 4; 26:60, 61; 1 Chr. 6:3; 24:1, 2]

2. date unknown. A son of Jeiel, Nadab and his family were leaders of the tribe of Benjamin living in Jerusalem. [1 Chr. 8:30; 9:36]

3. date unknown. The elder son of Shammai and a leader of the tribe of Judah. [1 Chr. 2:28, 30]

4. Second king of Israel after the monarchy split, he reigned 910-09 BC. Nadab was the son and successor of Jeroboam I. Just before he became king, Israel had been defeated by the forces of Judah and the southern part of its territory occupied. Thus weakened it came under pressure from the Philistines in the coastal plain. Nadab led his men against the Philistines, and laid siege to the town of Gibbethon, south-west of Gezer. Baasha, of the tribe of Issachar, seized the chance to carry out a successful coup, overthrowing Nadab and putting him and all his offspring to death. [1 Kgs. 14:20; 15:25-31]

NAHAM (Heb. 'comforter') date unknown. Brother-in-law of Hodiah, from the tribe of Judah. [1 Chr. 4:19]

NAHAMANI (Heb. 'compassionate') 6 century BC. A leader of Judah who returned to Judah with Zerubbabel from exile in Babylon. [Neh. 7:7]

NAHARAI *c.* 10 century BC. A soldier from Beeroth, he was armour-bearer to Joab and one of King David's chosen guard renowned for his bravery. [2 Sam. 23:37; 1 Chr. 11:39]

NAHASH (Heb. 'serpent') **1.** *c.* 10 century BC. King of the Ammonites who lived east of the river Jordan, he besieged the city of Jabesh-gilead. The inhabitants of the city offered to make a treaty and surrender to him. Nahash agreed, provided he could gouge out the right eye of every Jabeshite. Gaining seven days' truce, they sent frantic messages asking for help throughout Israel. Saul was coming in from the fields with his cattle when he learnt the grim plight of Jabesh-gilead. He mobilized a large force and marched to the relief of the beleaguered town. The Ammonite army was routed, and the city saved.

Nahash's son Shobi brought supplies to David when he fled from Absalom, and came to Mahaniam. [1 Sam. 11:1-3; 12:12; 2 Sam. 10:2; 17:27; 1 Chr. 19:1-2]

2. *c.* 11 century BC. Sister of Zeruiah, mother of Abigail, she was the grandmother of Amasa who commanded the army of Absalom. [2 Sam. 17:25]

NAHATH (Heb. 'rest') **1.** *c.* 16 century BC. Son of Reuel and a grandson of Esau, he was an Edomite leader. [Gen. 36:13, 17; 1 Chr. 1:37]

2. *see* TOAH

3. *c.* 8 century BC. A Levite appointed by King Hezekiah to supervise the bringing of offerings and tithes into the Temple. [2 Chr. 31:13]

NAHBI (Heb. 'secret') *c.* 13 century BC. Son of Vophsi, a leader of the tribe of Naphtali, Nahbi was one of the twelve men sent by Moses to spy out the Promised Land. [Num. 13:14]

NAHOR 1. date unknown. Son of Serug and grandfather of Abraham. [Gen. 11:22, 23; 1 Chr. 1:26]

2. *c.* 18 century BC. Brother of Abraham whose granddaughter Rebekah married Abraham's son Isaac. [Gen. 11:26, 27, 29; 22:20; 24:10, 15, 24, 47; 29:5; Josh. 24:2]

NAHSHON (Heb. 'diviner') *c.* 13 century BC. Leader of the tribe of Judah in the wilderness and a brother-in-law of Aaron, he was the son of Amminadab. [Exod. 6:23; Num. 1:7; 2:3; 7:12, 17; 10:14; Ruth 4:20; 1 Chr. 2:9-11]

NAHUM (Heb. 'comforted') *c.* 7 century BC. Hebrew prophet. In his brief prophetic Book, Nahum the Elkoshite (the place is unknown) is not concerned with the religious and moral welfare of his own people, like other Hebrew prophets. He confines himself to lashing out against Nineveh, the capital of the hated Assyrian empire, that dominated the Near East of his time. He calls it a 'bloody city, all full of lies and booty' (Nah. 3:1), and predicts its coming downfall in some of the most vivid and powerful descriptive passages in the Old Testament. The Book must have been written a few

years before the actual fall of the city in 612 BC.

Nahum describes the assault troops – the scarlet uniforms and shields and the flashing steel of the chariots: 'Horsemen charging, flashing sword and glittering spear, hosts of slain, heaps of corpses, dead bodies without end – they stumble over the bodies.' (Nah. 3:3) Fear and panic grip the inhabitants but there is no one to save the city from becoming 'Desolate! Desolation and ruin!' (Nah. 2:10) And when it has been destroyed

Assyrian war-chariots: detail from
the bronze gates of Shalmaneser III
at Balawat, 858 BC.

'all who hear the news of you clap their hands over you. For upon whom has not come your unceasing evil?' (Nah. 3:19)

Among the fragments of Dead Sea Scrolls found in the Qumran caves were portions of a commentary on Nahum, which has helped to establish the dates of the Scrolls and identify some of the obscure references. [Book of Nahum]

NAOMI (Heb. 'my pleasure') *c.* 11 century BC. Mother-in-law of Ruth.

The tender tale of the love between Naomi and her Moabite daughter-in-law Ruth is placed in the period of the judges. Naomi lived with her husband Elimelech in the small town of Bethlehem, where she had two sons, Mahlon and Chilion. When famine swept the country, the family moved to the neighbouring country of Moab on the fertile plateau east of the Dead Sea and settled there. Elimelech died and the two sons married Moabite girls, Orpah and Ruth. After ten years, both sons died and the bereft Naomi, hearing that the famine had ceased in the land of Israel, decided to return to her people.

To her daughters-in-law Naomi said, 'Go, return each of you to her mother's house. May the Lord deal kindly with you, as you have dealt with the dead and with me.' (Ruth 1:8) The two young widows at first refused to leave her. With melancholy sarcasm she

Assyrian archers, from a relief showing
the defeat of Lachish, 700 BC.

asked whether they expected her to marry again and produce sons as husbands for them. Orpah finally went 'back to her people and to her gods.' (Ruth 1:15) Naomi tried to persuade the tearful Ruth to do the same; but Ruth refused to part from her.

The two women set out alone along the arduous hundred-mile journey down the mountains, across the floor of the Jordan valley and up through the wilderness of Judea to Bethlehem. When they entered the town the people were very surprised and cried out, 'Is this Naomi?' (Ruth 1:19) Naomi, making a play on her name, said to them, 'Do not call me Naomi, call me Mara, for the Almighty has dealt very bitterly with me.' (Ruth 1:20) (*Mara* means 'bitter' in Hebrew.)

Ruth went to glean barley in a field belonging to Boaz, a wealthy relative of her dead father-in-law, Elimelech. Boaz treated her kindly and gave her extra food. With Boaz obviously attracted towards the gentle and appealing young widow, Naomi saw a prospect of gaining a happier and more secure life for her beloved daughter-in-law. Naomi said to Ruth, 'My daughter, should I not seek a home for you, that it may be well with you? Now is not Boaz our kinsman . . .?' (Ruth 3:1, 2) She had Ruth bathe and perfume herself and put on her best clothes. On Naomi's instructions Ruth waited until Boaz was asleep on the ground at the threshing floor and went to lie trustfully at his feet. When he woke up he was deeply moved to find her there.

Next day Boaz arranged to marry Ruth, in exercise of a kinsman's 'right of redemption' of a widow. A son was born to them called Obed, and to Naomi's great joy the baby was handed over to her care. Her women

left Naomi was given Ruth's son Obed to nurse. Neo-Hittite relief of a woman nursing a child.

neighbours assured Naomi that the boy would be 'a restorer of life and a nourisher of your old age.' (Ruth 4:15) Obed's son Jesse was the father of King David. [Book of Ruth]

NAPHISH *c.* 17 century BC. Son of Abraham's son Ishmael, he was a desert leader. [Gen. 25:13-15; 1 Chr. 1:31; 5:18-19]

NAPHTALI (Heb. 'wrestling') *c.* 16 century BC. The fifth son of Jacob.

Naphtali was the second son born to Bilhah, the maid Rachel gave Jacob her husband as a concubine. Together with his brothers, he was involved in the selling of Joseph into slavery in Egypt. Later he was one of the ten sons sent by Jacob to buy corn in Egypt where Joseph had become a leading figure at the Pharaoh's court. When Jacob went to settle in Egypt with all his family it included Naphtali's four sons.

On his deathbed Jacob blessed his sons in turn. Of Naphtali he said: 'Naphtali is a hind let loose, that bears comely fawns.' (Gen. 49:21)

Centuries later, in the conquest of Canaan under Joshua, the tribe of Naphtali was allocated an extensive territory stretching from the Jezreel valley and the Sea

Dishon, in the territory allotted to the tribe of Naphtali.

of Galilee to the northern border.

In the blessing attributed to Moses, he referred to Naphtali as 'satisfied with favour, and full of the blessing of the Lord.' (Deut. 33:23) [Gen. 30:8; 35:25; 46:24; 49:21; Exod. 1:4; Deut. 33:23; 1 Chr. 2:2; 7:13]

NAPHTUHIM date unknown. Son of Egypt and a grandson of Ham. [Gen. 10:13]

NATHAN (Heb. 'he gave') **1.** date unknown. Son of Ahai, descended from Jerahoneel, he was the father of Zabad. [1 Chr. 2:36]

2. *c.* 10 century BC. Hebrew prophet.

The prophet Nathan was a trusted adviser to King David. The Lord revealed to Nathan in a dream that he did not want the Temple built by David but by his son Solomon.

After the king had sent Uriah the Hittite to his death in battle, so that he could marry Uriah's wife Bathsheba, Nathan told a parable to the king, concerning 'two men in a certain city, the one rich and the other poor.' (2 Sam. 12:1) The rich man had a great many flocks and herds, while the poor man had only one cherished ewe-lamb reared in his home. One day a traveller came to the city and the rich man offered him

Nathan admonishing King David for having Uriah killed in order to obtain Bathsheba: from a 10th-century Greek Bible.

hospitality. Instead of killing one of his flock for the meal, he slaughtered the poor man's lamb. On hearing this story, David was greatly incensed and said the rich man should die 'because he did this thing, and because he had no pity.' (2 Sam. 12:6) Nathan promptly answered, 'You are the man.' (2 Sam. 12:7) He reminded David how much he had achieved with the Lord's help; yet he had done evil in the sight of the Lord, who now declared that 'Behold, I will raise up evil against you out of your own house.' (2 Sam. 12:11) The child born by Bathsheba fell ill and died.

When David was aged and ailing, the prophet got

word that the eldest prince Adonijah planned to usurp the throne. Nathan advised Bathsheba to go to the king, recall his promise that Solomon would succeed him, and tell him of Adonijah's designs. The prophet followed her and confirmed her words. David commanded Nathan and Zadok the priest to take Solomon on the royal mule to the spring of Gihon and anoint him king.

After David's death, Nathan's two sons were given high office by Solomon: Azariah was put in charge of the officials responsible for the twelve tax districts; while Zabud became Solomon's confidential adviser.

It is mentioned that Nathan chronicled the events of David's reign, but no such work has been found. [2 Sam. 7:2-17; 12:1-25; 1 Kgs. 1:8-45; 4:4-5; 1 Chr. 17:1-15; 29:29; 2 Chr. 9:29; 29:25; Ps. 51; Zech. 12:12]

3. *c.* 10 century BC. Father of Igal, a warrior in the army of King David; in the First Book of Chronicles he is described as the brother of Joel. [2 Sam. 23:36; 1 Chr. 11:38]

4. *c.* 10 century BC. A son of King David and Bathsheba. [2 Sam. 5:14; 1 Chr. 3:5; 14:4]

5. 5 century BC. A leader of Judah in Babylon, he was sent by Ezra to ask Iddo to send Levites to Jerusalem to minister in the Temple. [Ezra 8:16]

6. 5 century BC. A descendant of Binnui who divorced his non-Jewish wife in the time of Ezra. [Ezra 10:39]

NATHAN-MELECH *c.* 7 century BC. An official in the time of King Josiah whose name was given to a room in the Temple used for sun-worship. During the reforms Josiah took down the statues of horses – 'chariots of the sun' – that had been set there by earlier kings of Judah. [2 Kgs. 23:11]

NEARIAH (Heb. 'child of God') **1.** *c.* 8 century BC. A leader of the tribe of Simeon in the days of Hezekiah, king of Judah, he led an army of 500 men and drove out the Amalekites from Mount Seir, south-east of the Dead Sea, and settled there. [1 Chr. 4:42]

2. date unknown. Son of Shemaiah of the tribe of Judah, he was a descendant of King David. [1 Chr. 3:22, 23]

NEBAI (Heb. 'building') 5 century BC. A leader of Judah who signed the solemn covenant in the time of Nehemiah. [Neh. 10:19]

NEBAIOTH (Heb. 'heights') *c.* 17 century BC. Eldest son of Ishmael and the grandson of Abraham and Hagar, he was one of the twelve leaders who ruled from Egypt to Assyria. [Gen. 25:13; 28:9; 36:3; 1 Chr. 1:29]

NEBAT (Heb. 'view') *c.* 10 century BC. Father of Jeroboam, king of Israel, he died before his son's rebellion split the united monarchy. [1 Kgs. 11:26; 12:2, 15; 15:1; 16:3, 26, 31; 21:22; 22:52; 2 Kgs. 3:3; 9:9; 10:29; 13:2, 11; 14:24; 15:9; 17:21; 23:15; 2 Chr. 9:29; 10:2, 15; 13:6]

NEBO (Acc. 'the proclaimer') **1.** A Babylonian god, he was originally the Sumerian deity of wisdom

Nebuchadnezzar

and writing, and the cult of Nebo became very popular in Assyria and the Babylonian empire. His 'wisdom' related to the movement of the stars and the priests of Nebo were astrologers. His 'writing' was associated with the tables of fate upon which were inscribed the names of the people. The main centre of Nebo worship was his shrine at Borsippa, south-west of Babylon. [Isa. 46:1]

2. date unknown. Ancestor of a family who returned to Judah with Ezra and whose descendants divorced their non-Jewish wives. [Ezra 10:43]

NEBUCHADNEZZAR (Ass. 'Nabu protects my boundary stone') King of Babylon, 604-562 BC. The fall of Nineveh in 612 BC marked the end of the mighty Assyrian empire and its replacement by Babylonia as the dominant power of the Near East. In 605 BC a Babylonian army commanded by Nebuchadnezzar, the crown prince, marched into the area and decisively defeated the Egyptians at the battle of Carcemish. He advanced towards Egypt but turned back to assume the throne of Babylon when his father died. Judah became a vassal of Babylon.

In 598 BC Judah attempted to throw off the yoke of Babylon. Nebuchadnezzar advanced on Jerusalem and occupied it. He carried off the young King Jehoiachin and appointed his uncle Zedekiah to the throne.

Nine years later, in 587 BC, Zedekiah was drawn into a rebellion, against the advice of the prophet Jeremiah. Again Nebuchadnezzar besieged Jerusalem, which held out for two years and then fell. The city was destroyed, including the demolition of the Temple, the palace and the walls. Most of the inhabitants were carried off to exile in Babylon. Judah was annexed as a Babylonian province.

Nebuchadnezzar was the most powerful and energetic ruler of the new Babylonian empire. His capital, Babylon, became the greatest centre of trade, architecture, art and astronomy of the time.

The terraced roof gardens on top of his palace, the

Reconstruction of the Ishtar Gate of Nebuchadnezzar's palace at Babylon, with animal reliefs in glazed tiles.

'hanging gardens of Babylon', were listed by the Greeks as one of the seven wonders of the world. Also called Nebuchadrezzar. [2 Kgs. 24, 25; 1 Chr. 6:15; 2 Chr. 36; Ezra 1:7; 2:1; 5:12, 14; Neh. 7:6; Esther 2:6; Jer. 21; 22; 24; 25; 27-9; 32; 34; 37; 39; 43; 44; 46; 49-52; Ezek. 26; 29; 30; Dan. 1-5]

NEBUCHADREZZAR *see* NEBUCHADNEZZAR

NEBUSHAZBAN (Ass. 'Nabu saves') *c.* 6 century BC. One of the officers in the Babylonian army responsible for the destruction of Jerusalem, he was among those who committed Jeremiah to the care of Gedaliah, son of Ahikam, the Babylonian-appointed governor of Judah. His title was Rabsaris. [Jer. 39:13]

NEBUZARADAN (Ass. 'Nabu has given offspring') *c.* 6 century BC. Captain of the guard of Nebuchadnezzar, king of Babylon, he led a successful attack on Jerusalem and burnt the Temple, the king's palace and all the houses, and demolished the city walls.

Nebuchadnezzar ordered the Hebrews to worship the golden images on hearing music: 8th-century BC stone fragment from Nineveh, showing musicians.

He carried off the people of Jerusalem to exile in Babylon, but left some farmers to look after the vineyards and the field crops. He released the prophet Jeremiah who had advised the people to submit to the Babylonians and appointed Gedaliah, son of Ahikam, to rule over Judah. Five years later Nebuzaradan returned to Jerusalem and took another group of Jews into exile. [2 Kgs. 25:8-20; Jer. 39:9-13; 40:1-5; 41:10; 43:6; 52:12-26]

NECO *see* PHARAOH **9.**

NEDABIAH (Heb. 'God is generous') *c.* 6 century BC. Son of Jehoiachin, the last king of Judah, and a descendant of King David. [1 Chr. 3:18]

NEHEMIAH (Heb. 'God has consoled') **1.** 6 century BC. A leader of Judah who returned with Zerubbabel from Babylon. [Ezra 2:2; Neh. 7:7]
2. 5 century BC. Son of Azbuk, he helped rebuild the walls of Jerusalem in the days of Nehemiah. [Neh. 3:16]
3. *c.* 5 century BC. Jewish governor of Judea.

Nehemiah the son of Hacaliah was a member of the Judean exile community in Babylonia that came into existence at the time of the fall of Jerusalem. After Babylon had been conquered by the Persians in 539 BC, the Jewish minority was well treated and prospered. Nehemiah was appointed the royal cupbearer to King Artaxerxes I in Susa (Shushan) the capital. This was a position of honour and trust which brought Nehemiah into daily contact with the monarch.

Nearly a century earlier, the Persian king Cyrus had issued a decree permitting the Jewish exiles to return to Judea. Nehemiah relates in his personal memoirs how his kinsman Hanani arrived with some companions from Jerusalem and came to see him. He asked how the settlers in Judea were faring and was told: 'The survivors there in the province who escaped exile are in great trouble and shame; the wall of Jerusalem is broken down, and its gates are destroyed by fire.' (Neh. 1:3) Nehemiah was deeply affected by this report. A devout man, he fasted and prayed, recalling the Lord's promise to Moses to redeem the Children of Israel. That was in 445 BC, the twentieth year of the reign of his master Artaxerxes.

The resolve took shape in Nehemiah's mind to go to Jerusalem himself. A short while later, he was serving wine at the royal table when the king asked him why he looked so downcast. He replied: 'why should not my face be sad, when the city, the place of my fathers' sepulchres, lies waste . . .?' (Neh. 2:3) Nehemiah asked for permission to make a trip to Jerusalem, which was granted. The sympathetic ruler also gave him letters to the provincial governors along the route, an instruction to the keeper of the royal parks to provide him with any timber he might need for construction work in Jerusalem, and an armed escort for the journey of over a thousand miles across mountains, rivers and deserts.

On his arrival in Jerusalem, Nehemiah did not make himself known at once to the authorities. He rested three days, then got up at night and with a few men made a secret moonlight inspection tour of the ruined walls and gates of the city. Nehemiah then called together the Jewish leaders, and proposed that the work of rebuilding the fortifications be put in hand at

Excavations at Jerusalem
that reveal a section of
Nehemiah's reconstructed
city wall.

once. They responded eagerly: 'Let us rise up and build.'
(Neh. 2:18) The project was organized on a voluntary
basis, with specific parts of it allocated to some of the
surrounding towns and to guilds such as the goldsmiths
and perfume-makers. Each of the leading merchants
and priests undertook to be responsible for the section
of the wall opposite his own home.

There were leaders in neighbouring territories who
objected to the shattered fortifications of Jerusalem
being restored. One was Sanballat the provincial governor of Samaria, who claimed general authority over the
Judean district as well. The Samaritans had been hostile
to the return of the Jewish exiles from Babylon and at
an earlier stage had succeeded for a long time in holding
up the reconstruction of the Temple.

Sanballat's opposition was supported by Geshem,
ruler of the Edomites who had occupied the southern
part of Judah; and by Tobiah, head of a wealthy feudal
family of Jews in Transjordan, with relatives among the
Jerusalem notables. At first the three of them tried to
kill the project by ridicule: 'they derided us and
despised us and said, "What is this thing that you are
doing? Are you rebelling against the king?"' (Neh. 2:19)
Nehemiah answered stoutly that the building would go
on, and that 'you have no portion or right or

memorial in Jerusalem.' (Neh. 2:20) Sanballat continued to mock them, and asked whether these 'feeble
Jews' really wanted to 'revive the stones out of
the heaps of rubbish, and burned ones at that?' (Neh.
4:2) Tobiah added that even a fox would be able to
break down their stone wall.

But when the wall reached mid-height and the
builders were getting tired and discouraged, their
opponents threatened to stop them by force. Nehemiah
made security arrangements for the work to continue.
He posted an armed militia day and night, and also
made each of the workers carry a weapon. 'And each
of the builders had his sword girded at his side while he
built.' (Neh. 4:18) Since the working parties were strung
out in different sectors at some distance from each
other, he commanded that they should all rally when
they heard the trumpet sound. At night they remained
within the walls. Nehemiah records that during this
period neither he nor the members of his family nor his
bodyguard took off their clothes except for washing.

These vigorous precautions had their effect, and the
idea of armed intervention was dropped. Instead, his
enemies resorted to various intrigues. They invited
Nehemiah to meet them for a parley, but he distrusted
them and declined. Sanballat then sent Nehemiah a

letter, suggesting that the walls were being erected because Nehemiah planned to rebel against the Persian rulers and proclaim himself king. These rumours, the letter stated, would no doubt reach the Persian court, and Nehemiah had better come and discuss matters. Nehemiah replied that the rumours were unfounded, and a figment of Sanballat's imagination.

At this point Shemaiah, the high priest, urged Nehemiah to take sanctuary in the Temple and hide there, as his life was in danger. Nehemiah answered sharply that he had no intention of running away. He notes in his memoirs that the priest was no doubt in the pay of Tobiah, and that they were trying to frighten him.

In spite of every obstacle, the walls and gates were completed. On the appointed day the solemn dedication took place. After the purification ceremonies, two processions marched round the walls in opposite directions, each headed by priests and notables. They met at the Temple, where the thanksgiving service was followed by a feast.

Nehemiah appointed gatekeepers and sentries for the gates. He put his kinsman Hanani in charge of the city with instructions to see that all the gates were to be shut before sundown and reopened in the morning.

With the city secure behind its reconstructed walls, Nehemiah gave thought to increasing its population. He had a census taken of the inhabitants, and compared the results with the original lists of returnees from Babylon. He then invited the leading men of other Judean towns to move to Jerusalem, 'the Holy City'. From the rest of the Judean population, one person selected by lot out of every ten came to settle in the capital.

The list of the towns outside Jerusalem indicates areas of Jewish settlement which were not part of the Jerusalem district at an earlier period of the Return. It is probable that these were border areas of Hebrew settlement in the Negev, the Shephelah and to the north of Jerusalem that remained intact at the time of the fall of the city and the deportations to Babylon. If so, they became integrated again into Judea in Nehemiah's time.

In 433 BC, after twelve years in Jerusalem, Nehemiah returned to Persia and presented himself again to his royal master. During his absence the standards of religious observance declined in Judea and abuses crept in. Some time later Nehemiah came back to Jerusalem and carried out a series of sweeping reforms. They corresponded to the written covenant which the leading citizens had signed in a formal ceremony, probably under the supervision of Ezra the scribe.

On his return Nehemiah was horrified to find that the high priest Eliashib had placed at the disposal of Tobiah, a wealthy Jewish landowner, a room in the Temple court used for keeping sacrificial food, incense and vessels. Nehemiah ordered the furnishings to be flung out and the room restored to its proper use.

Most of the Levites and cantors in the service of the Temple had gone back to their villages and fields because the dues from the worshippers had not been paid. Nehemiah strongly reprimanded all concerned; the Temple staff returned to work and the tithes were promptly paid into the storehouses in the form of corn, oil and wine. Nehemiah placed four trustworthy officials in charge of gathering and distributing these dues.

He next clamped down on the desecration of the Sabbath. Farmers were bringing their produce into the city market on the holy day, and Phoenician traders were selling fish brought up from the coast. Nehemiah ordered the gates of the city to be shut before the Sabbath started and reopened only after the Sabbath was over. Traders who came and bivouacked next to the walls on the Sabbath were chased away.

Nehemiah denounced the practice of intermarriage with the surrounding peoples. In many cases, the children could only speak the foreign tongue and not Hebrew. To set an example, he expelled from Jerusalem Jehoiada the high priest's son, for having married the daughter of Sanballat the Samaritan leader.

Nehemiah was anxious to get due credit with the Lord for his diligence in restoring the purity of religion and in preserving the identity of the Jews. His memoir ends with the words: 'Remember me, O my God, for good.' (Neh. 13:31) [Book of Nehemiah]

NEHUSHTA (Heb. 'brazen') c. 7 century BC. Daughter of Elnathan of Jerusalem, she became the wife of Jehoiakim, king of Judah, and the mother of Jehoiachin, his successor. [2 Kgs. 24:8]

NEHUM (Heb. 'comfort') 6 century BC. A leader of the Jewish community in Babylon who returned with Zerubbabel and settled in Jerusalem. Also known as Rehum. [Ezra 2:2; Neh. 7:7]

NEKODA (Heb. 'sheep owner') **1.** date unknown. Ancestor of a family of Temple servants who returned to Judah with Zerubbabel from exile in Babylon. [Ezra 2:48; Neh. 7:50]

2. date unknown. Ancestor of a family of Judah who returned with Zerubbabel from exile but who could not trace their family tree and therefore could not prove that they were Jews. [Ezra 2:60; Neh. 7:62]

NEMUEL (Heb. 'God's day') **1.** see JEMUEL

2. c. 13 century BC. A son of Eliab, he was a leader of the tribe of Reuben and the brother of Dathan and

Abiram who conspired with Korah against Moses and Aaron in the wilderness. [Num. 26:9]

NEPHEG (Heb. 'sprout') **1.** *c.* 13 century BC. A son of Izhar of the tribe of Levi, he was a brother of Korah who led the revolt against Moses in the wilderness. [Exod. 6:21]

2. *c.* 10 century BC. A son of King David, born to him in Jerusalem. [2 Sam. 5:15; 1 Chr. 3:7; 14:6]

NEPHISIM date unknown. Ancestor of a family who returned to Judah with Zerubbabel from Babylon. In the Book of Nehemiah he is called Nephushesim. [Ezra 2:50; Neh. 7:52]

NEPHUSHESIM *see* NEPHISIM

NER (Heb. 'lamp') *c.* 11 century BC. Grandfather or uncle of King Saul. In the First Book of Samuel Ner is described as the son of Abiel and a brother of Saul's father Kish, but in the First Book of Chronicles Ner is described as the father of Kish and the grandfather of Saul. His son was Abner, the commander of King Saul's army. [1 Sam. 14:50, 51; 26:5, 14; 2 Sam. 2:8, 12; 3:23, 25, 28, 37; 1 Kgs. 2:5, 32; 1 Chr. 8:33; 9:36, 39; 26:28]

NERGAL The god of sun and war worshipped by the Assyrians and Babylonians and taken over by the men of Cuth who were settled in Samaria after the destruc-tion of the northern kingdom of Israel in 721 BC. [2 Kgs. 17:30]

NERGAL-SHAREZER (Bab. 'Nergal preserve the king') *c.* 6 century BC. An officer of Nebuchadnezzar who sat down in the middle gate after the fall of Jerusalem. He carried out Nebuchadnezzar's order to release the prophet Jeremiah from jail and treat him well. His title was Rabmag (Babylonian 'most wise prince').

His name was found on a cuneiform tablet excavated at Erech. He succeeded to the throne after killing his brother-in-law Evil-meredoch, became king of Babylon, and reigned four years, 560-56 BC. [2 Kgs. 25:27; Jer. 39:3, 13, 14]

NERIAH (Heb. 'God is my light') *c.* 7 century BC. A priest of Judah who was the father of Baruch, disciple of the prophet Jeremiah. He may be identical with Neriah, son of Mahseiah whose son Seraiah was the leader of Judah to whom Jeremiah addressed his prophecies after the fall of Jerusalem. [Jer. 32:12, 16; 36:4, 8, 14, 32; 43:3, 6; 45:1; 51:59]

NETHANEL (Heb. 'gift of God') **1.** *c.* 13 century BC. Son of Zuar, Nathanel was appointed chief of the contingent of Issachar in the army of the children of Israel in the wilderness. [Num. 1:8; 2:5; 7:18, 23; 10:15]

above Gypsum relief from the palace of Tiglath-pileser III in Nimrod, 8th century BC, showing Assyrian soldiers carrying off the gods of a captured town.

289

2. *c.* 10 century BC. Fourth son of Jesse of the tribe of Judah and a brother of King David. [1 Chr. 2:14]

3. *c.* 10 century BC. A priest who blew a trumpet during the ceremony of bringing the Ark of God to Jerusalem in the reign of King David. [1 Chr. 15:24]

4. *c.* 10 century BC. A Levite, he was the father of Shemaiah, the scribe who kept the records of the service of the Levites in the Tabernacle in the reign of King David. [1 Chr. 24:6]

5. *c.* 10 century BC. A son of Obed-edom who, with his seven brothers, served as gatekeepers of the Tabernacle in the reign of King David. [1 Chr. 26:4]

6. *c.* 9 century BC. A leader of Judah sent by King Jehoshaphat to teach the Law of God to the people of Judah. [2 Chr. 17:7]

7. *c.* 7 century BC. A leader of the Levites in the reign of Josiah, king of Judah, who donated large quantities of cattle for the special Passover offering. [2 Chr. 35:9]

8. 5 century BC. A descendant of Pashhur, a priest of Judah, he divorced his non-Jewish wife in the time of Ezra. [Ezra 10:22]

9. 5 century BC. Son of Hilkiah and head of a priestly family who lived when Joiakim was high priest, towards the end of Nehemiah's lifetime. [Neh. 12:21]

10. 5 century BC. A Levite who played musical instruments at the service of dedication of the rebuilt walls of Jerusalem in the time of Nehemiah. [Neh. 12:36]

NETHANIAH (Heb. 'given by God') **1.** *c.* 10 century BC. A son of Asaph, chief musician to King David, he and his brothers played musical instruments under their father's direction. Nethaniah took the fifth turn of service in the Tabernacle. [1 Chr. 25:2, 12]

2. *c.* 9 century BC. One of the Levites sent by King Jehoshaphat to teach the Law of God to the people of Judah. [2 Chr. 17:8]

3. *c.* 7 century BC. Son of Shelemiah, he was the father of Jehudi, the court official who read out Jeremiah's prophecies to the princes of Judah. [Jer. 36:14]

4. 6 century BC. Son of Elishama and a descendant of the royal family of Judah, he was the father of Ishmael who assassinated Gedaliah, the governor of Judah. [2 Kgs. 25:23, 25; Jer. 40:8, 14, 15, 16; 41:1-18]

NEZIAH date unknown. Ancestor of a family of Temple servants who returned to Judah with Zerubbabel from exile in Babylon. [Ezra 2:54; Neh. 7:56]

NIBHAZ One of the gods worshipped by the people of Babylon who were settled in parts of Samaria by the Assyrians after the capture of the northern kingdom of Israel. [2 Kgs. 17:31]

NIMROD date unknown. Son of Cush and a grandson of Noah, he was renowned as a great hunter and ruled over a large kingdom in what is now Iraq. The prophet Micah refers to the destruction of the land of Nimrod by a Jewish king from Bethlehem. [Gen. 10:9; 1 Chr. 1:10; Mic. 5:6]

NIMSHI *c.* 9 century BC. Grandfather of Jehu, commander of the army of King Joram who seized the throne of Israel. Jehu is also referred to as the son of Nimshi. [1 Kgs. 19:16; 2 Kgs. 9:2, 20; 2 Chr. 22:7]

NISROCH An Assyrian god in whose temple Sennacherib, king of Assyria, was murdered by two of his sons. [2 Kgs. 19:37; Isa. 37:38]

NOADIAH (Heb. 'revealed by God') **1.** 5 century BC. Son of Binnui, he was a Levite who assisted the priest, Meremoth, in weighing the gold, silver and precious vessels which Ezra brought back from Babylon to Judah. [Ezra 8:33]

2. 5 century BC. A prophetess hired by Tobiah and

Persian silver cup from the 2nd millennium BC, showing hunters with bows and arrows.

Sanballat to discourage Nehemiah from completing the work of rebuilding the walls of Jerusalem after the return from exile in Babylon. [Neh. 6:14]

NOAH (Heb. 'rest') **1.** *c.* 2000 BC. The son of Lamech, Noah was the tenth generation in descent from Adam. He was a just and God-fearing man, but lived in a period when 'the earth was corrupt ... filled with violence.' (Gen. 6:11) God told Noah that He had decided to destroy all living creatures with a great flood. Noah was ordered to build a wooden ark with three decks, according to certain precise measurements. It was stocked with every kind of food.

Before the flood began, Noah went into the ark with his wife, his three sons Shem, Ham and Japheth and their wives, and a male and female of each living creature (in the case of the 'clean' animals there were seven pairs of each). The Bible gives Noah's age at this time as 'six hundred years old' (Gen. 7:6).

Then the rains came: 'on that day all the fountains of the great deep burst forth, and the windows of the heavens were opened.' (Gen. 7:11) It poured for forty days and forty nights and the floodwater rose until it covered the mountain tops. The ark floated on the surface with its strange cargo while all other life perished on earth.

17th-century Persian manuscript showing Noah's ark coming to rest on Mount Ararat.

Noah was ordered to build a wooden ark. Terracotta plaque showing a woodworker, early 2nd millennium B.C.

After five months the floodwater started to recede and in the seventh month the ark came to rest on the top of Mount Ararat. Noah waited several more months while the water subsided. He then opened the window of the ark and sent out a raven which 'went to and fro'. (Gen. 8:7) He also despatched a dove which did not find dry land and came back to the ark. A week later the dove went forth the second time and brought back an olive leaf in its beak. The third time the dove did not return, and this meant that the earth was dry. A year after they had entered it, Noah and his family and all the living creatures emerged from the ark.

Noah built an altar and made sacrifices to the Lord, in thankfulness for his deliverance. The Lord made a covenant with him that the flood would not be repeated; that Noah and his descendants would be fruitful and people the earth again; and that all the living creatures that had been preserved in the ark would also multiply and serve man for food. The cycle of nature, the Lord promised, would be restored: 'While the earth remains, seedtime and harvest, cold and heat, summer and winter, day and night, shall not cease.' (Gen. 8:22) Every time there was a rainbow in the clouds, it would serve as a token of God's covenant with Noah.

Noah cultivated a vineyard and became drunk on his own wine. While he lay naked in his tent, his son Ham came in and stared at his father in this undignified position. He told his two brothers, Shem and Japheth, who entered the tent backwards carrying a garment and covered up Noah with their faces averted. When

Noah aroused himself from his stupor, he cursed Ham and Ham's son Canaan, saying that they would be servants to their brethren.

Noah died at the age of nine hundred and fifty years.

If Adam was the first Founding Father, Noah was the second, for with him the human race, made a fresh start. He had another minor distinction as the first producer of wine recorded in the Bible.

Noah's story is told with such charm and freshness of detail that he and his family, the wooden ark, the animals who went in two by two, and the dove with an olive leaf in its beak, have become the nursery fables and toys of countless generations of children.

The Hebrews believed that the races of the ancient Near East were each descended from one or other of Noah's three sons. Shem was the ancestor of the Semites inhabiting the fertile crescent and the Arabian desert. From Japheth came the Indo-European peoples to the north and west. The Hamites dwelt mainly in Africa (Egypt and Ethiopia). These three groups were re- presented in the Land of Canaan itself: the Hebrews were Semites, the Philistines in the coastal area were Western invaders identified with Japheth, and the fore-father of the local Canaanites was Canaan, the son of Ham.

The story of a great flood that destroyed most of mankind recurs in the folklore of primitive tribes in different parts of the world. The account in the Bible has many similarities with a Babylonian version appearing in the epic Gilgamesh, written on clay tablets in the 7th century BC, but believed to be a copy of a much earlier original. It is possible that the Babylonian story had its origin in a flood disaster in southern Mesopotamia in the 3rd millennium BC. [Gen. 5-10; 1 Chr. 1:4]
2. *c.* 13 century BC. A daughter of Zelophehad who claimed a share of her father's estate before Moses, since her father had no sons. [Num. 26:33; 27:1; 36:11; Josh. 17:3]

Babylonian cuneiform tablet telling the story of the flood: from Nineveh, 8th-6th centuries BC.

NOBAH (Heb. 'barking') date unknown. A leader of the tribe of Manasseh who settled east of the river Jordan, captured the region of Kenath and named it after himself. [Num. 32:42; Judg. 8:11]

NOGAH (Heb. 'bright') *c.* 10 century BC. One of the sons of King David, born to him in Jerusalem. [1 Chr. 3:7; 14:6]

NOHAH (Heb. 'rest') *c.* 16 century BC. Fourth son of Benjamin and a grandson of Jacob and Rachel. [1 Chr. 8:2]

NUN (Heb. 'fish') *c.* 13 century BC. Father of Joshua. *see* JOSHUA **1.**

O

OBADIAH (Heb. 'servant of God') **1.** date unknown. A son of Izrahiah, he and his five brothers were leaders of the tribe of Issachar and mighty warriors. [1 Chr. 7:3]
2. *c.* 10 century BC. One of the eleven army commanders of the tribe of Gad who left the army of King Saul and rallied to David at Ziklag. [1 Chr. 12:9]
3. *c.* 10 century BC. Father of Ishmaiah who was made ruler of the tribe of Zebulun during the reign of King David. [1 Chr. 27:19]
4. *c.* 9 century BC. The head of the royal household of King Ahab of Israel. He was a pious man and when Jezebel, the king's wife who was a worshipper of Baal, had begun to kill off the priests of the Lord, Obadiah had hidden a hundred in caves and they had survived. During a famine, Ahab told Obadiah that they would have to find pasture for the livestock or they would die. He went in one direction and sent Obadiah in another. Obadiah met the prophet Elijah and recognizing him, fell on his face in front of him. Elijah told Obadiah to take him to Ahab but the servant was terrified, knowing that Ahab had placed a price on the head of the prophet and would kill him for having spoken to him. But Eiljah insisted and Obadiah took the message to the king and Ahab agreed to meet Elijah. [1 Kgs. 18]
5. date unknown. Son of Azel of the tribe of Benjamin and a descendant of King Saul. [1 Chr. 8:38; 9:44]
6. *c.* 9 century BC. A leader of Judah who was sent by King Jehoshaphat to teach the Law of God in the cities of Judah. [2 Chr. 17:7]
7. 7 century BC. A Levite descended from Merari who was a supervisor of the work of repairing the Temple during the reign of Josiah, king of Judah. [2 Chr. 34:12]
8. 5 century BC. A leader of the tribe of Judah descended from Zerubbabel and the royal house of King David. [1 Chr. 3:21]
9. *c.* 5 century BC. Son of Shemaiah, and a descendant of Jeduthun, he was one of the first Levites who settled in Jerusalem following the return from exile in Babylon. Also called Abda. [1 Chr. 9:16; Neh. 11:17]
10. *c.* 5 century BC. Son of Jehiel and a descendant of Joab, he was a leader of Judah who returned to Jerusalem from exile in Babylon and brought with him two hundred and eighteen men. [Ezra 8:9]

11. 5 century BC. A priest of Judah who signed the covenant to observe the Laws of God in the days of Nehemiah. [Neh. 10:5]
12. *c.* 5 century BC. A Levite who was a porter at the gates of the Temple in Jerusalem in the time of Nehemiah. [Neh. 12:25]
13. *c.* 5 century BC. Post-exilic Hebrew prophet. The Book of the prophet Obadiah is the shortest one in the Old Testament: a single chapter of twenty-one verses.

The prophet Obadiah, from an anonymous Italian series of drawings of famous men, *c.* 1450.

Nothing is known of the personal history of the author, though the text suggests he probably lived in the 5th century BC, some time after the fall of Jerusalem (587 BC).

His oracle is directed against the Edomites, who moved up from the Dead Sea area and occupied the depopulated southern part of Judah, up to Hebron.

Obadiah fiercely denounces them for their behaviour in the darkest hour of his people.:

'For the violence done to your brother Jacob, shame shall cover you, and you shall be cut off for ever ... on the day that strangers carried off his wealth, and foreigners entered his gates and cast lots for Jerusalem, you were like one of them ... you should not have looted his goods in the day of his calamity. You should not have stood at the parting of the ways to cut off his fugitives ...' (Obad. 1:10, 11, 13, 14)

Obadiah looked forward to the day of the Lord, when the Hebrew nation would be restored to its independence and its former territory, and the heathen nations that oppressed them would be destroyed. On that day: 'The house of Jacob shall be a fire, and the house of Joseph a flame, and the house of Esau stubble ... and there shall be no survivor to the house of Esau.' (Obad. 1:18)

After that day of judgment 'the kingdom shall be the Lord's.' (Obad. 1:21) [Book of Obadiah]

OBAL *see* EBAL **2.**

OBED (Heb. 'servant') **1.** *c.* 11 century BC. The son of Boaz and Ruth, he was the father of Jesse and the grandfather of King David. [Ruth 4:17, 21; 1 Chr. 2:12]
2. *c.* 10 century BC. One of the chosen warriors in the army of King David famous for his bravery. [1 Chr. 11:47]
3. *c.* 10 century BC. A son of Shemaiah who was a porter at the gates of the Tabernacle during the reign of King David. [1 Chr. 26:7]
4. date unknown. Son of Ephlal of the tribe of Judah and the father of Jehu. [1 Chr. 2:37, 38]
5. *c.* 9 century BC. Father of Azariah, one of the five army commanders of Judah who, on the orders of the high priest Jehoiada, crowned Joash king of Judah and executed Joash's grandmother Athaliah, who had usurped the throne. [2 Chr. 23:1]

OBED-EDOM (Heb. 'servant of Edom') **1.** *c.* 10 century BC. Obed-edom was a Philistine from Gath who lived near Jerusalem in the time of King David. After the death of one of the Israelites for touching the Ark, David left it for three months in the house of Obed-edom: 'and the Lord blessed Obed-edom and all his household.' (2 Sam. 6:11) Obed-edom helped carry the Ark from his house to Jerusalem and later was appointed one of its guards. He had five sons, who also tended the Ark. [2 Sam. 6:10-12; 1 Chr. 13:13-14; 15:18, 21, 24; 16:38; 26:4, 8, 15; 2 Chr. 25:24]
2. 10 century BC. Son of Jeduthun, he was a gatekeeper for the Ark in the time of King David. He also played a musical instrument at the celebration when the Ark was brought to Jerusalem. [1 Chr. 15:18, 24; 16:5, 38; 26:4, 8, 15]
3. 8 century BC. A servant in charge of the gold and silver vessels in the Temple, he was captured by King Joash of Israel together with the vessels. [2 Chr. 25:24]

OBIL (Heb. 'camel-keeper') *c.* 10 century BC. The Ishmaelite officer of King David responsible for the king's camels. [1 Chr. 27:30]

OCHRAN (Heb. 'disturber') *c.* 13 century BC. Father of Pagiel and a member of the tribe of Asher. [Num. 1:13; 2:27; 7:72, 77; 10:26]

ODED (Heb. 'restoring') **1.** *c.* 10 century BC. Father of Azariah, the prophet who counselled King Asa of Judah. [2 Chr. 15:1-8]
2. *c.* 8 century BC. A prophet. After King Pekah invaded and defeated the kingdom of Judah, he carried off to Israel a large number of captives. Oded arrived in Samaria and intervened on behalf of the captives. Several of the leaders listened to him, and arranged for the prisoners to be treated well and returned. [2 Chr. 28:9-15]

OG *c.* 13 century BC. Og was the king of Bashan, east of the Sea of Galilee. He fought against Moses at Edrei, one of his main cities, was unexpectedly defeated, 'and they possessed his land' (Num. 21:35). This area was later assigned to the tribe of Manasseh.

In the Book of Deuteronomy they talk of his enormous iron bedstead (probably a black basalt tomb) which could be seen in Rabbath-ammon, the capital of Ammon. [Num. 21:33; 32:33; Deut. 1:4; 3:1-13; 4:47; 29:7; 31:4; Josh. 2:10; 9:10; 12:4; 13:12, 30, 31; 1 Kgs. 4:19; Neh. 9:22; Ps. 135:11; 136:20]

OHAD (Heb. 'strength') *c.* 16 century BC. Son of Simeon and a grandson of Jacob with whom he went down to Egypt. [Gen. 46:10; Exod. 6:15]

OHEL (Heb. 'tent') 6 century BC. Son of Zerubbabel who led the return from Babylon and a descendant of King David. [1 Chr. 3:20]

OHOLAH (Heb. 'tent') date unknown. Sister of Oholibah and a harlot whose name was used by the

Woman painting her face: fragment of the Egyptian so-called 'Obscene' Papyrus, 16th-11th centuries B C.

Oholiab

prophet Ezekiel to describe Samaria. [Ezek. 23:4, 11]

OHOLIAB (Heb. 'father is my tent') *c.* 13 century BC. Son of Ahisamach of the tribe of Dan, he was appointed assistant to Bezalel by Moses in the construction of the Tabernacle in the wilderness. [Exod. 31:6; 35:34; 36:1, 2; 38:23]

OHOLIBAH (Heb. 'my tent is in her') date unknown. Sister of Oholah and a harlot whose name was used by the prophet Ezekiel to describe Jerusalem. [Ezek. 23:4, 11]

OHOLIBAMAH (Heb. 'my tent is in them') **1.** *c.* 17 century BC. A wive of Esau, she was the daughter of Anah and the granddaughter of Zibeon the Hivite. [Gen. 36:2, 5, 14, 18]

2. date unknown. A leader of Edom descended from Esau. [Gen. 36:41; 1 Chr. 1:52]

OMAR (Heb. 'speaker') *c.* 16 century BC. Second son of Eliphaz, and a grandson of Esau, he was a chieftain of an Edomite clan. [Gen. 36:11, 15; 1 Chr. 1:36]

OMRI (Heb. 'pupil') **1.** date unknown. Son of Becher and a grandson of Benjamin, he and his brothers were leaders of the tribe and mighty warriors. [1 Chr. 7:8]

2. *c.* 10 century BC. Son of Michael, he was made ruler over the tribe of Issachar during the reign of King David. [1 Chr. 27:18]

3. Sixth king of Israel after the monarchy split, he reigned 885-74 BC. Omri was one of the ablest and most successful of the Israelite kings. Yet the Bible takes only brief and unsympathetic notice of him. The royal house he founded, continued by his son Ahab, was held in disfavour because of its ties with the pagan Phoenicians, and the religious controversies that swirled around the prophets Elijah and Elisha.

Omri first appeared as commander of the armed forces of Israel during the brief reign of Elah. While engaged in the siege of the Philistine town of Gibbethon, Omri was informed that a senior army officer, Zimri, had murdered the king and his household and seized the throne. Proclaimed king by his men, Omri immediately marched back and occupied the capital, Tirzah. With the collapse of his bid for power, Zimri set part of the palace on fire and was burnt to death.

The kingdom was now flung into a protracted fight for the succession between the supporters of Omri and those of Tibni son of Ginath, and it ended only with the latter's death.

The kingdom had been weakened by internal strife and lost much territory. As a wise general, Omri freed his hands for the struggle with Aram-Damascus (Syria) by making peace with Judah. This terminated the chronic border warfare between the two Hebrew kingdoms since the death of Solomon.

Omri secured another important ally by renewing the friendship with Tyre on the Phoenician coast. This alignment was strengthened by the marriage of Omri's

Tel el-Farah – the biblical Tirzah – showing houses from the time of King Omri.

crown prince Ahab to Jezebel, the daughter of Ethbaal, king of Sidon.

Omri regained lost territory east of the Jordan, and reconquered the kingdom of Moab, the fertile plateau east of the Dead Sea. This is confirmed by the stele of the Moabite king Mesha. It states that 'as for Omri, king of Israel, he humbled Moab many years . . .'

There was a growth of security and affluence in Israel in the period of Omri and his son Ahab, as well as in the kingdom of Judah. The palace at Hazor, the extensive stables at Megiddo, and the thick walls and the elaborate tunnels to external water springs at both places probably date from this age.

Omri's greatest achievement was the construction of the new capital, Samaria, later completed by Ahab. For the first six years of his reign Omri had continued to use the capital of Tirzah in the same vicinity. Samaria

Excavations at Hazor showing the 9th-century BC Israelite storehouse, with columns and casemate walls dating back to the 10th century.

was constructed on a prominent, solitary hill eight miles north-west of Shechem (Nablus) with a spectacular view to the sea twenty-three miles away. It commanded the ancient road to the coastal plain through the broad Vale of Barley. The site was bought from a certain Shemer for two talents of silver. The name Samaria (Hebrew 'Shomron') was supposed to be derived from Shemer, though it may also come from the Hebrew word for a watchtower. In due course the whole area became known as Samaria, and its inhabitants as Samaritans.

Various motives for the new capital could be attributed to Omri. He was conscious of the lustre of Jerusalem as the centre of Hebrew politics, religion and culture,

and wanted his own kingdom to have a capital worthy of comparison with that of Judah. No doubt too, he felt the compulsion of most energetic and affluent monarchs to perpetuate their fame in splendid buildings. Physical security also played a part – the hill Omri bought was very steep on three sides, and could be made almost impregnable. Recent excavations have revealed the remains of the great stone walls, the palaces, courtiers' homes, storehouses, large reservoirs and granaries dating back to Omri's period.

Omri died after twelve years on the throne and was buried in Samaria. He was succeeded by his son Ahab. His reign had been sufficiently important for the king-

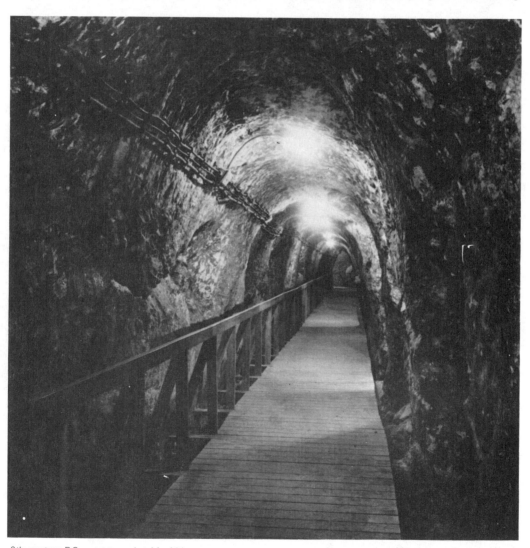

9th-century BC water tunnel at Megiddo.

The hills of Samaria. It was in this region, on a free-standing hill, that Omri established his capital.

dom of Israel to be referred to in documents of surrounding countries for more than a century afterwards as 'the house of Omri'. [1 Kgs. 16:16-28; 2 Kgs. 8:26; 2 Chr. 22:2; Mic. 6:16]

4. *c.* 6 century BC. Son of Imri, he was the father of Ammihud and his grandson Uthai was one of the first men of Judah to settle in Jerusalem after the return from exile in Babylon. [1 Chr. 9:4]

ON (Heb. 'strength') *c.* 13 century BC. Son of Peleth and a chief of the tribe of Reuben, he joined Korah's revolt in the wilderness against the leadership of Moses and Aaron. [Num. 16:1]

ONAM (Heb. 'strong') **1.** date unknown. Son of Shobal and the grandson of Seir, the Horite, he was a leader of an Edomite clan. [Gen. 36:23; 1 Chr. 1:40]
2. date unknown. Son of Jerahmeel and Atarah, and a leader of the tribe of Judah. [1 Chr. 2:26, 28]

ONAN *c.* 16 century BC. A son of Judah. Onan was the second son of Jacob's son Judah and of Bath-shua, a Canaanite woman. According to Jewish law, Judah told Onan that he had to marry his brother Er's widow Tamar and have a son by her that would carry on the line. Knowing the child would not be regarded as his, Onan spilled his seed on the ground. The Lord was displeased and slew him.

This story gave rise to the word 'onanism'. [Gen. 38:4-10; 46:12; Num. 26:19; 1 Chr. 2:3]

OPHIR (Heb. 'fruitful') date unknown. Son of Joktan and a descendant of Shem. [Gen. 10:29; 1 Chr. 1:23]

OPHRAH (Heb. 'fawn') *c.* 12 century BC. Son of Meonothai and grandson of Othniel, he and his father were leaders of the tribe of Judah. [1 Chr. 4:14]

OREB (Heb. 'raven') *c.* 12 century BC. A leader of Midian slain by the men of Ephraim, after Gideon had defeated them. The rock on which Oreb was killed became known as the 'rock of Oreb' and Oreb's head was brought to Gideon. [Judg. 7:24, 25; 8:3; Ps. 83:11]

OREN (Heb. 'pine') date unknown. Son of Jerahmeel and a leader of the tribe of Judah. [1 Chr. 2:25]

ORNAN *see* ARAUNAH

ORPAH *c.* 11 century BC. Orpah was a Moabitess who married Chilion the son of Naomi when he and his family lived in Moab. After Chilion died, and Naomi returned to Bethlehem, Orpah remained in Moab. [Ruth 1:4, 14]

OSORKON I *see* PHARAOH **7.**

OTHNI *c.* 10 century BC. A son of Shemaiah, he and his brothers, like their father, were gatekeepers of the Tabernacle. [1 Chr. 26:7]

OTHNIEL (Heb. 'my strength is God') *c.* 13-12 centuries BC. An Israelite judge. Othniel was the son of Kenaz and the nephew of Caleb the son of Jephunneh, whose daughter Achsah he was given in marriage as a reward for capturing the town of Kiriath-sepher.

Later, Othniel defeated Cushun-rishafaim the king of Mesopotamia who had oppressed the Israelites for eight years. Afterwards Othniel judged the people for forty peaceful years. [Josh. 15:17; Judg. 1:13; 3:9-11; 1 Chr. 4:13; 27:15]

OZEM 1. *c.* 10 century BC. Sixth son of Jesse and a brother of King David. [1 Chr. 2:15]
2. date unknown. Son of Jerahmeel and a leader of Judah. [1 Chr. 2:25]

OZNI *see* EZBON **1.**

P

PAARAI (Heb. 'opening') 10 century BC. The Arbite warrior in the army of King David noted for outstanding bravery. Also called Naarai. [2 Sam. 23:35; 1 Chr. 11:37]

PADON (Heb. 'escape') date unknown. Ancestor of a family of Temple servants whose descendants returned with Zerubbabel to Judah from exile in Babylon. [Ezra 2:44; Neh. 7:47]

PAGIEL (Heb. 'allotted by God') *c.* 13 century BC. Son of Ochran, he was appointed by Moses to count the tribe of Asher for military service and led the contingent of the tribe in the army of the children of Israel. [Num. 1:13; 2:27; 7:72, 77; 10:26]

PAHATH-MOAB (Heb. 'governor of Moab') **1.** date unknown. A leader of Israel and the ancestor of many who returned to Jerusalem from captivity in Babylon. [Ezra 2:6; 8:4; 10:30; Neh. 3:11; 7:11]
2. 5 century BC. One of the leaders who signed the solemn covenant in the time of Nehemiah. [Neh. 10:14]

PALAL (Heb. 'God will judge') 5 century BC. Son of Uzai, he helped rebuild the walls of Jerusalem in the days of Nehemiah and repaired the tower of the king's palace. [Neh. 3:25]

PALLU (Heb. 'famous') *c.* 16 century BC. A son of Reuben and a grandson of Jacob, Pallu was the father of Eliab, ancestor of Dathan and Abiram who joined Korah's revolt against Moses and Aaron. [Gen. 46:9; Exod. 6:14; Num. 26:5, 8; 1 Chr. 5:3]

PALTI (Heb. 'deliverance') **1.** 13 century BC. Son of Raphu of the tribe of Benjamin, he was one of the twelve men chosen by Moses to spy out the Promised Land. [Num. 13:9]
2. 10 century BC. Son of Laish from Gallim, he married King Saul's daughter Michal after Saul had driven away her legitimate husband David. When David became king, he forced Ishbosheth to take Michal from Palti and restore her to him. Palti wept at Michal's departure and followed her on her way to David, until ordered to return. Also called Paltiel. [1 Sam. 25:44; 2 Sam. 3:15]

PALTIEL (Heb. 'deliverance by God') **1.** *c.* 13 century BC. Son of Azzan and a member of the tribe of Issachar, he was chosen to make the division of

the land allocated to his tribe. [Num. 34:26]
2. *see* PALTI **2.**

PALTITE *see* HELEZ **2.**

PARMASHTA (Pers. 'stronger') 5 century BC. A son of Haman who conspired to kill all the Jews in Persia during the reign of Ahasuerus. [Esther 9:9]

PARNACH 13 century BC. Father of Elizaphan who represented the tribe of Zebulun and aided Moses in the division of the land of Israel among the tribes. [Num. 34:25]

PAROSH (Heb. 'flea') **1.** date unknown. Ancestor of a large family of Judah, some of whom returned with Zerubbabel and others with Ezra from exile in Babylon. Some helped Nehemiah to rebuild the walls of Jerusalem and joined him in signing the covenant to observe the Law. Several are recorded as having divorced their non-Jewish wives in the time of Ezra. [Ezra 2:3; 8:3; 10:25; Neh. 3:25; 7:8]
2. *c.* 5 century BC. One of the leaders of Judah in the days of Nehemiah who signed the covenant to observe the Laws of God. [Neh. 10:14]

PARSHANDATHA (Pers. 'prayer given') *c.* 5 century BC. A son of Haman who was chief minister of Ahasuerus, king of Persia, and who conspired to kill all the Jews in the land. [Esther 9:7]

PARUAH (Heb. 'gloomy') *c.* 10 century BC. Father of Jehoshaphat who was in charge of supplies to the palace for one month a year during the reign of King Solomon. [1 Kgs. 4:17]

PASACH (Heb. 'passed over') date unknown. One of the three sons of Japhlet and a leader of the tribe of Asher. [1 Chr. 7:33]

PASEAH (Heb. 'lame') **1.** date unknown. Son of Eshton, an early leader of the tribe of Judah. [1 Chr. 4:12]
2. date unknown. Ancestor of a family who returned with Zerubbabel to Judah from exile in Babylon. [Ezra 2:49; Neh. 7:51]
3. 5 century BC. Father of Joiada who helped repair the walls of Jerusalem in the time of Nehemiah. [Neh. 3:6]

PASHHUR (Heb. 'freedom') **1.** date unknown. Ancestor of a priestly family who returned with Zerubbabel to Judah from exile in Babylon; one descendant was a signatory to the solemn covenant, and others divorced their non-Jewish wives in the time of Ezra. [Ezra 2:38; 10:22; Neh. 7:41]

2. 6 century BC. Son of Immer and chief priest in the Temple, he was angered by Jeremiah's prophecy of the defeat of Judah, and had him put in stocks near the Temple area for a day. When he let him out, Jeremiah cursed him with the name 'Terror on every side' (Jer. 20:3) and prophesied that when Judah would fall to

Ostraca from the excavations at Arad, 9th-6th centuries BC, with the name 'Pashhur' written in Hebrew.

the Babylonians, Pashhur would be taken into captivity and die in exile in Babylon. [Jer. 20:1-6]

3. 6 century BC. A contemporary of Pashhur **1.**, he was the son of Malchiah. He was sent by King Zedekiah of Judah to ask Jeremiah what the outcome of Nebuchadnezzar's attack on Jerusalem would be. Jeremiah gave them a message of unrelieved gloom. After this Pashhur joined a group of men who complained to Zedekiah that Jeremiah was undermining the morale not only of the citizens of Jerusalem but also of the army. The king gave them permission to deal with the prophet as they saw fit. They tied him up with rope and lowered him into a empty water cistern so 'Jeremiah sank in the mire' (Jer. 38:6), but was later rescued by Ebed-melech the Ethiopian. Pashhur's descendants returned to Jerusalem from Babylonian exile. [1 Chr. 9:12; Neh. 11:12; Jer. 21:1, 3]

4. *c.* 6 century BC. Father of Gedaliah, one of the leaders of Judah who threw the prophet Jeremiah into a well. [Jer. 38:1]

5. *c.* 5 century BC. A leader of Judah who signed the covenant to observe the Laws of God in the time of Nehemiah. [Neh. 10:3]

PATHRUSIM (Egypt. 'from the southern land') date unknown. Son of Egypt and a grandson of Ham. [Gen. 10:14]

PEDAHEL (Heb. 'saved') *c.* 13 century BC. Son of Ammihud of the tribe of Naphtali, he was the leader of the tribe in the time of Moses selected to divide the part of Israel given to Naphtali among the members of the tribe. [Num. 34:28]

PEDAHZUR (Heb. 'saved by the rock') *c.* 13 century BC. A leader of the tribe of Manasseh, he was the father of Gamaliel who was responsible for numbering the tribe of Manasseh for service in the army of Israel in the wilderness. [Num. 1:10; 2:20; 7:54, 59; 10:23]

PEDAIAH (Heb. 'saved by God') **1.** *c.* 10 century BC. Father of Joel who was made ruler of the half-tribe of Manasseh west of the river Jordan in the reign of King David. [1 Chr. 27:20]

2. 7 century BC. Father of Zebidah, who married Josiah king of Judah and gave birth to a son, Jehoiakim. [2 Kgs. 23:36]

3. *see* SHEALTIEL

4. 5 century BC. Son of Parosh, he helped repair the walls of Jerusalem in the days of Nehemiah after the return from exile in Babylon. [Neh. 3:25]

5. date unknown. Son of Kolaiah and the father of Joed, he was an ancestor of Sallu, one of the first Benjaminites to settle in Judah after the return from exile in Babylon. [Neh. 11:7]

6. 5 century BC. A leader who stood at the side of Ezra when he read the Law of God to the people of Judah in the market-place. [Neh. 8:4]

7. 5 century BC. One of the four trustworthy Levites appointed by Nehemiah to distribute offerings among the Levites. [Neh. 13:13]

PEKAH (Heb. 'open-eyed') Eighteenth king of Israel after the monarchy split, he reigned 737-2 BC. Pekah, the son of Remaliah, was an army officer who carried out a coup with fifty Gileadite troopers, murdered King Pekahiah and seized the throne.

He made common cause with Israel's traditional enemy Aram-Damascus (Syria) against the expanding Assyrian power that threatened them both. Pekah and Rezin, king of Aram, tried to draw the kingdom of Judah into the coalition. Ahaz, king of Judah, rejected these overtures. With the support of Rezin, Pekah then invaded and defeated Judah, carrying off to Israel a large number of captives. They were returned due to the intervention of a prophet called Oded.

In 733 BC the Assyrian forces of Tiglath-pileser III invaded Israel from the north, breaking through the line of forts guarding the upper Jordan valley, and occupying Galilee and the coastal region. The invaders annexed the occupied territories and converted them into three Assyrian provinces, with governors stationed at Megiddo (for the Galilee), Dor (for the coast), and Gilead, east of the Jordan river. Many of the inhabitants of these territories were taken away to Assyria as captives. All that was left intact of Israel was the capital

Samaria and the hill region of Ephraim round it. This remnant of Israelite independence was to be finally wiped out a decade later.

Pekah did not survive the disastrous outcome of his challenge to Assyrian power. He was murdered and succeeded by Hoshea, son of Elah, who reverted to the policy of submission to Assyria.

The excavations at Hazor and Megiddo show extensive destruction dating from the same period, probably caused by the Assyrians. [2 Kgs. 15:25-32, 37; 16:1, 5; 2 Chr. 28:6; Isa. 7:1]

PEKAHIAH (Heb. 'God watches') Seventeenth king of Israel after the monarchy split, he reigned 738-7 BC. Pekahiah succeeded his father Menahem on the throne of Israel at a time when the kingdom was rapidly declining. It was internally unstable and already sucked into the orbit of Assyria, to which heavy tribute was paid. Pekahiah maintained this submissive policy for two years until he was murdered and supplanted by one of his army officers, Pekah, the son of Remaliah. [2 Kgs. 15:22-6]

PELAIAH (Heb. 'distinguished') **1.** 5 century BC. A Levite who explained the Law of God to the people of Judah after Ezra had read it in the market-place. He later signed the covenant to observe the Laws of the Lord in the time of Nehemiah. [Neh. 8:7; 10:10]

2. date unknown. Son of Elioenai of the tribe of Judah, he was a descendant of King David. [1 Chr. 3:24]

PELELIAH (Heb. 'judged') *c.* 5 century BC. Ancestor of a priest who returned from exile in Babylon and lived in Jerusalem in the time of Nehemiah. [Neh. 11:12]

PELATIAH (Heb. 'saved') **1.** *c.* 8 century BC. Son of Ishi, during the reign of King Hezekiah of Judah he commanded a force of 500 Simeonites who drove out the Amalekites from the hill-country of Seir south-east of the Dead Sea and settled there. [1 Chr. 4:42]

2. 6 century BC. Son of Benaiah, Pelatiah was one of two leaders in Jerusalem mentioned by name among the twenty-five who appeared in the vision of the prophet Ezekiel standing at the city gate and giving false counsel to the people. Ezekiel prophesied that Jerusalem would be destroyed, and in the vision Pelatiah dropped dead. [Ezek. 11:1-13]

3. 6 century BC. Son of Hananiah and a grandson of Zerubbabel who led the return from Babylon, he was a descendant of King David. [1 Chr. 3:21]

4. 5 century BC. A leader of Judah in the time of Nehemiah who signed the solemn covenant. [Neh. 10:22]

PELEG (Heb. 'divided') date unknown. Elder son of Eber and a great-grandson of Shem, he was called Peleg 'for in his days the earth was divided'. [Gen. 10:25; 11:16-19; 1 Chr. 1:19, 25]

PELET (Heb. 'refuge') **1.** date unknown. Son of Jahdai of the tribe of Judah and a descendant of Caleb son of Hezron. [1 Chr. 2:47]

Excavations at Hazor showing the level of building at the time of Pekah, king of Israel 737-2 BC.

2. 11 century BC. Son of Azmaveth, he and his brother Jeziel were among the Benjaminites to desert King Saul and rally to David at Ziklag. [1 Chr. 12:3]

PELETH 1. *c.* 13 century BC. A leader of the tribe of Reuben and the father of On, who joined Korah's rebellion against Moses and Aaron in the wilderness. [Num. 16:1]

2. date unknown. Son of Jonathan and a descendant of Jerahmeel, a leader of the tribe of Judah. [1 Chr. 2:33]

PELONITE *see* HELEZ **2.**

PENINNAH (Heb. 'pearl') 11 century BC. A wife of Elkanah, the father of the prophet Samuel, Peninnah had several children. Elkanah favoured his other wife, Hannah, even though she was childless until the birth of Samuel. Peninnah, jealous of Hannah, scoffed at her because of her childlessness. [1 Sam. 1:2, 4]

PENUEL (Heb. 'face of God') **1.** date unknown. An early leader of the tribe of Judah, he was the father of Gedor. [1 Chr. 4:4]

2. date unknown. Son of Shashak he was a leader of the tribe of Benjamin living in Jerusalem. [1 Chr. 8:25]

PERESH (Heb. 'clung') date unknown. Son of Machir and his wife Maachah, and grandson of Manasseh, his descendants settled in Gilead east of the river Jordan. [1 Chr. 7:16]

PEREZ (Heb. 'a breach') *c.* 16 century BC. A twin son of Judah and Tamar. Perez and his twin brother Zerah were conceived as the result of an incestuous relationship between Judah and his daughter-in-law Tamar. At the birth Zerah's hand appeared first and the midwife tied a scarlet thread round the wrist. But to the midwife's surprise Perez was born first. Later he had two sons and founded a tribe called Pharzites. Boaz the husband of Ruth was a descendant of his, as was King David. [Gen. 38:29; 46:12; Num. 26:20-1; Ruth 4:12, 18; 1 Chr. 2:4, 5; 4:1; 9:4; 27:3; Neh. 11:4-6]

PERIDA *see* PERUDA

PERIZZITES (Heb. 'villagers') An ancient tribe in Canaan at the time of the conquest by the Children of Israel under Joshua. Their land was taken over by the tribes of Ephraim and Manasseh. [Gen. 13:7; Josh. 17:15]

PERUDA (Heb. 'gay') 10 century BC. A servant of King Solomon, his descendants were among the first men of Judah to return with Zerubbabel from exile in Babylon. Also called Perida. [Ezra 2:55; Neh. 7:57]

PETHAHIAH (Heb. 'freed by God') **1.** 10 century BC. A priest in the days of King David who took the nineteenth turn of service in the Tabernacle in Jerusalem. [1 Chr. 24:16]

2. 5 century BC. A Levite who divorced his non-Jewish wife in the time of Ezra. Also among the Levites who called on the people of Judah to confess their sins and praise God on the public fast day proclaimed by Ezra. [Ezra 10:23; Neh. 9:5]

3. 5 century BC. Son of Meshezabel and a leader of the tribe of Judah, he was chief adviser to the king of Persia in the days of Nehemiah, on matters relating to the exiles of Judah who returned to Jerusalem. [Neh. 11:24]

PETHUEL (Heb. 'vision') *c.* 5 century BC. Father of the prophet Joel. [Joel 1:1]

PEULLTHAI (Heb. 'my works') 10 century BC. Son of Obed-edom and a gatekeeper of the Tabernacle in Jerusalem in the reign of King David. [1 Chr. 26:5]

PHARAOH (Egypt. 'the great house') **1.** *c.* 18-16 centuries BC. The Pharaoh who wished to take over Abraham's wife Sarah, who had been passed off as his sister, cannot be identified as the date is conjectural. [Gen. 12:14-20]

2. *c.* 16 century BC. The Pharaoh at whose court Joseph rose to eminence may have been an early ruler of the Hyksos dynasty (1720-1450 BC) but cannot be identified by name. [Gen. 37:36; 39:1; 40-1; 42:15, 45; 46:33, 47; 50:4-6]

above Scarab of Rameses II, found at Ashdod.

right Stone statue of Rameses II, 1301-1234 BC.

3. Pharaoh Rameses II (1301-234 BC) may have been the 'new king over Egypt, who did not know Joseph' (Exod. 1:8), who started to use the Israelites as forced labour for building the store-cities of Pithom and Rameses. [Exod. 1:8; 11-14; 5:4-19; 10:11, 16, 28]

4. *c.* 11 century BC. An unknown Pharaoh in the reign of King David (1025-970 BC) who gave political asylum to Hadad, a young Edomite prince. Pharaoh gave him a house and land, and the sister of his principal wife in marriage. [1 Kgs. 11:17-22]

5. The Pharaoh whose daughter was married to King Solomon (970-31 BC) must have been one of the lesser known rulers of Egypt in the last part of the 21st dynasty that ended in 945 BC. [1 Kgs. 3:1; 7:8; 9:16, 24; 11:1; Chr. 8:11; S. of S. 1:9]

6. Pharaoh Shishak I [Sheshonk] (945-25 BC) invaded the kingdoms of Judah and Israel in the fifth year of the reign of Rehoboam, king of Judah, which would be *c.* 926 BC. Jerusalem was spared by payment of a heavy ransom. The names of the towns occupied by Shishak are inscribed in the wall of the Temple of Karnak in Egypt. It was to his court that Jeroboam, later king of Israel, fled during the reign of Solomon. [1 Kgs. 11:40; 14:25, 26; 2 Chr. 12:2-9]

7. Pharaoh Osorkon I, successor to Shishak, may have been 'Zerah the Ethiopian' who invaded Judah from

Head of the Pharaoh Tirhakah,
c. 675 BC, from Thebes.

Green basalt statue of Shishak,
probably from Karnak. His position
indicates that he was originally
placed before a statue of Osiris.

the south about 900 BC and was repulsed by King Asa (911-870 BC). [2 Chr. 14:9-15; 2 Chr. 16:8]

8. Pharaoh Tirhakah (690-64 BC) of the 25th (Nubian) Dynasty, was 'Tirhakah, king of Ethiopia', whom Sennacherib went off to fight during the siege of Lachish in the reign of King Hezekiah of Judah. [2 Kgs. 18:21; 19:9; Isa. 19:11; 30:2-7]

9. Pharaoh Neco (609-593 BC) defeated and killed King Josiah of Judah at Megiddo in 609 BC and was himself defeated by the Babylonian crown prince Nebuchadnezzar at Carchemish in 605 BC. [2 Kgs. 23:28-35; 2 Chr. 35:20; 36:4]

10. Pharaoh Hophra (Apries) (588-66 BC) was defeated in 587 BC by the Babylonian army under Nebuchadnezzar, who temporarily raised the siege of Jerusalem to encounter the Egyptians. [Jer. 37:5, 11; 44:30]

PHICOL (Heb. 'strong') *c.* 17 century BC. The army commander of Abimelech who was king over an area of southern Israel in the days of Abraham. Phicol accompanied Abimelech when the latter made a covenant with Abraham. [Gen. 21:22; 26:26]

PHILISTINES An energetic people from the regions of the Aegean Sea, they reached Canaan in the 12th century BC, after Joshua's conquest, and settled along the coastal plain. They quickly established themselves, and were soon in conflict with the Israelites, a situation which lasted throughout the period of the judges. Their

Bronze statue of the Pharaoh Neco,
609-593 BC.

principal base of settlement and of power was the group
of five towns near the coast, Gaza, Ashkelon, Ashdod,
Ekron and Gath. By the middle of the 11th century BC
they had become a formidable force, their control of the
manufacture of iron tools and weapons giving them
arms superiority over the Israelites. Their destruction
in 1050 BC of Shiloh, the centre of Hebrew worship at
the time, and the capture of the Ark of the Covenant
were grievous blows to Israel, and they were followed
by the occupation of additional territory. Not until the
reign of Saul were they checked, after suffering a series
of defeats at the hands of the king and of his son
Jonathan. They were finally subdued by King David.
When the kingdom was divided after the death of King
Solomon, the Philistines partially reasserted themselves.
Following the Assyrian invasion under Sennacherib at
the close of the 8th century BC, they vanish from the
records. [Books of 1 Sam.; 2 Sam.; 1 Kgs.; 2 Kgs.; 1
Chr.; 2 Chr.]

PHINEHAS (Egypt. 'negro') **1.** *c.* 13 century BC.
High priest in the time of Moses. Phinehas was the son
of Eleazar and the grandson of Aaron, and on his
father's death he became high priest in his stead. When
the Children of Israel under Moses stopped at Shittim
(Abel-shittim) on the east of the Jordan river, they
began to dally with the gods of Moab and with Moabite
women. This angered the Lord and he threatened
to destroy the Israelites, and sent a plague. Moses
ordered the judges among his people to sentence
to death anyone bowing down to Baal of Peor, the
Moabite god. At this moment an Israelite came
into the camp with a Midianite woman. Phinehas
was so incensed that he 'took a spear in his hand and
went after the man of Israel into the inner room, and
pierced both of them . . .' (Num. 25:8) The plague was
stopped but not before twenty-four thousand had died.

After the tribes of Gad, Reuben and half of Manasseh
had settled on the east side of the Jordan, they built an
altar to the Lord. When the rest of the Israelites who
had now settled in the land of Canaan heard about it,
they grew afraid that this might anger the Lord again.
Phinehas was sent at the head of a delegation to arbitrate.
He decided that the altar on the east of the river Jordan
had been built with the best motives and that it might
remain without causing any harm to the rest of the
tribes. Phinehas was given a hill in the Ephraim range
in Samaria and brought his father there for burial.
[Exod. 6:25; Num. 25:7-11; 31:6; Josh. 22:13, 31; 24:33;
Judg. 20:28; 1 Chr. 6:4, 50; 9:20; Ezra 7:5; 8:2; Ps.
106:30]

2. *c.* 11 century BC. Wicked son of the priest Eli.
Phinehas and Hophni were priests at the sanctuary of
Shiloh, and sons of Eli, the chief priest. They were corrupt enough to be thus described: 'the sons of Eli were
worthless men; they had no regard for the Lord.' (1
Sam. 2:12) They abused their office by taking for themselves the best part of the meat for sacrifices and by
seducing women who came to the Temple. Eli remonstrated with them in vain, even though another
priest prophesied they would both die on the same day.

When the Israelites were being hard pressed in battle
by the Philistines at Aphek, the two priests were sent
there with the sacred Ark to rally them. They were
defeated and the Ark captured, with Phinehas and
Hophni among the slain. The shock of their death and
the loss of the Ark killed their father.

When Phinehas's wife, who was pregnant, heard the
news she began her labour, but when her son was born
she refused to look at him. She called him Ichabod –
'inglorious' – since 'The glory has departed from Israel.'
(1 Sam. 4:21) She then died. [1 Sam. 1; 2; 4]

3. 5 century BC. Father of Eleazar, a priest who
weighed the gold, silver and precious vessels for the
Temple brought back to Jerusalem from Babylon by
Ezra. [Ezra 8:33]

PILDASH *c.* 18 century BC. Son of Abraham's brother
Nahor. [Gen. 22:22]

PILHA (Heb. 'worship') 5 century BC. A leader of
Judah who joined Nehemiah in signing the solemn
covenant. [Neh. 10:24]

PILTAI (Heb. 'saved') 5 century BC. Head of a priestly

family in Jerusalem when Joiakim was high priest in the time of Nehemiah. [Neh. 12:17]

PINON date unknown. An Edomite leader. [Gen. 36:41; 1 Chr. 1:52]

PIRAM (Heb. 'wild ass') 13 century BC. King of Jarmuth in the days of Joshua who joined with four other kings to attack the Gibeonites because Gibeon had made an alliance with the children of Israel. Joshua rushed to the aid of the Gibeonites, destroyed the armies of the five kings and put them to death at Makkedah. [Josh. 10:3]

PISPA date unknown. Son of Jether and a member of the tribe of Asher. [1 Chr. 7:38]

PITHON (Heb. 'harmless') date unknown. Son of Micah of the tribe of Benjamin and a descendant of King Saul. [1 Chr. 8:35; 9:41]

POCHERETH-HAZZEBAIM (Heb. 'gazelle-hunter') 10 century BC. Ancestor of a family of Temple servants who returned with Zerubbabel to Judah from exile in Babylon. [Ezra 2:57; Neh. 7:59]

PORATHA *c.* 5 century BC. A son of Haman, the chief minister of Persia in the reign of Ahasuerus, who

Limestone relief of an Egyptian vizier and his wife, 7th century BC, from Thebes.

Puah was one of two Hebrew midwives in Egypt. Egyptian statuette of a maid dressing the hair of a woman nursing a child.

together with his sons was put to death on the discovery of their plot against the Jews. [Esther 9:8]

POTIPHAR (Egypt. 'belonging to the sun-god Ra') *c.* 16 century BC. Potiphar, an Egyptian officer and captain of the guard, bought Joseph, Jacob's favourite son, as a slave for his household from a band of Midianites who had found him in a well. Joseph proved his worth and Potiphar promoted him to 'overseer of his house and put him in charge of all that he had' (Gen. 39:4). Potiphar's wife made amorous overtures to Joseph, which he rejected. Angrily she complained to her husband that Joseph had made improper suggestions to her and Potiphar had him jailed. [Gen. 37:36; 39]

POTIPHERA (Egypt. 'belonging to the sun') *c.* 16 century BC. The Egyptian father-in-law of Joseph, and a priest of On. [Gen. 41:45, 50; 46:20]

PUAH (Heb. 'mouth') **1.** *c.* 16 century BC. A son of Issachar and a grandson of Jacob, he went down to Egypt with his grandfather. Also called Puvah. [Gen. 46:13; Num. 26:23; 1 Chr. 7:1]

2. *c.* 13 century BC. One of the two Hebrew midwives in the days when the Children of Israel were slaves to Pharaoh in Egypt. She and the other Hebrew midwife deliberately ignored Pharaoh's order to kill all Hebrew boys immediately after birth and excused herself by saying that Hebrew mothers always gave birth before the midwives arrived. The Lord rewarded her with riches. [Exod. 1:15]

3. *c.* 12 century BC. Father of Tola of the tribe of Issachar who was judge over Israel for twenty-three years. [Judg. 10:1]

PUL *see* TIGLATH-PILESER III

PURAH *c.* 12 century BC. Gideon's aide who at God's command secretly crawled with him into the camp of the Midianites and Amalekites and overheard a soldier tell his dream in which he saw the destruction of Midian, Israel's enemy. [Judg. 7:10-14]

PUT date unknown. A son of Ham and a grandson of Noah, he was the father of the people of Put, who were famous warriors. [Gen. 10:6; 1 Chr. 1:8]

PUTIEL *c.* 13 century BC. His daughter married Eleazar, the son of Aaron and nephew of Moses. [Exod. 6:25]

PUVAH *see* PUAH **1.**

R

RAAMA *see* RAAMAH

RAAMAH (Heb. 'shaking') date unknown. Son of
Cush and a descendant of Ham. Also called Raama.
[1 Gen. 10:7; 1 Chr. 1:9; Ezek. 27:22]

RAAMIAH *see* REELAIAH

RABMAG *see* NERGAL-SHAREZER

RABSARIS (Heb. 'chief of the eunuchs') **1.** *c.* 8
century BC. Title of a commander of the Assyrian
army of King Sennacherib who marched against
Jerusalem and demanded the surrender of King
Hezekiah. [2 Kgs. 18:17]

2. *see* NEBUSHAZBAN

3. *see* SARSECHIM

RABSHAKEH (Ass. 'chief cupbearer') *c.* 7 century BC.
The chief officer of Sennacherib, king of Assyria, he
was sent together with the commander-in-chief and the
chief eunuch to demand the surrender of Jerusalem from
King Hezekiah. A Hebrew delegation was sent to meet
them but no agreement was reached. Rabshakeh
shouted out in Hebrew to the crowd on the ramparts
that Hezekiah was deluding them if he relied on their
God to save them. The Assyrian demand was rejected,
and Rabshakeh returned to report to Sennacherib, who
had been besieging Lachish. [2 Kgs. 18, 19; Isa. 36, 37]

RACHEL (Heb. 'ewe') *c.* 18 century BC. Second wife
of Jacob.

Rachel was the younger daughter of Laban, Jacob's
uncle in Nahor, Mesopotamia. Jacob first met and fell
in love with her when she was watering her father's
sheep at a well. He had been sent there by his mother
Rebekah, who wanted him to escape the anger of
Esau his brother and to find a wife among her people.

Laban had two daughters: 'Leah's eyes were weak,
but Rachel was beautiful and lovely.' (Gen. 29:17)
Jacob said he would work seven years for Laban to earn
the hand of Rachel 'and they seemed to him but a few
days because of the love he had for her.' (Gen. 29:20)
But after the wedding feast, Laban managed to substitute Leah for Rachel and Jacob did not find this out
until next morning. Jacob had to work another seven
years to earn Rachel.

Though Jacob loved Rachel more than Leah, she
remained childless, while Leah had four sons. Rachel

Rachel was renowned for her beauty:
14th-century BC ivory female
head from Syria.

envied her sister and reproached Jacob: 'Give me
children, or I shall die!' (Gen. 30:1) He became angry
and asked her, 'Am I in the place of God, who has
withheld from you the fruit of the womb?' (Gen. 30:2)
In desperation Rachel gave Jacob her maid Bilhah and
adopted the two sons she had, Dan and Naphtali. Then
'God remembered Rachel' (Gen. 30:22), and she had a
son who was called Joseph.

When Jacob set out for his own land he was pursued
by Laban. Jacob denied stealing Laban's household
images. He did not know that 'Rachel had taken the
household gods and put them in the camel's saddle,
and sat upon them' (Gen. 31:34) so that Laban failed
to find them in the tents.

When Jacob and his family reached the outskirts of
Bethlehem en route to Hebron, Rachel gave birth to
another son, whom she called Benoni ('son of my sorrow') for she died in childbirth. Jacob changed the boy's
name to Benjamin, 'son of my right hand'. Rachel was

Mesopotamian terracotta of a woman playing a drum, from approximately the time of Rachel.

buried there, 'and Jacob set up a pillar upon her grave; it is the pillar of Rachel's tomb, which is there to this day.' (Gen. 35:20)

The traditional site of Rachel's tomb is today marked by a small white structure with a cupola, standing at the side of the main road before entering Bethlehem. It is venerated by Jews and Moslems as a holy place, and superstitious women wind threads of cotton round the tomb to secure healthy sons for their daughters.

In the Book of Jeremiah she is pictured as weeping for her children who were taken away in captivity to Babylon. [Gen. 29-31; 33; 35; 46; 48:7; Ruth 4:11; 1 Sam. 10:2; Jer. 31:15]

RADDAI (Heb. 'trampling') 11 century BC. Fifth son of Jesse of the tribe of Judah and a brother of King David. [1 Chr. 2:14]

RAHAB (Heb. 'wide') c. 13 century BC. A prostitute in Jericho who lived on the city wall. The two spies Joshua sent into the city found lodging in Rahab's house. She hid them from the authorities on a promise that the Israelites would spare her and her family. The spies agreed and instructed her to tie a scarlet thread to her window as a sign. She then lowered them with a rope through her window and down the outside of the wall.

When Jericho fell, the two young men were sent by Joshua to bring Rahab and her family to safety inside the Israelite camp. Jericho was then burnt to the ground. The descendants of Rahab 'dwelt in Israel to this day'. (Josh. 6:25) [Josh. 2:1-21; 6:22-3, 25]

RAHAM (Heb. 'mercy') date unknown. Son of Shema of the tribe of Judah and descendant of Caleb son of Hezron. [1 Chr. 2:44]

RAKEM (Heb. 'woven') date unknown. Son of Sheresh and a leader of the tribe of Manasseh. [1 Chr. 7:16]

RAM (Heb. 'exalted') **1.** date unknown. Son of Hezron of the tribe of Judah, father of Amminadab, and an ancestor of King David. [1 Chr. 2:9, 10; Ruth 4:19]

2. date unknown. Son of Jerahmeel and grandson of Hezron of the tribe of Judah. [1 Chr. 2:25, 27]

3. date unknown. Ancestor of Elihu son of Barachel the Buzite, the young man who debated angrily with Job and his three friends. [Job. 32:2]

RAMIAH (Heb. 'God is exalted') 5 century BC. A descendant of Parosh who divorced his non-Jewish wife in the time of Ezra. [Ezra 10:25]

RAPHA (Heb. 'tall') c. 16 century BC. Son of Benjamin and grandson of Jacob and Rachel, he was a leader of the tribe born after Jacob's family went down into Egypt. [1 Chr. 8:2]

RAPHAH (Heb. 'tall') date unknown. Son of Binea of the tribe of Benjamin, and a descendant of King Saul. Also called Rephaiah. [1 Chr. 8:37; 9:43]

Rachel's tomb, still in existence, at Bethlehem: 17th-century Dutch engraving.

RAPHU (Heb. 'healed') 13 century BC. Leader of the tribe of Benjamin whose son Palti was appointed by Moses as one of the twelve men sent to spy out the Promised Land. [Num. 13:9]

REAIAH (Heb. 'seen by God') **1.** c. 8 century BC. Son of Micah and grandfather of Beerah who was a Reubenite leader taken into captivity by Tiglath-pileser during the Assyrian conquest of the northern kingdom of Israel. [1 Chr. 5:5]

2. date unknown. Ancestor of a family of Temple servants who returned with Zerubbabel from exile in Babylon. [Ezra 2:47; Neh. 7:50]

3. *see* HAROEH

REBA (Heb. 'fourth') 13 century B.C. A leader of Midian killed on the plain of Moab by the children of Israel. [Num. 31:8; Josh. 13:21]

REBEKAH *c.* 17 century B.C. Wife of Isaac.

Rebekah, the second of the biblical matriarchs, was the daughter of Bethuel and the granddaughter of Nahor, Abraham's brother. This part of the family stayed behind in Paddan-aram (northern Syria) when Abraham moved to the land of Canaan with his wife Sarah and his nephew Lot.

Rebekah went one evening to fill her water-jar at the well. As she was returning, a stranger in charge of a string of laden camels stopped the comely young girl and asked for a drink. She gave it to him and offered to draw water for his camels as well. He bestowed upon her a gold earring and two gold bracelets.

The man was Abraham's trusted servant, sent to find a wife for his master's son Isaac from among his kinsfolk. Having earlier enlisted the help of an angel, he knew that this was the girl he sought. He enquired who her parents were and whether there was room in her home for him to lodge that night. She courteously invited him to do so.

The servant disclosed his mission to her family and gave them the gifts sent by Abraham. After some discussion, and with Rebekah's consent, it was settled that she should travel to distant Canaan to be the bride of her relative Isaac.

On nearing their destination, Rebekah saw a man walking through the fields towards them at dusk, and was told by the servant that this was Isaac. She alighted from the camel and veiled her face to meet him. Rebekah became Isaac's wife and he brought her to the tent of his late mother, Sarah.

Rebekah remained barren for many years, but after Isaac had pleaded with the Lord, she bore him twin sons, Esau and Jacob. During a famine, Rebekah moved with Isaac into the territory of Abimelech, king of the Philistine city of Gerar (between Beersheba and Gaza). Here she was passed off as Isaac's sister for fear that he might otherwise be killed because of her. On learning the truth, Abimelech was angry with Isaac, but gave orders that they should not be harmed.

Old and nearly blind Isaac asked his favourite son Esau, a skilled hunter, to bring him a dish of venison. He would then bestow his patriarchal blessing on Esau, the first-born. Rebekah overheard the conversa-

Rebekah and Eliezer at the Well,
by Esteban Murillo (1617-82).

above Rebekah drew water for Eliezer and his camels. Water decanter, 9th-6th centuries BC, from Megiddo.

below Rebekah veiled her face when she came to meet Isaac. The Bedouin women of today still wear veils.

tion and determined to secure the blessing for Jacob, the twin brother she loved best. She ordered Jacob to select two young kids from his flock and prepared a savoury dish of meat. Jacob carried the food to his father, after Rebekah gave him Esau's garment to wear and covered his smooth hands and neck with the fleece of the kids, for Esau was a hairy man. Isaac was misled into bestowing the blessing on Jacob, declaring he would succeed his father as head of the family and that his brethren would serve him. Hearing that Esau had threatened to kill Jacob in revenge, Rebekah persuaded Isaac to send Jacob away to her brother Laban, in distant Paddan-aram, so that he too could find a bride among his own people.

When Rebekah died, she was buried in the family tomb in the Cave of Machpelah in Hebron. [Gen. 22:23; 24:29; 35:8; 49:31]

RECHAB (Heb. 'rider') **1.** *c.* 11 century BC. Rechab and Baanah were the two fierce sons of Rimmon, from Beeroth. They served under Abner when he supported Ishbosheth, Saul's weakling son, against David. After Abner's death, realizing that Ishbosheth's cause was hopeless, Rechab and Baanah entered his house in the middle of the day. They slipped past the doorman, who was dozing over the chore of sorting wheat, and killed their master while he lay sleeping on his bed. The two brothers hacked off his head and brought it to David at Hebron, hoping to be well rewarded. The shocked David ordered his men to kill them both for having 'slain a righteous man in his own house upon his bed' (2 Sam. 4:11). Their hands and feet were cut off and they were hung up over a nearby pool. David ordered the head of Ishbosheth to be buried in the sepulchre of Abner in Hebron. [2 Sam. 4:2, 5-12]

2. 9 century BC. Descendant of the desert tribe of Kenites and father of the redoubtable Jonadab who supported Jehu in wiping out the remnants of the house of King Ahab of Israel and their priests and eradicating Baal worship from Samaria. Rechab's descendants abstained from drinking wine and, opposed to the materialism of city life, dwelt only in tents. Their asceticism was commended by the prophet Jeremiah. [2 Kgs. 10:15-23; 1 Chr. 2:55; Jer. 35]

3. 5 century BC. Father of Malchijah, ruler of the district of Beth-haccherem, who repaired the Dung Gate of Jerusalem. [Neh. 3:14]

REELAIAH (Heb. 'thunder of God') 6 century BC. A leader of Judah who returned to Jerusalem with Zerubbabel from exile in Babylon. Also known as Raamiah. [Ezra 2:2; Neh. 7:7]

REGEM (Heb. 'friend') date unknown. Son of Jahdai of the tribe of Judah and a descendant of Caleb son of Hezron. [1 Chr. 2:47]

REGEM-MELECH (Heb. 'friend of the king') 5

century BC. One of the Jewish leaders during the reign of Darius of Persia who was deputed by the people to enquire of the priests in Jerusalem whether the custom of mourning the destruction of the Temple would be continued since the Temple had been rebuilt. [Zech. 7:2]

REHABIAH (Heb. 'God has broadened') 13 century BC. Only son of Eliezer and a grandson of Moses, he was chief of the Levites. [1 Chr. 23:17; 24:21; 26:25]

REHOB (Heb. 'width') **1.** *c.* 10 century BC. Father of Hadadezer, king of Zobah, who was defeated and killed in battle by King David. [2 Sam. 8:3, 12]

2. 5 century BC. A leading Levite among the returned exiles who signed the covenant to observe the Laws of God in the time of Nehemiah. [Neh. 10:11]

REHOBOAM (Heb. 'increase of the nation') First king of Judah after the monarchy split, he reigned 931-13 BC.

When Solomon died, he was succeeded on the throne by Rehoboam, his forty-one-year-old son by an Ammonite wife, Naamah. The new king immediately ran into trouble with the northern tribes, headed by Ephraim, the traditional rival of Judah. At an assembly in the ancient city of Shechem (Nablus), the northern leaders confronted Rehoboam with a list of demands for relief of taxation and other burdens. He asked for three days to think the matter over, and consulted the courtiers who had been his father's chief counsellors. They urged him to take a conciliatory tone with the restive northerners, and to redress some of their legitimate grievances. But he was influenced by the more hawkish advice of younger men. On the third day he again met the assembly at Shechem and harshly rejected the petition that had been presented to him: 'My father made your yoke heavy, but I will add to your yoke; my father chastised you

with whips, but I will chastise you with scorpions.' (1 Kgs. 12:14)

This attempt to browbeat the northern tribes into submission was disastrous. Their accumulated resentment burst into open rebellion. The leaders cried: 'What portion have we in David? We have no inheritance in the son of Jesse. To your tents, O Israel! Look now to your own house, David.' (1 Kgs. 12:16)

Rehoboam realized how serious the revolt was when Adoniram, the court official in charge of the forced levies, was stoned to death by the northerners, and the king himself had to flee back to Jerusalem in his chariot.

The northern kingdom of Israel was proclaimed with Jeroboam as its ruler. Rehoboam's rump kingdom, Judah, was left with only the tribal areas of Judah and Benjamin. The united monarchy had split into two small and warring Hebrew states. Rehoboam prepared to recover the lost provinces by force, but was dissuaded by Shemaiah the prophet.

In the fifth year of Rehoboam's reign, the country was invaded by the Egyptian Pharaoh Shishak. The biblical chronicler attributes this visitation to the religious backsliding of Rehoboam under the influence of his foreign wives. After he had been three years on the throne, he and his people had started to revive pagan forms of worship, erecting 'high places, and pillars, and Asherim on every high hill and under every green tree' (1 Kgs. 14:23).

Shishak approached the capital after capturing the fortified Judean towns on the way. He accepted the treasures of the Temple and the palace as a ransom and the city was spared.

Probably as a result of Shishak's invasion, Rehoboam proceeded to construct a chain of fifteen fortified places to defend the approaches to his country from the

King Rehoboam: detail from a fresco by Hans Holbein the Younger, *The Presumption of King Rehoboam*, 1530.

east, west and south. The southern line of defence was along the edge of the hills, which implies that Rehoboam had lost control of the Negev desert, and with it Solomon's Red Sea port of Ezion-geber. The forts did not extend across the disputed northern frontier with Israel, perhaps because Judah hoped to push Israel back in this Benjaminite borderland.

Rehoboam's household was modest compared to that of his father Solomon, but large by any other standard. He had eighteen wives, sixty concubines, twenty-eight sons and sixty daughters. The wife he loved best was Maacah, the daughter of Abishalom. Rehoboam died after a reign of seventeen years and was succeeded by Abijah, his son by Maacah. [1 Kgs. 11:43; 12; 1 Chr. 3:10; 2 Chr. 9:31; 13:7]

REHUM (Heb. 'merciful') **1.** 6 century BC. A leader of Judah who returned with Zerubbabel from exile in Babylon. [Neh. 12:3]

2. see NEHUM

3. 5 century BC. A leading Persian official stationed in Samaria during the reign of King Artaxerxes who wrote to the king falsely accusing the returning Jewish exiles of rebellion. The letter led to a royal decree stopping the work of rebuilding and Rehum and his colleagues hastened to Jerusalem to enforce it. [Ezra 4:8, 9, 17, 23]

4. 5 century BC. Son of Bani of the tribe of Levi, he helped repair the walls of Jerusalem in the time of Nehemiah. [Neh. 3:17]

5. 5 century BC. One of the leaders of Judah who joined Nehemiah in signing the covenant to observe the Laws of God. [Neh. 10:25]

REI (Heb. 'friendly') 10 century BC. A loyal minister of King David, he did not join David's son Adonijah when he tried to make himself king. [1 Kgs. 1:8]

REKEM (Heb. 'flowered') **1.** 13 century BC. A chief of Midian who was killed when his army was defeated by the children of Israel under Moses in the plain of Moab. [Num. 31:8]

2. date unknown. Son of Hebron, leader of the tribe of Judah, and a descendant of Caleb. [1 Chr. 2:43-4]

REMALIAH (Heb. 'exalted by God') c. 8 century BC. Father of Pekah, the army general who assassinated King Pekahiah of Israel and usurped the throne. [2 Kgs. 15:25-7; 16:1, 5; 2 Chr. 28:6; Isa. 7:1, 4-5, 9; 8:6]

REPHAEL (Heb. 'healed by God') 10 century BC. Son of Shemaiah and grandson of Obed-edom, he and his family were gatekeepers of the Tabernacle in the reign of King David and outstanding warriors. [1 Chr. 26:7]

REPHAH (Heb. 'wealth') date unknown. Son of Beriah and a grandson of Ephraim. [1 Chr. 7:25]

REPHAIAH (Heb. 'healed by God') **1.** c. 16 century BC. Son of Tola, and a grandson of Issachar, he and his family were leaders of the tribe and mighty warriors. [1 Chr. 7:2]

2. see RAPHAH

3. 8 century BC. Son of Ishi of the tribe of Simeon who commanded a band of 500 men which drove the Amalekites out of Mount Seir, south-east of the Dead Sea, and settled there. [1 Chr. 4:42]

4. c. 6 century BC. A descendant of King David and probably a contemporary of Zerubbabel. [1 Chr. 3:21]

5. 5 century BC. Son of Hur, ruler of part of Jerusalem in the days of Nehemiah, he helped to rebuild the walls of Jerusalem. [Neh. 3:9]

REPHAIM (Heb. 'giants') Ancient race of giants living east of the land of Canaan. [Gen. 14:5; 15:20; Deut. 2:20]

RESHEPH (Heb. 'fire') c. 16 century BC. Son of Rephah and a leader of the tribe of Ephraim. [1 Chr. 7:25]

REU (Heb. 'friend') date unknown. Son of Peleg and a descendant of Shem. [Gen. 11:18-21; 1 Chr. 1:25]

REUBEN (Heb. 'see a son') c. 16 century BC. Reuben was the eldest son of Jacob and Leah. One day he found mandrakes in a field at harvest time and brought them to his mother, who gave them to Rachel, Jacob's favourite wife, in return for Jacob's favour that night.

Later Reuben incurred his father's displeasure by sleeping with Bilhah, one of Jacob's concubines.

When the jealous brothers wanted to kill their brother Joseph, Reuben saved him by having him left in a pit but when Reuben came to take him out, Joseph had disappeared. Reuben was one of the ten sons sent by Jacob to buy corn in Egypt where Joseph had become a leading figure in Pharaoh's court. Joseph demanded that the youngest child, Benjamin, should be brought back with Jacob's sons on their next visit. Jacob objected but Reuben offered to leave his own two sons as hostage for the safe return of Benjamin. When Jacob went to settle in Egypt with all his family, it included Reuben's four sons. On his deathbed Jacob blessed his sons in turn. Reuben he called: 'my might, and the first fruits of my strength, pre-eminent in pride and pre-eminent in power. Unstable as water . . .' (Gen. 49:3, 4)

Centuries later in the conquest of Canaan under Joshua, the tribe of Reuben obtained an area east of the Jordan, between the rivers Arnon and Jabbok.

In the blessing attributed to Moses, he said: 'Let Reuben live, and not die, nor let his men be few.' (Deut. 33:6) [Gen. 29:32; 30:14; 35:22, 23; 37:21, 22, 29; 42:22, 37; 46:8, 9; 48:5; 49:3; Exod. 1:2; 6:14; Num. 1:20; 16:1; 26:5; Deut. 11:6; Josh. 15:6; 18:7; 1 Chr. 2:1; 5:1]

REUEL (Heb. 'God is my friend') **1.** 16 century BC. Son of Esau and Basemath, and a leader in Edom. [Gen. 36:4, 10, 13; 1 Chr. 1 Chr. 1:35, 37]

2. date unknown. Son of Ibnijah and an ancestor of Meshullam, one of the first Benjaminites to settle in Jerusalem after the return from Babylon. [1 Chr. 9:8]

3. see JETHRO

4. see DEUEL

REUMAH *c.* 18 century BC. Concubine of Abraham's brother Nahor, and mother of four of Nahor's sons. [Gen. 22:24]

REZIN (Heb. 'firm') **1.** 8 century BC. King of Syria who, together with King Pekah of Israel, attacked King Ahaz of Judah when he refused to join them in revolting against their Assyrian masters. Ahaz called upon the Assyrian king Tiglath-pileser III for help and he marched on Damascus, destroyed Rezin's army and killed Rezin. [2 Kgs. 15:37; 16:5, 7, 9; Isa. 7:1, 4, 8; 8:6]
2. 6 century BC. Head of a family of Temple servants who returned with Zerubbabel from exile in Babylon. [Ezra 2:48; Neh. 7:50]

REZON 10 century BC. Son of Eliada and commander of the army of Hadadezer, king of Zobah. When King David captured Zobah, Rezon fled with a band of his followers. [1 Kgs. 11:23]

RIBAI (Heb. 'pleader') *c.* 10 century BC. A Benjaminite from Gibeah whose son Ittai was a warrior in the army of King David noted for outstanding bravery. [2 Sam. 23:29; 1 Chr. 11:31]

RIMMON (Heb. 'pomegranate') **1.** *c.* 11 century BC. Father of Baanah and Rechab who murdered Saul's son Ishbosheth in the hope of getting a reward from King David, but were put to death instead. [2 Sam. 4:2, 5, 9]
2. Hebraized form of Ramman, the Babylonian and also Syrian god of thunder. When the Syrian general Naaman was cured of leprosy by taking the advice of the prophet Elisha, he accepted the God of Israel as all powerful but nevertheless felt he should go with the king of Syria to worship in the temple of Rimmon. [2 Kgs. 5:18]

RINNAH (Heb. 'song') date unknown. One of the four sons of Shimon and a leader of the tribe of Judah. [1 Chr. 4:20]

RIPHATH (Heb. 'spoken') date unknown. Son of Gomer and a grandson of Japheth. Also called Diphath. [Gen. 10:3; 1 Chr. 1:6]

RIZIA (Heb. 'delight') date unknown. Son of Ulla of the tribe of Asher, he and his family were leaders of the tribe and mighty warriors. [1 Chr. 7:39]

RIZPAH (Heb. 'hot stone') *c.* 11 century BC. Concubine of King Saul.

Rizpah, the daughter of Aiah, was one of King Saul's concubines and the mother of two sons by him. After Saul's death, his general Abner was angered when Saul's son Ishbosheth charged him with having relations with Rizpah.

Towards the end of David's reign there was a three-year famine in the country. It was regarded as a belated punishment for Saul's slaying of a number of inhabitants of Gibeon, an Amorite hill-town five miles north-west of Jerusalem. The Gibeonites demanded as an act of atonement that David hand over to them Saul's seven children and grandchildren. David felt obliged to yield up to them the two sons Saul had had by Rizpah and five grandsons by Saul's eldest daughter. The Gibeonites hanged all seven. 'Then Rizpah the daughter of Aiah took sackcloth, and spread it for herself on the rock.' (2 Sam. 21:10) and she kept watch over the bodies of the children until the harvesting was finished and the rains came. When this was reported to David, he made peace with his troubled conscience by burying the bones of the children in the family tomb of their grandfather Kish, in the territory of Ephraim. [2 Sam. 3:7; 21:8-12]

ROHGAH (Heb. 'clamour') date unknown. Son of Shemer of the tribe of Asher, and one of the leaders of the tribe. [1 Chr. 7:34]

ROMAMTI-EZER 10 century BC. One of the fourteen sons of Heman, King David's musician. He and his family played musical instruments in the Tabernacle under their father's direction and Romamti-ezer took the twenty-fourth turn of service. [1 Chr. 25:4, 31]

ROSH (Heb. 'head') *c.* 16 century BC. A son of Benjamin and a grandson of Jacob and Rachel, he went down to Egypt at the same time as his grandfather Jacob. [Gen. 46:21]

RUTH (Heb. 'beloved') *c.* 11 century BC. The Moabite ancestress of King David.

The touching story of the love between the Israelite widow Naomi and her Moabite daughter-in-law is set in the time of the judges.

During a period of famine, Naomi with her husband Elimelech and their two sons, Mahlon and Chilion, left their home town of Bethlehem and moved eastwards, beyond the Dead Sea to the mountain plateau of Moab. There Elimelech died. The sons married Moabite girls, Orpah and Ruth. Ten years later, both sons also died, and Naomi decided to return to Bethlehem, but she urged her two widowed daughters-in-law to remain with their own families in Moab. When they clung to her and wept, she gently chided them, pointing out that she could not produce more sons to replace their dead husbands. Orpah went back to her family, but Ruth refused to be parted from Naomi saying 'for where you go I will go, and where you lodge I will lodge; your people shall be my people, and your God my God.' (Ruth 1:16)

The two destitute women reached Bethlehem at the beginning of the wheat and barley harvest. Ruth went into the fields to glean the ears of corn left by the reapers, hoping that a farmer would be kind to her. By chance, her gleaning brought her into a barley patch belonging to Boaz, a well-to-do relative of Naomi's late husband, Elimelech. Coming to the field from Bethlehem Boaz asked his foreman who the unknown young woman was and was told she was the Moabite who had come back with Naomi. Boaz felt drawn towards her.

Reaping corn in Moab, Ruth's land of origin.

He told her he had heard about her devotion to her mother-in-law whom she had followed to a strange land. He insisted that she remain in his field and share the food and water of his workers. He then quietly ordered the foreman to let Ruth glean even among the bound sheaves, and to leave handfuls of barley for her to gather and to ensure that she was not molested. At the end of the day Ruth returned to the town and handed to Naomi a whole bushel of barley, together with some of the food she had been given. Naomi told her that Boaz was one of her husband's relatives who might have a right of redemption over both of them as widows. (In the Israelite law of the time, a dead man's next-of-kin had the right to marry the widow, or 'redeem' her, and if he renounced that right it would pass on to the next nearest male relative.) Naomi urged Ruth to go on working in Boaz's field where she would be treated kindly and would not be molested. This Ruth did, gleaning the barley and wheat harvests.

Naomi heard that Boaz would be at the winnowing of the barley and would be spending the night on the threshing floor after the customary eating and drinking. On her mother-in-law's advice Ruth went there and waited until Boaz had laid himself down to sleep next to the barley heap. She quietly turned back the edge of his cloak and lay down at his feet. In the middle of the night Boaz awoke and was surprised to find her there. She told him who she was and added 'spread your skirt over your maidservant, for you are next of kin.' (Ruth 3:9) He praised her, saying that all Bethlehem knew she was a virtuous woman and did not go after

young men poor or rich. He explained that the right of redemption was held by another kinsman closer than he was. If the other did not exercise that right, he Boaz would do so and marry her. Before daybreak he sent her back to Naomi, after filling her cloak with barley.

That morning Boaz waited in the city gate for the other relative to pass by. They sat down together in the presence of ten elders whom Boaz had invited to join them as witnesses. Boaz asked the other man whether he was prepared as the next-of-kin to redeem the piece of land that had belonged to Elimelech and that his widow Naomi now wanted to sell. The other was willing to do so, until Boaz pointed out to him that he would also be required to marry Ruth, the Moabite, the widow of Elimelech's son and heir. The kinsman then re-nounced his right of redemption in favour of Boaz. The agreement was ratified in the customary way by his taking off one sandal and handing it to Boaz in the presence of the witnesses. Boaz then declared that he was acquiring the property and also Ruth to be his wife 'that the name of the dead may not be cut off from among his brethren . . .' (Ruth 4:10) All those present called down the blessings of the Lord upon the union.

Ruth gave birth to a son, Obed. The other women congratulated Naomi and expressed their admiration 'for your daughter-in-law who loves you, who is more to you than seven sons . . .' (Ruth 4:15)

In the course of time Obed had a son Jesse, who was the father of David. Ruth, the Moabite girl, was thus the great-grandmother of Israel's most illustrious king. [Book of Ruth]

Scenes from the story of Ruth and Boaz, from a 13th-century French illuminated manuscript.

S

SABTA *see* SABTAH

SABTAH date unknown. Son of Cush and a grandson of Ham, he was a desert chieftain. Also called Sabta. [Gen. 10:7; 1 Chr. 1:9]

SABTECA date unknown. Son of Cush and a grandson of Ham, he was a desert chieftain. [Gen. 10:7; 1 Chr. 1:9]

SACHAR (Heb. 'reward') **1.** *c.* 10 century BC. Father of Ahiam one of David's trusted warriors. Also known as Sharar. [2 Sam. 23:33; 1 Chr. 11:35]

2. *c.* 10 century BC. Son of Obed-edom a gatekeeper of the Ark in the time of King David. [1 Chr. 26:4]

SACHIA date unknown. Son of Shaharaim and a leader of the tribe of Benjamin. [1 Chr. 8:10]

SALLAI (Heb. 'basket-maker') **1.** 6 century BC. A leading priest who returned with Zerubbabel from exile in Babylon. His son Kallai was a chief priest of Judah in the days of Nehemiah. Also known as Sallu. [Neh. 12:7, 20]

2. 5 century BC. A chief of the tribe of Benjamin who returned to Judah from exile in Babylon and settled in Jerusalem. [Neh. 11:8]

SALLU (Heb. 'measured') **1.** *see* SALLAI 1.

2. 5 century BC. Son of Meshullam and a leader of the tribe of Benjamin who returned to Judah from exile in Babylon and lived in Jerusalem in the time of Nehemiah. [1 Chr. 9:7; Neh. 11:7]

SALMA (Heb. 'clothed') **1.** *c.* 13 century BC. A leader of Judah, son of Hur and grandson of Caleb, he was regarded as the founder of Bethlehem. [1 Chr. 2:51, 54]

2. *see* SALMON

SALMON (Heb. 'clothed') *c.* 11 century BC. Father of Boaz who married Ruth, the Moabitess, he was an ancestor of King David. Also called Salma. [Ruth 4:20, 21; 1 Chr. 2:11]

SALU (Heb. 'measured') *c.* 13 century BC. A leader of a Simeonite family in the wilderness whose son publicly consorted with a Midianite woman for immoral purposes and was killed by Phinehas the priest. [Num. 25:14]

SAMGAR-NEBO (Bab. 'sword of Nebo') *c.* 6 century BC. A prince of Babylon who sat in triumph in the middle gate of Jerusalem after the Babylonian army had broken through the walls of Jerusalem. [Jer. 39:3]

SAMLAH (Heb. 'cloth') date unknown. Fifth king of Edom, he succeeded Hadad. [Gen. 36:36, 37; 1 Chr. 1:47, 48]

SAMSON (Heb. 'man of the sun') *c.* 12 century BC. A judge of the tribe of Dan. It is attempted in the Book of Judges to fit Samson into the pattern of the tribal leaders called 'judges', and it is said that he 'judged Israel in the days of the Philistines twenty years' (Judg. 15:20). However, there is nothing in the narrative to indicate that he actually gave judgments or that he led his people in battle. He was not a judge, a military commander, or a religious leader – but a folk-hero of the

Persian lapis lazuli figure
of a man strangling a lion,
5th century BC.

315

kind that has captivated the popular mind down the ages, from Hercules to Superman, with feats of incredible strength.

Samson belonged to the tribe of Dan. At the time of Joshua's conquest of Canaan, that tribe was allocated a strip of territory extending westwards from the Judean hills across the Shephelah (lowlands) and the coastal plain. It thereby encroached into an area occupied by the Philistines, a sea-people recently arrived from the Aegean Islands and Crete (though some scholars say they came from the south and west coasts of Asia Minor). The Danites were unable to secure their hold on that territory, and most of them left and

Mesopotamian cylinder seal showing men fighting lions, 3rd millennium BC.

resettled in the north-eastern corner of the country, near Mount Hermon. Remnants of the tribe must have clung to their homes in the Judean foothills and continued to live insecurely side by side with the Philistines, who in Samson's time 'had dominion over Israel' (Judg. 14:4). It was in this context that he carried on his one-man border war, and that he met his death.

Samson's birth, like that of a number of Bible heroes, had a miraculous aspect. His father Manoah lived in the village of Zorah, situated in the undulating foothill region of the Shephelah. It overlooked the valley of Sorek (through which the railway line now climbs up to Jerusalem).

His mother was a pious woman who had been childless for many years. One day an angel appeared before her and told her she would conceive a son. He warned her not to drink wine or eat unclean food during her pregnancy. The child would be dedicated to God's service, and forbidden to cut his hair or touch strong drink. The prophecy was added that when he grew up, he would 'begin to deliver Israel from the hand of the Philistines' (Judg. 13:5).

As a young man Samson fell in love with a Philistine

left Sampson and Delilah,
by Andrea Mantegna
(*c*. 1431-1506).

girl from the village of Timnath, four miles from his home. He asked his father and mother to arrange the match. They first protested, urging him to marry someone of his own people, not knowing that Samson's wish 'was from the Lord; for he was seeking an occasion against the Philistines' (Judg. 14:4). But Samson persuaded them to come with him to the girl's home and talk to her family.

During this visit Samson encountered a young lion in the vineyards of Timnath and killed it with his bare hands. Passing there on his next visit he turned off the road to see what had happened to the lion's carcass, and found that a swarm of bees had settled in it. He scooped out the honeycomb, ate some of it and brought the rest home to his parents, without saying where he had got it.

As was the custom, Samson gave in his bride's village a wedding feast that went on for seven days. Thirty young Philistines were invited to attend. Samson put a riddle to them, for a wager of thirty pieces of fine linen and thirty garments. He said to them: 'Out of the eater came something to eat. Out of the strong came something sweet.' (Judg. 14:14) Unable to resolve the riddle, they threatened Samson's wife that if she did not coax the answer out of him and reveal it to them, they would burn her and her father's house. She reproached Samson with tears until he told her.

above left Philistine jug with bird and fish motifs from Azor, 12th century BC.
above right Philistine beer jug from Azor, 12th century BC.

On the last evening of the wedding feast, the Philistines gleefully produced the answer: 'What is sweeter than honey? What is stronger than a lion?' (Judg. 14:18) Samson was furious and rejoined, 'If you had not ploughed with my heifer, you would not have found out my riddle.' (Judg. 14:18)

Exploits against the Philistines

Samson stalked away and paid his wager by killing thirty Philistines at Ashkelon and taking the pieces of linen and garments from them. He then returned to his father's home. But his longing for his Philistine wife sent him back to her village, bearing a kid as a gift. Her embarrassed father refused to let him enter her room, explaining that she had meantime been given to the Philistine who had acted as the best man at the wedding. He offered Samson her pretty younger sister as a substitute. Samsom scorned this proposal, and claimed that this time he was clearly entitled to revenge himself on his wife's people.

He caught three hundred foxes, tied them together in pairs by their tails, put lighted torches between the tails and let them loose into the Philistine wheatfields. It was harvest time, and the fires destroyed the sheaves and the unreaped corn, as well as vineyards and olive groves.

The Philistines asked in consternation who had caused the damage. They were told that Samson had been getting his own back for what his wife's family had done to him. As a reprisal, the incensed farmers then set fire to the house of the Timnite, and he and his daughter perished in the flames.

Again Samson reacted violently, and 'he smote them hip and thigh with great slaughter' (Judg. 15:8). He then took refuge in a rock cleft at Etam, in the Judean hills.

By now what had started as a family incident at a wedding threatened to escalate into a war. The Philistines sent an armed force into the territory of the tribe of Judah with a demand that Samson be handed over to them. The men of Judah came to Samson's hiding-place and said to him: 'Do you not know that the Philistines are rulers over us? What then is this that you have done to us?' (Judg. 15:11) Samson retorted: 'As they did to me, so have I done to them.' (Judg. 15:11) All the same he agreed to let his fellow-countrymen bind him and hand him over, on a promise they would not try to kill him themselves. They tied him up with two new ropes and brought him to the place where the Philistines were waiting.

But when his enemies shouted in triumph, the spirit of the Lord came upon Samson and he snapped the cords that bound him, like 'flax that has caught fire' (Judg. 15:14). Catching sight of the jawbone of an ass, he snatched it up, went on a rampage among the Philistines and slew a thousand of them. The place where he tossed away the curious weapon was named Ramath-lehi ('the Hill of the Jawbone'). After these exertions, Samson was overcome with a burning thirst. The Lord opened a hollow in the ground from which water gushed, and he was able to drink his fill and revive.

Some time later, Samson went to spend the night with a harlot in Gaza. Word of his presence got around and a group of Gaza men set an ambush for him near the city entrance, waiting for him to emerge in the early morning (since the city gates were closed at night). Instead, he rose at midnight, wrenched off the gates together with the two posts and bar, and carried them on his back to a hilltop near Hebron, thirty-eight miles away.

Samson and Delilah

Samson once more indulged in his fondness for Philistine women. He fell in love with Delilah, who lived in the valley of Sorek near his home town. A group of the Philistine chiefs came to her and offered to pay her eleven hundred silver shekels each if she would wheedle out of Samson the secret of his abnormal strength, so that they could capture and hurt him. Pretending to satisfy her curiosity, Samson told her that he would be helpless if tied with seven freshly-made bowstrings. Concealing armed men in her room, Delilah tied her lover while he was sleeping, and then shouted, 'The Philistines are upon you, Samson!' (Judg. 16:9) He jumped up and snapped the cords with ease. The same story was repeated with unused ropes, and again when she wove the locks of his hair into a web of her loom and pegged it down. Each time he laughingly broke free, and the plot was thwarted.

Having failed three times, she nagged him until 'his soul was vexed to death' (Judg. 16:16). In the end he disclosed to her that as he had been dedicated to the service of God from birth, his strength would fail him if his hair was shorn. Convinced this time that she had heard the truth, she sent for the Philistines, who arrived with the money in their hands. When he was asleep, with his head in her lap, Delilah called on one of the men to cut off Samson's hair, 'and his strength left him' (Judg. 16:19). This time the Philistines were able to overcome and capture him. They put out his eyes, brought him to Gaza, and set him to work turning the millstone in the prison.

The legendary strongman had suddenly become an object of derision and sport, led around helplessly by a boy:

'Promise was that I
Should Israel from Philistinian yoke deliver:
Ask for this great deliverer now, and find him
Eyeless in Gaza at the mill with slaves,
Himself in bonds under Philistinian yoke.'

(Milton: *Samson Agonistes*)

But some assurance of divine grace crept back to him, as 'the hair of his head began to grow again after it had been shaved' (Judg. 16:22).

All the leading Philistines gathered in the temple of their god Dagon, to offer sacrifices and celebrate the capture of their enemy. (Dagon was a Canaanite corn god, whose cult was absorbed by the Philistines.) 'And when their hearts were merry, they said, "Call Samson, that he may make sport for us."' (Judg. 16:25) The temple was full, and three thousand more men and women crowded onto the roof to jeer at him.

Samson asked the boy to lead him by the hand to the two middle pillars supporting the roof. When he stood between them and felt them on either side with his hands, he entreated the Lord: 'remember me, I pray thee, and strengthen me, I pray thee, only this

once, O God, that I may be avenged upon the Philistines for one of my two eyes.' (Judg. 16:28) As his former power came surging back, he grasped the pillars, cried out, 'Let me die with the Philistines' and 'bowed with all his might' (Judg. 16:30). The pillars cracked and collapsed and the building crashed down, killing its occupants together with Samson.

The brawny fighter and the lover of women had become in his death a noble and tragic figure. His kinsfolk came to fetch his body and buried it in the tomb of his father, between Zorah and Eshtaol, in the foothills of his childhood.

Samson's name in Hebrew, Shimshon, is related to the word for the sun, *shemesh*; the locality in which he lived centred on the town of Beth-shemesh, which means 'house of the sun'; and his power resided in the

Death of Samson: engraving by Gustave Doré (?1832-83).

long hair radiating from his head, like the sun's rays. These facts, together with some of his exploits, prompted some Bible scholars to suggest that Samson originated as a mythical sun-god, such as appears in other ancient religions. Legends may have grown up around him; but the biblical story is so specific in time and place that Samson was undoubtedly a real person, pitting his great strength against the oppressors of his people. [Judg. 13-16]

SAMUEL (Heb. 'name of God') *c.* 11 century BC. The last of the judges. The judges were individuals who exercised influence over the tribes of Israel because of their strong personality, moral stature, and the belief that they had direct access to the Lord. They were able to rally the tribes in self-defence, and to settle disputes. Samuel, the reluctant king-maker, was the last and most dominant of these spontaneous leaders.

Samuel's father was Elkanah, from the town of Ramathaim-zophim, in the hill country of Ephraim. His mother, Hannah, was childless. On one of their annual pilgrimages to the religious centre at Shiloh, she vowed that if she was given a son, he would be given to God's service.

In due time Hannah bore a child she called Samuel, because the Lord had heard her. When he was weaned she brought the infant to the shrine at Shiloh and left him to be reared by the priests, as she had promised. The child Samuel helped with the religious services, wearing a linen ephod or priestly apron. Each year Hannah came with her husband to worship and brought the boy a coat she had made for him.

Twice one night Samuel thought he heard the voice of the aging high priest Eli and went to him, but was sent back to bed. The third time this happened Eli understood that it was the Lord calling to Samuel and told the boy to answer: 'Speak, Lord, for thy servant hears.' (1 Sam. 3:9) When Samuel did this, the Lord told him that Eli and his household would suffer for the misdeeds of his two sons, the corrupt priests Hophni and Phinehas. 'Behold, I am about to do a thing in Israel, at which the two ears of every one that hears it will tingle.' (1 Sam. 3:11) Next morning, at Eli's insistence, Samuel reported to him what he had heard. This experience was a turning point in Samuel's life. For the first of many times, the Lord had spoken directly to him. Samuel continued to serve in the shrine at Shiloh and his reputation spread through the country from Dan to Beersheba.

At the battle of Aphek, in the foothills, the Israelites were heavily defeated by their Philistine foes, and thousands of them were killed. Among the killed were Eli's two sons, who had been sent from Shiloh with the sacred Ark of the Covenant to rally the Israelite warriors. The Ark was captured. On hearing the news, Eli fell over backward with shock and died of a broken neck.

View of Shiloh
where the Tabernacle
once stood.

For the Philistines the Ark proved an awkward trophy. In the temple of Dagon at Ashdod, the great idol fell down before it and was broken. Plague broke out, and 'the hand of God was very heavy' (1 Sam. 5:11). The Ark was sent back in a cart drawn by 'two milch cows' to the Israelite town of Beth-shemesh in the foothills. From there it was brought to the sanctuary of Kiriath-jearim near Jerusalem, and remained at that spot for twenty years.

Samuel summoned the people to gather at Mizpah, a

Philistine fortress excavated
at Ashdod, with a Canaanite
city in the foreground.

below Terracotta figure of Ashtaroth, late Canaanite period. Samuel berated the Israelites for worshipping Canaanite deities.

hilltop north of Jerusalem. He attributed their misfortunes to religious backsliding and the worship of pagan Canaanite deities, and exhorted them to fasting and prayer. When a Philistine army again advanced upon them, Samuel interceded with the Lord who unleased a violent thunderstorm on the enemy. The Israelites were able to repel the Philistines and regain lost territory. Samuel marked the victory by setting up a stone to the Lord, and called the place Ebenezer ('the Stone of Help'). Samuel's leading position was now established. He settled at Ramah, six miles north of Jerusalem, 'and there also he administered justice to Israel' (1 Sam. 7:17).

Samuel the Kingmaker

When Samuel became old he appointed his two sons, Joel and Abijah, to be local judges in Beersheba. But they were corrupt, taking bribes and perverting justice. The elders of Israel complained to Samuel, saying: 'Behold, you are old and your sons do not walk in your ways; now appoint for us a king to govern us like all the nations.' (1 Sam. 8:5)

Till that time the twelve Hebrew tribes had had no earthly ruler, and were loosely held together by their common origin, history and religion. God was their king, and His commandments were their law. Outraged at the demand of the elders, Samuel warned them that a king would take their sons as soldiers and their daughters as servants; he would exact tithes from their herds and produce, and confiscate their best lands for his own use. The elders refused to be put off by this lecture and Samuel had to yield. He called the people together at Mizpah and upbraided them for their ingratitude to the Lord after all he had done for the Hebrew people. He then proceeded with the drawing of lots, whereby the choice was narrowed to the small tribe of Benjamin and finally fell on 'Saul the son of Kish' (1 Sam. 10:21) of Gibeah. Saul, who had hidden himself, was brought forth. He was very tall, 'taller than any of the people from his shoulders upward' (1 Sam. 10:23) and Samuel presented him to the populace. All shouted 'Long live the king.' (1 Sam. 10:24) Samuel then 'told the people the rights and duties of the kingship; and he wrote them in a book' (1 Sam. 10:25) and dispersed the gathering. Saul went quickly back to his father's house in Gibeah.

Into this account intrudes a different version. Looking for strayed asses, Saul came to a town where Samuel was visiting and decided to consult the seer. Guided by the Lord, the prophet took Saul up with him to the place of sacrifice, gave him the seat of honour at the table, and invited him to spend the night. Early next morning Samuel poured oil on Saul's head and told him that 'the Lord has anointed you to be prince over his heritage' (1 Sam. 10:1). After Saul had led a military expedition to relieve the Israelite town of Jabesh-gilead (east of the Jordan river) Samuel called the people together at Gilgal to 'renew the kingdom' (1 Sam. 11:14). There, amid the sacrifice of peace offerings to the Lord and great rejoicing, Saul was publicly acclaimed.

But the imperious old Samuel remained unreconciled to the change. He pointedly reminded the people that even if they now had a king, only the Lord could preserve them, as he had in the past. To drive home the

Israelite libation jar,
13th-11th century B.C.

point, he miraculously summoned up thunder and rain although it was still the dry harvest season. Having terrified his audience, he concluded: 'I will instruct you in the good and the right way. Only fear the Lord, and serve him faithfully with all your heart.... But if you still do wickedly, you shall be swept away, both you and your king.' (1 Sam. 12:23, 24, 25) These ominous words were the prelude to a bitter conflict between prophet and king that lasted for the rest of Samuel's life, and even after his death.

The Conflict with Saul

When Saul had reigned two years he felt ready to challenge the Philistines, who had gained a foothold in the hills north of Jerusalem. At Gilgal, down on the Jericho plain, Saul waited seven days for Samuel to come and make the ritual sacrifices to the Lord before battle. Then, feeling that he dared not tarry any longer, Saul made the burnt-offerings himself. The prophet then appeared, angrily denounced him and hinted that he would be replaced by someone else.

Having pushed back the Philistines, Saul sent an expedition against the Amalekites, the fierce nomad tribes of the southern desert. Samuel gave explicit instructions, in the Lord's name, to wipe out all of them, together with all their herds and flocks. Saul failed to obey these instructions to the letter. After vanquishing the Amalekites, he took captive their king, Agag, and allowed his men to bring back the pick of the cattle and sheep. He tried to appease Samuel's wrath by claiming that the animals were meant to be sacrificed to the Lord. Samuel retorted with scorn, 'Has the Lord as great delight in burnt offerings and sacrifices, as in obeying the voice of the Lord?' (1 Sam. 15:22)

As Samuel turned away Saul clutched at his mantle, which tore. Samuel promptly claimed this was a sign that the 'Lord has torn the kingdom of Israel from you this day' (1 Sam. 15:28). The prophet demanded that Agag be brought before him: 'And Samuel said, "As your sword has made women childless, so shall your mother be childless among women." And Samuel hewed Agag in pieces before the Lord in Gilgal.' (1 Sam. 15:33) After this bloody reproof, Samuel retired to his home in Ramah, and went into mourning for the king as if he were dead.

The Lord now called on Samuel to anoint the boy David the son of Jesse as the future king. The prophet went to Bethlehem, where David lived, on the pretext of conducting a religious ceremony in the town. That gave him a chance to see Jesse, and meet seven of his sons. The youngest one, David, was tending the sheep. He was sent for at the request of the prophet, who anointed him with oil.

Later, when David had become established at court and married Saul's daughter, the moody king became jealous of him and tried to kill him. David fled to Ramah and took refuge with Samuel. Saul sent messengers to bring him back and when they failed he went himself. But Saul was caught up in the religious fervour surrounding Samuel: 'And he too stripped off his clothes, and he too prophesied before Samuel, and lay naked all that day and all that night. Hence it is said, "Is Saul also among the prophets?"' (1 Sam. 19:24) This curious episode did not heal the breach between the king and the prophet.

The aged Samuel died and was buried at Ramah, and was mourned by all Israel.

Before his last battle against the Philistines at Mount Gilboa, Saul persuaded an old witch in·the hamlet of

Saul slain together with his sons. At these dread tidings, the king swooned away, and had to be revived and fed by his servants and the women of Endor. The next day the prediction came true.

Even in death Samuel had had the last and crushing word to the king he had raised up and then tried to cast down again. Saul had stood in awe of his mentor, and had never argued with him; yet the king had not acted as the docile instrument he was set up to be. The uncompromising dictates of a man of God had clashed with the more flexible attitudes of a ruler coping with

below Egyptian relief of mourners and funeral meats, *c.* 1350 BC.

above The traditional tomb of Samuel at Nebi Samuil, north of Jerusalem.

Endor to summon up from the grave the spirit of Samuel. When the apparition appeared of an old man covered with a mantle, Saul flung himself on the ground before him. The ghost demanded, 'Why have you disturbed me by bringing me up?' (1 Sam. 28:15) Saul replied humbly '... I have summoned you, to tell me what I shall do.' (1 Sam. 28:15)

Samuel's spirit was as unrelenting as the living prophet had been. He reminded Saul that he had disobeyed the Lord, who had rejected him. On the morrow, he revealed, the Israelites would be defeated and

p... ... military ... ... conflict between
th... ... ...-repeated conflict between
C... ... ... Book of ...amuel]

The books of Samuel

Th... ... and ... books of ...amuel were probably
a ... ... divided into two scrolls for con-
ve... ... The whole story of ...amuel is confined to the
Fi... book where it overlaps with the reign of Saul and
th... ... ... part of David's life. The Second Book of
Sa... ... not concerned at all with him but only with
th... reign of King David.

SANBALLAT (Ass. 'Sin save the life') *c.* 5 century
BC. Sanballat was a Horonite who lived in Beth-horon,
north of Jerusalem, and held a post in the Persian
government. He was vehemently opposed to the rebuilding of Jerusalem by Nehemiah and tried various
means to prevent it. He ridiculed the capacity of the
'feeble Jews' to build the walls, but when the work
went on and was almost finished, he tried to lure
Nehemiah from Jerusalem in order to kill him. When
this failed he threatened war against the Jews. This did
not stop the work as Nehemiah stationed armed men
to protect the builders. Finally Sanballat wrote a letter
accusing Nehemiah of conspiring to set himself up as
king of Judah. Later, on his second visit to Jerusalem,
Nehemiah banished Sanballat's son-in-law from Jerusalem, and Jewish folklore suggests that he became the
founder of the Samaritan sect. [Neh. 2:10, 19; 4:1-2, 7;
6:1-14; 13:28]

SAPH *c.* 10 century BC. A giant in the Philistine army,
killed in battle by a warrior in the army of King David.
Also called Sippai. [2 Sam. 21:18; 1 Chr. 20:4]

Present-day Samaritans at prayer
on Mount Gerizim above
Shechem (Nablus).

SARAH (Heb. 'princess') *c.* 18 century BC. Wife of
Abraham. Sarah was Abraham's half-sister and became
his wife before the family left Ur of the Chaldeans on the
long journey to Haran, and from there to Canaan. She
was the first of the four biblical matriarchs, the others
being Rebekah, Leah and Rachel.

Sarah's unusual beauty gave rise to two similar
episodes. When they journeyed to Egypt because of
famine, Abraham passed her off as his sister for fear
that he might otherwise be killed on her account.
Pharaoh took her into his harem, bestowing gifts on
her alleged 'brother'. But when the Lord afflicted

Sarah was the first biblical matriarch.
Mesopotamian diorite female head from
the end of the 3rd millennium BC,
from the Nin-Gal Temple at Ur.

Pharaoh and his household with plagues, he learnt the
truth and hastily restored Sarah to her husband, bid-
ding them go their way in peace. On a later journey
into the territory of Abimelech, ruler of Gerar near
Gaza, he too acquired Sarah after being told she was
Abraham's sister, but handed her back after the Lord
had disclosed the truth in a dream. (One of the Dead
Sea Scrolls discovered in 1948 is an apochryphal commentary on the story of Abraham, that dwells on
Sarah's beauty.)

The tragedy of Sarah's life was that she was barren.
Her childless state was particularly ironical because the
Lord kept telling Abraham that 'I will make your
descendants as the dust of the earth' (Gen. 13:16) and
that the whole land of Canaan would belong to his
descendants. Sarah suggested a solution that fitted in
with the customs of the period. She offered Abraham
her Egyptian slave-maid Hagar, who bore him a son
called Ishmael. Sarah could not conceal her jealousy
when Hagar conceived, and at one stage the pregnant
maid 'fled from her' (Gen. 16:6) but was persuaded to
return by an angel of the Lord.

When Abraham was ninety-nine, the Lord announced to him that Sarah would bear him a son. He was incredulous, for Sarah was then ninety, and long past child-bearing age. The announcement was later repeated by three strangers, angels in disguise, who visited Abraham at Mamre. Listening to the conversation from inside the tent, Sarah laughed scornfully to herself. But in due time the child was born and named Isaac, which in Hebrew means 'he laughed'.

Sarah remained sensitive about having a child in her old age. She wanted also to secure the inheritance for Isaac. When Hagar and Ishmael mocked her at Isaac's weaning feast, Sarah demanded of Abraham that he send them away. This he did reluctantly, after consulting the Lord.

Sarah lived to the ripe old age of one hundred and twenty-seven, and was buried by Abraham in the Cave of Machpelah at Hebron, which he bought to serve as a family tomb. Also called Sarai. [Gen. 11, 12, 16-18, 20, 21, 23; 49:31; Isa. 51:2]

SARAI *see* SARAH

SARAPH (Heb. 'burning') date unknown. A descendant of Shelah and leader of the tribe of Judah, he ruled over parts of Moab, east of the Dead Sea. [1 Chr. 4:22]

SARGON II (Ass. 'lawful king') King of Assyria, 721-04 BC. Sargon was an Assyrian general who seized the throne when King Shalmaneser V died during the siege of Samaria. The city fell to Sargon, thus ending the northern kingdom of Israel. According to Assyrian records, 27,290 Israelites were deported to other parts of the Assyrian empire, while colonists were brought in from elsewhere and settled in Israel, which then became a province of Assyria.

Judah and other neighbouring kingdoms remained vassal states paying tribute to Assyria. In 711 BC Sargon sent an army into the coastal plain of Philistia to quell a revolt at Ashdod, whose king was deposed and a governor appointed. Judah, as well as the Trans-jordan kingdoms of Edom and Moab, were probably linked with this revolt but seemed to have submitted to the Assyrians. Sargon was killed in 704 BC and was succeeded by his son Sennacherib. [2 Kgs. 17; Isa. 20:1]

SARSECHIM (Bab. 'master of wardrobes') *c.* 6 century BC. One of the Babylonian army commanders who conquered Jerusalem and sat in triumph at the middle gate of the city following its capture. His title was Rabsaris. [Jer. 39:3]

below left Lion killing a man, ivory, from Nimrod, 8th century BC. The Assyrians who were settled in Samaria under Sargon were killed by lions.

below right Relief of King Sargon II (721-05 BC), from his palace at Khorsabad.

SAUL (Heb. 'loaned') *c.* second half of 11 century BC. First Hebrew king.

Saul was the son of Kish, a man of substance in the tribe of Benjamin, and his wife Ahinoam. The family home was at Gibeah, three miles north of Jerusalem. Saul himself is described as 'a handsome young man . . . from his shoulders upward he was taller than any of the people' (1 Sam. 9:2). The kingly office was bestowed upon him by the prophet Samuel at a time when the Israelites were being hard pressed by their enemies, and felt desperately in need of a single leader under whom they could unite.

There are two different accounts in the First Book of Samuel of how Saul became king. According to the first, he was sent by his father with a servant to look for some asses that had strayed in the hill country north of Gibeah. They came to a town where Samuel was on a visit, and decided to consult him, since he was a renowned seer. Samuel had already been apprised by the Lord that Saul was destined to be king. He therefore showed the young man special favour, inviting him to eat with him and stay the night. At daybreak, Samuel sent him on his way after anointing him with oil and telling him the Lord had chosen him 'to be prince over his heritage' (1 Sam. 10:1). On the road Saul encountered various signs foretold by Samuel: two men told him the missing asses had been found, and three passing prophets gave him bread. When he met a company of prophets coming down from the high places with music, the spirit of God came upon him and he prophesied among them to the astonishment of all who knew him – hence the saying 'Is Saul also among the prophets?' (1 Sam. 10:11) On his return Saul encountered his uncle and told him about his meeting with Samuel but kept to himself what the prophet had said about the kingship.

The other account of Saul's selection pictures Samuel as yielding to popular pressure against his will. He called the people to a gathering where the drawing of lots determined that the choice should be from the tribe of Benjamin, then narrowed it down to Saul. The young man had hidden himself but was fetched and presented by Samuel to the people, who shouted, 'Long live the king.' (1 Sam. 10:24) Saul then went back to his home.

It took a military emergency to propel Saul into the leadership for which he had been marked. The Hebrew town of Jabesh-gilead, east of the Jordan river in the tribal area of Manasseh, was being heavily attacked by the Ammonites from further to the east. The townspeople sought surrender terms. Nahash the Ammonite king bluntly replied that he would spare them but take out their right eyes, in order to humiliate Israel. The elders prayed for time while they sent out appeals for help. Saul was coming from the fields with his cattle

when he learnt of the grim plight of Jabesh-gilead. He mobilized a large force and marched to the relief of the beleaguered town. Approaching at night, he launched a surprise attack at dawn. The Ammonite army was routed, and Jabesh-gilead was saved.

Saul Becomes King

This victory established Saul as a military leader. Samuel assembled all the people at Gilgal and Saul was crowned with ceremonial sacrifices and public rejoicing.

Saul defeating the Ammonites (top),
and anointed by Samuel (bottom).
13th-century French manuscript.

When Saul had been king two years, he felt ready to challenge the power of the Philistines. They were a formidable enemy – an alliance of five wealthy tribes, possessing an effective army equipped with chariots. The Israelites at this time were relatively poor and backward, and did not know how to smelt iron. 'Now there was no smith to be found throughout all the land

right 16th-century German engraving of David playing to Saul. Saul holds his spear in his hand ready to hurl it at David.

Iron daggers found in a Philistine tomb
at Tel Farah.

sure for some time, and Saul was able to campaign against other neighbouring peoples that had been harassing the Israelites. They included the Amorites and the Zobahites, Aramean peoples pressing down from the north; the Ammonites on the Trans-jordan plateau to the east; and the Amalekites in the southern desert.

The Conflict with Samuel

From the beginning of Saul's reign, his relations with Samuel were strained. The moment the king deviated from what he was told to do, the prophet turned fiercely upon him and rejected him. It was a one-sided quarrel. However strong and courageous Saul was in battle against his people's enemies, he was cowed by Samuel's wrath, and stood in awe of Samuel's claim to speak for God. He did not argue or resist when attacked by the prophet.

The trouble had started when the Philistine army had occupied Michmash. Saul waited for Samuel at Gilgal for seven days; then, unable to tarry any longer, Saul himself made the ritual burnt-offerings before battle. Samuel denounced him for this, and declared that the Lord 'has sought out a man after his own heart' (1 Sam. 13:14) to replace Saul.

It was perhaps to atone for this transgression and demonstrate his piety that Saul ordered his men to fast all day during the battle of Michmash that followed. Jonathan unwittingly broke the order by tasting

Egyptian glazed tile of a Philistine dignitary, c. 13th century BC.

of Israel; for the Philistines said, "Lest the Hebrews make themselves swords or spears"' (1 Sam. 13:19). In fact only Saul and his son Jonathan possessed these weapons; their men were a people's militia armed with pitchforks and other farm tools.

Saul decided to attack the Philistine garrison at Geba, just a few miles north of his capital of Gibeah. He selected and trained a force of three thousand men, left a thousand of them under the command of his eldest son Jonathan, and with the rest cut off the rear line of the Philistines. Jonathan's task force then struck at the enemy garrison and wiped it out.

The Philistine leaders reacted swiftly to this bold challenge. With an army of chariots, horsemen and foot-soldiers, they marched upon the occupied Michmash, not far from Saul's capital. The Israelites were overcome with fear. They hid in mountain caves and bushes, and many of them fled across the Jordan river. Saul's forces melted away, and he was left with only six hundred men.

It was Jonathan who saved the situation. Unknown to his father, he slipped away with his young armour-bearer, climbed up above a rocky pass, and surprised and killed a group of twenty Philistine soldiers moving through it. After this sudden counter-attack, panic spread among the Philistines, and the Hebrews came out of hiding and fell upon them as they fled.

The victory at Michmash relieved the Philistine pressome wild honey, and encouraged the hungry soldiers to kill and eat captured animals. Because of this sin, when Saul asked counsel of God 'he did not answer him that day' (1 Sam. 14:37). Saul declared that Jonathan must die, but readily yielded to the pleas of the people for the beloved son whose single-handed exploit had turned the tide of battle.

The next clash with Samuel took place after Saul's successful expedition against the Amalekites. Contrary to Samuel's injunction, Saul had spared and brought back as his captive the Amalekite king, Agag, and had allowed his men to take as booty the pick of the enemy's sheep and cattle. When Saul claimed that the animals were intended as a sacrifice to the Lord, Samuel scornfully replied, 'Behold, to obey is better than sacrifice, and to hearken than the fat of rams.' (1 Sam. 15:22) Saul begged Samuel to pardon him and appear at his side before the elders. The prophet refused, and turned to leave. Saul clutched at the edge of his robe; it tore, and Samuel promptly called this a sign that the Lord had rent the kingdom of Israel from Saul. Samuel relented about departing but demanded that the captive king be brought to him; and he 'hewed Agag in pieces before the Lord in Gilgal' (1 Sam. 15:33). After this bloody lesson, Samuel retired to his abode at Ramah, and did not see Saul again in his lifetime. Meanwhile, Samuel had secretly anointed someone else on the Lord's behalf to be the future king. He was the young David.

Saul and David

Two different accounts are given of how the young David first came to the notice of the king. According to one, Saul had become increasingly subject to fits of depression, for 'an evil spirit from the Lord tormented him' (1 Sam. 16:14). He was told by his servants that David the son of Jesse the Bethlehemite was a skilled player on the harp, and might be able to relieve his mood. Saul sent for the youth, was charmed by his music and his comely looks, and made him the king's armour-bearer. The other account suggests that David met Saul when he killed Goliath, and was then taken into the king's service.

Saul's jealousy was aroused when David's exploits made him popular. The women turned out to greet them on their return from battle, singing 'Saul has slain his thousands, and David his ten thousands.' (1 Sam. 18:7) This rankled with the king; 'And Saul eyed David from that day on.' (1 Sam. 18:9) In one of his black moods, Saul actually hurled a javelin at David who was playing for him. After that Saul tried to get rid of him by sending him out against the Philistines in command of a unit.

David handled himself wisely and his fame grew. Saul said, 'Let not my hand be upon him, but let the hand of the Philistines be upon him.' (1 Sam. 18:17) He

Philistine anthropoid
coffin found at
Beth-shean.

offered David the hand of his daughter in marriage, provided David slew a hundred Philistine soldiers and brought back their foreskins as evidence. David and his men slew two hundred, and he married Michal, the younger daughter.

One night Jonathan warned David to hide himself because his father Saul again intended to kill him. Jonathan interceded with Saul on David's behalf and the king appeared to relent and welcome David back. But Saul again tried to kill David, who escaped. Saul's men were sent in pursuit to David's home. Michal saved her husband by lowering him down through a window, and putting a dummy figure in his bed. David made his way to Ramah where he told Samuel what had happened. After the king's messenger had failed to capture David, the king came in person. But David was saved by the religious streak coming to the surface in Saul, who 'prophesied before Samuel' (1 Sam. 19:24).

From now on David was a fugitive from the king. He found refuge in the mountain caves of Adullam, south-west of Jerusalem, and became the leader of a band of about four hundred outcasts. When Saul heard that David had slipped out of his hands, he railed bitterly at his attendants and accused everyone of disloyalty, including Jonathan. Hearing the priests of the Shrine of Nob had helped David, he had them brought before him and killed, and their village wiped out.

Saul heard that David and his band were in the town of Keilah in the Adullam area, and saw a chance to trap them inside the walls. But the wily David slipped away again into the hills. At one point David was surrounded, but Saul had to abandon the chase and hurry back to meet a threat from the Philistines.

Saul resumed the hunt into the Engedi wilderness near the Dead Sea. By chance, Saul took shelter in a cave where David and some of his men were hiding. David could easily have killed the king, but all he did was to cut a piece from the hem of Saul's robe. On learning of this, Saul was deeply moved and said, 'You are more righteous than I; for you have repaid me good, whereas I have repaid you evil.' (1 Sam. 24:17) Saul made David swear that when he became king of Israel, he would not injure Saul's descendants or try to wipe out his name.

On another occasion, David penetrated into Saul's camp at night, but refrained from killing the sleeping king. On being awakened Saul called out, 'return, my son David, for I will no more do you harm, because my life was precious in your eyes this day; behold, I have played the fool, and have erred exceedingly.' (1 Sam. 26:21) This was the last encounter between them. David decided to put himself out of the king's reach by going into exile, and joined Achish, the Philistine king of Gath.

The Death of Saul

When Saul had reigned for twenty years, the Philistines once more massed an army to attack Israel, and advanced into the valley of Jezreel. The Israelite forces faced them from Mount Gilboa. Unable to reach the Lord for his guidance, Saul felt abandoned and fearful. In disguise, and accompanied by two trusted men-servants, he sought out a woman at Endor who was a famous medium. Though she pointed out that a royal decree had banned practices of witchcraft and magic in the kingdom, Saul persuaded her to summon the spirit of Samuel from the dead. What Samuel foretold was shattering. The Israelites would be defeated and Saul and his sons killed in battle. Saul lay on the ground in a swoon, till the woman and his two servants picked him up, seated him on the bed and made him eat some food. From his grave, Samuel had had the last word.

The Israelite forces were disastrously defeated on Mount Gilboa and put to flight. Saul's three sons, Jonathan, Abinadab and Melchishua were among the slain. The king himself was wounded by the Philistine archers and begged his armour-bearer to kill him rather than let him fall into the hands of the enemy. The armour-bearer was afraid to do so and Saul 'took his own sword, and fell upon it' (1 Sam. 31:4). The armour-bearer did likewise and died with his master.

Next day the Philistines found Saul's body on the battlefield. They cut off his head, hung his corpse and those of his sons on the wall of Beth-shean city, and exhibited his armour as a trophy in their main temple. When the grim tidings reached the men of Jabesh-gilead (the town Saul had saved at the beginning of his reign), they journeyed all night, recovered and brought back the bodies of Saul and his sons, cremated them and buried their bones under a tree, and fasted seven days in mourning.

David had in the meantime returned to the southern part of Judah, and was in the town of Ziklag when he was told of the disaster on Mount Gilboa. His lament for Saul and Jonathan is one of the most eloquent and moving passages in the Bible. (2 Sam. 1:19-27)

The valley of Jezreel, the scene of Saul's defeat and death, was the classic battleground of the Old Testament, and associated also with the stories of Deborah and Gideon. It was here that Bible prophecy located the final battle of the world at 'Armageddon' – a corruption of the Hebrew *Har Megiddo*, the Mount of Megiddo.

The Bible narrative gives King Saul less than due credit. The two decades of his reign fully justified the first Hebrew experiment in kingship. He gave the weak and poorly organized Israelite tribes the military and political cohesion needed to hold their enemies at bay. He thereby paved the way for the expansion of the kingdom under David. But his achievements are overshadowed in the story by personal conflicts: with his spiritual mentor, the aging and resentful Samuel; with his brilliant young protégé and rival David; and the conflict within himself, that made him erratic, unstable and subject to outbursts of violence. Though the later biblical chroniclers tended to favour David at Saul's expense, the latter emerges as a kingly figure and a leader of men, although a tragic prisoner of his own 'evil spirit'.

Archaeological excavations carried out from 1921 to 1933 at Tel el-Hosen, the 'mound of the fortress', which was the location of the Canaanite city of Beth-shean, brought to light the remains of six temples. Four were in the stratum belonging to the period when the city was subject to Egyptian rule. In them were found victory steles of Pharaoh Seti I and a monument and statue of Rameses II. Two temples date to the time when it was under Philistine authority, and are associated by scholars with the account of the death of Saul and Jonathan at nearby Mount Gilboa. [1 Sam. 9-11; 13-29; 31; 2 Sam. 1-7; 9; 12; 16; 19; 21; 22; 1 Chr. 5:10; 8:33; 9:39; 10; 15:29; 26:28]

SEBA date unknown. Son of Cush and a grandson of Ham, he was a leader of a desert tribe and an ancestor of the Sabeans. [Gen 10:7; 1 Chr. 1:9; Ps. 72:10; Isa. 43:3]

SEGUB (Heb. 'lifted up') **1.** date unknown. Son of Caleb the son of Hezron, he was the father of Jair, a leader of Judah who ruled over twenty-three cities in Gilead, east of the river Jordan. [1 Chr. 2:21, 22]

2. *c.* 9 century BC. Son of Hiel of Bethel, he died in fulfilment of Joshua's curse when his father rebuilt Jericho, during the reign of King Ahab. [Josh. 6:26; 1 Kgs. 16:34]

SEIR (Heb. 'the rugged') date unknown. The Horite

ruler of the part of the land of Edom named after him. [Gen. 36:20, 21; 1 Chr. 1:38; 2 Chr. 25:11, 14]

SELED (Heb. 'lifted up') date unknown. Son of Nadab of the tribe of Judah and a descendant of Jerahmeel, he died childless. [1 Chr. 2:30]

SEMACHIAH (Heb. 'sustained by God') *c.* 10 century BC. Son of Shemaiah and a grandson of Obed-edom, he and his family were gatekeepers of the Tabernacle in the reign of King David and renowned for their strength. [1 Chr. 26:7]

SENAAH (Heb. 'brambly') date unknown. Ancestor of the men of Judah who rebuilt the Fish Gate of Jerusalem in the time of Nehemiah. Also called Hassenaah. [Ezra 2:35; Neh. 3:3; 7:38]

SENNACHERIB (Acc. 'Sin [a god] replace the brothers') King of Assyria, 704-681 BC. Sennacherib succeeded to the throne of the Assyrian empire in 704 BC when his father Sargon II was killed. In 701 BC he invaded Judah, and took forty-six towns. The siege and capture of the fortified Judean city of Lachish is depicted in detail on four wall panels from the palace in Nineveh, Sennacherib's great capital city.

Hezekiah, king of Judah, sent a message of submission to Sennacherib at Lachish, with a huge sum in tribute. The Assyrian monarch was not satisfied but

Relief from Sennacherib's palace at Nineveh, with the inscription: 'Sennacherib, king of the universe, king of Assyria . . . while the booty of Lachish passed before him'.

The final edition of Sennacherib's
Annals, in cuneiform script, 691 BC.
The inscription talks of 'Hezekiah the Jew'
as a 'caged bird'.

demanded the surrender of Jerusalem. This was refused, and for reasons which are not clear, Sennacherib withdrew without laying siege to the city.

The rest of his reign was spent in constant campaigns in parts of the empire closer to Assyria. He was murdered by two of his sons in 681 BC. [2 Kgs. 18:13; 19:16; 20; 2 Chr. 32; Isa. 36, 37]

SEORIM (Heb. 'bearded') *c.* 10 century BC. A priest in the reign of King David who took the fourth turn of service in the Tabernacle in Jerusalem. [1 Chr. 24:8]

SERAH (Heb. 'lady') *c.* 16 century BC. Daughter of Asher and the granddaughter of Jacob and Zilpah, she went down to Egypt at the same time as her grandfather Jacob. Serah was the only woman mentioned in the genealogy of the tribes of Israel in the wilderness. [Gen. 46:17; Num. 26:46; 1 Chr. 7:30]

SERAIAH (Heb. 'warrior of God') **1.** *c.* 13 century BC. Son of Kenaz, brother of Othniel of the tribe of Judah, he was head of a family of craftsmen. [1 Chr. 4:13, 14]
2. *c.* 10 century BC. He was appointed secretary by David when he became king. Seraiah's two sons were secretaries to King Solomon. Also called Sheva,

Shisha and Shavsha. [2 Sam. 8:17; 20:25; 1 Kgs. 4:3; 1 Chr. 18:16]
3. 9 century BC. Grandfather of Jehu who was a leader of the tribe of Simeon. [1 Chr. 4:35]
4. *c.* 6 century BC. Chief priest of Judah in the reign of King Zedekiah, he was taken before the king of Babylon following the destruction of the Temple and put to death. [2 Kgs. 25:18, 21; 1 Chr. 6:14; Jer. 52:24, 27]
5. 6 century BC. A captain of the army who joined Gedaliah when he was made governor over the cities of Judah after the Babylonian conquest. [2 Kgs. 25:23; Jer. 40:8]
6. *c.* 6 century BC. One of the men King Jehoiakim ordered to seize the prophet Jeremiah and his scribe Baruch. [Jer. 36:26]
7. 6 century BC. Son of Neriah and quartermaster to King Zedekiah, he went with his master into exile in Babylon. The prophet Jeremiah ordered him to take with him a book containing the evil prophecies that would befall Babylon. When he finished reading this book, Seraiah was to tie a stone round the scroll and throw it into the Euphrates where it would sink. This would be a symbol of the coming destruction of the Babylonians. [Jer. 51:59-64]
8. 6 century BC. A leader of the Jewish captives in Babylon who returned to Jerusalem with Zerubbabel. Also called Azariah. [Ezra 2:2; Neh. 7:7; 12:1, 12]
9. 5 century BC. Father of Ezra the scribe. [Ezra 7:1]
10. 5 century BC. A priest who signed the solemn covenant in the days of Nehemiah. [Neh. 10:2]
11. 5 century BC. One of the priests who returned to Jerusalem following the exile in Babylon. Also called Azariah. [1 Chr. 9:11; Neh. 11:11]

SERED *c.* 16 century BC. A son of Zebulun and the grandson of Jacob and Leah, he went down to Egypt with his grandfather Jacob. [Gen. 46:14; Num. 26:26]

SERUG (Heb. 'branch') date unknown. Son of Reu and ancestor of Abraham. [1 Gen. 11:20-23; 1 Chr. 1:26]

SETH (Heb. 'founder') date unknown. Seth was the third son of Adam and Eve. He was born after his oldest brother Cain had killed Abel. In the Book of Genesis it is said that Seth was born when Adam was one hundred and thirty years old. He was the father of Enosh. [Gen. 4:26; 5:3-8; 1 Chr. 1:1]

SETHUR (Heb. 'hidden') *c.* 13 century BC. Son of Michael and a leader of the tribe of Asher, he was chosen by Moses as one of the twelve men sent to spy out the Promised Land. [Num. 13:13]

SHAAPH (Heb. 'division') **1.** date unknown. Son of Caleb and his concubine Maacah, he was a leader of the tribe of Judah and the father of Madmannah. [1 Chr. 2:49]
2. date unknown. Son of Jahdai and a leader of the

tribe of Judah descended from Caleb. [1 Chr. 2:47]

SHAASHGAZ (Pers. 'lover of beauty') 5 century BC. Chamberlain of Ahasuerus, king of Persia, into whose custody the king's concubines were delivered, he took charge of all the young girls from whom the king was to choose a new wife. [Esther 2:14]

SHABBETHAI (Heb. 'my rest') 5 century BC. A prominent Levite in the time of Ezra who helped explain the Law of God to the people of Judah after Ezra had read it out in the market-place, and supervised the administration of the Temple. [Ezra 10:15; Neh. 8:7; 11:16]

SHADRACH (Pers. 'command of Aku') c. 7 century BC. The Babylonian name given to Hananiah, one of the four princes of Judah taken off to Babylon by the orders of King Nebuchadnezzar in 607 BC. When the four refused to worship or serve the Babylonian gods, Nebuchadnezzar, in great rage, ordered them cast into the fiery furnace. They were delivered by an angel and walked out unhurt. [Dan. 1:7; 2; 3]

SHAGEE (Heb. 'erring') c. 10 century BC. Father of Jonathan, a warrior in the army of King David who was distinguished for his bravery. [1 Chr. 11:34]

SHAHARAIM (Heb. 'double warning') date unknown. Leader of the tribe of Benjamin, he sent away two of his wives, Hushim and Baara, and had seven sons by his wife Hodesh with whom he lived in Moab east of the river Jordan. [1 Chr. 8:8-11]

SHALLUM (Heb. 'reward') **1.** see SHILLEM.

2. c. 16 century BC. A grandson of Simeon and the father of Mibsam, he and his family were leaders of the tribe. [1 Chr. 4:25]

3. date unknown. Son of Sismai of the tribe of Judah and the father of Jekamiah. [1 Chr. 2:40, 41]

4. c. 10 century BC. Son of Kore the Levite and a descendant of Korah, he was chief of the porters at the gates of the Tabernacle in the reign of King David. His descendants performed similar services in the time of Ezra and Nehemiah. Also called Meshelemiah and Shelemiah. [1 Chr. 9:17, 19, 31; 26:1, 2, 9, 14; Ezra 2:42; Neh. 7:45]

5. 8 century BC. Fifteenth king of Israel after the monarchy split, he reigned for one month in 743 BC. This brief reign of Shallum the son of Jabesh was inglorious. Nothing is known about his background. He assassinated King Zechariah and seized the throne, but a month later was murdered and succeeded by Menahem, son of Gadi. [2 Kgs. 15:10-15]

Shadrach, Meshach and Abednego in the fiery furnace, from the *Nuremberg Bible*, 1483.

Assyrian helmet crests found at Lachish,
9th-6th centuries B.C.

6. *c.* 8 century BC. Father of Jehizkiah, a leader of Ephraim who insisted that the prisoners of Judah captured in battle by the army of Israel in the reign of Pekah should be returned to Judah. [2 Chr. 28:12]

7. *c.* 7 century BC. Husband of Huldah the prophetess, he was the son of Tikvah and the grandson of Harhas who was keeper of the king's wardrobe. [2 Kgs. 22:14; 2 Chr. 34:22]

8. *c.* 7 century BC. Son of Zadok and father of Hilkiah, the high priest in the reign of King Josiah, he was an ancestor of Ezra. [1 Chr. 6:12; Ezra 7:2]

9. *c.* 7 century BC. An uncle of Jeremiah, he was the father of Hanamel whose field in Anatoth Jeremiah redeemed though he knew the land of Israel was about to be conquered by the Babylonians. [Jer. 32:7]

10. *see* JEHOAHAZ **3.**

11. *c.* 6 century BC. Father of Maaseiah who was a gatekeeper of the Temple in Jerusalem in the time of the prophet Jeremiah. [Jer. 35:4]

12. 5 century BC. A Levite who was a porter at the gates of the Temple and who divorced his non-Jewish wife in the time of Ezra. [Ezra 10:24]

13. 5 century BC. A descendant of Binhui who divorced his non-Jewish wife in the time of Ezra. [Ezra 10:42]

14. 5 century BC. Son of Hallohesh and a ruler of part of Jerusalem, he and his daughters helped repair the walls of Jerusalem in the days of Nehemiah. [Neh. 3:12]

15. 5 century BC. Son of Colhozeh and ruler of the district of Mizpah, he repaired the Fountain Gate of Jerusalem and the wall of the Pool of Siloam in the time of Nehemiah. [Neh. 3:15]

SHALMAI (Heb. 'thanks') date unknown. Ancestor of a family of Temple servants who returned with Zerubbabel to Judah from exile in Babylon. Also called Shamlai. [Ezra 2:46; Neh. 7:48]

SHALMAN 8 century BC. An eastern ruler who captured and despoiled the city of Beth-arbel. It is thought by some scholars to be a reference to the Assyrian emperor Shalmaneser V. [Hos. 10:14]

SHALMANESER V (Ass. 'Sulman is leader') King of Assyria, 727-2 BC. When Tiglath-pileser III, king of Assyria, died in 727 BC, the throne was seized by Ululai, the governor of Babylon, who became Shalmaneser V.

At that time most of the kings in Palestine were tributaries of the Assyrian empire, including Hoshea, king of Israel. With Egyptian encouragement, he revolted against Assyrian domination. In 724 BC. Shalmaneser invaded Israel and took Hoshea captive. The Assyrians then besieged the strongly fortified hill capital of Samaria, which held out for two years. Before its fall, Shalmaneser died and was succeeded by Sargon II. (Possibly he is Shalman referred to by Hosea, Hos. 10:14.) [2 Kgs. 17:3-6; 18:9, 10]

SHAMA (Heb. 'heard') *c.* 10 century BC. One of the two sons of Hotham who were warriors in King David's army and distinguished for their bravery. [1 Chr. 11:44]

SHAMGAR (Heb. 'sword') *c.* 12 century BC. Son of Anath, and the third judge of Israel, he delivered Israel from the Philistines and once killed six hundred Philistines with an ox-goad. [Judg. 3:31; 5:6]

SHAMHUTH (Heb. 'destruction') *c.* 10 century BC. A captain in King David's army who commanded the army for the fifth month of each year. Also known as Shammah and Shammoth. [2 Sam. 23:25; 1 Chr. 11:27; 27:8]

SHAMIR (Heb. 'thorn') *c.* 10 century BC. Son of Micah of the tribe of Levi and a descendant of Izhar, he served in the Tabernacle in the reign of King David. [1 Chr. 24:24]

SHAMLAI *see* SHALMAI

SHAMMA (Heb. 'desolation') date unknown. Son of Zophah, he and his family were leaders of the tribe of Asher and mighty warriors. [1 Chr. 7:37]

SHAMMAH 1. 16 century BC. Son of Reuel and a grandson of Esau, he was an Edomite leader. [Gen. 36:13, 17; 1 Chr. 1:37]

2. *c.* 11 century BC. Son of Jesse and a brother of David, he fought in Saul's army against the Philistines. Also known as Shimei and Shimea. [1 Sam. 16:9; 17:13; 2 Sam. 13:3, 32; 21:21; 1 Chr. 2:13; 20:7]

3. *c.* 10 century BC. One of the three mighty men of King David, he fought the Philistines single-handed at Lehi in a lentil patch after all the men of Israel had fled. [2 Sam. 23:11, 33]

4. *see* SHAMHUTH

SHAMMAI (Heb. 'assessor') **1.** date unknown. Son of Onam and grandson of Jerahmeel, a leader of the tribe of Judah, he was the father of Nadab and Abishur. [1 Chr. 2:28]

2. date unknown. Son of Rekem of the tribe of Judah

and the grandson of Hebron, he was the father of Maon. [1 Chr. 2:44, 45]

3. date unknown. Son of Mered of the tribe of Judah by his wife Bithiah, the daughter of a Pharaoh. [1 Chr. 4:17]

SHAMMOTH *see* SHAMHUTH

SHAMMUA (Heb. 'heard') **1.** *c.* 13 century BC. Son of Zaccur and a leader of the tribe of Reuben, he was appointed by Moses as one of the twelve men sent to spy out the Promised Land. [Num. 13:4]

2. *c.* 10 century BC. One of the sons of King David born to him when he was king in Jerusalem. Also called Shimea. [2 Sam. 5:14; 1 Chr. 3:5; 14:4]

3. *see* SHEMAIAH **17.**

4. 5 century BC. The head of a priestly family descended from Bilgah, he was a chief priest of Judah towards the end of Nehemiah's lifetime. [Neh. 12:18]

SHAMSHERAI (Heb. 'hero') date unknown. Son of Jeroham, he was a leader of the tribe of Benjamin living in Jerusalem. [1 Chr. 8:26]

SHAPHAM (Heb. 'bare') date unknown. A leader of the tribe of Gad living in Bashan, east of the river Jordan. [1 Chr. 5:12]

SHAPHAN (Heb. 'rabbit') **1.** *c.* 7 century BC. Son of Azaliah and secretary of Josiah, his son Ahikam saved the prophet Jeremiah from being put to death at the order of King Jehoiakim. [2 Kgs. 22:3; 2 Chr. 34:8; Jer. 26:24; 36:10-12]

2. *c.* 6 century BC. Father of Jaazaniah, a leader of Judah condemned by Ezekiel for offering sacrifices to idols near the Temple. [Ezek. 8:11]

SHAPHAT (Heb. 'judge') **1.** *c.* 13 century BC. Son of Hori and a leader of the tribe of Simeon, he was one of the twelve men chosen by Moses to spy out the Promised Land. [Num. 13:5]

2. *c.* 10 century BC. The official of King David in charge of the royal herds that fed in the valleys. [1 Chr. 27:29]

3. *c.* 9 century BC. Father of the prophet Elisha. [1 Kgs. 19:16, 19; 2 Kgs. 3:11; 6:31]

4. *c.* 5 century BC. Son of Shemaiah and a member of the royal family of Judah descended from King David. [1 Chr. 3:22]

5. date unknown. A leader of the tribe of Gad living in Bashan, east of the river Jordan. [1 Chr. 5:12]

SHARAI (Heb. 'set free') 5 century BC. A descendant of Binnui who divorced his non-Jewish wife in the time of Ezra. [Ezra 10:40]

SHARAR *see* SACHAR **1.**

SHAREZER (Heb. 'prince') **1.** *c.* 7 century BC. One of the two sons of Sennacherib, king of Assyria, who murdered their father while he was at worship in the temple of Nisroch at Nineveh. [2 Kgs. 19:37; Isa. 37:38]

2. *c.* 6 century BC. One of the two leaders of a delegation of men of Judah who asked the prophet Zechariah if the people were still obliged to commemorate the

destruction of the Temple even after it had been rebuilt. [Zech. 7:2]

SHASHAI (Heb. 'noble') 5 century BC. A descendant of Binnui who divorced his non-Jewish wife in the time of Ezra. [Ezra 10:40]

SHASHAK date unknown. Son of Elpaal and a leader of the tribe of Benjamin. [1 Chr. 8:14, 25]

SHAUL (Heb. 'asked') **1.** date unknown. A king of Edom who came from Rehoboth on the Euphrates. [Gen. 36:37, 38; 1 Chr. 1:48, 49]

2. *c.* 16 century BC. Son of Simeon and his Canaanite wife, he went down to Egypt with his grandfather Jacob. [Gen. 46:10; Exod. 6:15; Num. 26:13; 1 Chr. 4:24]

3. *see* JOEL **3.**

SHAVSHA *see* SERAIAH **2.**

SHEAL (Heb. 'asking') 5 century BC. A descendant of Bani, he divorced his non-Jewish wife in the time of Ezra. [Ezra 10:29]

SHEALTIEL (Heb. 'asked of God') *c.* 6 century BC. Father of Zerubbabel who led the return to Judah from exile in Babylon. In the First Book of Chronicles, Zerubbabel's father is given as Pedaiah. [1 Chr. 3:17, 18, 19; Ezra 3:2, 8; 5:2; Neh. 12:1; Hag. 1:1, 12, 14; 2:21]

SHEARIAH (Heb. 'God's gate') date unknown. Son of Azel of the tribe of Benjamin and a descendant of King Saul. [1 Chr. 8:38; 9:44]

SHEAR-JASHUB (Heb. 'a remnant shall return') *c.* 8 century BC. The son of the prophet Isaiah whom God ordered to go with Isaiah to meet Ahaz, king of Judah, at the upper pool outside Jerusalem. His name is symbolic of Isaiah's prophecy that the kingdoms of Israel and Judah would be destroyed but a remnant would return to Judah. [Isa. 7:3]

SHEBA 1. date unknown. Son of Joktan, a descendant of Shem. [Gen. 10:28; 1 Chr. 1:22]

2. *c.* 16 century BC. Son of Jokshan and grandson of Abraham and Keturah, he was a desert chieftain. [Gen. 25:3; 1 Chr. 1:32]

3. date unknown. A leader of the tribe of Gad, living in Bashan, east of the river Jordan. [1 Chr. 5:13]

4. *c.* 10 century BC. Son of Bichri, he was a Benjaminite who stirred up a rebellion against David after the revolt of Absalom had been quelled. David sent his commander Joab after Sheba who took refuge in the city of Abel-beth-maacha in northern Galilee. Joab besieged the town and attacked the wall. A woman renowned for her wisdom called down to him, reminding Joab that this city had always been loyal to David. Joab agreed to withdraw his troops if she would hand over Sheba. The men of the city killed him and sent his head to Joab who immediately left and returned to King David. [2 Sam. 20]

SHEBANIAH (Heb. 'grown by God') **1.** *c.* 10 century

Inscription from a rock-cut tomb at Silwan, believed to refer to the tomb of Shebna the royal steward, berated by Isaiah for his elaborate sepulchre hewn out of rock.

BC. A priest who blew a trumpet during the celebrations when King David brought the Ark of God to Jerusalem. [1 Chr. 15:24]

2. date unknown. Ancestor of a priestly family of Judah that returned from exile in Babylon, his descendant Joseph was a priest in the time of Nehemiah. [Neh. 12:14]

3. 5 century BC. A Levite who prayed to God to forgive the people of Judah for their sins on the public fast day proclaimed by Ezra. He later signed the solemn covenant. [Neh. 9:4; 10:10]

4. 5 century BC. A Levite who called upon the people of Judah to praise God during the public fast day called by Ezra. He later signed the solemn covenant. [Neh. 9:5; 10:12]

5. 5 century BC. A priest of Judah who signed the solemn covenant in the time of Nehemiah. [Neh. 10:4]

SHEBER (Heb. 'breaking') date unknown. Son of Caleb and Maacah and a leader of the tribe of Judah. [1 Chr. 2:48]

SHEBNA (Heb. 'may God sit') *c.* 8 century BC. Official scribe to King Hezekiah, he took part in the negotiations between Judah and the attacking Assyrians in which the surrender of Jerusalem was demanded. No agreement was reached.

Hezekiah sent Shebna as part of a delegation to consult the prophet Isaiah, who told them that the Assyrians would not take Jerusalem, but would go away – which is what happened.

Later Shebna carved himself an elaborate rock tomb for which he was attacked by Isaiah. The prophet told him that the Lord would 'whirl you round and round, and throw you like a ball into a wide land; there you shall die' (Isa. 22:18). He also told him he would be replaced by Eliakim, son of Hilkiah, who would fill the post with honour. [2 Kgs. 18:18, 26, 37; 19:2; Isa. 22:15; 36:3, 11, 22; 37:2]

SHEBUEL (Heb. 'captive of God') **1.** *c.* 10 century BC. A descendant of Moses and leader of the family of Gershomites in the reign of King David, he was responsible for the administration of the treasury in the Tabernacle. Also called Shubael. [1 Chr. 23:16; 24:20; 26:24]

2. *c.* 10 century BC. A son of Heman, one of King David's chief musicians, he and his brothers played musical instruments in the Tabernacle under their father's directions and were responsible for the thirteenth turn of the service. Also called Shubael. [1 Chr. 25:4, 20]

SHECANIAH (Heb. 'dweller with God') **1.** *c.* 10 century BC. A priest in the reign of King David who was responsible for the tenth turn of service in the Tabernacle in Jerusalem. [1 Chr. 24:11]

2. *c.* 8 century BC. A priest of Judah in the reign of King Hezekiah who distributed the freewill offering among the priests and Levites in the cities of Judah. [2 Chr. 31:15]

3. 6 century BC. A leading priest who returned to Judah with Zerubbabel from exile in Babylon. [Neh. 12:3]

4. 5 century BC. A descendant of Zerubbabel, he was the father of Shemaiah and the head of a family which returned with Ezra from exile in Babylon. [1 Chr. 3:21, 22; Ezra 8:3]

5. 5 century BC. Son of Jahaziel, he was head of a family which returned with Ezra from exile in Babylon. [Ezra 8:5]

6. 5 century BC. Son of Jehiel, he suggested that the people of Judah could begin to make atonement for their sins by promising to divorce their non-Jewish wives. [Ezra 10:2]

7. 5 century BC. Father of Shemaiah, the priest who repaired the East Gate of Jerusalem in the time of Nehemiah. [Neh. 3:29]

8. 5 century BC. Son of Arah he was a leading citizen of Judah. His daughter married Tobiah the Samaritan leader who attempted to interfere with Nehemiah's work of rebuilding Jerusalem and whose relationship with Shecaniah brought him many allies among the leading families of Judah. [Neh. 6:18]

SHECHEM (Heb. 'shoulder') **1.** *c.* 16 century BC. Son of Hamor, a Canaanite leader, he fell in love with Jacob's daughter Dinah and seduced her. Shechem sent his father Hamor to Jacob to ask for her hand in marriage. Jacob and his sons agreed provided that all the males in his family and in his city were circumcised. This was done but before the men could recover from this painful operation, Simeon and Levi, full brothers

right The remains of the east gate of the temple at Shechem, now under excavation.

below Shechem was an important centre in the age of the patriarchs: reconstruction of the ancient courtyard temple.

of Dinah, entered the city and killed them all. [Gen. 33:19; 34:2, 4, 13; Josh. 24:32; Judg. 9:28]

2. date unknown. A leader of the tribe of Manasseh descended from Gilead, his family was numbered among the children of Israel in the wilderness. [Num. 26:31; Josh. 17:2]

3. *c.* 13 century BC. Son of Shemidah, he and his family were leaders of the tribe of Manasseh living in Gilead, east of the river Jordan. [1 Chr. 7:19]

SHEDEUR (Heb. 'God is my light') *c.* 13 century BC. Father of Elizur who was chosen by Moses in the wilderness to number the men of Reuben who were fit for the army. [Num. 1:5; 2:10; 7:30-35; 10:18]

SHEERAH (Heb. 'relation') *c.* 16 century BC. Daughter of Beriah and the granddaughter of Ephraim, her descendants built the towns of Lower and Upper Beth-horon and Uzzen-sheerah. [1 Chr. 7:24]

SHEHARIAH (Heb. 'seeks God') date unknown. Son of Jeroham, he was one of the leaders of the tribe of Benjamin living in Jerusalem. [1 Chr. 8:26]

SHELAH (Heb. 'prayer') **1.** date unknown. Son of Arpachshad and a grandson of Shem. [1 Chr. 1:18, 24]

2. *c.* 16 century BC. Youngest son of Judah, he went down to Egypt with his grandfather Jacob. [Gen. 38:5, 11, 26; 46:12; Num. 26:20; 1 Chr. 2:3; 1 Chr. 4:21]

SHELEMIAH (Heb. 'God rewards') **1.** *see* SHALLUM **4.**

2. *c.* 7 century BC. Son of Cushi and father of Nethaniah, his grandson Jehudi read out Jeremiah's prophecies of doom to Jehoiakim, king of Judah. [Jer. 36:14]

3. *c.* 7 century BC. Son of Abdeel, he was an officer of Jehoiakim, king of Judah, commanded to arrest the prophet Jeremiah and his scribe Baruch after the king had heard the prophecies of doom concerning Judah. [Jer. 36:26]

4. *c.* 6 century BC. Father of Jehucal who was sent by Zedekiah, king of Judah, to ask the prophet Jeremiah to pray for Judah during the Babylonian siege of Jerusalem. Later, he was among the Judean leaders who demanded the death of the prophet for spreading alarm and despondency and threw him in prison. [Jer. 37:3; 38:1]

5. *c.* 6 century BC. Son of Hananiah and the father of Irijah, a captain in the army of Zedekiah who falsely accused the prophet Jeremiah of deserting to the Babylonians during the siege of Jerusalem. [Jer. 37:13]

6. 5 century BC. Two descendants of Binnui who divorced their non-Jewish wives in the time of Ezra. [Ezra 10:39, 41]

7. 5 century BC. Father of Hananiah who helped repair the walls of Jerusalem in the time of Nehemiah. [Neh. 3:30]

8. 5 century BC. A priest of Judah who was appointed by Nehemiah to supervise the distribution of corn, wine and oil among the priests and Levites. [Neh. 13:13]

SHELEPH date unknown. One of Joktan's thirteen sons and a great-grandson of Shem. [Gen. 10:26; 1 Chr. 1:20]

SHELESH (Heb. 'strength') date unknown. Son of Helem, he and his family were leaders of the tribe of Asher and mighty warriors. [1 Chr. 7:35]

SHELOMI (Heb. 'my peace') *c.* 13 century BC. Father of Ahihud, a leader of the tribe of Asher who was chosen by Moses to divide up the area of the land of Israel allotted to his tribe. [Num. 34:27]

SHELOMITH (Heb. 'peace') **1.** date unknown. Daughter of Dibri of the tribe of Dan who married an Egyptian. Their son cursed God during a fight with a man of Israel and as a punishment was stoned to death. [Lev. 24:11]

2. *see* SHELOMOTH **2.**

3. *c.* 10 century BC. Son of Rehoboam king of Judah and his favourite wife Maacah. [2 Chr. 11:20]

4. 6 century BC. Daughter of Zerubbabel of the tribe of Judah who led the return from exile in Babylon. [1 Chr. 3:19]

5. *c.* 5 century BC. Son of Josiphiah, he returned with Ezra from exile in Babylon. [Ezra 8:10]

SHELOMOTH (Heb. 'peace') **1.** *c.* 10 century BC. A Levite descended from Gershom, he and his family ministered in the Tabernacle during the reign of King David. [1 Chr. 23:9]

2. *c.* 10 century BC. The head of a family of Levites, he and his son Jahath ministered in the Tabernacle in the reign of King David. Also known as Shelomith. [1 Chr. 23:18; 24:22]

3. *c.* 10 century BC. Son of Zichri the Levite, during the reign of King David he was in charge of the precious vessels taken in battle, which were dedicated to the Tabernacle. [1 Chr. 26:25-8]

SHELUMIEL (Heb. 'God's peace') *c.* 13 century BC. Son of Zurishaddai, he was head of the tribe of Simeon who helped Moses with the census in the wilderness. [Num. 1:6; 2:12; 7:36, 10:19]

SHEM (Heb. 'renown') date unknown. Eldest son of Noah. Shem and his wife went into the ark with his father Noah and the rest of the family. When they left the ark, Noah became a farmer, planted a vineyard, made wine out of his grapes and became drunk. Shem, together with his brother Japheth, covered their father as he lay in a drunken stupor in his tent, and tactfully turned their heads away so they should not see his nakedness. When Noah heard what Shem and Japheth had done for him he blessed them. Noah said: 'Blessed by the Lord my God be Shem.' (Gen. 9:26) Shem lived for five hundred years and had many sons who gave their names to states and cities in the region. He came to be regarded as the legendary ancestor of the Semites. [Gen. 5:32, 6:10, 9:18-27; 10:1, 21, 22, 31; 11:10, 11; 1 Chr. 1:1, 17, 24]

SHEMA (Heb. 'hearing') **1.** date unknown. Son of Hebron and a leader of the tribe of Judah. [1 Chr. 2:43-4]
2. date unknown. Grandfather of Bela, he was a leader of the tribe of Reuben. Also called Shemaiah. [1 Chr. 5:4, 8]
3. date unknown. A leader of the tribe of Benjamin who 'put to flight the inhabitants of Gath' (1 Chr. 8:13). Also known as Shimei. [1 Chr. 8:13, 21]
4. 5 century BC. A leader of Judah who stood at the side of Ezra when he read out the Law of Moses to the people. [Neh. 8:4]

SHEMAAH (Heb. 'God hears') *c.* 11 century BC. Father of Ahiezer and Joash, leaders of a band of Benjaminite archers who deserted from King Saul's army and joined David at Ziklag. [1 Chr. 12:3]

SHEMAIAH (Heb. 'God hears') **1.** date unknown. Father of Shimri, he was an ancestor of Ziza, one of the leaders of Simeon in the reign of Hezekiah, king of Judah. [1 Chr. 4:37]
2. *see* SHEMA **2.**
3. *c.* 10 century BC. A prophet during the reign of Rehoboam. Shortly after succeeding his father, King Solomon, Rehoboam faced a revolt of the northern tribes, who seceded and established a separate kingdom of Israel under the rule of Jeroboam. When Rehoboam assembled an army from the tribes of Judah and Benjamin to suppress the revolt and restore the united kingdom, Shemaiah warned him against it, calling upon him in the name of the Lord not to fight his 'kinsmen the people of Israel' (1 Kgs. 12:24). His words were heeded; there was no war; and Rehoboam ruled over a truncated kingdom, the kingdom of Judah.

Five years later, when the Egyptian Pharaoh Shishak attacked Judah, ravaged several of its cities and was marching on Jerusalem, Shemaiah again came to Rehoboam and told him that since he had deserted the ways of the Lord, the Lord had abandoned him. However, because Rehoboam took the prophet's words to heart and repented, Jerusalem did not fall but Judah became a tributary of Egypt. It is recorded that Shemaiah together with Iddo wrote an account of Rehoboam's reign. [1 Kgs. 12:22; 2 Chr. 11:2; 12:5, 7, 15]
4. *c.* 10 century BC. The head of a family of Levites descended from Elizaphan who took part in the ceremony of bringing the Ark of God to Jerusalem in the reign of David. [1 Chr. 15:8, 11]
5. *c.* 10 century BC. Son of Nethanel the Levite, he was a scribe in the reign of King David who wrote out the rota of service for the priests in the Tabernacle. [1 Chr. 24:6]
6. *c.* 10 century BC. Eldest son of Obed-edom, a family of porters at the gates of the Tabernacle in Jerusalem in the reign of King David. His sons were strong men dedicated to the service of the Tabernacle. [1 Chr. 26:4, 6, 7]

7. *c.* 9 century BC. A Levite sent by Jehoshaphat, king of Judah, to teach the Law of God to the people in the cities of Judah. [2 Chr. 17:8]
8. *c.* 8 century BC. A Levite descended from Jeduthun who obeyed the command of King Hezekiah to sanctify himself and cleanse the Temple. [2 Chr. 29:14]
9. *c.* 8 century BC. A Levite in the reign of Hezekiah, king of Judah, entrusted with the distribution of the offerings among the priests in the cities of Judah. [2 Chr. 31:15]
10. *c.* 7 century BC. A leading Levite who donated large quantities of cattle as part of the Passover sacrifice in the fourteenth year of King Josiah's reign. [2 Chr. 35:9]
11. 6 century BC. A priest of Judah who returned with Zerubbabel from exile in Babylon, and was the ancestor of Jehonathan, head of a priestly family in the days of Nehemiah. [Neh. 12:6, 18, 34]
12. *c.* 6 century BC. Father of the prophet Uriah of Kiriath-jearim who predicted the destruction of Jerusalem and was put to death by Jehoiakim, king of Judah. [Jer. 26:20]
13. *c.* 6 century BC. A false prophet of Judah who was taken into captivity in the days of the prophet Jeremiah. He wrote to the priest Zephaniah, son of Maaseiah, telling him that the exile in Babylon would soon end and asking him to rebuke Jeremiah for prophesying that the exile would last a long time. Jeremiah foretold that Shemaiah and his descendants would never live to see the return of the exiles to Zion. [Jer. 29:24-32]
14. *c.* 6 century BC. Father of Delaiah, one of the leaders of Judah who reported Jeremiah's prophecies of doom to King Jehoiakim. [Jer. 36:12]
15. *c.* 5 century BC. Son of Shecaniah and a leader of the tribe of Judah descended from King David. Shecaniah was keeper of the East Gate of Jerusalem and Shemaiah helped repair the walls at the time of Nehemiah. [1 Chr. 3:22; Neh. 3:29]
16. 5 century BC. Son of Hasshub the Levite and a descendant of Merari, he was one of the first Levites to settle in Jerusalem following the return from Babylon, and ministered in the Temple. [1 Chr. 9:14; Neh. 11:15]
17. 5 century BC. Son of Galal the Levite, he was the father of Obadiah, who was responsible for conducting the thanksgiving prayer in the Temple in the time of Nehemiah. Also called Shammua. [1 Chr. 9:16; Neh. 11:17]
18. 5 century BC. A descendant of Adonikam who returned with Ezra to Judah from exile in Babylon. [Ezra 8:13]
19. *c.* 5 century BC. One of the men sent by Ezra to Iddo at Casiphia to ask him to send Levites to Jerusalem to serve in the Temple. [Ezra 8:16]
20. 5 century BC. A descendant of Harim, the priest, who divorced his non-Jewish wife in the time of Ezra. [Ezra 10:21]

Mesopotamian terracotta of a harpist.
Shemaiah played musical instruments
during the dedication of the rebuilt walls
of the Temple.

21. 5 century BC. A descendant of Harim, a man of Israel, who divorced his non-Jewish wife in the time of Ezra. [Ezra 10:31]

22. 5 century BC. Son of Delaiah, he invited Nehemiah to meet him in secret inside the Temple, claiming that conspirators planned to kill Nehemiah. Guessing that Shemaiah had been hired by his enemies to frighten him, Nehemiah declined the invitation. [Neh. 6:10]

23. 5 century BC. A priest of Judah who signed the solemn covenant in the time of Nehemiah. [Neh. 10:8]

24. 5 century BC. One of the leaders of Judah who took part in the dedication of the rebuilt walls of Jerusalem at the time of Nehemiah. [Neh. 12:34]

25. 5 century BC. Grandfather of Zechariah, one of the priests who blew a trumpet at the ceremony dedicating the walls of Jerusalem in the days of Nehemiah. [Neh. 12:35]

26. 5 century BC. A Levite who played musical instruments during the dedication service for the rebuilt walls of Jerusalem in the days of Nehemiah. [Neh. 12:36, 42]

SHEMARIAH (Heb. 'preserved by God') **1.** *c.* 11 century BC. One of the Benjaminite archers who deserted the army of King Saul and rallied to David at Ziklag. [1 Chr. 12:5]

2. *c.* 10 century BC. A son of Rehoboam, king of Judah, by his wife Mahalath. [2 Chr. 11:19]

3. 5 century BC. A descendant of Harim, he divorced his non-Jewish wife in the time of Ezra. [Ezra 10:32]

4. 5 century BC. Son of Binnui, he divorced his non-Jewish wife in the time of Ezra. [Ezra 10:41]

SHEMEBER *c.* 18 century BC. King of Zeboiim in the days of Abraham, he was one of the five kings defeated in battle by Chedorlaomer, king of Elam, and his three confederate kings. [Gen. 14:2]

SHEMED date unknown. One of the three sons of Elpaal, a leading Benjaminite, whose descendants built the towns of Ono and Lod. [1 Chr. 8:12]

SHEMER (Heb. 'keeper') **1.** date unknown. A leader of the tribe of Levi descended from Merari, he was an ancestor of Ethan who served in the Tabernacle in the reign of King David. [1 Chr. 6:46]

2. *c.* 9 century BC. The owner of the hill which King Omri of Israel bought for two talents of silver and on which he built his capital city. He called it Samaria (Heb. *Shomron*) after Shemer. [1 Kgs. 16:24]

3. *see* SHOMER 1.

SHEMIDA (Heb. 'wise') *c.* 13 century BC. A leader of the tribe of Manasseh and the son of Gilead, he was head of a family who were numbered among the children of Israel with Moses in the wilderness. [Num. 26:32; Josh. 17:2; 1 Chr. 7:19]

SHEMIRAMOTH (Heb. 'heights of heaven') **1.** *c.* 10 century BC. A Levite who ministered in the Tabernacle in the reign of King David and played musical instruments when the Ark of the Lord was brought up to Jerusalem. [1 Chr. 15:18, 20; 16:5]

2. *c.* 9 century BC. A Levite sent by Jehoshaphat, king of Judah, to teach the Law of God in the cities of Judah. [2 Chr. 17:8]

SHEMUEL (Heb. 'heard by God') **1.** date unknown. Son of Tola and a grandson of Issachar, he and his family were leaders of the tribe and mighty warriors. [1 Chr. 7:2]

2. *c.* 13 century BC. Son of Ammihud and a leader appointed by Moses to divide up the part of the land of Israel allotted to the tribe of Simeon. [Num. 34:20]

SHENAZZAR (Ass. 'Sin [a god] protected') *c.* 6 century BC. Son of Jehoiachin, king of Judah, he and his family were taken into captivity when Judah was conquered by the Babylonians. [1 Chr. 3:18]

SHEPHATIAH (Heb. 'God judges') **1.** date unknown. An ancestor of Zebadiah, son of Michael, who returned with Ezra to Judah from exile in Babylon. [Ezra 8:8]

2. date unknown. Son of Mahalalel of the tribe of Judah and the father of Amariah, he was an ancestor of Athaiah, who settled in Jerusalem in the days of Nehemiah. [Neh. 11:4]

3. date unknown. Ancestor of a family of Temple servants who returned with Zerubbabel from exile in Babylon. [Ezra 2:57; Neh. 7:59]

4. date unknown. Ancestor of a family that returned with Zerubbabel to Judah from exile in Babylon. [Ezra 2:4; Neh. 7:9]

5. *c.* 11 century BC. One of several archers of the tribe of Benjamin who deserted the army of King Saul and rallied to David at Ziklag. [1 Chr. 12:5]

6. *c.* 10 century BC. A son of King David and Abital, he was born in Hebron. [2 Sam. 3:4; 1 Chr. 3:3]

7. *c.* 10 century BC. Son of Maachah, he was appointed ruler over the Simeonites in the reign of King David. [1 Chr. 27:16]

8. 9 century BC. A son of Jehoshaphat, king of Judah, who was killed by his eldest brother Jehoram when he succeeded to the throne. [2 Chr. 21:2]

9. *c.* 6 century BC. Son of Mattan and a leader of Judah, he was one of four who pressed King Zedekiah to put the prophet Jeremiah to death for urging surrender to the invading Babylonians. When the king gave them freedom to do what they liked with Jeremiah, they threw him into a cistern with the intention of letting him die there. [Jer. 38:1]

10. *c.* 5 century BC. Son of Reuel of the tribe of Benjamin and the father of Meshullam, one of the first men to settle in Jerusalem after the return from Babylon. [1 Chr. 9:8]

SHEPHI *see* SHEPHO

SHEPHO (Heb. 'bareness') date unknown. Son of Shobal and a grandson of Seir, the Horite. Also called Shephi. [Gen. 36:23; 1 Chr. 1:40]

SHEPHUPHAM *see* MUPPIM

SHEPHUPHAN *see* MUPPIM

Temple instruments, from a 17th-century German engraving.

SHEREBIAH (Heb. 'God's burning heat') 5 century BC. A Levite who returned from Babylon following Ezra's appeal to Iddo to send Levites to minister in the Temple in Jerusalem. He was entrusted with carrying the gold and silver vessels from Babylon back to Jerusalem and was responsible for the thanksgiving services in the Temple. He helped to explain the Law to the people and called upon them to repent of their sins. He signed the solemn covenant in the time of Nehemiah. [Ezra 8:18, 24; Neh. 8:7; 9:4, 5; 10:12; 12:24]

SHERESH (Heb. 'root') date unknown. Son of Machir and Maacah, and a grandson of Manasseh, he was a leader of the tribe. [1 Chr. 7:16]

SHESHAI (Heb. 'princely') c. 13 century BC. A descendant of the giant Anak, he was killed by Caleb following the invasion of the land of Israel under Joshua, and Caleb took possession of his lands at Hebron as part of his inheritance. [Num. 13:22; Josh. 15:14; Judg. 1:10]

SHESHAN (Heb. 'princely') date unknown. Son of Ishi and a leader of the tribe of Judah, he married his daughter to his Egyptian servant, Jarha. [1 Chr. 2:31-5]

SHESHBAZZAR (possibly Pers. 'fire-worshipper') c. 6 century BC. A member of the Judean royal house, he became leader of the first group of repatriated exiles after the decree of Cyrus, king of Persia, in 538 BC. He received the vessels of silver and gold that had been pillaged from the Temple by the Babylonians and were sent back by Cyrus with the returning Jews. There were forty-two thousand, three hundred and sixty of them, and Sheshbazzar was in charge of bringing them up to Jerusalem.

Although it is stated in one passage that he became governor of Jerusalem, his name fades out at the beginning of the account of the return from Babylon in the Book of Ezra, while Zerubbabel emerges as the leader of the settler community in Jerusalem. Since both of them were of royal blood, had Babylonian names and figured in the return, some scholars suggest that Sheshbazzar and Zerubbabel were really the same person. [Ezra 1:8, 11; 5:14, 16]

SHESHONK see PHARAOH **6**.

SHETHAR (Pers. 'star') c. 5 century BC. One of the seven princes of Persia and Media who sat at the table of King Ahasuerus. [Esther 1:14]

SHETHAR-BOZENAI (Pers. 'star of splendour') c. 6 century BC. A Persian official in Judah who wrote to Darius, king of Persia, telling him that the Jews under Zerubbabel were rebuilding the Temple in Jerusalem, and asking the king if they had authority to do so, as they claimed. When Darius replied that the Jews had permission and ordered that help be given to them, the Persian official hastened to carry out the order. [Ezra 5:3, 6; 6:6, 13]

SHEVA (Heb. 'warrior of God') **1**. date unknown.

Grandson of Caleb and son of Hezron and Maacah, he was a leader of the tribe of Judah and the father of Machbenah. [1 Chr. 2:49]

2. see SERAIAH **2**.

SHILHI (Heb. 'armed') c. 9 century BC. Grandfather of Jehoshaphat, king of Judah. [1 Kgs. 22:42; 2 Chr. 20:31]

SHILLEM (Heb. 'paid') c. 16 century BC. Son of Naphtali, he was a grandson of Jacob and Bilhah. Also called Shallum. [Gen. 46:24; Num. 26:49; 1 Chr. 7:13]

SHILSHAH (Heb. 'third') date unknown. Son of Zophah, he and his family were leaders of the tribe of Asher and mighty warriors. [1 Chr. 7:37]

SHIMEA (Heb. 'hearing') **1.** date unknown. Son of Uzzah the Levite, he was a descendant of Merari. [1 Chr. 6:30]

2. c. 11 century BC. Grandfather of Asaph, King David's musician. [1 Chr. 6:39]

3. see SHAMMAH **2**.

4. see SHAMMUA **2**.

SHIMEAH (Heb. 'hearing') date unknown. Son of Mikloth, he was one of the leaders of the tribe of Benjamin living in Jerusalem. Also called Shimeam. [1 Chr. 8:32; 9:38]

SHIMEAM see SHIMEAH

SHIMEATH (Heb. 'hearing') c. 9 century BC. Ammonite mother of Jozacar, an officer of Joash, king of Judah, who assassinated the king in revenge for the execution of Zechariah, son of the high priest Jehoiada. [2 Kgs. 12:21; 2 Chr. 24:26]

SHIMEI (Heb. 'famed') **1.** date unknown. Son of Gog, a Reubenite who lived in Aroer, east of the Jordan. [1 Chr. 5:4]

2. date unknown. Younger son of Gershom and the grandson of Levi, his descendants were leading Levites who ministered in the Tabernacle of King David in Jerusalem. [Exod. 6:17; Num. 3:18; 1 Chr. 6:17, 42; 23:7, 10]

3. date unknown. Son of Zaccur, he was a leader of the tribe of Simeon. [1 Chr. 4:26, 27]

4. date unknown. Son of Libni of the tribe of Levi, he was a descendant of Merari. [1 Chr. 6:29]

5. date unknown. Son of Jahath of the tribe of Levi and a grandson of Gershom, he was the father of Zimmah and an ancestor of Asaph, one of King David's chief musicians. [1 Chr. 6:42]

6. date unknown. Leader of the tribe of Benjamin who lived in Jerusalem. [1 Chr. 8:21]

7. see SHEMA **3**.

8. see SHAMMAH **2**.

9. c. 10 century BC. Shimei, the son of Gera, was a Benjaminite and a member of Saul's family, living at Bahurim, south-east of Jerusalem. When David came through the town fleeing from Absalom, Shimei threw stones and dirt at him, shouting, 'Begone, begone, you man of blood, you worthless fellow!' (2 Sam. 16:7) David restrained his men from killing the old man, and said, 'Behold, my own son seeks my life; how much more now may this Benjaminite!' (2 Sam. 16:11)

After the defeat of Absalom, Shimei came down to the Jordan ford to greet David, and begged for forgiveness. Again, David spared his life. But David did not forget the incident, and on his deathbed instructed Solomon: 'You shall bring his grey head down with blood to Sheol.' (1 Kgs. 2:9)

Three years later, Shimei went off to Gath after two runaway slaves. This broke his undertaking not to leave Jerusalem, and Solomon ordered him to be put to death. [2 Sam. 16:19; 19:16; 1 Kgs. 2:8, 9, 36-46]

10. *c.* 10 century BC. A leader of Israel who remained loyal to King David when Adonijah proclaimed himself king before his father was dead. [1 Kgs. 1:8]

11. *c.* 10 century BC. Son of Ela, he was one of the twelve officers of King Solomon responsible for supplying the provisions of the royal household. [1 Kgs. 4:18]

12. *c.* 10 century BC. An officer of King David who was responsible for supervising the king's vineyards. [1 Chr. 27:27]

13. *c.* 8 century BC. A Levite descended from Heman, King David's musician, he obeyed the call of Hezekiah, king of Judah, to sanctify himself and cleanse the Temple. [2 Chr. 29:14]

14. *c.* 8 century BC. Brother and deputy of Conaniah, leader of the Levites in charge of the offerings and tithes brought to the Temple in the reign of Hezekiah, king of Judah. [2 Chr. 31:12, 13]

15. 6 century BC. Son of Pedaiah of the tribe of Judah and the brother of Zerubbabel who led the Return of the Jews to Judah from exile in Babylon. [1 Chr. 3:19]

16. 5 century BC. A Levite, he divorced his non-Jewish wife in the time of Ezra. [Ezra 10:23]

17. 5 century BC. A descendant of Hashum, he divorced his non-Jewish wife in the time of Ezra. [Ezra 10:33]

18. 5 century BC. A descendant of Binnui, he divorced his non-Jewish wife in the time of Ezra. [Ezra 10:38]

19. *c.* 5 century BC. Son of Kish of the tribe of Benjamin and the father of Jair, his grandson Mordecai thwarted the plot during the reign of King Ahasuerus to kill all the Jews in the Persian empire. [Esther 2:5]

SHIMEON (Heb. 'one who hears') 5 century BC. A descendant of Harim, he divorced his non-Jewish wife in the time of Ezra. [Ezra 10:31]

SHIMON (Heb. 'wasteland') date unknown. A leader of the tribe of Judah, descended from Caleb son of Jephunneh. [1 Chr. 4:20]

SHIMRATH (Heb. 'watcher') date unknown. Son of Shimei, he was a leader of the tribe of Benjamin living in Jerusalem. [1 Chr. 8:21]

SHIMRI (Heb. 'vigilant') **1.** date unknown. Father of Jedaiah, he was the ancestor of Ziza, a leader of the tribe

of Simeon who settled in the rich valley of Gedor in the reign of Hezekiah, king of Judah. [1 Chr. 4:37]

2. *c.* 10 century BC. Father of Jediael who was one of the warriors in the army of King David and distinguished for his bravery. [1 Chr. 11:45]

3. *c.* 10 century BC. Son of Hosah, a Levite descended from Merari who served as a gatekeeper of the Tabernacle in the reign of King David. [1 Chr. 26:10]

4. *c.* 8 century BC. A Levite descended from Elizaphan who obeyed the command of Hezekiah, king of Judah, to sanctify himself and cleanse the Temple. [2 Chr. 29:13]

SHIMRITH (Heb. 'vigilant') 8 century BC. The Moabite mother of Jehozabad, an officer of Joash, king of Judah, who assassinated the king in revenge for the execution of Zechariah, son of the high priest Jehoiada. Also known as Shomer. [2 Kgs. 12:21; 2 Chr. 24:26]

SHIMRON (Heb. 'watch-place') *c.* 16 century BC. A son of Issachar and a grandson of Jacob and Leah, he went down to Egypt with his grandfather Jacob. [Gen. 46:13; Num. 26:24; 1 Chr. 7:1]

SHIMSHAI (Heb. 'bright') 5 century BC. A Persian scribe who served under Rehum, the Persian governor in Judah, he was one of the authors of a letter to King Artaxerxes calling upon him to order the Jews to stop rebuilding the walls of Jerusalem and suggesting they planned to rebel against the authority of Persia as soon as the walls were rebuilt. [Ezra 4:8, 17, 23]

SHINAB (Heb. 'splendour') *c.* 18 century BC. King of Admah in the days of Abraham, he was one of five kings defeated in battle by Chedorlaomer, king of Elam, and his three confederate kings. [Gen. 14:2]

SHIPHI (Heb. 'many') 8 century BC. Son of Allon of the tribe of Simeon, he was the father of Ziza, a Simeonite leader in the time of King Hezekiah who invaded and settled the Gedor valley. [1 Chr. 4:37]

SHIPHRAH (Heb. 'handsome') *c.* 13 century BC. One of the two Hebrew midwives in Egypt who did not obey Pharaoh's orders to kill all Hebrew boys at birth. [Exod. 1:15]

SHIPHTAN (Heb. 'judging') *c.* 13 century BC. Father of Kemuel, a leader of the tribe of Ephraim who was appointed by Moses to share out the part of the Promised Land allotted to his tribe. [Num. 34:24]

SHISHA *see* SERAIAH **2.**

SHISHAK *see* PHARAOH **6.**

SHITRAI (Heb. 'scribe') *c.* 10 century BC. A herdsman living in the Sharon plain in the reign of King David who was responsible for tending the royal herds in the Sharon area. [1 Chr. 27:29]

SHIZA *c.* 10 century BC. Father of Adina, commander of a force of men of the tribe of Reuben in King David's army who was renowned for his bravery. [1 Chr. 11:42]

SHOBAB (Heb. 'hostile') **1.** date unknown. Son of Caleb and his wife Jerioth, he was a leader of the tribe of Judah. [1 Chr. 2:18]

2. *c.* 10 century BC. Son of King David born to him when he was king in Jerusalem. [2 Sam. 5:14; 1 Chr. 3:5; 14:4]

SHOBACH (Heb. 'enlarging') *c.* 10 century BC. The general commanding the army of Hadadezer, king of Zobah in Syria, who was defeated and killed in battle by King David. Also called Shophach. [2 Sam. 10:16, 18; 1 Chr. 19:16-18]

SHOBAI (Heb. 'captive') date unknown. Ancestor of a family of Levites who returned with Zerubbabel to Judah from exile in Babylon and who served as gate-keepers of the Temple in Jerusalem. [Ezra 2:42; Neh. 7:45]

SHOBAL 1. *c.* 16 century BC. Youngest son of Judah and a grandson of Jacob. [1 Chr. 4:1, 2]

2. date unknown. Son of Seir, the Horite, and an Edo-mite chieftain. [Gen. 36:20, 23, 29; 1 Chr. 1:38, 40]

3. date unknown. Son of Hur and grandson of Caleb, he was a leader of Judah and regarded as the founder of Kiriath-jearim. [1 Chr. 2:50, 52]

SHOBEK (Heb. 'forsaken') 5 century BC. A leader of Judah who signed the solemn covenant in the time of Nehemiah. [Neh. 10:24]

SHOBI (Heb. 'captive') *c.* 10 century BC. Son of Nahash from Rabbah in Ammon, he brought food and equipment to King David and his army when they crossed the river Jordan to avoid attack from Absa-lom's rebel forces. [2 Sam. 17:27]

SHOHAM (Heb. 'onyx') *c.* 10 century BC. Son of Jaaziah, the Levite descended from Merari, he and his family ministered in the Tabernacle in Jerusalem in the reign of King David. [1 Chr. 24:27]

SHOMER (Heb. 'watchman') **1.** date unknown. Son of Heber, he and his family were leaders of the tribe of Asher and mighty warriors. Also known as Shemer. [1 Chr. 7:32, 34]

2. *see* SHIMRITH

SHOPHACH *see* SHOBACH

SHUA (Heb. 'wealth') **1.** *c.* 16 century BC. A Canaanite

Canaanite head, ivory, 13th-12th centuries BC, from Megiddo.

whose daughter Bath-shua married Judah and bore him three sons. [Gen. 38:2, 12; 1 Chr. 2:3]

2. date unknown. Daughter of Heber, a leader of the tribe of Asher. [1 Chr. 7:32]

SHUAH (Heb. 'pit') *c.* 17 century BC. A son of Abra-ham and his wife Keturah, he was a leader of a desert tribe. [Gen. 25:2; 1 Chr. 1:32]

SHUAL (Heb. 'fox') date unknown. Son of Zophah, he and his family were chiefs of the tribe of Asher and mighty warriors. [1 Chr. 7:36]

SHUBAEL *see* SHEBUEL **1.** and **2.**

SHUHAH (Heb. 'pit') date unknown. A chief of the tribe of Judah and the brother of Chelub. [1 Chr. 4:11]

SHUHAM *see* HUSHIM **1.**

SHUNI (Heb. 'resting') *c.* 16 century BC. A son of Gad and grandson of Jacob and Zilpah, he went down to Egypt with his grandfather Jacob. [Gen. 46:16; Num. 26:15]

SHUPPIM (Heb. 'serpents') **1.** *c.* 16 century BC. A descendant of Benjamin and a leader of the tribe. [1 Chr. 7:12, 15]

2. *c.* 10 century BC. A Levite in the reign of King David who served as a gatekeeper of the Tabernacle in Jeru-salem. He and Hosah were chosen by lot to be posted on the western side near the gate of Shallecheth. [1 Chr. 26:16]

SHUTHELAH (Heb. 'discord') **1.** *c.* 16 century BC. A son of Ephraim and grandson of Joseph. [Num. 26:35, 36; 1 Chr. 7:20]

2. date unknown. Son of Zabad and a leader of the tribe of Ephraim. [1 Chr. 7:21]

SIA *see* SIAHA

SIAHA (Heb. 'assembly') date unknown. Ancestor of a family of Temple servants who returned with Zerub-babel to Judah from exile in Babylon. Also called Sia. [Ezra 2:44; Neh. 7:47]

SIBBECAI (Heb. 'weaver') *c.* 10 century BC. A warrior in the army of King David who killed the Philistine giant, Saph. Sibbecai was commander of David's army for the eighth month of the year. Also called Mebunai. [2 Sam. 21:18; 23:27; 1 Chr. 11:29; 20:4; 27:11]

SIDON date unknown. Elder of Canaan's two sons and a grandson of Ham, he was the traditional founder of the great Phoenician port city of Sidon. [Gen. 10:15; 1 Chr. 1:13]

SIHON (Heb. 'sweeping away') *c.* 13 century BC. Amo-rite king in Transjordan in the time of Moses. When the Children of Israel reached the Arnon river east of the Dead Sea, they found that the country beyond it had recently been conquered by the Amorites under King Sihon. Moses sent messengers asking for leave to pass through and promising to stay on the King's Highway. Not only was his request turned down, but 'He gathered all his men together, and went out against Israel ...' (Num. 21:23) The battle took place at Jahaz and Sihon was beaten. The Israelites overran his land from the Arnon river to the Jabbok river, including Heshbon, Sihon's capital. His territory, together with that of Og, king of Bashan, who was also defeated, was allocated to the tribes of Reuben, Gad and half of Manasseh. Frequent references to the defeat of Sihon occur in the Old Testament. [Num. 21:21-34; 32:33; Deut. 1:4; 2:24-32; 3:2, 6; 4:46; 29:7; 31:4; Josh. 2:10; 9:10; 12:2; 13:8; Judg. 11:19-22; 1 Kgs. 4:19; Neh. 9:22; Ps. 135:11; 136:19; Jer. 48:45]

SIMEON (Heb. '[God] has heard') *c.* 16 century BC. Simeon was the second son of Jacob, by his wife Leah. Together with his brothers he was involved in the events that led to the selling of their brother Joseph into slavery in Egypt.

When Jacob was living at Shalem, his daughter Dinah was seduced by Shechem, a local young man. The father came and asked for Dinah's hand in marriage for Shechem. Jacob and his sons, concealing their rage, agreed provided that Shechem, his father, and all the men in the town should be circumcised. This was done, but before the men had recovered from the painful operation, Simeon and his brother Levi killed them all.

Later he was one of the ten sons sent by Jacob to buy corn in Egypt, where Joseph had become a leading figure at Pharaoh's court. Simeon was selected as the hostage to be left behind as a guarantee that the brothers would return with Benjamin, the youngest of Jacob's sons and Joseph's full brother. He was duly released when they all returned.

When Jacob went to settle in Egypt with all his family, it included Simeon and his six sons.

On his deathbed Jacob blessed all his sons in turn, but remembering the reprisal of Simeon and Levi over the seduction of their sister, he said: 'Simeon and Levi are brothers; weapons of violence are their swords . . . I will divide them in Jacob and scatter them in Israel.' (Gen. 49:5, 7)

In the conquest of Canaan under Joshua, the tribe of

Canaanite war chariots: drawing from a Late Canaanite stone relief.

Simeon was allocated an area in the south that included Beer-sheba. It seems to have disappeared soon after, perhaps by merging with local tribes. [Gen. 29:33; 34:25, 30; 35:23; 42:24, 36; 43:23; 46:10; 48:5; 49:5; Exod. 1:2; 6:15]

SIPPAI *see* SAPH

SISERA (Canaanite 'leader') **1.** *c.* 12 century BC. Sisera was the Canaanite commander of the army of Jabin, king of Hazor, who had conquered the Israelites and had treated them harshly for twenty years. The prophetess Deborah roused the Israelites to fight Sisera under Barak and he was defeated at the Kishon river. Sisera fled northwards on foot and arrived at the tent of a Kenite woman, Jael. She invited him in, fed him and, when he fell asleep, she killed him by driving a tent peg through his head.

In Deborah's song of victory, which is considered as an earlier version of the same story, there is a moving account of Sisera's mother looking through her lattice window, watching for her son's return. Her maids try and divert her by chattering about the booty Sisera will bring back with him. This account refers to Sisera as the king and not the commander. [Judg. 4:5 23; 5:20, 26-30; 1 Sam. 12:9; Ps. 83:9]

2. date unknown. Ancestor of a family of Temple servants who returned with Zerubbabel to Judah from exile in Babylon. [Ezra 2:53; Neh. 7:55]

SISMAI (Heb. 'famous') date unknown. Son of Eleasah of the tribe of Judah he was the father of Shallom. [1 Chr. 2:40]

Tel el-Farah in the Negev has been identified with Sharuhen, part of the territory of Simeon.

SITHRI (Heb. 'protected') *c.* 13 century BC. Son of Uzziel and a grandson of Kohath, he was a Levite leader in Egypt in the days of Moses and Aaron. [Exod. 6:22]

SO *c.* 8 century BC. 'So, king of Egypt', whose help King Hoshea of Israel (732-24 BC) sought against the Assyrians, was apparently not a Pharaoh but an Egyptian general or prince. [2 Kgs. 17:4]

SOCO date unknown. Son of Heber and a leader of the tribe of Judah. [1 Chr. 4:18]

SODI (Heb. 'secret') *c.* 13 century BC. A leader of the tribe of Zebulun, he was the father of Gaddiel who was chosen by Moses as one of the twelve men sent to spy out the Promised Land. [Num. 13:10]

SOLOMON (Heb. 'peaceable') Son and successor of King David, he reigned from 970-31 BC. In all the long array of Israelite kings, Solomon shares with David the pinnacle of renown. Yet father and son emerge from the biblical narrative with markedly different lives and personalities. David's story is a vivid human document of a shepherd boy's struggle to power. In contrast, Solomon was reared as a royal prince, had the sceptre thrust into his boyish hand by an aging father and an ambitious mother, and kept his realm free of war and internal strife. Compared to David, Solomon seems an aloof and intellectual figure.

Solomon's mother was the beautiful Bathsheba, with whom King David fell in love when he saw her bathing herself on a moonlit rooftop below the palace. He caused her husband Uriah the Hittite to be killed in battle, then married her. As retribution, the first child of David and Bathsheba died in infancy. Solomon was the second child of this marriage. As a mark of divine forgiveness, Nathan the court prophet gave him the additional name of Jedidiah, 'beloved of God'.

When David was aged and ailing, his eldest surviving son Adonijah made a bid for the throne, supported by two of the most powerful figures at the court: Joab the commander of the army and Abiathar, one of the two high priests. Bathsheba rushed to David to tell him that Adonijah was attempting to supplant him, and she was supported by Nathan. The king agreed that Solomon should at once be crowned. He sent Solomon on the royal mule to the spring of Gihon in the Kidron valley where the youth was anointed with oil from the sacred Tabernacle. The trumpets sounded, and everyone shouted, 'Long live King Solomon.' (1 Kgs. 1:39)

The dying David gave Solomon his last counsel. 'I am about to go the way of all the earth. Be strong, and show yourself a man.' (1 Kgs. 2:2) If Solomon wished to

left King Solomon: painting by Perugino (*c.* 1452-1524), from a frieze of Old Testament figures in the Collegio di Cambio, Perugia.

right Solomon's Temple, from a 17th-century Dutch engraving.

be a successful ruler, he should above all obey the Lord and observe his Laws. 'Then David slept with his fathers, and was buried in the city of David.' (1 Kgs. 2:10)

As a young and untried king, Solomon acted with surprising forcefulness in crushing the men who had turned against his father and had remained a threat to his own throne.

Adonijah had been spared, but now played into Solomon's hands. Through the queen-mother Bathsheba, he asked permission to marry Abishag of Shunam, the young girl who had nursed David in his old age. Solomon reacted sharply. Adonijah might as well have asked for the kingdom, he said. (To take a woman from the household of a dead or deposed king symbolized a claim to the succession.) Benaiah the captain of the palace guard was immediately sent to kill Adonijah.

Solomon told Abiathar the high priest that he too deserved to die for his support of Adonijah's attempt to take the throne, but his life would be spared because of the years of hardship he had shared with David. Instead, he was banished from the capital to the small village of Anathoth, near Jerusalem.

When the news reached David's nephew and general Joab, who had also supported Adonijah, he realized his danger and fled for sanctuary to the altar. Benaiah was sent to dispose of him too, but shrank from violating the sanctuary until Solomon firmly ordered him to do so. Joab was then struck down. Solomon justified this unprecedented act on the grounds that the blood-guilt was being wiped out for Joab's murder of Abner and Amasa during David's reign.

Shimei, the old Benjaminite who had cursed David, had been ordered to live in Jerusalem on pain of death if he should leave the city. One day he went to the Philistine city of Gath to look for two runaway slaves, and Solomon had him executed when he returned.

By these vigorous actions, 'the kingdom was established in the hand of Solomon' (1 Kgs. 2:46).

He went to Gibeon, an important sanctuary some six miles north-west of Jerusalem, and made a thousand burnt-offerings to the Lord. In a dream God asked him what he would like to be given. Solomon replied that he was a very young man, unskilled in leadership. 'Give thy servant therefore an understanding mind to govern thy people, that I may discern between good and evil.' (1 Kgs. 3:9) The Lord was pleased that the young king had not asked for long life, riches, and triumph over his enemies, and promised him these boons as well.

Solomon soon gave dramatic proof of his wisdom in judgment. There appeared before him two prostitutes living in the same house, each of whom had given birth to a son. One child died, and both claimed the surviving one as hers. The king ordered that a sword be brought

in and the baby cut in two, with half to be given to each of the women. At this one of them cried out: 'Oh, my Lord, give her the living child, and by no means slay it.' (1 Kgs. 3:26) The other one declared: 'It shall be neither mine nor yours; divide it.' (1 Kgs. 3:26) The king decreed that the first woman was the real mother and should have the baby. The story of this judgment spread through the land and established Solomon's fame.

The Bible states categorically that 'Solomon's wisdom surpassed the wisdom of all the people of the east, and all the wisdom of Egypt. For he was wiser than all other men.' (1 Kgs. 4:30, 31) It is further claimed that he composed three thousand proverbs and a thousand and five songs; and that he could discourse learnedly about all plants, animals, birds, reptiles and fish.

The borders of the Israelite empire had been firmly established by David, and Solomon did not add to them. They extended up to the Euphrates in the north and to the desert in the east and south. Aram (Syria) and the Transjordan kingdoms of Ammon, Moab, and Edom had been conquered by David and remained vassal states under Solomon. Two skilled and energetic peoples had retained their independence in enclaves along the coast: the Philistines to the south and the Phoenicians further north. Hiram, king of the Phoenician port-city of Tyre, had been a friend and ally of David, and this special relationship was retained by Solomon.

Administration and Trade

From the list of chief ministers in Chapter 4 of the First Book of Kings, it appears that Solomon ensured continuity in the conduct of the kingdom's affairs by relying mostly on the men who had served David, or by appointing their sons.

For administrative and tax purposes, the kingdom was divided into twelve districts, about half of them corresponding to the old tribal areas. Each district was placed in charge of a commissioner who was provided with an official residence, and thick-walled storehouses for the grain, oil and other products that served as taxes. Judah, which was the most important tribe and that of the royal house, was left out of this arrangement, and was presumably governed directly from Jerusalem.

Each district was to provide the food for the palace for one month a year. The text specifies the daily quota of flour and meal, oxen, sheep, deer, gazelles, roebucks and fowl, as well as barley and straw for the horses and other animals. It is reckoned that the quantity of food specified was sufficient for a household of five to six thousand persons.

Solomon's foreign policy rested on securing political alliances and developing trade with the surrounding countries. As had always been the custom with monarchs, diplomatic relations were cemented with suitable marriages. Solomon was a notable exponent of this harem statecraft, and early in his reign he brought off a political coup of the first magnitude by marrying the daughter of the Egyptian Pharaoh.

The kingdom of Israel lay astride the great trade routes between the Nile valley and the Euphrates basin, and lucrative revenue was derived from tolls and supplies for the laden caravans passing to and fro. Israelite merchants expanded their own foreign trade; the Bible mentions that they bought chariots in Egypt and horses in Cilicia (now southern Turkey), reselling them to the Hittites and the Syrians in the north-east.

Solomon's partnership with Hiram, king of Tyre, also opened up a southern sea route through the Gulf of Akaba into the Red Sea area. The Israelites were essentially a hill people, with a desert background, and they had no real knowledge of seafaring. But with the help of Hiram's shipwrights, Phoenician-type wooden vessels with flat bottoms and square sails were constructed at Solomon's port of Ezion-geber near Eilat, at the head of the Gulf. They were suitable for transporting the copper ore from King Solomon's mines, a few miles north of Ezion-geber, for export southwards. (These mines are being worked again in modern Israel three thousand years later.) Carrying Solomon's traders, and manned by Hiram's crews, the vessels reached the coasts of southern Arabia and East Africa. The richest country in that region was the land of Ophir, the exact location of which is still uncertain. Once in three years, the fleet

above Solomon and his many wives: 16th-century German engraving.
below The 'Tomb of Pharaoh's Daughter' at Silwan to the east of Jerusalem, so-called from an inscription found on the stonework. It originally had a pyramidal top.

Solomon

of ships brought back cargoes of 'gold, silver, ivory,
apes, and peacocks' (1 Kgs. 10:22). It is these voyages
that figure in John Masefield's poem *Cargoes*:

> 'Quinquireme of Nineveh from distant Ophir
> Rowing home to haven in sunny Palestine,
> With a cargo of ivory,
> And apes and peacocks,
> Sandalwood, cedarwood and sweet white wine.'

There is also a suggestion that Solomon may have sent
ships with the Phoenician trading fleets along the
Mediterranean coasts.

In the Red Sea region now penetrated by Israelite
shipping and commerce, there was a kingdom called

right 9th-century BC Assyrian relief, showing
Phoenician envoys bringing tribute.

below The meeting of King Solomon and
the Queen of Sheba : detail from the frescoes
by Piero della Francesca in the Church
of S. Francesco, Arezzo.

Sheba. It may have occupied the south-west corner of the Arabian peninsula at the southern entrance to the Red Sea in what is now Yemen; though the Ethiopians maintain that Sheba was on the African side in a locality now included in Ethiopia. Its inhabitants, the Sabeans, took advantage of their strategic position to become an enterprising trading nation along the sea-lanes and the inland caravan routes. They dealt in gold, gems, spices and other valuable commodities from the East and from Africa. In Solomon's time Sheba was ruled by a queen. She was intrigued by the reports of Solomon's legendary wisdom, and the growing wealth and power of Israel; and she no doubt also saw prospects of extending her people's commercial activities. The Queen of Sheba decided to pay a royal visit to the Israelite court in Jerusalem, and set out by camel caravan on the arduous fifteen-hundred-mile overland trek across deserts and mountains.

Solomon received the queen with due pomp, and she was dazzled by the brilliance and luxury of his household. She had come armed with cunning riddles and difficult questions to test him, and found him able to deal easily with them. She declared that 'Your wisdom and prosperity surpass the report which I heard.' (1 Kgs. 10:7) She then presented him with the lavish gifts she had brought – a great quantity of gold and precious stones and more spices than had ever been seen at one time in Israel. Solomon made gifts in return from the royal treasury and the queen set out again on the long journey home.

The story of King Solomon and the Queen of Sheba has given rise to much romantic folk-lore in Jewish, Moslem and Christian writings. Some of these tales suggest that the relations between them were less platonic than might appear from the biblical account. In Ethiopia it is a national legend that the Queen of Sheba bore Solomon a son, Menelek, who settled in what was then the land of Cush and became the founder of the royal house. The Emperor of Ethiopia bears the official title 'The Lion of Judah'; and the national emblem is a six-pointed star, corresponding to the Shield of David on the Israel flag.

left 8th-century BC relief from the palace of King Sargon of Assyria at Khorsabad, showing logs of wood being transported by ship.

below 20th-century popular Ethiopian painting, depicting the Queen of Sheba (right to left) travelling up the Nile; appearing before Solomon; and the two of them in bed.

Reconstruction of the Canaanite temple at Hazor, showing similarities with Solomon's Temple, particularly in its three main divisions.

Solomon

Solomon the Builder

Growing wealth, and freedom from external pressures, enabled Solomon to launch an ambitious building programme. In this he was fortunate in being able to draw on the aid of his Phoenician ally Hiram for designers, craftsmen, lumber and gold.

Solomon set about embellishing Jerusalem, the city David had captured from the Jebusites and had made the political and religious centre of the nation. On the rising ground to the north of David's city, Solomon laid out a series of terraces and courtyards holding a complex of sumptuous buildings, and enclosed by a great stone wall. In the complete programme the Temple stood at the highest point, on the site of the threshing floor that David had bought for this purpose for fifty shekels of silver. (It is today the platform known as the Haram-esh-Sharif, holding the Dome of the Rock and the El-Aksa Mosque.)

The Temple itself took seven years to build. Its dedication was one of the most solemn days in the history of Israel. The elders from all over the country assembled in Jerusalem to be present. The priests carried the sacred Ark from the Tabernacle where David had brought it after the capture of Jerusalem, and placed it in the Temple courtyard. The king offered sacrifices on the bronze altar. The chief priests then bore the Ark into the Holy of Holies. When they emerged, a dark cloud filled the Temple, denoting God's presence.

The palace complex took another thirteen years to build. Solomon also built fortresses at strategic points along the main highways passing through the country. Three regional centres for his chariot forces were the sites of important archaeological excavations in this century. They were Hazor, north of the Sea of Galilee, commanding the historic road to Damascus; Megiddo, controlling the pass from the coastal plain into the Jezreel Valley; and Gezer, lying astride the road from Joppa to Jerusalem.

Solomon's extensive building operations required a huge labour force. Eighty thousand men are stated to have worked on the buildings, in the stone quarries and as porters; while thirty thousand more were sent to Phoenicia in shifts of ten thousand a month, to fell timber from the cedar and pine forests in the Lebanese mountains, and transport it to the coast. Hiram's men floated the log-rafts down to the Israelite port of Joppa, and from there the timber was hauled up to Jerusalem.

Under the treaty arrangements between Solomon and Hiram, lumber and gold were bartered for Israelite wheat and oil. During twenty years a deficit accumulated, which Solomon was obliged to meet by ceding to Hiram a strip of territory in western Galilee along the plain of Acre, containing twenty towns. This area was known as the land of Cabul.

Revenue flowed into the royal exchequer from vari-

Reconstruction of the First Temple according to the biblical description.

ous sources: the heavy taxes, the profits from trade, tribute monies from the vassal states, tolls levied on the passing caravans, and the lavish gifts brought by distinguished foreign visitors. These resources were drained out again by Solomon's building programme, and by the luxury and splendour of the court. The biblical chronicler records with awe the king's throne of ivory and gold, and the golden drinking vessels. For an oriental potentate, an even more impressive status symbol was the size of his harem, given as seven hundred wives and three hundred concubines. 'Now King Solomon loved many foreign women: the daughter of Pharaoh, and Moabite, Ammonite, Edomite, Sidonian, and Hittite women.' (1 Kgs. 11:1) Even if the statistics are inflated, it was clearly an expensive household to maintain in royal style.

Erosion of the Kingdom

In the later years of Solomon's reign, the kingdom ran into increasing difficulties. In the Bible, they are ascribed to a lack of religious piety on the king's part, for which his foreign wives are held to blame. Solomon was broad-minded enough to give them facilities for worshipping their own assorted heathen gods. This could hardly have commended itself to the faithful. What was worse, they felt that the king himself did not remain immune to these idolatrous practices. 'For when Solomon was old his wives turned away his heart after other gods; and his heart was not wholly true to the Lord his God, as was the heart of David his father.' (1 Kgs. 11:4) He was accused of being drawn towards Ashtaroth the

Phoenician goddess, and to the 'abominations' that were the gods of Ammon and Moab, building shrines for them in the hills round Jerusalem. The Lord was angry with him and declared that the kingdom would be torn apart when he died. However, the historian would link to more mundane factors the erosion that started to show itself.

The vassal states became troublesome. Edom, the desert kingdom in the south, was less tractable than it had been under David. The revived Aram-Damascus kingdom in the north was a constant source of harassment. The Egyptians were regaining their influence over the Philistine part of the coastal plain.

Inside the country, discontent was growing. Solomon's subjects were proud of his fame, the splendour of his court and the magnificent new Temple and palace in Jerusalem. They had enjoyed decades of peace and prosperity. But they groaned under the burden of heavy taxes and forced labour. In addition, the traditional rivalry between Judah and the other tribes (especially Ephraim in the centre) still smouldered under the surface. An abortive plot against the king was instigated by Jeroboam, a young Ephraimite of good birth whom Solomon had put in charge of the labourers engaged in the Jerusalem construction work. The king learnt of the plot, and Jeroboam fled for his life to Egypt. (He later returned to become ruler of the northern kingdom.)

Solomon died after nearly forty years on the throne, and was buried in Jerusalem with David. His son Rehoboam succeeded to the throne, but the ten northern tribes revolted. The united monarchy started by Saul, expanded by David and consolidated by Solomon, irretrievably split apart. The two small successor states of Judah and Israel were to co-exist or clash for centuries, until each in turn was wiped out by imperial invaders from the north. [The main story of Solomon is told in 1 Kgs. 1-11 and 2 Chr. 1-9]

Solomon's Architecture

The Temple

No remains of Solomon's Temple have as yet been excavated; but the Bible account describes it with such loving detail that it can be visualized. The building itself was famous not for size (it was only about 100 feet by 30 feet), but for beauty and the splendour of its material and decoration. It was built of stone lined on the inside with cedarwood and gold. The interior was divided into three parts: the vestibule; the nave; and the inner sanctuary or Holy of Holies. The latter contained the sacred Ark of the Law, under the outstretched wings of two fifteen-foot cherubim of olive wood overlaid with gold leaf. In the space above their wings, the invisible spirit of God was said to hover. The entrance to the Temple was flanked by two great bronze pillars. In the courtyard in front of the building stood the bronze altar, and an enormous bronze bowl or 'molten sea' supported on

Bronze Phoenician basin-stand from Solomon's time, found in Cyprus: it fits the description of the ten stands made for the Temple.

the figures of twelve oxen. The pillars and the bowl were fashioned and cast by an artist of genius from Tyre, whose name was also Hiram.

Solomon's Temple stood for nearly four hundred years, until it was destroyed in the sack of Jerusalem in 587 BC by the Babylonian army under Nebuchadnezzar. Half a century later, in the reign of Cyrus, king of Persia, the Jews started returning from the Babylonian exile and began to build the Second Temple, completed in 515 BC. Herod the Great set out to reconstruct it on a grander scale in 20 BC. His temple was completed after his death, and just four years before the Romans razed it to the ground in AD 70. The Temple has never been rebuilt, and its most notable relic remains the Western (Wailing) Wall.

The Palace

The palace complex was just south of the Temple. First came the king's quarters and the quarters for the Egyptian Queen and the harem. Below that were the 'Porch of Pillars'; the 'Porch for the Throne'; and the large 'House of the Forest of Lebanon'. The latter buildings were used for official purposes: halls for meetings and special assemblies, the hall in which Solomon gave judgment, and the administrative offices.

The Chariot Cities

The excavations at Hazor, Megiddo and Gezer disclosed Solomonic fortifications of identical plan, presumably built by the same engineer. The casemate walls were eighteen feet wide, with the chambers within it used as guests' quarters or stores. The entrance gateway was fifty-five feet wide and of elaborate design. It was flanked by two square towers and led into a long vestibule with three rooms on either side. Both at Megiddo and Hazor the digs revealed underground tunnels leading to springs of fresh water. They were constructed in order to withstand a siege, like Hezekiah's tunnel in Jerusalem.

Solomon and the Wisdom Books

Solomon was Israel's greatest sage, renowned for his judicial insight, learning and literary skill, so that it could be said that 'he was wiser than all other men' (1 Kgs. 4:30, 31). It is not surprising that he came to be regarded as the father of Hebrew wisdom literature.

This kind of writing flourished in the ancient cultures of the Near East, in the form of proverbs, parables, fables, riddles, and poems. It was common in Egypt, Mesopotamia, and Assyria, and was associated with the local sages of Canaan, Edom and Arabia. The earliest Hebrew proverbs derived much from these sources in the area, but developed their own unique character.

It is not easy to define 'wisdom' in this context. Where the prophets were concerned with the covenant between God and his chosen people, and the priests with formal worship, the sages (Heb. *hachamim*) were more concerned with the individual human predicament. Their domain was the practical morality of daily life rather than abstract theology.

The Wisdom Books in the Hebrew Bible are Proverbs, Job and Ecclesiastes. Two more works – the Wisdom of Solomon (also known as the Book of Wisdom) and the Wisdom of Jesus the Son of Sirach (also known as Ecclesiasticus) – were included in the Greek and

Reconstruction of Megiddo as it was at
the time of Solomon.

above Solomon's four-entry city gate at Hazor, which fits the biblical description of the gate of the First Temple.

Latin Bibles, but classified as Apocrypha in the Protestant bible. Of these works, Solomon's name is associated with Proverbs, Ecclesiastes and Wisdom. The Song of Songs (or Song of Solomon) has also been attributed to his authorship; it appears together with the wisdom books in the Old Testament, but is of a different genre.

Proverbs

The Book as a whole is headed 'The proverbs of Solomon, son of David, king of Israel'. It is compiled from several collections of proverbs made at different times. The two main anthologies are introduced as 'The proverbs of Solomon' (375 maxims) and 'Proverbs of Solomon, which the men of Hezekiah king of Judah copied out' (128 maxims). The contents of these two collections may well go back to the time of Solomon, or even earlier.

Other sections of the Book include an introduction in which a father commends wisdom to his son; smaller

King Solomon on this throne, with a Lion of Judah on either side. From the *Speculum Humanae Salvationis*, late 14th century.

groups of 'sayings'; and an alphabetical poem at the end in praise of the good wife whose 'price is far above rubies'.

The standard form of the proverb (Heb. *mashal*) is a single sentence with the second half balancing the first. In the Hebrew, a very condensed language, the usual length of a proverb is from six to eight words. The main themes are the virtues of piety, industry, thrift, moderation, honesty and charitableness. A few familiar examples are:

'Go to the ant, O sluggard; consider her ways, and be wise.' (6:6)

'Like a gold ring in a swine's snout is a beautiful woman without discretion.' (11:22)

'He who spared the rod hates his son, but he who loves him is diligent to discipline him.' (13:24)

'A soft answer turns away wrath, but a harsh word stirs up anger.' (15:1)

'Better is a dinner of herbs where love is than a fatted ox and hatred with it.' (15:17)

'Pride goes before destruction, and a haughty spirit before a fall.' (16:18)

'Let a man meet a she-bear robbed of her cubs, rather than a fool in his folly.' (17:12)

'Wine is a mocker, strong drink a brawler; and whoever is led astray by it is not wise.' (20:1)

'If you have found honey eat only enough for you, lest you be sated with it and vomit it.' (25:16)

'If your enemy is hungry, give him bread to eat; and if he is thirsty, give him water to drink.' (25:21)

'Where there is no prophecy the people cast off restraint, but blessed is he who keeps the law.' (29:18)

Ecclesiastes

The unknown writer of this book refers to himself in Hebrew as Kohelet, meaning one who appears before an assembly or *kahal*. The word was translated in the Greek bible (Septuagint) as 'Ecclesiastes' and in English as 'the Preacher'.

Up to the first century AD the rabbis hesitated to accept into the Hebrew bible a work which seemed to many of them heretical and impious. It was included mainly because King Solomon was supposed to be the author. Solomon's name is not actually used, but the title reads 'The Words of the Preacher, the son of David, king in Jerusalem'. In the text the writer refers to himself as a king who has reigned in Jerusalem, is exceptionally wise and has enjoyed great wealth and luxury. However, it is now considered that these references are only literary allusions, meant to give the work the prestige attached to Israel's royal sage.

From the contents and language of the Book, it appears to have been written by a Jewish intellectual of the 3rd century BC during the Hellenistic period, before the Maccabean Revolt put fresh faith and confidence into the people. Kohelet has a brilliant but pessimistic and sceptical mind. He is obviously influenced by the contemporary Greek philosophers, such as Epicurus.

The tone is set in the opening passage: 'Vanity of vanities, says the Preacher, vanity of vanities! All is vanity. What does man gain by all the toil at which he toils under the sun?' (Eccles. 1:2, 3)

Injustice is rife in the world. The pursuit of power, wealth or pleasure cannot gain any lasting happiness, nor does achievement bring reward. Whatever is to happen to any man is predetermined. No man can comprehend God's will. Only one thing is certain – that death will come to all. 'For who knows what is good for man while he lives the few days of his vain life, which he passes like a shadow? For who can tell man what will be after him under the sun?' (Eccles. 6:12) His advice therefore is: 'So I say that there is nothing better than that a man should enjoy his work, for that is his lot; who can bring him to see what will be after him?' (Eccles. 3:22)

Whatever its meaning, life should be accepted as a fact: 'But he who is joined with all the living has hope, for a living dog is better than a dead lion.' (Eccles. 9:4) Kohelet's views are not all negative, and at times he contradicts his own pessimism. The aphorisms in the Book contain much sage counsel, based on worldly experience.

Ecclesiastes is one of the five Megilloth (Scrolls) that form part of the Jewish service on certain festivals. It is read in synagogues on the Feast of Tabernacles (Succoth).

The Song of Solomon

This dazzling love poetry, the only work of its kind in the Bible, opens with the words: 'The Song of Songs, which is Solomon's' (Heb. *Shir ha-Shirim*). Here the identification is with Solomon not as a sage but as a writer of songs and an oriental monarch credited with having a thousand wives and concubines in his harem.

However, the suggested link with Solomon is clearly no more than a poetic fiction. The work was probably woven together about the 3rd century BC though it must have drawn on more ancient oral sources. Its form is that of a series of short songs or poems designed to be chanted in turn by the bride and bridegroom at a wedding feast, in part as a dialogue and in part separately.

Religion has no visible place in the work and its inclusion in the bible is at first glance puzzling. But the attribution to Solomon had become an accepted tradition by the time the canon of the Hebrew bible was settled. Moreover, the rabbis read into the work an elaborate allegory of the relations between God (the bridegroom) and the people of Israel (the bride). For their part, the Christian Fathers saw in it an allegory of Jesus's relations with the Church.

However valid these religious interpretations may be,

the Song of Songs has been cherished for its own sake – above all for the sensuous delight of the language and imagery. It is filled with the rapture of love between man and woman, and with the lyricism of the Israel countryside in the springtime:

'O that you would kiss me with the
　　kisses of your mouth!
For your love is better than wine.'

(S. of S. 1:2)

'Sustain me with raisins,
　　refresh me with apples;
for I am sick with love.
O that his left hand were under my head,
　　and that his right hand embraced me!'

(S. of S. 2:5, 6)

'Your two breasts are like two fawns,
　　twins of a gazelle,
that feed among the lilies.'

(S. of S. 4:5)

'for lo, the winter is past,
　　the rain is over and gone.
The flowers appear on the earth,
　　the time of singing has come,
and the voice of the turtledove
　　is heard in our land.
The fig tree puts forth its figs,
　　and the vines are in blossom;
they give forth fragrance.
Arise, my love, my fair one,
　　and come away.'

(S. of S. 2:11-13)

The Wisdom of Solomon

Certain passages in this book are written as if Solo-

mon were speaking in the first person; but again, these references are a mere literary device. The work is a philosophical treatise written anonymously in the Greek language by a cultivated Alexandrian Jew, about the middle of the 1st century BC. The theme is traditional wisdom and its role in the history and outlook of the Jewish people. The author's object is plainly to counteract among his educated fellow-Jews the attraction of Hellenistic culture, philosophy and rationalism. This work is included in the Apocrypha.

SOPHERETH (Heb. 'scribe') c. 10 century BC. A servant of King Solomon, his descendants were among the people of Judah who returned with Zerubbabel from exile in Babylon. Also known as Hassophereth. [Ezra 2:55; Neh. 7:57]

SOTAI (Heb. 'fickle') c. 10 century BC. A servant of King Solomon, and ancestor of a family who returned with Zerubbabel from exile. [Ezra 2:55; Neh. 7:57]

SUAH (Heb. 'sweeping') date unknown. Son of Zophah of the tribe of Asher, he and his family were chiefs of the tribe and mighty warriors. [1 Chr. 7:36]

SUCCOTH-BENOTH A deity worshipped by the Babylonians who were settled in Samaria by the conquering Assyrian empire after the fall of the northern kingdom of Israel. [2 Kgs. 17:30]

SUKKIIM A tribe (possibly African) who joined Pharaoh Shishak of Egypt in his invasion of Judah during the reign of Rehoboam, king of Judah. [2 Chr. 12:3]

SUSI (Heb. 'my horse') c. 13 century BC. A leader of the tribe of Manasseh, he was the father of Gaddi who was appointed by Moses as one of the twelve men sent to spy out the Promised Land. [Num. 13:11]

T

TABBAOTH (Heb. 'rings') date unknown. Ancestral head of a family of Temple servants who returned to Judah with Zerubbabel from exile in Babylon. [Ezra 2:43; Neh. 7:46]

TABEEL (Heb. 'God is good') **1.** *c.* 8 century BC. Father of a pretender to the throne of Judah whom the kings of Syria and Israel planned to crown when they had overthrown King Ahaz. [Isa. 7:6]

2. *c.* 5 century BC. A Samarian leader who wrote a letter to Artaxerxes, king of Persia, protesting against the rebuilding of Jerusalem by the Jews. [Ezra 4:7]

TABRIMMON (Ass. 'Rimmon is good') *c.* 10 century BC. King of Syria, he was the son of Hezion and father of Ben-Hadad I who allied himself with King Asa of Judah against King Baasha of Israel. [1 Kgs. 15:18]

TAHAN (Heb. 'camp') **1.** *c.* 16 century BC. Son of Ephraim and head of the family of Tahanites. [1 Num. 26:35]

2. date unknown. Son of Telah and the father of Ladan, he and his family were chiefs of Ephraim. [1 Chr. 7:25, 26]

TAHASH (Heb. 'porpoise') *c.* 17 century BC. Son of Abraham's brother Nahor by his concubine Reumah and by Hebrew tradition the founder of an Aramean clan. [Gen. 22:24]

TAHATH (Heb. 'compensation') **1.** *c.* 16 century BC. Son of Bered of the tribe of Ephraim, he was father of Eleadah. [1 Chr. 7:20]

2. *c.* 15 century BC. Son of Eleadah of the tribe of Ephraim and the father of Zabad. [1 Chr. 7:20, 21]

3. *c.* 13 century BC. Son of Assir, a Levite descended from Kohath and the father of Uriel and Zephaniah, he was an ancestor of the prophet Samuel. [1 Chr. 6:24, 37]

TAHPENES (Heb. 'Egyptian wife of the king') *c.* 10 century BC. Queen of Egypt during the reign of King David, her sister married Hadad, the Edomite leader who fled from David to Egypt. [1 Kgs. 11:19, 20]

TAHREA *see* TAREA

TALMAI (Heb. 'makes furrows') **1.** date unknown. A descendant of the giant Anak from Hebron, he was killed by Caleb, leader of the tribe of Judah, after the invasion of Canaan by the Children of Israel under Joshua. [Num. 13:22; Josh. 15:14; Judg. 1:10]

2. *c.* 10 century BC. Father of Maacah who married King David and bore him Absalom. When Absalom killed his half-brother Amnon, he fled to his grandfather, Talmai. [2 Sam. 3:3; 13:37; 1 Chr. 3:2]

TALMON 6 century BC. Head of a family of Levites who returned to Judah with Zerubbabel from Babylon. Members of his family became gatekeepers of the Tabernacle in Jerusalem in the days of the high priest Joiakim. [1 Chr. 9:17; Ezra 2:42; Neh. 7:45; 11:19; 12:24]

TAMAR (Heb. 'date') **1.** *c.* 16 century BC. The wife of Judah's elder sons Er and Onan. Both men died before she had children, so when Judah refused to give her his

Judah and Tamar, by the Dutch painter Aert de Gelder (1645-1727).

third son in marriage, Tamar tricked Judah into sleeping with her by disguising herself as a prostitute, and bore him twin sons Perez and Zerah. [Gen. 38:6, 11, 13-30; Ruth 4:12; 1 Chr. 2:4]

2. *c.* 10 century BC. She was the beautiful daughter of

The rape of Tamar by Amnon caused the feud between Amnon and Absalom. Limestone nude statue of a woman from Nineveh, 11th century BC.

King David and his wife Maacah, and a full sister of Absalom.

Her eldest half-brother Amnon fell in love with her and pretending to be ill, he received David's permission for her to look after him. Amnon sent everyone out of his room, raped her and suddenly hating her, had her thrown out of his house. Tamar went in great distress to Absalom who looked after her. Two years later Absalom gave a feast, invited Amnon and killed him in revenge for the honour of his sister. [2 Sam. 13; 1 Chr. 3:9]

3. *c.* 10 century BC. Daughter of Absalom and the granddaughter of King David, she was known for her beauty. [2 Sam. 14:27]

TAMMUZ (Syrian 'sprout') An Accadian god whose worship spread throughout the ancient world – Babylonia, Assyria, Palestine and Phoenicia. He was worshipped by the people of Judah shortly before the destruction of the Temple. The prophet Ezekiel in his vision of 'abominations' describes women weeping for Tammuz at the very gates of the Temple in Jerusalem. [Ezek. 8:14]

TANHUMETH (Heb. 'comfort') *c.* 6 century BC. Father of Seraiah, one of the army commanders of Judah who rallied to Gedaliah when the Babylonians made him governor of Judah. [2 Kgs. 25:23; Jer. 40:8]

TAPHATH (Heb. 'drop') *c.* 10 century BC. Daughter of King Solomon, she married Ben-abinadab, one of the leaders of Israel who ruled over the area of Dor. [1 Kgs. 4:11]

TAPPUAH (Heb. 'apple') date unknown. Son of Hebron of the tribe of Judah and a descendant of Caleb son of Hezron. [1 Chr. 2:43]

TAREA *c.* 10 century BC. Son of Micah of the tribe of Benjamin and a descendant of King Saul. Also called Tahrea. [1 Chr. 8:35; 9:41]

TARSHISH (Heb. 'gold-coloured stone') date unknown. Son of Javan and a great-grandson of Noah, he was by Hebrew tradition the legendary founder of Tarshish. [Gen. 10:4; 1 Chr. 1:7]

2. date unknown. Son of Bilhan and a leader of the tribe of Benjamin. [1 Chr. 7:10]

3. *c.* 5 century BC. One of the seven princes of Persia and Media who sat at the table of King Ahasuerus. [Esther 1:14]

TARTAK One of the gods worshipped by the Avvites, an eastern tribe settled in Samaria by the Assyrians after they had exiled the population of the northern kingdom of Israel. [2 Kgs. 17:31]

TARTAN (Ass. 'officer') *c.* 8 century BC. A commander of the Assyrian army sent against the kingdom of Judah in the reign of King Hezekiah. Tartan had previously commanded the Assyrian army which captured the Philistine city of Ashdod. [2 Kgs. 18:17]

TATTENAI *c.* 6 century BC. The Persian governor of Judah in the days of Zerubbabel who questioned the right of Zerubbabel to repair the Temple and the walls of Jerusalem and wrote to the Persian Emperor, Darius, asking for instructions. When ordered by Darius to assist in repairing the Temple, he hastened to carry out the emperor's command. [Ezra 5:3, 6; 6:6, 13]

TEBAH (Heb. 'slaughter') *c.* 17 century BC. A son of Abraham's brother Nahor by his concubine Reumah and by Hebrew tradition the founder of an Aramean clan. [Gen. 22:24]

TEBALIAH (Heb. 'purged') *c.* 10 century BC. Son of Hosah, and a Levite descended from Merari, he was a gatekeeper of the Tabernacle in the days of King David. [1 Chr. 26:11]

TEHINNAH (Heb. 'entreaty') date unknown. Son of Eshton, a leader of the tribe of Judah who lived in Recah. [1 Chr. 4:12]

TELAH date unknown. Son of Resheph of the tribe of Ephraim and the father of Tahan, he was an ancestor of Joshua who led the Children of Israel into the Promised Land. [1 Chr. 7:25]

TELEM *c.* 5 century BC. A Levite gatekeeper at the Temple in the days of Ezra, who divorced his non-Jewish wife. [Ezra 10:24]

TEMA (Heb. 'desert') *c*. 18 century BC. Son of Ishmael, and a grandson of Abraham, he was leader of a desert clan. [Gen. 25:13-15; 1 Chr. 1:30]

TEMAH (Heb. 'mirth') date unknown. Ancestral head of a family of Temple servants who returned with Zerubbabel from exile in Babylon. [Ezra 2:53; Neh. 7:55]

TEMAN (Heb. 'south') *c*. 16 century BC. Eldest son of Eliphaz and a grandson of Esau, he was an Edomite leader. [Gen. 36:11, 15; 1 Chr. 1:36, 53]

TEMENI (Heb. 'southern') date unknown. Son of Ashhur, a leader of the tribe of Judah, and his wife Naarah. [1 Chr. 4:6]

TERAH *c*. 18 century BC. Father of Abraham, he left his native city of Ur in Babylonia intending to go to Canaan but settled in Haran in Syria. Terah worshipped idols and did not adopt his son's faith in God. [Gen. 11:24-32; Josh. 24:2; 1 Chr. 1:26]

TERESH *c*. 5 century BC. One of the two doorkeepers who plotted to assassinate King Ahasuerus of Persia. Their plot was discovered by Mordecai and the two conspirators were put to death. In the Greek Additions to the Book of Esther, in the Apocrypha, he is called Tharra. [Esther 2:21; 6:2]

TIBNI *c*. 9 century BC. Son of Ginath he tried to make himself king of the northern kingdom of Israel after the suicide of King Zimri. Some of the people supported Tibni and the rest supported the army commander Omri who eventually triumphed, and Tibni was put to death. [1 Kgs. 16:21, 22]

TIDAL *c*. 18 century BC. Tidal was king of Goiim (a word meaning 'nations') and one of the four Mesopotamian kings who defeated an alliance of five local kings from the Dead Sea area in the time of Abraham. They carried off a number of captives, including Abraham's nephew Lot, and much booty. Abraham pursued them and rescued the captives and booty.

None of these nine kings have been identified, and none of their countries or cities except Elam. [Gen. 14]

TIGLATH-PILESER III (Ass. 'my confidence is the son of Esarra') King of Assyria 745-27 BC. Assyria, on the Upper Tigris river in Mesopotamia, was for centuries the dominant imperial power in the Near East. Tiglath-pileser III, also known as Pul or Tilgath-pilneser, was one of its greatest conquerors. In 733-2 BC his armies swept westward, and in a series of campaigns conquered Philistia on the Mediterranean coastal plain, destroyed Damascus, and occupied most of the kingdom of Israel, turning Gilead, the Galilee and the coastal district into Assyrian provinces. Many of the inhabitants were deported to other parts of the Assyrian empire.

This took place in the reign of Pekah, king of Israel, who was murdered by Hoshea who then ruled over the rump of the kingdom as a vassal paying

Assyrian relief from Nimrod, showing Tiglath-pileser III standing in his chariot at the assault of the town of Ashtoreth in Gilead.

tribute to the Assyrians. Ahaz, the king of Judah, also came to present himself to Tiglath-pileser in Damascus, and to tender him tribute.

Tiglath-pileser died in 727 BC and the throne was seized by Ululai, the governor of Babylonia, who became Shalmaneser V. [2 Kgs. 15:19, 29; 16:7, 10; 1 Chr. 5:6; 2 Chr. 28:20, 21]

TIKVAH (Heb. 'hope') **1.** *c*. 7 century BC. Son of Harhas, keeper of the wardrobe of the king of Judah, he was the father-in-law of the prophetess, Huldah. Also called Tokhath. [2 Kgs. 22:14; 2 Chr. 34:22]
2. 5 century BC. Father of Jahzeiah who opposed Ezra in his appeal to the people of Judah to divorce their non-Jewish wives. [Ezra 10:15]

TILGATH-PILNESER *see* TIGLATH-PILESER

TILON date unknown. Son of Shimon of the tribe of Judah, he was descended from Caleb son of Jephunneh. [1 Chr. 4:20]

TIMNA 1. *c*. 16 century BC. Concubine of Esau's son, Eliphaz, she bore him Amalek. [Gen. 36:12]
2. *c*. 16 century BC. Son of Eliphaz, he was the grandson of Esau. [1 Chr. 1:36]
3. date unknown. Daughter of Seir, leader of the Edomite warriors, she was the sister of Lotan. [Gen. 36:22; 1 Chr. 1:39]
4. date unknown. One of the Edomite chiefs descended from Esau. [Gen. 36:40; 1 Chr. 1:51]

TIRAS (Heb. 'longing') date unknown. Son of Japheth, he was a grandson of Noah. [Gen. 10:2; 1 Chr. 1:5]

TIRHAKAH *see* PHARAOH **8.**

TIRHANAH (Heb. 'favour') date unknown. Son of Caleb the son of Hezron and his concubine Maacah, he and his family were leaders of the tribe of Judah. [1 Chr. 2:48]

TIRIA (Heb. 'dread') date unknown. Son of Jehallelel, he was a leader of the tribe of Judah descended from Caleb son of Jephunneh. [1 Chr. 4:16]

TIRZAH (Heb. 'pleasing') *c.* 13 century BC. One of the five daughters of Zelophehad who successfully claimed a share of their father's estate before Moses, since their father had no sons. [Num. 26:33; 27:1; 36:11; Josh. 17:3]

TOAH (Heb. 'bent') date unknown. Son of Zuph of the tribe of Levi and the father of Eliab, he was an ancestor of the prophet Samuel. Also known as Tohu and Nahath. [1 Sam. 1:1; 1 Chr. 6:26, 34]

TOBADONIJAH (Heb. 'good is the Lord my God') *c.* 9 century BC. A Levite sent by Jehoshaphat, king of Judah, to teach the Law of Moses to the people of Judah. [2 Chr. 17:8]

TOBIAH (Heb. 'the Lord is good') **1.** *c.* 5 century BC. A Transjordan Jew in the time of Nehemiah. Tobiah was the head of a wealthy family of landowners, with relatives among the Jerusalem notables. Together with Sanballat, the governor of Samaria, and Geshem, an Edomite chief, he opposed Nehemiah's plans to rebuild the walls of Jerusalem and suggested that it would be interpreted as a rebellious act against the king of Persia. The Judeans persisted and Tobiah sneered at their handiwork: 'if a fox goes up on it he will break down their stone wall!' (Neh. 4:3) As the work progressed Tobiah and his friends grew angry and tried to lure Nehemiah out of Jerusalem, but he felt they would harm him and refused to go.

Later, when Nehemiah returned from a visit to Babylon, he was horrified to find that the high priest had installed Tobiah in a room in the Temple courtyard. Nehemiah ordered all the household gear thrown out of the room and had it thoroughly cleansed and returned to its former function. [Neh. 2:10, 19; 4:3, 7; 6:1-19; 13:4-8]
2. date unknown. Ancestor of a family which returned from exile with Zerubbabel but could not trace their ancestry and therefore could not prove that they were Jewish. [Ezra 2:60; Neh. 7:62]

TOBIJAH (Heb. 'God's goodness') **1.** *c.* 9 century BC. A Levite sent by Jehoshaphat, king of Judah, to teach the Law of Moses to the people of Judah. [2 Chr. 17:8]
2. *c.* 6 century BC. A leader of Judah who returned from exile in Babylon and was commanded by the prophet Zechariah to provide gold and silver for a crown to be put on the head of Joshua, son of Jehozadak, the high priest, who would rebuild the Temple. He was told to keep the crown as a memorial in the Temple. [Zech. 6:10, 14]

TOGARMAH (Heb. 'bony') date unknown. Son of Gomer and a great-grandson of Noah. [Gen. 10:3; 1 Chr. 1:6; Ezek. 27:14; 38:6]

TOHU *see* TOAH

TOI (Heb. 'wandering') *c.* 10 century BC. The king of Hamath in the reign of King David, who sent his son Joram to congratulate David on his victory over his enemy Hadadezer, king of Syria. Also known as Tou. [2 Sam. 8:9; 1 Chr. 18:9, 10]

TOKHATH *see* TIKVAH

TOLA (Heb. 'worm') **1.** *c.* 16 century BC. A son of Issachar and a grandson of Jacob and Leah, he went down to Egypt with his grandfather Jacob. [Gen. 46:13; Num. 26:23; 1 Chr. 7:1, 2]
2. *c.* 12 century BC. The son of Puah of the tribe of Issachar, he became judge and ruler over Israel after the death of Abimelech. He ruled for twenty-three years from Shamir in the hills of Ephraim, then died and was buried in Shamir. [Judg. 10:1]

TOU *see* TOI

TUBAL (Heb. 'tumult') date unknown. Son of Japheth and a grandson of Noah, and by Hebrew tradition the father of the people Tubal, referred to in the Books of Isaiah and Ezekiel. [Gen. 10:2; 1 Chr. 1:5; Isa. 66:19; Ezek. 27:13; 32:26; 38:2; 39:1]

TUBAL-CAIN date unknown. Son of Lamech and Zillah a descendant of Cain, he was the 'forger of all instruments of bronze and iron'. [Gen. 4:22]

Tubal-cain, the first metalworker: relief from Florence Cathedral.

U

UCAL (Heb. 'power') date unknown. One of the two men to whom Agur's words were addressed. [Prov. 30:1]

UEL (Heb. 'God's will') 5 century BC. One of the twelve descendants of Bani who married a non-Jewish woman and divorced her in the time of Ezra. [Ezra 10:34]

ULAM (Heb. 'porch') **1.** date unknown. Eldest son of Eshek, a Benjaminite chief descended from King Saul. His descendants were renowned as mighty archers. [1 Chr. 8:39, 40]

2. date unknown. A chief of the tribe of Manasseh descended from Machir. [1 Chr. 7:16, 17]

ULLA (Heb. 'yoke') date unknown. A leader of the tribe of Asher, he and his three sons were mighty warriors. [1 Chr. 7:39]

UNNI (Heb. 'afflicted') *c.* 10 century BC. A Levite who played musical instruments in the celebrations when the Ark of God was brought by King David to Jerusalem. [1 Chr. 15:18, 20]

UNNO (Heb. 'afflicted') *c.* 6 century BC. One of the Levites who participated in the thanksgiving services in the Temple after the return from exile in Babylon. [Neh. 12:9]

UR (Heb. 'light') *c.* 10 century BC. Father of Eliphal, one of the warriors in the army of King David distinguished for his bravery. Also called Ahasbai. [2 Sam. 23:34; 1 Chr. 11:35]

URI (Heb. 'fire') **1.** *c.* 13 century BC. Son of Hur of the tribe of Judah and the father of Bezalel, the craftsman who constructed the Tabernacle of the Children of Israel in the wilderness. [Exod. 31:2; 35:30; 38:22; 1 Chr. 2:20; 2 Chr. 1:5]

2. *c.* 10 century BC. Father of Geber who was one of King Solomon's twelve officers responsible for providing the royal supplies. [1 Kgs. 4:19]

3. 5 century BC. One of the Levites who was a Temple gatekeeper and who divorced his non-Jewish wife in the time of Ezra. [Ezra 10:24]

URIAH (Heb. 'God is my light') **1.** *c.* 10 century BC. First husband of Bathsheba. Uriah, the Hittite, was one of the thirty chosen men who commanded David's army. While the king's army under Joab was besieging Rabbah, the Aramean capital, David took advantage of Uriah's absence to have an affair with his wife Bathsheba. When he discovered she was pregnant he sent a secret message to Joab, asking him to send Uriah home, so that he should be regarded as the father. Uriah, however, did not join his wife and spent that night and the next with the palace guard.

Fearful of the scandal if the adultery became known, David sent Uriah back to the front with a sealed letter to Joab, saying, 'Set Uriah in the forefront of the hardest fighting, and then draw back from him, that he may be struck down, and die.' (2 Sam. 11:15) Joab accordingly arranged a dangerous sortie and in this engagement Uriah was killed. David was then able to marry Bathsheba. [2 Sam. 11; 1 Kgs. 15:5; 1 Chr. 11:41]

The stoning of Uriah, from a 13th-century English Bible. Nathan (right) berates David and Bathsheba (left).

2. *c.* 8 century BC. The high priest of Judah in the reign of King Ahaz. At the king's request he designed an altar in Jerusalem on the model of the altar Ahaz had seen in Damascus, when he went to pay tribute to the Assyrian emperor, Tiglath-pileser. Uriah also carried out the king's command to offer sacrifices on the altar. When the prophet Isaiah denounced the iniquities of Israel he referred to Uriah as one of the witnesses to his prophecy of doom. [2 Kgs. 16:10-16; Isa. 8:2]

3. *c.* 6 century BC. Son of Shemaiah, he was a prophet from Kiriath-jearim. He foretold the destruction of Jerusalem at the same time as Jeremiah, and fled to Egypt to escape arrest by the enraged King Jehoiakim. The king sent agents to seize him in Egypt and he was brought back to Judah where he was executed. [Jer. 26:20-23]

4. *c.* 5 century BC. A Levite who stood at the right-hand of Ezra when he read the Law of Moses to the people of Judah after the return from exile in Babylon. [Neh. 8:4]

5. 5 century BC. Son of Hakkoz and the father of Meremoth, the priest who was head of the four leaders of Judah appointed by Ezra to weigh the gold and silver and precious vessels brought back from Babylon, and who also helped repair the walls of Jerusalem. [Ezra 8:33; Neh. 3:4]

URIEL (Heb. 'God is my light') **1.** 13 century BC. Son of Tahath, a Levite descended from Kohath, he was an ancestor of the prophet Samuel. [1 Chr. 6:24]

2. *c.* 10 century BC. Head of a family of Levites descended from Kohath who ministered in the Tabernacle in the reign of King David. He was one of the Levites ordered by King David to carry the Ark of God to Jerusalem. [1 Chr. 15:5, 11]

3. *see* ABISHALOM

UTHAI (Heb. 'helpful') **1.** *c.* 6 century BC. Son of Ammihud of the tribe of Judah, he was one of the first men of Judah to settle in Jerusalem following the return from exile in Babylon. Also called Athaiah. [1 Chr. 9:4; Neh. 11:4]

2. *c.* 6 century BC. Son of Bigvai he returned to Judah from exile in Babylon. [Ezra 8:14]

UZ 1. date unknown. Grandson of Shem, and son of Aram. [Gen. 10:23; 1 Chr. 1:17]

2. *c.* 18 century BC. Son of Nahor and Milcah, he was a nephew of Abraham. [Gen. 22:21]

3. date unknown. Son of Dishan, a Horite. [Gen. 36:28]

UZAI 5 century BC. Father of Palal who repaired part of the walls of Jerusalem in the days of Nehemiah. [Neh. 3:25]

UZAL (Heb. 'wanderer') date unknown. Son of Joktan and a descendant of Shem, he was a leader of a desert tribe. [Gen. 10:27; 1 Chr. 1:21]

UZZA (Heb. 'strength') **1.** date unknown. Son of Gera, a leader of the tribe of Benjamin. [1 Chr. 8:7]

2. date unknown. A Temple servant whose descendants

returned with Zerubbabel from exile in Babylon. [Ezra 2:49; Neh. 7:51]

3. *c.* 7 century BC. Owner of the garden in which the kings of Judah, Manasseh and Amon, were buried. [2 Kgs. 21:18, 26]

UZZAH (Heb. 'strength') **1.** date unknown. Son of Shimei, a Levite descended from Merari, he was the father of Shimea. [1 Chr. 6:29]

2. *c.* 10 century BC. Son of Abinadab of Gibeah, he took hold of the Ark of God to steady it while it was being transported to Jerusalem on King David's orders; he was killed immediately. [2 Sam. 6:3-8; 1 Chr. 13:7-10]

UZZI (Heb. 'my strength') **1.** *c.* 16 century BC. Son of Tola and a grandson of Issachar, he and his brothers were leaders of the tribe of Issachar and mighty warriors. [1 Chr. 7:2]

2. *c.* 16 century BC. Son of Bela and a grandson of Benjamin, he and his brothers were leaders of the tribe of Benjamin and mighty warriors. [1 Chr. 7:2]

3. date unknown. Son of Bukki, the priest, and father of Zerahiah, he was an ancestor of Ezra. [1 Chr. 6:5, 6, 51; Ezra 7:4]

4. 6 century BC. Son of Michri and father of Elah who was one of the first Benjaminites to settle in Jerusalem following the return from Babylon. [1 Chr. 9:8]

5. 5 century BC. Son of Bani, he was the overseer of the Levites in Jerusalem after the return from Babylon in the time of Nehemiah. [Neh. 11:22]

6. 5 century BC. Head of a priestly family descended from Jedaiah, he was a chief priest of Judah when Joiakim was high priest and took part in the ceremony of dedication of the walls of Jerusalem in the days of Nehemiah. [Neh. 12:19, 42]

UZZIA (Heb. 'God is [my] strength') *c.* 10 century BC. An Ashterathite who was a warrior in the army of King David distinguished for his bravery. [1 Chr. 11:44]

UZZIAH (Heb. 'God is [my] strength') **1.** date unknown. Son of Uriel of the tribe of Levi and a descendant of Kohath. Also called Azariah. [1 Chr. 6:24; 36]

2. *c.* 10 century BC. Father of Jonathan who supervised the storehouses of King David. [1 Chr. 27:25]

3. Tenth king of Judah after the monarchy split, he reigned 781-40 BC.

Uzziah was the son of King Amaziah of Judah and his wife Jecoliah of Jerusalem. He succeeded to the throne at the age of sixteen after his father was assassinated.

During Uzziah's long reign, Judah enjoyed greater military prowess and material progress than it had done for generations. This was paralleled by the expansion of the northern kingdom of Israel under Jeroboam II. At the peak of this period, in the middle of the 8th century BC, the two Hebrew states together controlled an area roughly corresponding to that of King David's empire of over two centuries earlier.

Uzziah

Uzziah was statesmanlike enough to repair the relationship with the kingdom of Israel after the brief war in his father's reign when the army of Israel had taken the Judean king captive and battered the walls of Jerusalem. With peace and co-operation between the two kingdoms, Israel was free to expand eastwards across the Jordan river and northward into Aram (Syria); while Judah could expand to the south and west.

Uzziah re-established control over the desert kingdom of Edom, in the Negev and southern Jordan. He could therefore rebuild the harbour town and copper-smelting centre of Ezion-geber (Eilat) originally constructed by King Solomon. Evidence of this period has been found including a signet ring inscribed with the name Jotham, in the excavations at Tel el-Kheleifeh in this vicinity.

Uzziah also extended the borders of the kingdom into the Philistine area of the coastal plain, capturing and annexing the cities of Gath, Jabneh and Ashdod. He repulsed the nomad tribes in the south, and defeated the Ammonites east of the Jordan, on whom he levied tribute. This extension of Judah's power and influence

Pottery cup in the form of a human head from Ashdod, dating from the time King Uzziah (781-40 BC) captured the city.

below King Uzziah developed the agriculture of Judah. The terraced slopes of the Judean hills near Jerusalem as they appear today.

brought about a large programme of military fortification.

In Jerusalem he strengthened the walls and constructed towers at the 'Corner Gate and at the Valley Gate and at the Angle' (2 Chr. 26:9). Devices were installed on the walls for discharging arrows and hurling rocks. Along the borders and the main highways, large forts were erected. Three such desert forts have been excavated at Kadesh-barnea on the Sinai border, at Tel Arad in the eastern Negev and at Khirbet Ghazzeh five miles south-east of Tel Arad. These stood on the ancient road to Edom. The army was re-organized, with full-time professional cadres of officers and instructors under the command of Hananiah. It is mentioned that the troops were equipped with shields, spears, helmets, coats of mail, bows and slings.

Uzziah put much effort into the development of the kingdom's agriculture, including the settlement of farming of some of the semi-arid areas he had acquired: 'He built towers in the wilderness, and hewed out many cisterns, for he had large herds, both in the Shephelah and in the plain, and he had farmers and vinedressers in the hills and in the fertile lands, for he loved the soil.' (2 Chr. 26:10)

The building activity and busy commerce in Jerusalem, and the rising standard of luxury are depicted in the disapproving utterances of the great contemporary prophets Isaiah, Amos and Hosea.

Uzziah's importance and prestige were demonstrated by his assuming leadership of a coalition of the kings of the region formed to block the Assyrian advance from the north under Tiglath-pileser III. This effort was unsuccessful. Assyrian power subdued Aram and Israel, and Uzziah had to concern himself with preserving the borders of his own kingdom. Judah was left as the strongest local state still holding out against Assyrian pressure. After the death of Jeroboam II of Israel, Judah under Uzziah filled to some extent the vacuum left by the rapid decline of Israel.

During his reign Uzziah was smitten with the dread disease of leprosy. According to the Second Book of Chronicles, this was a punishment for his presumption in personally burning incense on the altar in the Temple, a sacred function reserved for the priests. From then on Uzziah no longer appeared in public but remained secluded in his quarters. He remained in control of the affairs of the kingdom, together with his son and crown prince Jotham, who acted as co-regent and master of the household. This odd father-and-son rule continued for a number of years, until the death of Uzziah, when Jotham became king in his own right.

In the last century, the re-internment stone of King Uzziah was discovered in Jerusalem, and is now in the Israel Museum. Its Aramaic inscription in Hebrew letters reads: 'Hither were brought the bones of Uzziah,

Tombstone of King Uzziah, bearing the following inscription in Aramaic: 'Hither were brought the bones of Uzziah, king of Judah. Do not open.'

king of Judah. Do not open.' It dates to the 1st century BC, when Jerusalem was undergoing its expansion under Herod, and all graves, except for the tombs of the kings, were moved outside the city walls; but as a leper, Uzziah had not been buried in the royal tombs, and so his remains were re-interred at that time and appropriately marked by this limestone plaque. Also called Azariah. [2 Kgs. 14:21; 15:1-8, 13, 17, 23, 27; 2 Chr. 26; 27:2; Isa. 1:1; 6:1; 7:1; Hos. 1:1; Amos 1:1; Zech. 14:5]

4. *see* AMMIHUD **5.**

5. 5 century BC. Son of Harim the priest he divorced his non-Jewish wife in the time of Ezra. [Ezra 10:21]

UZZIEL (Heb. 'God is my strength') **1.** *c.* 16 century BC. A son of Bela and a grandson of Benjamin, he and his brothers were leaders of the tribe and mighty warriors. [1 Chr. 7:7]

2. date unknown. Son of Kohath and a grandson of Levi, one of his descendants of the same name was an uncle of Moses and Aaron and another was prominent in the reign of King David. [Exod. 6:18, 22; Lev. 10:4; Num. 3:19, 30; 1 Chr. 6:2; 15:10; 23:12, 20; 24:24]

3. *see* AZAREL **2.**

4. *c.* 8 century BC. A son of Ishi of the tribe of Simeon, he and his brothers commanded a band of 500 men, which drove out the Amalekites from Mount Seir, south-east of the Dead Sea, and settled there in the time of Hezekiah, king of Judah. [1 Chr. 4:42]

5. *c.* 8 century BC. A descendant of Jeduthun, the musician in the time of King David, he and his brother Shemaiah were among the Levites to carry out the command of Hezekiah, king of Judah, to repair and sanctify the Temple. [2 Chr. 29:14]

6. 5 century BC. Son of Harhaiah and a member of a Judean family of goldsmiths, he helped repair the walls of Jerusalem in the time of Nehemiah. [Neh. 3:8]

V

VAIZATHA *c.* 5 century BC. Youngest son of Haman the Agagite who plotted to kill all the Jews in the Persian empire in the reign of King Ahasuerus. When the plot was discovered Haman and his sons were put to death. [Esther 9:9]

VANIAH 5 century BC. A descendant of Bani who divorced his non-Jewish wife in the time of Ezra. [Ezra 10:36]

VASHTI (Pers. 'beautiful') 5 century BC. The queen of Persia who was ordered by her husband, King Ahasuerus, to appear before him at a feast to show off her beauty to his guests. She refused and as a punishment for her disobedience the king divorced her. [Esther 1:9-22; 2:1, 4, 17]

VOPHSI *c.* 13 century BC. Father of Nahbi of the tribe of Naphtali, who was one of the twelve scouts sent by Moses to reconnoitre the Promised Land. [Num. 13:14]

Z

ZAAVAN (Heb. 'unquiet') date unknown. Son of Ezer and a grandson of Seir the Horite, he was a leader of an Edomite tribe. [Gen. 36:27; 1 Chr. 1:42]

ZABAD (Heb. 'gift') 1. date unknown. Son of Tahath and a leader of the tribe of Ephraim. [1 Chr. 7:21]

2. date unknown. Son of Nathan and father of Ephlal, he was a great-grandson of Jarha, the Egyptian slave who married the daughter of his master Sheshan of the tribe of Judah. [1 Chr. 2:36, 37]

3. c. 10 century BC. Son of Ahlai, he was a valiant warrior in the army of King David. [1 Chr. 11:41]

4. see JOZACAR

5. 5 century BC. A descendant of Zattu who divorced his non-Jewish wife in the time of Ezra. [Ezra 10:27]

6. 5 century BC. A descendant of Hashum who divorced his non-Jewish wife in the time of Ezra. [Ezra 10:33]

7. 5 century BC. A descendant of Nebo who divorced his non-Jewish wife in the time of Ezra. [Ezra 10:43]

ZABBAI (Heb. 'limpid') 1. 5 century BC. A son of Bebai who divorced his non-Jewish wife in the time of Ezra. [Ezra 10:28]

2. 5 century BC. Father of Baruch who helped repair part of the walls of Jerusalem in the time of Nehemiah. [Neh. 3:20]

ZABDI (Heb. 'gift') 1. c. 13 century BC. Son of Zerah of the tribe of Judah, his grandson Achan disobeyed Joshua and took booty from Jericho after it was destroyed. Also called Zimri. [Josh. 7:1, 17; 1 Chr. 2:6]

2. date unknown. Son of Shimhi, he was a leader of the tribe of Benjamin who lived in Jerusalem. [1 Chr. 8:19]

3. c. 10 century BC. An official of King David who was in charge of the royal vineyards. [1 Chr. 27:27]

4. c. 5 century BC. Son of Asaph and father of Mica, his grandson Mattaniah was a Levite responsible for the thanksgiving prayer in the time of Nehemiah. Also called Zichri. [1 Chr. 9:15; Neh. 11:17]

ZABDIEL (Heb. 'gift of God') 1. c. 10 century BC. Father of Jashobeam who was commander of the army which served in the first month of the year during the reign of King David. [1 Chr. 27:2]

2. c. 5 century BC. Head of a group of priests who served in Jerusalem in the days of Nehemiah. [Neh. 11:14]

ZABUD (Heb. 'gift') c. 10 century BC. Son of the prophet Nathan, he was an important official and the king's friend in the reign of Solomon. [1 Kgs. 4:5]

ZACCAI (Heb. 'pure') 6 century BC. Head of a family who returned to Judah with Zerubbabel from exile in Babylon. [Ezra 2:9; Neh. 7:14]

ZACCUR (Heb. 'mindful') 1. c. 13 century BC. Father of Shammua of the tribe of Reuben who was one of the twelve men sent by Moses to spy out the Promised Land. [Num. 13:4]

2. c. 10 century BC. Son of Jaaziah, a Levite descended from Merari, he ministered in the Tabernacle in the reign of King David. [1 Chr. 24:27]

3. date unknown. Son of Hammuel, he was a leader of the tribe of Simeon. [1 Chr. 4:26]

4. c. 10 century BC. Son of Asaph, one of King David's leading musicians, he took the third turn of service in the Temple. He was the ancestor of Zechariah. [1 Chr. 25:2, 10; Neh. 12:35]

5. 5 century BC. A descendant of Bigvai, he returned to Judah from Babylon with Ezra. [Ezra 8:14]

6. 5 century BC. Son of Imri, he helped rebuild the walls of Jerusalem in the time of Nehemiah. [Neh. 3:2]

7. 5 century BC. A Levite who signed the covenant in the time of Nehemiah. [Neh. 10:12]

8. 5 century BC. Father of Hanan, a treasurer appointed by Nehemiah to distribute tithes. [Neh. 13:13]

ZADOK (Heb. 'just') 1. c. 10 century BC. High priest in the time of King David. Zadok, the son of Ahitub, was from a priestly family claiming Eleazar, Aaron's son and successor, as their ancestor. When David became king of the united monarchy Zadok was made one of his two high priests.

At the time of Absalom's revolt, Zadok and the other high priest Abiathar carried the Ark of the Covenant out of Jerusalem in readiness to follow David into the wilderness. But at David's request they turned back, and arranged to keep him informed of Absalom's actions, using their sons as runners.

Absalom entered Jerusalem and after a debate between his counsellors decided not to pursue David immediately. Zadok and Abiathar sent their sons secretly to find David and tell him not to tarry in the plains, but to cross the Jordan river at once.

After the defeat and death of Absalom, David used Zadok and Abiathar to encourage the leaders of Judah to ask for his return.

When David chose his younger son Solomon as his successor, he sent for Zadok and the prophet Nathan and told them to take Solomon on the royal mule and anoint him 'king at Gihon' (1 Kgs. 1:45). In reward for Zadok's faithful service to his father, King Solomon appointed Azariah, one of his sons, as high priest.

From that time until the Maccabees eight centuries

return of the Jews from Babylon. [1 Chr. 9:11]

6. 5 century BC. Son of Baana, he helped Nehemiah rebuild the walls of Jerusalem. [Neh. 3:4]

7. 5 century BC. Descendant of Immer, he was a priest and scribe who also helped rebuild the walls of Jerusalem in the days of Nehemiah, and was one of four trusted officers appointed to distribute the tithes of corn, wine and oil among the Levites. [Neh. 3:29; 13:13]

8. *c.* 5 century BC. A leader of Judah who signed the covenant to observe the Laws of God in the time of Nehemiah. [Neh. 10:21]

ZAHAM (Heb. 'hateful') *c.* 10 century BC. Son of Rehoboam, king of Judah, and a grandson of King

Hollow ivory tusk, trimmed with gold and with a human head at the end, used for anointing. Found at Megiddo, *c.* 2000 BC.

later the high priests were drawn from the Zadokian line. In his vision of the ideal commonwealth Ezekiel insists that the Zadokites are the only legitimate priests. [2 Sam. 8:17; 15:24-36; 17:15; 18:19, 22, 27; 19:11; 20:25; 1 Kgs. 1:26, 32-9; 44-5; 2:35; 4:2, 4; 1 Chr. 6:8, 53; 15:11; 16:39; 18:16; 24:3, 6, 31; 27:17; 29:22; 2 Chr. 31:10; Ezra 7:2; Ezek. 40:46; 43:19; 44:15; 48:11]

2. *c.* 10 century BC. A young officer who led twenty-two warriors from his clan to join David at Hebron and help him secure the kingdom of Israel from the house of King Saul. [1 Chr. 12:28]

3. *c.* 8 century BC. Father of Jerusha, wife of King Uzziah of Judah, and grandfather of Uzziah's successor, King Jotham. [2 Kgs. 15:33; 2 Chr. 27:1]

4. *c.* 8 century BC. A priest, son of Ahitub and father of Shallum, he was probably a descendant of Zadok and an ancestor of Jehozadak, a priest who was taken into Babylonian captivity. [1 Chr. 6:12]

5. *c.* 6 century BC. Son of Meraioth, he was an ancestor of Azariah, the first priest to settle in Jerusalem after the

Solomon, his mother was Mahalath, a granddaughter of King David. [2 Chr. 11:19]

ZALAPH (Heb. 'caper plant') 5 century BC. Father of Hanun who helped repair the walls of Jerusalem in the time of Nehemiah. [Neh. 3:30]

ZALMON *see* ILAI

ZALMUNNA (Heb. 'shadow') *c.* 12 century BC. One of the two Midianite chieftains who fled after the bulk of the Midianite army had been routed at Ain Harod by Gideon. Gideon caught up with them at Karkor, destroyed their forces and personally executed them in retaliation for their murder of his brother. [Judg. 8:5-21; Ps. 83:11]

ZANOAH (Heb. 'swamp') date unknown. Son of Jekuthiel, a leader of the tribe of Judah. [1 Chr. 4:18]

ZATTU 1. 6 century BC. Ancestor of a family of several hundreds who returned to Judah with Zerubbabel from captivity in Babylon. [Ezra 2:8; 10:27; Neh. 7:13]

2. 5 century BC. A leader of Judah who signed the covenant to keep the Laws of the Lord in the time of Nehemiah. [Neh. 10:14]

ZAZA (Heb. 'moving') date unknown. Son of Jonathan, a descendant of Jerahmeel of the tribe of Judah. [1 Chr. 2:33]

ZEBADIAH (Heb. 'portion of God') **1.** date unknown. Son of Beriah, he was a leader of the tribe of Benjamin living in Jerusalem. [1 Chr. 8:15]

2. date unknown. Eldest son of Elpaal, he was one of the leaders of the tribe of Benjamin living in Jerusalem. [1 Chr. 8:17]

3. *c.* 11 century BC. Son of Jeroham of the tribe of Benjamin, he and his brother joined David at Ziklag where he had taken refuge from Saul. [1 Chr. 12:7]

4. *c.* 10 century BC. Son of Meshelemiah, he and his family were gatekeepers at the Tabernacle in the reign of King David. [1 Chr. 26:2]

5. *c.* 10 century BC. Son of Asahel and nephew of Joab, he succeeded his father as commander of the army of King David which served in the fourth month of the year. [1 Chr. 27:7]

6. *c.* 9 century BC. A Levite sent by King Jehoshaphat to teach the Law of God to the people of Judah. [2 Chr. 17:8]

7. *c.* 9 century BC. Son of Ishmael, he was governor of the house of Judah 'in all the king's matters' in the reign of King Jehoshaphat. [2 Chr. 19:11]

8. 5 century BC. Son of Michael and a descendant of Shephatiah, he returned to Judah from exile in Babylon with Ezra. [Ezra 8:8]

9. 5 century BC. Descendant of Immer the priest, he divorced his non-Jewish wife in the time of Ezra. [Ezra 10:20]

ZEBAH (Heb. 'sacrifice') *c.* 12 century BC. One of the two kings of Midian who were defeated by Gideon and fled with the remnant of their army to Karkor. There Gideon captured the kings and put them to death. [Judg. 8:5-21; Ps. 83:11]

ZEBIDAH (Heb. 'given') *c.* 7 century BC. Daughter of Pedaiah of Rumah, she was the mother of Jehoiakim, king of Judah. [2 Kgs. 23:36]

ZEBINA (Heb. 'buying') 5 century BC. A descendant of Nebo, he divorced his non-Jewish wife in the time of Ezra. [Ezra 10:43]

ZEBUL (Heb. 'habitation') *c.* 12 century BC. Head of the city of Shechem during the reign of Abimelech. When Gaal the son of Ebed roused the Shechemites against Abimelech, Zebul sent secret word to the ruler who took timely action to crush the revolt. [Judg. 9:26-41]

ZEBULUN (Heb. 'dwelling') *c.* 16 century BC. Zebulun was the tenth son of Jacob and the sixth born to Leah. Together with his brothers he was involved in the events that led to the selling of their brother Joseph into slavery in Egypt. Later he was one of the ten sons sent by Jacob to buy corn in Egypt, where Joseph had become a leading figure at the court of Pharaoh. When Jacob went to settle in Egypt with all his family it included Zebulun and his three sons.

On his deathbed Jacob blessed all his sons in turn, and said: 'Zebulun shall dwell at the shore of the sea.' (Gen. 49:13)

In the blessing attributed to Moses, it is said: 'for they suck the affluence of the seas and the hidden treasures of the sand.' (Deut. 33:19)

In the conquest of Canaan under Joshua, the tribe of Zebulun was allocated the western Jezreel valley. [Gen. 30:20; 35:23; 46:14; 49:13; Exod. 1:3; 1 Chr. 2:1]

The Valley of Zebulun in Upper Galilee.

ZECHARIAH (Heb. 'God has remembered') **1.** date unknown. A leader of the tribe of Reuben related to Joel, chief of the tribe. [1 Chr. 5:7]

2. date unknown. Son of Pashhur, the priest, and father of Amzi, his descendant Adaiah lived in Jerusalem in the time of Nehemiah and served in the Temple. [Neh. 11:12]

3. date unknown. Son of Amariah of the tribe of Judah and father of Uzziah, his descendant Athaiah settled in Jerusalem after the return from exile in Babylon. [Neh. 11:4]

4. *c.* 11 century BC. Son of Jeiel and a leader of the tribe of Benjamin, he was an uncle of King Saul. Also called Zecher. [1 Chr. 8:31; 9:37]

5. *c.* 10 century BC. Eldest son of Meshelemiah the Levite, he was a gate-keeper at the northern entrance to the Tabernacle in the time of King David. [1 Chr. 9:21; 26:2, 14]

6. *c.* 10 century BC. A musician during the reign of King David who played the harp when the Ark of God was brought to Jerusalem, he was one of the Levites appointed by David to minister before the Ark of God. [1 Chr. 15:18, 20; 16:5]

7. *c.* 10 century BC. A priest who blew a trumpet to celebrate the bringing of the Ark of the Lord into Jerusalem by King David. [1 Chr. 15:24]

8. *c.* 10 century BC. Son of Isshiah, he was a Levite serving in the Tabernacle in King David's reign. [1 Chr. 24:25]

9. *c.* 10 century BC. Son of Hosah, he was a Levite who served as gatekeeper of the Tabernacle in the reign of King David. [1 Chr. 26:11]

10. *c.* 10 century BC. Father of Iddo who ruled over the half-tribe of Manasseh in Gilead in the reign of King David. [1 Chr. 27:21]

11. *c.* 9 century BC. One of the five princes of Judah who were sent by King Jehoshaphat to teach the Law in the cities of Judah. [2 Chr. 17:7]

12. *c.* 9 century BC. Father of Jahaziel who prophesied in the reign of King Jehoshaphat of Judah that God

Phoenician bronze incense burner from the time of Zechariah, showing a harpist.

would defeat the Ammonites and Moabites, and that King Jehoshaphat would not need to fight them. [2 Chr. 20:14]

13. *c.* 9 century BC. A son of Jehoshaphat, he and his five brothers were killed by their eldest brother, Jehoram, when he succeeded his father as king of Judah. [2 Chr. 21:2]

14. *c.* 9 century BC. Son of Jehoiada, the priest, in the reign of Joash, king of Judah. After his father's death he admonished the people for transgressing the Laws of God, and the angry king ordered him to be stoned to death in the Temple courtyard. [2 Chr. 24:20-22]

15. Fourteenth king of Israel after the monarchy split, he reigned for six months in 743 BC. Zechariah succeeded his father Jeroboam II and was assassinated six months later by Shallum, the son of Jabesh, who seized the throne. Zechariah's death ended the dynasty of Jehu which had reigned over Israel for nearly a century. [2 Kgs. 14:29; 15:8-12]

16. *c.* 8 century BC. Father of Abi who was the mother of Hezekiah, king of Judah. [2 Kgs. 18:2; 2 Chr. 29:1]

17. *c.* 8 century BC. A prophet consulted by Uzziah, king of Judah, who instructed the king how to serve God faithfully. [2 Chr. 26:5]

18. *c.* 8 century BC. A Levite descended from Asaph who obeyed King Hezekiah's command to sanctify himself and cleanse the Temple. [2 Chr. 29:13]

19. *c.* 8 century BC. Son of Jeberechiah, he was one of the reliable witnesses who attested to Isaiah's inscription of *Maher-shalal-hash-baz* (Heb. 'booty and shame

are imminent') which Isaiah then gave as a name to his newborn son. The inscription signified the impending destruction of Israel and Damascus by the Assyrians. [Isa. 8:2]

20. *c.* 7 century BC. A Levite descended from Kohath who helped supervise the work of repairing the Temple in the time of Josiah, king of Judah. [2 Chr. 34:12]

21. *c.* 7 century BC. A head priest serving in the Temple during the reign of Josiah, king of Judah, he received the Passover offerings donated by the leaders of Judah. [2 Chr. 35:8]

22. Second half of 6 century BC. Post-exilic Hebrew prophet. Zechariah the son of Berechiah prophesied in Jerusalem after the return from Babylonia. In 520 BC, in the second year of the reign of Darius the Great, he and the prophet Haggai pressed for the work to be resumed on the ruined Temple. It was completed within five years.

In the earlier chapters of the Book of Zechariah, the prophet has eight mystical visions full of symbolic images, as Ezekiel before him and Daniel afterwards. Mysterious horsemen come back from patrolling the earth; four horns represent hostile kingdoms and are destroyed; a man with a measuring rod comes to measure Jerusalem; the high priest Joshua is tried before a heavenly court and his filthy clothes are replaced by splendid robes; a golden lamp stands between two olive trees; an immense scroll flies through the air over the land; a woman representing wickedness sits in a great bowl and is carried off to Babylonia; four chariots are

One of Zechariah's visions was of four chariots. Miniature gold chariot and drivers, Persian, 6th-4th centuries BC.

The hill of Zion to
the south-west of the Old City
of Jerusalem.

drawn by red, black, white and piebald horses and go to
the four points of the compass. These visions are interpreted to reflect the political turmoil in the Persian
empire that followed the accession of Darius, and the
Messianic hopes for a restored and purified Jewish
kingdom.

In one of the visions Zechariah sees a crown placed
on the head of Zerubbabel, who is called a 'branch',
because he was a scion of the house of David.

Zechariah sees a future in which the Jews will live in
peace in their land, under the protection of the Lord:
'I will return to Zion, and will dwell in the midst of
Jerusalem, and Jerusalem shall be called the faithful
city, and the mountain of the Lord of hosts, the holy
mountain.' (Zech. 8:3)

The coming of the Messianic age is elaborated in the
last six chapters. Enemy nations will be subdued, and a
third of the Jewish nation will survive and live in freedom, and the Lord will be king over all the earth. This
part of the Book has no reference to the historical events
of Zechariah's time, and appears to have been written
by someone else at a much later date. [Neh. 12:16; Book
of Zechariah]

Herodian rock-cut tomb in
the Kidron Valley, traditionally known
as the tomb of Zechariah.

23. *c.* 6 century BC. Father of Joiarib, his descendant Maaseîah was one of the first men of Judah to settle in Jerusalem after the return from Babylon. [Neh. 11:5]

24. 5 century BC. A descendant of Parosh and a leader of Judah who returned with Ezra from exile in Babylon. [Ezra 8:3]

25. 5 century BC. Son of Bebai, he was one of the leaders of Judah who returned with Ezra from exile in Babylon. [Ezra 8:11]

26. 5 century BC. A leader of Judah sent by Ezra to Iddo at Casiphia to ask him to send Levites to Jerusalem to minister in the Temple. [Ezra 8:16]

27. 5 century BC. A descendant of Elam who divorced his non-Jewish wife in the time of Ezra. [Ezra 10:26]

28. 5 century BC. A leader of Judah who stood at the side of Ezra when he read the Law of Moses to the people of Judah. [Neh. 8:4]

29. *c.* 5 century BC. A priest of the family of Iddo when Joiakim was high priest over Judah, after the return from exile in Babylon. [Neh. 12:16]

30. 5 century BC. Son of Jonathan and a descendant of Asaph, he was a priest who blew a trumpet at the dedication ceremony for the rebuilt walls of Jerusalem in the time of Nehemiah. [Neh. 12:35, 41]

ZECHER *see* ZECHARIAH **4.**

ZEDEKIAH (Heb. 'God is [my] righteousness') **1.** 9 century BC. Son of Chenaanah, he was one of the four hundred 'prophets' of King Ahab of Israel who favoured the joint attack by Ahab and King Jehoshaphat of Judah on the Arameans occupying Ramoth-gilead. When the true prophet Micaiah (correctly) predicted disaster, Zedekiah struck him in the face. [1 Kgs. 22:11, 24; 2 Chr. 18:10, 23]

2. *c.* 7 century BC. Son of Hananiah, he was one of the princes of Judah who ordered Baruch, son of Neriah, to read out Jeremiah's prophecies of doom and then repeated them before King Jehoiakim. [Jer. 36:12]

3. Twentieth and last king of Judah after the monarchy split, he reigned 598-87 BC. The son of King Josiah and Hamutal, daughter of a certain Jeremiah from Libnah. Zedekiah (called Mattaniah till he mounted the throne) was appointed to the throne by the Babylonians when his nephew King Jehoiachin surrendered Jerusalem and was carried off into captivity. Zedekiah was then twenty-one years old. A Babylonian inscription from the reign of Nebuchadnezzar, referring to these events, states that 'he captured the city and took the king prisoner. A king of his own choice was set up in his midst.'

The Babylonians stripped away much of the territory held by Judah, and carried on a harsh indirect rule of the country. In 589 BC, when Zedekiah had been a puppet king for nine years, he revolted against the Babylonian overlords, together with two neighbouring states, Tyre and Ammon, with Egyptian encouragement. For the second time Nebuchadnezzar advanced

on Jerusalem with a large army. This time the city did not surrender and was kept under tight siege for two years. In the year 587, in the heat of midsummer, the northern wall of the starving city was breached by battering rams, and further resistance became hopeless.

That night, under cover of darkness, the king and some of his fighting men escaped through a gateway next to the royal garden and fled eastwards. They were pursued and captured on the Jericho plain. Zedekiah was brought before Nebuchadnezzar and forced to witness the slaying of his children. His eyes were then put out and he was hauled off in chains to Babylon, where he died. The city was sacked, the Temple destroyed and most of the inhabitants taken off into captivity. The independence of Judah had come to an end. [2 Kgs. 24:17-20; 25:1-7; 1 Chr. 3:15; 2 Chr. 36:10-21; Jer. 1:3; 21:1-7; 24:8; 27:3, 12; 28:1; 29:3; 32:1-5; 34:2-8, 21; 37:1, 3, 17, 18, 21; 38:5, 14-26; 39:1-7; 44:30; 49:34; 51:59; 52:1-11]

The 'Lachish Letters'

The remarkable 'Lachish Letters' relating to the Babylonian invasion of Judah at the beginning of the 6th century BC, were discovered at the archaeological excavations of the fortified Judean city of Lachish (Tel ed-Duweir) carried out between 1932 and 1938. Eighteen ostraca – inscribed potsherds – were found among the burnt debris in a guard-room of a bastion in the outer city wall. Three more were found elsewhere on the site.

Fragment of the 'Lachish Letters', written 588-7 BC.

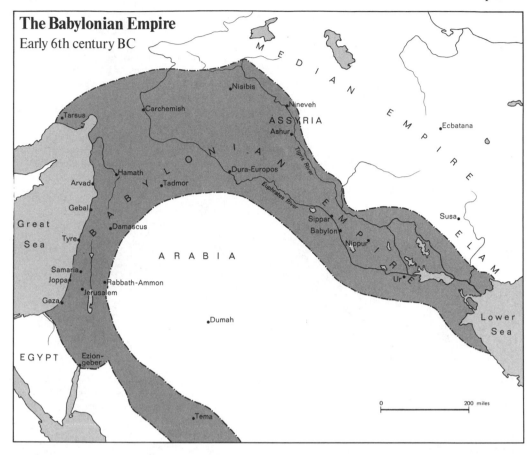

The Babylonian Empire
Early 6th century BC

The writing, in black ink on broken pottery, is classical Hebrew prose, and the lettering in early Hebrew script. They consist for the most part of reports written in the years 588-7 BC to Yaosh, military commander of the Lachish fortress, one of the last to fall to the Babylonians before the conquest of Jerusalem, by his subordinate officer Hoshaiah, who was in command of an outpost to the north of the city.

The letters reflect the pessimism evident in Jerusalem at the time, when king Zedekiah had Jeremiah brought from prison and 'questioned him secretly' about the immediate prospects. Referring to letters sent to him from Jerusalem. Hoshaiah is much alarmed and writes to 'my lord Yaosh':

'Who is thy servant but a dog that my Lord hath sent the letter of the king and the letters of the princes, saying, "Pray read them": And behold the words of the princes are not good, but to weaken our hands and to slacken the hands of the men who are informed about them ... truly since thy servant read the letters there hath been no peace for thy servant ....'

Other items of this Lachish correspondence deal with purely military matters.

4. 6 century BC. Son of Maaseiah, he was among those deported to Babylon with King Jehoiachin by Nebuchadnezzar, and he, together with Ahab, son of Kolaiah, aroused the anger of the prophet Jeremiah by their immorality and by raising false hopes among the exiles. Jeremiah cursed them and foretold that Nebuchadnezzar would have them burnt to death. [Jer. 29:21, 22]

5. 5 century BC. A leader of Judah who signed the solemn covenant in the time of Nehemiah. [Neh. 10:1]

ZEEB (Heb. 'wolf') c. 12 century BC. A prince of Midian who was killed by the men of Ephraim at the wine press of Zeeb, at the orders of Gideon. [Judg. 7:25; 8:3; Ps. 83:11]

ZELEK (Heb. 'chasm') 10 century BC. An Ammonite, he was a warrior in the army of King David distinguished for his bravery. [2 Sam. 23:37; 1 Chr. 11:39]

ZELOPHEHAD (Heb. 'protection from fear') c. 13 century BC. A leader of the tribe of Manasseh who died in the wilderness leaving six daughters but no sons. His

375

daughters asked Moses to give them their father's inheritance since they did not want their father's name to die out and Moses, after consulting God, agreed. [Num. 26:33; 27:1, 7; 36:2-11; Josh. 17:3; 1 Chr. 7:15]

ZEMIRAH (Heb. 'song') date unknown. Son of Becher, he was a leader of the tribe of Benjamin and a mighty man of valour. [1 Chr. 7:8]

ZEPHANIAH (Heb. 'God has protected') **1.** *c.* 13 century BC. Son of Tahath, a Levite descended from Kohath, he was an ancestor of Heman, musician to King David. [1 Chr. 6:36]

2. *c.* second half of 7 century BC. Hebrew prophet in the kingdom of Judah. Zephaniah the son of Cushi lived in the reign of King Josiah (640-09 BC), and was a contemporary and fellow-citizen of the great prophet Jeremiah. His words are recorded in the short Book bearing his name.

Since he was vehement against the idolatrous practices in Jerusalem – the star-worship copied from the Assyrians and the infiltration of local Canaanite deities – Zephaniah must have prophesied before the religious reforms of Josiah that started about 622 BC, He denounced the king's deceitful counsellors, dressed in foreign styles; the merchants in the new quarter of the town; the rapacious judges and the false men of religion: 'Her prophets are wanton, faithless men; her priests profane what is sacred, they do violence to the law.' (Zeph. 3:4)

Salt formations on the edge of the Dead Sea. Zephaniah declared that Moab and Ammon would be reduced to 'nettles and salt pits'.

The prophet also pronounced oracles against the neighbouring pagan peoples. The cities of the Philistines would be destroyed, 'The seacoast shall become the possession of the remnant of the house of Judah' (Zeph. 2:7). Moab and Ammon would be reduced to 'nettles and salt pits, and a waste for ever' (Zeph. 2:9). As for the mighty Assyrians, their capital Nineveh would be reduced to a ruin in which sheep would graze and birds would roost.

All this would happen in the 'day of the Lord' that loomed ahead, when the divine wrath would overtake Judah and the other nations: 'I will bring distress on men, so that they shall walk like the blind, because they have sinned against the Lord; their blood shall be poured out like dust, and their flesh like dung.' (Zeph. 1:17) After that great purge, Zion would be restored for the humble and penitent remnant of God's people. The pagan nations would also turn to the Lord, and his worship would become the universal faith of mankind. [Book of Zephaniah]

3. 6 century BC. Son of the priest Maaseiah and himself a priest and adviser to King Zedekiah in the final days of the kingdom of Judah, he opposed the policy of the prophet Jeremiah and favoured revolt against Babylon. With the Babylonian victory, he was among those carried off to Riblah and executed. [2 Kgs. 25:18; Jer. 21:1; 29:25, 29; 37:3; 52:24]

4. 6 century BC. Father of Josiah in whose home in Jerusalem the prophet Zechariah ordered that Joshua son of Jehozadak, the high priest, should be crowned as leader of the return to Judah. [Zech. 6:10, 14]

ZEPHI see ZEPHO

ZEPHO (Heb. 'watch') *c.* 16 century BC. Son of Eliphaz and a grandson of Esau, he was an Edomite leader of a desert tribe. Also called Zephi. [Gen. 36:11; 1 Chr. 1:36]

ZEPHON see ZIPHION

ZERAH (Heb. 'God's shine') **1.** *c.* 16 century BC. Son of Reuel and a grandson of Esau, he was an Edomite leader of a desert tribe. [Gen. 36:13; 1 Chr. 1:37]

2., *c.* 16 century BC. One of the twins born to Judah and Tamar. Just before he was born he thrust forth his hand and the midwife put a scarlet thread round his wrist. Actually his brother Perez was born first. [Gen. 38:28-30; Num. 26:20; Josh. 7:1, 24; 22:20; 1 Chr. 2:4, 6; 9:6; Neh. 11:24]

3. *c.* 16 century BC. Son of Simeon and a grandson of Jacob. Also called Zohar. [Gen. 46:10; Exod. 6:15; Num. 26:13; 1 Chr. 4:24]

4. date unknown. Father of Jobab, king of Edom. [Gen. 36:33; 1 Chr. 1:44]

5. date unknown. Son of Iddo and a descendant of Levi's son Gershom. [1 Chr. 6:21]

6. date unknown. Son of Adaiah the Levite, and an ancestor of King David's musician Asaph. [1 Chr. 6:41]

7. see PHARAOH 7.

8. *c.* 9 century BC. An Ethiopian commander who fought against Asa, king of Judah, with a huge army but was completely defeated. [2 Chr. 14:9]

ZERAHIAH (Heb. 'rising of God') **1.** date unknown. Son of Uzzi, he was a descendant of Aaron, the priest. [1 Chr. 6:6, 51; Ezra 7:4]

2. 5 century BC. Father of Eliehoenai, a leader of Israel who returned from exile in Babylon with Ezra. [Ezra 8:4]

ZERESH (Pers. 'gold') 5 century BC. Wife of Haman, chief minister of King Ahasuerus of Persia. When Mordecai refused to bow down to him, Haman plotted to kill all the Jews in the kingdom. Zeresh encouraged him to build a special gallows on which Mordecai would be hanged. The following day instead of persuading the king to order Mordecai hanged on a trumped-up charge, Haman was ordered by Ahasuerus to pay special honour to the Jew. That evening when Haman told Zeresh what he had been forced to do, she and their friends at once prophesied the fall of Haman and the success of Mordecai. [Esther 5:10, 14; 6:13]

ZERETH date unknown. Son of Ashhur, a leader of the tribe of Judah. [1 Chr. 4:7]

ZERI (Heb. 'balsam') *c.* 10 century BC. Son of Jeduthun, a chief musician in the Tabernacle during King David's reign, Zeri and his brothers played musical instruments under their father's direction; Zeri took the fourth turn of service. Also called Izri. [1 Chr. 25:3, 11]

ZEROR (Heb. 'tied') 11 century BC. Great-grandfather of King Saul, of the tribe of Benjamin. [1 Sam. 9:1]

ZERUAH (Heb. 'leprous') 10 century BC. Mother of King Jeroboam of the northern kingdom of Israel, she was the widow of Nebat an Ephraimite. [1 Kgs. 11:26]

ZERUBBABEL (Heb. 'seed of Babylon') *c.* 6 century BC. Judean prince associated with the return from the Babylonian exile.

Zerubbabel the son of Shealtiel (called 'son of Pedaiah' in the First Book of Chronicles) was a member of the royal house of King Jehoiachin of Judah who was carried off into captivity to Babylon in 598 BC. Forty years after the fall of Jerusalem, Babylon was captured by Cyrus king of Persia, and Judah became part of the Persian empire. The following year, in 538 BC, Cyrus issued an edict permitting the Judean exiles to return to their homeland if they wished, and to rebuild the Temple. Those who remained behind were to assist the repatriates with money and goods, and to give them voluntary donations for the Temple. A total of 42,360 Jews gathered together for the return, under the leadership of Sheshbazzar, also of the Judean royal dynasty. In listing the other prominent persons going on the journey, Zerubbabel's name is the first one mentioned. (Some scholars believe that he and Sheshbazzar were the same person.) When everything was ready, the caravan moved off slowly on the six-hundred-mile trek across the desert.

The two men who shared authority over the settler community were Zerubbabel and Jeshua the high priest. They now started to organize the rebuilding of the Temple. Masons and carpenters were gathered, and set to work under the supervision of the Levites. Cedar logs from Phoenicia (Lebanon) were imported by sea to Joppa, and paid for in foodstuffs and olive oil – as Solomon had done with the building of the First Temple more than four centuries earlier. When the foundations had been laid, a celebration took place. The priests were robed in their vestments, trumpets and cymbals were sounded, and prayers of thanksgiving loudly chanted. The shouts of joy mingled with the weeping of the old men who remembered the First Temple before it had been destroyed.

Before the work could proceed beyond the foundations, it was interrupted by the Samaritans. They were the mixed offspring of the Hebrews who had survived the destruction of the northern kingdom of Israel a century and a half earlier and the deportees brought in from other parts of the Assyrian empire. At first some of them claimed the right to help rebuild the Temple. But Zerubbabel bluntly refused: 'You have nothing to do with us in building a house to our God.' (Ezra 4:3)

After this rebuff, the Samaritans harassed and disrupted the work. Rehum the local governor of Samaria wrote a letter to the king of Persia. He contended the archives would show that Jerusalem had always been a trouble spot, and would be so again if it was restored: 'and learn that this city is a rebellious city, hurtful to kings and provinces . . .' (Ezra 4:15). The palace accepted this plea, and orders were given that the work was to be suspended.

Eighteen years later, after King Darius I had mounted the Persian throne, Zerubbabel and Jeshua called the leading citizens together and initiated another effort to resume the building of the Temple. This was done under strong moral pressure from two Jerusalem prophets, Haggai and Zechariah. Again complaints were made to higher authority. This time Tattenai the satrap (regional governor) came with his staff from Damascus to investigate the dispute personally. Tattenai's report to King Darius was objective. The Jewish settlers claimed, he wrote, that King Cyrus had expressly given authority to reconstruct the Temple that had stood on the site, and he asked for confirmation that this was true.

The reply from the king stated that Cyrus's permission was confirmed by a copy of a memorandum found at Ecbatana (the summer capital in Media of the Persian kings). Darius ordered that the building was to proceed and be paid for out of the revenue of the satrapy. What was more, the animals and supplies that would be needed for the sacrifices were to be provided from official sources. In return, prayers were to be offered for the

Persian horse head, terracotta, 6th-5th centuries BC, found at Achziv in western Galilee. The Persian king, Darius, provided horses for sacrifice in the Temple.

welfare of the king and the royal family. Anybody who disobeyed these orders would be severely punished.

After the work was resumed, Zerubbabel seems to have disappeared and his end is unknown.

The construction of the Second Temple took five years and was completed in 515 BC. It lasted for 585 years. The Temple was sumptuously remodelled by Herod the Great (37-4 BC) and destroyed by the Roman legions under Titus in AD 70. [1 Chr. 3:19; Ezra 2:2; 3:2, 8; 4:2, 3; 5:2; Neh. 7:7; 12:1, 47; Hag. 1:1, 12, 14; 2:2, 4, 21, 23; Zech. 4:6-10]

ZERUIAH (Heb. 'guarded') *c.* 11 century BC. Sister of King David, she was the mother of Joab, Asahel and Abishai. The name of her husband is not mentioned. [1 Sam. 26:6; 2 Sam. 2:13, 18; 3:39; 8:16; 14:1; 16:9, 10; 17:25; 18:2; 19:21, 22; 21:17; 23:18, 37; 1 Kgs. 1:7; 2:5, 22; 1 Chr. 2:16; 11:6, 39; 18:12, 15; 26:28; 27:24]

ZETHAM (Heb. 'olive') *c.* 10 century BC. Son of Ladan, he was a leader of the Gershom branch of Levites in the time of King David. [1 Chr. 23:8; 26:22]

ZETHAN (Heb. 'olive') date unknown. Son of Bilhan and a grandson of Jediael, he was a leader of the tribe of Benjamin and a mighty man of valour. [1 Chr. 7:10]

ZETHAR (Pers. 'star') *c.* 5 century BC. One of the seven chamberlains of King Ahasuerus who was commanded by the drunken king on the seventh day of a feast to bring Queen Vashti before his guests to show off her beauty. [Esther 1:10]

ZIA (Heb. 'moving') date unknown. A leader of the tribe of Gad who dwelt east of the Jordan. [1 Chr. 5:13]

ZIBA (Heb. 'statue') *c.* 10 century BC. A servant in the household of King Saul. After the death of Saul and Jonathan, David adopted Jonathan's crippled child Mephibosheth, and put Ziba in charge of the boy's property.

When David fled from Jerusalem after the rebellion of Absalom, Ziba met him with asses laden with provisions, and suggested that his master Mephibosheth had sided with Absalom. The angry David promptly told him he could have all Mephibosheth's property. After the defeat of Absalom, David discovered that Ziba had misled him and ordered half the lands to be returned to Mephibosheth. [2 Sam. 9:2-12; 16:1-4; 19:17-29]

ZIBEON (Heb. 'hyena') *c.* 16 century BC. Grandfather of Esau's wife, Oholibamah, he was a leader of a Horite tribe. [Gen. 36:2, 14, 20, 24, 29; 1 Chr. 1:38, 40]

ZIBIA (Heb. 'deer') date unknown. Son of Shaharaim of the tribe of Benjamin and his wife Hodesh, he was an early clan leader. [1 Chr. 8:9]

ZIBIAH (Heb. 'deer') 9 century BC. Wife of King Ahaziah of Judah and mother of King Joash, she was born in Beersheba. [2 Kgs. 12:1; 2 Chr. 24:1]

ZICHRI (Heb. 'my memorial') **1.** date unknown. Youngest son of Izhar of the tribe of Levi, he was a leader of the tribe. [Exod. 6:21]

2. date unknown. Son of Shimei, he was a leader of the tribe of Benjamin living in Jerusalem. [1 Chr. 8:19]

3. date unknown. Son of Shashak, he was a leader of the tribe of Benjamin living in Jerusalem. [1 Chr. 8:23]

4. date unknown. Youngest son of Jeroham, he was a leader of the tribe of Benjamin living in Jerusalem. [1 Chr. 8:27]

5. *c.* 10 century BC. A Levite, father of Shelomoth who was responsible for the treasures in the Tabernacle in the reign of King David. [1 Chr. 26:25]

6. *c.* 10 century BC. Father of Eliezer who was ruler over the tribe of Reuben in the reign of King David. [1 Chr. 27:16]

7. *c.* 9 century BC. Father of Amasiah, one of the army commanders of the kingdom of Judah in the days of King Jehoshaphat. [2 Chr. 17:16]

8. *c.* 9 century BC. Father of Elishaphat who joined the conspiracy organized by the priest Jehoiada to overthrow Athaliah, queen of Judah, and crown her grandson Joash as king. [2 Chr. 23:1]

9. *c.* 8 century BC. A warrior of the tribe of Ephraim in the army of Pekah, king of Israel, in his war against King Ahaz of Judah, he killed Maaseiah, the king's son, Azrikam, governor of the palace and Elkanah, the chief minister to the king of Judah. [2 Chr. 28:7]

10. 5 century BC. Father of Joel, he was a leader of those of the tribe of Benjamin who lived in Jerusalem in the days of Nehemiah. [Neh. 11:9]

11. 5 century BC. Head of a priestly family when Joiakim was high priest towards the end of Ezra's lifetime. [Neh. 12:17]

12. *see* ZABDI 4.

ZIHA (Heb. 'dried') **1.** 6 century BC. Head of a family who returned with Zerubbabel from Babylonian exile and who served in the Temple. [Ezra 2:43; Neh. 7:46]

2. 5 century BC. One of the two supervisors of those ministering in the Temple in the days of Nehemiah. [Neh. 11:21]

ZILLAH (Heb. 'shadow') date unknown. A wife of Lamech and mother of Tubal-cain. [Gen. 4:19, 23]

ZILLETHAI (Heb. 'shadow') **1.** date unknown. Son of Shimei, a leader of the tribe of Benjamin. [1 Chr. 8:20]

2. 11 century BC. One of the commanders of the tribe of Manasseh who left the army of King Saul and joined David at Ziklag. [1 Chr. 12:20]

ZILPAH (Heb. 'dropping') *c.* 18 century BC. The maid whom Laban gave to his daughter Leah when she married Jacob. Later when Leah thought she was past childbearing age she gave Zilpah to Jacob as a concubine. She became the mother of two of his sons, Gad and Asher. [Gen. 29:24; 30:9-12; 35:26; 37:2; 46:18]

ZIMMAH (Heb. 'wickedness') **1.** date unknown. Son of Jahath, he was a Levite descended from Gershom. [1 Chr. 6:20]

2. date unknown. Son of Shimei and father of Ethan, he

was a Levite descended from Gershom. [1 Chr. 6:42]
3. *c.* 8 century BC. Father of Joah, a Levite who sanctified the Temple in the days of Hezekiah, king of Judah. [2 Chr. 29:12]

ZIMRAN (Heb. 'sung') *c.* 18 century BC. Son of Abraham by his wife Keturah, he was leader of a desert tribe. [Gen. 25:2; 1 Chr. 1:32]

ZIMRI (Heb. 'singer') **1.** *c.* 13 century BC. Son of Salu, a leader of the tribe of Simeon, he took a Midianite woman into his tent in front of Moses and the people of Israel. They were both killed by Phinehas. [Num. 25:14]
2. *see* ZABDI 1.
3. Fifth king of Israel after the monarchy split, he reigned for seven days in 885 BC. During the brief reign in the northern kingdom of Israel of King Elah, Zimri was the 'commander of half his chariots' (1 Kgs. 16:9). In 885 BC, Zimri murdered Elah while he was drunk in the house of his steward in Tirzah, the capital. Zimri proclaimed himself king, but his rule lasted only seven days. When Omri, the general of the army, occupied the capital, Zimri set fire to the keep of the palace and died in the flames. Omri mounted the throne after a struggle for the succession. [1 Kgs. 16:9-20]
4. date unknown. Son of Jehoaddah of the tribe of Benjamin, he was a descendant of King Saul. [1 Chr. 8:36; 9:42]

ZINA *see* ZIZAH

ZIPH (Heb. 'that flows') **1.** date unknown. Son of Mareshah and a leader of the tribe of Judah. [1 Chr. 2:42]
2. date unknown. Son of Jehallelel, he was a leader of the tribe of Judah and the brother of Ziphah. [1 Chr. 4:16]

ZIPHAH (Heb. 'that flows') Son of Jehallelel and leader of the tribe of Judah, he was the brother of Ziph. [1 Chr. 4:16]

ZIPHION (Heb. 'watchman') *c.* 16 century BC. Eldest son of Gad, he went down to Egypt together with his grandfather Jacob. Also called Zephon. [Gen. 46:16; Num. 26:15]

ZIPPOR (Heb. 'bird') *c.* 13 century BC. Father of Balak, king of Moab, who hired the prophet Balaam to curse the children of Israel under Moses before they entered the Promised Land. [Num. 22:2, 10, 16; 23:18; Josh. 24:9; Judg. 11:25]

ZIPPORAH *c.* 13 century BC. Wife of Moses.

Zipporah was one of the seven daughters of Jethro, the Midianite priest with whom Moses found refuge after he killed an Egyptian and fled into the desert. He met Zipporah when she and her sisters were at the well near their home struggling to water their father's flocks. Moses drove off the rest and helped them draw the water from the well. In gratitude Jethro invited Moses to stay with him and gave him Zipporah in marriage.

When Moses set out for Egypt with his wife, his elder son Gershom and his newly-born second son Eliezer

Shepherds with their flocks at a well at Tel Malhata. Moses met Zipporah at a well in the Sinai.

(who had not yet been circumcised), he became ill. Zipporah hastily circumcised the infant with a sharp flint, believing that the Lord was angry with Moses and he would die if the rite were neglected.

Later Moses sent her and the children back to live with her father. They rejoined him when he returned to the desert, leading the Children of Israel towards the Promised Land. [Exod. 2:21; 4:25; 18:2]

ZIZA (Heb. 'plenty') **1.** *c.* 10 century BC. A son of King Rehoboam of Judah by his favourite wife, Maacah. [2 Chr. 11:20]

2. *c.* 8 century BC. Son of Shiphi, he was a leader of the tribe of Simeon in the days of King Hezekiah, who drove out the inhabitants of the rich Gedor valley and settled there. [1 Chr. 4:37]

ZIZAH (Heb. 'plenty') *c.* 10 century BC. Son of Shimei of the tribe of Levi, he served in the Tabernacle in the time of King David. Also called Zina. [1 Chr. 23:10, 11]

ZOBEBAH (Heb. 'slothful') date unknown. Son of Koz, a leader in the tribe of Judah. [1 Chr. 4:8]

ZOHAR (Heb. 'white') **1.** *c.* 18 century BC. Father of Ephron the Hittite from whom Abraham bought the field near Hebron containing the Cave of Machpelah. [Gen. 23:8; 25:9]

2. *see* ZERAH 3.

ZOHETH date unknown. Son of Ishi of the tribe of Judah, he was a descendant of Caleb son of Jephunneh. [1 Chr. 4:20]

ZOPHAH (Heb. 'vial') date unknown. Son of Helem, a descendant of Asher, he was one of the leaders of the tribe. [1 Chr. 7:35, 36]

ZOPHAI *see* ZUPH

ZOPHAR period of the Patriarchs. One of the three friends who remonstrated with Job.

Zophar the Naamathite joined two other friends to visit the afflicted Job. They were shocked at his changed appearance, and rent their clothes and put dust on their heads. They sat silently next to him for seven days and seven nights.

Then Job began to curse the day he had been born, and protest that his suffering was undeserved. Zophar and the others tried to console him, but when he persisted they pointed out that he must have committed

sins to have so heavy a punishment to bear. As Job continued to rail against the Lord, Zophar said to him sternly: 'oh, that God would speak, and open his lips to you. ... Know then that God exacts of you less than your guilt deserves.' (Job 11:5, 6) Job made no effort to conceal his impatience with his pious friends. 'So these three men ceased to answer Job, because he was righteous in his own eyes.' (Job. 32:1)

Finally the Lord spoke to Job out of a whirlwind and he was completely overwhelmed and humbled. Then the Lord turned on the three friends and told them he was angry with them 'for you have not spoken of me what is right, as my servant Job has' (Job 42:7). The Lord instructed them to offer up a burnt sacrifice 'and my servant Job shall pray for you, for I will accept his prayer' (Job 42:8). [Job 2:11; 11; 20; 42]

ZUAR (Heb. 'little') 13 century BC. Father of Nethanel who represented his tribe of Issachar when Moses selected one chief of each tribe to help him take a census of the children of Israel fit for military service. [Num. 1:8; 2:5; 7:18-23; 10:15]

ZUPH (Heb. 'honeycomb') *c.* 12 century BC. A Levite, son of Elkanah and ancestor of the prophet Samuel. Also called Zophai. [1 Sam. 1:1; 1 Chr. 6:26, 35]

ZUR (Heb. 'rock') **1.** *c.* 13 century BC. Father of Cozbi, a Midianite woman who was brought into the Israelite camp by Zimri. Cozbi and Zimri were killed by Phinehas the priest and Zur was killed in the subsequent war with the Israelites. [Num. 25:15; 31:8; Josh. 13:21]

2. *c.* 11 century BC. Son of Jeiel and a leader of the tribe of Benjamin living in Gibeon. [1 Chr. 8:30; 9:36]

ZURIEL (Heb. 'my rock is God') *c.* 13 century BC. Son of Abihail, a Levite descended from Merari, he was chief of the Merari Levites in the days of Moses, and his people were in charge of specific items of the Tabernacle including the equipment needed for its maintenance in the wilderness. [Num. 3:35]

ZURISHADDAI (Heb. 'my rock is the Almighty') *c.* 13 century BC. Father of Shelumiel who represented his tribe of Simeon when Moses selected one chief of each tribe to help him take a census of the children of Israel fit for military service. [Num. 1:6; 2:12; 7:36, 41; 10:19]

The Apocrypha

Introduction to the Apocrypha

'The Apocrypha' is the name given to a collection of fifteen Jewish books, or portions of books, written in the last two centuries BC and the 1st century AD. They were not included in the Hebrew canon of the Bible. The Greek Bible (Septuagint) included all of them except 2 Esdras. After centuries of uncertainty, it was laid down in the 16th century AD that these works should be accepted as part of the Latin (Vulgate) Bible, except for the Prayer of Manasseh and 1 and 2 Esdras, which were placed in an appendix after the New Testament. In the Protestant Bible, the Apocrypha were not treated as scriptural. They were printed as a separate section between the Old and New Testaments, and in modern editions usually appear in a separate volume. (On the position of the Apocrypha in the canon of various Christian Bibles, see also the main introduction to this volume, *The Books of the Old Testament*.)

A brief description follows of the Apocrypha, with the order, full titles and abbreviations as used in the Revised Standard Version.

The First Book of Esdras (1 Esd.)
A re-written Greek version of parts of Chronicles, Ezra and Nehemiah. It probably dates from the 2nd century BC. (Since they would be mainly repetitions, no entries from 1 Esd. have been included in the Apocrypha section.)

The Second Book of Esdras (2 Esd.)
An apocalyptic work, with its main part consisting of seven visions attributed to Ezra. It was written in Hebrew or Aramaic, probably at the end of the 1st century AD after the destruction of Jerusalem. (It has not been necessary to include any entries from 2 Esd. in this section.)

Tobit (Tob.)
A tale about a Jewish captive in Babylon who was blinded and had his sight miraculously restored. It was written in Hebrew or Aramaic about 200 BC.

The Apocrypha

Judith (Jdt.)
A story about a devout and patriotic young Jewish widow who delivered her people from the Assyrians. It was written in Hebrew in the late 2nd century BC.

The Additions to the Book of Esther (Ad. Est.)
Six additional passages inserted in the Book of Esther. They were probably written in Greek about the end of the 2nd century BC, in order to give the Book a more religious character, and to fill out the story by quoting documents.

The Wisdom of Solomon (Wis.)
A book in praise of traditional Hebrew wisdom, written in Greek in the 1st century BC by an unknown Alexandrian Jew. (See the note on the Wisdom Books under SOLOMON.)

Ecclesiasticus, or the Wisdom of Jesus the Son of Sirach (Sir.)
A treatise stressing the value of wisdom in the Hebrew way of life. It was written in Hebrew about 180 BC and was translated into Greek by the author's grandson about 130 BC. (See under JESUS, SON OF SIRACH in this section.)

Baruch (Bar.)
A prophetic work attributed to Jeremiah's scribe and disciple Baruch, prophesying the return of the Jewish exiles to their homeland. It was compiled from several Hebrew elements about the end of the 1st century AD. The work is placed in the Greek and Latin Bibles after Jeremiah and Lamentations.

The Letter of Jeremiah (Let. Jer.)
A document purporting to be an epistle from Jeremiah to his fellow-Jews, warning them against idolatry during their exile. The original was probably written in Hebrew or Aramaic not later than the 2nd century BC. Fragments in Greek have been found among the Dead Sea Scrolls. In the Latin Bible this Letter forms Chapter 6 of the Book of Baruch.

The Prayer of Azariah and the Song of the Three Young Men (S. of 3 Y.)
Liturgical insertions in Chapter 3 of the Book of Daniel. They were probably written in Hebrew in the 2nd century BC.

Susanna (Sus.)
A tale about the beautiful and virtuous wife of a Babylonian Jew who resisted the advances of two elders. The work was probably composed in Greek in the 2nd or 1st century BC. It appears in the Latin Bible as Chapter 13 of the Book of Daniel.

Bel and the Dragon (Bel)
These two popular tales ridicule idolatry. Daniel exposed the priests of the temple of Bel, slew a sacred reptile, and was miraculously delivered from the lions' den. The work was probably written in Greek in the 2nd or 1st century BC. It appears in the Latin Bible as Chapter 14 of the Book of Daniel.

The Prayer of Manasseh (Man.)

A fine penitential psalm attributed to Manasseh the sinful king of Judah. It was composed at some time during the last two centuries BC – whether in Hebrew, Aramaic or Greek is uncertain.

The First Book of the Maccabees (1 Macc.)

An important historical work concerning the Maccabean Revolt against Seleucid rule, covering the period 175-35 BC. The book was originally written in Hebrew about 100 BC, but survives only in a Greek translation.

The Second Book of the Maccabees (2 Macc.)

A different and more fervid account of the Maccabean Revolt, the book covers the period 175-61 BC, and starts with two letters to the Jews of Alexandria from their brethren in Jerusalem. It was written in Greek about 60 BC, and the author states it is condensed from a work in five volumes by one Jason of Cyrene.

The Apocrypha section contains characters that do not appear in the Old Testament, or about whom there is additional material in the Apocrypha – such as Daniel and Esther.

Who's Who in the Apocrypha

ABSALOM (Heb. '[my] father is peace') **1.** 2 century BC. The father of two captains in the Maccabean army – Mattathias and Jonathan. [1 Macc. 11:70; 13:11]
2. 2 century BC. An envoy sent by Judas Maccabeus to Lysias carrying a letter for King Antiochus. [2 Macc. 11:17]

ABUBUS *c.* 2 century BC. The father of Ptolemy, who was married to the daughter of Simon the high priest. [1 Macc. 16:11, 15]

ACCOS (a form of Heb. *hakkos*, 'thorn') *c.* 3 century BC. Grandfather of Eupolemus, who was sent by Judas Maccabeus on a mission to Rome about 162 BC. [1 Macc. 8:17]

ACHIOR (Heb. 'brother of light') *c.* 5 century BC. An Ammonite chief.

Achior was the leader of a group of Ammonite auxiliary forces, attached to the Assyrian army under Holofernes that was besieging Bethulia, where Judith lived. He advised Holofernes that the Israelite nation could not be defeated as long as it remained faithful to the Lord. The angry commander ordered him to be bound and left outside the gate of Bethulia, so that he would share its fate.

He was taken into the city and treated well by the inhabitants. When Judith returned with the severed head of Holofernes, Achior identified it. He then decided to become converted to the Jewish faith and was circumcised. [Jdt. 5:5-22; 6; 14:5-10]

ADUEL (Heb. 'God is an ornament') date unknown. Ancestor of Tobit, the son of Tobiel. [Tob. 1:1]

AHIKAR (possibly Aramaic 'precious brother') *c.* 8 century BC. Nephew of Tobit, and Assyrian royal treasurer.

Ahikar was the son of Tobit's brother Anael, and became one of the leading men at the Assyrian court, serving King Sennacherib and his successor Esarhaddon as chief cupbearer and royal treasurer.

Tobit had to flee from Sennacherib's anger when it became known that he had been retrieving and burying the bodies of Jews put to death by the king. When Esarhaddon ascended the throne, Ahikar was able to intervene on his uncle's behalf so that he could return to his home.

Coin of Alexander the Great, with the figure of Victory and the name 'Alexander'.

Tobit became blind and for the next two years was cared for by Ahikar who then moved to Elemais.

Biblical scholars have been struck by the resemblances between the Book of Tobit and a work called 'The Wisdom of Ahikar', that enjoyed a great vogue throughout the ancient Near East. It has been suggested that the Ahikar story was one of the main sources of the Tobit story, and that Tobit's puzzling deathbed reference to Ahikar and his brother Nadab can only be understood as an echo of the earlier work. [Tob. 1:21; 11:18; 14:10, 11]

ALCIMUS (from the Heb. 'God sets up') 2 century BC. High priest in Jerusalem in the reign of Demetrius I Soter.

Alcimus, a member of the priestly clan, aspired to become high priest in Jerusalem, and urged the new Seleucid ruler Demetrius I Soter to crush the Maccabean revolt. The king appointed him high priest, and sent a large force under his general Bacchides to instal him in office.

At first Alcimus by conciliatory talk and promises won over the orthodox sect of the Hasideans, who had supported the Maccabeans. But once he was established he had sixty of the Hasideans seized and killed, while Bacchides put a number of other Jews to death. These harsh measures made Alcimus unpopular, and Judas Maccabeus fanned the embers of revolt throughout Judea. Bacchides had returned to Antioch, leaving some of his troops in Jerusalem.

During the next few years, Alcimus was maintained in office only by the direct military support of the Seleucid armed forces. Alcimus remained high priest until 159 BC when he had a stroke and died. According to legend, Alcimus's death was a divine punishment for breaking down the inner wall of the Temple. [1 Macc. 7:5-25; 9:1-4, 54-57; 2 Macc. 14:3-13, 26]

ALEXANDER THE GREAT (Gk. 'defender of men') 356-23 BC. Alexander the Great is mentioned in the First Book of Maccabees since one of his generals founded the Seleucid kingdom of which Judea was a part at the time of the Maccabean revolt. [1 Macc. 1:1-9]

ALEXANDER BALAS (EPIPHANES) 2 century BC. King of the Seleucid Empire, 150-45 BC.

Alexander Balas, a claimant to the Seleucid throne, landed at Ptolemais (Acre) in 152 BC and gained control of the country by 150 BC. The high priest Jonathan, who had supported him, was made ethnarch (provincial governor) of Jerusalem. In 145 BC Alexander was in turn

Alexander the Great: detail from the 1st-century Pompeii mosaic of the Battle of Issus, at which he defeated the forces of the Persian king, Darius III.

defeated by another claimant, Demetrius II, with the help of Ptolemy VI of Egypt, whose daughter Cleopatra was married to Alexander. He fled into Arabia where he was killed by a tribal sheikh. [1 Macc. 10:1, 15-21, 23, 47-59, 68, 88; 11:1, 2, 8-12, 14-17, 39]

ANAEL *c.* 8 century BC. Brother of Tobit, he was the father of Ahikar, the royal treasurer of Esarhaddon. [Tob. 1:21]

ANANIAS (from the Heb. 'the Lord has been gracious')
1. Date unknown. Ancestor of Judith. [Jdt. 8:1]
2. *c.* 8 century BC. Descendant of the prophet Shemaiah. [Tob. 5:13]
3. *c.* 8 century BC. A relative of Tobit claimed as his father by the angel Raphael. [Tob. 5:12]

ANANIEL (from the Heb. 'God is gracious') date unknown. An ancestor of Tobit, he was of the tribe of Naphtali. [Tob. 1:1]

ANDRONICUS (Gk. 'conqueror of men') **1.** 2 century BC. One of the ministers of King Antiochus IV Epiphanes.

He was left in charge of affairs when the king hurried to Cilicia to restore order in the towns of Tarsus and Mallus. Menelaus, who had bought himself into the office of high priest in Jerusalem, was summoned at this time to Antioch for failing to pay the monies he owed. He purloined gold plate from the Temple and handed it to Andronicus as a bribe.

Onias, the venerable high priest who had been deposed, was living in the sanctuary at Daphne near Antioch, and denounced the sacrilege committed by Menelaus. The latter persuaded Andronicus to lure Onias out of the sanctuary and have him murdered. This crime stirred up great popular anger, and on his return the king sentenced Andronicus to death. [2 Macc. 4:31-8]
2. 2 century BC. A governor who was left at Gerizim by Antiochus Epiphanes when he fled to Antioch. [2 Macc. 5:23]

ANNA (from the Heb. 'grace') *c.* 8 century BC. The wife of Tobit.

Anna, like Tobit, was of the tribe of Naphtali. They were carried off as captives to Nineveh where Anna obtained work with a weaver after Tobit became blind. When she brought home a kid her employer had given her and Tobit accused her of stealing it, she jeered at him. Anna was filled with anxiety when their son Tobias set out on the long journey to Medea, and was the first to see him return with his bride Sarah. Anna lived to a ripe old age and was buried in Nineveh next to her husband. [Book of Tobit]

ANTIOCHIS 2 century BC. A concubine of King Antiochus IV Epiphanes, who gave her the revenues from the Cilician towns of Tarsus and Mallus as a gift. The inhabitants of these towns revolted, and Antiochus had to hurry off to restore order. [2 Macc. 4:30]

ANTIOCHUS (from the Gk. 'the opposed') **1. Antiochus III** ('the Great') King of the Seleucid Empire, 223-187 BC, he was the father of Antiochus Epiphanes. [1 Macc. 1:10; 8:8]
2. Antiochus IV Epiphanes (Gk. 'manifest [God]') King of the Seleucid Empire, 175-63 BC.

In the history of the Maccabean revolt, Antiochus IV

Silver coin of Antiochus IV,
with a figure of Zeus bearing a sceptre
and seated on a throne.

is the villain of the piece. The First Book of Maccabees details his religious persecution of the Jews which brought about the revolt; while the Second Book of Maccabees, a more emotional document, pictures him as a vicious tyrant. He seems to have been an able, dynamic and ambitious ruler, vain enough to adopt the title of Epiphanes 'god-manifest'. His detractors suggested that his additional name should have been Epimanes, 'the madman'.

Antiochus belonged to the Seleucid dynasty founded by one of the generals of Alexander the Great. The Seleucid empire covered, with its capital at Antioch in northern Syria, most of Asia Minor and finally, from 198 BC, included Judea.

Having been born and brought up in Athens, Antiochus was an intense admirer of all things Greek, and determined to impose the Greek religion, language and culture upon all his subject peoples. Many of the Jews assimilated the Hellenistic customs and way of life, but the more orthodox among them strongly resisted it, and clung to the ancestral faith and traditions.

Antiochus's greatest ambition was to conquer Egypt, which he tried to do in several campaigns from 170-67 BC. But he was frustrated by the rising power

Circular Hellenistic tower at Samaria, late 4th century BC, one of
the best preserved in the area.

of Rome, which was reaching into the eastern Mediterranean. On returning from his first Egyptian campaign,
he marched into Jerusalem and pillaged the Temple,
carrying away its gold vessels and even stripping the gold
ornaments from the walls. In a second campaign, a
Roman envoy curtly ordered Antiochus to withdraw his
forces from Egypt, and he was obliged to submit. This
repulse sharpened his fear of Roman domination, and
his compulsive urge to stamp out religious separatism
and enforce a uniform worship of the Greek deities.
The harsh steps he took to destroy the Jewish faith
provoked armed resistance.

One of his generals was sent to occupy Jerusalem. He
butchered many of its inhabitants, razed the walls, and
constructed a fortified citadel near the Temple. The
practice of Judaism was banned, including observance
of the Sabbath and the rite of circumcision. His desecration of the Temple was termed by Daniel 'the abomination of desolation'. The Greek soldiers sacrificed swine
on the altar, tore up the sacred scrolls of the Law, and
held drunken feasts to Bacchus. A statue of Jupiter was
set up in the Holy of Holies. Through intrigue and
bribery, a certain Menelaus had got himself appointed
to the key office of high priest, and served as a willing

tool of Antiochus's repressive religious policy.

The Second Book of Maccabees, more an indictment
than a sober history, relates a series of atrocities alleged
to have been committed by Antiochus and his sub-
ordinates during this period. One story concerns two
Jewish mothers who had circumcised their babies. They
were driven through the streets with the infants hanging
at their breasts, and then hurled over the city wall. In
another case, a mother was forced to witness her seven
sons tortured to death in turn for refusing to eat pork
and then she herself was murdered. A respected ninety-
year-old teacher of the Law, Eleazar, chose to be blud-
geoned to death rather than make even a pretence of
swallowing the forbidden meat.

Officials were sent around Judea to oversee observance of worship of Greek gods by the inhabitants. In
the village of Modi'in, one such official was defied and
killed by the local Jewish priest, Mattathias, who fled
into the Judean hills with his five sons, and operated as
a guerrilla band. The banner of revolt had been raised.

During the remaining years of Antiochus's rule, a
series of military expeditions failed to crush the Maccabean rebellion or to relieve the Syrian garrison cut off
in the citadel in Jerusalem. The Seleucid generals who

Quant alixandre roys
des macedonicus eust
prestant le royaume des
persiens et ordonne in
dre et qui mourut il laissa moult de
successeurs. Car antigon prist asie.

Seleucus prist babiloine et les atre
dentiron. Lisimacus tint lellespont.
Cassander conquist macedoine.
Ptholomce fil: de lagi posseda egypte.
Et ainsi comme tous ceulx a
auoient discncion entre eulx et que

Antiochus IV had a statue of Zeus set up in the Temple. Head of Zeus on one of his silver coins, minted 370 BC.

led the successive campaigns were Apollonius, Seron, Ptolemy Macron, Nicanor, Gorgias, and Lysias.

In 165 BC, two years after the revolt started, Antiochus led a campaign eastwards into Persia and Medea to exact tribute and replenish the empty royal coffers. Lysias was left in charge of the kingdom, and as tutor of the young crown prince.

In 163 BC, Antiochus fell ill and died at Tabae, in Persia, after sacking the Temple of Artemis at Elymais.

On his deathbed Antiochus appointed his close friend Philip as guardian of his young son and regent of the kingdom until he came of age. In Antioch, Lysias ignored this appointment and had the twelve-year-old boy immediately crowned king as Antiochus v Eupator. [1 Macc. 1 – 6:16; 2 Macc. 4:7; 9:5–28; 10:9]

3. 2 century BC. Father of Numenius, the envoy sent by Judas Maccabeus to Rome. [1 Macc. 12:16; 14:22]

4. Antiochus v Eupator (Gk. 'born of a noble father') Son of Antiochus IV Epiphanes, he was king of the Seleucid Empire, 163-2 BC. [1 Macc. 6:15, 17, 55; 7:2; 2 Macc. 9:25, 29; 10:10-13; 11:1, 14-36; 12:1; 13; 14:2]

5. Antiochus vi King of the Seleucid Empire, 145-39 BC. Antiochus vi, son of Alexander Balas, succeeded to the Seleucid throne as a boy after a confused power struggle. He made a number of concessions to Jonathan, the Maccabean high priest in Jerusalem, in order to win Jewish support. After three years Antiochus was killed by Trypho, a general who usurped the throne. [1 Macc. 11:40, 57-59; 13:31, 32]

left Antiochus IV (on horseback) commanding the slaughter of the inhabitants of Jerusalem. 15th-century French manuscript illumination.

6. Antiochus vii Sidetes (Gk. 'from Side [in Pamphylia]') King of the Seleucid Empire, 138-29 BC.

Antiochus vii Sidetes was the younger brother of the Seleucid king Demetrius ii, who had been ousted by his general Trypho.

Antiochus landed on the coast of Syria with a large army, quickly gained control, and besieged Trypho at Dor on the west coast of Palestine.

Before his invasion Antiochus had written to Simon the high priest in Jerusalem, offering him a number of concessions in exchange for his support. But the king later repudiated these promises. Pursuing Trypho from Dor, he left behind one of his generals, Cendebeus, who was defeated by Simon's two sons.

After the death of Antiochus vii in 129 BC, his successors were involved in bitter family feuds and lost control of Judea and the rest of Palestine. [1 Macc. 15:1-38]

ANTIPATER 2 century BC. Son of Jason, he was one of two envoys sent to Rome by Jonathan to renew the pact of friendship. [1 Macc. 12:16; 14:22]

Silver tetradrachm of Antiochus VI Dionysus, bearing his portrait, 145-2 BC.

APOLLONIUS (from the Lat. 'of Apollo') **1.** 2 century BC. Son of Gennaeus, he was a governor of a Jewish province in the time of Judas Maccabeus. [2 Macc. 12:2]

2. 2 century BC. A Seleucid general who was the military governor in Samaria at the time of the Maccabean revolt in 167 BC. He led a force to crush the insurgents. It was ambushed and routed by Judas Maccabeus on the steep incline of Lebonah along the main road through the hills from Samaria to Jerusalem. Apollonius was killed in this engagement, and Judas took his sword which he used for the rest of his life. The Maccabeans were greatly elated at this first success against regular troops. [1 Macc. 3:10-12]

3. 2 century BC. The son of Menestheus and governor of Coelsyria and Phoenicia. Apollonius of Tarsus was sent by Antiochus IV to Egypt for the coronation of Ptolemy VI Philometer. [1 Macc. 3:5, 7; 4:4, 21]

4. 2 century BC. A captain of the Mysians, he was sent by Antiochus IV to Jerusalem with 22,000 men and had a number of the Jewish inhabitants massacred by his troops on the Sabbath day. [2 Macc. 5:24-6]

5. 2 century BC. General of the Seleucid ruler Demetrius II (147-38 BC), he was sent with a strong army against Judea, then under the leadership of Jonathan, brother of Judas Maccabeus.

Apollonius camped at Jamnia on the coast plain, and challenged Jonathan to meet him in battle in open ground 'where there is no stone or pebble, or place to flee' (1 Macc. 10:73), that is, where Jews could not fight as guerrillas in familiar hill terrain. Jonathan felt strong enough to accept this challenge. He led a force of 10,000 men into the coastal plain, with his brother Simon bringing up reinforcements. The wily Apollonius feigned a retreat and drew the Israelites into a trap. They were attacked from the rear by cavalry units that had been concealed but stood their ground all day until Simon was able to counter-attack and rout the cavalry. Apollonius and his troops were pursued into Azotus (Ashdod), the outlying defences of which were captured and burnt.

After this victory the Maccabean army was regarded as the strongest military force in the area. [1 Macc. 10:69-87]

APOLLOPHANES 2 century BC. A commander in the Syrian army of Antiochus V Eupator. He was captured and killed when the fortress of Gazara was taken by Judas Maccabeus. [2 Macc. 10:37]

APPHUS (possibly from the Heb. 'cunning') see JONATHAN

ARETAS (from the Gk. 'goodness') 2 century BC. An Arabian prince who captured the high priest Jason when he was deposed and fled across the Jordan river, during the reign of Antiochus IV Epiphanes. [2 Macc. 5:8]

ARIARATHES 2 century BC. King of Cappadocia, he was one of the rulers who received a letter from the Roman consul Lucius, indicating Roman protection for Judea at the time when Simon the Maccabean was high priest in Jerusalem. [1 Macc. 15:22]

ARIOCH 6 century BC. King of the Elymeans who lived along the plain between the rivers Euphrates and Tigris. [Jdt. 1:6]

ARISTOBULUS c. 2 century BC. Member of a Jewish priestly family in Egypt and tutor to Ptolemy VII Physcon.

The second of the two letters to the Jews in Egypt which form a foreword to the Second Book of The Maccabees is addressed to him. The letter is undated and was probably written early in the 1st century BC. [2 Macc. 1:10]

ARIUS c. 3 century BC. King of Sparta, he sent an envoy with a letter to Onias I the high priest in Jerusalem, to conclude an agreement of alliance and friendship with the Jews. This was probably in the reign of the Seleucid king Seleucus IV. Jonathan the Maccabean leader and high priest later wrote to Sparta to renew this alliance. [1 Macc. 12:7, 20]

ARPHAXAD c. 6 century BC. King of Media.

According to the Book of Judith, Nebuchadnezzar king of Assyria is described as waging war against Arphaxad king of the Medes. Arphaxad fortified his capital Ecbatana with huge walls and towers and massive gates. He was defeated in battle by Nebuchadnezzar who captured the city and pursued Arphaxad into the mountains, where he slew him with a spear.

This account is imaginary. Nebuchadnezzar was in fact king of Babylon, after the end of the Assyrian empire; he did not wage a war against Media, and there is no record of a Median king called Arphaxad. The story of Judith was written in the 2nd century BC and the historical references are inaccurate. [Jdt. 1:1, 5, 13-15]

ARSACES 2 century BC. King of the Parthians, he was one of the rulers who received a letter from the Roman consul Lucius, indicating Roman protection for Judea at the time when Simon the Maccabean was high priest in Jerusalem.

He later defeated and captured the Seleucid Demetrius II, after the latter had been ousted from his throne. [1 Macc. 15:22]

ARTAXERXES see AHASUERUS (O.T. section)

ASIEL date unknown. An ancestor of Tobit and a member of the tribe of Naphtali. [Tob. 1:1]

ASTYAGES c. 6 century BC. King of Babylon, he was succeeded by Cyrus the Persian in 538 BC. [Bel. 1:1]

ATHENOBIUS 2 century BC. An official of the Seleucid ruler Antiochus VII. The king had demanded from Simon the high priest in Jerusalem the return of certain cities and areas captured and annexed by Judea. Athenobius was sent to negotiate these demands. Simon rejected them on the ground that the places in question were part of the ancestral Jewish territory and that their occupation by others had been unlawful. Athenobius returned and reported to his royal master who was very angry at the failure of the mission. [1 Macc. 15:28-36]

ATTALUS 2 century BC. King of Pergamum, he was one of the rulers who received a letter from the Roman consul Lucius, indicating Roman protection for Judea at the time when Simon the Maccabean was high priest in Jerusalem. [1 Macc. 15:22]

AURANUS 2 century BC. Described as 'a man advanced in years and no less advanced in folly' (2 Macc. 4:40), he was used by Lysimachus, brother of the corrupt high priest Menelaus, in an attempt to suppress the angry mob that attacked and killed Lysimachus for plundering the Temple. [2 Macc. 4:40]

AVARAN *see* ELEAZAR **4.**

AZARIAH (Heb. 'whom God aids') 2 century BC. One of the two senior commanders left in charge in Jerusalem in 163 BC while Judas Maccabeus and his brother Jonathan were campaigning east of the Jordan, and another brother Simon was in Galilee. Azariah and

Joseph were eager to prove themselves as generals, and contrary to Judas's instructions, they led an expedition against Jamnia in the coastal plain. Here they were routed by the redoubtable Seleucid general Gorgias, and fled back to Jerusalem. [1 Macc. 5:18, 55-62]

AZARIAS (from the Heb. 'whom God aids') *c.* 8 century BC. The name assumed by the angel Raphael.

The angel Raphael was sent by the Lord to Nineveh to cure Tobit of his blindness, and to help Sarah the daughter of Tobit's kinsman Raguel. Her seven successive husbands had been killed on the wedding night by the demon Asmodeus.

Pretending to be Azarias, a distant kinsman, he acted

Tobias and the Angel, by Antonio Pollaiuolo (*c.* 1432-98).

as companion and guide to Tobias, Tobit's son, who travelled to Media to reclaim some silver left there by his father twenty years before.

That night he and Tobias camped on the bank of the river Tigris. When Tobias bathed his feet, a huge fish appeared. The angel told Tobias to catch the fish and keep its liver, heart and gall as medicine.

At Ecbatana in Media Tobias married Sarah, the daughter of his father's kinsman Raguel. On the angel's advice, Tobias burnt the heart and liver of the fish and thereby drove away the demon Asmodeus. The demon fled to Upper Egypt where the angel caught and bound him.

At Tobias's request, Azarias travelled on by himself to fetch the silver.

On their return to Nineveh, Tobit's blindness was cured with the gall of the fish. He and his son wished to reward Azarias who revealed himself as an angel and refused their gift. He urged them to praise the Lord instead. [Book of Tobit]

BACCHIDES 2 century BC. Military commander under Seleucid kings Antiochus IV and Demetrius I.

Bacchides, a leading general and governor of the western part of the Seleucid kingdom, led three expeditions into Judea to subdue the Maccabean revolt. In 162 BC he established a garrison in Jerusalem. In 161 BC he defeated the Maccabeans in the battle of Elasa and Judas was killed. In 157 BC Bacchides failed to round up the Jewish partisans under Jonathan, but fortified the area around Jerusalem. [1 Macc. 7:8-20; 9:1-34, 43-53, 57-64, 68-73; 10:12; 2 Macc. 8:30]

BACENOR 2 century BC. Officer under Judas Maccabeus who fought against Gorgias. [2 Macc. 12:35]

BAGOAS (possibly from the Persian 'eunuch') c. 5 century BC. A eunuch, who was in charge of the personal household of Holofernes, commander of the Assyrian army invading Judea. It was he who took care of Judith in the Assyrian camp, and who discovered the headless corpse of Holofernes after Judith had killed him. [Jdt. 12:11-15; 13:1, 14:14-18]

BARUCH (Heb. 'blessed') c. 6 century BC. Disciple and scribe of the prophet Jeremiah.

The prophetic book attributed to Baruch, the disciple and scribe of Jeremiah, was probably written in Hebrew about the end of the 2nd century BC. According to the introduction, it purports to have been written by Baruch from exile in Babylonia after the fall of Jerusalem. It contains several sections to be read in temples on feast days. It includes a prayer on behalf of the exiles, a poem on the nature of wisdom; and a poem of complaint and hope spoken by a personified Jerusalem, to which the author replies with a promise of messianic recovery.

In the Greek and Latin Bibles, the Book of Baruch appears together with Jeremiah and Lamentations.

The letter of Jeremiah is a separate work, probably written in Hebrew in the Hellenic period. In the Latin Bible it appears as Chapter 6 of the Book of Baruch. see also BARUCH (O.T. section) [Book of Baruch]

BEN SIRA see JESUS, SON OF SIRACH

CALLISTHENES 2 century BC. A Syrian who with others set fire to the sacred gates of the Temple in the time of Antiochus IV Epiphanes. After the capture of Jerusalem by Judas Maccabeus, he was burnt to death in retaliation. [2 Macc. 8:33]

CENDEBEUS 2 century BC. A general under the Seleucid ruler Antiochus VII. The king beseiged Dor, on the coast, where the usurper Trypho had taken refuge. Trypho escaped and was pursued by Antiochus, who left Cendebeus in command of the coastal area, with a force of infantry and cavalry. He established his headquarters at Jamnia and fortified the town of Kidron as a forward position. From this area he started to raid and harass the adjacent districts of Judea. Simon, the high priest and Maccabean leader in Jerusalem, sent troops under his two eldest sons, Judas and John, against Cendebeus, who was defeated and chased into Azotus (Ashdod). see JOHN [1 Macc. 15:38-41; 16:1-10]

CHABRIS c. 5 century BC. The son of Gothoniel, he was one of the three magistrates or elders of the town of Bethulia where Judith lived. When the town was about to surrender to the Assyrian general Holofernes because of famine and thirst, Judith sent for the magistrates and berated them for their lack of faith in God. That night they let her out of the city gate, and she saved the country by beheading Holofernes. [Jdt. 6:15, 8:10, 10:6]

CHAEREAS 2 century BC. Commander of the fortress of Gazara, stormed by the forces of Judas Maccabeus, he was killed together with his brother Timothy after they were found hiding in a cistern. [2 Macc. 10:32-37]

CHALPHI (from the Heb. 'a child replacing one who has been lost') c. 2 century BC. Father of Judas, who was a captain in the Maccabean army under Jonathan the high priest. [1 Macc. 11:70]

CHARMIS c. 5 century BC. The son of Melchiel, he was one of the three magistrates or elders of the town of Bethulia where Judith lived. When the town was about to surrender to the Assyrian general Holofernes because of famine and thirst, Judith sent for the magistrates and berated them for their lack of faith in God. That night they let her out of the city gate, and she saved the country by beheading Holofernes. [Jdt. 6:15; 8:10; 10:6]

CLEOPATRA (Gk. 'sprung from a famous father') c. 2 century BC. Daughter of Ptolemy VI Philometer, she married Alexander Balas, a pretender to the Seleucid throne.

In a footnote to the Greek translation of the Book of Esther, it is stated that the translation was brought to Egypt in the fourth year of the reign of 'Ptolemy and Cleopatra'. There were four Ptolemies who had wives

Egyptian marble statuette of
a Queen Cleopatra, possibly
Cleopatra II, *c.* 170 BC.

Daniel: chalk drawing
by Peter Paul Rubens,
c. 1618.

called Cleopatra, but the reference appears to be to
Ptolemy VIII, and the date has, therefore, been fixed at
114 BC. [Ad. Est. 11:1; 1 Macc. 10:57, 58]

CRATES 2 century BC. Deputy to Sostratus, the
commander of the Syrian garrison in the citadel in
Jerusalem, in the reign of Antiochus IV Epiphanes, he
was a Cypriot and was transferred back to that island
when it came under the control of Antiochus. [2 Macc.
4:29]

DANIEL (Heb. 'God is my judge') *c.* 6 century BC.
Hebrew official at the Babylonian court.

Among the Apocrypha are two short works containing additional legends about the prophet Daniel –
the story of Susanna; and Bel and the Dragon. They
were originally written in Hebrew or Aramaic in the
second century BC. These two works were included in
the Septuagint (Greek Bible) and later in the Vulgate
(Catholic Bible), where they were added to the Book
of Daniel as Chapters 13 and 14.

Susanna

Susanna was the beautiful and virtuous wife of Joakim,
a respected leader of a Jewish community in Babylon.

397

above Priests receiving offerings of food. Relief from the Temple of Rameses II at Abydos, Egypt, 13th century B.C.

She aroused the lust of two elders or judges. When she repulsed their advances in Joakim's garden, they falsely accused her of adultery with an unknown young man, and she was condemned to death. The young Daniel was inspired by the Lord to intervene, and had the trial reopened. He then had the two elders brought forward separately. Under his interrogation they contradicted each other about the kind of tree under which they claimed to have seen Susanna lying with the young man. Her innocence was established, and the elders were put to death as perjurers.

'And from that day onward Daniel had a great reputation among the people.' (Sus. 64)

Bel and the Dragon

The story of the god Bel opens with Daniel already established as the friend and confidant of the king of Babylon. The king worshipped at the temple of Bel, and asked Daniel why he did not do so as well. Daniel replied that he worshipped the living God, not idols made with human hands. The king insisted that Bel was a living god, and pointed out that he consumed every day the quantities of food and wine placed before him (12 bushels of fine flour, 40 sheep, and 50 gallons of wine). Daniel smiled and said, 'Do not be deceived, O king; for this is but clay inside and brass outside, and it never ate or drank anything.' (Bel 7)

The indignant king took Daniel to the temple to test his blasphemous statement. The priests retired and the king himself set out the food and wine in the chamber of the god. He then sealed the door. But before that Daniel had instructed his servants to strew ashes over the floor. Next morning the king removed the seals, opened the door and saw that the food and wine had disappeared. However, Daniel pointed to the floor where the footprints of the seventy priests, with their wives and children, were clearly visible. When the king had them arrested, they confessed that there was a secret entrance under the table, and that they came in

The angel carries Habakkuk by the hair to bring Daniel food in the lions' den. From an early 13th-century German Bible.

King Darius III Codomannus of Persia in his war chariot: detail from the 1st-century BC mosaic of the Battle of Issus, Pompeii.

every night with their families to eat the offerings. The king ordered them to be put to death, and authorized Daniel to destroy the idol and the temple.

The Dragon

In Babylon a sacred dragon or snake was worshipped as a god. As had happened with the god Bel, Daniel ridiculed this cult and affirmed the faith of his Lord. When the king remonstrated with him, Daniel obtained authority to try and kill the dragon, without using any weapon. He mixed pitch, fat and hair, baked cakes with them, and fed these cakes to the dragon until it burst and died.

The destruction of the temple of Bel, followed by the killing of the sacred dragon, aroused popular anger against the king, who found himself and his family threatened. To appease the mob, the king agreed that Daniel should be thrown into the lion-pit – a method then used to execute wrongdoers. The seven lions were accustomed to feed on two condemned men and two

sheep each day, but this ration stopped while Daniel was in the pit.

In Judea, the prophet Habakkuk was on his way to the fields with a bowl of bread for the reapers. An angel appeared, took him by the hair, and carried him through the air to Babylon, putting him down next to the lion-pit. He called out 'Daniel! Daniel! Take the dinner which God has sent you.' (Bel 37) Daniel ate the food while Habakkuk was taken home the same way.

On the seventh day, the king came to the lion-pit to mourn his friend. To his astonishment Daniel was sitting in it, alive and well. The king draw him out, and gave praise to the Hebrew God who had saved him. Those who had accused Daniel were cast into the pit on the order of the king, 'and they were devoured immediately before his eyes'. (Bel 42) [Sus. 45-59, 60, 64; Book of Bel and the Dragon]

DARIUS III CODOMANNUS (from the Persian 'he who upholds the good') 4 century BC. The last king of Persia, 336-1 BC, he was defeated by Alexander the Great at Arbela in 331 BC, thereby bringing the Persian empire to an end. [1 Macc. 1:1]

DEMETRIUS 1. Demetrius I Soter (Gk. 'saviour') Ruler of the Seleucid kingdom, 162-50 BC.

Demetrius seized the Seleucid throne in 162 BC from his cousin Antiochus V.

Judea was in the throes of the Maccabean revolt, led by Judas. Demetrius appointed a loyal and pro-Hellenist high priest in Jerusalem, Alcimus, and sent a military force under his general Bacchides to install Alcimus. Part of the troops were left behind in Jerusalem as a garrison.

During the next few years Demetrius sent several more military expeditions against Judas and later against his brother and successor Jonathan.

From 155 BC, Demetrius tried to win over Judea in his struggle against a rival claimant Alexander Balas, who finally ousted him in 150 BC when Demetrius was killed in battle. [1 Macc. 7:1-9, 26; 8:31; 9:1, 57; 10:2-9; 15:22-50, 52, 67]

Head of Demetrius I Soter on a gold octodrachm, struck during the last six months of his short reign.

2. Demetrius II Nicator Ruler of the Seleucid kingdom, 145-38 BC and 129-5 BC.

Demetrius II, son of Demetrius I, wrested the Seleucid throne from his cousin Alexander Balas, with the help of an Egyptian army led by Ptolemy VI.

Demetrius marched south to Ptolemais (Acre) and summoned Jonathan, the high priest, who was besieging the Seleucid garrison in Jerusalem. Arriving with lavish gifts, Jonathan made a good impression on the king and was confirmed in his office, as well as being granted tax exemptions. Jonathan later came to the military aid of Demetrius, when the king was in trouble due to a revolt in his army. The disaffection was

led by an ambitious general, Trypho, who subsequently succeeded in overthrowing Demetrius and installing in his stead Antiochus VI, the young son of Alexander Balas (145-2 BC).

Demetrius continued his struggle to regain the throne and succeeded in doing so in 129 BC, after ten years' captivity in Medea. This time he reigned for four years during the period that John Hyrcanus, the son of Simon the Maccabee, was high priest in Jerusalem. [1 Macc. 10:67, 69; 11:9-12, 19, 28-53, 55, 63; 12:24, 34; 13:34-40; 14:1-3, 38; 15:1, 22]

DEMOPHON 2 century BC. A Syrian military governor in Palestine in the reign of Antiochus V who harassed the Jews. [2 Macc. 12:2]

DOSITHEUS 1. 2 century BC. A fighting commander in the Maccabean army, he distinguished himself in the campaign of Judas Maccabeus against Timothy in Gilead. He and another commander captured Timothy but released him for fear of reprisals against Jewish hostages. [2 Macc. 12:19, 24]

2. 2 century BC. In a later battle with the Idumeans, 'a certain Dositheus one of Bachenor's men' is described as a Jew of powerful physique, fighting on horseback. He seized Gorgias, the Syrian general, by his cloak and started to drag him away. A Thracian horseman rescued Gorgias by lopping off the arm of Dositheus. It is not clear whether he is the same person referred to in **1.** above. [2 Macc. 12:35]

3. *c.* 2 century BC. A Jewish priest who, together with his son Ptolemy, brought the Greek translation of the Book of Esther to Egypt in the fourth year of the reign of Ptolemy VIII and Cleopatra (probably 114 BC). The document is referred to in the text as 'Letter of Purim'. [Ad. Est. 11:1]

EDNA (Heb. 'delight') *c.* 8 century BC. Edna was married to Raguel, a kinsman of Tobit. Their home was in the city of Ecbatana in Media. They had an only child, Sarah, who had been married seven times, but each time the bridegroom had been killed on the wedding night by the demon Asmodeus. When Tobias, the son of Tobit, arrived on a visit, he too married Sarah, but with the help of an angel exorcized the demon.

After the death of Tobit and his wife Anna in Nineveh, Tobias and Sarah rejoined Raguel and Edna in Ecbatana and took care of them until they died. [Tob. 7:2, 8, 14-18; 8:12; 10:12; 11:1; 14:13]

ELEAZAR (Heb. 'God has helped') **1.** *c.* 3 century BC. The father of Sirach who was the father of Jesus the sage and scribe. [Sir. 50:27]

2. *c.* 2 century BC. The father of Jason who was sent by Judas Maccabeus as an envoy to Rome. [1 Macc. 8:17]

3. *c.* 2 century BC. A venerable and dignified teacher of the Law in Jerusalem. When Antiochus IV Epiphanes decreed the suppression of the Jewish faith and forcible conversion to Greek paganism, the ninety-year-old sage *left* Eleazar was a teacher of the Law. Pottery lamp in the form of a teacher reading a scroll, *c.* 333-63 BC, from Amka, north-east of Acre.

above Greco-Bactrian silver phaleron, showing a war elephant, Hellenistic period.

was ordered to eat pork in public, or undergo flogging. Out of respect for him, the officials in charge privately offered to let him swallow meat acceptable to him, while only pretending to eat the pork. He proudly rejected this subterfuge, declaring that in any case he only had a little while to live, and was not prepared to appear in the eyes of the younger generation as a traitor to his faith. He died of the effects of the flogging then meted out to him. [2 Macc. 6:18-31]

4. 2 century BC. The fourth son of Mattathias the priest who started the Maccabean revolt in the village of Modi'in in 167 BC. Also called Avaran.

Five years after the start of the revolt, the Maccabeans were defeated by the Seleucid general Lysias at the battle of Beth-zechariah, south of Jerusalem. During the battle, Eleazar wrongly concluded that the largest of the war elephants, which was richly decorated in the royal colours, carried the young king Antiochus V, who had accompanied Lysias on the campaign. Eleazar carried out a bold single-handed attack on the animal. He fought his way through the phalanx of soldiers surrounding it, reached the elephant and from below rammed his spear into its belly. The great beast toppled over dead, and Eleazar was crushed beneath it. [1 Macc. 2:5; 6:43-48; 2 Macc. 8:23]

ELIAB (Heb. 'God is father') date unknown. Ancestor of Judith. [Jdt. 8:1]

ELIJAH (Heb. 'my Lord is Jehovah') date unknown. Ancestor of Judith. [Jdt. 8:1]

ELKIAH date unknown. Ancestor of Judith. [Jdt. 8:1]

ESDRIAS 2 century BC. A commander under Judas Maccabeus, mentioned in the battle in Idumea against the Syrian general Gorgias. [2 Macc. 12:36]

ESTHER (Pers. 'star') *c.* 5 century BC. Jewish queen of King Artaxerxes (Xerxes I).

In the Greek or Septuagint version of the Book of Esther, additional passages were inserted in order to give the work a stronger religious tone, and to place more emphasis on the help of God in saving the Jews.

After Haman's edict ordering the extermination of the Jews, Mordecai asked Esther not only to speak to the king but also to 'invoke the Lord'. Esther took off her sumptuous robes, put on mourning, covered her head with ashes and dung, tore out her hair and addressed a fervent prayer to God, beseeching his intervention. In this inserted prayer Esther claimed that she got no pleasure out of her high position and the luxurious life of the court: 'thou knowest that I hate the splendour of the wicked and abhor the bed of the uncircumcised . . .' (Ad. Est. 14:15)

Esther and Mordecai, by Andrea Mantegna (c. 1431-1506).

Esther then took off her mourning attire and went in to the king, leaning on the arm of a maid because she felt weak and fearful. The added passage describes her interview with the king in greater detail, making Esther fall down in a faint, and God making the king well disposed towards her. This enabled Esther to bring about Haman's downfall and save her people. [Additions to the Book of Esther]

EUMENES (Gk. 'well-disposed') 2 century BC. King of Pergamum, 197-58 BC, he was an ally of the Romans when they defeated the Seleucid ruler Antiochus III at the battle of Magnesia (190 BC), and certain territories were ceded to him. He is mentioned in the eulogy to the Romans by Judas Maccabeus. [1 Macc. 8:8]

EUPOLEMUS (Gk. 'skilful in war') 2 century BC. Eupolemus, son of John, and grandson of Accos, was one of two envoys sent by Judas Maccabeus to propose an alliance with Rome; the other was Jason. They appeared before the Roman Senate about 162 BC, and a treaty of friendship and alliance was approved and inscribed on bronze for the envoys to take back as a permanent record. [1 Macc. 8:17-22; 2 Macc. 4:11]

GABAEL 1. date unknown. Gabael was an ancestor of Tobit, of the tribe of Naphtali [Tob. 1:1]

2. *c.* 8 century BC. Gabael, the son of Gabrias, was a relative of Tobit and lived in the Median town of Rages. Tobit, who had been employed by the king as a buyer of supplies in Media, had deposited ten talents of silver with Gabael. Then Assyria lost control of the trade routes to Media, and Tobit stopped journeying there.

Twenty years later, when Tobit was stricken with blindness and prayed for death, he sent his son to Media to collect the bags of silver. Tobias set out accompanied by the angel Raphael in the guise of a Jew called Azarias. They reached Ecbatana in Media, where Tobias married Sarah, the daughter of another kinsman of his father. Azarias travelled on his own to Rages, where Gabael produced and handed over the bags of silver with the seals still intact. He accompanied Azarias back to Ecbatana and took part in the wedding celebrations. [Tob. 1:14; 4:1, 20; 5:6; 9:2–6; 10:2]

GADDI *see* JOHN **3.**

GENNAEUS *c.* 2 century BC. Father of Apollonius, a Syrian governor and general in the reigns of Antiochus IV and Antiochus V. [2 Macc. 12:2]

GIDEON (Heb. 'hewer') date unknown. Ancestor of Judith. [Jdt. 8:1]

GORGIAS 2 century BC. Assyrian general under the Seleucid rulers Antiochus IV and Antiochus V.

Gorgias was one of three generals in command of the Seleucid army sent in 166 BC to crush the Maccabean revolt. While the main force remained in camp at Emmaus, in the Judean foothills, Gorgias led a detach-

Reconstruction of the great altar of Zeus at Pergamum, built *c.* 180 BC during the reign of Eumenes.

ment on a night march into the hills. But Judas Maccabeus and his men slipped away and captured the camp at Emmaus. Gorgias retreated southwards without giving battle.

Gorgias remained in command in the coastal district, and ignominiously repulsed an attack at Jamnia made by two Judean commanders, contrary to the orders of Judas.

In the Second Book of Maccabees, Gorgias is described as operating against Judea from the south, with the Idumeans. In battle, he was seized by the coat and dragged off by one of the Jews, but was saved by a Thracian horseman, who slashed off the arm of the assailant. [1 Macc. 3:38-40; 4:1-5; 5:59; 2 Macc. 8:9; 10:14; 12:32-37]

HASADIAH (Heb. 'beloved of God') date unknown. Ancestor of Baruch the disciple and scribe of Jeremiah. [Bar. 1:1]

HEGEMONIDES (possibly from the Gk. 'guide') 2 century BC. A senior officer in the Syrian army who was left in command of the district from Ptolemais (Acre) to Gerar, when King Antiochus V and his general Lysias had to rush back to Antioch from their Judean campaign. [2 Macc. 13:24]

HELIODORUS 2 century BC. Chief minister of the Seleucid ruler Seleucus IV Philopater, he was sent by the king to Jerusalem to confiscate the gold and silver in the Temple, but was driven off by an apparition in the form of a man on horseback in golden armour, and was severely flogged by two supernatural youths.

In 175 BC Heliodorus murdered his royal master and made an unsuccessful attempt to seize the throne. [2 Macc. 3:7-40; 4:1; 5:18]

HIERONYMUS 2 century BC. A Syrian military governor in Palestine in the reign of Antiochus V, he is mentioned as harassing the Jews. [2 Macc. 12:2]

HILKIAH (Heb. 'God's portion') 1. date unknown. Ancestor of Judith. [Jdt. 8:1]

2. date unknown. Ancestor of Baruch the disciple and scribe of Jeremiah. [Bar. 1:1]

3. *c.* 6 century BC. Father of Susanna, the beautiful and virtuous young wife who was falsely accused of adultery by two elders, but was acquitted when the young Daniel proved her innocence. This charming short tale is supposed to have taken place in a Jewish community in Babylon. [Sus. 1:2, 29, 63]

HOLOFERNES (from the Gk. 'to be deceitful') *c.* 5 century BC. Assyrian general in the Book of Judith.

Holofernes, the Assyrian commander-in-chief, reached Bethulia in Judea at the head of a huge army and laid siege to it. Judith, who lived in the town, came into the Assyrian camp with her maid and was brought before the general. Captivated by her beauty, he believed her story that she had fled the city to escape its fate. He gave orders that she and her maid should be allowed to cross

through the lines at night in order to pray. Judith had told him she would know from God when her fellow-townsmen had sinned by eating polluted food, thus exposing them to defeat.

Four days after Judith reached his camp, Holofernes gave a banquet for his retinue. He told his steward to persuade her to join them, 'For it will be a disgrace if we let such a woman go without enjoying her company, for if we do not embrace her she will laugh at us.' (Jdt. 12:12) Judith came to the feast dressed in all her finery, and the commander was filled with lust for her. He drank copiously, and by the time his staff withdrew and left the two of them alone, he was sprawled on the couch in a drunken sleep. Judith seized his sword and with two blows at the neck severed his head. She and her maid stole away with it, and safely reached Bethulia again.

The Assyrian troops panicked and fled, and Judea was saved. [Book of Judith]

HYRCANUS 2 century BC. The son of Tobias, a member of the wealthy Jewish land-owning family of Tobias, he had funds on deposit in the Temple. Onias the high priest explained this to Heliodorus, who had been sent by the Seleucid king to seize the Temple treasury. [2 Macc. 3:11]

ISRAEL (Heb. 'who prevails with God') date unknown. Ancestor of Judith. [Jdt. 8:1]

JASON (Gk. 'to heal') 1. 2 century BC. Son of Eleazar, he was one of two envoys sent by Judas Maccabeus to Rome to propose an alliance; the other envoy was Eupolemus. They appeared before the Roman Senate in about 162 BC, and a treaty of friendship and alliance was approved and inscribed on bronze for the envoys to take back as a permanent record.

This may be the same Jason mentioned as the father of Antipater, who was later sent by Jonathan on a similar mission to Rome. [1 Macc. 8:17-22; 12:16; 14:22]

2. *c.* 2 century BC. High priest in Jerusalem (175-2 BC)

Jason was the son of the high priest Simon II and the younger brother of the high priest Onias III. On the accession to the throne of Antiochus IV in 175 BC, Jason had himself appointed in place of his brother, by offering the new king a large sum of money.

Jason collaborated in introducing Hellenistic customs and undermining strict adherence to the ancestral Jewish faith. He constructed a gymnasium in the Temple area, and sent a sacrifice to the shrine of Hercules at Tyre in Phoenicia. When Antiochus came to Jerusalem, he was lavishly entertained by Jason, although he was generally detested by the Jews for his repressive religious measures.

Three years after becoming high priest Jason was in his turn ousted by the corrupt Menelaus, who had heavily bribed the provincial governor. Jason took

Jason built a gymnasium in the Temple area.
Hellenistic sculpture of the head of a young man,
probably an athlete with victory wreath.

refuge across the Jordan river among the Ammonites, from where he made an abortive attempt to regain his position in Jerusalem by force. Taking refuge again over the Jordan, he was captured by the Arabian chief Aretas, but escaped and reached Egypt. From there he went to Sparta where he died. [2 Macc. 1:7, 4:7-27; 5:5-10]

JATHAN *c.* 8 century BC. Descendant of the prophet Shemaiah. [Tob. 5:13]

JECONIAH *c.* 6 century BC. The name given in the Book of Baruch to the son of Jehoiakim, the Judean king carried away to captivity in Babylonia. In the introduction to his Book, Baruch claims to have read his work to Jeconiah (Jehoiachin). [Bar. 1:3]

JEHOIAKIM (Heb. 'God established') *c.* 6 century BC. High priest in Jerusalem in the time of the Babylonian exile. [Bar. 1:7]

JEREMIAH (Heb. 'God will elevate') 7-6 century BC. The prophet Jeremiah appeared in a dream to Judas Maccabeus and handed him a golden sword from the Lord with which to crush the enemies of the Jews. [2 Macc. 15:14, 15]

JESUS, SON OF SIRACH (Heb. 'God is salvation') *c.* 2 century BC. Author of the Wisdom Book that bears his name.

The work known as the Wisdom of Jesus the son of Sirach (or Joshua Ben Sira in the Hebrew form) was originally written in Hebrew in Palestine, early in the 2nd century BC. From the 3rd century AD the book also became known in the Christian church as 'Ecclesiasticus', a Latin word that simply means 'church book' – an indication of the liturgical importance attached to it.

In the preface added to the Greek version by the anonymous translator from the Hebrew, he states that he is a grandson of the author and that he settled in Egypt in the thirty-eighth year of the reign of King Euergetes. This would no doubt be Ptolemy VII Euergetes, and the date would thus correspond to 132 BC. The original may therefore have been written about half a century earlier. This would have enabled Jesus son of Sirach to know the renowned high priest Simon II, to whom a glowing tribute is paid in the book.

In his preface, the translator sums up the nature of the work: '. . . my grandfather Jesus, after devoting himself especially to the reading of the law and the prophets and the other books of our fathers, and after acquiring considerable proficiency in them, was himself also led to write something pertaining to instruction and wisdom, in order that, by becoming conversant with this also, those who love learning should make even greater progress in living according to the law.' (Sir., Prologue)

Jesus son of Sirach lived at a time when Judea was part of the Seleucid kingdom, ruled from Antioch. Among the Jews there was a strong current of assimilation to the Hellenistic way of life, in language, dress,

12th-century Italian manuscript illumination, showing Jesus son of Sirach addressing an audience, his scroll in his hand.

customs, religious practices and philosophical ideas. Jesus son of Sirach was clearly a learned teacher and devout Jew, not unfamiliar with Greek ideas, but keen to reaffirm the traditional Jewish concepts and values. His work is a synthesis of the trends in Hebrew thought that had evolved down the centuries: the formal system of the Mosaic Code, the deep religious emotion of the prophets, and the practical sagacity of the sages. The relationship of wisdom to religion is stated in the opening verse of the Book, 'All wisdom comes from the Lord and is with him for ever' (Sir. 1:1).

This Book belongs to the Hebrew wisdom literature, that includes Proverbs, Job, Ecclesiastes, and another apocryphal work written in Alexandria, the Wisdom of Solomon. Like Proverbs and Ecclesiastes, the Wisdom of Jesus son of Sirach does not form a unified and organic work. It is a loose anthology in fifty-one chapters containing short discourses, sayings and maxims on a variety of unrelated topics, and eulogies of national figures in Israelite history. It ends with a poem in which the author speaks of his lifelong quest for wisdom:

'My heart was stirred to seek her, therefore I have gained a good possession.

The Lord gave me a tongue as my reward, and I will praise him with it.
Draw near to me, you who are untaught, and lodge in my school.'

(Sir. 51:21-3)

Until recently the book was known only in its Greek translation. In 1896, an astounding collection of old Hebrew manuscripts came to light in the 'genizah' or storehouse for discarded sacred books, belonging to a Cairo synagogue. Two learned English ladies acquired some pages from the genizah, which included portions of Sirach in Hebrew. Some scholars maintained that these pages were not a copy of the original Hebrew, but were translated back from the Greek. However, in Professor Yigael Yadin's 1963-5 archaeological expedition on the Masada Rock next to the Dead Sea, one of the finds was twisted fragments of a scroll which turned out to be from the Wisdom of Jesus son of Sirach in Hebrew. It obviously belonged to the Zealots who died defending the Masada fortress against the Romans in AD 73. Since the text was almost identical with the genizah fragments, the latter may now be regarded as copied from the original Hebrew. [Book of Sirach]

Page of the Hebrew manuscript of the Book of Sirach found in the genizah hoard in Cairo in 1896.

JOAKIM 1. *c.* 6 century BC. Husband of Susanna, he was a rich and respected member of a Jewish community in Babylon. His home was a meeting place for the important members of the community and two of them, who were elders and judges, fell in love with Susanna. When she repulsed them, they falsely accused her of adultery. Her innocence was proved by the young Daniel and she was restored to Joakim and their children. [Sus. 1, 4, 6, 28, 29, 63]

2. *c.* 5 century BC. High priest in Jerusalem, and as such the national leader of Judea, he governed with the aid of an assembly of elders referred to as the Senate.

When the Assyrian army under Holofernes appeared in the northern part of the country, Joakim and the elders decided to resist. They issued orders that the towns and villages on the heights should be fortified, supplies of food stored, and the narrow passes into the hills defended.

The Assyrians besieged the town of Bethulia where Judith lived, and cut off the water supply. The situation was saved by her beauty and courage. She gained Holofernes's confidence, and cut off his head while he was in a drunken sleep. The Assyrian troops fled in panic and were pursued and slaughtered by the Israelites.

Joakim and the members of the senate travelled to Bethulia to help celebrate this victory, and to bestow praise on Judith for saving the country. In addressing her Joakim said: 'You are the exaltation of Jerusalem, you are the great glory of Israel, you are the great pride of our nation!' (Jdt. 15:9) [Jdt. 4:6-15; 15:8-10]

JOHN (from the Heb. 'the Lord has been gracious')
1. *c.* 3 century BC. Father of Mattathias. [1 Macc. 2:1]
2. *c.* 3 century BC. Father of Eupolemus, he obtained concessions for the Jews from Antiochus III. [1 Macc. 8:17; 2 Macc. 4:11]
3. 2 century BC. Eldest son of Mattathias. John (also known as Joseph and as Gaddi, meaning 'fortunate'), was the eldest of five sons of Mattathias the priest, the others being Simon, Judas, Eleazar and Jonathan. When Mattathias raised the banner of revolt in the village of Modi'in, in 167 BC, all his sons fled with him into the Judean hills, where they operated as a guerrilla band.

John does not seem to have possessed the qualities of leadership. After his father's death, he served first under Judas and then under Jonathan. John was sent by Jonathan to ask the friendly Nabateans, east of the Dead Sea, to take care of the baggage. His convoy was attacked by local tribesmen, who killed John and his men and made off with the baggage. Jonathan took his revenge by attacking a marriage procession of that tribe. [1 Macc. 2:2; 9:35-8; 2 Macc. 8:22]
4. 2 century BC. An envoy sent by Judas Maccabeus to Lysias with a letter for Antiochus V. [2 Macc. 11:17]

5. 2 century BC. High priest and ruler of Judea from 134-04 BC.

John Hyrcanus was the son of Simon, the last surviving brother of Judas Maccabeus, who was high priest and ethnarch of Judea from 143-34 BC. Simon made John commander of the Judean armed forces. John and his brother Judas routed the forces of Antiochus VII Sidetes, commanded by the Syrian general Cendebeus in the coastal plain near Jamnia. Not long after, Simon and two of his sons, Judas and Mattathias, were murdered by his son-in-law Ptolemy who was the military commander in Jericho. Ptolemy sought to make himself ruler of Judea. But John Hyrcanus, who was in charge of the garrison at Gazara, foiled an attempt to assassinate him. He became high priest and ruler in succession to his father.

By military and political successes, John was able to expand the territory of Judea, and to strengthen its autonomy.

The first Book of Maccabees ends with the death of Simon, the high priest and his succession by John Hyrcanus. [1 Macc. 13:53, 16]

JONATHAN (Heb. 'given by God') **1.** 2 century BC. Youngest son of Mattathias and Maccabean leader after Judas.

Jonathan (also called Apphus meaning 'favoured') was the youngest son of Mattathias, the priest of Modi'in who started the Maccabean revolt against Antiochus IV, in the year 167 BC. With his father and his brothers John, Simon, Judas and Eleazar, Jonathan fled into the hills and took part in the partisan activities. When Judas was defeated and killed in 161 BC, the surviving Maccabeans elected Jonathan as their new leader. They took refuge in the wilderness of Tekoa between the Hebron hills and the Dead Sea.

The Seleucid general Bacchides led a strong force in search of the Maccabeans, and trapped them at the northern end of the Dead Sea, between the Jordan river and the marshes. Jonathan and his supporters fought their way out and swam across the river to safety. After fortifying the area round Jerusalem, Bacchides returned to Antioch, and for the next two years the military pressure on the Maccabeans was relaxed. They took advantage of this respite to occupy the abandoned stronghold of Bethbasi, just south of Bethlehem. Bacchides returned and laid siege to this fortress. Jonathan slipped away with some of his men, and attacked the Seleucid force from the rear, with the help of local tribes. At the same time, Simon led a sortie from the fortress and set fire to the siege engines. After this setback Bacchides again withdrew to Syria. Jonathan sent envoys to negotiate a truce. As a result, he was able to establish his headquarters at Michmash, north of Jerusalem, and gradually to gain control of Judea, except for Jerusalem and the Beth-zur fortress south of

Bronze coin of Jonathan, obverse and reverse, with the inscription 'Yehonatan the King', 103-76 BC.

it. 'And Jonathan began to judge the people, and he destroyed the ungodly out of Israel.' (1 Macc. 9:73)

During the next few years, Jonathan skilfully exploited the dynastic struggle in the Seleucid kingdom between Demetrius I and the rival claimant Alexander Balas. Both sides sought Judean support by making far-reaching concessions to Jonathan. He was able to regain Jerusalem, become recognized as high priest and governor and expand the borders of Judea from Lydda to beyond the Jordan river. An army sent against Judea by a new ruler, Demetrius II, was defeated at Jamnia by Jonathan and Simon. Judea had become practically autonomous with its Seleucid power marked only by a small annual tribute and by the continued presence of a small garrison in the Jerusalem citadel.

In 144 BC, Jonathan fought another crucial battle against the forces of Demetrius II, which advanced into the Galilee highlands. At Hazor, in north-eastern Galilee, the Seleucid army set an ambush and caught the Judean forces in a pincer movement. A large part of Jonathan's army was routed, but he and his two commanders rallied the rest and fought back until the day was won.

Jonathan now sent two envoys to Rome, and obtained from the Senate a renewal of the treaty of alliance that had been negotiated at the time of his brother Judas. On their way home, the envoys stopped in Sparta (Greece) and delivered a message from Jonathan to his Spartan 'brothers' recalling a friendly letter that had been received from the Spartan king by an earlier high priest in Jerusalem.

Demetrius again despatched a large force against Judea. Jonathan marched up into Syria in order to meet the enemy in the district of Hamath, before they reached his own borders. They withdrew, and Jonathan marched back through Damascus, collecting on the way a small Jewish community that was in distress.

A ruthless and ambitious army commander called Trypho emerged as the strong man in Antioch, and planned to seize the throne. He decided that a strong Judea would be a threat to him, and led an army southward through Syria to subdue the Jews. On reaching Scythopolis (Beth-shean), he found Jonathan waiting

Beth-shean, where Jonathan's forces waited for Trypho; in the foreground is the Roman amphitheatre.

for him with 40,000 men, and shrank from the military confrontation. Instead, he lured Jonathan into Ptolemais (Acre) with false protestations of friendship, and there took him prisoner, killing his bodyguard.

This blow left the Jews confused and dejected. Simon, the second of the Maccabean brothers, now took command and rallied his people. Trypho advanced on Jerusalem from the south, but then abandoned the Judean campaign. On his way back, he had Jonathan put to death. It was the year 142 BC. The Jewish struggle for independence was to be carried on by Simon, the last of the five Maccabean brothers left alive. Simon had the body of Jonathan exhumed and brought to the family tomb at Modi'in for burial. [1 Macc. 2:5; 5:17, 24, 25; 9; 10; 11; 12:53; 13:8-25; 2 Macc. 8:22]

to prove themselves as generals, and contrary to Judas's instructions, they led an expedition against Jamnia in the coastal plain. Here they were routed by the redoubtable Seleucid general Gorgias, and fled back to Jerusalem. [1 Macc. 5:18, 55-62]

3. *see* JOHN 3.

JUDAS (Gk. from Heb. *Judah*) **1. Judas Maccabeus** (probably from the Heb. 'hammer') 2 century BC. Third son of Mattathias and leader of the Maccabean revolt.

Judas (the Greek form of *Judah*) was the third of five remarkable brothers, the others being John, Simon, Eleazar and Jonathan. Their father Mattathias was the priest of the village of Modi'in situated on the coastal plain seventeen miles north-west of Jerusalem. Judas afterwards acquired the nickname of Maccabeus ('the

Seleucid and Ptolemaic Empires
2nd century BC

2. 2 century BC. Son of Absalom, who was an officer under Simon the Maccabean. [1 Macc. 13:11]

JOSEPH (Heb. 'may [God] add [children]') **1.** date unknown. An ancestor of Judith, he was the son of Oziel. [Jdt. 8:1]

2. 2 century BC. Judean commander under Judas Maccabeus.

Son of Zechariah, he was one of two senior commanders who were left in charge in Jerusalem in 163 BC, while Judas Maccabeus and his brother Jonathan were campaigning east of the Jordan, and another brother, Simon, was in Galilee. Joseph and Azariah were eager

left Judas Maccabeus, the Jewish nationalist hero of the 2nd century BC: 16th-century French enamel medallion.

hammer') and as a result, the family and their followers became known as the Maccabeans.

Judea at that time was part of the realm of the able and ambitious Seleucid king Antiochus IV Epiphanes, who ruled from Antioch on the Syrian coast from 175-63 BC. He belonged to the dynasty founded by Seleucus, one of the generals amongst whom Alexander the Great had divided his empire 150 years earlier. From Alexander's time, Hellenistic influence had steadily increased in the whole region. The Greek language became fashionable as well as Greek dress, social customs, athletic pursuits and religious cults. In Judea this assimilationist trend was resisted by orthodox groups that clung firmly to the ancestral faith and the traditional way of life. Antiochus, an intense admirer of all things Greek, was determined to Hellenize the peoples over

The village of Upper Beth-horon, which commanded the great highway from the maritime plain into the mountains. Here Judas Maccabeus defeated the Syrian general Seron.

whom he ruled. This urge was sharpened by his abortive attempt to gain control of Egypt.

Antiochus took harsh measures to stamp out the Jewish faith. Its practice was banned, including Sabbath observance and the right of circumcision. Jerusalem was occupied and many of its inhabitants butchered. The Temple was desecrated with swine sacrificed on the altar and a statue of Jupiter set up in the Holy of Holies.

When one of the king's officials came to Modi'in to enforce worship of the Greek gods, he was killed by Mattathias who then fled into the hills with his sons and followers and launched a partisan movement. In this year of 167 BC the banner of revolt had been raised.

The Maccabeans established a guerrilla base in the Gophna hills, a rugged area of boulders, ravines and bush half-way between Jerusalem and Samaria, then the Seleucid provincial centre. They were joined by other outlaws, and raided the Jewish villages in the region, knocking down pagan altars, circumcising male children and fanning the spirit of rebellion.

In this mountain refuge, the dying Mattathias appointed Judas as the military leader. The old man was buried in the ancestral tomb at Modi'in. (Eighteen rock-cut tombs in the vicinity are by tradition associated with the Maccabeans.)

Apollonius, the military governor in Samaria, led out a force to crush the insurgents. It was ambushed and routed by Judas and his men on the steep incline of Lebonah at the edge of the Gophna hills. Apollonius

was killed; Judas took his sword and used it for the rest of his life. The Maccabeans were greatly elated at this first success against regular troops.

After this startling blow, the Seleucid authorities began to take the rebellion seriously. The countryside was aflame and Jerusalem practically cut off. The regional commander, Seron, now led an army against the Maccabeans. As the troops toiled up the path of Beth-horon from the coastal plain, the hearts of Judas's men sank at the overwhelming disparity in numbers. He said to them firmly, 'It is not on the size of the army that victory in battle depends, but strength comes from Heaven . . . we fight for our lives and our laws.' (1 Macc. 3:19, 21) Judas launched a surprise attack, broke through the advancing force, and pursued it southward towards the coast. The day was won and only then did Judas allow his followers to be diverted by the plunder: 'much gold and silver, and cloth dyed blue and sea purple, and great riches' (1 Macc. 4:23). This was in 165 BC, two years after the revolt had started in Modi'in.

In the following year, Lysias the regent himself commanded another expedition. He skirted round the foothills of the Shephelah and advanced towards Jerusalem from the south, where the terrain was easier and occupied by the loyal Idumeans. Judas waited for the Seleucid force at Beth-zur, on the highway between Bethlehem and Hebron. Here he launched a swift attack and the enemy was repulsed.

The access to Jerusalem from the south now lay open to the Maccabeans. They entered the city and cut off the garrison in the citadel. Judas devoted himself to restoring and purifying the Temple, which had been disused for three-and-a-half years and was in a state of neglect. 'And they saw the sanctuary desolate, the altar profaned, and the gates burned. In the courts they saw bushes sprung up as in a thicket, or as on one of the mountains. They saw also the chambers of the priests in ruins.' (1 Macc. 4:38)

When the building had been restored and a new stone altar constructed in place of the one that had been defiled, a day was set aside for the rededication of the Temple. This took place on the twenty-fifth day of Chislev, the ninth month of the Hebrew calendar. It was

a joyous occasion, with music, singing and prayers of thanksgiving and praise. It was ordained that every year on that day the feast of Hanukkah (dedication) would commence and would be observed for eight days.

A dramatic moment in the celebration was the rekindling of the great eight-branched Temple candelabrum. According to the accepted Jewish legend, a search in the Temple revealed only one small jar of the specially prepared oil that was used for the candelabrum, and had to be sealed by the high priest himself. It was only sufficient for one night, but by a miracle the oil replenished itself and lasted for the eight days. Hanukkah is also called the Feast of Lights.

15th-century Italian Hebrew manuscript, illustrating the lighting of the eight-branched candlestick to celebrate the rededication of the Temple.

Judas had Mount Zion fortified to withstand another attack, and also built a fortress at Beth-zur to block the road from Idumea. He then carried out a series of swift campaigns against hostile neighbours. First he marched southward against the Idumeans (Edomites), the 'sons of Esau' who had occupied southern Judea after the fall of Jerusalem. Having defeated them and taken booty, he attacked the Beonites, a marauding tribe near the Dead Sea, and swung eastward across the Jordan against the Ammonites.

The main expedition east of the Jordan was aimed at Gilead, to relieve and evacuate the Jewish communities trapped in a number of fortified cities there. They had written to Judas appealing for help. With his brother Jonathan and eight thousand men, Judas crossed the river and marched three days across the desert, through an area inhabited by friendly Nabateans. He conquered the town of Bozrah, in the land of Nob east of Gilead. The defending army commanded by Timothy fled towards the north-east, in the direction of the Sea of Galilee. The Maccabean forces followed them, and took and ravaged one town after another. In another pitched battle at Raphon, Timothy's reorganized troops were again routed.

top left Maccabean oil-press reconstructed in the Valley of the Cross in western Jerusalem.

top right Children in Israel celebrating the last day of Channukah with their menorah.

left Menorah of the Second Temple type with a Hebrew inscription, found engraved on a wall in the Sinai cliffs.

The Jewish inhabitants of Gilead were assembled, and evacuated through the Beth-shean valley and the Samarian hills to Jerusalem. At the same time, Simon with three thousand men swung through the Galilee highlands and brought the Jews to safety from that district.

Judas won one more battle against Timothy at Jazer, to the east of the Jericho ford, and the enemy commander was killed.

After his return from the successful Transjordan campaign, Judas carried out expeditions to the south and south-west of Jerusalem, capturing Hebron, destroying a pagan temple at Azotub near the coast, and setting fire to the ships in the ports of Joppa and Jamnia.

Antiochus Epiphanes died during a campaign in Persia, in 163 BC. Lysias had the young prince declared king as Antiochus V Eupator.

In Jerusalem, Judas laid siege to the citadel, which was still held by his Hellenist opponents. They appealed for help to the new king, and Lysias arrived in Judea with

above The hills of Hebron, where the Maccabeans were defeated by Lysias in 166 BC.

below The Gilead region and the Jordan Valley, where Judas and Jonathan defeated the forces of Timothy, commander of the Ammonites.

War elephants on a coin of
the founder of the Seleucid Empire,
Seleucus I (312-280 BC).

a large army, including some of the royal elephants
brought from India after the death of Alexander. Once
again, Lysias made a detour in order to march on
Jerusalem from the south through Idumean territory,
where the hills were less rugged. Battle was joined at
Beth-zechariah, half-way between Hebron and Jerusalem. Eleazar, the fourth of the Maccabean brothers,
attacked and slew one of the war elephants, but was
crushed when it toppled over on top of him. The
Judeans had to retreat before an overwhelming force.
Judas and his followers abandoned Jerusalem, and
took to the hills again in the Gophna region.

In 162 BC the throne was seized by another claimant,
Demetrius I. His general Bacchides occupied Jerusalem
and installed a Jewish priest Alcimus, as high priest and
governor. Later, a force commanded by the Seleucid
general Nicanor was sent to the aid of Alcimus. In 161
BC Nicanor was surprised by Judas at Adasa, and fell in
battle. The remnants of his men fled into the royal
fortress at Gazara in the foothills, pursued by the
Maccabeans and the local villagers. This victory was
later celebrated in Jewish tradition as 'the Day of
Nicanor'.

Realizing that he and his followers would not be able
to hold out indefinitely against Seleucid armies, Judas
decided to invoke the power of the Romans. He sent
two envoys to Rome, who appeared before the Roman
Senate and said: 'Judas, who is also called Maccabeus,
and his brothers and the people of the Jews have sent us
to you to establish alliance and peace with you . . .' (1
Macc. 8:20) The Romans were not averse to backing a
rebellion that weakened and disrupted the Seleucid
kingdom from within. The Senate approved a treaty and

a mutual defence pact with the Jews. At the same time,
a Roman message was sent to King Demetrius warning
him that further attempts to crush Judea might lead to
Roman intervention.

This development made it urgent for Demetrius to
quell the revolt and assert his authority over the Judean
province. Bacchides was despatched again with powerful forces. He marched through Galilee, Samaria and
Judea to Jerusalem, with Judas keeping out of his way.
Bacchides then set out to destroy the Maccabean
stronghold in the Gophna hills. Judas was left with no

13th-century French manuscript illumination, showing
(top) the massacre of the Jews by Antiochus IV, and
(bottom) a battle between the Maccabeans and Bacchides.

option but to attack greatly superior forces. At the
battle of Elasa, north of Jerusalem, Judas forced the
Seleucid right wing to retreat. The left wing counter-
attacked and cut off the Maccabeans, who were then
overrun. Judas himself was killed and his followers
scattered. His brothers Simon and Jonathan were able
to retrieve his body, and buried it in the family tomb at
Modi'in. 'And all Israel made great lamentation for
him; they mourned many days, and said "How is the
mighty fallen, the saviour of Israel!"' (1 Macc. 9:20-1)
In his place, his brother Jonathan was chosen as leader.

After the defeat and death of Judas, less determined

Omment la grnt des
uiufs quand les mace
doniens la tenoient
en seruitute reconnu
ulerite. et comment apres moult de
batailles midas leur duc fu most.

Nous lauons demonstre ou uolu
me de deuant cesti. Mais apres
la most de midas derichief les man
uais. et ceulx qui trespassoient la
loy uendrent contre les uiufs et de
toutes pars tresselonnement les

Ὁ ἍΓΙΟΣ ΠΑῦΛΟΣ

men would have given up what seemed a hopeless struggle. But the Maccabeans remained inspired by Judas's dauntless spirit, and were to carry on the fight in the years ahead.

For the Jews, Judas Maccabeus has remained a national hero and a symbol of a never-ending struggle for political and religious freedom. [1 Book of Maccabees; 2 Book of Maccabees]

2. 2 century BC. Son of Chalphi, he was one of the commanders under Jonathan the high priest and Maccabean leader. When Jonathan's forces were routed by the army of Demetrius II in the battle of Hazor in the Galilee, Judas was one of the few who fought on with him, until the others rallied and the enemy was defeated. [1 Macc. 11:70]

3. 2 century BC. Son of Simon the high priest. Together with his brother John, he commanded the Judean force that defeated the Syrian general Cendebeus near Jamnia on the coastal plain in the year 138 BC. Judas was wounded in this engagement. He was later murdered together with his father Simon and brother Mattathias by his ambitious brother-in-law Ptolemy the son of Abubus. [1 Macc. 16:2, 9, 14]

JUDITH (Heb. 'from Judah') *c.* 5 century BC. A patriotic widow who saved her people.

Judith was the young wife of Manasseh, a well-to-do farmer of the town of Bethulia, in the northern part of the hills of Ephraim in Judea. She was beautiful, intelligent and devout. One day her husband died of sunstroke during the reaping of the harvest. Judith did not remarry but remained in mourning, and lived quietly on the farm. She spent much of her time secluded in a shelter she had constructed on the roof of the house.

A huge Assyrian army, commanded by Holofernes, invaded Judea from the north and camped in the Esdraelon valley before Bethulia. The Judeans were in a state of great alarm, but the high priest Joakim and the senate in Jerusalem decided to resist. The Samarian towns and villages on the mountain tops were fortified; food was stored, and the narrow passes through the hill-country were guarded. For several days the high priest and the people, dressed in sackcloth and ashes, prayed and fasted at the Temple. 'So the Lord heard their prayers and looked upon their affliction.' (Jdt. 4:13)

Holofernes asked the leaders of his local auxiliary forces, 'Tell me, you Canaanites, what people is this that lives in the hill country? What cities do they inhabit? How large is their army, and in what does their power or strength consist? Who rules over them as king, leading their army? And why have they alone, of all who live in the west, refused to come out and meet me?' (Jdt. 5:3–4)

Achior, the Ammonite chief, related the history of the Hebrew nation and explained that it was under God's protection and could not be defeated. The angry Holofernes had him bound and thrown down near the gate of Bethulia so that he should share its fate. The city was surrounded and its water supply cut off. The invaders then settled down to wait for the inhabitants to surrender from hunger and thirst.

In Bethulia the water available from cisterns was strictly rationed, but gave out after thirty-four days of blockade. 'Their children lost heart, and the women and young men fainted from thirst and fell down in the streets of the city and in the passages through the gates;

Assyrian alabaster relief, showing Assyrians encamped in tents, 7th century B.C.

Judith taking leave of the Elders of Bethulia, by Paolo Veronese (*c.* 1528-88)

there was no strength left in them any longer.' (Jdt. 7:22)

The magistrates agreed to surrender if the Lord did not send help within five days. Judith upbraided them, pointing out that if Bethulia fell, the whole of Judea would be conquered and laid waste. She had her own plan to save them. After praying fervently to the Lord, she discarded her widow's weeds, dressed in her brightest clothes, put on her jewelry and perfumed herself. She then left the house with her maid and persuaded the city elders to open the gate for them. They were seen to cross the valley in the direction of the enemy camp.

Judith went out of Holofernes's camp to prepare her own food. 5th-century Boeotian terracotta of a woman kneading dough.

The two women reached the Assyrian outposts and were seized and questioned by the sentries. Judith told them that she had fled from the town to escape its fate. She had important information for the general, since she could tell him of secret routes whereby all the hill country could be occupied without losses. They were escorted to the tent of Holofernes who was lying down under a mosquito net richly decorated with jewels. He rose to greet her; Judith prostrated herself and was raised up by the attendants.

Judith told the commander that the hungry citizens of Bethulia would soon lose divine protection by eating prohibited food. They would then be helpless before the Assyrian advance. She would herself guide Holofernes all the way to Jerusalem and see him crowned king there. Captivated by her beauty, he believed her story. He promised that she would be properly treated and gave instructions to the guards to let Judith and her maid pass freely through the lines to pray to the Lord in the open. In this way she would find out when the Israelites had sinned.

For the next three days Judith went out each evening to the spring, bathed herself and prayed. She refused Holofernes's invitation to share his meals, as she had brought her own food prepared in accordance with Jewish dietary laws.

On the fourth day Holofernes invited his personal retinue to feast with him. Judith readily agreed to join them. Dressed in all her finery, she reclined in front of Holofernes on the fleeces her maid had spread for her. The Assyrian general could hardly control his passion for her. He ate and drank with abandon, and by the time all the attendants retired and left Judith alone with him, he lay sprawled drunk on the couch.

Praying silently for strength, Judith drew Holofernes's sword from the scabbard hung at the bed-head, grasped his hair and with all her force struck twice at his neck, lopping off the head. She rolled the body on to the floor and pulled down the rich canopy to take with her. As she went out, she handed the severed head to the waiting maid, who put it in the food-bag. The two of them left the camp unhindered, as if they were going out to pray as usual. They made their way across the valley and up the hill to the city gate of Bethulia.

Judith called out to the sentries, who let her in. Ussiah and the other elders were hurriedly summoned from their homes. Judith held up Holofernes's head and praised the Lord who had delivered her people through her. She swore that 'it was my face that tricked him to his destruction, and yet he committed no act of sin with me, to defile and shame me'. (Jdt. 13:16)

At dawn a number of armed Israelites sallied out from the gate, pretending they were about to attack the enemy camp. As Judith had foreseen, the Assyrians sprang to arms and the senior officers ran to the tent of the commander-in-chief. The steward went in to arouse him, and rushed out screaming that his master's body was lying on the floor decapitated. Consternation spread

through the camp, and the men started running away in panic. A great number were slaughtered in the pursuit, and huge quantities of abandoned baggage and supplies were distributed as booty.

The high priest Joakim and the members of the senate came personally from Jerusalem to visit Bethulia after the victory. They added their voices in praise of Judith, calling her 'the great glory of Israel' (Jdt. 15:9). Judith led the women in a dance of thanksgiving and sang a hymn to God: 'Woe to the nations that rise up against my people! The Lord Almighty will take vengeance on them in the day of judgment.' (Jdt. 16:17) The silver, furnishings and other belongings in Holofernes's tent were given to Judith. Having come to Jerusalem to share in the rejoicing, she handed these costly possessions over to the Temple as a gift.

Judith returned to Bethulia and resumed her quiet way of life on the farm, refusing all offers of marriage. The maid who had accompanied her in her amazing exploit was given her liberty. During the rest of Judith's lifetime Judea remained at peace and was not invaded by foreign armies. She died at the ripe age of 105 and was buried at the side of her husband Manasseh.

It is probable that the story was composed in the time of the Hasmonean ruler and high priest John Hyrcanus I (134-04 BC). In 108-7 BC John Hyrcanus besieged the city of Samaria, and a Seleucid (Syrian) army sent

left *Judith with the Head of Holofernes,* by Caravaggio (1583-1610).

The Apocrypha

to relieve it was defeated. The Book of Judith may have been inspired by this episode, which would account for its patriotic theme and spirit. Bethulia is an imaginary name. [Book of Judith]

LASTHENES 2 century BC. When Demetrius II, ruler of the Seleucid kingdom, reached an agreement with the Maccabean leader Jonathan, whereby Judea was exempted from tax levies, he sent Jonathan a copy of a letter of instruction to 'our kinsman Lasthenes' about the matter. He was presumably a high official in charge of the royal finances. The historian Josephus later suggested that Lasthenes was the Cretan commander of the mercenaries who helped Demetrius gain the throne by ousting King Alexander Balas. The word 'kinsman' in the letter was only a courtesy term used for a close associate. [1 Macc. 11:31, 32]

LUCIUS 2 century BC. Roman consul in the time of Simon the Maccabee.

When Simon succeeded his brother Jonathan as high priest and leader in Jerusalem, he sent a special envoy to Rome, with the gift of a gold shield, to renew the alliance maintained with the Romans by his brothers Judas and Jonathan. The envoy came back with the copy of a letter sent by Lucius to the rulers of the surrounding countries, including King Ptolemy in Egypt and King Demetrius in Antioch. The letter warned against making war upon 'our friends and allies the Jews' or harbouring traitors from Judea. The powerful protection of Rome assisted Simon in gaining autonomy for Judea under the Hasmonean dynasty to which he belonged. [1 Macc. 15:16-24]

LYSIAS 2 century BC. A Seleucid general in the reigns of Antiochus IV and Antiochus V.

When Antiochus IV was preparing a campaign against Persia in 165 BC, he left his kinsman Lysias in charge of the kingdom and as tutor to his young son Antiochus. The king died during this expedition, and Lysias had the boy assume the throne immediately as Antiochus V, while himself wielding the real power.

Lysias despatched an army to subdue the Maccabean revolt in Judea. Judas Maccabeus defeated this force at the battle of Emmaus.

In the next year, 164 BC, Lysias himself headed an expeditionary force against Judea. He marched down the coastal plain and made a detour in order to reach Jerusalem from the south through the Hebron hills, where the terrain was less difficult and the area was occupied by friendly Idumeans. Judas waited for the

Beth-zur, where Lysias was defeated by the forces of Judas Maccabeus in 166 BC.

Seleucid force at Beth-zur, on the highway between Bethel and Hebron. Here he launched a swift attack and the troops of Lysias were repulsed. The Maccabeans were now able to enter Jerusalem, and rededicate the Temple.

Two years later, Lysias again marched into Judea at the head of a large army. In the battle of Beth-zechariah, to the north of Beth-zur, the Maccabean forces under Judas were defeated, and his brother Eleazar was killed. Lysias occupied Jerusalem but withdrew northwards when his rival Philip seized Antioch, the capital. Later, he was defeated by another claimant to the throne, Demetrius I Soter, and both he and Antiochus V were killed by their own troops. [1 Macc. 3:32-60; 4:1-35; 6; 7:1-4; 2 Macc. 11:1-26; 12:1; 13:26; 14:1, 2]

LYSIMACHUS 1. 2 century BC. He was the brother of Menelaus the corrupt high priest in Jerusalem, in the reign of Antiochus IV Epiphanes. When Menelaus was summoned to Antioch, Lysimachus was left in charge of the Temple and plundered its treasury. In the public riots provoked by his actions, he was killed by the mob. [2 Macc. 4:29, 39-42]

2. *c.* 2 century BC. Lysimachus, an Alexandrian Jew, translated the canonical Book of Esther from Hebrew into Greek. [Ad. Est. 11:1]

MACCABEUS *see* JUDAS **1.**

MACRON *see* PTOLEMY **2.**

MANASSEH (Heb. 'forgetting') *c.* 5 century BC. Husband of the beautiful and brave Judith, he was a well-to-do farmer of the town of Bethulia, in Ephraim. During the time of the barley harvest, he suffered sunstroke and died. Judith was faithful to his memory, and refused to remarry. [Jdt. 8:2, 3, 7; 16:22-4]

MATTATHIAS (Heb. 'gift of the Lord') **1.** 2 century BC. Jewish priest of Modi'in who started the Maccabean Revolt.

Mattathias, the son of John, was a priest of the Joarib family in Jerusalem. He settled in the village of Modi'in, situated on the coastal plain half-way between the sea and the Judean hills. (It is not far from the present Lod airport.) He had five sons: John, Simon, Judas, Eleazar and Jonathan.

At that time there was religious persecution of the Jews by the Seleucid ruler Antiochus IV Epiphanes. The Temple in Jerusalem had been defiled, the practice of the Jewish faith banned, and the worship of Greek gods made compulsory.

Special commissioners were sent around the districts of Judea to enforce this programme of Hellenizing the Jews. One such official came to Modi'in. The villagers gathered in the square where an altar had been placed for a sacrifice to the Greek gods. Mattathias and his sons stood sullenly to one side. The officer called out to him, promising him riches and the favour of the king if he would set a lead as a respected figure in the community. Mattathias flung back defiantly: 'We will not obey the king's words by turning aside from our religion to the right hand or to the left.' (1 Macc. 2:22) At that moment an obsequious villager sidled forward to comply. This was too much for Mattathias who leapt upon him and killed him at the altar. He then spun round and killed the king's official. Mattathias rushed along the street shouting to the faithful to follow him. He and his sons and some of the townspeople fled into the Judean hills, abandoning their homes and possessions. Thus, in the year 167 BC, the banner of revolt was raised.

The Maccabeans (so named after the most famous of the sons, Judas Maccabeus), established a guerrilla base in the Gophna hills, north-west of Jerusalem. From here they raided the surrounding countryside, destroying pagan altars and arousing a spirit of resistance among the people.

It was in their mountain refuge that Mattathias died the following year, 166 BC. On his deathbed he exhorted his sons to carry on with the struggle for freedom: 'show zeal for the law, and give your lives for the covenant of our fathers' (1 Macc. 2:50). He told them to heed the counsel of the wise Simon, and to accept the strong and brave Judas as their military commander.

Mattathias was buried by his sons in the family tomb in Modi'in, and they carried on with the fight he had launched.

The descendants of Mattathias who ruled over Judea for more than a century, from 141 BC onwards, became

Ancient tombs at Modi'in, the village where Mattathias launched the revolt and where the Maccabees were buried in a mausoleum built by Simon.

Bronze coin of Mattathias Antigonus,
40-37 BC, the last Maccabean ruler, named after
the initiator of the Maccabean revolt.

known as the Hasmonean dynasty, from the name
associated with Mattathias's grandfather Simeon. [1
Macc. 2]

2. 2 century BC. The son of Absalom, he was one of the
commanders under Jonathan the high priest and
Maccabean leader. When Jonathan's forces were routed
by the army of Demetrius II in the battle of Hazor in
Galilee, Mattathias was one of the few who fought on
with him, until the others rallied and defeated the
enemy. [1 Macc. 11:70]

3. 2 century BC. Mattathias and his brother Judas were
murdered together with their father Simon, the high
priest, in the year 138 BC by their ambitious brother-in-
law Ptolemy, the son of Abubus. [1 Macc. 16:14-16]

4. 2 century BC. One of three envoys sent by the Syrian
general Nicanor to come to terms with Judas Maccabeus.
[2 Macc. 14:19]

MELCHIEL *c.* 5 century BC. Father of Charmis, a city
magistrate in the time of Judith. [Jdt. 6:15]

MENELAUS 2 century BC. High priest in Jerusalem,
172-62 BC.

In the reign of Antiochus IV, Menelaus succeeded by
bribery in ousting the high priest Jason and getting himself appointed instead. He arranged for the murder of
the revered former high priest Onias III who had denounced him.

Menelaus helped Antiochus IV despoil the Temple
and carry off its treasures. Later, charges were laid
against him before the king by leading citizens of
Jerusalem, but he saved himself by bribery.

Menelaus was apparently dismissed when Judas
Maccabeus entered Jerusalem and purified the Temple.
Eventually he was condemned to death by the Seleucid
general Lysias and executed by being thrown from a
a high water tower into hot ashes. [2 Macc. 4:23-34, 39,
43-50; 5:15, 23; 11:29-32; 13:3-8]

MENESTHEUS *c.* 2 century BC. Father of Apollonius
who was sent to Egypt for the coronation of Ptolemy VI
Philometor. [2 Macc. 4:21]

MERARI (Heb. 'bitter') *c.* 5 century BC. The father
of Judith. [Jdt. 8:1]

MICAH (Heb. 'who is like the Lord?') *c.* 5 century BC.
Father of Uzziah, chief city magistrate in the time of
Judith. [Jdt. 6:15]

MORDECAI (Heb. 'consecrated to Merodach') *c.* 5
century BC. Cousin and foster-father of Esther.

In the Septuagint (Greek) translation of the Book of
Esther, a number of additional passages were inserted,
some of which concern Mordecai (Gk. *Mardochaeus*).

In an introductory passage, Mordecai has an apocalyptic dream: the nations plan to destroy God's
people but the humble overcome the mighty.

The Greek text contains a prayer by Mordecai, asking
God for deliverance from Haman's edict. It also includes the text of a letter written by Mordecai in the
name of the king ordering provincial governors to give
the Jews arms for self-defence.

In a final passage, Mordecai recalls his dream, and
praises the Lord for safeguarding the Jews.

The object of these additions was clearly to inject a
religious note lacking in the canonical story of Esther.
see also MORDECAI (O.T. section) [Ad. Est. 11:2-12; 12;
13:8-17; 16:1-24; 10:4-13]

NADAB (Heb. 'God is willing') *c.* 8 century BC.
Nephew of Tobit and younger brother of Ahikar, he was
the son of his brother Anael. Tobit's deathbed instruction to his son Tobias contains an inexplicable reference
to an attempt by Nadab to murder his elder brother
Ahikar by shutting him up in a grave, but it is Nadab
who gets killed instead in the trap. This allusion has no
relation to anything else in the Tobit story, and is probably an echo of an earlier Near Eastern work, *The Wisdom of Ahikar*, which scholars regard as one of the main
sources of the Book of Tobit. [Tob. 11:18; 14:10]

NATHANAEL (Heb. 'God has given') date unknown.
Ancestor of Judith. [Jdt. 8:1]

NEBUCHADNEZZAR (Ass. 'Nabu protects my
boundary stone') date unknown. In the Book of Judith,
Nebuchadnezzar, king of Assyria, sent an army
under his general Holofernes to punish the Jews, who
had failed to help him in a war against Arphaxad the
king of Media.

This reference has no historical basis. Nebuchadnezzar was in fact the king of Babylon after the end of the
Assyrian empire, and he did not have a general called

Holofernes. [Jdt. 1; 2:1-13; 3:2, 8; 4:1; 6:2, 4; 11:1, 4, 7; 12:13, 14:18]

NICANOR (Gk. 'conqueror') 2 century BC. A Seleucid general under Antiochus IV Epiphanes and Demetrius I Soter. Nicanor, the son of Patroclus, was one of three generals appointed by Lysias in command of an army sent in 166 BC to crush the Maccabean revolt. This Syrian force was defeated by Judas Maccabeus at the battle of Emmaus, near the foot of the Judean hills, and Nicanor escaped in disguise.

In 162 BC, in the reign of Demetrius I Soter, Nicanor was sent to cut through to Jerusalem and reinforce the garrison there. He was driven back in the battle of Capharsalama. The following year, Nicanor was surprised by Judas at Adasa, and fell in battle. This victory was later celebrated in Jewish tradition as 'the Day of Nicanor', the 13th day of the Hebrew month of Adar. [1 Macc. 3:38-41; 7:27-50; 2 Macc. 8:9-35; 14:12-34, 37-40; 15:1, 6, 25-37]

NUMENIUS 2 century BC. Son of Antiochus, he was one of two envoys sent to Rome by Jonathan to renew the pact of friendship. [1 Macc. 12:16; 14:22-24]

ODOMERA 2 century BC. Nomad leader defeated by Jonathan. [1 Macc. 9:66]

ONIAS 1. Onias I *c.* 4 century BC. High priest in Jerusalem and ancestor of Simon the Just, a later high priest, he received a letter of friendship from Arius, king of Sparta. [1 Macc. 12:7, 8, 19; Sir. 50:1]

2. Onias III 2 century BC. Son of the high priest Simon II, he was himself high priest in Jerusalem during the reign of the Seleucid ruler Seleucus IV Philopator, 187-75 BC. He was venerated for his learning and piety; after his murder he appeared in a vision related by Judas Maccabeus to inspire his men before battle.

The king's chief minister Heliodorus was sent to Jerusalem to confiscate the gold and silver in the Temple, but was foiled through divine intervention in response to Onias's prayers.

When Antiochus IV Epiphanes came to the throne in 175 BC, Onias was ousted by his corrupt brother Jason, and retired to the sanctuary at Daphne, near Antioch. He was later murdered at the instigation of another high priest Menelaus. [2 Macc. 3:1, 31-35; 4:1-6, 7, 33-38; 15:12-16; Sir. 50:1]

OX *c.* 6 century BC. Grandfather of Judith. [Jdt. 8:1]

OZIEL date unknown. Ancestor of Judith. [Jdt. 8:1]

PATROCLUS 3 century BC. Father of Nicanor, the

The tel of Adasa, about seven miles from Beth-horon, where Nicanor was defeated by Judas Maccabeus.

Syrian general, who was killed in a battle against Judas Maccabeus. [2 Macc. 8:9]

PERSEUS 2 century BC. Last king of Macedonia, he was mentioned by Judas Maccabeus as having been defeated by the Romans. (This was at the battle of Pydna in 168 BC.) [1 Macc. 8:5]

PHASIRON date unknown. His descendants were killed in their tents by Jonathan Maccabeus. [1 Macc. 9:66]

PHILIP 1. 4 century BC. King of Macedonia, 359-36 BC, he was father of Alexander the Great. [1 Macc. 1:1]

2. 3 century BC. King of Macedonia, 220-179 BC, father of Perseus, he was conquered by the Romans. [1 Macc. 8:5]

3. *c.* 2 century BC. He was a trusted friend of Antiochus IV Epiphanes and accompanied him on the expedition to Persia in 165 BC. Antiochus IV fell ill in this campaign and before he died, he appointed Philip regent of the Seleucid kingdom, until his young son Antiochus should come of age. But Lysias, who had been left in the capital Antioch in charge of the kingdom, promptly had the boy crowned as Antiochus V Eupator, under his guidance.

In 162 BC, after Lysias had defeated Judas Maccabeus and entered Jerusalem, together with the king, they received news that Philip had returned from Persia with troops and occupied Antioch. Lysias hurried back and recaptured the city. Philip was either killed, or escaped to Egypt. [1 Macc. 6:14-18, 55-63; 2 Macc. 9:29]

4. *c.* 2 century BC. A Phrygian appointed by Antiochus IV Epiphanes as governor of Jerusalem. He is said to have been a brutal man, who had a number of Jews burnt alive for having secretly observed the Sabbath against the decrees of Antiochus.

After the Maccabean revolt, when Judas and his men were raiding the countryside round Jerusalem, Philip appealed for military aid. A Syrian army was despatched which Judas defeated at Emmaus in 165 BC. [2 Macc. 5:22; 6:11; 8:8]

POSIDONIUS 2 century BC. One of three envoys sent by the Syrian general Nicanor to come to terms with Judas Maccabeus. [2 Macc. 14:19]

PTOLEMY 1. Ptolemy VI Philometor King of Egypt, 180-45 BC. Ptolemy VI succeeded to the Egyptian throne in 180 BC, at the age of seven. His mother Cleopatra acted as regent until he was enthroned in 172 BC.

The Seleucid ruler Antiochus IV twice invaded Egypt. Ptolemy was defeated and taken prisoner but Antiochus was ordered to withdraw by the Romans.

After the death of Antiochus IV, Ptolemy took an active part in the dynastic struggle that followed: initially acknowledging Alexander Balas, to whom he then married his daughter Cleopatra, three years later. He led his forces into Palestine and helped Demetrius II to defeat his own son-in-law near Antioch in 145 BC.

Shortly afterwards Ptolemy himself died of wounds, and was succeeded by his younger brother Ptolemy VII Physcon.

Ptolemy VI was friendly towards the Jews, and is favourably mentioned in the Two Books of Maccabees. He permitted the high priest Onias IV to found a Jewish temple at Leontopolis (Tel-el-Yehudiyeh), near modern Cairo. It survived until about AD 73. [1 Macc. 1:18; 10:51-58; 11:1-18; 2 Macc. 4:21]

2. 2 century BC. Son of Dorymenes (also called Ptolemy Macron in 2 Macc.), he was made Governor of Cyprus by the Egyptian ruler Ptolemy VI Philometor (180-45 BC). He defected to the Seleucid ruler Antiochus Epiphanes who invaded Egypt.

He was one of the generals put in command of the Seleucid forces sent to crush the Maccabean revolt. This force was defeated by Judas Maccabeus at the battle of Emmaus in 165 BC.

Ptolemy was offered a large bribe to intercede with the King Antiochus IV on behalf of Menelaus, the corrupt high priest accused by several leading Jews.

After the death of Antiochus IV, Ptolemy appears to have been out of favour with the young successor Eupator. Having urged a more liberal policy towards the Jews, Ptolemy was accused by his enemies of disloyalty to the throne, and took his own life by poison. [1 Macc. 3:38; 2 Macc. 4:45, 46; 10:12, 13]

3. 2 century BC. Son of Abubus, he was married to the daughter of Simon the high priest and Maccabean leader. Simon appointed him military commander of the Jericho district. Simon arrived there on a visit, and at a banquet for him Ptolemy treacherously had him murdered together with two of his sons, Mattathias and Judas, and his retinue.

He then sent a message to King Antiochus VII, the Seleucid ruler in Antioch, offering to govern Judea under his rule.

John, the eldest son of Simon, was at the time in Gazara. Having received word of Ptolemy's treachery, he was able to forestall an attempt to assassinate him too. He then appointed himself as the ruler in succession to his father, under the name of John Hyrcanus I.

The fate of Ptolemy is unknown. [1 Macc. 16:11-22]

4. Ptolemy VII Physcon King of Egypt, 145-16 BC. Brother of Ptolemy VI. [2 Macc. 1:10]

5. Ptolemy VIII, Soter II, Lathyrus *c.* 2 century BC. In a footnote to the Greek translation of the Book of Esther, it is stated that the translation was brought to Egypt in the fourth year of the reign of 'Ptolemy and Cleopatra'. There were four Ptolemies who had wives called Cleopatra but the reference appears to apply to Ptolemy VIII, and the date has therefore been fixed at 114 BC. [Ad. Est. 11:1]

6. *c.* 2 century BC. With his father Dositheus the priest, he brought the Greek translation of the Book of Esther to Egypt in the fourth year of the reign of Ptolemy and Cleopatra (probably 114 BC). [Ad. Est. 11:1]

QUINTUS MEMMIUS 2 century BC. One of the two Roman legates who wrote a letter to the Jews at the time of Judas Maccabeus, confirming certain concessions made to them by the Seleucid general Lysias. [2 Macc. 11:34]

RAGUEL *c.* 8 century BC. Kinsman of Tobit.

Raguel was a relative of Tobit and lived in the city of Ecbatana, in Media. He was married to Edna, and their only child was the beautiful and intelligent Sarah. Their great tragedy was that Sarah had been possessed by the demon Asmodeus. She had been married seven times and each time the demon had killed the respective husband when he entered the bridal chamber on the wedding night.

Tobias, the son of Tobit, arrived in Ecbatana and was betrothed to Sarah. On the wedding night Raguel feared the worst, but the demon was exorcized with the help of the angel Raphael. Tobias returned to Nineveh with his bride. Many years later, after the death of Tobit and Anna, Tobias and Sarah went back to Ecbatana and took care of Raguel and his wife Edna for their remaining years. [Tob. 3:7, 17; 6:10, 12; 7; 8; 10:7-10; 11:1; 14:12, 13]

RAPHAIM date unknown. Ancestor of Judith. [Jdt. 8:1]

RAZIS 2 century BC. A devout and respected elder of Jerusalem, he was honoured with the title 'Father of the Jews'. In the persecution under Antiochus IV Epiphanes, the Syrian general Nicanor sent a detachment of troops to arrest Razis. The tower in which he had taken refuge was set alight and stormed. He stabbed himself with his sword, jumped off the tower wall into the street below and, bleeding profusely, dragged himself on to a rock. Tearing out his entrails, he flung them at the crowd, calling upon the Lord to give them back to him again. 'This was the manner of his death.' (2 Macc. 14:46) [2 Macc. 14:37-46]

RHODOCUS 2 century BC. A Maccabean soldier who gave military information to the enemy when the Jewish fortress of Beth-zur was being besieged by Syrian forces; he was caught and imprisoned. [2 Macc. 13:21]

SALAMIEL (possibly from the Heb. 'God is friendly') date unknown. Ancestor of Judith. [Jdt. 8:1]

SARAH (Heb. 'princess') *c.* 7 century BC. Wife of Tobias the son of Tobit.

Sarah, described as 'fair and wise', was the only child of Raguel, a kinsman of Tobit, and his wife Edna. They lived in Ecbatana, a city in Media. Sarah was married seven times but on each occasion when her husband entered the bridal chamber on the wedding night, he was killed by the demon Asmodeus.

Sarah's despair was brought to a head when her maid jeered at her, accusing her of strangling her seven hus-

bands. 'Why do you beat us? If they are dead, go with them.' [Tobit 3:9]

Tobias the son of Tobit arrived in Ecbatana, accompanied by the angel Raphael who was pretending to be a relative called Azarias. Tobias obtained Raguel's permission to marry Sarah. Acting on the angel's advice, he entered the room on the wedding night and drove away the demon by burning the heart and liver of a fish. He and Sarah then prayed to God to keep them safe. Later that night, when a maid was sent into the room with a light to see whether Tobias was still alive, she found the young couple sleeping soundly.

Two weeks later, after the wedding celebrations, Sarah set out with her husband on the journey back to Nineveh. She was met at the city gate by Tobit, whose sight had been miraculously restored.

Tobias and Sarah remained in Nineveh until after her parents-in-law had died, and then went back to her own parents in Ecbatana, together with their children. [Tob. 3:7-15; 6:10-12; 7; 8; 10:10-12; 11:7; 14:12]

SARASADAI (from the Heb. 'Shaddai [a name of God] is a rock') date unknown. Ancestor of Judith. [Jdt. 8:1]

SELEUCUS IV PHILOPATOR 2 century BC. Ruler of the Seleucid kingdom, 187-75 BC.

Seleucus IV succeeded his father Antiochus III (the Great) on the Seleucid throne in Antioch.

The king respected the religion of the Jews and the sanctity of the Temple, which he helped to maintain from his own revenues. However, on getting a report of great riches concealed in the Temple in Jerusalem,

Coin of Seleucus I, minted
300-290 BC, with elephant and anchor,
the badge of the Seleucid dynasty.

Seleucus sent his chief minister Heliodorus with an armed guard to collect the gold and silver for the royal treasury. Heliodorus returned to report that his attempt to do so had been thwarted by divine intervention and he himself severely flogged by two supernatural beings.

At one stage Onias the high priest came personally to appeal to the king against the intrigues of one Simon, who had instigated the story about the Temple treasure.

Seleucus was killed by Heliodorus in 175 BC, and the throne seized by his brother Antiochus IV Epiphanes. [2 Macc. 3:3; 4:7]

SENNACHERIB (Acc. 'Sin [a god] replace the brothers') 8 century BC. King of Assyria, 704-681 BC.

According to the Book of Tobit, Sennacherib succeeded Shalmaneser as king of Assyria. Tobit had to flee from him, because he had secretly buried Jewish bodies, and returned when Sennacherib was succeeded by Esarhaddon. This order of succession is historically inaccurate. [Tob. 1:15, 16, 18, 21]

SERON 2 century BC. Seleucid general under Antiochus IV. After Judas Maccabeus had defeated and killed Apollonius, the military governor of Samaria, in 166 BC, a larger Seleucid army was sent to crush the Maccabean revolt. It was led by Seron, the commander of the forces in Syria. His troops established a base in the coastal plain and advanced into the Judean hills up the steep pass of Beth-horon, in an effort to relieve the garrison cut off in Jerusalem. Judas and his men launched a surprise attack on the vanguard and routed it. The Seleucid army was pursued towards the coast. [1 Macc. 3:13-24]

SHALLUM date unknown. Ancestor of Jehoiakim the high priest. [Bar. 1:7]

SHALMANESER V (Ass. 'Sulman is leader') 8 century BC. King of Assyria, 726-2 BC.

Tobit was a member of the tribe of Naphtali in eastern Galilee and was taken captive in the time of Shalmaneser, king of Assyria. This may be a reference to Shalmaneser V who laid siege to Samaria the capital of the kingdom of Israel in 723 BC. It actually fell to his successor Sargon II in 721 BC, and after that the inhabitants were deported to other parts of the Assyrian empire.

Tobit states that his piety won him the favour of Shalmaneser, and he was employed by the king as a buyer of supplies in Media. This is an improbable statement, as Tobit's captivity could not have coincided with the short reign of Shalmaneser V. [Tob. 1:2, 13, 16]

SIMEON (Heb. '[God] has heard') 1. c. 3 century BC. Grandfather of the priest Mattathias who started the Maccabean revolt, to whom the Jewish historian Josephus and later writers attached the name of Hasmon. Thus the descendants of Mattathias who ruled over Judea became known as the Hasmonean dynasty. [1 Macc. 2:1]
2. *see* SIMON 2.

SIMON (Heb. '[God] has heard') 1. c. 3 century BC. High priest known as 'the Just'. [Sir. 50:1]
2. 2 century BC. Second son of Mattathias and leader of the Maccabean revolt after Jonathan.

Simon (also called Thassi and Simeon) was the second son of Mattathias, the village priest of Modi'in who started the revolt against Antiochus IV Epiphanes in 167 BC. With his father and his four brothers John, Judas, Eleazar and Jonathan, Simon fled into the hills and took part in the partisan movement. On his deathbed the next year, Mattathias made Judas the military commander and told the brothers to heed the wise counsel of Simon. For the next fourteen years Simon faithfully served first under Judas and then under Jonathan. From time to time, he took command of military expeditions such as that in 163 BC to rescue the oppressed Jews of Galilee, and another to capture the port of Joppa (Jaffa).

In 146 BC, Jonathan was captured through the deceit of the Seleucid general Trypho. Simon took charge and rallied the dejected Judeans. Trypho advanced on Jerusalem but then abandoned his Judean campaign and returned to Antioch, killing the captive Jonathan along the way.

The leading citizens of Jerusalem declared to Simon, 'You are our leader in place of Judas and Jonathan your brother. Fight our battles . . .' (1 Macc. 13:9) He was to lead them for the next twelve years, until 134 BC.

The power struggle for the Seleucid throne continued and, as Jonathan had done, Simon was able to take advantage of it. Trypho had proclaimed himself king, and Simon sent a message of support to the rightful ruler Demetrius II. In exchange, he obtained from Demetrius recognition of his status as high priest and ethnarch (governor), also suspension of the annual tribute and remission of the taxes. Judea was now autonomous, and in the year 142 BC 'the yoke of the Gentiles was removed from Israel, and the people began to write in their documents and contracts, "In the first year of Simon the great high priest and captain and leader of the Jews".' (1 Macc. 13:41, 42) Simon marked the new independence by beginning to mint and issue Judean coins.

Simon's next military step was the capture of the strongly fortified city of Gazara, on the edge of the coastal plain. He spared the inhabitants but evicted them, and resettled the place with loyal Judean subjects. In the next year, 141 BC, the citadel in Jerusalem was assaulted, and the starving garrison surrendered. This eliminated the last vestige of foreign rule, and was the occasion for public rejoicing 'because a great enemy had been crushed and removed from Israel'. (1 Macc. 13:51) Simon built himself a residence on the site. His son John had reached manhood and was made commander of the armed forces, with his headquarters in Gazara.

Like his brothers had done, Simon sent his ambassadors to Rome and to Sparta, to ensure that the alliances with these two powers remained in force. To the Romans he sent a golden shield as a gift.

In the meantime, Demetrius II had been succeeded by his son Antiochus VII, who deposed and pursued Trypho. He repudiated previous promises to Simon, and sent an envoy to him in Jerusalem with an ultimatum. Either Joppa, Gazara and the citadel in Jerusalem were to be handed over, or a huge sum of compensation was to be paid. Failing that, war would be declared. Simon rejected the demand, pointing out that the areas he had taken were part of the ancestral territory of the Jews that had wrongfully been occupied by their enemies.

The Seleucid general Cendebeus based an army in the coastal plain and harassed the adjacent Jewish districts. His troops were routed by the Judean forces led by Simon's two eldest sons, John and Judas. Simon did not long survive this success. He was treacherously mur-

dered together with his two sons Judas and Mattathias by his son-in-law Ptolemy, whom he had appointed military commander of Jericho. Ptolemy's bid for power was frustrated by Simon's eldest son John Hyrcanus, who became the new ruler.

The murder of Simon ended the story of the five remarkable Maccabean brothers, all of whom had been killed in battle or been murdered. The Hasmonean dynasty that derived from Mattathias lasted for 120 years, until Herod the Great.

Simon himself remains in Jewish tradition an example of a wise and statesmanlike national leader. He is eulogized for enlarging the borders of the nation, making peace in the land, providing for the needy, and strengthening the Law. [1 Macc. 2:3, 65; 9:33-42, 65-68; 10:74-83; 11:63-66; 12:33, 34, 38; 13; 14; 15; 16:1-3, 11-17] **3.** 2 century BC. Simon, of the clan of Benjamin, was the administrator of the Temple under the high priest Onias III. He quarreled with Onias about the regulation of the city market. In order to cause trouble for Onias,

Excavation of the eastern slope of Jerusalem, showing a tower rebuilt over 6th-century ruins in the 2nd century BC, under Maccabean rule.

Reconstructed model of the Second Temple with
the Hasmonean palace in the centre.

he went to Apollonius, the governor, and told him that
a huge amount of treasure was hoarded in the Temple.
Apollonius passed on this information to the king
Seleucus IV, who sent his minister Heliodorus with an
armed guard to seize the wealth. The attempt was foiled
by divine intervention.

Later Onias went personally to see the king in the
capital, Antioch, and asked him to put a stop to Simon's
intrigues and slanders so that peace could be restored to
Jerusalem. [2 Macc. 3:4; 4:1]

SOSIPATER (Gk. 'saving one's father') 2 century BC.
A fighting commander in the Maccabean army who
distinguished himself in the campaign of Judas Maccabeus against Timothy in Gilead. He and another
commander captured Timothy but released him for fear
of reprisals against Jewish hostages. [2 Macc. 12:19, 24]

SOSTRATUS 2 century BC. A Syrian commander of
the garrison in Jerusalem under Antiochus IV Epiphanes.
He was entrusted with the collection of taxes and of the
money promised by Menelaus for his appointment as
high priest. For neglecting his duties Sostratus was
recalled by the king. [2 Macc. 4:28, 29]

SUSANNA *c.* 6 century BC. A virtuous wife falsely
accused of adultery.

Susanna the daughter of Hilkiah was 'a very beautiful
woman and one who feared the Lord' (Sus. 2). She was
married to Joakim, a wealthy and respected member of
a Jewish community in Babylon. Their home was a
meeting place for the important men of the community.

Two elders or judges who frequented the house conceived a passion for Susanna. One day they pretended to
go home for the noon-day meal but each sneaked back
again. Coming face to face, they revealed their secret to
each other. They both knew that Susanna was accustomed to walk in the garden at that time of day, and hid
themselves so that they could spy on her.

It was a hot day. Susanna decided to bathe in the
garden and sent the maids back into the house to fetch

soap and olive oil. Unable to restrain their lust, the elders approached her and said, 'we are in love with you; so give your consent, and lie with us' (Sus. 20).

Susanna rejected their advances rather than sin against the Lord. She shouted for help and the servants rushed back. The elders then denounced her, and demanded that she be brought before the communal assembly to answer the charges against her. She came accompanied by her parents, family and children, with her tear-stained face covered by a veil. The two elders insisted that she be unveiled, since they wanted to feast their eyes on her beauty.

They gave evidence that they had been strolling in a corner of Joakim's garden when they saw Susanna enter, dismiss her maids and meet a young man who had been hidden. The two of them then lay together under a tree. The elders claimed they had rushed forward and seized the young man, but he had broken away and escaped. Susanna had refused to disclose his name.

Since the story of two such important citizens could not be doubted, Susanna was immediately condemned to death. She cried out to the Lord that she was innocent, and her appeal was heard. As she was being led out to her death, the young Daniel was inspired to protest. He called the assembly fools for condemning the woman without proper enquiry and demanded that the trial be reopened since the elders had given false

Susanna and the Elders, by Jacopo Tintoretto (1518-94). The two elders hide behind a bush to watch Susanna bathing.

evidence. The court reassembled and he was invited to state his case.

Daniel insisted that the accusers should be brought forward separately. He berated the first one for the unjust decisions he had given as a judge. He then asked under what kind of tree he had seen Susanna and the young man lying together. The witness answered that it was a clove tree. Daniel declared that he lied and his life would be forfeited. He told that elder to stand aside and ordered the other one brought in. Daniel denounced him for frightening women into consorting with him, and declared that this time his lust had betrayed him. When questioned about the kind of tree, this witness replied that it had been a yew.

Daniel's cross-examination convinced the assembly that the two elders had given false evidence. They were put to death, while Susanna was freed and restored to her rejoicing family. 'And from that day onward Daniel had a great reputation among the people.' (Sus. 64)

This charming short tale was written in Palestine about the 2nd century BC. It was included in the Septuagint (Greek Bible) and later in the Vulgate (Latin Bible), and it became attached to the Book of Daniel as Chapter 13 thereof. [Book of Susanna]

THASSI (Gk. 'zealous') *see* SIMON 2.

THEODOTUS 2 century BC. One of three envoys sent by the Syrian general Nicanor to come to terms with Judas Maccabeus. [2 Macc. 14:19]

TIMOTHY (Gk. 'man who honours God') 2 century BC. A leader of the Ammonites who fought against Judas Maccabeus.

In 163 BC Judas Maccabeus and his brother Jonathan marched across the Jordan river with an army of 8000 men, to rescue the persecuted Jewish communities in the land of Gilead. They were opposed by an Ammonite army commanded by Timothy. The Maccabeans made a three-day desert march through the territory of the friendly Nabateans, and appeared unexpectedly at the gates of Bozrah, in the land of Tob, east of Gilead, which they captured. They then continued at night towards Dathema, and launched a three-pronged attack on the army of Timothy, which fled. Judas then relieved the Jews in several other fortified towns.

Timothy regrouped his forces, but they were again routed in a pitched battle at Raphon, near the Sea of Galilee.

Judas was victorious in a later battle against Timothy at Jazer, across the Jordan river, east of Jericho. Timothy was killed in this battle. [1 Macc. 5:11, 34, 37-44; 2 Macc. 10:24-38]

TITUS MANIUS 2 century BC. One of the two Roman legates who wrote a letter to the Jews at the time of Judas Maccabeus, confirming certain concessions made to them by the Seleucid commander Lysias. [2 Macc. 11:34]

TOBIAS (from the Heb. 'God is [my] good')
1. *c*. 7 century BC. The son and only child of Tobit and Anna, of the tribe of Naphtali in eastern Galilee.

As a child Tobias was carried off with his parents into exile in Nineveh, the capital of Assyria. Here his father became a respected and well-to-do man in the community.

Tobit was stricken with blindness and believed he would soon die. He sent for Tobias, now a young man, and revealed to him that twenty years earlier a substantial sum of silver had been deposited with a kinsman called Gabael, who lived in the town of Rages in Media. Tobias was to find a reliable companion who knew the routes to Media, and travel there to collect the money.

The guide Tobias found called himself Azarias, but was actually the angel Raphael, who had been sent by the Lord to cure Tobit. The two of them set out on the journey, accompanied by the family dog. That night they camped by the river Tigris. Tobias went to bathe his feet in the water and a huge fish tried to grab his foot. On the angel's instructions, Tobias caught the fish and kept its gall, heart and liver to use as medicine.

They reached the city of Ecbatana in Media, where another relative, Raguel, lived. His daughter Sarah, also an only child, was beautiful and wise. As her nearest kinsman Tobias was entitled to claim the hand of Sarah in marriage. The angel undertook to speak to her father

Tobias catches the fish (top),
and returns with Sarah to Tobit (bottom):
from a 12th-century French Bible.

The Blindness of Tobit: drawing by Rembrandt van Rijn (1606-69). On the right stands the goat which Tobit accused his wife of stealing.

about it, but Tobias declined. Sarah had already been married seven times and each husband had been killed on the wedding night by the demon Asmodeus. The angel told Tobias not to be afraid; if he burnt the heart and liver of the fish in the bridal chamber, the demon would be driven away. They were warmly welcomed by Raguel and his wife Edna, though they were distressed to hear that Tobit had gone blind. Raguel agreed that Tobias should marry his daughter, but warned him about the demon. A marriage contract was drawn up and signed, and the bridal chamber prepared.

That night Tobias entered the chamber and burnt the fish's liver and heart on the incense burner. The demon fled to Upper Egypt, where he was caught and bound by the angel Raphael. Tobias and Sarah prayed to the Lord to keep them safe, and went to sleep. Finding that Tobias had survived, Raguel gave praise to the Lord, and prepared the wedding feast.

At Tobias's request, Azarias travelled on by himself to Rages, where Gabael produced the bags of silver Tobit had left with him, and gladly agreed to attend the wedding.

After two weeks, Tobias insisted that he should return to his parents without further delay, taking his wife with him. Raguel handed over to him half of all his possessions, as a wedding gift. On reaching home, Tobias rubbed the gall of the fish into his father's eyes, as the angel had told him to do, and Tobit's sight was restored.

Tobias agreed with his father that half the wealth he had brought back from Media should be offered to his travelling companion, as a reward for all he had done for them. Azarias disclosed that he was really the angel Raphael, sent by the Lord to cure Tobit and Sarah. They threw themselves on the ground in awe, and when they looked up the angel had disappeared.

Tobit lived on for nearly another half century. On his deathbed, he urged Tobias to depart from Nineveh, which was doomed to destruction for its wickedness. Tobias waited until his mother also died, then buried her with his father, and left with his wife and children to rejoin his parents-in-law in Media. He cared for Raguel and Edna, and buried them at Ecbatana when they died. He himself lived until after the fall of Nineveh to the Medes and Babylonians, and died greatly respected at the age of one hundred and seventeen. [Book of Tobit]

2. *c.* 2 century BC. Father of Hyrcanus, he had money kept on deposit in the Temple in Jerusalem. [2 Macc. 3:11]

TOBIEL (Heb. 'God is [my] good') *c.* 8 century BC. Father of Tobit. [Tob. 1:1]

TOBIT (Heb. 'my goodness') *c.* 8 century BC. A devout Jewish captive in Assyria.

Tobit the son of Tobiel was a God-fearing young man of the tribe of Naphtali in the eastern Galilee. After the Israelite monarchy divided, this area fell into the northern kingdom of Israel, which broke away from the Temple worship in Jerusalem and developed its own shrines. Tobit expressed disapproval of such apostasy and continued to make the pilgrimage to Jerusalem. When he came of age, he married Anna and had a son called Tobias.

The Assyrians invaded Israel and Tobit was carried off in captivity to Nineveh, the Assyrian capital, together with other members of his tribe. He gained the trust of the king and was employed by him as a buyer of supplies in Media, which lay to the east of Assyria. In connection with these journeys he deposited ten talents of silver – a considerable sum – with his kinsman Gabael, who lived at Rages in Media. When Sennacherib succeeded to the throne of Assyria the routes to Media passed out of Assyrian control and Tobit could no longer travel there.

He remained a devout and charitable man, and claimed with pride that 'I, Tobit, walked in the ways of truth and righteousness all the days of my life, and I performed many acts of charity to my brethren and countrymen . . .' (Tob. 1:3) He provided food and clothes for the poor; and would, as an act of piety, give a proper burial to any Jewish body found abandoned outside the city walls. When Sennacherib was repulsed in Judea and killed a number of Nineveh Jews in revenge, Tobit secretly retrieved and buried the bodies. Report of this act enraged the king and Tobit had to flee with his wife and son, leaving behind all his possessions.

Soon afterwards, Sennacherib was murdered and succeeded by his son Esarhaddon. Tobit's nephew Ahikar, who had become the royal treasurer, was able to arrange for his uncle's return.

At the Feast of Pentecost Tobit sent his son Tobias to find a poor man who could be invited to share the family meal. Tobias came back to report that he had seen in the market-place a Jew who had been strangled to death. Tobit rushed off to fetch the body, hid it until dark, and buried it. He was disturbed when the neighbours jeered at him and recalled that he had been forced to flee once for the same offense.

That night it was hot, and Tobit lay down to sleep next to the wall of the courtyard. The droppings from the sparrows on the wall fell right into his eyes, and produced white patches. The doctors treated him, but he went blind, to the distress of all his family.

His wife Anna earned money by weaving cloth for a merchant. One day her employer gave her a young kid as a present, in addition to her wages. When she brought it home the blind Tobit refused to believe her story, accused her of stealing the animal, and ordered her to return it at once. She taunted him: 'Where are your charities and your righteous deeds? You seem to know everything!' (Tob. 2:14) This incident depressed Tobit, and in a fit of despair he prayed to God to end his life.

Believing he might soon die, Tobit sent for his son and commanded him to give his father a decent burial, to take care of his mother, and to live righteously. He then told him about the silver he had deposited in Media with his relative Gabael, twenty years before. Tobias was to find a reliable travelling companion who knew the route, and fetch back the money, which would restore the family's means.

In Ecbatana, a city in Media, Tobit had another kinsman called Raguel. He and his wife Edna had an only child, a beautiful and virtuous daughter called Sarah. She had already been married seven times, but each husband had been killed when he entered the bridal chamber on the wedding night by the demon Asmodeus. Sarah too was in despair, and prayed for death after her serving-maid had jeered at her.

God sent the angel Raphael to help both Tobit and Sarah. Tobias went out to look for someone suitable to journey with him to Media and came face to face with a man who was the angel in human form. When questioned by Tobias, this man said he was a fellow-Jew, knew the routes to Media well, and actually used to lodge with Gabael. Tobias brought him into the house to meet his father, who asked him about his family background. He said his name was Azarias and he was the son of Ananias – another relative of Tobit whom he had known well as a young man in Israel. The delighted Tobit immediately engaged 'Azarias' to accompany Tobias, at a wage of one drachma a day and his travelling expenses. Tobias took leave of his parents and set out with the guide. The family dog ran after him and was taken along.

When some time had gone by without news of their son, Anna started wailing that he was dead. Tobit tried to reassure her, though becoming anxious himself. One day Anna cried out that she saw Tobias approaching with his companion. As the blind Tobias stumbled out through the courtyard door, Tobias came up to him and rubbed into his eyes the gall of a fish caught in the river on the way to Media. (The angel had told him this medicine would restore his father's sight.) Tobias pulled the white patches off the eyes of his father, who burst into tears and blessed the Lord: 'For thou hast afflicted

The healing of Tobit: drawing by Rembrandt van Rijn (1606-69). Tobias pulls the white patches off Tobit's eyes.

me, but thou hast had mercy upon me; here I see my son Tobias!' (Tob. 11:15)

The young man told his parents all that had happened on his journey. In Ecbatana he had married his relative Sarah, after exorcizing the demon Asmodeus by burning the liver and the heart of the same fish used to cure Tobit's blindness. His father-in-law Raguel, a well-to-do man, had bestowed half his possessions on Tobias. In addition, Gabael had come to the wedding and brought the bags of silver Tobit had once deposited with him. On nearing home Tobias had hurried ahead, and Sarah with the rest of his party were close behind.

Tobit went out to meet his daughter-in-law at the city gate. His fellow-citizens were astonished to see him striding through the streets full of vigour and no longer blind. A sumptuous marriage feast was held. 'So there was rejoicing among all his brethren in Nineveh.' (Tob. 11:17)

Tobit and Tobias offered the travelling companion Azarias half of all the wealth brought back from Media, as a reward for the services he had performed. He then disclosed to them that he was the angel Raphael. All he asked for reward was that Tobit and Sarah should give praise to the Lord and proclaim to everyone what had been done for them. 'It is good to guard the secret of a king, but glorious to reveal the works of God.' (Tob. 12:7) Father and son prostrated themselves to the ground, and when they looked up the angel had disappeared.

Tobit sang hymns of praise to the just and merciful God, prophesying that the Lord would gather his scattered people, and would restore the splendour of Jerusalem and its sanctuary.

He lived on in peace and honour for nearly half a century more, and died at the age of 112. On his deathbed he urged Tobias to depart with his family because Nineveh was doomed to be destroyed for its wickedness. When Anna his mother also died, Tobias buried her with his father in Nineveh, then left to join his parents-in-law in Media.

It is unclear to what period or country the Jewish author of the Book of Tobit belonged. Internal events suggest the 3rd century BC, after the start of the Hellenistic period but before the Maccabean revolt. It is likely that he lived in Egypt. The events are supposed to have taken place in the Assyrian empire several centuries earlier, but the author is curiously vague about the history and the geography which formed the background to the story. Tobit is described as a young man when the Israelite kingdom was split after the death of Solomon (931 BC); he was deported to Assyria (about 734 BC); while his son Tobias died after the fall of Nineveh (612 BC). The town of Rages in Media, where Tobit's kinsman Gabael lived, is stated to be in the hills two days journey from Ecbatana in the plain; in fact, Ecbatana was a winter capital in the mountains at an altitude of 6000 feet; while Rages was 200 miles away and much lower down. These discrepancies do not detract from a vivid human story mingling Jewish piety, a belief in demons and magic, and warm family sentiment. [Book of Tobit]

TRYPHO 2 century BC. An army commander who usurped the Seleucid throne.

Trypho was an ambitious army commander under the Seleucid rulers Alexander Balas and Demetrius II. He fomented a mutiny amongst the units that Demetrius was disbanding, seized control of the capital, Antioch, and in 145 BC installed the young son of Alexander Balas on the throne as Antiochus VI.

In an expedition to Judea, Trypho treacherously took Jonathan the Maccabean leader as his prisoner, and later killed him while retreating northwards. Jonathan's brother and successor, Simon the high priest, gave his support to Demetrius II, who continued his struggle to regain the throne. In 143 BC Trypho had Antiochus VI put to death and himself seized the throne.

In 138 BC Trypho was ousted in his turn by Antiochus VII Sidetes who pursued him to Dor on the Palestinian coast and set siege to the town. Trypho escaped by ship to Orthosia but was again pursued by Antiochus, and committed suicide. [1 Macc. 11:39, 40, 54-56; 12:39-49; 13:1, 12-24, 31-34; 15:10-14, 25, 37, 39]

UZZIAH (Heb. 'God is [my] strength') c. 5 century BC. Chief magistrate of Bethulia.

Uzziah, the son of Micah, was the chief magistrate or elder of the town of Bethulia in the hills of Ephraim, where Judith lived. It was besieged by an Assyrian army under Holofernes, and its spring of water was seized. After thirty-four days the townspeople, suffering from famine and thirst, demanded that Uzziah surrender to the Assyrians. He promised to do so if help from the Lord did not come within another five days.

Judith, a beautiful and devout young widow living on her deceased husband's farm, was outraged at this undertaking. She reproached Uzziah and his fellow-magistrates for their lack of faith in the Lord. At her request, they let her slip out of the city gate that night, accompanied only by her maid. Four days later, she returned from the Assyrian camp, bearing the severed head of Holofernes. Uzziah was aroused from his sleep and led the crowd in praise of Judith for delivering them. He then sent messengers 'to all the frontiers of Israel' (Jdt. 15:4), telling the men to rush out and destroy the enemy who were now in retreat. [Jdt. 6:15-21; 7:23-32; 8:9, 28-31, 35; 10:6; 13:18-20; 14:6; 15:4]

ZABDIEL (Heb. 'gift of God') 2 century BC. Leader of an Arabian tribe, he killed and decapitated King Alexander Balas, after he had been defeated by Ptolemy VI of Egypt, and sent his head to the king. [1 Macc. 11:17]

ZACCHAEUS (from the Heb. 'pure') 2 century BC. A captain in the Maccabean army, he took part in the siege of two strong Idumean fortresses. [2 Macc. 10:19]

ZEDEKIAH (Heb. 'God is [my] righteousness') date unknown. Ancestor of Baruch who was the disciple and scribe of Jeremiah. [Bar. 1:1]

Volume Two

Who's Who in the New Testament

Ronald Brownrigg

Advisory editors for this volume:

The Reverend Canon E. Every,
St George's Cathedral, Jerusalem

The Very Reverend Wolfgang E. Pax, OFM,
Convent of the Flagellation,
Via Dolorosa, Jerusalem

Contents

List of maps

Author's acknowledgments

I should like warmly to express my gratitude to the following for their academic advice and encouragement in the production of this book: The Reverend Anthony Harvey, Warden of St Augustine's College, Canterbury; The Reverend Canon Edward Every, St George's Cathedral, Jerusalem; The Very Reverend Wolfgang E. Pax, OFM, Convent of the Flagellation, Via Dolorosa, Jerusalem.

I want to thank the industrious picture-researchers, Elaine Varady in Jerusalem and Josephine Labanyi in London; also for their endless typing and proof-reading my friends Elna Charleson and Kathleen Clarke, of Blechingley, and Philip and Susan Richardson for their 'prophet's chamber'.

Most particularly I should like to mention John Curtis of Weidenfeld and Nicolson for his skill, perception and never failing good will, throughout this project.

Photographic acknowledgments

The author and publishers would like to thank the following museums, institutions and photographers for supplying the illustrations reproduced on the pages listed below. Those photographs not listed are the author's own.

Art Institute of Chicago 212 (bottom left); Barnabys Picture Library 78; Bayerische Staatsbibliothek, Munich 209, P-26; Bayerisches Nationalmuseum, Munich 206; Beirut Archaeological Museum 325; Biblioteca Medicea-Laurenziana, Florence 42, 85, 258 (left), 328 (bottom); Bibliothèque Municipale, Epernay 265; Bibliotheque Nationale, Paris 115 (top), 134 (bottom), 177, 193, 204, 222, 254, 278 (bottom), 281 (top), 356, 402; Bodleian Library, Oxford P-20, P-25, 296; Werner Braun 119, 153, 160 (bottom left), 166 (bottom), 172 (bottom), 176 (bottom left), 198, 211, 283 (bottom); British Museum 17, 27 (top), 28 (bottom), 35 (bottom), 46 (bottom), 50 (centre), 51 (centre: above and below), 109 (top), 142, 169 (bottom), 174, 196, 202, 207 (top), 221, 223, 232 (top), 242, 262, 263, 268 (top), 297, 302, 318 (bottom), 326, 358, 364, 388, 414, 420; British School at Rome 151; Photo Bulloz 14, 20, 116-7, 260-1, 279, 340, 390-1; Hillel Burger 363 (left); Camera Press 79 (right), 115 (centre), 188, 353; J. Allan Cash 86-7, 98, 110, 213 (top), 230 (top), 235, 205; City Museum of

7

Acknowledgments

Ancient Art, Haifa 259; Cleveland Museum of Art 200; Colchester and Essex Museum 60 (bottom); Courtauld Institute of Art, London P-27; Dean and Chapter of Durham 294 (right); Fitzwilliam Museum, Cambridge 274-5; Françoise Foliot 115 (top), 134 (bottom), 177, 193, 204, 222, 254, 278 (bottom), 281 (top), 356; Forum Museum, Rome 37 (top); John Freeman 158; Isabella Stewart Gardner Museum, Boston 163 (top); Sonia Halliday 39, 48, 49, 60 (top), 63, 79 (left), 90, 91, 113, 143, 191, 213 (bottom), 230 (bottom), 247, 257, 258 (right), 319, 320, P-29, P-30, 322, 323 (left), P-31, P-32; David Harris 46 (top), 68-9, 102 (bottom), 103, 104-5, 120 (top), 133 (bottom left), 138, 160 (top), 164, 176 (bottom right), 208, 272, (centre), 273 (bottom), 283 (centre), 305, 382 (bottom), 385, 387 (bottom), 412, 423, 432; Andrè Held 246, 339, 366, 367, 369 (bottom), 382 (top); Hirmer Verlag 334; Institut Royal du Patrimoine Artistique, Brussels 233 (top); Israel Department of Antiquities and Museums 35 (top right), 80, 84, 123, 130 (top), 284, 289, 351, 362 (top), 392, 393; Israel Government Press Office 47, 58 (top and centre), 59, 132 (bottom), 135, 169 (top), 219 (right); Israel Museum 34, 68-9, 104-5, 360, 361 (top right), 423; Israel Press 429; Kress Collection, University of Miami 384 (top); Kunsthistorischesmuseum, Vienna 178-9; Lincoln's Inn, London 108-9; Louvre, Paris P-19, 281 (bottom), 398-9; Lowe Art Gallery, Coral Gables, Florida 384 (top); Mansell Collection 23, 24, 25 (top and centre), 26, 28 (top), 29, 33, 36, 37 (bottom), 41 (top), 43, 44-5, 50 (top and bottom), 51 (top and bottom), 52, 56-7, 57 (right), 66, 73, 74, 76, 82, 92, 94, 95, 101, 102 (top), 111, 114, 128, 129, 144, 147 (right), 148, 150, 157, 171, 175, 176 (top), 182-3, 186-7, 201, 212 (bottom right), 215, 218-9, 226-7, 236, 240, 244, 249 (bottom), 266-7, 268 (right), 270, 271, 276-7, 278 (top), 282, 288, 295, 300, 314, 327 (bottom), 329, 330, 333 (left), 336, 337, 338, 344, 347, 355, 363 (bottom), 365, 378, 379, 380-1, 386, 401, 403, 406, 409, 413, 415, 416, 426, 430-1; Leonard von Matt 328 (top), 368, 371 (right); Metropolitan Museum of Art, New York 237; Middle East Archives 132 (top), 273 (top), 304, 315, 318 (top); Monastery of St John, Patmos 308; Musée des Beaux-Arts, Dijon 395; Museo Civico, Turin 27 (bottom); Museo Sacro Cristiano, Vatican 371 (left); Museum Boymans-van Beuningen, Rotterdam 290; Museum of Fine Arts, Boston 41 (bottom), 60 (top), 81, 253; Museum of the Sailor, Haifa 273 (bottom); National Galleries of Scotland 291, National Gallery, London 64-5, 71, 134 (top), 189 (below), P-21, P-22, P-23, 231, P-28, 357, 376, 405; Ny Carlsberg Glyptothek, Copenhagen 293; Öst. Nationalbibliothek, Vienna 306; Picturepoint 40, 77, 88, 89, 323 (right), 327 (top), 349; Pierpont Morgan Library, New York 162, 335; Pont. Comm. di Arch. Sacra, Vatican 32, 369 (top), 370; Paul Popper 145 (top), 362 (bottom); Zev Radovan 21, 61, 115 (bottom), 120 (bottom), 130, 133 (top and bottom right), 136, 137, 145 (bottom), 160 (bottom right), 170, 192 (top left), 212 (top), 214, 241, 268 (bottom left), 272 (top and bottom), 283 (top), 303, 324, 333 (right), 348, 361 (top), 384 (bottom), 387 (top), 410 (top), 427; Reifenberg Collection, Jerusalem 361 (centre right), 363 (left), 397, 432; Rheinisches Bildarchiv, Cologne 30, 341 (top); Roger-Viollet 402; Royal Institute of British Architects 35 (top left); David Rubinger P-17, 161; John Rylands Library, Manchester 316 (top); Schweiz. Landesmuseum, Zurich 181, 269; Ronald Sheridan 147 (left), 205 (right), 249 (top), 342; Staatliche Museen, Berlin 112, 410 (bottom); Staatsbibliothek, Bamberg 311, Stiftsbibliothek, St Gallen 220; Tate Gallery, London P-24; Teylers Stichting, Haarlem 255; Ufficio Tecnico, Vatican 373, 374; Universitätsbibliothek, Göttingen 233 (bottom); Universitätsbibliothek, Würzburg 67; University of Michigan Museum of Art 232 (bottom), 298-9; Victoria and Albert Museum, London 404; Walker Art Gallery, Liverpool 163 (bottom); Roger Wood 99, 325; Yigael Yadin 341 (bottom), 363 (top right).

Introduction

The scope of this work is comprehensive and includes all the people mentioned by name in the New Testament as well as some who remain unnamed like the centurions at Capernaum and Calvary, together with certain political and religious groups. The articles are necessarily limited and selective in content, but are primarily planned for the general reader, students and others needing concise, accurate and readable information. They are not intended for scholarly research, but are meant to answer questions raised by ordinary reading.

Considerable space has been given to those personalities thought to be essential to the New Testament story. Thus, such characters have been briefly introduced, their biography outlined without commentary and their significance assessed. In the process, some attention has been paid to sources of information and authorship, and, where relevant, to environment and archaeological evidence. Very little knowledge of places and persons has been assumed, and the reader is often reminded of names and dates, the topography and chronology of events.

The names have been compiled from the Revised Standard Version, but include some variants from the King James Version. The R.S.V. New Testament, the work of American scholars first published in 1946, was an authorised revision of the American Standard Version of 1901, itself a revision of the King James version published in 1611.

The derivation of each character's name, its origin from Hebrew, Greek or Latin, is given – where it is known and appears to be of interest. Relevant scripture references are listed at the end of each article and in some cases scripture passages are quoted at length. A table of abbreviations is to be found on page 19.

Repetition has been reduced to a minimum, so have cross-references, in the hope that each entry may stand on its own. No Old Testament names have been included, unless there is a New Testament character of the same name. The selection of groups and types of people, for example scribes and centurions, may appear to be arbitrary, but has tended towards those playing a major role in the life of the central character, Jesus. There is an article on the Essenes, who are not mentioned in the New Testament, since many of their ideas are reflected in the Gospels.

The background of the land

The Holy Land was the bridge between the riverside civilizations of the ancient world, spanning the routes between Egypt, Babylon, Persia, Greece and finally Rome. A buffer state, exposed to, yet detached from, these great civilizations, its history is one of constant political disaster and prophetic reconciliation.

The geography of the country is remarkably simple, consisting of consecutive parallels running north and south. From east to west, the pattern is coastal plain, foothills, spine, mountainous desert, descending to the Rift Valley far below sea-level through which runs the River Jordan. This north-south pattern is broken only by the fertile plain of Esdraelon, running south-east from Carmel to the Jordan. Below Carmel the coastal plain is reduced to a narrow bottleneck, avoided by armies of the ancient world. Instead of circumventing the cape of Carmel and risking ambush, the military and trade routes struck through the Carmel range from the coastal plain of Sharon to Esdraelon by narrow passes of considerable tactical importance.

The nature of the country tended to break up the population into small and closely-packed communities among the tangle of hills. The River Jordan, whose name means 'Descender', rises in the foothills of Mount Hermon and enters the Sea of Galilee at 680 feet below sea-level, before sinking deeper and deeper into the Rift Valley to empty itself into the Dead Sea at 1,300 feet below sea-level. Standing back from the coastal highways, the hill-country of Judea and Samaria, of limestone rock strata, is hard to cultivate and breeds a hardy, God-fearing people, whose livelihood depends largely upon the climate.

As the Land influenced the people, so it did also their writings. The awe and majesty of the scenery, in its ruthless immensity, provoke a sense of the nearness of God.

The Land was thus a well-prepared seed-plot for the sowing of the Word and Message of God. Bethlehem was the traditional city of David, from whose line the coming Messiah was expected. Nazareth, a cosmopolitan township overlooking the trade-routes through Esdraelon, provided a rugged schooling for an itinerant, open-air ministry. Capernaum and the lakeside of Galilee, with a crowded and hot-blooded population in the climate of the Rift Valley, were conducive to the spread of the Gospel, to be carried on the wind of the Spirit throughout the Roman world.

The time of Jesus's birth

'When the time had fully come,' said the Apostle Paul, 'God sent forth his Son, born of a woman, born under the Law . . .' The long process of progressive preparation, through the revelation of God and the reason of Man, culminated in a remarkable sequence of events. During the exile in Babylon, Hebrew prophecy flowered into a rich monotheism and universalism; religion was momentarily emancipated from nationalism; personal religion developed within the synagogue, apart from the Temple. With the return, the spiritual life and worship of the people prospered. The Canon of the Law and the Prophets was compiled and the Scribal interpretation developed.

The world at large was enriched by the universal ideals of Alexander and the philosophy of Aristotle. With the Ptolemaic domination of Greater Syria, Jewish communities fled to Egypt and throughout the eastern Mediterranean, taking their scriptures with them, establishing their synagogues and attracting their Gentile proselytes and God-fearers.

Under the Hellenistic persecution of the Seleucids, Judaism was further refined in the furnace of affliction. The Jews consoled and comforted themselves with apocalyptic hopes of the coming of a Messiah (Deliverer). Jewish philosophers, such as Philo in Alexandria, began to interpret the nature and purpose of their God in terms understandable to the pagan world – as the mind and reason that made sense of all created life.

With the advent of the Augustan age and stable government from Rome, law and order was established on land and sea; robbery and piracy were reduced to a minimum. Travel facilities and communications had never been better. Colloquial Greek was the *lingua franca* of the whole Mediterranean world. A sense of imperial unity and a wise colonial policy enabled a limited freedom in both local government and in matters of religion. East and West were united and Alexander's dream was realized. Into such a world and at such a time, Jesus was born. Nor is it a coincidence that the four years of good government prior to Nero's persecution marked the climax of the ministry of Paul the Apostle.

How the Gospels came to be written

On the day of Pentecost, the first Whitsunday – sometimes called the birthday – of the Christian Church, Peter proclaimed the gospel of Jesus. 'Men of Israel, hear these words: Jesus of Nazareth, a man attested to you by God with mighty works and wonders and signs which God did through him in your midst, as you yourselves know – this Jesus, delivered up according to the definite plan and foreknowledge of God, you crucified and killed by the hands of lawless men. But God raised him up, having loosed the pangs of death, because it was not possible for him to be held by it . . . Let all the house of Israel therefore know assuredly that God has made him both Lord and Christ.' (Acts 2:22-24, 36)

The first followers of Jesus preached 'Christ risen from the dead' and expected his early return to establish his kingdom. At first the apostles stayed in Jerusalem, which remained the headquarters of the Christian Church despite the siege and destruction in the years 69–70, until the end of the 1st century. An advance headquarters was established at Antioch, from which missionary enterprises were conducted throughout the whole Mediterranean world.

As the years passed, the surviving apostles were now scattered far and wide, sometimes under bitter persecution from outside the Christian community, sometimes faced with disunity and false teaching within the local Church congregations. All the original eye-witnesses to the life, death and resurrection of Jesus were growing older and some written record and authoritative account of the facts behind the Christian faith became essential to the sound progress and development of the Church. However much the scattered Christian communities treasured and exchanged their letters from Paul and other missionary apostles, these congregations needed an accurate record of the life and teaching of Jesus on which to base their own teaching and practical living.

Following a great fire in the city of Rome in the year 64, the Christians were blamed by the government and suffered a reign of terror under the Emperor Nero. Among the victims of this persecution were the two Apostles Peter and Paul, who had both been preaching and teaching about Jesus for some thirty years. Almost immediately after their death there began to be circulated 'The Gospel of Jesus Christ', which we now call the 'Gospel according to Mark'. An early Christian bishop linked this Gospel directly with the Apostle Peter. Papias in around the year 130 quoted the Elder as saying: 'Mark was the interpreter of Peter and wrote down accurately, but not in order, all that Peter remembered.' Fifty years later, Irenaeus said that after the death of Peter and Paul Mark wrote his Gospel to record the story while there were still eye-witnesses to the events in the life of Jesus. The result was a vigorous, vivid and dramatic series of episodes in the life of Jesus, whom the reader is encouraged to recognize as the 'Son of God', as well as the Jewish Messiah.

Mark's account, however, recorded little of the teaching of Jesus, of which there was already a separate account in circulation. Probably in answer to a demand for an enlarged edition of 'The Gospel of Jesus Christ', to include both narrative and teaching, two further Gospels were published within the next twenty-five years. Although their authors were very different people – Matthew, a Jew brought up on the Old Testament scriptures, and Luke, probably a Gentile of Greek culture and education – they both made extensive use of Mark's narrative and a contemporary collection of the teaching and sayings of Jesus. This last is sometimes called 'Q', being the first letter of the German *Quelle*, 'source'. The first three Gospels are grouped together as 'Synoptic', for they largely follow the substance, language and order of Mark and can thus be 'viewed together'. Nearly all of Mark's work is to be found in the other two: 90% in Matthew, 50% in Luke, and only 6% in neither. Again, in language Matthew and Luke are often identical with Mark and never agree to differ from him, though each sometimes revises him for the sake of reverence, brevity or accuracy. Both Matthew and Luke seem to have had also their own written sources of information, such as Matthew's Sermon on the Mount and the long parables peculiar to Luke's Gospel. Both seem to have drawn information from their own personal contacts or traditions; thus Luke's accounts of the birth of Jesus reflect the feelings of Mary, whereas those of Matthew describe the experience of Joseph.

The Fourth Gospel did not emerge until the end of the 1st century. It is quite different in style, order and even sometimes in substance. Looking back over almost a century, it aims at an interpretation rather than at a record of events. Recently, however, scholars have recognized an independent historical tradition and a knowledge of Judea in this gospel. John's readers in the sophisticated Greek city of Ephesus were far removed in time and space from the days and home of Jesus. This Gospel was written primarily to explain the place of Jesus, the Jewish Messiah, in God's wider and universal plan of salvation, to provoke belief in and response to his son Jesus as the Way, the Truth and the Life for all mankind.

Despite their differences in detail and presentation, the Gospels constitute a serious record of historical events, vouched for by honest and well-informed witnesses. They support each other in giving a clear portrait of Jesus within a framework of events entirely consistent with the history of his day.

The spreading of the Gospel

The Gospel according to Luke was followed by a second volume, addressed to the same person, in the same literary style, with the same motives and approach as the Gospel. 'Acts of Apostles', as it is correctly translated, is no exhaustive or consecutive history of the early Church, but rather a selection of adventures of certain apostles vividly and accurately recorded. Yet, apart from the Letters, the Book of Revelation and some occasional comments from heathen writers, Acts is the main source of information about the apostolic age. As an adventure book, it is full of people, of plots and intrigues; its hero is Jesus; its chief character is first Peter and then Paul, both working in the power of the Spirit of God. The zeal and enthusiasm of the early leaders of the missionary Church

Christ enthroned in majesty, with the symbols of the four evangelists.
Centre portal of the west front of Chartres Cathedral.

come alive in the condensed yet vivid narrative of the personal travelling companion of
the Apostle Paul. It is Paul's many friends and acquaintances who provide the greater part
of the entries in this book.

It was some six years after the crucifixion of Jesus that Paul experienced his sudden and
unique encounter with the risen Jesus and his commission as the apostle to the Gentiles.
In the momentous thirty years that followed, Paul carried the good news throughout the
Mediterranean world, establishing in many cities and towns small Christian communities
which survived, in spite of persecution and apparent isolation. It is the problems and controversies, the progress and practice of these early Christian congregations that are revealed
in Paul's remarkable correspondence which occupies so great a part of the New Testament.

Whether theological treatises or direct communications dealing with particular persons
in specific and concrete situations, the epistles of Paul bear the stamp of apostolic authority.
They are real letters to real people, often personally known to the writer, and they reveal
his own very real personality and genius for friendship. Composed and dictated in long-
hand, laboriously written between constant interruptions to his train of thought, compressed
no doubt by a shortage of time and papyrus, it is not surprising that the arguments are
sometimes hard to follow.

14

Besides all this, the vast distances travelled, his constant 'thorn in the flesh', the continual physical and mental strain, not least the severe bodily violence he suffered, are inevitably reflected in his correspondence. Paul's theology is deeply rooted in the crucible of his own conversion, his continuing experience of suffering, and in the life of the Christian community.

Interpretation of Jesus's message

At first glance the New Testament may appear almost equally divided into the historical account of Jesus and the interpretation of his message, between past events and present faith. On closer inspection, however, the Gospels are seen to include a great deal of interpretation and of faith. Each account, written well after the events of the crucifixion, the resurrection and the coming of the Spirit, inevitably interprets the good news for the benefit of its particular readers. Thus the Palestinian Jews, Mark and Matthew, provoke their readers to a recognition of the central character as the Messiah, who is also the Son of God. Luke, possibly a doctor-slave and Gentile, emphasizes the universality of the rule of the Messiah, whose love and forgiveness embrace all races and all levels of society. The Fourth Gospel, written at the close of the apostolic age, when the primitive hopes and momentum of the good news were somewhat spent, when Christianity could no longer be confined within Judaistic language and thought, is even more full of interpretation and of faith than the others. In John's presentation, as in that of Paul, it is not so much who Jesus *was* that matters, but rather what he has *become* to those who have experienced his spiritual presence within the believing community. Past events are overshadowed by present experience and future hopes.

Under the guise of historical narrative, John records a series of seven signs each demonstrating the difference that Jesus makes in the lives of his followers, as their Lord, their healer, their strength, their food, their guide, their light and their life. The frequent brief episodes and comments within the Synoptic Gospels are replaced by a few selected scenes with explanatory conversations or speeches; the many short parables give way to carefully worked out allegories and illustrations. Those of the 'Good Shepherd' and the 'True Vine' are explored at considerable length and depth. John's Gospel seems to record not just the impressions of eye-witnesses among the crowd, but rather the insight and the hindsight into these far-off events of the more mature faith of the apostles.

The writer expressed himself in terms and language understood by both the Jews and Greeks of his day, to claim that the very 'Word', 'Thought' or 'Mind' of God had become 'enfleshed' in the person of Jesus. As the Apostle Paul had already stated: 'In him the whole fulness of deity dwells bodily', so John proclaimed: 'The Word became flesh and dwelt among us, full of grace and truth; we have beheld his glory, glory as of the only Son from the Father.' Thus God communicated himself to mankind, revealing his glory in a supreme act of self-giving love, in Jesus. Both Paul and John perceived that it was God's plan, in this very act of revealing his love, to bring into being a new humanity – a new community – bound by a new commandment to love one another and empowered to do so by their union with himself.

The formation of the New Testament

The compilation of each Gospel from the oral tradition and written material from a variety of sources had been a lengthy and complicated process; so was the formation of the canon (literally 'measure') of the New Testament. This process took place in three stages: the writing (in a space of approximately sixty years) and preservation, the collection of such writings as were of apostolic authority by the catholic Church, and finally their recognition or rejection.

The primitive Christian Church was more concerned with preaching the good news than with recording it in writing. The kernel of the good news was therefore the story of the passion of Jesus 'crucified and risen from the dead', told as history and preached as gospel. To this were added accounts of his ministry, collections of his sayings, and practical guidance in Christian living.

Some compendium of instruction was necessitated by the growth in the number of converts, particularly Gentiles. Thus Paul and Barnabas would have set out on their missionary travels armed with the Old Testament, an account of the passion of Jesus, an outline of his ministry, and perhaps a collection of his sayings and parables.

The first book of the New Testament to be written may have been the letter (or sermon) of James. All Paul's letters had been written, however, before the first Gospel (of Mark) was in circulation, but they were not all collected into one group until considerably later. In the last half of the 1st century sections of Paul's correspondence found their way to libraries at the main centres of the Christian Church in Jerusalem, Antioch, Ephesus and Rome. All four Gospels were used in Rome by the early Christian apologist and martyr, Justin, in about the year 150: Irenaeus, bishop of Lyons, in 180 accepted the four Gospels without question.

The selection and recognition by the catholic Church of a canon of authorized and apostolic writings were precipitated by the independent selections of certain individuals and heretical sects wishing to promote their own personal interpretations of the Christian faith. During the 2nd century, most churches had come to acknowledge a canon which included the present 4 Gospels, Acts, 13 Letters of Paul, 1 Peter and 1 John, but they still disputed the inclusion of Hebrews, James, 2 Peter, 2 and 3 John, Jude and Revelation. The final stage of sifting, accepting and rejecting lasted well into the 4th century. Eusebius, bishop of Caesarea and 'Father of Church History', classified the Christian writings into three groups: recognized, disputed and spurious. It was not until 367 that the 27 books now contained in the New Testament were finally listed by Athanasius, bishop of Alexandria, as exclusively canonical. Formal sanction was accorded this list by the synod of Carthage in the year 397.

The original manuscripts have long disappeared, but there are nearly 5,000 ancient Greek manuscripts of all or parts of the New Testament. Of these the oldest, written on papyrus or parchment, number more than 300 and date from the 2nd to the 8th centuries.

Codex Sinaiticus, the celebrated 4th-century manuscript of the Greek Bible,
found in 1859 at the Monastery of St Catherine, near Mount Sinai.

List of abbreviations

The following abbreviations have been used for the books of the New Testament:

Matt.	Matthew	Eph.	Ephesians	Heb.	Hebrews
Rom.	Romans	Col.	Colossians	Jas.	James
Cor.	Corinthians	Thess.	Thessalonians	Pet.	Peter
Gal.	Galatians	Tim.	Timothy	Rev.	Revelation
Phil.	Philippians	Philem.	Philemon		

The following abbreviations have been used for the derivations of the names:

Aram.	Aramaic	Heb.	Hebrew
Gk.	Greek	Lat.	Latin

A

ABADDON (Heb. 'ruin', 'perdition', 'destruction') In the Old Testament books of Job and Proverbs, Abaddon has the general sense of death and destruction or even of Sheol, the place of the dead. The word occurs only once in the New Testament, in the vision of John the Divine on Patmos. John sees the fifth angel blow his trumpet and the bottomless pit open up to emit billowing clouds of black smoke. Within the smoke are seething swarms of locusts, like squadrons of war-horses. Against such a pest the world of men is defenceless. 'They have as king over them the angel of the bottomless pit; his name in Hebrew is Abaddon, and in Greek he is called Apollyon.' (Rev. 9:11)

Abaddon may be interpreted within the context of this vision as the master-mind of evil, directing the hosts of temptation to their targets in the world of mankind, who without divine grace fall an easy prey. [Rev. 9:11]

ACHAICUS (Gk. 'native of Achaia') A Corinthian Christian of the household of Stephanas, he was named after Achaia, the province of which Corinth was the capital.

Writing from Ephesus in about the year 55, during his Third Journey, to the Church in Corinth which he had founded some four years before, Paul affectionately and courteously closes his letter: 'I rejoice at the coming of Stephanas and Fortunatus and Achaicus, because they have made up for your absence; for they refreshed my spirit as well as yours. Give recognition to such men.' (1 Cor. 16:17)

Apparently the household of Stephanas included slaves and employees, such as Fortunatus and Achaicus. This was the first household to have been converted by Paul – and the only household to have been baptized by Paul – in Corinth, on his Second Journey in around the year 51. These three men had travelled to Ephesus on business, possibly carrying a letter to Paul from Corinth, and were probably present with Paul as he completed the dictation of his answering letter. In this, he commends to the loyalty of the Corinthians all such people who have dedicated themselves to serve the Christian community. [1 Cor. 16:17]

AENEAS (Gk. 'praise') A paralytic, bedridden for eight years, who was healed by the Apostle Peter at Lydda. 'Peter said to him, "Aeneas, Jesus Christ heals you; rise and make your bed."' Luke, the recorder of this incident in Acts, adds, 'And immediately he rose. And all the residents of Lydda and Sharon saw him, and they turned to the Lord.' [Acts 9:33-35]

AGABUS (Gk. from the Heb. 'to love') One of the prophets, acknowledged within the primitive Christian Church to rank next to the apostles, Agabus is twice recorded as exercising a prophetic ministry in the presence of Paul.

On the first occasion, Agabus and others had come down from Jerusalem to Antioch. Agabus foretold a severe famine, which actually occurred in the reign of the Emperor Claudius. In fact there were acute shortages of food in different parts of the Roman Empire over the period of years 41–54. Josephus, the Jewish historian, relates that there was a famine in Jerusalem during the procuratorship of Tiberias Alexander and that the poor were relieved by the generosity of Queen Helena of Adiabene between the years 46 and 48.

below Monumental portico of the necropolis of Queen Helena of Adiabene who emigrated from Mesopotamia to Jerusalem *c.* AD 45, and embraced Judaism.

left Angel and devil, from the 14th-century *Tapisserie de l'Apocalypse*, illustrating scenes from the Revelation of John the Divine.

On another occasion Agabus came down from Judea to Caesarea, to meet Paul in the house of Philip the deacon. This would have been in about the year 58, when Paul had returned by sea from Corinth to make his last visit to Jerusalem. Agabus acted in the same symbolic manner as the Old Testament prophets, binding his own hands and feet as a token that Paul would suffer a similar fate in Jerusalem – which indeed he did. [Acts 11:28; 21:10]

AGRIPPA *see* HEROD **5.** *and* **6.**

ALEXANDER (Gk. 'defender of men')
1. **Son of Simon of Cyrene**
2. **Relative of Annas, the high priest**
3. **Jewish spokesman at Ephesus**
4. **Convert turned apostate**
5. **Coppersmith from Asia**

1. One of the sons of Simon of Cyrene, 'the father of Alexander and Rufus', who was compelled by the Roman execution squad to carry the cross-piece for Jesus on his way to Calvary. Only Mark mentions the sons by name, perhaps because they had become Christians and were known to his readers. Mark's Gospel is said to have been written in Rome during the year 64-5. Paul, in the final chapter of his letter to the Christians in Rome, includes a greeting to 'Rufus, eminent in the Lord, also his mother and mine'. Whether this greeting and others were in fact addressed to Rome or to Ephesus, there cannot be any certain identification of this family with that of Simon of Cyrene. The respect of Paul for the mother of Alexander and Rufus, coupled with Mark's mention of them by name, would seem, however, to strengthen the tradition that Simon of Cyrene and his family were converted to Christianity. [Mark 15:21]

2. A relative of Annas, the high priest, in Jerusalem. This Alexander is only mentioned once among the members of high-priestly families, within the Sanhedrin. The Supreme Council was, on this occasion, convened in emergency to deal with the situation caused by the powerful preaching of the apostles in Jerusalem. Peter and others were arrested and detained overnight, possibly in the guardroom at the high priest's palace where Jesus himself had been imprisoned overnight. The modern church of 'St Peter in Gallicantu' probably covers the site of this house of Caiaphas and, on a series of levels cut into the rock of the cliff face, enshrines the courtroom of the Council, the guardroom complete with the whipping-block and staples for prisoners' chains, and a bottle-necked condemned cell.

This Alexander is reported to have met with the rulers, elders and scribes together with Caiaphas, John, and other Sadducees. Their decision was to warn the apostles and forbid them to preach in the name of Jesus, but for fear of the people they dared not punish them. [Acts 4:6]

3. A spokesman of the Jewish community in Ephesus. At the height of the confusion in the silversmiths' riot at Ephesus incited by Demetrius (*see* DEMETRIUS), the Jews tried to put forward Alexander as their spokesman, but he was howled down by the mob. Alexander's intention was to defend the two travelling-companions of the Apostle Paul, Gaius and Aristarchus, who had been dragged into the great theatre by members of the offended trade-guilds. When the excited crowd saw that the speaker was a Jew, rather than one of themselves, they began to chant in chorus 'Great is Diana of the Ephesians'. Alexander had seemingly attached himself to Paul but had then joined his fellow-countrymen in opposing Paul. (*see* ALEXANDER **4.** *and* **5.**) Luke adds that the majority of the crowd had no idea what it was all about and that after two hours of tumult the town clerk managed to obtain a hearing, conciliated his audience, and dispersed the disorderly meeting. [Acts 19:33]

4. A convert of Paul's, turned apostate. This Alexander may well have been the man involved in the silversmiths' riot (*see* ALEXANDER **3.**). He was a heretical teacher within the Christian community, probably at Ephesus or Troas, on the coast of Asia Minor, whom Paul found it necessary to excommunicate, as his teaching represented a real threat to the faith and loyalty of the local congregation. As Paul puts it in his first letter to Timothy, 'By rejecting conscience, certain persons have made shipwreck of their faith, among them Hymenaeus and Alexander, whom I have delivered to Satan that they may learn not to blaspheme.' (1 Tim. 1:19-20) In his last letter to Timothy, Paul is even more insistent in his warnings against false teachers. Timothy needs to be a 'sound workman', 'handling the word rightly', avoiding 'what is ignoble', and exercising a strict supervision of his congregation. [1 Tim. 1:20]

5. A coppersmith, probably from Troas or Ephesus, bitterly opposed to Paul. This Alexander may possibly have been the same as the heretical teacher, and even the same man who was involved in the silversmiths' riot at Ephesus. (*see* ALEXANDER **3.** *and* **4.**) If so, then the progressive opposition and hostility of this man to the work and person of the Apostle Paul may have culminated in the final arrest of Paul and the ending of his missionary activity. Certainly the final paragraph of Paul's last letter to Timothy implies that he had been arrested at Troas, for Timothy was asked to bring his cloak and scrolls left behind there. The letter could also imply that his arrest was due to the treachery of a certain Alexander. 'Alexander the coppersmith did me great harm; the Lord will requite him for his deeds. Beware of him yourself, for he strongly opposed our message. At my first defence no one took my part; all deserted me. May it not be charged against them!' [2 Tim. 4:14-16]

There would seem to be a case for identifying the last three Alexanders. The first Alexander was concerned in the silversmiths' riot in the year 57, though not specified as himself a craftsman. The last Alexander was described by Paul as a 'smith', using the general Greek word for a worker in copper or brass. The first Alexander was probably a renegade Christian convert of Paul's, yet put forward by the Jews as prepared to give evidence which was more likely to support their case than that of his former teacher. The second Alexander with his plausible but misleading teachings of the Christian faith was active, probably, during Timothy's ministry at Ephesus. Paul certainly felt the need to warn Timothy against this man and wrote to this effect from his first captivity in Rome, during the years 61–2. Three years or so later, after Paul's acquittal by the imperial tribunal and following the resumption of his missionary activities, his re-arrest and final deportation back to Rome, Paul again wrote to Timothy of a third Alexander. This man's bitter hostility and malicious gossip seem to have got Paul into trouble with the civic author-

The Pharos at Alexandria, one of the seven wonders of the ancient world.

ities; moreover he represented a potential menace to the future progress of the Christian Church. The character of this Alexander appears to have been all too consistent with that of the other two references. It would seem that in fact Paul was speaking from hard and bitter experience of a man whom he had known for a decade, and that all three Alexanders were one and the same man.

ALEXANDRIANS Traditionally before the dispersion of the Jews there were said to have been 480 synagogues in Jerusalem. These were the meeting-places for prayer and discussion – particularly about the Law – of many different peoples of Jewish faith. Alexandrian Jews had emigrated to Jerusalem to escape persecution. At the time of Stephen's martyrdom, it was the natives of Alexandria and Cyrene in Africa, and of the Roman provinces of Asia and Cilicia (the home of Saul the Persecutor who was to become Paul the Apostle), who took the initiative in Stephen's arrest. It was the members of these synagogues who took most offence at Stephen's teaching, but could not successfully dispute with his wisdom and enthusiasm.

In consequence, they instigated the crowd to accuse him of blasphemy against Moses and God, for the Jew the ultimate wickedness. The mob dragged Stephen off to the Council and accused him of speaking both against the Temple, as the official centre of worship, and against the Law. Members of the synagogue of the Alexandrians were among the foremost in securing his condemnation and stoning. [Acts 6:9]

ALPHAEUS 1. Alphaeus, father of Levi the tax-collector (better known as the Apostle Matthew). *see* MATTHEW, *and* ALPHAEUS **2.** [Mark 2:14]

2. Alphaeus, father of James the Younger. In the three Synoptic Gospels and in the Acts, the name of this Alphaeus is linked with that of James the Younger, but is not otherwise mentioned. If he was the same person as Alphaeus, father of Levi the tax-collector, Matthew and James the Younger would have been brothers.

The name 'Alphaeus' is derived from the same Aramaic word as the name 'Clopas' (John 19:25); it is possible that these two may have been one and the same person. In this case, 'Mary the wife of Clopas', who watched by the cross of Jesus, would have been the mother of James the Younger, if not also of Matthew.

The 2nd-century historian Hegesippus supposed that Clopas was the brother of Joseph the carpenter. If this were correct, together with the identification of Alphaeus with Clopas, then Alphaeus would have been uncle to Jesus. [Matt. 10:3; Mark 3:18; Luke 6:15; Acts 1:13]

AMPLIAS see AMPLIATUS

AMPLIATUS One of the Christians greeted warmly by Paul as 'my beloved in the Lord', at the close of his letter to the Christian congregation in Rome. The Aurelii family at Rome used this common surname and

Ceiling of vault in the Catacomb
of Domitilla, Rome. The cemetery
dates from the 1st century.

the Christian members of that family are buried in the
1st-century cemetery of Domitilla, on the Via Ardeatina.
Here, one tomb in an early style bears the single word
'Ampliati' in lettering of the 1st or 2nd century. The
identification is uncertain, but possible, as the position
and character of this tomb indicate a person held in
considerable respect. [Rom. 16:8]

ANANIAS (Gk. from the Heb. 'Jehovah has been
gracious')

1. False Christian at Jerusalem
2. Christian disciple at Damascus
3. High priest in Jerusalem

1. False Christian at Jerusalem. The hypocrite who sold
property, but appropriated some of the purchase-
money with the connivance of his wife Sapphira, and
only brought part of its value to give to the apostles
for the Church. The Apostle Peter rebuked him sharply.
'Ananias, why has Satan filled your heart to lie to
the Holy Spirit and to keep back part of the proceeds of
the land? While it remained unsold, did it not remain
your own? And after it was sold, was it not at your
disposal? How is it that you have contrived this deed in
your heart? You have not lied to men but to God.'
(Acts 5:3, 4) This terrible indictment caused his immediate death. Three hours later, his wife Sapphira

arrived and, after similar cross-examination and for the
same lie, was instantly punished by death. [Acts 5:1-5]
2. The Christian disciple in Damascus who welcomed
the baptized Saul. In a vision 'the Lord said to him,
"Rise and go to the street called Straight, and inquire in
the house of Judas for a man of Tarsus named Saul; for
behold, he is praying, and he has seen a man named
Ananias come in and lay his hands on him so that he
might regain his sight." But Ananias answered, "Lord,
I have heard from many about this man, how much evil
he has done to thy saints at Jerusalem; and here he has
authority from the chief priests to bind all who call upon
thy name." But the Lord said to him, "Go, for he is a
chosen instrument of mine to carry my name before the
Gentiles and kings and the sons of Israel; for I will show
him how much he must suffer for the sake of my name."'
(Acts 9:11-16) Then Ananias went to the house in
Straight Street 'and, laying his hands on him, he said,
"Brother Saul, the Lord Jesus who appeared to you on
the road by which you came, has sent me that you may
regain your sight and be filled with the Holy Spirit."
And immediately something like scales fell from his eyes
and he regained his sight. Then he rose and was baptized,
and took food and was strengthened.' (Acts 9:17-19)
That was in about the year 36.

Later, at his trial in Jerusalem in about the year 58,
Paul described before the Council his conversion and
baptism at Damascus. He emphasized the character of
Ananias, 'a devout man according to the Law, well
spoken of by all the Jews who lived there'. Ananias had
said, 'The God of our Fathers appointed you to know
his will, to see the Just One and to hear a voice from his
mouth; for you will be a witness for him to all men of
what you have seen and heard. And now why do you
wait? Rise and be baptized, and wash away your sins,
calling on his name.' (Acts 22:12-16) Paul wished to
show that those Jews who strictly kept the Law approved of him at the time of his conversion, and he spoke
with affection of Ananias. [Acts 9:10-17; 22:12-16]
3. The high priest in Jerusalem and chairman of the
Council at Paul's trial. At the order of the Roman
tribune, the Council met to draw up the charges against
Paul. When Paul began to defend himself, the high
priest, Ananias, commanded those who stood by to
strike him on the mouth. This drew from Paul a blistering rebuke, '"God shall strike you, you whitewashed
wall! Are you sitting to judge me according to the law,
and yet contrary to the law you order me to be struck?"
Those who stood by said, "Would you revile God's high
priest?" And Paul said, "I did not know, brethren, that
he was the high priest; for it is written, 'You shall not
speak evil of a ruler of your people'."' (Acts 23:3-5)

Five days later, the Roman governor, Felix, summoned Ananias and the elders to Caesarea. They
brought a barrister called Tertullus to act as prosecutor

above The Death of Ananias: tapestry based on a design of Raphael (1483-1520).

top left Detail from the Brescia Casket, ivory, *c.* 370, showing the 'young man' carrying out the dying Ananias. Junior members of the Church were given the manual tasks.

bottom left A house of Ananias, near Straight Street, is shown within the south-eastern Roman gate of the modern city of Damascus.

in presenting the charges against Paul. But all Felix could do was to confine Paul for the next two years, until he was succeeded by the new governor, Festus.

Ananias was murdered by his fellow-countrymen in Jerusalem, during the siege of the city by Titus in the years 69-70, in revenge for Ananias's pro-Roman tendencies. [Acts 22:12; 23:2; 24:1]

ANDREW (Gk. 'manly') One of the first disciples of Jesus and the brother of Simon Peter, Andrew appears in all the lists of the apostles. All three Synoptic Gospels – Matthew, Mark, and Luke – and the first chapter of the Acts describe the call of Simon Peter and Andrew, though Luke does not mention Andrew in his account of the event by name, but adds the story of the miraculous draught of fish and Peter's penitence. 'And passing along by the Sea of Galilee, he saw Simon and Andrew the brother of Simon casting a net in the sea; for they were fishermen. And Jesus said to them, "Follow me and I will make you become fishers of men." And immediately they left their nets and followed him.' (Mark 1:16-18)

After the exorcism of an unclean spirit in the synagogue at Capernaum, all three Gospels again record that Jesus entered the home of Peter. Mark adds, 'And immediately he left the synagogue, and entered the house of Simon and Andrew', implying that the house was directly outside the synagogue and that it was the home of both the brothers as well as of Peter's mother-in-law. An octagonal Byzantine shrine of

The calling of Peter and Andrew, from the early 6th-century mosaic
in the Church of S. Apollinare Nuovo, Ravenna.

'Peter's house' has long been shown opposite the entrance of the site of the synagogue at Capernaum. Recently, however, the Byzantine pavement has been lifted to permit the excavation of 1st-century houses beneath, thus confirming the occupation of the site in the life-time of Jesus.

Andrew was present on the Mount of Olives with the inner circle of Jesus's disciples, Peter, James, and John, when Jesus foretold the destruction of the Temple. The four disciples questioned him privately, 'Tell us, when will this be, and what will be the sign when these things are all to be accomplished?' (Mark 13:4) Mark uses their question to introduce the long discourse that follows in his Gospel and which is repeated in both Matthew and Luke.

There is no further reference to Andrew in the first three Gospels, apart from the list of apostles, where he is linked with Philip, as he is also in the list of apostles in the Upper Room before Pentecost.

Andrew and John the Baptist
The Fourth Gospel is far more specific about Andrew

and his particular function within the group of disciples. It seems that Andrew and another disciple, possibly Philip, were disciples of John the Baptist during his evangelistic mission by the River Jordan. It was thanks to the words of John the Baptist that his disciples first took notice of Jesus: 'John was standing with two of his disciples; and he looked at Jesus as he walked, and said, "Behold, the Lamb of God!" The two disciples heard him say this, and they followed Jesus. Jesus turned, and saw them following, and said to them, "What do you seek?" And they said to him, "Rabbi" (which means Teacher), "where are you staying?" He said to them, "Come and see." They came and saw where he was staying; and they stayed with him that day.' (John 1:35-9)

Early next morning Andrew met his brother Simon Peter and declared, 'We have found the Messiah', and introduced Simon Peter to Jesus. Jesus looked hard at Peter and said, '"So you are Simon the son of John? You shall be called Cephas" (which means Peter).' The writer goes on to speak of Philip, Simon

Peter, and Andrew as being natives of the fishing town Bethsaida.

The next reference to Andrew in the Fourth Gospel is in the story of the feeding of the five thousand. His friend Philip, possibly the caterer of the party, has just commented on the fact that two hundred denarii would hardly buy enough bread to give such a crowd a mere mouthful apiece. At this point in the dilemma, Andrew produces a little boy with his picnic meal of five barley loaves and two small fishes, saying, 'But what are they among so many?' Nevertheless, he introduces the boy to Jesus, who takes what the boy has to offer, says grace, and divides it for distribution by the disciples. And all are fed.

The last appearance of Andrew is before the Passover festival in Jerusalem, after the triumphal entry on the first Palm Sunday. Some Greeks came up to Philip with the request, 'Sir, we wish to see Jesus.' Philip promptly told his friend Andrew, and together they told Jesus. Andrew once again seems to have been the willing witness and missionary, introducing first his own brother, Peter, then the boy with the loaves and the fishes, and finally a Gentile delegation to Jesus.

St Andrew's Cross

A 3rd-century apocryphal *Acts of St Andrew* describes his ministry, persecution, imprisonment, and execution

The crucifixion of Andrew: miniature from the *Milan Book of Hours*, 15th century.

'Andrew the apostle', from the *Golden Legend* of William Caxton, 1493.

at Patrae, on the north-west coast of Achaia, in the year 60. He was said to have hung alive on the cross for two days, preaching to and encouraging his watchers. The 4th-century bishop of Caesarea and 'Father of Church History', Eusebius, relates that Andrew's ministry was among the backward and ruthless barbarians of Scythia – now the southern steppes of Russia and the Ukraine.

The *Muratorian Fragment*, the earliest list of New Testament writings, dating from the end of the 2nd century, connects Andrew vaguely with the writing of the Fourth Gospel.

Since about 750, Andrew has been the patron saint of Scotland, and his festival has always been kept in the Anglican Church as a time of prayer for missionaries and the mission of the Church. It was not until the 14th century that the tradition of his crucifixion on the 'X'-shaped cross appeared, presumably because the 'X' was the Greek 'Ch', the first letter of 'Christos', meaning 'Messiah'. [Matt. 10:2; Mark 1:14-18, 29; 3:18; 13:3; Luke 6:14; John 1:40-44; 6:8-12; 12:20-22; Acts 1:13]

ANDRONICUS (Gk. 'man of victory') One of the Christians greeted by Paul at the end of his letter to the Christian Church in Rome, Andronicus is linked with Junias. Paul refers to them as his 'kinsmen', probably meaning that at least they were fellow-Jews, if not blood-relatives. Paul also calls them his 'fellow-prisoners', though during which of his imprisonments is uncertain.

Detail of angel from a scene of
the crucifixion: fresco by Giotto in
the Arena Chapel, Padua, *c.* 1306.

Gethsemane. Angels rolled away the stone from the tomb and announced his resurrection. Angels encouraged his apostles after his ascension. Angels supported his followers. An angel led Peter out of prison. An angel stood by Paul throughout his shipwreck off the island of Malta. In the Revelation of John the Divine, the worship of the angels in heaven is the prototype of the worship of the Church. From St Augustine of Hippo to St Francis of Assisi and to Joan of Arc, the more simple and humble-minded Christians have felt that they enjoyed the guidance, comfort and protection of angels.

Catholic Christianity today teaches their existence, their pure spirituality and their creation before that of mankind – while the Protestants tend to disregard rather than define their place in the order of creation. The Eastern Churches are on the whole far more aware of the presence of the angels, for whom Monday is a weekly Orthodox day of commemoration. The Book of Common Prayer collect for Michaelmas well sums up Christian belief thus: 'God who hast ordained and constituted the services of Angels and men in a wonder-

The dead Christ supported by two angels:
17th-century ivory.

Paul goes on: 'They are men of note among the apostles, and they were in Christ before me.' This immediately places their conversion within five years of the crucifixion of Jesus and connects them with the Church in Jerusalem, rather than at Antioch. In fact they may well have been associated with the Stephen group of Hellenized Jews who dispersed to found branches of the Church in Antioch, Cyprus, and elsewhere in the eastern Mediterranean. It is just possible that Junias should be read as 'Junia', in the feminine, which would then suggest the wife of Andronicus and a woman apostle. [Rom. 16:7]

ANGEL (Gk. 'messenger') For centuries before Jesus, people felt protected, guided and advised by the angels of God – and not just Jewish people, but those of many races and cultures, whether from primitive superstition, oriental imagination, or from divine inspiration. The New Testament never questions the existence of angels, but simply states the fact. Jesus often spoke of them in the terms of his day and age. He told us that they rejoice over the penitent, they bear up souls to paradise, that the guardian angels of little children always see the Father's face, that the angels neither marry nor are given in marriage.

The angels, moreover, were closely linked with the crises of his own life. They announced the birth of his cousin John the Baptist to the old priest Zechariah and his own birth to Mary at Nazareth. Angels sang at his birth, in the fields of Bethlehem. Angels ministered to him during his temptation in the wilderness. Angels strengthened him during his agony in the Garden of

The Presentation in the Temple, by Taddeo Gaddi (d. 1366). Note the sage Anna on the left, the priest Simeon holding the child, and Joseph with the doves in his hand.

ful order; mercifully grant that, as thy holy angels always do thee service in heaven, so, by thy appointment, they may succour and defend us on earth.' *see* GABRIEL *and* MICHAEL [Matt. 1:20; 2:13, 19; 4:6, 11; 13:39; 16:27; 18:10; 25:41; 28:2, 5; Mark 1:13; 8:38; 13:27; 16:5; Luke 1:11, 18, 19, 26, 34; 2:9, 10, 13, 15; 22:43; 24:23; John 1:51; Acts 1:10; 5:19; 6:15; 8:26; 10:30; 27:23, 24; Rom. 8:38; 1 Cor. 6:3; 13:1; 2 Cor. 12:7;

Gal. 4:14; Eph. 3:10; Col. 1:16; 2:15; 2 Thess. 1:7; Heb. 1:4-14; 2:1-16; 13:2; 1 Pet. 1:12; 3:22; 2 Pet. 2:4; Jude 6; Rev. 2:1, 12, 18; 3:1, 7, 14; 5:2, 11; 22:6]

ANNA (Gk. from the Heb. 'grace') An elderly prophetess – in the tradition of Moses's sister Miriam (Exod. 15:20), Deborah (Judg. 4:4), and Huldah (2 Kgs. 22:14), who served in the Temple at Jerusalem, as did the aged priest Simeon, when the child Jesus was presented in the Temple by Joseph and Mary. Luke says that after only seven years of marriage she had been widowed, since when she had hardly left the Temple area, spending her time by day and night in fasting and prayer. 'And coming up at that very hour she gave thanks to God, and spoke of him to all who were looking for the redemption of Jerusalem.' (Luke 2:38) It would seem that Anna thanked God for living to see the baby Jesus, whom she openly pronounced to be the fulfilment of God's Messianic promises. [Luke 2:36-38]

ANNAS (Gk. from the Heb. 'gracious', 'merciful') This Jewish high priest was appointed at the age of 36, in the year 6, and nine years later was deposed by the Roman procurator of Judea, Valerius Gratus. Annas was succeeded by his son-in-law Caiaphas, a member of the priestly aristocracy, the wealthy class resident traditionally in the upper city of Jerusalem. The house of Annas to which Jesus was first taken after his arrest (according to the Fourth Gospel) had a spacious courtyard, a portress on the gate, and other servants. The traditional site of this building is now that of an Armenian church of the 15th century on the Western Hill outside the wall.

The hierarchy tended to fill all the chief positions from their own families as a matter of course. The ruling house of Annas held perhaps all the chief-priestly positions within its control, besides operating a flourishing trade in sacrificial victims within the court of the Gentiles, in the Temple. No less than eight members of this family held the supreme office of high priest: Annas himself, five sons, Caiaphas his son-in-law, and his grandson Matthias, from the year 65. Such a family virtually established the political as well as religious leadership of the nation.

Luke dates the beginning of the ministry of John the Baptist as 'within the high priesthood of Annas and Caiaphas'. John describes the arrest and escort of Jesus to Annas. It was here, according to the Fourth Gospel, that young John Bar-Zebedee (*see* ZEBEDEE) obtained entrance for Peter into the courtyard, where he thrice denied Jesus. There, 'the high priest then questioned Jesus about his disciples and his teaching. Jesus answered him, "I have spoken openly to the world: I have always taught in synagogues and in the Temple, where all Jews come together; I have said nothing secretly. Why do you ask me? Ask those who have heard me, what I said to them; they know what I said." When he had said this, one of the officers standing by struck Jesus with his hand, saying, "Is that how you answer the high priest?" Jesus answered him, "If I have spoken wrongly, bear witness to the wrong; but if I have spoken rightly, why do you strike me?" Annas then sent him bound to Caiaphas the high priest.' (John 18:19-24) As retired high priest, Annas would retain considerable prestige and influence.

German 18th-century engraving after the description of Josephus, of the garments worn by the high priest.

Luke again mentions Annas, first on account of his age and influence, in a list of 'rulers' in Jerusalem for a meeting of the Sanhedrin. This supreme court was convened to try the Apostles Peter and John for their healing of the lame man at the Beautiful Gate of the Temple. The court warned and acquitted the apostles without punishment. No further mention is made of Annas in the New Testament, though it was openly rumoured in his day that, as a wealthy man, he had lent money to the Romans and was so able to blackmail them into doing as he wished. Certainly he and his family were deep in a highly successful political intrigue and were able to claim the privileges and immunity of priesthood.

Jesus had few contacts with the aristocratic Sadducees, as he moved rather among the common people, but no doubt the Sadducees watched the development of his movement with increasing dislike and restlessness. [Luke 3:2; John 18:13-24; Acts 4:5-6]

ANTICHRIST (Gk. 'against' or 'instead of Christ') One who assumes the place and office of the Messiah, but is directly opposed to him, the man of sin epitomizing all that is impious and abominable.

Christian belief about the 'Last Things' or the 'End' inherited much from Judaism. Jewish apocalyptic thought posed a programme of events to come: the world was under the limited and temporary sway of evil powers, but at the 'End', God would establish his rule or kingdom and destroy the control or kingdom of the 'adversary'. It was an ancient belief, however, that this final victory would be preceded by the final desperate stand of the powers of evil. For this, one supreme adversary – either a man of diabolical power and wickedness, or a supernatural being from another world – would appear as a sort of Antichrist. In Mark's Gospel, the prediction of the end of the world put into the mouth of Jesus (Chapter 13) refers to 'desolating sacrilege' which will defile the Temple. Paul foretells 'the coming of the lawless one' (2 Thess. 2:9) who will set himself up in the Temple and claim to be God. The coming of the Antichrist was to herald the 'End' and at the second coming of the Messiah the Antichrist would be finally defeated.

John the Divine in his Book of Revelation sees the Antichrist as the 'Beast', the power of Rome, which desecrated and destroyed the Temple in the year 70. The author of the letters of John, most probably another John, tends to rationalize the ancient mythology of the 'Last Things' by thinking of Antichrist as not one but many opponents and false teachers. 'Children, it is the last hour; and as you have heard that antichrist is coming, so now many antichrists have come; therefore we know that it is the last hour. They went out from us, but they were not of us; for if they had been of us, they would have continued with us; but they went out, that it might be plain that they all are not of us. . . . Who is the liar but he who denies that Jesus is the Christ? This is the antichrist, he who denies the Father and the Son.' (1 John 2:18, 19, 22) 'For many deceivers have gone into the world, men who will not acknowledge the coming of Jesus Christ in the flesh; such a one is the deceiver and the antichrist.' (2 John 7) [1 John 2:18, 19, 22; 2 John 7]

ANTIPAS 1. An early martyr at Pergamum, the northernmost of the seven Christian parishes on the mainland of Asia Minor, encircling Ephesus.

Paul could have passed through Pergamum during his Third Journey, when travelling from Ephesus north to Troas on his way to Macedonia. These Christian congregations were possibly founded by teachers trained by Paul during his three-year stay in Ephesus in the years 54-7. Later, John the Divine inherited this ministry and, when deported to the island of Patmos as a Christian agitator, wrote to his beloved 'Seven Churches', referring to Antipas as 'Antipas my witness, my faithful one, who was killed among you, where Satan dwells'. [Rev. 2:13]

2. Antipas, Herod *see* HEROD ANTIPAS

APELLES (Gk. abbreviation for 'Apollonius') One of the Christian converts greeted by Paul, as 'approved in Christ', at the close of his letter to the Christian congregation in Rome. A variant reading in an important manuscript, the *Codex Sinaiticus*, identifies Apelles with Apollos – but without further confirmation. The name 'Apelles' is frequently found in Jewish inscriptions and in the works of Philo, Josephus, and Horace. [Rom. 16:10]

APOLLOS A learned Alexandrian Jew, who arrived with others at Ephesus in the year 53, during Paul's absence at Antioch between his Second and Third Journeys.

Apollos and his twelve companions were teachers of the 'baptism of John' but had never received baptism in the name of Jesus. Apollos himself was an erudite and eloquent scholar of the Old Testament scriptures and an enthusiastic teacher with an accurate knowledge of the story of Jesus; but he had little knowledge of the purpose and progress of the Christian movement. Aquila and Priscilla, left at Ephesus by Paul, heard him speaking in the synagogue and immediately recognized the potential power of his message – once he had grasped the significance of what he was already trying to teach. They took him aside and completed his Christian education, explaining the 'Way of God' more perfectly. As he was bound for Corinth, they also commended him to the newly-founded Christian community there, where his forceful preaching and illustrations from the scriptures of the Messiahship of Jesus were of immediate use.

After Apollos's arrival in Corinth, Paul reached Ephesus to find the little group of disciples of John the Baptist, who after instruction received baptism in the name of Jesus. Paul laid his hands upon them and they received the gift of the Spirit.

Meanwhile Apollos made a deep impression, probably by the allegorical style (in the Alexandrian tradition) and expertise of his preaching. The Corinthian community had little sense of unity and quickly came to regard Apollos as a rival, rather than a successor to Paul, as the pastor of their immature little Christian congregation. To many of them Apollos's gift of exposition and oratory compared favourably with the blunt technique and insignificant physical appearance of Paul. Consequently, some of the Corinthian congregation remained loyal to Paul; others were attracted and overwhelmed by the preaching of Apollos; yet others rallied to the name of Peter.

Paul dealt with their party-spirit frankly, in his Corinthian correspondence, upbraiding them for their

Agape or 'love feast', the early Christian celebration of the Last Supper: wall-painting from the 3rd-century Greek Catacomb of Priscilla at Rome.

lack of spirituality as 'men of flesh' and 'babes in Christ'. 'For when one says, "I belong to Paul," and another, "I belong to Apollos," are you not merely men? What then is Apollos? What is Paul? Servants through whom you believed, as the Lord assigned to each. I planted, Apollos watered, but God gave the growth. . . . He who plants and he who waters are equal, and each shall receive his wages according to his labour. For we are fellow workers for God; you are God's field, God's building.' (1 Cor. 3:4-9) 'So let no one boast of men. For all things are yours, whether Paul or Apollos or Cephas or the world or life or death or the present or the future, all are yours; and you are Christ's; and Christ is God's.' (1 Cor. 3:21-23)

After working with Paul in Ephesus during his long teaching mission, Apollos returned to take charge of the Corinthian congregation and, according to Jerome, the 4th-century biblical scholar, became the first bishop of Corinth.

A final reference in the letter addressed to Titus asks him to send Apollos to meet Paul at Nicopolis, on the Adriatic coast of Greece, though the Pauline authorship of this request is very uncertain. [Acts 18:24; 19:1; 1 Cor. 1:12; 3:4-6; Titus 3:13]

APOLLYON (Gk. 'destroyer') *see* ABADDON

APPHIA (Gk. from the Phrygian 'beloved') The mistress and hostess of the well-to-do household in which the Christian congregation gathered at Colossae. Together with Philemon, who was apparently her husband, and Archippus, probably their son, Apphia was an addressee of Paul's personal plea that they should forgive and welcome back the runaway slave, Onesimus. (*see* PHILEMON) According to tradition, Apphia and her family were martyred at Colossae during the persecutions in the time of the Emperor Nero. [Philem. 2]

AQUILA (Lat., Gk. 'eagle') Aquila and his wife Priscilla, always called 'Prisca' by Paul, were very close friends of the Apostle Paul. Aquila, originally a Jew from Pontus in Asia Minor, had migrated to Rome. In the year 49 he had been exiled, with his wife, by the edict of Claudius expelling all Jews from the imperial city. They met Paul, probably in the following year, at Corinth, where they had a business as tentmakers, in which trade Paul also earned a living. Paul went to live with them, probably working under Aquila, either in canvas or leather.

It is not certain whether Aquila and Priscilla were Christians before their expulsion from Rome, or whether they were converted at Corinth. They soon, however, became partners with Paul in Christian evangelism, as well as in the tent trade. In about the year 52, they sailed with Paul from Cenchrae, the Aegean port of Corinth, for Syria; but they seem to have stopped at Ephesus, where they awaited Paul on his return from Antioch. They may well have been opening a branch of their business in Ephesus, for Paul was able to spend the next two years there in a concentrated teaching mission. It was during this time that an Alexandrian Jew called Apollos, who had been baptized after the manner of John the Baptist, but had not experienced the gift of the Holy Spirit, arrived in Ephesus. An eloquent and learned man, Apollos argued powerfully in the Jewish synagogue for the Messiahship of Jesus. When Aquila and Priscilla heard him, they took him aside and instructed him more accurately in the Christian faith. Later, Paul gave him charge of the Christian congregation at Corinth.

Whether Aquila and Priscilla were involved in the silversmiths' riots at Ephesus, or in some other dangers there, is unknown. Paul, however, includes in his greetings to the Christian congregation at Rome 'Prisca and Aquila, my fellow workers in Christ Jesus, who risked their necks for my life, to whom not only I but also all the churches of the Gentiles give thanks'.

Following the death of the Emperor Claudius, the edict of banishment was no longer in force and Aquila and Priscilla probably returned to Rome. On the other hand, they probably retained their business in Ephesus and travelled freely between the two cities. This would explain Paul's greeting to them, at the end of his last letter to Timothy, when he had left Timothy as his representative in Ephesus and was himself writing from prison in Rome.

It is interesting that of the six times that Aquila and his wife are mentioned in the New Testament, four times Priscilla's name is put first – twice by Luke and twice by Paul. This might be taken to imply that she was a more prominent member of the Church than her husband Aquila [Acts 18:2, 18, 26; Rom. 16:3; 1 Cor. 16:19; 2 Tim. 4:19]

ARABIANS (Heb. 'steppe') At the feast of Pentecost – for the Jew, the giving of the Law; for the Christian, the giving of the Spirit – Arabians, Elamites, Medes, Parthians are included in the list of nationalities enumerated as present in Jerusalem. The gift of the Spirit enabled the apostles of the early Christian Church to make themselves understood in all languages. The Greek implies that each heard his own dialect. This miracle was thought to be symbolical of the coming universality of the gospel of Jesus.

On their return home to many Jewish communities throughout the eastern Mediterranean, those who had heard the preaching of the apostles might well have taken with them the news of a Messiah. [Acts 2:11]

ARCHELAUS (Gk. 'ruling the people') *see* HEROD ARCHELAUS

ARCHIPPUS (Gk. 'master of the horse') Described by Paul as a 'fellow soldier', he was probably in charge of Church affairs at Colossae, in the absence of Epaphras, the pastor and evangelist. Paul indeed sent him a message, 'And say to Archippus, "See that you fulfil the ministry which you have received in the Lord." '

The letter to Philemon is addressed also to Apphia and to Archippus, 'and the church in your house'. It has been suggested that Apphia was the wife of Philemon and that Archippus was their son – besides being the responsible leader in the Colossian Church at that time. This might mean that Paul's plea to the father and

The Descent of the Holy Spirit, by Andrea da Firenze. In the foreground are the different nationalities who witnessed the descent of the Holy Spirit.

Obverse and reverse of a bronze coin of Aretas IV, minted at Petra 9 BC-AD 40, showing the Nabatean king and his wife.

family of Archippus, to forgive and welcome back the runaway slave Onesimus, was in fact addressed to the most influential Christian family at Colossae, in whose house the local congregation met for worship. *see* PHILEMON [Col. 4:17; Philem. 2]

AREOPAGITE (Gk. 'member of the court of Areopagus', i.e. of Mars Hill) *see* DIONYSIUS

ARETAS (Gk. 'pleasing' or 'virtuous') The Nabatean king, the fourth of that name (9 BC-AD 40), whose daughter was married to and divorced from Herod Antipas; he ruled Damascus at the time of the conversion of Paul, and his governor there tried to arrest the future apostle.

The capital of his kingdom was Petra, some 170 miles south of Amman. This city of rock is famous for its complex of fantastic hills and chasms, and for the multiplicity of its monuments carved in the rose-red sandstone of an exquisite, natural, and strategic setting.

The Nabateans began as a wandering Bedouin tribe living on the plunder of caravans from Arabia. From Petra they sallied forth on to the 'King's Highway', first to pillage and then to protect. In fact, they were the forerunners of the protective racketeers, extorting high taxes for providing escorts to passing caravans. Thus their city of Petra became a prosperous trading metropolis, perhaps identifiable with Sela, Nebaioth and the strong city of Edom. The Nabatean kingdom, famous also for its agriculture and its architecture, with familiar egg and arrow motifs, reached the height of its history under its kings, particularly Aretas IV.

The power of the Nabateans extended over the caravan routes south and east of Judea from the 7th century BC to the 2nd century AD. Their influence may be inferred from references in the New Testament. Antipas, son of Herod the Great and tetrarch of Galilee, had married the daughter of Aretas, but divorced her in favour of Herodias, his brother Philip's wife. It was opposition to this liaison that cost John the Baptist his life (Matt. 14:3). Aretas promptly revenged his daughter by invading Antipas's territory and Antipas was able to escape only with the help of Roman forces.

Paul relates that 'At Damascus, the governor under King Aretas guarded the city of Damascus in order to seize me, but I was let down in a basket through a window in the wall, and escaped his hands.' (2 Cor. 11:32-33) The Roman Emperor Caligula had apparently limited the power of the Jewish high priests and, not trusting Antipas, had given the control of the Hellenistic city of Damascus to Aretas, who had put the city in the charge of a governor. Why the governor co-operated with the Jewish enemies of Paul is not known. There is today an unconvincing site of Paul's descent in the basket, but the atmosphere of the story is more vividly illustrated by the ancient brick walling, with its Turkish overhanging lattice windows, nearby. [2 Cor. 11:32]

ARISTARCHUS (Gk. 'the best ruler') A faithful fellow-traveller and constant companion of the Apostle Paul, Aristarchus is first mentioned together with Gaius. They were both Macedonians; Aristarchus came from Thessalonica and was probably a convert from Judaism.

At the very height of the silversmiths' riot at Ephesus, towards the close of Paul's teaching ministry in about the year 57, Aristarchus and Gaius were seized by the mob and dragged into the great theatre. The silversmiths felt their trade in shrines and images of Artemis (Diana of the Ephesians) threatened by the teachings of Paul, and stirred up the crowd to demonstrate against Paul and his companions. In the resultant confusion, Aristarchus and Gaius seem to have borne the brunt of the grievance and Paul was warned not to come to their rescue. The town clerk finally called an end to the disorder and we may assume that Aristarchus and Gaius escaped, if a little the worse for wear.

The following year, they are both mentioned among the representatives of Christian congregations accompanying Paul, and the money-offering for the relief of the poor, from Troas to Jerusalem. Only Aristarchus, however, is recorded as sailing with Paul and Luke from Caesarea, on Paul's long and eventful voyage to Rome.

It is probable that, during Paul's long imprisonment in Rome, his friends took turns in keeping him company and sharing captivity along with him. This would account for Paul's mention in his later letters of different 'fellow prisoners'. Certainly when Paul wrote his letter to the Christian Church at Colossae, Aristarchus was his companion in prison. By the time Paul writes his personal letter to Philemon, it is Epaphras whom he mentions as his fellow-prisoner, whereas Aristarchus is listed, together with Mark, Demas, and Luke, as a fellow-worker.

Thus all five references to Aristarchus, covering a period of seven critical years in the life of Paul, seem to refer with little doubt to one and the same faithful and staunch companion of the apostle. [Acts 19:29; 20:4; 27:2; Col. 4:10; Philem. 24]

ARISTOBULUS (Gk. 'the best counsellor') His

above left Reconstruction of the Temple of Artemis at Ephesus, with a huge statue of the goddess on the right.
above right Roman copy of a Hellenistic statue of the goddess of fertility, Artemis. Marble, 2nd century AD, found at Caesarea.

below Column drum from the Temple of Artemis of Ephesus, 4th century BC.

family was greeted by Paul at the close of his letter to the Christian congregation in Rome. The name 'Aristobulus' was also that of a grandson of Herod the Great, resident in Rome earlier in the 1st century. It is possible that Paul's friend had been a slave in the household of Herod Aristobulus. [Rom. 16:10]

ARTEMAS (Gk. 'gift of Artemis') A companion of Paul during his stay at Nicopolis, on the Adriatic coast of Greece, perhaps after his release from his first captivity in Rome, and during the years 64-5. Paul intended to send Artemas or Tychicus to Titus in Crete, and wanted Titus to return and spend some of the winter with him at Nicopolis. According to tradition, Artemas became bishop of Lystra in the Roman province of Galatia, in the south of Asia Minor. [Titus 3:12]

ARTEMIS The great goddess of the Ephesians, whose name and cult were the oriental equivalent of the Roman huntress-goddess, Diana. Artemis was represented as the many-breasted goddess of fertility. In the times of the Apostle Paul and of John the Divine of Patmos, the vast temple of Artemis in Ephesus was one of the seven wonders of the world and a centre of pilgrimage as

Mars Hill, looking towards the Acropolis: the traditional meeting place
of the Athenian council of elders where St Paul gave his sermon in *c.* AD 51.

famous as Jerusalem. To the progress of the early
Christian Church in Asia, the cult of Artemis presented
the most profound and incipient opposition. Today,
the vast sanctuary complex of the Temple of Artemis
below the acropolis is buried under layers of sand,
rubble and silt. The Roman historian Pliny relates
that the temple was destroyed seven times. It was
completely sacked by the Goths in the year 263. Some
of its columns were used in the building of the church of
S. Sophia, at Constantinople. *see* EPHESIANS [Acts
19:28, 34]

ASYNCRITUS (Gk. 'incomparable') The first of a list
of five men, mentioned in a special greeting from Paul at
the close of his letter to the Christian congregation in
Rome. Perhaps Asyncritus, his fellows, and 'the brethren who are with them' formed a household or small
group within the larger Christian community. [Rom.
16:14]

ATHENIANS Within the New Testament, the men of
Athens present a rather disdainful audience on Mars
Hill to the Apostle Paul on his Second Journey, in
about the year 51.

Paul was making his way south from Thessalonica to
Corinth, but left his companions up in Macedonia,
while he probably sailed down the coast of Achaia to
land at Piraeus, the port of Athens, and passed over the
isthmus to Corinth.

Three hundred years previously, Athens had been the
intellectual centre of the world. The Athenians, therefore, were hardly likely to be impressed by the insignificant figure and rough-and-ready oratory of the Jew
from Tarsus who impertinently proclaimed: 'Men of
Athens, I perceive that in every way you are very religious. For as I passed along, and observed the objects of
your worship, I found also an altar with this inscription, "to an unknown God". What therefore you

worship as unknown, this I proclaim to you.' (Acts 17:22-23)

The altar probably 'belonged' to a goddess of the mystery cults; Paul, stirred by the progressive philosophy of the Athenians, preached in the synagogues and the market-place. At the request of Epicurean and Stoic philosophers, Paul gave an exposition of his teaching before the Council of the Areopagus on Mars Hill. It was a masterpiece of tact, insight, and condensation but in practical terms it was a complete failure. The Greek conception of the human body was of a tomb imprisoning the spirit of the man. They rejected out of hand any mention of the resurrection of the body. They did not believe resurrection would lead to redemption and liberation. Paul made few converts and, filled with disappointment, made his way in fear and trembling to Corinth. [Acts 17:21-23]

AUGUSTUS (Gk. 'majesty') Gaius Octavius was born at Rome in 63 BC, the great-nephew of Julius Caesar. At the age of 20, on the assassination of Caesar, he learned that he had been adopted as Caesar's heir. He conquered his rival, Anthony, at the battle of Actium in 31 BC and held supreme power in the Roman world for the next 45 years. The Senate awarded him the title of 'Augustus', which has continued to grace the age of progress and peace marked by his reign. On his death in AD 14, he was succeeded by his stepson, Tiberius.

Luke dates the census which required Joseph and Mary's presence at Bethlehem as being in the reign of

above The Roman Emperor Augustus, wearing the veil of a priest: marble, 1st century AD.

below Mars Hill seen from the *Agora* or market-place of ancient Athens.

Augustus. An imperial enrolment, such as Luke describes, was not in accordance with Roman practice, though provincial enrolments, for taxation purposes and carried out by the governor, were well known. It is just possible that such a census was instigated by Herod the Great, but no Roman census was held until after Judea came under direct Roman rule in AD 6. Unless, however, Luke was mistaken, this was not perhaps the census that resulted in the birth of Jesus taking place in Bethlehem some twelve years previously, within the lifetime of Herod the Great who died in 4 BC.

It was in honour of Augustus that Herod built both Caesarea, on the Mediterranean coast, and Samaria in the hill country. The Greek name for Samaria, *Sebastos*, means 'Augustus'. [Luke 2:1]

B

BARABBAS (Gk. from the Heb. 'son of a father' or 'teacher') The Jewish prisoner whose release was demanded, according to a customary Passover amnesty, by the crowd in preference to the release of Jesus offered by Pilate, the Roman procurator, in the year 30.

All four Gospels mention Barabbas and the Apostle Peter refers to him as a 'murderer' in a speech to the people of Jerusalem, shortly after Pentecost. Matthew and Mark record that the chief priests incited the mob to call for Barabbas rather than Jesus. 'Now at the feast he used to release for them one prisoner whom they asked. And among the rebels in prison, who had committed murder in the insurrection, there was a man called Barabbas. And the crowd came up and began to ask Pilate to do as he was wont to do for them. And he answered them, "Do you want me to release for you the King of the Jews?" For he perceived that it was out of envy that the chief priests had delivered him up. But the chief priests stirred up the crowd to have him release for them Barabbas instead.' (Mark 15:6-11)

Luke describes Barabbas as 'a man who had been thrown into prison for an insurrection started in the city, and for murder'. (Luke 23:19) In John's more detailed and exact account, probably taken from the official records of the trial of Jesus, Pilate does not even mention Barabbas. After considerable cross-examination of the prisoner Jesus, Pilate, aware that the case was being fraudulently presented and that he was expected to act as a destructive tool of the Sanhedrin, looked for a means of escape. He suggested the offer of the customary Passover amnesty; but he had forgotten Barabbas. Again he went to the Jews and told them, '"I find no crime in him. But you have a custom that I should release one man for you at the Passover; will you have me release for you the King of the Jews?" They cried out again, "Not this man, but Barabbas!" Now Barabbas was a robber.' (John 18:38-40) John emphasizes the tragedy of their choice by his choice of word for Barabbas; the word 'robber' is better translated 'bandit'.

A number of early manuscripts of Matthew's Gospel give Barabbas a forename. Possibly very early in the life of the original manuscript a copyist transcribed the Greek words 'to you' ('release *to you* Barabbas') as the abbreviation for the common name Jesus, or Joshua.

So, in such manuscripts, the words of Pilate to the people appear as: 'Whom do you want me to release, Jesus Barabbas or Jesus who is called the Messiah?' The dramatic force of the choice thus offered to the people is heightened by the identical names of the prisoners. It was noted in the 3rd century by the biblical scholar Origen.

The Barabbas incident has become permanently incorporated in Christian tradition with the story of the trial of Jesus. It is, however, all too possible to perceive here the polemical purpose to blame not only the Jewish priests but the Jewish people for the death of Jesus. And yet the choice of Barabbas rather than of Jesus would have been absolutely consistent with the contemporary political situation.

Barabbas was almost certainly a Zealot (*see* ZEALOTS) and a member of the *Sicarii*, the guerrillas or commandos, literally 'dagger-men', dedicated to the expulsion of the hated Roman occupation forces. Jesus, on the other hand, in teaching and practice was an exponent of non-resistance, appearing even at his own arrest and trial to yield feebly to the occupying power. Faced with such a choice, the crowd without hesitation, even with enthusiasm, chose the violent nationalist rather than the patient idealist, so useless to the nationalist cause. To coin Jesus's own dictum, they took the sword and perished by the sword, in Roman hands. It may be that the rabble outside the Antonia Fortress (*see* PILATE) included a group of the partisans of Barabbas and this may account for their clamorous insistence for his release. In any case Pilate's device to free Jesus was self-defeating, for the crowd demanded the release of their real rebel. In a sense, the choice was and is symbolical. The world still chooses violence and banditry. [Matt. 27; Mark 15; Luke 23; John 18]

BAR-JESUS (Gk. from the Heb. 'son of Jesus', 'son of Joshua') A Jewish sorcerer in the retinue of the Roman proconsul, Sergius Paulus, at Paphos, on the island of Cyprus.

When Paul, Barnabas, and Mark visited Cyprus in the year 46, on the first of Paul's journeys, they fell in silenced the opposition and so impressed the governor that he accepted and believed the gospel proclaimed by Paul. [Acts 13:6]

BAR-JONAH (Gk. from the Heb. 'son of Jonah', 'son of John') *see* PETER

BARNABAS (Gk. from the Heb. 'son of exhortation', 'son of consolation') This Cypriot Jew, of the tribe of Levi, is described by Luke in Acts as 'a good man, full of the Holy Spirit and of faith', as a result of whose devotion and encouragement 'a large company was added to the Lord'. Barnabas was instrumental in introducing the newly-converted Paul to the leaders of the Christian Church both in Jerusalem and in Antioch. Together with Paul he conducted a mission to the churches of Galatia, and later with Mark firmly established the Christian Church in the island of Cyprus.

When the early Christian community in Judea was setting up a system of stewardship of money and property, Barnabas sold his only piece of land and presented the proceeds to the apostles for distribution to needy members of the congregation. He showed the same generosity in his personal relationships. When Paul arrived in Jerusalem after his conversion, and probably after a period of retirement in the desert to the east of Damascus, the disciples in Jerusalem gave him a cool reception, for they could not believe that Paul, until lately the 'grand inquisitor' and arch-persecutor of the Church, was really a disciple of Jesus. Barnabas, who may indeed have known Paul in Tarsus, trusted and sponsored Paul, taking charge of him and introducing him personally to the leaders of the Church in Jerusalem.

Because of the persecution of Hellenized Christians in Judea after the stoning of Stephen, the Gentile Christian community had scattered throughout the Levant as far as Phoenicia and Syria. Whether because of the Hellenized Christians from Cyprus and Jerusalem, or through Paul himself, or by means of both, the Church was firmly established at Antioch, capital of Syria, which was to become the headquarters of Paul's future journeys. The leaders in Jerusalem sent Barnabas to superintend the Church at Antioch, and Barnabas in turn chose Paul as his assistant, collecting him from Tarsus. For a whole year they conducted a teaching mission together. It was at that time that the possibly derisive title of 'Christians' was first given to the members of the Church at Antioch.

In all this success, Barnabas did not forget his old friends in Jerusalem. There the stewardship experiment was breaking down under the strain of poor crops and other difficulties in maintaining regular support. The Antiochene Christians had started a Judean relief fund. Barnabas and Paul were chosen for the happy task of delivering their contributions to Jerusalem, whence they returned to Antioch, bringing with them John Mark. There the spontaneous success of the young Christian

15th-century mural of Barnabas, at Platanistasa in the island of Cyprus, his homeland.

with a false prophet and sorcerer, who belonged to the suite of the Roman proconsul. It is quite in keeping with what is known of Roman colonial life that a learned Jew should have been attached to his household, that is, one who combined his philosophy with the exercise of magic or divination. When Sergius Paulus invited Paul and Barnabas to present 'the word of God' to him, Elymas Bar-Jesus attempted to baulk the teaching of the Christian gospel to his Roman master. Paul pronounced a curse upon him, as it were 'beating him at his own game' and inducing a temporary blindness, which both

Church promoted new enterprise and it was natural that the same pair, Barnabas and Paul, should be sent off on what has now come to be called the First Journey, in the year 45 or 46.

On a journey that was to cover 1,400 miles, they set off down the Orontes valley to sail from the port of Seleucia for Salamis, the eastern harbour of Cyprus. There were many Jews working in the copper-mines of Cyprus and a number of Hellenized Christians had come to Cyprus after the persecution in Jerusalem in the year 36. Now, ten years later, Barnabas and Paul landed on the island and proceeded to Paphos, seat of the Roman proconsul Sergius Paulus, who may have been a God-fearing attendant at the local synagogue. One of the proconsul's household was a Jewish magician called Elymas Bar-Jesus, who tried to prevent the preaching of the Christian gospel to his master. Paul very quickly and mercilessly exposed him, and the proconsul accepted Paul's teaching about Jesus.

Crossing over to the mainland of Pisidia, on the south coast of Asia Minor, they landed at Attalia and set off inland, climbing the western spurs of the rugged Taurus range, infested with robbers and other hazards. A few miles inland, John Mark (*see* MARK) left them and returned to Jerusalem. The rest arrived at Antioch, the capital of Pisidia – not of Syria – a hundred miles north from the coast, an important centre with a large Jewish

Ruins of a Roman colonnaded street at Salamis in Cyprus, the port at which Paul and Barnabas landed on their First Journey.

community. In their synagogue, Paul delivered an address (fully recorded in Acts 13) to both Jews and Gentiles. By the following morning, opposition had crystallized and Paul and Barnabas were expelled from the city – but not before Paul had convinced many pagans, who were later to form the core of the Christian community in Pisidian Antioch.

Paul and Barnabas now turned eastwards and after nearly a hundred miles of rough travelling came to Iconium – a city of Lycaonia now called Konya. Here again their visit followed the same pattern and a Church was formed before – under threat of being stoned – Paul and Barnabas went on to Lystra, 25 miles towards the coast. Here there was no synagogue, so Paul spoke in the open air and healed a cripple. When the crowd realized what had happened, they declared Paul and Barnabas to be gods and attempted to offer them sacrifices.

Barnabas, however kindly, must have had a commanding presence, because in this amusing if (for a Jew) highly embarrassing incident at Lystra, the crowd decided that Barnabas must be Jupiter, lord of the gods, while to the talkative and eloquent Paul they assigned the subordinate role of Mercury.

After a most successful journey, the two reported to headquarters in Jerusalem and had to face a barrage of questions about the freedom with which they had admitted pagans into the Church by baptism, without causing them first to be circumcised. In the end it was decided that the free admission of Gentiles to the Church would be allowed, if they would conform with certain particular social customs of the Jews.

On the next journey, because Barnabas proposed to take Mark with them, the party split up and Paul chose to go with other companions. Barnabas went to Cyprus with Mark.

In any case, the dispute did not end the friendship between Paul and Barnabas. Even on his last journey, when he was writing to the Corinthians, Paul shows that they had kept in touch. He mentions Barnabas as an example, with himself, of apostles who still maintain themselves by working at their old trade and refuse to live on the charity of the Church. It may be said that without the sympathy and encouragement of Barnabas, the vital contributions of Paul and Mark to the Christian faith and the New Testament might never have been made. [Acts 4:36; 11:22, 25, 30; 12:25; 13:1-50; 14:12-20; 15:2-37; 1 Cor. 9:6; Gal. 2:1, 9, 13; Col. 4:10]

BARSABBAS (Gk. from the Heb. 'son of Sabbas' or 'born on the Sabbath') **1. Justus Barsabbas** (sometimes called Joseph) The unsuccessful candidate proposed together with Matthias to fill the gap left by the death of the traitor Judas, and so to complete the number of the twelve apostles of Jesus. *see* MATTHIAS [Acts 1:23] *above* Sacrifice offered to Zeus, *c.* 9 BC, from the *Ara pacis*, Rome. To the citizens of Lystra, Barnabas recalled the fatherly figure of Zeus.

left Bronze statuette of Zeus, 1st century AD, with a thunderbolt in his right hand, his left hand raised to hold a sceptre.

2. Judas Barsabbas One of two eminent and respected members of the first General Assembly or Christian Council in Jerusalem, held in the year 49 or 50, who were commissioned to convey their decision or decree to the Church in Antioch.

The Council, under the chairmanship of James the brother of Jesus, had received a deputation from the Judean Church stating that circumcision was necessary for salvation.

The Council repudiated the Judaizers and refused to impose the Law on the Gentiles, only forbidding specific offensive practices. Their decision was conveyed to the Church at Antioch by the official delegates Judas and Silas, accompanying Paul and Barnabas on their return. 'So when they were sent off, they went down to Antioch; and having gathered the congregation together, they delivered the letter. And when they read it, they rejoiced at the exhortation. And Judas and Silas, who were themselves prophets, exhorted the brethren with many words and strengthened them.' (Acts 15:30-32)

Judas Barsabbas is carefully distinguished from

Justus with the same patronymic, the near-apostle of twenty years before. (*see above*) [Acts 15:22, 27, 30-32]

3. Joseph Barsabbas *see* BARSABBAS 1. and MATTHIAS

BARTHOLOMEW (Gk. from the Aramaic 'son of Tolmai' or 'Talmai') This name is mentioned in the Gospels of Matthew, Mark, and Luke, within the lists of the twelve apostles, where each time Bartholomew is linked with Philip. Otherwise he is listed in Acts among the apostles present at the election of a substitute apostle for the traitor Judas. As the name Bartholomew is simply a patronymic indicating that he was the son of Tolmai, he must also have had a personal name. This is

Eusebius, bishop of Caesarea, and Ammonius, bishop of Alexandria, from the *Rabula Gospels*, written in Aramaic *c.* AD 586.

often identified as 'Nathanael', by which name the writer of the Fourth Gospel calls the apostle-companion of Philip in both his first and last chapters. Here, Nathanael is introduced to Jesus by Philip and is said to come from Cana of Galilee. The identification of Nathanael with Bartholomew has been widely accepted by biblical scholars from the 9th century to the present day.

Eusebius, the early 4th-century historian and bishop of Caesarea, records that an Alexandrian traveller in India discovered a *Gospel of Matthew*, written in Hebrew and left behind by 'Bartholomew, one of the apostles'. According to tradition, Bartholomew was flayed alive in Armenia. He is often represented in art with his skin over his arm and the knife in his hand. *see also* NATHANAEL [Matt. 10:3; Mark 3:18; Luke 6:14; Acts 1:13]

BARTIMAEUS (Gk. from the Heb. 'son of Timaeus') The blind beggar at Jericho, healed by Jesus on his final journey to Jerusalem. All the first three Gospels relate the story of the blind man by the roadside at Jericho, though Matthew duplicates the central character into two blind men; only Mark mentions his name and parentage, and Luke, unlike the other two, says that Jesus was on the way to Jericho.

The story is significant, and full of dramatic irony, for, apart from Peter at Caesarea Philippi, and also certain 'evil spirits' in possession of people whom Jesus healed, this blind man is the first person mentioned in Mark's Gospel to recognize the identity of Jesus as Messiah. He is sitting by the edge of the road, probably begging, when he hears the hubbub of the approaching crowd. Hearing that 'Jesus of Nazareth is passing by', the blind man calls out not 'Jesus of Nazareth', but 'Jesus, Son of David, have mercy on me!', thus using the title reserved for the expected Messiah/Deliverer. At this point, all three Gospels portray the bystanders telling him to be quiet, but depict the blind man calling all the more insistently 'Son of David, have mercy'. Now, Jesus comes to a standstill and calls for the blind man, who stands up, drops his cloak and comes, guided through the crowd, to Jesus. Jesus asks him what he wants him to do for him, and Bartimaeus asks, 'Master, let me receive my sight'. The irony lies in the fact that the blind man is the only member of the public who has the insight to recognize the Messiahship of Jesus, and yet he asks to receive his sight. Jesus's answer immediately pinpoints his faith as the real source of his sight, 'Go your way;

right St Bartholomew holding his flayed skin and a knife, from the ceiling of the Sistine Chapel by Michelangelo (1475-1564).

overleaf Jesus restoring sight to the blind, putting clay in the eyes of one man while the other washes it away. 11th-century wall-painting from S. Angelo in Formis, near Capua.

your faith has made you well.' Whereupon Bartimaeus, now seeing, follows Jesus with the crowd.

Bartimaeus is one of very few persons miraculously healed and restored who are mentioned by name in the first three Gospels. [Mark 10:46-52]

BE-ELZEBUL (*or* BEELZEBUB) (Heb. 'Baal' or 'Lord of the flies') Be-elzebul (in the original Greek) was the ancient pagan god worshipped by the Philistines at Ekron. The word 'baal' was a Canaanite term for 'lord' and the whole word meant 'Lord of heaven'. The Hebrews came to think of him as the prince of the demons and changed his name to Beelzebub, 'Lord of the flies', equating him with the devil. Thus the scribes from Jerusalem said of Jesus: 'He is possessed by Be-elzebul, and by the prince of the demons he casts out the demons.' Jesus at once replied: 'How can Satan cast out Satan? If a kingdom is divided against itself, that kingdom cannot stand. And if a house is divided against itself, that house will not be able to stand. And if Satan has risen up against himself and is divided, he cannot stand, but is coming to an end.' (Mark 3:22-26) *see* SATAN [Matt. 10:25; 12:24-27; Mark 3:22; Luke 11:15]

BELIAL (Gk. from the Heb. 'vain fellow', 'fool', 'good-for-nothing') An Old Testament term of scorn. 'Sons of Belial' were 'useless' and sometimes 'wicked' fellows. In the intertestamental period, the term became synonymous with Satan. In the writings of the Apostle Paul, the term implied 'antichrist'. *see* SATAN [2 Cor. 6:15]

BELOVED DISCIPLE *see* JOHN **3.**

BERNICE (Gk. 'victorious') This daughter of Herod Agrippa I and great-granddaughter of Herod the Great was present with her brother Herod Agrippa II to hear

left Coin of Titus, the Roman general, later emperor, who destroyed Jerusalem in AD 70 and to whom Bernice was mistress.

above White marble statue found at Caesarea, considered by some to be that of Blastus, royal chamberlain to Herod Agrippa I.

Paul's defence at Caesarea. The procurator, Festus, wished to draw up the charges against Paul before despatching him to Rome, and invited the opinion of Agrippa. The impression of Agrippa and Bernice given by Luke in the Acts of the Apostles is a pleasing one of Roman aristocrats of Jewish birth, courteously attentive, genuinely interested, and well-informed of the political and religious implications of Paul's defence.

Paul's respect for Agrippa is sincere. He says: 'I think myself fortunate that it is before you, King Agrippa, I am to make my defence today against all the accusations of the Jews, because you are especially familiar with all customs and controversies of the Jews.' And Agrippa's comment at the end of Paul's eloquent speech may well have been equally sincere. 'And Agrippa said to Paul, "In a short time you think to make me a Christian!"' (Acts 26) Bernice seems to have been included in the discussion which followed and may well have influenced Festus's report to Rome, which appears to some to have resulted in Paul's acquittal after two years under house-arrest.

The constant companionship of this brother and sister, Herod Agrippa II and Bernice, caused considerable scandal, as recorded in the satires of Juvenal. Both, however, in the family tradition, were skilled and courageous diplomats. Bernice risked her life for the Jews during the massacre by the infamous procurator Gessius Florus. Agrippa did his best to avert the Jewish War. Bernice is also said to have married King Ptolemy of Sicily, and to have been the mistress of the Emperor Titus. [Acts 25:13, 23; 26:30]

BLASTUS (Gk. 'sprout') The royal chamberlain to Herod Agrippa I, who arranged an audience for the people of Tyre and Sidon, at Caesarea, to settle their differences with the king.

The story told by Luke in Acts is interesting because it is partly corroborated by Josephus in his *Antiquities*. Both sources record an important gathering at Caesarea, at which the audience with true oriental flattery acclaimed Agrippa as a god. Both describe his royal robes, his oration, and his miserable death. The complete independence of Luke's account is indicated by the fact that he alone mentions Blastus, the king's chamberlain. Luke alone records the solution of the feud by the submission of the two cities to the chamberlain. For his master was the ruler of Galilee, upon which the food-supply of the Phoenician coastal cities depended.

Josephus's account adds some interesting details: 'The king went to Caesarea . . . and gave a spectacle in honour of Caesar, at which all the chief personages were present. On the second day of the show, Herod put on a marvellously woven robe of silver, which shone wondrously when the rays of the sun caught it. Thereupon his flatterers cried out, "Be propitious; if we reverenced thee hitherto as a man, from henceforth we acknowledge thee to be more than mortal." The king did not rebuke them, but as he looked up he saw an owl sitting on a rope, and realized that the bird which had once been a messenger of good fortune to him was now an omen of evil. He was seized with violent internal pains, and told his friends that he, whom they saluted as a god, was about to depart from life. He lingered in agony for five

2nd-century Roman aqueduct, which conducted sweet water from the region of Mount Carmel to the Roman military base and port of Caesarea.

days, and died, to the great grief of his countrymen at Caesarea.'

Although Blastus and the feud with the coastal cities do not figure in Josephus's account, yet the 'persuasion' of Blastus, possibly by bribery, the consequent overtures for peace and the resultant reconciliation are typical within the context of the royal magnanimity of such a festal occasion. [Acts 12:20]

BOANERGES (Gk. from the Heb. 'sons of thunder') The name given by Jesus to the two sons of Zebedee, James and John, recorded only by Mark.

The lists of the disciples of Jesus reveal the nickname given to John and his brother James as 'Boanerges'. This means 'sons of thunder' and presumably refers to their angry temperaments, or glowering faces. 'Son of' implies 'having the quality of' thunder. Whether the nickname implies honour or rebuke, it is certain that John and sometimes his brother too were reproved by Jesus. John once said to Jesus at Capernaum, 'Master, we saw a man who is not one of us casting out devils in your name; and because he was not one of us we tried to stop him.' But Jesus said, 'You must not stop him: no one who works a miracle in my name is likely to speak evil of me. Anyone who is not against us is for us.'

The 'sons of thunder', the brothers James (left) and John (right): from the apse of the 12th-century chapel at Eski Gumus, Cappadocia.

When James and John asked Jesus to reserve the seats of honour on either side of him at his Messianic banquet in heaven, Jesus replied, 'You do not know what you are asking.' And he went on to ask if they could share his destiny. They confidently affirmed that they could, whereupon Jesus answered, 'The cup that I must drink you shall drink . . . but as for the seats at my right hand or my left, these are not mine to grant. . . .' James was in fact the first of Jesus's apostles to suffer martyrdom, as early as AD 44, under Herod Agrippa. John and James received a further rebuke from Jesus when his messengers were not welcome in a Samaritan village, and the 'sons of thunder' suggested, perhaps typically, 'Lord, do you want us to call down fire from heaven to burn them up?' Jesus and his disciples shared the rigours of his itinerant ministry, often forced to go without shelter: 'The Son of Man has nowhere to lay his head'.

Despite their temperament and Jesus's frank rebukes, the two brothers, James and John, together with Peter, formed an inner circle within the group of disciples and it is these three whom Jesus took with him on at least three important occasions. They accompanied him into the house for the raising of Jairus's daughter; they were permitted to witness the glory of Jesus's transfiguration on the mountain; they were chosen to support him and to witness his agony in the Garden of Gethsemane. [Mark 3:17]

C

CAESAR The title of the Roman emperors until the 3rd century AD, denoting to the people of the provinces the concept of the imperial throne rather than its particular occupant.

The name originally was that of a Roman family, prominent from the 3rd century BC, whose most well-known member was Julius Caesar, the conqueror of Gaul (102-44 BC). Julius Caesar adopted Octavius as his heir, thereby conferring on him and his successors the title of 'Caesar', to which the Senate added for Octavius, in 31 BC, the title 'Augustus'.

Always acknowledging the doubt in dating the writings, the emperors during the events of the New Testament were:

Augustus (27 BC-AD 14) – Jesus was born and grew up.

Tiberius (AD 14-37) – Jesus taught in Galilee and Judea; Jesus was crucified, rose, and ascended; the Christian Church received the Spirit at Pentecost; Paul was converted.

Caligula (Gaius) (AD 37-41) – Paul was received by the Christian leaders in Jerusalem; the Church was established at Antioch in Syria.

Claudius (AD 41-54) – The First Journey of Paul and Barnabas to Cyprus and Galatia; the first Council of Jerusalem; the Second Journey of Paul and Silas to Europe; Paul's Letters to Thessalonica, Galatia, and Corinth.

Nero (AD 54-68) – The Third Journey of Paul; the Teaching Mission at Ephesus; Paul's return to arrest in Jerusalem; Paul's trials and imprisonment under Felix and Festus; Paul's appeal to Caesar and journey to Rome; Paul's captivity, trial and possible release; (the writing of Mark's Gospel?); the writing of 1 Peter, James, and Jude; the remainder of Paul's Letters, except Timothy and Titus; the arrest and martyrdom of Peter and Paul.

Galba (AD 68-9), *Otho* (AD 69), *Vitellius* (AD 69), *Vespasian* (AD 69-79) – The fall of Jerusalem; the establishment of the Christian congregation at Pella; the writing of the Gospel of Matthew.

Titus (AD 79-81) – The writing of the Gospel of Luke; (the writing of the Letters to Timothy and Titus?).

Domitian (AD 81-96) – The writing of the Fourth Gospel;

top to bottom Marble statue of the Emperor Augustus, great-nephew and heir of Julius Caesar. Coin of the Emperor Tiberius, bearing his portrait. Claudius, portrayed as Jupiter.

top to bottom Bust of Nero, the Roman emperor notorious for his persecution of the early Christian community in Rome.
Coin of Vespasian, with his portrait.
Bust of the Emperor Titus.
Busts of Domitian and his wife Longina.

the exile of John to Patmos; the three Letters of John; (the second Letter of 'Peter'?); the Revelation of John. *see also* ROMANS [Matt. 22:17; Mark 12:14; Luke 2:1; 20:22-25; John 19:12; Acts 17:7; 25:8-21; Phil. 4:22]

CAIAPHAS Joseph, surnamed Caiaphas, was the Jewish high priest (AD 18-37) by whose calculation and cunning Jesus was arrested, convicted, and crucified by the Roman authorities in Jerusalem.

He married the daughter of Annas the high priest (AD 6-15). It was customary for a priest to marry the daughter of a priest, especially among the priestly aristocracy and the priests of Jerusalem, whose prestige and education gave them a superior standing. The high priests tended to appoint their sons and sons-in-law into the more lucrative posts in the Temple, consequently it was not surprising that Caiaphas succeeded his father-in-law, who virtually founded a dynasty of high priests.

The ruling house of Annas held perhaps all the chief-priestly positions within its control, besides operating a flourishing trade in sacrificial victims in the court of the Gentiles, within the Temple. No less than eight members of this family held the supreme office of high priest: Annas himself, five sons, Caiaphas his son-in-law, and his grandson Matthias, from the year 65. Such a family virtually established the political as well as the religious leadership of the nation. Both Caiaphas and his father-in-law, Annas, were appointed from Rome but removed from office by the Roman procurator, in the case of the unpopular Caiaphas by Vitellius. The patriarchal figure of Annas long continued as the 'power behind the throne'. Luke dates the beginning of the ministry of John the Baptist as 'within the high priesthood of Annas and Caiaphas'.

Jesus, a threat to the Council

The Fourth Gospel describes the arrest and escort of Jesus to the house of Annas from where, after an unsuccessful examination, he was sent to Caiaphas, the officiating high priest who convened the Sanhedrin for the trial and sent Jesus to Pilate. Mark, on the other hand, does not specify the high priest by name, but Matthew does. In any case, it was Caiaphas who presided at the Sanhedrin's trial of Jesus.

The Sadducees had long watched Jesus and the development of his movement with increasing dislike and restlessness, as they had done that of John the Baptist. Again and again the messengers of Caiaphas had tried to trap Jesus into self-conviction, until they had begun to ask themselves, 'What are we to do? For this man performs many signs. It we let him go on thus, every one will believe in him, and the Romans will come and destroy both our holy place and our nation.' (John 11:47-48) But Caiaphas had answered them: '"You know nothing at all; you do not understand that it is expedient for you that one man should die for the people, and that the whole nation should not perish." He did not

Christ before Caiaphas, by Fra Angelico (*c.* 1400-55)

say this of his own accord, but being high priest that year he prophesied that Jesus should die for the nation, and not for the nation only, but to gather into one the children of God who are scattered abroad. So from that day on they took counsel how to put him to death.' (John 11:49-53)

No doubt the outcome of their consultations was a very clever and crafty solution, possibly the product of the fertile cunning of Caiaphas himself. This was to hand Jesus over to the Roman authorities: in any case they could not execute him. They could, however, label him guilty of treason and a danger to the imperial

security and let the Romans cope with him. They could then convince their people that it was better for one man to die for the whole nation. Thus in one act they would destroy Jesus, put the blame on the Romans, and pretend their own loyalty to the Roman authority in the process.

Very shortly followed the incident involving the expulsion of the dealers from the Temple and the overthrowing of the kiosks of the money-changers, nicknamed 'the booths of Annas'. This was a clear threat to the vested interest and authority of Caiaphas himself, for the Temple was a thriving trading-colony and an excellent source of income from the sale of sacrificial animals and offerings, augmented by an exorbitant rate of exchange on the Temple coinage needed to purchase them. Josephus, in his *Antiquities*, says, 'Such was the shamelessness and effrontery which possessed the high priests, that they were actually so brazen as to send their servants to the threshing-floors to receive the tithes due to the priests, so it happened at that time that those of the priests who in olden days were maintained by the tithes now starved to death.'

Only a fear of the common people restrained the Temple authorities from arresting Jesus then. On the first Palm Sunday, the day of Jesus's final entry into Jerusalem, the city was in an uproar and many expected him to declare himself the 'Son of David' at the Passover festival. Caiaphas must have realized that it was 'now or never', and that he must act before the beginning of the feast.

Caiaphas at the trial of Jesus

Caiaphas may well have feared the miraculous power of Jesus as well as being nervous of the reaction of the crowds of Galilean pilgrims, with whom Jesus was a popular hero. Hence the marks of haste in the arrest and trial of Jesus: the arrest in the dark, the nocturnal trial, the witnesses badly prepared. It was illegal to try a capital charge at night; it was illegal for the president (Caiaphas) to invite the prisoner to convict himself; it was illegal for him not to be acquitted once the witnesses had disagreed. Of the charges: Jesus's threat to destroy the Temple was manifestly unproven; Jesus's claim to be the Messiah was the direct outcome of the coercion of the high priest Caiaphas, who, seeing the charges fail, intervened to cross-examine the prisoner himself.

Invoking the most solemn oath binding on any Jew, Caiaphas 'stood up in the midst, and asked Jesus, "Have you no answer to make? What is it that these men testify against you?" But he was silent and made no answer. Again the high priest asked him, "Are you the Christ, the Son of the Blessed?" And Jesus said, "I am; and you will see the Son of Man sitting at the right hand of Power, and coming with the clouds of heaven." And the high priest tore his mantle, and said, "Why do we still need witnesses? You have heard his blasphemy. What is your decision?" And they all condemned him as deserving death.' (Mark 14:60-64)

The conviction for blasphemy in the Sanhedrin was disregarded in favour of the more appealing charge of treason, when the case was referred to Pilate. The very speed and expedition of the arrangements for the trial in the early hours of the morning before Pilate reflects the pressure and power of the influential high priest, Caiaphas. This was most probably not the first time that Caiaphas had presented a threat to the procuratorial reputation of Pilate, who was ultimately exiled

for his tactless and inept brutality. He was a child in the hands of Caiaphas, and the argument: 'If you release this man, you are not Caesar's friend; everyone who makes himself a king sets himself against Caesar' was the final twist of the screw necessary to secure conviction. (*see* PILATE)

Caiaphas in Acts

Caiaphas figures several times in the story of the early Church. Twice he presided over examinations of Peter, John, and the other apostles, in connection with their preaching and healing activities in the Temple. Finally, on the advice of the Pharisee Gamaliel, Caiaphas had them beaten, warned, and discharged. He also presided at the trial of Stephen and took the initiative in the persecution of Hellenist Christians that followed the stoning of Stephen. Indirectly, Caiaphas contributed thereby to the diaspora of these potential Christian missionaries throughout the Mediterranean. Caiaphas was also the high priest who commissioned Saul (later to become the Apostle Paul) with letters of authority to persecute Christians as far as Damascus, then under his ecclesiastical authority.

The house of Caiaphas

A possible site of the house of Caiaphas in the upper city, on the Western Hill of Jerusalem, provides many vivid illustrations of all the paraphernalia of the high priest's palace: the store-house, treasury, palace, court of justice, guardroom, and cells.

Various churches have been built on this site to commemorate the trial and imprisonment of Jesus by Caiaphas, as well as St Peter's denial and repentance. The Pilgrim of Bordeaux in 533, commenting on the ruins of the high priest's palace, wrote: 'In the same Valley of Siloam, you go up to Mount Zion and (in the same valley) you see the spot where the House of Caiaphas stood.' Between 457 and 459, a fine basilica dedicated to St Peter was built on the ruins by the Empress Eudocia. In 530, Theodosius went from the Cenacle to the House of Caiaphas, 'which is now St Peter's Church'.

The present church includes at least three different storeys or levels, being built on a steep, if not almost sheer, hillside. Perhaps the one man-made feature common to both the city of the 1st century and that of the Byzantine age, and still to be seen, is that magnificent rock-hewn staircase ascending the hillside from the Pool of Siloam. It was on to this equivalent of the city highway that the palace of the high priest faced.

The main west doorway of the present church leads into the top level, and from a balcony outside the east end the visitor can look down on the vast storage-chambers below the palace. Staircases lead down into corn-stores; oil-stores are lined with plaster and have round bottle-necks. There is a complete grinding-mill here, with an underground rock-hewn stable for the

above Wet and dry storage chambers for offerings in oil and grain from the remains of the high priest's palace, at the Church of St Peter in Gallicantu, Jerusalem.

left 1st-century stone stairway from the Pool of Siloam rising up the Western Hill and passing the high priest's palace.

donkey that operated it. Complete sets of weights and measures, used only by the priests, have been discovered in this 'treasury', also a huge stone door-lintel inscribed: 'This is Korban or offering'. Such facilities on such a scale indicate the storage of Temple dues.

Within the church, over the high altar, is an illustration of the trial which was conducted in the rock-hewn courtroom on the next level below the church. The prisoner is standing on a raised platform or dock, in the centre and with his back to the wall, chained by the wrists to escorts sitting on either side of him. It is easy to picture this scene on the lower level, facing westwards into the hillside in which are cut staircases and galleries. On one of these Peter must have sat with the soldiers, warmed himself by the fire, and denied knowing his master. On either side of the wall, behind the raised rock platform, the corners of the courtroom are cut square to a height of almost ten feet.

In the very centre of the courtroom is the mouth of the bottle-necked prison, into which the condemned prisoner could be lowered after trial.

Descending to a third level there is a complete guardroom, all round the walls of which are still the staples for the prisoners' chains. On one side is a small window opening on to the bottle-necked condemned cell. Below this window, and left projecting from the floor when

the guardroom was excavated out of the rock, is a block on which the guard stood to peer down into the gloom of the cell below him. On the opposite side of the guardroom is the whipping-block. Here, tied up by the wrists with leather thongs through staples at the top, a belt round his waist secured to a staple at each side, the prisoner would be stretched up taut and helpless. At his feet were two bowls carved in the rock, one for salt to disinfect his scars, one for vinegar to revive him. Here, the apostles of the early Church received the legal number of 'forty lashes less one' (thirteen on each shoulder from the back and thirteen on the chest from the front), were commanded not to preach Jesus as Christ, then sent home. Yet they returned daily to the Temple to teach and to preach this very thing, despite the threats and warnings of Caiaphas. [Matt. 26:3; Luke 3:2; John 11:49; 18:13, 14, 24, 28; Acts 4:6]

CANAANITE (Gk. from the Aramaic 'native of Cana') see SIMON

CANDACE (Gk. from the Ethiopian) The general title of the queens of Meroe in Ethiopia, then meaning Nubia in the area of the upper Nile. The story of the Ethiopian eunuch, treasurer to the Candace, probably himself a pilgrim visiting Jerusalem, his conversion and baptism by Philip the Evangelist on the road to Gaza, is included by Luke in Acts immediately before the conversion of Paul. see also ETHIOPIAN [Acts 8:27]

CARPUS (Gk. from the Heb. 'harvest') The Christian in whose house at Troas Paul left his cloak and scrolls, following his arrest, perhaps through the treachery of Alexander the coppersmith, possibly between the years 64 and 67. Paul wrote from Rome to Timothy in Ephesus, asking him to collect his things from Carpus 'and above all the parchments', before his execution.

Tradition claims that Carpus became bishop of Beroea. [2 Tim. 4:13]

The courtroom of the high priest's palace, complete with galleries and staircases cut in the rock-face of the Western Hill.

CENTURION (Lat. 'hundred')
1. **Centurion at Capernaum**
2. **Centurion at Calvary**
3. **Cornelius, centurion at Caesarea**
4. **First centurion at the Antonia Fortress**
5. **Second centurion at the Antonia Fortress**
6. **Julius, centurion of the Augustan cohort**

The centurion was a non-commissioned officer in charge of a hundred soldiers in the Roman army. He was always promoted from the ranks and was the equivalent of a company sergeant-major. There were sixty centurions to each legion of 6,000 men. Just as sergeant-majors are a byword for comic swagger and policemen for their alleged flat feet, so, according to Juvenal, centurions were caricatured for their fat calves and hob-nailed boots. Julius Caesar mentions several centurions who earned his praise for their loyalty and initiative. Polybius, the Greek historian of Rome, in his well-known description of the army, says of the 'centurions' that they are not expected to be so much 'venturesome seekers of danger, as men who can command, steady in action, and reliable; they ought not to be over-anxious to rush into the fight, but when hard-pressed, they must be ready to hold their ground and die at their posts'.

No less than six centurions are mentioned in the New Testament, and they all stand out very creditably in the narrative. Of these, two are linked with the life of Jesus: the centurion at Capernaum in Matthew and Luke, and the centurion in charge of the crucifixion squad appearing in all three Synoptic Gospels, Matthew, Mark, and

above Roman soldiers crossing a pontoon bridge, from Trajan's Column, Rome.

right Stone relief of a Roman soldier, from the column of Nero, Mainz.

above Reconstruction of the 2nd-3rd-century synagogue at Capernaum, the carvings of which bear Jewish religious and Roman military symbols.

top right The Ark of the Covenant, from the synagogue at Capernaum.

centre right The manna pot in the wilderness, from the synagogue at Capernaum.

bottom right Eagles back to back, the regimental crest of the Tenth Legion, Capernaum.

Luke. One other centurion, Cornelius, was converted by Peter, and three others are linked with Paul.

1. Centurion at Capernaum He sent a message to Jesus begging his help. Luke says that the centurion had a servant – presumably the equivalent of a batman – who was desperately ill. Matthew adds that he was paralysed and in great pain. In Luke's account, the centurion himself never appears, but the Jewish elders commend him and his request to Jesus. The centurion's friends then bring the message that he is not worthy to receive Jesus into his house – 'Lord, do not trouble yourself . . . But say the word, and let my servant be healed,' runs the message. Jesus then says to the crowd following him, 'I tell you, not even in Israel have I found such faith.' And when the messengers get back to the house they find the servant in perfect health.

It is strange that at a solemn moment of the Catholic Mass of the Latin Rite the priest, before receiving Communion, says the words of that Roman centurion. Three times he repeats, 'Lord, I am not worthy that thou shouldst come under my roof, but speak the word only . . .' Some scholars think that the story in John's Gospel (4:46) of the cure of the nobleman's son records the same incident, retold in the manner and for the purpose of the later writer. Certainly he shows that the act of healing took place over a distance of 20 miles, from Cana to Capernaum.

This centurion was probably one of the Gentiles who attended worship at the Jewish synagogue, a 'God-fearer', as Paul called them. Luke describes how the elders reported that 'he loves our nation, and he built us our synagogue'. Today, at Capernaum, is to be seen a 3rd-century reconstruction into which are incorporated both Roman and Jewish designs. This synagogue has been partially restored; it was well built of white limestone, contrasting vividly with the black lava of the surrounding houses. The prayer hall was rectangular, nearly 80 feet long and 53 feet wide. To the east of the prayer hall was an open courtyard, entered by two doors, on the south side. Both hall and courtyard were colonnaded, the columns in the hall supporting the gallery, those in the courtyard forming a cloister facing a doorway into the hall. Through this doorway the Gentile 'God-fearers' might listen to the synagogue service.

The whole building was elaborately decorated with carved stone ornaments. Its walls may have been covered with frescoes, like those of the nearly contemporary Dura synagogue, built in AD 244. As Professor Albright has pointed out, the catacombs in Rome and the necropolis at Beth She'arim demonstrate the dependence of early Christian art on Jewish frescoes of the Roman period. What is really striking at Capernaum is the variety of the motifs, particularly the mixture of Jewish and Roman symbols. Among the former are the *menorah* (the seven-branched candle-stick), the *shofar* (the ram's horn), the *magen David* (the shield of David), the Ark of the Covenant, the manna pot, and that old symbol of the land, the palm-tree.

Among the Roman symbols, two have particular significance for the Christian. The first is the regimental crest of the Tenth Legion, two eagles back to back and beak to beak. The second is the Roman army's equivalent of the Victoria Cross: it was awarded to a soldier who saved the life of an officer in battle. It is a victor's laurel-wreath tied in a circle with a reef-knot and enclosing a round sea-shell. The eagles in the regimental crest are holding the same laurel-wreath in their beaks. What is the explanation of this combination of symbols?

Although this is a late 2nd-century or early 3rd-century building, Professor Albright is certain that it stands on the site of an earlier synagogue. This latter may possibly have been that in which Jesus worshipped, taught, and healed. It may well be that carvings of this synagogue were moved on to the later building. Coupled with the story in Luke's Gospel, this could explain how the regimental crest of a Roman legion came to adorn the very keystone of a Jewish synagogue. [Luke 7:1-10]

2. Centurion at Calvary As commander of the Roman

Roman military decoration, awarded for saving the life of an officer in battle, Capernaum

execution squad, he gives us the only independent eye-witness account of the conduct of Jesus up to the moment of his death. What this rough and honest soldier exclaimed came from the depth of his own military and human experience.

As a Roman soldier he was trained in the hard school of courage, endurance, and fortitude in uncomplaining suffering. He had had the opportunity to watch the prisoner – if he was in charge of him – from his trial before Pilate; he would have watched the scourging, the mocking, the barrack-room horseplay with the crown of thorns. He would have whipped back the mob thronging the Via Dolorosa of cobbled streets, out through the Judgment Gate to the rocky mound of execution. He would have watched the falls beneath the weight of the cross, the stripping, the nailing, and the hideous moment when the cross was reared and the tortured body dropped to hang upon the nails. Then he would have shared the hours of waiting for the end – the

1st-century AD marble statue of a Roman officer's armour. The metal cuirass had a leather lining culminating in broad strips with fringed ends.

publicly in the Temple with four other men under a vow of purification, which he did. But Paul was soon recognized by some Asiatic Jews, who accused him of 'teaching men everywhere against the people and the law and this place'. The mob dragged Paul out of the Temple to kill him. The Tribune and commander of the Antonia Fortress 'turned out the guard' to Paul's rescue, put him under protective custody, and attempted to retire with him up the stairway into the fortress. Despite the violence of the mob, Paul obtained permission to speak to them and in a mercurial speech related his own Jewish background as a Pharisee at the feet of Gamaliel, his own ardent persecution of the Christian communities, his own remarkable conversion on the road to Damascus, and finally his own vocation to the Gentiles.

At this point the mob went berserk, and the commander ordered Paul to be taken into the fortress for examination under the lash. When he was already strapped up, Paul turned to the centurion on duty and asked, 'Is it lawful for you to scourge a man who is a Roman citizen, and uncondemned?' At once the centurion informed the commander – 'What are you about to do?' – that Paul was a Roman citizen. The commander questioned his citizenship and arranged for a confrontation between Paul and the Jewish Sanhedrin for the next day. [Acts 22:25]

5. Second centurion at the Antonia Fortress The meeting with the Sanhedrin (*see above*) broke up in

Tombstone of a centurion, AD 43-9, from Colchester, England.

agonized conversations, first with the two thieves and then with the mother and the 'son'. He was there in the darkness; he heard the cry of desolation – and he heard the final cry of triumph, 'It is finished'.

And out of this experience – however little he may have grasped what was going on, or the significance of what he himself was doing as executioner – he gave his personal verdict of utter admiration. He allowed himself bravely and honestly to be heard, in complete insubordination, contradicting and criticizing his superior authority – the Roman governor: 'Certainly this man was innocent!'; 'Truly this was the Son of God!' [Matt. 27:54; Mark 15:39; Luke 23:47]

3. Cornelius, centurion at Caesarea *see* CORNELIUS

4. First centurion at the Antonia Fortress When Paul came to Jerusalem after his Third Journey, James, the first bishop of Jerusalem, warned him that his loyalty to the Jewish Law was being questioned. James recommended that Paul associate himself

above Model of the Roman fortress of Antonia.
right Procession carrying the cross along the Via Dolorosa to Calvary passing over the site of the Antonia Fortress.

confusion, Paul being supported by the Pharisees but condemned by the Sadducees. Again, the commander took Paul into protective custody. Some of the Jews, however, held a meeting and made a solemn vow to hunger-strike until such time as they should have killed Paul. They planned to ambush him on the way to the Sanhedrin, but Paul's nephew got wind of the plan and warned him. Paul called one of the centurions and asked him to conduct his nephew to the commander, who at once acted on the information. Summoning two centurions, he arranged for the despatch of Paul, under infantry and cavalry escort, to Caesarea, with a letter of explanation to the governor, Felix. [Acts 23:17, 23]

6. Julius, centurion of the Augustan cohort *see* JULIUS
CEPHAS (Gk. from the Aramaic 'rock' or 'stone')
see PETER
CHLOE (Gk. 'verdant') The Corinthian woman, the members of whose household, possibly her slaves, informed Paul at Ephesus of the party strife within the Christian Church at Corinth. [1 Cor. 1:11]

CHRIST (Gk. 'anointed', 'Messiah')
The Messianic hope

The title 'Messiah', in the Hebrew *Mashiah* and in the Greek *Christos*, from which we derive the term 'Christ', is found in the Old Testament as an adjective meaning anointed or consecrated to an office. Kings, priests and prophets were thus anointed. The king was the 'Anointed of the Lord'. The prophet Nathan told King David that his house would remain on the throne; from this prophecy expectations arose about future kings descended from David. But an anointed king does not come into all the pictures to be found in the Old Testament of a better world coming in the future. In many prophetic utterances God is said to be the only true king of Israel. However, for some time before the period in which the New Testament books were written, the ideal future king of Israel was called the Messiah.

Jewish expectations underwent considerable change in periods of persecution of the Jewish people. In the reign of Antiochus Epiphanes (175-163 BC), according to many scholars, the Book of Daniel was written and in this the 'People of the saints of the Most High', the future possessors of the kingdom which God will establish, are represented symbolically by a human figure: 'One like a son of man came with the clouds of heaven'. The Book of Enoch, generally thought to have been written about the same period, envisaged a superhuman being, the 'Elect One', waiting in heaven to descend upon the world in judgement. The writer of eighteen psalms attributed to Solomon, generally believed to have been written about 70-40 BC, perpetuated the idea of a Davidic king who would rule from Jerusalem. The last two of these psalms refer to the 'righteous and pure Davidic king who will build up Jerusalem', who will punish sinners, subdue the nations hostile to Israel and rule in righteousness.

In the time of Jesus expectation was divided between a warrior king who would, as a political ruler, introduce the reign of God on earth, and a supernatural deliverer, a figure from the world beyond the sky, the 'Son of Man' of the Book of Daniel or the 'Elect One' of the Book of Enoch. The followers of Jesus believed that he had fulfilled Messianic expectation in his ministry and by his death and resurrection. In this redemption and deliverance, according to their perception of the matter, he had fulfilled their expectation. The writers of the Gospels of Matthew and Luke had evidently expected the Messiah to be of the family of David and they traced the ancestry of Jesus, through Joseph, back to David, although such a genealogy may seem to us

left The Transfiguration of Christ: 19th-century Russian icon. Jesus, now recognized by his followers as the Messiah, is flanked by the Old Testament prophets Moses (left) and Elijah (right).

The Last Supper: 13th-century mural from Karanlik Kilise, Cappadocia. Judas dips in the dish to receive the sop.

inconsistent with the story of the virgin birth of Jesus which they also included in their Gospels.

Jesus as Messiah

All four Gospels state that Jesus knew himself to be the Messiah. The Gospels differ from one another in their presentation of the style or kind of Messiahship which he envisaged and of the extent to which he actually claimed Messiahship. Jesus is never represented as saying that he was the Messiah, using that actual word. Nor is he represented as denying that he was the Messiah. In the Gospels of Mark, Matthew and Luke, generally known as the Synoptic Gospels, it appears that Jesus tried to keep secret his identity as Messiah, ordering those who recognized him to remain silent about it. Especially in the Gospel of Mark the dramatic irony of this secret is to be found in the fact that it was only the evil spirits possessing the mentally handicapped who did recognize him, until the last few months of his life. Then Peter and other disciples said to him, 'You are the Christ', only to be ordered to keep silent and say nothing about it. At his examination in front of the high priest, when asked under oath the question, 'Are you the Christ, the Son of the Blessed?', Jesus answered, 'I am',

overleaf The Agony in the Garden, by Giovanni Bellini (c. 1430-1516). The kneeling figure of Christ looks up to the angel who extends to him the cup of suffering.

Mosaic from St Mark's, Venice, showing
the crucified Christ, flanked by Mary and John
and the Roman soldiers.

according to Mark's Gospel. The Gospels of Matthew
and Luke state that he said, 'You have said so' or, 'you
say that I am'. This has been said to introduce an element of ambiguity into the frank admission recorded
in the Gospel of Mark. But whatever ambiguity there is
in the phrase used in the Gospels of Matthew and Luke
may belong to the original Aramaic words of Jesus.

The purpose of Jesus in keeping the 'Messianic
Secret' seems to lie in the radical difference between his
conception of the Messianic function and the current
conceptions and expectations. Public recognition would
inevitably have resulted in general misunderstanding
of his purpose. Thus when he chose to enter Jerusalem
on a donkey, as a man of peace, he was acclaimed as a
conquering hero.

The Gospel of John, often called the Fourth Gospel,
is unlike the other three Gospels and was written later.

It describes an open acknowledgment by the disciples
of Jesus that he was the Messiah, even at the beginning
of his ministry. Before Jesus invited his disciples to be
with him, Andrew said to Peter, 'We have found the
Messiah' and Nathanael addressed Jesus as 'Son of God
and King of Israel'. Martha said to Jesus that she knew
that he was the Messiah. When the woman of Samaria
mentioned the Messiah to Jesus he said to her, 'I who
speak to you am he'. It is thought by many scholars that
when this Gospel was written the words 'Christ' and
'Jesus' had in the writer's circle almost become two
names of one person. But the Gospel of John concludes that 'These things are written that you may
believe that Jesus is the Christ, the Son of God'.

Jesus as the Son of Man

Jesus applied to himself the title of 'Son of Man', to be
found in his speeches eighty times within the Gospels,
always with reference to Jesus himself. Outside the
Gospels it is used little in the New Testament; but
Stephen, among the first Christian martyrs, uses it at
his trial as a title of Jesus. (Acts 7:56) Jesus certainly
seems to have applied the title to himself in a prophetic
and authoritative or official context. Before telling a
paralytic to take up his pallet and walk, since his
paralysis was healed, Jesus declares that 'The Son of
Man has authority on earth to forgive sins.' (Mark 2:10)
On another occasion, defending his disciples who had
plucked ears of grain on the Sabbath Day, he said, 'The
Son of Man is lord even of the Sabbath.' (Mark 2:28)
He uses the title in the context of his quotations from
the Suffering Servant passages in the Book of Isaiah.
Thus he says, 'The Son of Man . . . came not to be
served but to serve and to give his life as a ransom for
many.' (Mark 10:45) In the Fourth Gospel the title is
used in a prediction of his death on the cross, 'as Moses
lifted up the serpent in the wilderness, so must the Son
of Man be lifted up'. (John 3:14) Finally, according to
the Synoptic Gospels of Mark, Matthew and Luke,
Jesus when confronting the high priest at his trial
quoted from the prophecy in the Book of Daniel, 'You
will see the Son of Man sitting at the right hand of
Power and coming with the clouds of heaven.'

Jesus as the Suffering Servant

According to all the Gospels, Jesus associated his
Messiahship and his identity as the Son of Man with
his future sufferings and his death. From his baptism
and temptation onwards, Jesus saw in the passage which
we find in the Book of Isaiah about the 'Suffering Servant of the Lord' the mode of his Messiahship.

In the Gospel of Mark, Jesus predicts his passion in
detail. 'Behold, we are going up to Jerusalem; and the
Son of Man will be delivered to the chief priests and the
scribes, and they will condemn him to death, and
deliver him to the Gentiles: and they will mock him, and
spit upon him, and scourge him, and kill him: and after

three days he will rise.' The Gospel of Luke describes Jesus directly quoting from the Book of Isaiah on the way to the place where he was arrested. 'For I tell you that this scripture must be fulfilled in me, "And he was reckoned with transgressors": for what is written about me has its fulfilment.' At the Last Supper, Jesus had said, 'I am among you as one that serves.'

Perhaps the many indirect allusions to the Suffering Servant passages are more significant than the direct quotations. For example, Jesus said to his disciples: 'For the Son of Man came not to be served but to serve, and to give his life a ransom for many.' (Mark 10:45) The costly suffering of the obedient servant of the Lord in the Suffering Servant passages is well described by the word 'ransom'. There are several places in these passages where the word 'many' is used and the suffering of the servant is said to be beneficial to many nations and many individual people. (Isa. 52:14, 15; 53:11, 12)

The actions of Jesus described in the Gospels and the teaching about human conduct attributed to him in the Gospels seem to be related to these prophetic passages. He is silent at his trial before Pilate: 'Like a lamb that is led to the slaughter, and like a sheep that before its shearers is dumb, so he opened not his mouth.' (Isa. 53:7) He was treated as a criminal, yet was buried in the tomb of a rich man, Joseph of Arimathea. 'And they

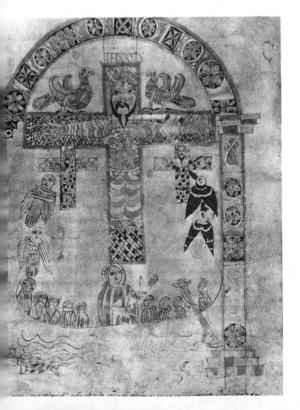

The crucifixion, from a late 8th-century Celtic manuscript. The two thieves hang on either side, while beneath Mary stretches up her hand.

made his grave with the wicked and with a rich man in his death.' (Isa. 53:9) The teaching of Jesus about non-resistance reflects the action of the Suffering Servant in offering 'cheeks to those who pulled out the beard'. (Isa. 50:6) So the follower of Jesus is to turn the left cheek to those who strike him on the right cheek. (Matt. 5:39)

All the imagery used in the New Testament to portray the Messianic function of Jesus is derived from the Old Testament. But in the Old Testament, outside the Suffering Servant passages, the conception of the Messiah and the conception of vicarious suffering are not combined or united. It may be said, in general terms, that the Messiah belongs to the future, while suffering, whether it is vicarious or not, belongs to the present age. Jesus identified the Suffering Servant with the Messiah, in the context of his own life and time, combining the two conceptions.

Jesus the Son of God

In Hebrew, phrases such as 'son of' and 'father of' may indicate the character of a person, rather than parenthood. Jesus called the devil the 'Father of Lies'. (John 8:44) 'Sons of Belial' is a common biblical term for evil men. So also the phrase 'son of Righteousness' can describe an honest man and a godly man can be called 'son of God'. Jesus pronounced the peacemakers blessed, 'for they shall be called sons of God'. (Matt. 5:9) Hosea the prophet referred to Israel as God's son and Nathan the prophet addressed the anointed king of Israel as God's son. (Hos. 11:1; 2 Sam. 7:14)

In the days of Jesus the term the 'Son of God' was used for the Messiah. It is so used in the first words of the Gospel of Mark: 'The beginning of the Gospel of Jesus Christ, the Son of God.' In that Gospel, when Peter recognizes Jesus as the Messiah, he says: 'You are the Christ.' In the Gospel of Matthew, at the same point, the words are: 'You are the Christ, the Son of the Living God.' Jesus is reported in the Gospels of Matthew and Luke as saying: 'No one knows the Son except the Father and no one knows the Father except the Son'. It is the belief of Jesus that he was the Son of God which has given to his followers their most vivid idea of the Fatherhood of God. It is reported in all the Synoptic Gospels that, when Jesus was baptized by John the Baptist and on the occasion when he was transfigured in the presence of three of his disciples, he heard a voice from heaven. The words of that voice were: 'You are [or 'This is'] my beloved Son, in whom I am well pleased.' The words seem to come from two passages in the Old Testament, one of which refers to the King-Messiah (Ps. 2:7) while the other concerns the Suffering Servant (Isa. 42:1). It was this union of 'Sonship' with

overleaf 18th-century German engraving of Jerusalem, showing the death of Judas, the Crucifixion, the Resurrection and the Ascension.

'Suffering Service' that made the conception of the Messianic function in the mind of Jesus, as he is pictured in all the Gospels, radically different from all other conceptions of the Messiah. The inauguration of the kingdom of God was the function of the Messiah according to Jesus, as well as in the popular conceptions; but the kingdom of God was seen according to a different pattern. The contrast is shown in the story of the temptation of Jesus in the wilderness, at the beginning of his public ministry according to the Synoptic Gospels, when he rejected popular conceptions of the Messiah as an economic benefactor or a political ruler overcoming the enemies of his people by miracles.

In the parable of the vineyard, his assessment of his situation and his purpose are revealed. It describes a man planting a vineyard, fencing it, ditching it and building a tower to protect it, before letting it to tenants and going abroad. In due time he sends a series of servants to collect the produce due to him from the vineyard. Each time the tenants maltreat or kill his servants. He still has someone left to send, his beloved son. Last of all he sends his son and they kill him and throw his body out of the vineyard. In this story given in the Synoptic Gospels (Mark 12:1-8; Matt. 21:33-39; Luke 20:9-15) Jesus accuses his opponents among the priests and scribes of disregarding the messages of the prophets of the past and makes a prediction of a violent death for himself, similar to the deaths of many prophets. Jesus believed that his task, as the Son of God, was to reveal the loving purpose of his Father to his

Aerial view of Jerusalem, showing the Old City and Temple area in the centre, the city of David and the Western Hill in the foreground, Gethsemane on the Mount of Olives to the right.

Christ in Majesty, by Fra Angelico (*c.* 1400-55), depicting Christ with the stigmata of crucifixion, surrounded by a choir and orchestra of angels.

people. 'I, when I am lifted up from the earth, will draw all men to myself.' (John 12:32) It was his consciousness of his sonship to God and his vivid experience of God's fatherly purpose that shaped his Messianic destiny to save by suffering. He went to his death in the certainty that it was the will of God, completely aware of what was coming to him, completely accepting it and utterly determined that nothing should prevent the will of God being done. Throughout the Passion, he is the master of the situation, in the Upper Room, in Gethsemane, before the high priest, before Pilate and finally on the cross. The writer of the Gospel of John, the Fourth Gospel, declares that it is the belief of the followers of Jesus that the death of Jesus was according to the purpose of God for the world, 'that whoever believes in him may have eternal life. For God so loved the world that he gave his only Son, that whoever believes in him should not perish, but have eternal life.'

Jesus Christ as God Incarnate

The disciples of Jesus and their successors in the Christian Church came to believe that Jesus had created a new relationship between man and God, through his life and teaching, his death and his resurrection. His achievement could not be fitted into the traditional picture of the Messiah. They believed that he had not just brought a new message about God; in him God had come to save and to draw mankind to himself, by love and by the example of his self-sacrifice. He had come into human history from a 'beyond', from the heart of God himself, to redeem mankind that men might live with him as fellow sons of God. As Athanasius wrote in the 4th century: 'He became human, that we might become divine.'

The Christian doctrine of the incarnation, that God became Man in the Person of Jesus, is not to be identified with the belief that Jesus had no human father, which is the Christian doctrine of the virgin birth. The Muslim believes in the virgin birth, without believing in the Incarnation. In modern times many Christians consider the doctrines of the incarnation to be true, while doubting the historical character of the story of the virgin birth. The speeches attributed to Peter in the Acts of the Apostles, the Letters of Paul and the Gospel of John do not use the virgin birth as an argument for the Messiahship of Jesus. Paul writes that 'God sent forth his Son, born of woman, born under the law'. (Gal. 4:4) But this need not be a reference to the virgin birth; it implies that the Son of God whom Paul proclaims to the Gentiles is a man and a Jew. The doctrine of the virgin birth was taken by the Church from the Gospels of Matthew and Luke, where it dominates the accounts of the infancy of Jesus. Some Christian scholars regard these accounts of the infancy as the expression in the form of a story of the idea that Jesus as the Son of God came into history and not out of history, having in him a new life and a new hope, which the world itself could not produce. [The Suffering Servant passages in the Book of Isaiah are Isa. 42:1-4; 49:1-6; 50:4-9; 52:13; 53:12] *see* JESUS, JOHN, LUKE, MARK, MATTHEW, COLOSSIANS, HEBREWS

CHUZA The domestic administrator or steward at the court of Herod Antipas, whose wife Joanna was one of the women – together with Mary of Magdala, Susanna, and others – who accompanied Jesus and the Twelve on his teaching tour of Galilee. These women provided for the disciples 'out of their means'. No doubt Chuza was a man of some income and substance and may well have told Antipas about the miraculous ministry of Jesus. For Luke records that 'Herod the tetrarch heard of all that was done, and he was perplexed, because it was said by some that John had been raised from the dead, by some that Elijah had appeared, and by others that one of the old prophets had risen. Herod said, "John I beheaded; but who is this about whom I hear such things?" And he sought to see him.' (Luke 9:7-9) [Luke 8:3]

CLAUDIA One of the four who sent their personal greetings at the close of Paul's final letter to Timothy in Ephesus, perhaps the last he ever wrote. From the grouping of the names, Claudia may possibly have been the wife of Pudens and the mother of Linus. Paul is writing from prison, presumably in Rome, after his conviction, and expecting execution. This family, not elsewhere mentioned in the New Testament, may have ministered to the final needs of Paul, along with the 'beloved physician' Luke, Paul's fellow-prisoner to the end. [2 Tim. 4:21]

CLAUDIUS The Roman emperor, AD 41-54, mentioned twice by name in Acts. First, Luke established the date of the fulfilment of a prophecy of famine, foretold by the prophet from Jerusalem, called Agabus, which famine 'took place in the days of Claudius'. (*see* AGABUS)

Secondly, Luke comments on the arrival in Corinth from Rome of two Jews, Aquila and his wife Priscilla, 'because Claudius had commanded all the Jews to leave Rome'. This edict of the expulsion of Jews from Rome took effect in the year 49. (*see* AQUILA)

It was during the reign of Claudius that the first two missionary journeys set forth from Antioch, by then the headquarters of the Gentile Christian mission, and that the first Christian Council was held in Jerusalem. [Acts 11:28; 18:2]

CLAUDIUS LYSIAS The Roman tribune commanding the troops of the Antonia Fortress, at the time of the assault on Paul by the Jews in the Temple area, on his final visit to Jerusalem. The tribune is faced with constant responsibilities and decisions in the face of the tremendous emotional forces at play in a highly combustible situation. Throughout, he conducts himself and disposes his forces with skill and efficiency. His report, however, to his superior, the governor Felix at Caesarea, abbreviates and manipulates the record of events in such a manner as to give a logic to his actions that was not originally there. Only in the opening address of this

report is the tribune's name revealed as Claudius Lysias, after two whole chapters of fast-moving events in which the tribune plays the leading role.

On his arrival in Jerusalem, Paul, in deference to the wishes of the Jewish leaders of the Christian Church, had agreed to undergo a week's ritual purification in the Temple, with four other men under a vow, to show that he personally kept the Law. When the week's ritual was almost completed, some Asian Jews had recognized Paul and, stirring up the crowd, had accused him of bringing Greeks into the Temple. They would have lynched Paul, if the guard had not turned out to protect him and hustle him up the steps of the Antonia Fortress. Paul, speaking in Greek and declaring his Roman citizenship, requested a final opportunity to address the mob, which he did in Aramaic.

The tribune himself seems to have taken command and in considerable force to have charged the mob, thinking that the dishevelled figure of Paul was that of a dangerous Egyptian brigand, who had only recently brought an army of assassins (literally 'dagger-men') against the city. His astonishment to hear a request in educated Greek from a 'Jew of Tarsus, a citizen of no mean city' must have been considerable, and so he gave permission for Paul to speak. Luke's description of the riot and the scenes that followed is a masterpiece and certainly the work of an eye-witness of the events.

At this point, Paul 'motioned with his hands to the people; and when there was a great hush, he spoke to them in the Hebrew language [dialect] saying: "Brethren and fathers, hear the defence which I now make before you . . ."'

When he described his own conversion, all listened in silence, but when he declared his commission to the Gentiles he was shouted down. The tribune accordingly took him into the fortress for scourging in preparation for his interrogation. Not until Paul was actually strapped up for this literally crippling torture did he say to the centurion standing by: '"Is it lawful for you to scourge a man who is a Roman citizen, and uncondemned?" When the centurion heard that, he went to the tribune and said to him, "What are you about to do? For this man is a Roman citizen." So the tribune came and said to him, "Tell me, are you a Roman citizen?" And he said, "Yes." The tribune answered, "I bought this citizenship for a large sum." Paul said, "But I was born a citizen." So those who were about to

above Roman sculpture of a soldier on horseback,
armed with a short stabbing sword and shield.

examine him withdrew from him instantly; and the
tribune also was afraid, for he realized that Paul was a
Roman citizen and that he had bound him.' (Acts 22:25-
29)

The tribune had put himself in a difficult situation,
for Paul had influential relatives in Jerusalem, and had
just brought an enormous sum of money to the city for
the relief of the poor, which had been collected in several
different Roman provinces. The next day, therefore, the
tribune ordered a meeting of the high priests and the
whole Council and placed Paul before them.

Within the Council, Paul skilfully divided the
Pharisees from the Sadducees, by claiming to be a
Pharisee and basing his claim to orthodoxy on the
resurrection of the dead, a doctrine unacceptable to the
Sadducees. Paul was withdrawn from the debate that
followed and returned to the fortress. Some forty
zealous opponents of Paul vowed to fast until they had
killed Paul. Information, however, of their plot reached
the Roman tribune and he sent Paul with both an
infantry and cavalry escort, at nine o'clock that night,

The supper at Emmaus at the house of Cleopas: painting by Caravaggio (1583-1610).

down to Antipatris, a Roman staging-post on the way to the coast. On the following day the cavalry took Paul on to Caesarea and presented him to the Roman governor, Felix, with a covering letter from the tribune.

The tribune's letter has every appearance of being genuine, being as brief and objective as it is misleading of the real motives of the man, but it fulfilled its purpose admirably. 'Claudius Lysias to his Excellency the governor Felix, greeting. This man was seized by the Jews, and was about to be killed by them, when I came upon them with the soldiers and rescued him, having learned that he was a Roman citizen. And desiring to know the charge on which they accused him, I brought him down to their council. I found that he was accused about questions of their law, but charged with

nothing deserving death or imprisonment. And when it was disclosed to me that there would be a plot against the man, I sent him to you at once, ordering his accusers also to state before you what they have against him.' (Acts 23:26-30)

Had Claudius Lysias been an incompetent and corrupt official, he might well have connived at Paul's death at any one of a number of moments in this sequence of events. Yet he took every precaution to ensure Paul's protection until the governor should decide his innocence or guilt. Thus Claudius Lysias became one of several who together enabled Paul to reach Rome. [Acts 21, 22, 23. By name Acts 23:26]

CLEMENT A fellow-worker with Paul and others at Philippi 'whose names are in the book of life', commended by Paul in the final and happy chapter of his letter to the Christian congregation in Philippi. Clement is such a common Roman name that the 3rd-century theologian Origen's identification of this Philippian Clement with Clement, bishop of Rome at the turn of the 1st century, is barely possible. [Phil. 4:3]

CLEOPAS One of two disciples walking over the hills from Jerusalem to a village called Emmaus on the first Easter Day. While they were discussing the events of the last few days, Jesus joined them, walking and talking with them, but they did not recognize him. 'And he said to them, "What is this conversation which you are holding with each other as you walk?" And they stood still looking sad.' (Luke 24:17) Then Cleopas answered, '"Are you the only visitor to Jerusalem who does not know the things that have happened there in these days?" And he said to them, "What things?" They said to him, "Concerning Jesus of Nazareth, who was a prophet mighty in deed and word before God and all the people, and how our chief priests and rulers delivered him up to be condemned to death, and crucified him. But we had hoped that he was the one to redeem Israel. Yes, and besides all this, it is now the third day since this happened. Moreover, some women of our company amazed us. They were at the tomb early in the morning and did not find his body; and they came back saying that they had even seen a vision of angels, who said that he was alive. Some of those who were with us went to the tomb, and found it just as the women had said; but him they did not see."' (Luke 24:18-24) Jesus, still unrecognized, turned to them and said, '"O foolish men, and slow of heart to believe all that the prophets have spoken! Was it not necessary that the Christ should suffer these things and enter into his glory?" And beginning with Moses and all the prophets, he interpreted to them in all the scriptures the things concerning himself.' (Luke 24:25-27)

As they drew near to their destination, Jesus made as if to continue further on his journey, but they persuaded him, 'Stay with us, for it is toward evening and the day is now far spent.' (Luke 24:29) And so he turned in to eat with them. As the guest, he was invited to give thanks before the meal. 'When he was at table with them, he took the bread and blessed, and broke it, and gave it to them. And their eyes were opened and they recognized him; and he vanished out of their sight. They said to each other, "Did not our hearts burn within us while he talked to us on the road, while he opened to us the scriptures?" And they rose that same hour and returned to Jerusalem.' (Luke 24:30-33)

Perhaps the companion of Cleopas was his wife, though surely Luke, of all people, would have said so. In any case, they were probably Judean rather than Galilean disciples.

There are no less than four sites for Emmaus, though all with differing merits and at varying distances from Jerusalem. The Roman *stadia* was approximately equivalent to the modern furlong, but the number of *stadia* differs in some of the major manuscripts. An unlikely site is that of Kaloniyeh (so named after a colony of Roman veterans), only half the recorded distance from Jerusalem. Another site is at Qubeibe, 60 *stadia* (or 7 miles) away, as quoted in most of the major biblical manuscripts; this was a small town on the Roman road (still to be seen) from Jerusalem to Caesarea. This site is supported only by the Crusaders and the Franciscans. Yet another site, favoured by the Crusaders, with a magnificent church built over the Roman masonry and water-supply for the detachment of the Tenth Legion from Fretensis in Sicily, is to be found at Abu Ghosh. Again, this site is the correct distance away from Jerusalem and on another and perhaps earlier Roman road to the coast.

Paradoxically, the earliest traditional and archaeological evidence, probably 4th-century Byzantine as well as Crusader, supports a location at Amwas (Arabic for Emmaus), one hundred and sixty *stadia* from Jerusalem, as quoted in *Codex Sinaiticus*, which was known to both Bishop Eusebius of Caesarea and to Jerome, who translated the Vulgate. Over the hills from Jerusalem, however, Amwas is only 15 miles. Therefore, this site is within reach of the possibility of the double journey from and back to Jerusalem in an afternoon.

Wherever the Emmaus appearance of the risen Jesus took place, Luke's narrative of this story of Cleopas and his companion is of great value as typical of the post-resurrection experience of Jesus's disciples. Excavations at Amwas and Qubeibe prove that the whole region supported some sort of agricultural community. Cleopas, therefore, was not likely to have been a dreamer, but a sober business man. As Luke himself says: 'To them he presented himself alive after his passion by many proofs, appearing to them during forty days, and speaking of the kingdom of God.' (Acts 1:3) [Luke 24:18]

CLOPAS The husband of Mary, whom John describes as watching by the cross of Jesus. 'Standing by the cross of Jesus were his mother, and his mother's sister, Mary the wife of Clopas, and Mary Magdalene.' (John 19:25) The 2nd-century historian, Hegesippus, supposed that Clopas was the brother of Joseph the carpenter, and brother-in-law to Mary the mother of Jesus. Were this correct, Clopas would have been uncle to Jesus. [John 19:25]

COLOSSIANS Colossae was one of three cities within the fertile valley of the River Lycus, about 100 miles inland and to the eastward of Ephesus. All three cities were probably evangelized by Epaphras, a convert of Paul, trained during Paul's long and systematic period of teaching at Ephesus, in the course of his Third Journey.

Christ in Judgment: 12th-century mosaic from the apse of the Cathedral
of Monreale, Sicily.

Paul's letter to the Christian community at Colossae
was primarily concerned with countering a peculiar type
of false teaching, which devalued the importance of
Jesus in God's plan for the world. This was probably a
local heresy, the result of a wish to incorporate into
Christian theology the best of both pagan and Jewish
philosophies. Paul roundly declared Jesus Christ the
supreme power for salvation, the ultimate reality, and
the all-sufficient redeemer and intermediary between
God and man.

A letter from captivity

The so-called 'pastoral epistles' to Timothy and Titus
belong to a period of Paul's imprisonment after his first
trial and acquittal in Rome. The letters to Philippi,
Colossae, Philemon, and the circular letter now entitled 'to the Ephesians' may have been written during
any of three previous imprisonments, at Ephesus,
Caesarea, and Rome. The last two each lasted at least

two years, while the first, to which Paul refers on three
occasions (1 Cor. 15:32; 2 Cor. 1:8-10; Rom. 16:3, 4),
seems to have been very brief, however critical and
severe.

There is some doubt as to during which imprisonment
Paul wrote his letter to the Colossians. Together with a
personal letter to Philemon, himself a Colossian, the
two letters were written at the same time and despatched
to Colossae by the same messenger, Tychicus. Both
letters include greetings from Epaphras, Luke the
physician, Demas, Aristarchus, and Mark, nephew of
Barnabas. Both refer to Paul's prison chains. Together
with his letter to Philemon, Paul returns the fugitive
slave, Onesimus. It might seem more probable that Paul
despatched Onesimus the comparatively short distance
of 100 miles from Ephesus to Colossae, rather than from
Caesarea or from Rome. Again, both letters are sent by
Paul and Timothy, Paul's companion during his time

at Ephesus. Moreover, those who send greetings also belong to the band of Paul's associates on his Third Journey and stay in Ephesus in the years 56 and 57. But there is no evidence that Paul's imprisonment in Ephesus was long enough for him to receive reports and send considered answers. During his first long imprisonment in Rome in the years 61-63, he was only under house arrest and his friends had free access to him. The vast cosmopolitan city of Rome was a notorious hideout for runaway slaves such as Onesimus.

Heresy at Colossae

Wherever Paul was imprisoned at the time, he was visited by Epaphras with a report from Colossae, favourable except for one ominous detail. Certain strange teachings were gaining ground, and Epaphras himself was not sufficiently confident to deal with them. Paul therefore wrote to correct this false doctrine and at the same time gave some practical advice on domestic relations. It seems that the teachers at Colossae had tried to combine within Christianity what they considered to be the best in both Judaism and Hellenism. On the one hand they stressed the demands of the Mosaic Law, the keeping of festivals, of the Sabbath, and of the hygiene laws. On the other, they devalued the material and physical, regarding the human body with contempt, not considering the physical birth and death of the Man Jesus as able to secure the reconciliation of the world with God. They questioned the uniqueness of Jesus Christ in God's scheme of salvation, which they felt could only be achieved by supernatural means. We do not know exactly what form this heresy took. We only have Paul's reply, which seems an attempt to combat pagan theosophy and to reaffirm the total sufficiency of Jesus Christ within God's purpose and scheme of salvation.

Stressing the role of Jesus

The theme of the letter to the Colossians is to be found more fully expressed within the circular letter now known to us as the Letter to the Ephesians. (*see* EPHESIANS) The importance of this letter to the Colossians is that it includes the first known Christian statement of the cosmic significance of Jesus. This is all the more remarkable, appearing as it does more than thirty years before the *Logos* declaration of Jesus as the source of universal life, in the prologue of the Fourth Gospel. (*see* JOHN **4.**)

'He is the image of the invisible God, the first-born of all creation; for in him all things were created, in heaven and on earth, visible and invisible, whether thrones or dominions or principalities or authorities – all things were created through him and for him. He is before all things, and in him all things hold together. He is the head of the body, the church; he is the beginning, the first-born from the dead, that in everything he might be pre-eminent. For in him all the fullness of God was

pleased to dwell, and through him to reconcile to himself all things, whether on earth or in heaven, making peace by the blood of his cross.' (Col. 1:15-20)

Such a magnificent formal statement is followed rapidly by personal witness of his own sufferings, by which Paul claims to make up all that still has to be endured by Jesus for the sake of his body, the Church.

Then Paul warns his readers to hold to the true faith in Jesus, rather than to any false teaching: 'As therefore you received Christ Jesus the Lord, so live in him, rooted and built up in him and established in the faith, just as you were taught, abounding in thanksgiving. See to it that no one makes a prey of you by philosophy and empty deceit, according to human tradition, according to the elemental spirits of the universe, and not according to Christ. For in him the whole fullness of deity dwells bodily, and you have come to fullness of life in him, who is the head of all rule and authority.' (Col. 2:6-10)

Paul warns his readers against forms of asceticism: 'Therefore let no one pass judgment on you in questions of food and drink or with regard to a festival or a new moon or a sabbath. These are only a shadow of what is to come; but the substance belongs to Christ. . . . If with Christ you died to the elemental spirits of the universe, why do you live as if you still belonged to the world? Why do you submit to regulations?' (Col. 2:16, 17, 20)

Paul's closing exhortation concerns general rules of Christian behaviour and the morals of home and household relationships. Finally, he adds to the dictated letter a message in his own bold hand: 'Remember my fetters. Grace be with you.' [Col. 1-4]

CORINTHIANS It was at Corinth, during his Second Journey, that Paul conducted a mission (from perhaps the winter of the years 49 and 50 to the summer of the year 51), described by Luke in Acts 18:1-18. Later,

Looking north from the height of Acro-Corinth, the isthmus of Corinth was flanked by the ports of Lechaeum and Cenchreae.

Ruins of the *Agora* (market place) of ancient Corinth, with Acro-Corinth, the fortress which protected the city, in the background.

during his Third Journey, he conducted a considerable correspondence with the Christian community at Corinth, writing from Ephesus between the years 54 and 57, during which time he also paid a brief visit to Corinth. Although Paul built up a flourishing Christian congregation at Corinth, which he left in the care of Apollos, a learned Alexandrian Jewish convert, the Corinthian Church played a relatively small part in the later history of the Christian Church in the eastern Mediterranean.

Corinth was an important and wealthy city astride the Isthmus of Corinth and controlling the ports on either side, Lechaeum on the west, Cenchreae on the east. Corinth was the capital of the Roman province of Achaia, the southern part of Greece, and the seat of the Roman proconsul. It was a city of great commerce, wealth, and squalor, renowned for its culture and notorious for its immorality. Lying on the great trade-route between Rome and the East, with a very mixed commercial and cosmopolitan community, Corinth was of strategic importance in the spreading of Christianity throughout the eastern Mediterranean. Travellers could avoid the dangerous voyage round the Peloponnese by crossing the Isthmus of Corinth from harbour to harbour. The international character of the city fostered the development of a variety of cults from as far away as Egypt and Phoenicia. The chief shrine, however, was the temple of the Greek goddess of Love – Aphrodite – although the cult was debased by foreign influences. The priestess-prostitutes of Aphrodite at Corinth are said to have numbered a thousand.

Paul came to Corinth after his highly unsuccessful visit to Athens. Filled with disappointment, in fear and trembling he made his way over the isthmus to the city

top left Stairway entrance to the fortress of
Acro-Corinth.
bottom left Ancient road along the Isthmus of Corinth.

above right The Fountain of Peirene, Corinth, which
supplied the public baths and still flows
through the aqueducts among the ruins of the city.

in the winter of 49-50. There he remained for eighteen
months, living and working as a tentmaker with Aquila
and his wife Priscilla, Jews expelled from Rome by the
edict of Claudius in the year 49. On the arrival of
Timothy and Silas, they taught both Jews and Greeks in
the synagogue and then in a private house. As a result,
a large Church was formed at Corinth, mostly from the
poor and slave classes. During this time Paul, receiving
Timothy's report from Thessalonica, sent his first letter
to that Church about the second coming of Jesus.
Following further reports he sent his second letter,
warning the Thessalonians not to use the teaching of
justification by faith as an excuse for lawlessness, but to
persevere in faith and well-doing. In both these letters,
Paul's intensity and affection are conveyed and reveal
the power of his personality.

With the arrival of a new proconsul of Achaia, called
Gallio, in the year 51, certain members of the Jewish
community at Corinth accused Paul of teaching
religion 'contrary to the Law'. Gallio refused to adjudicate, but the time had come for Paul and his party
to move on. Sailing from Cenchreae, the eastern harbour
of Corinth, he reached Ephesus, on the west coast of
Asia Minor. After a brief preliminary visit to the
synagogue and promising to return on his next journey,
Paul sailed for Caesarea, where he greeted the Christian
Church on his way north by road to Antioch. This
Second Journey of 2,800 miles must have taken three
years, the greater part of which was spent at Corinth.

Broadside against immorality

The following is one of many theories of the circumstances of Paul's correspondence with Corinth.

The oriental cult of Aphrodite flourished in the city
and ports of Corinth. (left) Kneeling marble
Aphrodite. 1st century BC; (right) Aphrodite
of the Melos type.

During his time in Ephesus, Paul had heard news
from Corinth that made it necessary for him to write to
warn that Christian community against associating with
immoral persons. He then probably wrote what is now
to be found in 2 Cor. 6:14-7:1. Shortly afterwards, he
received an official letter from the Corinthian Church
asking advice on specific matters, such as the celebration
of the Eucharist and the doctrine of the resurrection.
Paul had also heard that a party spirit prevailed in that
community and that a particularly grave case of immorality had arisen within the Church. Paul dealt with
these questions in a letter now known to us as 1 Corinthians, which he sent by sea, while Timothy took the
land route to deal with the situation in person. Neither
the letter nor Timothy's visit achieved the desired effect,
and Paul himself sailed for Corinth. Even he was not
able to secure a reform within the Corinthian Christian
community and, after being grossly insulted, he sailed
back to Ephesus. From there, he wrote a 'severe letter',
his third, part of which is probably to be found in 2
Cor. 10-13, which was carried by Titus, an older
and more experienced man than Timothy. This letter
demanded a proper respect both for Christian morality
and for Paul, as founder of the Church in Corinth.

When Paul finally closed his ministry at Ephesus, he
travelled north overland to Troas, whence he sailed
once again for Macedonia to visit Philippi, Thessalonica,
and Beroea. Somewhere *en route* he met Titus, who at
last brought him the good news that the Corinthian
Church was ready to conform, and that they had already
by a majority vote censured the person who had insulted
Paul. Paul immediately wrote his fourth letter, to be
found in 2 Cor. 1-9. In this last letter, he forgave
his antagonist, closed the controversy, and arranged for
a collection to be taken for the poor at Jerusalem. Paul
seems to have travelled overland to Corinth, where he
spent the winter months, in which time he wrote his
letter to the Christian Church in Rome, to prepare them
for his coming and to secure their support for a journey
to Spain.

Paul's plan to sail directly from Corinth for Jerusalem,
taking his poor-relief collection, was thwarted by some
threat of ambush. Consequently he returned overland
to Macedonia.

'Temples of the living God'

Only a fragment of Paul's first letter is to be found in 2
Cor. 6:14-7:1, but the theme is crystal clear: an appeal
for purity and the consecration of life to God. 'We are
the temple of the living God.' As the membership of the
Christian Church had been drawn from a motley of
pagans with a variety of standards of conduct, many
such problems were to arise in the newly-formed Christian community. Here, in this fragment of the initial
letter, we get only a glimpse at the sort of problems to
be dealt with at length in the later letters.

The second letter – our 1 Corinthians – must have
been sent soon after the first. A member of Chloe's
household (1 Cor. 1:11) brought Paul depressing news
of the faction rife in Corinth, and a letter (1 Cor. 7:1)
arrived, asking for Paul's ruling on a variety of points
concerning the ordering of worship and relationships
with the pagan society within the city. Our first letter to
the Corinthians is Paul's reply: an effort to deal with
these disciples and their problems.

The early Corinthian Church had little sense of unity,
little sense of sin, or of the need for salvation. Paul's
successor as pastor of the embryo Christian Church at
Corinth had been the Alexandrian Apollos, and his gifts
of exposition and oratory had compared favourably
with Paul's technique. Some of the congregation remained faithful to Paul, others were attracted to the
preaching of Apollos, yet others rallied to the name of
Peter. To all these Paul now preached Christ's leadership alone. 'Is Christ divided? Was Paul crucified for
you? Or were you baptized in the name of Paul?' (1 Cor.
1:13), and again, 'For Jews demand signs and Greeks
seek wisdom, but we preach Christ crucified, a stumbling
block to Jews and folly to Gentiles, but to those who

Etruscan sarcophagus, 3rd century BC,
showing a loving husband and
wife, illustrating Paul's teaching to
the Church at Corinth.

are called, both Jews and Greeks, Christ the power of God and the wisdom of God.' (1 Cor. 1:22-24)

Paul goes on to comment on a case of incest within the Christian congregation, which had cheerfully tolerated a liaison between a man and his stepmother. The man must be excommunicated. Such sin should be hunted out of the Christian household, as the Jews hunted out leaven before their Passover. 'Cleanse out the old leaven that you may be a new lump, as you really are unleavened. For Christ, our paschal lamb, has been sacrificed. Let us, therefore, celebrate the festival, not with the old leaven, the leaven of malice and evil, but with the unleavened bread of sincerity and truth.' (1 Cor. 5:7, 8) And this must be a personal choice: 'For what have I to do with judging outsiders? Is it not those inside the church whom you are to judge? God judges those outside. "Drive out the wicked person from among you."' (1 Cor. 5:12, 13)

Paul then complains of Christians going to law against each other in the pagan courts, which is further evidence of their lack of unity. 'I say this to your shame. Can it be that there is no man among you wise enough to decide between members of the brotherhood, but brother goes to law against brother, and that before unbelievers?' (1 Cor. 6:5-7) He warns his flock against immorality of all kinds. To 'become one' means surely to establish a close personal relationship. To do so with a harlot who has served in the pagan temple is forbidden to a Christian, who is linked with his Lord and is of one spirit with Christ Jesus. 'Do you not know that your body is a temple of the Holy Spirit within you, which you have from God? You are not your own; you were bought with a price. So glorify God in your body.' (1 Cor. 6:19, 20)

Then Paul deals one by one with the questions which he has been asked. As a bachelor, Paul points out the advantages of celibacy that Christian loyalties may be first and foremost to God. Those who need to marry should do so and there can be no question of divorce, says Paul, citing Jesus's own teaching. Paul's discouragement of marriage was most likely due to the current expectation of the End.

A thorny question was that of food offered to idols. Much of the meat sold in the markets had been offered as sacrifice in the pagan temples, and Paul gave three simple rulings. Christians could buy meat in the open market without scruple, but if the host at a dinner-party declared that the meat was sacrificial meat, then a Christian guest must refuse for the sake of his pagan friend, that nothing must be allowed to become an obstacle to his conversion. Any attendance at pagan feasts by Christians was expressly forbidden.

Because of the different backgrounds among the Christian community there was a variety of conduct, even at the *agape* or 'common meal' eaten together

2nd-century *bas-relief* of heathen sacrifice, from the Arch of Constantine, Rome, showing the Emperor Trajan sacrificing to Hercules.

before the Eucharist. The Gentile Christians did not have the same sacramental respect for all meals which the Jewish Christians had. Consequently their conduct at the meal was sometimes a scandalous preparation for the Eucharist that followed. Paul reminded them sharply of the sacramental nature of the Last Supper, declaring that 'Whoever, therefore, eats the bread or drinks the cup of the Lord in an unworthy manner will be guilty of profaning the body and blood of the Lord' (1 Cor. 11:27), and sums up, 'So then, my brethren, when you come together to eat, wait for one another – if any one is hungry, let him eat at home – lest you come together to be condemned. About the other things I will give directions when I come.' (1 Cor. 11:33-34)

One of the questions raised in the letter to Paul must have concerned the 'speaking with tongues' during religious fervour. Paul listed the various spiritual gifts within the Church, such as preaching, teaching, believing, healing, miracles, prophecy, and lastly the 'gift of tongues'. He showed that the spiritual community, or Body of Christ, like the human body, has different members with different functions. The test of their reality was whether they contributed to the corporate life of the Church as a whole. And Paul went on to extol the greatest gift – love – using the Greek word *agape*, denoting the highest form of self-giving love, like that of Jesus himself.

'Love is patient and kind; love is not jealous or boastful; it is not arrogant or rude. Love does not insist on its own way; it is not irritable or resentful; it does not rejoice at wrong, but rejoices in the right. Love bears all things, believes all things, hopes all things, endures all things. Love never ends; as for prophecies, they will pass away; as for tongues, they will cease; as for knowledge, it will pass away. . . . So faith, hope, love abide, these three; but the greatest of these is love.' (1 Cor. 13:4-8, 13)

The final question Paul answers concerns the resurrection. The Greek conception of the human body was of a tomb imprisoning the spirit of man, and so they rejected out of hand any mention of the resurrection of the body, which the Jews and the Christians accepted. Paul gives a long testimony of the Easter faith of the early Christian Church. He reminds his readers what he had taught them about the resurrection and gives what must be the earliest record of the resurrection appearances of Jesus, through which mankind was redeemed to share in the resurrection. The resurrection of the body would involve both a difference and a continuity between the earthly personality and the risen 'body'. As the seed is sown in one form but grows up to be a plant, so the individual soul will retain the individual's personality in some recognizable spiritual form. God gives his creations bodies suitable for their environment; the physical body of flesh and blood in this life will be replaced by an immortal body in the life to come.

'When the perishable puts on the imperishable, and the mortal puts on immortality, then shall come to pass the saying that is written: "Death is swallowed up in victory. O death, where is thy victory? O death, where is thy sting?" The sting of death is sin, and the power of sin is the law. But thanks be to God, who gives us the victory through our Lord Jesus Christ.' (1 Cor. 15:54-57)

Paul closes this letter with final commendations and greetings, after outlining his plan for a collection of money to be taken for the Church in Jerusalem. He saw this as a way of uniting both the Jewish and the Gentile elements in the Churches he had founded in Asia and Europe. He planned to take a representative group of Gentile and Jewish Christians to deliver the offering to the Mother Church in Jerusalem. The letter ends with a prayer in the form of a versicle and a response that may have been part of the liturgy, perhaps between the *agape* and the Eucharist: 'The grace of the Lord Jesus be with you. My love be with you all in Christ Jesus.'

Paul's 'severe' letter

Neither Paul's second letter to Corinth nor the personal visit of Timothy managed to clear up the situation in the Corinthian Church, and Paul, disturbed by the news,

decided to visit Corinth himself. But even he was unable to achieve a reform within the Christian community, and, after being publicly insulted, he sailed back to Ephesus. There he wrote a third letter and sent it back by the hand of Titus, an older and more experienced man than Timothy.

The four chapters we have of this letter were perhaps only the beginning of it. If we had the rest, we might have known why it was so effective in bringing the Corinthian congregation to heel. It appears to begin with an appeal, 'by the meekness and gentleness of Christ', at the 10th chapter of 2 Corinthians; but the military metaphors in which it proceeds show that it is little less than a declaration of war. 'For though we live in the world we are not carrying on a worldly war, for the weapons of our warfare are not worldly but have divine power to destroy strongholds. We destroy arguments and every proud obstacle to the knowledge of God, and take every thought captive to obey Christ, being ready to punish every disobedience, when your obedience is complete.' (2 Cor. 10:3-6)

Paul proceeds to vindicate himself against charges of being arrogant and self-seeking, however pitiable a public speaker he may be. It seems that one of the apostles, passing through Corinth, accepted hospitality as by right of his apostleship. In consequence, some Corinthians seem to have denied that Paul, who worked for his living, was in fact a genuine apostle at all. 'I think that I am not in the least inferior to these superlative apostles. Even if I am unskilled in speaking, I am not in knowledge; in every way we have made this plain to you in all things. Did I commit a sin in abasing myself so that you might be exalted, because I preached God's gospel without cost to you? I robbed other churches by accepting support from them in order to serve you.' (2 Cor. 11:5-8)

In a deliberately sarcastic passage, Paul challenges the Corinthians, if they did take him for a fool, to listen to some of his folly. Then, after a caustic apology for boasting, he gives them an autobiographical account of his life and sufferings for Jesus. 'But whatever any one dares to boast of – I am speaking as a fool – I also dare to boast of that. Are they Hebrews? So am I. Are they Israelites? So am I. Are they descendants of Abraham? So am I. Are they servants of Christ? I am a better one – I am talking like a madman – with far greater labours, far more imprisonments, with countless beatings, and often near death. Five times I have received at the hands of the Jews the forty lashes less one. Three times I have been beaten with rods; once I was stoned. Three times I have been shipwrecked; a night and a day I have been adrift at sea; on frequent journeys, in danger from rivers, danger from robbers, danger from my own people, danger from Gentiles, danger in the city, danger in the wilderness, danger at sea, danger from false brethren; in toil and hardship, through many a sleepless night, in hunger and thirst, often without food, in cold and exposure. And, apart from other things, there is the daily pressure upon me of my anxiety for all the churches. Who is weak, and I am not weak? Who is made to fall, and I am not indignant? If I must boast, I will boast of the things that show my weakness. The God and Father of the Lord Jesus, he who is blessed for ever, knows that I do not lie.' (2 Cor. 11:21-31)

But Paul had learned that his weaknesses and sufferings for Jesus's sake were a source of strength, and his severe language changes to an appeal as he declares, 'I will all the more gladly boast of my weaknesses, that the power of Christ may rest upon me. For the sake of Christ, then, I am content with weaknesses, insults, hardships, persecutions, and calamities; for when I am weak, then I am strong.' (2 Cor. 12:9, 10) '. . . since you desire proof that Christ is speaking in me. He is not weak in dealing with you, but is powerful in you. For he was crucified in weakness, but lives by the power of God. For we are weak in him, but in dealing with you we shall live with him by the power of God. Examine yourselves, to see whether you are holding to your faith. Test yourself. Do you not realize that Jesus Christ is in you? – unless indeed you fail to meet the test!' (2 Cor. 13:3-5)

Paul concludes with the promise of a third visit to Corinth, on which he duly set out from Ephesus, via Troas and Macedonia. There, on his way, Titus met him with the good news that the Corinthian Church was ready to reform and that they had already, by a majority vote, censured the person who had insulted Paul. He therefore immediately wrote his fourth letter,

Incense shovel, with bronze handle in the form of a Corinthian fluted column and capital, 1st century, found at Dura, near Hebron.

from Macedonia – our 2 Corinthians 1-9 (omitting 6:14-7:1).

A paean of praise

Paul sent his own apostolic greeting, to which he added the greetings of Timothy. He thanked God for the sufferings and the comfort that both he and the Corinthian congregation shared in Christ Jesus. He refers to some dire and distressing danger he had undergone when in Asia, asking for their continued prayers. (This was probably some persecution Paul had endured in Ephesus, but which is not recorded in the Acts.) The second chapter of this fourth letter gives a vivid picture of Paul's concern for the Church at Corinth. He had dispatched his 'severe' letter in great anxiety. 'For I wrote you out of much affliction and anguish of heart and with many tears, not to cause you pain but to let you know the abundant love that I have for you.' (2 Cor. 2:4)

Paul simply could not bear to wait in Ephesus for their reply to his 'severe' letter, so he went up to Troas to meet Titus. There was no sign of him there, so Paul crossed by sea to Macedonia, where at last Titus met him with an answering letter and a reassuring report. Paul accordingly broke into a paean of praise, his anxiety dispersed by the good news. The rest of his journey he compares to a triumphal and sacrificial journey in which incense is burned with the fragrance of the knowledge of Christ. Paul here feels that in a sense he himself is the victim being burned and offered up for the life of his beloved Corinthians. 'But thanks be to God, who in Christ always leads us in triumph, and through us spreads the fragrance of the knowledge of him everywhere. For we are the aroma of Christ to God among those who are being saved and among those who are perishing, to one a fragrance from death to death, to the other a fragrance from life to life. Who is sufficient for these things?' (2 Cor. 2:14-16)

For a moment Paul is almost embarrassed by his self-recommendation, and then tells his Corinthians that they themselves are his best reference. 'Are we beginning to commend ourselves again? Or do we need, as some do, letters of recommendation to you, or from you? You yourselves are our letter of recommendation, written on your hearts, to be known and read by all men; and you show that you are a letter from Christ delivered by us, written not with ink but with the Spirit of the living God, not on tablets of stone but on tablets of human hearts.' (2 Cor. 3:1-3)

Paul proceeds to defend the apostles and to describe his own trials and hopes. He is essentially a realist, whose every word is tested in the fire of experience. 'For

right The Apostle Paul teaching the crowd, with his halo and executioner's sword, Italian manuscript, 15th-16th centuries.

Non in comessatioib[us] et ebrietatib[us]. Non i cubilib[us] τ impudicitiis Non in contentione τ emulatione. Sed induimini d[omi]n[u]m iesum xpm

Rees. Quecumq[ue] scrip ta sunt : ad n[ost]ram doctrinam script sunt : ut per patientia[m] et consolatio[n]em scrip turarum spem habeam[us]. Deus aut[em] patientie et solatii : det nob[is] idipm[m] sapere in alterutru[m]. s[ecundu]m iesum xpm : Vt unan[i] mes uno ore honoifi cetis deum τ patre[m] do[mi]ni n[ost]ri iesu xpi. Propt[er] q[uo]d suscipite invicem : sicut τ xps suscepit nos

Fratres scientes q[ui]a hora est iam nos de somno surgere. Nunc aute[m] propior e[st] n[ost]ra salus quam cum credidim[us]. Nox p[ro]cessit : dies aut[em] appropinquauit. Abi ciamus ergo op[er]a tene brarum : τ induamur arma lucis sic ut i die honeste ambulemus

what we preach is not ourselves, but Jesus Christ as Lord, with ourselves as your servants for Jesus's sake .... But we have this treasure in earthen vessels, to show that the transcendent power belongs to God and not to us. We are afflicted in every way, but not crushed; perplexed, but not driven to despair; persecuted, but not forsaken; struck down, but not destroyed; always carrying in the body the death of Jesus, so that the life of Jesus may also be manifested in our bodies. For while we live we are always being given up to death for Jesus's sake, so that the life of Jesus may be manifested in our mortal flesh.' (2 Cor. 4:5, 7-11)

Paul, the tentmaker, compares the body to the canvas tent that is to be replaced by 'a building from God, a house not made with hands, eternal in the heavens'. (2 Cor. 5:1) He appeals to the Corinthians in Christ's name to be reconciled to God while they have time. Finally, he outlines his plan for taking up a col-

Ruins of the Roman amphitheatre at Caesarea, where the centurion Cornelius was stationed.

lection from the missionary congregations for the Mother Church in Jerusalem. He says that this is not obligatory for them, but that he is testing the genuineness of their love against the keenness of others. 'For you know the grace of our Lord Jesus Christ, that though he was rich, yet for your sake he became poor, so that by his poverty you might become rich . . . So give proof, before the churches, of your love and of our boasting about you to these men.' (2 Cor. 8:9, 24) [Acts 18; First and Second Letters to the Corinthians]

CORNELIUS (Gk. 'of a horn') Cornelius was a centurion of the Italian cohort, the equivalent of a regiment, stationed in Caesarea a year or two after the crucifixion of Jesus. He is described as 'a devout man who feared God with all his household, gave alms liberally to the people, and prayed constantly to God'. (Acts 10:2) He was probably a pious Roman who, disillusioned by polytheism and disappointed by pagan philosophy, had gravitated spiritually towards Judaism.

At three o'clock one afternoon, Cornelius distinctly saw in a vision an angel who told him that his prayers and alms had been accepted by God and that he was to

Excavations at the port
of Amnisos, on the island
of Crete.

had not yet been baptized. Whereupon Cornelius and his whole household were baptized 'in the name of Jesus Christ'.

This is a unique chapter in the story of the early Church, just because it brought to a head the controversy between Peter and the 'circumcision party' at Jerusalem. It was not until the first Council of Jerusalem, under the chairmanship of James the brother of Jesus, that the issue was finally settled with only minimal demands being made of Gentile Christians. (Acts 15) This was largely the result of reports from Paul and Barnabas, together with Peter's own account of the conversion of Cornelius, the Roman centurion. [Acts 10:1-31]

CRESCENS (Gk. 'increasing') A companion of Paul in his final imprisonment, who left him to visit Christian churches in Galatia. Tradition claims that he became bishop of Chalcedon, in northern Asia Minor, the scene of the fourth Ecumenical Council of the Christian Church in the year 451. [2 Tim. 4:10]

CRETANS The long island of Crete in the eastern Mediterranean forms a natural bridge with the island of Cythera on the north-west and those of Salmone and Rhodes on the north-east; a bridge between Europe, Asia Minor and Phoenicia. There was a large community of Jews in Crete, some of whom came to attend the festival of Pentecost in Jerusalem, heard and understood the message of the apostles of Jesus. The Apostle Paul, on his way from Caesarea, sailed 'under the lee of Crete off Salmone. Coasting along it with difficulty . . . to a place called Fair Havens, near which was the city of Lasea.' Against Paul's advice, the captain and owner of the ship preferred to sail further round the island to the more commodious harbour of Phoenix for the winter. Although they kept inshore along the coast, they were blown offshore by a north-east gale and, being forced off course, never actually landed in a Cretan harbour. (Acts 27:7-15)

There is no record in Acts or allusion in his letters to any visit of Paul to Crete, though, writing to Titus, he says, 'This is why I left you in Crete, that you might amend what was defective, and appoint elders in every town as I directed you.' (Titus 1:5) Paul well knew the proven tact and experience of Titus, from his successful dealings with the demanding task of organizing the Church in Corinth. If the letter to Titus was in fact written by Paul, then it is just possible that Paul visited Crete after his release from captivity in Rome. There are many other directions in which Paul might have preferred to conduct a final Christian mission. He had no high opinion of Cretans, as his advice to Titus shows (if indeed the letter is his). 'One of themselves, a prophet of their own, said, "Cretans are always liars, evil beasts, lazy gluttons." This testimony is true. Therefore rebuke them sharply, that they may be sound in the faith, in-

send to Joppa (Jaffa) to fetch Simon, called Peter, staying with Simon the Tanner, whose house was by the sea. Cornelius dispatched a soldier and two slaves to Joppa. Just before they arrived the next day, Peter at noon fell into a trance, in which he too had a vision. A great sheet was let down from the sky, full of strange animals and birds; a voice called to him, saying, 'Rise, Peter; kill and eat,' to which Peter answered, 'No, Lord; for I have never eaten anything that is common or unclean.' The voice replied, 'What God has cleansed, you must not call common.' This sequence was repeated three times before the sheet was taken up into the sky again. While Peter was puzzling out the meaning of his vision, the messengers of Cornelius arrived on the doorstep, calling out to know whether Simon, called Peter, was staying there. It was then that the Spirit told him, 'Behold, three men are looking for you. Rise and go down, and accompany them without hesitation; for I have sent them.' So Peter went to greet them and asked them why they had come; the next day he set off with them and with six brothers from Joppa to go to Caesarea.

It is interesting to note that the centurion at Caesarea, like the centurion at Capernaum, sends others with a message for help.

On Peter's arrival, Cornelius, his family and friends were assembled and waiting. Cornelius prostrated himself at Peter's feet, then each explained their visions and Peter added, 'Truly I perceive that God shows no partiality, but in every nation any one who fears him and does what is right is acceptable to him.' (Acts 10:34-35) Peter than announced the good news of Jesus, his life, death, and resurrection, and proclaimed the eternal purpose of God in sending Jesus to be the Saviour. While he was speaking, the Spirit came to all who were listening, to the astonishment of Peter and his Jewish companions from Joppa, because these Gentiles stead of giving heed to Jewish myths or to commands of men who reject the truth. . . . They profess to know God, but they deny him by their deeds; they are detestable, disobedient, unfit for any good deed.' (Titus 1:12-14, 16) [Acts 2:11; Titus 1:12]

CRISPUS (Gk. 'curled') The ruler of the Jewish synagogue in the pagan city of Corinth, who became a Christian and was probably baptized by Paul the Apostle during his eighteen-month stay in about the years 51 and 52. Tradition records that he became bishop of Aegina. [Acts 18:8; 1 Cor. 1:14]

CYRENIANS (Gk. 'wall') Traditionally there were 480 synagogues in Jerusalem. These were the meeting-places for prayer and discussion – particularly about the Law – of many different peoples of Jewish faith. At the time of Stephen's martyrdom, it was the natives of Alexandria and Cyrene in Africa and of the Roman provinces of Asia and Cilicia (the home of Saul the Persecutor, who was to become Paul the Apostle), who took the initiative in Stephen's arrest. It was the members of these synagogues who took most offence at Stephen's teaching, but could not successfully dispute with his wisdom and enthusiasm.

In consequence, they instigated the crowd to accuse him of talking blasphemy against Moses and God, for the Jews the ultimate wickedness. The mob dragged Stephen off to the Council, and accused him of speaking both against the Temple and against the Law. Members of the synagogue of the Cyrenians were foremost among those who secured Stephen's condemnation and stoning. [Acts 6:9]

CYRENIUS *see* QUIRINIUS

Early Byzantine church at Phaestos, Crete. St Paul may have visited Crete, which was the home of an early Christian community.

D

DAMARIS An Athenian woman, mentioned by name with only one other Athenian, called Dionysius the Areopagite, as believing and joining with Paul on the occasion of his visit to Athens. The great bishop of Constantinople in the 4th century, John Chrysostom, in his *Priesthood* declared that Damaris was the wife of Dionysius. *see* DIONYSIUS [Acts 17:34]

DEMAS (Gk. 'popular') Linked with Luke as a loyal prison-companion of Paul in Rome, on at least one occasion, Demas has yet left a doubtful reputation behind him because of a disparaging reference in the last letter to Timothy.

He was certainly with Paul at the time of his writing the captivity letters – his letters to the Christian congregation at Colossae and to Philemon, a member of that congregation. In both these letters, Paul sends the greetings of Demas, along with those of Luke. 'the beloved physician'. In the final letter to Paul, if indeed it was written by Paul at all, to Timothy, Demas is mentioned with some bitterness. He is there said to have stayed with Paul for some time and then to have forsaken him, having returned to his wordly business.

In his *Pilgrim's Progress*, John Bunyan depicts Demas as the type of half-hearted Christian who goes part of the way and then turns back. If the pastoral letters to Timothy are not authentically Pauline, then some early tradition must have branded Demas with disloyalty. [Col. 4:14; Philem. 24; 2 Tim. 4:10]

DEMETRIUS (Gk. 'belonging to Demeter') **1.** The silversmith at Ephesus who, suffering a slump in his sales of silver shrines and trinkets of the goddess Artemis, blamed Paul's teaching and stirred up his fellow-tradesmen to make a riotous demonstration.

For the significance of Artemis in Ephesus, *see* ARTEMIS.

Demetrius must have catered for a very considerable pilgrim and tourist trade entirely centred on the vast temple and cult of the goddess Artemis, for Ephesus was the Benares of the eastern Mediterranean. It was probably the month of the festival, the *Artemision*; the people would be keeping holiday and the city would be crowded with visitors and customers for the purchase of the shrines and images of the sanctuary. The Ephesians

and even the provincials of Asia, however, had been so affected by the mission of Paul and his companions that there was little sale for these objects of devotion.

Demetrius, therefore, appealed to the pockets of the silversmiths and the piety of the people. Paul's teaching was bad for both trade and religion. The great goddess Artemis herself was threatened: 'Men, you know that from this business we have our wealth. And you see and

The Arcadian Way at Ephesus, looking from the direction of the harbour towards the great theatre, the scene of the silversmiths' riot.

hear that not only at Ephesus but almost throughout all Asia this Paul has persuaded and turned away a considerable company of people, saying that gods made with hands are not gods. And there is danger not only that this trade of ours may come into disrepute but also that the temple of the great goddess Artemis may count for nothing, and that she may even be deposed from her magnificence, she whom all Asia and the world worship.' (Acts 19:25-27)

In the riot that followed, Paul was conspicuous by his absence. It was two of his travelling companions who were dragged into the theatre, until the town clerk called for order and dismissed the assembly, appealing to Demetrius to bring the matter to court rather than cause such a commotion. [Acts 19:24, 38]

2. The bearer of the third letter of John the Elder to Gaius, reproving one Diotrephes for flouting the authority of the elder, calling for his reader's support and quoting Demetrius as a witness in the writer's cause. [3 John 12]

DEVIL (Gk. 'slanderer') *see* SATAN, BE-ELZEBUL, BELIAL

DIANA *see* ARTEMIS

DIDYMUS (Gk. 'twin') Each of the three times that Thomas is mentioned in the Fourth Gospel he is called 'the Twin'. The word *Didymus*, to be found in the King James Version, is not a surname but a Greek translation of the Hebrew for Thomas, which itself means 'Twin'. *Didymus* was probably the nickname by which Thomas was known to Greek Christians in Asia Minor. It is possible that this disciple's real name was not known, but that he was in fact just called 'the Twin', in whatever language. *see* THOMAS [John 11:16; 20:24, 26; 21:2]

DIONYSIUS A member of the Council of the Areopagus (the High Court of Athens that used to meet on Mars Hill), called Dionysius, is mentioned by name with only one other Athenian, a woman called Damaris, as believing and joining with Paul on the occasion of his visit to Athens.

The Areopagus (Mars Hill) would have been admirably suited to public meetings, being a low but large outcrop of rock just below the main stairway entrance to the Acropolis, in full view of the Parthenon and the statue of Athena. Here the ancient religion of the Greeks was confronted by the Christian Faith, presented by an insignificant little Jew.

The theatre at Ephesus, which held 25,000 spectators and was almost new in the days of Paul.

At the request of Epicurean and Stoic philosophers, Paul gave an exposition of his teaching before the Council of the Areopagus. It was a masterpiece of tact, insight, and condensation but in practical terms it was a complete failure. The Greek conception of the human body was of a tomb imprisoning the spirit of the man, therefore they rejected out of hand any mention of the resurrection of the body. Paul made few converts on this occasion, of which Dionysius was, however, traditionally one and destined to become the first bishop of Athens and to be martyred under the Emperor Domitian. [Acts 17:34]

DIOTREPHES (Gk. 'nurtured by Zeus') A domineering elder, if not leader of the Christian congregation to which Gaius, the addressee of 3 John, belonged. Diotrephes appears from this letter to have flouted the writer's authority as an elder and to have been highly critical of him. The writer is more concerned, however, with Diotrephes's refusal to receive messengers from him and with his hostility to all of those who offer hospitality to his messengers. He writes to thank Gaius for giving them a welcome and providing for their needs, in spite of the threats of Diotrephes. [3 John 9]

DORCAS (Gk. 'gazelle') *see* TABITHA

DRUSILLA The Jewish wife of the Roman procurator Felix, himself born a Greek and made a freedman by the Roman Emperor Claudius, of whom Felix and his brother Pallas were favourites. Drusilla, the youngest of the three daughters of Herod Agrippa I, at the age of fourteen had been married to Azizus, king of Emesa (Homs) in Syria. Azizus accepted circumcision in order to obtain her. With the help of a Syrian sorcerer, Drusilla was persuaded to desert her husband and marry Felix, for whom she bore a single son, later killed in an eruption of Mount Vesuvius.

During a period of violent Jewish resistance to the occupying Roman forces in Palestine, the Emperor Claudius appointed Felix as procurator in the year 52, because of his tolerant disposition to Jewry and of his Jewish wife, Drusilla. This, however, only served to strengthen the position of the Zealot party and their fanatical loyalty to the Law and the Temple, and to correspondingly weaken the independence of the young Christian Church. In about the year 58, following the return to and arrest of the Apostle Paul in Jerusalem, Paul appeared before Felix at Caesarea in the presence of his wife Drusilla. A Syriac text of this passage implies that Drusilla herself was interested in Paul, and induced Felix to have Paul brought to him. It seems that Paul had virtually convinced Felix of his innocence and certainly he was well treated, if kept under arrest for the rest of Felix's procuratorship. Drusilla accompanied Felix when he was recalled to Rome to answer for his misgovernment. [Acts 24:24]

Marble bust of a young girl, 1st century AD, probably Roman.

E

ELAMITES (Gk. 'inhabitants of Elamais') *see* ARABIANS

ELDERS Whether within the Jewish or Christian communities, the elder had a double function – both to rule and to teach.

The elders of ancient Israel were called by Moses to direct the affairs of the community, to make decisions and announcements of importance. The elders announced the institution of the Passover, and they accompanied Moses up Mount Sinai to meet with God. On the settlement in Canaan, elders functioned in each town and were consulted by the central government. On the return from exile in Babylon, the elders continued to function locally but formed a third grade of laymen within the Sanhedrin or central council of justice.

From the Gospels, it is clear that they were still the leaders of religious life in three clear respects. In local affairs, they were of considerable influence. It was the elders of Capernaum who came to Jesus to ask him to help the Roman centurion, 'for he loves our nation, and he built us our synagogue'. (Luke 7:5) In matters of biblical interpretation, too, the elders inherited a tradition handed down from the earliest times. This 'tradition of the elders' took the form of an endless extemporization and extension of the Old Testament Law to enable its application in all circumstances. It began as an oral tradition added to the written Law, but in the hands of the scribes it was preserved in writing, constantly extended and transmitted to include the whole range of conduct in every possible situation. Consequently, it had become near impossible of fulfilment and was often criticized by Jesus as a burden too heavy to bear. 'So, for the sake of your tradition, you have made void the word of God,' he said, referring to the fact that any man could allocate his earnings to the Temple, according to the tradition of the elders, and in so doing avoid supporting his parents as demanded by the Law of Moses. (Matt. 15:1-9)

It was the elders who questioned Jesus's authority in turning the dealers out of the Temple. (Mark 11:27) The elders gave judgment at the trial of Jesus. The elders in consultation with the high priest and scribes drew up the charges for the trial before Pilate, as the lay members of the Sanhedrin.

Within the early Christian Church, the presbyters or elders were among the first officers to be appointed. In the pastoral epistles, the functions of the Christian elders are clearly seen. 'Let the elders who rule well be considered worthy of double honour, especially those who labour in preaching and teaching; for the scripture says, "You shall not muzzle an ox when it is treading out the grain," and, "The labourer deserves his wages." Never admit any charge against an elder except on the evidence of two or three witnesses.' (1 Tim. 5:17-19)

Titus is called upon to appoint elders in every town on the island of Crete. At least ten years, however, before these letters were written Paul had himself already appointed elders at Ephesus, to whom on his last journey to Jerusalem he gave these final instructions: 'Take heed to yourselves and to all the flock, in which the Holy Spirit has made you guardians, to feed the church of the Lord which he obtained with his own blood. I know that after my departure fierce wolves will come in among you, not sparing the flock; and from among your own selves will arise men speaking perverse things, to draw away the disciples after them. Therefore be alert, remembering that for three years I did not cease night or day to admonish every one with tears. And now I commend you to God and to the word of his grace, which is able to build you up and to give you the inheritance among all those who are sanctified.' (Acts 20:28-32) [Matt. 15:2; 16:21; 21:23; 26:57; 27:1, 20; Mark 7:3; 8:31; 15:1; Acts 4:5, 8, 23; 6:12; 11:30; 14:23; 15:4, 6, 22, 23; 16:4; 20:17; 1 Tim. 5:1, 17, 19; Titus 1:5; Jas. 5:14; 1 Pet. 5:1; 2 John 1; 3 John 1; Rev. 4:4, 10; 5:5, 6, 8, 11, 14; 7:11, 13; 11:16; 19:4]

ELIZABETH (Gk. from the Heb. 'God is my oath') Elizabeth, the mother of John the Baptist, was visited by her cousin Mary, mother of Jesus, when they were both expecting their first babies. The story of the parents and birth of John the Baptist is recorded only by Luke.

Elizabeth was the wife of a village priest called Zechariah. They were both of priestly descent, she from Aaron, he from Abijah. Both were devout and scrupulous in their observance of the Law; but they were

Elizabeth

The Visitation, by Rogier van der Weyden, 1435-8, showing the meeting of Mary (left) with Elizabeth (right).

childless, for Elizabeth was barren and they were getting on in years. The twenty-four families of the 'sons of Aaron' were responsible in rotation for service in the Temple at Jerusalem. Within each family the individual priest was chosen by lot to tend the brazier on the altar of incense in front of the Most Holy Place. When Elizabeth's husband Zechariah was carrying out this privileged task, he received a vision in which the Archangel Gabriel made him a promise: 'Do not be afraid, Zechariah, for your prayer is heard, and your wife Elizabeth will bear you a son, and you shall call his name John.' (Luke 1:13) It was Elizabeth who at the child's circumcision was to insist on his being named 'John' rather than 'Zechariah' after his father.

After his service in the Temple, Zechariah returned home. Elizabeth conceived and remained in retirement for five months, saying 'Thus the Lord has done to me in the days when he looked on me, to take away my reproach among men.' (Luke 1:25) Meanwhile, Elizabeth's cousin Mary of Nazareth had had a vision and the promise of a son, Jesus. The Archangel Gabriel had told Mary the news of Elizabeth. 'And behold, your kinswoman Elizabeth in her old age has also conceived a son; and this is the sixth month with her who was called barren. For with God nothing will be impossible.' (Luke 1:36-37)

Mary promptly set out to visit her cousin Elizabeth at her home in the 'hill country, to a city of Judah'. Elizabeth met her with the words, 'Blessed are you among women, and blessed is the fruit of your womb! And why is this granted me, that the mother of my Lord should come to me? For behold, when the voice of your greeting came to my ears, the babe in my womb leaped for joy.' (Luke 1:42-44)

At this point Luke introduces the paean of praise that has come to be included in the liturgies of all the Christian Churches as the 'Magnificat'. In nearly all manuscripts it is put into the mouth of Mary, but in a few it is attributed to Elizabeth.

The feast of the Visitation, kept within the Eastern and Western Churches, is a commemoration of the significant role of these two women in God's plan of redemption, as perceived by Luke, who stresses the agency of the Holy Spirit in the life of Elizabeth as well as in the life of Mary. The visitation would have been the most natural event. Mary would have welcomed an opportunity to escape from prying eyes and malicious tongues in Nazareth, and the three months' rest with her cousin would have been a most welcome retreat. Elizabeth, the older woman, herself going through the same experience, would have been a great comfort and support to the young peasant girl Mary, plunged so unexpectedly though so willingly into pregnancy.

Apart from the normal course of personal relations,

The Birth of John the Baptist, by Fra Filippo Lippi, 1452-4, in the choir of Prato Cathedral.

each woman had an added incentive to seek the society of the other. Each knew that there was something altogether exceptional about the promise of her child. Elizabeth's age, quite apart from her husband's vision, had alerted her to the marvel that was happening to her. Mary's virginity, together with the message of the angel, had left her in no doubt that she was being used as a willing agent in the hand of God.

They understood quickly the respective roles they had to play, and what would be the relative positions of their children. With the advantage of hindsight we are inclined to read rather more than is warranted into the words addressed by the angel Gabriel to Elizabeth's husband in the Temple. But there may have been enough to suggest to Zechariah that work of a preparatory nature would be the destiny of his son-to-be. Perhaps some communication had already passed between Mary and Elizabeth, so that the older woman knew of the wonderful circumstances attending Mary's pregnancy. In any case, Elizabeth had no hesitation in joyfully accepting the minor role for her child, and so establishing, even before their birth, the position of John as the forerunner and of Jesus as the Messiah.

When the time came, the two boys were born within six months of each other, in towns within sight of each other. Joseph and Mary had come to Bethlehem for the census; the home of the priest Zechariah and Elizabeth was below Mount Orah in Ein Karem, the 'Gracious Spring'. Before the time of the Russian pilgrim Daniel in 1107 the birthplace of John was located, within the village, in a cave that is now shown in the Franciscan Church of St John. On the other side of the valley is the Franciscan Church of the Visitation, within the crypt of which is shown the spring that according to a medieval tradition appeared at the meeting-place of Mary with Elizabeth. This is the spring which gives a name to the town today. In the wall of the crypt is a hollowed rock in which, according to another medieval tradition, the child John was concealed at the time of the Massacre of the Innocents by Herod's order. An apse of the Crusader Church of the Visitation can be seen in the upper church today, which is covered in murals.

The Russian Convent of Elizabeth, surrounded by little whitewashed cottages, rises among the trees on the slopes of Mount Orah above the Church of the Visitation at Ein Karem. On the feast of the Visitation, the Russian nuns from the Garden of Gethsemane used until 1947 to bring icons representing Mary to meet their sisters of Ein Karem with icons representing Elizabeth. At the village well, called Mary's Spring, they would touch icons together in a kiss of greeting, before carrying them in procession up the flower-strewn steps to the Convent of Elizabeth. [Luke 1]

ELYMAS (Gk. from the Aramaic 'powerful') *see* BAR-JESUS

EPAENETUS (Gk. 'praised') One of the Christians greeted warmly by Paul, at the close of his letter to the Christian Church in Rome. Paul refers to him as 'My beloved Epaenetus, who was the first convert in Asia for Christ'. Some manuscripts read 'in Achaia' rather than in Asia, referring to the mainland of Greece, rather than that of Turkey. This would seem to conflict with Paul's nomination of Stephanas and his household (1 Cor. 16:15) as the first Christians in Achaia. As one of the leading Christians at Ephesus, Epaenetus may well have visited the congregation in Rome. [Rom. 16:5]

EPAPHRAS A Christian probably taught by Paul during his long and systematic period of teaching at Ephesus, in the course of his Third Journey over the years 54-7. Epaphras took a leading part in the evangelization of the cities within the fertile valley of the River Lycus, 100 miles east and inland from Ephesus, particularly Colossae, Laodicea, and Hierapolis.

Some years later, Epaphras reported to Paul, in prison in Rome, on the good progress of the Church at Colossae. Paul wrote back to Colossae a letter in which he corrected some false teaching and gave some practical advice. He mentions Epaphras twice, first paying tribute to him as the evangelist and faithful steward of the gospel message, secondly praising his prayerful and pastoral concern for his fellow Colossians. 'We always thank God, the Father of our Lord Jesus Christ, when we pray for you, because we have heard of your faith in Christ Jesus and of the love which you have for all the saints, because of the hope laid up for you in heaven. Of this you have heard before in the word of the truth, the gospel which has come to you, as indeed in the whole world it is bearing fruit and growing – so among yourselves, from the day you heard and understood the grace of God in truth, as you learned it from Epaphras our beloved fellow servant. He is a faithful minister of Christ on our behalf and has made known to us your love in the Spirit.' (Col. 1:3-8)

A short time before the writing of this letter, a great earthquake had taken place in the Lycus valley; it is just possible that Epaphras's journey to Rome may have been with the specific purpose of requesting some Christian aid for the victims of this disaster. The historian Tacitus records that financial help from Rome was offered on a large scale. Paul thus mentions Epaphras at the close of his letter to Colossae: 'Epaphras, who is one of yourselves, a servant of Christ Jesus, greets you, always remembering you earnestly in his prayers, that you may stand mature and fully assured in all the will of God. For I bear him witness that he has worked hard for you and for those in Laodicea and Hierapolis.' (Col. 4:12, 13)

It is probable that, during Paul's long imprisonment in Rome, his friends took turns in keeping him company and sharing his captivity with him. This would account for Paul's mention in his later letters of different 'fellow-prisoners'. Certainly when Paul wrote his letter to the Christian Church at Colossae, Aristarchus was his companion in prison. By the time Paul writes his personal letter to Philemon, it is Epaphras whom he mentions as his fellow-prisoner.

Epaphras is shown to have been a very useful and faithful friend both to Paul personally and to the development of the Christian Church in Asia. [Col. 1:7; 4:12; Philem. 23]

EPAPHRODITUS (Gk. 'lovely') The messenger of the Christian congregation at Philippi entrusted with a gift of money for Paul during his first imprisonment in Rome, who was also the bearer of Paul's letter back to Philippi.

Epaphroditus stayed some time with Paul, perhaps taking a turn with others in sharing his captivity. During that time of caring for Paul, he himself became severely ill. On his recovery, Paul decided to send him back to the congregation at Philippi with the letter that we know as the Letter to the Philippians. (see PHILIPPIANS) In that letter, among other things, Paul thanks them for their very acceptable gift, referring to their record of generosity over some ten years of acquaintance. 'Yet it was kind of you to share my trouble. And you Philippians yourselves know that in the beginning of the gospel, when I left Macedonia, no church entered into partnership with me in giving and receiving except you only; for even in Thessalonica you sent me help once and again. Not that I seek the gift; but I seek the fruit which increases to your credit. I have received full payment, and more; I am filled, having received from Epaphroditus the gifts you sent, a fragrant offering, a sacrifice acceptable and pleasing to God. And my God will supply every need of yours according to his riches in glory in Christ Jesus.' (Phil. 4:14-19)

Paul's letter includes a personal discharge and warm commendation of Epaphroditus, revealing the depth of Paul's pastoral relationships, even during the rigours of his imprisonment. 'I have thought it necessary to send to you Epaphroditus my brother and fellow worker and fellow soldier, and your messenger and minister to my need, for he has been longing for you all, and has been distressed because you heard that he was ill. Indeed he was ill, near to death. But God had mercy on him, and not only on him but on me also, lest I should have sorrow upon sorrow. I am the more eager to send him, therefore, that you may rejoice at seeing him again, and that I may be less anxious. So receive him in the Lord with all joy; and honour such men, for he nearly died for the work of Christ, risking his life to complete your service to me.' (Phil. 2:25-30) [Phil. 2:25; 4:18]

EPHESIANS Ephesus was the headquarters of Paul's great Third Journey. It was later the centre of the mission and pastoral activities of John the Divine. From Ephesus, Paul conducted his correspondence with the Christian community at Corinth and possibly also wrote his letter to the congregation at Philippi. To the Church at Ephesus, along with other congregations in Asia, Paul wrote a circular letter or encyclical when under house-arrest during his first visit to Rome. This so-called Letter to the Ephesians is a magnificent exposition of the 'mystery' of God's purpose in history and of the new life within the Christian Church. It has been called 'the very crown of all his epistles'.

Paul in Ephesus

Paul spent three years – perhaps 54-7 – at the very heart of Greco-Roman civilization, at Ephesus, the great city of paganism in Asia. Its temple of Diana was the centre of pagan worship for all the Mediterranean lands. The proud title of this great commercial and religious centre was 'Neocorus' – temple-keeper or sacristan – of Artemis. Ancient writers considered that this Benares (place of pagan pilgrimage) of the ancient world outshone even the gardens of Babylon and the Colossus of Rhodes. Its temple was the centre of a dark, licentious, and mysterious oriental culture, very different from the healthy-minded open-air huntress-goddess known in Greece as Artemis and in Rome as Diana. Wherever the deity of a race was female, women took a prominent part in the life of the place and people. Asia Minor had been the land of the fabled moon-worshipping Amazons. Consequently the Temple of Artemis enjoyed the services of an army of virgin-prophetesses, eunuch-priests, choristers, vergers, and even acrobats – in a spate of infamous and immoral excess. Ephesus – in the early Christian era – was a city of magic and necromancy, the home of a superstition so ancient and deeply rooted that it outlived the gods of Olympus.

To the little Christian communities founded along the coast-line, in the 50s, the Temple of Artemis at Ephesus was an infernal counterpart to the Temple at Jerusalem. A vast stone staircase led up past the many-breasted statue of the Ephesian Artemis to the glistening colonnade and façade. The Temple was the size of St Paul's Cathedral in London but the same shape and style as the Parthenon in Athens, white marble colonnades without, dark and numinous within, containing no statue but a single colossal meteorite.

Before the 4th century BC, the Temple of Artemis had formed the centre of the city. When the harbour became silted up, the city was moved a mile and a half towards the sea, and a sacred pilgrim's way linked the city to the sanctuary. In the 6th century AD, the city was moved back to the acropolis where it was more easily defensible than on the low marshland by the river. Little stands on the acropolis today but the magnificent Byzantine Basilica of St John. The Greco-Roman city remains, however, form a magnificent complex of temples, libraries, baths, gymnasia, and theatres, linked by a splendid marble street which still today runs from the

The Marble Street at Ephesus which leads the length of the city ruins.
In the distance can be seen the site of the ancient harbour.

Magnesia Gate to the Roman *Agora* or market-place.

Here, Paul spent the first three months of his ministry teaching in the synagogue. When the final break with the Jewish community occurred, he moved to the lecture-room of Tyrannus. There he worked daily in teaching and discussion among Jews and Greeks, over a period of two whole years, in the siesta hours of noon to four in the afternoon. Remarkable progress followed this systematic instruction, accompanied also by a ministry of healing. Both Jews and Greeks came to respect the name of Jesus, rather than the magical arts of Diana. Paul despatched teachers to Colossae and Macedonia; at this time also the Seven Churches of Asia, mentioned by John in the Book of Revelation, were founded. (*see* JOHN **9.**) Paul, when he closed his ministry in Ephesus, travelled overland to Troas,

crossed into Macedonia and, visiting his Greek congregations, made his way down to Corinth for the winter months of the year 57-8. In the spring, wishing to reach Jerusalem by Pentecost, Paul summoned the elders of the Church at Ephesus to meet him on the coast at Miletus, where he bade them a fond farewell.

It is not certain that Paul managed to return to Asia and Ephesus, following his release from his first captivity in Rome. His letters to Philemon and Timothy, however, imply that he did so, before being finally arrested at Troas some 150 miles north of Ephesus.

Paul's letter: a masterpiece

Until very recently there has been no doubt that this was an authentic letter of Paul and indeed his masterpiece. Its thought and language are echoed in Peter's first letter written in the 1st century, and the letter was often quoted by the Fathers of the Church in the 2nd century. The letter reveals a careful reconsideration of some of the themes explored in his earlier letters, together with a splendid and original statement of God's purpose for man as seen in the establishing of the universal Church of Jesus Christ. Doubts as to the letter's genuine Pauline authorship spring from its difference in style and approach from the earlier letters. Such peculiarities, however, whether intentional or even unconscious, may be due to the fact that the whole letter is in the form and language of a prayerful meditation. Consequently ideas follow one upon the other, born of the inspiration of the moment and with little regard for punctuation. It has been said that in his letter to the Romans Paul flies off at a tangent, but that in his letter to the Ephesians he ties himself in knots! It is within the context of a meditation that he borrows ideas from his own letter to the Colossians, but tends to modify and develop his conclusions. No editorial comment or recent criticism can conceal the distinctly Pauline stamp on the thinking and expression of this letter.

The destination of this letter is perhaps less certain than its authorship. At least three of the most ancient manuscripts omit the address 'at Ephesus' within the opening verse. In the year 140, the heretical writer Marcion substitutes the address 'to the Laodiceans'. We know from Paul's letter to the Colossians (4:16) that he did in fact write a letter to the Laodiceans and that he suggested that the congregations at Colossae and Laodicia should exchange letters after they had read their own. Both letters were sent by the hand of Tychicus and his route would inevitably take him to many other Asian congregations during the course of his journey. It may well be, therefore, that what we know as the letter to the Ephesians was a circular letter of which perhaps half a dozen copies were carried by Tychicus. The bearer may have been instructed to fill in the blank address before delivering each copy of the letter, but probably failed to do so on at least one copy. This theory is widely accepted; it explains the somewhat abstract and impersonal nature of the letter, almost devoid of greetings for any one person among the multitude of Paul's friends at Ephesus.

God's purpose: unity through the Church

The letter is clearly the result of a private meditation of the writer, but is expressed with practical ends in view. He is concerned with the sectarianism within the Christian congregations – made up as they were of Jews and Gentiles of different nationalities and backgrounds. The letter is in two clearly marked sections, expressing two aspects of a single theme. The first three chapters describe God's purpose to unite all things through his Church. If the Church is to be the unifying factor within God's world, it must itself be united. The duties of the individual Christian churchman are analysed in the final chapters of the letter, in the light of the unifying purpose for which the Church exists. The whole letter is woven together into a single prayer for world-wide reconciliation in Jesus. Out of a divided humanity God has made a united community in the Christian Church. Jesus is the 'principle' of reunion; his Church is to be the 'instrument' of reconciliation.

'For he has made known to us in all wisdom and insight the mystery of his will, according to his purpose

The Marble Street at Ephesus looking towards the great theatre.

which he set forth in Christ as a plan for the fullness of time, to unite all things in him, things in heaven and things on earth.' (Eph. 1:9-10)

Paul is deeply aware of the age-old warfare between good and evil. It is against this background that he sees the hidden purpose of God from the beginning to 'unite all things in him, things in heaven and things on earth'. When men grasped the 'mystery' of this inner purpose of God, then they held the clue to all his doings. 'Having the eyes of your hearts enlightened, that you may know what is the hope to which he has called you, what are the riches of his glorious inheritance in the saints, and what is the immeasurable greatness of his power in us who believe, according to the working of his great might which he accomplished in Christ when he raised him from the dead and made him sit at his right hand in the heavenly places.' (Eph. 1:18-20)

Meanwhile, the Church of Jesus is the continuation of his life and work in God's world. The life of the risen Lord is expressed through his Church. As he assumed a human body for his earthly life, so now he works his purpose through his eternal Body, the Church. He has solved the problem of the mutual alienation of Jew and Gentile by the creation of this single and united Body. 'For he is our peace, who has made us both one, and has broken down the dividing wall of hostility, by abolishing in his flesh the law of commandments and ordinances, that he might create in himself one new man in place of the two, so making peace, and might reconcile us both to God in one body through the cross, thereby bringing the hostility to an end.' (Eph. 2:14-16)

The first section of this letter closes with a magnificent prayer for all the congregations of the Church who may receive it. It is hard to realize that the entire Christian Church at this time consisted of a few thousand people meeting in small groups in the back streets of such cities as Antioch, Ephesus, and Rome. To Paul, however, the Church was God's instrument to carry out his infinite purpose of reconciliation, planned from the beginning of time, guided and energized by his indwelling Spirit. 'For this reason I bow my knees before the Father, from whom every family in heaven and on earth is named, that according to the riches of his glory he may grant you to be strengthened with might through his Spirit in the inner man, and that Christ may dwell in your hearts through faith; that you, being rooted and grounded in love, may have power to comprehend with all the saints what is the breadth and length and height and depth, and to know the love of Christ which surpasses knowledge, that you may be filled with all the fullness of God.' (Eph. 3:14-19)

The Christian's duty

In Paul's eyes, the essential unity of the Church has been planned and provided for in Jesus, but it can only come into being by every individual member co-operating in the purpose of Jesus. All their actions must be directed towards love, peace, and understanding. Each in his own family circle and community must be a centre of reconciliation, as Jesus is for the whole world. Each is to hold close to the person and teaching of Jesus, that they may draw their strength and unity from him.

'I therefore, a prisoner for the Lord, beg you to lead a life worthy of the calling to which you have been called, with all lowliness and meekness, with patience, forbearing one another in love, eager to maintain the unity of the Spirit in the bond of peace. There is one body and one Spirit, just as you were called to the one hope that belongs to your call, one Lord, one faith, one baptism, one God and Father of us all, who is above all and through all and in all.' (Eph. 4:1-6)

Each individual member of the Church has been given different spiritual gifts and abilities, 'for the equipment of the saints, for the work of the ministry, for building up the body of Christ, until we all attain to the unity of the faith and of the knowledge of the son of God, to mature manhood, to the measure of the stature of the fullness of Christ.' (Eph. 4:12, 13) Meanwhile, however, there is a need for organization in the Church, for sound teaching and frank speaking. 'Rather, speaking the truth in love, we are to grow up in every way into him who is the head, into Christ, from whom the whole body, joined and knit together by every joint with which it is supplied, when each part is working properly, makes bodily growth and upbuilds itself in love.' (Eph. 4:15, 16)

Finally, Paul comes to the practical details of the new life in Christ. He deals with personal relationships: truth, honesty, decency, and forgiveness. He deals with the morals of the Christian home and family, husbands and wives, parents and children, masters and slaves. He closes with an exhortation to all his readers to stand their ground against evil in the strength of the 'armour of God', and begs their support for himself in prison, 'an ambassador in chains'.

So ends what is perhaps the most remarkable of all Paul's letters. For Paul, Jesus is the central principle of existence, because the whole visible creation exists not for its own sake, but simply to unfold the divine purpose shown in Jesus. Those who, like Paul, know Jesus, share the hidden plan of God for his universe. By their response to the law and life of Jesus, in their homes and in their communities, men co-operate with God in his eternal purpose. [Eph. 1-6]

EPICUREANS The Greek philosophers who, together with the Stoics, questioned the teachings of Paul in Athens, and brought him to speak publicly on the Aeropagus, during his Second Journey in the years 50-2.

The Epicureans followed the teachings of a Greek thinker called Epicurus, 342-270 BC, who claimed that reality lay in the world of nature rather than in the

Bust of Epicurus, from Herculaneum.

reason of man. In a world of matter and space, the pursuit of happiness was the primary and attractive purpose of man. For Epicurus and his early followers, who lived in small communities of friends, happiness lay in intellectual and spiritual exercises, but for lesser mortals in more basic satisfactions. Consequently the high intellectual standards of the founder of this philosophy degenerated into lower and more common forms of pleasure-seeking.

It was hardly surprising, therefore, that Paul's teaching about God as the Maker and 'Lord of heaven and earth', who now calls 'all men everywhere to repent', who has 'fixed a day on which he will judge the world in righteousness' by someone already appointed 'by raising him from the dead', did not much appeal to the Epicureans. [Acts 17:18]

ERASTUS (Gk. 'beloved') This name occurs three times in the New Testament, each person of that name being linked with the work of the Apostle Paul. All three references may be to one and the same person, who may well have been a Corinthian.

1. A helper of Paul during his long ministry in Ephesus, on his Third Journey. Erastus and Timothy were sent by Paul into Macedonia, while Paul himself stayed on in Ephesus. Following the riot of the silversmiths, Paul took leave of his friends in Ephesus and then followed Timothy and Erastus to Macedonia. [Acts 19:22]

2. A representative of Paul remaining at Corinth, after Paul's arrest and second journey to Rome. In his final letter to summon Timothy from Ephesus to Rome, Paul outlines the whereabouts of his representatives and leaders of the Christian Church in the eastern Mediterranean. Among these, perhaps, were some who had accompanied him on this final journey towards Rome. He had left Trophimus ill at Miletus; Erastus had remained at Corinth; only Luke was still with him in Rome. [2 Tim. 4:20]

3. The city treasurer of Corinth, who joined with Paul in sending greetings, at the close of Paul's letter to the Church in Rome. His name is grouped with those of Gaius and Quartus. [Rom. 16:23]

ESSENES (Gk. from the Syriac 'holy ones') The Essenes were a Jewish sect which grew up in the two centuries before the Christian era. One branch of this sect settled at Qumran. Recently they have found new fame as the probable writers of the Dead Sea Scrolls and the pioneers of a monastic community in the wilderness of Judea.

Community in the wilderness

A schismatic movement of priests broke away from the worship of the Temple and from the theocratic rule of the Maccabean high priesthood. They did so because they considered that the Maccabees were not entitled to be high priests, not being of the correct tribe of Levi. The Hasmoneans had simply claimed the high priesthood as the spoils of conquest in war. If, therefore, the priesthood was invalid, so were its sacrifices in the Temple at Jerusalem.

During the Greek domination, there had been many cultic innovations and the calendar had had to be remodelled to the more exact lunar cycle. The conservative Essenes considered this calendar invalid together with its appointed sacrifices. In their eyes, consequently, there was feasting on fast days and fasting on feast days, with which God was displeased. The Essenes were highly apocalyptic and, following the Book of Daniel, expected an early end of the world. Remembering the Mosaic experience in the wilderness as a necessary means of purification, they retired to form a monastic community at Qumran, in the wilderness of Judea, overlooking the Dead Sea. There they prepared for the final battle between good and evil. We can not be certain, however, that the Qumranis were truly representative of the Essenes.

So, led by a Teacher of Righteousness, as a community of guaranteed purity – of the individual, of the priesthood and of the calendar – they set up a framework of monasticism as early as 150 BC. Surprisingly enough, however, this sect is not mentioned by name in the New Testament. The name 'Essenes' probably comes from the Syriac 'holy ones', 'pious ones'.

Until 1947, comparatively little was known about this sect and the principal sources of information were from outside the community at Qumran, which may have been the headquarters of the Essenes. From the Jewish philosopher Philo, born in 20 BC, the Roman writer Pliny, and the Jewish historian Josephus, both writing about AD 110, the Essenes were known to be a priestly

above The Jewish historian Josephus, 19th-century engraving.
below Caves at Qumran near the monastery, to which the last scrolls to be hidden were hastily transported before the arrival of Roman troops.

Ruins of the Essene monastery at Qumran, on a marl plateau
between the cliffs and the Dead Sea.

order of about 4,000 in number, isolating themselves in communities and observing a strict discipline of conduct, ritual purity, and communal living, being bound together by the sharing of a sacred meal.

The Dead Sea Scrolls

In the summer of 1947, a young Arab shepherd chanced upon a cave, near the Wadi Qumran, containing several parchment scrolls carefully wrapped in linen cloths and stowed in tall, wide-necked jars. These scrolls were examined and proved to be part of the library of an Essene community. It was not long before archaeologists discovered and excavated a monastic settlement on the nearby plateau overlooking the Dead Sea. The discovery of ten other scroll caves followed, the last of which was found in 1956. These proved to contain 500 different documents from a great library, of which some biblical fragments go back to the 3rd century BC. Until then, the earliest Hebrew manuscripts of the Old Testament were of the 9th century AD. These 'Dead Sea Scrolls', as they have come to be called, throw much light on the transmission of the Bible text over a period of nearly a thousand years. The scrolls concerning the monastic life and discipline of the Essene community reveal many of the ideas, customs, and hopes that appear later in the New Testament. Perhaps the most important

significance of these scrolls is that they portray, more vividly than before, the Jewish background of the early Christian Church and of the New Testament.

There are parallels between some of the ideas expressed in the scrolls and some in the four Gospels, particularly in the Fourth Gospel. Among these are 'eternal life', 'light', and the 'spirit of truth'. There is, too, the same conflict of opposites, such as 'truth and error', 'spirit and flesh', 'light and darkness'. Perhaps the John who wrote this Gospel was influenced by the Essenes, their practices and their terminology, as was possibly John the Baptist. The Essenes seem to have been possessed enthusiastically, if not obsessed, by their vivid expectation of the coming of the Messiah and the end of the world. They believed that the world was to end by a final conflict between the forces of good and evil, after which God would establish his kingdom of righteousness.

Community and fortress

The ruins of the Essene monastery at Qumran stand on a projecting spur of a marl plateau above the floor of the Rift Valley. The spur is surrounded by precipitous ravines and joined by a narrow neck to cliffs which form a steep scarp overlooking the Dead Sea. From the valley a path leads up on to the spur, passing through a cemetery of over a thousand tombs in orderly rows. Each body lies, head to the south and hands crossed, at a depth of at least six feet on a slab within a single tomb. The path leads up to the main gate and directly ahead in the cliff-face is the gorge or waterfall of the Wadi Qumran. From this, the remains of a broad water-canal can be seen entering the north-west of an enclosed compound. This conduit feeds seven large cisterns scattered throughout the settlement. These cisterns are mostly rectangular with steps leading down into them; they were probably indispensable as baptisteries for the ritual ablutions of the community. On the west side is the reconstructed watch-tower which affords both an excellent bird's-eye view of the monastery layout and also commands views of several miles north to the head of the Dead Sea and south along the narrow valley between the cliffs and the water's edge. Perhaps it was its situation and strategic position that caused the capture of the monastery and its adaptation as a fortress by the Romans in AD 68.

South of the tower rose a long double-storeyed building, the top floor of which was the scriptorium. A long table ran the length of the wall complete with inkwells and a bench; here probably the scrolls were written or

The *Manual of Discipline,* one of the Dead Sea Scrolls describing the faith and practice of the Qumran community.

copied. The largest room in the monastery, more than sixty-five feet long, was within the south wall of the settlement and served as an assembly hall and dining-room or refectory. Opposite the entrance was a raised dais, from which a speaker could address the meeting. Next to the dining-hall was the pantry, discovered complete with about a thousand dishes and platters stacked according to size, but shattered by the collapse of the roof. Whether, however, this was caused by earthquake or during the Roman assault remains a matter of conjecture. These large structures were surrounded by a number of smaller rooms, with the functions necessary to an isolated community: there are still clearly to be distinguished a laundry, a pottery, a kitchen, a bakery, a mill, and food stores. The most

impressive and essential item of all remains the water system, penetrating the length and breadth of the walled enclosure by a series of canals and conduits linking tanks and basins from the waterfall of the wadi to the farthest cistern. Two or three miles to the south of the settlement is still a fresh and plentiful spring, where once the Essenes had considerable plantations and fields which enabled them, even in the desert, to be self-sufficient through their own careful and skilful agricultural efforts.

All members lived outside the monastery proper in settlements, under canvas or in caves, coming in to eat, work, and worship. They shared a variety of skills within the community. There were farmers, potters, writers, and healers using roots and herbs, who claimed to be able to cast out evil spirits. The Jewish historian Josephus says that there were astrologers and interpreters of dreams. The women lived in the camp outside the walls, but the leaders of the community were probably celibate. Some members married, but put their wives outside the community when they became pregnant. Twice every day, the community gathered in the assembly hall to sing hymns and give thanks to God. They sat down in a strict order of priority: the priest reading the scriptures, the overseer expounding them, members of the Council of Twelve in front, the 'many' sitting in rows behind them with the unbaptized novices at the back. On the Sabbath they ate a ritual meal of bread and wine. On important festivals, they held a love-feast, which was for them a foretaste of the none too distant last days, when the Messiah and Prince of Israel would arrive to conquer the world and invite the faithful to share his triumph.

Every other Jewish sect is mentioned in the New Testament, but nothing is said either of the Essenes or their remote headquarters at Qumran, either within the New Testament or the Mishnah. Their omission appears to remain an unsolved mystery. Despite their disciplines of secrecy, Jesus must have known something about them, their teaching, and their Messianic expectation. Indeed, at his own baptism only a few miles from Qumran, he became acutely aware of his own Messianic vocation, which was so different from the apocalyptic and nationalistic conception of Messiahship in his day among the Essenes and other religious groups.

The significance of the Essenes is that their writings have not only bridged a gap in the literary history of the Jewish people, but that they have provided a background canvas against which the transition from the Old to the New Testament era will become progressively and more clearly understood. [There is no mention of the Essenes by name in the New Testament.]

ETHIOPIAN The only Ethiopian mentioned in the New Testament was the eunuch, treasurer to the Candace of Ethiopia, converted and baptized by Philip the Evangelist on the road to Gaza. The man was possibly a court official from the train of the queen at Meroe, in Nubia, and probably himself also a Jew, though, being a eunuch, he was outside the covenant and forbidden by the Law to enter the congregation. (Lev. 21:20; Deut. 23:1)

The story told by Luke in Acts is of an incident completely isolated from the rest of the narrative. Philip is described as intercepting the chariot on the road from Jerusalem to Gaza. The site is still pointed out to pilgrims on the road to Hebron. The Ethiopian Jewish eunuch was returning from a pilgrimage to Jerusalem and was reading aloud as he journeyed, from the prophet Isaiah. Philip ran up, heard what he was read-

ing, and asked him if he really understood. He answered, '"How can I, unless someone guides me?" And he invited Philip to come up and sit with him. Now the passage of the scripture which he was reading [from the 'Suffering Servant' songs of the Second Isaiah] was this:

"As a sheep led to the slaughter
or a lamb before its shearer is dumb,
so he opens not his mouth.
In his humiliation justice was denied him.
Who can describe his generation?
For his life is taken up from the earth."

And the eunuch said to Philip, "About whom, pray, does the prophet say this, about himself, or about some one else?" Then Philip opened his mouth, and beginning with this scripture he told him the good news of Jesus. And as they went along the road they came to some water, and the eunuch said, "See, here is water! What is to prevent my being baptized?" And he commanded the chariot to stop, and they both went down into the water, Philip and the eunuch, and he baptized him.' (Acts 8:32-8)

This well-known 53rd chapter of Isaiah is rarely, if at all, applied to the Messiah in Hebrew literature, although it is constantly quoted of the Christ in the New Testament. (Matt. 8:17; Luke 22:37; John 12:38; Acts 3:18; 1 Pet. 2:22, 24; Heb. 9:28; Rev. 13:8; 14:5)

It is not possible to link the conversion of the Ethiopian eunuch with the foundation of the Christian Church in what is now Ethiopia, but when, in the 4th century, Frumentius and Edesius, missionaries from Tyre, set about the conversion of Ethiopia, they found there already an early form of the Christian faith. [Acts 8:27]

EUBULUS (Gk. 'of good counsel') A Christian in Rome, known to Timothy, whose greetings Paul sent to Timothy in Ephesus, when he, Paul, was imprisoned in Rome and awaiting execution. [2 Tim. 4:21]

EUNICE (Gk. 'conquering well') The mother of Timothy, a lieutenant of Paul destined to become bishop of Ephesus, Eunice was a Christian Jewess married to a Greek (Acts 16:1) and living with her family at Lystra. Paul may well have persuaded Timothy, his mother Eunice, and his grandmother Lois, to become Christians on the very first visit to Lystra with Barnabas in the year 46. (Acts 14:8-20) Certainly Timothy knew of Paul's stoning by the Jews on that occasion. (2 Tim. 3:11) When Paul passed through Lystra again, on his Second Journey some four years later, he collected Timothy from his home and family. Because he wanted to use Timothy for evangelism among the Jews, who knew that his father was a Greek, Paul personally took Timothy and circumcised him, to convince them of his adherence to the Jewish Law.

Paul, in his correspondence with Timothy, acknowledges generously the careful training of Timothy in the

Jewish faith and scriptures, within his own home and family. 'I am reminded of your sincere faith, a faith that dwelt first in your grandmother Lois and your mother Eunice and now, I am sure, dwells in you.' (2 Tim. 1:5) And again, 'Continue in what you have learned and have firmly believed, knowing from whom you learned it and how from childhood you have been acquainted with the sacred writings which are able to instruct you for salvation through faith in Christ Jesus.' (2 Tim. 3:14-15)

Presumably Eunice remained at Lystra, for Paul did not send her greetings in his letters to Timothy at Ephesus. [2 Tim. 1:5]

EUODIA (Gk. 'prosperous journey' or 'fragrance') One of two women members of the Christian congregation at Philippi who had been disagreeing. Probably news of their quarrel was brought to Paul in prison by Epaphroditus. In the letter which Epaphroditus now took back to Philippi, Paul wrote this appeal, 'I entreat Euodia and I entreat Syntyche to agree in the Lord. And I ask you also, true yokefellow, help these women, for they have laboured side by side with me in the gospel together with Clement and the rest of my fellow workers, whose names are in the book of life.' (Phil. 4:2, 3) The 'true yokefellow' referred to might well be an elder in their congregation, or may be read as the proper name 'Syzygus'. [Phil. 4:2]

EUTYCHUS (Gk. 'fortunate') A boy member of the Christian congregation at Troas who, listening to a long sermon from the Apostle Paul, was overcome by sleep and fell from a second- or third-storey window. Paul ran downstairs and hugged him, though he was taken for dead, and declared, 'Do not be alarmed, for his life is in him.' Paul then returned to the upper room, where he 'broke the bread' and talked until daybreak before leaving. The boy revived, much to the comfort of the congregation.

The description of this assembly throws some light on the form of early Christian Eucharist. The points of particular interest include the fact that it was the first day of the week, that is, late Saturday or Sunday night, the use of many lamps either for light or ritual, the assembly in an upper dining-room or cenacle, the division between a liturgy of the Word and a liturgy of the Eucharist. The preaching of the Word in the sermon was separated from the breaking of the bread and the meal that followed, by the rescue and restoration of the boy Eutychus. [Acts 20:9]

F

FELIX (Gk. from the Lat. 'happy') Procurator of Judea
53-60, during the critical period of revolts of the Zealots
and *Sicarii*, Felix conducted the first trial of Paul the
Apostle at Caesarea, and left him in custody two years
later for his successor, Porcius Festus.

Antonius Claudius and his brother Pallas were Greek
subjects, made freedmen by the Emperor Claudius, 41-
54. They became favourites first of Claudius and then of
Nero, 54-68. Antonius, who had received the name of
Felix, enters the New Testament story of the early
Christian Church on his appointment as procurator of
Judea in the year 53. The impression of him given by
Luke's narrative in Acts, particularly in his dealings
with Paul, is one of dilatory inefficiency. There is no
need to doubt Luke's eyewitness account and careful
report of these events. Other historians of the time are
far less generous and more caustic in their assessment of
his character.

The Jewish historian, Josephus, describes Felix's
heavy hand in suppressing the constant disorder within
his territory. Felix appears to have been compromised
in the murder of the high priest, Jonathan, and to have
sent other priests for trial to Rome, despite his appointment by Claudius on the grounds of his sympathy with
Jewry and his marriage to a Jewish princess. (*see*
DRUSILLA) Josephus wrote two accounts of Felix, one
in the *War* about 80, one ten years later in the *Antiquities*
which enumerates the 'crimes' of Felix. The Roman
historian, Tacitus, accused Felix of fomenting strife
between the Jews and Samaritans for his own personal
profit and said that Felix 'revelled in cruelty and lust,
and exercised the powers of a king with the outlook of a
slave'. Suetonius regarded Felix as a military ad-
venturer, who married three queens in the course of his
adventurous career.

Luke's narrative in Acts, of the trial of Paul by Felix,
gives perhaps the earliest and most independent eye-
witness impression of Felix. Both the prosecution and
the defence felt that he would respond to flattery and
began accordingly. However impressive the prosecutor
Tertullus may have been, the defence of Paul, trained in
the famous law school of Tarsus, was more than a match
for him. Felix, 'having a rather accurate knowledge of

Felix

right Obverse and reverse of a coin issued at Caesarea under the procurator-ship of Felix (AD 53-60)

below Paul before Felix, by William Hogarth (1697-1764). On the left is the prosecutor, Tertullus.

Roman columns built into the Crusader masonry at Caesarea, then the Roman provincial capital, port and military base.

predecessor (*see* FELIX) had left the Apostle Paul unconvicted after two years in custody, but now under close arrest. The chief priests demanded Paul's transfer to Jerusalem for trial, but arranged for him to be ambushed *en route*. Festus in turn requested them to accompany him down to Caesarea and there to accuse Paul.

Ten days later, at Caesarea, Festus presided at a tribunal at which many serious charges were brought against Paul, who denied them all with the words, 'Neither against the law of the Jews, nor against the temple, nor against Caesar have I offended at all.' (Acts 25:8) Festus, apparently to placate the Jews, then invited Paul to accompany him to Jerusalem for trial, not by the Jews but by himself as procurator. At this point Paul felt he had no alternative but to make his appeal to Caesar, the ancient right of all Roman citizens since the year 449 BC. 'I am standing before Caesar's tribunal, where I ought to be tried; to the Jews I have done no wrong, as you know very well. If then I am a wrongdoer, and have committed anything for which I deserve to die, I do not seek to escape death; but if there is nothing in their charges against me, no one can give me up to them. I appeal to Caesar.' (Acts 25:10, 11) After consulting his advisers, Festus answered, 'You have appealed to Caesar, to Caesar you shall go.'

Some days afterwards, King Agrippa and his sister Bernice arrived at Caesarea with pomp to welcome the new procurator. Festus took the opportunity to present Paul's case to the king, in order to enable him, as procurator, to draw up a report of the charges against Paul. Paul rose to the occasion with a magnificent defence calculated to appeal to the Jewish sympathies of Agrippa and Bernice, and summing up the Christian gospel as a proclamation of the fulfilment of Messianic prophecy. 'For this reason the Jews seized me in the temple and tried to kill me. To this day I have had the help that comes from God, and so I stand here testifying both to small and great, saying nothing but what the prophets and Moses said would come to pass: that the Christ must suffer, and that, by being the first to rise from the dead, he would proclaim light both to the people and to the Gentiles.' (Acts 26:21-23)

At this point, Festus loudly declared, ' "Paul, you are mad; your great learning is turning you mad." But Paul said, "I am not mad, most excellent Festus, but I am speaking the sober truth." ' (Acts 26:24-25) After further exchanges between Agrippa and Paul, the king and the governor withdrew and agreed together, ' "This man is doing nothing to deserve death or imprisonment." And Agrippa said to Festus, "This man could have been set free if he had not appealed to Caesar." ' (Acts 26:31-32) Despite Agrippa's considered verdict of 'not guilty', Festus could not legally disregard Paul's own appeal to Caesar and made the necessary arrangements for his

the Way', as Luke puts it, adjourned the trial until the arrival of the Roman tribune from Jerusalem. (*see* CLAUDIUS LYSIAS) Paul must have convinced Felix of his innocence, for the procurator behaved kindly, allowing him some liberty and permitting Paul's friends to care for his needs.

A few days later, Felix sent for Paul and, together with his Jewish wife Drusilla, listened to Paul speaking about the 'faith in Christ Jesus'. As Paul argued about 'justice and self-control and future judgment', Felix became alarmed and dismissed him, thinking perhaps that Paul would bribe him to secure release. After two years in protective custody, Paul was left by Felix under close arrest. Felix had in fact been recalled to Rome to stand his own trial for misgovernment, and, seeking favour with the Jews, left Paul in prison.

Felix suffered banishment, and lost his only son by Drusilla in the great eruption of Mount Vesuvius in the year 79. [Acts 23, 24]

FESTUS (Gk. 'joyful') The Roman procurator who succeeded Felix in Judea, of whom little is known before this particular appointment by the Emperor Nero. Porcius Festus, according to the Jewish historian Josephus, did what he could to restore peace by the vigour of his methods, but died only two years after his appointment.

On his arrival at Caesarea, Festus soon started for Jerusalem to consult with the leading Jews, for his preescort and journey as a prisoner to Rome.

There is no comparison between the inefficient pro-crastination of Felix and the efficient despatch of Festus, who died unexpectedly at his post two years later. [Acts 25, 26]

FORTUNATUS (Gk. 'blessed', 'fortunate') Fortuna-tus was a Christian member of the household of Stephanas in Corinth.

Writing from Ephesus in the year 55, during his Third Journey to the Church in Corinth which he had founded some four years before, Paul closes his letter: 'I rejoice at the coming of Stephanas and Fortunatus and Achaicus, because they have made up for your absence; for they have refreshed my spirit as well as yours. Give recognition to such men.'

Apparently the household of Stephanas included slaves and employees, such as Fortunatus and Achaicus. This was the first household to have been converted by Paul – and the only household to have been baptized by Paul – in Corinth, on his Second Journey in the year 51. These three men had travelled to Ephesus on business, possibly carrying a letter to Paul from Corinth, and were probably present with Paul as he completed the dictation of his answering letter. [1 Cor. 16:17]

FREEDMEN (*also* LIBERTINES) (Gk. 'free') 'Liber-tine' is a Latin word for freedman, referring to a Roman Jew who had obtained his liberty. Following Pompey's capture of Jerusalem in the year 63 BC, many captives had been deported to Rome, where by now they or their children had obtained their liberty to return home. It seems that there was in Jerusalem a synagogue of such men, though some scholars, such as Moffat, would transpose 'Libertine' into 'Libyan' within this context, in order to form a list of three groups of Jews from Africa: Libyans, Cyrenians, and Alexandrians.

Traditionally there were 480 synagogues in Jerusalem. These were the meeting-places for prayer and discus-sion – particularly about the Law – of many different peoples of Jewish faith. At the time of Stephen's martyrdom, it was the natives of Alexandria and Cyrene in Africa and of the Roman provinces of Asia and Cilicia (the home of Saul the Persecutor who was to become Paul the Apostle) who took the initiative in Stephen's arrest. It was the members of these synagogues who took most offence at Stephen's teaching, but could not successfully dispute with his wisdom and enthusiasm.

In consequence, they instigated the crowd to accuse him of talking blasphemy against Moses and God, for the Jew the ultimate wickedness. The mob dragged Stephen off to the Council and accused him of speaking both against the Temple as the official centre of wor-ship, and against the Law. Members of the synagogue of the Freedmen were first mentioned among those who secured Stephen's condemnation and stoning. [Acts 6:9]

The spoils of Jerusalem, from Titus's Arch. The Jews captured at the fall of Jerusalem to Pompey had by the 1st century AD become free to return to Jerusalem.

G

GABRIEL (Heb. 'man of God') One of the seven archangels, the messenger of divine comfort, Gabriel is accorded a place in Jewish theology second only to Michael. Appropriately, his feast-day is the day before that of the Annunciation of the Blessed Virgin Mary. Only in the Book of Enoch is he given the status of archangel (Chapters 9, 20 and 40). Twice in the Book of Daniel he appears to interpret visions. Twice in Luke's Gospel he appears to announce miraculous births: first to Zechariah, the priest in the Temple, the birth of John the Baptist, forerunner and cousin of Jesus; second to Mary, the mother of Jesus.

On the occasion of Zechariah's turn of duty in the Temple in Jerusalem, when he was chosen for the great privilege of entering the sanctuary to burn incense there, the congregation remaining outside at prayer, Zechariah received a vision.

He saw an angel standing by the altar of incense, and he was overcome with fright. He heard the angel speaking to him: '"Do not be afraid, Zechariah, for your prayer is heard, and your wife Elizabeth will bear you a son, and you shall call his name John. And you will have joy and gladness, and many will rejoice at his birth; for he will be great before the Lord, and he shall drink no wine nor strong drink, and he will be filled with the Holy Spirit, even from his mother's womb. And he will turn many of the sons of Israel to the Lord their God, and he will go before him in the spirit and power of Elijah, to turn the hearts of the fathers to the children, and the disobedient to the wisdom of the just, to make ready for the Lord a people prepared." And Zechariah said to the angel, "How shall I know this? For I am an old man, and my wife is advanced in years." And the angel answered him, "I am Gabriel, who stand in the presence of God; and I was sent to speak to you, and to bring you this good news. And behold, you will be silent and unable to speak until the day that these things come to pass, because you did not believe my words, which will be fulfilled in their time."' (Luke 1:13-20)

The visit of Gabriel to the peasant girl Mary at Nazareth is told also with consummate artistry by Luke. 'In the sixth month the angel Gabriel was sent from God to a city of Galilee named Nazareth, to a virgin betrothed to a man whose name was Joseph, of the house of David; and the virgin's name was Mary.' (Luke 1:26-27) In a single sentence, the sender, the messenger,

right The Archangel Gabriel: 7th-century mosaic from Kiti, Cyprus.

below Late 15th-century German tapestry, showing the annunciation.

and the receiver are introduced: God Almighty, the angel Gabriel and the girl betrothed to the village carpenter. 'And he came to her and said, "Hail, O favoured one, the Lord is with you!" But she was greatly troubled at the saying, and considered in her mind what sort of greeting this might be. And the angel said to her, "Do not be afraid, Mary, for you have found favour with God."' (Luke 1:28-30) The divine choice of Mary implies her utter devotion and dedication; even the angel delivers his message with reverence and humility: 'Hail Mary, full of grace'; she is disturbed and ashamed at the extravagant greeting.

Then the burden of the message (is it a command or an invitation?): 'And behold, you will conceive in your womb and bear a son, and you shall call his name Jesus. He will be great, and will be called the Son of the Most High; and the Lord God will give to him the throne of his father David, and he will reign over the house of Jacob for ever; and of his kingdom there will be no end.' (Luke 1:31-33) Mary's reply is no refusal, but only an enquiry as to how she is to accept. 'And Mary said to the angel, "How can this be, since I have no husband?"' (Luke 1:34) It is only then that the messenger can unfold the divine plan of the sender. 'And the angel said to her, "The Holy Spirit will come upon you, and the power of the Most High will overshadow you; therefore the child to be born will be called holy, the Son of God."' (Luke 1:35) Momentarily, the divine plan for the redemption of mankind waited upon the acceptance of this little Jewish girl, before she sealed her acceptance with that stupendously humble *fiat*: 'And Mary said, "Behold, I am the handmaid of the Lord; let it be to me according to your word." And the angel departed from her.' (Luke 1:38) [Luke 1:19, 26]

GADARENES (Gk. 'inhabitants of Gadara') One of three names for the people in whose country Jesus cured a savage and untamable demoniac, who lived in the tombs and mountains overlooking the Lake of Galilee. The unclean spirits were exorcized from the man, whose very name was Legion (they were so many), and at their own request were allowed to go into a herd of pigs, who immediately ran over the cliff into the lake and were drowned. The proximity to the pagan cities of the Decapolis would account for the presence of the pigs.

The story is virtually the same in all three Synoptic Gospels, though the original narrative in Mark is understandably more graphic in detail, but the names, or cities, of the people concerned vary. Thus in Mark it is the country of the Gerasenes, from the city of Gerasa (the modern Jerash) 50 miles south-east of the Lake of Galilee, beyond Ajlun. This, however, is obviously a mistaken identification by Mark, the Palestinian, who seems to have been muddled between the various cities of the Decapolis, for Gerasa is too far from the lakeside

6th-century mosaic from S. Apollinare Nuovo, Ravenna, showing Jesus curing the demoniac, with the pigs running over the cliff.

above Jesus exorcizing devils, who ride on the backs of pigs: from an early Greek Bible.

left Roman colonnaded street in the city of Gerasa, now Jerash in Jordan, once a Greco-Roman colony and one of the Ten Towns.

bottom left Mosaic pavement and columns on the top of Mount Susita, overlooking the Lake of Galilee on the site of the city of Hippos, one of the cities of the Decapolis.

to be appropriate. Then, in Matthew, it is the country of the Gadarenes, from the city of Gadara (possibly identified with Um Keis, whose ruins are on a steep hill) 5 miles south-east of the lake and south of the Yarmuk River. Like Gerasa, Gadara was a city of the Decapolis with its own hot springs, baths, and public buildings, though on a far smaller scale than those still to be seen at Jerash. 'The country of the Gadarenes' is a more likely identification with the story.

Luke's Gospel poses yet a third possibility in some manuscripts, some of which have 'the country of the Gergesenes' instead of either Gerasenes or Gadarenes. Gergesa has been identified with the ruins of Khersa, well to the north of Hippos and the modern Ein Gev, at the only point on the east coast where the steep slopes reach right down to the shore. It is possible that Gergesa, a smaller town, may have been under the jurisdiction of the city of Gadara, the 'best fortified city in Perea', and that the area of Gergesa was rightly called 'the country of the Gadarenes'. Certainly the cliffs of Khersa illustrate the dramatic events of the story very well indeed. [Matt. 8:28; Mark 5:1; Luke 8:26]

GAIUS (Gk. 'the name of a Christian') **1.** One of the

converts baptized personally by Paul at Corinth. [1 Cor. 1:14]

2. A prominent member of the Christian community at Corinth, who joined his greetings to those of Paul, at the close of Paul's letter to the Church in Rome. Paul was staying in his house while the letter was being written, and his house seems to have been the meeting-place for Christians at Corinth, or perhaps a lodging-house for Christians travelling over the Isthmus of Corinth. [Rom. 16:23]

3. A Macedonian travelling-companion of Paul, arrested in Ephesus during the silversmiths' riot. Gaius and Aristarchus were dragged into the great theatre, still to be seen at Ephesus, which was the scene of a vast demonstration in the name of Artemis (Diana) of the Ephesians, whose famous temple was the cathedral shrine of paganism in the eastern Mediterranean. Paul was dissuaded from venturing into the theatre at the height of the commotion. The assembly was dismissed by the town clerk and, presumably, Gaius and Aristarchus were released, if a little the worse for wear. [Acts 19:29]

4. A Galatian from Derbe, who accompanied Paul from Corinth to Jerusalem, as one of the many representatives of the newly-founded churches, chosen to deliver the money collected for the poor of Jerusalem. The name of Aristarchus is also listed, which implies that possibly both the men arrested at Ephesus travelled with Paul to Corinth and later returned to Jerusalem with him. [Acts 20:4]

5. The addressee of the last letter of John the Elder. This man lived on after the turn of the 1st century, that is, well after the life of Paul. He was a respected and influential member of some congregation in Asia Minor, within range of Ephesus, the probable home of John the Elder who encouraged his continued support and leadership. [3 John 1]

GALATIANS Paul's letter to the Galatians has been described as the *Magna Carta* of Christian freedom. His plea for freedom from legalistic codes presents timeless Christian principles. Paul's attack on the influence of extraneous religious practices on the belief in God, as revealed through Jesus, is nowhere so clearly stated as in this letter. He singled out the danger of the rigid observance of external rules as a fundamental stumbling-block of his day; and it is still a relevant issue in the Christian Church today.

There were two Galatias in New Testament times: the old kingdom of Galatia along the south coast of the Black Sea, and the Roman province of Galatia, an enlargement of the kingdom and bordering the Mediterranean to include those towns visited by Paul and Barnabas on the First Journey. Paul's letter was intended either for the Christian Churches of the Roman province at Iconium, Lystra, and Derbe, or for other

Christian communities further north which Paul visited briefly during his Second Journey on the way to Ephesus. It is possible that his letter to the Galatians was written either from Syrian Antioch on his return from the Second Journey, or from Ephesus during his Third Journey, between the years 53 and 57.

His letter to the Galatians is second only in writing among Paul's letters to the Thessalonian correspondence. It reveals many valuable details of Paul's earlier life and activity, with which the parallel accounts in Acts are not always easily reconciled. It may be that Luke's history of the early Church in Acts was written as a brief for the legal defence of Paul in Rome, but even its powerful and polished presentation does not carry the same authority as the more personal and spontaneous witness of Paul's own letters. Luke's description of

The Last Judgment, tympanum of the Church of Ste Foy, Conques, early 12th century, incorporating Abraham (central figure, bottom left) into the Christian schema.

Paul's visit to the Galatian Churches with their particular problems is wholly compatible, however, with the contents of the letter of Paul which was intended to tackle those problems.

The challenge to orthodoxy

Paul had heard that agents of a party among the Jewish Christians had 'furtively crept in to spy on the liberty we enjoy in Christ Jesus and wanted to reduce us all to slavery'. The emissaries of that party were insisting that Paul's Gentile converts in Galatia should be circumcised and keep the Mosaic Law, as a necessary condition for entering the Christian Church. To Paul this demand seemed a complete contradiction of the free grace of God and a denial of the sufficiency of redemption through Jesus. 'We ourselves, who are Jews by birth and not Gentile sinners, yet who know that a man is not justified by works of the law but through faith in Jesus Christ, even we have believed in Christ Jesus, in order to be justified by faith in Christ, and not by works of the law, because by works of the law shall no one be justified. . . . For I through the law died to the law, that I might live to God. I have been crucified with Christ; it is no longer I who live, but Christ who lives in me; and the life I now live in the flesh I live by faith in the Son of God, who loved me and gave himself for me. I do not nullify the grace of God; for if justification were

117

through the law, then Christ died to no purpose.' (Gal. 2:15, 16; 19-21)

Paul saw in the demands of these Jewish Christians the danger that Christianity would become a party among believers in Judaism rather than a universal faith. Paul was willing that Jewish Christians should continue to keep their ancient national customs, but they should not try to impose them on Christians of other cultures and nations. Such observances were not necessary for salvation.

The Council of Jerusalem (described in Acts 15) had already ruled on this issue with an absolute minimum of regulation. 'And when they perceived the grace that was given to me, James and Cephas and John, who were reputed to be pillars, gave to me and Barnabas the right hand of fellowship, that we should go to the Gentiles and they to the circumcised; only they would have us remember the poor, which very thing I was eager to do.' (Gal. 2:9, 10) Paul, seeing clearly that some of the Jewish Christians wanted to turn the Christian Church into a select circle within Judaism rather than the universal society intended by Jesus, held the whole Christian Church to the decision of the Council. In order to convince the Jewish Christians from their own scriptures, Paul justified his action by a careful exposition of Old Testament·history.

First, he boldly cites the blessing and faith of Abraham, father of the Jewish race: 'Thus Abraham "believed God, and it was reckoned to him as righteousness". So you see that it is men of faith who are the sons of Abraham. And the scripture, foreseeing that God would justify the Gentiles by faith, preached the gospel beforehand to Abraham, saying, "In you shall all the nations be blessed." So then, those who are men of faith are blessed with Abraham who had faith.' (Gal. 3:6-9) Paul then quotes the Book of Deuteronomy to show that the law brings a curse upon all who fail to keep it in full, but states that Jesus has redeemed man by taking that curse upon himself, through the shameful death of crucifixion. The Book of Leviticus says, 'Cursed be everyone who hangs on a tree.' This was done, says Paul, 'that in Christ Jesus the blessing of Abraham might come upon the Gentiles, that we might receive the promise of the Spirit through faith'. (Gal. 3:14)

In other words, the promise of Abraham is fulfilled in the death and resurrection of Jesus. And since the Law was given 430 years later than the promise, it is secondary to the promise which has been fulfilled in Jesus. In fact, says Paul, the Law served the purpose of a tutor or guardian for mankind, until mankind 'came of age' with the coming of Jesus.

'Now before faith came, we were confined under the law, kept under restraint until faith should be revealed. So that the law was our custodian until Christ came,

that we might be justified by faith. But now that faith has come, we are no longer under a custodian; for in Christ Jesus you are all sons of God, through faith. For as many of you as were baptized into Christ have put on Christ. There is neither Jew nor Greek, there is neither slave nor free, there is neither male nor female; for you are all one in Christ Jesus. And if you are Christ's, then you are Abraham's offspring, heirs according to promise.' (Gal. 3:23-29)

Finally, Paul takes the analogy of 'coming of age' one step further. If faith in Jesus is the condition of adoption into the family of Abraham and of the inheriting of the promise to Abraham, so the Spirit of Jesus in people's hearts makes them both the sons and heirs of God himself. 'But when the time had fully come, God sent forth his son, born of woman, born under the law, to redeem those who were under the law, so that we might receive adoption as sons. And because you are sons, God has sent the Spirit of his Son into our hearts, crying, "Abba! Father!" So through God you are no longer a slave but a son, and if a son then an heir.' (Gal. 4:7) [Gal. 1-6]

GALILEANS (Gk. from the Heb. 'circuit') The mixed population of the Roman-ruled district between the Mediterranean and the Lake of Galilee, ruled successively by Herod Antipas (4 BC-AD 39) from Sepphoris and then Tiberias, by Agrippa I (39-44) and, after a short time within the Roman province of Syria, by Agrippa II (48-53).

The name Galilee, from the Hebrew *galil* meaning 'circuit', is applied to any well-defined region. Galilee of the Gentiles, *Galil ha-Goim*, the 'Region of the Gentiles', was the name given to the northern province of Israel, because it was surrounded on three sides by foreigners. Following the return from Babylon, the district remained largely Gentile, but by the 1st century BC was thoroughly Judaized. The words 'of the Gentiles' were dropped from the title of the district, which then became proudly known as 'The Region'.

The most striking feature of Galilee, in the time of Jesus, was the system of roads crossing the district in all directions, from the Levant to Damascus and the East, from Jerusalem to Antioch, from the Nile to the Euphrates. The fertility and the good communications of the district resulted in the growth of a considerable population, engaged in local industry and commerce, concentrated largely upon the lakeside. Unlike Judea, whose desert borders exerted an austere influence on that province, Galilee was surrounded by pagan and colonial townships, which poured upon Galilee the full influence of Greek life and leisure.

The Lake of Galilee is fed by the river Jordan from the north, from the melting snows of Hermon and the springs of Banias.

above The Lake of Galilee and surrounding hills, looking south from Tabgha, the Seven Springs, near the traditional sites of the feeding of the five thousand and the commission of Peter.

left Remains of the prayer hall of the synagogue at Chorazin, a town north of Capernaum and denounced with Capernaum by Jesus.

Methods of fishing on the Lake of Galilee: (*opposite, top left*) the drop net cast over a shoal of fish, used by Simon and Andrew; (*opposite, top right*) the drag net paid out from the stern of a boat; (*opposite, bottom left*) the deep net used by partners with two or more boats at night in deep water; (*opposite, bottom right*) mending nets, the task from which Jesus called the disciples James and John.

All these features – the wealth of water, the extreme fertility, the great highways, the considerable population, the Greek influences – were crowded into the Rift Valley, in tropical heat, round a blue and lovely lake. These were the conditions in which Jesus taught and worked – and under which Christianity began to grow. It takes very little imagination today, as one looks down on the rather sleepy and deserted lakeside, to picture the nine cities round the lake, each of not less than 15,000 inhabitants. Of these cities, Tiberias and Magdala were on the western shore, Gadara and Hippos on the eastern hills, Bethsaida, Capernaum, and Chorazin to the north, but the remaining two are unlocated.

The catalogue of towns around the lake conjures up for us an almost unbroken line of buildings. Little remains of the city walls, houses, synagogues, wharves, and factories; of the castle, temples, and theatres of Tiberias, the bath-houses at Hammath, the hippodrome of Tarichae, the amphitheatre and the Greek villas at Gadara. All this was once imposed on the simple open-air life of fields, roads, and boats that we see in the Gospels.

Jesus drew his disciples from the hardy fisherfolk of Galilee. He called them out of a highly temperamental and turbulent population, concentrated within the deep trench and intense heat of the Rift Valley, which further served to inflame the spirit of nationalism and revolt among the Galileans. Jesus, however, went to a trade which had no private wrongs and which was content to work from day to day, whose members had the time and opportunity to escape from the crowds to the fishing-grounds out on the lake in peace. So it is not the jargon of the fanatics or brigands, or of the Zealots hiding in the highlands of Galilee, but the speech of the fishermen and their simple craft that have become the language and symbolism of Christianity. Even the Gospels reflect a Judean disrespect for the rugged rustics and strangers of Galilee, referring to Peter's Galilean *patois*, which betrayed him at the trial of Jesus. Pilate's mingling of Galilean blood with their sacrifices was a foretaste of the frightful suppression of the Zealot revolt in 66, when the lake ran red with the blood of Galileans.

At Bethphage on the Mount of Olives there was a Galilean settlement, indicated by the discovery of a 1st-century ossuary with the name 'Galileans', in 1923. The inhabitants of Bethany were also mostly Galileans, therefore Jesus when visiting Mary, Martha and Lazarus stayed with his compatriots. This fact may also explain the ease with which the disciples were able to procure the donkey for the triumphal entry of Jesus into Jerusalem, on Palm Sunday. The men at the crossroads were probably fellow-Galileans. [Mark 14:70; Luke 13:1; 22:59; 23:6; John 4:45; Acts 2:7]

GALLIO The proconsul of Achaia, appointed by the Emperor Claudius in the year 52, who declined to adjudicate when the Jews brought Paul before the tribunal at Corinth, in the course of his Second Journey.

Lucius Junius Gallio's appointment, which incidentally pinpoints the end of Paul's visit to Corinth and his return via Ephesus and Caesarea to Antioch, is one of very few certain dates in the apostolic period. This is because Gallio's appointment was included in an inscription discovered at Delphi, in Greece, in 1905.

The Apostle Paul had spent 18 months in Corinth, working with Aquila and Priscilla, both tentmaking and building up the young Christian Church in that very pagan city. No doubt, as elsewhere, the Jewish synagogue had provided both the pulpit and the congregation for Paul's preaching. Certainly, it was the Jews, probably led by their synagogue ruler, Sosthenes, who took Paul up before the tribunal, saying, 'This man is persuading people to worship God contrary to the Law.' Before Paul could even answer the charge, Gallio the proconsul, as the judge, dismissed the case with these words, 'If it were a matter of wrongdoing or vicious crime, I should have reason to bear with you, O Jews; but since it is a matter of questions about words and names and your own law, see to it yourselves; I refuse to be a judge of these things.' (Acts 18:14, 15) And Gallio ordered the court to be cleared.

Gallio's decision was that the prosecution had no case, but the charge against Paul was a cunning one and quite different from that brought by the Jews at Thessalonica. There, they accused Paul and his followers of 'acting against the decrees of Caesar, saying that there is another king, Jesus', at which the magistrates were somewhat disturbed, but must have realized that the accusation was absurd. Here, at Corinth, the Roman proconsul Gallio was asked to decide whether Paul's teaching was contrary to the Law and put him beyond the pale of Judaism, and particularly outside the toleration by the Roman law afforded to Jews. Gallio, however, had the philosophical temperament of his Stoic brother Seneca, and was far too good a lawyer to entertain such a charge. He simply acquitted Paul and cleared the court.

Immediately the Greeks, perhaps even those who had listened to Paul from the God-fearers' courtyard attached to the synagogue, seized Sosthenes the ruler of the synagogue and very possibly Paul's chief prosecutor. They beat Sosthenes in front of the tribunal, but Gallio 'paid no attention' or, as one text put it, 'pretended not to see'.

Gallio was the elder brother of the Stoic philosopher Seneca. [Acts 18:12, 17]

GAMALIEL (Gk. from the Heb. 'reward of God') The great and highly respected Pharisee and doctor of the Law, at whose feet the Apostle Paul claimed to have been educated in Jerusalem, 'according to the strict manner of the Law of our fathers'. Gamaliel was one of the seven rabbis to be honoured with the supreme title of *Rabban*.

Gamaliel was the pupil and grandson of Hillel, who together with his rival Shammai formed the last great 'pair' to hand down the tradition of the Law. Each of them held a distinctive interpretation and had a following or school of interpretation. The school of Hillel, and, of course, Gamaliel, represented the realist, the liberal, and the merciful application of the Law, as exemplified by the outlook of the Pharisees. That of Shammai represented the more rigid, the theoretical and the unimaginative attitude of the Sadducees to the Law.

When Peter and John, among the apostles in Jerusalem, were arrested in the Temple area for preaching the Messiahship of Jesus, it was the influential Pharisee Gamaliel who took the initiative in securing their release. He prevailed upon the Sadducees in the Sanhedrin, or Council of Justice, by using an argument that was both typically generous and also highly practical: 'Men of Israel, take care what you do with these men'; then Gamaliel proceeded to remind the Council of others whose Messianic claims had perished with them and their followers in the past, and he declared, 'So in the present case I tell you, keep away from these men

and let them alone; for if this plan or this undertaking is of men, it will fail; but if it is of God, you will not be able to overthrow them. You might even be found opposing God!' (Acts 5:35-39)

It is perhaps not surprising that the firebrand and persecutor of the early Christian Church, Saul of Tarsus, should have mellowed to the generous wisdom of 'Paul, the aged'. Paul was justifiably proud of being a Jew and a Pharisee, trained in the lecture-room of the great Gamaliel of whom the Talmud says: 'Since the Rabban Gamaliel died, the glory of the Law has ceased.' [Acts 5:34; 22:3]

GAZELLE *see* TABITHA

GENTILES (from the Heb. 'nation', 'people') The Hebrew word *goy* usually implies a non-Israelite people. The Greek *ethnos*, used as a translation for *goy*, indicates 'nation', and as such the word appears mostly in the Revised Standard Version, though in the King James Version the word 'Gentile' is more common. This word 'Gentile' was used of all non-Jews who were considered 'outside the mercy' of the God of Israel.

Jesus and Gentiles

In the 1st century, most Jews believed that the only hope for the Gentiles was for them to accept the Jewish Law. If they did so, being circumcised and making the

Herodian tablet from the outer court of the Temple with Greek inscription warning Gentiles against entering the Inner Temple.

Threshold and doorstops between the prayer hall and the Gentiles' courtyard
in the synagogue at Capernaum.

necessary offering, keeping the Sabbath and food laws and regulations of conduct, they were called 'proselytes'. Other Gentiles were attracted to the Jewish belief in one God and attended worship in the Gentile courtyard of the synagogues, but were not circumcised. Such were called 'God-fearers', of which one was certainly the centurion at Capernaum, who built the synagogue there. (Luke 7)

Although Galilee of the Gentiles was ringed round (that is the meaning of the word) by Gentile districts, Jesus had remarkably little contact with foreigners during his public ministry. There is record of only one crossing of the border into Phoenicia on the Syria coastline, and a single visit to the Decapolis, the league of ten Greco-Roman colonial cities east of Jordan. Indeed, the more Hebrew Gospel of Matthew specifically describes Jesus's instructions to his disciples, 'Go nowhere among the Gentiles, and enter no town of the Samaritans, but go rather to the lost sheep of the house of Israel.' (Matt. 10:5, 6) At the end of the same Gospel, however, Jesus's final commission to his apostles is all-embracing and universal, 'All authority in heaven and on earth has been given to me. Go therefore and

make disciples of all nations, baptizing them in the name of the Father and of the Son and of the Holy Spirit.' (Matt. 28:18, 19)

In spite of this, the leaders of the early Christian Church in Jerusalem seem to have been at first rather unwilling to extend their message to the Gentiles. Their early conservatism proved a considerable obstacle to the missionary policy of Paul, though many of the apostles subsequently travelled extensively throughout the Mediterranean and beyond.

In spite of Matthew's portrayal of a rather exclusive ministry, the personal attitude of Jesus to Gentiles seems to have been highly sympathetic and pastoral. (*see* SYRO-PHOENICIAN, SAMARITAN, CENTURION, LEGION *and* PILATE) For reasons of practical policy, his immediate mission was to his own people and confined largely to Galilee. There, the climatic conditions and the intensity of the population were ideal for his purpose of selecting and training a group of disciples. The Rift Valley of the lakeside was a trench well dug to receive the Word of God and the humid climate calculated to germinate seeds quickly in a warm emotional soil.

Jewish people, as their scriptures and history reveal,

were prepared in a way that no other nation was to expect a saviour or deliverer. Other nations contributed to the preparation by the spread of a common Greek language throughout the Mediterranean, and of the Roman communications-system and security of travel by land and sea. Hence the time, the place and – above all – the people to receive the gospel; the Jewish people were to be 'the sacred school of the knowledge of God and of the spiritual life for all mankind'. Though Jesus's mission was primarily to his own people, it was of vital importance that they should be prepared to share the good news with the Gentile world.

It was necessary to his purpose that his own people should recognize and discharge their mission to their neighbours. The parable of the Good Samaritan, in answer to the question 'Who is my neighbour?', is of great significance to the propagation of the gospel to the world. The priest and the Levite represent the particularist element in the ecclesiastical system, but it was the foreigner who behaved like a neighbour. How much more should the true Israelite behave like a neighbour to his Samaritan cousins, rather than foster a policy of apartheid towards foreigners.

When Jesus cleared the Temple area of the merchants buying and selling, with the words 'Is it not written, "My house shall be called a house of prayer for all the nations"? But you have made it a den of robbers.' (Mark 11:17), only Mark included the important words 'for all nations'. It is Luke, however, possibly the only Gentile evangelist, who brings out the destiny of the Gentiles within the purpose of God. Luke records the words of Simeon at the presentation in the Temple, that the child Jesus is to be 'a light to lighten the Gentiles', as well as to be 'the glory of Israel his people'. Both Luke and Matthew record the words of Jesus: 'You will weep and gnash your teeth, when you see Abraham and Isaac and Jacob and all the prophets in the kingdom of God and you yourselves thrust out. And men will come from east and west, and from north and south, and sit at table in the kingdom of God.' (Luke 13:28-29) Luke alone quotes Jesus as explaining the purpose of his crucifixion and resurrection, 'that repentance and forgiveness of sins should be preached in his name to all nations, beginning from Jerusalem.' (Luke 24:47)

On the day of Pentecost, Peter was crystal-clear in his instructions to potential new recruits to the following of Jesus: '"Repent, and be baptized every one of you in the name of Jesus Christ for the forgiveness of your sins; and you shall receive the gift of the Holy Spirit. For the promise is to you and to your children and to all that are far off, every one whom the Lord our God calls to him." And they devoted themselves to the Apostles' teaching and fellowship, to the breaking of bread and the prayers.' (Acts 2:38-39, 42) Thus, in theory baptism replaced circumcision, the Eucharist

took the place of the Passover, and the weekly commemoration of the resurrection (the first day of the week) replaced the Sabbath (the seventh day).

Just as Israel had been known as 'the people of God', so this new community thought of itself as 'the Church of the Messiah', bound together by a paschal and personal experience of salvation by the action of Jesus. The young Christian Church felt that it owed allegiance to a new covenant, ratified in the blood of Jesus on the cross, a covenant, however, not restricted to Jews alone but to the world at large. The practical, ritual and social difficulties of extending the membership of the hitherto Judeo-Christian Church to Gentiles were faced and largely solved by the Apostle Paul.

Apostle to the Gentiles

Paul's attitude to the Gentiles sprang from his own conversion, experience, and direct commission as the Apostle to the Gentiles. As he declared to the Galatian Churches: God 'called me through his grace, was pleased to reveal his Son to me, in order that I might preach him among the Gentiles . . .' (Gal. 1:15, 16) In the vision of Ananias, the Lord had said to him, 'Go, for he is a chosen instrument of mine to carry my name before the Gentiles and kings and the sons of Israel; for I will show him how much he must suffer for the sake of my name.' (Acts 9:15, 16)

The Apostles Peter and Barnabas at Antioch, the headquarters of the Gentile Church, were intellectually convinced that there could be no distinction within the Christian Church between Jew and Gentile, but they wavered under the heavy barrage of criticism by Jewish Christians in Jerusalem. The end of Paul's letter to the Galatians reflects the early tensions between the two main parties within the infant Church: those followers of Jesus, who like him had been born and bred Jews, and who felt that one could not be a Christian without also being a Jew; and those followers of Jesus – whether Jew or Greek or Turk – who could not bear the double yoke of being a Jew as well as a Christian. The first are sometimes called Judaizers, the second Hellenists.

On the return of Paul and Barnabas to Antioch from their First Journey in Asia Minor, they found that emissaries from the Jerusalem Church had raised the whole question of the relation of Christian converts from paganism to the Jewish Law. Christian Pharisees put forward the view that since the Christian Church was the direct heir of ancient Israel, converts from paganism should in the ordinary way become Jews by submitting to the rite of circumcision and accepting the obligations of the Law. Antioch took a different view. Paul and Barnabas went up to Jerusalem, and the matter was discussed. Paul's account of the conference is somewhat different from that given in Acts, which perhaps represents the Jerusalem account of the matter. In Paul's view, he was given a perfectly free hand. According to Acts 15, certain minimum restrictions on Gentile converts were laid down. But in any case the issue was in substance a victory for the more liberal party. The demand that converts from paganism should be circumcised and subject themselves to the Mosaic Law was set aside. Paul evidently took this to imply that henceforward Gentile Christians stood on exactly the same footing as Jews, enjoying full rights of intercourse with Jewish Christians.

Following Paul's rebuke to Peter for withdrawing from 'table-fellowship' with Gentile Christians while in Antioch, where Jewish and Gentile Church members seem to have practised 'open communion', Paul defended integration as a vital principle. It may be that his change of missionary partners from Barnabas the Cypriot to the Roman citizen Silas strengthened his hand. His classical statement of 'justification by faith' in the letter to the Christians at Rome explains his reasons. 'For man believes with his heart and so is justified, and he confesses with his lips and so is saved. The scripture says, "No one who believes in him will be put to shame." For there is no distinction between Jew and Greek; the same Lord is Lord of all and bestows his riches upon all who call upon him. For, "every one who calls upon the name of the Lord will be saved".' (Rom. 10:10-13)

Paul is careful, however, to emphasize the part of his own people in God's plan of salvation and the debt owed to them by Gentiles. 'Now I am speaking to you Gentiles ... but if some of the branches were broken off, and you, a wild olive shoot, were grafted in their place to share the richness of the olive tree, do not boast over the branches. If you do boast, remember it is not you that support the root, but the root that supports you.... You have been cut from what is by nature a wild olive tree, and grafted, contrary to nature, into a cultivated olive tree.' (Rom. 11:13, 17, 18, 24)

The universalism of the Second Isaiah thus finally flourished within the second generation of the Christian Church. 'Here there cannot be Greek and Jew, circumcised and uncircumcised, barbarian, Scythians, slave, free man, but Christ is all, and in all.' (Col. 3:11) [Matt. 4:15; 6:32; 10:5, 18; 12:21; 20:19, 25; Mark 10:33; Luke 18:32; 21:24; 22:25; John 7:35; Acts 7:45; 9:15; 10:45; 11:1, 18; 13:46, 48; 14:2, 27; 15:3-23; 18:6; 21:19, 21, 25; 22:21; 26:20, 23; 28:28; Rom. 1:13; 2:14, 24; 3:29; 9:24, 30; 11:11-25; 15:9-27; 16:4; 1 Cor. 1:22-24; 10:20, 32; 12:2, 13; Gal. 2:2-15; 3:14; Eph. 2:11; 3:1-8; 4:17; Col. 1:27; 1 Thess. 2:16; 4:5; 1 Tim. 2:7; 1 Pet. 2:12; 4:3; 3 John 7 (in some cases translated as 'Greeks' or 'pagans' in the RSV)]

GERASENES (Gk. 'inhabitants of Gerasa') *see* GADARENES

GERGESENES (Gk. 'inhabitants of Gergesa') *see* GADARENES

GRECIANS *see* GREEKS

GREEKS The two words for Greeks are used in the New Testament to indicate three different groups of people. The word 'Hellenes' is used to describe those of Greek descent in the narrow sense: Timothy's father was a Greek. (Acts 16:1, 3) Paul in the synagogue at Corinth persuaded both Jews and Greeks. (Acts 18:4) Paul thought himself sent to Greeks and barbarians and Romans. (Rom. 1:14) The same word 'Hellenes', however, can imply anyone not of Jewish extraction, in a more general sense: Greeks attending the Jewish Passover asked to see Jesus. (John 12:20) Paul declared the gospel to be the power for salvation to Jews and also to Greeks. (Rom. 1:16) For him there was no distinction between Jews and Greeks, for they all had the same Lord. (Rom. 10:12) There was 'neither Jew nor Greek ... slave nor free' for all were 'one in Christ Jesus'. (Gal. 3:28) (*see* GENTILES)

The word 'Hellenists' was used of Greek-speaking Jews of the Diaspora. These Hellenists complained that their widows were neglected in the welfare distributions at Jerusalem, whereas those of the Hebrew-speaking Jews were not neglected. The newly converted Paul disputed hotly with the Hellenist Jews at Jerusalem. (*see* STEPHEN)

The people of Greece

The Greeks of New Testament times were living at least 400 years after the Golden Age of Greece. They were proud, eager, restless and elegant folk with a noble record of art, literature, and philosophy. They had a love of the beautiful and a poetic imagination that peopled Olympus with gods and goddesses. The whole civilized world looks to the ancient Greeks with wonder and gratitude. Never was any nation more rich in culture or more proud of its heritage. (*see* STOICS *and* EPICUREANS)

By the 1st century, however, their best days were over, their political integrity was lost, their religion ineffective, and their mode of life frivolous and corrupt. Though with real piety they kept up their religious rites and their mystery cults held a strong fascination, they had lost their religious belief. Their mythology had become a fairy tale. 'Men had climbed up into Olympus and found no gods there.' The Greeks were lonely and hungry for a faith by which to guide their lives. Their mysteries and philosophy reflected the seriousness and earnestness of spiritual searching.

Despite Paul's disappointing reception at Athens, the Christian gospel secured a strong bridge-head into Europe and established Christian communities in many Greek cities. More than half the letters in the New Testament are written to or from these communities, the fruits of Paul's Second, Third and perhaps subsequent Journeys. (*see* PAUL, *also* CORINTHIANS, THESSALONIANS, PHILIPPIANS)

The language of Greece

Although Greece became a Roman colony from 146 BC, Greek remained the *lingua franca* of the Mediterranean and the Romans did not enforce the use of Latin outside Italy. Greek was the one language that could carry the traveller from the River Euphrates to Spain. All Roman officials understood and spoke Greek, and it was the commercial language of the Mediterranean world. Thus Christianity was preached in Greek and the New Testament written in Greek, which remained the language of the Christian Church until the middle of the 2nd century.

Jesus, whose mission was primarily to his own people, knew Greek (as we know from his private interrogation by Pilate), but preached and taught in Aramaic, quoting the Old Testament scriptures in Hebrew. Paul, the Apostle to the Gentiles, probably spoke to his Palestinian Jewish hearers in the Hebrew dialect Aramaic, but to those of the dispersion in Greek, quoting the Septuagint translation of the Old Testament. Indeed, these travelling Jews helped to spread the Greek language, and such Jewish authors as Philo and Josephus wrote in Greek.

The colonial cities of Greece

To the east and south of the Lake of Galilee was the Decapolis, a league of ten cities of Greek culture. These were the wealthy, leisure-loving, Greek-speaking, pagan communities – vastly different from the busy Jewish lakeside townships. Each of these had its own territory, stretching in some cases over a considerable area, each with its own constitution, rights and privileges. They were associated by common interests, culture, and obligations. They were mostly founded in the early days of Macedonian conquest, but owed their independence to the Roman general Pompey and came directly under the authority of Rome. A league of Greek cities surrounded by an unsympathetic Jewish population, they were bound together by their common Hellenism in culture, way of life, and religion.

The cities of the Decapolis were Scythopolis, the ancient Beth-shean on the western side of the Jordan, guarding the entrance to the Plain of Esdraelon; on the eastern side Hippos, Gadara and Pella, whose territories were contiguous; on the road which ran south from Pella were Dium, Gerasa, and Philadelphia – the ancient Rabbath Ammon; on the road west from Gadara, Raphana and Kanatha, which lay at the foot of the Jebel Hauran; finally, to the north was Damascus.

The sites of these cities are remarkable at the present day for the striking ruins of the empire that they preserve. Their theatres, their amphitheatres, their temples still stand in ruined magnificence; their aqueducts stretch for miles across the country; their bridges and their roads survive as memorials of the past.

We know of at least one visit of Jesus to the territory of the Ten Towns, on which occasion he cured the man whose name was Legion, gave speech to the deaf mute, and fed the five thousand. [Rom. 1:14, 16; 10:12; Gal. 2:3; 3:28; Col. 3:11; John 12:20; Acts 14:1; 17:4, 12; 18:4; 19:10, 17; 20:21; 21:28; 1 Cor. 1:22, 24]

The Decapolis

H

HEBREWS The letter to Hebrew Christians is an eloquent and scholarly homily in classical Greek, addressed to a group of educated Christians of Jewish origin who were possibly in danger of relapsing. It is not likely to have come from the pen of Paul the Apostle, though he may perhaps be responsible for the appendix, a final exhortation which forms the last chapter. The letter is a carefully written thesis with a long-sustained argument step by step for the pre-eminence of Christianity over Judaism.

Who wrote the letter?

The document appears to come from outside the main stream of primitive Christian theology, but it was already in use by the year 96 and quoted in the letter of Clement of Rome to the Corinthians. It reflects the influence of Paul's earlier letters, particularly those to Corinth and Rome, rather than that of his later letters. This might date it between the years 65 and 95. It was excluded from the first known list of works forming the canon of the New Testament, called the *Muratorian Fragment* and written in Rome about 170. It is, however, to be found in the 3rd-century *Chester Beatty Papyrus* and the great manuscripts of the 4th century, *Codex Sinaiticus* and *Codex Vaticanus*.

In the 2nd and 3rd centuries any possible Pauline authorship was denied, though at Alexandria scholars declared it to be indirectly Pauline; that is, 'translated' by Luke or perhaps 'remembered' by another friend. From the 4th century until the studies of Luther, Erasmus, and Calvin, its Pauline authorship was accepted. Today, it is considered obviously *un*-Pauline in its theology of salvation in Christ, in its literary style, its excellent classical Greek, and deliberate arrangement. The author's declaration (2:3) of his conviction through the witness of early disciples contrasts strangely with Paul's conviction through his direct conversion. As the great Alexandrian scholar of the 3rd century, Origen, remarked, 'Who wrote the epistle? God only knows!'

There are several to whom the authorship has been attributed over the centuries. Luke the physician, whose Greek but not his style showed similarity, obviously shared some parallel ideas on universalism, also found in Stephen's speech (Acts 7). Barnabas was credited by the African scholar Tertullian early in the 3rd century with an epistle to the Hebrews. Priscilla and her husband Aquila have been named as the authors by the German theologian Harnack within this century. Silvanus, secretary to Peter, has been suggested because of the literary similarity of the first letter of Peter and the common use of such illustrative ideas as 'pilgrim', 'shepherd', and 'sprinkling'. Apollos, the Alexandrian Jew 'mighty in the scriptures', has been more plausibly supported by Luther. Apollos, as we know from Acts 18, was 'learned' and 'eloquent', 'for he powerfully confuted the Jews in public', showing by the scriptures that the Messiah was Jesus. (Acts 18:28) Apollos, too, was an orator capable of the conventional rhythm, careful assonance and alliteration to be found in the epistle. Apollos could have shared a knowledge of the wisdom of Solomon and the philosophy of Philo, and he could have been steeped in the Platonic influence and the allegorical interpretation found in the mystical figure of Melchizedek.

The purpose of the letter

The title of this letter 'to the Hebrews' is first found in Tertullian in the early 3rd century. The contents would seem to indicate that it was written to a definite local community of Jewish Christians, perhaps in Asia Minor, the 'home of Gnosticism'. The letter might have fulfilled several purposes. It could have been designed to reconcile Jewish Christians to the destruction of Jerusalem and the Temple in the year 70. It could have been

Title page to a life of the 3rd-century African scholar Tertullian, 1669.

Mosaic from S. Maria Maggiore, Rome, showing Melchizedek as the Priest-King of Salem offering bread and wine to Abraham, returning from the slaughter of the kings.

and victim, of the New Covenant. Like Melchizedek, 'priest of God Most High', Jesus appears without antecedents on the stage of history, as the mediator representing Man to God, and God to Man. The recurrent ceremonial on the Day of Atonement illustrates the need of continuous sacrifice under the old dispensation. In sacrifice, the offerer lays his hand upon the victim, symbolizing its substitution for his own life. Jesus used no substitute, but, as the only pure offering once and for all time, he led the way as both victim and human high priest. His was a voluntary substitution of himself for his people; his was a vicarious suffering but not a vicarious punishment. Now, as Man seated at the right hand of God, by his very presence he intercedes for mankind. The writer goes on to appeal for his readers' repentance, for their assurance of forgiveness and for their obedience to God's will, after the example of Jesus.

The author's idealism is shown by his frequent comparison of the phenomena of human experience with spiritual conceptions of eternal reality. He draws his illustrations from such parallel examples as: the Heavenly and Eternal Jerusalem, as compared with its earthly counterpart; the Tabernacled presence of God within Jesus, as compared with the Tabernacle of Moses; the full revelation of God in Jesus, as compared with a Judaism which does not accept him as Messiah.

Like Mark and John, the author insists that Jesus's life and death have inaugurated the kingdom, or rule of God. For him, the spiritual world is a present reality, but not yet realized or recognized. So, for him, there are two worlds in the present rather than two ages, one in the present and one in the future.

One of the least attractive features of this letter is its severity, founded perhaps on the Old Testament conception of sacrifice which avails only for sins of ignorance. The writer holds no hope of forgiveness for those who sin after Christian conversion knowing what they are doing, yet purposefully and high-handedly turning their backs on what is right. He offers only an uncompromising warning that such apostasy is tantamount to idolatry, 'seeing they crucify to themselves the Son of God afresh'.

This letter is the first known systematic interpretation of the Old Testament from the Christian point of view. At an early date the Church recognized its worth. Christians of all ages have been inspired by the great chapter on faith (Chapter 11) as well as by the author's profound interpretation of the significance of the person and work of Jesus the Messiah. *see also* ISRAELITES [Heb. 1-13]

HELLENISTS (Gk. 'Greek-speaking Jews') *see* GREEKS

HERMAS The last of a list of five men mentioned in a special greeting from Paul at the close of his letters to

written to prepare them for this event. It could have been meant to prevent them from deserting Christianity. On the other hand, the letter might have been written for Gnostics, who were insisting on the need of some angel mediation, in addition to that of Jesus. Perhaps their contempt for material things had prevented them from appreciating the sacrifice of the man Jesus; and the author wished to emphasize that God's Son had assumed flesh and blood to become the Son of Man.

Whatever his exact intention when he started, the author moves rapidly and imperceptibly from one leading idea to another. The work is full of quotation, allegory and illustration. The main outline of argument is interrupted by frequent digression or emphasis on the practical implication of what he is saying. The value of the work is not in its logical presentation but in its passion for Jesus – as Jesus the Messiah and the Saviour, who deserves devoted service. The writer is concerned to show the sufficiency of Christianity and to give the right place in the scheme of revelation, creation, and world order to Jesus. He is the pre-existent Son of God. He represents the mind, the will and the purpose of God. He is supreme, standing far above the angels, being made perfect through his sufferings and now crowned with glory.

The argument of the letter

Speaking, as he is, to Christians of Hebrew background, the author works through the ideas of 'priesthood', 'sacrifice', and 'atonement'. He compares the functions of the Aaronic high priest and the sacrificial system of the Old Covenant with the function of Jesus, both priest

Statue of Hermes,
2nd century AD,
from Ascalon.

the Christian congregation in Rome. Perhaps Hermas,
his fellows and 'the brethren who are with them' formed
a household or small group within the larger Christian
community.

Hermas was a common slave's name. Paul's friend is
not to be confused with the writer of the 2nd-century
work on penitence and forgiveness called *The Shepherd*,
himself a slave in Rome. [Rom. 16:14]

HERMES (Gk. 'messenger') Hermes is the Greek
name for the messenger of the gods, translated sometimes as 'Mercury', in Acts 14:12, where the voluble
and mercurial character of Paul is contrasted with the
dignified appearance and bearing of Barnabas, who
was mistaken for Zeus, the father of the gods.

The third of a list of five men, mentioned in a special
greeting from Paul at the close of his letter to the Christian congregation in Rome. Perhaps Hermes, his fellows
and 'the brethren who are with them' formed a household or small group within the larger Christian community. [Rom. 16:14]

HERMOGENES (Gk. 'born of Hermes') A Christian
disciple who, with Phygelus and others in Asia, deserted Paul on his last arrest, perhaps at Troas and
through the betrayal of Alexander the coppersmith.
The last letter to Timothy conceals the drama of Paul's
disastrous departure from Asia and arrival under arrest
in Rome where, already convicted, he awaits execution.
Many Asian Christians, under the threat of arrest for
their association with Paul, simply did not manage to
remain loyal. Among these, Paul mentioned by name
those whose desertion represented the greatest disappointment, particularly Phygelus and Hermogenes.
[2 Tim. 1:15]

HEROD (Gk. 'sprung from a hero') Herod was the
family name of the senior officer in the court of the
Hasmonean prince Hyrcanus II, called Antipater, in
the year 63 BC. He was the military governor of Idumea
(called Edom in the Old Testament). The Idumeans had
been conquered by John Hyrcanus in about 120 BC
and forcibly converted to Judaism. This Antipater was a
skilled politician, who established his two sons within
the court of Hyrcanus, before being murdered in the
year 43 BC. One of these sons, Herod the Great, so successfully courted Roman favour that he was the first to
be called 'King of the Jews', and his descendants became the puppet rulers for Rome in Greater Syria
throughout the 1st century of the Christian era.

Since the capture of Jerusalem by Pompey in 63 BC,
the whole of Syria had become part of the Roman
Empire. When Julius Caesar was besieged by the
Egyptians at Alexandria, he escaped largely owing to
the support of Jewish troops despatched by Antipater.
As a reward, Antipater was given Roman citizenship
and became procurator of all Jewish territory in Syria.
His sons became governors – Phasael in Judea and
Herod in Galilee. Despite the murder of Julius Caesar
in 44 BC, the rise and fall of Antony, and the shift of
power to Octavian, under whose august rule began the
golden age of the *Pax Romana*, the family of Antipater
remained in power.

1. Herod the Great
2. Herod Archelaus
3. Herod Antipas
4. Herod Philip
5. Herod Agrippa I
6. Herod Agrippa II

Phasael Tower in the remains of the Herodian Palace
or Citadel, Jerusalem. Called after Phasael, son of
Antipater, brother of Herod the Great.

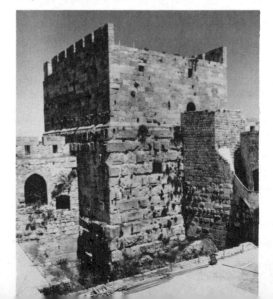

FAMILY TREE OF THE HERODS

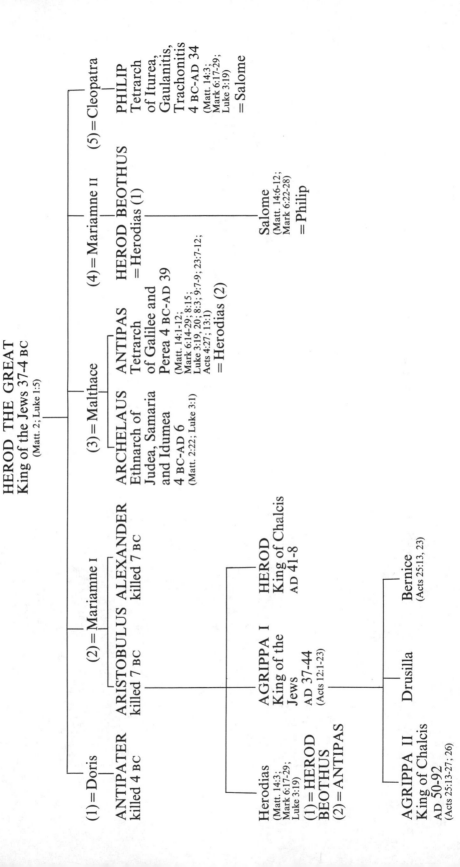

HEROD THE GREAT
King of the Jews 37–4 BC
(Matt. 2; Luke 1:5)

(1) = Doris

(2) = Mariamne I

(3) = Malthace

(4) = Mariamne II

(5) = Cleopatra

ANTIPATER
killed 4 BC

ARISTOBULUS
killed 7 BC

ALEXANDER
killed 7 BC

ARCHELAUS
Ethnarch of
Judea, Samaria
and Idumea
4 BC–AD 6
(Matt. 2:22; Luke 3:1)

ANTIPAS
Tetrarch
of Galilee and
Perea 4 BC–AD 39
(Matt. 14:1-12;
Mark 6:14-29; 8:15;
Luke 3:19, 20; 8:3; 9:7-9; 23:7-12;
Acts 4:27; 13:1)
= Herodias (2)

HEROD BEOTHUS
= Herodias (1)

PHILIP
Tetrarch
of Iturea,
Gaulanitis,
Trachonitis
4 BC–AD 34
(Matt. 14:3;
Mark 6:17-29;
Luke 3:19)
= Salome

AGRIPPA I
King of the
Jews
AD 37-44
(Acts 12:1-23)

HEROD
King of Chalcis
AD 41-8

Herodias
(Matt. 14:3;
Mark 6:17-29;
Luke 3:19)
(1) = HEROD
BEOTHUS
(2) = ANTIPAS

Salome
(Matt. 14:6-12;
Mark 6:22-28)
= Philip

Drusilla

Bernice
(Acts 25:13, 23)

AGRIPPA II
King of Chalcis
AD 50-92
(Acts 25:13-27; 26)

left Herodian masonry within the south wall of the Mosque of Abraham over the Cave of Machpelah at Hebron.

below The fortress on Masada rock, seen from the north. Built by the high priest Jonathan *c.* 36 BC, it was enlarged by Herod the Great.

opposite, above The south-east corner of the Temple area exterior wall, showing vast Herodian masonry.

opposite, bottom right The spring of Robinson's Arch, part of a viaduct from the Western Hill to the Temple area. This arch, the first of three, springs from the Herodian wall of the Temple area.

opposite, bottom left Herodian masonry now excavated far below the height of Robinson's Arch at the south-west exterior wall of the Temple area.

1. Herod the Great King of the Jews (37-4 BC) Through his political acumen and his consummate diplomacy, Herod extended his authority from Galilee to become ruler of all the Jewish territories and, when in Rome in the year 40 BC, was appointed king of Judea. Although Herod liked to be regarded as a true Jew in spite of his Edomite ancestry, he had much sympathy with Greek culture and literature. He was a great builder, not only of the Temple in Jerusalem and the shrine above the Patriarchal Cave of Machpelah in Hebron, and his many palace-fortresses at Samaria, Jericho, Bethlehem, Masada, Machaerus, and the Antonia Fortress in Jerusalem, but also of other monuments as far afield as Damascus, Antioch, and Byblos.

Herod was a clever politician consistently backed by the Romans, and an efficient but unpredictable ruler, absolutely unscrupulous where his own interests and security were involved, and absolutely merciless when he felt his own safety was threatened. He executed one of his wives and two of his sons. He has been described as 'an unhappy man with two souls', the one of a modern man of Hellenistic culture, but with a longing to retire into the desert (his castles are all on the borders of the wilderness), and the other soul that of a ruler with Messianic aspirations.

It was perhaps to mitigate his unpopularity that he built the Temple. He died in the year now computed as

above The Massacre of the Innocents, by the Italian painter, Gerolamo Mocetto.

below The Massacre of the Innocents, from the *Très beaux heures* of the Duc de Berry, early 15th century.

The four-towered fortress of the Herodium, the palace-tomb of Herod the Great, near Bethlehem. Note the staircase and courtyard.

4 BC, and we know from the First Gospel that Jesus was born in his reign. Herod is described, on the arrival of the wise men in Jerusalem, as sending them to Bethlehem with instructions to return with news of the child born 'King of the Jews' – the title given by Rome to Herod himself. The murderous massacre of the innocents at Bethlehem, following his discovery of his deception by the wise men, accords well with the character of Herod in his old age. He was in fact buried at his summer palace near Bethlehem, and it would have been surprising if he had not been disturbed at the thought of a rival born so near to his own summer residence.

The Gospel of Matthew depicts the arrival of the 'wise men from the East' at Jerusalem, asking, 'Where is he who has been born king of the Jews? For we have seen his star in the East, and have come to worship him.' The Gospel goes on to describe the disturbing effect of their question upon Herod and his enquiries

as to where the Messiah was expected to be born. The chief priests and scribes quoted for him the prophet Micah to the effect that the Messiah is to be born 'in Bethlehem in Judea'. Whereupon Herod summoned the wise men, asked the exact date on which the star had appeared, and sent them on to Bethlehem, saying, 'Go and search diligently for the child, and when you have found him bring me word, that I too may come and worship him.' After visiting the house in Bethlehem and offering their gifts, however, the wise men were warned in a dream to avoid Herod and return home by a different way.

On their departure, Joseph was also warned in a dream of Herod's intention to destroy the child. Joseph's flight to Egypt with Mary and the child was rapidly followed by the massacre of all children of two years old and under within the district and town of Bethlehem. On Herod's death, Matthew records, the holy family returned to Nazareth. Josephus in the *Wars* (1:33-35)

gives a grim picture of the physical and mental degeneration of the aging king – deluded, violent, and
vicious. The Gospel story of the birth of Jesus falls
within Herod's final years, and accords well with the
description of Herod's character as recorded by
Josephus.

On Herod's death, at his own wish his kingdom was
partitioned among three of his surviving sons: Judea,
Samaria, and Idumea to Archelaus as ethnarch; Galilee
and Perea to Antipas as tetrarch; Iturea, Gaulanitis,
and Trachonitis to Philip. None of these had the diplomatic ability of their father. [Matt. 2:1-23; Luke 1:5]

2. Herod Archelaus Ethnarch of Judea, Samaria, and
Idumea (4 BC-AD 6) The oldest surviving son of Herod
the Great, Archelaus is mentioned in the 'birth stories'
of the First Gospel as reigning in Judea on the return
of Mary and Joseph from Egypt. It seems that Archelaus
inherited all that was worst in the character of his father.
He ruled for ten years, before being charged in Rome
with misgovernment and banished to Gaul. He was
replaced by a Roman procurator, under Augustus a
three-year appointment but under Tiberius consider-

above The family tomb of the Herods, the entrance
tunnel closed by a rolling stone.
below Reconstruction of the palace and gardens in
which Jesus appeared before Herod Antipas.

ably longer, and in the case of Pontius Pilate ten years. Pilate presided at the trial of Jesus and condemned him to crucifixion. He, too, was recalled to Rome on a charge of oppression, and was convicted and banished in the year 36 to Vienne, and died ten years later. [Matt. 2:22]

3. Herod Antipas Tetrarch of Galilee and Perea (4 BC-AD 39) The second surviving son of Herod the Great, Antipas had John the Baptist imprisoned, and on the request of Herodias, his brother Philip's wife, ordered John's execution. Jesus called Antipas 'that fox' when warned by some Pharisees that Antipas wished to kill him. Antipas is reputed to have been idle, vicious, and extravagant. Luke records that Jesus was taken before Antipas at his trial. Pilate, hearing that Jesus came from Antipas's territory and knowing he was in Jerusalem for the Passover, sent Jesus to him for questioning, but Jesus refused to answer him and was returned to Pilate.

Antipas built the castle and town of Tiberias, his capital, on the north-west coast of the Sea of Galilee. Luke uses his title of tetrarch, literally the 'ruler of a quarter' of the total kingdom of his father. Mark more informally calls him 'king', which title Antipas requested from the Emperor Caligula without success in the year 39. Antipas was summoned to Rome and banished that same year. He married and divorced the daughter of Aretas, king of Arabia, and later married Herodias, the wife of Philip, his half-brother and tetrarch of Iturea, Gaulanitis, and Trachonitis.

The Jewish historian Josephus records that Aretas avenged the divorce of his daughter by defeating Antipas in AD 36. He also records Antipas's execution of John the Baptist, but does not mention John the Baptist's denunciation of Antipas's marriage to his brother Philip's wife. The Gospels of Mark and Matthew may have been mistaken in linking Herodias with Philip; Josephus says she was first married to an uncle in Rome, and confirms her marriage later to Antipas. [Matt. 14:1-12; Mark 6:14-29; Luke 3:19, 20; 8:3; 9:7-9; 23:7-12; Acts 4:27; 13:1]

4. Herod Philip Tetrarch of Iturea, Gaulanitis, and Trachonitis (4 BC-AD 34) Philip was the youngest and the most efficient of the three sons of Herod the Great, retaining his position until his death in the year 34. It was during a visit to his territory near Caesarea Philippi that Jesus was first recognized and named by his disciples as the Messiah. A strong tradition links the transfiguration of Jesus not only with Mount Tabor but also with Mount Hermon, on whose southern slopes Philip had built a temple in honour of Caesar Augustus, upon the site of an earlier shrine to the god Pan.

Philip is linked in the Gospels of Matthew and Mark with Herodias, before her marriage to Antipas. According to Josephus, Herodias was first married to

Shrines to the god Pan in the face of the cliff at Caesarea Philippi, linked with the travels of Jesus at the time of his transfiguration.

another member of the Herod family in Rome. Philip is known to have married Salome, his niece, the daughter of Antipas and Herodias. [Matt. 14:3; Mark 6:17-29; Luke 3:19]

5. Herod Agrippa I King of Iturea, Gaulanitis, Trachonitis, and later of Galilee and Perea (AD 37-44)

The Kingdom of Herod Agrippa I

Agrippa, so called after the famous minister and lieutenant of the Emperor Augustus, was the son of Aristobulus, brother of Herodias and grandson of Herod the Great. Educated in Rome and the companion of the young prince Caligula, according to Josephus Agrippa dissuaded Caligula from erecting his imperial statue in the Temple at Jerusalem. On Caligula's accession as emperor, Agrippa inherited the territory of his uncle Philip. On the exile of Antipas and Herodias, Agrippa also ruled Galilee and Perea. He survived the murder of Caligula, and received from Claudius the sovereignty of Judea, Samaria, and Idumea. In fact, he now controlled the whole of what had been his grandfather's kingdom.

Luke, in the Acts of the Apostles, records the first royal persecution of the Christian Church as the work of Agrippa, in which he had James Bar-Zebedee executed and also imprisoned Peter. Luke further describes Agrippa's hideous death (at the age of only 34) at Caesarea, in the act of ratifying a treaty with the cities of Tyre and Sidon. Josephus confirms Luke's account and rates Agrippa as the last great Jewish monarch in the diplomatic tradition of his grandfather Herod the Great. [Acts 12:1-23]

6. Herod Agrippa II King of Chalcis (AD 50-92) The second Agrippa, the young son of the first, and great-grandson of Herod the Great, was given the Lebanese ethnarchy of Chalcis by the Emperor Claudius. To this was added Galilee, Iturea, Gaulanitis, and Trachonitis in the year 53. In about the year 60, Paul appeared before Agrippa at the request of Festus, the Roman procurator, who wished to draw up the charges against Paul before sending him to Rome.

Luke's account in Acts gives some indication of the respect in which Agrippa was held by both Romans and Jews. Festus lays Paul's case before Agrippa with much

Excavation beneath the present Damascus Gate at Jerusalem, revealing Herodian masonry that may belong to an extension of the city wall by Herod Agrippa I in the year 41.

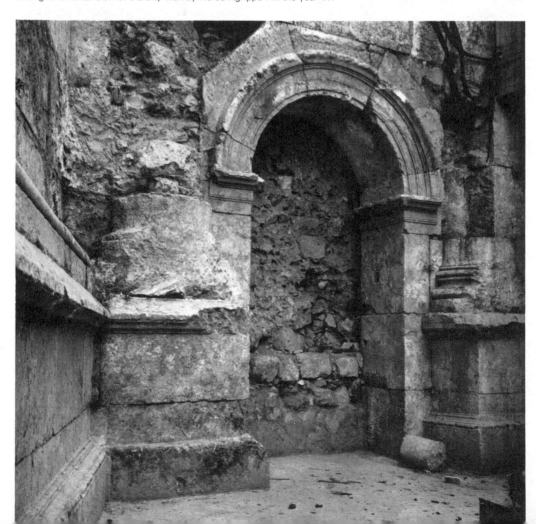

deference: 'But I found that he had done nothing deserving death; and as he himself appealed to the emperor, I decided to send him. But I have nothing definite to write to my lord about him. Therefore I have brought him before you, and, especially before you, King Agrippa, that, after we have examined him, I may have something to write.' (Acts 25:25-26) Paul, too, pays tribute to Agrippa in the opening words of his defence: 'I think myself fortunate that it is before you, King Agrippa, I am to make my defence today against all the accusations of the Jews, because you are especially familiar with all customs and controversies of the Jews.' (Acts 26:2, 3) Agrippa's generous reply and Paul's comment reflect the mutual admiration and concern of the two men: 'In a short time you think to make me a Christian!' 'Whether short or long,' Paul replies, 'I would to God that not only you but also all who hear me this day might become such as I am – except for these chains.' (Acts 26:28-29)

Agrippa lived on in Caesarea, surviving the disastrous revolt and destruction of his own people in the years 66-70. With his retirement to Rome and his death there in the year 92, the Herodian dynasty came to an end, having played no little part in the earliest years of the Christian era and the life of the Christian Church. [Acts 25:13-27; 26:1-32]

HERODIANS The political party so named for its support of the Herod family is described by Josephus, the Jewish historian, as wanting to put Herod on the throne instead of the Maccabean Antigonus in 40 BC. The Herodians are mentioned on two occasions in the Gospels; on both they are linked with the Pharisees in opposing Jesus. Evidently the religious leaders wanted to be rid of a popular leader who was challenging the whole system of Jewish religious and social control. Therefore they were willing to join hands with the political forces which wished to maintain the Herodian dynasty and the *Pax Romana*.

On the first occasion that the Herodians are mentioned, Jesus had cured a man with a withered hand, on the Sabbath and within the synagogue at Capernaum. This incident aroused the anger of the Pharisees, for healing was classified as work and Jesus had technically defiled the Sabbath. Mark says that the Pharisees at once began to plot with the Herodians to destroy Jesus.

On the second occasion, within the Temple at Jerusalem, Jesus had just told the provocative and transparently clear parable of the 'Wicked Husbandmen'. This parable was an allegory accusing the leaders of the Jews down the centuries of persecuting the prophets and finally of planning to reject and kill the Messiah himself. In order to trap Jesus into convicting himself of treason, the Herodians and Pharisees again combined, this time to ask his opinion of paying taxes to Caesar. The tax in question was a tribute collected from each inhabitant of Judea, Samaria, and Idumea and much resented by the Jewish population. Its payment would be supported by the Herodians, who were careful to cultivate the Roman favour upon which the Herodian dynasty depended. The tax was paid with a silver denarius which, in contrast to the copper coins put out by the procurator of Judea, bore the name or head of the emperor. Anyone who recommended the payment of so unpopular a tax would have been rejected by the crowds, but to repudiate payment was tantamount to treason, for which Jesus could have been immediately arrested. His answer, however, took the Pharisees and Herodians completely by surprise. '"Why put me to the test, you hypocrites? Show me the money for the tax." And they brought him a coin. And Jesus said to them, "Whose likeness and inscription is this?" They said, "Caesar's." Then he said to them, "Render therefore to Caesar the things that are Caesar's, and to God the things that are God's."' (Matt. 22:18-21) [Matt. 22:16; Mark 3:6; 12:13]

HERODIAS This granddaughter of Herod the Great is notorious for the sordid scheme by which she secured the execution of John the Baptist.

Both her father, Aristobulus, and her grandmother, Mariamne I, were assassinated by order of Herod, the former in the year 6 BC and the latter in 29 BC. Herodias married her uncle, Herod Beothus, a private citizen in Rome according to Josephus, and they had a daughter called Salome. The Gospel of Mark, followed by that of Matthew, indicates that she married Philip, the tetrarch of Iturea, Gaulanitis, and Trachonitis, but this was probably a case of mistaken identity between two different 'Philips'. Certainly, Josephus does not record her association with Philip the Tetrarch, but he does mention her marriage to a member of the Herod family called Philip in Rome, and later to Herod Antipas. In order to marry Herodias, Antipas divorced his own wife, the daughter of the Nabatean King of Arabia, Aretas IV. The latter invaded Antipas's territory in revenge, and inflicted such a crushing defeat on Antipas that he had to seek the help of Roman troops. Popular opinion seems to have regarded this defeat as a divine punishment of Antipas for his execution of John the Baptist a short time before.

The account of the death of John the Baptist in Mark's Gospel reads like a popular legend of the prophet rebuking the king, along the lines of the Old Testament story of Elijah rebuking Ahab for appropriating Naboth's vineyard. John fearlessly condemned Antipas for taking Philip's wife, who was his own niece and consequently by law forbidden to be his wife. No doubt John also condemned Herodias for deserting her first husband to form an adulterous alliance with her uncle Antipas. Certainly, it was Herodias who bore a grudge against John, though her husband Antipas is said to have respected and even to have protected him.

'But an opportunity came when Herod on his birthday gave a banquet for his courtiers and officers and the leading men of Galilee. For when Herodias's daughter came in and danced, she pleased Herod and his guests; and the king said to the girl, "Ask me for whatever you wish, and I will grant it." And he vowed to her, "Whatever you ask me, I will give you, even half of my kingdom." And she went out, and said to her mother, "What shall I ask?" And she said, "The head of John the baptizer." And she came in immediately with haste to the king, and asked, saying, "I want you to give me at once the head of John the Baptist on a platter." And the king was exceedingly sorry; but because of his oaths and his guests he did not want to break his word to her. And immediately the king sent a soldier of the guard and gave orders to bring his head. He went and beheaded him in the prison, and brought his head on a platter, and gave it to the girl; and the girl gave it to her mother.' (Mark 6:21-28)

According to Josephus the execution took place in the fortress of Machaerus beyond Jordan; John's burial is supposed to have been at Samaria, where his tomb was honoured from the 4th century.

Herodias later encouraged Antipas to seek from the emperor the title of 'King', like the newly-crowned Herod Agrippa. The latter, however, reached Rome first and brought charges against Antipas. These led to his exile in Gaul, whither Herodias accompanied him in the year 39. [Matt. 14:3; Mark 6:17, 19, 22; Luke 3:19]

HERODION A Christian greeted by Paul, at the close of his letter to the Church in Rome, as 'my kinsman'. [Rom. 16:11]

HYMENAEUS (Gk. 'pertaining to Hymen, the god of marriage') A heretical teacher within the Christian community, probably at Ephesus or Troas, on the coast of Asia Minor, whom Paul found it necessary to excommunicate, as his teaching represented a real threat to the faith and loyalty of the local congregation. As Paul puts it in his first letter to Timothy, 'By rejecting conscience, certain persons have made shipwreck of their faith, among them Hymenaeus and Alexander, whom I have delivered to Satan that they may learn not to blaspheme.' (1 Tim. 1:19, 20)

In his last letter to Timothy, Paul is even more insistent in his warnings against false teachers. Timothy needs to be a 'sound workman', 'handling the word rightly', avoiding 'what is ignoble', and exercising a strict supervision of his congregation. 'Remind them of this, and charge them before the Lord to avoid disputing about words, which does no good, but only ruins the hearers. Do your best to present yourself to God as one approved, a workman who has no need to be ashamed, rightly handling the word of truth. Avoid such godless chatter, for it will lead people into more and more ungodliness, and their talk will eat its way like gangrene. Among them are Hymenaeus and Philetus, who have swerved from the truth by holding that the resurrection is past already. They are upsetting the faith of some. But God's firm foundation stands.' (2 Tim. 2:14-19)

Exactly what the false teaching of Hymenaeus and Philetus was cannot be exactly or certainly determined. It is likely, however, to have been some early and high-flying Gnosticism, like the Colossian heresy, robbing the resurrection of Jesus of its reality and substituting some allegorical explanation. Paul saw clearly that a purely mystical interpretation of the life and person of Jesus represented a real threat to the Christian faith in the true humanity of the Son of God, who came, lived, died, rose, and returned to God, as 'the first fruits of the human race'. [1 Tim. 1:20; 2 Tim. 2:17]

I

ISRAELITES (Heb. 'who prevails with God') The community of Israel was made up of its clergy, the priests and Levites, and its laity, the Israelites. The social community of Judaism was conscious of its descent and inheritance. Even the simple Israelite knew his immediate ancestors and to which tribe he belonged.

The Apostle Paul was himself a true Israelite, 'a descendant of Abraham, a member of the tribe of Benjamin'. (Rom. 11:1) Paul's threefold description of himself as a Hebrew, an Israelite, and descended from Abraham (2 Cor. 11:22) emphasizes his claim to be a full-blooded Jew.

He perceived, however, that God's promises were made not to Abraham's physical descendants merely as such, but to those whom God should choose. He declared that God's right to choose was not limited to Jews, but that God's promises were extended to apply to those Gentiles who believed; for righteousness is achieved by faith, rather than by inheritance. As a true Israelite, Paul was deeply and emotionally involved in the tragedy of Israel's rejection of the Messiahship of Jesus and that of God's seeming rejection of Israel. (Rom. 9:8-26)

The letters of Paul compare clearly the Old Testament idea of Israel and Paul's own theory of a New Israel, which he illustrates in many different ways.

From creation, the disobedience of the first man, Adam, resulted in mankind's universal expectation of death. Jesus, 'the firstborn among many brethren' (Rom. 8:29), by his obedience to the point of dying, gained for all mankind the promise of life. 'As in Adam all die, so also in Christ shall all be made alive.' (1 Cor. 15:22) In Paul's philosophy of history, Jesus is the pivot and focal point. The old community narrows down to vanishing-point in the death of Jesus. The new community widens out from his resurrection. Both the Apostles Peter and Paul use for Jesus the metaphors of the 'foundation' and the 'cornerstone' on which a new community is to be built. As the twelve patriarchs were the founder-members of the Old Israel, so the twelve apostles were the founder-members of the New Israel. Paul's belief in the special vocation of Israel nevertheless continued; she was like the cultivated olive tree while the Gentiles were like wild olives grafted on to the original tree.

To Paul, however, the real Israel is the responsive 'remnant'. Those who accept Jesus as their Messiah and Lord become the New Israel, by virtue of their response. A person becomes a New Israelite by faith, rather than by descent. 'Thus Abraham "believed God, and it was reckoned to him as righteousness". So you see that it is men of faith who are the sons of Abraham. And the scripture, foreseeing that God would justify the Gentiles by faith, preached the gospel beforehand to Abraham, saying, "In you shall all the nations be blessed." So then, those who are men of faith are blessed with Abraham who had faith.' (Gal. 3:6-9) A person becomes a New Israelite not by circumcision, but by re-creation. 'For neither circumcision counts for anything, nor uncircumcision, but a new creation. Peace and mercy be upon all who walk by this rule, upon the Israel of God.' (Gal. 6:15, 16) In fact, any who share the faith of Abraham are the New Israelites. 'Therefore remember that at one time you Gentiles in the flesh, called the uncircumcision by what is called the circumcision, which is made in the flesh by hands – remember that you were at that time separated from Christ, alienated from the commonwealth of Israel, and strangers to the covenants of promise, having no hope and without God in the world. But now in Christ Jesus you who once were far off have been brought near in the blood of Christ. For he is our peace, who has made us both one.' (Eph. 2:11-14)

Later writers have extemporized at length on this theme of the Old and the New Israel. The writer of the Book of Revelation, in his vision of a new heaven and a new earth, saw 'the holy city, new Jerusalem, coming down out of heaven from God, prepared as a bride adorned for her husband'. (Rev. 21:2) He continues: 'And I saw no temple in the city, for its temple is the Lord God the Almighty and the Lamb. And the city has no need of sun or moon to shine upon it, for the glory of God is its light, and its lamp is the Lamb. By its light shall the nations walk; and the kings of the earth shall bring their glory into it, and its gates shall never be shut by day – and there shall be no night there;

they shall bring into it the glory and honour of the nations.' (Rev. 21:22-26) The same idea of a city of God laid up in heaven occurs in the writings of both Clement and Augustine. Subsequent Christian theologians have likewise tended to bring the future into the present, to project the New Jerusalem into this world and to identify the Christian Church with 'Holy Zion'.

In the earthly city of Jerusalem, from Byzantine times a false tradition transferred the name of Zion from the ancient Davidic city site on Ophel to the Western Hill. The mass of Christian monuments and churches on the Western Hill became loosely and confusingly referred to as on 'Mount Zion'. Thus the Christian Church has appropriated topographically as well as theologically the inheritance and title of Zion. *see also* NATHANAEL, called by Jesus 'an Israelite indeed, in whom is no guile!' [John 1:47; Rom. 9:4; 11:1; 2 Cor. 11:22]

Title-page of William Blake's poem *Jerusalem* (1804-20).
For Blake, Jerusalem was no longer the earthly city but a mystical symbol.

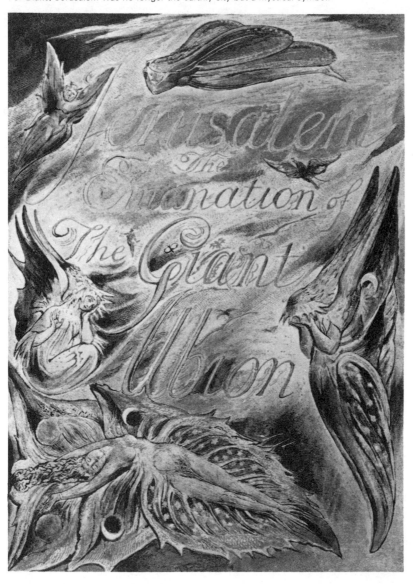

J

JAIRUS (Gk. from the Heb. 'whom Jehovah enlightens') The head of the local sanhedrin or court of elders, supervising the synagogue worship and life of the community at Capernaum, whose little daughter, aged twelve years, Jesus healed or restored to life.

The story of this miracle occurs only in the Synoptic Gospels, where the original account in Mark is abbreviated in Luke, and considerably more abbreviated in Matthew, who omits even the name of Jairus. The account emphasizes the need of faith to release the healing power of Jesus.

The 'ruler' or president of the synagogue came to Jesus in desperate need. His only daughter was dying. He prostrated himself before Jesus and begged him to come back to his house. 'My little daughter is at the point of death. Come and lay your hands on her, so that she may be made well, and live.' (Mark 5:23) Perhaps because Jairus was a well-known and important person, the crowd gathered and followed.

Taking advantage of the press of people, a woman with an incurable haemorrhage – involving probably a ceremonial uncleanness requiring an official expiation –

The raising of Jairus's daughter by Jesus, 14th-century mural from Kariye Camii, Istanbul. Jairus and his wife stand on the right.

The raising of Jairus's daughter, from a 4th-century ivory casket. Jesus takes the dead girl by the hand.

came up behind Jesus and touched the fringe of his robe. She said to herself, 'If I touch even his garments, I shall be made well.' (Mark 5:28) Jesus felt that power had gone out of him, and at once turned round and asked, 'Who touched my garments?' He realized that this was due to no accidental jostling by the crowd, but to someone's longing for healing, and he insisted that they declare their need.

As Jesus looked round, the woman, knowing that she could not escape his notice but that she was now instantly cured, came forward, fell at his feet and owned up. Whereupon Jesus answered: 'Daughter, your faith has made you well; go in peace, and be healed of your disease.' (Mark 5:34)

By now, they were approaching Jairus's house, and while Jesus was still speaking someone arrived to tell Jairus: 'Your daughter is dead. Why trouble the Teacher any further?' (Mark 5:35) Taking no notice, Jesus simply turned to Jairus and said, 'Do not fear, only believe.' When they reached the house to find everyone weeping and wailing, Jesus said, 'Why do you make a tumult and weep? The child is not dead but sleeping.' (Mark 5:36, 39) They scornfully laughed at him, knowing the girl was dead. Jesus then turned them all outside, allowing only the parents and his closest followers, Peter, James and John, to remain. Then in the presence of these five whose faith he could trust, Jesus commanded the child to get up. Mark records his actual words in Aramaic, '*Talitha cumi* – Little girl, I say to you, arise.' (Mark 5:41) At once, she rose up and

walked, and they were all astonished. Jesus bound them all to silence and told them to give her something to eat.

Nowhere better is the need and power of faith illustrated than in this double miracle story of the woman who believed that just to touch him would cure her, and of the man who went on believing – Jairus, the ruler of the synagogue at Capernaum. *see also* CENTURION [Matt. 9:18-25; Mark 5:22-43; Luke 8:41-55]

JAMBRES (Gk. Iambres) Together with Jannes, according to rabbinical tradition, the names of the magicians at the court of Pharoah, who withstood and reproduced the miracles of Moses and Aaron, trick for trick, as the latter begged Pharaoh to release the Hebrews from Egypt. Although not mentioned by name in the book of Exodus, Paul quoted Jannes and Jambres as the type of men who 'oppose the truth, men of corrupt mind and counterfeit faith; but they will not get very far, for their folly will be plain to all' – as was that of Jannes and Jambres. [2 Tim. 3:8]

JAMES (the English form of 'Jacob' from the Heb. 'heel-catcher' or 'supplanter')

1. James, son of Zebedee (the Great)
2. James, son of Alphaeus
3. James, son of Clopas (the Younger)
4. James, father or brother of Judas (not Iscariot)
5. James, brother of Jesus
6. James, author of the General Letter

1. James, son of Zebedee (the Great) James and John, the two sons of Zebedee, were called by Jesus while mending their fishing-nets by the Lake of Galilee. Luke says that the brothers were partners with Simon and Andrew, sons of John. James is throughout linked with his brother John. Together with Peter, they constituted the innermost circle of Jesus's companions, the eye-witnesses of his life, work, death, and resurrection. They were present at the raising of Jairus's daughter, the transfiguration on the mountain, and the agony in the garden. For their zeal and spirit, well-illustrated in their desire to destroy an inhospitable Samaritan village, they were nicknamed 'Boanerges', the 'sons of thunder'.

They were, however, effectually harnessed to Jesus's purpose and his continuing energy and activity within the Church. John, in the early chapters of the Acts (3, 4), is described as the companion of Peter at Jerusalem, in a ministry of preaching and healing, for which they were arrested and taken before the Sanhedrin. Later the same two apostles conducted a preaching mission in the villages of Samaria (Acts 8), after which John is no longer mentioned apart from 'the apostles which were in Jerusalem'.

Barely fifteen years after their calling by the lakeside, James became the political victim of Herod Agrippa I, being executed shortly before Agrippa's own death. 'About that time Herod the king laid violent hands upon some who belonged to the church. He killed James the brother of John with the sword; and when he saw that it pleased the Jews, he proceeded to arrest Peter also.' (Acts 12:1-3) James's martyrdom, described in a single sharp sentence of seven Greek words, is the only absolutely reliable (and the only biblical) record of the death of any one of the twelve apostles. James was also the first to drink his master's cup of death and to be baptized with his master's baptism of suffering, as his master had promised him. (Mark 10:35-40)

According to a 17th-century tradition, without any scriptural support, James is said to have visited Spain before his martyrdom. Another Spanish tradition records the translation of James's body to Santiago de Compostela in north-west Spain, where the shrine is still a centre of pilgrimage. In the Middle Ages, Compostela became the centre of the Christian national movement opposed to the Muslim occupation. The 12th-century Armenian Cathedral of St James, on the Western Hill in the Old City of Jerusalem, encloses the traditional shrine of the head of James, the first apostle-martyr. [Matt. 4:21; 10:2; 17:1; Mark 1:19, 29; 3:17; 5:37; 9:2; 10:35, 41; 13:3; 14:33; Luke 5:10; 6:14; 8:51; 9:28, 54; Acts 1:13; 12:2; Gal. 2:12]

2. James, son of Alphaeus This James, like James son of Zebedee, was one of the twelve apostles appearing in the company listed in the Gospels of Matthew, Mark, and Luke, and was among those present in the Upper Room at Jerusalem after the ascension for the election of a twelfth apostle in place of Judas. In the apostles' rolls recorded in Matthew and Mark, this James is

top The so-called 'Tomb of St James' in the Cathedral of Santiago de Compostela, Spain.

above Entrance to the Armenian patriarchal Cathedral of St James, Jerusalem.

linked with Thaddaeus. Mark also records that Levi – by which name he is referring to Matthew – is a 'son of Alphaeus'. (Mark 2:14) From this it may be inferred that there was a family link between these three members of the twelve – James, Thaddaeus, and Matthew.

Nothing further is known about James, son of Alphaeus, nor is there sufficient evidence to identify him with either James the brother of Jesus, or James the Younger. [Matt. 10:3; Mark 3:18; Luke 6:15; Acts 1:13]

3. James, son of Clopas (the Younger) He is mentioned in only one parallel passage occurring in Matthew, Mark and Luke as the son of that Mary who, with Mary of Magdala and Salome (Luke includes Joanna), witnessed the crucifixion of Jesus. It is Mark who calls him 'the younger', which may refer to his age or his size. The Fourth Gospel does not refer to this Mary as 'Mary, the mother of James', but as 'Mary, the wife of Clopas'. (John 19:25) The context, however, is identical, and this establishes that the parents of James 'the younger' were Clopas and Mary; but there is no further reference to him by name. [Matt. 27:56; Mark 15:40; Luke 24:10]

4. James, father or brother of Judas (not Iscariot) This James was the father of one of the apostles, sometimes called 'Judas', sometimes 'Thaddaeus'. Judas is listed among the twelve apostles only by Luke, both in his Gospel and in the Acts. The corresponding name within the Gospels of Mark and Matthew is that of Thaddaeus, which is omitted by Luke. The Fourth Gospel refers to him as 'Judas, not Iscariot'. It is, therefore, reasonable to identify Thaddaeus and Judas as the same person, with this James as his father. The actual wording in Luke's list is 'Judas son of James', implying either that James was his father or his brother. If this Judas was the writer of the letter of Jude, the last within the New Testament, then he does in fact refer to himself as 'Jude, a servant of Jesus Christ and brother of James'. [Luke 6:16; Acts 1:13]

5. James, brother of Jesus This James was one of four brothers or cousins or half-brothers of Jesus. (For a discussion of their exact relationship *see* JOSEPH 2.) The conversion of James, 'the brother of the Lord', to belief in Jesus as the Messiah, may well have taken place as a result of the special appearance of Jesus to him after the resurrection, mentioned by Paul. (1 Cor. 15:7) Within ten years he became the acknowledged leader of the Christian Church in Jerusalem. Paul, in the autobiographical chapters of his letter to the Galatian Church, describes how, immediately after his conversion (AD 35-6) and subsequent retreat into the wilderness, he spent a fortnight in Jerusalem with Peter and James. Even Peter himself on his release from imprisonment by Herod Agrippa I (AD 44) asked his friends to 'Tell this to James and to the brethren.' (Acts 12:17) Paul also in his letter to the Galatians

narrates how, fourteen years after his conversion, he discussed his mission to the Gentiles with James, Cephas. and John, 'who were reputed to be pillars' of the Church.

Though the initiative of the Christian Church had by now moved from Jerusalem to Antioch, the headquarters of the Church remained at Jerusalem. There, at the centre of Judaism, among the Jewish Christians there existed a powerful party opposed to the welcome of Gentiles who did not observe the Law of Moses. James, however, was held in great respect by both parties for his personal sanctity and his political acumen. Paul and Barnabas had been sent from Jerusalem to plead the case for the welcome of Gentile Christians. Peter also championed their cause, declaring that as all men are saved by their faith in Jesus and by his grace, the Church had no right to impose other restrictions.

James, chairman of the Council and by now regarded as the equivalent of the first bishop of the Church in Jerusalem, gave a ruling. Pagans who turned to God were told only to abstain from food offered to idols, from the meat of strangled animals, and also from fornication. This probably included marriages between near relatives as forbidden by Jewish Law. Thus the Council refused to impose the Law on the Gentiles, only forbidding specific offensive practices. Thus vindicated, Paul and Barnabas continued their work at Antioch. James and other Christians of Jewish origin continued to keep the Law of Moses as their way of life.

When possibly at the close of the year 58 Paul arrived for the last time in Jerusalem, James and the elders of the Christian Church were apprehensive of his coming, for they pointed out, 'You see, brother, how many thousands there are among the Jews of those who have believed; they are all zealous of the Law, and they have been told about you that you teach all the Jews who are among the Gentiles to forsake Moses, telling them not to circumcise their children or observe the customs.' (Acts 21:20-22) At James's suggestion, Paul agreed to undergo a week's ritual purification in the Temple. This, however, only led to Paul's arrest and his long 'Via Dolorosa', from which not even James could rescue him and which took him all the way to Rome.

The Jewish historians Josephus and Hegesippus, both natives of Palestine, record James's execution at the instigation of the high priest and the Sanhedrin, shortly after the death of Festus, the procurator who

right The south-east corner of the Temple wall where it towers above the Kidron Valley, the traditional site of the martyrdom of James, the brother of the Lord.

far right St James being led to Martyrdom, by Andrea Mantegna (*c.* 1431-1506). Fresco in the Eremitani Church, Padua.

despatched Paul to Rome in the year 62. James was thrown down into the Kidron ravine from the top of the Temple area wall, and mercifully 'clubbed' out of his misery by a fuller from Siloam, in the valley below.

Before the destruction of the city of Jerusalem in the year 70, the Christian community had left the city and had settled at Pella, beyond the River Jordan. Within a few years they returned, but it was not until early in the 4th century that the vast Byzantine basilica of 'Holy Zion' was built on the site of the Upper Room, which was the first Christian synagogue and headquarters of James, 'the brother of the Lord'. [Matt. 13:55; Mark 6:3; Acts 12:17; 15:13; 21:18; 1 Cor. 15:7; Gal. 1:19; 2:9]

6. James, author of the General Letter This letter has been called the 'Pastoral Encyclical of James of Jerusalem'. Although traditionally ascribed to James, the brother of Jesus, this homily addressed to the 'twelve tribes in the Dispersion' is perhaps more likely to be the work of an unknown teacher, writing some time shortly before the year 90. The Church to whom he refers is governed by elders. There is no mention of bishops and deacons. Only in the 4th century was this letter included in the canon of the New Testament in the west, and then simply because its address was taken to contain an allusion to James the brother of the Lord – 'James, a servant of God and of the Lord Jesus Christ'.

The writer combines the function of preacher and prophet with a remarkable forcefulness. His message is highly practical and positive, delivered with a wealth of authority. He begins with an exhortation to his readers to treat all trials and persecutions as a privilege, rather than to blame God for them. He is emphatic that true religion must not only be a matter of faith, but of practice: 'But be doers of the word, and not hearers only, deceiving yourselves. For if any one is a hearer of the word and not a doer, he is like a man who observes his natural face in a mirror; for he observes himself and goes away and at once forgets what he was like. But he who looks into the perfect law, the law of liberty, and perseveres, being no hearer that forgets but a doer that acts, he shall be blessed in his doing. . . . Religion that is pure and undefiled before God and the Father is this: to visit orphans and widows in their affliction, and to keep oneself unstained from the world.' (Jas. 1:22-25, 27)

Christians are not to distinguish between classes of people, for the poor have a rich calling from God. The supreme law of scripture is that 'you must love your neighbour as yourself'. To break the law at one point is to be guilty on all counts. What are good wishes without

The Martyrdom of St James,
by Andrea Mantegna.

good deeds? 'So faith by itself, if it has no works, is dead. But some one will say, "You have faith and I have works." Show me your faith apart from your works, and I by my works will show you my faith. . . . Was not Abraham our father justified by works, when he offered his son Isaac upon the altar? You see that faith was active along with his works, and faith was completed by works.' (Jas. 2:17, 18, 21, 22)

The writer is swift to condemn uncontrolled language; the tongue, though a tiny part of the body, is vital to its control, as the bit in a bridle or the rudder of a ship. 'So the tongue is a little member and boasts of great things. How great a forest is set ablaze by a small fire! And the tongue is a fire. The tongue is an unrighteous world among our members, staining the whole body, setting on fire the cycle of nature, and set on fire by hell. . . . But no human being can tame the tongue – a restless evil, full of deadly poison. With it we bless the Lord and Father, and with it we curse men, who are made in the likeness of God. From the same mouth come blessing and cursing.' (Jas. 3:5, 6, 8-10)

He diagnoses the disunity among his readers: 'What causes wars, and what causes fightings among you? Is it not your passions that are at war in your members? You desire and do not have; so you kill. And you covet and cannot obtain; so you fight and wage war. You do not have, because you do not ask. You ask and do not receive, because you ask wrongly, to spend it on your passions.' (Jas. 4:1-3)

The excellent Greek, forceful style, and facile morality of this letter tend to conceal that it has many parallels with the Sermon on the Mount in its demands for perfection. [Jas. 1-5]

JANNES *see* JAMBRES

JASON (Gk. 'to heal') There are two men of this name mentioned in the New Testament, who may in fact have been one and the same person.

1. A Jewish Christian at Thessalonica, with a Greek name, sheltered Paul and his followers in his house. There, the Jewish community, full of resentment at Paul's preaching about Jesus as the Messiah, searched Jason's house. Not finding Paul, they dragged Jason and some others before the 'People's Assembly' and accused them of proclaiming Jesus as a rival to the emperor. The City councillors made Jason and the rest give security, before setting them free. [Acts 17:5-9]

2. A Jewish Christian in Rome mentioned at the close of Paul's letter to the Christian community in Rome. Paul describes him as 'my compatriot' – that is, fellow-Jew.

Whether the final chapter of Paul's letter to Rome included messages to Christians at Ephesus or in Rome, the Jason who linked his greetings with that of Paul may well have been the same man of Thessalonica. [Rom. 16:21]

JESUS (Gk., Heb. 'God is salvation') Jesus is universally recognized to have been the Jewish rabbi who, in the period before the destruction of the Temple by the Roman armies, gathered disciples by his teaching and was condemned as a troublesome imposter by priests and other leading men among the Jews of Jerusalem, though his own disciples believed him to be the Messiah. There is little information about him to be found outside the books of the New Testament; but that little is enough to fix the figure of Jesus, the founder of Christianity, in a definite historical setting. The Roman world knew, through a letter of Pliny when he was governor of Bithynia and through an allusion in the works of the historian Tacitus, that Jesus was believed by his followers to be the Messiah of the Jews and the Son of God and also that he was an object of their worship as well as the founder of the Christian community. Jewish traditions recorded in the Talmud depict Jesus as a rabbi, list his disciples and allude to his condemnation for 'practising sorcery and leading Israel astray', as well as his execution on the eve of the Passover feast.

In the books of the New Testament apart from the Four Gospels, there is a considerable amount of evidence about the life of Jesus, particularly in the letters of Paul, who was a personal friend of Peter and other apostles knowing Jesus during his public ministry. In the Acts of the Apostles the speeches of Peter contain an account of the ministry and passion of Jesus, as well as an affirmation of his resurrection. Thus Peter said to Cornelius and others that his message to them was: 'The word which was proclaimed throughout all Judea, beginning from Galilee after the baptism which John preached: how God anointed Jesus of Nazareth with the Holy Spirit and with power; how he went about doing good and healing all that were oppressed by the devil, for God was with him. And we are witnesses to all that he did both in the country of the Jews and in Jerusalem. They put him to death by hanging him on a tree; but God raised him on the third day. . . .' (Acts 10:37-40a)

The Four Gospels

The Gospels, the principal source of our information, are probably the survivors of a considerable body of literature about Jesus which existed in the 1st century AD. They give written form to the oral tradition of the infant Christian Church. This tradition was developed, in the speeches and writings of the Christians of the first generation, in order to present the story of Jesus to those outside the Christian community and also to teach those who followed Jesus to apply his teaching in

The Turin Shroud, allegedly bearing the imprint of the features of a scourged and crucified man, if not of Jesus himself.

The earliest portrait of Jesus from a ceiling in the Catacomb of Domitilla, not later than the 3rd century. The Jewish features had not yet become stylized nor had the halo been introduced.

their lives. This was done not by making a complete biography of Jesus but by a careful selection of episodes in his ministry, with a full and continuous account of his passion and the events which followed it. Each evangelist or writer of a Gospel adapts the tradition to the needs of his particular readers; but it is possible to trace, in each Gospel, the general course of events from the baptism of Jesus by John the Baptist to the resurrection of Jesus. Each Gospel was written by a believer in Jesus and all the writers of the Gospels interpret what they record, having in mind their particular purposes and the needs of their readers.

The Gospel of Mark and the Gospel of John present a notable contrast in their presentations of the life and work of Jesus. Mark's account is generally thought to have been written between 64 and 67 AD, earlier than the other three Gospels. The Gospels of Matthew and Luke seem to have been written later and they contain a great deal of material also found in the Gospel of Mark. This first Gospel to be written in Greek is thought by many scholars to have been composed in Rome, at the time of crisis following the death of the Apostles Peter and Paul and during a persecution of the Christians in Rome. It is thought to contain the recollections of Peter, whose interpreter Mark is said to have been. It was written as a statement of the facts about Jesus for

Palestine at the appearance of Jesus

Mediterranean Sea

Tyre

Caesarea Philippi

ITUREA

TETRARCHY UNDER PHILIP
4 BC – 34 AD

TRACHONITIS

SYRO-PHOENICIA

Ptolemais

GALILEE

TETRARCHY UNDER
HEROD ANTIPAS
4 BC – 39 AD

GAULANITIS

Bethsaida Julias

Sea of Galilee

Tiberias

Hippus

Sepphoris

Gadara

Dora

Caesarea

Scythopolis

DECAPOLIS

Sebaste

Gerasa

TERRITORY UNDER
THE PROCURATORS OF JUDEA
FROM 6 AD

JUDEA AND

SAMARIA

PEREA

TETRARCHY UNDER
HEROD ANTIPAS
4 BC – 39 AD

Joppa

Philadelphia

Jericho

Jerusalem

Azotus

Ascalon

Dead Sea

Machaerus

Gaza

Hebron

IDUMEA

Beersheba

NABATEANS

0   20 miles

use in the presentation of the message of the Christian community. It forms a group with the Gospels of Matthew and Luke; these three are often called the Synoptic Gospels.

The author of the Gospel of John, often called the Fourth Gospel, wrote for the Christians of the second generation, at a time when almost all those who remembered the life and death of Jesus had died. It has often been said that he assisted Christianity to continue to be a living faith, by proclaiming the Jesus of history and the Jesus of inward experience to be one. In order to do this in a manner which the world of his time could understand, he virtually adapted the story he had to tell to the form of a Greek tragedy. He combined, by the use of his imagination, narrative and symbolism, words and actions of Jesus and his thoughts about their meaning. In another respect he differs from the writers of the Synoptic Gospels. They describe the ministry of Jesus in Galilee, followed by his passion and resurrection in Jerusalem. John lays the scene of a great part of the ministry of Jesus in and near Jerusalem. There are some indications in the Gospels of Mark, Matthew and Luke that Jesus conducted more of his ministry in Judea and Jerusalem than they actually record; in this way they confirm the account given in the Gospel of John. No writer of a Gospel would have claimed to have supplied a complete and accurate biography of Jesus. But Mark, at a time when biography was in vogue in Rome, wrote a coherent life of Jesus the Christ, while the author of the Gospel of John presented to the Greek-speaking world scenes from the life of Jesus the Son of God. (*see* JOHN, LUKE, MARK, MATTHEW)

The birth stories

No account of the circumstances of the birth of Jesus is found either in the Gospel of Mark or in the Gospel of John. According to the Gospels of Matthew and Luke, Jesus was born in Bethlehem before the death of Herod the Great in 4 BC, probably not more than three years earlier. The Gospel of Matthew begins with a genealogy tracing the ancestry of Jesus back to Abraham. Composed in a Hebraic manner, this genealogy consists of three divisions, each containing fourteen generations. The Gospel of Luke has a different genealogy of Jesus, going back to God the universal Father of Mankind, through David, Abraham and Adam. Both include David and both refer to Joseph, the betrothed husband of Mary, rather than to Mary herself.

The belief that Jesus had no human father, but was conceived in the womb of Mary his mother by the action of the Holy Spirit (the Christian doctrine of the Virgin Birth) is clearly stated both in the Gospel of Matthew and in the Gospel of Luke, where it is expressed in the story of the annunciation of Mary. 'The angel Gabriel was sent from God to a city of Galilee named Nazareth, to a virgin betrothed to a man whose name was Joseph, of the House of David; and the virgin's name was Mary. And he came to her and said, "Hail, O favoured one, the Lord is with you." But she was greatly troubled. . . . And the angel said to her, "Do not be afraid, Mary, for you have found favour with God, and behold you will conceive in your womb and bear a son, and you shall call his name Jesus . . ."' To this Mary replies, '"How can this be, since I have no husband?" And the angel said to her, "The Holy Spirit will come upon you, and the power of the Most High will overshadow you; therefore the child to be born will be called holy, the Son of God. . . . For with God nothing will be impossible." And Mary said, "Behold, I am the handmaid of the Lord; let it be to me according to your word." And the angel departed from her.' It is noteworthy, however, that the speeches attributed to Peter in the Acts of the Apostles, giving the outlines of the life of Jesus the Christ, make no mention of the Virgin Birth and that the Gospels of Mark and John do not use it in support of the idea of the Messianic function of Jesus. The Christian Church has taken this doctrine from the Gospels of Matthew and Luke. (Matt. 1:18-25; Luke 1:26-38)

Matthew alone describes the dilemma of Joseph finding his spouse to be with child and his reassurance by an angel in a dream. This story could have come from Joseph. Many of the stories in the Gospel of Luke could have come from Mary the mother of Jesus. The Gospel of Matthew is concerned to show the birth of Jesus as the fulfilment of prophecy, in order to prove his

The modern Church of the Annunciation built by the Franciscans in 1955, protecting the traditional grotto of the annunciation and the remains of a 2nd-century synagogue-church with Christian graffiti.

Bethlehem from the south. The tel of the Old Testament town is to the right.

Messiahship. He writes for a Christian community having Jews and Gentiles in its membership, so that he shows the child Jesus being welcomed by the Gentile wise men from the east, as King of the Jews. Only secular authority, represented by Herod the Great and his son Archelaus, is seen to reject Jesus. (Matt. 2:3-12, 22) This Gospel quotes Isaiah (7:10-14) to confirm the Virgin Birth, Micah (5:2) to indicate Bethlehem as the place of the birth of the Messiah, Jeremiah (31:15) in connection with the massacre of the children by Herod (Matt. 2:16) and Hosea as predicting the flight of Joseph and Mary with the child to Egypt. They return from Egypt 'to fulfil what the Lord had spoken by the prophet, "Out of Egypt have I called my son"'. The Gospel of Luke alone tells the story of the birth of John the Baptist, the cousin of Jesus, and the announcements by angels of the births of John and Jesus to the father of John, Zechariah, and Mary the mother of Jesus, with the meeting between the two mothers,

Mary and Elizabeth. These stories are beautifully told and many believe that the writer of the Greek Gospel of Luke took them from an Aramaic document which he translated. He introduces into his story of the births of John and Jesus three songs, composed in a Hebraic manner. These may have been translations from Hebrew or Aramaic and are known and used in the Christian Church as hymns. In Western Christendom they are called the *Magnificat* (Luke 1:46-55), the *Benedictus* (Luke 1:68-79) and the *Nunc Dimittis* (Luke 2:29-32). In the last of these the old man who blesses the child Jesus in the Temple at Jerusalem says that he is to be 'a light for revelation to the Gentiles and for glory to thy people Israel'.

Both accounts of the birth of Jesus place it in Bethlehem. The Gospel of Luke says that the original home of Mary was at Nazareth in Galilee and that she and Joseph went to Bethlehem in response to the demands of a Roman census. During their stay in

top Bethlehem cave stables, formed by the erosion between the limestone strata of the hillside, often accommodating cattle, donkeys or camels.
above Camel manger of a cave stable near Bethlehem. The circle of stone and mud is filled with straw.

above right Cave stable beneath a living room at Bethlehem, the house being built over a natural cave basement.
right Courtyard of the Sultan's Inn, dating from the 9th century, showing upper rooms, stable door, tethering chain and cistern head.

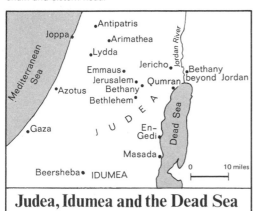

Joppa
Antipatris
Arimathea
Lydda
Mediterranean Sea
Emmaus
Jerusalem
Azotus
Bethany
Bethlehem
Jericho
Qumran
Bethany beyond Jordan
Jordan River
J U D E A
Dead Sea
Gaza
En-Gedi
Masada
0   10 miles
Beersheba   IDUMEA

Judea, Idumea and the Dead Sea

155

above The village of the Watching, Beit Sahur, a mile towards the wilderness east of Bethlehem. Beyond the village is a basin of fields which constituted the night flocking-area of the district.

left Shepherds in Bethlehem standing before a stable door; the steps lead up to the house above.

right *The Adoration of the Shepherds,* by the Flemish painter Hugo van der Goes (d. 1482).

above Camel riders in the Arabah: the three kings were forced to take a different route back to their own country to avoid Herod.

Bethlehem the child is born, visited by shepherds who have seen an angelic vision, circumcised on the eighth day after his birth and presented in the Temple at Jerusalem on the fortieth day. His parents, Mary and Joseph, then return with him to Nazareth. However, Luke says that Joseph went to Bethlehem because it was his own city, to which his family belonged. The Gospel of Matthew does not mention Nazareth until the return of the family from their escape into Egypt and seems to imply that they had a house in Bethlehem, into which the wise men from the east brought their gifts. There are some modern critical scholars who consider that the tradition about the birth of Jesus in Bethlehem grew out of the need to prove his Messiahship and that he is more likely to have been born in Nazareth. They draw our attention to a comment recorded in the Gospel of John: 'When they heard these words, some of the people said, "This is really the prophet". Others said, "This is the Christ." But some said, "Is the Christ to come from Galilee? Has not the scripture said that Christ is descended from David, and comes from Bethlehem, the village where David

left The three kings bring their gifts to the child Jesus: 19th-century stained-glass window from St Peter, Mancroft, Norwich.

was?" So there was a division among the people over him.'

The Bethlehem tradition soon crystallized in the Church and a cave in Bethlehem was pointed out as the birthplace of Christ. This is not mentioned in the Gospels. But about AD 155 Justin Martyr, a Christian whose birthplace was Neapolis in Samaria, wrote in Rome: 'Should anyone desire other proof for the birth of Jesus in Bethlehem ... let him consider that in harmony with the Gospel story of his birth a cave is shown in Bethlehem where he was born and a manger in the cave where he lay wrapped in swaddling clothes.' The apocryphal Christian *Protoevangelium* of James, said to have been written during the 2nd century AD, referred to the Cave of the Birth of Jesus. At the close of the 3rd century AD Eusebius, bishop of Caesarea, wrote: 'The inhabitants of the place bear witness of the story that has come down to them from their fathers and they confirm the truth of it and point out the cave in which the Virgin brought forth and laid her child.' The Church of the Holy Nativity was built over this cave in Bethlehem, on the initiative of the Empress Helena, the mother of the Emperor Constantine, in AD 325. From that time forward there is no question of the site being lost, although the church building was destroyed and rebuilt two centuries later.

above 19th-century print of the town of Bethlehem, viewed from the north.
left The Church of the Nativity crowning the hill of ancient Bethlehem, seen from a bell-tower in the new town.
below left The courtyard of the Church of the Nativity at Bethlehem.
below The silver star marking the traditional place of the nativity, inscribed with the words: 'Here Jesus Christ was born of the Virgin Mary', presented by the Ottoman sultan in 1852.
right A Russian nun venerates the traditional place of the birth of Jesus.

above The Child Jesus disputing in the Temple, by Paris Bordone, *c.* 1560.

below Christ discovered in the Temple and questioned by his parents: painting by Simone Martini (1284-1344).

The boyhood and youth of Jesus

About the childhood of Jesus in Nazareth there is only one story in the Gospels. During a visit made by the family to Jerusalem when he was twelve years old, his parents found him 'in the Temple, sitting among the teachers, listening to them and asking them questions'. His mother said to him, 'your father and I have been looking for you anxiously.' To this Jesus replied, 'Did you not know that I must be in my Father's house?' (An alternative translation is, 'that I must be occupied with my Father's affairs'.) The Gospel of Luke goes on to say, 'Jesus increased in wisdom and in stature and in favour with God and man.' In the Gospel of Mark (and also in the Gospel of Matthew, dependent on Mark at this point in all probability) we are told that Jesus was known as 'the carpenter, the son of Mary, and brother of James and Joses and Judas and Simon', in Nazareth. The Gospel of Matthew says that Jesus was 'the carpenter's son'.

Jesus was educated. Unlike the other religions of the time, the religion of the Jews was essentially recorded in the Book of the Law and the Books of the Prophets,

left The circumcision of Jesus, the presentation in the Temple, and Jesus among the doctors: from a late 11th-century north Italian Gospel manuscript.

163

above left Nazareth from the south, showing the new
Basilica of the Annunciation in the centre.
below left The Plain of Esdraelon from the slopes of
Mount Tabor, near Nazareth.
above Village street in the old quarter of Nazareth,
showing the central drainage system.
right The market-place at Nazareth, in the time of Jesus
frequented by merchants travelling on the trade routes
through Esdraelon.
below Arab women at a well near Nazareth. The village
well is still the centre of the community.

written in a language which people understood and which all children were taught to read. Jewish children were taught to hear, understand and study their sacred books. A synagogue was to be found in every village or town and schools attached to the synagogues were attended by all boys. The teachers were the rabbis, from whom the children learned the Law and its meaning, Hebrew history and the Hebrew language.

Nazareth overlooks that great highway and battle-field of history, the Plain of Esdraelon, which is the only flat corridor through the mountain ranges between the Mediterranean and the east. Thus through the plain below the hillside town many armies have march-ed, from the empires of Egypt, Assyria and Babylon, from Persia and from Macedonia and Rome. The plain continued to be the scene of battles until modern times. Through this plain passed the trade route between Damascus and Egypt, known as 'The Way of the Sea'. In and near Nazareth, a market town of Galilee not far from this great road, caravans of silk and spices passed camels laden with grain and fish. The peasants of Galilee mingled with the merchants and travellers of the east. It has been contended that this made them, or at least some of them, adopt a more or less cos-mopolitan outlook. Jesus may have watched the bar-gains driven in the market-place and listened there to the stories and gossip of the day. It was a rough and ready schooling for the hazards of an itinerant ministry, of open-air preaching and heckling by his opponents in the years of his public life.

The baptism of Jesus by John and his temptation in the desert

It was as a man, 'about thirty years of age' (Luke 3:23), that Jesus came down to the fords of the River Jordan to be baptized by John. He associated himself with the revivalist message of John the Baptist. John, the son of Zechariah and Elizabeth, the cousin of Mary according to the Gospel of Luke, 'came into all the region round about Jordan, preaching a baptism of repentance, for the forgiveness of sins'. According to the Gospel of Matthew his message was 'Repent, for the kingdom of heaven is at hand.' This became the message of Jesus after John was imprisoned by Herod Antipas. The story of the baptism of Jesus by John, as the Gospel of

left, top to bottom The traditional living-quarters of the Holy Family, beneath the workshop of Joseph, include silos for storage beneath the floor, staples for ropes and a central 'table'.

top right The Jordan Valley from the outlet of the Kelt Gorge, Brook Cherith, showing the oasis of Jericho on the left.
bottom right The place of the baptism of Jesus by John the Baptist in the River Jordan.

Mark describes it, is much more than an indication of the acceptance by Jesus of the message of John. It is an account of a personal experience of Jesus, a revelation to him both of his Messiahship and of the method of his Messiahship. 'And when he came up out of the water, immediately he saw the heavens opened and the Spirit descending upon him like a dove; and a voice came from heaven, "Thou art my beloved Son; with thee I am well pleased."' (Mark 1:10, 11) Jesus must have told this story himself and cannot have failed to point out that the words of the voice were quoted from the Psalms and the Book of Isaiah. The first words come from Psalm 2, generally believed to refer to the King-Messiah: 'The Lord hath said unto me, "Thou art my son"' (cf. Ps. 2:7: 'I will tell of the decree of the Lord; He said to me "You are my son".') The other words of the voice came from the Suffering Servant passages of the Book of Isaiah, which Jesus repeatedly quoted during his ministry. (Isa. 42:1-4: 'Behold my servant, whom I uphold, my chosen, in whom my soul delights.') Jesus constantly used the Suffering Servant passages of the Book of Isaiah to convince his disciples that he had come into the world in order 'to give his life as a ransom for many'. (Mark 10:45 and compare Isa. 53:11, 12)

It would seem that at his baptism Jesus became supremely aware of his Sonship as the Messiah of his people and of the cost in suffering that his calling would demand from him. From that moment, as Peter said in his speech to Cornelius, 'God anointed Jesus of Nazareth with the Holy Spirit and with power'. (Acts 10:38) But the immediate effect of this experience was to drive him into the wilderness, to face the consequences of this new realization. There in an inward mental struggle he rejected various ways of winning the loyalty of men without winning their hearts. These took the form of three temptations. The first was the temptation to bribe a following by the offer of material gain, turning stones into bread to feed the hungry crowds. Another temptation was to astound men by a display of supernatural powers, leaping from the top of the Temple at Jerusalem and floating over the Kidron Valley supported by the angels of God. Thirdly, Jesus was tempted to make a compromise with the forces of evil by imposing his own personal will in opposition to the purpose of God for him; this is expressed in the offer of 'all the kingdoms of the world', in return for an act of prostration before Satan. (Luke 4:1-12; Matt. 4:1-11)

After his temptation, according to the Gospel of Luke, Jesus went back to Galilee, 'in the power of the Spirit . . . and a report concerning him went out through all the surrounding country. And he taught in their synagogues, being glorified by all.'

Whether the setting of the wilderness, the wild beasts, the devil and the angels was symbolical or not, the

above The Mount of Temptation dominating the oasis of Jericho and the Jordan Valley.

traditional place of the baptism of Jesus in the Jordan is the ford at Hajlah, not far from the mouth of the river at the north end of the Dead Sea. It is among the lowest points on the earth's surface; on the west of it is the mountainous wilderness of Judea, the traditional site of the temptation of Jesus. It seems that for some time John the Baptist lived on the east bank of the Jordan, perhaps to avoid conflict with the authorities in Judea and Jerusalem and because the regular flow of clean water from the Wadi el-Kharrar into the Jordan facilitated baptisms. Here too was an ideal place, off the road yet accessible from the ford. In the earlier centuries of the history of Christianity tradition seems to have placed the baptism of Jesus on the east bank of the Jordan. But the Greek Orthodox Monastery of St John, on the west bank, contains remains of a Christian shrine of the Byzantine period. Arculf, a pilgrim to the Jordan about 670, describes a small chapel at a lower level than the monastery and a stone bridge from the west bank of the river to a cross in the middle of the stream to indicate the actual place of the baptism of Jesus.

For the place of the temptation of Jesus, a tradition indicates a mountain about 820 feet high on the edge of the Jordan valley, overlooking ancient Jericho (Tel es-Sultan). The mountain is called *Sarantarion Horos* in Greek and *Mons Quarantana* in Latin, because of the forty days of the fast kept by Jesus. A pilgrim of the period of the Crusades, named Theodoric, describes a path leading up the mountain, first to a chapel dedicated to St Mary, the mother of Jesus, and then to an altar in the form of a cross, close to which was shown the

Jesus's journeys: Nazareth and Galilee

Jotapata

Chorazin •
Capernaum •
Bethsaida Julias

Gergesa

Magdala

Sea of Galilee

Sepphoris
Cana

Tiberias •
Hammath

Hippus

Nazareth

Mt. Tabor

Sennabris •

Tarichae

Gadara •

Nain

Shunem •

Jordan R.

0   5 miles

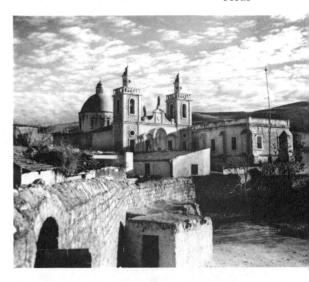

above The Latin Church of the Miracle of the Marriage Feast in Cana, Galilee, the traditional site of the changing of water into wine.

below The Miracle at Cana, 15th-century French ıvory showing Jesus in two scenes, one with his mother, one with the servants drawing the water.

place, halfway up the mountain, where Jesus sat on the rock. On the summit of the mountain was shown the seat of Satan the tempter. This site commands a magnificent view of the Jordan Valley and of the mountains of Moab, although not of 'all the kingdoms of the world'.

The kingdom of God

This was the opening theme of the teaching and preaching of Jesus. He declared that: 'The time is fulfilled, and the kingdom of God is at hand.' (Mark 1:15) From the beginning of their life as a nation, the Israelites had believed themselves to be under the rule of God. During their history, before and after their exile in Babylon, they came to think of the kingdom of God as including all nations, although the other nations did not acknowledge the rule of God. Over his own people God was the supreme ruler; but he was opposed by the other nations and this opposition would in the end be overcome. During and after the exile of the Jews in Babylon, the recovery of the independence of Israel was expected to be achieved under a prince of David's line, the Anointed of the Lord or the Messiah. Then God would reign in the whole world. The prophets of Israel had foretold a day of judgment and purging by suffering which would precede and usher in the universal rule of God. When the Jews were in the grip of alien occupation and persecution, under the empires of Babylon, Persia, Greece and Rome, they hoped for the triumph of the kingdom or empire of God, after the fall of all these empires, as the result of a supernatural intervention in human history. The writers of the Book of Daniel and

Galilee, Samaria, Phoenicia and Syria

SYRIA

Sidon
Sarepta
Tyre
SYRO-PHOENICIA
Mt. Hermon
Caesarea Philippi
Mediterranean Sea
GALILEE
Ptolemais
Chorazin
Capernaum
Bethsaida Julias
Cana
Magdala
Tiberias
Nazareth
Mt. Tabor
Nain
Gadara
Megiddo
Caesarea
TEN TOWNS
Jordan R.
SAMARIA
Samaria
Mt. Gerizim
Sychar
Gerasa
Joppa
Antipatris
0   25 miles

the Book of Enoch foretold a 'Son of Man', descending through the clouds to establish the kingdom of God in the future, at the end of the period in which the world is dominated by the 'Beasts' which are the Gentile empires. This hope of supernatural deliverance is called 'apocalyptic', as it meant that God would reveal or unveil his purpose for his people ('apocalypse' means 'revelation').

The arrival of Jesus in Galilee, declaring that: 'The time is fulfilled, and the kingdom of God is at hand' (Mark 1:15), had a tremendous impact on the simple people and drew all of them, including the Scribes and Pharisees and Zealots, coming from all directions to hear his message. Jesus believed in the present sovereignty of God and the future universal manifestation of that sovereignty. But he also insisted that the power of the kingdom of God was already at work in the world, through his own coming. Jesus declared that the rule of God comes here and now, insofar as it is acknowledged, and becomes a reality at once to those who accept it. 'But if it is by the Spirit of God that I cast out demons, then the Kingdom of God is come upon you.' (Matt. 12:28) 'But blessed are your eyes, for they see, and your ears, for they hear. Truly I say to you, many prophets and righteous men longed to see what you see, and did not see it, and to hear what you hear, and did not hear it.' (Matt. 13:16, 17) At Nazareth Jesus read a passage from the Book of Isaiah, concerning the Messiah: 'The

Spirit of the Lord is upon me, because the Lord has anointed me to bring good tidings to the afflicted; he has sent me to bind up the broken-hearted, to proclaim liberty to the captives, and the opening of the prison to those who are bound: to proclaim the year of the Lord's favour.' (Isa. 61:1-2) (Cf. Luke 4:18-19: 'Because *he* has anointed me to preach good news to the poor. He has sent me to proclaim release to the captives and recovering of sight to the blind, to set at liberty those who are oppressed, to proclaim the acceptable year of the Lord.') He then rolled up the scroll and declared: 'Today has this scripture been fulfilled in your hearing.' (Luke 4:21) When the Pharisees asked him to tell them when the kingdom of God would come, he replied, 'Behold, the kingdom of God is in the midst of you.' (Luke 17:21)

There is no inconsistency in this triple conception of the kingdom or rule of God the Father as eternal, present and also to be fully recognized in the future. According to the Gospel of John, Jesus identified the kingdom of God with eternal life. To accept the rule of God, to enter the kingdom of God and to inherit eternal life are the same. In the Gospel of John, except in the story of Nicodemus, the term 'the kingdom of God' is not used. The term 'eternal life' is constantly used instead of 'the kingdom of God' in John's Gospel, according to some scholars. This may have been because it was more comprehensible to the Greek world and less easily confused with Jewish national aspirations. The Zealots in their battle with Rome may well have said that they fought for the kingdom of God. But it is likely that Jesus used both phrases – with a similar meaning. The word 'kingdom' is found at crucial points in the Gospel of John. The word translated as 'eternal' in that Gospel, the Greek *aionia*, is derived from *aion*,

The traditional site on the slopes of Little Hermon of the village of Nain, where Jesus raised the widow's son.

The healing of the paralytic at Capernaum: 6th-century mosaic from S. Apollinare Nuovo, Ravenna.

translated 'age' or 'world', which is often found in the other three Gospels. The end of this *aion* and the beginning of the future or coming *aion* signify the time of the Messiah, which is the manifestation of the kingdom of God. Life (in Greek *zoe*) as the object of man's spiritual search and the gift of God is emphasized in all the Four Gospels.

In the Synoptic Gospels, especially in the Gospel of Matthew, many of the parables of Jesus begin with the phrase, 'The kingdom of God is like . . . .' It grows fast like the mustard-seed. It acts like leaven in the lump of God's world. It is like hidden treasure, worth selling everything in order to obtain it. It is like a dragnet full of every kind of fish, from which the contents must ultimately be sorted out. So at the final judgment at the end of the *aion* men will be sorted out. According to the Gospel of Mark, Jesus said to his disciples: 'To you has been given the secret of the kingdom of God, but for those outside everything is in parables.' 'To his own disciples he explained everything.'

The miracles attributed to Jesus in the Gospels are regarded by the writers as signs of the coming of the kingdom of God. In the time of Jesus there was no dispute about the possibility of miracles and the reality of supernatural power was assumed. Two Greek words

sometimes translated by the word 'miracle' appear in one sentence of a speech of Peter in Jerusalem, on the feast of Pentecost following the death and resurrection of Jesus. 'Jesus of Nazareth, a man attested to you by God with mighty works [Greek *dynameis*] and portents and signs [Greek *semeia*] which God did through him, as you yourselves know,' is the subject of Peter's speech. The first word used, *dynameis*, meant 'acts of power'; the word translated 'signs' (*semeia*) alluded to the meanings of these acts of power. In modern times miracles are events thought to be beyond the known power of natural causes and therefore attributed to the supernatural by those who believe in it. In the days of Jesus, miracles were also signs of divine power of which the true importance lay in what they might signify. The parables of Jesus were homespun stories of real life with an inner spiritual meaning which could be perceived only by those whose listening and thinking was in tune with the mind of the teacher. The miracles of Jesus seem to have been acted parables; they and the stories about them have a meaning which could not be grasped except by those who believed in Jesus. According to the Gospels the Pharisees still asked Jesus for a sign, after seeing all his miracles. Jesus said to his disciples, 'To you it has been given to know the secrets of the kingdom

171

above Weighing out fish at the north-west of the Lake of Galilee, near the traditional site of the feeding of the five thousand.

right Jesus calling his first disciples: Peter and Andrew on the left, James and John on the right. 11th-century German Bible.

below Mosaic of the Loaves and Fishes in the Byzantine Church of the Multiplication, whose altar stands over the rock associated with the miracle.

of heaven, but to them it has not been given.' (Matt. 13:11) The writer of the Gospel of Matthew adds, as a comment, a quotation from the Book of Isaiah: 'You shall indeed hear but never understand, and you shall indeed see but never perceive. For this people's heart has grown dull, and their ears are heavy of hearing, and their eyes they have closed, lest they should perceive with their eyes, and hear with their ears, and understand with their heart, and turn for me to heal them.' (Matt. 13:14, 15; cf. Isa. 6:9, 10) Without faith in Jesus in the minds and hearts of the eye-witnesses, the miracles of Jesus were not an effective means of showing his identity as the Messiah. Mark records that Jesus 'could do no mighty work' at Nazareth, 'because of their unbelief'.

Physical disease was then regarded as the manifestation of evil. Talking about a man who had been born blind, the disciples of Jesus asked him, 'Who sinned, this man or his parents, that he was born blind?' The answer of Jesus is significant: 'It was not that this man sinned, or his parents, but that the work of God might be made manifest in him. We must work. . . .' (John 9:2-4) In other words, we are to cure evils rather than to search for their causes. Among the contemporaries of Jesus the leper was considered to be unclean, spiritually as well as physically; and as such he was rejected. Thus Jesus, by curing the body, showed his power to heal the spirit. As the diseases of body and spirit were thought to be interdependent, those who had faith in Jesus believed him to have power over the bodies and spirits of men.

When Jesus healed the paralytic who was carried to him at Capernaum, seeing the patient on a pallet he said, 'My son, your sins are forgiven.' The scribes then accused him of blasphemy, saying: 'Who can forgive sins, but God alone?' Jesus asked them, 'Which is easier, to say to the paralytic, "Your sins are forgiven", or to say, "Rise, take up your pallet and walk"? But that you may know that the Son of Man has authority on earth to forgive sins.' Jesus then said to the paralytic, 'I say to you, rise, take up your pallet and go home.' (Mark 2:5-11)

A prophecy about the Messiah in the Book of Isaiah (Isa. 61) stated that his coming would be accompanied

overleaf, left 'When I was hungry, you fed me, when thirsty you gave me drink, when naked you clothed me, when sick and in prison, you visited me. Ivory bookcover, 12th century.

overleaf, right The Good Shepherd, from the 2nd-century Catacomb of Domitilla, Rome.

above *The Transfiguration*, by Titian (*c.* 1490-1576).

left Mount Tabor, in Esdraelon, the scene of the transfiguration according to Byzantine tradition.
below Mount Hermon in Syria, to which the Gospels may be said to refer in the story of the transfiguration.

by the healing of disease and the liberation of men from the power of evil. Mental illness, like physical illness, was regarded as spiritual in origin. It was described as the possession of a person who was ill by evil spirits or demons. The exorcists of the time of Jesus employed magical formulas and spells, of a religious character. Jesus cast out demons by his own authority, ordering them to go out of the person possessed by them. This power was believed to demonstrate his Messiahship. 'If it is by the finger of God that I cast out demons, then the kingdom of God is come upon you,' he said in an argument with his opponents. (Luke 11:20) The demons are represented as recognizing his Messianic power, as they cry out with a loud voice, 'What have you to do with us, O Son of God? Have you come here to torment us before the time?' (Matt. 8:29) On another occasion the evil spirit shouts, 'I know who you are, the Holy One of God.' Jesus orders the demons to be silent. (Mark 1:24, 25)

The miracles of Jesus in raising the dead, as they are found in the Gospels, have the same meaning. Power to restore life to the dead body is symbolical of divine power to give eternal life. The story of the raising of the daughter of Jairus, a ruler of the synagogue at a town in Galilee, comes at the climax of a series of miracles. Delay in the arrival of Jesus results in the death of the child and a message is brought to her father to say that it is too late for the healer to come. But for Jesus death is no ground for despair and he says to the child's father, 'Do not fear, only believe.' (Mark 5:31) In the raising of the daughter of Jairus there is no public display; the faith of the eye-witnesses is essential, so those present are only the parents of the

overleaf Christ and the Woman taken in Adultery, by Titian (c. 1490-1576).

child and his own disciples. The lesson to be learnt by the discerning readers of the Gospels may be that eternal life is not to be found only beyond the grave, but it is to be grasped by a spiritual rebirth, within this present life. Jesus said, in a conversation with Martha, the sister of Lazarus, before the raising of Lazarus in the Gospel of John: 'I am the Resurrection and the Life; he who believes in me, though he die, yet shall he live. . . .' (John 11:25, 26)

The miracles of Jesus within the world of the forces of nature are also reported in the Gospels as signs of the kingdom of God. In many passages of the Hebrew Bible a storm at sea is a symbol of demonic forces, a fearsome monster epitomizing the uncontrollable forces against God. The story of the miracle by which Jesus calmed the stormy water in the Lake of Galilee may have a meaning related to this biblical imagery. The power of God is pre-eminently shown in Jesus's control of the sea. 'A great storm of wind arose, and the waves beat into the boat, so that the boat was already filling. But he was in the stern, asleep on the cushion; and they woke him and said to him, "Teacher, do you not care if we perish?" And he awoke and rebuked the wind, and said to the sea, "Peace! Be still!" And the wind ceased, and there was a great calm. He said to them, "Why are you afraid? Have you no faith?" And they were filled with awe and said to one another, "Who then is this, that even wind and sea obey him?"' (Mark 4:37-41) Indeed, their own Jewish tradition might have supplied the answer: 'This is God'. After Jesus is seen miraculously

below Jesus healing the two blind men of Jericho: from an early Greek Bible.

walking on the water of the lake, the Gospel of Mark comments that his followers were 'utterly astounded'. (Mark 6:51) The Gospel of Matthew, in giving an account of the same incident, adds that 'Those in the boat worshipped him, saying, "Truly you are the Son of God."' (Matt. 14:33)

The Suffering Messiah

see CHRIST

The purpose of the passion of Jesus

According to all the Four Gospels, Jesus foretold his own arrest, condemnation and crucifixion and believed that these were required in order that the Messianic purpose of his life might be carried out. The famous German historian of religion Albert Schweitzer thus answered the question: what did Jesus himself believe about his future suffering and death? 'Jesus considered himself the spiritual ruler of mankind and he bent history to his purpose. He cast himself upon the wheel of the world and it crushed him, yet he hangs there still. That is his victory.' This was written by one who did not believe in the resurrection of Christ. Certain historians of religion attribute to the Christian community, as represented by the writers of the Four Gospels, the association between the life of Jesus and the Suffering Servant passages in the Book of Isaiah, together with the purposeful element in the story of the sufferings of Jesus. Schweitzer, disagreeing with them, attributed it to Jesus himself, fully conscious of the

Jesus's journeys: Galilee and Jerusalem

top The modern church at Bethany, the traditional site of the house of Martha and Mary.
centre The doorway on the right leads into a rock-hewn tomb, the traditional site of the raising of Lazarus from the dead.
above The crossroads between Bethany, Bethlehem, Jerusalem and the Mount of Olives, from where the disciples were to take the donkey back to Jesus.
right Christ mounted on an ass: south German painted wooden sculpture, *c.* 1200.

overleaf The triumphant entry of Jesus into Jerusalem: 12th-century mosaic from St Mark's, Venice.

consequences of his actions, including his death on the cross, and seeking to fulfil prophecy by forcing events to take place with this purpose in view.

According to the Gospels, Jesus made many references to the Suffering Servant passages in the Book of Isaiah in his teaching. (*see* CHRIST) He asked the disciples James and John this question: 'Are you able to drink the cup that I drink, or to be baptized with the baptism with which I am baptized?' (Mark 10:38) On another occasion 'he is reported in the Gospel of Luke as saying, 'I came to cast fire upon the earth; and I would that it were already kindled! I have a baptism to be baptized with; and how I am constrained until it is accomplished!' (Luke 12:49, 50)

Jesus went up to Jerusalem on the last journey before his arrest and death, knowing that the kindling of fire on the earth depended on his drinking of the cup of suffering, according to his own belief about himself. The passion was not a martyrdom which he endured passively; it was the accomplishment of his own set purpose, an act of his own will. He need not have gone to Jerusalem and challenged the authorities by his actions there. He need not have stayed in the Garden of Gethsemane to await his arrest; in the Garden his vivid foreknowledge of the end cost him an agony of anticipation. According to the Gospel of John he said, 'For this reason the Father loves me, because I lay down my life, that I may take it again. No one takes it from me, but I lay it down of my own accord. I have power to lay it down, and I have power to take it again. . . .' (John 10:17, 18)

Jesus is represented as knowing himself to be the Messiah, although keeping his conviction a secret, told only to those disciples whom he was certain of not misleading about the nature of his work and purpose. He went to his death in the certainty that it was the will of God, completely aware of what was coming to him, completely accepting it and utterly determined that nothing should prevent the will of God being done.

The passion of Jesus

The Passion narratives, continuous and coherent, occupy a considerable part of each of the Four Gospels. All the Gospels state that there was a meeting of Jewish leaders in which the downfall of Jesus was planned. The Gospel of John describes, in some detail, a meeting of chief priests and leaders of the Pharisees after the raising of Lazarus, at which they discussed the matter in these terms: '"What are we to do? For this man performs many signs. If we let him go on thus, everyone will believe in him, and the Romans will come and destroy both our holy place and our nation." But one of them, Caiaphas, who was high priest that year, said to them, "You know nothing at all; you do not understand that it is expedient for you that one man should die for the people, and that the whole nation should not

perish." . . . So from that day on they took counsel how to put him to death.' (John 11:47-53) There was a real danger of Roman intervention, in the form of a general attack on the Jews, if anyone claiming to be the Messiah had enough support to make him seem to be a danger to the Romans. For the Messianic hope was popularly associated with the end of Roman rule. Certainly there were other motives for an attack on Jesus. The chief priests and the party of the Sadducees might see his expulsion of the traders from the Temple at Jerusalem as a threat to their private interests, as well as to public security. To the party of the Pharisees and the leaders of the scribes and rabbis, his attitude to the traditional interpretation of the Law might appear subversive and dangerous.

The Gospels all give accounts of the treachery of Judas, one of the twelve disciples of Jesus, who betrayed him. The Gospel of Luke implies that the information given by Judas made it possible for the arrest of Jesus to be made secretly, avoiding an uproar among the crowds of people in Jerusalem for the Passover festival. It is also probable that evidence was given by Judas of the Messianic claim of Jesus, at his examination before the chief priests. The motives of Judas were mercenary according to all the Four Gospels. But it is possible that he had simply lost faith in Jesus and wished to provide for his own safety. Some imaginative writers have suggested that he tried to force the hand of Jesus, provoking him by treachery into an open declaration of his Messiahship, without being aware of the fatal consequences.

According to all the Gospels, Jesus ate a last supper with his disciples, on the night before his death. There is a difference between the Gospels about the date of this in the Jewish calendar. The Synoptic Gospels appear to identify the Last Supper with the Passover feast. The Gospel of John represents Jesus as crucified on the day of the Passover feast and places the Last Supper on the previous evening. However, the description of the Last Supper in the Gospels of Mark and Matthew may suggest that it is not the Passover feast, although the name of the Passover is given to it. A hymn is mentioned; but Mark and Matthew put the breaking of the bread before the cup is passed round. In the Gospel of Luke the cup comes before the breaking of the bread; this may indicate the Passover feast. John's account of the date is considered by many to be historical; a man with a group of followers who might be expected to defend him would not be arrested on the night of the Passover. The Synoptic Gospels seem to imply that the arrest was not intended to be on the feast of the Passover (which includes the previous evening). 'They said, "Not during the feast, lest there be a tumult of the people."' (Mark 14:2; Matt. 26:5) The Jewish leaders are described in the Gospel of John

Jesus

as fearing to be defiled, if they entered the Roman governor's headquarters for the trial of Jesus before Pilate. The Passover feast was still in the future at that point. The bodies of Jesus and of the thieves crucified with him were removed from the crosses late in the afternoon, before sunset, on the day of the crucifixion, so that there would be no evidence of the execution when the Sabbath of the Passover festival began. The symbolical significance of the date of the crucifixion, according to the Gospel of John, is remarkable. At noon, as the crucifixion took place, the Passover lambs were killed in the Temple. The resurrection, on the first day of the week, coincided with the offering of the first-fruits in the Temple. So in the letter of Paul to the Corinthian Christians he can write 'Christ, our paschal lamb, has been sacrificed' and 'Christ has been raised from the dead, the first fruits of those who have fallen asleep.' (1 Cor. 5:7; 15:20)

above left The place from where Jesus wept over Jerusalem as he descended the Mount of Olives.

top The Golden Gate, built one hundred years after Jesus's crucifixion on the site of the gate by which he entered the Temple on the first Palm Sunday.

left Model of the Temple. Jesus would have entered the gate on the right, passed through the court of the Gentiles and into the court of the Israelites.

above Rough track back over the Mount of Olives to Bethany, where Jesus returned each night.

Jesus

The atmosphere at the Last Supper must have been heavy with a sense of the impending passion of Jesus combined with all the sacrificial associations of the Passover. The Gospel of John does not describe the supper itself, for the writer has already included in his Gospel, in the passage after the feeding of the five thousand (John 6:25-59), a long account of the teaching of the Church about Jesus as 'the bread of life'. He, however, tells the wonderful story of Jesus washing the feet of his disciples after the supper, giving a last example of loving humility. The writers of the Synoptic Gospels relate the actions of Jesus, as they described them in their accounts of the feeding of the five thousand and other similar happenings during the ministry of Jesus in Galilee. 'Taking the loaves . . . he looked up to heaven, and blessed and broke the loaves and gave them to the disciples.' (Mark 6:41) But this time the actual words of Jesus are given. 'Take; this is my body,' he said, as he gave the bread. 'This is my blood of the covenant which is poured out for many,' he said, giving the cup of wine. To his followers, the bread was a sign and more than a sign; like the live coal from the altar brought to the prophet Isaiah at his call, it was to purge them, that they might share his atoning power. Nor could they fail to remember the blood sprinkled by Moses, first upon the altar and then upon the people of Israel, 'the blood of the covenant which the Lord has made with you', at the foot of Mount Sinai. Thus Jesus

above Jesus sent his disciples to meet a man carrying a pitcher of water, who would show them a house with an upper room in which to prepare the Passover.

right The Communion of the Apostles, by the Flemish painter Giusto di Gand.

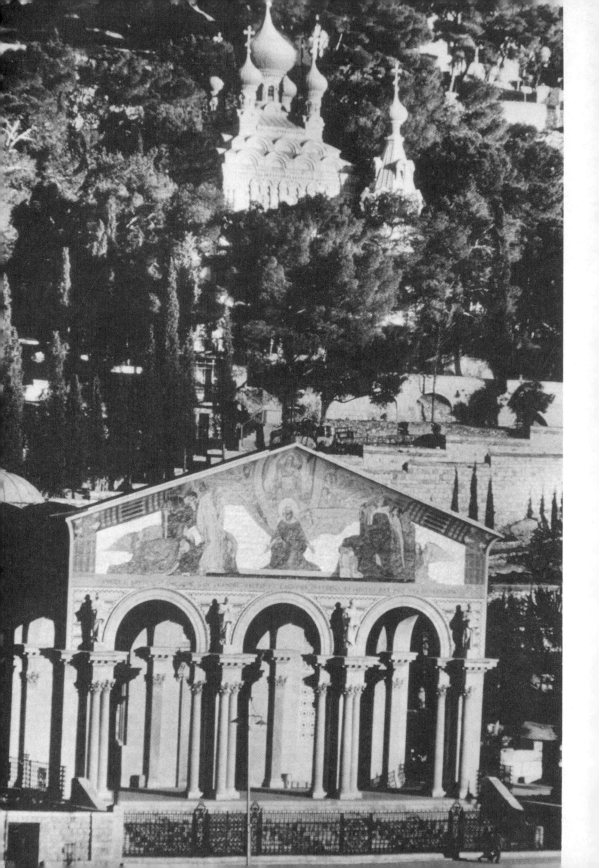

Jesus

is said to have instituted what became in the Christian community the Holy Eucharist, the sacrifice of the New Testament, the means of communion between him and his followers. For this purpose he had evaded arrest until then. As the Gospel of Luke records his words, he said at the Last Supper: 'I have earnestly desired to eat this Passover with you before I suffer.'

The arrest and trials of Jesus

Judas had already slipped out into the darkness when, with a sense of foreboding, Jesus and his remaining disciples went down into the Kidron Valley and crossed the brook to reach the Garden of Gethsemane. It is probable that this was their regular resting-place and their meeting-place, before they came into the city together or returned from the city to their lodgings at Bethany or elsewhere for the night. The Gospel of Luke indicates that on occasions they used to spend the night on the Mount of Olives. The Gospel of John says 'across the Kidron valley . . . there was a garden, which he and his disciples entered. Now Judas, who betrayed him, also knew the place; for Jesus often met there with his

above Jesus told his disciples to watch while he prayed. From among the olive trees they could watch the city gate.
opposite The Garden of Gethsemane, enclosing the Russian Church of St Mary Magdalene (above) and the Franciscan Church of All Nations (below).
below The Agony in the Garden, by Andrea Mantegna (*c.* 1431-1506). To the right, the Temple police led by Judas emerge from the city.

above The path round the corner of the city wall across the Roman bridge over the Kidron, which Judas probably took to enter the Garden of Gethsemane.

disciples.' Although no doubt he could have returned over the hill to Bethany, Jesus remained there, purposefully, to await his arrest. In a final human agony of anticipation, he submitted himself to the divine will. On the arrival of Judas with those who were sent to arrest Jesus, he was identified and apprehended and his disciples fled. From the Garden of Gethsemane the prisoner and his escort returned to the Western Hill of Jerusalem, passing down the Kidron, in at the Fountain Gate and up the ancient stairway that led from the Pool of Siloam to the palace of the high priest, in which the scribes and elders were assembled.

At a place which many believe to have been the site of the house of Caiaphas the high priest, there are striking remains of ancient buildings that illustrate the story of the trial of Jesus there. On this site, under the Church of St Peter, there are remains of buildings at several levels, cut into the rocky face of the hill. Above is the courtroom, with a raised dock at one end and the bottle-neck of a cell for the condemned in the centre of the rock floor. Below this is the guardroom, with whipping-block and with staples for the prisoners' chains. Further down is the cell for the condemned, where Jesus may have spent the night before his crucifixion in the darkness, remembering the words of Psalm 88: 'I am reckoned among those who go down

to the pit . . . in the regions dark and deep . . . afflicted and close to death . . . I am helpless. . . .'

The descriptions in the Gospels of the trial or examination before the religious authorities vary considerably. The Gospels of Mark and Matthew agree closely; the Gospels of Luke and John give different accounts. The Gospel of Mark, followed by that of Matthew, describes the trial of Jesus before the 'whole Council' (the Sanhedrin) as taking place on the night of his arrest. The first charge of blasphemy was that he had said that he would destroy the Temple. The witnesses did not agree and the charge was not proved. The next charge was that he had claimed to be the Messiah. Judas could have given evidence on this charge and perhaps did so. Peter was sitting within earshot and could have been pressed into giving evidence. Perhaps that is why he was asked three times and denied three times that he knew anything about Jesus. Jesus, when directly questioned on this charge by the high priest, said 'I am,' according to the Gospel of Mark, and 'You have said so,' according to the Gospels of Matthew and Luke. According to the Gospel of John he refused to answer about his disciples and his teaching. But in the three other Gospels his answer to the question of the high priest about his Messianic claim includes a reference to 'the Son of Man sitting at the right hand of power and coming with the clouds of heaven'. This brought about his conviction for blasphemy. According to the Gospels of Matthew and Mark, 'they all condemned him as deserving death'. The Council met early on the following morning to formulate the charges which they were to present before Pilate the Roman governor. He was waiting for the prisoner and his accusers at the Praetorium. According to the somewhat different account in the Gospel of Luke the trial at the house of the high priest was not held until the morning after the arrest of Jesus. This would be lawful, whereas it was unlawful to hold a trial during the night. Peter denies that he knows Jesus, not during his trial, but in the course of the night before it. At the trial there is no mention of the charge that Jesus said he would destroy the Temple. The Council does not condemn Jesus to death on the charge of claiming to be the Messiah, the one charge mentioned. Jesus is mocked before the trial by the servants of the high priest, in the account given by Luke; in the Gospels of Matthew and Mark the members of the Council appear to mock him during the trial.

The Praetorium was probably within the Antonia Fortress. This is described thus by the great Dominican scholar Vincent: 'This gigantic quadrilateral, cut almost entirely out of the rocky hill, covered an area of 150

right The betrayal: 13th-century wall-painting from Karanlik Kilise, Cappadocia.

opposite, above left 1st-century stone staircase leading up the Western Hill from the Pool of Siloam to the high priest's palace.

opposite, above right Guardroom of the high priest's palace, from which the sentries could look down into the prisoner's cell, the only entrance to which was through a bottle-neck in the ceiling (*opposite, below left*) The prisoner was strung up to the whipping-block (*opposite, below right*) by leather thongs round the wrists. The two bowls in the rock below were for salt and vinegar to disinfect his wounds and to revive him.

above Jesus before Caiaphas: early 15th-century French manuscript illumination. Caiaphas, as high priest, is depicted with a bishop's mitre.

Jerusalem in the time of Jesus

ROMAN TRIAL
ANTONIA
FORTRESS

TOMB OF JOSEPH
OF ARIMATHEA

GOLGOTHA
CRUCIFIXION

GETHSEMANE

HEROD'S PALACE

TEMPLE

Mount of Olives

JEWISH TRIAL
HIGH PRIEST'S
PALACE

LAST SUPPER
UPPER ROOM

POOL
OF SILOAM

Kedron Ravine

Hinnom Valley

metres east to west, by 80 metres north to south. It was protected by powerful corner towers and enclosed installations as complex and diverse as a palace and camp. The outstanding but characteristic feature of this complex was, without doubt, the courtyard, about 2,500 metres square, serving as a place of meeting between the city and the Antonia. Extending over deep water cisterns, covered with a massive polished pavement, surrounded by tall cloisters, this courtyard was really the heart of the fortress whose activity it regulated. . . . Pilate had his tribunal set up within the courtyard, transformed for the occasion into the Praetorium, called indeed the "Pavement" *par excellence.*' Where could one find more appropriate a setting for the place where Pilate pronounced the sentence which sent Jesus on his way to Calvary? On to this Pavement the prisoner and his escort proceeded, while the crowd of those not entering the castle for fear of ceremonial defilement on the day of the Passover were left standing in and around the great double gateway. Pilate, seated in his curial chair at the head of a stairway, may well have gazed down on the Pavement in disgust.

According to the Gospels of Mark and Matthew, Jesus was accused by the chief priests of treason against the Roman authority in declaring himself to be the King of the Jews. The description is one of a perfunctory routine. The Gospel of Luke, however, gives

detailed and specific charges: 'We found this man perverting our nation, and forbidding us to give tribute to Caesar, and saying that he himself is Christ a king. . . . He stirs up the people, teaching throughout all Judea, from Galilee even to this place.' The high priest intends to place the responsibility for the death of Jesus on the shoulders of Pilate, claiming that he himself is a loyal supporter of the Roman administration. He wants to make the case of Jesus seem to be similar to that of any other self-appointed leader of an uprising against authority. In the Gospel of Luke the crowd, incited by the chief priests, demands the release of Barabbas, 'a man who had been thrown into prison for an insurrection started in the city, and for murder'. According to the other Synoptic Gospels and the Gospel of John, Pilate offered to release either of the two prisoners, Barabbas or Jesus, as it was customary to release a prisoner on the day of the Passover feast. The assembled crowd, no doubt under the influence of the priests and the Council, demanded the release of Barabbas and the crucifixion of Jesus. After making a feeble gesture of protest, Pilate condemned Jesus to the customary sequence of execution: scourging, mocking and crucifixion. Luke seems particularly anxious to show that the Roman governor did not want to crucify Jesus. Pilate believes in his innocence and declares it three times. An attempt is made to pass Jesus over to the jurisdiction of Herod, to whom Pilate sends him; but Herod, after ridiculing him, returns him to Pilate. Luke mentions no mocking by the soldiers in the Praetorium, described in the Gospels of Mark and Matthew. Pilate finally offers to flog Jesus and then to release him; but he is faced with something like a riot among the crowd and so releases Barabbas and condemns Jesus to death.

The Gospels were written, in all cases, either shortly before the war between the Jews and the Roman Empire of AD 66-70 or during the period after that war. The Romans associated the Christians with the Jews, although recognizing a difference between the two communities. The conviction of Jesus by a Roman governor and his death by a Roman form of capital punishment, crucifixion, were facts about the account of Jesus given by the Christians. They were an embarrassment to those who sought to stop the Roman persecution of Christianity. This may well have influenced the way in which the trials of Jesus were presented to the readers of the Gospels. The Council of the Jews, the Sanhedrin, was described as morally responsible for the sentence of death pronounced by the Roman governor. But Pilate may well have been influenced by the stories of the cleansing of the Temple by Jesus and his alleged intention to destroy the Temple. Though aware of the lack of evidence for any charge of treason, he must have been afraid of Messianic claims, since all associated the coming of the Messiah with the end of the Roman rule. He could not dismiss the charge of treason, if Jesus refused to refute it and remained silent. Having secured his own conviction for blasphemy, before Caiaphas, Jesus did nothing to secure his own release, before Pilate. The Gospel of John gives an account of a conversation between Jesus and Pilate, about the nature of the kingship of Jesus. It is not possible to know how such a conversation could have been recorded. It may well have been meant by the writer of the Gospel to explain the situation to his readers a generation later. Jesus declared, 'My kingship is not of this world; if my kingship were of this world, my servants would fight ... but my kingship is not from the world. ... You say that I am a king. For this I was born and for this I have come into the world, to bear witness to the truth. Everyone who is of the truth hears my voice.' (John 18:36, 37)

The crucifixion of Jesus

The crowd continued to call for the crucifixion of Jesus until Pilate pronounced the desired judgment, washed his hands publicly and returned to his quarters. After the necessary preparations three prisoners, Jesus and two bandits or robbers, formed a procession on the Pavement with their escort and passed out of the Antonia Fortress through the great double gate with its two guardrooms, one on each side, the prisoners carrying their huge crosses along the way to Calvary, known later among Christians as the *Via Dolorosa*.

The Gospels of Mark and Matthew agree in their accounts of the crucifixion, although Matthew adds the earthquake in which 'the rocks were split'. A remarkable fissure in the whole height of what now remains of a great rock has been treated since *c.*350 as evidence for the truth of this story in the Gospels and for the authenticity of the traditional site of the place which local Christian tradition regards as Calvary. The description of the crucifixion in the Gospel of Mark is a stark and grim account of the death of the strong and silent Son of God, the Master still in control of the situation, 'bending history to his purpose'. It is unrelieved by the pity and sympathy shown in the Gospel of Luke. Jesus is too weak to carry his cross. He refuses the drugged wine, choosing to remain conscious. The soldiers strip him, crucify him and then share out his clothing. The passers-by jeer at him, taunt him, and tell him to get down from the cross, if he has miraculous powers. Those crucified with him revile him. The only words he is heard to utter are 'My God, my God, why hast thou forsaken me?' But supernatural events accompany his death, the sudden descent of the darkness and the split in the curtain in the Temple, which should hide but then reveals the Holy of Holies. The only man to recognize Jesus as the Son of God at the moment of his death is the Roman centurion in charge of his execution.

top Spanish statue of the scourged Jesus in the guardroom of the Antonia Fortress.
above The gaming boards at the foot of the troops' staircase, cut in the pavement, used for the popular game of 'King'.

left Ecce Homo: engraving by Albrecht Dürer (1471-1528). A turbanned Pilate presents Jesus, crowned with thorns, to the crowd.
above right Model of the Via Dolorosa, showing the city wall, leading from the Antonia Fortress in the foreground to Calvary outside the wall.
above left City wall from the time of Jesus, later adapted as the façade of the Constantinian Basilica of the Holy Sepulchre and Resurrection.
right The Via Dolorosa today, climbing up towards Calvary.

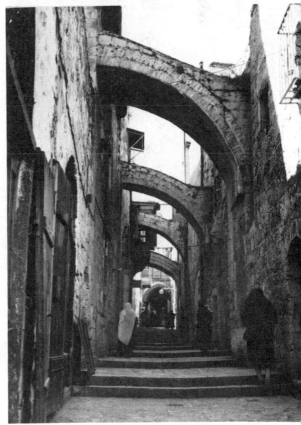

The account in the Gospel of Luke has been contrasted with the other accounts of the crucifixion, as an appeal to the pity of the readers. Crowds follow Jesus to his crucifixion, including wailing women and sympathetic watchers. One of the bandits who are crucified with Jesus is penitent and confesses his own guilt, recognizing the innocence of Jesus. The Roman centurion says that 'Certainly this man was innocent'. This description has been characterized as that of a martyr's death, surrounded by sympathy. The Gospel of Mark tells the story of a man willing to die. Mark's story carries with it a Christian interpretation. For every event a prediction is found in the Psalms and the Prophets of Israel. The words ascribed to Jesus are taken from the beginning of Psalm 22, which he may be thought to have been saying in prayer. The end of that Psalm is a picture of the universal reign of God: 'Yea, to him shall all the proud of the earth bow down ... men shall tell of the Lord to the coming generation, and proclaim his deliverance to a people yet unborn, that he hath wrought it.'

The burial regulations of the Book of Deuteronomy (21:23) demanded that crucified criminals – or indeed any executed criminals – should be buried before sunset. This may have been especially important when the Passover Sabbath began in the evening, and the Romans respected local laws and customs in such matters. If the body of Jesus had not been claimed, it might have been buried in a common grave. But Joseph of Arimathea begged the permission of Pilate to bury Jesus in his own tomb cut in the rock. Mark says: 'Joseph of Arimathea, a respected member of the Council, who was also himself looking for the kingdom of God, took courage and went to Pilate and asked for the body of Jesus.' The Gospel of Matthew describes Joseph of Arimathea as 'a rich man . . . and a disciple of Jesus'. Luke says that he was 'a member of the Council, a good and righteous man, who had not consented to their purpose and deed'. John calls him 'a disciple of Jesus, but secretly', who, together with Nicodemus, another secret friend of Jesus, anointed the body of Jesus, and buried it in a new tomb very near the place of his crucifixion.

The tomb was in a garden or grove of trees, presumably the private property of Joseph of Arimathea. Even if Herod Agrippa, at the building of the 'Third Wall' in the year 43, enclosed the garden within the walled city, it would have been untouched as a place of burial and the Christians, even if they did not own it, could have pointed it out to one another. Even the destruction of Jerusalem in the year 70 would not cause tombs cut in the rock or rocks split by earthquakes to disappear. When the city was rebuilt by the Romans in the year 138, after the Bar-Kokhba rebellion of 135, it is certain that the traditional site of the death and burial of Jesus Christ was covered by a terrace on which a Roman forum and temples of the deities of Rome were built. Recent archaeological investigation seems to show that the place which Christian tradition regards as Calvary was in a deep quarry, probably used for the defence of the 'Second Wall'. In this quarry the rock split by an earthquake is 32 feet higher than the level of the natural rock on all sides of it. What remains of it is 14 feet square. There were several tombs cut in the rock in the sides of the quarry. The Roman builders in the year 138 filled this trench with earth and built upon it, as their walled city was to be on both sides of the line of the 'Second Wall'. They may well have done this without intending the desecration of a holy place, belonging to a new community of which they knew little or nothing. But it was said by Christians in later centuries that the

top An Armenian deacon mounts the steps up to the Chapel of Calvary, on a level with the top of the rock.
above The rock of the mound of Calvary, revealing an earthquake fissure.
overleaf, left Christ on the Cross, by El Greco (c. 1545-1614).
overleaf, right Unfinished *Pietà* by Michelangelo.

left Aerial view of Jerusalem, showing the Church of the Holy Sepulchre (right), which encloses both the sites of Calvary and of the Tomb.

Emperor Hadrian felt it to be necessary thus to desecrate, systematically and thoroughly, the sites of the crucifixion and resurrection of Jesus Christ. In this way he marked the sites for the Christian excavations in 323-5, when the first Church of the Holy Resurrection of Christ was built, by the orders of the first Christian Roman emperor, Constantine the Great. The shrines then built included the rock split by an earthquake at Calvary (still to be seen in the church) and the tomb identified as the Holy Sepulchre of Jesus Christ. The traditional tomb was destroyed to a very great extent in the 11th century; the shrine contains remains of it.

This is the central shrine in the church which Western Christians call the Church of the Holy Sepulchre, known to local Christians and to Eastern Christendom as the Church of the Holy Resurrection.

The resurrection

The followers of Jesus of Nazareth believed that he had shown himself to be alive. In the New Testament we find three ways of presenting the resurrection of Jesus Christ. First of all the Christian community or Church exists and the life of that community is the continuation of the life of Jesus of Nazareth. Secondly, followers of Jesus of Nazareth say and write that on the first day of

left Pietà: drawing by Michelangelo (1475-1564).
below 15th-century Russian icon showing the entombment.

overleaf Early 15th-century French manuscript illumination, symbolizing the victory over sin and death achieved by the crucifixion.

above Tomb closed by a rolling stone, among spring
flowers, near Jerusalem today.

right Within the Tomb of Jesus today: the single slab
or *loculus* is as described by Eusebius, who was
present at the excavation of the original tomb.

the week, the day after the Sabbath which followed his
death, his tomb was found to be empty. Thirdly, many
of the followers of Jesus state in the books of the New
Testament that during the six weeks after his death he
appeared to them and showed them that he was alive.

All the Four Gospels record visits made to the tomb
of Jesus by his disciples, who found it to be empty. The
Gospels of Luke, Matthew and John, as well as the
Acts of the Apostles and the First Letter of Paul to the
Corinthians, record appearances of Jesus after the
resurrection. The Gospel of Mark says that women who
were disciples of Jesus bought spices after sunset on the
Sabbath day following the crucifixion, in order to
anoint his body. Very early in the morning on the first
day of the week they came to the tomb of Jesus. They
found that the stone in the entrance of the tomb was
rolled back. 'And on entering the tomb, they saw a
young man sitting on the right side, dressed in a white
robe; and they were amazed. And he said to them, "Do
not be amazed; you seek Jesus of Nazareth, who was
crucified. He has risen, he is not here; see the place
where they laid him. But go, tell his disciples and Peter
that he is going before you to Galilee; there you will see
him, as he told you." And they went out and fled from
the tomb, for trembling and astonishment had come
upon them; and they said nothing to anyone, for they
were afraid.' (Mark 16:5-8) At this point the Gospel of
Mark ends. It is universally recognized that the verses

which follow are a later addition, an attempt to
finish an unfinished work which appears differently in
various manuscripts. The writer of the Gospel of Mark
may have stopped at that point, with the words 'they
were afraid', or may have added something now lost.

The Gospel of Matthew says that the Council of the
Jews asked Pilate to put a guard on the tomb of Jesus,
that he told them to send their own men as guards.
This they did and sealed the entrance of the tomb.
There was an earthquake during the night, 'For an angel
of the Lord descended from heaven and came and rolled
back the stone, and sat upon it. . . . And for fear of him
the guards trembled and became like dead men.' When
the women who were disciples of Jesus came early
next morning, it was this angel who gave them the
message recorded in the Gospel of Mark as given by 'a
young man'. As they went away, 'Behold, Jesus met
them and said, "Hail". And they came up and took
hold of his feet and worshipped him.' Jesus repeats the
command of the angel: 'Go and tell my brethren to go
to Galilee.' The guards report the matter to the chief
priests, who instruct them to say that while they were
asleep the disciples of Jesus stole his body. The disciples
then meet Jesus at an appointed place in Galilee.

In the Gospel of Luke, when the women enter the
tomb and are perplexed to find that the body of Jesus
is not there, two men suddenly appear beside them.
'The men said to them, "Why do you seek the living

among the dead? Remember how he told you, while he was still in Galilee, that the Son of Man must be delivered into the hands of sinful men, and be crucified, and on the third day rise." And they remembered his words. . . .' When the Gospel of Luke describes appearances of Jesus after his resurrection, they occur in Judea, first on the road to Emmaus and then at Jerusalem in the Upper Room. He shows the scars of his crucifixion and eats with his disciples.

The Gospel of John gives an account coming from the women, and particularly from Mary of Magdala, together with the recollections of the Apostle Peter and of another disciple, 'the one whom Jesus loved'. The women went to the tomb early in the morning, found it empty and ran to summon the men. When Peter and the other disciple came to the tomb, they looked into it. Peter went into the tomb, in which he had seen that there was no dead body, and it is reported that 'he saw the linen cloths lying, and the napkin, which had been on his head, not lying with the linen cloths, but rolled up in a place by itself.' The disciple other than

above The Resurrection, drawing by Michelangelo (1475-1564).

Peter, 'the one whom Jesus loved', grasped what had happened, as soon as he went in: 'he saw and believed'. But Peter did not grasp it, 'for as yet they did not know the scripture, that he must rise from the dead'. They went home. Meanwhile Mary of Magdala saw two angels in white sitting in the tomb. When they asked her why she was weeping, she said that some people had taken the dead body of Jesus away and had hidden it in some unknown place. Turning round outside the tomb, she suddenly saw through her tears the figure of someone whom she imagined to be the gardener and begged him to tell her where the body of Jesus could be found. It was Jesus and he called her by her name, 'Mary'. She fell at his feet and said to him in Hebrew, 'Rabboni' (Master). 'Jesus said to her, "Do not hold me, for I have not yet ascended to the Father; but go to my brethren and say to them, I am ascending to my Father and your Father, to my God and your God."'

On the evening of that day and also a week later Jesus appeared to his disciples in Jerusalem. He showed them the marks of the nails in his hands and in his side, where the lance of a soldier had pierced his body. He is reported as saying to one of them, Thomas, who needed proof, 'do not be faithless, but believing. . . . Have you believed

left The ascension of Jesus, 5th-century ivory panel. While the three Marys and disciples wait round the tomb. God stretches down a hand to raise Jesus up to heaven.

above Empty *loculus* in the Garden Tomb, Jerusalem.

207

above The Mount of Olives seen from the Russian tower of the Ascension, showing the minaret and Byzantine enclosure of the Ascension in the foreground

because you have seen me? Blessed are those that have not seen and yet believe.'

In the last chapter of the Gospel of John, which many scholars regard as a kind of appendix, coming after the original end of the book, there is the story of the appearance of Jesus on the shore of the Sea of Galilee. After a fruitless night of fishing in deep water, Peter and seven other disciples of Jesus were approaching the shore at dawn when a voice hailed them, saying, 'Children, have you any fish?' They answered, 'No.' The voice then said, 'Cast the net on the right side of the boat, and you will find some.' They did so and there were so many fish in the net that they could not haul it into the boat. It was then that the disciple, 'the one whom Jesus loved,' recognized the voice of Jesus and said, 'It is the Lord'. Peter jumped into the water, while the others brought the boat to the land, dragging with it the net full of fish. On the beach Jesus gave them bread and fish and ate with them. 'They saw a charcoal fire, with fish lying on it, and bread. . . . Jesus came and took the bread and gave it to them and . . . the fish.' Afterwards he questioned Peter three times and three times ordered him to take care of the other disciples. 'Simon, son of John, do you love me more than these? . . . Feed my lambs. . . . Do you love me? . . . Tend my sheep. . . . Do you

love me? . . . Feed my sheep.' It seems that Jesus is regarded by the authors of the Gospel of John as thus making Peter the leader of the Church. The fact that Peter had three times denied all knowledge of Jesus at the time of his trial before the chief priests is overlooked. The promise given to Peter according to the Gospel of Matthew is confirmed.

The Book of the Acts of the Apostles is a sequel to the Gospel of Luke, written by the same author. It is said there that Jesus presented himself alive (to the apostles whom he had chosen) 'after his passion by many proofs, appearing to them during forty days'. In the same book, in the speech of Peter to Cornelius, he says that God raised Jesus from the dead 'and made him manifest, not to all the people but to us who were chosen by God as witnesses, who ate and drank with him after he rose from the dead'.

The ascension

Only the author of the Gospel of Luke relates the story of the ascension of Jesus Christ into heaven from the Mount of Olives. In the Gospel he writes, 'Then he led them out as far as Bethany, and lifting up his hand he blessed them. While he blessed them, he parted from them.' In the Acts of the Apostles there is more description, 'And when he had said this, as they were looking on, he was lifted up, and a cloud took him from their sight . . . they were gazing up into heaven as he went. . . . Then they returned to Jerusalem from the mount called Olivet. . . .'

The Gospel of John, however, uses the word 'ascend'. Jesus in that Gospel says to Mary of Magdala, 'I am ascending.' And on an earlier occasion asks, 'What if you were to see the Son of Man ascending where he was before?' Paul in his letter to the Ephesians writes, about the risen Jesus Christ, 'he also ascended far above all the heavens, that he might fill all things. And his gifts were that some should be apostles, some prophets, some evangelists, some pastors and teachers.'

According to the Gospels there is a great difference between the appearance of Jesus Christ during the six weeks after his crucifixion and all later visions of him seen by his followers. After the time which may be called his ascension, he is seen, 'sitting at the right hand of God', in a state which is outside earthly space and time. Before the ascension, he is in Judea or in Galilee, and he is present in a bodily form. He is not a spirit, in the sense of a vision. Yet he promises that he will be with his followers. As he says in the Gospel of Matthew, 'Lo I am with you always, to the close of the age.' Matt., Mark, Luke, John, and all books of the New Testament] *above* The ascension of Jesus, with the angels promising his return to Mary and the apostles, from the 11th-century *Book of Pericopes*, Bamberg.

Jesus Justus

JESUS JUSTUS *see* JUSTUS

JESUS BARABBAS *see* BARABBAS This name is not to be found in any extant manuscript, though the great biblical scholar Origen records having seen the name in the first half of the 3rd century.

JOANNA The wife of Chuza, the steward or domestic administrator of Herod Antipas, Joanna was among the women who helped Jesus financially in Galilee. She was also a witness of the empty tomb on Easter morning. *see* CHUZA [Luke 8:3; 24:10]

JOHN (Gk. from the Heb. 'God has been gracious') The various men who are thought to have been called 'John' are dealt with separately. John the Evangelist may also have been the author of at least one, if not all three, of the Letters. John, son of Zebedee, might also have been the beloved disciple.

1. **John the Baptist**
2. **John, son of Zebedee**
3. **John, the beloved disciple**
4. **John the Evangelist**
5. **John the Elder**
6. **John, father of Peter**
7. **John, relative of Annas**
8. **John Mark, the Evangelist**
9. **John the Divine**

1. John the Baptist John was the cousin and forerunner of Jesus. In the prophetic tradition he appeared out of the wilderness, heralding the coming of the Messiah and proclaiming the baptism of repentance for the forgiveness of sins. At the River Jordan, he recognized Jesus as the Messiah, baptized him, and pointed him out to his own disciples as 'the Lamb of God'. The story of John the Baptist is the drama of a man aware of his own mission and greatness, yet willing to step aside and act as a signpost to one even greater than himself. John was imprisoned and executed by Herod Antipas in about the year 30.

Miraculous birth

Born in the hill-country of Judea, John was the son of elderly parents, Zechariah, a priest, and Elizabeth, daughter of a priestly family and a relative of Mary, the mother of Jesus. Luke tells the story of John's birth. Both his parents were worthy in the sight of God, but they were childless. When it was Zechariah's turn to serve in the Temple at Jerusalem, he was attending to the altar of incense in the sanctuary when he had a vision of an angel. The angel announced that his prayer had been heard and that Elizabeth was going to have a son, whose name was to be John. 'And you will have joy and gladness, and many will rejoice at his birth; for he

left 17th-century Russian icon of John the Baptist. The background details include the vision of Zechariah, the birth and execution of John, and the River Jordan full of birds and beasts.

above The traditional birthplace and home of John the Baptist, the village of Ein Karem.

will be great before the Lord . . . and he will go before him in the spirit and power of Elijah, to turn the hearts of the fathers to the children, and the disobedient to the wisdom of the just, to make ready for the Lord a people prepared.'

When the old priest asked, 'How shall I know this?' the angel replied, 'I am Gabriel, who stand in the presence of God; and I was sent to speak to you, and to bring you this good news. And behold, you will be silent and unable to speak until the day that these things come to pass, because you did not believe my words, which will be fulfilled in their time.' When he returned home at the end of his duties, his wife Elizabeth conceived. Six months later, the angel was sent to Mary in Nazareth to make a similar announcement of the birth of Jesus. Mary set out at once to visit Elizabeth over the hills of Judea, and stayed with her some three months before returning to Nazareth. Meanwhile, Elizabeth's baby arrived, was circumcised, and named 'John'.

His father recovered his power of speech and blessed God, saying, 'And you, child, will be called the prophet of the Most High; for you will go before the Lord to prepare his ways.'

The two boys were born within six months of each other, in towns within sight of each other. Joseph and Mary had come to Bethlehem for the census; the home of the priest Zechariah and Elizabeth was below Mount Orah in Ein Karem, the 'Gracious Spring'. Before the time of the Russian pilgrim Daniel, in 1107, the birth-

above The wilderness of Judea, scene of the ministry of John the Baptist. The wilderness descends from the east of the Mount of Olives into the Rift Valley to the Dead Sea.

far left St John in the Wilderness, by Giovanni di Paolo, *c*. 1450.

left John the Baptist, wearing a coat of camel hair, preaches the 'Lamb of God'. Detail from the ivory throne of Archbishop Maximianus, Ravenna, 6th century.

above The River Jordan between the traditional place
of baptism and its exit into the Dead Sea

right The baptism of Jesus, 16th-century mural from
Bellieu, Bulgaria. Jesus stands on the serpent.

place of John was located, within the village, in a cave
that is now shown within the Franciscan Church of St
John. On the other side of the valley is the Fransciscan
Church of the Visitation, in the crypt of which is shown
the spring that according to tradition appeared at the
meeting-place of Mary with Elizabeth. This is the spring
which gives a name to the town today. The life of the
young John was hidden for nearly thirty years in the
wilderness, from which he emerged to fulfil his vocation.

'Crying in the wilderness'

Luke carefully states that it was in the year 28 that John
began his public ministry of baptizing in the River
Jordan, and preaching the baptism of repentance for
the forgiveness of sins. Mark includes the prophecy of
Isaiah, 'Behold, I send my messenger before thy face,
who shall prepare thy way.' All four evangelists see
John's coming as a fulfilment of Isaiah's prophecy:
'The voice of one crying in the wilderness: Prepare
the way of the Lord, make his paths straight . . .',
but only the first three Gospels describe the power of
John's message, which drew all Judea and all the people
of Jerusalem. They describe his dress of camel-skin and

213

his diet of locust-beans and wild honey, in the pattern of the Bedouin today. The theme of John's teaching was revivalist: the Messiah is coming, people need the spiritual preparation of repentance. Baptism was the traditional Jewish symbolism for cleansing from sins; the Greek word for 'repentance' means 'a change of heart'. John's baptism by water was to prepare people for the Messiah's baptism by the Spirit of God; with the coming of the Messiah, his work was done.

Matthew and Mark tell the story of John's imprisonment and death retrospectively, as though they occurred before the public ministry of Jesus. They tell how John was imprisoned by Herod Antipas for denouncing Herod's marriage with Herodias, his brother Philip's wife. John's courage rivalled that of the prophet Elijah in his denunciation of Ahab and Jezebel. Biblical prophecy depends on the human acceptance of God's terms for its fulfilment. Since John's message was to be accepted – which generally it was – then his ministry became that foretold in the name of Elijah. Both of them were forerunners, and both of them concentrated their courage on the spot where it could witness most dramatically for righteousness – the royal palace.

When in prison, John sent his disciples to Jesus with the question, 'Are you he who is to come?' His question may have indicated his doubt, but more likely his hope that he was to have a successor and that he had not been a failure after all. Jesus's answer, mentioning his performance of the works predicted for the Messiah, should have reassured him. Matthew and Mark describe John's execution, at Herod's command, to fulfil a rash promise to Herodias's daughter, Salome. This took place, according to Josephus, the Jewish historian of the 1st century, in Herod's fortress of Machaerus, an isolated Hasmonean outpost east of the Dead Sea.

John's disciples

A rather different picture of John the Baptist is given in the Fourth Gospel. John is shown as the witness and forerunner of the Messiah, whom he recognizes by the descent of God's Spirit in the form of a dove. As John said, 'He who sent me to baptize with water said to me, "He on whom you see the Spirit descend and remain, this is he who baptizes with the Holy Spirit." And I have seen and have borne witness that this is the Son of God.' (John 1:33, 34)

The Fourth Gospel has only this account of Jesus's baptism by John, and omits the fact that Jesus began to preach only after John's imprisonment. In this Gospel, the ministry of the two men is simultaneous, until Jesus attracts the most disciples and John withdraws. As John himself put it, 'He who has the bride is the bridegroom; the friend of the bridegroom, who stands

The Madeba mosaic, showing a ferry above the place of baptism, to the left, north of the Dead Sea.

Herod's Banquet, by Antonio di Salvi. John the Baptist's head is brought to Herod, while Salome dances.

and hears him, rejoices greatly at the bridegroom's voice; therefore this joy of mine is now full. He must increase, but I must decrease.' (John 3:29, 30)

The reason for this deliberate subordination of John in the Fourth Gospel is likely to be that, even at the end of the 1st century when this Gospel was written, there were still some disciples of John who considered John more important than Jesus himself. The writer of this Gospel describes John the Baptist from the first as surrounded by disciples, who were soon to become the core of Jesus's own band of followers. The evangelist shows clearly that they did so at the suggestion of John himself, who pointed them to Jesus as 'the Christ', and 'the Lamb of God'. Luke tells us that John had taught his disciples how to pray. Matthew describes how they fasted. We know, too, something of their loyalty to John as their leader, through his imprisonment and execution to his burial. Twenty years later, there were still disciples of John, among them the learned Alexandrian Jew Apollos, who met Paul in Ephesus and later became the first bishop of Corinth.

The place of baptism

John the Baptist's activities were based on at least two points on the River Jordan, one accessible to the people of Samaria, one to the people of Judea. The former is likely to have been in the area of Salem (John 3:23), Tel er-Ricra, probably at the five wells of Aenon ('the place of the spring'), located at Ed-Der. The southern place of baptism, described by St John as at Bethabara (meaning 'ford-house' or 'ferry-house'), is probably less than a mile from the accepted place of baptism today. It is unlikely that there was a proper village there, but rather a few huts for those operating the ferry, the customs, and the frontier business between Judea and Perea. There would probably have been a lodging-house or caravanserai. The Madeba mosaic shows the ferry above the place of baptism, with a house standing on piles, presumably designed with a view to floods.

Early tradition has always represented the place where Jesus was baptized by his cousin John as being the spot shown today: the ford at Hajlah. It seems that John lived for some time beyond Jordan, perhaps to avoid the authorities of Judea and Jerusalem, perhaps because of the regular and clean flow of the Wadi el-Kharrar from the east into the Jordan. It was an ideal place for his purpose, off the road yet easily approached from the ford. In 1902, at the outlet of the Wadi el-Kharrar two small buildings dating back to Byzantine times stood on arches, presumably at one time in the water – one of them nearly 33 feet square. The pilgrim Theodosius, in the year 530, found a Church of John the Baptist, built by order of the Emperor Anastasius, at this point on the east bank. This church apparently rested on arches built out over the water. A cross on a marble pillar stood in the river to mark the place of baptism. Antoninus, forty years later, found only the pillar. Perhaps the floods had carried away the foundations of the little church. The coming of the Persians put an end to other shrines on the east bank of the Jordan.

On the west bank, a monastery of St John had existed since the time of Justinian, if not before. This, too, appears on the Madeba mosaic and in the writings of Antoninus and Arculf. For centuries, this was the focus of Christian pilgrimage from Jerusalem. The present church, erected in 1882 on this site, includes Byzantine remains. Arculf, in 670, described a small chapel under the monastery and a stone bridge leading out over the water to a cross at the place of baptism.

John and Qumran

Many scholars have wished to establish a direct connection between John the Baptist and the monastic community at Qumran, whose scrolls have been found in caves near the Dead Sea. It is possible that John was one of the Essenes, who pursued the ideal of purity and holiness in the isolation of the desert. It is probable that John was influenced, directly or indirectly, by their practices – particularly by their ritual washings and cleansings, not to mention their formation of a company of disciples seeking to 'fly from the retribution that is coming'. (*see* ESSENES)

Certainly, Jesus himself adopted and prescribed the practice of baptism as the means of Christian initiation. Jesus also proclaimed much the same gospel as John: 'The time has come. The kingdom of God is close at hand. Repent and believe.' Yet for Jesus, John was the

The Lake of Galilee provided fish for the nine or ten towns, each of 15,000 inhabitants, which encircled it. Fishermen set out from Tiberias, nets loaded in the sterns of their boats.

last of the prophets and forerunners of the *old* world, which had given place to the *new* order with the coming of the Christ. Hence Jesus's final appraisal of John: 'I tell you, among those born of women none is greater than John; yet he who is least in the kingdom of God is greater than he.' (Luke 7:28) [Matt. 3; 4:12; 9:14; 11:2-18; 14:2-10; 16:14; 17:13; 21:25-32; Mark 1:4-14; 2:18; 6:14-29; 11:27-32; Luke 1:13-80; 3:2-20; 7:18-35; 9:7, 19; 11:1; 16:16; 20:4-6; John 1:6-40; 3:23-36; 4:1; 5:33-36; 10:40, 41; Acts 1:5, 22; 10:37; 11:16; 13:24, 25; 19:3, 4]

2. John, son of Zebedee John was the son of Zebedee, the Galilean fisherman possibly from Bethsaida, and of Salome, whom some traditions describe as the sister of Mary, the mother of Jesus. John and his brother James were fishermen, whom Luke describes as partners with Peter and Andrew. John, his brother James, and Peter formed the inner circle of the disciples of Jesus. John is mentioned twice in the Acts as accompanying Peter, both in healing and in confirming the faith of the primitive Church. He is also one of the three 'pillars of the Church' whom Paul met at Jerusalem.

John may have been one of the unnamed disciples of John the Baptist at the Jordan who, together with Andrew and Peter, later became disciples of Jesus. Jesus called John and his brother while they were in their boat mending their nets. They promptly left their father Zebedee in the boat with the men he employed. Salome is listed as one of the women who 'looked after' Jesus in Galilee. It seems, therefore, that Zebedee's family was of some substance. John appears to have been sufficiently acquainted with the high priest's palace in Jerusalem to know the girl portress and to be able to persuade her to admit Peter at the time of the trial of Jesus. Perhaps the tradition, expressed in the building by the Crusaders in Jerusalem of a small chapel dedicated in the name of 'Zebedee's fish-shop', indicates the presence in Jerusalem of members of his family. It is not impossible that they might have been purveyors of Galilean fish to the high priest's household. Certainly, the disciples of Jesus were men of varying means.

The lists of the disciples of Jesus reveal the nickname given to John and his brother James as 'Boanerges', 'sons of thunder', presumably because of their angry temperaments, or glowering faces. 'Son of' implies 'having the quality of' thunder. Whether the nickname implies humour or rebuke, it is certain that John and his brother were reproved by Jesus. John once said to Jesus at Capernaum, '"Master, we saw a man casting out demons in your name, and we forbade him because he does not follow with us." But Jesus said to him, "Do not forbid him, for he that is not against you is for you."' When James and John asked Jesus to reserve for them the seats of honour on either side of him at his

Fishing on the Lake of Galilee, the home of James and John, sons of Zebedee: the drag-net is hauled ashore.

Messianic banquet in heaven, Jesus replied, 'You do not know what you are asking.' And he went on to ask if they could share his destiny. They confidently affirmed that they could, whereupon Jesus answered, 'The cup that I drink you will drink . . . but to sit at my right hand or at my left, is not mine to grant . . .' James was in fact the first of Jesus's apostles to suffer martyrdom, at the command of Herod Agrippa, and a writer of the 5th century records the martyrdom of John as early as AD 44. John and James received a further rebuke from Jesus when his messengers were not welcome in a Samaritan village, and the 'sons of thunder' suggested, 'Lord, do you want us to bid fire come down from heaven and consume them up?' Jesus and his disciples shared the rigours of his itinerant ministry often without shelter: 'The Son of Man has nowhere to lay his head.'

Despite their temperament and Jesus's frank rebukes, the two brothers, James and John, together with Peter, formed an inner circle within the group of disciples, and it is these three whom Jesus takes with him on at least three important occasions. They accompany him into the house for the raising of Jairus's daughter; they are permitted to witness the glory of Jesus's transfiguration on the mountain; they are chosen to support him and to witness his agony in the Garden of Gethsemane. Apart from one question to Jesus asking when his prophecy of the destruction of the Temple was going to be fulfilled, John is not further mentioned by name throughout the story of the Passion. It is possible, however, that he may have been the person referred to in the Fourth Gospel as 'the beloved disciple'. If so, then a very great deal is to be known of his character and the

The Last Supper, by Andrea del Castagno (1423-57). The 'beloved disciple' leans on the breast of Jesus.

important part played by him in the Upper Room, at Calvary, at the empty tomb, and in Galilee. *see also* JOHN **3.** *and* JOHN **4.** [Matt. 4:21; 10:2; 17:1; Mark 1:19, 29; 3:17; 5:37; 9:2, 38; 10:35, 41; 13:3; 14:33; Luke 5:10; 6:14; 9:28, 49, 54; 22:8; Gospel of John; Acts 1:13; 3:1, 11; 4:13, 19; 8:14; 12:2; Gal. 2:9; 1, 2, and 3 John; Revelation to John]

3. John, the beloved disciple The term 'the disciple Jesus loved' is used only by the writer of the Fourth Gospel and on only four occasions, all during or following the Passion of Jesus. The first scene is set in the Upper Room on the night of the Last Supper, after the meal. Jesus, having washed the disciples' feet, sat down with them and warned them of his forthcoming betrayal, 'Truly, truly, I say to you, one of you will betray me.' The disciples looked at each other wondering who it could be. 'The disciple whom Jesus loved' was reclining next to Jesus. Simon Peter signed to him and said, 'Tell us who it is of whom he speaks'; so leaning back on Jesus's breast he said, 'Lord who is it?' 'It is he to whom I shall give this morsel when I have dipped it.' He dipped the piece of bread and gave it to Judas.'

The second occasion is on Calvary when the crucifixion is completed and the long agony has begun. 'When Jesus saw his mother, and the disciple whom he loved standing near, he said to his mother, "Woman, behold, your son!" Then he said to the disciple, "Behold, your mother!" And from that hour the disciple took her to his own home.'

The third occasion when the term was used is early on Easter morning when Mary of Magdala has been to the tomb only to find it empty and the stone rolled away. 'So she ran, and went to Simon Peter and the other disciple, the one whom Jesus loved, and said to them "They have taken the Lord out of the tomb...."' So Peter set out with the other disciple. They ran together, but the other disciple, running faster than Peter, reached the tomb first; he bent down and saw the linen cloths lying on the ground but did not go in. Peter who was following now came up, went right into the

The closing verses or epilogue of the Gospel state: 'This is the disciple who is bearing witness to these things, and who has written these things; and we know that his testimony is true.'

From these four scenes it seems inconceivable that this intimate friend should have been outside the twelve, if even outside the inner circle of Peter, James and John. Apart from the list of fishermen on this final expedition in the last chapter of the Gospel, there is not a single reference to John, son of Zebedee. It is unlikely that a disciple so often mentioned within the other three Gospels should be unconsciously omitted from the Fourth Gospel, even though he was often rebuked! It is likely that John, son of Zebedee, was the 'disciple Jesus loved', even if the Gospel of John was written by another hand.

It must have been the work of someone whose affection and respect for John, son of Zebedee, was considerable and who was willing to undersign all he said. In fact the authority for the Gospel is that of John, son of Zebedee, even if the authorship is not. *see also* JOHN **2.** *and* JOHN **4.**

The Coenaculum, the site of the Last Supper, a Crusader building on the site of the Byzantine Basilica of Holy Zion.

tomb, saw the linen cloths on the ground and also the cloth that had been over his head rolled up in a place by itself 'Then the other disciple, who reached the tomb first, also went in, and he saw and believed. . . .'

The final scene is some time later on the Lake of Galilee after a fruitless night's fishing with Peter and the others. As they bring the boat into the north shore, a voice calls, 'Cast the net on the right side.' They do so and enclose so vast a haul of fish that they cannot even land it. At that moment 'the disciple whom Jesus loved' said to Peter: 'It is the Lord!' After landing the catch and eating breakfast on the beach, Peter is solemnly thrice commissioned by Jesus to feed his sheep. Then Jesus predicts Peter's own destiny of crucifixion: '"When you are old, you will stretch out your hands, and another will gird you and carry you where you do not wish to go." And after this he said to him, "Follow me." Peter turned and saw following them the disciple whom Jesus loved, who had lain close to his breast at the supper . . . and said to Jesus, "Lord, what about this man?" Jesus said to him, "If it is my will that he remain until I come, what is that to you? Follow me!"''

4. John the Evangelist Whoever the actual author of the Fourth Gospel was, the depth and the effect of his work places him second in importance only to Paul among the members of the primitive Christian Church. It was this man who, writing in the very last years of the 1st century when all eye-witnesses to the life of Jesus were dead, expressed a wonderful union between the belief in an historical outward act of God and a living inward experience of the risen Jesus. His book is a meditation in the manner of the Jewish *Midrash*, but in Christian form. In parts, it is very early indeed, especially the narrative of the passion of Jesus. It has affinities too with the Qumran literature of the Dead Sea Scrolls and may perhaps have been based on a Palestinian Aramaic original, now lost.

From the internal evidence, already discussed in the two preceding articles concerning John, son of Zebedee, and the beloved disciple, together with the external evidence of the early Church Fathers, we may draw some conclusions about the authorship of the Fourth Gospel. Then turning to the content and matter of the Gospel, we can examine the purpose and method of its writing, its relationship to the other Gospels, its presentation of Jesus and its effect upon the Christian Church.

Who wrote the Fourth Gospel?

Internal evidence appears to identify the author with John, son of Zebedee, particularly the four passages concerning 'the disciple Jesus loved'. By a process of elimination it can be confirmed that this phrase refers to John, son of Zebedee, who is not otherwise mentioned in the Gospel, except perhaps as the companion of Peter and the disciple of John the Baptist. If John, son of Zebedee, is the author, however, 'the disciple Jesus loved' is a strangely immodest title for an author to apply to himself. If, however, the Gospel had been dictated to scribes, in the first person, they could have replaced the words "I, John' with 'the disciple whom Jesus loved'. Were the actual author to be other than John, son of Zebedee, from whom, however, the information was received, such a title would be possible. Were the actual author to have respected John, son of Zebedee, as being loved by Jesus more openly than the other disciples, such a title would be understandable. Now, the final appendix to the Gospel specifically identifies the authority for the Gospel with the 'disciple Jesus loved' and therefore with John, son of Zebedee. These verses also imply that the actual author was himself a disciple of John, son of Zebedee. Of course, these verses might have been added some years afterwards, but they appear in all extant manuscripts of this Gospel.

The external evidence at first appears conflicting; some of the early Fathers of the Church, such as

left John the Evangelist, portrayed with his eagle-symbol in a late 8th-century Celtic Gospel.

above The opening of the Gospel of St John, from the early 8th-century *Lindisfarne Gospels*.

Irenaeus of Lyons (130-200) and Clement of Rome (*c.* 100), argued for John, son of Zebedee, as the author when at Ephesus. However, Papias, bishop of Hieropolis (60-130), said that there were *two* Johns, the apostle who was dead and the elder who was still alive. Dionysius, a later bishop of Ephesus, confirmed that there were two tombs at Ephesus, both ascribed to a John. In any case, a strong tradition connected the Gospel with Ephesus. The conclusion seems to be again that the authority for this Gospel was that of John, son of Zebedee, but that it was either written or edited by an elder, also living at Ephesus and also called John. The 2nd and 3rd Letters of John are both addressed from 'the Elder' and are probably entirely the work of this second John. The First Letter resembles, more than the 2nd and 3rd, the style and content of the Gospel and may therefore be the work of John, son of Zebedee. *see also* JOHN 2. *and* JOHN 3.

Need for a written record

It may help to compare the backgrounds of the Gospels of Mark and John, the first and the last Gospels within the New Testament to be written. Both Gospels were

above John the Evangelist, from the 15th-century
Psalter of the Duc de Berry.

written during periods of crisis and emergency. Both were written for specific and vital purposes. Without both, the course of Christianity might have been rather different. Mark was faced with the death of the two great pillars of the apostolic Church. Peter and Paul had made the events and teaching *live* before their cosmopolitan congregations – as only inspired eye-witnesses and men with personal experience and knowledge can. Upon their death, it was essential that some written record – based upon their teaching – should be made available for the work of the Church. Who was better equipped to undertake the task than the man who had been a travelling companion to Paul and a secretary to Peter – the task of writing 'the beginning of the good news of Jesus Christ, the Son of God'. Mark must have been saturated with the apostolic preaching and tradition and with what was most required.

After some 70 or 80 years the apostolic age was at an end and the eye-witnesses of the Word made Flesh no longer among men to inspire and proclaim. The primitive hopes and momentum were spent; moreover Christianity had to be adapted to the needs of the Hellenistic world. Christianity had to unite her belief in an historical act of God with her present inward ex-

perience. John set out to fulfil two objects – one purely religious, the other practical.

First he set out to impress the belief that Jesus was not only the Messiah and the Son of Man of Jewish tradition, but also the Son of God – a title more understandable and far more significant to the Gentile world. Men must 'believe' in the actual historic person of Jesus and 'have life' by a realization of the purpose of his life, which is not merely a thing of the past, but an everliving fact of the present. Jesus's life on earth was but the beginning of a larger and ever-enduring life open to all believers; for the historical person of Jesus can be revealed to any true believer, now and always. Secondly John had a practical object – to meet some of the questions and accusations levelled at Christianity by his Gentile contemporaries and to support and build up the idea of the Christian Church.

John himself had a strong and certain conception of both the person and life of Christ, and not unnaturally interpreted facts accordingly. To him, facts were valuable because they supported or illustrated the beliefs he wished to impress. He therefore selected and concentrated upon a few episodes which bear witness to the divinity of Christ. Similarly, he adapted and modified his selected material, reading a meaning into words and incidents independent of their actual circumstances. To him the outward event was often a mere shell, covering a hidden message, which was only apparent to the believer.

Consequently John did not, like Mark, record by narrative and dialogue events as they happened – but he adapted and matched narrative to dialogue, and vice-versa, to achieve his purpose. Therefore, both narrative and dialogue are in the same style and it is sometimes impossible to distinguish editorial comment from narrative or dialogue. The teaching of Jesus, combined with editorial comment, makes up long discourses. Through the calculated combination of narratives and discourses, John adapted to the needs of his readers the Gospel message, as it was recorded by Mark or as he, John, had seen and heard it.

John sought to interpret the Jewish ideas of the 'Messiah' and the 'kingdom' in such terms as 'truth' and 'eternal life'. This is well illustrated in the private conversation at the trial in which Pilate asked Jesus, 'Are you King of the Jews?' [the Messiah]. 'Jesus answered, "My kingship is not of this world. . . ." Pilate said to him, "So you are a king?" Jesus answered, "You say that I am a king. For this I have come into the world, to bear witness to the truth. Every one who is of the truth hears my voice."'

right Carpet-page from the Gospel of St John,
from the *Lindisfarne Gospels,*
early 8th century.

John the Evangelist

The Word of God

The prologue – the first eighteen verses of the Fourth Gospel – is a poem about the 'Word' of God. John opens his prologue as the book of Genesis. The Greek words 'In the beginning' can equally mean 'In principle' or 'At the root of the Universe' – thus implying not just an event in time, but also an eternal reality: 'In the beginning was the Word, and the Word was with God, and the Word was God. He was in the beginning with God; all things were made through him, and without him was not anything made that was made. In him was life, and the life was the light of men. The light shines in the darkness, and the darkness has not overcome it.'

The Greek term *Logos* or 'Word' has a long history. As early as the 6th century BC an Ephesian philosopher, Heraclitus, had used it to explain the order and sense within the world. 'Though this "Word" – this fundamental law – exists from all time, yet mankind is unaware of it, both before they hear it and in the moment that they hear it.' For him, the *Logos* was the pantheistic principle of reason within the universe, which explained its logic or sense. Later, the Stoics took over the idea and popularized it as the dynamic principle of reason operating within the world. Greek and Roman philosophers developed the idea that the *Logos* was the mind of God, the means of communion between God and man. Philo, the Jewish philosopher of Alexandria, born about 20 BC, made the *Logos* a bridge between the God of Israel and the Gentile world. The *Logos* or 'Word' of God is responsible for the creation of the world, as well as being the inspiration of the prophets and the means of covenant and continued communication between God and his people. Philo almost personified the *Logos* as the image and instrument of God, referring to the *Logos* as the 'firstborn son' or the 'Wisdom' of God.

The writer of the Fourth Gospel does not use the term 'Wisdom', but identifies Jesus with the *Logos* or 'Word' of God. Mark began his Gospel with John the Baptist. John began the Fourth Gospel with the Creation. The gospel was uttered in the 'Word' of God, but Jesus is the gospel and the 'Word' that began the creation of the Word itself. The *Logos* was no new thing. It existed before creation. The world in its entirety was his creation. The Psalmist wrote: 'By the word of the Lord the heavens were made and all their hosts'. (Ps. 33) So the gospel concerns all men. It is the light of all men. It is identical with the author of life, but it was rejected and the darkness did not understand it, nor indeed quench it.

The exception to that darkness was the witness of John the Baptist, who was typical of the prophets. 'There was a man sent from God, whose name was John. He came for testimony, to bear witness to the light, that all might believe through him. He was not the light, but came to bear witness to the light.' The Light was there to be seen, yet man did not see it. Even his own people did not recognize or receive him. There were some, however, who accepted the *Logos* and underwent a new birth as 'sons of God'. This new creation, like the old, was brought about by the *Logos*. To Jesus was owed both creation and re-creation. He was and is both the creative 'Word' and the sacramental presence of God with us.

'The true light that enlightens every man was coming into the world. He was in the world, and the world was made through him, yet the world knew him not. He came to his own home, and his own people received him not. But to all who received him, who believed in his name, he gave power to become children of God; who were born, not of blood nor of the will of the flesh nor of the will of man, but of God. And the Word became flesh and dwelt among us, full of grace and truth; we have beheld his glory, glory as of the only Son from the Father.'

For the writer of the Fourth Gospel, the 'grace and truth' of Jesus even replaced the covenant of the Law. (Exod. 34:27) This record of John was confirmed by the apostles and all Christians who received 'grace upon grace'. 'And from his fullness have we all received grace upon grace. For the law was given through Moses; grace and truth came through Jesus Christ. No one has ever seen God; the only Son, who is in the bosom of the Father, he has made him known.'

The presentation of Christianity in the Fourth Gospel is seen most clearly when contrasted with that of the first three Gospels – as typified by the Gospel of Mark.

The most striking difference in the teaching of Jesus, as recorded in these two Gospels, is in what is said about Jesus himself. Mark's Jesus did not demand any opinion of himself, or belief in himself. His message was similar to that of John the Baptist (as Mark records him). He preached repentance, a change of heart and conduct. He hid his Messiahship until Peter's confession at Caesarea Philippi, and even then forbade his disciples to tell it to others. His disciples gradually grew to recognize him as the Son of Man, the Messiah, who would come in glory to judge the world – his verdict depending upon the conduct of men, not upon the belief of men and certainly not upon their recognition of him. Jesus does not openly admit his Messiahship until standing before the high priest. Even then, there is no question of his divinity; his disciples acknowledge his Messiahship, as Enoch's supernatural or Daniel's human 'Son of Man', but not as the Son of God. That is left to the Gentile Roman centurion.

The disciples' recognition of Jesus as Son of God must have taken place some time between his resurrection and Peter's first recorded sermon in Jerusalem (Acts 2), perhaps on the occasion, recorded in John, of Thomas's confession 'My Lord and my God'. Even so, the conviction of the apostles of Jesus's divinity must also have been a process accelerated by the action of the Holy Spirit among them at Pentecost.

John's portrait of Jesus is very different from that of Mark. Mark, except in his prologue, does not himself call Jesus 'Son of God'. He may continually hint at it to his readers as though to say, 'But you and I know that only God can do such miracles,' but he does not represent Jesus or his disciples referring to Jesus as Son of God. John represents Jesus as openly admitting his Messiahship, from his meeting with John the Baptist onwards. John the Baptist immediately recognized him. Jesus did not simply preach repentance and good conduct; he preached himself as the Son of God. He openly claimed a unique relationship with God. Salvation was not a matter of conduct, but of belief in himself. (John 3:16) The disciples were not fully convinced till after the resurrection – perhaps at the confession of the most practical, if obstinate, member of their party, Thomas. John, anxious to present Jesus both as an historical personality and as the Son of God, both flesh and *Logos*, emphasized his true humanity as 'the Word made flesh'. Jesus is tired, hungry and thirsty at the well, where the Samaritan woman, seeing him without rope and tackle, 'pulls his leg' – before drawing water for him. He weeps at Lazarus's tomb. Simultaneously, John emphasized his divinity, for he is miraculously satisfied when the disciples bring him food to the well, and John implies that he wept at their lack of faith.

Both Mark and John regard miracles as signs or evidence of God's power and presence in Jesus, whether expressed as acts of power or as signs. Both show Jesus apparently unwilling to do unnecessary miracles. Both indicate that faith is essential – Mark at Nazareth; John at Bethany. In Mark, sheer compassion appears to prompt Jesus, as in the case of the feeding of the five thousand, yet he uses every miracle to point a lesson – even though on most occasions only the spiritually-minded or believing witnesses can grasp the real significance of the event. In John, the purposes of all miracles recorded are the glory of God and the production of faith in men.

Mark records Jesus doing miracles, as far as possible, in the presence of a few eye-witnesses. John does not hesitate to portray Jesus calling out to Lazarus 'in a loud voice', for the benefit of bystanders and the glory of God. John, however, does not include more than six

miracles: changing water into wine at Cana, healing the officer's son at Capernaum and the paralytic at the public baths of Bethesda, feeding the five thousand, giving sight to the blind man, and the raising of Lazarus. He has carefully chosen these miracles to exclude the more common practice of exorcism. John has included the more striking and unique miracles, emphasizing them accordingly: 'Thou hast kept the good wine until now', 'Born blind', and 'Four days in the tomb'.

In one other respect, John has contributed information – not forthcoming from the Synoptic Gospels – about the locality of Jesus's teaching. John lays nearly the whole scene of the ministry in the Jerusalem district and not up in Galilee. There are indications in the Synoptic Gospels that Jesus did conduct more of his ministry in Judea than they in fact record. Scribes and Pharisees from Jerusalem (Luke 5:17; Mark 3:7; 7:1) went up to Galilee to hear Jesus. Judas was a native of Kerioth in Judea. Jesus's friendship with Mary, Martha, and even with Joseph of Arimathea must have been the result of more than one or two previous visits. Jesus's lamentation over Jerusalem implies that he had on many occasions preached there. Perhaps the chronological order of Mark may be more accurate than that of John, but it is probable that Jesus did spend a great deal more of his life and ministry in Judea than Mark records. Neither of the evangelists would have claimed to have written a complete and accurate biography of Jesus. The material was not available, but Mark – writing at a time when biography was in vogue in Rome – arranged his material into as coherent a 'life of Christ' as he could. John preferred to write 'Scenes from the life of Jesus, the Son of God'.

Mark's account – in spite of its slightly pro-Roman outlook – is generally thought to be remarkable for its utter simplicity, honesty, and fidelity to tradition. The incorporation of so much of Mark's material in later Gospels is ample proof of its worth. Its value and usefulness, at the time of crisis following the death of the apostolic leaders and amid the persecutions of Christians in Rome, must have been incalculable – not only for devotional purposes as the sacred memoirs of the earliest leader of the apostles, but also as a balanced and clear statement of the facts for evangelistic use.

John, however, writing long after the events in the life of Jesus and aware of the mistakes made by clinging to such reminiscences as Mark's Gospel contained, without any real inward impulse or spiritual reality, assisted Christianity to continue as a *living* faith. He transplanted Christianity before the roots had time to wither, proclaiming the Jesus of history and the Jesus of inward experience to be *one*. In order to do so in such a manner as the Hellenistic world could understand, he had virtually to adapt the gospel story to that of a Greek tragedy. He had to combine, by means of a reverent use of his imagination, both historicity and symbolism, both the words and actions of Jesus, and also the very thoughts. [Gospel of John]

5. John the Elder This John was author of at least one of the letters attributed to John. He was an anonymous and venerable father of the Christian Church at Ephesus in the first half of the 2nd century AD.

Links with the Fourth Gospel

From the 2nd century onwards, the traditional view of the authorship of the writings in the New Testament attributed to John was that they were all the work of the Apostle John, son of Zebedee. Many modern scholars still support his authorship of the Letters of John on the following grounds: Most of the themes in the Letters have a place also in the Gospel. There is a general affinity of theological outlook, both insisting on the necessity of Jesus's coming 'in the flesh', both speaking of judgment, forgiveness, God's love for mankind, the mutual love and obedience enjoined upon men, together with God's promise of the gift of his Spirit to men. The styles of the Gospel and of the First Letter are similar. A list has been compiled of at

The Good Shepherd: 5th-century mosaic at Ravenna. The allegory of the Good Shepherd is told only in the Fourth Gospel, though it awakens echoes of passages in the Synoptic Gospels.

least fifty phrases in the First Letter which have close parallels in the Gospel. Both use the method of anti-thesis, or contrast, of darkness and light, flesh and spirit, truth and falsehood. The First Letter of John claims to have been written by an eye-witness who has 'seen, heard, and handled' Jesus the 'Word' of God. If we assume the author of the Gospel was the Apostle John, this is just the sort of claim we might expect him to make. Even if we decide that the Gospel was not written by the apostle, we can still claim apostolic authorship for the First Letter of John.

Within the last thirty years, however, this assumption of the traditional view has been strongly criticized and the identification of authorship challenged. In the matter of the styles of the Gospel and Letters, while there is a certain similarity, the differences are shown to be great. In the Gospel, there are thirty key words, closely related to the central ideas and constantly recurring – these do not occur in the Letters.

As compared with the rest of the New Testament, there is a decided affinity of thought and standpoint, but there are fundamental divergencies of outlook between the Gospel and the Letters of John. The Gospel has many quotations and many implicit allusions to the Old Testament. Its author displays an acquaintance with Jewish ideas and practices and his work reflects the strong influences of Judaism, both Rabbinic and Hel-lenistic. The Letters, on the other hand, have no quotations from the Old Testament and one single re-ference to it. (1 John 3:12) There are no other books in the New Testament which have so little mention of the Hebrew Bible as the Letters of John.

In the Gospel, Hellenistic and Hebraic ideas are united, but in the Letters, the Hellenistic element has freer play. There are various points where the Letters represent a theological outlook nearer to primitive Christianity than that of the Gospel. The Letters hold out the prospect of a near second coming of Jesus and of the end of the world. They take no account of the re-interpretation of the coming again of Jesus, in the Holy Spirit and in the Church at Pentecost, as is so clearly implied in the Gospel. The ideas within the Letters, about the effects of Jesus's death and the theology of man's redemption, resemble the proclama-tion of the very primitive Christian Church, rather than the cosmic significance of the 'Word', the *Logos*, the 'Mind' of God made flesh – expressed so clearly in the prologue of the Gospel. The conception of the 'Spirit of God' within the Letters remains too much within the limits of rather primitive Christian belief.

So, in regard to their ideas of eschatology, atonement, and the Spirit, the outlook of the Letters is very different from that of the Gospel. It might be possible to hold that the same man wrote the First Letter, first, and the Gospel much later – but the Gospel is presupposed within the Letter. Without the Gospel the Letters would hardly be intelligible and the Gospel provides the necessary background to the Letters. Such dif-ferences combine to show that the First Letter is the work of an admiring disciple of the evangelist, who has absorbed much but not all of his theology. It is a strange coincidence, however, that two contemporary writers, living in the same area, should share such similarities of style, outlook, theology, and purpose.

Who was John?

The writer of the Letters was not named in the text, but since the Letters were known to Polycarp, bishop of Smyrna, Papias, bishop of Hieropolis, and Irenaeus, a native of Smyrna who became bishop of Lyons – all

227

of whom lived in the first half of the 2nd century AD – the Letters were certainly known in Asia Minor by that time. Since the Letters presuppose a situation within the Churches to which they were written similar to that at Corinth in the year 96 in the time of Clement, the third bishop of Rome after Peter, and whose own letters tackle the same sort of problems, the Letters of John were probably written at the turn of the 1st century. The Church was no longer being persecuted, following the succession of Nerva, also in the year 96; so the Church emerged to face a new set of conditions, including a spirit of unrest and development.

In the Second and Third Letters, the author describes himself as the 'elder'. Literally, this just meant 'old man'. It also bore a technical sense in the early Church after Jewish custom, as the title of one of the board of 'elders' who ministered to a local congregation. The authority with which this elder speaks, however, is more than local. There seems to have been another quasi-technical use of the term 'elder' current for a short time in Asia. Christians in this province seem to have spoken of 'elders' when they referred to a group of teachers, who formed a link between the apostles and the next generation. Apparently they were a small group, and it was quite possible for one of these teachers to be spoken of as '*the* Elder'. Irenaeus several times referred to things he had learned from 'the Elder' and 'the Elder the disciple of the Apostles'. It is unlikely that 'the Elder' is to be identified with the Apostle John, for why refer to himself as 'elder' rather than 'apostle'?

The argument in the Third Letter turns altogether on the question of the writer's authority. If he were an apostle would he not have silenced his opponent Diotrephes by claiming the authority of an apostle? Papias talks of 'John the Elder'. Irenaeus quotes the First and Second Letters, over the name of 'John the Apostle'. It is, therefore, likely that the true author of the First and Second Letters was 'John the Elder', whose grave along with that of 'John the Apostle' was shown at Ephesus in the 3rd century.

Papias called the Elder 'a disciple of the Lord', that is, a survivor of the group who had known and followed Jesus in his lifetime. Irenaeus says that this 'disciple of the Lord' survived until the time of Trajan and was known to other elders in Asia. Irenaeus thought that this disciple was also in fact the apostle, but it seems more likely that this disciple John was not an apostle so much as one of the elders. He must have been nearly ninety if he had been a disciple of Jesus – but that is the claim of the opening verse of the First Letter.

The message of the First Letter

The Letter opens with a similar sort of preface to that of the Gospel, using similar words such as 'the beginning' and the *Logos*. In this preface the writer declares the purpose of his letter. The body of the letter consists of three clear and simple expositions: on the nature of Christianity, life in the family of God, and the certainty of the Christian faith. The letter ends with a brief postscript and encouragement to prayer.

On the nature of Christianity, the writer severely criticizes false ideas of religious experience and stresses the need for repentance: 'If we say we have no sin, we deceive ourselves', but 'the blood of Jesus Christ cleanses us from all sin'. The writer declares the following: Jesus intercedes for his followers in heaven, as perfect man he is the ideal advocate. Love is the essence of Christianity and distinguishes it from paganism. The Antichrist is coming soon. The time is short. Men must act now. Christians must not be perverted by teaching which denies the divinity of Jesus, but they may be assured that the gospel story is true and no lie.

Concerning life within the family of God, Christians are the children of God, the Father. The writer stresses the gravity of sin and declares the incompatibility of sin with God. Love is the bond of the family: 'We know that we have passed out of death into life, because we love the brethren.' That is his love for us through Jesus, and man's love for his fellow-men. True love demands action. The writer stresses the dangers of false teaching, which denies the reality of the incarnation, the fact that the 'Word' or 'Mind' of God became flesh in the person of Jesus. God himself is love; through love he sent his son to die for man, who should respond with love to God and to his fellow-men.

Concerning the certainty of the Christian faith, the writer declares that there are three signs of God's indwelling: the Spirit, confession that Jesus is the son of God, and love: 'God is love, and he who abides in love abides in God, and God abides in him.' Love is that attitude of mind which should pervade all Christian conduct. By far the greatest contribution to theology of this First Letter is its unprecedented and unequalled expression of the true nature of Christian love, and the perception of the all-important truth that God himself is love personified. This love is the bond that binds the family of God to each other and to the Father.

The Second and Third Letters

The Second Letter, thinly disguised in the form of a private letter, is a pastoral message addressed to a single Christian congregation, by a person who calls himself 'The Elder'. The writer encourages his readers against those who spread propaganda for a false doctrine which denies the reality of the incarnation of God in Jesus. This heretical teaching seems to present a real threat to the local Christian Church.

The Third Letter is a genuine piece of personal correspondence, giving a vivid glimpse into the life of the local Church and full of human interest. The Elder seems to be responsible for a circuit of local churches. His representatives carry the gospel to the pagan population, with the financial and moral support of the Christian communities in the neighbourhood. In one church, his agents have met with opposition and a very divided reception. The opposition was led by one Diotrephes, who carried the day and drove out his agents; they returned to the Elder to report. In this situation the Third Letter was written. The Elder plans a personal visit to the offending community; he writes to a loyal supporter, Gaius, and entrusts the letter to one Demetrius, who is universally respected within the circuit of churches. The agents return with this letter to resume their interrupted mission, under the loyal protection of Gaius and duly warned against Diotrephes. The outcome of the Letter and the success or failure of the Elder's agents is not known. [1st, 2nd and 3rd Letters of John]

6. John, father of Peter Simon Peter's father was sometimes called by the Greek form of his Hebrew name, Jona(h). (Matt. 16:17) He was the father of at least two sons, Andrew and Peter, and his home was at Bethsaida, the 'fisher home', to the north of the Lake of Galilee. Perhaps, like his sons, he was a man of piety and of skill in deep-water fishing.

This John is mentioned three times in the Gospels, on each occasion linked with his son Peter. On the first occasion, recorded in the first chapter of the Fourth Gospel, the scene was the ministry of John the Baptist, by the River Jordan, when the Baptist told his own disciples, who included the two fishermen brothers, and Philip of Cana, that the man from Nazareth was Jesus, 'the Chosen One of God'. Early the following morning, Andrew met his brother Peter and said to him, 'We have found the Messiah' and he introduced Peter to Jesus. 'Jesus looked at him, and said, "So you are Simon the son of John? You shall be called Cephas" (which means Peter).'

On the second occasion, Jesus had taken his followers into the quiet and lovely mountainous scenery on the southern slopes of Mount Hermon, in the neighbourhood of the source of the River Jordan at Caesarea Philippi, the shrine and city of Pan. There, in retreat from the bustle of the lakeside, Jesus had asked his followers, 'Who do the people say that I am?' Peter had answered for his companions, 'You are the Christ, the Son of the living God.' In response to this profession of faith, Jesus proclaimed Peter's pre-eminence among his followers, 'Blessed are you, Simon Bar-Jona! For flesh and blood has not revealed this to you, but my Father who is in heaven. And I tell you, you are Peter, and on this rock I will build my Church.' So this John's son was to become the leader of the apostles and the first bishop of Rome.

On the last occasion, recorded in the final chapter of the Fourth Gospel, the scene is by the lakeside, after the resurrection of Jesus, when seven of his followers have discovered him on the beach, along the north shore, when they returned from a night's fishing. They have had breakfast together, cooked on a charcoal fire, and Jesus has called Peter over to test and to commission him. 'Simon, son of John, do you love me more than these?' to which Peter replied, 'Yes, Lord; you know that I love you.' Jesus then said to him, 'Feed my lambs.' A second time Jesus said to him, 'Simon, son of John, do you love me?' and Peter had given him the same answer and been told 'Tend my sheep.' Then Jesus said to him a third time, 'Simon, son of John, do you love me?' Peter was upset at this third question – perhaps corresponding to his threefold denial of Jesus during the trial at the house of Caiaphas – and again declared, '"Lord, you know everything; you know that I love you." Jesus said to him, "Feed my sheep."'

These three occasions, on which Jesus described Peter formally as the son of his father John, were the landmarks in the gospel narratives of Peter, his naming as the Rock, his appointment as the Rock on which the Church was to be built, and finally his threefold testing and commission to feed and care for the flock of Christ. This last event has been commemorated by successive chapels of the Primacy on the rocks of the north shore of Galilee. The column-bases of a medieval church are visible in the clear water offshore; they enclose an enormous rock which projects out over the water, as well as the modern little basalt chapel of the Primacy. This great rock was known to medieval pilgrims as the *Mensa Christi*, the 'Table of the Lord'. It still stands in its striking simplicity a silent witness to the Galilee resurrection tradition. [Matt. 16:17; John 1:42, 43; John 21:15-17]

7. John, relative of Annas This John is only mentioned once among the members of high-priestly families, within the Sanhedrin. The Supreme Council was, on this occasion, convened in emergency to deal with the situation caused by the powerful preaching of the apostles in Jerusalem. Peter and others were arrested and detained overnight, possibly in the guardroom at the high priest's palace where Jesus himself had been imprisoned overnight. The modern church of St Peter in Gallicantu possibly covers the site of this house of Caiaphas and, on a series of levels cut into the rock of the cliff face, enshrines the courtroom of the Council, the guardroom complete with the whipping block and staples for prisoners' chains and a bottle-neck condemned cell.

This John is reported to have met with the rulers, elders, and scribes, together with Annas, Caiaphas, Alexander, and other Sadducees. Their decision was to warn the apostles and forbid them to preach in the name of Jesus, but for fear of the people they dared not punish them. [Acts 4:6]

8. John Mark, the Evangelist *see* MARK

9. John the Divine Author of the Book of Revelation.
Of all the preceding Johns who might or might not have
been the writer of the Fourth Gospel and one or more
of the Letters, there can be remarkably little certainty of
authorship. St John 'the Divine', as the Authorized
Version of the Bible calls him, cannot perhaps be
identified with John the Apostle and son of Zebedee
with any greater certainty. If, however, John Bar-
Zebedee lived for any length of time into the reign
of the Roman Emperor Domitian (AD 81-96), it is
possible that he was the 'Seer of Patmos' whose visions
the Book of Revelation records.

Patmos and Ephesus

It is possible with some imagination to reconstruct the
events which led to the revelation of such visions to such
a man and their remarkable record in writing. Towards
the end of the 1st century, a Roman quinquereme – a
large galley with five banks of oars – slipped through
the surf and spray into the harbour of the rocky island
of Patmos. Patmos is one of a number of small islands
off the Turkish coast and yet from its rocky heights one
can pick out the approximate direction of each of the
seven parishes to which the writer of Revelation sent
messages. While the galley-slaves lay exhausted across
their oars, a long chain of convicts bound for the penal
settlement threaded its way up the rocks to the sound of
the lash. These men were deported for life to work in
the stone quarries, to sleep in the caves, and live in the
confines of the island of Patmos. Among them was one
John, condemned as a Christian agitator for his activities
in the seven cities of the mainland, of which the chief
was Ephesus.

John had made his home at Ephesus and loved his
adopted city, having come to speak its language and
think in terms of its mentality. He was in heart but not

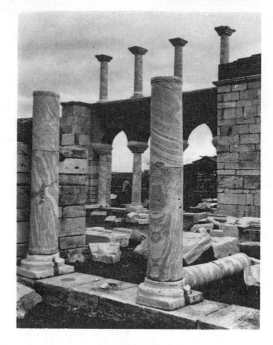

above The great 6th-century Basilica of St John
which crowns the citadel at Ephesus.

right John the Divine, eagle at his side, his previous
writings at his feet, records his visions of the
Apocalypse while a prisoner on the island of Patmos.
Painting by Velazquez (1599-1660).

below Fragment of the original 6th-century reliefs
from the Basilica of St John at Ephesus.

Ephesus
1st century AD

TEMPLE
OF ARTEMIS

GATE OF
CORESSUS

ROMAN
BATHS AGORA
STADIUM

Bay of
Ephesus

THEATRE-
GYMNASIUM

OLD CITY

THEATRE

Mt. Pion

THE CITY WALL

TEMPLE
OF SERAPIS

HELLENISTIC
AGORA

RESIDENTIAL
QUARTER

GATE OF
MAGNESIA

Mt. Coressus

TRADITIONAL
GRAVE OF LUKE

0   250 yards

opposite, below John on the island of Patmos : painting by Joos van Cleve, *c.* 1525.
opposite, above Two scenes from the vision of John the Divine by Albrecht Dürer: the four horsemen of the Apocalypse; and the angel sealing the Devil up in the Bottomless Pit.
above The Mystic Adoration of the Lamb, by Hubert and Jan Van Eyck (1422-41).
below The adoration of the Lamb: 10th-century manuscript illumination.

in soul a citizen of Ephesus, the cathedral city of paganism in Asia.

To the worship of Artemis at Ephesus, immensely old and mystical, was added the modern emperor worship, as a political expedient in an age that was frankly sceptical of the old gods. To give divine honour to the emperor, however, and admit the claim of the state upon the soul was impossible for the Christian and the Jew, bound by the commandment 'Thou shalt have none other gods but me'. Thus, the sacrifice to the emperor became the passport of the loyal citizen, but to refuse this sacrificial homage meant death. The more Christians resisted, the more they were feared and the more cruelly they were persecuted. Nevertheless, from the earliest visits of Paul, in the fifties, to the time of John, Asia became the nursery of Christendom. Indeed, in the year 431 Ephesus was the place of a great Council of the Christian Church.

Ruins of Pergamum, one of the Seven Churches of Asia, which John could see from his island prison of Patmos.

Asia Minor

Towards the end of the 1st century, this John, having spent his life for his seven precious parishes whose Christian communities he may have helped to found, had had to leave them to struggle for survival against the fanatical pagan cults. There on Patmos, where today the huge Orthodox Monastery of St John crowns the rocky hilltop, John, inspired by the skyscapes, wrote the message of God's denunciation of evil, sending his love, his longing and his encouragement to his beloved 'Churches of Asia'. It is not surprising that his visions of a 'new heaven and a new earth' have 'no more sea' and 'no more thirst'. He ends, 'He who testifies to these things says, "Surely I am coming soon." Amen. Come, Lord Jesus!'

The record of visions

One of the most striking features of the book is the oddness and crudity of its Greek style, completely obscured in the Authorized Version. The spasmodic lack of regard for syntax and grammar in the Book of Revelation is in marked contrast with the smoothness and correctness of the Greek of the Fourth Gospel. Perhaps the only possible explanation is that John wrote a record of his ecstatic experiences during his visions. Only this, says one translator, could account for the incoherence, the repetition, and the incredible piling up of words. It seems that the Gospel and the Revelation are the works of different Johns.

The Revelation has been described as an inspired picture-book which, by an accumulation of magnificent poetic imagery, makes a powerful appeal to the reader's imagination. Many of the strange beasts, symbols, and apocalyptic figures of the visions would have been much better understood by Christians for whom the

book was first written than they are for us today, but some are still clear. In the prologue, the writer declares that he is 'John, who bore witness to the word of God and to the testimony of Jesus Christ, even to all that he saw.' The first three chapters consist of John's greetings to his beloved Seven Churches of Ephesus, Smyrna, Pergamum, Thyatira, Sardis, Philadelphia, and Laodicea. His messages are inspired by a vision of seven golden lamp-stands surrounding a figure of Jesus, who says, 'Fear not, I am the first and the last, and the living one; I died, and behold I am alive for evermore, and I have the keys of Death and Hades. Now write what you see . . .' And to each Church, the message of God flows to encourage or to reproach.

Then follows a series of prophetic visions. The first describes the preparations for the Day of Judgment. God entrusts the future of the world to the Lamb, who is worthy to break the seven seals of the scroll of the book of life. God's servants are to be preserved and rewarded; their prayers bring the Great Day nearer. The great battle between good and evil is symbolized by a struggle between the woman and the dragon. The sovereignty of God is absolute and his ultimate purpose is to destroy all forms of evil. He is in control of history.

The second of the prophetic visions shows the coming punishment of evil, epitomized in all that is Roman – pagan cults and the idolatrous emperor-worship – while the songs of victory are sung in heaven. The third prophetic vision reveals the coming destruction of the pagan nations, the chaining up of Satan for a thousand years before the final battle of the End. The last of the visions is of the heavenly, Messianic Jerusalem, through the centre of which flows the river of life of which all the thirsty are invited to drink. Over and over again, the nearness of the End is proclaimed, 'The time is close . . . very soon now, I shall be with you again'.

So, John, the convict among the stone quarries of Patmos, aware of the vast forces of evil ranged against Christianity in his time, at one moment opened a door in heaven and at another lifted the cover off the bottomless pit. For he lived in an age of blood and fire. He was not a vindictive man, but he wrote 'in the spirit' with a frightening sense of the reality of good and evil, a reality whose bitterness burned, but whose sweetness was inexpressible. [Revelation to John]

JOSEPH (Gk. from the Heb. 'may God add [children]') This much-used Jewish name was that of five different persons in the New Testament.

1. **Joseph, father of Jesus**
2. **Joseph, brother of Jesus**
3. **Joseph of Arimathea**
4. **Joseph Barsabbas**
5. **Joseph Barnabas**

Joseph's dream, and Joseph and the angel helping Mary along the road to Bethlehem. Detail from the 6th-century ivory chair of Archbishop Maximianus, Ravenna.

1. Joseph, father of Jesus This Joseph was the spouse of the Virgin Mary at the time of the annunciation of the angel Gabriel and the conception of Jesus. Joseph subsequently married Mary and, on the birth of the child, adopted him as his son. The few references within the Gospels suggest that he was a humble, kindly, generous, and conscientious parent who probably taught Jesus the carpenter's trade. Perhaps Jesus's respect for Joseph is, in some measure, reflected in his deliberate adoption of the affectionate title of *Abba* – 'Daddy' – for God, and in his deep personal apprehension of the fatherhood of God.

Joseph's dilemma
Matthew describes how Joseph discovered that his espoused Mary was pregnant, and the dilemma in which this placed Joseph. 'Being a just man and un-

willing to put her to shame', he had already made up his mind to put her away informally, when in a dream he was reassured by an angel. 'Joseph, son of David, do not fear to take Mary your wife, for that which is conceived in her is of the Holy Spirit: she will bear a son, and you shall call his name Jesus, for he will save his people from their sins.' Thus reassured of her virginal conception, Joseph took Mary to his home and, when the child was born, duly named him 'Jesus'. Matthew adds as a credential to his account the prophecy of Isaiah (7:14): 'Behold, a virgin shall conceive and bear a son, and his name shall be called Emmanuel'. which Matthew explains means 'God with us'.

The child was born in Bethlehem in Judea, during the reign of Herod the Great (perhaps in what is known as the year 6 BC). Some time later (anything up to two years) some wise men came to Jerusalem from the east (probably astrologers from Persia or Arabia). On their arrival they asked, 'Where is he who has been born king of the Jews? For we have seen his star in the East, and have come to worship him.' (Matt. 2:2) After a somewhat guarded reception by Herod, and again guided by the star which for them had portended the birth of a king, the wise men came 'into the house' in Bethlehem where the family lived, offered their gifts, and returned without further contact with Herod.

After the wise men had left, Joseph was warned by the angel to 'Rise, take the child and his mother, and flee to Egypt, and remain there till I tell you; for Herod is about to search for the child, to destroy him.' (Matt. 2:13) Again Matthew adds a prophetic credential to the story, quoting Hosea (11:1) – 'Out of Egypt have I called my son'. Joseph's escape was amply justified by Herod's massacre of the children in Bethlehem. Only after Herod's death did Joseph – guided again by the angel – return with his family to Israel. Distrusting Herod's successor Archelaus, Joseph took his family up to Galilee and settled in the town of Nazareth. Matthew again adds the prophetic 'He shall be called a Nazarene.' This is indeed the first mention of Nazareth by Matthew.

Considerably later in his narrative, and perhaps some thirty years later in time, Matthew describes Jesus's return to Nazareth in the course of his public ministry. Surprised at his wisdom and power, the members of the synagogue congregation exclaim, 'Is not this the carpenter's son? Is not his mother called Mary? And are not his brothers James and Joseph and Simon and Judas? And are not all his sisters with us? Where then did this man get all this?' (Matt. 13:55, 56) The Greek word for carpenter can be applied to the trade of building and repairing in wood, stone, or metal. No further mention of Joseph appears in Matthew's Gospel.

Luke's version: the cares of fatherhood
Luke describes Mary at the time of the annunciation as 'a virgin betrothed to a man whose name was Joseph,

Joseph the Carpenter: detail of the Campin Altarpiece by the Flemish painter Robert Campin (1406-44).

of the house of David'. Unlike Matthew, Luke describes Mary and Joseph as living in Nazareth. Only the census, for which everyone went to his own town for registration, took them to Bethlehem, because Joseph 'was of the house and lineage of David'. So it was in Bethlehem that Mary gave birth to her son, 'and wrapped him in swaddling cloths, and laid him in a manger, because there was no place for them in the inn'. Here the shepherds hurried in to find 'Mary and Joseph, and the babe lying in a manger'. At the child's circumcision, 'he was called Jesus, the name given by the angel before he was conceived in the womb'.

Forty days after the birth, both parents are described as taking the child to the Temple for him to be presented and redeemed by sacrifice. Both the 'father' and mother are described standing there, wondering at what was said about him by the old priest Simeon. When the ceremony was completed and the Law fulfilled, they 'returned into Galilee, to their own city, Nazareth'.

Luke further describes the regular Passover visits of the parents to Jerusalem, with particular reference to the visit when the boy Jesus was twelve years old (perhaps to celebrate his 'confirmation' as a 'son of the Law'). When they had mislaid the boy on the first day of the return journey, and had discovered him among the doctors in the Temple, his mother said, 'Son, why have you treated us so? Behold, your father and I have been looking for you anxiously.' 'How is it that you sought me?' he replied. 'Did you not know that I must be in my Father's house?' But they did not understand what he meant. 'And he went down with them and came to Nazareth, and was obedient to them; and his mother kept all these things in her heart.' (Luke 2:48-51)

Luke's account of Jesus's later visit to the synagogue at Nazareth evokes the comment 'Is this not the carpenter's son?' But there is no gospel mention of the survival of Joseph after the Jerusalem Passover visit, when Jesus was twelve years old. In John's Gospel, both Philip (talking to Nathanael) and the Jews at Capernaum identify Jesus as the 'son of Joseph', and at Capernaum they claim to know his father and mother. (John 6:42)

Certainly, the accounts of Matthew and Luke disagree as to the original home of Joseph, and even, in their genealogies, as to his father's name. But in most other respects their accounts can be considered complementary rather than contradictory. It has been suggested that this may be because Matthew's primary source of information for his birth narrative was the person or family of Joseph, whereas Luke's account certainly reflects the thoughts and feelings of Mary.

Was there a family partnership?

The apocryphal infancy gospel called after James, the brother of Jesus, but likely to have been written in the 2nd century, declares Joseph to have been elderly at the time of his marriage to Mary. His comparatively early death might account for there being no mention of him at the crucifixion, and it would certainly help to explain why the public ministry of Jesus did not begin until he was nearly thirty years old, if he was needed for family and business reasons within his own home.

In the 4th and 5th centuries, an apocryphal *History of Joseph the Carpenter* accounted for a growing veneration of Joseph within the Eastern Churches, as the pattern of domestic holiness. His feast was introduced into the Roman calendar in 1479 and his name inserted in the Litany of the Saints in 1729. He is usually represented in art, staff in hand, with the boy Jesus. [Matt. 1:16-24; 2:13; Luke 1:27; 2:4-51; 3:23; 4:22; John 1:45; 6:42]

2. Joseph (also Joses, or Joset), brother of Jesus When Jesus returned to Nazareth in the course of his public ministry, and spoke in the synagogue there, the congregation recognized him as the 'carpenter's son' and claimed to know his family, naming four brothers and mentioning his sisters. Luke in the birth stories refers to Jesus as Mary's 'first-born son' (2:7). Some of the Church Fathers, wishing to uphold the perpetual virginity of Mary, suggested that these brothers and sisters were the children of a previous marriage of Joseph. Others, including the 4th-century biblical scholar Jerome, have suggested that the normal Greek words used for 'brothers' and 'sisters' could be intended to include 'cousins'. It must be admitted that oriental customs can be quoted to support this. However, we may see a purpose in the selection of the words used.

Mark, no doubt followed by Matthew and Luke, describes Jesus teaching at Capernaum and, hearing that his mother and brothers have arrived and are asking for him, he replied, '"Who are my mother and my brothers?" Looking around on those who sat about him, he said, "Here are my mother and my brothers! Whoever does the will of God is my brother, and sister, and mother."' (Mark 3:33-35) John describes how, at the feast of Tabernacles when the Jews were out to kill Jesus and he had to remain in Galilee, his brothers failed to understand his purpose and message, saying to him, '"Leave here and go to Judea, that your disciples may see the works you are doing. For no man works in secret if he seeks to be known openly. If you do these things, show yourself to the world." For even his brothers did not believe in him.' (John 7:3-5) Luke, however, relates how Mary the mother of Jesus 'with his brothers' remained loyal in their prayers along with the apostles in Jerusalem after the ascension of Jesus.

Of this brother Joseph – unlike Jesus's brother James, whom we know to have become the first bishop in Jerusalem – there is no further mention. [Matt. 13:55; 27:56; Mark 6:3; 15:40, 47]

3. Joseph of Arimathea Each of the Gospels contributes to the picture of Joseph of Arimathea. Mark describes him as 'a respected member of the council' (that is, the Sanhedrin), 'who was also himself looking for the kingdom of God'. Matthew simply calls him 'a rich man'. Luke vouches for him as 'a good and righteous man', and adds that he had 'not consented to their [the members of the Sanhedrin] purpose and deed'. John calls him 'a disciple of Jesus, but secretly, for fear of the Jews'.

All four Gospels record that after the crucifixion of Jesus, Joseph went to Pilate and asked for the body of Jesus, obtained permission, took it down, wrapped it in a linen cloth, and laid it in a tomb. Mark adds that Pilate 'granted the body to Joseph. And he bought a linen shroud', and finally 'rolled a stone against the door of the tomb'. Matthew adds that it was Joseph's own personal tomb. Luke adds that no one had ever been laid in the tomb till then. He also adds that the women returned home to prepare spices and ointments, which they later took to the tomb on the first day of the week, after the Sabbath.

It is interesting, however, that Paul makes no mention of Joseph of Arimathea in his speech at Pisidian Antioch, during his First Journey. He says that it was the Jews who 'took him down from the tree, and laid him in a tomb'. (Acts 13:29) The traditional site of Joseph's home town Arimathea is Ramlah, near Lydda, on the coastal plain south-west of Jerusalem. According to the apocryphal *Gospel of Nicodemus*, Joseph helped to found the first Christian community at Lydda.

In 1135 the Englishman William of Malmesbury, in a history of the ancient church of Glastonbury in Somerset, recorded the legend of Joseph of Arimathea's voyage to England, bringing the holy chalice, or grail, used at the Last Supper. A number of legends surround the 'Holy Grail' and the 'Glastonbury Thorn', a species of Levantine hawthorn flowering twice a year and still to be seen today. [Matt. 27:57, 59; Mark 15:43, 45; Luke 23:50; John 19:38]

4. Joseph Barsabbas, nicknamed Justus *see* BARSABBAS *and* MATTHIAS

5. Joseph Barnabas *see* BARNABAS

JOSES (Gk. form of 'Joseph') **1.** The brother of Jesus *see* JOSEPH **2.**

2. 'Surnamed by the apostles "Barnabas"' *see* BARNABAS

JUDAS (Gk. from the Heb. 'praised', 'celebrated')

1. Judas Iscariot

2. Judas Barsabbas

3. Judas of Damascus

4. Judas of Galilee

5. Judas, brother of Jesus

6. Judas, son of James

1. Judas Iscariot The traitor disciple, who betrayed and enabled the arrest of his master, Jesus.

Owing to the lapse of time between the events of the gospel story and their recording, the story of Judas gathered accretions and interpretations. It is not possible with any certainty to draw from the Gospels a single and concurrent account of Judas's place among the twelve. Therefore, the events in which he was involved will be mentioned with reference to the comments of each evangelist, then his possible motives will be discussed, and finally certain obvious misconceptions will be disposed of.

Always an outsider?

On lists in all three Synoptic Gospels, Judas appears last with the epithet 'who betrayed him'. He is described as 'Iscariot', which might possibly be an Aramaic adaption of *Sicarius*, the Latin for 'dagger-man', implying that Judas was a Zealot partisan. 'Iscariot' is more likely, however, to mean simply *Ish* ('man') *Kerioth*, from Kerioth, a town in southern Judea. In which case, Judas would have been the only non-Galilean among the twelve and, therefore, the 'odd man out'; certainly he seems to have been essentially lonely and misunderstood.

John frankly calls him 'a thief' or 'betrayer', 'possessed by the devil', or 'the son of perdition'. It is as though the evangelists could not paint him black enough in retrospect. After all, they had all at one time or another denied or deserted their master and the blackness of Judas might make their own greyness less noticeable. Jesus himself, however, is acknowledged to have been a clear reader of personality and he must have first called Judas, and then have appointed him as the treasurer or accountant of the little company. Jesus is hardly likely to have given Judas the job if it was to be a source of temptation to him, nor is Judas likely to have joined a band of itinerant and penniless preachers if he was a greedy and petty pilferer.

Jesus must have seen in Judas a potentially useful member of his team, and Judas must have seen in Jesus the potential fulfilment of Messianic prophecy. Christians, particularly in the west, have long speculated on the reasons for the original choice of Judas, his suicide, his motives and the relatively small amount of blood-money paid to him. One theory is that Judas was probably the most passionate nationalist of the group, of shrewder stuff than the rustic Galileans swift to recognize the potential of Jesus, 'mighty in works and deeds', to be the Messiah long awaited by such as he.

Judas, more than the others perhaps, seems to have misunderstood or disregarded Jesus's interpretation of his own Messiahship. Faced with a slow and steady process of disillusionment and disappointment, at what so many of Jesus's followers considered to be lost opportunities (John says they wanted to make him

The kiss of betrayal: anonymous 12th-century painting of the betrayal of Jesus.
To the left, Peter cuts off Malchus's ear.

'King'), Judas's impatience seems to have grown until he himself grasped the initiative.

Whether intending perhaps to force Jesus into declaring himself Messiah, at the height of the Passover feast, when support was ready to hand – or whether driven to a pathetic revenge for his deep personal disappointment and frustration, Judas acted the traitor. Three years' close acquaintance with Jesus may well have convinced Judas of Jesus's Messiahship, but also of a genuine inability to declare himself. Judas, by pushing Jesus at the tactical moment, may well have felt that he was acting for Jesus's own good; for Judas's ideal of Messiahship did not include Jesus actually allowing himself to be killed. Once, however, the plot was under way, there was no brake to apply.

The betrayal

All three Synoptic Gospels declare that Judas himself approached the chief priests 'in order to betray Jesus to them'. They were glad and promised to reward him. Matthew adds that they gave him thirty silver pieces, the equivalent of under ten dollars or four pounds sterling – that is, the purchase-value of a foreign slave in Old Testament times, or the amount claimed by a Jewish slave if his master drew blood in New Testament times. If Judas was as greedy as is often supposed, he could have extorted far more from the high priests.

At the Last Supper with his disciples, the night before the Passover feast, Jesus gave a clear warning of his impending betrayal: 'And as they were at table eating, Jesus said, "Truly, I say to you, one of you will betray me, one who is eating with me." They began to be sorrowful, and to say to him one after another, "Is it I?" He said to them, "It is one of the twelve, who is dipping bread in the same dish with me. For the Son of Man goes as it is written of him, but woe to that man by whom the Son of Man is betrayed! It would have been better for that man if he had not been born."' (Mark 14:18-21) Matthew adds that Jesus identified Judas as his betrayer. 'Judas, who betrayed him, said, "Is it I, Master?" He said to him, "You have said so."' (Matt. 26:25)

The Fourth Gospel, substituting the story of the feet-washing for that of the Last Supper, describes the conversation that followed in considerable detail. The warning is all the more poignant, following the lesson in humility illustrated by Jesus's washing of his disciples' feet, including those of Judas. 'Truly, truly, I say to you, a servant is not greater than his master; nor is he who is sent greater than he who sent him. If you know these things, blessed are you if you do them. I am not speaking of you all; I know whom I have chosen; it is that the scripture may be fulfilled, "He who ate my bread has lifted his heel against me".' (John 13:16-18)

Now the betrayer must be dissuaded or dismissed, but first Jesus gives Judas the place of honour next to himself and hands him a chosen morsel of food, concealing his treachery from all but the 'beloved disciple' seated on Jesus's other side. 'The disciples looked at one another, uncertain of whom he spoke. One of his disciples, whom Jesus loved, was lying close to the breast of Jesus; so Simon Peter beckoned to him and said, "Tell us who it is of whom he speaks." So lying thus, close to the breast of Jesus, he said to him, "Lord, who is it?" Jesus answered, "It is he to whom I shall give this morsel when I have dipped it." So when he had dipped the morsel, he gave it to Judas, the son of Simon Iscariot.' (John 13:22-26)

Judas seems to have rejected Jesus's last gesture of friendship, for, as John says, 'Satan entered into him'. So Jesus said, 'What you are going to do, do quickly,' and Judas went out literally and figuratively into the dark, for 'it was night'.

The Synoptic Gospels go on to describe the walk down to Gethsemane, the agony in the Garden, and then the arrival of Judas with the Temple police. Judas had given them a sign by which they would recognize Jesus – ' "The one I shall kiss is the man; seize him and lead him away safely." And when he came, he went up to him at once, and said, "Master!" And he kissed him. And they laid hands on him and seized him.' (Mark 14:44-46) The description of the arrest in the Fourth Gospel is rather one of purposeful surrender. 'Then

The Garden of Gethsemane on the Mount of Olives, where Judas led the Temple police to arrest Jesus.

Jesus, knowing all that was to befall him, came forward and said to them, "Whom do you seek?" They answered him, "Jesus of Nazareth." Jesus said to them, "I am he." Judas, who betrayed him, was standing with them. When he said to them, "I am he," they drew back and fell to the ground. Again he asked them, "Whom do you seek?" And they said, "Jesus of Nazareth." Jesus answered, "I told you that I am he; so, if you seek me, let these men go."' (John 18:4-8)

Judas is not mentioned at the trial before the Council, though undoubtedly he must have given his evidence, probably of Jesus's acceptance of the title of Messiah from Peter at Caesarea Philippi: 'Thou art the Christ'. But it required two witnesses to convict and Peter himself contrived to remain out of sight in the gallery, partially recognized by his Galilean accent in spite of his denial. Again Judas is mercifully not mentioned at the later trial before Pilate, or at the crucifixion, though his presence and his feelings are all too clearly revealed in the events that followed.

Matthew's account of Judas's pathetic remorse and suicide is based on the Old Testament prophecy of Zechariah (11:12, 13): 'When Judas, his betrayer, saw that he was condemned, he repented and brought back the thirty pieces of silver to the chief priests and the elders, saying, "I have sinned in betraying innocent blood." They said, "What is that to us? See to it yourself." And throwing down the pieces of silver in the temple, he departed; and he went and hanged himself.' (Matt. 27:3-5) Luke's account in Acts of an accidental death, known to all the people in Jerusalem, seems more

5th-century ivory casket, showing both the crucifixion of Jesus and (left) Judas hanging from a tree.

likely to be accurate. Both accounts, however, link the death of Judas with a cemetery for foreigners in Jerusalem, called Akeldama, 'The Field of Blood', the site of which is today still to be seen south of the Western Hill, across the Valley of Hinnom.

What was his motive?

The synoptists made no effort to analyse the motive of Judas. The Fourth Gospel, rather unworthily perhaps, simply accuses him of greed and theft, quoting Judas's reaction to the anointing of Jesus by Mary of Bethany with precious ointment – ' "Why was this ointment not sold for three hundred denarii and given to the poor?" This he said, not that he cared for the poor but because he was a thief, and as he had the money-box he used to take what was put into it.' (John 12:5-6) This motive does not seem to fit the facts of Judas's selection by Jesus as a disciple, nor his appointment as treasurer, presumably for his business acumen. This is not to deny the evil inspiration which, as John says, was the basic cause of Judas's treachery. Whether he was misguidedly trying to force Jesus's hand to declare his Messiahship, for nationalistic motives, or was simply jealous, as a shrewd southerner, of his rustic Galilean rivals, such as Peter and John, we may never know. We may be sure, however, that Judas was no puppet predestined to play a necessary part in the betrayal of Jesus. Judas was essentially a free agent, acting from his own motives at any given moment.

Another enigma of the story is not why but what Judas actually betrayed. Was it just a convenient place of arrest away from the Passover crowds? Was it Jesus's secret admission to his Messianic identity? This alone could and did result in his conviction, but it came from his own lips 'I am' with all the purposefulness of the 'Son of Man who came to give his life a ransom for many'. [Matt. 10:4; 26:14, 25, 47; 27:3; Mark 3:19; 14:10, 43;

Luke 6:16; 22:3, 47; John 6:71; 12:4; 13:2, 26-29; 18:2-5; Acts 1:16, 25]

2. Judas Barsabbas *see* BARSABBAS

3. Judas of Damascus The owner of the house, in the street called Straight, where Ananias was told to enquire for Saul of Tarsus, following his conversion on the road to Damascus.

'The Lord said to him in a vision, "Ananias." And he said, "Here I am, Lord," ' and the Lord directed him to find Saul in the house of Judas, saying that Saul also had had a vision – but of Ananias entering and laying hands upon him to restore his sight. It was not surprising that Ananias timidly demurred, saying, 'Lord, I have heard from many about this man, how much evil he has done to thy saints at Jerusalem; and here he has authority from the chief priests to bind all who call upon thy name.' (Acts 9:13, 14) But the Lord reassured him and Ananias departed, and entered the house and, laying his hands on him, said, ' "Brother Saul, the Lord Jesus who appeared to you on the road by which you came, has sent me that you may regain your sight and be filled with the Holy Spirit." And immediately something like scales fell from his eyes and he regained his sight.' (Acts 9:17, 18)

Judas, the Jewish host of Saul, the future Christian apostle, played no small part in the critical days following Saul's conversion. [Acts 9:11]

4. Judas of Galilee A Galilean patriot from Gamala who raised a revolt in bitter opposition to the census, or enrolment, ordered by the Roman Emperor Augustus, during the governorship of Quirinius in AD 6. It was on the occasion of the incorporation of Judea into the Roman province of Syria and it was probably the first Roman provincial census, by Roman methods, to be held in Judea. The Galilean uprising was cruelly suppressed by the Romans, its leader Judas killed, and 2,000 of his followers were crucified. The momentum, however, survived underground in the form of a constant guerrilla movement, whose members were known as Zealots.

The great rabbi and Pharisee Gamaliel cited the suppression of Judas and his followers to persuade the Sanhedrin that false Messiahs and their followers similarly perish, without the direct action of the Council. It was wiser to leave the apostles of the early Christian Church, for if that movement was of God, it would survive and prosper, regardless of any intervention by the Council. [Acts 5:37]

5. Judas, brother of Jesus Writer of the General Letter of Jude. This Judas is among the family of Jesus mentioned by the congregation of the synagogue at Nazareth, when they were impressed by the wisdom and works of Jesus. ' "Is not this the carpenter, the son of Mary and the brother of James and Joses and Judas and Simon and are not his sisters here with us?" And they took offence at him.' (Mark 6:3) John commented on the fact that in the last year of Jesus's life, his own brothers did not believe in him. Of the four brothers, nothing certain is known further about Joseph or Simon, but James became the leader and first bishop of the Christian Church in Jerusalem, and Judas the author of a brief letter, which survives within the New Testament.

This letter was written round about the year 80, as a warning against false teachers in the Church. The writer calls himself 'Jude, a servant of Jesus Christ, and brother of James'. James, leader of the Church at Jerusalem for some twenty years, was obviously known to his readers. There seems little reason to doubt the author's claim to his relationship. The destination of the letter cannot be determined, but it appears to have been somewhere where the interpretation of the gospel and Christian life was far too free and undisciplined. The writer had to encourage his readers to 'contend for the faith which was once for all delivered to the saints. For admission has been secretly gained by some who long ago were designated for this condemnation, ungodly persons who pervert the grace of our God into licentiousness and deny our only Master and Lord, Jesus Christ.' (Jude 4)

Jude's warning is remarkably clear: these false teachers are immoral, covetous, anti-authority, 'Worldly people, devoid of the Spirit'. 'These are grumblers, malcontents, following their own passions, loud-mouthed boasters, flattering people to gain advantage. But you must remember, beloved, the predictions of the apostles of our Lord Jesus Christ; they said to you, "In the last time there will be scoffers, following their own ungodly passions." It is these who set up divisions, worldly people, devoid of the Spirit.' (Jude 16-19) Then the writer presses home his own advice, 'But you, beloved, build yourselves up on your most holy faith; pray in the Holy Spirit; keep yourselves in the love of God; wait for the mercy of our Lord Jesus Christ unto eternal life.' (Jude 20-21)

Finally the letter ends quite beautifully with this farewell: 'Now to him who is able to keep you from falling and to present you without blemish before the presence of his glory with rejoicing, to the only God, our Saviour through Jesus Christ our Lord, be glory, majesty, dominion, and authority, before all time and now and for ever.' (Jude 24-25)

This letter is particularly interesting because it shows the strength of Old Testament Jewish traditions within the faith and life of the Church. Both Jude and his brother James were zealous observers of the Law, as well as leaders of Christian thinking. Jude speaks in terms of disobedient angels 'in eternal chains in the nether gloom until the judgment of the great day'. 'But when the archangel Michael, contending with the devil, disputed about the body of Moses, he did not presume to pronounce a reviling judgment upon him, but said, "The Lord rebuke you." But these men revile whatever they do not understand, and by those things that they know by instinct as irrational animals do, they are destroyed. Woe to them! For they walk in the way of Cain, and abandon themselves for the sake of gain to Balaam's error, and perish in Korah's rebellion.' Such passages seem very far from the central themes of the Christian gospel, but show how very Jewish in their thinking some of the early Christian writers (such as the author of 2 Peter also) must have been.

For those concerned with the exact relationship of Jude to Jesus, see JOSEPH 2. [Letter of Jude]

6. Judas, son of James One of the twelve, but not Iscariot. Judas is listed among the twelve apostles only by Luke, both in his Gospel and in the Acts. The corresponding name in the Gospels of Mark and Matthew is that of Thaddaeus, which is omitted by Luke. The Fourth Gospel refers to him as 'Judas, not Iscariot', when at the Last Supper he asks Jesus: 'Lord, how is it that you will manifest yourself to us, and not to the world?' It is, therefore, reasonable to identify Thaddaeus and Judas as the same person, with James as their father. (The name Lebbaeus is included as an alternative to Thaddaeus only in some minor manuscripts at Matt. 10:3, and also in the Western Text only at Mark 3:18, but Lebbaeus is not to be found in the Revised Standard Version.) The actual wording in Luke's list is 'Judas, son of James', implying either that James was his father or his brother. If this Judas was the writer of the Letter of Jude, the last in the New Testament, then he does in fact refer to himself as 'Jude, servant of Jesus Christ and brother of James'. [Luke 6:16; John 14:22; Acts 1:13. Thaddaeus: Matt. 10:3; Mark 3:18]

JUDE see JUDAS **5**. and **6**.

JULIA One of the Christians greeted by Paul at the close of his letter to the Church in Rome. Julia is linked with the name of Philologus, perhaps her husband, in a group or household of five, 'and the saints that are with them'. Both names were common among Roman slaves. [Rom. 16:15]

JULIUS Julius was a centurion in the Augustan cohort, a corps of officer-couriers. He was in charge of Paul and other political prisoners sailing for Rome from Caesarea.

Julius was considerate enough to allow Paul to go ashore at Sidon to visit friends, but he disregarded Paul's warning not to sail from Crete so late in the year, instead taking the advice of both the captain and the ship's owner. Driven before a storm for fourteen days, the ship was virtually out of control when at last soundings indicated that land was near. The crew attempted to escape in the ship's boat, but at Paul's suggestion Julius made the soldiers cut the ropes and let the boat drop away. When the ship finally ran aground, the soldiers prepared to kill the prisoners, lest they escape. Julius, however, 'wishing to save Paul', would not let them, and ordered all who could swim to jump overboard and the rest to follow on planks and wreckage. In this way all came safe and sound to land.

Paul, indeed, knew only too well what a shipwreck was like (2 Cor. 11:25), and Luke, who was with him on this occasion, describes Paul's constant initiative and encouragement in emergency. Certainly, Julius may well have recognized the experience of Paul and, by accepting Paul's advice to jettison the ship's boat, ensured that the crew remained on board to beach the ship. Thus without Julius the centurion's respect for Paul's judgment, Paul might have perished before reaching Rome; and, indeed, all the centurions of Paul's acquaintance protected him. [Acts 27:1-44]

JUNIA(S) One of the Christians greeted by Paul at the end of his letter to the Christian Church in Rome. Junias is linked with Andronicus. Paul refers to them as his 'kinsmen', probably meaning that at least they were fellow-Jews, if not blood-relatives. Paul also calls them his 'fellow-prisoners', though during which of his imprisonments is uncertain. Paul goes on: 'They are men of note among the apostles. They were in Christ before me.' This immediately places their conversion within five years of the crucifixion of Jesus and connects them with the Church at Jerusalem rather than at Antioch. In fact, they may well have been associated with the Stephen group of Hellenized Jews who dispersed to found branches of the Church in Antioch, Cyprus, and elsewhere in the eastern Mediterranean. It is just possible that Junias should be read as 'Junia', in the feminine, which would then suggest the wife of Andronicus and a woman apostle. [Rom. 16:7]

JUPITER (Lat. *Jupiter*, Gk. *Zeus*) *see* ZEUS

JUSTUS (Gk. 'just') **1.** The surname of Joseph Barsabbas *see* BARSABBAS

2. The surname of Titius, a devout proselyte at Corinth, to whose house, next to the Jewish synagogue, Paul removed when virtually ejected from the synagogue by the opposition of the Jews. It was essential that Paul had somewhere to preach his message that Jesus was the Messiah, and the violent opposition of the Corinthian Jews provoked him to a change of policy, marked by his declaration, 'Your blood be upon your heads! I am innocent. From now on I will go to the Gentiles.' And from that moment, he moved into the house of the Gentile – and possibly Roman – convert Titius Justus. [Acts 18:7]

3. The surname of Jesus, one of Paul's companions at Rome during his first imprisonment at the time of his writing to the Christian community at Colossae. [Col. 4:11]

Stone *bas-relief* of a Roman galley, with soldiers and perhaps a prisoner on board.

L

LAODICEANS (Gk. *Laodikeis*) Laodicea, together with Hierapolis and Colossae, was one of the three cities within the fertile valley of the River Lycus, about 100 miles east and inland from Ephesus. All three cities were probably evangelized by Epaphras, a convert of Paul from Ephesus. He was probably trained within a missionary team during Paul's long and systematic period of teaching at Ephesus, in the course of his Third Journey. Some forty years later, the writer of the Book of the Revelation of John the Divine reprimands the Laodiceans for their 'lukewarmness' and lack of enthusiasm for the cause of the Seven Christian Churches in Asia.

Laodicea was a wealthy city founded in the middle of the 3rd century BC. Within the Lycus Valley, Laodicea was on one of the trade-routes of Asia, which ensured its commercial prosperity. The city was a leading banking centre, where Cicero cashed drafts in 51 BC, and which no doubt financed the reconstruction following the great earthquake of AD 60. Laodicea's refusal of relief from the senatorial earthquake fund may be quoted in John's comments in the book of Revelation. 'To the angel of the church in Laodicea write ... I know your works: you are neither cold or hot ... for you say, I am rich, I have prospered, and I need nothing; not knowing that you are wretched, pitiable, poor, blind, and naked.' (Rev. 3:14-17) The Lycus Valley also produced a glossy black wool for cloaks and carpets. Laodicea had a famous medical school, which pioneered the use of collyrium as an eye-ointment. 'The words of the Amen, the faithful and true witness' in the Book of Revelation says, '"because you are lukewarm. ... I will spew you out of my mouth"', a reference to the emetic qualities of warm soda-water from the springs of Hierapolis. By the time of John of Patmos, under the Emperor Domitian, Laodicea had become the capital of the province of Phrygia.

Some thirty years earlier Paul, writing from his imprisonment in Rome to the Christian community at Colossae, sent his affectionate greetings and encouragement to the Christian community at Laodicea. 'Paul, an apostle of Christ Jesus by the will of God, and Timothy our brother, To the saints and faithful brethren in Christ at Colossae: Grace to you and peace from God our Father. We always thank God, the Father of our Lord Jesus Christ, when we pray for you, because we have heard of your faith in Christ Jesus and of the love which you have for all the saints, because of the hope laid up for you in heaven. Of this you have heard before in the word of the truth.' (Col. 1:1-5) This letter continued with a magnificent statement, calculated to deal with a local heresy diluting Christian theology with pagan and Jewish philosophy. Paul roundly declared Jesus the Messiah as the supreme power for salvation, the ultimate reality and all-sufficient redeemer, and intermediary between God and man.

At the end of the letter to Colossae, Paul wrote, 'And when this letter has been read among you, have it read also in the church of the Laodiceans; and see that you read also the letter from Laodicea.' (Col. 4:16) The letter to the Laodiceans does not appear to have survived within the New Testament. It has, however, been suggested that the Letter to the Ephesians may supply the clue. The destination of this letter is perhaps less certain than its authorship. At least three of the most ancient manuscripts omit the address 'at Ephesus' in the opening verse. In the year 140, the scholar Marcion substitutes the address 'to the Laodiceans'. We know from Paul's letter to the Colossians (4:16) that he did in fact write a letter to the Laodiceans, and that he suggested that the congregations at Colossae and Laodicea exchange letters after they had read their own. Both letters were sent by the hand of Tychicus and his route would inevitably take him to many other Asian congregations during the course of his journey. It may well be, therefore, that what we know as the letter to the Ephesians was a circular letter of which, perhaps, half a dozen copies were carried by Tychicus. The bearer may have been instructed to fill in the blank address before delivering each copy of the letter, but probably failed to do so on at least one copy, of which the letter to the Laodiceans may have been one. [Col. 21:1; 4:13-16; Rev. 3:14]

LAZARUS (Gk. from the Heb. 'helped by God')
1. The beggar in the parable of the Rich Man and

Lazarus. He is the only character in all the parables of Jesus to be given a name. This parable may or may not allude to some contemporary incident, known to Jesus's hearers. It is one of a whole sequence of parables recorded only in Luke's Gospel and for the most part addressed to the Pharisees and Scribes, illustrating God's fatherly care for every kind of person. In the parable of the Marriage Feast, it is the poor, the maimed, the blind and the lame who are the guests. The Lost Sheep and the Lost Coin reflect his care for the very last, lost sinner. The Prodigal Son demonstrates the longing of the father to forgive. The story of the Judge and the Widow shows his care for the deprived and oppressed, that of the Pharisee and the Publican his mercy on the outcast and rejected.

Jesus insisted that it was impossible to serve two masters in this life. 'You cannot serve God and mammon.' When the Pharisees scoffed at him, he answered, 'You are those who justify yourselves before men, but God knows your hearts; for what is exalted among men is an abomination in the sight of God.' (Luke 16:13, 15) It was then that he told them the parable of the Rich Man and Lazarus.

It is a tragedy in three acts, with two chief characters: the Rich Man, often called for convenience by the Latin word *Dives*, meaning 'wealthy', and the beggar called Lazarus, a Hebrew word meaning 'he whom God helps'.

In the first act, the scene is the home of Dives, a well-to-do man of the world and a respectable pillar of society. Neither his character nor his means of income

The raising of Lazarus, painted in gold on glass, from Rome, 4th century.

are questioned. At his gate, however, lies Lazarus the beggar, a mass of sores, ill-clad and hungry. Every now and then he is given the leavings of the rich household, but even then his claims are disputed by the dogs, who add to his misery and degradation. To Dives, this familiar figure of Lazarus had come to be accepted as part of the street scenery, and he simply does not *see* the beggar at his gate. There is no bitterness, but only blindness. And so the first act closes.

In the second act, the scene is the next world, described in terms of popular Jewish thought. There is Paradise and Hades within sight and hearing of each other, but separated by a deep gorge. Dives has been buried in a manner appropriate to his status: Lazarus's burial is not mentioned, but his soul had an escort of angels. In Paradise Abraham presides at the feast; reclining on the couch next to him in the place of honour is the one-time beggar Lazarus; while Dives in Hades on the other side of the gorge is in torment and begs for water. Abraham reminds him that he has had *his* good time and now it is the turn of Lazarus; nothing can be done about it. The gulf that separated them both on earth seems to be still there in the next world, but now it is eternal.

In the third act, the scene is the same. Dives now accepts his position, but pleads for others in danger of sharing his fate. They like him have not been properly warned. Abraham, however, does not agree. People have all the warning they need. If they do not listen now, they will not be persuaded even by a resurrection or return from the next world. There the parable ends without comment, explanation, or judgment.

The Fourth Gospel, however, may be said to provide an epilogue. It shows that Lazarus *of Bethany* was in fact raised from the dead, but the Pharisees and Scribes to whom the parable was told did not believe or repent, and nor apparently did they do so following the resurrection of Jesus himself. [Luke 16:19-31]

2. The brother of Martha and Mary in Bethany, an intimate friend of Jesus whose 'home from home' was their house whenever he came up to Jerusalem, particularly for the Passover festival. Lazarus was raised from the dead by Jesus and became a walking witness of the divine power and calling of Jesus, which represented such a threat to the vested interests and security of the high priests and their Council.

The story to be found within the Fourth Gospel has been variously described as the true account either of an actual miracle, or of an historical event which has been later elaborated into the reason for the decision of the Jewish leaders to kill Jesus. Finally the story has also been assessed as an entirely fictitious tale used as a vehicle for introducing some particular points of Christian teaching, not unconnected with the parable in Luke's Gospel. There are some to whom the Fourth

15th-century mural of the raising of Lazarus, from Platanistasa, Cyprus,
showing Mary and Martha in the foreground and Jesus's disciples on the left.

Gospel, written perhaps as much as thirty years after
the Synoptic Gospels, appears to be a meditation on,
rather than a record of, historical events. On the other
hand the chronology of the ministry and particularly
the passion of Jesus within the Fourth Gospel are
presented in a convincing sequence and timetable.

The story in John's Gospel, therefore, may best be
regarded as that of an actual miracle, not recorded by
the synoptists, but typically adapted to the teaching
purposes of the writer. The synoptists clearly see the
driving of the merchants from the Temple as the final
cause for the plot to kill Jesus, but they describe Jesus
lodging in Bethany during the earlier part of that
Passover week. In the Fourth Gospel, the 'cleansing of
the Temple' is associated with an earlier visit of Jesus

to Jerusalem, and the person and household of Lazarus
play a key role in the events that lead to the Passover
plot.

The story opens with the illness of Lazarus, whose
sisters at once send for Jesus, saying, 'Lord, he whom
you love is ill.' Jesus is apparently on the far side of
the River Jordan and comments: 'This illness is not
unto death; it is for the glory of God, so that the Son
of God may be glorified by means of it.' Jesus remains
there two more days before suggesting a return to
Judea. The disciples question his wisdom: 'Rabbi, the
Jews were but now seeking to stone you, and are you
going there again?' Jesus answers, 'Our friend Lazarus
has fallen asleep, but I go to awake him out of sleep.'
To talk of 'sleep' was a recognized euphemism for

Looking east towards the wilderness and Jericho, a typical village household in Bethany today

'death' and Jesus makes the situation very clear: 'Lazarus is dead; and for your sake I am glad that I was not there, so that you may believe.'

On his arrival, Jesus finds that Lazarus died four days ago and that many Jewish friends have come to comfort the two sisters. Martha, leaving Mary at home, comes to meet Jesus with the words, 'Lord, if you had been here, my brother would not have died. And now I know that whatever you ask from God, God will give you.' Jesus answers, 'Your brother will rise again.' 'I know that he will rise again,' returns Martha, 'in the resurrection at the last day.' 'Jesus said to her, "I am the resurrection and the life; he who believes in me, though he die, yet shall he live, and whoever lives and believes in me shall never die. Do you believe this?" She said to him, "Yes, Lord; I believe that you are the Christ, the Son of God, he who is coming into the world."' (John 11:21-27) (This passage forms the first gospel for the Requiem Mass in the Catholic Church of the Latin Rite today.)

Martha then went to call her sister and Mary greeted him with exactly the same first words as those of her sister Martha. Jesus, seeing her weeping and her Jewish friends with her, was deeply moved and asked, 'Where have you laid him?' Seeing Jesus weep too, some of the friends asked, 'Could not he who opened the eyes of the blind man have kept this man from dying?' Jesus came to the tomb and told them to take away the stone. Martha reminded him that after four days there would be a smell, but they did so; and Jesus began to pray, '"Father, I thank thee that thou hast heard me. I knew that thou hearest me always, but I have said this on account of the people standing by, that they may believe that thou didst send me." When he had said this, he cried with a loud voice, "Lazarus, come out." The dead man came out, his hands and feet

bound with bandages, and his face wrapped with a cloth. Jesus said to them, "Unbind him, and let him go."' (John 11:41-44)

Many of the Jews present are reported to have believed in Jesus as the Messiah, but others went and reported the matter to the Pharisees, who with the chief priests immediately called together the Council to plan his downfall. Jesus himself escaped to the town of Ephraim overlooking the wilderness.

Not a week later, however, Jesus had returned to Bethany for the Passover week, and the writer of the Fourth Gospel adds, 'When the great crowd of the Jews learned that he was there, they came not only on account of Jesus but also to see Lazarus, whom he had raised from the dead. So the chief priests planned to put Lazarus also to death, because on account of him many of the Jews were going away and believing in Jesus.' (John 12:9–11) The following day the crowds came out from Jerusalem to greet his triumphant entry with palm branches, and the evangelist again comments, 'The crowd that had been with him when he called Lazarus out of the tomb and raised him from the dead bore witness. The reason why the crowd went to meet him was that they heard he had done this sign.' (John 12:17, 18)

Today the village of El-Azariah (the Arabic form of Lazarion, the House of Lazarus), nestles under the Mount of Olives, facing east towards the wilderness and the Jordan Valley. It was above the now empty spur that the village of Bethany stood in the time of Jesus. Today, there are two new churches, one Greek Orthodox, the other Franciscan. The latter covers the remains of a 4th-century church built over the tomb of Lazarus, then within the cemetery of Bethany. The village has since grown up around the church of the tomb. Jerome tells us that already at the beginning of the 4th century a church had been built over it. In the

248

11th century the site was covered by a mosque, and a little later the Latin custodian of the holy places in the Holy Land obtained permission to open a new entrance into the tomb.

It is strange that there is no further mention of Lazarus and his family in the history of the early Christian Church at Jerusalem. According to an Eastern tradition, he and his sisters were put in a leaking boat, on the Mediterranean, but reached the island of Cyprus, where Lazarus became bishop of Kitium. In the year 890, his supposed relics were transferred to Constantinople. In Crusader times, pilgrimage to the house of Mary, Martha, and Lazarus at Bethany was revived and a legend became popular in the west that Lazarus had been bishop of Marseilles and was martyred under Domitian. [John 11:1-44; 12:2, 9, 10, 17]

LEBBAEUS (Gk. 'hearty'). The name Lebbaeus is included as an alternative to Thaddaeus only in some minor manuscripts at Matt. 10:3, and also in the Western Text only at Mark 3:18, but Lebbaeus is not to be found in the Revised Standard Version. *see* THADDAEUS [Matt. 10:3]

LEGION This Latin word, used for a regimental unit of 6,000 soldiers in the Roman army, was adopted as

Tombstone of a Roman soldier of the Tenth Legion, found in Jerusalem.

his name by the demoniac living on the east shore of Galilee and possessed by unclean spirits, for, said he, 'we are many'. The actual name occurs only in the Mark and Luke Gospels, though the story is told in all the three Synoptic Gospels.

Jesus and his disciples crossed to the 'other side'. (*see* GADARENES) As they disembarked, they were met by a savage demoniac possessed by many unclean spirits, who lived within the tombs on the hillside. Mark's account is particularly vivid of a wild figure whom no one could bind, not even with chains and fetters. 'For he had often been bound with fetters and chains, but the chains he wrenched apart, and the fetters he broke in pieces; and no one had the strength to subdue him. Night and day among the tombs and on the mountains he was always crying out, and bruising himself with stones. And when he saw Jesus from afar, he ran and worshipped him; and crying out with a loud voice, he said, "What have you to do with me, Jesus, Son of the Most High God? I adjure you by God, do not torment me." For he had said to him, "Come out of the man, you unclean spirit!" And Jesus asked him, "What is your name?" He replied, "My name is Legion; for we are many."' (Mark 5:4-9)

In primitive communities, mental illness is naturally interpreted as possession by evil spirits who need to be tamed by force. The use of chains for this purpose was common in medieval Europe to restrain the evil in the person, which appeared to reduce him to the level of a savage animal. In the primitive thinking of 1st-century Palestine, the power to suppress evil spirits could only come from God, the all-good. Therefore anyone able to exercise such power over evil received his power from God, and the miracles of Jesus were consequently

Two Roman legionaries, from the *Mostra augustea*, Mainz.

interpreted as proofs of his Messiahship and divine commission. It is interesting, if ironical, that his Messiahship, in the Synoptic Gospels, is never publicly recognized and proclaimed except by the handicapped members of the community, whether blind or possessed. It is blind Bartimaeus at Jericho who begs, 'Jesus, Son of David, have mercy.' It is the demented 'Legion' who begs, 'Jesus, Son of the Most High God, I adjure you by God, do not torment me.' Matthew adds the significant words, 'Have you come here to torment us before the time?', meaning before the prophesied coming of the Messiah.

Jesus then said, 'Come out of the man, you unclean spirit,' and he asked him, 'What is your name?' for the knowledge of the name of a person enabled control over him (Jacob at Penuel). The man replied, 'My name is Legion; for we are many,' and the word 'legion' is still used to indicate a vast number. The psychologist can infer much from this story, for the man was cut off from the community by his own choice, a schizophrenic whose multiple personalities were well described by the name of 'Legion'.

The man begged Jesus eagerly not to send his many spirits 'out of the country', and as there was a large herd of pigs feeding on the hillside, the spirits begged Jesus, 'Send us to the swine, let us enter them.' So Jesus agreed, and the story continues, 'And the unclean spirits came out, and entered the swine; and the herd, numbering about two thousand, rushed down the steep bank into the sea, and were drowned in the sea.' (Mark 5:13)

The story is a conflation of both what people thought they saw was happening and of their current ideas about what should happen. They believed in the existence of evil spirits and in their need to be transplanted to animals, if driven out of men – rather like bacteria needing to feed on flesh in order to survive. The actual reason behind the headlong flight of the pigs over the cliff may well have been a combination of the neglectful curiosity of their herdsmen, the shouting of the man, and the sudden movement of the people from the nearby township. The result was the same. 'The herdsmen fled, and told it in the city and in the country. And people came to see what it was that had happened. And they came to Jesus, and saw the demoniac sitting there, clothed and in his right mind, the man who had had the legion; and they were afraid. And those who had seen it told what had happened to the demoniac and to the swine. And they began to beg Jesus to depart from their neighbourhood.' (Mark 5:14-17)

As Jesus was getting into the boat, the man who had been possessed begged Jesus that he might come with him, but Jesus refused, saying, 'Go home to your friends, and tell them how much the Lord has done for you, and how he has had mercy on you.' (Mark 5:19)

And the man went off and began to tell in the Ten Cities how much Jesus had done for him. [Mark 5:9; Luke 8:30]

LEVI (Gk. from the Heb. 'joined'). **1.** Son of Alphaeus, mentioned by the name of Levi in the story of his call by Jesus, in Mark and Luke. Though both Matthew and Luke followed the Marcan version of the story almost verbatim, yet Matthew changes the name of 'Levi' to that of 'Matthew'. When, however, the three synoptists list the twelve apostles, all three omit the name of 'Levi', but include the name of 'Matthew'. In Matthew's Gospel, 'Matthew' is called 'the publican'. Furthermore, in the list of apostles present at Pentecost, there is no mention of the name 'Levi', but only of 'Matthew'. Therefore, it is sound to assume that 'Levi' became known as 'Matthew' and that the two names refer to one and the same tax-collector, called by Jesus from his desk at the frontier town of Capernaum. *see* MATTHEW [Mark 2:14; Luke 5:27, 29]

2. Son of Jacob, the Patriarch mentioned in the letter to Hebrew Christians as the father of the priestly tribe. [Heb. 7:9]

3. Son of Melchi and father of Matthat mentioned by Luke within the genealogy of Jesus. [Luke 3:24]

LEVITE(S) The Levites were the descendants of the priests of the high places deposed by the religious reformers of the 8th century BC, whose views are expressed in the Book of Deuteronomy. By the 1st century, the Levites were an inferior clergy, lower in rank than the priests and fulfilling the mass of minor tasks essential to the maintenance of worship in the Temple. In theory, the Levites were the descendants of Levi, one of the twelve patriarchs and sons of Jacob. The tribe of Levi appears early to have lost favour and even perhaps its tribal distinction. Moses was a Levite and used his own tribe to purge the people of Israel after the 'golden calf' incident. Later, the Levites became known as professional priests. They were not allocated a tribal territory, but lived in the cities of other tribes.

In the 1st century, from among the descendants of Levi, the priesthood were the descendants of Aaron, and the high priests – a privileged class within the priesthood – were the descendants of Zadok, the high priest who anointed Solomon king. The lowest strata of this ecclesiastical hierarchy was that of the Levites, who were limited to the inferior duties, taking no part in the offering of sacrifice and forbidden access to the central Temple building.

Divided into twenty-four weekly courses, they served the needs of the Temple in their turns, there being some 10,000 Levites in all. Some performed the instrumental music of the Temple, others formed the choir, others were doorkeepers; others acted as servers, dressing the high priest in his vestments, assembling the scrolls, and cleaning such parts of the Temple as they were allowed to enter. The Temple police and guards were provided from among the Levites; these patrolled the courts of the Temple by day and night, enforcing the discipline of admission to the correct courts and exacting punishment from offenders.

There were of course many sons of Levi who did not wish to fulfil the traditional functions of Levites within the Temple and followed other pursuits, crafts and trades, even as Scribes and Pharisees.

The Levite in the parable of the Good Samaritan

Jesus told the story in answer to the lawyer's quibble, 'Who is my neighbour?' The story described the reaction of three travellers to seeing a wounded man by the roadside. 'Now by chance a priest was going down that road; and when he saw him he passed by on the other side. So likewise a Levite, when he came to the place and saw him, passed by on the other side.' At this point, the hearers, who thought of their community in terms of Priests, Levites, and Israelites – as perhaps Christians today of bishops, clergy, and lay people – might have been confident that the hero would be an Israelite. Their shock and consternation when the hero turned out to be a hated Samaritan – one publicly cursed in the synagogue and whose evidence was inacceptable in a court of law – can be easily imagined. The parable did not exactly answer the question of the lawyer, 'Who is my neighbour?' but it illustrated graphically that neighbourhood was unlimited, by race or religion. The only criterion for neighbourliness is need. [Luke 10:32]

The Levites sent to interrogate John the Baptist

'And this is the testimony of John, when the Jews sent priests and Levites from Jerusalem to ask him, "Who are you?" He confessed, he did not deny, but confessed, "I am not the Christ." And they asked him, "What then? Are you Elijah?" He said, "I am not." "Are you the prophet?" And he answered, "No." They said to him then, "Who are you? Let us have an answer for those who sent us. What do you say about yourself?" He said, "I am the voice of one crying in the wilderness, 'Make straight the way of the Lord,' as the prophet Isaiah said."' [John 1:19-23]

The Levitical priesthood compared with that of Jesus

The writer of the letter to Hebrew Christians argued for the superiority of the priesthood of Jesus, as descended from Melchizedek, to that of the Levites descended from Aaron. The writer points out that Abraham the forefather of Levi paid tithes to Melchizedek, whose order was therefore superior to that of Levi. [Heb. 6:20; 7:11]

LINUS One of the four who sent their personal greetings at the close of Paul's final letter to Timothy in Ephesus, perhaps the last he ever wrote. From the grouping of the names, Linus may well have been the

son of Pudens and Claudia. Paul is writing from prison, presumably in Rome, after his conviction and expecting execution. This family, not elsewhere mentioned in the New Testament, may have ministered to the final needs of Paul, along with the 'beloved physician', Luke, Paul's fellow-prisoner to the end. [2 Tim. 4:21]

LOIS The grandmother of Timothy, a lieutenant of Paul destined to become bishop of Ephesus. Eunice was a Christian Jewess married to a Greek (Acts 16:1) and living with her family at Lystra. Paul may well have persuaded Timothy, his mother Eunice, and his grandmother Lois to become Christians, on the very first visit to Lystra with Barnabas in the year 46 (Acts 14:8-20). Certainly Timothy knew of Paul's stoning by the Jews on that occasion (2 Tim. 3:11). When Paul passed through Lystra again, on his Second Journey some four years later, he collected Timothy from his home and family. Because he wanted to use Timothy for evangelism among the Jews, who knew that his father was a Greek, Paul personally took Timothy and circumcised him, to convince them of his adherence to the Jewish Law.

Paul, in his correspondence with Timothy, acknowledges generously the careful training of Timothy in the Jewish faith and scriptures within his own home and family. 'I am reminded of your sincere faith, a faith that dwelt first in your grandmother Lois and your mother Eunice and now, I am sure, dwells in you.' (2 Tim. 1:5) And again, 'Continue in what you have learned and have firmly believed, knowing from whom you learned it and how from childhood you have been acquainted with the sacred writings which are able to instruct you for salvation through faith in Christ Jesus.' (2 Tim. 3:14, 15)

Possibly Lois had died, or Eunice remained with her at Lystra, for Paul did not send her greetings in his letters to Timothy at Ephesus. [2 Tim. 1:5]

LUCAS see LUKE

LUCIUS There are two men of this name mentioned in the New Testament, who may in fact have been one and the same person. The first is listed among the leaders of the progressive Christian Church in Antioch as prophet and teacher. These also included Barnabas, Simeon Niger, Manaen, a member of the court of Herod the tetrarch, and Saul. This Lucius came from Cyrene, on the north coast of Africa.

The second reference to Lucius comes in the final greetings at the close of Paul's letter to the Christian community in Rome. Paul describes him as 'my kinsman'.

Whether the final chapter of Paul's letter to Rome included messages to Christians at Ephesus or at Rome, the Lucius who linked his greetings with those of Paul may well have been the same man of Cyrene. [Acts 13:1; Rom. 16:21]

LUKE Although Luke is mentioned only twice by name within the New Testament, by the year 170 he was acknowledged as author of both the Third Gospel and the Acts of the Apostles. His character emerges very clearly from these writings as that of a highly sensitive and sympathetic person of wide interests and perception. He was possibly an early Gentile convert to Christianity, who may himself have met Jesus. He became the loyal and indefatigable secretary, doctor, and companion of the Apostle Paul. Luke was perhaps a Syrian by birth, hailing from the city of Antioch on the Mediterranean. He was possibly a slave, educated, and trained in medicine within some Greco-Roman household in an eastern Mediterranean country. Some recent scholarship has suggested, however, that Luke was a Jew, whose writings were translated from a Semitic language.

From the 'we' sections of the Acts (16:10-17; 20:5-15; 27:1-37; 28:1-14) which describe his adventures with Paul (and which may be parts of Luke's own travel diary), we can deduce some biographical details about him. He accompanied Paul on his Second Journey across the Aegean from Troas in Asia Minor to Philippi in Greece. On Paul's Third Journey, six years later, he returned with Paul from Philippi to Jerusalem. And he accompanied Paul on his final journey from Caesarea, seat of the procurator of Judea, all the way to Rome. There he loyally remained with Paul throughout his captivity.

Much of the early history of the development of Christianity, as recorded in the Acts, revolves round the Church at Antioch, where Luke was an early member of the Christian community. Antioch also had the honour of being both the birthplace of the name 'Christian' and the headquarters of the mission to the Gentiles. Indeed, Antioch was second only to Jerusalem in the early history of Christianity. Of the glories of this one-time capital of Syria which straddled the River Orontes, few remain today. There are some massive sections of ancient city walling, some arches of Trajan's aqueduct, and the rather scanty remains of a theatre and stadium. The ancient city, in the time of Paul and Luke, extended over the slopes and plateau of Mount Silpius to the south of the smaller modern town.

right St Luke painting the Virgin, by Rogier van der Weyden (1399-1464).
below Luke acted as doctor and companion to St Paul on his journeys. Greek *bas-relief*, showing a physician treating patients.

The Eastern Mediterranean

BITHYNIA
PONTUS
Ancyra
GALATIA
PHRYGIA
Antioch
Iconium
PAMPHYLIA Derbe
CILICIA
Attalia Perga
Tarsus
Seleucia Antioch
CYPRUS Salamis
Paphos
SYRIA
Mediterranean Sea
Sidon
Tyre
Ptolemais
Caesarea
Joppa
JUDEA Jerusalem
ARABIA
Alexandria
EGYPT
100 miles

out his purpose in a brief prologue addressed to 'Theophilus' (which means 'God-lover') – probably a Roman nobleman, identified by some as Flavius Clemens, fourth cousin of the Emperor Domitian.

The writer of both Luke and Acts appealed to the Romans, emphasizing the universal elements in Jesus's actions and teachings. His genealogy attempts to trace the ancestry of Jesus back to Adam, whereas Matthew begins with Abraham. Luke's description of the passion of Jesus is more generous to the Roman authorities than those of Matthew and Mark. He translates carefully into Greek all Hebrew terms, laying less stress on the fulfilment of Old Testament prophecy in the life of Jesus, which he tells as a message of universal salvation for all men. Much of the teaching of Jesus he describes as given over the supper-table, full of compassion, kindness, and self-identification with the needs of the people concerned.

The parables included in Luke's Gospel lay stress on these characteristics in the personality of Jesus and in the conduct subsequently required in his followers. In fact, Luke's portrait of Jesus may reflect the colours to be found in the artist himself. These include – as in the parable of the Prodigal Son and the conversation

4th-century bust of Constantine the Great, ivory set in gold. Constantine transported the relics of Luke to his capital, Constantinople.

In other documents Luke is referred to as being unmarried, writing his Gospel in Greece, and dying at the age of 84. In 356, Constantine II had his relics translated from Thebes in Boeotia to Constantinople, where they were later preserved in the Church of the Apostles. Later legends describe Luke variously as one of the seventy disciples sent out by Jesus, as living in Bithynia, Alexandria, and Achaia, as dying a natural death, and as being martyred in the time of Domitian. Luke is the patron saint of both doctors and artists. In the Middle Ages, pictures of Mary, the mother of Jesus, were ascribed to him, both at the Syrian Church in Jerusalem, at Santa Maggiore in Rome and in several other places.

Luke's Gospel

Luke's writings form at least a quarter of the New Testament. In a two-volume work, he tells the story of Christianity from the birth of Jesus until the gospel reached the whole of the Mediterranean world. As there is no reference in his writings to the martyrdom of Paul, both the Gospel and Acts might well have been completed before that event (AD 64). However, Luke's description of the fall of Jerusalem – in 70 – is less likely to be simply a prediction than those in the other Gospels. This may indicate a date after 70. The authorship of Luke has not been seriously disputed, being supported by Justin Martyr and a succession of bishops and scholars, including Polycarp, Papias, Clement, Irenaeus, and Tertullian. The author of the Gospel sets

The Prodigal Son, pen and ink drawing by Rembrandt van Rijn, *c.* 1642.

with the penitent thief on the cross – forgiveness and affection towards sinners. Luke shows clearly Jesus's neighbourliness and his respect for foreigners in the parable of the Good Samaritan, and his concern for the outcasts and the poor in the parable of the Rich Man and Lazarus, the healing of the Ten Lepers, the story of Zacchaeus, and the parable of the Pharisee and the Publican.

Luke's Gospel records – as none of the others do – Jesus's sensitivity towards women and children. He gives the names of many women concerned with the gospel story, including Mary, Elizabeth, Anne, Mary Magdalene and Susanna. Luke has a great interest in children. He tells us about the birth of Jesus in great detail, about the child whom Jesus took and 'put him by his side' before the disciples as an example of simple faith, and about the children brought to Jesus. If Luke was a slave, that might account for his surprisingly uncompromising presentation of Jesus's teaching about the dangers of wealth. For Luke, poverty was a virtue;

where Matthew records Jesus's words, 'Blessed are the poor in spirit,' Luke unequivocally records, 'Blessed are *you* poor.' Where Matthew records, 'Blessed are those who hunger and thirst for righteousness,' Luke records, 'Blessed are you that hunger now.' Luke even describes Jesus as demanding total renunciation of a man's family as a condition of discipleship.

Luke is also the evangelist of prayer. He tells us about Jesus's prayers; how he taught men to pray, and that he prayed before he chose his disciples. Jesus, we are told, prayed at his baptism, and the transfiguration, in Luke, takes place during prayer. Luke makes it very plain that the Holy Spirit is ruling and guiding the disciples. He alone gives the full story of the nativity of John the Baptist and of the conception of Jesus as the action of the Spirit of God. A strong sense of the supernatural alongside a gracious humanity lends great charm to his Gospel, and to his portrayal of Jesus. The Gospel of Luke has been called 'the most beautiful book in the world'.

'The reign of Christ'

The theme of the Gospel has been summed up as 'the reign of Christ, how it is established and how it must be maintained'. Luke, with supreme literary skill and artistry, puts a Jewish story in a world-wide setting: the hero of the story is not just the Jewish Messiah but the king of the universe.

Luke claims to be – and is – carefully systematic in his presentation of the facts. Nowhere else does any New Testament writer so clearly declare his aims or marshal his evidence in favour of the world-wide significance of Jesus the Messiah. The Messiah comes as God's answer to the faith and expectation of the people. Luke alone places the lovely hymns which reflect the Messianic expectation of the Jews in the mouths of Zechariah, Mary, and Simeon. These hymns now form canticles within the liturgy of the Christian Church, as the *Benedictus* – 'Blessed be the Lord God of Israel, for he has visited and redeemed his people' – the *Magnificat* – 'My soul magnifies the Lord, and my spirit rejoices in God my Saviour' – and the *Nunc Dimittis* – 'Lord, now lettest thou thy servant depart in peace, according to thy word; for mine eyes have seen thy salvation'.

The prayer of the old priest Zechariah is heard: he is the father of John the Baptist, the forerunner of the Christ, and in the *Benedictus* he proclaims that the saviour of the House of David, promised of old, is at hand. The prayer of Mary is heard: she has found favour with God and is the mother of the Saviour, and in the *Magnificat* she declares that the promise to Abraham is to be fulfilled. And Simeon proclaims in the *Nunc Dimittis* that the infant Messiah is to be a 'light for revelation to the Gentiles, and for glory to thy people Israel'.

Luke himself quotes the prophet Isaiah: 'all flesh shall see the salvation of God'. The first sermon which Jesus preaches in Nazareth after his baptism shows that even in the time of Elijah and Elisha God was not to be confined within the bounds of any narrow Jewish nationalism. Jesus finds greater faith in a Roman centurion than he has found in any Jew. He prophesies the rejection of the Jews and the call of the Gentiles: 'And men will come from east and west, and from north and south, and sit at table in the kingdom of God.' Repentance for the forgiveness of sins will be preached to all the nations. Indeed, Luke's universalism is clearly seen in every page of his Gospel.

It is therefore on the canvas of universalism that Luke paints the figure of Christ as King and his claims to the throne. 'Of his kingdom there will be no end,' said the angel to Mary. 'I must preach the good news of the kingdom of God to the other cities also,' said Jesus in Capernaum. On Palm Sunday, Jesus entered Jerusalem as a king, refusing to check his disciples for exclaiming, 'Blessed is the King who comes in the name of the Lord!' At the Last Supper, he promised a reward for his apostles: 'You are those who have continued with me in my trials . . . so do I appoint for you that you may eat and drink at my table in my kingdom.'

Before Pilate, Jesus was accused by elders of claiming to be 'Christ a king'. Pilate asked him, 'Are you the King of the Jews?' The soldiers mocked him on his cross with the words, 'If you are the King of the Jews, save yourself!' The penitent thief on the nearby cross appealed to him, 'Jesus, remember me when you come in your kingly power.' After the resurrection and on the road to Emmaus, Jesus explained that the Christ had to suffer in order to enter into his glory. The Gospel of Luke is the record of his royal progress and the fulfilment of prophecy, through his passion and resurrection, to his ascension and enthronement.

The Acts – Christianity's first chronicle

Of all the writings of the New Testament, the Acts of the Apostles, Luke's second volume, most closely resembles a work of secular history, being provided with constant indications of time and place. The Acts is a selection of events illustrating the first encounter of the kingdom of God in Jesus with the Roman Empire. Drawing upon all kinds of sources and information besides his own personal experience, Luke describes how the gospel – the good news of Jesus and the universal kingdom of God – spread from Jerusalem all over the Roman Empire and finally reached Rome itself. It is a masterly summary of the preaching and movements of the early Christian teachers, under the guidance and power of the Holy Spirit. The letters of Paul reveal the Acts as a very skilled selection of events illustrating the growth of the early Church.

According to a commentary on Luke written about 160-80, the Acts was written in Achaia after the death of Paul, about 64-5. Eusebius argued for an earlier date – perhaps 62 – following Paul's first Roman captivity. Some contemporary scholars suggest a date after the publication of the works of the Jewish historian Josephus, which they find reflected in both the Gospel and the Acts, perhaps 90-5. Both works may include eye-witness accounts by the author, particularly the 'we' passages in Acts, but Luke also had access to oral and written traditions.

These last possibly included a manuscript in Aramaic or Hebrew, which Luke seems to have translated word *above* 12th-century wall-painting from Eski Gumus, Cappadocia, showing St Luke, with his Gospel and ox-symbol, appearing from behind the figure of Christ.

by word into Greek to form the basis of the first two chapters of the Gospel. He certainly used Mark's Gospel, half of which he includes almost word for word, though excluding any reference to almost three chapters of that Gospel – a remarkable omission (Mark 6:45-8:28). Luke also probably used some 200–250 verses of a 'Sayings' collection – given the name of 'Q' for *Quelle*, German for 'source'. There is also a considerable corpus of gospel parables and stories, peculiar to Luke.

The Acts is a literary masterpiece as much as is the Gospel. The birth of the early Church and the career of Paul are related with great skill and efficiency. The speeches of Peter, Stephen, and Paul are magnificent, and though there is less beauty in the Acts, some passages are incomparable – particularly the conversions of Cornelius, Paul, and the elders of Miletus – and, of course, the description of the shipwreck at Malta.

As Luke, 'the beloved physician', is one of the most attractive personalities in the New Testament, so his two-volume work must have provided effective Christian 'propaganda' within the Roman patrician circle for *above left* Canon tables from an early Aramaic Gospel of Luke.

above right Luke the Evangelist, surrounded by scenes from his Gospel, from a Carolingian manuscript.

whom he wrote. His own particular contribution to the gospel and the presentation of the character of Jesus is best seen in the beautiful parables which only Luke records. Luke is, however, first and foremost the evangelist of the incarnation, which is to him not a theological conception, but a reality. He presents the Jewish background, birth and childhood of Jesus. In places, his Gospel is more Jewish than the others. For Luke, Jerusalem is the centre of the story and the scene of the triumphs of Jesus, whether as a child of twelve years in the Temple or at his Messianic entry into the Temple on Palm Sunday, the establishment of his Kingdom by the cross of Calvary or the commission of his followers in the Upper Room and on Olivet. [Gospel of Luke; Acts of the Apostles; Col. 4:14; 2 Tim. 4:11]

LYCAONIAN The local dialect of the people of Lystra and Derbe, spoken by the people of Lystra when they mistook Barnabas and Paul for the gods Zeus and Hermes, during Paul's First Journey through Anatolia. *see* ZEUS [Acts 14:11]

LYDIA The rich lady from Thyatira who met Paul by

the little River Ganga, outside Philippi, a Roman colony and city founded by Alexander the Great in Macedonia. Lydia's household was the first in Europe known to have been converted and baptized.

Paul found few Jews at Philippi and no synagogue. He probably waited some days until the Sabbath and then went to the river, where he might expect any local Jews to be at prayer. There, he met a few women who gathered regularly for prayer; among these was Lydia, who was in the purple-dye trade and came from the city of Thyatira, 100 miles or more north of Ephesus in Asia Minor. Paul and his companions sat down and talked to the women who had gathered; Lydia listened and opened her heart to what Paul said; she was herself a pagan and only loosely attached to the little Jewish community. She insisted on being baptized by Paul, together with her household, and begged the three visitors, Paul, Timothy, and Silas, to accept hospitality. 'If you have judged me to be faithful to the Lord, come to my house and stay.'

above Portrait of a young man in a white robe with purple dye stripes, from Fayum, Egypt. Lydia was in the purple-dye trade.

On the way from Lydia's house to the prayer-meeting, a fortune-telling slave-girl called out after Paul and the others, 'These men are servants of the Most High God, who proclaim to you the way of salvation.' She did this each day, until Paul lost his temper and ordered the fortune-telling spirit to leave the woman. But when her owners realized that they would not make any more money out of her, they seized and dragged Paul and Silas into the market-place, where they charged them before the magistrates with causing a disturbance. The crowd joined in, and the magistrates had them stripped and flogged. After many lashes, they were thrown into prison and committed to the safe-keeping of the gaoler, who put them in the inner prison and fastened their feet in the stocks.

That night, while Paul and Silas were praying and singing, there was an earthquake, which opened the cells and released the prisoners. The gaoler, presuming his charges had escaped, was only just prevented by Paul from committing suicide. In gratitude the gaoler took Paul and Silas to his home, where they preached to, converted and baptized his whole family – who, in turn, fed them and washed their wounds.

At daylight, the magistrates sent the order for their release, to which Paul typically replied, 'They have beaten us publicly, uncondemned, men who are Roman citizens, and have thrown us into prison; and do they now cast us out secretly? No! Let them come themselves and take us out.' (Acts 16:37) The magistrates duly arrived, and begged them to leave the town.

As soon as they left the prison, they went to the house of Lydia to meet and encourage the newly-formed Christian congregation, then left on their way to Thessalonica. It was to this little Christian community at Philippi, based on the house of Lydia, that Paul wrote later, when in prison in Rome or perhaps Ephesus, a letter full of happiness, gratitude, affection and reassurance. Lydia was certainly a key person in the foundation of the Christian Church at Philippi. [Acts 16:14, 40]

LYSANIAS One of the rulers in power at the beginning of the ministry of John the Baptist, the non-Jewish Lysanias is included as tetrarch of Abilene, a district in Syria north of Herod Philip's territory and between the cities of Chalchis and Damascus. The Jewish historian, Josephus, records that the territories of both Philip and Lysanias were given to Herod Agrippa in AD 37 by the Roman Emperor Caligula. Luke did his best to date the events of his Gospel by reference to current political affairs. [Luke 3:1]

LYSIAS *see* CLAUDIUS LYSIAS

overleaf The three Magi awakened by an angel; above their bed is the Star of Bethlehem. Carving by Gislebertus from Autun Cathedral, early 12th century.

M

MACEDONIAN The mysterious man of Macedonia in Paul's vision at Troas, during his Second Journey, who encouraged Paul to cross the Aegean into Europe, with the words 'Come over to Macedonia and help us.'

The narrative of Luke, within the Acts, from this moment onwards is written in the first person plural, '*We* sought to go on into Macedonia, concluding that God had called *us* to preach the gospel to them.' (Acts 16:10) As this is the first of the 'we' passages, indicating the presence of Luke himself, it has often been thought that Luke first joined Paul either at Troas or at Philippi in Macedonia. In which case, it is just possible that the Macedonian in Paul's dream or vision might have been Luke himself, but Paul had many Macedonian friends including Gaius, Aristarchus, Secundus, Sopater, Epaphroditus, and also Lydia.

Macedonia, an insignificant Greek kingdom, constantly involved in tribal war, was unified by Philip II (359-36 BC), whose son Alexander led the conquering armies of Macedon as far as the Ganges and overthrew the Persian Empire. Macedonia had become part of the Roman Empire in 167 BC. [Acts 16:9]

MAGDALENE (Gk. from Heb. 'tower of God') *see* MARY OF MAGDALA

MAGI (Gk. 'wise men', 'sages') The wise men were the first Gentiles to worship the child Jesus as the Messiah or 'King of the Jews'. Following a star, they came from the east to Bethlehem with gifts of gold, frankincense, and myrrh. The Greek word used in Matthew's Gospel is that for 'wise men' (R.S.V.), translated 'astrologers' in the New English Bible. The Arabic *Gospel of the Infancy*, one of the many apocryphal Gospels, starts the birth narrative with the words:

'And it happened when the Lord Jesus was born in Bethlehem of Judea at the time of King Herod, the Magicians arrived from the east in Jerusalem, as Zoroaster had predicted: and they had offerings with them – gold, frankincense, and myrrh, so they worshipped Him and offered their offerings.'

Some early legends linked the wise men with Zoroaster, and this association still persisted when in AD 614 Persian invaders spared the Justinian Church of the Nativity because there was a frieze, over the great triple doorway entrance, of the wise men, of whom one was in Persian costume. Certainly Persia and Mesopotamia were famous for their magical practices.

The 2nd-century theologian Tertullian refers to the wise men as 'almost kings', and by the 6th century the tradition of their kingship was widespread. The 3rd-century theologian Origen declared that they were three wise men, probably because of their three gifts. Again, by the 6th century they had been given the names 'Caspar, Melchior, and Balthasar'. In the Middle Ages, they were venerated as saints and their relics were said to have been taken by Frederick Barbarossa to Cologne Cathedral in the year 1162.

It has been suggested that gold, frankincense, and myrrh could well have come from Arabia and that there had been Jews there since the fall of Samaria and

The Magi, watched by an angel, bring gifts to Mary and the child Jesus: 6th-century ivory. Note the Phrygian caps of the Magi.

Magi

Jerusalem. The text 'wise men from the East came to Jerusalem' does not clearly reveal whether they were oriental astrologers or whether they arrived from east of Jerusalem. Both Tertullian and the Palestinian martyr Justin, early in the 2nd century, thought the Magi came from Arabia, like the 'kings of Arabia and Saba' bringing gifts, in the prophecy of Isaiah (Isa. 60:6). Certainly there were Arab tribes called after the stars, and one tribe called 'Planeteers' who claimed that it was their ancestors who visited 'the prophet Jesus the Messiah'.

However legendary the origin of Matthew's account and whatever accretions it may have gathered, the story is well told and true to life, and accounts for Herod's unsuccessful attempt to kill the child Jesus. Many had their stars and other men saw their risings. The observation of a particular star heralding the birth of a unique personality may have coincided with the conjunction of the planets Saturn and Jupiter in the year 7 BC, or (less likely) the appearance of Halley's Comet in 11 BC. Neither, however, would be likely to 'come to rest over the place where the child was'!

The personality of Herod the Great seen in the story exactly coincides with his historical character. On the arrival of the Magi, asking, 'Where is he who has been born King of the Jews?', Herod was 'troubled and all Jerusalem with him', as well they might be from previous experience of their elderly, morose, cruel, and suspicious ruler. Herod's ruse to send the wise men to discover the whereabouts of the child and to call for their report, just in order that he could assassinate a potential rival 'king of the Jews', was typical of the tyrant. 'Then Herod summoned the wise men secretly and ascertained from them what time the star appeared; and he sent them to Bethlehem, saying, "Go and search diligently for the child, and when you have found him bring me word, that I too may come and worship him."' (Matt. 2:7, 8)

Herod's summer palace was on a hilltop within a mile or so of Bethlehem; he is unlikely to have relished the advent of a rival in the nearest town. His fury at the evasion of the Magi, and their return to their own country 'by another way', rather than passing through Jerusalem, was also characteristic of him. His subsequent massacre of the innocents, the male children of 'two years old and under' (perhaps the wise men had first seen the star some time before) was also absolutely in accordance with his known character and practice.

The great significance of the coming of the wise men, to the writer of Matthew's Gospel, was that they were the vanguard of the Gentile worshippers of Jesus the Messiah. It is on the theme of Jesus's world-wide commission to his disciples that this Gospel ends: 'Go therefore and make disciples of all nations, baptizing them in the name of the Father and of the Son and of

Malchus, in the foreground, has his ear restored: 15th-century French ivory of the betrayal of Jesus.

the Holy Spirit . . .' (Matt. 28:19) [Matt. 2:1-11]

MALCHUS The slave of the high priest, whose right ear Peter cut off with a sword during the skirmish that took place at the arrest of Jesus in the Garden of Gethsemane. Malchus must have been one of the party of Temple police and others, armed with swords and staves, detailed to execute the arrest.

Only the Fourth Gospel gives the names both of the slave 'Malchus' and his assailant 'Peter', although all three Synoptic Gospels describe the event. In the Fourth Gospel the story of the arrest is rather that of a surrender, and Jesus's words to Peter are, 'Put your sword into its sheath; shall I not drink the cup which the Father has given me?' Luke the doctor's account mentions the fact that Jesus 'touched his ear and healed him'. [John 18:10, also by implication Matt. 26:51; Mark 14:47; Luke 22:50]

MANAEN (Gk. from the Heb. 'comforter') This man is listed among the prophets and teachers of the Christian Church in Antioch, who were 'guided by the Spirit' to select and despatch Paul and Barnabas on the First Journey, to Cyprus and Galatia. These leaders at the headquarters of the Christian Church included Barnabas, himself a Cypriot Jew, Simeon, Lucius from Cyrene, and Manaen, a one-time companion of Herod Antipas.

Luke describes Manaen as literally 'nourished together' with Herod the Tetrarch, implying that he was a foster-brother or child-companion at the court of Herod. His link with the family of Herod may well be due to the fact that an older Manaen, who was a well-known Essene, had been befriended by Herod the Great, having predicted, when Herod was only a child, that he would become 'king of the Jews'. The young Manaen of Antioch known to Luke may well have been a grandson of the Essene Manaen, brought up with Herod's children and later, perhaps, a particular friend of Herod Antipas.

Luke seems to have been remarkably well-informed about the Herod family, even mentioning Joanna, the wife of the steward of Herod Antipas, who helped Jesus and his disciples in Galilee. Perhaps Manaen was the source of Luke's information; they certainly shared a considerable acquaintance with Antioch. [Acts 13:1]

MARK *or* **JOHN MARK** (Gk. from the Lat. 'large hammer') Mark, a young man in his early teens during the ministry of Jesus, became a friend and companion of the Apostle Paul, and later of the Apostle Peter. After their martyrdom in Rome, Mark wrote his Gospel, which is said to reflect the mind and memory of Peter.

Mark's Jewish name was John and his adopted Roman surname was Marcus – just as the Jew Saul adopted the Roman name of Paulus. Mark is mentioned at least ten times in the New Testament, in three different groups of passages. First he appears as the son of Mary, a leading Christian woman in Jerusalem, at whose house the early Church met for prayer. Here was the natural meeting-place of the apostles and disciples in Jerusalem, and Peter went there on his escape from prison. A tradition links this house with the Upper Room, in which Jesus ate the Last Supper, and regards Mark as the son of the 'good man of the house'. Some have suggested that he was the 'young man' who fled naked from the Garden of Gethsemane at the time of Jesus's arrest. It is possible that Judas, having left the disciples at the Last Supper in the Upper Room, returned there to arrest Jesus, only to find him gone to Gethsemane; and that young Mark heard the knocking at the door and slipped out of bed to go and warn Jesus in Gethsemane.

In about the year 46 Paul and Barnabas took the Palestinian John Mark, then a young man, on their First Journey, from Antioch to Cyprus and Perga in Pamphylia, where Mark decided to return home to Jerusalem. Paul and Barnabas, an older cousin to Mark, had taken him 'to assist them'; the same word in Luke 4:20 is translated as 'attendant'; no motive is given for his return, and his reasons clearly failed to satisfy Paul. In 49 a violent disagreement took place between Barnabas and Paul as to whether they should take Mark with them on their Second Journey. This resulted in Paul and Barnabas separating, Paul taking Silas overland through Syria and Cilicia on his long journey of three years' duration, while Barnabas sailed with Mark for the island of Cyprus.

We next hear of Mark some ten years later, reconciled to Paul, a 'fellow-worker', a comfort to Paul in his imprisonment, and a useful assistant. We hear of a possible visit of Mark to the Church at Colossae (Col. 4:10), but do not know whether it materialized. The final reference to Mark comes in the closing greeting of the first letter of Peter from Rome, who entrusts his letter to the hand of Silvanus and adds the greetings of 'my son Mark', rather as Paul refers to Timothy. It is possible that Mark was the companion and spiritual 'son' of Peter, before and after his attendance on Peter in Rome.

Certainly the key to the origins of the Second Gospel

may lie in this relationship, and Papias (60–130), bishop of Hierapolis in Asia Minor, states that 'Mark, having become the interpreter of Peter, set down accurately though not in order, everything that Peter remembered of the words and actions of the Lord'. Irenaeus, in about 185, wrote: 'After the deaths of Peter and Paul, Mark, the disciple and interpreter of Peter, himself handed down to us in writing the things that Peter had proclaimed.' At the time of the martyrdom of Peter and Paul, during the persecutions of Nero, Mark must still have been in his early fifties. Eusebius states that he went to Alexandria and became its first bishop. From there, as a prize of war, his relics were taken to Venice and transferred to the Doges' Chapel, now the Cathedral of St Mark's. The Egyptian Church assigns its principal liturgy to his name, but among the Alexandrian Christian writers both Clement and Origen make no reference to Mark's residence in Egypt.

Author of the Second Gospel

The internal evidence of his Gospel confirms the other historical evidence about the man. He was certainly a Jew. He knew his scriptures, and he knew how to use them. He knew Aramaic, the colloquial language of Palestine. He understood Jewish life and thought, and was well aware of the political and geographical divisions of the age. He used such terms as Pharisees, Sadducees, Scribes, elders, priests, Temple, and synagogue with ease and accuracy. On the other hand, though a Jew by birth, he worked for the Church among the Gentiles. The version of the scriptures which he quoted is the Greek Septuagint. It has been said that 'while the cloth which he used came from Galilee and Judea, the threads with which the garment was sewn, and the pattern which was followed, were those of the great Hellenistic world of the 1st century'.

We can guess the motives which led to the composition of a 'Gospel of Jesus Christ' – the title is found in the very first verse – in the reign of terror for Christians after their condemnation for the great fire in Rome during the winter of the year 64-5. Christians needed to be reminded of the sufferings of Jesus as an example and inspiration to them in their own persecution. The Gospel has been called 'a Gospel for Martyrs'. When the last eye-witnesses to the life of Jesus were being killed or were dying, it was essential that the facts of his life should be set down in writing for the benefit of the early Church. It seems that Mark's Gospel was the first published account of the life, work, and death of Jesus – and it soon became an accepted work, forming the basis of the Gospels of both Matthew and Luke, and was also known to the writer of the Fourth Gospel.

right Mark writing his Gospel, inspired by a winged lion with scroll, from a 9th-century manuscript.

Mark preaching in Alexandria, by Gentile and Giovanni Bellini
(1429-1507 and 1430-1517).

Of the 660 verses in Mark's Gospel, 600 are to be found in Matthew's Gospel, and 350 in Luke's Gospel, and only 60 in neither. The verbal agreement between Mark's and the other two Gospels is striking, though at times Matthew and Luke adjust the language of Mark for reasons of reverence, accuracy, brevity, or propriety. Matthew and Luke, however, never combine to contradict the order of events as recorded by Mark. Such

similarities in substance, language, style, grammar, and chronological order are easily explained by the priority of Mark's Gospel.

Compared with the later Gospels, Mark's is shorter, more direct and informal, written in the simple Greek used throughout the Mediterranean world. At first sight, this Gospel appears to consist of a series of events loosely strung together. There is little continuous biographical narrative; some stories are full of vivid dramatic detail, while others are abrupt in their brevity. The episodes gradually combine to present a clear picture of the public life of Jesus. There is no account of the birth of Jesus, only a brief introduction about the 'forerunner' or 'herald', John the Baptist, before the hero Jesus arrives from Nazareth full-grown to be baptized by his cousin in the River Jordan.

Within 20 verses, Jesus has begun to select his team of disciples and to preach, teach, and heal in the synagogues of Galilee. At once he makes friends and enemies. Controversy with the Scribes and Pharisees (Chapter 3) is followed by a group of parables (Chapter 4), which in turn is followed by a series of miracles (Chapter 5). A careful ordering of the episodes presents a sequence of stages which lead steadily up to a climax. The opposition grows, and Jesus retires from the lakeside, crossing the border into a foreign land, to complete the teaching and training of the twelve. At last they grasp his real identity as the expected Messiah, and from that moment Jesus is able to tell them of the real purpose of his life and of the ordeals, both for him and for them, which lie ahead. 'The Son of Man came not to be served but to serve, and to give his life as a ransom for many.' It is as though the whole Gospel hinges on their recognition of Jesus as the Christ, and the last half of the Gospel is the fulfilment of his purpose in the final journey to Jerusalem and the events which follow there.

Mark's portrait of Jesus

The personality of Jesus comes through clearly to the reader – from his words and actions, and the response they arouse in others; his great energy, firmness, and friendliness, his power of command, his severity, his sympathy, and his tremendous courage. Against the background of a ruthless Roman occupation, of a priestly and privileged aristocracy, a religious leadership based on a legal code and tradition – amid political firebrands, religious fanatics, a depressed people, and wild hopes of deliverance – the whole story becomes vivid and its outcome inevitable.

The last three chapters, unlike the earlier ones, tell in continuous narrative and much detail how Jesus was arrested, tried, and executed. It is the tale of a good man, progressively encircled by his opponents, betrayed by a friend, denied and deserted by his disciples, trapped by plotting priests, condemned by a weak judge, and executed with all the shame and agony of crucifixion. Yet through all the grim details, the purpose, dignity, and royalty of the central figure would seem to justify the assessment of Albert Schweitzer that 'Jesus bent history to his purpose, flung himself upon

top left Mark the Evangelist, from a page in the *Lindisfarne Gospels*, c. 700.
left The door of the Syrian Jacobite Church of John Mark in Jerusalem, associated by a Byzantine tradition with the room of the Last Supper.
above St Mark's Square, Venice.

the wheel of the world. It crushed him, yet he hangs there still. That is his victory.'

One of the intriguing features of Mark's Gospel is that in it, though the conscious fulfilment of Messianic prophecy and the forcing of events to that end may be traced throughout, the secret of Jesus's *identity* as Messiah is concealed almost until the end. The reader is taken into the author's confidence with the title, 'The gospel of Jesus Christ, the Son of God'. Jesus himself is told by the divine voice at his baptism, 'Thou art my beloved Son,' but all the characters in the story are left to draw their own conclusions. The disciples do so only shortly before the crucifixion. The centurion in charge of the execution squad recognizes Jesus – but by then Jesus has admitted his identity to the high priest at his trial before the Sanhedrin; indeed, he admitted it in order to secure his own conviction.

Such is the dramatic irony of this Gospel that the readers can share the knowledge of the identity of its hero with the writer, because they know the answer to such questions as 'Who can forgive sins but God alone?' or 'Who then is this, that even wind and sea obey him?' Yet even at the crucifixion it is only the supernatural events – the darkness and the rending of the veil of the Temple – that witness to the identity of Jesus as the strong, silent, and purposeful 'Son of God'.
[Acts 12:12, 25; 15:37-39; Col. 4:10; Philem. 24]

MARTHA (Gk. from the Aram. 'lady', 'mistress') One of two sisters of Lazarus of Bethany, intimate friends of Jesus, whose 'home from home' was their house whenever he came up to Jerusalem, particularly for the Passover festival.

Only Luke and John mention the sisters by name, but both Gospels give the same impression of their respective characters, as may be seen in this very perceptive and sensitive passage from the pen of Luke, 'the beloved physician'. 'Now as they went on their way, he entered a village; and a woman named Martha received him into her house. And she had a sister called Mary, who sat at the Lord's feet and listened to his teaching. But Martha was distracted with much serving; and she went to him and said, "Lord, do you not care that my sister has left me to serve alone? Tell her then to help me." But the Lord answered her, "Martha, Martha, you are anxious and troubled about many things; one thing is needful. Mary has chosen the good portion, which shall not be taken away from her."' (Luke 10:38-42) The name of Martha still epitomizes the practical and efficient but over-busy and intolerant housekeeper. The hospitality of the Orient indeed requires the housekeeper to be over-busy.

For the significance of the household of Mary, Martha, and Lazarus to the story of the passion of Jesus, and for the story of the raising of Lazarus, *see* LAZARUS [Luke 10:38-42; John 11:1-44]

Martha, sister of Lazarus and Mary of Bethany: wing-panel from an early 16th-century altarpiece, by an unknown artist of the Lombardy School.

MARY (Gk. from the Heb. 'obstinacy')
1. **Mary, mother of Jesus**
2. **Mary of Magdala**
3. **Mary, mother of James and Joses**
4. **Mary, wife of Clopas**
5. **Mary of Bethany**
6. **Mary, mother of John Mark**
7. **Mary, member of the Christian Church at Rome**

1. Mary, mother of Jesus A devout Jewish girl perhaps in her mid-teens betrothed to Joseph, a carpenter in Nazareth of Galilee, she was chosen by God to be the mother of Jesus. Through her willing obedience to God's will and purpose of redemption, she has come to be regarded as foremost among the Christian saints.

According to the Acts of the Apostles Mary, mother of Jesus, shared with the apostles the events of Pentecost, after the ascension of Jesus. Mary occupies a unique place in the affection and devotion of many Christians, both in the East and the West. Mary is to them what Abraham is to both Jews and Moslems: the person whose obedience to and acceptance of God's call and commission brought blessing to his people. To Christians also, Mary was the ark by which God became present among his people, in the person of Jesus. Consequently, the place of her birth, traditionally a cave beneath the Church of St Anne, her mother, and the tomb in which she rested in the Kidron ravine at Gethsemane before her assumption into heaven are greatly venerated in Jerusalem.

Mary's background
According to a 2nd-century apocryphal infancy narrative, called the *Protoevangelium* (literally 'first gospel') of James, Mary was the child of elderly parents, Joachim and Anna, in Jerusalem. This would accord with her priestly family connections noted by Luke (1:36). The 6th-century Roman emperor, Justinian, built a basilica at Constantinople in honour of her mother; both her parents were, and are, commemorated

left Mary with the Christ child, from the Catacomb of Priscilla at Rome, 3rd century.
below Joachim and Anna, parents of Mary the mother of Jesus, meet at Jerusalem: fresco by Giotto in the Arena Chapel, Padua.

top The traditional grotto of the nativity of Mary, Jerusalem. (*centre*) Excavations at the Pool of Bethesda, the site of a Byzantine basilica of St Mary of the Sheepmarket. (*bottom*) Byzantine column-bases of a large church shown on the Madeba mosaic as near the traditional site of the home of Mary and her parents.

in Eastern Christendom from medieval times. There is another tradition, supported by two references in early apocryphal Christian writings to 'Mary the Galilean', that her birthplace was at Sepphoris in Galilee.

At Jerusalem the history of the Church of St Anne is closely linked with that of the Pool of Bethesda (John 5). Both in Aramaic and Hebrew the word 'Bethesda' means 'House of Mercy'. St Jerome and Bishop Eusebius interpreted it as 'House of Effusion', which is also the meaning of the word 'Anna'. A large Byzantine basilica appears on the Madeba mosaic map of Jerusalem. The site of the pool is still under excavation, beside the surviving Crusader church of St Anne.

It would seem that Mary went from Jerusalem to live at Nazareth, as indicated in the Gospel of Luke. Beneath the new Latin Church of the Annunciation, as late as March 1960, have been found Greek *graffiti* of 'Hail Mary', dating back to the 2nd century. This enormous church covers the site of Crusader, Byzantine, and even earlier synagogue-style churches, all in their turn built to venerate the visit of the angel to the peasant girl Mary.

The Orthodox Church has a tradition that the annunciation took place not only at the site of the present Latin basilica, but also at Mary's Well over which it has built its own church.

This tradition comes from the apocryphal *Gospel of St James*, which has of course no sort of canonical authority. In that Gospel, we are told: 'One day when the Virgin Mary was found as usual at the fountain to draw water, there, where the young woman of the Orient cannot elsewhere be seen in public, an angel appeared and saluted her. She was afraid and fled to her house where she started to spin, when suddenly the angel appeared to her again to announce the divine message.' It is likely enough that Mary went to the present well to draw her water, since it was the city's only water supply.

'Hail, O favoured one!'

Luke relates the story of the visit of the angel to the peasant girl Mary with consummate artistry. 'In the sixth month the angel Gabriel was sent from God to a city of Galilee named Nazareth, to a virgin betrothed to a man whose name was Joseph, of the house of David; and the virgin's name was Mary.' (Luke 1:26-27) In a single sentence, the sender, the messenger and the receiver are introduced: God Almighty, the angel Gabriel, and the girl betrothed to the village carpenter. 'And he came to her and said, "Hail, O favoured one, the Lord is with you!" But she was greatly troubled at the saying, and considered in her mind what sort of greeting this might be. And the angel said to her, "Do not be afraid, Mary, for you have found favour with God." ' (Luke 1:28-30)

The divine choice of Mary implies her utter devotion and dedication; even the angel delivers his message with reverence and humility, 'Hail Mary, full of grace within the presence and favour of the Lord God'; she is disturbed and ashamed at such an extravagant greeting.

Then comes the burden of the message (is it a command or an invitation?): 'And behold, you will conceive in your womb and bear a son, and you shall call his name Jesus. He will be great, and will be called the Son of the Most High; and the Lord God will give to him the throne of his father David, and he will reign over the house of Jacob for ever; and of his kingdom there will be no end.' (Luke 1:32-33) Mary's reply is no refusal, but only an enquiry as to how she is to accept. 'And Mary said to the angel, "How can this be, since I have no husband?" ' (Luke 1:34) It is only then that the messenger can unfold the divine plan of the sender. 'And the angel said to her, "The Holy Spirit

above The Orthodox Church of Mary's Well, Nazareth, showing the Crusader arcading and present water supply.

below 19th-century engraving of Mary's Well at Nazareth, once the only water supply of the town.

The annunciation to Mary by the Angel Gabriel: painting by the Venetian painter, Domenico Veneziano (d. 1461).

will come upon you, and the power of the Most High will overshadow you; therefore the child to be born will be called holy, the Son of God."' (Luke 1:35) Momentarily, the divine plan for the redemption of mankind waited upon the consent of this little Jewish girl, before she sealed her acceptance with that stupendously humble *fiat*: 'And Mary said, "Behold, I am the handmaid of the Lord; let it be to me according to your word". And the angel departed from her.' (Luke 1:38) God's plan had already been transformed into action.

Mary is the personification of the part of Israel which was ready to 'hear the word of God and do it'. Thus she became the 'brother, sister and mother' of the Messiah.

The virgin birth

see JESUS

The visitation

By way of encouragement, the angel Gabriel had announced to Mary the news of her cousin Elizabeth. 'And behold, your kinswoman Elizabeth in her old age has also conceived a son; and this is the sixth month with her who was called barren. For with God nothing will be impossible.' (Luke 1:36) Mary promptly set out to visit her cousin Elizabeth at her home in the 'hill country of Judea'. Elizabeth met her with the words, 'Blessed are you among women, and blessed is the fruit of your womb! And why is this granted me, that the mother of my Lord should come to me? For behold, when the voice of your greeting came to my ears, the babe in my womb leaped for joy.' (Luke 1:42-44)

It is at this point that Luke includes the paean of praise that has come to be included in the liturgies of all the Christian Churches as the *Magnificat*. In nearly every manuscript it is put into the mouth of Mary, but in a few it is attributed to Elizabeth. It is still to-day the custom of the oriental woman to sing, about her work.

The feast of the Visitation, kept within the Eastern and Western Churches, is a commemoration of the significant role of these two women in God's plan of redemption, as perceived by Luke, who emphasizes the agency of the Holy Spirit in the life of Elizabeth as well as of Mary. The visitation would have been the most natural event, for Mary would have welcomed an opportunity to escape from prying eyes and malicious tongues in Nazareth. The three months' rest with her cousin would have been the most welcome retreat. The

older woman, Elizabeth, herself going through the same experience, would have been of great comfort and support to the young peasant girl, Mary, plunged so unexpectedly though so willingly into pregnancy.

These considerations are on the most ordinary level of personal relations. But in this case there was something far removed from the ordinary that would give each an added incentive to seek the society of the other. Each knew that there was something altogether exceptional about the promise of her child. Elizabeth's age, quite apart from her husband's visions, had alerted her to the marvel that was happening to her. Mary's virginity, combined with the angelic annunciation, had left her in no doubt that she was being used as a willing agent in the hand of God.

It is impossible to say how they understood so quickly the respective roles they had to play and what would be the relative positions of their children. It is, of course, possible that some communication had already passed between Mary and Elizabeth, so that the older woman knew already of the wonderful circumstances attending the pregnancy of Mary. In any case, Elizabeth had no hesitation in joyfully accepting the minor role for her own child, and so establishing even before their birth the position of John as the forerunner of Jesus the Messiah.

When the time came, the two boys were born within six months of each other, in towns within sight of each other. Joseph and Mary had come to Bethlehem for the census; the home of the priest Zechariah and Elizabeth was below Mount Orah in Ein Karem, the 'Gracious Spring'. This is the spring that according to medieval tradition appeared at the meeting-place of Mary with Elizabeth, and it gives its name to the town today.

The birth stories

According to the Gospels of Matthew and Luke, Jesus was born in Bethlehem before the death of Herod the Great (4 BC) but probably not more than three years earlier. The birth stories have been described as 'too manifestly legendary in character to contain any reliable data' and there is a division of opinion as to whether these stories are contradictory or complementary, perhaps as a result of the lapse in time before their recording.

Luke alone relates the promise of the birth of Jesus's cousin, John the Baptist, the annunciation by the Angel Gabriel to Mary in Nazareth of the birth of Jesus, followed by the visitation by Mary to her cousin Elizabeth in Judea, and the birth of John the Baptist. These stories are beautifully told either from oral tradition in the Greek style, or possibly from an Aramaic document, which would account for their Hebrew phraseology translated into Greek.

Both Matthew and Luke record the birth of Jesus in Bethlehem but give different reasons for doing so. Luke

says that the original home of Mary and Joseph was at Nazareth in Galilee, and that they came to Bethlehem in response to the demands of a Roman census because Joseph was of David's family and therefore had to report to the City of David. Luke describes the visit of the shepherds, the circumcision on the eighth day, and the presentation after forty days, followed by their return home to Nazareth. Matthew, however, does not mention Nazareth until their return from Egypt to settle there for the first time. Matthew seems to imply that Joseph and Mary already lived in Bethlehem; he describes the visit of the wise men taking place in their 'house'. 'When they saw the star, they rejoiced exceedingly with great joy; and going into the house they saw the child with Mary his mother, and they fell down and worshipped him. Then, opening their treasures, they offered him gifts, gold and frankincense and myrrh. . . . Now when they had departed, behold, an angel of the Lord appeared to Joseph in a dream. . . . And he rose and took the child and his mother by night, and departed to Egypt. . . . But when Herod died, behold, an angel of the Lord appeared in a dream to Joseph in Egypt, saying, "Rise, take the child and his mother, and go to the land of Israel, for those who sought the child's life are dead."' 'And he went and dwelt in a city called Nazareth.' (Matt. 2:10, 11, 13, 14, 19, 20, 23)

There are some who consider that the tradition of the birth of Jesus in Bethlehem grew out of the need for credentials to prove his Messiahship and that he was more likely to have been born in Nazareth. 'Would the Christ be from Galilee? Does not scripture say that the Christ must be descended from David and come from the town of Bethlehem?'

Certainly, the Bethlehem tradition very soon crystallized within the early Church. Justin Martyr of Nablus and Rome wrote in AD 155: 'Should anyone desire other proof for the birth of Jesus in Bethlehem, according to Micah's prophecy and the history described by the disciples in the Gospels, let him consider that in harmony with the gospel story of his birth, a cave is shown in Bethlehem where he was born and a manger in the cave where he lay wrapped in swaddling clothes.' So, too, the early apocryphal *Protoevangelium* of James referred to the cave. At the close of the 3rd century Eusebius, bishop of Caesarea, writes: 'The inhabitants of the place bear witness of the story that has come down to them from their fathers, and they confirm the truth of it and point out the cave in which the Virgin brought forth and laid her child.' The first Church of the Nativity was built over this cave on the initiative of the Empress Helena, mother of the Emperor Constantine, in 325. From then onwards, there is no real question

The Nativity of the Child Jesus, by Giotto, from the lower Church of St Francis at Assisi.

Madonna and child, surrounded by apostles, saints and angels, by the Sienese painter Duccio (c. 1255/60-1378/9).

of the site having been lost. There is a continuous chain of evidence from the building of the first church to the present day.

The purification and presentation

As Mary and Joseph had fulfilled the Law of Moses by the circumcision and naming of the child Jesus on the eighth day, so Mary, in dutiful patience and obedience, fulfilled the forty days of her purification, before coming up to Jerusalem to make her thanksgiving. 'And when the time came for their purification according to the law of Moses, they brought him up to Jerusalem to present him to the Lord (as it is written in the law of the Lord, "Every male that opens the womb shall be called holy to the Lord") and to offer a sacrifice according to what is said in the law of the Lord, "a pair of turtledoves, or two young pigeons."' (Luke 2:22-24)

The first-born son of every Jewish family had to be presented within the Temple at Jerusalem forty days after birth. In pagan times, the first son was sacrificed to the tribal god, as the first-fruit of the family. Now, the Mosaic Law had altered this primitive custom by demanding the offering of five shekels, in order to 'redeem' or buy back the child from God, to whom his life was owed.

So it was that the parents of Jesus took him up to Jerusalem to present him to the Lord, as is demanded in the Book of Exodus (13:2): 'Every first-born male must be consecrated to the Lord'. Mary and Joseph took with them the poor man's offering demanded in the Book of Leviticus (5:7) at purification: 'a pair of turtledoves or two young pigeons'.

On this occasion, an upright and devout Jew called Simeon who looked forward to the deliverance of Israel met them in the Temple. He had been shown that he would not die without seeing 'the anointed one of God'. Taking the child Jesus in his arms, he blessed God, saying, 'Lord, now lettest thou thy servant depart in peace, according to thy word, for mine eyes have seen thy salvation which thou hast prepared in

Gold coin of the Empress Helena, mother of Constantine the Great, who in AD 325 built the first Church of the Nativity at Bethlehem.

the presence of all peoples, a light for revelation to the Gentiles, and for glory to thy people Israel.' (Luke 2:29-32)

As Simeon gave the child Jesus back into the arms of his mother and blessed the parents, he uttered the rather enigmatic prophecy, 'Behold, this child is set for the fall and rising of many in Israel, and for a sign that is spoken against (and a sword will pierce through your own soul also), that thoughts out of many hearts may be revealed.' (Luke 2:34-35) This has generally been taken to refer to the anguish caused to Mary the mother of Jesus at his crucifixion.

The visit to Jerusalem

When her son was twelve years old and ready to be initiated as a 'Son of the Law', Mary and Joseph took him up to Jerusalem for the feast of Passover. 'And when the feast was ended, as they were returning, the boy Jesus stayed behind in Jerusalem. His parents did not know it, but supposing him to be in the company they went a day's journey, and they sought him among their kinsfolk and acquaintances; and when they did not find him, they returned to Jerusalem, seeking him. After three days they found him in the temple, sitting among the teachers, listening to them and asking them questions; and all who heard him were amazed at his understanding and his answers. And when they saw him they were astonished; and his mother said to him, "Son, why have you treated us so? Behold, your father and I have been looking for you anxiously." And he said to them, "How is it that you sought me? Did you not know that I must be in my Father's house?" And they did not understand the saying which he spoke to them. And he went down with them and came to Nazareth, and was obedient to them; and his mother

kept all these things in her heart.' (Luke 2:43-51)

His reply did not hurt her so much as perplex her. She did not understand, but once again, she took it to her heart. Over and over again, Mary was to feel she had lost her son, in the Temple, in his crowded Galilean ministry, on the cross, even perhaps after the ascension, and there were times when she simply could not reach or understand him. Such humbling grief, loss, and love are well expressed in Michelangelo's *Pietà* in St Peter's, Rome.

Mary's home and family

Nazareth, the market-town of southern Galilee, was also a religious centre, and surrounded by scenery recalling the Old Testament judges, prophets, and kings. It overlooked the 'Way of the Sea', one of the main trade-routes between Damascus and Egypt. Here, caravans of silks and spices passed camels laden with grain and fish. Here, the rough and rustic Galilean peasant mingled with the merchants and travellers of the east in a truly cosmopolitan community. The living-conditions of the Holy Family in this hillside town of Nazareth are best illustrated by the so-called 'Workshop of St Joseph', a Franciscan church built on the site of a Byzantine church, whose baptistry and cave-crypts are still to be seen.

Here would have been the home of the Holy Family: a single-roomed cottage used as a workshop by day and as a bedroom by night. Up above on the flat roof, a booth of green branches would have given shade or shelter on summer evenings. Underneath, in a cave-basement, formed between the limestone strata of the rising hillside, was the living-room. Here, in the centre of the cave, a flat raised surface provided the low table. Round this, reclining or squatting on the floor, the

The flight into Egypt, with the massacre of the Innocents on the left and the presentation in the Temple on the right: relief from Moissac, France, early 12th century.

family may have eaten its simple meals. In the centre of the wall was a small niche, once blackened by the oil lamp for which it was designed. In the floor were the round openings down into the grain silos, carved out of the rock below floor-level. Above each silo, carved in the cave wall, are still the staples through which the rope passed to lower a basket or bucket into the silo below.

The exact composition of the family that occupied such accommodation has been a matter either of doubt or of dogma among Christians.

When Jesus returned to Nazareth in the course of his public ministry and spoke in their synagogue, the congregation recognized him as the 'carpenter's son' and claimed to know his family, naming four brothers and mentioning his sisters. Luke in the birth stories refers to Jesus as 'Mary's first-born' (2:7). Some of the Fathers of the Church, wishing to uphold the perpetual virginity of Mary the mother of Jesus, have suggested that the normal Greek words used for 'brothers' and 'sisters' could be extended to include 'cousins'. Oriental customs can be quoted to support this. Other Christians, however, have seen a purpose in the selection of the Greek words used.

Certainly, the Catholic and Orthodox attitude to Mary, as a symbol of human sanctity and purity, has some roots in the mentality of religious people in the Near East – when the books of the New Testament were written. This attitude is not simply and solely an import from the Greek or European world.

The great majority of Christians, however, believe that Jesus was the only son of Mary. This view is perhaps supported by three pieces of evidence in the New Testament: (1) Luke 1:34: If Mary is going to have children by her husband, why is she astonished at being told that she will have a son? The dialogue is written, in its Greek form, by Luke; but it is written on the assumption that Mary and Joseph are known to have had no children. (2) John 19:25-27: Mary is placed in the charge of the beloved disciple, on the assumption that she is a widow without children other than Jesus. (3) John 19:25 read with Matthew 27:56, Mark 15:40 and Luke 24:10: James the younger and Joses are sons of Clopas and of Mary the sister of Mary the mother of Jesus. But James and Joses are among the 'brothers' of Jesus in Mark 6. The *Protoevangelium* of James, supposed to be written about AD 150, makes James the son of Joseph by a wife who died before he was betrothed to Mary. The theological importance of Jesus having 'brothers and sisters' is not affected by their exact relationship to him.

Mark, no doubt followed by Matthew and Luke, describes Jesus teaching at Capernaum and hearing that his mother and brothers have arrived and are asking for him. He replied, 'Who are my mother and my brothers?' And looking round at those sitting in a circle about him, he said, 'Here are my mother and my brothers! Whoever does the will of God is my brother, and sister, and mother.' (Mark 3:33-35) John describes how, at the feast of Tabernacles when the Jews were out to kill Jesus and he had to remain in Galilee, his brothers failed to understand his purpose and message – saying to him, '"Leave here and go to Judea, that your disciples may see the works you are doing. For no man works in secret if he seeks to be known openly. If you do these things, show yourself to the world." For even his brothers did not believe in him.' (John 7:3-5) Luke, however, relates how Mary the mother of Jesus 'with his brothers' remained loyal in their prayers along with the apostles in Jerusalem, following the ascension of Jesus.

The miracle at Cana

This is the first of the seven signs or miracles upon which the writer of the Fourth Gospel allegorizes and extemporizes to compare the new gospel of Jesus with the dispensation of the Old Testament. Although the historical reliability of the events and conversations within the story may be questioned, somewhere behind John's account there was probably an actual historical incident involving Jesus and his mother Mary at a wedding. In any case, as a 1st-century reconstruction or illustration of the relationship between mother and son, it is important.

'On the third day there was a marriage at Cana in Galilee, and the mother of Jesus was there; Jesus also was invited to the marriage, with his disciples.' (John 2:1, 2) Mary was already at the wedding, perhaps in some position of responsibility, when Jesus and six of his friends turned up, no doubt straining the planned provision of food and drink. She was quick to draw his attention to the fact, but he had already noticed it.

'When the wine failed, the mother of Jesus said to him, "They have no wine." And Jesus said to her, "O woman, what have you to do with me? My hour is not yet come."' (John 2:3, 4) His answer is not rude, but in the Greek is perfectly respectful and can be even tender. He used the same word to her from the cross: 'Woman, behold thy son.' So, too, his seeming refusal includes an implicit understanding and assurance: 'It is all right. It is not my time yet.' Mary at once understood and knew that he would do what might be needed.

'His mother said to the servants, "Do whatever he tells you".' (John 2:5) Seeing the large water-pots which supplied water for both washing up and toilet facilities, Jesus said to the servants, 'Fill the jars with water.' 'Now draw some out, and take it to the steward of the feast.' When the water reached the tables, it had become wine; so the bride's family was saved from disgrace and Mary's trust was justified. There were to be many times during his intense, itinerant ministry when her confidence in him would be sorely strained. She was not likely to grasp the full purport of his life and work perhaps until after his crucifixion and resurrection.

At the cross of Jesus

Of the four evangelists, only John mentions Mary at the crucifixion. Certainly she must have shared Jesus's disgrace and degradation, his pain and thirst. Her anguish was part of the tragedy and must have contributed to the sufferings of her son. Consequently he did not want her to see the agony of death itself, so he commended her to the care of the beloved disciple. 'But standing by the cross of Jesus were his mother, and his mother's sister, Mary the wife of Clopas, and Mary Magdalene. When Jesus saw his mother, and the disciple whom he loved standing near, he said to his mother, "Woman, behold, your son!" Then he said to

right Jesus meeting his mother Mary on the way to Calvary, the Fourth Station of the Cross: early 15th-century French manuscript illumination.

below The *Avignon Pietà* (*c.* 1450). Mary mourns over the broken body of Jesus.

Mary, mother of Jesus

Mary, mother of Jesus

the disciple, "Behold, your mother!" And from that hour the disciple took her to his own home.' (John 19: 25-27)

If, as the story tells us, she went with that disciple to his own home and left the scene of crucifixion, she would have been spared the memory of the end and she would have spared him the added anguish of knowing that she was there watching his final agony. At this moment, if not many times before, the prophecy of the old priest Simeon at the presentation in the Temple was fulfilled: 'A sword shall pierce thine own soul.' And inevitably it was her own son who held the sword.

Mary in later life

There are two clearly contrary theories or traditions as to where Mary lived her last years. One is that she remained in Jerusalem to live in the house of John Bar-Zebedee, traditionally on Mount Zion. The other is that she accompanied John on a journey to Ephesus, where she lived to the end of her life. Both theories are supported by local tradition.

In Jerusalem, Mary is venerated by Christians and Muslims and respected by Jews. The eastern gate into the Old City is called in Arabic the *Bab Sit Miriam*, the 'Gate of the Lady Mary'. The area inside and outside that part of the city has long been associated with Mary.

East of the viaduct on which the Jericho road crosses the Kidron is an ancient church, now almost buried by the accumulation of centuries of rubble in the bottom of the ravine. A tradition records how the body of Mary, the mother of Jesus, was brought here from the house of St John on Mount Zion for burial. An extension of this same tradition records how from here she was carried bodily into heaven, three days after her burial. As in the case of the Holy Sepulchre, her rock tomb was isolated and left standing within a basilica, built about the year 440. It is perhaps this basilica that is to be seen on the Madeba mosaic, outside the eastern wall, in the Kidron Valley.

The Church in the Byzantine Empire, including Ephesus, seems to have accepted this tradition before 787 and Ephesus as the place of Mary's burial has very little traditional support. The Church of the Tomb of Mary is an integral part of Gethsemane. It was used by Christians of many different nations and rites in the 15th, 16th and 17th centuries, and there is a Muslim *mihrab* in the building, showing the direction of Mecca. This is in honour of Mary, but also because of the Islamic tradition that Jesus was taken up into heaven from Gethsemane, his arrest, suffering, trial and death being illusionary. The building was, for some time before 1757, under Latin control, and Latins at

left The *Pietà* by Michelangelo, in St Peter's Rome, *c.* 1501.

top The gate on the east side of the Old City of Jerusalem, called by the Arabs the 'Gate of the Lady Mary'.
centre The Crusader porch of the Church of the Tomb of Mary, within the Kidron ravine, near Gethsemane.
bottom Candles on the stairs leading down to the traditional tomb of Mary.

1st-century limestone ossuary inscribed in Hebrew with the names of 'Miriam' and 'Joanna'.

various times before 1757 used the tomb itself as an altar. The Eastern communities, before 1757, had the use of various altars in the building. After 1757 the building came under the joint control of the Greek Orthodox and Armenian Patriarchates and the tomb is used as an altar, daily, by both these communities. The Copts and the Syrian Orthodox officiate on altars in the building regularly; but these altars are in the possession of the Armenians. It is the Latins on the other hand who hold the Cave of the Agony, just outside the door of the church.

From Byzantine times, a large church on the Western Hill, called 'Christian Zion', was said to cover several sites. These included the Upper Room and place of feet-washing, later to become the headquarters and first synagogue of the Christian community, the house of John, and later also the place of the supposed 'falling asleep' of Mary.

The history of the Zion Church is hard to unravel. Bishop Epiphanius, a native of Palestine in the 4th century, referring to documents of the 2nd century, wrote: 'Hadrian . . . found the whole city razed to the ground and the Temple of God destroyed and trodden underfoot. There were only a few houses standing and the House of God, a little building in the place where the disciples on their return from the Mount of Olives, after the Saviour's ascension, assembled in the Upper Room'. It was the 'little building', mentioned by Epiphanius and restored by Bishop Maximus, that was transformed into the great basilica called 'Holy Zion' by Archbishop John early in the 5th century. Burned down by the Persians in 614, the 'mother of all churches' was restored by Modestus, the Christian patriarch of Jerusalem, 20 years later. We know also that the

patriarchs of the 7th century venerated within the same church a stone, on which tradition related that the mother of Jesus 'fell asleep'.

In 685, Bishop Arculf made a drawing or plan of the church on a wax tablet, showing in this one building, facing east, the cenacle or supper-room on the southeast side (once within the house of St Mark) and the rock of the dormition on the north-west side (once within the house of St John). This accords exactly with the location of the cenacle and the dormition shrines today. The Crusaders built, over the remains of the earlier church, a large church with three aisles and dedicated it to 'St Mary of Mount Zion'.

Today a great modern church and the Benedictine Monastery of the Dormition stand on part of this traditional site, while remains of a shrine of the cenacle or room of the Last Supper are nearby, on top of the shrine of the 'Tomb of David'.

The Ephesian theory is that, following the early persecutions, the Diaspora of Hellenistic Christians, and Peter's departure from Jerusalem, John took Mary the mother of Jesus to Anatolia, on the west coast of Asia Minor. Paul's failure to mention John or Mary's presence in Ephesus is sometimes put forward as an objection to this theory, but it must be pointed out that he also made no mention of Peter's mission to Rome, although Peter died there before Paul.

In the 5th century, Pope Celestine I referred to Ephesus as the home of Mary the mother of Jesus and of John. Hippolytus of Thebes in the 7th century mentioned that Mary had lived for eleven years at Ephesus before her death. This tradition survived the Muslim occupation of Ephesus in 1090 and thrived among the scattered Christian community in surrounding villages. Since the end of the last century, a small shrine in the Byzantine style, some miles to the south of the ruins of Ephesus, has been a place of Latin pilgrimage and devotion, as symbolizing a home of Mary in Ephesus. The preponderance of scholarly opinion and archaeological evidence supports the 3rd-century tradition of Mary's life and death in Jerusalem, rather than in Ephesus.

The gentle saint

Homage, but not worship, is rightly accorded to the mother of Jesus. She was the willing and obedient instrument of the purpose of God. She made a home for God, in the person of Jesus, first within her own body and then in the cottage at Nazareth. She carried him and gave him birth. She fed, cleaned, and clothed him over his helpless years. She cared for and cultivated his character through a formative decade of years. Under her influence he 'increased in wisdom and in stature, and in favour with God and man'. (Luke 2:52)

Unlike some other members of his family, Mary maintained her love and confidence in him, under seemingly impossible strains. She was found among the twelve at Pentecost, a totally reconciled and respon-

sible leader within his Church, dedicated to continue his work.

She never dominated him, but enabled him to be himself, even though there were times when she felt 'He is beside himself' (Mark 3:21). Though constantly puzzled and driven to ponder and treasure up her problems in her own heart, she never thwarted his divine progress. Though at times he appeared to go his own way, yet she maintained the unity of her family until the end. If Jesus's tremendous sense and experience of the loving fatherhood of God was the basic theme of all his teaching, what must his respect have been for his human mother? 'Hail Mary! full of grace, the Lord is with thee. Blessed art thou among women.'

Perhaps the last to be written about Mary the mother of Jesus is to be found in the vision of John the Divine of Ephesus. 'A woman clothed with the sun, with the moon under her feet, and on her head a crown of twelve stars; she was with child . . . and the dragon stood before the woman . . . that he might devour her child when she brought it forth. She brought forth a male child, one who is to rule all the nations with a rod of iron, but her child was caught up to God and to his

The house of the Virgin Mary at Ephesus, a shrine of Byzantine style on a traditional site of her last home with St John.

above The beach of Magdala, on the north-west shore of Galilee. Magdala was once the largest of the lakeside cities.

throne, and the woman fled into the wilderness, where she has a place prepared by God.' (Rev. 12:1-6) [Matt. 1; 2; 13:55; Mark 6:3; Luke 1:26-56; Acts 1:14]

2. Mary of Magdala The Synoptic Gospels describe Mary of Magdala as one of the women from Galilee who gave financial help and domestic service to Jesus and his disciples, and who was present at the crucifixion and burial of Jesus. The Fourth Gospel gives Mary of Magdala pride of place as the first witness of the resurrection and the risen Christ.

The lakeside town of Magdala, whose excavated ruins and water-conduits border the west shore of Galilee north of Tiberias, is approximately marked by its successor, Megdel or Magdal. It was the largest of some ten sizeable towns round the lake in the time of Jesus.

The first three Gospels give little evidence of Mary's

left Russian icon of Mary as Queen of Heaven, surrounded by scenes of miracles attributed to her influence.

character. Only Luke comments that 'seven demons had gone out' of her, but there is no evidence that Jesus had exorcized her and she was probably an epileptic, for epilepsy was commonly attributed to possession by evil spirits. This reference in Luke's Gospel immediately follows the story of a sinful woman who anointed the feet of Jesus during a meal at the house of Simon the Pharisee. The tradition of the Church has from early times identified Mary of Magdala with the woman living an immoral life in the city. Rightly or wrongly, Mary has become for all Christians the type of passionate penitent.

The story of Simon the Pharisee recorded by Luke has many distinctive features. The scene is set in Galilee, not Bethany. The woman is locally notorious, with a bad name in the town. She comes purposefully to make an act of penitence to Jesus: 'and standing behind him at his feet, weeping, she began to wet his feet with her tears, and wiped them with the hair of her head, and kissed his feet, and anointed them with the ointment'. (Luke 7:38)

Simon the Pharisee condescendingly looks on, assuming that a prophet like this rabbi Jesus would at least have the insight to perceive the sort of woman she was and therefore drive her away. When both the woman herself and Simon have waited long enough for their true motives to be tested, Jesus, reading their minds, says to the Pharisee, '"Simon, I have something to say to you." And he answered, "What is it, Teacher?" "A certain creditor had two debtors; one owed five hundred denarii, and the other fifty. When they could not pay, he forgave them both. Now which of them will love him more?" Simon answered, "The one, I suppose, to whom he forgave more." And he said, "You have judged rightly."' (Luke 7:40-43) Then turning to the woman whose uninhibited penitence and emotional abandon contrasted clearly with the veiled criticism and discourteous condescension of the Pharisee, Jesus said, '"Do you see this woman? I entered your house, you gave me no water for my feet, but she has wet my feet with her tears, and wiped them with her hair. You gave me no kiss, but from the time I came in she has not ceased to kiss my feet. You did not anoint my head with oil, but she has anointed my feet with ointment. Therefore I tell you, her sins, which are many, are forgiven, for she loved much; but he who is forgiven little, loves little." And he said to her, "Your sins are forgiven . . . your faith has saved you; go in peace."' (Luke 7:44-50)

Luke is not slow to perceive and to compare the passion of penitence and the coldness of reason. With his deep sensitivity, Luke well knows that the basis of all forgiveness is love, and that the spring of love is often just this sense of forgiveness.

Again, and not surprisingly perhaps, Mary of Magdala has also been identified with Mary of Bethany, the sister of Martha and Lazarus. The Fourth Gospel describes Jesus at supper in the household at Bethany during the Passover week, following the raising of Lazarus. 'There they made him a supper; Martha served, and Lazarus was one of those at table with him. Mary took a pound of costly ointment of pure nard and anointed the feet of Jesus and wiped his feet with her hair; and the house was filled with the fragrance of the ointment.' (John 12:2, 3) Certainly these two Marys were very similar in temperament.

Yet again, Mary of Magdala has been identified with the woman with the alabaster cruse who anointed Jesus in the house of Simon the Leper at Bethany, as recorded in Mark's and copied in Matthew's Gospel. All these anointings have their variations on the theme of the reformed sinner or passionate penitent, yet not

Mary of Magdala: wooden statue by Donatello (1386-1466). She is traditionally portrayed with her hair reaching to her knees.

one of them can be linked with the slightest degree of certainty with Mary of Magdala. They may indeed refer to different women on different occasions. Whereas the Western Church, in the feast of Mary of Magdala on 22 July, makes no distinction between the three women, the Eastern Church regards each as a different person.

Both Mark and Matthew describe her, together with Mary the mother of James and Joses, and with Salome, 'looking on from afar' at the crucifixion, then attending the entombment in the rock-hewn sepulchre belonging to Joseph of Arimathea. All three Synoptic Gospels mention the two Marys arriving at the tomb early on the Easter morning. 'And when the sabbath was past, Mary Magdalene, and Mary the mother of James, and Salome, bought spices, so that they might go and anoint him. And very early on the first day of the week they went to the tomb when the sun had risen. And they were saying to one another, "Who will roll away the stone for us from the door of the tomb?" And looking up, they saw that the stone was rolled back; for it was very large. And entering the tomb, they saw a young man sitting on the right side, dressed in a white robe; and they were amazed. And he said to them, "Do not be amazed; you seek Jesus of Nazareth, who was crucified. He has risen, he is not here; see the place where they laid him. But go, tell his disciples and Peter that he is going before you to Galilee; there you will see him, as he told you." And they went out and fled from the tomb; for trembling and astonishment had come upon them; and they said nothing to any one, for they were afraid.' (Mark 16:1-8)

Only John, however, tells the story of Mary's meeting with the risen Jesus in the garden. John does not mention the other women, but only Mary of Magdala's dawn visit to the empty tomb, and her summoning of Peter and John. They confirmed her story and went home. 'But Mary stood weeping outside the tomb, and as she wept she stooped to look into the tomb; and she saw two angels in white, sitting where the body of Jesus had lain, one at the head and one at the feet. They said to her, "Woman, why are you weeping?" She said to them, "Because they have taken away my Lord, and I do not know where they have laid him." Saying this, she turned round and saw Jesus standing, but she did not know that it was Jesus. Jesus said to her, "Woman, why are you weeping? Whom do you seek?" Supposing him to be the gardener, she said to him, "Sir, if you have carried him away, tell me where you have laid him, and I will take him away." Jesus said to her, "Mary." She turned and said to him in Hebrew, "*Rabboni!*" (which means Teacher). Jesus said to her, "Do not hold me, for I have not yet ascended to the Father; but go to my brethren and say to them, I am ascending to my Father and your Father, to my God

and your God." Mary Magdalene went and said to the disciples, "I have seen the Lord"; and she told them that he had said these things to her.' (John 20:11-18)

Although Mary may not in fact have been the woman who anointed Jesus in a passion of penitence, or from a realization of forgiveness, yet John's story of her meeting with Jesus tends to confirm this aspect of her character. She passes from the depths of despair in her loss of her master to the height of ecstasy in her recognition of his risen presence. Jesus has affectionately to rebuke her with words which mean 'Stop clinging to me!' She was clearly as uninhibited and reckless in her devotion to Jesus as any of the women in the 'anointing' stories.

Among the legends that surround the person of Mary of Magdala, two are of particular interest. According to an early tradition within the Greek Orthodox Church, she accompanied John to Ephesus, where she died and her body was taken later to Constantinople. A groundless 9th-century tradition links her with the journey of Martha and Lazarus by sea to the south of France, where in the Middle Ages her tomb was claimed to be at Aix-en-Provence. [Matt. 27:56-61; 28:1; Mark 15:40-47; 16:1-9; Luke 8:2; 24:10; John 19:25; 20:1-18]

3. Mary, mother of James and Joses This Mary was the constant companion of Mary of Magdala, in the first three Gospels being linked with Mary Magdalene both in Galilee and in Jerusalem.

Mary, the mother of James the younger and of Joses, was one of the women who gave Jesus and his group of disciples both financial assistance and domestic care, during their arduous itinerant ministry. With them also,

Alabaster cruse, with wide rim and small lug handles, 586-330 B.C, reminiscent of the vase of ointment broken by the penitent sinner.

The Three Marys at the Open Sepulchre, by Hubert and Jan Van Eyck (1422-41). Mary the mother of Jesus, Mary of Magdala and Mary the mother of James and Joses are greeted by the angel.

she was a witness at the crucifixion and entombment of Jesus; she shared with them the surprise and shock of finding the stone rolled away from the tomb on the first day of the week. 'And when the sabbath was past, Mary Magdalene, and Mary the mother of James, and Salome, bought spices, so that they might go and anoint him. And very early on the first day of the week they went to the tomb when the sun had risen. And they were saying to one another, "Who will roll away the stone for us from the door of the tomb?" And looking up, they saw that the stone was rolled back, for it was very large. And entering the tomb, they saw a young man sitting on the right side, dressed in a white robe; and they were amazed.' (Mark 16:1-5) She heard the message of the 'young man' within the tomb: 'And he said to them, "Do not be amazed; you seek Jesus of Nazareth, who was crucified. He has risen, he is not

here; see the place where they laid him. But go, tell his disciples and Peter that he is going before you to Galilee; there you will see him, as he told you."' (Mark 16:6, 7) The reaction of the women is variously reported, Mark saying that they were too frightened to tell anyone, Matthew recording their meeting with Jesus on their way home, Luke including their delivery of the message to the apostles, who simply did not believe them! 'And they remembered his words, and returning from the tomb they told all this to the eleven and to all the rest. Now it was Mary Magdalene and Joanna and Mary the mother of James and the other women with them who told this to the apostles; but these words

right Jesus in the house of Martha and Mary, by Jan Vermeer, *c.* 1655. Jesus commends 'the best part' chosen by Mary, that of listening.

290

Mary, mother of James and Joses

seemed to them an idle tale, and they did not believe them.' (Luke 24:8-11)

The Fourth Gospel mentions Mary of Magdala as the only woman visiting the tomb on the Easter morning, but specifically mentions among the watchers by the cross of Jesus 'his mother, and his mother's sister, Mary the wife of Clopas, and Mary Magdalene'. If the characters in this account can be identified with those at the crucifixion as recorded in the Synoptic Gospels, then this 'Mary, the mother of James and Joses' was also the wife of Clopas. [Matt. 27:56; 28:1; Mark 15:40, 47; 16:1; Luke 24:10; John 19:25; 20:1]

4. Mary, the wife of Clopas This Mary is only mentioned in the Fourth Gospel, as present at the crucifixion of Jesus, together with his mother and her sister and Mary of Magdala. The equivalent person mentioned in the Synoptic Gospels is Mary, the mother of James. If these two characters are identical, then this Mary and her husband Clopas were the parents of James the Younger and of Joses. see MARY 3. [Matt. 27:56; 28:1; Mark 15:40, 47; 16:1, 8; Luke 24:10; John 19:25]

5. Mary of Bethany One of two sisters of Lazarus of Bethany, intimate friends of Jesus, whose 'home from home' was their house whenever he came up to Jerusalem, particularly for the Passover festival.

Only Luke and John mention the sisters by name, but both Gospels give the same impression of their respective characters as may be seen in this very perceptive and sensitive passage from the pen of Luke, 'the beloved physician'. 'Now as they went on their way, he entered a village; and a woman named Martha received him into her house. And she had a sister called Mary, who sat at the Lord's feet and listened to his teaching. But Martha was distracted with much serving; and she went to him and said, "Lord, do you not care that my sister has left me to serve alone? Tell her then to help me." But the Lord answered her, "Martha, Martha, you are anxious and troubled about many things; one thing is needful. Mary has chosen the good portion, which shall not be taken away from her."' (Luke 10:38-42) The name of Martha still epitomizes the practical and efficient but over-busy and intolerant house-keeper, as opposed to that of Mary the contemplative who has chosen the better part.

For the significance of the household of Mary, Martha, and Lazarus to the story of the Passion of Jesus and for the story of the raising of Lazarus see LAZARUS 2.

Later in the week following the raising of Lazarus, John describes Mary anointing the feet of Jesus with oil at a supper at which Martha served and Lazarus was at table. John's account appears to be a conflation of Mark's story of the anointing at the house of Simon the Leper, in Bethany, and Luke's story of the anointing at the house of Simon the Pharisee, in Galilee. Tradition

has linked Mary of Magdala with the woman 'with a poor reputation in the city' in Luke's story, at the house of Simon the Pharisee. [Luke 10:38-42; John 11:1-44; 12:1-8]

6. Mary, mother of John Mark This Mary was the owner of the house which became the first Christian synagogue, or meeting-place, in Jerusalem. Very probably tradition is right in identifying the Upper Room as the scene of both the Last Supper and the first meeting of the apostles of Jesus, following the ascension. The instructions of Jesus on Maundy Thursday clearly indicate a sizeable and suitable room at a secret rendezvous. 'And he sent two disciples, and said to them, "Go into the city, and a man carrying a jar of water will meet you; follow him, and wherever he enters, say to the householder, 'The Teacher says, Where is my guest-room, where I am to eat the passover with my disciples?' And he will show you a large upper room furnished and ready; there prepare for us." And the disciples set out and went to the city, and found it as he had told them; and they prepared the passover.' (Mark 14:13-16) Again, after the ascension 'they returned to Jerusalem from the mount called Olivet, which is near Jerusalem, a sabbath day's journey away; and when they had entered, they went up to the upper room, where they were staying. . . . All these with one accord devoted themselves to prayer, together with the women and Mary the mother of Jesus, and with his brothers.' (Acts 1:12-14)

It is not surprising, therefore, that Peter, after his escape from prison, should make his way at once to this secret headquarters of the early Church. 'He went to the house of Mary, the mother of John whose other name was Mark, where many were gathered together and were praying. And when he knocked at the door of the gateway, a maid named Rhoda came to answer.' (Acts 12:12, 13) Peter's first thought would have been to report to James, the leader of the Judeo-Christian community, and he seems to have expected to find James at Mary's house. She seems to have been a widow of some substance, for the house was in her name and she had servants. Again, Peter's voice was well known to the girl Rhoda, so he was probably a frequent caller.

If the Apostle Barnabas was an uncle or cousin to John Mark, then this Mary of Jerusalem may have been a sister or aunt to Barnabas. As he was a Cypriot Jew and appointed leader of the early Church in Antioch, Mary would probably have had connections far beyond the Jerusalem Church and would have been known at least by name in Syria and Cyprus.

One traditional site of the house of Mary, the mother of John Mark, on the Western Hill of Jerusalem within the Old City walls, is today occupied by the Syrian Orthodox Bishopric headquarters, church and convent. The attraction of this church for Christian pilgrims is

Head of an elderly
woman of the
1st century A.D.

that its Syrian liturgy is a form of Aramaic, the language spoken by Jesus and his disciples.

According to the strongest tradition, however, the cenacle or supper-room was on the very top of this Western Hill and in the immediate vicinity of the Tomb of David. Subsequent Christian monuments and churches in this area are somewhat confusingly referred to, from Byzantine times onwards, as being on 'Mount Zion'. Christians came to regard their 4th-century 'Zion Church' as the 'mother of all churches', because they cherished on this site memories of the Last Supper, the washing of the feet, the resurrection appearances of Jesus to his followers, and the outpouring of his spirit at Pentecost. Bishop Epiphanius, a native of Palestine in the 4th century, and referring to documents of the 2nd century, wrote: 'Hadrian ... found the whole city razed to the ground and the Temple of God destroyed and trodden underfoot. There were only a few houses standing and the House of God, a little building in the place where the disciples on their return from the Mount of Olives, after the Saviour's Ascension,

assembled in the Upper Room. This [church] was built in the part of Zion which had escaped destruction, together with some buildings round about and seven synagogues that stood alone on Zion like cottages, one of which remained standing down to the time of . . . the Emperor Constantine.'

St Cyril of Jerusalem, in 348, refers to the 'Upper Church of the Apostles where the Holy Spirit descended upon them'. The Spanish nun Aetheria, in 385, identified the site as the scene of both the Easter appearances of Jesus and of the events at Pentecost. She described the special services held in this church on these great festivals. The pilgrim Theodosius, in 530, adds the fact that the Upper Room was in the house of Mark the Evangelist. This was the first synagogue of the Church and their headquarters in Jerusalem. [Acts 12:12]

7. Mary, member of the Christian Church at Rome This Mary was mentioned early in Paul's list of greetings and picked for particular comment, along with Persis, as a hard worker within the Christian community at Rome. [Rom. 16:6]

293

MATTHEW (Gk. from Heb. 'gift of God') Matthew was the tax-collector who was called by Jesus from his desk at the frontier-town of Capernaum. He became one of the twelve apostles and was, by tradition, the author of the First Gospel, written for Jews by a Jew to present Jesus as the Messiah. Very little about Matthew the man can be discovered from the New Testament, unless he is the author of the First Gospel. Apart from his call, all other references to Matthew are found only within lists of apostles. The Gospel attributed to Matthew is in fact carefully compiled from at least three sources. Matthew the tax-collector may have been responsible for one source, or for their skilful collation.

The calling of Matthew

The call of Matthew is related in each of the first three Gospels, though the name given him in Mark and Luke is 'Levi'. As Simon was called Peter, 'the Rock', and Thomas called Didymus, 'the Twin', so probably Levi became known as Matthew, 'the gift of God'. He was called by Jesus rather later than the fishermen Peter,

above The jetties at Capernaum today, once the scene of the call of Matthew from his customs-ledger.

Andrew, James, and John, although his immediate response and following would indicate some previous acquaintance with and confidence in Jesus. Jesus's choice of Matthew was an unexpected one, for he was one of the tax-collectors or publicans, so-called from the Latin *publicani*, referring to people employed in collecting the state, or public, revenue. (*see* TAX-COLLECTORS) Perhaps by the quayside or the roadside, the shadow of Jesus fell across the customs ledger of Matthew, the publican. In the words of Matthew's Gospel, 'He said to him, "Follow me." And he rose and followed him.' (Matt. 9:9)

The Gospel story goes on to describe a supper held at

Matthew's house, attended by many publicans and others, with Jesus as the guest of honour. Luke's Gospel points out that this party was particularly for Jesus, and held at Matthew's house. At once the Pharisees and Scribes rebuked Jesus to his disciples, accusing him of eating and drinking with publicans and sinners. To which Jesus replied, 'Those who are well have no need of a physician, but those who are sick. Go and learn what this means, "I desire mercy, and not sacrifice." For I came not to call the righteous, but sinners.' (Matt. 9:12-13)

According to Papias (*c*. 60-130), bishop of Hieropolis in Asia Minor, Matthew made a collection of the sayings of Jesus in Hebrew. According to Eusebius (*c*. 260-340), bishop of Caesarea, Matthew preached to the Hebrews. Various traditions record his martyrdom – in Ethiopia, in Persia, or in Pontus on the Black Sea.

The Gospel

This is in part a manual of Christian teaching, in which Jesus the Messiah is shown to be both the fulfilment of God's purpose revealed in the Hebrew Scriptures and the Lord of the Christian Church in the New Testament. It is an account of the ministry of Jesus from the pen of a rabbi, completed in the last quarter of the 1st century. It was traditionally held to be the oldest of the four Gospels, and consequently is placed first in the New Testament. From the beginning of the 4th century it was consistently attributed to Matthew. But its contents seem to show it to be the work neither of an apostle nor of an eye-witness. The narrative of the life of Jesus in it is based on the Gospel of Mark, into

right Unfinished statue of Matthew by Michelangelo (1475-1564).
below Initial 'L' at the beginning of Matthew's Gospel, from an 11th-century Norman Bible.

which has been inserted much material, mostly about the teaching of Jesus, in five long discourses. For example, Chapters 3 and 4, being narrative largely from Mark, are followed by Chapters 5, 6, and 7 of the 'long discourse' or the Sermon on the Mount. Chapters 8 and part of 9, taken from Mark, are followed by more chapters of teaching.

The Gospel is a skilfully compiled and comprehensive work, combining at least two other written documents, of which one, containing an account of the teaching of Jesus, may be the record made by Matthew himself, and the reason behind the attribution of the whole Gospel to him. Matthew's training in accountancy and record-keeping may have been very useful to Jesus and the twelve. In this Gospel, the teaching of Jesus is carefully collected, divided according to subjects, and inserted at appropriate points in Mark's narrative. Ninety-five per cent of Mark's Gospel is included in that of Matthew. The incidents recorded by Mark are sometimes shortened in Matthew, with some loss of vividness and graphic description. Matthew consciously adjusts Mark's bluntness, for the sake of reverence and

Matthew writing his Gospel: 15th-century Moldavian manuscript illumination.

propriety, on many occasions. For example, in this Gospel, it is the disciples and not Jesus who forget to take food when they cross over the lake. Jesus did no miracles in Nazareth, according to Matthew, because of the people's lack of faith. Mark had written 'he could do no mighty work there'. Matthew does not include the terrified cry of the disciples to Jesus in the storm on the lake: 'Do you not care if we perish?'

This Gospel has certain specific points of interest with regard to the character of Jesus as the Messiah, the teacher, and the lawgiver of the Church. It was written after the controversy within the early Christian Church about the admission of Gentile Christians, resolved in the year 42 by the first Council of Jerusalem. Before that time, the Judeo-Christian Church was divided into two parties, clashing over their attitudes to the observance by the Gentiles of the Law of Moses. A 'circumcision party' held that all Christians must keep the Jewish Law and be circumcised. The other party among the Judeo-Christians considered the Law of Christ sufficient for the Gentiles. The Gospel-writers seem to reflect this division of opinion in their presentation of the Law of Moses as taught by the Pharisees, and of its interpretation and fulfilment by Jesus.

The writer of the First Gospel sought to prove that Christianity was the fulfilment of Judaism, and that Jesus's mission was primarily to the Jews, whose failure to respond to it had been followed by its extension to the Gentiles. He sought to show the teaching of Jesus to be the new Law, and the Christian Church of Jews and Gentiles to be the new Israel. There is a recurring emphasis on the fulfilment of the Old Testament in the person of Jesus, the 'son of David'. Mark often alluded to the Old Testament prophecies; Matthew used them independently of their original context in what may seem to be a somewhat artificial fashion, showing their fulfilment in Jesus. Perhaps these Messianic 'proof-texts' were part of a collection in circulation within the early Church and this collection was the work of Matthew himself, mentioned by Papias in the 2nd century.

Unlike Mark, Matthew does not say that the Messiahship of Jesus was hidden. The voice at his baptism proclaims to all, 'This is my beloved Son.' The disciples, seeing Jesus walking on the water, declare 'Truly you are the Son of God,' long before Peter confesses, 'You are the Christ.' Matthew adds to the story of Peter's confession given in Mark, the words spoken by Jesus, 'And on this rock [Peter] I will build my church,' implying that the secret of Jesus's identity and of his victory through suffering is to be enshrined in the community of his followers, the Church.

The great contribution of Matthew to the total picture of Jesus in the Gospels is his careful record of the teaching of Jesus about the principles upon which life is to be lived under the rule of God. The teaching of Jesus about these principles is carefully grouped into five discourses – a sort of Christian Pentateuch – as follows: the Sermon on the Mount (Chapters 5, 6 and 7); the Instructions to the Apostles (Chapter 10:5-42); a Collection of Parables (Chapter 13:1-52); Relationships within the Church (Chapter 18:1-35); the Discourse on the End of the World (Chapters 24 and 25). This account of the teaching of Jesus Christ was a source of guidance to the early Church; it can still be read as one continuous instruction, set within the story of the life, death and resurrection of Jesus.

The Sermon on the Mount

The Sermon on the Mount has won universal recognition as a supreme statement of the ethical duties of man. It is a statement of the Christian standard of life, but makes a general appeal to the human conscience of all men. It does not, at first sight, seem to vary from what is best in the ethics of Confucius, of the Buddha, or indeed of the Pharisees of Jesus's own day. The Sermon is not so much a detailed statement of principles as a series of illustrations of the way in which those principles work in actual living. The principles are twofold.

The first is self-renunciation: 'If any man would come after me, let him deny himself and take up his cross and follow me. For whoever would save his life will lose it, and whoever loses his life for my sake will find it.' (Matt. 16:24-25) The second is service: 'Whoever would be great among you must be your servant, and whoever would be first among you must be your slave.' (Matt. 20:26-27) Jesus offers himself as the supreme illustration: '. . . The Son of Man came not to be served but to serve, and to give his life as a ransom for many.'

The Sermon on the Mount begins with a list of spiritual qualities and the rewards that accompany them: 'Blessed are the poor in spirit, for theirs is the kingdom of heaven . . .' The task of the disciples in the world is illustrated by the metaphors of salt and light. Their true piety can be seen in *secret* giving, praying and fasting. Their trust in God's providence is to be that of the birds and the flowers. They are to go on asking from God, who loves to give to those who ask him. They are not to criticize, like a man with a log in his own eye seeing a splinter in that of his neighbour.

The 'golden rule' is given: 'Whatever you wish that men would do to you, do so to them; for this is the law and the prophets.' And the Sermon ends with a terrifyingly simple story of the man who builds his house on the rock of obedience and action, contrasted with the man who builds his house on the sands of apathy and inaction. 'And when Jesus finished these sayings, the crowds were astonished at his teaching, for

Matheus apostolus

The martyrdom of Matthew, from William Caxton's *Golden Legend*, 1493.

he taught them as one who had authority, and not as their scribes.' As Moses on Mount Sinai gave the Ten Commandments, so Jesus on the mountain in Galilee gave the new law, not commandments so much as ideals. The existence of the Law of Moses made the Tradition of the Scribes necessary, for it was only by a traditional interpretation of the Law that it could be applied to any particular day and circumstance. For instance, if keeping the Sabbath involved not working, it was necessary for tradition to define what constituted work in that day and age.

For Jesus, the Law was to be obeyed by willing assent to principles. For a system of written law, he substituted a law of the heart. 'You have heard that it was said to the men of old, "You shall not kill: and whoever kills shall be liable to judgment."' And again, 'You have heard that it was said, "You shall not commit adultery." But I say to you that every one who looks at a woman lustfully has already committed adultery with her in his heart.' The old Law sought to cure the disease of sin by treating its symptoms as seen in the outward action. Jesus tried rather to prevent sin at the

overleaf The Parable of the Unmerciful Debtor, by the Flemish painter Jan van Hermessen. This parable comes to us only from the pen of Matthew.

stage of intention, and to deal with evil in the heart before it reached the hand.

The ethical teaching of Jesus in the Sermon on the Mount is unique. Matthew's careful record and selection is invaluable, not only to the Christian but to all people of faith and for all time. As Matthew, at the beginning of his Gospel, tells the story of the wise men from the east coming to the king and saviour of mankind, so he ends with Jesus's commission to his apostles to 'Go therefore and make disciples of all nations.' [Matt. 9:9; 10:3; Mark 3:18; Luke 6:15; Acts 1:13]

MATTHIAS (Gk. from Heb. 'gift of Jehovah'). The twelfth apostle of Jesus elected to fill the gap left by the death of the traitor Judas.

In the presence of some 120 disciples of Jesus, the Apostle Peter outlined the brief ministry of Judas Iscariot among the twelve and recorded his violent death. Peter then called for the replacement of Judas from among the men who had been associated with the first disciples, from the baptism of John to the ascension of Jesus. It was important that there should be twelve apostles, to witness to the fact of the resurrection of Jesus. There had to be twelve to correspond to the twelve tribes of Israel. Indeed, in some ancient manuscripts, a tribe is assigned to each apostle. The necessary qualifications were his human witness of the resurrection and his divine selection, so two certain witnesses were proposed of which one was chosen by lot, after earnest prayer for the guidance of the Holy Spirit. This method had been used for the selection of Saul as the first king of Israel, a thousand years previously. Now, for the two candidates Justus Barsabbas and Matthias, 'They cast lots for them, and the lot fell on Matthias; and he was enrolled with the eleven apostles.'

Tradition numbers both candidates among the seventy disciples sent out two by two, during the early ministry of Jesus, but neither of them are mentioned elsewhere in the New Testament, nor is there any knowledge of their subsequent ministries. [Acts 1:23, 26]

MEDES *see* ARABIANS

MERCURY *see* HERMES

MICHAEL (Heb. 'who is like God') The greatest of the archangels and guardian of Israel. In early Hebrew thinking, angels were the agents and instruments of the will of God upon earth. They executed his will and delivered his messages. (*see* ANGEL) During their exile in Babylon (586-36 BC), the Jews were influenced by Babylonian and Persian ideas of a transcendent God

left Matthias was elected to make up the number of disciples to the symbolical figure of twelve, after the defection of Judas Iscariot. The twelve apostles, carrying their crowns, surround this 5th-century mosaic from Ravenna of the baptism of Jesus.

above 6th-century mosaic of Michael the Archangel, from the Basilica of S. Apollinare in Classe, Ravenna.

working within his creation through a host of angelic intermediaries. By the 2nd century BC, Michael and the archangels were attributed with great supernatural powers.

The Book of Daniel refers to Michael as the 'Prince', protector of God. The letter of Jude (verse 9) refers to him as the 'archangel contending with the devil' and declares that Michael 'disputed about the body of Moses'. Jude was referring to a Jewish tradition of the 'Assumption of Moses', according to which Michael, though provoked to anger by Satan who had charged that Moses being a murderer was not worthy of burial, yet did not condemn Satan but gently rebuked him. In the warlike vision of John the Divine Michael is depicted as the champion of Israel who has conquered the devil and his angels and driven them out of heaven and down to earth. 'Now war arose in heaven, Michael and his angels fighting against the dragon; and the dragon and his angels fought, but they were defeated and there was no longer any place for them in heaven. And the great dragon was thrown down, that ancient serpent, who is called the Devil and Satan, the deceiver of the whole world – he was thrown down to the earth, and his angels were thrown down with him.' (Rev. 12:7-9)

Within the Christian Church, the festival of Michaelmas Day embraces Michael and all the angels. Michael is always represented with a sword, standing over the dragon. [Jude 9; Rev. 12:7-9]

MNASON A wealthy Cypriot Jew of the Diaspora, with whom Paul and some of his party stayed on their arrival in Jerusalem, at the close of his Third Journey. Paul, with the representatives of many Christian communities in the eastern Mediterranean, planned to hand over personally to the leaders of the Church in Jerusalem the very considerable fund of money collected for the poverty-stricken congregation in the Holy City. Accommodation was arranged for them with one of the earliest Christian converts, Mnason, rather than with any of the elders of the Church, perhaps because these latter anticipated the reception that awaited Paul. [Acts 21:16]

Michael and his angels in combat with the dragon and the devils of Hell: 14th-century Tuscan manuscript illumination.

N

NARCISSUS (Gk. 'daffodil') 'Greet those in the Lord who belong to the family of Narcissus,' says Paul in his final greetings at the close of his letter to the Christian congregation in Rome.

There was in fact a certain freedman, Tiberius Claudius Narcissus, who exercised considerable authority under the Emperor Claudius, but who was put to death on the accession of Nero. The custom was that his property and slaves would pass into the hands of the emperor, though his slaves would retain the name of their previous master. This seems to have been confirmed in this case by inscriptions referring to 'Narcissiani'. It seems that the household slaves of Narcissus may indeed have been among the 'saints of Caesar's household' to whom Paul refers in his letter to the Church at Philippi. (Phil. 4:22) [Rom. 16:11]

NATHANAEL (Heb. 'God has given') The personal name of Bartholomew, one of the twelve apostles. Nathanael is mentioned by his personal name only in the Fourth Gospel, where he is shown to have been introduced to Jesus by Philip and where he is said to have come from Cana in Galilee. Under the name of Bartholomew, meaning 'son of Tolmai', he is listed among the apostles together with Philip in the Gospels of Matthew, Mark, and Luke, and also as being present at the election of a substitute apostle for the traitor Judas, in the opening chapter of Acts. The identification of Bartholomew and Nathanael has been widely accepted by biblical scholars from the 9th century to the present day.

The Fourth Gospel describes how Jesus was on the way back to Galilee from his own baptism by John the Baptist in the Jordan Valley. On his way, he passed through the village of Cana, where Nathanael lived. His friend Philip, who had himself been a disciple of John the Baptist, called in to see Nathanael and to say, 'We have found him of whom Moses in the law and also the prophets wrote, Jesus of Nazareth, the son of Joseph.' Nathanael thought of Nazareth, the next place up the road from Cana, as a rather insignificant and uncouth little town. So he asked with some scepticism, '"Can anything good come out of Nazareth?" Philip said to him, "Come and see."'

In the quaint little village of Cana, Nathanael was an earnest and sincere Jew, who was looking forward to the coming of the Messiah. It was his custom, as it was of many orthodox Jews, to sit under the family fig-tree whenever he wished to be quiet and pray.

Now it so happened that the day Philip went to bring him to Jesus, this is exactly what he had been doing. He had been reading about the patriarch Jacob and his cunning. He had been reading about the dream of the ladder and the angels going up and down between heaven and earth. Perhaps, too, he had read of Jacob wrestling with the angel and winning the name of 'Israel', which means 'who prevails with God'. At any rate, he, Nathanael, had begun to wrestle with the idea that this new teacher from Nazareth could be the long-expected Messiah, for whom Philip and he had been waiting. So he said, 'Not from Nazareth, surely?' and Philip answered, 'Come and see,' and so they went. As Nathanael approached, Jesus read his thoughts and said to him, 'Behold, an Israelite indeed, in whom is no guile!' Nathanael was absolutely stunned and said, 'How do you know me?' Jesus answered, 'Before Philip called you, when you were under the fig-tree, I

Bethel, scene of Jacob's dream of the 'ladder between heaven and earth' — the subject of Nathanael's meditation on the day of his meeting with Jesus.

saw you.' That is, 'My sympathy had reached you, before your friend broke in with the news that confirmed your thoughts and prayers'. Nathanael could only exclaim, 'Rabbi, you are the Son of God! You are the King of Israel!'

It is as though Jesus, called by the title that would be nailed to his cross, again addressed Nathanael along these lines: 'Are you believing because I saw you under the fig-tree? Is that why you believe? No, of course not! It is because of your honest wrestling with your doubts. You are a true son of Jacob. Now I promise you greater things. Jacob saw a ladder set up to heaven and the "angels of God ascending and descending on it". You will see heaven opened and the angels of God ascending and descending upon the Son of Man. Now you are looking at him of whom that ladder is just a picture. You see him who is the link between heaven and earth.'

The final reference to Nathanael in the Fourth Gospel relates that, after the resurrection of Jesus and together with six others, he was fishing in the Lake of Galilee, when the risen Jesus appeared to them. They had been out all night on the lake and returned at dawn to find Jesus standing on the beach, though they did not at first recognize him. He called out to them, '"Children, have you any fish?" They answered him, "No." He said to them, "Cast the net on the right side of the boat, and you will find some." So they cast it, and now they were not able to haul it in, for the quantity of fish.... But the other disciples came in the boat, dragging the net full of fish, for they were not far from the land, but about a hundred yards off. . . . Jesus said to them, "Come and have breakfast." Now none of the disciples dared ask him, "Who are you?" They knew it was the Lord. Jesus came and took the bread and gave it to them, and so with the fish. This was now the third time that Jesus was revealed to the disciples after he was raised from the dead.' (John 21:5, 6, 8, 12-14)

Nathanael, the orthodox Jew from Cana of Galilee, traditionally carried his apostolic witness of the resurrection of Jesus as far as India and was finally flayed alive at Albanopolis in Armenia. He is often depicted with his skin over his arm and the knife in his hand. [John 1:45-51; 21:2]

NAZARENE(S) (Gk. 'sprung from Nazareth', a patrial name applied to Jesus) Literally inhabitants of Nazareth, a town in Galilee, which was the home of Jesus and his family from his birth, traditionally at Bethlehem, until the start of his lakeside ministry, based on Capernaum. Matthew's Gospel, unlike that of Luke, makes no reference to Nazareth until the death of Herod the Great and his succession by Archelaus, ruler of Judea in 4 BC. Matthew then declares that Joseph, being warned in a dream, did not return to Bethlehem but withdrew to the district of Galilee. 'And he went and dwelt in a city called

General view of the town of Nazareth from the hilltop, looking south towards Little Hermon, rising from the plain of Esdraelon.

Nazareth, that what was spoken by the prophets might be fulfilled, "He shall be called a Nazarene".' (Matt. 2:23) The writer thus justifies the choice of Nazareth by a prophecy that is to be found nowhere in the Bible.

The town of Nazareth is not mentioned in the Old Testament, but it may be that Matthew had in mind a Hebrew phrase in the prophecies of Isaiah (9:1) and wished to show that Jesus was the *Nezer*, or 'branch', which was to spring from the stump of the fallen tree of Jesse. Naturally, however, the name 'Nazarene' was linked with the town of Nazareth.

Nazareth ranks with Jerusalem as one of the three main Christian holy cities of Palestine. Yet Nazareth's standing is very different from that of the two other towns. They were from the first marked out as Christianity's most important centres, and as such the victims of hostility towards it. Pagan temples were built over their holy places, though these had, in fact, the unintentional consequence of preserving and pinpointing their sites. Nazareth, on the other hand, was in the first centuries of Christianity strangely neglected by its friends and enemies alike. Origen, for instance, in the 3rd century lived for several years at Caesarea – only some thirty miles away – but never, it seems, took the trouble to visit Nazareth.

Thereafter, Jesus is referred to as 'of Nazareth' by friends and foes alike. The crowd tell blind Bartimaeus: 'Jesus of Nazareth is passing by.' The maid in the high priest's palace at the trial of Jesus points to Peter, saying, 'This man was with Jesus of Nazareth.' (Matt. 26:71) Peter at Pentecost declares: 'Jesus of Nazareth, a man attested to you by God with mighty works and wonders and signs.' (Acts 2:22) Healing the lame man at the Beautiful Gate of the Temple, Peter orders, 'In the name of Jesus Christ of Nazareth, walk!' (Acts 3:6) Stephen's accusers say: 'We have heard him say that this Jesus of Nazareth will destroy this place [the Temple] and will change the customs which Moses delivered to us.'

Finally, the hired prosecutor of Paul, the Roman orator Tertullus, charged Paul before Felix at Caesarea, 'For we have found this man a pestilent fellow, an agitator among all the Jews throughout the world and a ringleader of the sect of the Nazarenes.' (Acts 24:5) The new sect had early received the popular nickname of 'the Nazarenes', a term of reproach like the word 'Christians'.

Nazareth became in the years after Jesus's death a predominantly Jewish town, unlike Bethlehem which became Christian at an early date. When in 614 the Jews joined with the Persians in attacking the Christians, the Jews of Nazareth provided one of the largest contingents in that force.

Until recently it used to be thought that there were no Christians at all in Nazareth in these early years; certainly it was assumed that there was no Christian church there up to the time of Constantine, when one was built by Joseph of Tiberias at Constantine's command. Recent excavation, however, has shown that this was not so. In March 1960, when workmen were preparing to lift a mosaic pavement for preservation from the south wing of the Byzantine convent which had just then been uncovered, they came upon some bases, columns and a beautifully worked double arch which were all clearly of pre-Byzantine date. On some of these were graffiti of which one included the invocation 'XE MARIA', the Greek for 'Ave Maria'. There is now no doubt that though Christians in Nazareth in these early years were few, yet they did exist and did erect a Christian church there of a synagogue type. The only member of this community whose name has come down to us is that of Conon, who suffered martyrdom in the middle of the 3rd century. During the persecution of Decius, Conon is reported to have said to his judges in Phrygia: 'I am of Nazareth, a relative of the Lord whom I serve, as did my ancestors'.

Successive Byzantine, Crusader and Franciscan churches on the traditional site of the annunciation have now been succeeded by a vast modern church. In this are preserved the remains of the 'Ave Maria' graffiti and the synagogue churches, and the traditional cave of the annunciation. Elsewhere are shown the traditional Latin site of the 'Workshop of Joseph', over cave-basements purporting to have been the home of the Holy Family, also the Greek churches over the sites of Mary's Well and of the synagogue. *see* MARY **1**. [Matt. 2:23; Acts 24:5]

NEREUS This man and his sister are included in a long list to whom Paul sent greetings in the final chapter of his letter to the Church in Rome. It is possible that these greetings may have been addressed also to the Church in Ephesus. Perhaps 'Philologus and Julia, Nereus and his sister, Olympas, and all the saints who are with them' may refer to a single household.

A 4th-century tradition of the Roman Church associates Nereus and Achilleus with the Roman princess Domitilla, the Emperor Vespasian's niece. Domitilla was burnt, as a Christian, by order of her cousin, the Emperor Domitian. The apocryphal *Acts of Nereus and Achilleus* describe the deportation of Domitilla and two eunuchs of her household, Nereus and Achilleus, to the island of Terracina, where the princess was burnt and the other two were beheaded. Their remains are believed to be in the cemetery of St Domitilla, at Rome on the Via Ardeatina. The inscription on their tomb indicated that they were soldiers. [Rom. 16:15]

Capital from the Crusader church built at Nazareth by Tancred, prince of Galilee.

Christ and Nicodemus: pen and ink drawing by Rembrandt van Rijn (1609-69).

NICANOR (Gk. 'conqueror') *see* NICOLAUS

NICODEMUS (Gk. 'victor over the people') The Pharisee, 'a ruler of the Jews' and a member of the Sanhedrin or Great Council, who first came to Jesus by night. Later, he defended Jesus in the Council, protesting against their judgment of him without a hearing. Finally he, together with Joseph of Arimathea, administered the last rites to the body of Jesus before burial. Only the Fourth Gospel mentions Nicodemus.

On the first occasion John begins to describe a meeting and conversation between Nicodemus and Jesus, but the conversation soon develops into a discourse by Jesus without record of any response from Nicodemus. It is hard also to assess where the discourse ends and John's own comment begins, but the re-

appearance later of Nicodemus in the Gospel reveals the impact of their meeting on Nicodemus.

The meeting was at Jerusalem and by night, possibly in the Garden of Gethsemane, Jesus's regular meeting-place with his disciples on the Mount of Olives overlooking the city. Nicodemus, the highly-placed ecclesiastic, was typically cautious and diplomatic. He knew Jesus at least by reputation, he was genuinely impressed; he recognized that this new movement was from God. He was unwilling to commit himself and openly lend his support, because he would then lose influence in the Council and among the Pharisees. So he came by night, secretly, introducing his enquiry by a sincere but diplomatic compliment, 'Rabbi, we know that you are a teacher come from God; for no one can do these signs that you do, unless God is with him.' (John 3:2)

Jesus promptly cut him short, sweeping his compliment aside and striking at the root of Nicodemus's problem. Diplomacy and sympathy are out of place; so is an admiration for Jesus's powerful signs and teaching. Only one thing matters, and that is a new start, for anyone longing for the kingdom of God. 'Truly, truly, I say to you, unless one is born anew, he cannot see the kingdom of God.' (John 3:3)

The Greek words mean both 'born anew' and 'born from above'. New birth can only come from above, it is not something a man can do for himself, as Nicodemus is quick to point out. 'How can a man be born when he is old? Can he enter a second time into his mother's womb and be born?' (John 3:4) After all, Nicodemus had inherited a long tradition as a Pharisee. He had tested his tradition in a long life of experience, disciplining his conduct, speech and thinking. How could he now break away from all this to begin again?

Jesus, however, was adamant and Nicodemus must have grasped what he meant when he insisted, 'Truly, truly, I say to you, unless one is born of water and the Spirit, he cannot enter the kingdom of God. That which is born of the flesh is flesh, and that which is born of the Spirit is spirit. Do not marvel that I said to you, "You must be born anew." The wind blows where it wills, and you hear the sound of it, but you do not know whence it comes or whither it goes; so it is with every one who is born of the Spirit.' (John 3:5-8) To Nicodemus, the words 'born of water' must have implied the baptism of John the Baptist in the River Jordan.

The words 'born of the Spirit' should have recalled John's promise of the baptism 'by spirit and fire' to be administered by his successor. New birth, new life could only be gained by the baptism of repentance, and then discipleship with Jesus among those in whom the birth and life were already stirring with the Spirit of God. The Spirit was like the desert wind, a powerful unseen force, no one knowing from where it came, or whither it would go next.

For the Pharisee, this made things even more difficult. God had given the Law; devout men had drawn up in great detail its application. God had made a covenant with his people, to be carefully kept. Any talk of an unpredictable wind was destructive of institutional religion, so Nicodemus said to Jesus, 'How can this be?' And Jesus answered: 'Truly, truly I say to you, we speak of what we know, and bear witness to what we have seen; but you do not receive our testimony. If I have told you earthly things and you do not believe, how can you believe if I tell you heavenly things? And as Moses lifted up the serpent in the wilderness, so must the Son of man be lifted up.' (John 3:9, 11, 12, 14) And with this first prediction of the passion, the account

of the meeting with Nicodemus with Jesus fades into the meditations of the writer.

As Jesus's ministry proceeded, his credentials as Messiah were constantly questioned, his place of birth, his ancestry, and his message. The officers of the Council brought back reports of his teaching and signs, much impressed by him. 'No man ever spoke like this man.' The Pharisees and priests, however, poured scorn upon them as deceived and the crowds as credulous and ignorant of the Law. 'Are you led astray, you also? Have any of the authorities or of the Pharisees believed in him? But this crowd, who do not know the law, are accursed.' (John 7:46, 47-49) It was at this point that Nicodemus, still concealing his loyalties, postpones judgment on a matter of legal principle. 'Does our law judge a man without first giving him a hearing and learning what he does?' (John 7:51) At which his fellow Pharisees asked whether he was also a Galilean because he sympathized with this Galilean upstart.

Finally, Nicodemus appears with Joseph of Arimathea at the burial of Jesus. Joseph had bravely begged the body from Pilate to ensure a decent burial. Nicodemus came bringing a hundred pounds weight of myrrh and aloes to embalm his body. These two 'took the body of Jesus, and bound it in linen cloths with the spices, as is the burial custom of the Jews. Now in the place where he was crucified there was a garden, and in the garden a new tomb where no one had ever been laid. So because of the Jewish day of Preparation, as the tomb was close at hand, they laid Jesus there.' (John 19:40-42)

It is not possible to know the extent and depth of Nicodemus's discipleship, though many traditions credit him with becoming a faithful follower of Jesus in later years. [John 3:1-9; 7:50; 19:39]

NICOLAUS (Gk. 'conqueror of the people') Nicolaus, Nicanor, Parmenas, Prochorus and Timon were men 'of good repute, full of the Spirit and of wisdom', selected by the Hellenists to be some of the seven deacons, most of whom were Hellenistic Greek-speaking Jews, and commissioned by the apostles with prayer and the laying-on of hands; they supervised the daily distribution of bread to the Hellenist widows and poor in Jerusalem.

The earliest members of the Christian Church in Jerusalem had been mostly pious Jews, who had continued to visit the Temple and to observe the Jewish Law. The original disciples of Jesus, perhaps from Galilee or from the neighbourhood of Jerusalem, were Aramaic-speaking. Now, as others, both Jews and foreigners, had come to settle in the city, sometimes residing near the Temple, the Christian Church had acquired new members from these newcomers. Christian evangelism had been particularly successful among the Hellenistic Jews, who spoke Greek instead of Aramaic. Consequently, there developed in Jerusalem two classes of Christian believers, the Hebrews and the Hellenists, both accepting the Messiahship of Jesus.

The welfare and relief of the needy have always been a characteristic of Judaism and the Law insists on providing for the fatherless and the widow, the slave and the stranger. The Christian community gladly accepted such obligations, as may be seen from the very considerable fund for poor-relief that Paul brought back to Jerusalem from his Mediterranean congregations. There developed, however, a sense of resentment among the Hellenists that their widows were being neglected in the daily distribution at Jerusalem. This threatened to cause some friction between these two groups, the Hebrews and the Hellenists.

The twelve apostles immediately took action, summoning the community as a whole body and ruling, 'It is not right that we should give up preaching the word of God to serve tables. Therefore, brethren, pick out from among you seven men of good repute, full of the Spirit and of wisdom, whom we may appoint to this duty. But we will devote ourselves to prayer and to the ministry of the word.' (Acts 6:2-4) The whole Christian community approved this course of action and they chose seven men to undertake the domestic and financial administration of the poor-relief. These seven deacons, as they later came to be called, were apostles commissioned by prayer and the laying-on of their hands. Whatever the terms of their commission, certain of them are known to have been heavily involved in evangelistic work, particularly Stephen and Philip.

The names of the seven – Stephen, Philip, Prochorus, Nicanor, Timon, Parmenas, and Nicolaus – all indicate a Greek background, though most of them must have been of Jewish birth.

Nicanor, Parmenas and Timon are not mentioned elsewhere in the New Testament, nor has any legend or tradition concerning them survived, except that they were among the seventy disciples with Jesus in Galilee. Prochorus has been named as the writer of a late and apocryphal *History of the Apostle John*. According to a medieval legend, John dictated his Gospel to Prochorus.

The last, Nicolaus, Luke specifically describes as a 'proselyte of Antioch', meaning that he was born a pagan but had accepted the Jewish faith before being converted to Christianity by his new belief in the Messiahship of Jesus.

This Nicolaus of Antioch is not likely to have been responsible for the heretical doctrines of the Nicolatians, hated within the Christian community at Ephesus and held by some also in the congregation at Pergamum at the close of the 1st century. (Rev. 2:6, 15)

St John dictating his Gospel to Prochorus in a cave on the island of Patmos. Illumination from a 14th-century Greek Gospel manuscript.

The Nicolatians taught that Christians were free to eat food offered to idols and to practise immorality in the name of religion. They survived into the 3rd century and are mentioned by Irenaeus, bishop of Lyons, c. 200, by Clement, a theologian of Alexandria, c. 215, and by Tertullian, a Father of the African Church, c. 220. [Acts 6:5]

NIGER (Lat. 'black') *see* SIMEON

NYMPHA(S) A wealthy matron, or man, of the city of Laodicea in the Lycus Valley, east of Ephesus (*see* LAODICEA), whose house was large enough to serve as the meeting-place of one of the groups into which the Church in a large city was divided. Paul sends his greetings to 'the brothers at Laodicea, and to Nympha and the church in her house'. It is not certain from the manuscripts whether the person here named is Nympha, a woman, or Nymphas, a man. [Col. 4:15]

OLYMPAS One of the Christian converts greeted by Paul, at the close of his letter to the Christian congregation at Rome. Olympas is listed within a group, which includes Philologus and Julia, Nereus and his sister, 'and all the saints that are with them'. [Rom. 16:15]

ONESIMUS (Gk. 'useful') The runaway slave from Colossae, converted by Paul in Rome and returned to his master Philemon with a 'covering letter' (the most personal one from the pen of Paul to survive), begging the welcome in Christ Jesus of 'my child, Onesimus'.

During his captivity Paul was approached by an escaped slave called Onesimus. The Greek name means 'useful'. This slave had run away from his master Philemon in Colossae and had made his way to the vast cosmopolitan city of Rome, a notorious hide-out for fugitive slaves. There, in destitution and danger, the hunted man had sought out the imprisoned Apostle Paul and had attached himself to him as his personal attendant. Paul came to know Onesimus's story, his unsatisfactory record as a slave to Philemon, whom he had robbed as well as deserted and to whom now his very life was forfeit on both accounts. Useless as Onesimus had been to Philemon, he became invaluable to Paul and had apparently matured considerably in Christian commitment, for he was prepared to return, at risk of his life, to his deserted master Philemon.

The sole purpose of Paul's 'covering letter' is to return Philemon's property with a plea not only for his forgiveness of Onesimus but for his reception now in the status of a brother in Christ Jesus. Paul's letter is amazing in its tact, its tenderness, and utter charm. It presumes to seek the pardon of a slave for the most serious and the most easily identified offences against the common law, both theft and escape. Speaking as a Christian apostle to one for whose conversion he is indirectly responsible, he does not begin to dictate, but delicately touches on their mutual obligations.

He gently poses his petition for Onesimus as an old man might for his son. He even implies that he would have wished Philemon to return Onesimus to Rome in order to serve him in prison on behalf of Philemon. 'Accordingly, though I am bold enough in Christ to command you to do what is required, yet for love's sake I prefer to appeal to you – I, Paul, an ambassador and now a prisoner also for Christ Jesus – I appeal to you for my child, Onesimus, whose father I have become in my imprisonment. (Formerly he was useless to you, but now he is indeed useful to you and to me.) I am sending him back to you, sending my very heart. I would have been glad to keep him with me, in order that he might serve me on your behalf during my imprisonment for the gospel; but I preferred to do nothing without your consent in order that your goodness might not be by compulsion but of your own free will.' (Philem. 8-14)

Paul proceeds next to his daring request not only for Onesimus's forgiveness, but that he should be welcomed back as a brother. Then Paul underwrites whatever sum of money Onesimus owes to his master; taking the pen from his secretary – probably Timothy – Paul himself writes his bond in the required legal terms: 'I, Paul, . . . will repay it . . .' but adds, 'to say nothing of your owing me even your own self.' [Col. 4:9; Philem. 10]

ONESIPHORUS (Gk. 'profit-bringer') A hospitable and loyal friend of Paul, who rendered him good service at Ephesus and who eagerly searched out Paul during his last imprisonment in Rome. Onesiphorus and his household were not ashamed of Paul's chains and constantly brought him food, drink, news, and encouragement. Paul in his last letter to Timothy blesses Onesiphorus: 'May the Lord grant him to find mercy from the Lord on that Day [of Judgment] and you well know all the service he rendered at Ephesus.'

When in prison at Caesarea, in Rome, and probably at Ephesus also, Paul was often allowed visitors. Indeed, in Rome, Christian companions seem to have taken in turn the privilege of sharing his cell as fellow-prisoners. The emotional temperature of parts of that final letter indicate the strain under which Paul spent the delay, perhaps years, between his probable betrayal by Alexander the coppersmith at Troas, his trial and sentence to death, and his final execution in Rome. At the very close of his letter Paul sends his farewell greetings not to Onesiphorus, but to his family and household in Ephesus, as though perhaps Onesiphorus is still visiting Paul and his constant attendant, Luke, in Rome, if indeed Onesiphorus was still alive. [2 Tim. 1:16; 4:19]

P

PARACLETE (Gk. literally 'called to one's side', hence 'advocate') *see* SPIRIT OF GOD

PARMENAS (Gk. 'constant') *see* NICOLAUS

PARTHIANS *see* ARABIANS

PATROBAS The fourth of a list of five men, mentioned in a special greeting from Paul at the close of his letter to the Church in Rome. Perhaps Patrobas, his fellows and 'the brethren who are with them' formed a household or small group within the larger Christian community. The historian Tacitus describes the freeing of a Patrobas, one of Nero's slaves, and his execution under Galba. [Rom. 16:14]

above The Apostle Paul: 5th-century mosaic portrait from the mausoleum of Galla Placidia in Ravenna.

PAUL (Gk. from Lat. 'little') It was through the driving energy and unshakeable faith of Paul, the great Apostle to the Gentiles, that the Christian Church became an organized and established force within the Roman Empire. He hardly looked the part. 'A man rather small in size, bald-headed, bow-legged, with meeting eyebrows, a large, red and somewhat hooked nose,' he was described by a writer in the 2nd century, Onesiphoros, in the apocryphal *Acts of Paul and Thecla*.

Yet the power of the man was unmistakeable. 'Strongly-built,' the account ran on, 'he was full of grace, for at times he looked like a man, at times like an angel.' The frescoes on Roman catacombs seem to confirm this description. Such was the apostle who inspired courage and brotherhood into the early, struggling Christian communities in Palestine, Syria, and the Greek cities of the eastern Mediterranean provinces.

By the time of his martyrdom in Rome in AD 67, Paul had helped to create a world-wide Church in the space of a mere thirty-seven years after the crucifixion of Christ. And perhaps the two most remarkable facts about this remarkable man are that he was a citizen of the Roman Empire, and that his first contact with Christianity was as one of its most ferocious persecutors. Not for him the unique, personal faith of the apostles who had known Jesus: dazzled and blinded in a searing vision on the Damascus road, he became a Christian only after a shattering experience which transformed his entire mental outlook and way of life.

Roman citizen, Hellenized Jew

Paul's story is known to us from the account in the Acts of the Apostles supplemented by his own letters, but there must have been many events in his life which are unrecorded. It is possible that Luke's second volume, the Acts, was written as an apologia for Paul before his trial in Rome – indeed, Luke begins his narrative in Jerusalem and ends in Rome, with Paul still under house-arrest. Of Paul's letters, the writer of the 2nd-century letter attributed to Peter said, 'Some things in

right Paul (left) and Jesus, originally part of a Byzantine ivory book-cover of the Emperor Henry II and the Empress Cunigunde.

Year	Outside Events	Events in Paul's Life	Letters Written	Reference
6 BC	Birth of Jesus Schooling in Nazareth			
10 AD?		Birth of Paul Schooling in Tarsus		
26	Galilean ministry of Jesus starts			
28		Rabbinic student in Jerusalem		
30	Crucifixion, Resurrection and Ascension of Jesus			
36	Pilate resigns procuratorship	Persecution of Hellenist Christians Paul appointed to Damascus		Acts 7, 8
	Stoning of Stephen	Conversion on road to Damascus		Acts 9:22, 26
	Aretas ruling Damascus	Retirement to Arabia. Return to Damascus		Gal. 1:17 Gal. 1:17; Acts 9:20
39	Herod Antipas exiled by Caligula	Visit to Jerusalem		Gal. 1:18; Acts 9:26
		Return to Tarsus		Acts 9:30
		Unrecorded mission to Syria and Cilicia		Gal. 1:21
44	Death of Herod Agrippa I Judea again a procuratorial province	Assistant to Barnabas at Antioch		Acts 11:26
46		First Journey to Cyprus and Galatia, with Barnabas		Acts 13, 14
48-53	Herod Agrippa II. Inspector of the Temple at Jerusalem		Galatians (one theory)	
49	Expulsion of Jewish-Christians from Rome by Claudius	Council of Jerusalem		Acts 15
50		Second Journey, with Silas to Europe	1 and 2 Thessalonians	Acts 16
51-2	Gallio at Corinth			Acts 18:12
52-60	Felix procurator of Judea	Return to Antioch, via Caesarea	Galatians (one theory)	Acts 18:22
53		Third Journey		
54	Nero succeeds Claudius	Mission at Ephesus	1 and 2 Corinthians	Acts 19:1-20 1
57		Second Visit to Corinth; return via Troas and Miletus	Romans	Acts 20; 21:1-14
58		Arrival in Jerusalem		Acts 21:15
		Arrest and imprisonment at Caesarea		Acts 21:27; 22; 23
		Trial before Felix		Acts 24
60	Festus succeeds Felix as procurator of Judea	Trial before Festus. Appeal to Caesar		Acts 25
		Appearance before Agrippa		Acts 26
		Departure for Rome		Acts 27
		Winter on Malta, arrival at Rome		Acts 28:1-16
61-2		Under house arrest in Rome	Colossians, Ephesians, Philemon, Philippians	Acts 28:16-31
62	Albinus succeeds Festus as procurator of Judea	Release and visit to perhaps Asia, Macedonia, Achaia, Spain	1 Timothy, Titus	
64-7	Nero's persecution of Christians in Rome	Re-arrest, perhaps in Troas Imprisonment and execution in Rome	2 Timothy	2 Tim. 1:12; 4:13 (Eusebius, 4th century

NB The dating of all events and writings is approximate only.

Paul's letters are hard to understand.' Without some knowledge of the circumstances, the motives, and the addressees, this is very true. But once the situation in which the letter was written is understood, the warmth of Paul's message is immediately felt.

Within the Acts, Paul is called by his Hebrew name, Saul, until his clash on the island of Cyprus with the wizard Bar-Jesus. Then Luke writes, 'Saul, who is also

called Paul, filled with the Holy Spirit, looked intently at him. . . .' In the letters, he always calls himself 'Paul'. As a Roman citizen, he was probably called by both names from birth, for double names were common among Jews of the dispersion. The change from 'Saul' to 'Paul' – from the Hebrew to the Greco-Roman – was particularly appropriate at the time he began to be apostle to the Gentiles.

Everything Paul achieved was the result of his three-fold background. He was of Roman citizenship, of Greek culture, and of Jewish faith. Born in Tarsus in the first years of the Christian era, he inherited his Roman citizenship from his Jewish father, and always showed distinct pride in his birthplace. It was, as he said, 'no mean city'. Tarsus was a Hellenized city, famous for its university, its gymnasium, theatre, art school, and stadium. It was, however, in a strategical position to the north-east of the Mediterranean, between the Cilician Gates and the coast, and often suffered siege and destruction. Within this environment of typically Greek institutions, Paul grew up to speak and think in the colloquial Greek of the eastern Mediterranean.

Tarsus was a provincial capital of the Roman Empire, and Roman citizenship and a sense of identification with Rome played a decisive part in Paul's life. It gave him the right to vote, and a dignity which in a number of emergencies he was quick to claim. He was exempt from degrading punishments, even down to the manner of his martyrdom: whereas Peter was crucified, Paul was beheaded with the sword. A Roman citizen also had the right to appeal to the emperor himself, and when Paul felt that he could not retain security or obtain justice by other means, he could and did 'appeal to Caesar'.

Yet Paul was above all a Jew. To the end of his life he retained a deep and abiding love for his 'brethren, my kinsmen by race'. 'For I could wish that I myself were accursed and cut off from Christ for [their] sake ... to them belong the patriarchs, and of their race, according to the flesh, is the Christ. God who is over all be blessed for ever. Amen.' The son of a devout Jew, Paul proclaimed himself to be of pure Jewish blood, 'a Hebrew born of Hebrews'. He was originally named Saul, and like his namesake King Saul he was a member of the tribe of Benjamin and acutely aware of his Jewish religious and cultural heritage.

Early years: the scourge of the Christians

A Pharisee and the son of a Pharisee, destined for the Rabbinate, Paul had a strict upbringing in the synagogue school, his education based almost entirely on the Old Testament scriptures. From the age of thirteen, as a 'Son of the Law', he would have joined together with his father in the adult worship in the synagogue at Tarsus. About AD 28, at something over the age of eighteen, Paul went to Jerusalem to study theology under Gamaliel, a member of the Sanhedrin of much wisdom and moderation. He must have been a keen student of the scriptures and Rabbinate learning: his letters include some two hundred scriptural quotations.

When in Jerusalem, Paul probably lived with his sister. By the age of about thirty, he was an acknowledged defender of Judaism. It was about this time that the Greek-speaking element in the Jewish-Christian community at Jerusalem provoked considerable persecution from the Jewish authorities. Stephen, foremost among these Hellenized Jewish-Christians, was using scripture to support the Messiahship of Jesus and to indict the authorities for their reliance upon the Temple. Stephen's teaching particularly incensed Paul, who entered whole-heartedly into the persecution which followed.

Stephen's martyrdom – he was stoned publicly, without procuratorial consent – possibly indicates the interregnum following Pilate's resignation, and may therefore have been in AD 36. The fact of an Arabian governor ruling in Damascus at the time of Paul's conversion indicates a period of hostility between Herod Antipas and King Aretas of Petra – also in the year 36. It was at this time that there was a brief persecution of Christians in Jerusalem, followed by a dispersal of Hellenized Jewish-Christians to Antioch and Damascus – in the Gentile world. The high priest at Jerusalem, whose authority appears to have at that time extended as far as Antioch and Damascus, willingly commissioned Paul to travel north and arrest any followers of 'The Way' that he could find. And Paul, refusing even to consider the Messiahship of Jesus, whose followers claimed that he had 'risen from the dead', set out for Damascus, filled with a fanatical determination to defend the honour of God and to destroy this heresy.

Paul's blinding vision

Riding over the spine of Judea and Samaria, perhaps Paul may have passed through Nazareth, the home of the prophet-Messiah whose claims he rejected, through Capernaum, up the Jordan Valley on the road to Damascus. Then suddenly, outside the city, he was blinded by a light from heaven and fell to the ground, hearing a voice saying, 'Saul, Saul, why do you persecute me? I am Jesus, whom you are persecuting; but rise and enter the city, and you will be told what you are to do.' His companions led him, blind and helpless, into Damascus, where he fasted for three days. By a vision, a Christian disciple, Ananias, was instructed to visit him at the house of Judas in Straight Street, there to welcome and baptize him, and then to unfold and complete the divine commission of the Apostle to the Gentiles. Paul tells the story of his conversion both before the Sanhedrin in Jerusalem and before Herod Agrippa at Caesarea; he clearly records the words of Ananias: 'Brother Saul ... the God of our fathers appointed you to know his will, to see the Just One and to hear a voice from his mouth; for you will be a witness for him to all men of what you have seen and heard.' (Acts 22:14, 15)

Paul's acceptance of Jesus as the Messiah was very different from that of the other apostles. They had already known Jesus, as disciples, as their master and teacher. They claimed apostolic authority as witnesses of Jesus's resurrection. Paul, however, probably never

The Conversion of St Paul, by Michelangelo (1475-1564), from the ceiling of the Sistine Chapel. Jesus stretches down his hand, while Paul, covering his eyes, falls to the ground.

saw Jesus in the flesh; he became a Christian and an apostle, without ever having been a disciple. In fact, Paul hardly mentions the earthly life and teaching of Jesus, but he is fascinated by the significance of his death and resurrection. For he, Paul, had come face to face with Jesus, 'whom God has raised up', as Peter proclaimed.

Paul's conversion was remarkable for the *total* reversal that it involved in his thinking and the complete redirection of his whole life. In the very act of bitter persecution, he was called and commissioned as Apostle to the Gentiles, and called by the very person whose followers he was persecuting. It is not surprising that the grace and mercy of God towards all men forms the keystone of Paul's teaching. If anyone had experienced the totally undeserved and unconditional mercy of God, it was Paul on the road to Damascus. He discovered that the Christians were right in their recognition of the Messiah. He recognized the agent of his conversion as the risen Jesus, who identified himself to the Pharisee Paul with the words, 'I am Jesus, whom you are persecuting.'

In Paul's conversion are to be found the seeds of his very distinctive Christian teachings: justification by faith rather than by works, and salvation through the mercy of God in Jesus. His interpretation of the cross of Jesus was that it is the glory of God and the means of man's redemption, and – above all – the reconciliation of all men. All this was developed through his personal experience and living with the Christian community, to which he brought all his loyalty, intellect, and skill as a Pharisee. It was Paul who developed and applied a full theology of the sacraments, baptism, and communion by which members of the Christian Church were to be initiated, nourished, and governed by the Spirit of God. And this Spirit was inseparable from the continued presence of Jesus among his followers.

The new apostle

Paul's movements after his conversion are in some doubt, for Luke's narrative in the Acts of the Apostles does not include Paul's retirement or retreat into the desert, mentioned in the beginning of his letter to the Church in Galatia. There Paul says: 'I did not confer with flesh and blood, nor did I go up to Jerusalem to those who were apostles before me, but I went away into Arabia; and again I returned to Damascus.'

When Paul did return to Damascus, the essentials of his teaching and message were already crystal-clear: God's promise to Abraham has been fulfilled in the resurrection of Jesus. The risen Jesus is the climax of history, for he is both Messiah and God. God comes to all people, as he came to Paul, in the person of Jesus. This aggressive preaching provoked fury and consternation among Jews at Damascus; they enlisted the support of Aretas, whose Nabatean kingdom then

Damascus from the air, a green oasis set in a mountainous desert.

included Damascus, to secure Paul's arrest. Luke describes his escape: 'His disciples took him by night and let him down over the wall, lowering him in a basket.' (Acts 9:25) The date of his escape must have been before AD 40, because King Aretas died in that year.

The ancient city of Damascus lies to the south-east of the modern city. The street called Straight was the old east-west main traffic artery. The Roman-period east gate has been recently excavated, at the end of Straight Street. The overhanging perimeter walls, though of much later date, give a vivid impression of the possibility and method of Paul's escape, as he described it: 'At Damascus, the governor under King Aretas guarded the city of Damascus in order to seize me, but I was let down in a basket through a window in the wall and escaped his hands.' (2 Cor. 11:32, 33)

Three years after his conversion, Paul went up to Jerusalem to meet Peter, and stayed with him for fifteen days. 'But I saw none of the other apostles,' he wrote to the Galatians, 'except James the Lord's brother. . . . Then I went into the regions of Syria and Cilicia. And I was still not known by sight to the Churches of Christ in Judea.' (Gal. 1:19-22) Luke describes the cold reception and suspicion with which the Church leaders in Jerusalem greeted Paul, and relates that it was Barnabas who secured Paul's acceptance. Luke also declares that Paul's own preaching provoked such opposition that the Church leaders persuaded him to leave Jerusalem and, taking him to Caesarea, put him on a ship going to Tarsus.

npr̄ hoc domos· ⁊ fr̄atres· ⁊ sorores· ⁊ ma
s· ⁊ filios· ⁊ agros· cum p̄secutionibus· ⁊
seculo futuro · uitam æternam·

above 11th-century Latin manuscript, showing the blinded Paul being led into the city of Damascus, and then being lowered over the wall in a basket.

The Roman gate at the end of the 'Street called Straight', at the south-east corner of the city of Damascus.

Not till fourteen years later did Paul return to Jerusalem.

Luke's narrative in the Acts now turns to the activities of Peter and his conversion of the Roman centurion Cornelius and his household. Paul says that he 'went into' Syria and Cilicia. If he did attempt some unrecorded work at that time, it might well explain some of the punishments and perils of which we have no other account. 'Five times I have received at the hands of the Jews the forty lashes less one,' he wrote to the Corinthians. 'Three times I have been beaten with rods; once I was stoned. Three times I have been shipwrecked; a night and a day I have been adrift at sea; on frequent journeys, in danger from rivers, danger from robbers, danger from my own people, danger from Gentiles, danger in the city, danger in the wilderness, danger at sea, danger from false brethren.' (2 Cor. 11:24-27)

The capital of Syria was Antioch, third city in the world after Rome and Alexandria. Whether through the teaching work of the Hellenized Christians from Cyprus and Jerusalem, or of Paul himself, or of both, the Christian Church was firmly established at Antioch and the city was to become the headquarters of Paul's future journeys. The Church leaders in Jerusalem sent Barnabas to superintend the Church at Antioch, and Barnabas in turn chose Paul as his assistant, collecting him from Tarsus. For a whole year, they taught together. It was at that time that the derisive title of 'Christians' was first given to the members of the Church at Antioch – and gladly accepted.

Of the glories of the one-time capital of Syria which straddled the River Orontes, little remains. There are some massive sections of ancient city walling, some arches of Trajan's aqueduct, and the rather scanty remains of a theatre and stadium. The ancient city extended over the slopes and plateau of Mount Silpius, to the south of the smaller modern town.

Warned of famine by visitors from Jerusalem, the Church at Antioch held a collection for the Christians at Jerusalem and sent it by the hands of Barnabas and Paul.

It is difficult to reconcile Paul's account and Luke's account (Acts 11) of Paul's visit to Jerusalem. If, in fact, the letter to the Galatians was written before the Council, then the task of putting his case in writing in his letter to the Galatians may have helped to crystallize the issues and conclusions in Paul's thinking. Shortly afterward, Paul and Barnabas, together with the other delegates from the Church at Antioch, set out for a conference with the leaders of the Church in Jerusalem (Gal. 2). It seems likely that this informal conference took place at the time of the visit of Paul and Barnabas to present the offering from Antioch (Acts 11). The Acts account makes no mention of this discussion, but perhaps the author has passed over in silence a dispute that was not settled until later, preferring instead to give a full account at the time of the settlement (Acts 15). This would be in keeping with his tendency in Acts, to minimize the controversies that developed within the community, and to give the impression that the harmony of the fellowship was never disturbed more than briefly. But since this conference with the apostles was of prime importance for Paul's side of the argument in the Galatian letter, he related it there in some detail.

In his letter to the Church in Galatia, Paul implies that he discussed with the Church leaders in Jerusalem the adaptation of the creed and teaching to the need of the Gentile Christians in Antioch. As a result, Paul declared, his own work was approved and the *universal* significance of Jesus's life and teaching was recognized. On their return to Antioch, the spontaneous success of the young Christian Church generated a new enterprise. Under the guidance of the Holy Spirit, we are told, Paul embarked on the first of his great journeys, accompanied by Barnabas – their destination being the island of Cyprus.

The wizard of Cyprus

On a journey that was to cover 1,400 miles, they set off down the Orontes Valley to sail from the port of Seleucia to Salamis, the eastern harbour of Cyprus. There were many Jews working in the copper-mines of Cyprus, and a number of Hellenized Jewish-Christians had come to the island after the persecution in Jerusalem in the year 36. Now, ten years later, Paul and

The First Journey of Paul

46-48 AD

GALATIA

Sardis

PHRYGIA · Antioch

LYCAONIA

Ephesus

PISIDIA

·Iconium

Lystra·

CILICIA

·Derbe

Tarsus·

PAMPHYLIA

Attalia· ·Perga

Miletus

Rhodes

Seleucia· ·Antioch

Mediterranean Sea

CYPRUS ·Salamis

SYRIA

Paphos·

0   100 miles

Barnabas arrived, and they made direct for Paphos, seat of the Roman proconsul Sergius Paulus, who may have been a God-fearing attendant at the local synagogue. One of the proconsul's household was a magician called Elymas Bar-Jesus, who attempted to bar from his master the preaching of the Christian gospel. Paul very quickly and mercilessly exposed him, and the proconsul accepted Paul's message about Jesus.

From this moment Paul was recognized as the leader of the venture. His Jewish name Saul was replaced by his Greco-Roman name of Paul – which may or may not reflect his physical appearance as short of stature. Certainly the Latin word *paulis* can describe the 'runt' of a litter!

Crossing to the south coast of Asia Minor, Paul and Barnabas landed at Attalia and headed inland, crossing the western spurs of the Taurus Mountains, infested with robbers and other dangers. A few miles inland, John Mark (*see* MARK) left them and returned to Jerusalem. The others arrived at Antioch, the capital of Pisidia (not of Syria), 100 miles inland, an important centre with a large Jewish community. In their synagogue, Paul delivered an address (fully recorded in Acts

above Roman aqueduct at Antioch in Pisidia, founded by Seleucus Nicator in the 3rd century BC and fortified by the Romans, an important cross-roads of imperial highways.
left Paul being stoned at Lystra: from a 5th-century ivory casket.

13) to both Jews and Gentiles: 'Men of Israel, and you that fear God, listen . . . brethren, sons of the family of Abraham, and those among you that fear God, to us has been sent the message of this salvation.' (Acts 13:16, 26) It would seem that the pattern of Paul's work was immediately established. On arrival, he went straight to the synagogue, if there was one; there in the prayer-hall he spoke loud enough to be heard in the God-fearers' court. Afterwards he adjourned to a friendly household to answer questions. But after one night in Pisidian Antioch, opposition had crystallized. Paul and Barnabas were expelled from the city – but not before Paul had convinced many Gentiles, who were later to form the core of the Christian community in that place. It seems clear that they were accepted as followers of the Messiah, without undertaking all the obligations of the Law, by the apostolic decision of Paul.

Paul and Barnabas now turned east, and after nearly 100 miles of rough travelling reached Iconium (modern-day Konya). Here again their visit followed the same pattern, and a Church was formed before Paul and Barnabas were forced to move on under threat of being stoned. They reached Lystra, 25 miles towards the coast. Here there was no synagogue, so Paul spoke in the open and healed a cripple. When the crowd realized what had happened, they declared Paul and Barnabas to be gods and attempted to offer them sacrifices, considering the tall and dignified figure of Barnabas to be Zeus, father of the gods, and Paul, the shorter, mercurial character, to be Hermes, messenger of the gods. Very soon, however, hostile Jews arrived from Iconium and Antioch and turned the mob against them. Paul was stoned and dragged outside the town. He recovered, however, and ventured back into the town for the night before escaping next morning along the road to Derbe.

There, after a useful and unmolested visit, Paul and Barnabas decided very bravely not to cut down to the coast, but to return by the same route, appointing elders to report progress within these new Christian communities, and encouraging them all to persevere in their new-found faith. Paul's letter to the Church in Galatia (if it is directed to the Church in Lystra, Derbe and Iconium) reflects the bitter issues left to be settled within these communities – particularly those between Jewish-Christians and Christians of Gentile origin.

Having sailed from Attalia, Paul and Barnabas returned to Syrian Antioch, to find the Christian community there divided by the insistence on the part of a deputation from the Church in Jerusalem that circumcision was necessary for salvation. Once again, the Church at Antioch despatched Paul and Barnabas to Jerusalem, this time to present the case for the Gentile Christians. James, the brother of Jesus and the first bishop of Jerusalem, gave a ruling. The pagans who turned to God were told merely to abstain from food

ITALIA

Adriatic Sea

Amphipolis • Philippi
Thessalonica • Neapolis
Beroea • Apollonia
MACEDONIA
Troas

ACHAIA
Rhegium
SICILIA
Syracuse
Corinth
Cenchreae
Athens
Aegean Sea

BITHYNIA AND PONTUS

MYSIA

• Thyatira

PHRYGIA
GALATIA
LYCAONIA
• Iconium
CILICIA
Derbe • Tarsus

PISIDIA

• Ephesus

Rhodes

Antioch
Seleucia

CYPRUS

SYRIA

CRETE

Mediterranean Sea

Damascus
Sidon •
Tyre

Caesarea

Jerusalem

Cyrene

CYRENAICA

0   150 miles

**The Second
Journey of Paul**
49-52 AD

offered to idols, from blood from the meat of strangled
animals, and from fornication. Thus the Council of
Jerusalem refused to impose the Law on the Gentiles,
only forbidding certain specific practices, which still
continue to be forbidden by the Canons of Eastern
Christendom. The Council's delegates Judas and Silas
conveyed the decision to the Church at Antioch,
accompanying Paul and Barnabas on their return.

Thus vindicated, Paul and Barnabas continued their
work at Antioch. However, they as Jewish-Christians
continued to keep the Law of Moses as their own rule of
life. When on one occasion Peter withdrew from table-
fellowship with Gentiles, fearing to offend the 'circumcision' party, he was corrected by Paul for undermining
the equal status of all the Christians.

Westward to Europe

The probable date of the Jerusalem Council was AD
49-50, and next spring Paul and Barnabas planned to
revisit together the young Churches in Cyprus and
Galatia. They disagreed, however, on whether or not
John Mark, Barnabas's nephew, should accompany
them and finally they divided forces, Barnabas sailing
with Mark for Cyprus while Paul took Silas to
encourage the Galatian Churches.

Paul and Silas travelled by road, round the coast and
over the pass of the Cilician Gates to Derbe and Lystra,
where Timothy was added to the team. Because Timothy
was the son of a Greek married to a Jewess, Paul did
insist on his circumcision in order to remove obstacles
to his working among Jews. They revisited Iconium
and Antioch, but this time, driven by some positive

Ancient port of Assos, near Troas in western
Turkey, a possible port of call on Paul's Second
and Third Journeys.

319

Paul's prison at Philippi. Paul bore the scars
of the flogging which he received at Philippi for
the rest of his life.

spiritual guidance, they did not turn south to the coast. They made their way through Phrygia to Troas, on the north-west coast of Asia Minor – and there, guided by the vision of a Macedonian calling for help, Paul took ship across the Aegean, sailing via Samothrace to Europe.

Taking to the Via Egnatia, that great military highway which linked Rome to the East, the party moved inland to Philippi, a Roman colony and city founded by the father of Alexander the Great. There being few Jews and no synagogue, Paul stayed with a devout Jewess named Lydia, a dealer in dyed cloth, whose household was the first in Europe to be converted and baptized. Paul was enabled to conduct house-meetings near the River Ganga – but soon an unpleasant incident cut short their stay in Philippi. A soothsaying slave-girl with an evil spirit began following them, and Paul commanded the spirit to leave her. Her employers, who made considerable profits from her fortune-telling, had Paul and Silas arrested.

Under pressure from the mob, the magistrates had Paul and Silas stripped, flogged, thrown into gaol, and put in the stocks. That night, however, an earthquake released all the prisoners. The unfortunate gaoler was about to commit suicide when Paul called him and told him about Jesus. He and his family were converted; they took their prisoners home to feed them before returning them to the prison. When the order of release arrived the following morning, Paul insisted on the magistrates themselves freeing them. Although Paul never forgot his degradation and suffering at Philippi, his letter to the Church there is full of affection and thanksgiving.

The party then travelled seventy miles westward along the Via Egnatia to Thessalonica, chief port of the northern Aegean. For three consecutive Sabbaths Paul preached in the synagogue, proving Jesus to be the Messiah, and enjoyed some success among both Jews and Gentiles. With the help, however, of a market-place mob his Jewish opponents stormed the house of one Jason, a Jew of the dispersion with whom Paul was staying, and charged Paul with proclaiming Jesus as a rival emperor. Finding only Jason himself, they dragged him before the city council, who made Jason pay security before releasing him. This Jason may well be the relation of Paul mentioned in his letter to the Romans.

Under cover of dark, Paul and Silas escaped to Beroea, again travelling westward along the highway. Perhaps the fact that Paul's stay among the Thessalonians was cut short to a bare three weeks may explain their wrong ideas about the return of Jesus, corrected by Paul in his correspondence to them from Corinth. At Beroea they were welcomed in the synagogue, but were once again hounded by trouble-makers, this time from Thessalonica. Silas and Timothy remained at Beroea for some time before turning back, Timothy to Thessalonica, Silas to Philippi.

Paul now made a lone journey to Athens, which three centuries before had been the intellectual centre of the world. There, stirred by the idolatry of the Athenians, Paul preached in the synagogue and the market-place. At the request of Epicurean and Stoic philosophers, Paul gave an exposition of his teaching before the Council of the Areopagus on Mars Hill. It was a masterpiece of tact, insight and condensation but practically it was a complete failure. His message conflicted with the Greek conception of the human body as a tomb imprisoning the spirit of man, and his audience repudiated the idea of the resurrection of the body. Paul made few converts in Athens. Filled with disappointment, he travelled across the isthmus in fear and trembling for his reception at Corinth.

Corinth was a city of great commerce, wealth, and squalor, renowned for its culture and notorious for its immorality. Here Paul remained for eighteen months, working as a tentmaker with Aquila and his wife Priscilla, Jews expelled from Rome by the edict of

The Third Journey of Paul 53-57 AD

Claudius in the year 49. On the arrival of Timothy and Silas, they taught both Jews and Greeks, in the synagogue and then in a private house. As a result, a large Church was formed at Corinth, mostly from the poor and slave classes. During that time Paul, hearing Timothy's report from Thessalonica, sent his first letter to that Church about the second coming of Jesus. After further reports he sent them his second letter, warning the Thessalonians against misconceptions about the End and urging them not to use the teaching of justification by faith as an excuse for lawlessness, but rather to persevere in faith and good works. Both these letters convey Paul's intensity and affection, and reveal the power of his personality.

With the arrival in the year 51 of a new proconsul of Achaia, named Gallio, certain members of the Jewish community accused Paul of teaching religion 'in a way that breaks the Law'. Gallio refused to adjudicate, but the time had come for Paul and his party to move on. He reached Ephesus, on the west coast of Asia Minor, made a brief visit to the synagogue, and after promising to return on his next journey, sailed for Caesarea, where he greeted the Church on his way north to return to Antioch.

This Second Journey of 2,800 miles must have taken three years – probably AD 50-2, the greater part of which was spent at Corinth.

Mission to Ephesus

After a short stay at Antioch Paul was on his travels again, heading up through the Cilician Gates, through Cilicia and Galatia, encouraging the young Christian communities, until he reached Ephesus – a journey of some 500 miles over rugged country. About this time an Alexandrian Jew, Apollos, and a dozen others arrived in Ephesus. They were disciples of John the Baptist, but they had never received the Holy Spirit or been baptized in the name of Jesus. After their instruction by Aquila and Priscilla, Paul baptized them and laid his hands on them, and they 'spoke with tongues and prophesied'.

For the next three years – perhaps between 54 and 57 – Paul was involved in a concentrated mission at Ephesus, the chief city of paganism in Asia, whose temple of Artemis – 'Diana of the Ephesians' – was a great centre of paganism in the Mediterranean world. To the small Christian communities founded along the coastline of Asia, the Temple of Diana (*see* ARTEMIS) at Ephesus was an infernal counterpart to the Temple at Jerusalem. (*see* EPHESIANS) Paul spent the first three months of his ministry teaching in the synagogue. When the inevitable break within the Jewish community occurred, he moved to the lecture-room of Tyrannus. There he remained in teaching and discussion with both Jews and Greeks, for a period of two whole years, in the siesta hours of noon to four in the afternoon.

Remarkable progress followed his systematic instruction, which was also accompanied by a ministry of healing. Both Jews and Greeks came to respect the name of Jesus, rather than the magical arts of Diana.

From Ephesus, Paul sent well-trained teachers to Colossae and Macedonia, and it was at this time also that some of the Seven Churches of Asia, mentioned by John in the Book of Revelation, were founded. (*see* JOHN THE DIVINE)

Soon, however, the Christian success provoked fierce opposition, particularly from the commercial, pleasure-loving pagans of the fertility-cult of Diana. This culminated in the financially-prompted riot – raised by Demetrius the silversmith and other craftsmen whose trade in silver shrines and trinkets of Diana was threatened by a slump brought about by the teaching of Paul. These merchants took their grievance to the market-place, stirred the crowd into seizing two of Paul's Macedonian companions, and dragged them into the nearby theatre. In the uproar that followed, the situation was only saved by the tact of the town clerk, who had the men released and dispersed the crowd; but relations were now so strained that Paul decided to close his ministry in Asia Minor. He sent Timothy and Erastus on to Macedonia, and planned to follow them.

Rebukes for the Corinthians
During his time in Ephesus, Paul had heard news from Corinth that made it necessary for him to write a letter of warning (2 Cor. 6:14; 7:1) to that Christian com-

Many-breasted statue of Artemis, goddess of fertility, from Ephesus, 2nd century AD.

munity against immorality. Shortly afterwards, he received an official letter from the Corinthians asking advice on specific matters of doctrine, which Paul answered in a letter now known as 1 Corinthians. This he sent by sea, while Timothy took the land route to deal with the situation in person.

Neither the letter nor Timothy's visit achieved the desired effect, and Paul himself sailed for Corinth. Even he failed to reform the Corinthian Church, and after being grossly insulted he sailed back to Ephesus. From there, he wrote a 'severe letter', his third (possibly 2 Cor. 10-13), which was carried by Titus, an older and more experienced man than Timothy. This letter demanded a proper respect both for Christian morality and for Paul himself, as the founder of the Christian Church in Corinth.

When Paul finally closed his ministry in Ephesus, he travelled overland north to Troas, whence he sailed once again for Macedonia to visit Philippi, Thessalonica, and Beroea. Somewhere *en route*, he met Titus who at last brought him the good news that the Corinthian Church was ready to conform, and that they had already by a majority vote censured the culprit. Paul immediately wrote his fourth letter to Corinth (possibly to be found in 2 Cor. 1-9) omitting the content of his previous letter. In this last letter he forgave his antagonist, closed the controversy, and arranged for a collection to be taken for the poor Christians at Jerusalem. Paul seems then to have travelled overland to Corinth, where he spent the winter months, in which time he wrote his letter to the Church in Rome, to prepare them for his coming and to secure their support for a journey to Spain.

Paul's plan to sail directly from Corinth for Jerusalem, taking his poor-relief collection, was thwarted by some threat of ambush. Consequently he returned overland to Macedonia, perhaps collecting Luke in Macedonia and meeting his other escorts in Troas, whence he had first sailed for Europe some eight years before. Luke describes a Saturday or Sunday evening Eucharist in a first-floor room, at which Paul preached so long that a boy called Eutychus (the name means 'lucky') dozed off and fell out of the upper window, but was picked up and restored by Paul.

Wishing to reach Jerusalem by Pentecost, Paul summoned the elders of the Church of Ephesus to meet him on the coast at Miletus, where he bade them a fond farewell, sharing with them his apprehension of the fate that awaited him in Jerusalem. At Patara, on the southern tip of Asia Minor, they boarded a cargo vessel bound for Tyre. They sailed down the Phoenician coast, stopping a day at Acre (Ptolemais), and then on to Caesarea, where they enjoyed the hospitality of Philip the Evangelist. Once again, Paul received a prophetic warning of the sufferings in store for him in Jerusalem,

3rd-century Christian church on the citadel of ancient Assos, testifying to the success of Paul's ministry there.

the third heaven – whether in the body or out of the body I do not know, God knows. . . . And to keep me from being too elated by the abundance of revelations, a thorn was given me in the flesh, a messenger of Satan, to harass me, to keep me from being too elated. Three times I besought the Lord about this, that it should leave me; but he said to me, "My grace is sufficient for you, for my power is made perfect in weakness." I will all the more gladly boast of my weaknesses, that the power of Christ may rest upon me. For the sake of Christ, then, I am content with weaknesses, insults, hardships, persecutions, and calamities; for when I am weak, then I am strong.' (2 Cor. 12:2, 7-10)

What Paul's 'thorn in the flesh' was we may never known, whether physical, such as malaria or dysentery, or some particular source of personal temptation. How true, however, of himself were Paul's words: 'But we have this treasure in earthen vessels, to show that the transcendent power belongs to God and not to us. We are afflicted in every way, but not crushed; perplexed, but not driven to despair; persecuted, but not forsaken; struck down, but not destroyed; always carrying in the body the death of Jesus, so that the life of Jesus may also

The theatre at Miletus, Paul's last port of call in Asia on his way back to Jerusalem at the end of his Third Journey.

but he proclaimed himself ready not only for arrest but for death 'for the name of the Lord Jesus'. On arrival in Jerusalem, Paul lodged at the home of a Cypriot Christian called Mnason.

Burning faith and energy

Paul's journeys can be traced in his letters, as well as in the Acts of the Apostles. From the early letters to the Christian communities in Thessalonica, Galatia, Corinth, and Rome, his very distinct personality emerges, under every kind of physical and emotional strain, sometimes beyond his endurance. Often the briefest references are the most revealing of his perseverance. For two years, day by day, he taught right through the four long, hot hours of the siesta at Ephesus. Later, at Caesarea, he was to remain two whole years in prison, awaiting trial, through the idle and greedy procrastination of the Roman procurator, Felix, who expected a bribe.

Only in his last letter to the Church at Corinth does Paul himself hint at the cost of his calling. 'I know a man in Christ who fourteen years ago was caught up to

The ruins of the fortress of Antipatris, the
staging-post on Paul's journey under escort
from Jerusalem to Caesarea, for trial before
the procurator Felix.

be manifested in our bodies. For while we live we are
always being given up to death for Jesus's sake, so that
the life of Jesus may be manifested in our mortal flesh.'
(2 Cor. 4:7-11)

Prisoner for Christ

On his arrival in Jerusalem, towards the close of the
year 58, and nearly 30 years after the passion of Jesus,
Paul began his own Via Dolorosa, amid the fickle fury
of the crowds, the same feebleness of the Roman procurator, and the same fertile cunning of the religious
authorities. Even James and the elders of the Christian
Church were apprehensive of his coming, for they
pointed out, 'You see, brother, how many thousands
there are among the Jews of those who have believed;
they are all zealous for the law, and they have been told
about you that you teach all the Jews who are among
the Gentiles to forsake Moses, telling them not to circumcise their children or observe the customs.' Paul
agreed to undergo a week's ritual purification in the
Temple, with four other men under a vow for whose
expenses he paid, to show that he personally kept the
Law. When the week's ritual was almost completed,
some Asian Jews recognized Paul and, stirring up the
crowd, accused him of bringing Greeks into the Temple.
They would have lynched Paul if the guard had not
turned out to protect him and hustle him up the steps of
the Antonia Fortress. Paul, speaking in Greek and
declaring his Roman citizenship, requested a final
opportunity to address the mob, which he did in
Hebrew.

When he described his own conversion, all listened in
silence, but when he declared his mission to the Gentiles

he was shouted down. Taken into the fortress for
flogging, in preparation for his interrogation, Paul
claimed exemption by his citizenship, was taken into
protective custody, and appeared before the Sanhedrin
the following day.

Within the Council, Paul skilfully divided the Pharisees from the Sadducees by claiming to be a Pharisee
and basing his claims to be a Pharisee on the resurrection of the dead, a doctrine unacceptable to the Sadducees. Paul was withdrawn from the debate that
followed and returned to the fortress. Some forty men
vowed to fast until they had killed Paul. Information of
their plot reached the Roman commander and he sent
Paul, under both an infantry and a cavalry escort, that
night down to Antipatris, a Roman staging-post on the
way to the coast. The next morning, after travelling all
through the night, the infantry returned to Jerusalem,
and the cavalry took Paul on to Caesarea to present him
to the procurator Felix. When his accusers from Jerusalem brought a prosecutor called Tertullus down to
Caesarea, Felix heard the case. Paul successfully challenged the charge of disturbance and profanation of the
Temple, but he was retained in custody for the two
remaining years of Felix's term of office. Felix, anxious
to gain favour with the leaders of the Jews, left Paul in
close confinement.

The new procurator, Festus, was approached on the
matter by the Jewish chief priests, who demanded Paul's
transfer for trial before the Council in Jerusalem. Festus,
however, invited the accusers to Caesarea, and during
the hearing asked Paul if he was willing to return to
Jerusalem for trial. That left Paul with only one alternative: as a Roman citizen to appeal to the emperor

**Paul's voyage
to Rome**

59-62 AD

0   100 miles

himself. Festus had no choice but to accept his appeal and send him, under escort, to Rome. In order to arraign the charges, he took the opportunity to present Paul to Herod Agrippa II, the secular head of the Jewish people. Paul's eloquent speech evoked Agrippa's comment, 'In a short time you think to make me a Christian!...this man could have been set free if he had not appealed to Caesar.'

Probably in the autumn of the year 60, Paul and other prisoners in the charge of a centurion called Julius (*see* JULIUS) boarded a coaster which sailed round the eastern Mediterranean, calling in at Tyre and Myra on the

Roman ship, carved on the lid of a Phoenician sarcophagus. Paul embarked at Caesarea on a ship from Adramyttium, on the west coast of Asia Minor.

south coast of Asia Minor. There they transferred to a larger ship of the grain fleet based on Alexandria, which took them along the south coast of Crete to the small port of Fair Havens. Though it was late autumn and the time of rough weather, the captain, supported by the centurion and ignoring a warning from Paul, decided to run for the larger harbour of Phoenix, further west along the Cretan coast. The ship was driven hopelessly off course by a hurricane 'north-easter', passing the island of Cauda and scudding south-west towards the coast of Africa. After a fortnight's running helplessly before the wind, the ship was wrecked on the island of Malta. Largely owing to the initiative and common-sense of Paul, whose fourth experience of shipwreck this was, all hands were saved. For three months they enjoyed the hospitality of the Maltese, before sailing in another Alexandrian vessel for Puteoli, via Syracuse in Sicily, Rhegium on the toe of Italy, and through the Straits of Messina. After a week at Puteoli they went on to Rome on foot. Christians came out to meet the party at the Appian Market, to accompany and encourage them on the final stage of their journey. On arrival in Rome, Paul was allowed to rent a house and receive visitors, though constantly guarded for two years under house-arrest.

Letters from captivity

During this time, Paul wrote what have come to be called the 'captivity letters'. The first of these was probably to the Church at Colossae, about 100 miles inland from Ephesus and founded during Paul's long stay in that city. This letter is in the nature of a denouncement

St Paul's Island off St Paul's Bay, Malta: the traditional site of his shipwreck on the journey to Rome. The statue is of Paul.

of heresy with a scholarly defence of Paul's teaching of the Atonement – that Jesus is the only mediator necessary between man and God. A second letter addressed to the Church at Ephesus, following rather the same theme, may in fact have been originally written to the Laodiceans, a Christian community on the road between Ephesus and Colossae (mentioned in Col. 4:16).

left Paul's shipwreck, alongside scenes from the lives of the saints, from a late 13th-century French *Bible moralisée*.

below The ancient Appian Way, along which Paul and his companions travelled from the port of Puteoli to Rome.

Portrait of Nero, with laurel wreath, on a bronze coin minted in AD 64-6. It was under Nero's persecution of Christians at Rome that Paul was martyred.

Both these letters were sent by the hand of Tychicus, as was the personal letter to Philemon begging the life of his runaway slave Onesimus, who had been so 'useful' (a pun on the meaning of the slave's name) to Paul in his captivity. This last letter gives the impression that Paul expected his release and planned to revisit Asia.

Whether Paul was released, and whether he fulfilled his ambition to visit Spain, as expressed in his letter to the Romans (15:24), and implied by Clement some forty years later, we cannot be certain, nor do we know whether he returned to the eastern Mediterranean. The so-called 'pastoral epistles' of 1 and 2 Timothy and Titus provide the only possible clues, being probably written after the first term of imprisonment, if they are the work of Paul. From them it would appear that Paul *did* revisit Asia, Achaia, and Macedonia. His final paragraph of advice in his second letter to Timothy could imply that he was finally arrested at Troas, for Timothy is asked to bring the cloak and scrolls left there.

A final betrayal?

It could also imply that his arrest was due to the treach-ery of one 'Alexander, the coppersmith', who 'did me great harm'. Certainly this letter indicates that the end is near: 'No one took my part; all deserted me. May it not be charged against them! But the Lord stood by me and gave me strength to proclaim the word fully, that all the Gentiles might hear it. So I was rescued from the lion's mouth.'

Eusebius, the 'Father of Church History', and 4th-century bishop of Caesarea, records that Paul was again taken to Rome and killed in Nero's persecution in the year 67. Tertullian, the 'Father of the African Church' in the 2nd century, records that he was beheaded. St Gregory the Great and later writers site his execution on the left bank of the Tiber, some three miles from Rome on the road to the port of Ostia. The place became known as the 'Three Fountains', following the legend that where Paul's head bounced three times, three fountains appeared. His body was traditionally believed to be buried in a cemetery nearer Rome, by the Ostia Way, on the site of which now stands the Basilica of St Paul Outside the Walls – dedicated to the most powerful personality in the history of the Christian Church. [Under the name of SAUL: Acts 8:1; 9:1-30; 13:1-12. Under the name of PAUL: Acts 13:13-28; Letter to the Romans; 1 Cor. 1:12, 13; 3:4, 5, 22; 16:21; 1 Thess. 2:18; 2 Thess. 3:17; 1st and 2nd Letters to Timothy; Titus; Philem. 9; 2 Peter 3:15]

PAULUS *see* SERGIUS PAULUS

PERSIS (Gk. 'Persian woman') One of the women warmly greeted by Paul at the close of his letter to the Christian congregation in Rome, as 'beloved' and 'one who has worked hard in the Lord'. Her name was common among female slaves. [Rom. 16:12]

right The Martyrdom of St Paul, by Giotto (?1267-1337). Paul's head falls to the ground at his feet.
below The martyrdom of SS Peter and Paul, from a 15th-century Italian manuscript. Paul, as a Roman citizen, was beheaded, whereas Peter was crucified upside-down.

S · PE   TRVS ·

PETER (Gk. from the Aram. 'rock'; original name in Gk. *Simon*, 'hearing') Simon called Peter was a master fisherman on the Lake of Galilee, who became one of the earliest disciples of Jesus. He became one of Jesus's closest friends and was the first to recognize Jesus as the Messiah. He is particularly remembered for his three-fold denial of Jesus, his repentance, and his threefold commission by Jesus to 'feed my sheep'. This rustic Galilean fisherman, whose character resembled shifting sand rather than the rock from which Jesus named him 'Peter', did in fact become the natural leader of the twelve apostles. Later, his leadership seems to have been superseded by Paul, but Peter is the traditional first bishop of Rome, and his tomb is reputed to have been excavated below the high altar of the basilica of St Peter at Rome.

A wealth of human qualities

Of all the personalities in the New Testament, perhaps we know most about the character of Peter. He is the more attractive for his constant mistakes and forgiveness, his boisterous and impetuous enthusiasm, and for his good intentions and self-confidence that so soon seemed to disappear. At first he seems to have been a surprising choice as the 'Rock' upon which Jesus was to found his Church, but he justified his choice by an example that has inspired and encouraged Christians down the centuries.

The sources of information about Peter include the Gospels, Acts, Galatians, and tradition. He was the son of a certain John, or more probably Jonah. He was a native of Bethsaida, literally a 'fisher home', near the Lake of Galilee. He was living at Capernaum, however, at the beginning of the ministry of Jesus, together with his wife and her family, reasonably near the synagogue. Living in the district of Galilee (*Galil* in Hebrew means a region or encircled area) surrounded by Gentiles, Peter may have spoken colloquial Greek, but his native language would be Aramaic and his Galilean accent was quite obvious in Jerusalem at the trial of Jesus. When Peter and John were described by the Sanhedrin, the supreme Council, as 'uneducated, common men', this applied to their lack of Rabbinic training.

Peter and Andrew his brother were fishermen by trade and in partnership with Zebedee and his sons. Jesus drew his disciples from the fishermen of Galilee, whose best fishing-grounds were at the north-east of the lake, where the Jordan River deposited its silt. He drew his followers from the hardy men who braved the west wind's sudden squalls, funnelled down through the Gulf of Pigeons above Magdala. In a highly-concentrated

left Peter enthroned: central panel of a 13th-century altarpiece by an artist of the school of Guido da Siena.

below Fishing with drag-net off the north-west coast of the Sea of Galilee, near the home of Peter and Andrew at Bethsaida.

population, often inflamed by a spirit of nationalism, Jesus went to a trade which had no private wrongs. He called men, not from their dreams, but from work they were content to do from day to day, till something higher should touch them. And so it has come to pass that not the jargon of fanatics and brigands, but the speech of the fishermen and their simple craft has become the language and symbolism of Christianity.

In the Gospels, Peter's character appears to be at variance with the nickname of the 'Rock', given to him by Jesus. Whether his name was to describe his physique or his temperament, that name was prophetically confirmed by Jesus at Caesarea Philippi and amply justified by his granite-like leadership of the apostles from Pentecost onwards. He was always a man of action, but from his calling by Jesus to his denial of Jesus he was a man of impulse and aggressive energy, of childlike simplicity and daring, alternating with a weak and cowardly instability.

The turning-points in Peter's life were the appearance of Jesus to him after the resurrection, and Jesus's threefold question and commission to him to 'feed my sheep'. Certainly from Pentecost onwards he was the true and undoubted leader of the Church, facing without fear the consequent persecution and punishment, and doing so with an inspiring courage and humility. This humility is strikingly illustrated in the Gospel of Mark, which shows him in a far less favourable light than do the other three Gospels! This is striking when it is remembered that Mark's Gospel has been said by Irenaeus, as early as the year 85, to have been based on the reminiscences of Peter, the 'mind behind' the Second Gospel. (*see also* MARK)

A sincere pupil

The word 'disciple' means a 'pupil', and Peter was certainly prepared to learn and was deeply concerned about his faith. Peter and his brother Andrew were probably both disciples of John the Baptist during his ministry of teaching and baptism by the River Jordan. Peter was introduced to Jesus by Andrew, and Jesus greeted him, 'So you are Simon the son of John? You shall be called Cephas' – the Aramaic equivalent of the Greek 'Peter', meaning 'rock'. The evangelists used the Greek name 'Peter', which became his personal name and was applied to no one else in the New Testament. It is probable that Peter, Andrew, and Philip – all from the same town, Bethsaida – returned with Jesus to Galilee, attended the wedding at Cana, and were impressed by the miracle of the changing of the water into wine (John 2:11), before resuming their fishing on the lake. When Jesus himself arrived at Capernaum to begin his lakeside ministry, on leaving the synagogue with James and John he went straight to the house of Peter and Andrew, where he cured Peter's mother-in-law of a fever.

Some time later, Jesus used Peter's boat from which to speak to the crowds on shore. There are little bays on the north coast of the lake which form natural auditoria, with the water of the lake acting as a sounding-board. On this occasion Jesus prevailed upon Peter's greater experience, persuading him to shoot his nets in daylight after a fruitless night's fishing. The two pairs of brothers, James and John, Andrew and Peter, were completely overcome by the remarkable catch which they then made, and they were called by Jesus to follow him in full-time training to become 'fishers of men'.

From then onwards, Peter's house at Capernaum became the headquarters of Jesus's lakeside ministry, and Peter's boat was always at his disposal. The selection of the team of twelve disciples was completed, and Peter was always included at the head of the list. Perhaps this was not so much because he was acknowledged as leader by the other disciples, as the result of the fact that his household was the headquarters of the group and that he and Andrew were its first members.

With James and John, Peter formed an inner circle of three, who alone were allowed to accompany Jesus into the house for the raising of Jairus's daughter, to witness the transfiguration, and to share the agony in the Garden of Gethsemane. Peter was often the spokesman of the twelve, and was their natural leader. He walked on the water. He spoke loyally for the others when Jesus's teaching about the 'Bread of Life' scandalized them. He expressed the conviction of the twelve when he made his great confession at Caesarea Philippi: 'You are the Christ, the Son of the living God.' At once Jesus replied, 'You are Peter, and on this rock I will build my church, and the powers of death shall not prevail against it. I will give you the keys of the kingdom of heaven . . .' Peter's confession of faith, however, was followed by a sharp rebuke, because he refused to listen to Jesus's first prediction of his passion. In his capacity as leader, Peter was approached by the tax-collectors for the Temple tribute due from Jesus and his disciples. He was constantly voicing the questions of the twelve about the limits of forgiveness, and about the destruction of the Temple.

Peter's role in the passion story was considerable. Together with John, he was entrusted with the preparations for the Last Supper, in which Jesus clearly confirmed his leadership 'when you have turned again', and at once foretold the threefold denial, which Peter passionately contradicted; Peter also protested at the feet-washing, and then impetuously demanded that Jesus wash him completely. Peter beckoned John to ask Jesus the identity of the betrayer; and although chosen to keep watch with James and John in the Garden of Gethsemane, Peter slept with them. At the moment of arrest, however, it was Peter who struck out in defence of Jesus with his sword – only to be rebuked by Jesus.

above Peter's threefold denial of Jesus in the high priest's palace, followed by the cock crowing. Panel from the 5th-century doors of S. Sabina, Rome.

When all the rest fled, Peter followed at a distance to the high priest's palace, where he was admitted to the court after the intervention of John with the portress. There he was accused of being one of Jesus's followers, denied three times that he knew Jesus – then remembered Jesus's prediction and bitterly repented. Luke adds that 'the Lord turned and looked at Peter'. If Mark's account of the trial before the Sanhedrin may be said to reveal the lack of witnesses of Jesus's admission to being the Christ, for which he was condemned as a blasphemer, then perhaps Peter's denial might well have prevented Peter himself being forced to give evidence of Jesus's Messiahship.

Various churches have been built on the possible sites of the high priest's palace to commemorate the trial and imprisonment of Jesus by Caiaphas, as well as Peter's denial and repentance. Some place the site on top of the Western Hill, near the Armenian chapel, others prefer the remains covered by the Church of St Peter in Gallicantu, 'of the cock-crowing'. Here the story can be vividly reconstructed. Within the present church, over the high altar, is an illustration of the trial, which was conducted in the rock-hewn courtyard on the next level below the church. The prisoner is standing on a raised platform or dock, in the centre and with his back to the wall, chained by the wrists to escorts seated on either side of him. It is easy to picture this scene on the lower level, facing westwards into the hillside in which are cut staircases and galleries. On one of these Peter must have sat with the soldiers, warmed himself by the fire, and denied knowing his master.

On either side of the wall, behind the raised dock platform, the corners of the courtyard are cut square to a height of ten feet. In the very centre of the courtroom is the mouth of a bottle-necked prison, into which the condemned prisoner could be lowered after trial. Descending to a third level, there is a complete guardroom, all round the walls of which are still to be found the staples for the prisoners' chains (some consider this to have been a stable in Byzantine times). On one side there is a small window opening on to the bottle-necked condemned cell. Below this window, and left projecting

below, top Modern Church of St Peter in Gallicantu (St Peter of the Cock-crowing), which encloses a possible site of the high priest's palace on the Western Hill.
below, bottom Among the remains of the high priest's palace are the storage chambers for the trespass offerings in grain and oil.

from the floor when the guardroom was excavated from the living rock, is a block on which the guard stood to peer down into the gloom of the cell below him.

On the opposite side of the guardroom is the whipping-block. Here, tied up by the wrists with leather thongs through staples at the top, a belt round his waist secured to a staple at each side, the prisoner would be stretched up, taut and helpless. At his feet were two bowls carved in the rock, one for salt to disinfect his wounds, one for vinegar to revive him. Here, both Peter and John received the legal sentence of 'forty lashes less one', thirteen on each shoulder from the back, and thirteen on the chest from the front, were commanded not to preach Jesus as Christ, and then sent home. Yet they returned daily to the Temple to preach this very thing.

The Gospels do not mention Peter from the night of Jesus's trial to the morning of his resurrection, but the writer of the first Letter of Peter says that he was 'a witness of the sufferings of Christ' (1 Pet. 5:1). On Easter morning, Peter and John ran to the tomb, to find it empty. Both Luke and Paul report that Jesus appeared specially to Peter alone on the day of the resurrection.

Certainly he shared with several others the appearance by the Lake of Galilee. Then John recognized Jesus; but Peter swam ashore to share the breakfast cooked on the fire of coals. There, Peter's love was thrice tested for his threefold denial: 'Simon, son of John, do you love me?' Peter then received his threefold commission to shepherd the flock of God. There, too, he received the prediction of his martyrdom. And there today the remains of the medieval chapel of 'Peter's Primacy' enclose a vast rock which projects out into the clear waters of the lake. The rock, known as the 'Table of the Lord', is still in its striking simplicity a silent witness to the resurrection tradition in Galilee, and to the commission of Peter as 'prince of the apostles'.

Peter takes command

After Jesus's ascension, at which he 'sent out' his apostles into the world, Peter at once assumed the leadership of the apostles. He suggested the choice of a replacement for Judas. He spoke for the apostles on the day of Pentecost, with great inspiration and effect. He was the first of the apostles to perform a miracle in the name of Jesus – healing the cripple at the Beautiful

below Detail from a 4th-century sarcophagus in the Vatican grottoes below St Peter's, showing Jesus giving Peter a scroll of the Law.

right Peter, holding his key, presides over the apostles at Pentecost: from an early 13th-century German missal.

Gate of the Temple. He conducted the defence of John and himself before the Sanhedrin, and pronounced the condemnation of Ananias and Sapphira. He was soon renowned for his miracles done in the name of Jesus, and he and John were sent to Samaria where, through the laying-on of their hands, the Holy Spirit came to the baptized believers.

It was Peter who healed Aeneas, the paralytic at Lydda, and he raised to life Dorcas, the woman of many good works in Joppa. While in Joppa (now Jaffa), Peter received a vision convincing him, as he admitted, that 'God shows no partiality, but in every nation any one who fears him and does what is right is acceptable to him.' He then converted and baptized Cornelius, a Roman centurion, and his whole household at Caesarea.

above Peter freed from prison by the angel: detail from a 13th-century altarpiece by an artist of the school of Guido da Siena.
below Peter healing the son of the prefect of Antioch: an incident not recorded in the Acts. Painting by Masaccio (1401-28) and Filippino Lippi (1457-1504).

above The old Basilica of St Peter, Rome: anonymous fresco in the Church of St Martin on the Mount, Rome. Note the flagellation of Jesus, top right.

At the Council of Jerusalem, he upheld his decision to do this and was supported by Paul and Barnabas.

We know little of Peter's work outside Palestine. Paul mentions Peter's visit to Antioch (Gal. 2:11-21), where he yielded to the demands of certain Jewish-Christians, in dissociating himself temporarily from the Gentiles. Peter seems to have visited Corinth (1 Cor. 1:12), and he may well have been engaged in evangelism in Rome itself before Paul's arrival. (Rom. 15:20-22) Certainly, Eusebius and Origen declare that he went to Rome and, as an old man, suffered martyrdom by crucifixion head downwards, during the reign of Nero, probably in AD 64.

The site of the present St Peter's Church in Rome, and of the first Constantinian basilica there, has been venerated by Christians from the earliest times as the site of the tomb of Peter. The first memorial over his grave was built in about 160. A vast five-aisled basilica was built by Constantine on the Vatican Hill above the traditional site of the grave. Two series of excavations instituted by Pope Paul XII, from 1940-51 and from 1953-7, have established what if anything has survived of the original grave. The apostle's body was certainly buried on the Vatican Hill, at a spot close to the gardens of Nero and their famous circus or sports stadium. The

337

grave must have been a plain earth trench covered with large tiles. This whole area later came in time to be one of the largest burial-grounds in Rome and the apostle's grave became hemmed in by others, dating back to about the year 70 or 80. There are 2nd- or early 3rd-century Greek *graffiti*, cut in a dividing wall above the traditional site of the grave, which refer to Peter.

The First Letter

Of the two letters ascribed to Peter, the first is more likely to reflect the teaching and message of Peter himself than the second, which was written and attributed to him at least a hundred years after his death. The first is a message to the Churches in northern Asia Minor to help them meet the shock of sudden and violent persecution, to strengthen and reassure them in the faith, and to encourage them to remain firm in their allegiance to God. After the greeting there follows a long, perhaps baptismal discourse, unlike a simple letter in form or content, and without any personal or local references. This may have been a separate composition, with its own introduction and conclusion in the form of a sermon on the nature of the Christian life.

It assumes a basic knowledge of the Christian faith and it instructs the readers accordingly about baptism, regeneration, the nature of God, the sufferings of Jesus, and the Christian hope. The references to suffering and trials are of a general nature and do not indicate existing persecution. The mere profession of Christianity does not incur punishment, indeed those innocent of any wrongdoing can expect to be vindicated by the Roman magistrate. The Greek is excellent, the tone calm and tranquil.

The letter then begins to reflect an atmosphere of tension. The style is simple and direct, the language quick and nervous. Suffering is now a stark reality and their faith is put to the test; they are being persecuted for the very name of Christian by the authorities. Now is their judgment, their opportunity to share the sufferings of Christ in the brotherhood of his Church, that they may share his glory. The letter closes with greetings from the Church in Rome (here called Babylon), and from 'Mark my son'. The bearer was Silvanus.

There is a disagreement among scholars about the authorship of this letter. Some accept that it was written by Peter, explaining its style and language as the work of Silvanus, the secretary. In that case the persecution referred to must be Nero's of AD 64. But that persecution did not extend to the provinces of Asia Minor and Christianity did not reach Pontus by the Black Sea before 65. There was persecution of Christians under the Emperor Trajan (98-117) in Bythinia and Pontus, where the governor was Pliny the Younger. Pliny's

own records of examinations under torture both of men and women have survived and accord with the description in 1 Peter. The letter is first described by Polycarp in 135, so must have been written between 64 and 135. It may perhaps be the composite work of Peter, Silvanus, and another writer, adapting it to the needs of a later persecution, using the name of Peter as a suitable martyr-apostle to encourage the suffering Christians of his time. The letter is important as not teaching the doctrine of a single author, but as a systematic presentation of the faith of the early Christian Church.

The Second Letter

This letter was undoubtedly written in the 2nd century

above Roman statue in St Peter's, Rome. The head was replaced by one of Peter in the 13th century, and the hands by ones holding keys in the 14th century.

left The Martyrdom of St Peter, by Caravaggio (1583-1610).

under the name of Peter, in order to discredit views which the author thought unapostolic. The Greek style and the general tone is absolutely different from 1 Peter. Eusebius, writing in the 4th century, roundly declares that of all the writings in the name of Peter, 'only one epistle is genuine'. Certainly, this letter, 2 Peter, is dependent upon that of Jude. References to all Paul's letters also show that it was not written until after they had been collected into one corpus. The letter denounces false teachers with all the authority of an apostle. The inclusion within the New Testament of this letter is not based upon its authorship, but upon its intrinsic value recognized by the Church as the authentic voice of apostolic teaching. [Matt. 4:18; 10:2; 14:29; 16:6-23; 17:1; 26:37; Mark 3:16; 5:37; 8:32, 33; 9:2; 14:33; Luke 6:14; 8:51; 9:20-28; John 21:2-20; Acts 1:13, 15; 2:14, 38; 3:1-12; 4:13, 19; 5:3, 8, 9, 15, 29; 9:32-40; 10:5-48; 11:2-18; 12:3-18; 15:6-14; 1st and 2nd Letters of Peter]

PHANUEL (Gk. from the Heb. 'face of God') The father of the prophetess Anna and a member of the tribe of Asher. Anna was among those faithful Jews who, being in the Temple at Jerusalem at the time of the presentation of Jesus, 'gave thanks to God' and spoke of Jesus to all who were looking for the redemption of Jerusalem. [Luke 2:36]

PHARISEES (Gk. 'separated ones') At the time of Jesus, the Pharisees were the most powerful religious group among the Jews and his constant opponents. Jesus continually denounced their external observance of the Law, their multitude of petty traditions, and particularly their self-righteousness.

The Pharisees were the successors of the 'Holy Ones' who had fought for religious freedom during the Greek occupation of Palestine from 332 BC. Like the 'Holy Ones' the Pharisees had 'separated' themselves by their pious efforts to maintain the Law. Though they were themselves mostly middle-class, they had become essentially the people's party, very different from the Sadducees, the party of the chief priests, who held aloof from the passionate enthusiasm of the Pharisees for righteousness. Unlike the Sadducees, they believed in angels and spirits as intermediaries between God and man, in resurrection after death, and in retribution in the world to come. Also unlike the Sadducees, the Pharisees held that the Tradition of the Elders was an authoritative interpretation of the Old Testament Law of Moses. They would not revolt against Gentile rule; if God was in charge of history, they held, it was not man's place to force his hand. Whereas the Zealot party burned to establish a national kingdom by force of arms, the Pharisees waited for God's intervention through the Messiah.

St Peter, holding the keys of the Kingdom: carving from Moissac, France, early 12th century.

18th-century German drawing of a Pharisee, based on the description of Josephus.

Though probably few in number – perhaps 6,000 at the time of Jesus – the Pharisees were much admired by the man in the street for their austerity, both for their hatred of pagan rule and for their challenge to the rule of the chief priests. They fostered synagogue life and worship, calling people back to a study of the Law and its application to their own time. They consisted mainly of businessmen, shopkeepers, and teachers – but with some priests also.

Their 'fellowships' held regular meetings and prescribed rules for the admission of new members. These rules included the observance of seven 'hours of prayer', the Pharisaic interpretation of a tithe of one-tenth of all possessions to the Temple, fasting twice a week on the days when traditionally Moses ascended and came down from Mount Sinai, and performing scores of ritual washings and offerings, besides the complicated code of food laws and Sabbath regulations. All these were, of course, additions to the Mosaic commandments of the Law. The Pharisees regarded with scorn all those who did not come up to their own rigorous standards. Such people the Pharisees relegated to the depressed class of 'sinners', contact with whom rendered the Pharisee himself 'unclean'.

Opposition-group to Jesus

In the Gospel narratives the Pharisees are often linked with the Scribes, through whom they exerted their influence upon the minds of the people, for the Scribes presided in the local courts and taught in the local schools. It was inevitable that many Pharisees were bitterly opposed to Jesus, and constantly denounced by him. They rejected his claims to Messiahship. (John 9:16, 22) He condemned their ostentation, their hypocrisy, their doctrine of salvation by works, their impenitence and their lovelessness, which were so far from his own life and his teaching of the free forgiveness and love of God, culminating as it did in his death on the cross.

In the Gospels, the picture of the Pharisee is painted almost completely black and reflects the bitterness which later developed between the Christian Church and Rabbinic Judaism. This is particularly the case with Matthew's Gospel, where the denunciations of Scribes

Remains of a phylactery, a leather box containing small scrolls of the Law, from the Essene community at Qumran, 1st century AD.

and Pharisees are especially virulent. But it is unlikely that these fierce and wholesale criticisms were directed by Jesus himself against the whole party, rather than against unworthy members of it. Indeed, some Pharisees played vital roles in the early Christian Church, including Nicodemus (John 3:1; 7:50, 51; 19:39), Gamaliel, who publicly defended the Apostles before the Sanhedrin (Acts 5:34-40), Joseph of Arimathea (Matt. 27:57; Mark 15:43; Luke 23:50; John 19:38), and certainly the Apostle Paul. (Phil. 3:5) Paul uses the title 'Pharisee' of himself, as a name of honour and respect: 'As to the law [I am] a Pharisee.'

The conflict between Jesus and the Pharisees occurred mainly in Galilee. During the passion of Jesus in Jerusalem, they remained in the background, the lead in the attack upon Jesus being taken by the Sadducees, although they combined with the Herodians to ask him a question about the payment of taxes to Rome. Luke records three occasions when Jesus was invited to meals in the houses of Pharisees. His conversation in the house of Simon the Pharisee (Luke 7:36) sums up the difference between his philosophy and that of those Pharisees who were scandalized at the company he kept.

On this occasion a woman with a bad reputation came in, and sitting behind Jesus anointed his feet, thereby according Jesus the treatment which Simon, his host, had neglected to offer his guest. When Simon criticized Jesus, thinking that surely he should have recognized the kind of woman she was and driven her away, Jesus replied with this parable: ' "A certain creditor had two debtors; one owed five hundred denarii, and the other fifty. When they could not pay, he forgave them both. Now which of them will love him more?" Simon answered, "The one, I suppose, to whom he forgave more." ' Then Jesus compared Simon's own lack of courtesy with the almost embarrassing attentions of the woman, explaining: 'Her sins, which are many, are forgiven, for she loved much; but he who is forgiven little, loves little.'

The letter of the Law

Perhaps the first point of basic disagreement between Jesus and certain of the Pharisees was in the interpretation of the Law of Moses, in the matter of Sabbath observance. When Jesus healed a man with a withered hand on the Sabbath (Mark 3:1-6), he challenged the Pharisees to say whether it was lawful to do good on such a day. He allowed his disciples to pluck and rub ears of corn, thus technically reaping and threshing on the Sabbath day (Mark 2:23-6). He justified his actions by declaring, 'The sabbath was made for man, not man for the sabbath; so the Son of man is lord even of

'Whited sepulchres' outside the city and over the Kidron ravine, on the lower slopes of the Mount of Olives.

the sabbath.' Jesus, thus quoting Deut. 5:12-15, indicated that the institution of the Sabbath was for man's benefit. He did not deny that his action was a breach of the Law, but justified it as meeting human need.

The Pharisees also criticized Jesus for allowing his disciples to eat without washing their hands, thus disobeying the Levitical hygienic regulations. Jesus declared, 'What comes out of a man is what defiles a man. For from within, out of the heart of man, come evil thoughts, fornication, theft, murder, adultery, coveting, wickedness, deceit, licentiousness, envy, slander, pride, foolishness. All these evil things come from within, and they defile a man.' (Mark 7:20-23) Jesus, as a loyal Jew, respected the Law of Moses and sought to fulfil it, but his idea of fulfilment was not that of many contemporary Scribes. He kept the Commandments; but he summarized their content in two positive principles: 'You shall love the Lord your God with all your heart, and with all your soul, and with all your might', (Deut. 6:5) and 'You shall love your neighbour as yourself.' (Lev. 19:18)

It is likely that the condemnation of the Pharisees by Jesus as reported in the Gospels has been over-emphasized, particularly in the Gospel of Matthew. It must be remembered that this Gospel was probably written at a time when the Judeo-Christians were divided into two parties. This division was based on and expressed in contradictory attitudes towards the observance by Gentiles of the Law of Moses. A 'circumcision party' held that all Gentile Christians must keep the Jewish Law and be circumcised. Many rejected this demand, considering the Law of Jesus sufficient for the Gentile Christians. The Gospel-writers appear to reflect this division of opinion in their presentation of the controversy between Jesus and the Pharisees. [Matt. 5:20; 9:14, 34; 15:1, 12; 16:1-12; 19:3; 23:2-29; Mark 2:16, 18, 24; 3:6; 8:11, 15; 12:13-17; Luke 5:30, 33; 6:2, 7; 7:36, 37, 39; 11:37-53; 12:1; 14:1-6; 16:14; John 1:24; 3:1; 7:32, 47, 48; 11:47, 57; Acts 15:5; 23:6-9; 26:5; Phil. 3:5]

PHILEMON (Gk. 'loving') This well-established member of the Christian Church at Colossae was the recipient of a personal letter from Paul the Apostle. It is the only surviving letter of Paul's vast personal correspondence, and the only letter in the New Testament addressed to an individual rather than to a community.

Philemon was evidently a wealthy man, the owner of slaves, able to entertain the local Christian congregation in his house. Paul's opening sentence to him refers to himself as 'a prisoner for Christ Jesus', and addresses Philemon as 'our beloved fellow worker'. The greeting embraces 'Apphia our sister', probably Philemon's wife, and 'Archippus our fellow soldier', probably Philemon's son. From Paul's reference to Archippus in his letter to the Church at Colossae (Col. 4:17), Archippus

was a leader of their congregation. (*see* COLOSSIANS)

Writing in captivity, Paul had a particular reason and a favour to ask of his friend Philemon at Colossae. He also needed to write a general letter to the Colossian Church to counter certain false teaching, of which he had received reports from Epaphras, their first evangelist. Both letters were written at the same time and despatched from the same town to the same destination by the same messenger, Tychicus. In both letters Paul links with his own greeting the name of Timothy, his companion during his stay in Ephesus. In both letters he sends also greetings from Epaphras, Luke the physician, Demas, Aristarchus, and Mark the nephew of Barnabas. It is just possible that these letters were written during Paul's brief imprisonment in Ephesus, sometime during the years 54 and 57, but they are more likely to have been written during his long and leisurely period of house-arrest in Rome during the years 61-3.

Advocate for a slave

During his captivity Paul was approached by an escaped slave called Onesimus. The Greek name means 'useful'. He had run away from his master Philemon in Colossae and had made his way to the teeming capital of Rome, a notorious hide-out for fugitive slaves. There, in destitution and danger, the hunted man had sought out the imprisoned Apostle Paul and had attached himself to him as his personal attendant. Paul came to know Onesimus's story, his unsatisfactory record as a slave to Philemon, whom he had robbed as well as deserted – and to whom his very life was now forfeit on both accounts. Useless as Onesimus had been to Philemon, he became invaluable to Paul in his captivity. He had been taught by Paul and had apparently matured considerably in Christian character, for he was prepared to return – at the risk of his life – to the service of his deserted master, Philemon.

The sole purpose of Paul's 'covering letter' is to return Philemon's property with a plea not only for his forgiveness of Onesimus but for his new reception as a brother in Christ Jesus. Paul's letter is amazing in its tact, its tenderness, and its utter charm. It presumes to seek pardon for a slave for the most serious and the most easily identified offences against the common law: theft and flight. Speaking as a Christian apostle to one for whose conversion he is indirectly responsible, he does not begin to dictate, but delicately touches on their mutual obligations. The letter is a priceless memorial to the pastoral skill and affection of the apostle, in a way that his more theological treatises can never be.

Here, in the Greek style, is the opening thanksgiving and prayer addressed to Philemon: 'I thank my God always when I remember you in my prayers, because I hear of your love and of the faith which you have toward the Lord Jesus and all the saints, and I pray that the sharing of your faith may promote the knowledge of all

the good that is ours in Christ. For I have derived much joy and comfort from your love, my brother, because the hearts of the saints have been refreshed through you.'

Then he gently begins his petition for Onesimus, as a father might for his own son. He even implies that he would have wished Philemon to return Onesimus to Rome in order to serve him in prison on behalf of Philemon. 'Accordingly, though I am bold enough in Christ to command you to do what is required, yet for love's sake I prefer to appeal to you – I, Paul, an ambassador and now a prisoner also for Christ Jesus – I appeal to you for my child, Onesimus, whose father I have become in my imprisonment. (Formerly he was useless to you, but now he is indeed useful to you and to me.) I am sending him back to you, sending my very heart. I would have been glad to keep him with me, in order that he might serve me on your behalf during my imprisonment for the gospel; but I preferred to do nothing without your consent in order that your goodness might not be by compulsion but of your own free will.'

Paul then proceeds to his daring request not only for Onesimus's forgiveness, but that he should be welcomed back as a brother, as Paul himself might expect to be received! Paul takes responsibility for whatever sum of money Onesimus owes to his master: taking the pen from his secretary (probably Timothy), Paul himself writes his bond in the required legal terms: 'I, Paul, write this with my own hand, I will repay it ...' but adding, 'To say nothing of your owing me even your own self.'

Thus Paul closes his letter, in complete confidence of Philemon's willingness to do even more than he asks. Paul even asks on his own account that Philemon prepare his guest-chamber, as Paul expects shortly to be free to return to Asia. That Philemon preserved this letter and that it has been included in the New Testament surely shows that he granted Paul's request, though whether Onesimus returned to Rome, or Paul ever visited Colossae, we may never know for certain. According to tradition Philemon and his wife Apphia were martyred at Colossae and Onesimus became bishop of Ephesus.

This beautiful letter should surely convince all who accuse Paul of changing the simple message of Jesus into a complicated system of doctrine, that behind all his teaching lay the basic truth declared in the Sermon on the Mount.

This letter, too, is a milestone on the road to the emancipation of slaves; the principle that a slave be treated as a brother, that both Christian master and slave were the servants of Christ, and that all men are

Philip the Apostle,
by Peter Paul Rubens (1577-1640).

spiritually equals – this was ultimately and inevitably to destroy both the system and practice of slavery. [Letter to Philemon]

PHILETUS (Gk. 'worthy of love') A heretical teacher within the Christian community, probably at Ephesus or Troas, on the coast of Asia Minor, whom Paul found it necessary to excommunicate, as his teaching represented a real threat to the faith and loyalty of the local congregation.

In his last letter to Timothy, Paul is most insistent in his warnings against false teachers. Timothy needs to be a 'sound workman', 'handling the word rightly', avoiding 'what is ignoble', and exercising a strict supervision of his congregation. 'Remind them of this, and charge them before the Lord to avoid disputing about words, which does no good, but only ruins the hearers. Do your best to present yourself to God as one approved, a workman who has no need to be ashamed, rightly handling the word of truth. Avoid such godless chatter, for it will lead people into more and more ungodliness, and their talk will eat its way like gangrene. Among them are Hymenaeus and Philetus, who have swerved from the truth by holding that the resurrection is past already. They are upsetting the faith of some. But God's firm foundation stands.' (2 Tim. 2:14-19)

Exactly what the false teaching of Hymenaeus and Philetus was cannot be exactly or certainly determined. It is likely, however, to have been some early Gnosticism, like the Colossian heresy, robbing the resurrection of Jesus of its reality and substituting some allegorical explanation. Paul saw clearly that a purely mystical interpretation of the life and person of Jesus represented a real threat to the Christian faith in the true humanity of the Son of God, who came, lived, died, rose and returned to God, as 'the first fruits of the human race' [2 Tim. 2:17]

PHILIP (Gk. 'lover of horses') **1. Philip the Apostle** Within the gospels of Mark, Matthew, and Luke, Philip's name occurs only in the list of apostles, linked with that of Nathanael Bar-Tolmai. In the Acts, his name is listed with Thomas among the apostles present at the election of Matthias in the Upper Room before Pentecost. The Fourth Gospel, however, describes a number of incidents involving Philip, from which some estimate of his character and personality may be deduced.

Philip was almost certainly a disciple of John the Baptist, because Jesus called him from among the crowds on the banks of the River Jordan where John was baptizing. The previous day, Jesus had met Andrew, who had introduced to Jesus his brother Simon Peter. All three of them – Andrew, Peter, and Philip – came from the same town, Bethsaida, on the Lake of Galilee, and were fishermen. It was probably a day or two later that Philip brought his friend Nathanael to Jesus.

Nathanael was a native of Cana, the rival and neighbouring town to Nazareth. Consequently, his sarcastic comment on Philip's enthusiastic acclamation of Jesus as Messiah had been, 'Can anything good come out of Nazareth?' Philip's reply was 'Come and see,' and the interview with Jesus evoked Nathanael's confession, 'Rabbi, you are the Son of God! You are the King of Israel!'

It seems from the story of the feeding of the five thousand that Philip was responsible for the provisioning of the party of disciples, or for their picnic rations. Certainly he was staggered at the idea of feeding such a crowd, when Jesus suggested buying bread for them. 'Two hundred denarii would not buy enough bread for each of them to get a little,' Philip answered, perhaps with more simplicity than accuracy! No doubt he was as horrified as the others when Jesus said, 'Make the people sit down,' and equally astonished at the outcome.

During Jesus's final visit to Jerusalem before the crucifixion, some Greeks had come up for the Passover. They approached Philip with the request, 'Sir, we wish to see Jesus.' Philip told Andrew and together they went to tell Jesus. Perhaps Philip again invited his enquirers to 'Come and see'.

Again, at the Last Supper, Philip's words to Jesus are recorded in the Fourth Gospel. Jesus has just reassured his disciples that wherever he is going they will follow, and has promised them 'I am the way, and the truth, and the life; no one comes to the Father, but by me. If you had known me, you would have known my Father also; henceforth you know him and have seen him.' Philip asks, 'Lord, show us the Father, and we shall be satisfied.' Jesus answers, 'Have I been with you so long, and yet you do not know me, Philip? He who has seen me has seen the Father ... he who loves me will be loved by my Father, and I will love him and manifest myself to him.'

It seems that Philip was a sincere person, very approachable and very practical, but not yet during Jesus's ministry so much a leader as a 'contact man', whose very simplicity called forth words of Jesus that are still deeply treasured: 'He who has seen me has seen the Father.'

Traditions contradict each other about Philip's later life. A 2nd-century Ephesian tradition says that he died at Hierapolis, where there is a beautiful Byzantine church, a hundred miles inland from Ephesus. A later tradition claims that Philip was crucified; thus in medieval art he is depicted either with five loaves or a cross. [Matt. 10:3; Mark 3:18; Luke 6:14; John 1:43-48; 6:5-7; 12:21, 22; 14:8-21; Acts 1:13]

2. Philip the Deacon and Evangelist This Philip is mentioned only in the Acts, first as the second of the seven deacons elected to administer charity in the daily distribution at Jerusalem, and secondly as a successful Christian evangelist in Samaria and Caesarea.

Deacon

He was a man 'of good repute, full of the Spirit and of wisdom', selected by the Hellenistic Greek-speaking Jews, and commissioned by the apostles with prayer and the laying-on of hands; he supervised the daily distribution of bread to the Hellenist widows and poor in Jerusalem.

The earliest members of the Christian Church in Jerusalem had been mostly pious Jews, who had continued to visit the Temple and to observe the Jewish Law. The original disciples of Jesus, perhaps from Galilee or from the neighbourhood of Jerusalem, were Aramaic-speaking. Now, as others, both Jews and foreigners, had come to settle in the city, sometimes residing near the Temple, the Christian Church had acquired new members from these newcomers. Christian evangelism had been particularly successful among the Hellenistic Jews, who spoke Greek instead of Aramaic. Consequently, there developed in Jerusalem two classes of Christian believers, the Hebrews and the Hellenists, both accepting the Messiahship of Jesus.

The welfare and relief of the needy have always been a characteristic of Judaism and the Law insists on providing for the fatherless and the widow, the slave and the stranger. The Christian community gladly accepted such obligations, as may be seen from the very considerable fund for poor-relief that Paul brought back to Jerusalem from his Mediterranean congregations. There developed, however, a sense of resentment among the Hellenists that their widows were being neglected in the daily distribution at Jerusalem. This threatened to cause some friction between these two groups, the Hebrews and the Hellenists.

The twelve apostles immediately took action, summoning the community as a whole body and ruling, 'It is not right that we should give up preaching the word of God to serve tables. Therefore, brethren, pick out from among you seven men of good repute, full of the Spirit and of wisdom, whom we may appoint to this duty. But we will devote ourselves to prayer and to the ministry of the word.' (Acts 6:2-4) The whole Christian community approved this course of action and they chose seven men to undertake the domestic and financial administration of the poor-relief. These seven deacons, as they later came to be called, the apostles commissioned by prayer and the laying-on of their hands. Whatever the terms of their commission, certain of them are known to have been involved in teaching and evangelistic work, particularly Stephen and Philip.

The names of the seven – Stephen, Philip, Prochorus, Nicanor, Timon, Parmenas and Nicolaus – all indicate a Greek background, though most of them must have been of Jewish birth.

St Philip exorcizing the Devil, by Filippino Lippi (1457-1504).

Evangelist

Following the martyrdom of Stephen and the persecution of Hellenistic Christians, Philip went to Samaria to preach to the people about the Messiah. 'And the multitudes with one accord gave heed to what was said by Philip, when they heard him and saw the signs which he did. For unclean spirits came out of many who were possessed, crying with a loud voice; and many who were paralysed or lame were healed. So there was much joy in that city.' (Acts 8:6-8)

Philip the Deacon became a successful evangelist, converting a magician called Simon. 'But when they believed Philip as he preached good news about the kingdom of God and the name of Jesus Christ, they were baptized, both men and women. Even Simon himself believed, and after being baptized he continued with Philip. And seeing signs and great miracles performed, he was amazed.' (Acts 8:12, 13) Philip's evangelistic efforts were confirmed by a visit from the Apostles Peter and John, as a result of which the Christians in

347

Samaria were the first to receive the gift of the Holy Spirit by the 'laying on of hands with prayer'.

Philip is next described as intercepting the chariot of the chief treasurer of the queen of Ethiopia, on his way down from Jerusalem to Gaza. This court official was returning from a pilgrimage to the Holy City and was reading from the prophet Isaiah as he journeyed. Philip asked him if he knew about whom he was reading. The passage was from the Suffering Servant songs of the Second Isaiah: 'As a sheep led to the slaughter or a lamb before its shearer is dumb, so he opens not his mouth. In his humiliation justice was denied him. Who can describe his generation? For his life is taken up from the earth.' (Acts 8:32, 33) The man turned to Philip and asked, 'About whom, pray, does the prophet say this, about himself or about some one else?' Starting, therefore, with this text of scripture, Philip 'told him the good news of Jesus'. Further along the road, the Ethiopian was baptized by Philip at his own request. Later 'Philip was found at Azotus, and passing on he preached the gospel to all the towns till he came to Caesarea.' (Acts 8:40)

In about the year 58, it was at Caesarea that Paul and Luke were entertained by Philip and his four daughters, on Paul's final and fateful journey to Jerusalem. Certainly Philip and Paul had much in common, particularly their purpose in presenting the gospel of Jesus to the Gentiles. As with Philip the Apostle, traditions concerning the later life of this Philip are conflicting, but it is likely that he became a bishop in Lydia, the northern district of Asia Minor. [Acts 6:5; 8:5-40; 21:8]

The fountain of St Philip near Beth-zur, traditionally identified as the place where Philip baptized the Ethiopian eunuch.

3. Philip the Tetrarch *see* HEROD PHILIP

PHILIPPIANS The first European Christian community was founded in the year 50 by the Apostle Paul on his Second Journey, and was to receive from him a letter written some years later in prison at either Ephesus or Rome.

Luke and Philippi

Sailing from Troas to Neapolis via Samothrace, Paul and his companions arrived for the first time at Philippi. His companions were Silas, Timothy, and Luke, whose narrative at this point in Acts 16 suddenly changes from 'they' to 'we', implying that Luke the chronicler actually joined the party at Troas. When Paul sailed back from Philippi to Troas some five years later, returning to Jerusalem at the close of his Third Journey, Luke's narrative again resumes the first person plural, the 'we' section, which continues right back to Jerusalem. It is not therefore unlikely that Luke – though perhaps by birth a Syrian of Antioch – lived for some years at Troas or Philippi. At that time, too, there was at Philippi an excellent school of medicine, at which Luke the physician may have received his training. Certainly his detailed and vivid description of the events of Paul's first visit to Philippi is as graphic as any other passage in the Acts.

Luke's account reflects a touch of civic pride in what he calls 'Philippi, which is the leading city of the district of Macedonia, and a Roman colony'. The city, founded by Philip of Macedon, father of Alexander the Great, in the 4th century BC, had been built upon an ancient and strategic site near some gold-mines. It was near by that Octavius and Mark Antony defeated the forces of Brutus and Cassius in the year 42 BC, following the murder of Julius Caesar. Philippi had become a military centre of communication with the famous Via Egnatia, linking the Adriatic with the Aegean, passing through the centre of the city, whose inhabitants were very conscious of their Roman colonial status. Indeed, the population would have included many Latin-speaking Italian veterans. Today, the ruins of Philippi and the military highway are still to be found eight miles northwest of the modern Kavalla, once the port of Neapolis.

Paul at Philippi

Paul found few Jews and no synagogue at Philippi. There was, however, a devout woman called Lydia, from the town of Thyatira in Asia Minor, who was in the purple-dye trade. When Paul and his companions were praying and preaching outside the gates of the city by the riverside, on the Sabbath, Lydia accepted Paul's witness and was converted. She and her household were baptized and insisted on the visitors going to stay in her house. It was to this Christian community in Philippi that Paul wrote later, when in prison, a letter full of happiness, gratitude, affection, and reassurance – reflecting little bitterness for the rough

Basilica at Philippi, the first European city to be visited by the Apostle Paul.

treatment he and Silas had received at Philippi, being arrested, beaten, and imprisoned without trial. (*see also* PAUL for the events during his Second Journey and visit to Philippi.)

An earlier letter?

Until this century, it was not doubted that this letter was, together with the other 'captivity epistles' – Colossians, Philemon, Ephesians, Timothy, and Titus – written from Rome, particularly in view of Paul's reference in this letter to both his imprisonment and his expected release. Lately, however, it has been pointed out that this letter has far more in common with Paul's earlier letters, reflecting the same problems in his Jewish relationships as are found in Galatians, and the same mood of danger and emergency to be found in 2 Corinthians.

A good argument for the writing of the letter from Ephesus is the amount of traffic implied between Philippi and the place of writing. Paul sends Timothy and expects him to return with news from Philippi. He plans to send Epaphroditus back to Philippi as soon as his recovery from illness is complete. If Paul were writing in Rome, it would be 850 miles and a month's journey one way to Philippi. Yet Paul expects Timothy to complete the return trip between the giving of the verdict and his possible execution. 'Even if I am to be poured as a libation upon the sacrificial offering of your faith, I am glad and rejoice with you all. Likewise you also should be glad and rejoice with me. I hope in the Lord Jesus to send Timothy to you soon, so that I

may be cheered by news of you.' (Phil. 2:17-19) 'I hope therefore to send him just as soon as I see how it will go with me; and I trust in the Lord that shortly I myself shall come also.' (Phil. 2:23, 24) On the other hand, from Ephesus to Philippi is 250 miles and less than a week's journey. So we might perhaps conclude that the letter to Philippi was sent from Ephesus in the year 56 or 57, rather than from Rome some years later.

Anxiety at Philippi

Epaphroditus had brought a gift of money from Philippi to help Paul, and although Paul appears to have acknowledged it the Philippians had written again, perhaps displeased with what they considered a lack of appreciation. Paul's letter, which we have, is his reply to their second communication. Epaphroditus has been unwell and is anxious to return home, so Paul plans to send him as the bearer of the letter and explains why Epaphroditus is returning. Paul knows the anxiety at Philippi for his own welfare and assures his friends there that he will send news soon by Timothy, if indeed he does not come himself.

The basic reason for writing, however, is to encourage the Philippians, themselves under persecution, to unity and steadfastness in their faith. Although Paul is himself in prison and apparently awaiting trial for his very life, yet his letter is full of happy confidence, affection, and reassurance. The words 'joy' and 'rejoice' occur no less than fourteen times within the four brief chapters of this letter, which must have given great comfort to its readers – besides some truly inspiring insights into Christian truth.

Unity in humility

What more beautiful expression of confidence could there be than Paul's opening greeting? 'I thank my God in all my remembrance of you, always in every prayer of mine for you all making my prayer with joy, thankful for your partnership in the gospel from the first day until now. And I am sure that he who began a good work in you will bring it to completion at the day of Jesus Christ.' (Phil. 1:3-6) What more sincere expression of his affection than this? 'For God is my witness, how I yearn for you all with the affection of Christ Jesus. And it is my prayer that your love may abound more and more, with knowledge and all discernment, so that you may approve what is excellent, and may be pure and blameless for the day of Christ.' (Phil. 1:8-10)

It seems that there are two parties within the Christian community of the city in which he is imprisoned. The one is inspired to speak out by his example and courage. The other is concerned to speak out in order to bring down even more trouble on Paul in his captivity. 'What then?' asks Paul. 'Only that in every way, whether in pretence or in truth, Christ is proclaimed; and in that I rejoice.' (Phil. 1:18) Then his anxiety gets the better of his good spirits: 'I am hard pressed between the two,' he says. 'My desire is to depart and to be with Christ, for that is far better. But to remain in the flesh is more necessary on your account.' (Phil. 1:23-24)

Perhaps the most uplifting passage is his plea for unity in humility. 'Have this mind among yourselves, which you have in Christ Jesus, who, though he was in the form of God, did not count equality with God a thing to be grasped, but emptied himself, taking the form of a servant, being born in the likeness of men. And being found in human form he humbled himself and became obedient unto death, even death on a cross. Therefore God has highly exalted him and bestowed on him the name which is above every name, that at the name of Jesus every knee should bow, in heaven and on earth and under the earth, and every tongue confess that Jesus Christ is Lord, to the glory of God the Father.' (Phil. 2:5-11)

Then, incensed with those Judaizers who insisted on circumcision in addition to Christian baptism, Paul roundly declares, 'Look out for the dogs, look out for the evil-workers, look out for those who mutilate the flesh. For we are the true circumcision, who worship God in spirit, and glory in Christ Jesus, and put no confidence in the flesh. Though I myself have reason for confidence in the flesh also. If any other man thinks he has reason for confidence in the flesh, I have more: circumcised on the eighth day, of the people of Israel, of the tribe of Benjamin, a Hebrew born of Hebrews; as to the law a Pharisee, as to zeal a persecutor of the church, as to righteousness under the law blameless. But whatever gain I had, I counted as loss for the sake of Christ. Indeed I count everything as loss because of the surpassing worth of knowing Christ Jesus my Lord. For his sake I have suffered the loss of all things, and count them as refuse, in order that I may gain Christ.' (Phil. 3:2-8)

It is a remarkably turbulent letter, as Paul's equilibrium is upset by some sudden provocation or anxiety added to the strain of his captivity. Yet he always seems to recover his tranquillity. 'Therefore, my brethren, whom I love and long for, my joy and crown, stand firm thus in the Lord, my beloved. . . . Rejoice in the Lord always; again I will say, Rejoice. Let all men know your forbearance. The Lord is at hand. Have no anxiety about anything, but in everything by prayer and supplication with thanksgiving let your requests be made known to God. And the peace of God, which passes all understanding, will keep your hearts and your minds in Christ Jesus.' (Phil. 4:1, 4-7) [Phil. 1-4]

PHILOLOGUS (Gk. 'fond of learning) One of the Christians greeted by Paul at the close of his letter to the Church in Rome. Philologus is linked with the name of Julia, perhaps his wife, in a group or household of five, 'and all the saints who are with them'. Both names were common among Roman slaves. [Rom. 16:15]

PHLEGON (Gk. 'burning') The second of a list of five men, mentioned in a special greeting from Paul at the close of his letter to the Church in Rome. Perhaps Phlegon, his fellows, and 'the brethren who are with them' formed a household or small group within the larger Christian community. [Rom. 16:14]

PHOEBE (Gk. 'bright', 'radiant') 'Our sister Phoebe', as Paul called her, was the bearer of his letter to the Church in Rome, from her home town Corinth. She was in fact a deaconess or church-worker in the port of Cenchrae, on the east side of the Corinthian isthmus which faces the Aegean.

Paul asks for a special welcome to be given her 'in the Lord', and a 'welcome as befits the saints', and to help her with anything she needs. For Phoebe had been of great service both to Paul individually and to the Church as a whole.

The terms in which Paul speaks of Phoebe and her patronage indicate that she was of some wealth and social position within the community, as well as of some importance within the local congregation. [Rom. 16:1]

PHYGELUS A Christian disciple who, with Hermogenes and others in Asia, deserted Paul on his last arrest, perhaps at Troas and through the betrayal of Alexander the coppersmith. The last letter to Timothy conceals the drama of Paul's disastrous departure from Asia and arrival under arrest in Rome where, already convicted, he awaits execution. Many Asian Christians, under the threat of arrest for their association with Paul, simply did not manage to remain loyal. Among these, Paul mentioned by name those whose desertion represented the greatest disappointment, and particularly Phygelus and Hermogenes. [2 Tim. 1:15]

PILATE, PONTIUS Pontius Pilate was the fifth Roman procurator of Judea, Samaria, and Idumea, governing from the year 26 to 36, during which time he was officially responsible for the condemnation of Jesus on a charge of sedition, to be crucified in about the year 30. A good deal is known about Pilate, not just from the four Gospels, but from the contemporary Jewish secular historians Josephus and Philo, and also from the 4th-century Church historian Eusebius.

The name 'Pontius' was his family name and he came from a Roman family. The name 'Pilate' from the Latin *pilatus* means a 'pikeman', or one armed with the *pilum* or javelin. There are several legends about his origin, of which one is that he was the bastard son of Tyrus, king of Mainz, and was sent to Rome. There, so the story runs, he committed murder and was exiled to Pontus in Asia Minor, where he made good and was rewarded with the governorship of Judea. It is far more likely, however, that as the son of an eminent

Roman family he underwent the usual diplomatic training, succeeding through other minor posts to the procuratorship of Judea – not a very coveted appointment in any case, and directly responsible to the emperor himself.

On his appointment in the year 26, some three years before the crucifixion of Jesus, he was about the same age as Jesus, in his early thirties. He was a proud, hot-tempered, obstinate and aristocratic young man, capable of childish behaviour when his will was crossed and as military-minded as his name suggests. His official residence was at the Roman port and colonial

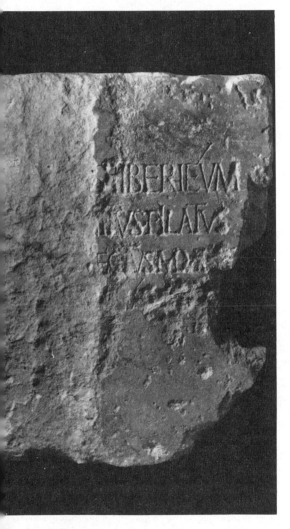

Dedicatory inscription of Pontius Pilate, carved in limestone, commemorating the completion of the Tiberium, at Caesarea.

city of Caesarea on the Mediterranean coastline. At Jewish festivals and other potential emergencies, however, the procurator 'stood to' with his troops in Jerusalem – particularly at the time of Passover, when riots were frequent. Over all but Roman citizens the procurator's power was absolute. As one who had only recently reached the governorship, he was determined to make a success of it, and to keep the notoriously turbulent and nationalistic Jews in order.

His wife was Claudia Procula, granddaughter of the Emperor Augustus and illegitimate daughter of Claudia, third wife of the Emperor Tiberius. She was a princess royal, sophisticated, cultured, and sensitive. Perhaps it was through her that Pilate got this particular appointment, rather than for his diplomatic tact. The governors of Judea did not usually get permission to take their wives, and although many women would have welcomed an excuse to stay in the comfort and society of Rome, Claudia was with him even in Jerusalem.

Events in Pilate's life before his appearance in the Gospels illustrate his character and capabilities. When he arrived in Judea, he discovered that there was no statue of the Roman emperor in Jerusalem. In fact it was the only city within the empire where people did not bow to the emperor's statue in the city square. Consequently, Pilate, concerned only to maintain the authority of Rome rather than to understand the outlook and problems of the Jews, decided to make an impression. When he entered Jerusalem for the first time, the Roman soldiers marched into the city with their images of the emperor on their standards. For the Roman with a dozen gods, this was one thing; for the Jew who believed in only one God, who did not allow graven images even of himself, this was an outrage. The Emperor Augustus had previously promised to grant Jerusalem immunity from such demands of the imperial cult. Having reached the Roman fortress, Pilate ordered the images to be put up on the walls facing down into the Temple, and returned himself to Caesarea. If the Jews attacked the fortress, he thought, they could be punished for revolt.

Outwitted by the high priest

Pilate, however, was a child in cunning compared with the high priest Caiaphas. The next day Jews streamed out of the city on their way down to Caesarea. They gathered others as they went and arrived 7,000 strong to surround Pilate's procuratorial residence. Pilate refused to listen to their deputation. For a whole week, the 7,000 picketed the palace, and every time Pilate emerged it was to find thousands of Jews at prayer for his own soul. At last his nerve was broken, and he gave orders for the Jews to gather in the *Agora* or market-place, where he would speak to them. Meanwhile his troops surrounded the square prepared to butcher the gathering crowd. The Jews, however, soon grasped the situation and, preferring to die than to suffer the images overlooking the Temple, they knelt down and waited, but the order was never given for the massacre and Pilate was humiliated.

A second incident showed a similar lack of sympathy on Pilate's part. He never met the demands of the Jews until their protests threatened to end in violence, likely to be reported back to Rome and thus endanger his own position. On this occasion, Pilate wanted to provide a fresh water-supply for Jerusalem by constructing in the grand manner an aqueduct to carry water six miles from some ancient reservoirs to the south of Jerusalem, beyond Bethlehem. The problem was not one of engineering so much as of the necessary funds. Pilate decided to raid the Temple treasury in order to finance the project. As each Jewish male paid three dollars or one guinea in Temple tax each year, there was a general uproar. Pilate sent his troops in plain clothes and armed with cudgels to suppress the riot, and himself gave the agreed signal for action. Thousands were trodden to death in the resulting panic and a very lurid account of the incident reached Rome. No doubt it was the high priest's intelligence and information service that procured for Pilate a very severe reprimand from Rome on this occasion.

Pilate's aqueduct is still to be seen following the contours of the hillsides, its stone vertebrae still showing signs of a lining with lead and lime mortar.

There is yet another incident, briefly mentioned by Luke (13:1), of Pilate's responsibility for the killing of some Galileans, when they were actually offering sacrifice in the Temple. In spite of such lapses into violence, Pilate must have been a strong and able administrator, for he remained ten years in office, while his four predecessors had governed only twenty years between them. Philo in fact describes Pilate as 'inflexible, merciless and obstinate' – not quite the impression given in the Gospels, where he appears as the pawn of Caiaphas. Both these aspects of his character can be reconciled, for the trial of Jesus took place in only the third year of his appointment, and his frustration and consequent lack of mercy appears to have progressively increased. He was not supported in his attitude by an imperial decree in the year 36, imposing a policy of greater tolerance and consideration towards Jews throughout the Roman Empire. As a result of this, he had to acquiesce to a demand from the Pharisees to remove the golden shields of portraits of the emperor and others, which had for years adorned the walls of Herod's citadel.

Soon after this further humiliation, Pilate made his final and fatal mistake. A crowd of Samaritans gathered for a religious ceremony on Mount Gerizim, their traditional place of sacrifice. Pilate interpreted their religious unrest as an act of revolt and brutally wiped out a neighbouring village in reprisal. The Samaritans complained to Vitellius, the Roman legate of Syria, and, as a result, Pilate was summoned to Antioch, examined, ordered to return to Rome, and finally exiled from Italy.

Pilate's judgment seat

The term 'praetorium' is the name of the judicial seat of the Roman governor or praetor at any given moment. He established his praetorium simply by hanging his shield at the gate and posting his tribune on guard, whether in Jerusalem or Caesarea, at Herod's Palace or at the Antonia Fortress.

A Hasmonean fort once stood to the west of the Temple area to protect it from assault. Here Herod built a vast fortress with the triple purpose not of protecting the Temple so much as suppressing riots and preserving order within the Temple courtyards, and securing the external defence of the city at its most vulnerable point. The fact that he called it after Mark Antony, the Roman conqueror of Syria and Palestine, indicates his true purpose – that the Antonia should successfully muzzle Jerusalem and her Jewish life. As Josephus, the contemporary Jewish historian, said, 'The city was dominated by the Temple and the Temple by the Antonia.'

Less than a hundred years ago, the Dominican archaeologist Père Vincent described the fortress thus: 'This gigantic quadrilateral, cut almost entirely out of the rocky hill, covered an area of 150 metres east to west, by 80 metres north to south. It was protected by powerful corner towers and enclosed installations as complex and diverse as a palace and camp. The outstanding but characteristic feature of this complex was, without doubt, the courtyard, about 2,500 metres square, serving as a place of meeting between the city and the Antonia. Extending over deep water-cisterns, covered with a massive polished pavement, surrounded by tall cloisters, this courtyard was really the heart of the fortress whose activity it regulated. . . . Pilate had his tribunal set up within the courtyard, transformed for the occasion into the Praetorium, called indeed the "Pavement" *par excellence*. Where could one find more explicit evidence, more expressive and appropriate a setting for the place where Pilate pronounced the sentence which sent Jesus on his way to Calvary?'

Leaving the high priest's palace, prisoner and escort, followed by the crowd, must have passed on over the great viaduct across the Tyropoaen Valley. They must have left the city by the 'Fish Gate' and climbed the steep slope which ran alongside the ramparts of the north wall, to appear before the great double gate of the Antonia. This vast fortress, defended by a moat and scarp from the open country beyond, had its main gate outside the city wall, as though fearing

Model of 1st-century Jerusalem, showing the massive four-towered fortress of
the Antonia on the right, probably the scene of the trial of Jesus by Pilate.

less from without than within the city walls. And with
good reason too, for though it dominated the Temple
area, it was from here that trouble could be expected.
Within the four corners of the great fortress, crammed
with troops at such a time as Passover, Pilate had his
own procurator's quarters in a little central tower
facing down on to the Pavement.

To water thousands in a fortress often under siege
must have demanded a phenomenal supply. This was
yet another function of the Pavement, whose water
runnels still lead down into the cavernous vaults below,
where cistern-tops yet bear the marks of lock and
chain, and whose counter-weights and pulleys are still
to be seen.

On to this Pavement prisoner and escort proceeded,
while the crowd, for fear of defilement before Passover,
crammed by the thousand into the great double gateway. Pilate, seated in his curial chair at the head of his
private stairway, must have gazed down upon the
Pavement in disgust, having blotted his colonial copy-
book more than once and knowing himself to be outwitted by Caiaphas.

At the trial of Jesus

There are three rather different accounts of the trial of
Jesus. Mark's version is closely followed by Matthew
and is probably the earliest account, based on the
memories of the Apostle Peter and published some
thirty years after the event. This account reflects the
undeniable fact that Jesus was convicted by the Roman

authority, represented by Pilate. This fact was of some
embarrassment to Christian propaganda throughout
the Roman Empire. Morally the account holds the
Jewish Sanhedrin and Caiaphas responsible, but the
form and execution of the punishment was Roman and
therefore the responsibility of Pilate.

After a second meeting of the Sanhedrin, early on
the Friday morning, Jesus was bound and brought to
Pilate. He was charged not with blasphemy, for which
he had been sentenced by the Sanhedrin, but with the
treason of claiming to be 'the King of the Jews'. 'And
Pilate asked him, "Are you the King of the Jews?"
And he answered him, "You have said so." And the
chief priests accused him of many things. And Pilate
again asked him, "Have you no answer to make? See
how many charges they bring against you." But Jesus
made no further answer, so that Pilate wondered.'
(Mark 15:2-5)

To Pilate, Jesus's case appeared similar to that of
Barabbas, another agitator with a more violent record;
therefore he offered to release Jesus, who was seemingly a popular favourite. The crowd, swayed by the
Sanhedrin, demanded the release of Barabbas and the
crucifixion of Jesus. 'And Pilate said to them, "Why,
what evil has he done?" but they shouted all the more,
"Crucify him." So Pilate, wishing to satisfy the crowd,
released for them Barabbas; and having scourged Jesus,
he delivered him to be crucified.' (Mark 15:14, 15)

There is no further mention of Pilate in Mark's

account, which throws little light on the feelings and motives of Pilate. He might have been expected to dismiss the case, without adequate evidence or cause for conviction. The prisoner silently refuses to refute the charge. Pilate, seemingly aware of the falseness of the accusation of treason, the 'envy' of the high priests and the insincerity of the people, yet delivered Jesus to be scourged and crucified. The writer is in fact more concerned with the purposeful progress of Jesus through his passion than with the characters of any of the personalities responsible.

Luke's version is noticeably different and he may have had access to an earlier and more accurate source than Mark. Writing, as he was, to the Roman aristocrat Theophilus, Luke tried to show that Rome – represented by Pilate – was responsible neither for the conviction nor the crucifixion of Jesus.

The threefold charge before Pilate is very specific: 'And they began to accuse him, saying, "We found this man perverting our nation, and forbidding us to give tribute to Caesar, and saying that he himself is Christ a king."' (Luke 23:2) However convinced of the innocence of the prisoner, Pilate could not disregard so detailed a charge of treason against the state. After some cross-examination of the prisoner, 'Pilate said to the chief priests and the multitudes, "I find no crime in this man." But they were urgent, saying, "He stirs up the people, teaching throughout all Judea, from Galilee even to this place."' (Luke 23:4, 5)

Hearing that Jesus was a Galilean, Pilate grasped his opportunity to pass the prisoner over to Herod Antipas, who happened to be in his castle at Jerusalem for the Passover festival. Herod, however, was more aware of the political and ecclesiastical issues involved in the case than was Pilate and, after making a fool of the prisoner, returned him to Pilate. Luke thus attributes the mocking of Jesus to the soldiers of Herod rather than those under Pilate's command.

Pilate, now faced with a second trial, attempted for the second time to acquit the prisoner. 'Pilate then called together the chief priests and the rulers and the people, and said to them, "You brought me this man as one who was perverting the people; and after examining him before you, behold, I did not find this man guilty of any of your charges against him; neither did Herod, for he sent him back to us. Behold, nothing deserving death has been done by him; I will therefore chastise him and release him." But they all cried out together, "Away with this man, and release to us Barabbas."' (Luke 23:13-18)

When the crowd called for the release of Barabbas and the crucifixion of Jesus, 'He said to them, "Why, what evil has he done? I have found in him no crime deserving death; I will therefore chastise him and release him." . . . And their voices prevailed. So Pilate

gave sentence that their demand should be granted.' (Luke 23:22-24) Luke makes no mention of a scourging and places the blame for Pilate's forced conviction of the prisoner, despite his threefold attempt at reprieve, firmly on Caiaphas and the Sanhedrin. Luke's portrait of Pilate is that of a humane judge, unable to resist the pressure of the angry and riotous crowds.

John's version, though published at the end of the 1st century, after the death of Peter and almost all the others involved, is completely fresh and independent of the other accounts. How John got the record of the case before Pilate no one can tell; perhaps one of the officials told him, or even Pilate's wife, Procula; perhaps he himself risked ceremonial defilement before the Passover, entered the fortress, and heard the trial himself. Certainly John's account is beyond the art of fiction and carries the hallmark of truth, not least in its portrayal of the character of Pilate and particularly in his personal interrogation of the prisoner.

John's topography of the praetorium and the *Gabbatha*, or Pavement, is easily understood. Because Caiaphas and the Sanhedrin feared ritual defilement before the Passover, they refused to enter on to the Pavement, but waited in the great double gateway. It was, as John says, 'early' – something before six o'clock – and Pilate was thus forced to go out and deal with them in the chill of the morning air. He would be uncomfortably reminded of religious scruples with which he felt scant sympathy. He demanded the written charge: 'What accusation do you bring against this man?' and was bluntly told: 'If this man were not an evildoer, we would not have handed him over.' In other words, the case had already been tried in their court and they were merely asking for the death-sentence to be confirmed. 'Pilate said to them, "Take him yourselves and judge him by your own law." The Jews said to him, "It is not lawful for us to put any man to death."' (John 18:31)

No doubt, irritated by such a clumsy attempt to steam-roller him, Pilate insisted on hearing the full case. Then he went inside and up into his private apartments in the central tower, followed by the prisoner now escorted by Romans. Pilate was unlikely perhaps to have been prepared to receive a prisoner quite so early in the morning, unless Caiaphas had warned him the night before of the nature and urgency of the case. Pilate would be expecting a charge of sedition and a prisoner capable of leading a dangerous revolt. He must have been surprised at the quiet figure before him, for he said 'Are you the King of the Jews?' ['Are you the Jewish Messiah?'] And the somewhat unconvincing rebel, Jesus, answered, 'Do you say this of your own accord, or did others say it to you about me?'

Christ before Pilate, by Tintoretto (1518-94).

Then, with all the scorn and contempt of Rome for a subject race, 'Pilate answered, "Am I a Jew? Your own nation and the chief priests have handed you over to me; what have you done?" ' (John 18:35) Vigorously, 'Jesus answered, "My kingship is not of this world; if my kingship were of this world, my servants would fight, that I might not be handed over to the Jews; but my kingship is not from the world." ' (John 18:36) In other words: 'My kingdom does not belong to your kind of world.' Not surprisingly, Pilate could make nothing of that, except that somehow the prisoner was admitting to being a king and thus pleading 'guilty'. 'Pilate said to him, "So you are a king?" Jesus answered, "You say that I am a king. For this I was born, and for this I have come into the world, to bear witness to the truth. Every one who is of the truth hears my voice." ' (John 18:37) However exasperated Pilate was by such a seemingly irrelevant and abstract answer, he must have grasped the utter harmlessness, if not the sincerity, of the prisoner.

Aware now that the case was being fraudulently presented and that he was expected to act as a destructive tool of the Sanhedrin, he looked for a means of escape. He suggested the offer of the customary Passover amnesty; but he had forgotten Barabbas. 'He went out to the Jews again and told them, "I find no crime in him. But you have a custom that I should release one man for you at the Passover; will you have me release for you the King of the Jews?" They cried out again, "Not this man, but Barabbas!" Now Barabbas was a robber.' (John 18:39, 40)

Foiled in his purpose by the Barabbas fiasco, fearing the gathering crowd, Pilate had to think again. Here, Luke introduced the Herod episode as an abortive attempt by Pilate to escape from giving judgment. Perhaps it was the return of the prisoner in his mock regalia from Herod that suggested Pilate's next move. Pilate saw that he must do something to conciliate the Sanhedrin and invite the sympathy of the crowd. Therefore, in the hope of avoiding the death sentence, Pilate had the prisoner scourged. The scourge was a 'cat-o-

nine-tails' loaded with crude pellets of lead and bone. The place of the scourging cannot now be known, but it probably took place in view of the people on the Pavement and at a column or post designed and used for the purpose.

After the scourging, John describes how the soldiers took him to their guardroom or quarters, before returning him to Pilate. It was in the guardroom that they had their opportunity to vent their detestation, as occupation forces, upon this representative of a subject race who had called himself a king. Just how they did so is well illustrated by carvings in the Pavement at the foot of the troops' stairways. Among a variety of knuckle-boards and hopscotch designs covering several flagstones, there are the following signs: the 'B' for *Basilicus*, meaning 'King', a rough and prickly crown, and finally a sabre. This is evidence of a game called 'King', described by Plautus as derived from the Saturnalia, in which a burlesque king is chosen, mockingly honoured and saluted, before being killed. So, in the crucifixion squad, each soldier would adopt as his stake one of the condemned prisoners. The winner in the game of bones would crown his own 'stake' with a crown of thorns in a mocking guardroom ceremony. The king, thus crowned, would receive his soldier's homage, his swagger-stick as sceptre and his military cloak as a royal robe. All the guardroom would hail him '*Basilicus Judaiorum*!' This indeed gives meaning to the Gospel account of the mocking.

When the prisoner was returned to Pilate in a condition to draw pity from the crowd, Pilate presented him, with the words '*Ecce Homo*!' – 'Behold the Man!' – or more contemptuously perhaps, 'See, here the fellow is!' He had, however, underestimated the determination and cunning of Caiaphas, as he must have realized when the crowd still demanded the death penalty. In his frustration and annoyance, Pilate once again attempted to 'pass the buck': 'Take him yourselves and crucify him, for I find no crime in him.' This finally stung the Sanhedrin into stating their real case against the prisoner, for which they had themselves convicted him of blasphemy. 'The Jews answered him, "We have a law, and by that law he ought to die, because he has made himself the Son of God." When Pilate heard these words, he was the more afraid.' (John 19:7, 8)

Once again entering the praetorium, Pilate attempted to re-examine the prisoner, who had just been brutally scourged. His sudden fear may have been due to his growing apprehension that his prisoner was perhaps out of the ordinary. The sceptic had become perplexed

above Pilate shows Jesus, crowned with thorns, to the people: from the *Très beaux heures* of the Duc de Berry, early 15th century.

right Ecce Homo, by Rembrandt van Rijn (1609-69) Pilate asks the crowd to free Jesus, but they demand Barabbas.

Pilate washing his hands (left) and (right, seated) at the trial. 5th-century ivory.

and superstitious; he wished to test the prisoner's claim to divine origin: 'Where are you from?' But the prisoner remained silent. When Pilate reminded him of his procuratorial power of life and death, the prisoner calmly rejected both Pilate's authority and indeed Pilate's significance in the situation. 'Jesus answered him, "You would have no power over me unless it had been given you from above; therefore he who delivered me to you has the greater sin."' (John 19:11) The real issue was between the prisoner and Caiaphas, in whose hands Pilate was merely a tool.

The truth of this was clearly shown within the next and final moments of this so-called trial. Pilate, more than ever convinced of the prisoner's innocence and harmlessness, once again went out to the crowd. But before he could even speak the Jews 'yelled' (the literal translation): '"If you release this man, you are not Caesar's friend; every one who makes himself a king sets himself against Caesar." When Pilate heard these words, he brought Jesus out and sat down on the judgment seat at a place called The Pavement, and in Hebrew, *Gabbatha*. Now it was the day of Preparation of the Passover; it was about the sixth hour. He said to the Jews, "Here is your King!" They cried out, "Away with him, away with him, crucify him!" Pilate said to them, "Shall I crucify your King?" The chief priests answered, "We have no king but Caesar."' (John 19:12-15)

Outmanoeuvred by a people whom he had not even begun to understand, his already precarious reputation in Rome dangerously threatened, deafened by the clamourous blood-lust of the crowd, Pilate's resistance collapsed. He signed the death warrant and handed the prisoner over for crucifixion. Perhaps he gained some revenge by his choice of words in the title nailed to the cross of Jesus in Hebrew, Latin and Greek: 'Jesus of Nazareth, the king of the Jews'.

'The chief priests of the Jews then said to Pilate, "Do not write, 'The King of the Jews', but, 'This man said, I am the King of the Jews.'"' Pilate answered, "What I have written I have written."' (John 19:21-22) Perhaps he felt some slight compensation in later granting the prisoner's corpse a decent burial.

Various traditions relate the execution of Pilate by Nero, his banishment to Vienne, his taking of his own life. The Abyssinian Church has made a saint of him. The Apostles' Creed has branded him throughout the universal Church by the words describing Jesus as 'crucified also for us under Pontius Pilate'. [Matt. 27; Mark 15; Luke 3:1; 13:1; 23:1-52; John 18, 19; Acts 3:13; 4:27; 13:28; 1 Tim. 6:13]

PORCIUS FESTUS (Gk. 'festal', 'joyful') *see* FESTUS

PRISCA (Gk. from the Lat. 'ancient') *see* AQUILA

PRISCILLA (Gk. from the Lat. 'ancient') *see* AQUILA

PROCHORUS (Gk. 'leader of the chorus') *see* NICOLAUS

PUBLICANS (Lat. 'civil servants') *see* TAX-COLLECTORS

PUBLIUS The 'chief man', a Greek term for a high official on the island of Malta, who received and entertained Paul and the ship's company for three days, on the occasion of their shipwreck in the autumn of the year 60, during the voyage to Rome, where Paul was to appear before the imperial tribunal.

Near their place of landing on the rocky coastline, traditionally called St Paul's Bay, Publius owned an estate and offered them hospitality there. It so happened that the father of Publius was laid up with fever and dysentery, so Paul visited him and prayed over him, then, putting his hands on him, healed him. Other islanders consequently brought their sick to be cured and in return gave Paul presents. The following spring, after the entire company had wintered on the island, Julius, the centurion in charge of the escort, put his prisoners on another Alexandrian ship, bound for Puteoli on the Italian coast south of Rome. [Acts 28:7, 8]

PUDENS (Gk. 'modest') One of the four who sent their personal greetings at the close of Paul's final letter to Timothy in Ephesus, perhaps the last he ever wrote. From the grouping of the names, Pudens may well have been the husband of Claudia and father of Linus. Paul is writing from prison, presumably in Rome, after his conviction, and expecting execution. This family, not elsewhere mentioned in the New Testament, may have ministered to the final needs of Paul, along with the 'beloved physician', Luke, Paul's fellow-prisoner to the end. [2 Tim. 4:21]

PYRRHUS (Gk. 'fiery red') The father of Sopater of Beroea, near Thessalonica in Macedonia. Sopater was one of the representatives chosen to accompany Paul on his return to Jerusalem with the poor-relief collection from the various Christian Mediterranean communities. Fearing an ambush if he travelled via Corinth, Paul travelled overland through Macedonia, in the spring of a year around 58, as far as Troas on the coast of Asia Minor and so by sea to Caesarea and Jerusalem, with an escort of seven men, of whom the first, and perhaps the leader, was Sopater, son of Pyrrhus. [Acts 20:4]

QUARTUS (Gk. from the Lat. 'fourth') A Christian in Corinth who asked to send greetings to the Church in Rome, at the close of Paul's letter to that congregation. His name is the last among a long list of greetings and is linked with those of Gaius and Erastus. An ancient tradition also lists him among the seventy early disciples, whom Jesus sent out two by two, during his Galilean ministry (Luke 10:1). [Rom. 16:23]

QUIRINIUS Governor of Syria, according to Luke, at the time of the enrolment decreed by Caesar Augustus, which compelled Joseph and Mary to register at his family town Bethlehem, where Jesus was born.

Luke's efforts to record the exact date and circumstances of the birth of Jesus do not seem in complete accord with the historical facts. It was not Roman custom to decree a census throughout the whole empire, but for taxation purposes a particular province might be enrolled, under the arrangements of the governor of that province. The first Roman census of Palestine did in fact take place in AD 6, on the occasion of Judea being incorporated into the Roman province of Syria, which was on the occasion of the dismissal of Archelaus and his replacement by a Roman procurator. This Roman type of census and the subsequent degree of taxation appear to have been a new and bitter experience for the Jews, for it aroused enormous resentment and a revolt led by Judas of Gamala, cruelly suppressed by the Roman authority. At that time, in AD 6, Quirinius was indeed governor of Syria and possibly Luke may have thought that the birth of Jesus coincided with that census.

On the other hand, Luke dates the early ministry of John the Baptist as in the fifteenth year of the Emperor Tiberius, who only succeeded Augustus in AD 14. So Luke dates the beginning of both John and Jesus's ministries and calling of the disciples in the year 29. If Jesus was born in AD 6, he would have begun his ministry at about the age of 23, which seems too young. Matthew, however, states that Herod the Great was ruler at Jerusalem at the birth of Jesus and at the time of the slaughter of the innocents, perhaps up to two years later. As Herod the Great died in 4 BC, this could mean that Jesus was born between 6 and 4 BC. By Luke's reckoning, he would then have been about 33 years old at the start of his ministry.

It is, of course, possible that Herod conducted his own census in the last year or so of his reign, and that Luke muddled this with a Roman census in the time of Quirinius, AD 6-9. An Egyptian papyrus from AD 104 includes an ordinance for such a census. The presence of the woman was also required, in order to ascertain the number in each family. [Luke 2:2]

R

RHODA (Gk. 'rose') The servant-girl who acted as portress at the house of Mary the mother of John Mark in Jerusalem, and who recognized the voice of the Apostle Peter outside the door, but in her surprise and joy failed to let him in.

Herod Agrippa, in a personal persecution of the infant Christian Church, had already executed James the brother of John, and now had Peter arrested with the intention of presenting him to the Jews after Passover. Peter was imprisoned under a strong guard of sixteen soldiers; meanwhile the little Christian community prayed hard for his release. The very night before his trial, Peter was miraculously led out of his cell and through the prison gates by an angel, who left him in the street outside. Only then did Peter quite grasp what had happened and said to himself, 'Now I am sure that the Lord has sent his angel and rescued me from the hand of Herod and from all that the Jewish people were expecting.' (Acts 12:11)

Peter at once made his way to Mary's house, the headquarters of the Christians on Mount Zion and the first synagogue of the Christian congregation. While they were at prayer within, Peter knocked on the door and Rhoda came to answer. Recognizing his voice, in her joy she did not open the door, but ran in to say that Peter was at the gate. 'They said to her, "You are mad." But she insisted that it was so. They said, "It is his angel!" But Peter continued knocking; and when they opened, they saw him and were amazed. But motioning to them with his hand to be silent, he described to them how the Lord had brought him out of the prison.' (Acts 12:15-17) [Acts 12:13]

Bronze Roman coin, minted at the Roman provincial capital of Caesarea, showing a man ploughing.

ROMANS The Romans were the rulers of Palestine throughout the New Testament period and for many centuries to come. Throughout the lives of Jesus and Paul, the Romans remain for the most part a power in the background, which emerges to dispense justice with a terrifying certainty. It was the Roman occupation forces who, as a matter of historical fact, crucified Jesus and, after long imprisonment, despatched Paul for trial to Rome. It was the Romans who exiled John in a penal colony on the rocky island of Patmos. And it was in Rome that the headquarters of the Christian Church was to be established by the end of the 2nd century.

The Roman Empire was a highly important factor in the successful spread of Christianity during the 1st century. The *Pax Romana* – the law and order on land and sea – lent security to the travels of the first apostles. As the Jewish synagogue provided a means of access to the minds of religious people, both Jews and Gentiles, so too the coloquial Greek (*lingua franca*) of the Roman world facilitated the transmission of the gospel. Christianity was by the Romans long regarded as a form of Judaism and enjoyed the privileges accorded to Judaism since the days of Julius Caesar. It was not until the persecution of Christians by the Emperor Nero, from AD 64, that there was any great conflict between Christianity and the Roman state.

Roman rule in Palestine

Since the capture of Jerusalem by Pompey in the year 63 BC, the whole of Syria had become a part of the Roman Empire. When Julius Caesar was besieged by the Egyptians at Alexandria, he escaped largely owing to the support of Jewish troops despatched by Antipater, the father of Herod the Great. As a reward, Antipater was given Roman citizenship and became procurator of all Jewish territory in Syria. His sons became governors, Phasael in Judea and Herod in Galilee. Despite the murder of Caesar in 44 BC, the rise and fall of Antony, and the shift of power to Octavian, under whose august rule began the golden age of the *Pax Romana*, the family of Antipater remained in power. Herod extended his authority from Galilee to become tetrarch of all the Jewish territories and, when in Rome in 40 BC, was appointed king of Judea.

far left Tenth Legion inscription on a column found at Jerusalem.
top left The Roman Emperor Tiberius on a coin issued by Herod Philip.
bottom left Head of the Emperor Domitian on a bronze coin of Herod Agrippa II, AD 86.

below Ruins of Jerash, Greco-Roman city of the Decapolis. The façade of the Byzantine cathedral, through which are seen the columns of the 1st-century Temple of Artemis.

top Late Roman glass found at Nahariya, on the coast of northern Israel.
above The Roman theatre at the city of Caesarea, named after Augustus Caesar, now a state theatre.

With the help of a Roman army, he made himself master of Jerusalem in 37 BC. In spite of domestic tragedies and private crimes, Herod proved himself a great builder, a clever politician, and an able ruler – though unpredictable and unpopular to the end of his days. (*see* HEROD **3.**)

On Herod's death, at his own wish his kingdom was partitioned among three of his surviving sons: Judea, Samaria and Idumea to Archelaus as ethnarch; Galilee and Perea to Antipas as tetrarch; Gaulanitis and Trachonitis to Philip. None of these, however, had the

diplomacy of his father. Archelaus is mentioned in the 'birth stories' of the First Gospel as reigning in Judea on the return of Mary and Joseph from Egypt. He ruled for ten years, before being charged in Rome with misgovernment and banished to Gaul. He was replaced by a Roman procurator, under Augustus a three-year appointment but under Tiberius considerably longer, and in the case of Pontius Pilate ten years. Pilate presided at the trial of Jesus and condemned him to crucifixion. He was recalled to Rome on a charge of oppression, convicted and banished in the year 36. The procurators were subordinate to the Roman legates of Syria, of whom one, Quirinius, is mentioned by Luke. The procurators resided in the military base and port of Caesarea, and were in command of 3,000 mercenaries, of which one cohort was permanently stationed in Jerusalem.

In spite of the appointment of the Herodian rulers, from the dismissal of Archelaus it was the Roman procurator who wielded the greatest power. Though he commanded mainly mercenary troops, he could call for the legions stationed in Syria. The Jews retained the right to administer their Jewish Law through their Scribal courts and their supreme Council, the Sanhedrin, but they could not execute the death sentence. The procurators had power to bring about the appointment and dismissal of the high priests. They could deploy their troops to support the collection of oppressive taxes. They became progressively more tactless and ruthless in dealing with the fanatical opposition of their subjects. The main cause of friction between the Jewish people and their Roman masters, however, was a difference in ideals. The new, pagan, materialistic state-worship was bound to conflict with the ancient Jewish *left* Bronze coin of the First Jewish Revolt, AD 66-70, used for paying Temple dues; the inscription refers to the 'freedom of Zion'.

above Remains of the Roman camp above the cave of Simon Bar Kokhba, the leader of the revolt against the Romans in the year AD 135.

faith. However much the Jews appreciated Roman law and order, they could not stomach the loss of liberty involved in maintaining the *Pax Romana*. Hence the rising tide of nationalism and resentment against the Roman authority as controlling the Holy City and indirectly the Temple itself. The Romans did not understand the puritanical fanaticism of the Jews, who in turn regarded the Romans as enemies both of their state and their religion.

For the most part, the Roman governors and procurators aimed at honest and impartial treatment of the provincials within their territories, but they were apt to be rigid, unimaginative and unsympathetic with peoples they did not understand. They found it particularly difficult to accept the point of view of the Jews, whose instincts and whose whole existence were bound up with their religion. The Romans were accustomed to despise the oriental cults of the eastern Mediterranean, and they found little difficulty in superimposing the additional cult of emperor-worship, as a token of loyalty to the ruling power. Faced with the racial pride, the national tradition, and religious fanaticism of the Jews, the Romans tried to meet the situation with concessions. They officially waived the demand for sacrifice to the emperor. For the most part they respected the sanctity of Jerusalem, though certain procurators were less conciliatory than others. Because the country was small and, politically, seemingly insignificant, the procurators appointed were 'little men' drawn from a lower social order. Felix, who imprisoned Paul without judgment for two years, was the brother of a freed slave. Not one procurator carried an ancient Roman name and it is not surprising that they were unequal to their task.

Claudius tried the brief experiment of appointing a native Jewish prince, Agrippa, who only survived to rule three years, and was replaced by a procurator. Even Tacitus, the Roman historian, admits that the methods of the procurators were too much for the patience of the Jews and, in AD 66, the revolt began. After some initial guerrilla successes, resistance was systematically worn down by the Roman general Vespasian before he was acclaimed emperor by his troops at Caesarea and returned to Rome. It was his son Titus who invested

above Detail from Trajan's column of Roman troops after an action. In the foreground, the wounded are being tended.

and besieged Jerusalem, burned the Temple, and destroyed the city in AD 70.

The gospel message and the whole life of Jesus are to be seen against a background of Roman military occupation and seething revolt. Only in the passion narratives is this political situation made explicitly clear, but there are various implications in earlier events. Jesus told his hearers in the Sermon on the Mount to be prepared to go a second mile with those who could compel them to go one mile. He was referring to the Roman soldier, who had the right to compel any native countryman to carry his military pack. Luke describes how Jesus was told about Galileans 'whose blood Pilate had mingled with their sacrifices' – thus implying the putting-down by the Romans of some petty revolt over the time of a Jewish festival. John describes the fear of the priests and Pharisees who said about Jesus, 'If we permit him to act thus the Romans will come and destroy both our Holy Place [the Temple] and our nation.' When Jesus entered Jerusalem on the first Palm Sunday, he foresaw and foretold the siege and destruction of the city. 'For the days shall come upon you, when your enemies will cast up a bank about you and surround you, and hem you in on every side, and dash you to the ground, you and your children within you, and they will not leave one stone upon another in you; because you did not know the time of your visitation.' (Luke 19:43-44)

The question of whether it was right to pay taxes to Caesar was a highly dangerous one. On Jesus's answer could depend either a complete loss of popularity for saying 'Yes' or a certain charge of treason for saying 'No'. In fact, he answered, 'Render to Caesar the things that are Caesar's and to God the things that are God's.'

The cold, callous cruelty of Roman justice is well illustrated by the narrative of the crucifixion, particularly as described by Mark. The scourging, the mocking in the guardroom, the method of crucifixion, all followed a common routine of execution calculated to induce fear and subjection. This impression is, however, in the Gospels relieved by the character of certain individuals – notably two centurions. One had built the synagogue in which Jesus taught at Capernaum, and displayed such faith in Jesus's ability to heal his son (or servant)

Coin portrait of Augustus Caesar, in whose reign Jesus was born.

that Jesus was astonished and declared, 'Not even in Israel have I found such faith.' The other centurion was in charge of the execution squad at the crucifixion and, seeing the courageous death of Jesus, declared, 'Truly this man was the son of God!' The words of the first centurion are still used by the priest at every Catholic Mass of the Latin Rite: 'Lord, I am not worthy that thou shouldest come under my roof, but speak the word only. . . .' The second centurion, to whom tradition has given the name Longinus and credited with conversion to Christianity, figures in the regular Western Catholic devotion called 'The Stations of the Cross'.

Romans and the early Church

The Third Gospel and the Acts, both the work of Luke, a highly educated and sensitive man, possibly a Gentile, were written to commend the Christian religion to the Greco-Roman public and authorities. These works are frankly tolerant of the Roman part in the crucifixion and of the Roman influence on the growth of the infant Church. They in turn set out to demand a tolerance for the Christian faith, in spite of the execution of its founder by a Roman procurator. Most of the letters of the New Testament were written by a Roman citizen, Paul, so here too we would expect to find a respect for Roman authority. If the writer of the first letter attributed to Peter was in fact Silas (otherwise called Silvanus), he too was a Roman citizen. As the writings of Paul were completed before the first outbreak of Christian persecution in Rome, under the Emperor Nero in AD 64, these documents indicate little Roman opposition to the early Christian Church. In Acts, the Roman centurion, Cornelius, converted by Peter at Joppa, and Julius, Paul's escort and protector on his way to Rome, play a vital part in the story. The Roman civil colonial authorities in Galatia, Philippi, Corinth, and Ephesus, however, appear to have been unpredictably uncaring or severe, and the Judean procurators uniformly ineffective, but there is no persecution.

Other New Testament writings, attributed to the period between AD 64 and the end of the 1st century, are marked by an insistence on the fact of persecution and the need for steadfast endurance. This is particularly to be seen in 1 Peter and Revelation. It was, nevertheless, in this period that the Christian Church at Rome grew in size and status, partly because being in the world's capital city, it was bound to become important, and partly because it was founded by the two great apostles, Peter and Paul. [John 11:48; Acts 16:12, 21, 37, 38; 22:25-27, 29; 23:27; 28:17]

Letter to the Romans

The first of Paul's letters, as they appear in the New Testament, is the longest and most influential, written at the height of the apostle's career. It conveys the richness of his personal experience of Jesus and the full maturity of his thinking. It is also his first work of

Peter and Paul being led to prison in Rome: painting by Hans Süss von Kulmbach (*c.* 1480-1522).

Christian theology. Calmly and systematically, Paul sets forth the gospel which he has been preaching, often in situations of danger and difficulty which did not permit either calm or system. The general theme is the good news about Jesus and the reconciliation he has procured.

The letter was written in the winter months of 57-8 from Corinth, during Paul's Third Journey. It is unique in being addressed by Paul to a Christian community barely established and not yet visited by him. Consequently it is much less personal than his other letters, since he is not acquainted with those to whom he writes. It is rather more of a treatise than a letter – a treatise in

which he works out at some length the line of thought more hastily expounded in his letter to the Galatians.

The letter to the Romans seems to have had a three-fold objective: to prepare his way for a visit to Rome; to enlist the help of Roman Christians for his mission in the West; and to provide a detailed exposition of the gospel. It is a document any Church would value; it was probably sent to other Christian communities besides that in Rome. Paul dictated his letters, but often added covering notes and greetings, sometimes in his own bold handwriting. The first fifteen of the letter's sixteen chapters are likely to constitute the original letter as sent to Rome, while the last three verses of Chapter 16 might well have been Paul's covering note accompanying the letter to Rome. It is also likely that a copy of the original letter would have been retained at Corinth.

Finally, the remarkable and lengthy series of individual greetings in the final chapter is hardly likely to have been included in his letter to Rome, a city which he had not yet visited. It is far more appropriate for a letter to the Christian community at Ephesus, where Paul had already spent three years and must have had countless friends. Many of the names of those greeted can in fact be linked with Ephesus. Moreover, the first postscript following the greetings is the sort of warning that would have been far more appropriate and natural in a letter to Ephesus than in one to Rome.

Paul warns against false and perverse teaching, contrary to what has already been taught. A similar warning was later addressed to the congregation at Colossae, and Paul personally warned the elders of Ephesus at their farewell meeting with him at Miletus (Acts 20:15-17). Therefore, it is possible that most of Chapter 16

was Paul's covering letter, enclosed with a copy of his treatise to Rome, that was sent to Ephesus. Again, an early editor would have grafted the Ephesian greeting on to the end of the letter to Rome, closing the whole with the final doxology.

Message of salvation

Paul was brought up in observance of the Jewish Law. For him, God was essentially the God of righteousness. If God is absolute moral perfection, truth and goodness – then no form of evil can come near him without dissolving, like darkness in the sunlight. Paul tackles the problem of how man, who deliberately and constantly sins, can ever approach God and share life with him. The Law of Moses offers one solution. If men will fully obey the Law, they will be free from moral taint and they will be able to approach God. Paul, however, points out that unfortunately men have failed to obey either the Law revealed to Israel on Sinai, or the universal law of human conscience. Whether they have broken the whole Law or only a small part of it, all men are guilty and come short of God's perfection. The Mosaic

The martyrdom of Peter at Rome, watched by the Emperor Nero. Panel from the bronze doors of St Peter's, Rome.

The traditional tomb of St Peter, over which Constantine the Great built the first basilica of St Peter's in the 4th century. From the 1st century onwards, the area became a Christian cemetery.

Law, which should be a signpost to God, had become nothing but a warning notice.

The gospel message is that God himself has dealt with this problem by coming himself, in the person of Jesus, to this world. God, as Jesus, became 'Representative Man', and himself deliberately accepted the eventual consequences of evil by his own suffering and death on the cross. Anyone who entrusts his life to Jesus can now be accepted by God, through God's own personal act of atonement. Now, both salvation from the consequences of sin, and salvation that we may come into the presence of God in his holiness, has become a matter of 'believing' and not of 'achieving', gained by 'faith' rather than by 'works'.

Greeting and introduction

Paul's greeting includes his own credentials as 'a servant of Jesus Christ, called to be an apostle, set apart for the gospel of God'. He then gives a simple definition of the person and work of Jesus, as Messiah and Son of God: 'the gospel concerning his Son, who was descended from David according to the flesh and designated Son of God in power according to the Spirit of holiness by his resurrection from the dead, Jesus Christ our Lord, through whom we have received grace and apostleship to bring about the obedience of faith for the sake of his name among all the nations, including yourselves who are called to belong to Christ Jesus.' (Rom. 1:3-6)

Paul goes on to thank God for the Christian community in Rome, traditionally founded by Peter, but more probably founded by some of the 120 disciples addressed by Peter at Pentecost. Paul outlines his plan to come to Rome, despite delays, in order to bring them the Good News, for he says, 'I am not ashamed of the gospel: it is the power of God for salvation to every one who has faith, to the Jew first and also to the Greek' (Rom. 1:16), and he quotes the prophet Habakkuk: 'He who through faith is righteous shall live.'

Warning for Jews and Gentiles

Paul denounces the Gentiles for their reliance upon their own reasoning and the Jews for their reliance upon the Mosaic Law. Of the Gentiles he said, 'Claiming to be wise, they became fools, and exchanged the glory of the immortal God for images resembling mortal man or birds or animals or reptiles ... though they know God's decree that those who do such things deserve to die, they not only do them but approve those who practise them.' (Rom. 1:22, 23, 32) Of the Jews Paul says, 'Therefore you have no excuse, O man, whoever you are, when you judge another; for in passing judgment upon him you condemn yourself, because you, the judge, are doing the very same things. . . . Do you suppose, O man,

367

that when you judge those who do such things and yet do them yourself, you will escape the judgment of God?' (Rom. 2:1, 3) Both must repent. 'There will be tribulation and distress for every human being who does evil, to the Jew first and also to the Greek, but glory and honour and peace for every one who does good, to the Jew first and also to the Greek. For God shows no partiality.' (Rom. 2:9-11) Paul then boldly asks: 'Then what advantage has the Jew?' Equally boldly Paul answers: 'Much in every way. To begin with, the Jews are entrusted with the oracles of God.' But it is not enough, for 'all men, both Jews and Greeks, are under the power of sin', and he goes on to answer from the Book of Psalms:

'None is righteous, no, not one;

no one understands, no one seeks for God.

All have turned aside, together they have gone wrong;

no one does good, not even one.' (Rom. 3:1, 2, 9-12) The Mosaic Law does not justify but simply convicts of sin. It is only faith in Jesus that avails. Paul cites Abraham, the father of the faithful, as an example of a man justified by his faith. 'The promise to Abraham and his descendants, that they should inherit the world, did not come through the law but through the righteousness of faith. If it is the adherents of the law who are to be the heirs, faith is null and the promise is void.' (Rom. 4:13, 14) The promise depends on faith and is freely available to all Abraham's descendants, not only his descendants by Law, but also by faith. Abraham was indeed made 'the father of many nations'. His faith was a model of the Christian faith.

Freedom from sin

Salvation, therefore, comes by faith, as the response of man to the grace of God through Jesus and his cross, and by no human achievement of righteousness in obedience to a code of laws. But because the grace of God is all-sufficient, this does not entitle Christians to continue in their old evil habits without fear. Paul illustrates this from the practice of baptism, the initiation into the Christian life, showing that it necessarily involves a death to the old sinful self and a rising to the new self. This does not make the Christian unable to sin, but it means that he no longer *belongs* to sin: he now belongs to Jesus, whose grace will inspire him to good conduct. That is why the Christian must keep himself holy, to present himself to God. 'So you must also consider yourselves dead to sin and alive to God in Christ Jesus.' (Rom. 6:11) Paul then launches into a direct psychological analysis of the experience of this

left The imperial city of Rome soon emerged as the chief centre of Christianity. Medallion of Peter and Paul, founders of the Church at Rome, painted in gold on glass, 4th century.

top A requiem inscription to a young Christian girl, Romana, with the *Chi-Rho* symbol, 3rd century, from the Catacomb of Marcus and Marcellianus, Rome.
above Detail of the baptism of Jesus by John the Baptist from a 3rd-century Roman sarcophagus.

salvation of sin. 'We know that the law is spiritual; but I am carnal, sold under sin. I do not understand my own actions. For I do not do what I want, but I do the very thing I hate. . . . Wretched man that I am! Who will deliver me from this body of death? Thanks be to God through Jesus Christ our Lord!' (Rom. 7:14, 15, 24, 25)

The universal Spirit

Paul goes on to compare those who live on a physical level with no expectation of further satisfaction when this is exhausted, and those who live by the Spirit of God. For Paul, this is the Spirit of Jesus that possesses his followers and makes them both the children and heirs of God. 'For all who are led by the Spirit of God are sons of God. . . . When we cry, "Abba! Father!" it is the Spirit himself bearing witness with our Spirit that we are children of God.' (Rom. 8:14-16)

At this point Paul – alternately the satirist, the philosopher, the rabbi, and the psychologist – now speaks with the vision of a poet, as he shows the function of the *universal* Spirit in the redemption of all created life. Paul explains that the story of the world is not yet complete, for Creation was purposefully made incomplete by the intention of God himself. The very gift of free-will and self-determination to man and the resultant risk of creating someone who may choose to crucify and

above Wood panel bearing the portrait of Paul, from Rome, 8th-9th centuries.

above Roman bronze bucket engraved with the figures of Jesus and the apostles, 4th-5th centuries.

left Decorated Christian tombs in the Catacomb of SS Peter and Marcellinus, 4th century.

reject you, is the only way to create a family of children, and not of robots. Indeed this very incompleteness of creation necessarily involves a process analagous to re-birth or re-creation. In this process, painful as it is, God himself is involved and is agonized – for the Spirit of God is within *all* and through all created life.

Paul himself was so filled and radiant with the Spirit, so truly alive, that he did not fear death. He had discovered a depth of life in the Spirit through his own experiences of betrayal and crucifixion. He had in a sense been down to hell, yet had survived, and in doing so had discovered the joy and purpose of living; so that he could truthfully exclaim, 'It is no longer I who live, but Christ who lives in me.' And again: 'Who shall separate us from the love of Christ? Shall tribulation, or distress, or persecution, or famine, or nakedness, or peril, or sword? ... No, in all these things we are more than conquerors through him who loved us. For I am sure that neither death, nor life, nor angels, nor principalities, nor things present, nor things to come, nor powers, nor height, nor depth, nor anything else in all creation, will be able to separate us from the love of God in Christ Jesus our Lord.' (Rom. 8:35, 37-39)

The tragedy of Israel

The next three chapters of Paul's treatise are devoted to this subject and are a vindication of God's dealings with the Jews. Paul, as a student of the Hebrew Bible, begins by outlining the privileges, promises, and responsibilities of Israel within it. He is deeply, emotionally involved in the tragedy of Israel's rejection of the Messiahship of Jesus. 'My conscience bears me witness in the Holy Spirit, that I have great sorrow and unceasing anguish in my heart. For I could wish that I myself were accursed and cut off from Christ for the sake of my brethren, my kinsmen by race. They are Israelites, and to them belong the sonship, the glory, the covenants, the giving of the law, the worship, and the promises; to them belong the patriarchs, and of their race, according to the flesh, is the Christ. God who is over all be blessed for ever. Amen.' (Rom. 9:2-5)

Paul claims that God has kept his promise, that God is not unjust, but that he retains a freedom of choice in disposing of his blessings. He tries to show that the rejection of the Messiah by Israel has been foretold by the prophets and foreseen by God – and that even this can be gathered up into God's purpose. Now, however, the order of events which Israel had been brought up to expect would be reversed. No longer would the Jews be saved first and the Gentiles saved later. The rejection of the Messiah by Israel would result in the salvation of the Gentiles.

'So I ask, have they stumbled so as to fall? By no means! But through their trespass salvation has come to the Gentiles, so as to make Israel jealous. Now if their trespass means riches for the world, and if their failure means riches for the Gentiles, how much more will their full inclusion mean! Now I am speaking to you Gentiles. Inasmuch then as I am an apostle to the Gentiles, I magnify my ministry in order to make my fellow Jews jealous, and thus save some of them.' (Rom. 11:11-14)

Paul, seeing that in fact the Church has been unsuccessful among the Jews, turns to the Gentiles. Writing to the very centre of the Roman Empire, he seeks to attract in the Church a nucleus of Gentiles from all parts of the world, in the hope that it will 'make my fellow Jews jealous'. For Paul, the Jews are still the chosen people – the olive-tree on to which the pagans have been grafted, and which awaits the regrafting of Israel. 'For if you have been cut from what is by nature a wild olive tree, and grafted, contrary to nature, into a cultivated olive tree, how much more will these natural branches be grafted back into their own olive tree.' (Rom. 11:24)

Charity and unity

Having disposed of some outstanding theological problems, Paul now declares that God brings those who are justified by their faith in Jesus into a new order of life in the Spirit. From this spiritual life, men derive the power to lead a good life and to display the righteousness of God in their Christian living. Similarly, by the indwelling of the Spirit, God's righteousness reshapes the conduct of men in society. Christians are therefore called to surrender their lives to God. 'I appeal to you therefore, brethren, by the mercies of God, to present your bodies as a living sacrifice, holy and acceptable to God, which is your spiritual worship. Do not be conformed to this world but be transformed by the renewal of your mind, that you may prove what is the will of God, what is good and acceptable and perfect.' (Rom. 12:1, 2)

Christians must behave in humility and charity, acknowledging their various individual contributions to the Christian community, like the different faculties which contribute to the health of the human body. 'For as in one body we have many members, and all the members do not have the same function, so we, though many, are one body in Christ, and individually members one of another.' (Rom. 12:4, 5)

Paul's standard of Christian behaviour, like that of Jesus's Sermon on the Mount, is based on love and non-resistance. He demands that Christians submit themselves to the civil authority – and this at a time when nationalist feeling was building up to the crisis of the revolt in AD 66. Paul reminds his readers that the return of Jesus may be soon and that they are to be awake, ready, and waiting. They are to be tolerant of the behaviour of others, and gentle with the scruples of their brethren, not scoffing at their eating habits or their festival days. 'Why do you pass judgment on your brother? Or you, why do you despise your brother? For we shall all stand before the judgment seat of God. ... So each of us shall give account of himself to God.' (Rom. 14:10, 12)

Paul exhorts Jewish and Gentile Christians to live in harmony and fellowship together. Their aim should be peace, the welfare and unity of the corporate life of the whole Church. 'May the God of hope fill you with all joy and peace in believing, so that by the power of the Holy Spirit you may abound in hope.' (Rom. 15:13)

Farewells and future plans

Paul outlines his plans to visit Rome *en route* for Spain, and asks for help and good wishes. First, however, he has to take the money contributed by the Christians in Greece to Jerusalem. It was appropriate, Paul said, that the Greeks – spiritual debtors to the Jewish-Christians – should contribute to their material needs. As soon as he

Early Christian *graffiti* in the pre-Constantinian necropolis beneath St Peter's, including (top, centre) the *Chi-Rho* monogram, based on the first letters of Christ in Greek.

has delivered this gift to Jerusalem, he will set out for Spain and visit them in Rome. 'I appeal to you, brethren, by our Lord Jesus Christ and by the love of the Spirit, to strive together with me in your prayers to God on my behalf, that I may be delivered from the unbelievers in Judea, and that my service for Jerusalem may be acceptable to the saints, so that by God's will I may come to you with joy and be refreshed in your company. The God of peace be with you all. Amen.' (Rom. 15:30-33)

As suggested above, the final chapter of the letter is probably Paul's covering letter when despatching a copy of his Roman letter to Ephesus. Certainly it is full of personal greetings, less likely perhaps to have been

Christian votive offering in gold, found beneath St Peter's, Rome, 6th-7th centuries.

addressed to the Roman congregations which he had not yet visited. The primary purpose of the covering letter is the introduction of the deaconess Phoebe to the Ephesian congregation. He sends greetings to Aquila and Prisca, who in Ephesus had risked their own lives for Paul, together with an early Asian convert, Epaenetus, and a host of other friends. Paul's secretary, then Tertius, adds his own greeting.

Paul closes with a final doxology that may perhaps have been transferred from the end of the original letter to the Romans. 'Now to him who is able to strengthen you according to my gospel and the preaching of Jesus Christ, according to the revelation of the mystery which was kept secret for long ages but is now disclosed and through the prophetic writings is made known to all nations, according to the command of the eternal God, to bring about the obedience of faith – to the only wise God be glory for evermore through Jesus Christ. Amen.' (Rom. 16:25-27) [John 11:48; Acts 16:21, 37, 38; 28:17; Rom. 1-16]

RUFUS (Gk. 'red') **1.** One of the sons of Simon of Cyrene, 'the father of Alexander and Rufus', who was compelled by the Roman execution squad to carry the cross-piece of the cross for Jesus on his way to Calvary. Only Mark mentions the sons by name, perhaps because they had become Christians and were known to his readers. Mark's Gospel is said to have been written in Rome during the year 64-5. Paul, in the final chapter of his letter to the Christians in Rome, includes a greeting to a Rufus, but there is no certain identification with the son of Simon of Cyrene. [Mark 15:21]

2. 'Rufus, eminent in the Lord, also his mother and mine.' Whether this greeting and others were in fact addressed to Rome or to Ephesus, there cannot be any certain identification of this family with that of Simon of Cyrene. The respect of Paul for the mother of Alexander and Rufus, coupled with Mark's mention of them by name, would seem, however, to strengthen the tradition that Simon of Cyrene and his family became Christians. [Rom. 16:13]

S

SADDUCEES (Gk. 'followers of Zadok' [Solomon's High Priest]) The Sadducees were a politico-religious party, holding the highest offices in church and state. They were prepared to compromise, for the sake of peace, with the Roman occupation forces, and consequently they frowned on the passive resistance of the Pharisees and on the aggressive nationalism of the Zealot freedom fighters. In return, they were allowed by the Romans to retain their power in the Temple and in the supreme Council, the Sanhedrin, and they guarded their position zealously. Indeed, the office of high priest was the appointment of Rome – much to the shame of the Jews – but Annas the Sadducee had so exerted his influence that six high priests in succession had been members of his own family, and Caiaphas, the seventh, was his own son-in-law. The importance of Caiaphas in the trial of Jesus gives some indication of the intrigue, the prestige, and the privileges of the Sadducees.

The high priests held the monopoly of the sale of animals for sacrifice, for which payment had to be made in Temple currency and on which they levied a rate of exchange. They also levied a tithe, or one-tenth of all their possessions, for the upkeep of the Temple, paid by every Jewish member of the population. The 'cleansing of the Temple' by Jesus represented a dangerous threat to both their authority and to their vested interests. This was the one occasion when Jesus accompanied his teaching with a violent demonstration to support his words: 'It is written, "My house shall be a house of prayer"; but you make it a den of robbers.' This undoubtedly took place within the eastern arcade of the Temple area, called Solomon's Porch, which was used at that time for limited public commerce.

Worldly self-interest

The worldly interests of the Sadducees led them in the same direction as the principles of their religion. Their very conservatism did not allow them to appreciate new doctrines such as resurrection. As wealthy aristocrats enjoying a privileged position in both church and state, they were indifferent to any hopes of a delivering Messiah. They were satisfied with their security under Roman patronage, and were very material in their pleasures. They did not believe in any after-life, except among the shades of Sheol, and so they set out to enjoy this life. For them there was no prospect of rewards or punishment in any future existence, nor was there time for troublesome traditions on earth. The Law was enough for them; there was no need to accept the new ideals of angels and spirits mediating between God and man. Scripture was the only authority for them, the 'hard-hearted rich', even if the 'pious poor' Pharisees preferred to saddle themselves with both scripture *and* tradition – even if, too, the masses of the people followed the Pharisees. They, the Sadducees, advocated a solid common-sense morality and political reality: for them any form of enthusiasm was unnecessary.

Jesus had few dealings with the Sadducees; they were not as influential in Galilee as they were in Jerusalem. John does not mention the Sadducees at all, but Matthew, Mark, and Luke all relate the question of the Sadducees to Jesus, on the day following his Palm Sunday triumphal entry into Jerusalem. Following the Pharisees' question about the tribute money, and before the Scribes' question about the primary commandment, the Sadducees put their question about the resurrection. They probably hoped to ridicule both Jesus and the Pharisees by this story, for they did not believe in any resurrection.

'Teacher,' they asked, 'Moses wrote for us that if a man's brother dies, having a wife but no children, the man must take the wife and raise up children for his brother. Now there were seven brothers; the first took a wife, and died without children; and the second and the third took her, and likewise all seven left no children and died. Afterward the woman also died. In the resurrection, therefore, whose wife will the woman be? For the seven had her as wife.' Perhaps this was a stock question of the Sadducees; Jesus answered it in God's words to Moses himself: 'But that the dead are raised, even Moses showed, in the passage about the bush, where he calls the Lord the God of Abraham and the God of Isaac and the God of Jacob. Now he is not God of the dead, but of the living; for all live to him.' (Luke 20:28-38)

Agents of Jesus's death

Although the Sadducees are not often mentioned by

Crucifix by the Master of San Francesco, showing Salome, the wife of Zebedee, among the women on the left.

name in the story of the passion, they are always included in references to the high priests. Caiaphas, as a matter of historical fact, was the architect of Jesus's crucifixion, and it is probable that it was the action of the Sadducees in the Sanhedrin that secured the conviction. It had been the Pharisees and high priests who had asked in the Council, when confronted by Jesus's progress in preaching, despite their efforts to trip him up, 'What are we to do? For this man performs many signs. If we let him go on thus, every one will believe in him, and the Romans will come and destroy both our holy place and our nation.' It had been Caiaphas the Sadducee who replied, 'It is expedient for you that one man should die for the people.' (John 11:47-50)

That meant, of course, let him be handed over to the Roman authority, for in any case the Jews could not execute him. So in one act the Sadducees would destroy Jesus, put the blame on Rome, and pretend their own loyalty to Roman law and order. And from the day of that plot, 'they took counsel how to put him to death'. (John 11:53) see also ANNAS, CAIAPHAS, and SANHEDRIN [Matt. 3:7; 16:1, 6, 11, 12; 22:23, 34; Mark 12:18; Acts 4:1; 5:17; 23:6-8]

SALOME (Gk. from Heb. peaceful') **1. Salome, wife of Zebedee** Only Mark mentions this Salome by name as a watcher at the crucifixion of Jesus and as a visitor to his tomb on the Easter morning. Matthew mentions by name each of the other women, found in Mark, using the same order, 'Mary Magdalene, Mary the mother of James and Joses', but includes instead of the word 'Salome', the description: 'the mother of the sons of Zebedee'. More certain identification is not possible. Luke merely calls them 'the women'. All three Synoptic Gospels state that they had followed Jesus from Galilee and looked after him. All the women were early involved in the lakeside ministry of Jesus, Mary at Magdala, the other Mary and Salome both as mothers of his earliest disciples, Salome as the mother of James and John, who with Peter formed the inner circle of the twelve.

At some point during the Galilean ministry, these two brothers James and John came with a personal request to Jesus. Mark makes it clear that they presented their plea for themselves, but Matthew, perhaps to preserve the propriety and dignity of the apostles, puts the question into the mouth of the 'mother of the sons of Zebedee'. 'Then the mother of the sons of Zebedee came up to him, with her sons, and kneeling before him she asked him for something. And he said to her, "What do you want?" She said to him, "Command that these two sons of mine may sit, one at your right hand and one at your left, in your kingdom." But Jesus answered, "You do not know what you are asking. Are you able to drink the cup that I am to drink?" They said to him, "We are able." He said to them, "You will drink my

cup, but to sit at my right hand and at my left is not mine to grant, but it is for those for whom it has been prepared by my Father."' (Matt. 20:20-23) Indeed, it was Salome's first son James who drank of his master's cup, scarcely fifteen years later, when as a political victim of Herod Agrippa I, he was executed during an early persecution of the young Christian Church.

Salome, whose husband Zebedee must have been of some substance and status in the lakeside fishing trade, would have been a very useful member of the little group of women who provided for the needs of Jesus and his disciples, not only in Galilee, but also on their journeys to Jerusalem. [Mark 15:40, 41; 16:1 and, by implication, Matt. 20:20-23]

2. Salome, daughter of Herodias This great-granddaughter of Herod the Great is chiefly remembered for the sordid scheme by which she danced for Herod Antipas and secured the execution of John the Baptist, at the instigation of her mother Herodias.

Salome's father was her great-uncle Herod Boethus, a private citizen in Rome and son of Herod the Great. Her mother was a granddaughter of Herod the Great, who contrived the assassination of both her father and grandmother. Salome's mother, Herodias, later married Herod Antipas, and the Gospels of Mark and Matthew mistakenly link her also with Philip the tetrarch, the brother of Antipas. Josephus, however, records the third marriage of Salome's mother Herodias with another Philip within the Herod family at Rome.

The account of the death of John the Baptist in Mark's Gospel reads like a popular legend of the prophet rebuking the king, along the lines of the Old Testament story of Elijah rebuking Ahab for appropriating Naboth's vineyard. John fearlessly condemned Antipas for taking Philip's wife, who was his own niece and consequently by law forbidden to be his wife. No doubt John also condemned Herodias for deserting her first husband to form an adulterous alliance with her uncle Antipas. Certainly, it was Herodias who bore a grudge against John, though Antipas is said to have respected and protected him.

'But an opportunity came when Herod on his birthday gave a banquet for his courtiers and officers and the leading men of Galilee. For when Herodias's daughter came in and danced, she pleased Herod and his guests; and the king said to the girl, "Ask me for whatever you wish, and I will grant it." And he vowed to her, "Whatever you ask me, I will give you, even half of my kingdom." And she went out, and said to her mother, "What shall I ask?" And she said, "The head of John the baptizer." And she came in immediately with haste to the king, and asked, saying, "I want you to give me at once the head of John the Baptist on a platter." And the king was exceedingly sorry; but because of his oath and

Salome, daughter of Herodias

Herod's Banquet, fresco by Fra Filippo Lippi (*c.* 1406-69) in Prato Cathedral. Salome dances (left) and (right) brings the head of John the Baptist to Herodias.

his guests he did not want to break his word to her. And immediately the king sent a soldier of the guard and gave orders to bring his head. He went and beheaded him in the prison, and brought his head on a platter, and gave it to the girl; and the girl gave it to her mother.' (Mark 6:21-28)

The execution took place, according to Josephus, in the fortress of Machaerus beyond Jordan; his burial is supposed to have been at Samaria, where his tomb was honoured from the 4th century.

Richard Strauss's opera *Salome,* based on the play by Oscar Wilde, ends fancifully with the flogging to death of Salome at the close of Antipas's banquet. Salome at that time was less than sixteen years old and, according to the Jewish historian Josephus, later married Philip, the tetrarch of Iturea, Gaulanitis and Trachonitis. This Salome's name does not appear

left Salome dancing with the head of John the Baptist, 14th-century mosaic in St Mark's, Venice.

in the Gospels, except by implication as 'the daughter of Herodias'. *see* HEROD [Matt. 14:6; Mark 6:22]

SAMARITANS The capital of the northern kingdom of Israel, built by Omri, father of Ahab, stands on a hill 'bought from Shemer for two talents of silver' (hence the name Samaria), and is still to be seen a few miles north of the modern city of Nablus. The name Samaria came to be used for the district occupied by the ten northern tribes, bounded by Galilee, Jordan, and Judea.

During the lifetime of Jesus, Samaria was ruled until 4 BC by Herod the Great; he left it to Archelaus, who was deposed in AD 6 by the Romans, and they in turn appointed a series of procurators, answerable to the governor of the Roman province of Syria.

Tradition of independence

The history of Samaria is that of five distinct occupations: 1) Israelite, 2) Assyrian, 3) Persian, 4) Greek, 5) Roman. The Israelite city and royal capital of the northern kingdom was destroyed in 721 BC. The Assyrian colonial and administrative centre of Sargon for

379

the next 400 years left little trace but for some crude walling on the acropolis. The Assyrian conquerors deported the leading inhabitants of the city, but imported settlers from Mesopotamia, who intermarried with the surviving population. These settlers practised their own religion, but were later instructed by an Israelite priest sent from Babylon. When, some two centuries later, the Jewish exiles were allowed to return and re-occupy Jerusalem, they found Judah under the administration of the governor of Samaria, appointed by the Persian Empire. They found their lack of political independence hard to bear, particularly as their religious scruples were offended by what they considered a debased form of Judaism, diluted with Assyrian customs, practised among the Samaritans. Nehemiah gained independence for Judah with its newly built Temple in Jerusalem.

The Samaritans built their own sanctuary on Mount Gerizim in about 400 BC, overlooking the ancient sanctuary at Shechem, Jacob's Well, and the traditional tomb of Joseph, from whom they claimed descent. By the 1st century, this sanctuary was in ruins. When the Jewish community accepted within their scriptures

previous pages Jesus and the woman of Samaria. 6th-century mosaic from S. Apollinare Nuovo, Ravenna.
above The Samaritan woman and Jesus at the well. Early 3rd-century mural from the catacomb of Calixtus, Rome.
below Roman theatre at Samaria, viewed over the wall of the Greek acropolis.

the Prophets and other writings of the Old Testament, the Samaritans did not do so, but confirmed their loyalty to the Five Books of Moses alone.

The woman of Samaria

Within the New Testament, this political and religious tension between Jew and Samaritan is well reflected in the Fourth Gospel account of the meeting of Jesus with the woman at Jacob's Well. On his way back from Jerusalem to Galilee by way of the highlands of Samaria, during his second day's travelling, Jesus rested at Jacob's Well and sent his disciples on to the next village to buy lunch. It was over his midday rest that he had that wonderful conversation with the much-married woman of Samaria, who teased him for his thirsty request for a drink: 'The Samaritan woman said to him, "How is it that you, a Jew, ask a drink of me, a woman of Samaria? For Jews have no dealings with Samaritans." ' (John 4:9) Jesus took his opportunity to teach her and answered, 'If you knew the gift of God, and who it is that is saying to you, "Give me a drink," you would have asked him, and he would have given you living water.' (John 4:10)

She was by now plainly puzzled, but intrigued, and answered him, the Jewish rabbi, almost facetiously, 'Sir, you have nothing to draw with, and the well is deep; where do you get that living water? Are you greater than our father Jacob, who gave us the well and drank from it himself, and his sons, and his cattle?' (John 4:11-12) Today the well is still 105 feet deep and its identification is unquestioned. The biblical scholar Jerome describes the building of a church there in the 4th century, and the Bordeaux Pilgrim as early as 333 identified the well by its proximity to Joseph's Tomb. Since then the site has had an unbroken tradition.

Jesus said to her, 'Every one who drinks of this water will thirst again, but whoever drinks of the water that I shall give him will never thirst; the water that I shall give him will become in him a spring of water welling up to eternal life.' (John 4:13-14) Again puzzled and practical, for it is a good half-mile's carry back from the well to her village, with a full pitcher on her head, 'The woman said to him, "Sir, give me this water, that I may not thirst, nor come here to draw." ' (John 4:15)

Jesus then suggested that she call her husband, but she, fearing exposure, denied she had a husband. Jesus, however, read her thoughts so clearly that she eagerly asked him, as a seer, to give his ruling on the vital question separating Jews and Samaritans. 'Sir, I perceive that you are a prophet. Our fathers worshipped on this mountain; and you say that in Jerusalem is the place where men ought to worship.' (John 4:19-20) Jesus gave his prophetic answer, 'Woman, believe me, the hour is coming when neither on this mountain nor in Jerusalem will you worship the Father. . . . God is

spirit, and those who worship him must worship in spirit and truth.' (John 4:21, 24)

The woman still did not understand him and, expecting an obscure answer perhaps from such a prophet, she looked forward to the coming of the Christ who, when he came, would make it all plain. 'I know that Messiah is coming (he who is called Christ); when he comes, he will show us all things.' (John 4:25) Immediately Jesus completed his pastoral instruction with that stupendous affirmation: 'I who speak to you am he.' [John 4:7, 9]

The Good Samaritan

In answer to a certain lawyer's question, 'Who is my neighbour?' Jesus told the parable of the Good Samaritan, recorded in Luke's Gospel. The setting of the story would be well-known to his hearers. 'A man was going down from Jerusalem to Jericho, and he fell among robbers, who stripped him and beat him, and departed, leaving him half dead.' (Luke 10:30) The road drops down over the Mount of Olives, from 3,000 feet above sea-level to 1,300 feet below sea-level within a distance of 24 miles. It passes through a dry and arid wilderness of crags and boulders, which has always provided a wonderful hiding-place for brigands. At a point exactly halfway down, there is an old khan (or inn) overlooked today by the ruins of Roman and Crusader staging-posts. In the centre of its courtyard is a Roman well, which has for centuries been the local water-supply of the surrounding caravanserai. Many of Jesus's hearers would know that route all too well and may even have shared the experience of the man who 'fell among thieves'.

The story continues, depicting three travellers on the same road and their reactions to the naked and wounded man by the roadside. 'Now by chance a priest was going down that road; and when he saw him he passed by on the other side. So likewise a Levite, when he came to the place and saw him, passed by on the other side.' At this point, the hearers, who thought of their community in terms of Priests, Levites, and Israelites – as perhaps Christians today of bishops, clergy, and lay people – might have been confident that the hero would be an Israelite. Their shock and consternation when the hero turned out to be a hated Samaritan – one publicly cursed in the synagogues and whose evidence was unacceptable in a court of law – can be easily imagined.

'But a Samaritan, as he journeyed, came to where he was; and when he saw him, he had compassion, and went to him and bound up his wounds, pouring on oil and wine; then he set him on his own beast and brought him to an inn, and took care of him. And the next day he took out two denarii and gave them to the innkeeper, saying, "Take care of him; and whatever more you spend I will repay you when I come back."' (Luke 10:33-35) The parable did not exactly answer the

question of the lawyer, 'Who is my neighbour?' but it illustrated graphically that neighbourhood was unlimited, by race or religion. The only criterion for neighbourliness is need.

Hostility – and gratitude

Luke gives two further accounts of Samaritans.

Jesus and his disciples were on their way from Galilee to Jerusalem and sent messengers to make the necessary arrangements for accommodation along the route. They came to a Samaritan village but were not welcomed because they were Jews and were on the way to Jerusalem. James and John, the hot-blooded 'sons of thunder', immediately asked Jesus: 'Lord, do you want us to bid fire come down from heaven and consume them?' Jesus turned and checked the brothers; they went on to another village.

According to Josephus, 'it was a custom of Galileans proceeding to the feasts at the holy city to journey through Samaritan territory'. (*Antiquities*, xx, 6:1) On one occasion Josephus records that in the Samaritan village of Gema 'A Galilean, one of a large company of Jews journeying to the festival, was murdered.' (*Wars*, II, 12:3) The Jews despised the Samaritans as 'the foolish nation that dwells in Shechem' (Ecclesiasticus 1:25), and the Samaritans repaid them with scorn.

On another journey to Jerusalem on the same route, Jesus healed ten lepers. Luke says that 'he was passing along between Samaria and Galilee. And as he entered a village, he was met by ten lepers' (Luke 17:11, 12). The pilgrim route to Jerusalem would cross the border into Samaria at Jenin where the road across the Plain of Esdraelon cuts south through the foothills into the vale of Dothan. Jenin, once called Ain Gannim, 'the gardens', is associated with a 15th-century tradition with the village of the ten lepers. In the neighbouring hamlet of Burkein, the Arabic-speaking Greek Orthodox congregation worship in a Church of the Ten Lepers, which they hold to be the site of the miracle. Gardens would indicate an appropriate and refreshing spot for the midday halt. It was also a crossroads at which pilgrims would gather from three different directions, those coming from the lakeside via Beth-shean, from Nazareth across the plain of Jezreel, and from the coast by the road among the Carmel range.

The lepers kept their distance and attracted Jesus's attention by shouting, ' "Jesus, Master, have mercy on us." When he saw them, he said to them, "Go and show yourselves to the priests." ' For Jewish lepers this would mean a visit to the Temple at Jerusalem, for they could only be pronounced clean after the necessary sacrificial

top left The Good Samaritan, by Domenico Campagnola. *bottom left* Crusader staging post in the wilderness of Judea, half-way along the Roman road between Jerusalem and Jericho.

Samaritan priests celebrating the Passover on the top of their holy mountain Gerizim, above Nablus.

rites. 'And as they went, they were cleansed,' says Luke, the physician. 'Then one of them, when he saw that he was healed, turned back, praising God with a loud voice; and he fell on his face at Jesus's feet, giving him thanks. Now he was a Samaritan.' (Luke 17:13-16) Jesus at once contrasted the gratitude of the Samaritan with the forgetfulness of the nine Jews. 'Were there not ten cleansed? Where are the nine? Was no one found to return and give praise to God except this foreigner? ... Rise and go your way; your faith has made you well.' (Luke 17:17-19)

It is interesting to note that Pontius Pilate's recall to Rome in the year 36 was to answer charges of high-handed and savage repression of a Samaritan rising, on which charges he was found guilty and banished.

Samaria proved to be highly responsive to early Christian evangelism. In about the year 35, Philip, one of the seven deacons, was so successful as an evangelist that the Church in Jerusalem despatched the two Apostles Peter and John to consolidate this activity and officially establish the Christian community in Samaria.

Today, there are two Samaritan communities, numbering perhaps 200 souls in all. One is to be found in the area of the town of Nablus, on the slopes of Mount Gerizim, on which they continue to celebrate their Passover every spring. Within their synagogue, they treasure a very ancient Pentateuch. The other and smaller community is at Holon, near Tel Aviv. [Matt. 10:5; Luke 9:52; 10:33; 17:16; John 4:9, 39; 8:48]

SANHEDRIN (Gk. 'council') This supreme assembly of post-exilic Judaism was an aristocratic senate, composed of representatives of the priesthood and laity who from the 4th century BC, in the Persian and Greek occupations, came to the forefront of the Jewish people.

The Sanhedrin at Jerusalem was in origin and effect the first authority in the land, and the highest court of law to which the provincial courts turned for decisions in particularly difficult cases. The Sanhedrin's com-petence and reputation extended throughout world Jewry, though its greatest influence was in Judea. They held court at Jerusalem, within the Temple area, on the south of the priests' court in the 'Chamber of Hewn Stone'. The Temple police were at their disposal and probably effected the arrests of Jesus in Gethsemane and of the Apostle Paul within the Temple courts. The Sanhedrin also examined candidates for ordination to the priesthood, checking the purity of their priestly descent and their bodily fitness – as well as their other qualifications.

Jesus Christ before Caiaphas: fresco in the Arena Chapel, Padua, by Giotto (?1267-1337). Caiaphas debates with members of the Sanhedrin.

When Judea became a Roman province in AD 6, the Sanhedrin became the chief political agency, controlling the affairs of the eleven districts into which the Romans divided the land, and linking every town and village administratively to Jerusalem.

The presidency of the Sanhedrin, as a matter of privilege, belonged to the high priest. The Council consisted of 71 members, falling into three main groups: the chief priests (sometimes called the 'rulers', Acts 4:5, 6), the elders (sometimes called the 'principal men of the people', Luke 19:47), and the scribes. These three groups or grades correspond with those who questioned the authority of Jesus for cleansing the Temple. (Mark 11:27)

The first group – the chief priests – included those who held the most important offices in the Temple: the anointed high priest and retired high priests, the Captain of the Temple, often the high priest's deputy, the leaders of the 24 weekly courses, the Temple overseers, and the Temple treasurers.

The hierarchy tended to fill all the chief positions from their own families as a matter of course. The ruling house of Annas held perhaps all the chief-priestly positions within its control, besides operating a flourishing trade in sacrificial victims within the court of the Gentiles, in the Temple. No less than eight members of this family held the supreme office of high priest: Annas himself, five sons, Caiaphas his son-in-law, and his grandson Matthias, from the year 65. Such a family virtually established the political as well as religious leadership of the nation.

Among the ruling priests, within the Sanhedrin and present at the trial of Peter and John in the early 30s, were Annas the elderly and influential former high priest, his son-in-law Caiaphas, the ruling high priest, Jonathan, probably a captain of the Temple, a son of Annas, who succeeded Caiaphas, an unknown priest called Alexander, and others who held high-priestly office in Jerusalem. The family that ruled the Sanhedrin clearly held the leadership of the whole people.

The second group – the elders – were descended from those ancient ruling families who had held the leadership within the tribes and after the settlement in Canaan. The heads of these dominant families had directed the settlement and administration of the exiles in Babylon. After their return, the heads of such families had acted as representatives of the people, negotiating with the provincial governors, and directing the reconstruction of the Temple in the time of Ezra. The Sanhedrin grew out of the union of this secular nobility with the priestly aristocracy of those times.

Within the lifetime of Jesus one representative of this group was Joseph of Arimathea, a rich landowner, in whose tomb at Jerusalem the body of Jesus was buried. Josephus, the Jewish historian writing in the 1st century,

top Entrance of the 2nd-century Tombs of the Sanhedrin, Jerusalem.
above Interior of the Tombs of the Sanhedrin, Jerusalem.

describes the elders variously as 'notables', 'most eminent citizens', and 'leading men'. He describes the three groups within the Sanhedrin as the 'principal citizens, the chief priests, and the most notable Pharisees'. These elders were usually the heads of patrician families whose precedence was based on centuries-old privilege. They were usually men of great wealth; the Roman procurator was careful to choose such as his tax officials, for their office might involve them in considerable financial sacrifice. These were charged with assessing citizens for taxation and guaranteeing the correct payment from their own resources.

These first two groups within the Sanhedrin, the chief priests and the patricians, combined to hold the highest offices in church and state. In politics and religion, too, they combined from the 2nd century BC to form the politico-religious party called the 'Sadducees'. (*see* SADDUCEES) In the reign of the Hasmonean Queen Alexandra, beginning in 76 BC, the Pharisees gained a foothold in the Sanhedrin and gradually won the confidence and support of the people. In the century after Jesus, the political power of the high priests came to an abrupt end in the year 70, and the new class of Pharisaic Scribes overtook the more ancient class of priestly and lay nobility, founded on the privilege of birth.

The rise of this new upper class of Scribes, the third group within the Sanhedrin, was largely due to their knowledge of scripture and administrative capacity. Jewish communities usually chose Scribes rather than laymen for the office of judge or synagogue-ruler, simply because of their expertise in scriptural exegesis and tradition, as well as in civil and criminal jurisdiction. Thus many important appointments previously held by priests and laymen passed into the hands of the Scribes. Among such were Nicodemus (John 3:1; 7:50), Gamaliel (Acts 5:34), and, of course, the Apostle Paul (Acts 26:10, 11). (*see also* SCRIBES *and* PHARISEES)

The Sanhedrin is linked, in the pages of the New Testament, mainly with the trials of Jesus (*see also* CAIAPHAS *and* ANNAS), of Peter and John, of Stephen, and of the Apostle Paul. [Mark 14:53-56; 15:1; Acts 4:5, 23; 6:12, 15; 22:30; 23:1, 6-9]

SAPPHIRA (Aram. 'beautiful') The wife of the hypocrite who sold property, but appropriated some of the purchase-money, and only brought part of its value to give to the apostles for the Church. The Apostle Peter rebuked him sternly. This terrible indictment caused his immediate death. Three hours later, Sapphira arrived and, after similar cross-examination and for the same lie, was instantly punished by death. Whether legend or truth, this story reflects little mercy in Peter's dealings with this guilty couple. It seems that Luke, the narrator, may have regarded the sin of Ananias and Sapphira as a 'sin against the Holy Spirit'. [Acts 5:7-11]

SATAN (Heb., Gk. 'accuser' or 'adversary') In the early books of the Old Testament, the word is used in a general sense to denote an opponent or enemy. The first occasion it is used of a supernatural being is in the Book of Job, when the Satan – it is not yet a proper name – acts as the public prosecutor before God in heaven of his righteous servant Job. In the prophecies of Zechariah he plays the same part of accuser of the high priest Joshua. In the First Book of Chronicles Satan appears, a proper name for the first time, as the tempter of David.

According to one Jewish tradition, the Jews brought back the names of the angels from Babylon, but neither in Persian religion nor in Palestine was the belief in angels and demons a sudden growth. The many gods of the ancient oriental world were not completely eradicated by the growth of the belief in a single true God. Some of these old gods were down-graded into angels

17th-century French ivory: the temptation of Jesus to turn stones into bread by Satan – in ordinary clothes but with pointed ears and clawed feet.

and agents of the one supreme God; others were degraded into demons and devils. Among these latter was a supernatural being – the Satan – whose function was to point out men's failings to God.

Jewish theology was somewhat influenced by Persian dualism, that is, the thought that there existed opposing kingdoms of good and evil, the one loyal to God, the other subject to the prince of devils, whether he was called Satan, Beelzebub, or by his Persian name Asmodeus. (Beelzebub was simply a degeneration of the Phoenician god Baal-Zebul, 'Lord of the Flies'.) The concept of Satan as public prosecutor may have developed from the function at the Persian court of an official called the 'King's eye', whose business it was to inform the king about his subjects.

In the text of the New Testament, the term Satan – transliterated from the Hebrew word – designates a personal devil. He is, however, known by various other names and descriptions, of which the most common in the Gospels is 'the devil', from the Greek word *diabolos*, meaning 'slanderer'. Elsewhere he is called 'Abaddon' or 'Apollyon' (Rev. 9:11), 'Deceiver of the whole world' (Rev. 12:9), 'Accuser' (Rev. 12:10), 'Adversary' (1 Pet. 5:8), 'Belial' (2 Cor. 6:15), 'The prince of the power of the air' (Eph. 2:2), 'the great dragon' and 'that ancient serpent' (Rev. 12:9). The Fourth Gospel includes many references to him by Jesus, as 'the evil one', 'the father of lies', 'a murderer from the beginning who has nothing to do with the truth, because there is no truth in him'. The writer of Jude describes him as the arch-enemy of the archangel Michael, cast out of heaven to roam the earth, as 'the prince of this world', a title thrice given him in the Fourth Gospel. This suggests the Jewish conception of the inherent evil of the present age and the good time expected in the age to come.

The first three Gospels describe the inward struggle of Jesus to face the implications and manner of his Messiahship in the form of three direct temptations by the devil in person.

The key to the understanding of the 'temptations' is to be found in the words of the divine voice at Jesus's baptism: 'Thou art my beloved Son; with thee I am well pleased.' (Mark 1:11) It was this fresh awareness of his sonship to God traumatically linked with that very clear reference to the Suffering Servant from Isaiah 52 (a reference repeated in all the Synoptic Gospels) that 'drove Jesus into the wilderness'. In that threatening environment, the evil one appeared, to offer him the means of escaping the cost of his Messiahship. The devil suggested various means of his gaining acceptance of God's kingdom among men but through the wrong means, the age-old means of coercing men's loyalty without first winning their hearts. These means included the bribery of the crowds by turning stones into bread, the spectacle and display of power in floating off the

wing of the Temple down into the Kidron Valley, and finally the compromise of good with evil to secure the best of both worlds. All these Jesus rejected, using the words of scripture to confront and to confound the devil.

However literally we may interpret this experience, Jesus himself clearly recognized the existence and power of a kingdom of evil under the control of a supreme personality to whom he referred as 'Satan' or 'Be-elzebul'. The principal function of the Messiah was to destroy the works of Satan (Mark 1:24, 34; 3:11, 15). In the expulsion of devils or exorcism by his disciples during the mission of the seventy, Jesus saw the overthrow of Satan's power. (Luke 10:18) His disciples, too, interpreted Jesus's acts of exorcism as attacks on the power and influence of the devil.

After 'casting out a demon' from a dumb man, the scribes from Jerusalem accused Jesus of exorcizing by the power of 'Be-elzebul, the prince of demons'. To them Jesus gave a very practical answer, 'But he, knowing their thoughts, said to them, "Every kingdom divided against itself is laid waste, and house falls upon house. And if Satan also is divided against himself, how will his kingdom stand? For you say that I cast out demons by Be-elzebul. And if I cast out demons by Be-elzebul, by whom do your sons cast them out? Therefore they shall be your judges. But if it is by the finger of God that I cast out demons, then the kingdom of God has come upon you."' (Luke 11:17-20)

He then told a parable clearly illustrating that his arrival as Messiah was about to establish the kingdom of God in this world and would inexorably seize control, hitherto in the hands of the 'strong man', the 'prince of this world': 'When a strong man, fully armed, guards his own palace, his goods are in peace; but when one stronger than he assails him and overcomes him, he takes away his armour in which he trusted, and divides his spoil.' (Luke 11:21, 22)

The Apostle Paul shared the contemporary belief in the reality of the devil, whom he linked with the serpent in the garden of Eden, 'But I am afraid that as the serpent deceived Eve by his cunning, your thoughts will be led astray from a sincere and pure devotion to Christ'. (2 Cor. 11:3) 'For while your obedience is known to all ... I would have you wise as to what is good and guileless as to what is evil; then the God of peace will soon crush Satan under your feet.' (Rom. 16:19, 20)

The Book of Revelation contains a detailed account of the devil's persecution of the early Church, under the figure of the 'woman clothed with the sun, with the moon under her feet' whose new-born child is threatened by the dragon. The 'dream-picture' goes on to explain that the dragon, defeated in heaven, has been cast out into the earth. There, for a limited time, the war between good and evil will continue. 'Now war arose in

Satan

The Last Judgment from the west front of Autun
Cathedral, 12th century. On the left the righteous
are received by the angels, on the right the
damned are tortured by the devils of Hell.

Satan

heaven, Michael and his angels fighting against the dragon; and the dragon and his angels fought, but they were defeated and there was no longer any place for them in heaven. And the great dragon was thrown down, that ancient serpent, who is called the Devil and Satan, the deceiver of the whole world – he was thrown down to the earth, and his angels were thrown down with him. . . . Rejoice then, O heaven and you that dwell therein! But woe to you, O earth and sea, for the devil has come down to you in great wrath, because he knows that his time is short!' (Rev. 12:7-9, 12) [Matt. 12:26; Mark 8:33; Luke 10:18; 22:3; Acts 5:3; 26:18; Rom. 16:20; 1 Cor. 5:5; 2 Cor. 2:11; 12:7; 2 Thess. 2:9; 1 Tim. 1:20; Rev. 2:24; 20:7]

SAUL (of Tarsus) (Heb. 'asked of God') *see* PAUL

SCEVA The arch-priest or high priest, whose seven sons at Ephesus attempted exorcism in the name of 'Jesus whom Paul preaches', with disastrous results to themselves.

Luke, in Acts, describes Paul's long teaching activity in Ephesus, accompanied by an extraordinary sequence of healings and exorcisms of unclean spirits. Ephesus was a noted centre for magic and itinerant exorcists, both pagan and Jewish. Perhaps the 'sons of Sceva' were not literally brothers, but members of a guild of exorcists, led by a priest with the Latin name of Sceva. The patient upon whom they misused the name of Jesus, however, turned on them in insane fury and drove them away, stripped and wounded.

Luke goes on to describe the effect of this encounter: 'And this became known to all residents of Ephesus, both Jews and Greeks; and fear fell upon them all; and the name of the Lord Jesus was extolled. Many also of those who were now believers came, confessing and divulging their practices. And a number of those who practised magic arts brought their books together and burned them in the sight of all; and they counted the value of them and found it came to fifty thousand pieces of silver. So the word of the Lord grew and prevailed mightily.' (Acts 19:17-20) [Acts 19:14]

SCRIBES (Gk. from Heb. 'man of letters') The Scribes were the expert lawyers, who interpreted and extemporized the written Law by a mass of their own traditions. They were the acknowledged and respected teachers of the Law, both in the schools and in the courts.

Before the exile of the Jews to Babylon, the Scribes had been the public writers and secretaries. They had copied the Law and other manuscripts; in doing so they had become the leading authorities and interpreters of the Law. Ezra the Scribe, in the post-exilic period, had instructed the returned exiles in the study of the Law. So it was that the Scribes developed gradually into a professional class, devoted to the copying, exposition, and application of the Law. Then, during the Hellenistic period, when the Law and its observance were

Writing desks from the scriptorium at Qumran, 1st century A.D.

threatened by pagan and Greek influence, it was the Scribes, together with the Pharisees, who became the defenders and teachers of the Law to the common people, and even the magistrates.

By the time of Jesus, the Scribes had developed a complicated system of traditions to ensure the correct application of the Law. They had come to demand and to receive the deep respect of the people. The very title 'Rabbi', meaning 'My Teacher', by which some were known indicates the honour in which they were held. In the Gospels they are often linked with the Pharisees, whose convictions some Scribes shared as Pharisees. There were, however, Scribes within the Sanhedrin, the supreme Council, both Pharisaic and apparently Sadducean Scribes. These are mentioned among the members of the court which convicted Jesus of blasphemy in Jerusalem.

In Galilee, too, the Scribes were highly critical of Jesus's activities, particularly at Capernaum, where the synagogue congregation compared Jesus's authoritative preaching with the less inspired efforts of their Scribes. The Scribes objected strongly to Jesus's words of forgiveness to the paralytic, saying, 'Who can forgive sins but God alone?' Again, they complained at his eating with Matthew the publican and his colleagues. In the Gospel of Luke, Jesus replies to them with the parables of the lost and the found: the Lost Sheep, the

Lost Coin, and the Prodigal Son – implying that he, Jesus, was sent to seek and to save those who were lost.

In Jerusalem, the Scribes were among the delegation that questioned Jesus's authority to drive the merchants out of the Temple. On at least two occasions an individual Scribe spoke to Jesus; when he was in the Temple, a Scribe asked which was the first commandment. Receiving and approving of Jesus's answer, he said: 'You are right, Teacher; you have truly said that he is one, and there is no other but he; and to love him with all the heart, and with all the understanding, and with all the strength, and to love one's neighbour as oneself, is much more than . . . sacrifice.' To which Jesus replied, 'You are not far from the kingdom of God.' Again, it was another Scribe who asked, 'Teacher, what shall I do to inherit eternal life?' then having partly answered his own question, the Scribe asked, 'And who is my neighbour?' It was in answer to this question that Jesus told him the story of the Good Samaritan and added, 'Go and do likewise.'

For the most part, however, the Gospels (and particularly that of Matthew) show Jesus in outspoken condemnation of the Scribes, together with the Pharisees. He saw that their mass of petty traditions often contradicted the spirit of the Law, however much they preserved the letter of the Law. He felt that the Scribes, by their systematic codification, robbed the common people of any freedom of interpretation, according to their own conscience. The Scribes, he felt, 'set a fence around the law'. It is perhaps not surprising that many Scribes became his most bitter opponents and called forth from him a devastating denunciation – for their hypocrisy, their blindness, and their neglect of justice, mercy, and good faith. They sought to win for

Inkwells from the scriptorium at Qumran, still containing dried ink. 1st century AD.

men the kingdom of Heaven by the meticulous observance of a written code. Jesus, in his Sermon on the Mount, set forward the two principles of self-sacrifice and service.

But the teaching of the Scribes had many virtues, as may be seen in the *Mishnah*, the earliest collection of Scribal teaching. It was a genuine attempt on the part of devoted scholars to interpret the Law so that men could be saved from unintentional transgression. There was much reference to other rabbis' opinions and little originality, but a vast amount of painstaking scholarship. The existence of the Law of Moses made the tradition of the Scribes necessary; for it was only by a traditional interpretation of the Law that it could be applied to the particular day and circumstances. For instance, if keeping the Sabbath involved not working, it was necessary for tradition to define what constituted work in that day and age. For Jesus, however, the Law was a matter of principles to be obeyed by a willing assent. *see also* PHARISEES [Matt. 5:20; 7:29; 16:21; 17:10; 20:18; 21:15; Mark 1:22; 2:6, 16; 8:31; 9:14; 10:33; 11:18; 12:28, 35, 38; 14:1; Luke 5:30; 6:7; 11:53; 20:1, 19; 22:2; 23:10; John 8:3; Acts 4:5; 6:12; 23:9]

SCYTHIAN (Gk. 'inhabitants of Scythia', but coloquially 'savages') The classical term for uncivilized foreigners, emanating from the name of the savage tribes in the steppe-lands beyond the Carpathians and the Caucasus, that is, to the north-east of the Roman Empire.

The Apostle Paul, writing to the Christian community at Colossae in Asia Minor, says that Christians have to put aside all the unworthy passions that belong to their baser nature. They are to have a new nature, formed after God's own likeness. Within this new Christian manhood there are to be no arbitrary divisions, as in the Roman world of Paul's day, where 'man is a wolf to his fellow man'. All men, says Paul, are made in the image of God. Divisions and antagonists have no meaning for the Christian. 'Here there cannot be Greek and Jew, circumcised and uncircumcised, barbarian, Scythian, slave, freeman, but Christ is all, and in all.' (Col. 3:11) The pairs of words used are opposites, except for 'barbarian', the Greek term of vilification for any foreigner, and 'Scythian', the Roman equivalent. Both terms imply that these peoples neither spoke the language nor shared the culture of the Greeks and Romans, who consequently regarded them as totally uncivilized. [Col. 3:11]

SECUNDUS (Gk. from the Lat. 'second') One of two Thessalonian representatives chosen to accompany Paul on his return to Jerusalem with the poor-relief collected from the various Christian communities in the Mediterranean. Fearing an ambush if he travelled via Corinth, Paul travelled overland through Macedonia, in the spring of the year 58, as far as Troas on the coast of Asia Minor, and so by sea to Caesarea and Jerusalem, with an escort of seven men, of whom Secundus was one. [Acts 20:4]

SERGIUS PAULUS The Roman governor of the island of Cyprus converted by Paul at Paphos on his First Journey.

When Paul, Barnabas, and Mark visited Cyprus in the year 46, on the first of Paul's Journeys, they fell in with a false prophet and sorcerer, who belonged to the suite of the Roman proconsul. It is quite in keeping with what is known of Roman colonial life that a learned Jew should have been attached to his household, that is, one who combined his philosophy with the exercise of magic or divination.

When Sergius Paulus invited Paul and Barnabas to present 'the word of God' to him, Elymas Bar-Jesus attempted to balk the teaching of the Christian gospel to his Roman master. Paul pronounced a curse upon him, as it were 'beating him at his own game', and inducing a temporary blindness, which both silenced the opposition and so impressed the governor that he accepted and believed the gospel proclaimed by Paul.

The name of Sergius Paulus occurs in the writings of Pliny the Elder about twenty years after this event; the name is also found in the works of the 3rd-century physician Galen. Two inscriptions have been found which include his name: the first contemporary with his lifetime and discovered in Cyprus, the second concerning the Christian family of a Sergius Paul in Asia Minor, at a rather later date. [Acts 13:7]

SILAS (Aram. from Heb. 'asked of God') A Roman citizen and companion of Paul on his Second Journey, AD 50-1, as far as to Corinth. Silas was still at Corinth when Paul wrote to the Christian community at Thessalonica, but then disappears entirely from the letters of Paul. He reappears as the emanuensis of Peter in Rome, perhaps thirteen years later. He is both the writer and bearer of Peter's letter to a group of Christian congregations in Asia Minor.

Silas first appears as one of two distinguished prophets, probably Jews of the Diaspora, commissioned as official delegates to convey the decision of the Council of Jerusalem to Antioch, in the year 49. The delegates were to deliver a written letter and to give orally this message, 'For it has seemed good to the Holy Spirit and to us to lay upon you no greater burden than these necessary things: that you abstain from what has been sacrificed to idols and from blood and from what is strangled and from unchastity. If you keep yourselves from these, you will do well. Farewell.' (Acts 15:28-29)

Silas and Judas gathered the community at Antioch and discharged their duty, with a wealth of advice and encouragement. They then returned, with greetings from Antioch, to Jerusalem. Silas, however, must have returned to Antioch by the spring of the year 50. Paul

and Barnabas at Antioch had meanwhile planned to revisit together the young Churches in Cyprus and Galatia, but they disagreed on the question as to whether John Mark, Barnabas's nephew, should accompany them. Finally, they divided forces and Barnabas sailed with Mark for Cyprus, while Paul took Silas to encourage the Galatian Churches. The name Silas is the Aramaic form of Saul. He is called Silvanus in the correspondence with the Thessalonians, and was the bearer of Peter's first letter to the Church in Asia. Like Paul, Silas also was a Roman citizen.

Timothy was added to the team. Because Timothy was the son of a Greek married to a Jewess, Paul insisted on his circumcision, in order to remove obstacles to his working among Jews. Passing through Iconium and Antioch, impelled by some positive spiritual guidance, they did not turn south to the coast, but made their way through Phrygia and Troas, a port of the north-west coast of Asia Minor. Again, guided this time by the vision of a Macedonian calling for help, Paul sailed via Samothrace, over the Aegean, to Neapolis in Europe.

Taking to that great military highway, the Via Egnatia, which linked Rome and the east, Paul, Silas, and Timothy moved inland to Philippi, a Roman colony and city founded by the father of Alexander the Great. There being few Jews and no synagogue, Paul stayed with a devout Jewess called Lydia, a dealer in dyed cloth, whose household was the first in Europe to be converted and baptized. Paul was enabled to conduct house-meetings near the River Ganga.

Soon, however, an unpleasant incident put an end to their stay in Philippi. A certain soothsaying slave-girl with an evil spirit began following them, and Paul commanded the spirit to leave her. Her employers, who made considerable profit from her fortune-telling, had Paul and Silas arrested. Under pressure from the mob, the magistrates had Paul and Silas stripped, flogged, thrown into gaol, and put in the stocks. That night an earthquake released all the prisoners, and the gaoler was about to commit suicide when Paul called him and spoke to him about Jesus. He and his family were converted; they took their prisoners home to feed and care for them before returning them to the prison. When, the following morning, the magistrates sent the order for their release, Paul and Silas insisted on the magistrates themselves freeing them. Although Paul never forgot his degradation and suffering at Philippi, his letter to the Church there was full of affection and thanksgiving.

The party travelled seventy miles westwards along the Via Egnatia to Thessalonica, the historical city and chief port of the Aegean. Paul preached on three consecutive Sabbaths in the synagogue, proving Jesus to be the Messiah, with some success among both Jews and Gentiles, men and women. With the help, however, of a

The Presentation in the Temple, by the Flemish painter Melchior Broederlam (1381-?1409), showing Simeon and Anna on either side of the child. On the right is the flight into Egypt.

market-place mob, the Jewish community stormed the house of one Jason, a Jew of the Diaspora, and accused him together with Paul and Silas of disloyalty to the Roman emperor, in declaring a rival king, Jesus. As a result, Paul and Silas left that night for Beroea, travelling west along the Via Egnatia.

When they arrived they went to the Jewish synagogue, where they were received with eagerness and much examining of the scriptures. Many believed and accepted the message of Paul and Silas; soon, however, Jews arrived from Thessalonica and, jealous of their success, incited the mob against them. Paul then set off to the coast, to make his way by sea to Athens, while Silas and Timothy remained some time at Beroea, with instructions to meet him at Corinth.

Some time later, they joined Paul at Corinth in an intense teaching mission, first within the synagogue and then in a Gentile household next to the synagogue. After eighteen months, following further friction with the Jews, Paul sailed from the port of Cenchreae, via Ephesus, and so to Antioch. Silas disappears from the story some time towards the end of the year 52. We know that he remained some considerable time with Paul at Corinth, because both the letters to the Christian community at Thessalonica are addressed, 'Paul, Silvanus, and Timothy, to the Church of the Thessalonians in God the Father and the Lord Jesus Christ: Grace to you and peace.'

How soon Silas began to work with Peter either in Greece, Asia or Rome, we may never know. One theory is that, by the year 64, he was in Rome writing a letter for Peter – in far better Greek than was possible for Peter – to a group of Churches in northern Asia Minor. This letter (1 Peter) included a systematic presentation of the Christian faith within the early Church, together with a message of encouragement to Churches under the shock of sudden and violent persecution. The whole is unlike a letter in form or content, but is a highly efficient composition. The Greek is excellent, the style deliberate and elaborate, the sentences balanced and polished, the tone calm and tranquil.

Although Luke's specific references to Silas are few and far between, he must have been a tremendously competent and useful member both of Paul's teaching team and also of the staff of the Apostle Peter in Rome. [Acts 15:22-40; 16:25, 29; 17:4, 10, 14, 15; 18:5; 2 Cor. 1:19; 1 Thess. 1:1; 2 Thess. 1:1; 1 Pet. 5:12]

SILVANUS *see* SILAS

SIMEON (Heb., Gk. 'hearing') **1. Simeon, the priest** The first-born son of every Jewish family had to be presented within the Temple at Jerusalem forty days after birth. In earlier, pagan times, the first son had often been sacrificed to the tribal god, as the first-fruit of the family. Now the Hebrew Law had adapted this primitive custom by demanding the offering of

5 shekels, in order to 'redeem' or buy back the child from God, to whom his life was owed.

The parents of Jesus took him up to Jerusalem to present him to the Lord, as demanded in the book of Exodus (13:2) : 'Consecrate to me all the first-born; whatever is the first to open the womb among the people of Israel, both of man and of beast, is mine.' Mary and Joseph took with them the purification offering demanded in the Book of Leviticus (5:7) – 'two turtle-doves or two young pigeons'.

On this occasion, an upright and devout Jew called Simeon, who looked forward to the deliverance of Israel, met them in the Temple. He had been shown that he would not die without seeing 'the Lord's Christ'. Taking the child Jesus in his arms, he blessed God, saying: 'Lord, now lettest thou thy servant depart in peace, according to thy word; for mine eyes have seen thy salvation which thou hast prepared in the presence of all peoples, a light for revelation to the Gentiles, and for glory to thy people Israel.' (Luke 2:29-32)

Simeon's song has for over 1,500 years formed part of the evening offices of the Christian Church as the *Nunc Dimittis*.

As Simeon gave back the child Jesus into the arms of his mother and blessed the parents, he uttered the rather enigmatic prophecy: 'Behold, this child is set for the fall and rising of many in Israel, and for a sign that is spoken against (and a sword will pierce through your own soul also), that thoughts out of many hearts may be revealed.' (Luke 2:34-35)

This has generally been taken to refer to the anguish caused to Mary, mother of Jesus, at his crucifixion. So, too, the promise of universal salvation in Simeon's song, as recorded by Luke, 'a light for revelation to the Gentiles', may have been inspired by the Suffering Servant songs of the Second Isaiah. [Luke 2:25-35]

2. Simeon, called 'Niger' [R.S.V. Symeon] This man is listed among the prophets and teachers of the Christian Church in Antioch, who were 'guided by the Spirit' to select and despatch Paul and Barnabas on the First Journey to Cyprus and Galatia. These leaders at the headquarters of the Christian Church included Barnabas, himself a Cypriot-Jew, Simeon 'Niger', Lucius from Cyrene, Manaen, a one-time companion of Herod Antipas, and Paul the Apostle. [Acts 13:1]

3. Simeon, referring to Simon Peter [R.S.V. Symeon] *see* PETER

SIMON (Heb., Gk. 'hearing') There are no less than nine men of this name to be found within the New Testament.

1. Simon Peter

2. Simon, 'the Cananaean' or 'the Zealot'

3. Simon, brother of Jesus

4. Simon, the leper

5. Simon, the Pharisee

6. Simon, father of Judas Iscariot

7. Simon of Cyrene

8. Simon, the sorceror

9. Simon, the tanner

1. Simon Peter *see* PETER

2. Simon, 'the Cananaean' or 'the Zealot' In the lists of the twelve apostles, Mark and Matthew call him 'the Cananaean', an Aramaic word meaning 'the zealous one' (not connected with Canaan, or with the village of Cana in Galilee). Luke uses the Greek word, 'the Zealot'. In each case, the implication may be that this Simon was a member of the Zealot party, the fanatical nationalist group whose guerrilla activities were designed to drive out the Roman occupation forces, but in fact provoked many bloody reprisals. The rise of the Zealots may be traced to the revolt of Judas of Gamala in AD 6; their story culminated in the disastrous revolt of AD 66, resulting in the fall and destruction of Jerusalem by the Romans in the year 70.

The Zealots found most of their support among the hot-headed Galileans, whose tropical climate and temperament provided fertile soil for both political and religious dissent. Simon may well have come from the lakeside, like so many other early followers of Jesus. Luke, in both his Gospel and the Acts, links Simon with Judas among the apostles. Nothing further is known with certainty about these two, but an apocryphal work *The Passion of Simon and Jude* describes their preaching and martyrdom in Persia. They are still linked together on their combined feast-day in the Western Church on 28 October. [Matt. 10:4; Mark 3:18; Luke 6:15; Acts 1:13]

3. Simon, brother of Jesus This Simon is among the family of Jesus mentioned by the congregation at Nazareth, when they were impressed by Jesus's preaching. 'Is not this the carpenter, the son of Mary and brother of James and Joses and Judas and Simon, and are not his sisters here with us?' (Mark 6:3) John commented on the fact that in the last year of Jesus's life his own brothers did not believe in him. We do not know, however, whether Simon, like his brother James, later became a member of the Christian Church. *see also* JOSEPH **2**. [Matt. 13:55; Mark 6:3]

4. Simon, the leper The term 'leper' is used generally to apply to one with any skin disease, and Simon was a former sufferer who had been cured either by Jesus or by someone else. Mark and Matthew describe Simon the leper as living in Bethany, where he entertained Jesus at his house.

During the meal a woman came in with an alabaster jar of precious ointment, called nard. She broke the jar and poured the ointment on the head of Jesus. This may be interpreted as being a singular honour to the guest, or – more specifically – as symbolic of the anointing of the Messiah. Some of those present complained at what

Bronze coin, obverse and reverse, of the leader of the Jewish revolt, Simon Bar Kokhba, AD 135, showing the Jewish emblem of the seven-branched palm-tree.

they considered a waste of good ointment, worth 300 silver denarii (a year's wages for a working man), that could have been given to the poor. Jesus, however, defended the woman with these words: 'Let her alone; why do you trouble her? She has done a beautiful thing to me. For you always have the poor with you, and whenever you will, you can do good to them; but you will not always have me. She has done what she could; she has anointed my body beforehand for burying. And truly, I say to you, wherever the gospel is preached in the whole world, what she has done will be told in memory of her.' (Mark 14:6-9)

This story in Mark and Matthew is sometimes linked and compared with a story in Luke's Gospel. (*see* SIMON **5**.) The writer of the Fourth Gospel appears to use Mark's account of the anointing at Bethany as the basis of a similar story, and he seems to have incorporated some features from Luke's account, too. John puts the story in the context of Holy Week. The hosts are Mary, Martha, and Lazarus. Mary is the woman with the ointment. Judas Iscariot complains at the waste of money and Jesus's reply is nearly identical, 'Let her alone, let her keep it for the day of my burial. The poor you always have with you, but you do not always have me.' (John 12:7, 8) [Matt. 26:6; Mark 14:3]

5. Simon, the Pharisee He may have been identical with Simon 'the leper', whose story is recorded by Mark and

overleaf The Meal in the House of Simon the Pharisee, by Paolo Veronese (c. 1528-88). The woman washes the feet of Jesus.

Simon, the Pharisee

Simon, the Pharisee

Matthew, but the story of Simon the Pharisee as recorded by Luke has many distinct features and probably refers to another person and occasion.

The scene is set in Galilee, not Bethany. The woman is locally notorious – 'a woman of the city, who was a sinner' – and comes with the intention of making an act of penitence to Jesus. 'Standing behind him at his feet, weeping, she began to wet his feet with her tears, and wiped them with the hair of her head, and kissed his feet, and anointed them with the ointment.' (Luke 7:38)

Simon the Pharisee condescendingly looks on, assuming that a prophet like this rabbi Jesus will at least have the insight to see the sort of woman she is and therefore drive her away. When both the woman herself and Simon have waited long enough to have their true motives tested, Jesus, reading their minds, says to the Pharisee, ' "Simon, I have something to say to you." And he answered, "What is it, Teacher?" "A certain creditor had two debtors; one owed 500 denarii, and the other 50. When they could not pay, he forgave them both. Now which of them will love him more?" Simon answered, "The one, I suppose, to whom he forgave more." And he said to him, "You have judged rightly." ' (Luke 7:40-43) Then, turning to the woman whose uninhibited penitence and emotional abandon contrasted so clearly with the veiled criticism and discourteous condescension of the Pharisee, Jesus says, ' "Do you see this woman? I entered your house, you gave me no water for my feet, but she has wet my feet with her tears and wiped them with her hair. You gave me no kiss, but from the time I came in she has not ceased to kiss my feet. You did not anoint my head with oil, but she has anointed my feet with ointment. Therefore I tell you, her sins, which are many, are forgiven, for she loved much; but he who is forgiven little, loves little." And he said to her . . . "Your faith has saved you; go in peace." ' (Luke 7:44-48)

Luke is not slow to notice and to compare the passion of penitence and the coldness of reason. With his deep sensitivity, Luke well knows that the basis of all forgiveness is love, and that the spring of love is often just this sense of forgiveness. [Luke 7:36-50]

6. Simon, father of Judas Iscariot Only the Fourth Gospel mentions the father of Judas. The family of the traitor-disciple hailed from the village of Kerioth, in southern Judea; hence the title *Ish-Kerioth*, meaning 'man of Kerioth'. [John 6:71; 13:2, 26]

7. Simon of Cyrene This Simon was the passer-by compelled to carry the cross of Jesus to the place of execution. Matthew and Luke describe him as of Cyrene, part of Libya in North Africa. Mark records that he was the father of Alexander and Rufus, rather as though these two sons had become Christians and were known to his readers, perhaps in Rome. Luke and Mark both say that Simon of Cyrene had 'come in from the coun-

try', as though he were on a Passover pilgrimage, either all the way from Cyrene or from the neighbouring countryside of Jerusalem. All three Synoptic Gospels state that he was pressed into the unpleasant job of carrying the cross-piece for the exhausted Jesus on his way to Calvary.

As the Roman routine of interrogation included a preliminary flogging and, once the prisoner was condemned, inevitably a scourging followed, it was not surprising that despite the encouragement of the lash many criminals collapsed on their way to execution. The drugged wine offered by the Guild of the Women of Jerusalem, at the Judgment Gate, served the double purpose of reviving and anaesthetizing the prisoners – yet this Jesus refused.

The writer of the Fourth Gospel specifically states that Jesus 'went out, bearing his own cross' to Golgotha, and makes no mention of Simon of Cyrene. Perhaps this was to contradict some rumour of the substitution of Simon for Jesus – not only in the carrying of the cross, but in the actual crucifixion. [Matt. 27:32; Mark 15:21; Luke 23:26]

8. Simon, the sorcerer After the stoning of Stephen and the persecution of Hellenized Christians in Jerusalem, Philip the Deacon carried out a mission to Samaria. His preaching and healing impressed the Samaritan community, among whom Simon Magus was a magician of considerable power and influence. Simon had for a long time worked his magic with such success that the people said, 'This man is that power of God which is called Great.' (Acts 8:10)

But Philip so impressed the Samaritans that they accepted his message of 'good news about the kingdom of God and the name of Jesus Christ'. They were baptized, including Simon the sorcerer, who 'continued with Philip. And seeing signs and great miracles performed, he was amazed' – hoping, perhaps, to learn more of this remarkable new power.

The apostles in Jerusalem followed up Philip's success by sending Peter and John to Samaria to teach and to confirm the Samaritans by the gift of the Holy Spirit, imposed by the laying-on of their hands. Simon was again highly impressed and tried to bribe the apostles with money, saying, 'Give me also this power, that any one on whom I lay my hands may receive the Holy Spirit.' Peter answered, ' "Your silver perish with you, because you thought you could obtain the gift of God with money! You have neither part nor lot in this matter, for your heart is not right before God. Repent therefore of this wickedness of yours, and pray to the Lord that, if possible, the intent of your heart may be forgiven you. For I see that you are in the gall of bitterness and in the bond of iniquity." And Simon answered, "Pray for me to the Lord, that nothing of what you have said may come upon me." ' (Acts 8:19-24)

Simon of Cyrene carrying the cross of Jesus: 6th-century mosaic
from S. Apollinare Nuovo, Ravenna.

Peter's blistering rebuke seems to have taken effect in
the resultant penitence of Simon. Post-apostolic traditions, however, credit this Simon with being the 'father
of Christian heresy'. He is said by the historian Justin
Martyr to have gone to Rome in the time of the Emperor
Claudius (AD 41-54) and to have been the father of
Gnosticism. [Acts 8:9-24]

9. Simon, the tanner After the conversion of Paul and
his first visit to Jerusalem, Peter lived for some time in
Joppa, lodging with a leather-tanner called Simon. It
was to the house of this Simon that the Roman centurion Cornelius was sent to summon Peter to Caesarea.

It was on the roof of Simon's house at Joppa that
Peter had his vision of the clean and unclean animals,
and his commission to accept the first Gentile members
of the Christian Church. (*see also* CORNELIUS) The
traditional site of the house of Simon the tanner was,
until very recently, shown overlooking the harbour of
ancient Joppa. [Acts 9:43; 10:6, 17, 32]

SOPATER A Christian from the town of Beroea, in
northern Greece, the son of Pyrrhus. He is the first mentioned of the companions of Paul on his final journey
from Corinth to Jerusalem. The companions were
representatives of the cities whose Christian congregations had subscribed to the relief of the community in
Jerusalem. [Acts 20:4]

401

SOSIPATER A Jewish-Christian in Rome, mentioned in the final greetings at the close of Paul's letter to the Christian community in Rome. Paul describes him as 'my compatriot', that is, a fellow-Jew.

Whether the final chapter of Paul's letter to Rome included messages to Christians at Ephesus or at Rome, the Sosipater who linked his greetings with those of Paul may well have been the same man as Sopater of Beroea. *see* SOPATER [Rom. 16:21]

SOSTHENES 1. The ruler of the synagogue at Corinth in the years 51 and 52, at the time of Paul's long stay there on his Second Journey, Sosthenes was also probably Paul's chief accuser before the new proconsul, Gallio, though whether he later became the Christian 'brother Sosthenes', Paul's emanuensis for his first letter to the Christian Church, is a matter of guesswork.

The Apostle Paul had spent 18 months in Corinth, working with Aquila and Priscilla, both tentmaking and building up the young Christian Church in that very pagan city. No doubt, as elsewhere, the Jewish synagogue had provided both the pulpit and the congregation for Paul's preaching. Certainly it was the Jews, probably led by their synagogue ruler Sosthenes, who took Paul up before the tribunal, saying, 'This man is persuading men to worship God contrary to the Law.'

The coming of the Holy Spirit, in the shape of a dove. From the *Grandes Heures d'Antoine Vérard*.

Before Paul could even answer the charge, Gallio the proconsul, as the judge, dismissed the case with these words, 'If it were a matter of wrongdoing or vicious crime, I should have reason to bear with you, O Jews; but since it is a matter of questions about words and names and your own Law, see to it yourselves; I refuse to be a judge of these things.' (Acts 18:14, 15) And Gallio ordered the court to be cleared.

Gallio's decision was that the prosecution had no case, but the charge against Paul was a cunning one and quite different from that brought by the Jews at Thessalonica. There, they accused Paul and his followers of 'acting against the decrees of Caesar, saying that there is another king, Jesus,' at which the magistrates were somewhat disturbed, but must have realized that the accusation was absurd. Here at Corinth the Roman proconsul, Gallio, was asked to decide whether Paul's teaching was contrary to the Law and put him outside the pale of Judaism and, particularly, outside the toleration by the Roman law afforded to Jews. Gallio, however, had the philosophical temperament of his Stoic brother Seneca, and was far too good a lawyer to entertain such a charge. Furthermore, it was outside the competence of any Roman governor to decide whether a Jew had committed an offence against the Jewish Law, and Gallio rightly refused to try the case. He simply acquitted Paul and cleared the court.

Immediately the Greeks, perhaps even those who had listened to Paul from the God-fearers' courtyard attached to the synagogue, seized Sosthenes, the ruler of the synagogue, and very possibly Paul's chief prosecutor. They beat Sosthenes in front of the tribunal, but Gallio 'paid no attention' or, as one text puts it, 'pretended not to see'. [Acts 18:17]

2. The Christian 'brother' who acted as Paul's emanuensis for his first letter to the Church at Corinth from Ephesus. 'Sosthenes' was an uncommon name and this man may well have been the ruler of the synagogue at Corinth. (*see* SOSTHENES 1.) Certainly this man was well-known in the Corinthian community only three years after the incident involving the first Sosthenes, and was probably trusted with the taking of a letter back to the Christian congregation at Corinth. [1 Cor. 1:1]

SPIRIT OF GOD The Holy Spirit is the life and activity of God at work in the world of nature and also in and through people. The Hebrew word for 'spirit' is the same as that for 'breath' or 'wind', and can even imply 'life', just as the English word 'spirit' forms the root of others, such as 'inspire', 'expire', and 'respiration', meaning 'breath in life'.

The Old Testament is a record of God's transmission of his life and energy among his people. His universal spirit has first given life and then, as man has evolved and has become able to absorb it, a knowledge of God.

The spirit of God descends on Jesus at his baptism by John in the Jordan. Detail from the dome of the 5th-century Arian baptistry at Ravenna.

This inspiration has taken place through the minds of those men in each age who have responded by their prayer and reason to God's progressive self-revelation. To such men as the Hebrew prophets and sages, God was gradually able through his Spirit to show his character, enabling the building-up of assessment within the minds of his people. They in turn looked forward to a more personal manifestation in the coming of his Chosen One, the Messiah.

Paul, acknowledging Jesus as the Messiah, wrote, 'God has shone in our minds to radiate the light of the knowledge of his glory on the face of Christ', and again, 'God was in Christ reconciling the world to himself.' The writer of the Fourth Gospel interpreted the coming of Jesus as the incarnation of the activity of God: 'And the Word became flesh and dwelt among us, full of grace and truth; we have beheld his glory, glory as of the only Son from the Father.'

At Pentecost, after Jesus had ceased to be seen among his followers, they underwent a spiritual experience which they identified as the coming of the Spirit, but with a new power, which they somehow associated with their master Jesus. They came to believe that his life and work continued, by the power of the Spirit within his Church.

Jesus and the Spirit

It was through the 'overshadowing' of the Spirit that Mary conceived the child Jesus. At his baptism the Spirit descended upon him in the form of a dove, the bird of peace, so many of which can still be seen flying down the River Jordan.

Immediately the Spirit drove him into the wilderness where he was tempted to escape from his Messianic calling, but from which he returned 'in the power of the Spirit' to begin his preaching in Galilee. In the synagogue at Nazareth he reads the Messianic prophecy of Isaiah 61: 'The Spirit of the Lord is upon me. . . .' He announces that he casts out devils by the Spirit of God and that the kingdom of God has arrived.

In the Fourth Gospel the teaching about the Spirit appears in characteristic form within the long discourse that follows the Last Supper. Here the writer uses the term *paraclete*, meaning literally an 'advocate', and referring to the task of helping Jesus's disciples after he has 'gone'. 'And I will pray the Father, and he will give you another Counsellor, to be with you for ever, even the Spirit of truth. . . .' (John 14:15-17) During his life on earth, Jesus had been their *paraclete*, revealing and teaching the truth. The world does not recognize the Spirit which replaces Jesus, and therefore does not receive the Spirit. The Spirit continues to do what Jesus did. The Spirit would remind and help his disciples and work through them.

Jesus tells the disciples that their grief at his departure is mistaken, for his going makes possible the sending of the Spirit. The Spirit will vindicate Jesus in the eyes of the world through his followers. The Spirit will guide the disciples to the truth and to a progressively fuller understanding of the truth in Jesus. As Jesus revealed God, the Father, so the Spirit will reveal Jesus. 'These things I have spoken to you, while I am still with you. But the Counsellor, the Holy Spirit, whom the Father will send in my name, he will teach you all things, and bring to your remembrance all that I have said to you.' (John 14:25, 26) Through the Spirit, the followers of Jesus will proclaim to the world the triumph of Jesus, the judgment of sinners, and the dethroning of evil. After the resurrection, Jesus breathes upon his disciples in the Upper Room, saying, 'Receive the Holy Spirit,' as if imparting to them his own personality. Indeed, for John, 'Life in the Spirit' begins at the resurrection rather than at Pentecost.

The apostles and the Spirit

The story of Pentecost in the Acts probably reflects the feelings, rather than the facts, on this occasion. The apostles had met together in the Upper Room, when 'suddenly a sound came from heaven like the rush of a mighty wind, and it filled all the house where they were

11th-century Byzantine ivory panel, showing the ascension. Before his departure, Jesus forewarned his disciples of the coming of the Spirit.

Pentecost, by Giotto (?1267-1337). The Spirit is here represented by both the dove and the tongues of flame.

sitting. And there appeared to them tongues as of fire, distributed and resting on each one of them. And they were all filled with the Holy Spirit and began to speak in other tongues, as the Spirit gave them utterance.' (Acts 2:2-4)

Certainly this spiritual experience generated a tremendous feeling of enthusiasm, which fired their hearts and minds, so that their message was understood by the cosmopolitan crowds in Jerusalem for the feast of Weeks. As a result 3,000 were recorded as being bap-

tized and added to the 120 disciples. Following Peter's cure of the cripple at the Beautiful Gate of the Temple, and the questioning and release of Peter by the Sanhedrin, the apostles met in prayer to thank God. As they prayed (after what was perhaps the first crisis following Pentecost) the house where they were assembled rocked; they were all filled anew with the Spirit of God and began to proclaim the word of God boldly.

Pentecost, originally a harvest festival, became for later Judaism a feast of the giving of the Law, the

Torah. For the Christian Church, however, the Holy Spirit replaced the Torah as God's supreme gift to man. The writer of the First Gospel regarded the Sermon on the Mount as the new Torah. Luke, the author of both the Third Gospel and the Acts, talked of the 'Sermon on the Plains' – keeping the Mountain of Zion for the giving of the Spirit – as the new Torah. A Jewish-Christian in Jerusalem might well have seen the events of Pentecost as the proclamation of the Torah for the proselytes of the world. The miraculous activity of the Spirit vindicated the truth of the gospel message and the authority of the apostles to preach it.

Then, gradually, came a reduction of emphasis on the miraculous power of the Spirit. His personification as the prophetic, inspiring, and guiding power among them was steadily accepted by the leaders of the primitive Church, who could say with complete faith: 'It has seemed good to the Holy Spirit and to us' to do this or that, and they did so both with confidence and success. They were able by the laying-on of their hands to transmit the gift of the Spirit to others. While Peter was still speaking to the Roman centurion Cornelius and his family at Caesarea, the Holy Spirit came down on all his listeners. The Jewish believers were astonished to see that the Gentiles present shared this experience, even the speaking in strange languages. Peter at once ordered their baptism, the first Gentile baptism within the hitherto Judeo-Christian Church.

Paul's interpretation

The Spirit occupies a central place in Paul's theology. The key to its understanding lies in Paul's vision, at his conversion, of Jesus in his glory – 'I am Jesus'. From that moment Paul's own life was transfigured with a wonderful spiritual strength. As he said to the Church at Philippi, 'Our commonwealth is in heaven, and from it we await a Saviour, the Lord Jesus Christ, who will change our lowly body to be like his glorious body, by the power which enables him even to subject all things to himself.' (Phil. 3:20-21) No wonder Paul described Jesus as 'life-giving spirit', seeing the function of Jesus as being identical with that of the Spirit, though he tried to distinguish between the persons by such phrases as 'the Spirit of Him who raised Jesus from the dead', and 'God has given us the pledge of the Spirit'. The new life that Paul discovered through Jesus he could only speak of – as did the primitive Christian Church – as 'life in the Spirit', compared with the old life in the flesh.

To Paul, this 'life in the Spirit' meant the dwelling of Jesus within the Christian heart.

The Holy Trinity: fresco from S. Maria Novella, Florence, by Masaccio (1401-28). God the Father and God the Son are linked by God the Holy Spirit in the traditional form of a dove.

Our reconciliation with God is made possible only by the saving sacrifice of Jesus, together with our response. Our response is prompted and guided by the Spirit. We are justified – that is, judged to be righteous – by our faith in Jesus. We are made holy by the action of the Spirit within us. The primitive Church identified the Spirit as the inner impetus which pointed them to the perfect life of Jesus, and also gave them power to live that life 'in Christ Jesus'.

After Pentecost, there was a tendency in the Christian community to perceive the working of the Spirit only in the cruder expressions of speaking in tongues and relapsing into ecstasies and wild emotions. It was Paul who insisted that the real tokens of the Spirit were to be found in the steady, normal life of faith, and in the secret inward assurance of the children of God. 'Since the Spirit is our life, let us be directed by the Spirit.'

Paul is adamant that the power of the Spirit is fundamentally shown in love and charity: 'The love of God has been poured into our hearts by the Holy Spirit which has been given us.' It is this love, says Paul, that builds up the Body of Christ, his Church, and holds it together in unity, as a 'fellowship of the Holy Spirit'. This communion of the Christian community is expressed within the Eucharist of the Church. [Mark 1:8; Luke 4:18; 12:12; John 4:24; 16:13; 20:22; Acts 2:17; 11:15, 16; 2 Cor. 3:17; Gal. 5:16-18, 22, 25; Eph. 4:30; 1 Thess. 5:19; Heb. 9:14; 1 John 5:7; Rev. 1:10; 22:17; and elsewhere throughout the New Testament]

STACHYS (Gk. 'head of grain') One of the Christians warmly greeted by Paul, as 'my beloved', at the close of his letter to the Church at Rome. [Rom. 16:9]

STEPHANAS (Gk. 'crown' or 'wreath') Stephanas was a Corinthian Christian and householder, one of the first converts and founder-members of the Church at Corinth.

Writing from Ephesus in the year 55, during his Third Journey, to the Church in Corinth which he had founded some four years before, Paul closes his letter: 'I rejoice at the coming of Stephanas and Fortunatus and Achaicus, because they have made up for your absence; for they have refreshed my spirit as well as yours. Give recognition to such men.'

Apparently the household of Stephanas included slaves and employees, such as Fortunatus and Achaicus. This was the first household to have been converted by Paul – and the only household to have been baptized by Paul – in Corinth, on his Second Journey in the year 51. These three men had travelled to Ephesus on business, possibly carrying a letter to Paul from Corinth, and were probably present with Paul as he completed the dictation of his answering letter. [1 Cor. 1:16; 16:15, 17]

STEPHEN (Gk. 'crown' or 'wreath') Stephen was one of the seven Greek-speaking or Hellenist disciples of

407

Jesus who were chosen to assist the apostles in the distribution of gifts to widows, after a dispute about this matter between the members of the first Christian Church in Jerusalem. These seven men are commonly called the seven deacons, although the word 'deacon' does not actually appear in the account of their appointment. The word is used because it was their duty to serve (Gk. *diakonein*) at the tables where gifts were distributed.

Stephen is described as a man full of faith, grace and spiritual power who, after his appointment to office in the church, 'did great wonders and signs among the people'. (Acts 6:8) There was a disputation between him and other Hellenists in Jerusalem, members of the synagogue called the Synagogue of the Freedmen, as well as Jews coming from Egypt and Asia Minor; these would of course be Hellenists and the debate would have been in Greek; no doubt it concerned Jesus. After this his opponents 'secretly instigated men who said, "We have heard him speak blasphemous words against Moses and God."' At the trial of Stephen before the Council evidence was given by 'false witnesses' who said, 'This man never ceases to speak words against this holy place and the law; for we have heard him say that this Jesus of Nazareth shall destroy this place, and will change the customs which Moses delivered to us' (Acts 6:13, 14). 'This place' undoubtedly signifies the Temple and the charge is like the charge brought against Jesus, that he said that he would destroy the Temple. (Mark 14:28; Matt. 26:61)

Stephen makes a long speech in his own defence. As reported in the Acts of the Apostles, he reviews the history of the people of God from the days of Abraham to those of King David and King Solomon. About the Temple he says, 'David ... found favour in the sight of God and asked leave to find a habitation for the God of Jacob. But it was Solomon who built a house for him. Yet the Most High does not dwell in houses made with hands.' This is followed by a quotation from the Book of Isaiah, 'Heaven is my throne, and earth my footstool. What house will you build for me, says the Lord, or what is the place of my rest? ...' (Acts 7:46-50, and compare Isa. 66:1, 2) It may be that this was taken to be an attack on the Temple, although the prophet quoted was most certainly a worshipper in the Temple. Stephen may be reacting to signs of opposition to what he is saying when he goes on, in an attack on the men standing around him, 'You stiff-necked people, uncircumcised in heart and ears, you always resist the Holy Spirit. As your fathers did, so do you.'

This leads on to a reference to Jesus, 'the Righteous One, whom you have now betrayed and murdered'. To this there was more opposition. 'They were enraged, and they ground their teeth against him.' Stephen, seeing a vision, declared, 'Behold, I see the heavens opened,

and the Son of Man standing at the right hand of God.' (Acts 7:56) This is like the statement of Jesus to the chief priests, 'But from now on the Son of Man shall be seated at the right hand of the power of God.' (Luke 23:69, and compare Mark 14:62, Matt. 26:64) This is treated as blasphemy. 'They cried out with a loud voice and stopped their ears and rushed together upon him. Then they cast him out of the city and stoned him; and the witnesses laid down their garments at the feet of a young man named Saul. And as they were stoning Stephen, he prayed, "Lord Jesus, receive my spirit." And he knelt down and cried with a loud voice, "Lord, do not hold this sin against them."' These last words are like some of the last words of Jesus, as reported in the Gospel of Luke, 'Father, forgive them. . . .' (Acts 7:59, 60; Luke 23:34)

The author of Acts no doubt wishes to suggest that the death of Stephen helped to prepare the conversion of Saul, who becomes the Apostle Paul. He describes its immediate result as a general flight from Jerusalem of the disciples of Jesus, except for the apostles who remained in the city. A widespread persecution of the Hellenist section of the Christian Church followed. The disciples scattered not only throughout Judea and Samaria (the whole Samaritan community 'received the word of God') but they carried the gospel message from Jerusalem across the entire Mediterranean world.

There are two different traditions about the place outside Jerusalem where Stephen was stoned. In the year 415, his body was identified. A priest named Lucian had a dream in which he thought that he saw Gamaliel and was told by him that Stephen was buried at Geth Gemal, some 22 miles south-west of Jerusalem. A body found in a tomb there was brought to Jerusalem and buried in the Zion Church on the Western Hill. In the year 460 the Empress Eudocia built a basilica and a monastery for the training of deacons outside the north gate of the city. These were dedicated to the memory of Stephen and his relics were brought to the basilica, to be buried under the altar. The buildings were destroyed in 614, rebuilt some years later, restored in the period of the crusades and finally demolished in the 12th century. Stephen being associated with them, the gate now known as the Damascus Gate, or the Shechem Gate, was called St Stephen's Gate and his death was commemorated near it. In 1881 the Dominicans acquired the site of the basilica built by the Empress Eudocia and they built the Church of St Stephen over the ancient remains which they found there. Beside it is the renowned *Ecole biblique et archéologique française*. It should, however, be remembered that when Stephen

The Stoning of St Stephen, by Giulio Romano. Stephen gazes up at the vision of Jesus at the right hand of God the Father.

The traditional site of the stoning of St Stephen in the Kidron ravine. On the right is the Greek Orthodox Oratory of St Stephen.

was stoned there was no city wall or city gate in the neighbourhood of the Damascus or Shechem Gate, which belongs to the 'Third Wall'.

Another tradition places the stoning of Stephen in the Kidron valley; there is a Greek Orthodox Church on this traditional site at Gethsemane, where the road to Jericho crosses the valley. Stephen's name has been given, in modern times, to the east gate of the city, north of the Temple site. This gate, built by the Sultan Beibars and also called the Gate of the Lions, is named by the Eastern Christians and by the Muslim community the Gate of the Lady Mary, *Bab Sit Miriam*, on account of its proximity to the traditional sites of the birth and burial of Mary the mother of Jesus.

Stephen became one of the most popular of all the saints during the Middle Ages, especially in Western Christendom. His feast followed immediately after Christmas Day and in the canon of the Mass according to the Roman rite his name was commemorated. [Acts 6:5-8:2; 11:19; 22:20]

STOICS The Greco-Roman philosophers who, together with the Epicureans, questioned the teachings of Paul in Athens and brought him to speak publicly on the Areopagus, during his Second Journey in the years

50-2. Tradition, but without evidence, claims that the Stoic philosopher and statesman Seneca conducted a long correspondence with the Apostle Paul. Stoicism was essentially the philosophy of the 'Establishment' and upheld the official moral standards of the Roman Empire.

In origin, Stoicism was a school of philosophy founded at Athens by the Jew Zeno, 335-263 BC, and had many famous Roman and Greek exponents. The Stoics believed in law, the law of nature and the law of

Bust of Seneca, the Stoic philosopher, who is traditionally supposed to have conducted a correspondence with Paul the Apostle.

conscience. God was the immanent all-pervading energy by which the world was created and sustained. Nature is controlled and ordered by an indwelling and divine *logos* or reason. The essence of man is his mind and capacity to understand this reasonable order within the world. The good man is the wise man, who accepts his fate, detaches himself from the world outside himself and masters his own reactions to that world. Thus, in theory and often in practice, the Stoic achieved a self-centred freedom, happiness, and self-sufficiency, but without pity, pardon, or feeling. For the Stoic, God was an impersonal energy, and sin was an error in judgment that could be corrected.

It was not surprising, therefore, that Paul's teaching about God as the 'maker and Lord of heaven and earth', who now calls 'all men everywhere to repent', who has 'fixed a day on which he will judge the world in righteousness' by someone already appointed 'by raising him from the dead', was hardly likely to appeal to the Stoics. Such doctrines of a personal God demanding a personal obedience, or a personal judgment by a risen person, were foreign to the thinking of the Stoic philosophers. [Acts 17:18]

SUSANNA (Heb., Gk. 'lily') Mentioned by Luke as one of the band of women who provided for the needs of Jesus and his disciples, during their itinerant ministry in Galilee, from out of their own means. [Luke 8:3]

SYMEON *see* SIMEON **2.** *and* **3.**

SYNTYCHE (Gk. 'fortunate') One of two women members of the Christian congregation at Philippi who had been disagreeing. Probably news of their quarrel was brought to Paul in prison by Epaphroditus. In the letter which Epaphroditus now took back to Philippi, Paul wrote this appeal, 'I entreat Euodia and I entreat Syntyche to agree in the Lord. And I ask you also, true yokefellow, help these women, for they have laboured side by side with me in the gospel together with Clement and the rest of my fellow workers, whose names are in the book of life.' (Phil. 4:2, 3) The 'true yokefellow' referred to might well be an elder in their congregation, or may be read as the proper name 'Syzygus'. [Phil. 4:2]

SYRIANS All the people living north of Palestine, as far as the Euphrates, were named in biblical Hebrew '*Aram*', translated loosely as 'Syrians' or 'Arameans'. In nomadic groups they emerged from Mesopotamia, moving westwards in the 12th century BC. In the time of David, Solomon, and the Kings, there were several small kingdoms or city-states often at war with Israel. The language of these peoples is to be found in sections of the Books of Ezra and Daniel; later various Aramaic dialects were used in different parts of greater Syria, in Mesopotamia and Persia. Syria was the meeting-place of different cultures and religions, of Judaism, Hellenism, Gnosticism, and those of Persia and the East.

In the year 312 BC, a Syrian empire was founded by Seleucus, a general of Alexander the Great, and greatly extended by Antiochus the Great a century later. In a decisive battle of the Panium in 198 BC, near the sources of the Jordan, Antiochus defeated the army of Ptolemy V of Egypt and ended the Ptolemaic occupation of Palestine. He was finally defeated by the Romans in 190 BC at the battle of Magnesia, and Palestine and Jerusalem came under Syrian domination. His successor Antiochus Epiphanes provoked the Maccabean revolt by appointing a Hellenist-Jewish high priest and introducing the Hellenistic state religion. The Syrian armies finally withdrew in 145 BC, and yielded to Judah's demand for independence.

From 64 BC Syria became a Roman province, whose governor ruled from the ancient Seleucid capital at Antioch, on the Orontes. After Rome and Alexandria, Antioch was the third city of the Roman Empire, with a population of half a million, and of great political, economic, and cultural importance, with the fine Mediterranean seaport of Seleucia some sixteen miles away. The Roman procurators of Judea and Samaria were directly responsible to the governors of Syria, and it was the Roman governor of Syria, Vitellius, who finally dismissed Pontius Pilate and sent him to Rome on the charge of cruelty. It was from bases in Syria that Vespasian launched his troops into Galilee in the year 67 and directed the siege of Jerusalem.

Within the New Testament narrative, Luke mentions Jesus's brief reference to 'Naaman the Syrian' to illustrate how the Jews had consistently rejected their prophets and were likely to reject him as Messiah. 'A prophet is not without honour except in his own country.' But when Jesus referred to the Gentile widow of Zarephath in Sidon, and Naaman the Syrian general, as examples of a more ready faith in the prophets Elijah and Elisha, the people of Nazareth were sufficiently enraged to attempt to stone him.

The greatest significance of Syria and Syrians within the story of the Christian Church is, without doubt, the fact that Saul the Persecutor was converted into Paul the Apostle on the road to Damascus, and that Antioch became the headquarters and centre of Christian activity among the Gentiles throughout Asia. It is possible that Luke the Evangelist hailed from Antioch and many scholars would say that the Gospel of Matthew was written in Syria. [Luke 4:27]

SYRO-PHOENICIAN The Phoenicians were a seafaring people, inhabiting the coastal strip north of the port of Acre and west of the Lebanon range. They were the people who in about 1500 BC had begun to develop a cuneiform alphabet of 30 letters, and they made extensive use of writing. They were primarily a nation of traders with a wide field of activity within the Mediterranean area, founding the city of Carthage in Tunisia, sailing as far as Spain and even to the south-west of

The Syro-Phoenician woman kneeling at the feet of
Jesus: Crusader capital from the church built at
Nazareth by Tancred, prince of Galilee.

Britain. The Phoenician cities of Byblos, Tyre, and
Sidon transacted commerce with merchants from Egypt,
Mesopotamia, Asia Minor, Cyprus, and Crete. Solo-
mon recruited Phoenicians to man his navy, and used
Phoenician labour in the construction of his Temple.
Ahab married the Tyrian princess Jezebel.

From the 4th century BC, following the famous adventures of the Carthaginian general Hannibal and the
Punic colonists, the *Syro*-Phoenicians were so-called
to distinguish them from the Africans.

In the 1st century, the Phoenician coast was part of
the Roman province of Syria. Jesus visited the district
of Tyre and Sidon on the one occasion that we know he,
the Jewish rabbi, crossed the border into foreign territory. Although he was in search of peace and quiet, after
his busy ministry among the crowds at the lakeside of
Galilee, he was accosted by a Syro-Phoenician woman
appealing to him to heal her daughter. Both Mark and
Matthew recount the story, though apparently they
draw from different sources and their accounts are
complementary.

Mark indicates that she was Greek by religion, Matthew that she was a Canaanite. She probably spoke in
the common Greek of the Mediterranean world. Her
little daughter was 'possessed by an unclean spirit' (the
common term for describing epilepsy). She must have
known the reputation of this Jewish rabbi, for she entreated him, crying repeatedly, 'Have mercy on me,
O Lord, Son of David.' Jesus, however, did not answer
her. She continued to pester Jesus until his embarrassed
disciples begged him to 'send her away, for she is
crying after us.' Jesus answered, 'I was sent only to
the lost sheep of the house of Israel.'

At this point, the woman knelt in front of him, saying,
'Lord, help me.' Jesus then answered her, 'It is not
fair to take the children's bread and throw it to the
dogs,' meaning 'It is not right to spend the message
for your own people on Gentiles.' Jesus's choice of
words shows that he had his tongue in his cheek. He
spoke with affection and humour. The sense of the
words is rather: 'It is not fair to throw the kid's bread
to puppies.'

The woman caught the tone of his banter and answered him in the same vein. The sense of her answer is:
'Yes, Lord, but the pups can lick up the crumbs under
the master's table.' She thus accepted his decision, yet
trusted him and believed that she would be comforted
by someone who spoke and thought on her own level.
Then Jesus responded to her need: 'O woman, great
is your faith! Be it done for you as you desire,' and
her daughter was instantly cured. Or, as Mark puts it,
' "For this saying you may go your way; the demon
has left your daughter." And she went home, and found
the child lying in bed, and the demon gone.' (Mark
7:29, 30) [Matt. 15:21-28; Mark 7:26]

T

TABITHA (Aram. *Tabeitha*; Gk. *Dorcas*, meaning in Greece, 'roe'; in Syria and Africa, 'gazelle') A woman whose life had been 'full of good works and acts of charity' fell ill and died at Lydda, where her body was laid out in an upper room. The Christian disciples at Lydda, hearing that Peter was in the nearby coastal town of Joppa, sent two men to fetch him without delay.

When Peter arrived in the upper room, all the local widows were wailing and displaying the clothes that Tabitha had made. He put them all outside, then knelt and prayed; finally, turning to the body, he said, 'Tabitha, rise.' Luke, the recorder of this incident, adds, 'She opened her eyes, and when she saw Peter sat up. And he gave her his hand and lifted her up. . . . And

The Raising of Tabitha, by Masolino (*c.* 1383/4-?1447). The woman on the right holds up the handiwork of Tabitha.

Peter raising up Tabitha: early 5th-century ivory casket.

it became known throughout all Joppa, and many believed in the Lord.' (Acts 9:40-42)

This story has remarkable similarities to the raising of Jairus's daughter, as recorded in Mark 5:38-42 and Matt. 9:25, particularly the weeping and the putting out of the women from the death chamber, and the Aramaic words spoken by Peter. Jesus had said to Jairus's daughter, '*Talitha cumi*' ('daughter, arise') and Peter '*Tabitha cumi*'. Luke adds that her name could be translated 'Dorcas' or 'Gazelle'. [Acts 9:36, 40]

TAX-COLLECTORS (from the Lat. 'civil servants') These are the 'publicans' mentioned in the Synoptic Gospels, so called from the Latin *publicani*, referring to people employed in collecting the state, or public, revenue. The collection of taxes within the provinces of the Roman Empire was auctioned in Rome to financial companies. The highest bid was accepted, and the companies sold their rights to collect in different areas of the province to smaller speculators. The result was often an exorbitant rate of taxation, far exceeding the original bid to the imperial colonial administration.

Consequently the publicans were highly unpopular members of society, particularly as they could call upon the support of the Roman colonial governor and his military forces. Those Jews who were willing to earn a living by extorting high rates from their fellow compatriots, in order to pay their Roman masters, were doubly despised and disliked. Moreover, as their business transactions brought them into close and constant touch with Gentiles and they were deemed to be dishonest anyway, publicans were regarded as sinners and outside the Law.

The chief source of taxation tended to be the frontier customs, which were usually collected in the towns astride the main roads leading to the frontiers. Thus Capernaum and Jericho were both towns in which Jesus

was likely to meet publicans, besides in Jerusalem and the provincial towns.

The Jordan River formed the natural frontier between the territory of Herod Antipas in Galilee and that of Herod Philip in Gaulanitis. Capernaum, the nearest lakeside town west of the frontier, was the natural frontier customs-post astride the main road to Damascus. Jericho was the town nearest the river and on the main trade route to Gerasa, Philadelphia, and the southern towns of the Decapolis. It was here that Jesus met the tax-superintendent Zacchaeus. Indeed, it has been recently suggested that the present name of the site of Capernaum, 'Tel-Hum', may be a corruption of the Greek word for 'custom house', *telonium*.

Certainly there must have been a busy harbour with boats from neighbouring ports loading and off-loading the dried fish and local wares of Galilee, the silks and spices of Damascus, the fruit and produce of the plain of Gennesaret. It was here perhaps by the quayside or the roadside that the shadow of Jesus fell across the customs ledger of Matthew, the publican. In the words of Matthew's Gospel: 'He said to him, "Follow me." And he rose and followed him.' (*see* MATTHEW)

Luke alone tells the delightful story of the chief tax-collector, Zacchaeus, who was very rich because the Jericho taxes constituted a fruitful source of income and he had contracted for the right of collecting the revenues of that district. When Jesus came to Jericho, probably among the crowds of pilgrims on the way up to Jerusalem for the Passover festival, Zacchaeus wanted to meet him. He was, however, a little man, and he therefore went on ahead and climbed into a tree overlooking the road along which Jesus was likely to come. As Jesus came level with him, he looked up, and called to him, 'Zacchaeus, make haste and come down; for I must stay at your house today.' (Luke 19:5) Zacchaeus made haste to come down and received Jesus joyfully.

When the crowds saw what had happened, they were resentful and murmured, '"He has gone in to be the guest of a man who is a sinner." And Zacchaeus stood and said to the Lord, "Behold, Lord, the half of my goods I give to the poor; and if I have defrauded any one of anything, I restore it fourfold." And Jesus said to him, "Today salvation has come to this house, since he also is a son of Abraham. For the Son of man came to seek and to save the lost."' (Luke 19:7-10)

Luke brings out very clearly Jesus's application of the word 'lost' to the publicans, as though their livelihood made them inevitably 'sinners'. Luke described how the 'tax-collectors and sinners' were attracted to Jesus and came near to listen to him. But the Pharisees and Scribes grumbled to the disciples, 'Why does your teacher eat with tax-collectors and sinners?' In answer, Jesus told them parables, all with the same theme of 'lost and found'. 'What man of you, having a hundred sheep, if he has lost one of them, does not leave the ninety-nine in the wilderness, and go after the one which is lost, until he finds it? And when he has found it, he lays it on his shoulders, rejoicing. And when he comes home, he calls together his friends and his neighbours, saying to them, "Rejoice with me, for I have found my sheep which was lost."' (Luke 15:4-6)

'Or what woman, having ten silver coins, if she loses one coin, does not light a lamp and sweep the house and seek diligently until she finds it? And when she has found it, she calls together her friends and neighbours, saying, "Rejoice with me, for I have found the coin which I had lost." Just so, I tell you, there is joy before the angels of God over one sinner who repents.' (Luke 15:8-10)

The third parable is that of the prodigal son and his elder brother. The prodigal demanded his share of his father's property, went and wasted it in a far country, but 'came to himself' and returned in penitence to his father. The father, in forgiveness, fêted him, saying, 'Bring quickly the best robe, and put it on him; and put a ring on his hand, and shoes on his feet; and bring the fatted calf and kill it, and let us eat and make merry; for this my son was dead, and is alive again; he was lost, and is found.' (Luke 15:22-24)

The elder son, however (and here Jesus undoubtedly was referring to the resentful Scribes and Pharisees), complained that the father had forgiven the prodigal (indicating the publicans who were repentant and attentive to Jesus). The elder son jealously answered him: 'Lo, these many years I have served you, and I never disobeyed your command; yet you never gave me a kid, that I might make merry with my friends. But when this

The Pharisee and the publican: 6th-century mosaic from S. Apollinare Nuovo, Ravenna. The Pharisee stands upright and prays 'with himself'. The publican does not lift up his head, but 'beats his breast'.

son of yours came, who has devoured your living with harlots, you killed for him the fatted calf!' (Luke 15:29, 30)

The father sums up the lesson of all three parables, that the Scribes and Pharisees should rejoice at and not resent the new-found penitence of the publicans. 'It was fitting to make merry and be glad, for this your brother was dead, and is alive; he was lost, and is found.' (Luke 15:32)

There is no doubt that Luke correctly interpreted Jesus's sense of vocation, in dealing with the publicans and sinners, 'to seek and to save the lost'.

The well-known parable of the Pharisee and the publican, also to be found in Luke's Gospel (18:9-14) tends to caricature both men. The Pharisee is depicted parading his virtues, while the publican is shown in penitence imploring God's mercy. 'The tax-collector, standing far off, would not even lift up his eyes to heaven, but beat his breast, saying "God be merciful to me a sinner".' Jesus's hearers might well have been amused at this portrait and surprised to hear that 'this man went down to his house justified, rather than the other'. [Matt. 5:46; 21:31; Mark 2:14-17; Luke 3:12; 7:27, 29, 30, 34; 15:1; 18:9-14; 19:1-10]

TERTIUS (Gk. from the Lat. 'third') The man who actually wrote the letter to the Christian Church in Rome, at Paul's dictation, added his own personal greeting at what he must have thought the end of Paul's greetings. Paul, however, added a further three names. It was Paul's custom, at the end of his letters, to take the pen from the hand of his emanuensis and add a final message in his own bold handwriting. (cf. Gal. 6:11; Col. 4:18; 2 Thess. 3:17) [Rom. 16:22]

TERTULLUS The Roman prosecuting attorney, employed by the Sanhedrin to present their case against the Apostle Paul before the procurator Felix at Caesarea in the year 60.

It was not unusual for Roman advocates, used to Roman court procedure, to be hired by the people resident in Roman provinces. Tertullus made a very competent speech for the prosecution, opening with a compliment to Felix to win his goodwill. 'Since through you we enjoy much peace, and since by your provision, most excellent Felix, reforms are introduced on behalf of this nation, in every way and everywhere we accept this with all gratitude. But, to detain you no further, I beg you in your kindness to hear us briefly.' (Acts 24:2, 4) He then declared Paul to be a perfect pest as (1) an agitator, (2) a ringleader of the Nazarenes, and (3) as a desecrator of the Temple. Finally he invited Felix to examine Paul himself to ascertain the truth of these charges. The speech, whether as spoken by Tertullus, or condensed by Luke, is a masterpiece of brevity. Paul's defence of himself, however, was more than a match for the prosecution, for Paul was equally

well-trained in the famous law school of Troas. [Acts 24:1, 2]

THADDAEUS (Gk. from the Heb. 'large-hearted', 'courageous') One of the twelve apostles of Jesus, whose name is to be found only in the Gospels of Mark and Matthew. Elsewhere (in Luke, John, and Acts) the equivalent name is Judas.

The Fourth Gospel refers to one of the twelve as 'Judas (not Iscariot)', when at the Last Supper he asks Jesus: 'Lord, how is it that you will manifest yourself to us and not to the world?' It is, therefore, reasonable to identify Thaddaeus and Judas as the same person, with James as their father. (The name Lebbaeus is included as an alternative to Thaddaeus only in some minor manuscripts at Matt. 10:3, and also in the Western Text only at Mark 3:18, but Lebbaeus is not to be found in the Revised Standard Version.) The actual wording in Luke's list is 'Judas, son of James', implying either that James was his father or his brother. If this Judas was the writer of the Letter of Jude, the last in the New Testament, then he does in fact refer to himself as 'Jude, a servant of Jesus Christ and brother of James'. [Matt. 10:3; Mark 3:18]

THEOPHILUS (Gk. 'lover of God') The unknown addressee of both the Gospel of Luke and the Acts of the Apostles. The title given him in the Gospel, 'Most excellent', elsewhere (Acts 23:26) used to 'His Excellency the governor Felix', procurator of Judea, indicates a specific person of some social prominence. The title would well have fitted a Roman official of equestrian rank.

Bronze statue of a Roman orator in action. Tertullus acted as prosecutor at Paul's trial before Felix.

This man had heard by repute about Jesus and his followers, and probably had requested further information. He received two scrolls, one about the birth, life, ministry, death and resurrection of Jesus, the other a selection of events connected with the society formed by the followers of this Jesus, particularly Peter and Paul.

The writer of these two volumes, Luke, tried to give an accurate account of the life of Jesus and the growth of the early Church that would appeal to Romans. He, himself possibly a Gentile, presents to his probably Roman reader the universal importance of the Gospel of Jesus. He does not lay the blame for the execution of Jesus primarily upon the Romans, but upon the Jews; nor does he present Jesus as a criminal condemned for crimes against the state and the authority of Rome. Rather, Luke presents Jesus as a Jew with a message of world-wide interest and significance, yet misunderstood and convicted by his own people, despite the efforts of the Roman authorities in power.

The theory that the Acts were originally written as a brief for the defence of Paul before the imperial tribunal presents some chronological difficulties, as the Gospel is not likely to have been completed before Paul's execution. Nevertheless, this double work must have been of considerable value to the progress of the Christian Church in Rome, of which it is only reasonable to suppose that Theophilus became an influential and well-instructed Christian. [Luke 1:3; Acts 1:1]

THESSALONIANS (Gk. 'inhabitants of Salonika') Thessalonica, the modern Salonika, was, in Paul's time, the capital of Macedonia. The Thessalonians were evangelized by Paul, Silas, and Timothy on the Second Journey, and the events are described in Acts 17: 'Now when they had passed through Amphipolis and Apollonia, they came to Thessalonica, where there was a synagogue of the Jews. And Paul went in, as was his custom, and for three weeks he argued with them from the scriptures, explaining and proving that it was necessary for the Christ to suffer and to rise from the dead, and saying, "This Jesus, whom I proclaim to you, is the Christ." And some of them were persuaded, and joined Paul and Silas; as did a great many of the devout Greeks and not a few of the leading women.' It was not long, however, before the Jews accused Paul and his companions of breaking 'the decrees of Caesar, saying that there is another king, Jesus'. It is likely that Paul's stay lasted much longer than three weeks – more likely three months, during which time he was supported by gifts of money from Christians at Philippi (Phil. 4:16), and these must have taken some time in collection and delivery. When Paul moved on to Beroea and word of his success reached Thessalonica, his opponents followed him and hunted him out of town again, so he went on to Athens and to Corinth.

It seems that Paul was anxious about the young Thessalonian Christian community, mostly Gentiles and persecuted by members of the synagogue. Paul's own character had been impugned and he had been accused of deception, immorality, and fraud, so he sent Timothy back from Beroea to keep them 'firm and strong in the faith' and prevent them from being unsettled. Timothy returned to Paul in Corinth with good reports of the Thessalonians, their faith in Jesus, and their love for Paul. Paul then wrote his first letter (1 Thess.) in AD 51, to send his gratitude and affection for their perseverance. He also answered two questions: one about those who die before the Second Coming of Jesus, and the other about the time of his coming. 'But we would not have you ignorant, brethren, concerning those who are asleep, that you may not grieve as others do who have no hope. For since we believe that Jesus died and rose again, even so, through Jesus, God will bring with him those who have fallen asleep. For this we declare to you by the word of the Lord, that we who are alive, who are left until the coming of the Lord, shall not precede those who have fallen asleep. For the Lord himself will descend from heaven with a cry of command, with the archangel's call, and with the sound of the trumpet of God. And the dead in Christ will rise first; then we who are alive, who are left, shall be caught up together with them in the clouds to meet the Lord in the air; and so we shall always be with the Lord. Therefore comfort one another with these words.' (1 Thess. 4:13-18)

As for the hour of Christ's coming, Paul wrote: 'But you are not in darkness, brethren, for that day to surprise you like a thief. For you are all sons of light and sons of the day; we are not of the night or of darkness ... but, since we belong to the day, let us be sober, and put on the breastplate of faith and love, and for a helmet the hope of salvation. For God has not destined us for wrath, but to obtain salvation through our Lord Jesus Christ, who died for us so that whether we wake or sleep we might live with him. . . . May the God of peace himself sanctify you wholly; and may your spirit and soul and body be kept sound and blameless at the coming of our Lord Jesus Christ.' (1 Thess. 5:4, 5, 8-10, 23)

The newly-founded congregation continued to make progress in real unity and love, still in the face of considerable opposition and persecution from the synagogue. Paul, therefore, wrote again to encourage them to persevere. 'So then, brethren, stand firm and hold to the traditions which you were taught by us, either by word of mouth or by letter. Now may our Lord Jesus Christ himself, and God our Father, who loved us and gave us eternal comfort and good hope through grace, comfort your hearts and establish them in every good work and word.' (2 Thess. 2:15-17)

Paul also tells them not to get excited too soon or to

be alarmed by any rumour that they have missed the second coming of Jesus. They are to follow the example of Paul and his companions, in working day and night for the Lord. 'For we hear that some of you are living in idleness, mere busybodies, not doing any work. Now such persons we command and exhort in the Lord Jesus Christ to do their work in quietness and to earn their own living. . . . If any one refuses to obey what we say in this letter, note that man, and have nothing to do with him, that he may be ashamed. Do not look on him as an enemy, but warn him as a brother.' (2 Thess. 3:11, 12, 14, 15)

The patience, affection, and pastoral skill of Paul are shown very clearly in the Thessalonian correspondence, together with a vivid impression of his personality. He ends his second letter with a prayer and farewell wishes: 'Now may the Lord of peace himself give you peace at all times in all ways. The Lord be with you all. I, Paul, write this greeting with my own hand. This is the mark in every letter of mine; it is the way I write. The grace of our Lord Jesus Christ be with you all.' (2 Thess. 3:16-18)

The Thessalonian Church was renowned for its orthodoxy and steadfastness in the years that followed. Its early martyrs included the three sisters SS Agape, Chionia, and Irene, with St Demetrius, later patron of the city; and the first bishop of Thessalonica was probably Gaius. [Acts 17:1-9, 11, 13; 20:4; 27:2; 1st and 2nd Letters to the Thessalonians]

THEUDAS (Gk. 'gift of God') A Jewish fanatic who with his 400 followers revolted against Roman authority in Palestine during the early years of the 1st century; they were ruthlessly wiped out.

The great Pharisee and rabbi Gamaliel quoted the stories of both Theudas and Judas the Galilean as unsuccessful leaders of pseudo-Messianic movements, in a speech to the Sanhedrin at the trial of the Apostles Peter and John. Gamaliel's advice was to leave the apostles alone and to trust God either to further or to destroy the movement, rather than themselves to take any drastic action against the Christian leaders at that time.

Judea was in those years seething with revolts and pretenders, and it is historically impossible to know the names of all the leaders involved. Josephus mentions a Theudas, who led a very much larger body than 400 in an uprising in AD 44, but Gamaliel's speech was made some years before that. Gamaliel's second and presumably later example, Judas of Galilee, led his revolt in the year 6, so the Theudas to whom he referred was probably active before that date. That is, of course, unless the whole reference to Theudas is an inaccurate and later interpretation of the writer or some editor. Luke, the writer of Acts, was not able to check his dates as can a modern historian. [Acts 5:36]

THOMAS (Gk. from Aram. 'twin') The loyal and practical, down-to-earth, 'seeing-is-believing' disciple of Jesus, whose doubts of the resurrection dissolved in the presence of his risen master.

The name of Thomas is included in the lists of apostles in each of the Synoptic Gospels and in the roll of those who, in the Upper Room after the ascension of Jesus, elected a replacement for Judas and received the Spirit at Pentecost. Nothing further is mentioned about him in the New Testament outside the Fourth Gospel, where he is called 'the Twin'. John, however, mentions four different occasions when the presence of Thomas was significant to the gospel story.

The first occasion was when Jesus had been hounded out of Jerusalem to seek safety in some quiet village, possibly Ephraim among the hills several miles to the north of the city and overlooking the wilderness of Judea. Suddenly the news of the illness of Lazarus of Bethany arrived; Jesus at once decided to go back to him at Bethany, within two miles of Jerusalem. Thomas was frightened, but loyal. He knew well the danger involved, but volunteered to accompany him in very blunt if realistic terms: 'Let us also go, that we may die with him.' (John 11:16)

The second incident took place at the Last Supper, in the Upper Room on the Western Hill, on Maundy Thursday night. Jesus had been preparing his disciples for his coming departure: 'And when I go and prepare a place for you, I will come again and will take you to myself, that where I am you may be also. And you know the way where I am going.' (John 14:3, 4) Thomas at once interrupted him, 'Lord, we do not know where you are going; how can we know the way?' (John 14:5) It was not as though the others knew any more than Thomas, but he was not the sort to let his master get away with something that he, Thomas, did not understand. No doubt Christians should be thankful for Thomas's question, which evoked such an answer. 'Jesus said to him, "I am the way, and the truth, and the life; no one comes to the Father, but by me. If you had known me, you would have known my Father also; henceforth you know him and have seen him."'

The third occasion was in the same room, but after the resurrection of Jesus. On the Easter night, Thomas had not been with the others when Jesus first came to them. When the others had told him, Thomas had not been able to believe them. Perhaps he felt they had succumbed to wishful thinking or had seen a ghost. His reply to them was quite typical of the man, absolutely practical: 'Unless I see in his hands the print of the

The Apostle Thomas reaching out his hand to thrust it into the side of the risen Jesus. Detail from an embroidered medieval cope.

Doubting Thomas, being shown the side
and stigmata of Jesus in the Upper Room.
5th-century ivory casket.

nails, and place my finger in the mark of the nails, and
place my hand in his side, I will not believe.' (John 20:25)

A week later, the disciples were again all together in
the Upper Room and this time Thomas was with them.
Though the doors were barred for fear of the Jews,
again Jesus was there. Thomas's doubts and demands
provided both Jesus and the evangelists with just the
opportunity that was needed, to bring home the reality
of the resurrection to the disciples both then and now.
Jesus called Thomas over to touch the scars of crucifixion: 'Put your finger here, and see my hands; and
put out your hand, and place it in my side; do not be
faithless, but believing.' (John 20:27)

In that moment Thomas must have seen both the
body on the cross, hanging by hands and feet, the side
opened by the soldier's spear, *and* his living friend and
master. As these two figures fused together, so Thomas
leapt the gap between loyalty to a friend and adoring
faith in God himself. His ponderous pessimism and
lonely doubts disappeared, and he identified his friend
as both 'My Lord and my God!'

The final reference to Thomas is among the seven
disciples who went fishing on the Lake of Galilee, when
at dawn they met Jesus on the shore, and landed a miraculous draught of fish. Thomas is mentioned only
second to Simon Peter in this final post-resurrection
story of Jesus.

Later traditions claim that Thomas found his way to
Persia and south India, where he was reputedly the
founder of the ancient Mar Thoma Church, in Travan-
core and Cochin, now called Kerala. He is credited with
an apocryphal gospel, that in fact dates from the 2nd
century. [Matt. 10:3; Mark 3:18; Luke 6:15; John 11:16;
14:5; 20:24-28; 21:2; Acts 1:13]

TIBERIUS The Roman emperor whose years of rule
(AD 14-37) include the ministry and crucifixion of Jesus.
In fact, Luke dates the beginning of Jesus's public life
as 'in the fifteenth year of the reign of Tiberius Caesar'.

Born in 42 BC, son of the Empress Livia, wife of
Augustus, by her first husband Tiberius Claudius Nero,
this Tiberius Julius Caesar Augustus served with military honours in Europe and the East. As Augustus his
step-father had no heir, Tiberius was his successor.
Augustus, however, disliked and distrusted him, and
Tiberius was a lonely and unpopular figure, despite his
able administration and determination to continue the
foreign and domestic policy of his august predecessor.

It was in honour of the Emperor Tiberius that Herod
Antipas built Tiberias, during the lifetime of Jesus, near
the hot springs already famous throughout the Roman
world. A great castle built to accommodate his court
dominated the town from the hillside.

The local Jewish population avoided the artificial
pagan township and despised Herod's oriental court.
To them also, the town was unclean because it was
built on the site of a cemetery. In the 2nd century,
the rabbis officially declared the purity of the site
and, thereafter, Tiberias became the seat of the
Sanhedrin. [Luke 3:1]

TIMAEUS (Gk. from Heb. 'to be unclean') Father of
the blind beggar Bartimaeus at Jericho, whose sight was

The martyrdom of Thomas, from William Caxton's
Golden Legend, 1493.

restored by Jesus. Bartimaeus was the first person publicly to proclaim the Messiahship of Jesus. *see* BARTIMAEUS [Mark 10:46]

TIMON *see* NICOLAUS

TIMOTHY (Gk. 'honouring God') The closest companion and messenger of Paul the Apostle, Timothy was called by Paul his 'dear and faithful child in the Lord', his 'brother', or his 'fellow-worker'. Timothy appears to have been entirely at Paul's disposal from Paul's visit to Lystra on the Second Journey until the time of Paul's death in Rome, a period of perhaps 17 years.

Timid nature, weak health

A much younger man than Paul (who knew his grandmother Lois), Timothy was by nature reserved and timid. 'When Timothy comes, see that you put him at ease among you, for he is doing the work of the Lord, as I am. So let no one despise him. Speed him on his way in peace, that he may return to me; for I am expecting him with the brethren.' (1 Cor. 16:10, 11) Paul nevertheless commissioned Timothy to strengthen the recalcitrant Corinthians in their faith and in their loyalty to Paul; and he writes in the same vein to the persecuted Thessalonian congregation, 'We sent Timothy, our brother and God's servant in the gospel of Christ, to establish you in your faith and to exhort you, that no one be moved by these afflictions. You yourselves know that this is to be our lot.' (1 Thess. 3:2, 3)

For all his shyness, Timothy could be trusted above many others for his pastoral concern and his gentle tact in dealing with awkward situations. When in prison, Paul wrote to the Christian community at Philippi, 'I hope in the Lord Jesus to send Timothy to you soon, so that I may be cheered by news of you. I have no one like him, who will be genuinely anxious for your welfare. They all look after their own interests, not those of Jesus Christ. But Timothy's worth you know, how as a son with a father he has served with me in the gospel.' (Phil. 2:19-22) Although Timothy may have been subject to 'frequent ailments' (1 Tim. 5:23), he seems to have been constantly ready to undertake dangerous journeys on difficult errands for Paul. His deliberate action leading to his martyrdom (some thirty years after Paul's) shows a similar courage, if not quite the same aggressive initiative as that of the apostle.

Timothy was a native of Lystra in Lycaonia, a town visited twice by Paul and Barnabas on their First Journey. On the first occasion Paul had been stoned and left for dead, so Timothy was under no illusions as to the cost and danger of discipleship. A few years later, when Paul returned to Lystra, this time with Silas, Timothy was already a respected member of the Christian congregation, as was his grandmother Lois and his mother Eunice, both Jewesses. His father, however, was a Gentile, and Timothy consequently was uncircumcised. Perhaps to placate the Jewish community, or – more

likely – because circumcision was still imposed by the Jewish Law, Paul decided that Timothy should undergo the operation rather than be hindered in his ministry. Certainly his Jewish mother would have seen to his education in the Old Testament scriptures.

Paul and Silas took Timothy along with them on their journey over to Macedonia. Somehow Timothy escaped the very rough treatment suffered by Paul and Silas at Philippi, and he does not seem to have been involved in the episode which incensed the Jews at Thessalonica. When Paul went on to Athens, Silas and Timothy stayed for some time at Beroea and Thessalonica before joining Paul at Corinth. We do not know at what point in Timothy's career he was ordained by the laying-on of hands by Paul and others. We do not know whether he accompanied Paul back to Antioch between the Second and Third Journeys. But we do know that Timothy and another disciple named Erastus were Paul's 'helpers' during his long teaching ministry at Ephesus, which may well have been interrupted by some crisis involving danger. Timothy acted as Paul's messenger to carry the Corinthian correspondence from Ephesus, and his name is linked with Paul's in letters to Thessalonica, Colossae, and Philippi.

At the end of Paul's Third Journey, Timothy was among the large group of disciples who met Paul at Troas and shared a Eucharist the night before Paul sailed for Jerusalem. But we do not know whether Timothy accompanied Paul or shared any of his imprisonment at Caesarea. It seems that Luke acted as Paul's secretary and companion until his arrival in Rome; from then onwards there is little evidence of Paul's movements, let alone those of his companions. If Paul's letter to Philippi or to Colossae, whether to the congregation or to Philemon, were written in Rome, then certainly Timothy was with Paul in Rome.

Whether the letters to Timothy were written by Paul or not, it is certain that Paul sent Timothy as his representative to Ephesus, to teach for some considerable time. We know that Paul sent for Timothy to bring his scrolls and cloak before winter set in – but not whether Timothy arrived before Paul's execution. The final chapter of the letter to Hebrew Christians may just possibly have been an appendix added by Paul himself. Its last message is that Timothy has been set free from some imprisonment and that Paul hopes he will arrive in time to be with him.

Eusebius, the 4th-century historian and bishop of Caesarea, records that Timothy became the first bishop of Ephesus. An apocryphal *Acts of Timothy*, dating from the same period, describes his martyrdom on 22 January in the year 97, when protesting at the licentious festivities in honour of Diana of the Ephesians. His relics are believed to have been translated to Constantinople in the year 356. [Acts 16:1; 17:14, 15; 18:5; 19:22;

20:4; Rom. 16:21; 1 Cor. 4:17; 16:10; 2 Cor. 1:1, 19; Col. 1:1, 1 Thess. 1:1; 3:2, 6; 2 Thess. 1:1; 1st and 2nd Letters to Timothy; Philem. 1; Heb. 13:23]

Timothy, Letters to

The two brief letters to Timothy and the one to Titus concern Church organization and discipline rather than doctrine. They reflect the situation in the Christian Church at the close of the 1st century.

Together with the letter to Titus, the letters to Timothy have, since the 18th century, been called the 'pastoral epistles', being primarily addressed to pastors. All three are in full agreement in their religious and ethical teaching; they deal virtually with the same problems in the same words. They were clearly written in a period not covered by the narrative in the Acts of the Apostles; they cannot be 'fitted in' to Paul's life as related in the Acts. They show little of Paul's power of thought and expression, nor of his depth and originality.

If Paul is to be considered as their author, we must suppose that Paul was released from his first imprisonment in Rome, as Agrippa anticipated. The second letter to Timothy does indicate some continuation of ministry in Asia before his final arrest, trial, and execution.

Briefly, the arguments against their Pauline authorship are these. The first letter purports to be sent from Macedonia to Ephesus, but the only time (Acts 19:22) Paul went from Ephesus to Macedonia, he sent Timothy on ahead of him. The letter to Titus in Crete, calling him to meet Paul in Nicopolis, on the west coast of Achaia, presupposes a long period of teaching activity in Crete. But there is no mention in the Acts of Paul conducting such a mission, nor would there have been time for him to make more than a cursory visit to Crete from Corinth. The last letter to Timothy presupposes another imprisonment in Rome, and purports to be written on the eve of Paul's martyrdom. This letter, however, has passages which are far more personal and typical of Paul in style and language. The letter's final chapter would seem to include a genuine fragment of some Pauline letter, with so vivid a description of his situation and feelings as he awaits execution that it may well be the last message he ever sent.

'For I am already on the point of being sacrificed; the time of my departure has come. I have fought the good fight, I have finished the race, I have kept the faith. Henceforth there is laid up for me the crown of righteousness, which the Lord, the righteous judge, will award me on that Day, and not only to me but also to all who have loved his appearing. Do your best to come to me soon. For Demas, in love with this present world, has deserted me and gone to Thessalonica; Crescens has gone to Galatia, Titus to Dalmatia. Luke alone is with me. Get Mark and bring him with you; for he is very useful in serving me. Tychicus I have sent to Ephesus. When you come, bring the cloak that I left with Carpus at Troas, also the books, and above all the parchments. Alexander the coppersmith did me great harm; the Lord will requite him for his deeds. Beware of him yourself, for he strongly opposed our message. At my first defence no one took my part; all deserted me. May it not be charged against them! But the Lord stood by me and gave me strength to proclaim the word fully, that all the Gentiles might hear it. So I was rescued from the lion's mouth. The Lord will rescue me from every evil and save me for his heavenly kingdom. To him be the glory for ever and ever. Amen.' (2 Tim. 4:6-18)

From the evidence, therefore, we may conclude that the 'pastoral epistles' are the work of an admirer of Paul who, employing Paul's theology and vocabulary, used both his name and brief notes of his correspondence in a desire to impress his readers with the need to hold fast to Paul's teachings of faith and practice.

The Church of the period in which the author is writing is not as it was in Paul's day. It no longer consists of scattered and struggling little communities, held together by the occasional visits of apostolic leaders. The conditions described in these 'pastoral epistles' indicate a more firmly-established and organized Church, officered by bishops, deacons, and elders. These letters give a useful picture of the Church at the close of its apostolic age, when as an institution it is taking shape, when its practices are becoming a system, and its beliefs are being formulated into a creed.

The letters do not constitute a systematic 'Manual of Church Order', but they are much concerned with the duties of Church leaders. 'Now a bishop must be above reproach, the husband of one wife, temperate, sensible, dignified, hospitable, an apt teacher, no drunkard, not violent but gentle, not quarrelsome, and no lover of money. He must manage his own household well, keeping his children submissive and respectful in every way.' (1 Tim. 3:2-4) 'Deacons likewise must be serious, not double-tongued, not addicted to much wine, not greedy for gain; they must hold the mystery of the faith with a clear conscience. And let them also be tested first; then if they prove themselves blameless let them serve as deacons.' (1 Tim. 3:8-10) 'Do not rebuke an older man but exhort him as you would a father; treat younger men like brothers, older women like mothers, younger women like sisters, in all purity. Honour widows who are real widows.' (1 Tim. 5:1-3)

The writer is also concerned to preserve the faith, as 'deposited' by the Apostle Paul, as a bastion against all false teaching. 'But as for you, continue in what you have learned and have firmly believed, knowing from whom you learned it and how from childhood you have been acquainted with the sacred writings which are able to instruct you for salvation through faith in Christ

Jesus. All scripture is inspired by God and profitable for teaching, for reproof, for correction, and for training in righteousness, that the man of God may be complete, equipped for every good work.' (2 Tim. 3:14-17)

Perhaps the greatest contrast between this writer and Paul himself is that, unlike Paul (whose ethics are based on the guidance of the Holy Spirit), the writer appears primarily guided by the need for prudence and good order within the Church. And indeed his wise, practical councils have helped to mould both the organization and the ethical teaching of the historical Church through the centuries.

His outlook is exactly shared by Clement of Rome, in the letter to the Corinthian Church written in the year 96. He is quoted by Ignatius, bishop of Antioch at the close of the 1st century. Thus it is probable that the pastoral letters belong to the end of the 1st century. [1st and 2nd Letters to Timothy]

TITIUS *see* JUSTUS **2.**

TITUS (Gk. *Titos*, a praenomen only, the surname being lost) A Greek Christian for nearly twenty years associated with the Apostle Paul, for whom he acted successfully in Corinth. Titus became a leader of the Church in Corinth, in Dalmatia, on the Adriatic, and finally Crete. He was also the addressee of one of the pastoral letters attributed to Paul.

No mention of Titus is made by Luke in the Acts of the Apostles, but Paul frequently refers to him in the Corinthian correspondence, once in his last letter to Timothy. Titus is first introduced in the Letter to the

Circumcision of a child, from the *Regensburg Pentateuch, c.* 1300. The question whether or not Christians should adhere to the Jewish custom of circumcision divided the early Christian Church.

Galatians as on the delegation from Antioch accompanying Paul and Barnabas to Jerusalem round about the year 49. Opinions differ as to whether this visit is that recorded in Acts 11, or that in Acts 15, for the Council.

The Council was called to deliberate the necessity of circumcision for all Christians and the observance of the Law of Moses by Gentile Christians, for salvation. Many Christians in Jerusalem resented the acceptance of Gentile Christians, particularly within the headquarters of the Church, at Antioch in Syria. The accounts of the Council vary. Luke says that the Apostle Peter, speaking out of his personal experience (*see* CORNELIUS), supported the Antiochene delegation and secured a generous judgment from James and the elders of the Church. Paul implies that he himself had forced the issue by taking the Gentile Christian Titus, who was not circumcised, to be a test case. 'Then, after fourteen years, I went up again to Jerusalem with Barnabas, taking Titus along with me. I went up by revelation; and I laid before them (but privately before those who were of repute) the gospel which I preach among the Gentiles, lest somehow I should be running or had run in vain. But even Titus, who was with me, was not compelled to be circumcised, though he was a Greek.' (Gal. 2:1-3)

Some years later during his Third Journey and while he was at Ephesus, Paul had bad news of the Church at Corinth. He heard that a party spirit prevailed in the community and that a particularly grave case of immorality had arisen within the Church. Paul dealt with these questions in a letter now known to us as 1 Corinthians, which he sent by sea, while Timothy took the land route to deal with the situation in person. Neither the letter nor Timothy's visit achieved the desired effect, and Paul himself sailed for Corinth. Even he was not able to secure a reform within the Corinthian Christian community and, after being grossly insulted, he sailed back to Ephesus. From there, he wrote a 'severe letter', his third, possibly to be found in 2 Cor. 10-13, which was carried by Titus, an older and more experienced man than Timothy. This letter demanded a proper respect for Christian morality and for Paul himself, as founder of the Christian Church in Corinth. In this letter, Paul wrote, 'Did I take advantage of you through any of those whom I sent to you? I urged Titus to go....' (2 Cor. 17, 18)

Paul was so anxious about the outcome of his appeal to the Corinthian Church to mend its ways that he had barely closed his ministry at Ephesus before setting out via Troas, to intercept Titus on his return from Corinth through Macedonia. Somewhere *en route* he met Titus, who at last brought him the good news that the Corinthian Church was ready to conform, and that they had already by a majority censured the person who had insulted Paul. Paul immediately wrote his fourth letter, to be found in 2 Cor. 1-9, omitting the content of his preliminary letter. In this last letter, he forgave his antagonist, closed the controversy, and arranged for a collection for the poor Christians at Jerusalem.

In this letter, Paul warmly expressed his relief and gratitude at the report of Titus. 'When I came to Troas to preach the gospel of Christ, a door was opened for me in the Lord; but my mind could not rest because I did not find my brother Titus there. So I took leave of them and went on to Macedonia.' (2 Cor. 2:12, 13) 'But God, who comforts the downcast, comforted us by the coming of Titus, and not only by his coming but also by the comfort with which he was comforted in you, as he told us of your longing, your mourning, your zeal for me, so that I rejoiced still more. For even if I made you sorry with my letter, I do not regret it (though I did regret it), for I see that that letter grieved you, though only for a while. As it is, I rejoice, not because you were grieved, but because you were grieved into repenting. . . . I do not mean that others should be eased and you burdened, but that as a matter of equality your abundance at the present time should supply their want, so that their abundance may supply your want, that there may be equality. As it is written, "He who gathered much had nothing over, and he who gathered little had no lack." ' (2 Cor. 7:6-9; 8:13-15)

Paul clearly valued the pastoral skill and tact of his veteran comrade, Titus, without whose efforts the story of the Christian community in Corinth might have been very different. It was to Titus therefore that Paul committed the care of that congregation, and the task of completing the collection for poor-relief, giving him this final letter to deliver to Corinth. 'Accordingly we have urged Titus that as he had already made a beginning, he should also complete among you this gracious work. . . . Thanks be to God who puts the same earnest care for you into the heart of Titus. For he not only accepted our appeal, but being himself very earnest he is going to you of his own accord. . . . As for Titus, he is my partner and fellow worker in your service; and as for our brethren, they are messengers of the churches, the glory of Christ.' (2 Cor. 8:6, 16, 17, 23)

The last reference to Titus is to be found in Paul's final letter to Timothy. Paul, re-arrested, condemned, and awaiting execution, is depressed by the scattering of his followers, even though for the most part they are concerned with the continuation of his work throughout the Mediterranean Churches. Titus, at Paul's request, had gone to Dalmatia on the east coast of the Adriatic, probably to Nicopolis.

The pastoral letter addressed to Titus and attributed to Paul, if written by the apostle, must belong to the period between Paul's two imprisonments in Rome. In this letter, Titus is represented as left in charge of the

organization of the Christian Church on the island of Crete where, according to the historian Eusebius, he became the first bishop. His traditional burial-place is at Gortyna, the ancient capital of Crete, though his head is venerated as a relic in St Mark's, Venice. *see also* CRETANS

(For discussion on the date, authorship, origin and contents of the pastoral letters, *see* TIMOTHY) [2 Cor. 2:13; 7:6, 13, 14; 8:6-23; 12:18; Gal. 2:1, 3; 2 Tim. 4:10; Titus 1:4]

TROPHIMUS (Gk. 'nourishing') A Gentile Christian from Ephesus, one of Paul's escorts on his final visit to Jerusalem, where he was indirectly the cause of Paul's arrest. Trophimus began to accompany Paul on his final journey to Rome, but fell ill and stayed at Miletus, on the south-west coast of Asia Minor.

As one of the two Asian representatives, Trophimus the Ephesian was chosen to accompany Paul on his return to Jerusalem with the poor-relief collection from the various Christian communities on the Mediterranean. Fearing an ambush if he travelled via Corinth, Paul went overland through Macedonia, in the spring of the year 58, as far as Troas on the coast of Asia Minor, and so by sea to Caesarea and Jerusalem, with an escort of seven men. They met the others at Troas, returned by sea to Caesarea, and went up to Jerusalem.

There, at the suggestion of James, the leader of the Christian Church in Jerusalem, Paul was advised to undergo a week's ritual purification in the Temple and to pay the expenses of four companions who with him were under a vow, to reassure the Jews of his adherence to the Law of Moses. When the week was nearly up, some Jews from Asia who had seen him in the Temple, but had also met him in the city with Trophimus the Ephesian, jumped to the hasty conclusion that Paul had taken Trophimus into the Temple. They dragged Paul out of the Temple and intended to lynch him, but he was rescued by the Antonia guard, who took him into protective custody. From this moment, Paul was never free until after his release by the imperial tribunal at Rome. Thus, indirectly, Trophimus was responsible for Paul's arrest, imprisonment, and appeal to Ceasar at Rome.

We next hear of Trophimus several years later, after Paul's acquittal and return to Asia, his re-arrest possibly at Troas, and his return in chains to Rome. Writing his final letter to Timothy, Paul comments that, on their way back to Rome – perhaps via Ephesus – Trophimus became ill at Miletus and had to be left there.

According to tradition, Trophimus was martyred during Nero's persecution at Rome, after the year 64. [Acts 20:4; 21:29; 2 Tim. 4:20]

TRYPHAENA (Gk. 'dainty') One of two Christian women greeted by Paul at the close of his letter to the congregation in Rome as 'workers in the Lord'. The similarity of their names (both from a common root in

424

the Greek word for 'luxurious living') gives rise to the supposition that Tryphaena and Tryphosa were sisters, if not twins. Both names are found in Latin inscriptions of the period, for members of the imperial household. Tryphaena was sometimes used of Jewish women, and was the name of the queen from Pontus, in Asia Minor, who befriended the early Christian virgin Thecla, in the apocryphal *Acts of Paul and Thecla*. [Rom. 16:12]

TRYPHOSA *see* TRYPHAENA

TYCHICUS (Gk. 'fortuitous') An Ephesian convert and one of the two Asian representatives chosen to accompany Paul on his return to Jerusalem with the poor-relief collection from the various Christian communities on the Mediterranean. Fearing an ambush if he travelled via Corinth, Paul went overland through Macedonia in the spring of the year 58 as far as Troas on the coast of Asia Minor, with an escort of seven men. They met the others at Troas, returned by sea to Caesarea, and went up to Jerusalem. Three men – Aristarchus, Timothy, and Tychicus – were later Paul's fellow-prisoners in Rome.

Tychicus is not mentioned as having accompanied Paul on his voyage to Rome. He was, however, commissioned by Paul to deliver the letter to the Christian Church in Colossae, together with Onesimus, the escaped slave of his master Philemon, to whom Paul restored him. (*see* PHILEMON) Tychicus, besides taking the general letter to the Church at Colossae and the personal letter to Philemon, was also the bearer of several copies of a circular letter to various churches in Asia, of which the epistle to Ephesians was one. (*see* EPHESIANS)

It would seem that Tychicus was the man who was capable of dealing with doctrinal questions arising from Paul's various letters to the Church in Asia. Paul commends him warmly to the Christian congregations at Colossae, Ephesus, and wherever else the circular letter was to be delivered in Asia. 'Tychicus will tell you all about my affairs; he is a beloved brother and faithful minister and fellow servant in the Lord. I have sent him to you for this very purpose, that you may know how we are and that he may encourage your hearts, and with him Onesimus, the faithful and beloved brother, who is one of yourselves. They will tell you of everything that has taken place here.' (Col. 4:7-9)

In both these letters, Paul wrote to correct some strange and heretical teachings that were gaining ground within the Asian Churches, particularly perhaps within the Lycus Valley and the area of Ephesus. News of these strange doctrines was reported to Paul in prison by Epaphras, one of the evangelists trained by Paul at Ephesus on his Third Journey. He reported that certain teachers at Colossae, trying to combine within Christianity what they considered to be best in both Judaism and Hellenism, emphasized on the one hand such

demands of the Jewish Law as the keeping of festivals and of the Sabbath and the hygiene laws. On the other hand, they devalued the material and physical, regarding the human body with contempt, not thinking that the physical birth and death of the Man Jesus was able to secure the reconciliation of the world with God. They questioned the uniqueness of Jesus Christ in God's scheme of salvation, which they felt could only be achieved by supernatural means.

Tychicus was entrusted with Paul's remarkable replies. The Letter to the Colossians was undoubtedly the first draft of Paul's attempt to combat this theosophy, and to restate the all-sufficiency of Jesus the Messiah within God's scheme of salvation. The circular letter, our Letter to the Ephesians, was possibly a carefully and purposefully revised form of the first letter into a magnificent exposition of the 'mystery' of God's purpose in history, and of the new life within the Christian Church. Tychicus was the bearer of the 'very crown of all Paul's epistles'.

These letters were probably despatched from Rome in the year 61 or 62. Following Paul's release, return to Asia Minor, rearrest and return in chains to Rome, he again mentions Tychicus in his letters to Titus and Timothy. To the former he suggests sending either Tychicus or Artemas as an assistant. To the latter, in the final report of the disposition and whereabouts of his companions, Paul tells Timothy that he has sent back Tychicus to Ephesus. Tychicus is one of the quiet but key figures in the history of the Asian communities, who have been described as the 'seed-plot of the Christian Church'. [Acts 20:4; Eph. 6:21; Col. 4:7; 2 Tim. 4:12; Titus 3:12]

TYRANNUS (Gk. 'tyrant') The teacher at Ephesus in whose lecture-room, or school, Paul taught over a period of two years, in the siesta hours of noon to four.

For three months, Paul had taught fearlessly in the synagogue, arguing the Christian message and persuading people of the Messiahship of Jesus. The opposition, however, hardened and Paul decided to withdraw from the synagogue – as he had done at Corinth also – into some alternative accommodation. It must have required an enormous effort of endurance to continue, throughout the middle of the day in the heat, teaching for two whole years. As a result, however, all the interested Jews and Greeks of Asia benefited from a period of continuous teaching. This accounts for the sound foundation of the Seven Churches in Asia, which later became known as the 'seed-plot' of Christianity in the time of John the Divine.

No doubt Tyrannus had heard Paul in the synagogue and offered his own accommodation to the apostle. He was possibly himself a proselyte to the Jewish faith or an attendant in the Gentile courtyard of the synagogue. [Acts 19:9]

U–Z

URBANUS One of the Christians greeted by Paul as 'our fellow-worker in Christ', at the close of his letter to the Church in Rome. Urbanus was a common slave name, often found within the emperor's own household. [Rom. 16:9]

WISE MEN *see* MAGI

ZACCHAEUS (Gk. from Heb. 'pure') Luke alone tells the delightful story of the chief tax-collector, Zacchaeus, who was very rich because the Jericho taxes constituted a fruitful source of income and he had contracted for the right of collecting the revenues of that district. When Jesus came to Jericho, probably among the crowds of pilgrims on the way up to Jerusalem for the Passover festival, Zacchaeus wanted to meet him. He was, however, a little man, and he therefore went on ahead and climbed into a tree overlooking the road along which Jesus was likely to come. As Jesus came level with him, he looked up, and called to him, 'Zacchaeus, make haste and come down; for I must stay at your house today.' (Luke 19:5) Zacchaeus made haste to come down and received Jesus joyfully.

When the crowds saw what had happened, they were resentful and murmured, ' "He has gone in to be the guest of a man who is a sinner." And Zacchaeus stood and said to the Lord, "Behold, Lord, the half of my goods I give to the poor; and if I have defrauded any one of anything, I restore it fourfold." And Jesus said to him, "Today salvation has come to this house, since he also is a son of Abraham. For the Son of man came to seek and to save the lost." ' (Luke 19:7-10)

Luke brings out very clearly Jesus's application of the word 'lost' to the publicans, as though their livelihood made them inevitably 'sinners'. Luke described how the 'tax-collectors and sinners' were attracted to Jesus and came near to listen to him, but the Pharisees and Scribes grumbled to the disciples, 'Why does your teacher eat with tax-collectors and sinners?' (Matt. 9:11) In defence of Zacchaeus, Jesus called him 'a son of Abraham', a good Jew, despite his profession.

left The Entry of Jesus into Jerusalem,
by the Sienese painter Barna Senese, showing a man who has climbed a tree to watch Jesus pass by.

In Jericho of the New Testament period, houses with ossuaries have been found, belonging to rich men. Jericho was then as now a popular winter resort, near to which Herod had a magnificent water-garden at the mouth of the Kelt Gorge. [Luke 19:1-10]

ZACHARIAS (Gk. from Heb. 'whom Yahweh remembered') *see* ZECHARIAH

ZEALOTS (Gk. 'zealous one') The name given to those Jews who, from Maccabean times in the 1st and 2nd centuries BC to the fall of the fortress of Masada in the spring of AD 73, were impelled by a fanatical nationalism. Considering themselves the agents of God to deliver their nation from the foreign oppressors, under a banner of 'No rule but the Law – No King but God', they became increasingly violent in their resistance both to the Roman occupation forces and to their own people who sympathized with Hellenism.

Following the example of the Maccabean resistance to the efforts of the Seleucid king, Antiochus Epiphanes, to force Greek customs and religion upon the Jews,

above The rugged ranges of Upper Galilee, a natural hide-out for Zealot partisans from the occupying forces of Rome.

Judas the Galilean of Gamala led a considerable revolt in protest at the introduction of a Roman census on the incorporation of Judea in AD 6. (*see* JUDAS **4**.) Theudas led another uprising in about the year 42. (*see* THEUDAS) Both these were quoted by the Pharisee Gamaliel as unsuccessful if patriotic attempts at a national deliverance impelled by religious motives.

The Gospels (Luke 6:15) give only one specific reference to the name Zealot (*see* SIMON **2**.) but include many incidents involving the probable activities of the Zealot party. Among these is the report of certain Galileans 'whose blood Pilate had mingled with their sacrifices'. Galilee, its climate and people, was fertile soil for discontent and revolt. (*see* GALILEANS) There is a similar comment on some eighteen men who were killed when a tower in Siloam fell on them, perhaps while they were undermining some Roman fortification. Jesus said of the Galileans: 'Do you think that these Galileans were worse sinners than all of the other Galileans, because they suffered thus? I tell you, No; but unless you repent you will all likewise perish.' (Luke 13:2, 3) And of the other victims he said, 'Of those eighteen upon whom the tower in Siloam fell and killed them, do you think that they were worse offenders than all the others who dwelt in Jerusalem? I tell you, No; but unless you repent you will all likewise perish.' (Luke 13:4, 5)

Perhaps Barabbas, who was released by Pilate instead of Jesus, was a Zealot leader, a mistaken claimant for the Messiahship who left his followers to suffer, while accepting his own release. The remark of one of the bandits crucified with Jesus implies a possible comparison between Barabbas and Jesus on his cross: 'Are you not the Christ? Save *yourself and us*!' Perhaps Judas Iscariot also was a Zealot, whose impatient aspirations for his master as Messiah led him in desperation to betray him in order to force Jesus's hand. For neither theory is there material evidence (*see* BARABBAS *and* JUDAS **1**.), but it would have been surprising if the Zealots had not at least considered exploiting Jesus for their cause. John clearly says that the people wanted to make Jesus king in Galilee, and that his movements were restricted by the threat of such demonstrations.

The Jews who conspired to assassinate Paul at Jerusalem were perhaps Zealots, acting in defence of the Law. 'When it was day, the Jews made a plot and bound themselves by an oath neither to eat nor drink till they had killed Paul. There were more than forty who made this conspiracy. And they went to the chief priests and elders, and said, "We have strictly bound ourselves by an oath to taste no food till we have killed Paul."' (Acts 23:12-14)

In the years that followed, partly as a result of the Hellenistic policies of the Emperor Nero, partly from the corrupt and harsh administration of the Roman procurators, the persistent trouble-making of the Zealots reached a climax. Open hostility broke out in the year 66, when Gessius Florus, the governor, demanded funds from the Temple treasury. The Jews refused and suspended the daily sacrifice for the emperor; from then onwards the Zealots led the people in open revolt, resulting in the cruel suppression of Galilee and the disastrous siege of Jerusalem. There, with the Zealots divided into two opposing factions, the aristocrats on the west hill, the commoners on the east of the city under John of Gischala, with the Romans under Titus along the Mount of Olives, the Antonia Fortress was taken, the Temple burnt and the city sacked. Of the remaining Zealot fortresses, Herodium (near Bethlehem) and Machaerus (beyond Jordan) rapidly fell, but Masada survived until the spring of 73. The ruins of Masada and the suicidal story of this last stronghold bear witness to all that was best and all that was worst in the character of the Zealots. [Luke 6:15]

ZEBEDEE (Gk. from Heb. 'my gift') The father of James and John, who together with Peter made up the inner circle of Jesus's disciples, and husband of Salome, Zebedee was a fisherman of some substance, employing a hired crew and at least one sizeable boat for deepwater fishing. He allowed and enabled his wife Salome to give financial help to Jesus and his disciples. He may himself have been a disciple with his two sons, first of John the Baptist and then of Jesus.

A particularly interesting possibility is that the firm of 'Zebedee and Sons, of Galilee' was contracted to supply fish to the high priest's palace in Jerusalem. This would account for the welcome of John Bar-Zebedee by the portress at the high priest's courtyard. 'Simon Peter followed Jesus, and so did another disciple. As this disciple was known to the high priest, he entered the court of the high priest along with Jesus, while Peter stood outside at the door.' (John 18:15-16) There exists a traditional site, in the upper city of Jerusalem, of the 'fish-shop of Zebedee', on which the Crusaders built a little cruciform church, now occupied by an Arab coffee-house.

Luke (5:3) describes Jesus borrowing Simon Peter's boat, from which to speak to the crowds on shore, and goes on to tell the story of the miraculous draught of fishes that Peter found in the deep water. They had let down their nets, but these were bursting with the quantity of the shoal they had thus enclosed. They had to signal to their partners to come and help them bring the catch on board. Having filled both boats, they began to sink with the sheer weight of fish. No wonder Simon Peter, the expert deep-water fisherman, was astonished, and Luke adds, 'so were also James and John, sons of Zebedee, who were partners with Simon'. It was after such an experience that the two sets of brothers, Simon and Andrew, James and John, must have decided to

The fortress of Masada Rock from the north-east; this was the scene of the final heroic Zealot stand against the Roman armies in the spring of AD 73.

leave their homes to follow Jesus. As Mark puts it, 'And going on a little farther, he saw James the son of Zebedee and John his brother, who were in their boat mending the nets. And immediately he called them; and they left their father Zebedee in the boat with the hired servants, and followed him.' (Mark 1:19, 20)

If Simon and Andrew came from Bethsaida at the north-west of the lake, it is probable that Zebedee's home was on that part of the coastline, though their best fishing-grounds were along the north-west shore.

429

Here the silt from the exit of the River Jordan, flowing down from the slopes of Hermon, still attracts the fish and provides their food. It is a mistake to think of the fisher-disciples of Jesus as all poor, simple, rustic peasants; Zebedee and his family were of great skill and considerable business acumen and substance. *see* SALOME **1.** *and* BOANERGES [Matt. 4:21; 10:2; 20:20; 26:37; 27:56; Mark 1:20; 3:17; 10:35; Luke 5:10; John 21:2]

ZECHARIAH *or* **ZACHARIAH** (Gk. from Heb. 'whom Yahweh remembered') Only Luke names the parents of John the Baptist and tells the story of John's birth. Zechariah, his father, belonged to the Abijah section of the priesthood. He and his wife Elizabeth, also a descendant of Aaron, were devout and scrupulous in their observance of the Law, but they were childless and both of them were getting on in years.

The twenty-four families of the 'sons of Aaron' were responsible in rotation for service in the Temple at Jerusalem. Within each family, two individuals were chosen by lot each day to tend the brazier on the altar of incense in front of the Most Holy Place, one in the morning and one in the evening. On the occasion that Zechariah was chosen for the great privilege of entering the sanctuary to burn incense there, the congregation remaining outside at prayer, Zechariah received a vision.

He saw an angel standing on the altar of incense and he was overcome with fright. He heard the angel speaking to him. 'Do not be afraid, Zechariah, for your prayer is heard, and your wife Elizabeth will bear you a son, and you shall call his name John. And you will have joy and gladness, and many will rejoice at his birth; for he will be great before the Lord, and he shall drink no wine nor strong drink, and he will be filled with the Holy Spirit, even from his mother's womb. And he will turn many of the sons of Israel to the Lord their God, and he will go before him in the spirit and power of Elijah, to turn the hearts of the fathers to the children, and the disobedient to the wisdom of the just, to make ready for the Lord a people prepared.' (Luke 1:13-17) To this Zechariah replied, ' "How shall I know this? For I am an old man, and my wife is advanced in years." And the angel answered him, "I am Gabriel, who stand in the presence of God; and I was sent to speak to you, and to bring you this good news. And behold, you will be silent and unable to speak until the day that these things come to pass, because you did not believe my words, which will be fulfilled in their time." ' (Luke 1:18-20) When at last Zechariah went out of the sanctuary to greet the people, he was unable to speak and could only make signs to them. They perceived that he had received a vision within the sanctuary.

In due time, he returned home, and his wife Elizabeth conceived. Six months later, Mary, the future mother of Jesus and cousin of Zechariah's wife Elizabeth, visited

and stayed with them for some three months. It was not, however, until after the birth of his child, his circumcision and naming, that Zechariah received back his power of speech. At the ceremony of circumcision on the eighth day, their family and friends were going to name the child 'Zechariah' after his father. Elizabeth, however, insisted on his being called 'John', despite their protests that no one else in the family had that name. Finally they appealed to Zechariah, the father,

The Patriarch Zechariah in the Temple: fresco by Domenico Ghirlandaio (1449-94) in the Church of S. Maria Novella, Florence.

who wrote on a tablet: 'His name is John', as the angel Gabriel had instructed him. At that instant, his power of speech returned. Luke records him as praising God in a prophetic poem, which has since become part of the liturgy of the Christian Church. It is full of Old Testament phrases and reflects the Messianic hopes of pious Jews of that time. It looks forward to the coming deliverance of the Lord Most High, whose forerunner and prophet the little child, John, was to become.

'Blessed be the Lord God of Israel,
    for he has visited and redeemed his people,
    and has raised up a horn of salvation for us

in the house of his servant David,
as he spoke by the mouth of his holy prophets from
of old,
that we should be saved from our enemies,
and from the hand of all who hate us;
to perform the mercy promised to our fathers,
and to remember his holy covenant,
the oath which he swore to our father Abraham, to
grant us
that we, being delivered from the hand of our enemies,
might serve him without fear,
in holiness and righteousness before him all the days
of our life.
And you, child, will be called the prophet of the Most
High;
for you will go before the Lord to prepare his ways,
to give knowledge of salvation to his people
in the forgiveness of their sins,
through the tender mercy of our God,
when the day shall dawn upon us from on high
to give light to those who sit in darkness and in the
shadow of death,
to guide our feet into the way of peace.'

(Luke 1:68-79)

According to a later tradition, Zechariah was murdered in the Temple at the command of Herod. *see*
ELIZABETH [Luke 1:5-79; Matt. 23:35; Luke 11:51]

ZENAS A lawyer whose services, together with those
of the biblical scholar Apollos, Paul requested in his
letter to Titus. Paul, writing probably from Macedonia
to Titus in Crete at the end of the year 64, following his
release from prison in Rome, asks Titus to meet him at
Nicopolis on the Dalmatian coast of the Adriatic. We
do not know why Paul needed the services of the lawyer
Zenas at Nicopolis. [Titus 3:13]

ZEUS (Gk. *Zeus*, Lat. *Jupiter*) The chief and father-
figure of the gods of Olympus, known to the Greeks as
'Zeus' and to the Romans as 'Jupiter', whose messenger
or spokesman was known as 'Hermes' to the Greeks
and 'Mercury' to the Romans.

During the First Journey of Paul in the years 46-8, he
and Barnabas had arrived at Lystra, a city of Lycaonia
in Pisidia, in the Roman province of Galatia, now
central Asia Minor. Here there was no synagogue,

so Paul preached in the open air. There was a man outside the Temple, a cripple from birth, who had never
walked. He was probably placed at the entrance to the
local temple of Zeus to attract sympathy and alms from
the worshippers. 'He listened to Paul speaking; and
Paul, looking intently at him and seeing that he had
faith to be made well, said in a loud voice, "Stand upright on your feet." And he sprang up and walked.'
(Acts 14:9, 10)

When the crowd saw what had happened, they were
convinced that these visitors were more than mere
mortals, and shouted out in their own Lycaonian dialect, 'The gods have come down to us in the likeness
of men!' They called Barnabas 'Zeus', perhaps for
his tall and dignified appearance, and they called Paul
'Hermes', 'because he was the chief speaker'. The priest
of the temple of Zeus, who emerged from his temple 'in
front of the city, brought oxen and garlands to the gates
and wanted to offer sacrifice with the people'. Seeing the
visitors outside his temple and the cripple healed, the
priest assumed that Zeus with Hermes had visited his
own shrine and had worked this miracle of healing.

At this point, Paul and Barnabas, who had not understood what was happening nor the shouting in the local
dialect, suddenly grasped the situation, tore their clothes
in the traditional manner of displaying grief and cried
out to the people, 'Men, why are you doing this? We
also are men, of like nature with you, and bring you
good news, that you should turn from these vain things
to a living God who made the heaven and the earth and
the sea and all that is in them. In past generations he
allowed all the nations to walk in their own ways; yet he
did not leave himself without witness, for he did good
and gave you from heaven rains and fruitful seasons,
satisfying your hearts with food and gladness.' (Acts
14:11-18)

The Roman writer, Ovid, tells the beautiful story of
an aged couple, Baucis and Philemon, who lived in the
neighbouring district of Phrygia and were similarly
visited by Zeus and Hermes. The gods granted their
wish that they should tend the temple of Zeus together
and that neither should outlive the other. On their death,
at the entrance to the temple two trees appeared, whose
leaves whispered together in the wind. [Acts 14:12]

Reverse side of a Hadrianic
coin, minted in Aelia
Capitolina (Jerusalem)
c. 130, showing Zeus (Jupiter)
seated, Hera (Juno) right,
and Athena (Minerva) left.